The Handbook of
Forensic Psychology

The Handbook of Forensic Psychology

Second Edition

Edited by
Allen K. Hess
Irving B. Weiner

John Wiley & Sons, Inc.

New York • Chichester • Weinheim • Brisbane • Singapore • Toronto

This publication is designed to provide accurate and authoritative information in regard to the subject matter covered. It is sold with the understanding that the publisher is not engaged in rendering professional services. If professional advice or other expert assistance is required, the services of a competent professional person should be sought.

Library of Congress Cataloging-in-Publication Data:

The handbook of forensic psychology / Irving B. Weiner and Allen K.
  Hess. — 2nd ed.
    p. cm.
  Includes bibliographical references and index.
  ISBN 0-471-17771-7 (cloth : alk. paper)
   1. Psychology, Forensic—Handbooks, manuals, etc. I. Weiner,
Irving B. II. Hess, Allen K., 1945–
RA1148.H36   1999
614'.1—dc21   98-23732

Contributors

Anne M. Bartol, Ph.D.
Castleton State College
Castleton, Vermont

Curt R. Bartol, Ph.D.
Castleton State College
Castleton, Vermont

Paul Brinson, M.Ed.
Fort Worth, Texas

James N. Butcher, Ph.D.
University of Minnesota
Minneapolis, Minnesota

Christopher E. Chin, M.A.
Georgia State University
Atlanta, Georgia

Charles R. Clark, Ph.D.
Private Practice
Ann Arbor, Michigan

Simona Ghetti, M.A.
University of California
Davis, California

Stephen Golding, Ph.D.
University of Utah
Salt Lake City, Utah

Gail S. Goodman, Ph.D.
University of California
Davis, California

Annette Hahn, M.A.
University of Denver
Denver, Colorado

Alfred B. Heilbrun, Jr., Ph.D.
Emory University
Atlanta, Georgia

Allen K. Hess, Ph.D.
Auburn University-Montgomery
Montgomery, Alabama

Kathryn D. Hess, M.S., M.P.A.
Montgomery, Alabama

Larry Heuer, Ph.D.
Barnard College
Columbia University
New York, New York

Matthew T. Huss, M.S.
University of Nebraska-Lincoln
Lincoln, Nebraska

William G. Iacono, Ph.D.
University of Minnesota
Minneapolis, Minnesota

Thomas R. Litwack, J.D., Ph.D.
John Jay College of Criminal Justice
New York, New York

William L. Marshall, Ph.D.
Queen's University
Kingston, Canada

Joan McCord, Ph.D.
Temple University
Philadelphia, Pennsylvania

Gary B. Melton, Ph.D.
University of South Carolina
Columbia, South Carolina

Michael A. Milan, Ph.D.
Georgia State University
Atlanta, Georgia

Kathryn B. Miller, M.A.
University of Minnesota
Minneapolis, Minnesota

Max J. Mobley, Ph.D.
Department of Corrections
Pine Bluff, Arkansas

Quang Xuan Nguyen, M.A.
Georgia State University
Atlanta, Georgia

Christopher J. Patrick, Ph.D.
Florida State University
Tallahassee, Florida

Steven Penrod, J.D., Ph.D.
University of Nebraska-Lincoln
Lincoln, Nebraska

Jianjian Qin, M.A.
University of California
Davis, California

Allison D. Redlich, M.A.
University of California
Davis, California

Daniel J. Reschly, Ph.D.
Vanderbilt University
Nashville, Tennessee

Jennifer K. Robbennolt, J.D., Ph.D.
Princeton University
Princeton, New Jersey

Ronald Roesch, Ph.D.
Simon Fraser University
Burnaby, British Columbia

Jennifer M. Schaaf, M.A.
University of California
Davis, California

Alan W. Scheflin, LL.M.
Santa Clara University School of Law
Santa Clara, California

Louis B. Schlesinger, Ph.D.
University of Medicine and Dentistry
  of New Jersey
Newark, New Jersey

Jennifer L. Skeem, M.S.
University of Utah
Salt Lake City, Utah

Ralph Slovenko, J.D.
Wayne State University Law School
Detroit, Michigan

David Spiegel, M.D.
Stanford University School of Medicine
Stanford, California

Herbert Spiegel, M.D.
John Jay College of Criminal Justice
New York, New York

John T. Super, Ph.D.
Manatee Sheriff's Department
Bradenton, Florida

Alan J. Tomkins, J.D., Ph.D.
University of Nebraska-Lincoln
Lincoln, Nebraska

Kimberly S. Tyda, M.A.
University of California
Davis, California

Robert J. Van Der Velde, J.D.
Auburn University-Montgomery
Montgomery, Alabama

Irving B. Weiner, Ph.D.
University of South Florida
Tampa, Florida

Patricia A. Zapf, M.A.
Simon Fraser University
Burnaby, British Columbia

Preface

LIKE THE first edition of *The Handbook of Forensic Psychology*, the second edition is aimed at three audiences. We intend that professionals who want to develop expertise in the forensic application of their practices and who want to enhance the knowledge base of their current forensic practice will find the chapters fulfilling. We expect that scholars who need a reference or source book for the myriad of questions that arise in forensic psychology find thoughtful consideration given to the issues. We want students with a thirst for knowledge about the scholarship and applications of forensic psychology to be both fulfilled and stimulated to learn more after reading this book.

The preface to the first edition described forensic psychology as a "rapidly emerging professional specialty." Some 11 years later, we can confidently state that forensics is a maturing part of psychology. Forensic psychology can be defined by three aspects: (1) the application of basic psychological processes to legal questions; (2) research on legal issues, such as the definition of privacy or how juries make decisions; and (3) knowledge of legal issues.

Both law and psychology have been enriched by the application of psychological knowledge to legal issues. For example, no profession is more adept at examining physiological processes and determining whether we can detect truth and falsehood via lie detectors than can physiological psychologists. Who better than cognitive psychologists can determine the constancy and malleability of memory? Psychologists apply knowledge of child development and family dynamics to domestic law issues. Many chapters in this book are concerned with the artful application of basic science to the legal arena.

Other chapters concern the analysis of legal questions. For example, psychologists have examined the functioning of juries; translated the definitions of competency, diminished capacity, insanity, and disabilities into psychological terms; and conducted research on concepts of privacy, all of which are intended to articulate psychological research into a more just legal system.

Finally, psychologists have been concerned with how the law affects their clinical practice. For example, how does a psychotherapist decide that a client is dangerous and in need of extratherapeutic controls? What kinds of conflicts arise in marital or family therapy when divorce or custody proceedings intrude into the therapeutic efforts of the psychologist? What conflicts of interest arise when the psychologist is called to court, either as a fact witness or an expert witness?

This second edition has kept the same principles that guided the first edition. The chapters provide a comprehensive overview of the central topics in forensic psychology and detailed guidelines for the effective application of psychological knowledge to psycholegal practice. The authors were invited to write chapters based on their accomplishments as scholars and practitioners.

Before we began the second edition, we wanted to be sure there was enough new material to warrant a new edition. The chapters are not just updated versions of the first edition but have been rewritten. A cursory look at any chapter will show the largest number of references are within 5 to 10 years old. Each author reviewed the enduring issues but clothed these issues with the most recent developments in forensic psychology.

This book is organized in six parts. Part One, "The Context of Forensic Psychology," provides a historical account of forensic psychology, an analysis of how psychology and law are similar and how they clash, and a primer on how to navigate the legal literature. Part Two, "Applying Psychology to Civil Proceedings," addresses several key areas of practice including domestic law, educational handicaps and personal injury, and civil competency determinations. Part Three, "Applying Psychology to Criminal Proceedings," addresses assessing violence; evaluating eyewitness testimony; recommending probation and parole; assessing jury competence; determining criminal competency, capacity, and sanity; consulting with police; and understanding lie detection and hypnosis as applied to criminal justice questions. Part Four, "Communicating Expert Opinions," advises the reader about effectively presenting psychological information. Written reports for court can differ in crucial aspects from traditional clinical reports. Presentation of psychological data in legal arenas requires an examination of the relationship of the psychologist and the attorney who hired the psychologist, of the nature of psycholegal data and of how information can be potently presented in the court. Part Five, "Intervening with Offenders," reviews effective treatment programs, describes how to conduct psychotherapy with inmates, details the identification and rehabilitation of sex offenders, and provides a prevention philosophy that is interventive. Part Six, "Professional Issues," describes a framework for ethical practices in all phases of forensic psychology and depicts options available to those interested in education and training in forensic psychology.

We are grateful to a number of people including the scholars and practitioners who contributed to the rich and growing literature in forensic psychology. We were fortunate to have outstanding Wiley editors, Herb Reich, JoAnn Miller, and Kelly Franklin, working with us on the first and second editions. The chapter authors are fine representatives of our profession and made editing their chapters an enriching experience. We are most grateful for the support of our families throughout the project. Kathryn, Tanya, Clara, and Joel Hess provide a wellspring of support and intellectual stimulation of inestimable value.

ALLEN K. HESS
Montgomery, Alabama

IRVING B. WEINER
Tampa, Florida

Contents

PART ONE

THE CONTEXT OF FORENSIC PSYCHOLOGY

CHAPTER 1

History of Forensic Psychology

CURT R. BARTOL and ANNE M. BARTOL

In the introductory paragraph to our chapter in the first edition of this *Handbook,* we asserted that psychologists often do not care about the history of their profession and are, not infrequently, drawn to contemporary issues and theories, and even to fads. In the years since the first edition was published, it has become clear that psychologists do indeed care, as is apparent from the numerous articles published in professional journals. Nevertheless, many psychologists today would doubtless share the sentiments of Stanley Brodsky (1996), who candidly began a recent article with the comment: "I am a dreadful historian" (p. 5). Brodsky proceeded to demonstrate, however, through his insights into earlier events, that he was not a dreadful historian at all. In fact, Brodsky has played a key role in the history of forensic psychology, a topic we will return to later.

Psychology, like all disciplines, needs to be aware of its past. It needs to understand whence it came in order to assess where it is going. A perusal of journals and books published at the turn of the 20th century, for example, may spark interest in a concept long forgotten or a predecessor whose theories and research deserve to be revisited. On the other hand, delving into early works like that of Henry H. Goddard (1914) is a sober reminder of the damage that can be wrought in the exercise of professional skills.

Forensic psychology is being viewed broadly here. It is both (a) the research endeavor that examines aspects of human behavior directly related to the legal process (e.g., eyewitness memory and testimony, jury decision making, or criminal behavior), and (b) the professional practice of psychology within or in consultation with a legal system that encompasses both criminal and civil law and the numerous areas where they intersect. Therefore, forensic psychology refers broadly to the *production* and *application* of psychological knowledge to the civil and criminal justice systems. As such, it includes activities as varied as courtroom testimony, performing child custody evaluations, screening of law enforcement candidates, provision of clinical services to offenders and staff in correctional facilities, research and theory building in the area of criminal behavior, and the design and implementation of intervention and prevention programs for youthful offenders.

Forensic psychology is distinguished from forensic psychiatry, which has its own rich and well-documented history. This chapter reviews the achievements of psychologists from the end of the 19th century to the late 1970s, when forensic psychology came of age (Loh, 1981). In the early years, European psychologists dominated the field, and some of their work will be highlighted. Beginning with World War I, the review will focus on the forensic psychology discussed and practiced on this continent. Readers interested in more detail about the issues and individuals discussed might check landmark summaries of psychology and law published by Whipple (1909, 1910, 1911, 1912, 1913, 1914, 1915, 1917), Hutchins and Slesinger (1929), Louisell (1955, 1957), Tapp (1976), Loh (1981), and Monahan and Loftus (1982).

IN THE BEGINNING

Do chestnut or oak trees lose their leaves earlier in autumn?
Do horses in the field stand with head or tail to the wind?
In which direction do the seeds of an apple point?
What was the weather one week ago today?

When J. McKeen Cattell posed these questions to 56 college students at Columbia University in March 1893, he was probably conducting one of the first studies, albeit an informal one, on the psychology of testimony. The questions he asked his students were similar to those that "might naturally be asked in a court of justice" (Cattell, 1895, p. 761). His subjects were allowed 30 seconds to consider their answers, then told to write their responses. They were also asked to indicate their degree of confidence in each answer.

When Cattell conducted his informal study, it was reasonably well established that courtroom eyewitness testimony was unreliable and incomplete. French and German psychologists were familiar with the powerful influence of suggestion over sensation and perception. The specific conditions under which testimony was inaccurate were not known, however. Furthermore, as Cattell (1895) noted, "An unscrupulous attorney can discredit the statements of a truthful witness by cunningly selected questions. The jury, or at least the judge, should know how far errors in recollection are normal and how they vary under different conditions" (p. 761). But Cattell himself was surprised at both the degree of inaccuracy he uncovered and the wide range of individual differences in the levels of confidence expressed by the students. Answers to the weather question, for example, were "equally distributed over all kinds of weather which are possible at the beginning of March" (p. 761). Some subjects were nearly always sure they were correct, even when they were not; others were consistently uncertain and hesitant in their answers, even when they were correct.

Cattell's study probably was the genesis of modern forensic psychology, because it sparked the interest of other researchers in the psychology of testimony. Joseph Jastrow immediately replicated Cattell's "experiment" at the

University of Wisconsin and obtained similar results (Bolton, 1896). Aside from this brief flirtation, however, American psychologists did not immediately embrace the study of legal issues.

Psychologists in Europe seemed more intrigued. First, Alfred Binet (1900) replicated Cattell's project in France. In addition, he summarized relevant experiments on the psychology of testimony that were being conducted in Europe and called for a *"science psycho-judiciaire"* (Binet, 1905; Binet & Clarparede, 1906). Most significant for the historical development of forensic psychology, however, was the apparent fascination Cattell's experiment and Binet's work held for (Louis) William Stern, who had received his PhD in psychology at the University of Berlin under the tutelage of Herman Ebbinghaus. In 1901, Stern collaborated with the criminologist F. V. Liszt in an attempt to lend realism to the Cattell design. Stern and Liszt conducted a "reality experiment" in a law class, staging a bogus quarrel between two students over a scientific controversy. The argument accelerated until one student drew a revolver (Stern, 1939). At this point, the professor intervened and asked for written and oral reports from the class about aspects of the dispute. Although the witnesses were law students who, Stern asserted, should have known the pitfalls of testifying, none could give a faultless report. The number of errors per individual ranged from 4 to 12. Moreover, the researchers found that inaccuracies increased with respect to the second half of the scenario, when excitement and tension were at their peak. They concluded—tentatively—that "emotions reduce accuracy of recall."

Stern became an active researcher in the psychology of testimony over the next few years (1906, 1910). He also helped establish the first journal on the psychology of testimony, *Betrage zur Psychollogie der Aussage* (Contributions to the Psychology of Testimony), which he edited and which was published at Leipzig. The journal was superseded in 1908 by the much broader *Zeitschrift fur Angewande Psychologie*, the first journal of applied psychology. In his *Aussage* research, Stern concluded, among other things, that "subjective sincerity" does not guarantee "objective truthfulness"; that leading and suggestive questions contaminate the accuracy of eyewitness accounts of critical events; that there are important differences between adult and child witnesses; that lineups are of limited value when the members are not matched for age and physical appearance; and that interceding events between an initial event and its recall can have drastic effects on memory. It can be concluded, therefore, that modern forensic psychology began with empirical research on the psychology of testimony.

As a parallel phenomenon, European, particularly German, psychologists at the turn of the century were beginning to be used as "expert witnesses" in criminal cases, and they often applied the knowledge gained from the newly established psychological laboratory. They testified both on matters of fact, such as reporting the results of a particular experiment, and on matters of opinion. Perhaps the earliest such testimony occurred in 1896, when Albert von Schrenck-Notzing testified at the trial of a Munich man accused of murdering three women (Hale, 1980). The murders had received extensive and sensational press coverage in the months prior to the trial, and Schrenck-Notzing (1897) opined that this pretrial publicity, through a process of suggestion, probably led numerous witnesses to "retroactive memory-falsification."

Witnesses could not distinguish between what they had seen and what the press reported had happened. He supported his opinion with accounts of laboratory research on memory and suggestibility. Although the accused was convicted on the basis of solid evidence, Schrenck-Notzing's direct application of the psychology of suggestion to court processes helped stimulate the interest of German jurists and psychologists (Hale, 1980).

European psychologists at the turn of the 20th century and until World War I also were delving into the area of guilt deception, the precursor of the lie detection of today. In 1904, psychologists in Germany, Austria, and Switzerland were developing a lie detection test for use in criminal investigations. The test was a word association/reaction time task, and key words were embedded in a list of innocuous words. Presumably, the slower the reaction time in recognizing the key words, the more likely the respondent was lying. Barland (1988), who has reviewed this history in impressive detail, notes that this approach did not catch on. It was inefficient and time consuming, and it often yielded inconclusive results.

This chapter reviews developments in five major areas of forensic psychology: (a) courtroom testimony, (b) cognitive and personality assessment, (c) correctional psychology, (d) police psychology, and (e) criminal psychology. Readers will undoubtedly recognize a considerable overlap in some of these categories.

COURTROOM TESTIMONY

American psychologists at the turn of the 20th century remained comparatively uninterested in applying research on topics related to law. They were just beginning to explore the broad psychological landscape and had little inclination to specialize in law-related matters. This reticence was probably also an effect of the influence of Wilhelm Wundt, who had trained many of the American pioneers in his Leipzig laboratory (Cattell being the first). Wundt, a philosopher and an experimentalist, was wary of applying psychology before sufficient research had been conducted. He believed that the premature use of partial information could be disastrous. His students often took this caveat quite seriously, although some, like Cattell, eventually began to link the laboratory to the world outside.

One of Wundt's not-so-cautious students was the German psychologist Hugo Munsterberg, who arrived in the United States in 1892 (at the invitation of William James) to direct the psychology laboratory at Harvard University. Munsterberg spent 24 years, until his sudden death in December 1916, trying to persuade the public that psychology had something to offer virtually every area of human endeavor. Now acknowledged as the father of applied psychology, he believed psychological knowledge could be applied to education, industry, advertising, music, art, and, of course, law. His claims were often exaggerated, however, and his proposals were rarely empirically based. He usually published in popular magazines rather than scholarly journals (some of his colleagues called his a "Sunday-supplement psychology"). He also incessantly promoted himself and his native Germany, a practice that alienated him increasingly from his colleagues and the public as World War I approached. Not surprisingly, the legal community vehemently resisted his intrusion into its territory (Hale, 1980). The great legal commentator John H. Wigmore found it necessary to assail Munsterberg in a satirical and devastating law review article (Wigmore, 1909). Wigmore's attack was prompted by the publication of Munsterberg's controversial best-seller *On the Witness Stand* (1908), in which Munsterberg proclaimed that the time was ripe to apply psychology to the practical needs of the legal system.

In 1914, Munsterberg published a study of group decision making. He used Harvard and Radcliffe students as subjects for the work, which he titled "The Mind of the Juryman." In a conclusion not atypical of the times, he commented that "the psychologist has every reason to be satisfied with the jury system as long as the women are kept out of it" (1914, p. 202; cited in Moskowitz, 1977). He based his conclusion on a finding that the female students in his study were less accurate in their final decisions than the male students. Interestingly, as will be noted shortly, one of his own students later arrived at a very different conclusion.

Munsterberg has been accused of being more an opportunist than a trailblazer (Kuna, 1978), and it is tempting to blame his brashness for the tenuous and occasionally hostile initial relationship between psychology and law. Nonetheless, he undeniably pushed his reluctant American colleagues into the practical legal arena and made a seminal contribution to forensic psychology. Readers are left to make their own judgments as to whether his contributions represent a false start.

During these years, European psychologists continued to interact much more regularly with the legal system than their American counterparts. In 1911, several psychologists testified at a Belgian murder trial in which a man was accused of raping and killing a nine-year-old girl. Two of the child's playmates had apparently seen the murderer but gave inconsistent and contradictory accounts. Among the psychologists retained by the defense was J. Varendonck, who designed a series of experiments based on questions suggested by information obtained at the preliminary hearing. Varendonck's subjects were children of approximately the same age as the two witnesses (ages 8 to 10). He found they were inaccurate in their recall of important events. Over the objection of the prosecution, he was allowed to present the results of these experiments as well as the general research on the psychology of testimony that was available at that time. The jury found the defendant not guilty.

Varendonck, it should be noted, was vehemently opposed to *any* use of child witnesses in the courtroom. In contrast, both Binet (1900) and Stern (1939) believed that errors in recollection, whether by children or adults, were more a reflection of leading and suggestive courtroom questioning than of any "natural" tendency to distort reality.

In 1922, Karl Marbe, a psychology professor at the University of Wurzburg, became the first psychologist to testify at a civil trial. He offered an expert opinion on the psychological issue of reaction times as applied to a train wreck near Mullheim. Professor Marbe was asked to testify as to the probable effect of alcohol both on the mental status of the engineer and on the reaction time of the fireman and guard applying the brakes. Based on reaction-time experiments, Marbe testified that the train could not have been stopped in time to avert a disaster. During the same year, Marbe also testified in a criminal trial similar to the one in which Varendonck had challenged the credibility of child witnesses. Several German adolescent girls had accused their teacher of sexually molesting them. Marbe persuaded the jury that the statements of the girls were unreliable, and the teacher was exonerated.

World War I placed in abeyance most of the exploration in applying psychology to law, although the war and early postwar years saw a few landmarks in American forensic psychology, including the gradual acceptance of psychologists as expert witnesses, particularly on matters of fact. The first psychologists were also appointed to law school faculties during these years.

Psychologist Donald Slesinger, a protégé of Robert M. Hutchins, made his mark during the years immediately following World War I. Although he had no formal legal training, Slesinger was appointed by Acting Dean Hutchins as a one-year Sterling Fellow to the Yale Law School in 1927. The following year he became a research assistant. In 1929, he was appointed associate professor and taught a course in the psychology of evidence, which appears to qualify him as the first psychologist granted faculty status in an American law school. In 1930, Slesinger followed Hutchins to the University of Chicago where he served as Professor of Law, and, briefly, as Dean of the Law School.

Several years earlier, psychologist William Marston had been the first to receive a faculty appointment as Professor of Legal Psychology. He joined the faculty at American University in 1922. Marston was by far the most influential psychologist associated with the legal system during this era. A student of Munsterberg but without his mentor's penchant for alienating the legal community, he received a law degree in 1918 and a PhD in 1921, both from Harvard. Marston's interests were multifaceted. He was even the originator, cartoonist, and producer of the successful comic strip "Wonder Woman," under the pen name of Charles Moulton—a dubious distinction, to be sure. Although admitted to the Massachusetts bar, Marston soon gave up his law practice to concentrate on psychology.

As a laboratory assistant in psychology at Radcliffe College, Marston had discovered a significant positive correlation between systolic blood pressure and lying (Marston, 1917), which became the basis of the modern polygraph. Although his continuing work in lie detection (Marston 1920, 1921, 1925) represents one of his major contributions to the forensic area, it was by no means the only one. He frequently consulted with attorneys, police, and other criminal justice personnel, and his evidence was determinative in the acquittals of several defendants accused of murder. It is likely, therefore, that Marston, along with Terman and psychologists associated with the New York City Psychopathic Clinic, qualifies as one of the first psychological consultants to the criminal justice system, particularly to law enforcement.

Marston also conducted the first serious research on the jury system (Winick, 1961). Using subjects in simulated jury conditions, he found in a series of studies (Marston, 1924) that written evidence was superior to oral evidence; that free narration, while less complete, was more accurate than cross examination or direct questioning; that a witness's caution in answering was a good indicator of accuracy; and that female jurors considered evidence more carefully than male jurors (contrast with Munsterberg's conclusions about female jurors, mentioned earlier). Because of his legal background and his cautious style, Marston's ideas and research were more acceptable to the legal community than Munsterberg's had been, although there is little evidence that the legal system put his findings to extensive use. This is not surprising because his recommendations, had they been implemented, would have required fundamental changes in court procedures and were inapposite to the adversarial process.

Legal Psychology: Taking Stock

Throughout the development of forensic psychology, various reviewers took on the task of documenting its progress. Hutchins and Slesinger, for example, coauthored numerous summary articles on the status of legal psychology (1927, 1928a, 1928b, 1928c, 1929). Slesinger, with Marion Pilpel in 1929, surveyed 48 articles written by psychologists on issues relating to forensic psychology that had appeared in professional journals up to that time. Eleven were concerned with the psychology of testimony, ten with deception, seven with intelligence and crime, and six with criminal behavior. The remainder focused on general topics such as the scientific method or legal research. Fifteen of the 48 articles had been written by German psychologists.

Like applied psychology in general, forensic psychology experienced some remission between the two world wars and did not recoup its energy until the late 1940s and 1950s. In addition to Marston's work, the period did see scattered research by Weld (Weld & Danzig, 1940; Weld & Roff, 1938) on how juries formed opinions and verdicts, a master's thesis on the relationship between narrative and interrogative methods of questioning (Cady, 1924), another study on questioning and testimony (Snee & Lush, 1941), and a survey of legal and psychological opinions about the validity of some of Wigmore's rules of evidence (Britt, 1940).

Loh (1981) notes a revived interest in psychology and law during the late 1920s and the 1930s, but this interest was almost exclusively on the part of lawyers, who produced such books as *Legal Psychology* (Brown, 1926), *Psychology for the Lawyer* (McCarty, 1929), and *Law and the Social Sciences* (Cairns, 1935). Wigmore (1940), the foremost authority on rules of evidence, paved the way for the use of test data in the courtroom, noting that the psychometrist introducing test evidence would stand "on the same footing as the expert witness to insanity" (cited by McCary, 1956, p. 9), as long as such tests were recognized as valid and feasible by the general scientific community.

In 1931, Howard Burtt (who was also a former student of Munsterberg) wrote *Legal Psychology*—the first textbook in the area written by a psychologist. Burtt's primary interest was industrial psychology, however, and he himself did not conduct much research on legal issues. Although the book made a valuable contribution to the academic psychological literature, it had little discernible influence on the legal profession or on applied psychology in general. In 1935, Edward S. Robinson published *Law and the Lawyers*, which predicted that jurisprudence would become one of the family of social sciences and argued that all of its fundamental concepts must be brought into line with psychological knowledge. The book was lambasted by lawyers and essentially ignored by psychologists. In hindsight, contemporary scholars have found Robinson's ideas much more palatable (e.g., Horowitz & Willging, 1984; Loh, 1981).

Acceptance of Psychologists as Expert Witnesses

It is generally believed that American psychologists have served as expert witnesses since the early 1920s (Comment, 1979), but, as we have seen, they clearly provided information to the courts, particularly the civil courts, before that time. According to Rogers (1910, 1918), the results of experimental research on visual perception were routinely accepted in trademark infringement cases, although not necessarily in the form of direct testimony. This was apparently considered a "safe" undertaking, since the psychologists were not infringing on the territory of the "medical experts"—physicians and psychiatrists—who routinely testified on matters of criminal responsibility. As Louisell (1955) notes, however, because trial court records are generally unavailable and only appellate decisions are published, the testimony of psychologists, particularly in civil cases, may have been less rare than the paucity of documentation would indicate. We do know that psychological testimony was almost inevitably *rejected* in criminal cases involving the defendant's mental state. "As a general rule, only medical men—that is, persons licensed by law to practice the profession of medicine—can testify as experts on the question of insanity; and the propriety of this general limitation is too patent to permit discussion" (*Odom v. State*, 1911; cited in Comment, 1979, n. 14).

The first published case in which an American psychologist qualified as an expert appears to be *State v. Driver* in 1921. The occasion was only a partial victory for forensic psychology, however. A West Virginia trial court accepted the chief psychologist of the State Bureau of Juvenile Research as an expert on the matter of juvenile delinquency. However, it rejected his testimony, based on psychological test data, that a 12-year-old attempted-rape victim was a "moron" (an unfortunate term coined by Henry H. Goddard, who will be discussed below) and could not be presumptively believed. In agreeing with the trial court, the West Virginia Supreme Court noted: "It is yet to be demonstrated that psychological and medical tests are practical, and will detect the lie on the witness stand" (*State v. Driver*, 1921, p. 488). Although some commentators interpreted *Driver* as a major loss for psychologists wishing to achieve status as expert witnesses, Louisell (1955) noted that the decision was not a rejection of psychologists per se, but only of the particular evidence offered by one psychologist. Nevertheless, it was not until much later, specifically the 1940s and 1950s, that psychologists testified in courts of law on a regular basis, at least in some jurisdictions.

Loh (1981) attributes this acceptance to an increase in professionalization, "the rapid growth of mental health professions during this period, and the formulation of legal doctrines of insanity consistent with modern psychiatry" (p. 323). Psychologists offered opinions and presented data relevant to subjects as diverse as the influence of pretrial publicity on potential witnesses and juries, the effects of pornography on adolescents, the effect of certain educational practices on children, and the likely influence of advertisements on consumers (Greenberg, 1956; Loh, 1981; Louisell, 1955). This is not to say that there was widespread acceptance of the idea that psychologists deserved a niche in the courtroom. Resistance to the idea, or at best a cautious approach, consistently characterized much of the legal literature (Comment, 1979).

In the early 1940s and the postwar era, appellate courts began to support the use of qualified psychologists as expert witnesses on the issue of mental responsibility for criminal and tortious conduct. The first influential decision was *People v. Hawthorne* (1940), a Michigan case. Hawthorne had been tried for the murder of his wife's lover and had pleaded not guilty by reason of insanity. The trial court refused to qualify as an expert witness a professor of psychology from Michigan State Normal College who had a PhD and an impressive list of credentials. In finding that the trial court had erred in not accepting the psychologist as an expert, the Michigan Supreme Court ruled that the standard for determining expert status was not a medical degree but the extent of the witness's knowledge. It advised trial courts to evaluate carefully the merits of a potential witness's claim to expertise, noting that the psychologist's ability to detect insanity could not be presumed inferior to that of a "medical man." The dissenters, however, believed that because insanity was a disease, only a person with medical training should qualify as an expert.

Later, in *Hidden v. Mutual Life Insurance Co.* (1954), the Fourth Circuit Court of Appeals allowed psychological expertise to be applied to a *civil* case. The insured argued that a disabling nervous condition prevented him from engaging in any gainful occupation and entitled him to disability benefits. A clinical psychologist with a doctoral degree administered a battery of projective tests and testified on his behalf. Not only did he report on the test results, but he also gave the opinion that the plaintiff deserved the benefits. When the lawyer for the insurance company objected, the trial judge instructed the jury to disregard the entire opinion testimony on the grounds that the psychologist did not qualify as an expert. The Fourth Circuit Court of Appeals ruled that the psychologist should have been qualified as an expert to express his opinion about the plaintiff's mental condition.

While some psychologists were struggling to be accepted as experts on questions of mental status, competence, and criminal responsibility, others during this era were joining the crucial legal battle against school segregation by testifying and consulting with attorneys in the numerous state cases that would ultimately culminate in the 1954 landmark ruling, *Brown v. Board of Education*. Richard Kluger (1975), in his informative and exhaustive case study, details the contributions of psychologists and other social scientists. David Krech and Helen Trager, social psychologists who had published articles on racial attitude tests, and Horace B. English, an expert on child psychology, testified at some of the school segregation trials. The most noteworthy contribution was that of Kenneth Clark and Mamie Clark, who conducted the now-famous "doll research" to gauge the effects of segregation. Kenneth Clark then gave factual testimony reporting the results of this research (Kluger, 1975). When the NAACP, appealed *Brown* and three other segregation cases to the U.S. Supreme Court, Kenneth Clark coordinated the social science involvement in the brief-writing process, which culminated in the now-famous "Social Science Appendix."

Meanwhile, psychologists were continuing to make enough inroads testifying on the issue of criminal responsibility that psychiatrists felt the need to protect their turf. In 1954, the Council of the American Psychiatric Association, the Executive Council of the American Psychoanalytical Association, and the American Medical Association joined in the resolution stating that only physicians were legitimate experts in the field of mental illness for purposes of courtroom testimony. Other individuals could participate only if their testimony was coordinated by medical authority. The resolution greatly influenced trial courts (Miller, Lower, & Bleechmore, 1978), which became reluctant to accept independent psychological testimony.

Finally, in *Jenkins v. United States* (1962), the Court of Appeals for the District of Columbia gave its own direct, although conditional, support to the use of psychologists as experts on the issue of mental illness. Although the court was sharply divided, its decision remains the predominant authority for the use of psychologists in the area of criminal responsibility.

COGNITIVE AND PERSONALITY ASSESSMENT

During the years in which Munsterberg was proselytizing about psychology's usefulness in the courtroom, another American psychologist was quietly making inroads into a different forensic area. In 1909, clinical psychologist Grace M. Fernald worked with psychiatrist William Healy to establish the first clinic specifically designed for youthful offenders: the Juvenile Psychopathic Institute. It was initially developed to serve the newly established Juvenile Court of Chicago by offering clinical diagnoses of "problem" children. Fernald, who received her doctorate from the University of Chicago in 1907, was probably the first clinical psychologist to work under the supervision of a psychiatrist (Napoli, 1981), as well as one of the earliest psychologists to specialize in the diagnosis and treatment of juvenile delinquency. The Institute, which extended its services rapidly to include treatment and research as well as diagnoses, became a public agency in 1914 and was renamed the Institute for Juvenile Research.

Fernald and Healy used the relatively new Stanford–Binet Intelligence Scale to test delinquents, but they soon realized the importance of obtaining "performance" measures as well. This prompted them to develop the Healy–Fernald series of 23 performance tests, which they began to use in 1911. The two eventually went their separate ways. Fernald became a specialist in mental deficiency and testing and taught psychology at UCLA for 27 years, until her retirement in 1948.

During the first third of the 20th century, most psychologists providing services to the courts were psychometrists associated with clinics. The drudgery of day-to-day testing (often under the watchful eyes of a physician or psychiatrist) made applied psychology, as it was then known, less than appealing as a profession. Often, however, it was the place where female psychologists were most accepted. In the 1930s, for example, fewer than one-third of all American psychologists were women, but women comprised over 60% of all applied psychologists (Napoli, 1981).

The work of Henry H. Goddard during this time period must be regarded with embarrassment. A student of G. Stanley Hall, Goddard paved the way for the massive intelligence testing of immigrants, residents of mental institutions, prisons, and juvenile training schools. His followers consulted with the juvenile courts and dutifully administered these tests to the children of the poor who arrived at their door. Goddard's warning that "feeble-minded" individuals should not be allowed to roam about freely in society because of their innate proclivity toward antisocial behavior contributed significantly to the continual incarceration of individuals during their reproductive periods as well as to the sterilization of residents in juvenile facilities (Kelves, 1984).

CORRECTIONAL PSYCHOLOGY

Lindner (1955) pinpoints 1913 as the date of the first instance of psychological services being offered within a U.S. correctional facility—specifically, a women's reformatory in New York State. The precise nature of the services and the identity of the psychologist(s) who provided them are not known. In December 1916, a psychopathic laboratory was established at the New York City Police Department for the express purpose of examining persons detained before trial (Keller, 1918). The staff included psychiatrists, neurologists, social workers, and psychologists; their task was to conduct hasty pretrial evaluations. According to E. I. Keller, a consulting psychologist to the clinic, detainees arrived for testing at 9 A.M. "The disadvantage is the lack of time, for all prisoners [sic] must be examined in time to get them to court by noon or earlier, and many courts are situated in distant parts of the city" (p. 85). Staff members had to conduct the evaluation in less than three hours.

The main function of psychologists employed in some capacity in the state and federal correctional systems during the 1910s and early 1920s was apparently the detection of "feeblemindedness" among offenders, a condition thought to lead to a life of crime (Giardini, 1942; Watkins, 1992). The first inmate classification system developed by psychologists in the United States was apparently instituted in New Jersey in 1918 (Barnes & Teeters, 1959; Watkins, 1992). New Jersey also became the first state to hire a full-time correctional psychologist. The first state to provide comprehensive psychological examinations as part of all admissions to its prison system and all applications for parole was Wisconsin in 1924 (Bodemar, 1956).

In the late 1930s, Darley and Berdie (1940) surveyed 13 federal and 123 state prisons and learned that they employed a total of 64 psychologists who called themselves "prison psychologists." Although all considered themselves clinical psychologists, only about half had PhD's in psychology. Later, Raymond Corsini (1945) expressed concern that there was as yet "no history of prison psychology." He estimated that during the 1940s approximately 200,000 individuals were confined in U.S. correctional facilities, and they were served by a mere 80 psychologists. Their work consisted of (a) testing (personality, aptitude, and academic progress); (b) giving educational, vocational, and personal guidance (usually at the inmates' request); and (c) maintaining working relationships with all members of the prison staff.

Psychological services to corrections facilities in Canada appeared much later, perhaps not until the early 1950s. Watkins (1992) notes that Canadian correctional psychology made its first appearance in the literature in 1952 in a series of newsletters published by the Ontario Psychological Association. The newsletters focused on psychology within the Ontario provincial corrections programs and the national correctional service. The first correctional psychologist employed in the national system in Canada was in 1955 at St. Vincent de Paul Penitentiary (later renamed Laval Institution) in the province of Quebec (Watkins, 1992). Interestingly, correctional psychologists in Canada were employed primarily to classify inmates and were usually not a component of the mental health treatment afforded to inmates.

In the 1960s, correctional psychology as a subdiscipline of forensic psychology began to emerge. Although there were exceptions, psychologists in correctional facilities had thus far focused more on classification than on treatment, because the demand for diagnostic services was great and the obstacles relative to respecting confidentiality and achieving the trust of inmates were difficult to surmount. In the 1960s, rehabilitation as a correctional goal gained favor, and positions for psychologists increased. The turnover rate was high, primarily because psychologists often had not received proper preparation for this environment (Watkins, 1992).

Stanley Brodsky, probably more than any other single individual, was most instrumental in launching modern correctional psychology and providing it with consistent support. His two-year term as president of the American Association of Correctional Psychologists (AACP) helped provide the impetus to move correctional psychology into a recognized and viable profession. During 1972 and 1973, the AACP played a key role in setting up a series of conferences on psychologists in the criminal justice system. The proceedings were published in a landmark volume edited by Brodsky (1973): *Psychologists in the Criminal Justice System*. The publication date of this influential book could arguably be called the official launch date of modern correctional psychology. Brodsky also became the founding editor of the international journal *Criminal Justice and Behavior*, launched in 1974 and sponsored by the AACP. Brodsky's leadership and enthusiasm also helped build, at the University of Alabama, one of the earliest doctoral programs specifically designed to prepare clinical psychologists to work within the criminal justice system.

Robert Levinson, in the Federal Bureau of Prisons, and Asher Pacht, in Wisconsin, also made noteworthy contributions. Pacht created a model, widely used today, whereby mental health services were integrated completely into a state prison system. Levinson, as the first Chief of Psychology Services in the Federal Bureau of Prisons, launched an objective classification system for security and custody purposes, developed unit management, and implemented Herbert C. Quay's Adult Internal Management System (AIMS) in corrections. Pacht's and Levinson's approaches have since been adopted both nationally and internationally in a variety of correctional settings.

Under Levinson's leadership, the Federal Bureau of Prisons began to employ at least one full-time psychologist at every major federal facility and to hire new staff at the doctoral level. Paid summer internships were also offered to students in doctoral programs in psychology as inducement to learn about opportunities in correctional settings (Levinson, personal communication, July 1, 1997).

Interestingly, Levinson saw the role of psychologists in corrections as more akin to community psychology than to clinical psychology. The prison setting demanded more than doing private practice in a clinical setting. This community model helped take correctional psychology away from the medical umbrella and the oversight of the psychiatric profession. Correctional psychologists in the Federal Bureau of Prisons became part of the Correctional Programs Division, where they offered not only clinical but also educational, classification, and research services.

POLICE PSYCHOLOGY

Louis Terman (1917) was the first American psychologist to use "mental tests" as screening devices in the selection of law enforcement personnel. On October 31, 1916, at the request of the city manager of San Jose, California, he administered an abbreviated form of the Stanford–Binet to 30 police and fire department applicants. They ranged in age from 21 to 38, with a median age of 30. Only four had attended high school, and none had gone beyond the sophomore year. Terman found that most of the applicants functioned near the dull-normal range of intelligence (68–84 on the Stanford revision of the Binet–Simon Intelligence Scale); only three obtained an IQ over 100, the score considered average for the general population. Based on his experience with the intellectual capabilities of school-age children, Terman suggested—somewhat arbitrarily—that applicants with IQs under 80 were not fit for police work or firefighting. The city manager agreed, and 10 applicants were immediately excluded from further consideration.

A contemporary of Terman, psychologist Louis Thurstone, was also interested in the value of mental testing to police screening. Thurstone (1922) administered the newly developed Army Intelligence Examination (Army Alpha) to 358 members of the Detroit Police Department, all of whom were male. Officers at all ranks scored below average; in fact, the more experienced the police officer, the lower was his intelligence score. The average score for the 307 patrol officers was 71.44; the 34 sergeants averaged 54.71; and the 17 lieutenants averaged 57.80 (Army Alpha mean = 100, standard deviation of 15). Thurstone concluded that law enforcement did not attract intelligent individuals. He also surmised that the more intelligent individuals who entered police service left for other occupations where their abilities and intelligence were better utilized.

Law enforcement officers were vindicated somewhat, however, when Maude A. Merrill (1927) administered the Army Alpha to a group of already employed officers and applicants. They scored at the average level (the sample's mean IQ was 104). The differences between her findings and those of Terman and Thurstone were probably due to department leadership factors, recruitment procedures, and selection ratios (Terrio, Swanson, & Chamelin, 1977).

In the years between the two World Wars, psychologists gradually became more involved in the screening of law enforcement personnel. Wilmington, Delaware, and Toledo, Ohio, appear to share the distinction of being the first two cities to require ongoing psychological screening for use in police selection, in the form of mental and personality tests (Gottesman, 1975; Oglesby, 1957). The year was 1938.

The aforementioned psychologists were among the first to study the cognitive capacities of police officers and candidates, but there is no indication that they consistently participated in the screening and selection of law enforcement personnel. At this point, we have no information about who might have been the first psychologist to assume this regular role. As late as 1939, Donald Paterson (1940) could identify only one professional psychologist—L. J. O'Rourke—who had actively investigated the validity of the civil service examination system, even though the Civil Service Commission had adopted routine competitive exams as far back as 1883.

During the late 1940s and the 1950s, psychologists continued to consult with police departments. The psychological screening initiated by the Wilmington and Toledo Police Departments was adopted by other cities: Jacksonville in 1947, Berkeley in 1949, Oakland in 1950, New Orleans in 1952, and Pasadena, Philadelphia, Milwaukee, and Cleveland in 1953 (Gottesman, 1975; Oglesby, 1957). In June 1952, the Los Angeles Police Department began to administer a battery of psychological tests (MMPI and Rorschach) and a psychological interview (Rankin, 1957, 1959). The 1957 Rankin article was the first to appear in the literature attesting to any ongoing program of psychological assessment for police applicants (Gottesman, 1975).

During the late 1960s, personality assessment, psychological screening, and police psychology in general received an immense boost when the President's Commission on Law Enforcement and the Administration of Justice (1967) strongly recommended widespread use of psychological measures to determine the emotional stability of all potential officers. This recommendation was followed by the 1968 National Advisory Commission on Civil Disorder's strong endorsement that psychological screening would improve the emotional quality of individuals entering law enforcement (Scrivner, 1994). In keeping with the Commission's recommendations, Congress provided funds through the Law Enforcement Assistance Administration (LEAA) for law enforcement agencies to retain the services of mental health professionals. In 1973, the Police Task Force Report of the National Commission on Criminal Justice Standards and Goals encouraged the establishment of a behavioral sciences unit or consultant for all law enforcement agencies.

Shortly before then, in December 1968, Matin Reiser was hired by the Los Angeles Police Department as a full-time police psychologist. The evidence to date indicates that Reiser was the first full-time psychologist whose responsibilities were strictly police-related. Reiser himself (1982) is not entirely certain that he was the first full-time police psychologist in the country. In 1969, he presented a paper at the Western Psychological Association Convention in

Vancouver, entitled "The Police Department Psychologist." This presentation may represent the "official" launch of contemporary North American police psychology. The paper was published in 1972. Reiser continued to be the most prolific writer on police psychology during the early 1970s. In 1972, in cooperation with the California School of Professional Psychology and the Los Angeles Police Department, he helped establish what is believed to be the first clinical internship in police psychology in the United States. By 1977, at least six other law enforcement agencies had hired full-time psychologists (Reese, 1986, 1987).

Viteles (1929) noted that police departments in Germany were using psychologists in a variety of capacities as early as 1919. Chandler (1990) reports that, in 1966, the Munich Municipal Police Department employed a full-time in-house psychologist to train officers to deal with various problems they encountered while on patrol.

CRIMINAL PSYCHOLOGY

In the early years of the 20th century, psychologists began to offer psychological perspectives on criminal behavior and to speculate about the causes of crime. Given the extensive early emphasis on testing, it is not surprising that the theories often centered on the measurable mental capacities of offenders.

Psychologists like Goddard had repeatedly found that most juvenile and adult offenders were mentally deficient, which led to the conclusion that a primary "cause" of crime and delinquency was intellectual limitation. In large part, this belief reflected the pervasive influence of Darwinism, which contended that humans differ only in degree from their animal brethren (and that some humans were closer to their animal ancestry than others). The mentally deficient were considered both intellectually and morally less capable of adapting to modern society. Thus, they presumably resorted to more "primitive" ways of meeting their needs, such as crime. These unfortunate conclusions, which did not take into account social conditions, cultural differences, or socialization processes, lent support to unconscionable practices such as lengthy incarcerations of the disadvantaged, confused, and powerless.

In the history of psychology, few scholars have ventured to offer comprehensive theories on crime or delinquent behavior. Those who have (e.g., Eysenck, 1964) were often strongly influenced by Darwinian thinking. Therefore, theoretical orientations focusing on mental deficiency or biological and constitutional dispositions have dominated early psychological criminology.

In the early 1960s, a psychological criminology distinct from psychiatric and more extensive than psychometrics began to show signs of life. Hans Toch (1961), who was also making significant contributions to correctional psychology, edited one of the first books on psychological criminology: *Legal and Criminal Psychology*. Some may argue that Hans Gross published the first criminal psychology book in 1898 *(Kriminal psychologie)*, the same year in which he was appointed Professor in Ordinary for Criminal Law and Justice Administration at the University of Czernowitz. However, Gross was a lawyer—by training, in practice, and in spirit—and eventually became a successful judge.

His book details his observations of offenders, witnesses, jurors, and judges, but relies very little on psychological research. This is not surprising; psychology in 1898 was far from being an integrated discipline with a rich body of knowledge. Nevertheless, it is significant that Toch's book, published over 60 years later, represents the earliest attempt to integrate, in an interdisciplinary fashion, the empirical research of psychologists relevant to criminal behavior and legal issues.

British psychologist Hans J. Eysenck, in *Crime and Personality* (1964), formulated the first comprehensive theoretical statement on criminal behavior advanced by a psychologist. Shortly afterward, Edwin Megargee (1966) presented data from his dissertation and proposed heuristic statements regarding undercontrolled and overcontrolled personalities and their relationships to violence. Toch (1969) followed with *Violent Men*. The relationship between aggression and violence continued to be studied under the leadership of Leonard Berkowitz (1962), Albert Bandura (Bandura, 1973; Bandura & Walters, 1959), and Robert Baron (1977). The psychopath became the subject of vigorous theory building and research at the hands of Robert Hare (1970) and others (e.g., Quay, 1965).

CONCLUSION

In the 1970, a literature and research explosion occurred in all areas of forensic psychology, which had, as Loh (1981) observes, "come of age." In 1965, just over 100 English-language articles and books related to forensic psychology had been published (Tapp, 1976). By the mid-1970s, the numbers were well into the thousands. Professional journals exclusively devoted to forensic psychological research and issues were beginning to emerge in North America. *Criminal Justice and Behavior* led the way in 1974, followed by *Law and Psychology Review* (a journal published by law students and graduate psychology students at the University of Alabama) beginning in 1975, *Law and Human Behavior* in 1977, *Behavioral Sciences & the Law* in 1982, and *Psychology, Public Policy, and Law* in 1995. Great Britain has followed suit with *Criminal Behavior and Mental Health* (launched in 1990), *Psychology, Crime & Law* (1994), and the British Psychological Society's *Legal and Criminological Psychology* (1996).

During the 1970s, interdisciplinary and specialized training in forensic psychology was introduced at the doctoral, master's, internship, postdoctoral, and continuing education levels (Melton, 1987, and this volume; Ogloff, Tomkins & Bersoff, 1996). The first successful interdisciplinary psychology/law program was developed by Bruce Sales at the University of Nebraska—Lincoln in 1974 (Ogloff et al., 1996). Other universities soon followed in this endeavor—some more successfully than others. Another indication of the growth in forensic psychology is professional certification of practitioners in forensic psychology, a development that began in 1978. The American Board of Forensic Psychology currently lists 155 Diplomates in Forensic Psychology.

Forensic psychology has seen a rapid expansion in other parts of the globe, particularly in Europe and Australia. Blackburn (1996), in the first issue of *Legal and Criminological Psychology*, asserts, "The growth in the number of forensic psychologists has been among the most prominent developments in the burgeoning application of psychology to law during the last two decades" (p. 3). He notes that, although the growth has been most apparent in the United States, there has been a parallel growth throughout Europe over the past 20 years. For example, forensic psychology in Spain has developed rapidly over the past five years (Martin, 1997). Interestingly, the subject area most studied in Spanish forensic psychology has been juries, even though juries are not yet in force in the Spanish judicial system (Martin, 1997). Although the Spanish Constitution of 1978 did reestablish the jury system, at this writing it has yet to be put into effect.

After an uncertain beginning and some stagnation during the post-World War II era, it is clear that forensic psychology is well established. All indicators suggest forensic psychology—as an umbrella term for psychology and law, correctional psychology, police psychology, and the psychology of juvenile and adult offending—has an extremely promising future as we move into the next millennium. In the following chapters, other contributors will assess forensic psychology's current status and the promise it holds for a future generation of researchers, practicing psychologists, theorists, and legal practitioners.

REFERENCES

Bandura, A. (1973). *Aggression: A social learning analysis.* Englewood Cliffs, NJ: Prentice-Hall.

Bandura, A., & Walters, R. H. (1959). *Adolescent aggression.* New York: Ronald Press.

Barland, G. H. (1988). The polygraph test in the USA and elsewhere. In A. Gale (Ed.), *The polygraph test: Lies, truth and science* (pp. 73–96). London: Sage.

Barnes, H. E., & Teeters, N. K. (1959). *New horizons in criminology* (2nd ed.). New York: Prentice-Hall.

Baron, R. A. (1977). *Human aggression.* New York: Plenum Press.

Berkowitz, L. (1962). *Aggression: A social-psychological analysis.* New York: McGraw-Hill.

Binet, A. (1900). *La suggestibilité.* Paris: Schleicher.

Binet, A. (1905). La science du termoignage. *L'Annee Psychologique, 11,* 128–137.

Binet, A., & Clarparede, E. (1906). La psychologie judiciaire. *L'Anne Psychologique, 12,* 274–302.

Blackburn, R. (1996). What *is* forensic psychology? *Legal and Criminological Psychology, 1,* 3–16.

Bodemar, O. A. (1956). Correctional psychology in Wisconsin. *Journal of Correctional Psychology, 1,* 7–15.

Bolton, F. E. (1896). The accuracy of recollection and observation. *Psychological Review, 3,* 286–295.

Britt, S. H. (1940). The rules of evidence—An empirical study in psychology and law. *Cornell Law Quarterly, 25,* 556–580.

Brodsky, S. L. (1973). *Psychologists in the criminal justice system.* Urbana: University of Illinois Press.

Brodsky, S. L. (1996). Twenty years of *Criminal Justice and Behavior:* An observation from the beginning. *Criminal Justice and Behavior, 23,* 5–11.

Brown, M. (1926). *Legal psychology.* Indianapolis, IN: Bobbs-Merrill.

Brown v. Board of Education, 347 U.S. 483 (1954).

Burtt, H. E. (1931). *Legal psychology.* New York: Prentice-Hall.

Cady, H. M. (1924). On the psychology of testimony. *American Journal of Psychology, 35,* 110–112.

Cairns, H. (1935). *Law and the social sciences.* New York: Harcourt, Brace.

Cattell, J. M. (1895). Measurements of the accuracy of recollection, *Science, 2,* 761–766.

Chandler, J. T. (1990). *Modern police psychology: For law enforcement and human behavior professionals.* Springfield, IL: Thomas.

Corsini, R. (1945). Functions of the prison psychologist. *Journal of Consulting Psychology, 9,* 101–104.

Darley, J. G., & Berdie, R. (1940). The fields of applied psychology. *Journal of Consulting Psychology, 4,* 41–52.

Eysenck, H. J. (1964). *Crime and personality.* London: Routledge & Kegan-Paul.

Giardini, G. I. (1942). The place of psychology in penal and correctional institutions. *Federal Probation, 6,* 29–33.

Goddard, H. H. (1914). *Feeblemindedness: Its causes and consequences.* New York: Macmillan.

Gottesman, J. (1975). *The utility of the MMPI in assessing the personality patterns of urban police applicants.* Hoboken, NJ: Stevens Institute of Technology.

Greenberg, J. (1956). Social scientists take the stand: A review and appraisal of their testimony in litigation. *Michigan Law Review, 54,* 953–970.

Hale, M. (1980). *Human science and social order: Hugo Munsterberg and origins of applied psychology.* Philadelphia: Temple University Press.

Hare, R. D. (1970). *Psychopathy: Theory and research.* New York: Wiley.

Hidden v. Mutual Life Insurance Co., 217 F.2d 818 (4th Cir. 1954).

Horowitz, I. A., & Willging, T. E. (1984). *The psychology of law: Integration and applications.* Boston: Little, Brown.

Hutchins, R. M., & Slesinger, D. (1927). Some observations on the law of evidence—Consciousness of guilt. *University of Pennsylvania Law Review, 77,* 725–740.

Hutchins, R. M., & Slesinger, D. (1928a). Some observations on the law of evidence—The competency of witnesses. *Yale Law Journal, 37,* 1017–1028.

Hutchins, R. M., & Slesinger, D. (1928b). Some observations of the law of evidence—Spontaneous exclamations. *Columbia Law Review, 28,* 432–440.

Hutchins, R. M., & Slesinger, D. (1928c). Some observations of the law of evidence—Memory. *Harvard Law Review, 41,* 860–873.

Hutchins, R. M., & Slesinger, D. (1929). Legal psychology. *Psychological Review, 36* 13–26.

Jenkins v. United States, 307 F.2d 637 (D.C. Cir. 1962) *en banc.*

Keller, E. I. (1918). Psychopathic laboratory at police headquarters, New York City. *Journal of Applied Psychology, 2,* 84–88.

Kelves, D. J. (1984, October 15). Annals of eugenics II. *The New Yorker,* pp. 52–125.

Kluger, R. (1975). *Simple justice.* New York: Knopf.

Kuna, D. P. (1976). The psychology of advertising, 1896–1916. *Dissertation Abstracts International, 37,* 3048B. (University Microfilms No. 76-26, 875)

Kuna, D. P. (1978). One-sided portrayal of Munsterberg. *American Psychologist, 33,* 700.

Lindner, H. (1955). The work of court and prison psychologists. In G. J. Dudycha (Ed.), *Psychology for law enforcement officers.* Springfield, IL: Thomas.

Loh, W. D. (1981). Perspectives on psychology and law. *Journal of Applied Social Psychology, 11,* 314–355.

Louisell, E. W. (1955). The psychologist in today's legal world: Part I. *Minnesota Law Review, 39,* 235–260.

Louisell, E. W. (1957). The psychologist in today's legal world: Part II. *Minnesota Law Review, 41,* 731–750.

Martin, E. G. (1997, February). *Psychology and law.* Available: www.ucm.es/OSTROS /Psyap/hispania/garrido.htm

Marston, W. M. (1917). Systolic blood pressure changes in deception. *Journal of Experimental Psychology, 2,* 117–163.

Marston, W. M. (1920). Reaction-time symptoms of deception. *Journal of Experimental Psychology, 3,* 72–87.

Marston, W. M. (1921). Psychological possibilities in deception tests. *Journal of the American Institute of Criminal Law and Criminology, 11,* 551–570.

Marston, W. M. (1924). Studies in testimony. *Journal of Criminal Law and Criminology, 15,* 5–32.

Marston, W. M. (1925). Negative type reaction-time symptoms of deception. *Psychological Review, 32,* 241–247.

McCary, J. L. (1956). The psychologist as an expert witness in court. *American Psychologist, 11,* 8–13.

McCarty, D. G. (1929). *Psychology for the lawyer.* New York: Prentice-Hall.

Megargee, E. I. (1966). Undercontrolled and overcontrolled personality types in extreme antisocial aggression. *Psychological Monographs, 80*(No. 3).

Melton, G. B. (1987). Training in psychology and law. In I. B. Weiner & A. K. Hess (Eds.), *Handbook of forensic psychology.* New York: Wiley.

Merrill, M. A. (1927). Intelligence of policemen. *Journal of Personnel Research, 5,* 511–515.

Miller, H. L., Lower, J. S., & Bleechmore, J. (1978). The clinical psychologist as an expert witness on questions of mental illness and competency. *Law and Psychology Review, 4,* 115–125.

Monahan, J., & Loftus, E. F. (1982). The psychology of law. *Annual Review of Psychology, 33,* 441–475.

Moskowitz, M. J. (1977). Hugo Munsterberg: A study in the history of applied psychology. *American Psychologist, 32,* 824–842.

Munsterberg, H. (1908). *On the witness stand: Essays on psychology and crime.* New York: McClure.

Munsterberg, H. (1914). *Psychology and social sanity.* New York: Doubleday.

Napoli, D. S. (1981). *Architects of adjustment.* Port Washington, NY: Kennikat.

Odom v. State, 174 Ala. 4, 7, 56 So. 913, 914 (1911).

Oglesby, T. W. (1957). Use of emotional screening in the selection of police applicants. *Public Personnel Review, 18,* 228–231, 235.

Ogloff, J. R. P., Tomkins, A. J., & Bersoff, D. N. (1996). Education and training in psychology and law/criminal justice. *Criminal Justice and Behavior, 23,* 200–235.

Paterson, D. G. (1940). Applied psychology comes of age. *Journal of Consulting Psychology, 4,* 1–9.

People v. Hawthorne, 293 Mich. 15, 291 N.W. 205 (1940).

President's Commission on Law Enforcement and the Administration of Justice. (1967). *Task force report: The police.* Washington, DC: United States Government Printing Office.

Quay, H. C. (1965). Psychopathic personality: Pathological stimulation-seeking. *American Journal of Psychiatry, 122,* 180–183.

Rankin, J. H. (1957). Preventive psychiatry in the Los Angeles Police Department. *Police, 2,* 24–29.

Rankin, J. H. (1959). Psychiatric screening of police recruits. *Public Personnel Review, 20,* 191–196.

Reese, J. T. (1986). Foreword. In J. T. Reese & H. Goldstein (Eds.), *Psychological services for law enforcement* (p. v). Washington, DC: United States Government Printing Office.

Reese, J. T. (1987). *A history of police psychological services.* Washington, DC: United States Government Printing Office.

Reiser, M. (1972). *The police psychologist.* Springfield, IL: Thomas.

Reiser, M. (1982). *Police psychology: Collected papers.* Los Angeles: LEHI.

Robinson, E. S. (1935). *Law and the lawyers.* New York: Macmillan.

Rogers, O. (1910). The unwary purchaser: A study in the psychology of trademark infringement. *Michigan Law Review, 8,* 613–644.

Rogers, O. (1918). An account of some psychological experiments on the subject of trademark infringements. *Michigan Law Review, 18,* 75–95.

Schrenck-Notzing, A. (1897). *Uber suggestion und erinnerungsfalschung im berchthold-process.* Leipzig: Johann Ambrosius Barth.

Scrivner, E. M. (1994). *The role of police psychology in controlling excessive forces.* Washington, DC: National Institute of Justice.

Slesinger, D., & Pilpel, M. E. (1929). Legal psychology: A bibliograpy and a suggestion. *Psychological Bulletin, 12,* 677–692.

Snee, T. J., & Lush, D. E. (1941). Interaction of the narrative and interrogatory methods of obtaining testimony. *Journal of Psychology, 11,* 225–236.

State v. Driver, 88 W.Va. 479, 107 S.E. 189 (1921).

Stern, L. W. (1906). Zur psychologie der aussage. *Zeitschrift fur die qesamte Strafrechswissenschaft, 23,* 56–66.

Stern, L. W. (1910). Abstracts of lectures on the psychology of testimony. *American Journal of Psychology, 21,* 273–282.

Stern, L. W. (1939). The psychology of testimony. *Journal of Abnormal and Social Psychology, 40,* 3–20.

Tapp, J. L. (1976). Psychology and the law: An overture. *Annual Review of Psychology, 27,* 359–404.

Terman, L. M. (1917). A trial of mental and pedagogical tests in a civil service examination for policemen and firemen. *Journal of Applied Psychology, 1,* 17–29.

Terrio, L., Swanson, C. R., Jr., & Chambelin, N. C. (1977). *The police personnel selection process.* Indianapolis, IN: Bobbs-Merrill.

The psychologist as expert witness: Science in the courtroom? (1979). *Maryland Law Review, 38,* 539–615.

Thurstone, L. L. (1922). The intelligence of policemen. *Journal of Personnel Research, 1,* 64–74.

Toch, H. (Ed.). (1961). *Legal and criminal psychology.* New York: Holt, Rinehart and Winston.

Toch, H. (1969). *Violent men: An inquiry into the psychology of violence.* Chicago: Aldine.

Viteles, M. S. (1929). Psychological methods in the selection of patrolmen in Europe. *Annals of the American Academy, 146,* 160–165.

Watkins, R. E. (1992). *An historical review of the role and practice of psychology in the field of corrections.* Ottawa: Correctional Service of Canada.

Weld, H. P., & Danzig, E. R. (1940). A study of the way in which a verdict is reached by a jury. *American Journal of Psychology, 53,* 518–536.

Weld, H. P., & Roff, M. (1938). A study in the formation of opinion based upon legal evidence. *American Journal of Psychology, 51,* 609–628.

Whipple, G. M. (1909). The observer as reporter: A survey of the "psychology of testimony." *Psychological Bulletin, 6,* 153–170.

Whipple, G. M. (1910). Recent literature on the psychology of testimony. *Psychological Bulletin, 7,* 365–368.

Whipple, G. M. (1911). Psychology of testimony. *Psychological Bulletin, 8,* 307–309.

Whipple, G. M. (1912). Psychology of testimony and report. *Psychological Bulletin, 9,* 264–269.

Whipple, G. M. (1913). Psychology of testimony and report. *Psychological Bulletin, 10,* 264–268.

Whipple, G. M. (1914). Psychology of testimony and report. *Psychological Bulletin, 11,* 245–250.

Whipple, G. M. (1915). Psychology of testimony. *Psychological Bulletin, 12,* 221–224.

Whipple, G. M. (1917). Psychology of testimony. *Psychological Bulletin, 14,* 234–236.

Wigmore, J. H. (1909). Professor Munsterberg and the psychology of testimony: Being a report of the case of *Cokestone v. Muensterberg. Illinois Law Review, 3,* 399–445.

Wigmore, J. H. (1940). *Evidence in trials at common law.* Boston: Little, Brown.

Winick, C. (1961). The psychology of juries. In H. Toch (Ed.), *Legal and criminal psychology.* New York: Holt, Rinehart and Winston.

CHAPTER 2

Defining Forensic Psychology

ALLEN K. HESS

IN THE past several decades, collaboration between psychology and law has grown prodigiously. The number of journals, textbooks, and continuing education workshops available in forensic psychology has increased; the American Psychological Association (APA) Division 41, the American Psychology–Law Society, has more than 2,000 members; postdoctoral credentialing boards offer diplomate status in forensic psychology; and 2 of the 11 elected members of the 1995–1997 APA Board of Directors hold degrees in both psychology and law.

In recent years, there has been a shift in the focus of clinical psychology from investigating neurotic and schizophrenic conditions to studying legal issues generally and criminal behavior specifically. As the public's interest in crime increased, clinical psychologists broadened their interests to include forensic questions and criminal behavior. Journals such as *Behavioral Sciences and the Law, Criminal Justice and Behavior, Law and Human Behavior, Journal of Personality Disorders,* and *Psychology, Public Policy and Law* are devoted to forensic psychology. Increasingly, *Ethics & Behavior, Journal of Abnormal Psychology, Journal of Consulting and Clinical Psychology,* and *Professional Psychology* publish articles devoted to forensic psychology concerns. Given the growth in collaboration, it is important to examine both the ways psychology and law relate to each other and the ways they differ. The two disciplines have much to offer each other. However, the two have differing philosophical assumptions that need to be described in order that collaborative efforts are not stymied by conflicts due to a failure to understand these differences.

The first section of this chapter describes three ways psychology and law interact: (a) the practice of psychology in legal settings, (b) the effects of the law on the practice of psychology, and (c) research and scholarly inquiry as applied to legal issues. The second section describes epistemological differences between

I am grateful to Chana Barron, Kathryn D. Hess, Robert M. Weinberg, Irving B. Weiner, and Peter Zachar for their helpful commentary about this chapter.

law and psychology. Both lawyers and psychologists need to understand these differences for their collaborations to meet with success.

THREE WAYS PSYCHOLOGY AND LAW INTERACT

Psychology in Legal Settings

We can establish a functional definition of forensic psychology by describing the three ways psychology and law interact. Some psychologists practice in a legal setting and must be aware of and knowledgeable about legal issues. The expert witness serves as an example of the psychologist in a legal context. The expert witness must be familiar with legal standards, definitions or tests, and the procedures by which the law operates (e.g., see Hess & Brinson, Chapter 4; Roesch, Zapf, Golding, & Skeem, Chapter 12; Clark, Chapter 13; Golding, Skeem, Roesch, & Zapf, Chapter 14; Hess, Chapter 19, in this volume). He or she must be aware of specific ethical parameters that govern forensic psychology practice, particularly where such practice differs from traditional clinical or experimental practices (see Hess, Chapter 24, in this volume). For example, psychologists who conduct research in prison settings need to know that prison officials have total authority to restrict access to prisoners except for approved family and friends and legal and spiritual counsel (*Pell v. Procunier*, 1974). The successful psychologist realizes the strictures of working with incarcerated populations and informs his or her research team about the protocol for conducting research in the prison.

The psychologist may find his or her research in clinical questions frequently applied to legal questions. For example, Eisendrath (1996) ably distinguishes between factitious disorders, malingering, and other forms of abnormality such as conversion, hypochondriasis, and somatization in Munchausen cases. Traditionally, such distinctions help clinicians develop treatment plans. However, distinctions such as Eisendrath's have important implications for legal questions such as disability determination, for competency and sanity questions, and for testimonial reliability (credibility).

Many of the following chapters involve the artful application of psychology in legal contexts. These chapters illustrate the advances in research and practice in such areas as domestic law, child eyewitness competence, lie detection, assessing jury competence, predicting violence and recommending parole, psychotherapeutic intervention, assessing disabilities, applying hypnosis, and police psychology.

Law's Effects on the Practice of Psychology

Psychologists must be aware of the way law has increased its influence on their daily functioning, whether in clinical practice, in academia, or in research contexts. For example, the *Tarasoff* (1976) decision had a major impact on the conditions of confidentiality clinicians could offer clients. In the two decades since *Tarasoff*, the law has refined the duty to warn third parties of a client's threats of violence. When a patient threatens violence to a third party, the courts have defined the duty of care standard (*Perreira v. State*, 1989), established a "zone of danger" regarding who might be a foreseeable victim (*Hamman v. County of Maricopa*, 1989), and identified what determines the remoteness of time between a threat and an overtly violent act (*In re Hofmaster*, 1989). The psychologist must continue to follow refinements in the law as they affect practice and, because state law and local custom shape legal and ethical practice, to learn about the law as applicable where the psychologist practices. For example, recently the number of disciplines that offer psychotherapy and counseling to the public has multiplied; the psychologist who receives or makes referrals needs to know about relevant law such as *Jaffee v. Redmond* (1996), which defined which professions can offer the protection of privilege to clients.

As clinical practices involve greater numbers of personnel such as secretaries, billing clerks, office managers, psychological assistants, associates, and partners, practitioners need to know the degree to which their staff is covered by the practitioner's ability to offer privilege. *Oregon v. Miller* (1985) described both the umbrella (nurses, receptionists, typists) of privilege that covers a professional's support staff and the time when privilege begins. In *Oregon v. Miller*, Miller's brother advised him to talk with mental health professionals after Miller had strangled his allegedly homosexual partner. Miller told the secretary-receptionist answering his phone call that he had killed someone and needed to talk with a professional. Dr. Saville talked with him for 10 to 15 minutes, assuring him that the conversation was confidential; then Miller gave his name and she stalled while police traced the phone number from which he was calling. Absent a clear and present danger (the victim was dead by then), psychotherapist privilege began when the circumstances showed that Miller held the belief that the communication was made for the purposes of diagnosis and treatment, even in the first minutes of the initial and sole conversation.

When hiring personnel, psychologists functioning as employers need to know about employment law; when managing a suicidal client, they need to know what constitutes the appropriate standard of care; when terminating psychotherapy, the clinician needs to know what would be actionable as patient abandonment; and when teaching, the instructor needs to know about issues such as what constitutes grounds for student or professor misconduct and what are the parameters of disclosure of student records (Office of Juvenile Justice and Delinquency Prevention, 1997). Psychologists as employers, clinicians, and teachers need to know about the Americans with Disabilities Act (1990) so they can better serve prisoners, students, faculty, staff members, and clients who need reasonable accommodations for their impairments (Greenlaw & Kohl, 1992). Although practicing in a legal manner does not constitute a forensic psychology practice, psychologists who become expert in legal parameters of practice to the degree that they offer services regarding legal practice questions are practicing forensic psychology.

There are many resources to guide the psychologist interested in the ethical, moral, and lawful practice of forensic psychology. Several chapters in this volume concern writing reports (see Weiner, Chapter 18), practicing principled forensic psychology (see Hess, Chapter 24), treatment (see McCord, Chapter 20; Milan, Chin, & Nguyen, Chapter 21; Mobley, Chapter 22; and Marshall, Chapter 23), assessing competence (see Slovenko, Chapter 7; and Roesch, Zapf, Golding,

& Skeem, Chapter 12), and using legal source materials to answer particular questions (see Van Der Velde, Chapter 3). There are other excellent sources to answer legal questions about practice issues, including journals (e.g., *Professional Psychology, Ethics & Behavior,* and *Psychology, Public Policy and Law*), books (Bersoff, 1995; Corey, Corey, & Callanan, 1993; Keith-Spiegel & Koocher, 1985; Rinas & Clyne-Jackson, 1988; Steininger, Newell, & Garcia, 1984; Swenson, 1993), codes of professional conduct (e.g., American Psychological Association, 1992; Committee on Ethical Guidelines for Forensic Psychologists, 1991), and newsletters and reports (e.g., Appelbaum/Grisso Report, Mental Health Report, Register Report of the National Register of Health Service Providers, and the APA Monitor's Judicial Notebook), and legal sources.

Academicians have been drawn into the legal arena regarding their rights to conduct research and to disseminate their findings. For example, the case of Dr. Paul Fischer should alert the psychologist to the degree that legal parameters can affect research. At dinner, his 2-year-old son sucked on a straw pretending that it was a cigarette and told his father how he was going to puff away when he was older. Fischer, a family medicine practitioner, constructed a little card game and tested it on 229 3- to 6-year-old children in day care, having obtained parental consent with the usual provision that neither the parent nor the child would be identified. Fischer found that 33% of the 3-year-old children and 91% of the 6-year-old children correctly placed Joe Camel on the picture of cigarettes. In contrast, fewer than 61% of the 6-year-old children correctly identified the Marlboro Man (*"Doctors Whose Study,"* 1997). The *Journal of the American Medical Association* published Fischer's paper. R. J. Reynolds subpoenaed Fischer's records, notes, and the names, addresses, and telephone numbers of the 229 children and their parents in the course of their defense in a lawsuit in which Fischer's research was mentioned in passing. A series of legal actions followed, with RJR asserting the need for the raw research data, Fischer asserting the need to preserve the promised confidentiality, and the Medical School of Georgia and the Georgia State Attorney failing to back Fischer. Under Georgia's open records law, Fischer was deemed a public employee and his records considered to be public records. Does the researcher who guarantees confidentiality stand on solid ground when relying on professional codes of ethics rather than the state law and the policies of the institution in which he or she works? Can researchers and their professional associations influence state law and institutional policy? Can the researcher separate the identification information of research participants from the raw data to assure the confidentiality of the participants?

In a case involving lecturing about controversial issues, Dr. Whitfield publicly taught about recovered memory of sexual abuse, using the case of Jennifer Freyd as an example. Her parents sued Whitfield for defamation, claiming that his intent was malicious, that his information was erroneous, and that his degree should have made him aware of the falsity of their adult daughter's claims about them. The judge held that such a guarantee of the truth of their hypotheses would stifle the very debate that leads to scientific knowledge (*"Judge Protects,"* 1997, p. A8). Lecturers have a broad freedom to express their views, but this freedom needs to be weighed against legal limitations such as defamation and the personal destructiveness their statements might have. Could Whitfield's points in his lecture be made without distressing the Freyds? What may be legally permissible may not always be right.

Legal issues extend to all psychologists' practices, whether they occur in academia, business, the lecture circuit, or the clinical office. Some might feel "belegaled" by the growing legal strictures concerning psychological practice (Simon, 1987), but the increased sensitivity to various interests and issues should help practitioners elevate their professional functioning, not limit it. Practitioners are advised not to become quasi-attorneys but rather to be aware of legal issues to remain current in their practices. Practitioners should hone their skills by keeping up with the literature, seeking consultation and supervision before questions become critical (an ongoing peer supervision group can be inestimably helpful), and practicing as if a videotape of their activities will be reviewed in court (Weiner, 1995). The best safeguard from legal troubles is to be constantly mindful of the best standards of care and practice in one's profession, to be aware of relevant state and case law, and to try to anticipate the consequences of one's activities.

PSYCHOLOGICAL RESEARCH ON LEGAL ISSUES AND PROCESSES

The third area concerns scholarly inquiry into what has been termed "psycholegal issues." For example, Saks, Hollinger, Wissler, Evan, and Hart (1997) address the important issue regarding variability of civil jury awards, a synonym for tort reform, a burning issue for legislatures and media across the country, but an issue that has received little scientific study. Mock jurors were presented six different ways of awarding damages: a cap condition indicating the maximum amount allowed by law, an average award information cue, an award interval or range cue, an average-plus-interval condition, an exemplar condition, and a control condition, all presented over the three injury-severity levels. The researchers found that the cap condition, advocated by many who want to limit awards, actually increased both the variability of awards at the three levels of injury severity and the size of awards in low and intermediate levels of injury cases, the very cases that make up the bulk of civil injury litigation. The authors consider the adverse effect on distributive justice and the way anchoring and assimilation theory would result in a more just system of civil injury awards.

Stinson, Devenport, Cutler, and Kravitz (1996) applied psychology to study the question of whether the presence of lawyers provided a safeguard for the defendant at lineups. They used videotaped lineups and found that public defenders were sensitive to the use of foils (people known to be innocent) but were less sensitive to instructional bias, where the witness is led to understand that the perpetrator is among the lineup members (a biasing factor). Attorneys rated simultaneous lineups as less biased than sequential lineups, in contrast to the literature that holds sequential lineups, though not often used, are less biasing than simultaneous lineups.

A key assumption in a jury case is that jurors will weigh the evidence against legal standards issued in the instructions by the judge. Smith (1991) found that uninstructed people hold incorrect legal information, that these misunderstandings influence their verdicts, and that this prototype information is resistant to change by typical instruction. Smith asserts that for our legal system to function according to the law rather than by lay (mis)conceptions of the law, instruction must be effective in changing prototype information.

Psychologists have applied research methodologies to a number of legal questions and practices. Literature concerning juror selection and jury dynamics, privacy, and discretion show applications of psychology studying the law.

Jury Processes and Juror Competence

Attorneys have long held that a trial verdict may have been determined before the opening statements are uttered if the attorney has wisely selected the jurors. In the 1970s, two brothers named Berrigan were accused of antiwar activities and conspiring to kidnap Secretary of State Henry Kissinger. Their trial established the practice of scientific jury selection (SJS) by social scientists (Diamond, 1990). Despite efforts and expenses devoted to SJS, Diamond concluded that research shows from 16% to fewer than 5% of trial outcomes can be attributed to SJS. Perhaps SJS continues because of attorney anxiety and because it shows that the attorney left no stone unturned in his or her client's advocacy, but it may leave the psychologist offering a service without any demonstrated validity. Diamond suggests that social scientists may be making a more substantive, and ethical, contribution if they explore such issues as the possibility of community bias that can support a motion for a change of venue or if consultants help attorneys identify the presentation of arguments that may be more effective with jurors. For example, Diamond, Casper, Heiert, and Marshall (1996) showed that jurors did not spend much time talking about the attorneys, and that they did focus on attorney behavior, were affected by what the witnesses presented, were persuaded by the strength and effectiveness of cross-examination, and were open to changing their verdicts as the trial unfolded.

How can psychological research inform the legal system about jurors and juries? Kuhn, Weinstock, and Flaton (1994) showed that there are significant individual differences among jurors in reasoning skills, showed how juror reasoning processes are activated, and showed that competent jurors choose moderate verdicts and are less certain in their judgments than less competent jurors. Kuhn et al. offered suggestions about training competence in jurors because competent jurors follow the judicial instructions by weighing alternatives. Forsterlee and Horowitz (1997) found that note takers, in contrast with non-note-taking jurors, demonstrated better cognitive performance, were more effective decision makers, and were less distracted by nonprobative evidence. Cooper, Bennett, and Sukel (1996) showed that mock jurors were more persuaded by highly expert witnesses than less expert witnesses when testimony was highly complex, but when testimony was simpler, the content of the testimony was telling in contrast to the expertise level of the witnesses. They demonstrated the Rosenthal effect, in that judges' biases were transmitted to mock student and nonstudent jurors but that this biasing effect was titrated when simplified jury instructions were given.

Jurors are exposed to stress both in the juror selection process and in the trial process. Hafemeister, Ventis, Levine, Constanza, and Constanza (reported by DeAngelis, 1995) showed that a juror might be exposed to graphic evidence in heinous murder, rape, assault, and personal injury cases, and might be sequestered, and that these stresses can affect verdicts. Towell, Kemp, and Pike (1996) showed that masking affected the nonverbal communication between witness and juror and reduced juror recall of information in pixilated and shadowed masks but not in photo-negative masks and that juror certainty remained high even when jurors' recall was reduced.

Kagehiro (1990a) examined the objections to quantifying the standards of proof in instructing juries. She found no basis to the objections that jurors would be overly certain and prone to conviction if the standards of proof employed statistical anchors and that such instructions would weaken the legal definition. In fact, Kagehiro found that quantifying the standards of proof—greater than 90% certainty for "beyond a reasonable doubt," 75% certainty for "clear and convincing" evidence, and more than 50% of the evidence for a "preponderance of the evidence"—was consistent with the law's intended effect in setting legal standards; further, the juries' findings for the plaintiffs decreased as the standards of proof became stricter. Statistical instruction alone and in combination with legal definitions were superior to the traditional definitions alone in achieving the law's purpose, the increased comprehension of the legal instructions upon which verdicts are based. Consider that the standards for liability, ranging from "reckless indifference," "reckless disregard," and "callous disregard" to "gross negligence," "outrageous conduct," and "a shock to the conscience" would be more easily understood with more metric definitions. Justice will be better served if legislation is informed by psychological research concerning scaling techniques as a way to clarify jury instructions.

Training more competent jurors would address an important societal problem, that of the perception of jury incompetence that has contributed to the erosion of trust in the jury system. Moreover, the jury research we have just sampled shows that juror selection might be a dead end but there are much more exciting and useful lines of research that psychologists are developing to improve jury performance (see Robbennolt, Penrod, & Heuer, Chapter 10).

Privacy and Identity

Psychological and legal concerns about questions of privacy are becoming increasingly important. The electronic information bases are compounding the problem of identity theft. Bronti Kelly's life was tormented. Despite a résumé replete with sales experience, he was rejected hundreds of times in a four-year search for sales jobs. When Kelly was hired, the employer would terminate him within days to return Kelly to the treadmill of the job seekers. He lost his apartment, filed for bankruptcy, lived in a parking garage to shield himself from the elements, and was rejected by welfare because he had no permanent address. Despondent, he blamed himself (Kalish, 1997). Kelly reported losing his wallet in 1990; this resulted in his identification papers being used by someone who engaged in arson, burglary, and shoplifting. Although Kelly was on active military duty when he was supposed to have committed crimes, his record was never cleared. Eventually, the identity theft was discovered, although the records of criminal activity seem to persist in the "system."

Pedersen (1997) examined aspects of the concept of privacy and found that people use solitude for creative efforts, for concealment to secure personal information, and to contemplate who they are, what they want to be, how to experiment with new behaviors without social condemnation, and for rejuvenation. Sex differences in privacy needs can account for differences in how males and females experience intrusion (Pedersen, 1987). Sheffey and Tindale (1992) found that female-dominated work situations (termed "traditional") rather than male-dominated or mixed work settings (termed "nontraditional and integrated") differed in the threshold for a determination of appropriate versus harassing sexual behavior. Larger status discrepancies produced more severe judgments of inappropriateness. Stockdale (1993) reviewed research that shows men perceive women's friendliness as more sexually charged than women intend and examined factors contributing to these differences. Sheffey and Tindale (1992) warn about the complexities in litigating charges based on complex subjective judgments and urge managers to be mindful of these factors in constructing their sexual harassment policies and training programs.

Kagehiro (1990b) wondered whether people understood their Fourth Amendment consent rights: that voluntariness for consent means absence of governmental coercion and not informed consent, that such consent waives the requirement of a warrant, and that consent can be waived by a third party without an individual's permission or knowledge when the premises are in possession and control of another (as often happens with a roommate or suite mate). Furthermore, she wanted to know how a third party, such as a judge reviewing a motion to dismiss evidence, would perceive the degree to which a person who waived his or her rights against search and seizure was free from coercion and acted voluntarily.

Kagehiro (1990b) found that observers attributed more voluntariness than did consenters in waiving the consenter's rights to the ability of the consenter to revoke consent, to ask for information during the entry and search process, and for these judgments to be affected by the formality of the request (e.g., "Why don't you let me take a peek in your purse so we can resolve this problem easily," versus "Empty the contents of your purse on the floor now"). These results are consistent with the actor-observer bias that has been well established in attribution theory research. Kagehiro's subjects did understand that civil and criminal justice authorities had no more rights of entry than did social or commercial parties, but their view of "common authority" and "exclusive use" differed from legal rulings. The subjects perceived co-residents' rights to consent as more circumscribed than the courts have held and that the parties' presence influenced these judgments, whereas the courts have held a person's presence as less telling when someone who has access to the area waives the person's rights while they are present.

Finally, courts hold that a wider range of people can waive privacy rights than subjects believe. Kagehiro (1990b) found that students view both the suspect's relationship to a third party and the third party's control over the space to be important, but the courts emphasize the third party's place control. This means that a person's house sitter, babysitter, house painter, or even drop-by acquaintance with place control has more authority over our privacy than we may assume. Interestingly, responses from a police detective sample were more similar to the students' views than they were to the court's holdings, perhaps demonstrating an intuitive sense of privacy consistent with lay expectations. Kagehiro further cautions that the court's understanding of privacy holds a more concrete view of the world than reality suggests when one considers the cultural differences in privacy among many of our ethnic groups and the nontraditional constitution of the American household.

Bomser et al. (1995) ramble down the information superhighway in their review of the legal issues concerning privacy and security of copyrighted and trademarked work, personal communications, defamation, and even the antitrust impact on access, privacy, and security of our business and personal data. Tracey (1998) cautions the clinician about the perils of electronic devices such as cellular and cordless phones, fax machines, photocopiers, answering machines, and pagers as threats to our clients' confidentiality. Who we are, how we determine our lives, and the penetrability of our identities are crucial issues affected by judgments regarding privacy. Vitek (1997) described privacy and civility as linked within "placed communities." For Vitek, the people that share an event in time, place, and emotional commitment constitute a placed community that is defined by shared values and a sense of civility. For example, a community that celebrates a marriage knows that the married couple will be sexually engaged later that evening; nonetheless, the act remains private. The sense of being in a placed community involves the shared values of affection, restraint, and propriety. Vitek's concern is that as modern life involves greater rootlessness leading to a lessened sense of community ties, there is an attenuation of shared values and the respect for privacy that we need (Vitek & Jackson, 1996).

Discretion

Shaver, Gilbert, and Williams (1975) described the concept of discretion. At every step in the legal system, decisions are made that involve a complex of factors described by Konecni and Ebbesen (1982). This subjectivity is trenchantly captured by Goble (1955): "facts are true only as judged by a selected system of references." Figure 2.1 shows the choice points in the processing of a criminal case: the decision by the perpetrator to commit an offense, the victim's recognition and subsequent declaration to authorities (a separate decision) to report the offense, the police's decision to make an arrest, the prosecutor's decision to pursue charges, the grand jury's bringing an indictment, an arraignment, a trial, sentencing, and finally the system's disposition of an imposed sentence.

Let us examine discretion at two points in Figure 2.1: factors influencing how a person determines that he or she is a victim and dimensions of judicial discretion. If a person does not perceive that he or she was a crime victim, there will most likely be no crime reported, as depicted on the left side of Figure 2.1. The veracity of memory and repression, particularly of childhood sexual offenses, is a highly controversial issue. Positions include the view that all memory is a contemporary reconstruction of events, the idea that memory can be distorted, and the idea that memory is recorded almost as a mechanical process (the last view is largely archaic and mostly held by the lay public).

Brainerd, Reyna, and Brandse (1995) use fuzzy trace theory to show that in certain circumstances false memories can be more firmly established than true memories because the implanted memory might be better embedded in a supporting set of memory traces. Pezdek, Finger, and Hodge (1997) show that false memories can be successfully embedded when the event is plausible or consistent with the person's experience. Tromp, Koss, Figueredo, and Tharan (1995) found that rape memories were less clear and vivid, were less meaningfully ordered, were less well remembered, and were less often thought of or discussed in contrast with unpleasant and pleasant memories. Tromp et al.'s findings have implications for both testimony and psychotherapeutic intervention. Dissociative disorders are often implicated as trauma's consequences. Eich, Macaulay, Loewenstein, and Dihle (1997) studied nine dissociative identity disordered people and found that priming with word-stem completion occurred in the same personality state, and priming in a picture-fragment completion was robust between personalities; thus, we must be sensitive to the conditions under which memory is assessed. Karon and Widener (1997) review the arguments of those skeptical about recalled memory (e.g., Newman & Baumeister, 1996) and a well-documented body of clinical findings about World War II and repressed memories, some of which can be fifty years old (Viederman, 1995).

Holmes, Offen, and Waller (1997) tackle the question of why so few male victims of childhood sexual abuse receive help for abuse-related issues in adulthood. They conclude that society's myths that few males are sexually abused and that those who are do not show much of an adverse effect are incorrect. Instead, Holmes et al. see society as having no legitimizing social construct regarding male sexual abuse, so that the clinician does not see, hear, or ask about male sexual abuse. Nor does the victim feel any legitimacy in either recognizing or discussing the abuse. Discretion operates through what society construes as legitimate: in this case, that girls are sexual abuse targets but boys are not. Blumenthal (1998) reviews gender differences in the perception of sexual harassment, a difference that can affect the victim's reporting of a purported event, the investigator's filing of a complaint, the prosecutor's arraigning of an alleged perpetrator, a judge's acceptance of charges, and the jurors' determination of guilt. Memory and social perception play crucial roles in the criminal justice system, invite more research (see Goodman, Redlich, Qin, Ghetti, Tyda, Schaaf, & Hahn, Chapter 9), and illustrate the complexities of the psychological processes mediating discretion.

Before leaving discretion, let us briefly examine judicial discretion, a topic receiving attention in *General Electric v. Joiner* (1997). In Figure 2.1, the judge has a wide latitude in handling charges. He or she can exercise discretion in granting or denying bail; in assigning counsel for indigents and in accepting counsel; in limiting, reducing, or dismissing charges; in admitting or dismissing evidence; in accepting or rejecting a jury's verdict; and in sentencing. *General Electric v. Joiner* serves as an example of judicial discretion. *Joiner* affirmed the judge's role as the gatekeeper who applies the law in determining what constitutes admissible scientific evidence. The standard for such judgments is that of "abuse of discretion." Such abuse occurs only when the judge acts with disregard to logic and with disregard to settled law in the application of the law to

What is the sequence of events in the criminal justice system?

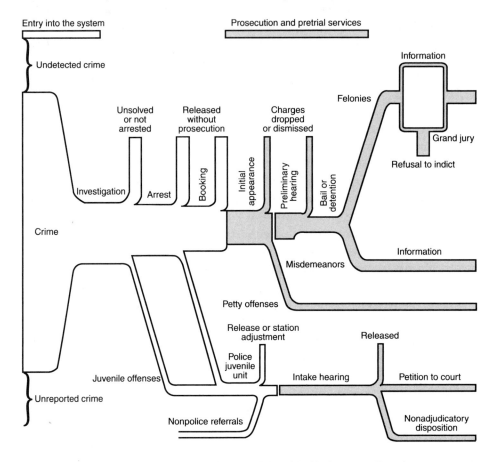

Note: This chart gives a simplified view of caseflow through the criminal justice system. Procedures vary among jurisdictions. The weights of the lines are not intended to show the actual size of caseloads.

Figure 2.1   Discretionary Points in the Criminal Justice System.

Source: From *Report to the Nation and Justice,* Bureau of Justice Statistics, U.S. Department of Justice, October 1983, pp. 42–45.

the offered testimony. Discretion is broadly defined and exercised with regard to nonscientific testimony, too. Is the following an abuse of discretion?

JUDGE: Mr. G. cooperated with you in every way?
OFFICER: Very cooperative.
JUDGE: And you had your gun out during the entire period?
OFFICER: That is correct, sir.
JUDGE: Where was the gun pointed, sir—at his stomach, midsection, head?
OFFICER: It was nestled right down the back of his neck.
JUDGE: Did you say anything to Mr. G., by the way, sir, concerning what would happen if he tried to move or get away?
OFFICER: I said I would blow his head off.

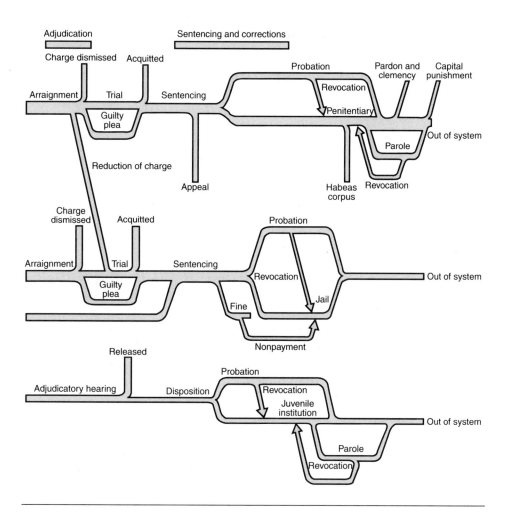

JUDGE: It was during this time, when Mr. G. had that .38 special cradled on the back of his neck, that you told him his rights under Miranda? Is that correct?

OFFICER: Yes, sir.

THE JUDGE'S RULING: I think it is a very unusual circumstance to have a gun pointed at the back of someone's head during the course of statement. No question . . . that it raises substantial question as to whether any statement was voluntary; however . . . I think the officer acted reasonably under the circumstances. . . . The defendant could have just as well said, "I have nothing to say," and that would have been the end of it. . . . So I would not find the statement involuntary, even though a gun was pointed at the back of the defendant's head (*Harper's Magazine*, 1987, p. 26).

As mentioned above, discretion permeates the legal system, has received attention by psychologists, and remains an area richly deserving of much more attention. Discretion is seen as sound when it appears reasonable or tied to logical application of the law in weighing evidence. Let us consider this fundamental concept of the law, reasonableness, and how psychological inquiry can help explicate reasonableness.

Reasonable Man Hypothesis

The law's benchmark is cognitive. What would we expect of the "reasonable man"? Hess (1987) and Redmount (1965) claim that psychologists should contribute to defining reasonableness. Consider three cases. In the first, a woman strikes a man on the jaw so hard that she knocks him out. Did she act unreasonably? If she were an airline hostess and a sudden drop during the flight caused the man to panic, start screaming, and lose control to the point that the passengers began to panic, then she might have acted not only reasonably but heroically.

Courtney Love, a rock music star, was charged with slugging two fans at her concert in Orlando, Florida, in 1995. The judge dismissed the two counts of battery because the fans were not exposed to any more violence than one should expect at a rock concert. What is a reasonable risk of exposure to violence seems to depend on the setting or context. What normative expectations does the public or the reasonable man have regarding risk in various settings? Are decisions regarding the definition of a social situation at least in part psychologically determined?

The third case concerns the au pair trial in which Louise Woodward was tried for causing the death of a child in her care. Much was made of the fact that the British-born and -raised 19-year-old Woodward did not display appropriate emotion during the police interrogation, the prosecutors' questioning, or the trial itself. Television commentators riveted their attention to this "insight." However, they did not take into account cultural differences in emotional expression; they did not include in their commentary her reaction to the guilty verdict, instead attributing her emotion to that of a person reacting not to the crime but to her conviction; and they did not attend to Woodward's parents' seemingly stoic reaction to their daughter's wailing at the verdict. What was a reasonable response by Louise Woodward? What expectations for emotional display did the jurors hold, and to what would they have attributed her emotional response had she displayed any? Was her stoicism judged within the jurors' or the media commentators' particular cultural emotional histories with little regard to Woodward's upbringing in a culture given to little public emotional expression? Could consulting forensic psychologists have been useful to Woodward's attorneys in witness preparation and in constructing their presentation to the jury in light of their client's seeming lack of emotion?

A FUNCTIONAL DEFINITION OF FORENSIC PSYCHOLOGY

Forensic psychology can be defined by the functions described above: providing psychological services in the justice or legislative systems, developing a specialized knowledge of legal issues as they affect the practice of psychology, and conducting research on legal questions involving psychological processes. Defining forensic psychology using these three functions has limitations. Any typology, and one as speculative as this one, serves at best as a guide and suffers the cases on the border between types. Walzer and Miltimore (1993) address the specific case in which disciplined health care professionals are mandated to enter controlled supervision, monitoring, and psychotherapy. Would the treating psychotherapist be practicing in a legal arena? or be practicing psychology in accord with legal mandates? or be engaging in a rich research area, as Conner (1996) has done in concluding that the willing client is not a precondition for successful psychotherapy? or be blending all three categories? Psychology in the law, psychology by the law, and psychology of the law comprise forensic psychology.

FUNDAMENTAL DISTINCTIONS BETWEEN PSYCHOLOGY AND LAW

As psychologists and lawyers work together with greater frequency, there are more chances for misunderstandings to occur. It is useful to consider distinctions that can become troublesome if not recognized. These differences arise from historical and philosophical sources that shaped the two professions. They are summarized in Table 2.1 and explicated below.

Epistemology: Objectivity versus Advocacy

The task of the psychologist offering expert testimony is to seek the truth. The scientist is supposed to be as delighted in the disproof as in the proof of a favored theory, because then science will be closer to finding law describing the nature of and mechanisms underlying the phenomenon in question. The law recognized this goal of science, as can be seen in one of the four prongs of the *Daubert v. Merrill* (1993) decision that replaced the Frye test regarding admissibility of expert testimony. The prong relies on Karl Popper's criterion of falsifiability of scientific theories; that is, a theory should be so operationally specific that it can be tested and found false. (This is an interesting example of the penetration of the philosophy of science into the court's thinking.) The goal of science, for Popper, is the construction of theories that are successively more accurate representations of nature.

On the other hand, the Anglo-American concept of law grew out of the trial by ordeal; that is, if one party were not telling the truth or did not have God on his or her side, then trial and tribulation would reveal which party was on the side of Right and which was in league with the Devil. Thus, the combat between good and evil was replayed in the adversarial trial in which a person could be tested. As we were weaned from the rack and the dunking chair between the 15th and 19th centuries, advocates in courts replaced the more physical tests with argumentation. It has become the task of the attorney to present the most telling case for his or her client (Stern, 1998). This advocacy proceeds through carefully crafted rules and procedures. The search for justice is more important than truth in the particular case. Stern writes that *"Fair* [italics in the original] refers to a case well tried by both parties with an opportunity to present evidence and arguments. It is hoped that from such fairness the truth

Table 2.1
Epistemological Differences between Psychology and Law

Dimension	Psychology	Law
Epistemology	Objectivity: Psychologists presume to progressively approach an ultimate truth. Any bias in theory or research is assumed to be balanced by competing theories, discovered by rigorous critique, and determined true or false by replication.	Advocacy: Truth in a case will be determined by the vigorous advocacy of the "stronger" facts that are more consistent with the prevailing law.
Causation of behavior	Deterministic: The behavioral sciences hold that behavior has causes that are known or potentially knowable.	Free will: Both the public and the law hold that people determine their fate. Responsibility in most cases is vested in the individual.
Nature of "law"	Descriptive: Research will reveal the underlying natural order or lawful relationships between variables, ideally realized in a formula, such as the relationship between anxiety and performance, or by typologies that are predictive of behavior, such as the type of person who would succeed in police work or on parole.	Prescriptive: Law directs behavior, clearly states what is proscribed or banned and authorizes punishment to enforce the proscriptions.
Knowledge	Empirical: Based on nomothetic or normative data gathered through methodologies described with sufficient detail to enable replication of the findings.	Rational: Based on idiographic or detailed case data from which similarities to other cases and to compelling logic from the law supports one's argument.
Methodology	Experimental: Control through experimental design or statistical regression allows the scientist to eliminate rival hypotheses so that conclusions can be deduced about the main variables under investigation.	Case Method: Analyses of the particulars in a case allows the investigator to draw parallels to other cases or to construct a narrative that encompasses the details into a tightly woven whole.
Criteria	Conservative: The usual criterion is $p < 0.5$ or that results must occur fewer that 1 time in 20 to be accepted.	Expedient: To resolve the case at hand, the criterion may be a "preponderance" or more than 50%, "clear and convincing" or more that 75%, or "beyond a reasonable doubt" or more than 90% of the weight of the evidence to produce a verdict.
Principles	Exploratory: Encourages a multiplicity of theories that are falsifiable or that can be tested and found wanting.	Conservative: The predominant theory in a case prevails based on the coherence of the facts to statutes and to stare decisis or precedent cases.
Latitude of courtroom behavior	Limited: Restricted to the rules of evidence and the attorney's questions or, in amicus curiae (friend of the court) briefs, to the questions posed by the attorneys or judge.	Broad: Within the rules of procedure and evidence, and within courtroom decorum, can introduce a wide variety of evidence in a desired sequence with as vigorous a style as befits a successful presentation of the case.

will emerge—but this is not always the case" (p. 103). For example, the basis for the exclusionary rule, and the public's angst over this rule, is founded on the idea that excluding evidence obtained in a way that violates the rules of evidence and procedure is better than including it, no matter how probative, compelling, or definitive that evidence is regarding the guilt of an alleged perpetrator. The law is structured so that it does not reward violation of the rules of justice.

Causation of Behavior

The task of behavioral science is to find causes for actions. These causes can be internal, as in the case of biological factors, or external, as in the case of environmental influences. In both cases, the scientist seeks deterministic explanations. From a legal perspective, one cannot be held accountable for a cause beyond one's control. A biologically based failing or a social learning regimen that compromised the individual's ability to control his or her own decision making would be deterministic in the sense that free will could not be exercised and individual legal responsibility would be negated.

The law holds a person with moral sense legally responsible. Definitions of moral sense most often involve the cognitive ability to understand moral issues and the freedom from defects to exercise that understanding. If the law is to work, it must hold individuals responsible or there would be an excuse for every human action. Just as a person may attribute positive actions to his or her own traits, negative events could be externally attributed.

Lawyers and the laity share the assumption that people exercise free will. Such attributions influence life or death determinations, as shown in Sundby's (1997) research. He studied the effects of expert witnesses, lay experts, and friends and family members as witnesses in the penalty phase of capital murder cases. Professional experts were viewed negatively by jurors in two-thirds of the cases but mentioned as positively influential by one-fifth of the juror references, a difference more pronounced in defense witnesses seeking to help avoid the death penalty for the guilty party than in prosecution expert witnesses. Consider a juror's reaction to an anthropologist's testimony that the defendant's background impelled his violence when he found someone else had fathered his daughter. The juror exclaimed, "Give me a break! Like we're supposed to believe it was just one of those macho things" (p. 1133). Another juror reacted to a social scientist's explanation about eyewitness identification errors, which are instances of external factors affecting a person's sincerely felt judgments, as "insulting"; another called the expert a "charlatan . . . [who said] you can't trust your own perceptions" (p. 1133). Even jurors who had similar drug experiences, described during the juror selection process and probably accepted by the defense as potentially empathic, said, "Yeah, well, I went through that and I didn't end up a killer," and "I've done this stuff . . . I've used it . . . Even so, when you do the drugs you know it's illegal, you know it's wrong, so I just believe you're responsible for your actions" (p. 1137). The presumption of personal responsibility seems augmented by what social psychologists would term the fundamental attribution error. Suffice it to say, "experts' explanations of human behavior that run contrary to notions of free will are hard to sell to the jury" (p. 1139).

THE NATURE OF "LAW"

Psychology uses the term "law" in the sense of descriptive laws. Law is something hidden in nature, a truth to be discovered, as with the law of gravity. For example, Latane (1981) wondered whether the failure of people to report a crime they witness can be understood in social psychological terms. Intrigued by the Kitty Genovese case in which at least 39 people heard her screams as she was murdered, Latane wanted to see whether the witnesses' failure to report a crime followed a lawful relationship. He found the diffusion of responsibility, or the impact of the victim's entreaty, was a function of the message's strength, immediacy, and the number of other potential interveners present. This multiplicative function is expressed in the psychophysical power function where the nth person has less impact on the witness than the nth − 1 person present at a crime scene, accounting for the diffusion of responsibility phenomenon. The task of science is to find lawful relationships, or empirical generalizations.

After research establishes lawful relationships, the practitioner fits the relevant scientific findings to the specific case. For the forensic psychologist this means, for example, whether cross-racial eyewitness identification research findings are applicable to the particulars in the specific case; whether the expert witness's perception that a parent's temper in a particular case renders him or her less fit to discharge parental responsibilities than other alternatives or whether the clinical judgment is inadequate because it is based on speculation rather than established empirical foundations.

Lawyers use the term law in a prescriptive sense. Behavior has a value that calls for its elicitation or, more often, its inhibition. Society values charity, so it codifies charity as meriting a tax deduction. If an HIV carrier knowingly has sex with unsuspecting partners, we codify and prosecute such activity, because we deem it harmful. That codification is what the law needs because it deals with specific cases. For larger unresolved issues, the law often waits for science to develop methods such as DNA testing or truth-detecting devices. The courts can wait for social changes; this is happening with the case of workplace sexual relations, which became an issue with the advent of women ascending organizational hierarchies. The court waits for the ripening of cases that lead to changes in the law by legislative means or by landmark court decisions.

KNOWLEDGE

Knowledge is justified belief that is normative and replicable. The laws are public and the method sections in research reports should be detailed enough to allow for others to repeat the experiments or to confirm or fail to find the phenomenon at issue. Although the single case study can reveal a phenomenon's existence or help us see the process underlying the phenomenon, the law of large numbers helps us increase the power of our statistical analyses in a nomothetic study, enabling us to reveal the generalizability of an effect.

The law is based on statutes covering classes of behaviors, but it operates through the single case. The application of the law is doctrinal, operates on a case-by-case basis, and relies on settled law, stare decisis, or the previously decided case. The law must decide the case, whereas the psychologist can defer a decision in the face of ambiguous results in favor of conducting more research. The goal of law is closure of important issues. Brandeis wrote, "it is more important that the applicable rule of law be settled than it be settled right" (cited in Wrightsman, Nietzel, & Fortune, 1994, p. 18). Hess (1987) opined that the law, or certainly court television and the incessant drumbeat of the talk shows, is contemporary society's version of the Middle Ages' morality plays. Plea bargaining is an example of the law's satisfaction with a case being closed, although many people feel justice was violated by the "cutting of a deal." A sense of veridicality or of a just world with a balance of crime and punishment seems to underlie this feeling people hold about plea bargaining.

Currently, psychology and law are sharing more from each other's traditional knowledge bases. Psychologists in the legal arena increasingly rely on the case method, as can be seen in the following chapters that cite cases with the same ease as they cite empirical studies. Increasingly, courts have admitted research findings from social scientists as evidence, and lawyers are learning about experimental design and statistical analyses just as psychologists are learning about case citations. Still, there is a fundamental difference in what psychologists and lawyers consider an adequate basis for knowledge.

METHODOLOGY

Methodology is tied to knowledge. Psychology has roots in both philosophy and science, but the latter has been its dominant model. With physical and biological sciences as psychology's model, psychology studies phenomena through the use of controls, be they experimental or statistical. The critical difference between science and art is that science can use controlled studies, or hold certain conditions constant while varying other conditions. Historians can speculate about counterfactual conditions, such as what might have happened if Cleopatra did not have her alluring charms or if Hitler had listened to Rommel about the Calais versus Normandy landing site for the D day invasion of continental Europe. A lawyer can wonder about whether his or her client would have killed someone but for the alcohol and work stress the client experienced that presumably led to the murder. Neither the historian nor the lawyer can replicate the conditions and use a control group to see whether their alternative hypotheses are correct. However, psychologists can conduct studies to determine the effects of punishment on group performance or the effectiveness of a Minnesota Multiphasic Personality Inventory (MMPI) or an inkblot indicator in predicting suicide, or, in the case of counterfactual conditions, set up studies about the effects of hindsight bias (Roese, 1997).

Benjamin, Rogers, and Rosenbaum (1991) provide an early and exemplary example of psychological research in the court. The Coca-Cola Company was charged under the then new Federal Food and Drug Act of 1906 with marketing and selling an adulterous beverage containing an ingredient harmful to health, caffeine. The government and Coca-Cola both assembled an array of medical expert witnesses, but because the charges involved caffeine's role as "a drug that makes one forget he is tired" (p. 596) and previous research was confined to motor responses and lacked experimental controls, Coca-Cola sought a psychologist's services. Hollingworth, lacking money and because he "had as yet no sanctity to preserve" (Benjamin et al., 1991, p. 593), accepted the assignment with several conditions. Aware of the suspicions with which people view privately sponsored research, of the "unclean" or stigmatized nature of applied research (p. 594), and of the potential for the misuse of the research in advertising, Hollingworth structured the agreement so that he could publish the research in academic journals whatever the results and that Coca-Cola could not use the research in its advertising.

Hollingworth used a multimethod approach, testing several cognitive processes alone and in combination, including perception, association, attention, motor speed and steadiness, judgment and discrimination, assessed by color naming, identifying word opposites, daily diary records of sleep, health and alertness, mental calculations, and discrimination reaction times as dependent measures. He hired his wife, Leta Stigger Hollingworth, to conduct the research. She ran blind testing sessions: examiners did not know the caffeine dosages that they gave to the subjects, and subjects did not know what dosage they ingested. Using placebos, employing counterbalanced administrations of dosages, controlling for diet, and measuring the effects of the caffeine through the course of the day, the Hollingworths generated some 64,000 data points. In contrast to the Hollingworths' research, one of the government's medical witnesses testified that caffeine produces congested cerebral arteries in rabbits. Cross-examination revealed that the researcher killed his test animals by hitting them on the head with a stick, "congesting" the arteries. Research presented by the government and by Coca-Cola, excepting the Hollingworths', was replete with flawed experimental designs, misinterpreted results, failure to use quantitative measures where possible, use of excessive quantities of caffeine atypical of customary use, and administering caffeine with other drugs confounding the caffeine effects (note that the same arguments and errors are made in more contemporary cases, such as whether massive doses of saccharine were fed to mice in the 1970s controversy concerning a saccharine-cancer causal relationship). Observers of the trial and leading medical journals hailed the Hollingworth research for its rigor, scope, and findings. It was still being cited 22 times in a literature search of the *Science Citation Index* and *Social Science Citation Index* for the 1983–1988 period (Benjamin et al., 1991, footnote 48).

Those familiar with court cases will not be surprised that the case did not go to the jury. The judge ruled that caffeine was not an added, adulterated ingredient but was natural to the drink, directing a verdict in favor of the defendant. Harry Hollingworth was elected president of the American Psychological Association in 1927. He helped industrial psychology shed some of academia's scorn and contributed to industrial-organizational psychology's uninterrupted involvement with the law to this day.

CRITERIA

Changes in systems are costly. Consequently, psychological research adopted a standard that calls for results so unusual that only 1 time in 20 can we attribute the differences obtained to a chance occurrence and then require replication of the results. Of course, many factors affect this standard, including faulty research designs, inclusion of so many variables that significant findings are inevitable (familywise error rates), serendipitous findings, and unscrupulous researchers who falsify data, making replication another touchstone for psychological research. Psychologists presenting research or clinical findings in legal arenas parenthesize their work by citing limiting conditions, or they will be highly vulnerable on cross-examination and may be misrepresenting both their work and the state of certainty in the field.

Whereas the legal system needs the immediate resolution of the case at issue, a decision resulting from research in science often requires expensive retooling of a system. For example, research that showed student ratings of their professors highly correlated with the ease of the professors' grades and lax course requirements may require reconsideration of the value of student ratings in determining promotion, tenure, and salary determination, as well as the development of alternative measurement strategies (Greenwald, 1997). Research showing the superiority of a method of teaching children to read requires expensive retraining of teachers; if the research is flawed, a generation of children may suffer. Consequently, research uses conservative statistical criteria.

The law requires resolution in the particular case. Shorn of the luxury of deferring a decision, the courts established standards for cases based on the gravity of the charges and outcomes. Consequently, legal thresholds consist of a preponderance of the evidence in favor of one side (more than 50%), clear and convincing evidence (what Kagehiro, 1990a, equates to 75% certainty), and evidence beyond a reasonable doubt (Kagehiro's 90% level of certainty). Note that the most compelling level of legal evidence approaches only the minimal level of difference that psychological research accepts.

PRINCIPLES

In some ways, the principles undergirding law and psychology are reciprocal to their respective criteria. The conservative scientific criteria are balanced by the encouragement of alternative hypotheses and a multiplicity of theories that vie to explain phenomena. The law, too, is an exercise in developing alternative hypotheses to explain the facts and matters of law in a way that is compatible with victory for the side propounding each theory.

Although encouraging alternative explanations on the individual case level, the law tends to be conservative with regard to legal principles. The law moves when circumstances are compelling. Otherwise, stare decisis or the precedent rules. Appellate courts may elect not to hear a case because the issues are not yet "ripe"; they await more case law, law review papers, and discussion in other forums before considering an issue ripe. For example, commentators have speculated that the number of blacks on the Nicolle Simpson–Ron Goldman murder trial jury led to the acquittal of O. J. Simpson, a black man accused of killing two white people. However, if the jury did engage in nullification, or the ruling by a jury on their sense of justice gainsaying the law, this issue has not ripened enough for the Supreme Court to hear. Whether jury nullification occurred, how often it occurs, whether there are concrete cases available to consider, and whether jury discretion is adequately defined are questions that could gather momentum and call for the law's attention.

LATITUDE OF COURTROOM BEHAVIOR

The forensic psychologist's practice encompasses three roles: the expert witness, the consultant, and the amicus curiae, or friend of the court. As an expert witness, the psychologist is confined to presenting evidence through the questioning by the attorney retaining the expert and through cross-examination by the opposing counsel. The opposing counsel tries to diminish the impact of the expert's testimony or even to use it to discredit the side that hired the expert. The consulting psychologist can help an attorney build a case, select jurors, and prepare materials for motions or strategies of presenting evidence (including witness preparation) and attacking adverse evidence. The psychologist serving as an amicus curiae might conduct research, review literature, conduct attitude surveys in cases involving change of venue due to a prejudiced jury pool, or help construct briefs to persuade the court regarding a psychological issue. Occasionally, the judge will hire a consulting psychologist, as in the case of a court monitor who examines whether a school or prison under court order is meeting the court's edicts. Each of these roles serves the attorney or the judge who retained the psychologist and requires the psychologist to work within the parameters established by the rules of evidence and procedure, the attorney's direction, and the judge's wishes.

The attorney, on the other hand, has great latitude to gather evidence to the limits of the client's resources, to develop a theory most favorable to the client, to secure witnesses, to file motions, to conduct voir dire, to order the sequence of presentation of witnesses and evidence, and to choose the tone of the advocacy. The psychologist may advise, but the attorney controls the decisions in managing the legal case.

CONCLUSION

Munsterberg presented psychology as having an immense contribution to make to the courts; Wigmore disabused Munsterberg and psychology of the idea that either one was ready to make an impact on the justice system (see Bartol & Bartol, Chapter 1). The question facing us is not *whether* psychology and the law are ready for psychology to have an influence throughout the legal system. Research reviewed in this chapter and in this volume makes it clear that the science and artful application of psychology to legal issues has matured to the point where it would be remiss of society, of the law, and of attorneys to ignore these developments. The questions facing us concern *how* such collaborations are to be managed: How do we promote psycholegal research? How do we establish relationships with appropriate bodies so that legal practice and legislation can be informed by psychological research? How can we improve the standards of practice of forensic psychology?

REFERENCES

Americans with Disabilities Act, Public Law 101-336, 104 Stat. 327 (1990).

Benjamin, L. T., Rogers, A. M., & Rosenbaum, A. (1991). Coca-Cola, caffeine, and metal deficiency: Harry Hollingworth and the Chattanooga Trial of 1911. *Journal of the History of the Behavioral Sciences, 27,* 42–55.

Bersoff, D. N. (1995). *Ethical conflicts in psychology.* Washington, DC: American Psychological Association.

Blumenthal, J. A. (1998). The reasonable women standard: A meta-analytic review of gender differences in the perceptions of sexual harassment. *Law and Human Behavior, 22,* 33–58.

Bomser, A. H., Costa, J. G., Friedman, J. R., Pomerantz, S. A., Post, J. A., Prowda, J. B., Weiner, S. H., & White, C. L. (1995). A lawyer's ramble down the information superhighway. *Fordham Law Review, 64,* 697–850.

Brainerd, C. J., Reyna, V. F., & Brandse, E. (1995). Are children's false memories more persistent than their true memories? *Psychological Science, 6,* 359–364.

Committee on Ethical Guidelines for Forensic Psychologists. (1991). Specialty guidelines for forensic psychologists. *Law and Human Behavior, 15,* 655–665.

Conner, T. A. (1996). Ethical and clinical issues in involuntary psychotherapy. *Psychotherapy, 33,* 587–592.

Cooper, J., Bennett, E. A., & Sukel, H. L. (1996). Complex scientific testimony: How do jurors make decisions? *Law and Human Behavior, 20,* 379–394.

Corey, G., Corey, M. S., & Callanan, P. (1993). *Issues and ethics in the helping professions* (4th ed.). Monterey, CA: Brooks/Cole.

Daubert v. Merrell Dow Pharmaceuticals, Inc., 113 S. Ct. 2786 (1993).

DeAngelis, T. (1995, June). Juror stress can influence final verdict. *APA Monitor,* 5–6.

Diamond, S. S. (1990). Scientific jury selection: What social scientists know and do not know. *Judicature, 73,* 178–183.

Diamond, S. S., Casper, J. D., Heiert, C. L., & Marshall, A. (1996). Juror reactions to attorneys at trial. *Journal of Criminal Law & Criminology, 87,* 17–47.

Doctor whose study tied Joe Camel to kids goes on an odd journey. (1997, February 21). *Wall Street Journal,* p. A1.

Eich, E., Macaulay, D., Loewenstein, R. J., & Dihle, P. H. (1997). Memory, amnesia and dissociative identity disorder. *Psychological Science, 8,* 417–422.

Eisendrath, S. J. (1996). When Munchausen becomes malingering: Factitious disorders that penetrate the legal system. *Bulletin of the American Academy of Psychiatry and Law, 24,* 471–481.

Exner, J. E., Jr. (1993). *The Rorschach: A comprehensive system: Vol. 1. Basic foundations* (3rd ed.). New York: Wiley.

Foley, L. A. (1993). *A psychological view of the legal system.* Madison, WI: Benchmark & Brown.

Forsterlee, L., & Horowitz, I. A. (1997). Enhancing juror competence in a complex trial. *Applied Cognitive Psychology, 11,* 305–319.

General Electric Company v. Joiner, 118 U.S. Ct. 512 (1997).

Goble, G. W. (1955). Nature, man and law. *American Bar Association Journal, 41,* 403.

Greenberg, M. S., & Ruback, R. B. (1982). *Social psychology of the criminal justice system.* Monterey, CA: Brooks/Cole.

Greenlaw, P. S., & Kohl, J. P. (1992). The ADA: Public personnel management, reasonable accommodation and undue hardship. *Public Personnel Management, 21,* 411–427.

Greenwald, A. G. (1997). Validity concerns and usefulness of student ratings of instruction. *American Psychologist, 52,* 1182–1186.

Halverson, A., Hallahan, M., Hart, A. J., & Rosenthat, R. (1997). Reducing the biasing effects of judges' nonverbal behavior with simplified jury instruction. *Journal of Applied Psychology, 82,* 590–598.

Hamman v. County of Maricopa, No. CV-87-0070-PR, Arizona Supreme Court, January 15, 1989.

Haney, C. (1980). Psychology and legal change: On the limits of a factual jurisprudence. *Law and Human Behavior, 4,* 147–200.

Harper's Magazine. (1987, April). p. 26. (Excerpted from C. M. Sevilla's "Great moments in courtroom history," *Champion,* December 1986.)

Hess, A. K. (1987). Dimensions of forensic psychology. In I. B. Weiner & A. K. Hess (Eds.), *Handbook of forensic psychology* (pp. 22–49). New York: Wiley.

Holmes, G. R., Offen, L., & Waller, G. (1997). See no evil, hear no evil, speak no evil: Why do relatively few male victims of childhood sexual abuse receive help for abuse-related issues in adulthood? *Clinical Psychology Review, 17,* 69–88.

In re Hofmaster, No. C1-88-2177, Minnesota Court of Appeals, January 17, 1989.

Jaffee v. Redmond, 116 S. Ct. 1923, 1996 WL 315841 (U.S. Ill.). June 13, 1996.

Judge protects scientists' statements. (1997, August 8). *Chronicle of Higher Education,* p. A-8.

Kagehiro, D. (1990a). Defining the standard of proof in jury instructions. *Psychological Science, 1,* 194–200.

Kagehiro, D. (1990b). Psycholegal research on the fourth amendment. *Psychological Science, 1,* 187–193.

Kalish, D. E. (1997, September 24). Thief tainted man's identity: Dogged by bogus data computers bred years of stigma. *The Record,* p. B1.

Karon, B. P., & Widener, A. J. (1997). Repressed memories and World War II: Lest we forget! *Professional Psychology, 28,* 338–340.

Keith-Spiegel, P., & Koocher, G. P. (1985). *Ethics in psychology.* Hillsdale, NJ: Erlbaum.

Konecni, V. J., & Ebbesen, E. B. (1982). The criminal justice system: A social psychological analysis. San Francisco: Freeman.

Kuhn, D., Weinstock, M., & Flaton, R. (1994). How well do jurors reason? Competence dimensions of individual variation in a juror reasoning task. *Psychological Science, 5,* 289–296.

Latane, B. (1981). The psychology of social impact. *American Psychologist, 36,* 343–356.

Lillard, A. S. (1997). Other folks' theories of mind and behavior. *Psychological Science, 8,* 268–274.

Newman, L. S., & Baumeister, R. F. (1996). Toward an explanation of the UFO abduction phenomenon: Hypnotic elaboration, extraterrestrial sadomasochism, and spurious memories. *Psychological Inquiry, 7,* 99–126.

Office of Juvenile Justice and Delinquency Prevention. (1997). *Sharing information: A guide to the Family Educational Rights and Privacy Act and Participation in Juvenile Justice Programs.* Washington, DC: U.S. Department of Justice.

Oregon v. Miller. 300 Or. 203, 709 P. 2d 225. Decided November 5, 1985.

Pedersen, D. M. (1987). Sexual differences in privacy preferences. *Perceptual and Motor Skills, 64,* 1239–1242.

Pedersen, D. M. (1997). Psychological functions of privacy. *Journal of Environmental Psychology, 17,* 147–156.

Pell v. Procunier. 417 US 817 (June, 24 1974).

Perreira v. State, No. 87SC75, Colorado Supreme Court, February 6, 1989.

Pezdek, K., Finger, K., & Hodge, D. (1997). Planting false childhood memories: The role of event plausibility. *Psychological Science, 8,* 437–441.

Redmount, R. S. (1965). The use of psychologists in legal practice. *The Practical Lawyer, 11,* 23–38.

Rinas, J., & Clyne-Jackson, S. (1988). *Professional conduct and legal concerns in mental health practice.* Norwalk, CT: Appleton & Lange.

Roese, N. J. (1997). Counterfactual thinking. *Psychological Bulletin, 121,* 133–148.

Saks, M. J., Hollinger, L. A., Wissler, R. L., Evans, D. L., & Hart, A. J. (1997). Reducing variability in civil jury awards. *Law and Human Behavior, 21,* 243–256.

Shaver, K. G., Gilbert, M. A., & Williams, M. C. (1975). Social psychology, criminal justice, and the principle of discretion: A selective review. *Personality and Social Psychology Bulletin, 1,* 471–484.

Sheffey, S., & Tindale, R. S. (1992). Perceptions of sexual harassment in the workplace. *Journal of Applied Social Psychology, 22,* 1502–1520.

Simon, R. I. (1987). Epilogue: We are belegaled. In *Clinical psychiatry and the law* (pp. 467–487). Washington, DC: American Psychiatric Association.

Smith, V. L. (1991). Prototypes in the courtroom: Lay representations of legal concepts. *Journal of Personality and Social Psychology, 61,* 857–872.

Steininger, M., Newell, J. D., & Garcia, L. T. (1984). *Ethical issues in psychology.* Homewood, IL: Dorsey Press.

Stern, P. (1998). *Preparing and presenting expert testimony in child abuse litigation: A guide for expert witnesses and attorneys.* Thousand Oaks, CA: Sage.

Stinson, V., Devenport, J. L., Cutler, B. L., & Kravitz, D. A. (1996). How effective is the presence-of-counsel safeguard? Attorney perceptions of suggestiveness, fairness, and correctability of biased lineup procedures. *Journal of Applied Psychology, 81,* 64–75.

Stockdale, M. S. (1993). The role of sexual misperceptions of women's friendliness in an emerging theory of sexual harassment. *Journal of Vocational Behavior, 42,* 84–101.

Sundby, S. E. (1997). The jury as critic: An empirical look at how capital juries perceive expert and lay testimony. *Virginia Law Review, 83,* 1109–1188.

Swenson, L. C. (1993). *Psychology and law for the helping professions.* Belmont, CA: Brooks/Cole.

Tarasoff v. Regents of the University of California, Supp. 131. *California Reporter, 14* (1976).

Towell, N. A., Kemp, R. I., & Pike, G. E. (1996). The effects of witness identification masking on memory and person perception. *Psychology, Crime & Law, 2,* 333–346.

Tracey, M. (1998, January/February). Be aware of malpractice risks when using electronic office devices. *The National Psychologist,* p. 17.

Tromp, S., Koss, M. P., Figueredo, A. J., & Tharan, M. (1995). Are rape memories different? A comparison of rape, other unpleasant, and pleasant memories among employed women. *Journal of Traumatic Stress, 8,* 607–627.

Viederman, M. (1995). The reconstruction of a repressed sexual molestation fifty years later. *Journal of the American Psychoanalytic Association, 43,* 1169–1195.

Vitek, W. (1997). Privacy's place: The role of civility and community in a technological culture. *Ethics & Behavior, 7,* 265–270.

Vitek, W., & Jackson, W. (Eds.). (1996). *Rooted in the land: Essays on community and place.* New Haven, CT: Yale University Press.

Walzer, R. S., & Miltimore, S. (1993). Mandated supervision, monitoring, and therapy of disciplined health care professionals: Implementation and model regulations. *Journal of Legal Medicine, 14,* 565–596.

Weiner, I. B. (1995). How to anticipate ethical and legal challenges in personality assessments. In J. N. Butcher (Ed.), *Clinical personality assessment: Practical applications* (pp. 95–103). New York: Oxford University Press.

Wrightsman, L. S., Nietzel, M. T., & Fortune, W. H. (1994). *Psychology and the legal system* (3rd ed.). Monterey, CA: Brooks/Cole.

CHAPTER 3

Accessing Legal Literature

ROBERT J. VAN DER VELDE

WITH THE growing involvement of the legal system in every facet of American life and the increasingly important intermingling of psychology and law, a working knowledge of the law upon which issues are decided and access to legal resource materials are ever more important to the social scientist and practitioner. This chapter surveys the types of law and then looks at the use of the law library and resource materials available to the researcher and practitioner.

SOURCES OF LAW

There are basically four types of law that mirror the organization of the American system of government: constitutional, legislative (statutory law), administrative (regulatory law), and judicial (case law or common law). As a general rule, most legal resource materials offer information on only one type of law from one particular source. Accordingly, a researcher needs to have a working knowledge of a variety of source materials so that research topics can be thoroughly reviewed.

CONSTITUTIONAL LAW

Constitutional law is not limited to the U.S. Constitution, which is, of course, the supreme law of the land. Each state is governed by a constitution that is supreme within its borders. The Tenth Amendment to the U.S. Constitution provides that all powers not delegated to the federal government and not specifically prohibited to the states are reserved to the states or to the people. In matters not preempted by the U.S. Constitution or federal law, state constitutional law is supreme.

Municipalities and counties are, in most cases, organized under charters. These charters are, in effect, constitutions for these political entities. The charter is superior to all ordinances enacted by these entities but is inferior to state and federal law.

STATUTORY LAW

Statutory law is derived from enactments by legislative bodies. Federal statutes are enacted by the U.S. Congress, state statutes by the legislatures of the various states, and ordinances by local governments. Statsky (1975) explains how the researcher may find statutory law. Statutory law is compiled in two ways: (a) *session laws*, which collect the statutes in chronological order, and (b) *statutory codes*, which rearrange these statutes according to subject matter. At the federal level, session laws are found in the *United States Statutes at Large (Stat.)*. The codified versions of statutes are found in the *United States Code (U.S.C.)*, published by the Government Printing Office, and in two commercially published compilations, *United States Code Annotated (U.S.C.A.)*, published by West Publishing Company, and the *United States Code Service (U.S.C.S.)*, published by the Lawyers Cooperative Publishing Company. Both the *U.S.C.A.* and *U.S.C.S.* are *annotated codes*, meaning that along with each statute the publisher has included short summaries of cases and other research aids.

Federal statutes are inferior only to the U.S. Constitution and are superior to all other laws. State statutes are enacted by legislatures and are binding within the state's borders if not in conflict with federal law or the state constitution. At the state level, in most cases the state government publishes session laws, and various private publishers compile and publish the state code.

ADMINISTRATIVE LAW

Administrative law is created by state and federal agencies through the issuance of regulations or by decisions made by the administrative body to settle disputes in the subject area that it regulates. For example, the Internal Revenue Service issues not only tax regulations but also administrative rulings on disputed claims. Both are forms of administrative law that bind taxpayers. As another example, administrative agencies grant a variety of licenses, from drivers' licenses to licenses for professional practice, and the rules and regulations pertaining to the issuance and revocation of licenses are forms of administrative law that affect nearly everyone. Where state and federal agencies share responsibilities for regulating certain activities, state administrative law is inferior to federal administrative law.

As with statutes, administrative rules are often arranged chronologically in *administrative registers* and according to subject matter in *administrative codes*. Federal administrative rules are published in the *Federal Register (Fed. Reg.)*, a daily publication of the Government Printing Office. Federal administrative rules are also organized each year in the *Code of Federal Regulations (C.F.R.)*. At the state level, some states publish compilations of administrative rules, but in other states the only source for this material may be the agency that promulgates the rule.

Federal administrative agency decisions may be published by the agency and compiled by the government and, occasionally, by commercial publishers.

Publication at the state level varies considerably, with many state agency decisions available only from the agency issuing the decision.

Judicial Law

Judicial law or case law is the law developed through the history of the judicial system from the cases decided by the courts in the past. The courts generally operate on what is known as a common law system. The common law is the product of a history of court decisions. Each court, building on the decisions of prior courts, strives to treat similar cases in a consistent manner, providing a base for common law. This principle of using prior decisions in deciding cases is called precedent or stare decisis (Latin for "stand by what has been decided"). Because not all issues that may arise within our legal system are specifically covered by statute, judges frequently rely on precedent in making their decisions or rulings.

Each court within the U.S. judicial system has a defined jurisdiction. This jurisdiction is defined not only geographically but also by subject matter. Generally, state courts consider state law and issues arising within their geographical borders. Federal courts handle issues involving federal laws, constitutional issues, cases where the federal government is a party, and controversies between citizens of different states.

Each state has its own common law history and its own case law, just as the federal court system has its own case law and common law history. Each court, whether state or federal, has a defined geographical district and handles only matters arising within that district. Prior to initiating research at the law library, a determination as to the jurisdiction involved must be made by the researcher. For example, a decision of the highest court of Florida will probably not be binding on the courts of Nebraska, though it may be considered persuasive to a Nebraska court if the courts of that state have not decided a similar issue.

The body of American case law consists of about five million decisions. More than 40,000 reports of court decisions are added to this collection each year. These reports are primarily decisions of federal and state appellate courts. Generally, decisions of state trial courts are not published, with a few exceptions. Most of the federal decisions that will have an impact on the research of the social scientist will be decisions of the U.S. District Courts, the U.S. Courts of Appeals, and decisions of the U.S. Supreme Court.

The U.S. District Courts are the trial courts of the federal system. Many of the decisions of the U.S. District Courts are published in the *Federal Supplement (F. Supp.)*, published by West Publishing Company. West also publishes several reporters serving specialized areas of federal law, such as the *Bankruptcy Reporter, Military Justice Reporter, Social Security Reporter, Education Law Reporter,* and *Federal Rules Decisions.*

Appeals from decisions of the U.S. District Courts are taken to the U.S. Courts of Appeals. The Courts of Appeals are organized into thirteen circuits. Eleven circuits handle appeals from several states in each circuit. There is a separate circuit for appeals from the District of Columbia, and the Court of Appeals for the Federal Circuit decides patent appeals and certain other specialized appeals. The decisions of the U.S. Courts of Appeals are published in the *Federal*

Reporter (F., F.2d, or F.3d) by West Publishing Company. Until recently, almost all written opinions of the courts of appeals were published in the *Federal Reporter*. However, because of the growing volume of federal litigation, each circuit has now adopted guidelines restricting the number of opinions actually published, so that as many as two-thirds of all federal appellate decisions go unpublished.

The opinions of the U.S. Supreme Court are presently published in five different publications: *The United States Reports* (official edition), *The United States Supreme Court Reports* (Lawyers' Cooperative Publishing Company), *Supreme Court Reporter* (West Publishing Company), *United States Law Week* (Bureau of National Affairs), and *Supreme Court Bulletin* (Commerce Clearing House). U.S. Supreme Court decisions are also available on the Internet, usually within an hour of being handed down by the Court, and may be downloaded at the Cornell Law Library site at http://supct.law.cornell.edu/supct.

The official edition *(U.S.)* has been published since 1817. The Supreme Court generally has only one term of court each year, beginning in October and ordinarily completed in June. This is known as the October Term. The opinions are initially issued separately as "slip" opinions immediately after being handed down to provide quick dissemination. They are subsequently published in "advance sheets" containing a compilation of the most recent decisions prior to binding. After the end of the October Term each year, the advance sheets are replaced by bound volumes.

The United States Supreme Court Reports (L.Ed.), privately published by the Lawyers' Cooperative Publishing Company and the Bancroft-Whitney Company, contains, in addition to the opinions of the Supreme Court, editorial treatments prepared by the publishers summarizing the cases in headnotes that precede the opinion. Summaries of the attorneys' briefs submitted to the Court are occasionally included for selected important cases.

The Supreme Court Reporter (S.Ct.), published by West Publishing Company, begins with opinions published in 1882 and contains a summary of each case and headnotes preceding each of the opinions.

Because the decisions of the Supreme Court are immediately law of the land, their impact is paramount. State and federal courts must follow these decisions as precedent. Accordingly, it is important that lawyers and lay persons have immediate access to these opinions. *United States Law Week (U.S.L.W.)* and *Commerce Clearing House Supreme Court Bulletin* are publications designed to disseminate these opinions as soon as they are handed down by the Court. Each of these publications receives the slip opinions on the day they are announced and mails copies immediately to subscribers. The *U.S.L.W.* is a publication of two or more volumes by the Bureau of National Affairs in Washington. The publication contains Supreme Court opinions in their complete text in looseleaf form. In addition to current opinions, the volumes contain the minutes of all sessions of the Court held during the week, a listing of cases docketed or scheduled to be filed, a summary of cases recently filed, a summary of the oral arguments of the cases argued each week before the Court, and an index of cases pending. *The Supreme Court Bulletin* is a publication of the Commerce Clearing House and is also in looseleaf form.

State court decisions are generally published in official and unofficial reports. The most frequently consulted and generally most available are the publications of the National Reporter System, published by West Publishing Company. The opinions of the state appellate and trial courts are found in seven regional reporters arranged by geographical divisions (*Atlantic, North Eastern, North Western, Pacific, South Eastern, South Western,* and *Southern Reporters*). In addition to the seven regional reporters, New York and California have their own individual reporters, which are included in the National Reporter System. Each bound volume contains two tables of cases: the first a single alphabetical list of all cases in the volume, and the second a separate alphabetical listing of all cases by states or courts.

To adequately treat the proper citation of court reports would require a rather lengthy volume and, accordingly, citation format only will be summarized here. State decisions are generally cited with both the official and unofficial state reporter citations. For example: *Wagner v. Roche Laboratories,* 77 Ohio St. 3d 116, 671 N.E.2d 252 (1996) is a case that appears in volume 77 of the third series of the *Ohio State Reports* (the official reporter) beginning at page 116, and in volume 671 of the second series of the *Northeastern Reporter,* beginning at page 252. In recent years, many states have discontinued publication of official reporters. With regard to these more recent decisions, the citations will omit the official citation and appear as follows: *Wooten v. Houston County Health Care Authority,* 681 So.2d 147 (Ala. Civ. App. 1995), a case found in volume 681 of the *Southern Reporter,* second series, beginning at page 147, and decided by the Alabama Court of Civil Appeals.

Federal decisions are cited in a similar fashion, with the volume, page, court, and year of decision, such as *Eddmonds v. Peters,* 93 F.3d 1307 (7th Cir. 1996), a case decided by the U.S. Court of Appeals for the Seventh Circuit, found in volume 93 of the *Federal Reporter,* third series, beginning at page 1307.

THE LAW LIBRARY

Law libraries can be found on law school campuses and in most larger municipalities. Generally, most courthouses contain law libraries. Local public libraries may contain general introductory works and a few primary resources but will usually be inadequate for research. Federal and state courthouse libraries are rarely officially open to the public but are often available with the consent of the librarian on duty. Most law school libraries are open to the public. These libraries are usually the best for general research, as they contain the widest variety of resource materials. In smaller communities, most law offices will have limited libraries; of course, access to these libraries must be obtained by permission. Although law librarians usually cannot dispense legal advice, they can be good sources of information for practitioners about navigating through the legal research process. Law librarians will also assist the novice legal researcher in defining search terms and in locating research tools.

ANALYZING THE FACTS

The first step for the practitioner or researcher is to assemble the pertinent facts about the case or the area to be researched. Once these facts are gathered, the researcher may then compile a list of key terms to use for further research. Price (1989), Olson (1988), and Wren and Wren (1983), for example, illustrate how these key terms enable the researcher to locate pertinent law. A common method used to analyze facts suggested by West Publishing Company is to identify categories as follows:

Parties involved in the case: This category involves identifying the status of the parties (i.e., membership in a class or group, such as minors, inmates, or mental incompetents) and their relationships to one another (such as therapist-patient, parent-child).

Places where the facts arose, and objects or things involved: Place refers not just to a physical place where the facts occurred (such as a hospital or school), but also to the jurisdiction involved, including whether the issue is one of state law, federal law, or both. As to the objects or things involved, the researcher should identify synonyms to use in a search (such as "treatment facility" as well as "hospital") so that relevant authorities are not missed.

Basis of the case or issue involved: This category addresses the legal theory on which the case is based. Experience will be the best guide for the researcher in properly identifying the legal issue involved.

Defense to the action or issue: This category deals with the claims the person being sued may use to defeat the claim, such as a statute of limitations defense for actions that are time-barred.

Relief sought: This category deals with identifying what it is that the plaintiff seeks to obtain, such as money damages, injunctive relief, or a discharge of a contract.

Once the researcher has identified key terms using these categories, there should be a long list of terms to explore using reference material available in most law libraries. For example, the practitioner may seek cases in which courts detail the standards for releasing an individual from confinement for treatment after acquittal by reason of insanity. The *parties* involved would include the patient but also could include the therapist or the institution in which the patient is being held. The *places* include the location of the institution, but also issues of state law (such as the state's rules for criminal procedure) and federal law (such as the patient's constitutional rights to due process). The *basis* or *issue* could include whether the process by which the state makes the determination to release an individual from confinement is sufficient to protect both the individual and the community. The *relief* sought is the individual's liberty. Each of these terms and their synonyms provide fertile areas for the researcher to explore using a variety of references.

REFERENCE SOURCES

Generally, research sources fall into two categories: primary sources and secondary sources. Court decisions, statutes, rules and regulations, and documents that establish the law on a particular issue are considered primary sources of law, as discussed above. Secondary sources consist of those sources that summarize, discuss, or explain primary sources of law. Most legal researchers begin their work with one or more of the secondary sources discussed below.

If the topic or subject of research involves general legal principles, the researcher may want to begin with treatises or legal encyclopedias. Treatises are books written by experts in certain areas of the law and cover the entire subject, such as criminal law, probate law, or civil rights. In a child custody case, for example, a review of a treatise on domestic law may be helpful. Treatises can explain the basic concepts of law and can provide useful instruction in more specialized areas. For example, a highly regarded treatise on the federal rules of evidence, including the use of psychological experts, is *Weinstein's Federal Evidence: Commentaries on the Rules of Evidence for the United States Courts* (McLaughlin, 1997). A practitioner interested in similar state rules might consult a treatise focusing on state law, such as *Weissenberger's Ohio Evidence* (Weissenberger, 1996).

Most law libraries will also contain one or more legal dictionaries and encyclopedias. Legal dictionaries, such as *Black's Law Dictionary*, provide definitions (and pronunciations) of unfamiliar legal terms. Legal encyclopedias are arranged by subject, providing statements as to general law supported by references to case authorities.

Corpus Juris Secundum (C.J.S.) is published by West Publishing Company. Its intent is to set out American case law from the first reported cases to the present. This work supersedes *Corpus Juris (C.J.)*, an earlier edition, with references being made to the earlier edition for the earlier case law. This set, like most law books, is kept up-to-date by replacement volumes and annual pocket supplements that are inserted in the back covers of each volume. In using any legal encyclopedia, it is important to check the pocket supplements or the applicable replacement volumes to make sure the material reviewed is up-to-date. As with other encyclopedias, *C.J.S.* is arranged alphabetically by subject matter, with short articles containing citations to pertinent authorities. An alphabetical list of topics is included in the beginning of the first volume of the general index and preceding the text of each volume. For example, the topic "mental health" is found in volume 57. Detailed subtopics include discussions of a wide variety of legal issues pertaining to mental health, such as 57 *C.J.S. Mental Health* § 240, entitled "Restoration to Mental Health and Release from Confinement." This section explains the standards by which courts make decisions to order the release of persons confined for treatment after being acquitted by reason of insanity, including references to statutes and judicial decisions in a number of states.

American Jurisprudence (AmJur) is published by the Lawyers' Cooperative Publishing Company and the Bancroft-Whitney Company. It began publication in 1936. Revised in 1962, *American Jurisprudence Second (AmJur2d)* was completed in 1976, superseding *AmJur*. *AmJur2d* contains an index volume arranged topically.

Other encyclopedias, notably *AmJur Proof of Facts, AmJur Proof of Facts Second, American Jurisprudence Trials, AmJur Pleadings and Practice Forms, Annotated*, and *AmJur Legal Forms Second*, are available, but these are technical encyclopedias designed to assist in preparing a case for trial and will probably be of little benefit to the nonlawyer.

Some states have encyclopedias devoted to their own laws. California, Florida, New York, Ohio, and Texas have encyclopedias published by the Lawyers' Cooperative Publishing Company and Bancroft-Whitney Company that follow the form of *AmJur2d*. Illinois, Maryland, and Michigan have encyclopedias published by West Publishing Company that are similar in form to *C.J.S.*

Legal periodicals provide additional resource material. There are three groups of legal periodicals: (a) law reviews, (b) bar association publications, and (c) special subject and interest periodicals. Law reviews are distinctive in that their editorial management is controlled by student editors. These reviews will contain a number of selected articles dealing with various topics, primarily in newly developing fields of law or changes in the law.

Bar association periodicals range from publications such as the *American Bar Association Journal* to some that are merely newsletters of local bar associations. Articles contained in the more familiar publications concern subjects of current interest to the general legal profession.

Subject and interest legal periodicals are journals devoted to a specific area of law. Generally published by private companies or law schools, they are aimed at practicing attorneys specializing in particular fields of law. *Insurance Law Journal, Journal of Psychiatry and Law,* and *Journal of Legal Medicine* are some of these. Some law schools publish a general law review and more specialized publications. For example, the *Columbia Law Review* contains articles on a broad range of topics, but law reviews such as *Columbia Journal of Environmental Law, Columbia Journal of Gender and the Law,* and *Columbia Journal of Law and Social Problems* publish articles on narrower topics. Most libraries will not contain all of these publications. Smaller law libraries generally contain only locally or regionally published reviews or periodicals. The serious researcher who desires access to a wide range of legal periodicals should seek out a law school library.

Comprehensive periodical indexes are available to provide entry into legal periodicals. The *Index to Legal Periodicals* is the most comprehensive index available. Coverage is limited strictly to legal periodicals published in the United States, Great Britain, Canada, Australia, and New Zealand. The index is arranged alphabetically by both topic and author. In using the *Index* it is important to search for articles covering the same topic in two or more subjects because this index tends to contain inconsistent subject indexing. For example, articles regarding mental capacity may be found under "Mental Health," "Insanity," "Psychiatry," and "Psychology," to name a few. Although many other indexes or digests of periodicals are available, the *Index to Legal Periodicals* is the most comprehensive. Many libraries subscribe to the *Index* in both print and electronic form.

Case digests are helpful research tools because they index case law. The digests published by West Publishing Company offer the most comprehensive system for locating cases by subject matter. West has organized all areas of American law into topics, arranged alphabetically, and further subdivided by key number. The key number identifies a narrow subtopic of the law. West editors provide short summaries, called headnotes, for each area of law discussed within each decision in the West reporters. Each case contains at least one headnote for each issue discussed in the case. Some complex decisions dealing with multiple issues may generate a hundred or more headnotes, although most decisions are summarized in a few. Each headnote is identified by the topic and key number and then gathered for publication into digests. For example, the broad topic of mental health is divided into hundreds of subtopics, each with its own key number. Under the subtopic "Disabilities and Privileges of Mentally Disordered Persons" there is a category for "Crimes"; under that category, key number 439 identifies cases dealing with "Confinement after acquittal on ground of mental disorder," and key number 440 is used for cases dealing with "Discharge from Confinement." Thus, a researcher may locate decisions on a narrow subtopic by referring to the digests containing all of the headnotes about that area of law.

West's federal digests cover cases from all federal courts. Headnotes from U.S. Supreme Court cases appear first in each topic, followed by appellate court and district court cases. The most recent edition, *Federal Practice Digest, Fourth,* the current edition, begins with 1991.

West's digest system also provides state digests for opinions of state courts in all states except Utah, Nevada, and Delaware. West also combines headnotes from state and federal courts into its *American Digest System.* The *American Digest Century Edition* provides coverage for cases from the beginning of the Republic to 1896. The *Decennial Digest* includes cases from 1896 to the present. Each issue of the *Decennial Digest* was designed to cover a 10-year period, but because of the growing volume of case law, "decennial" digests are now issued every five years.

Each of the West digests includes several useful research tools. The table of cases lists all of the cases included in the digest. The digests also include a descriptive word index used to locate the precise key number for each topic and a topical outline that lists the various subtopics, so that the researcher can easily locate the appropriate key number and examine all of the headnotes under that key number.

If the researcher is searching for a statute rather than a judicial opinion, several avenues are available. If following a cite provided by another source, the most recent edition of the code should be found to locate the volume containing the appropriate title and sections. For example, the federal law prohibiting sex discrimination in employment is found at 42 U.S.C. § 2000e. Title 42 of the U.S. Code, made up of several volumes, contains all federal statutes dealing with "Public Health and Welfare," including the 1964 Civil Rights Act. Section 2000e contains the provision regarding employment discrimination. This same section may be found by locating "Discrimination," "Employment," or "Sex Discrimination" in the general index to the code. The *U.S.C.A.* and *U.S.C.S.* services, as discussed above, will contain not just the code section but references to the headnotes of decisions interpreting the section of the statute.

If one is interested in a particular act and its name but not its location is known, four routes may be taken. *Cases by Popular Name* is a single volume edited to include only the names of acts and cases that the editors consider most important. It is organized alphabetically and updated by pocket parts that, as in most other legal publications, supplement the volume to provide the most recent information. The *U.S.C.* has an "Acts Cited by Popular Name" table beginning on page 1 in a volume called *Popular Names and Tables,* which provides a citation to a statute by its popular name. For example, Title 25, U.S.C. §§ 455–455ge can be located in this table under its popular name, the Indian Education Assistance Act. The *U.S.C.A.* has a "Popular Name Acts" list at the beginning of each volume, but this list includes only the popular acts included in the title covered by that volume. The *U.S.C.S.* has its complete popular name table in one of the tables volumes that follow the general index volumes.

Shepard's Citations, published by Shepard's/McGraw-Hill, is also an invaluable tool for the legal researcher. It provides a list of references that have cited or interpreted the case or law in question. *Shepard's* lists every case published in an official or unofficial reporter by its citation and allows the researcher to determine where a case or statute has been cited. *Shepard's* also indexes the subsequent history of cases, so that the researcher can quickly identify whether a case has been affirmed, modified, or reversed on appeal. There are *Shepard's* citators for every state. *Shepard's* citators are also available on CD-ROM, where a red traffic light appears if the user enters a citation of a case that has been overruled. It is vital for the researcher to examine each decision using *Shepard's* so that cases that have been overruled are not relied upon. For example, in *Rabidue v. Osceola Refining Co.,* 805 F.2d 611 (6th Cir. 1986), the Sixth Circuit concluded that for sexual harassment to be unlawful employment discrimination it must be so severe as to have "affected seriously [the] psychological well-being" of the employee. That conclusion was overruled by the Supreme Court in *Harris v. Forklift Systems, Inc.,* 510 U.S. 17 (1993). The *Harris* court concluded that concrete psychological harm was not required to establish unlawful sexual harassment, but was one factor that could be considered in determining whether the law had been violated. Thus, the *Harris* court overruled the *Rabidue* decision, and *Shepard's* citator indicates as much. Unless the careful researcher had "Shepardized" the *Rabidue* decision to find the *Harris* case, a subtle but important development in the law of psychological aspects of sexual harassment would have been missed.

COMPUTER-ASSISTED LEGAL RESEARCH

Rapidly developing technology has given the researcher new tools for legal research, including online services, CD-ROMs, and the Internet (Wren & Wren, 1988).

The two main competing online services for legal research are Lexis®, a service of Reed Elsevier Inc., and Westlaw®, a service of West Publishing Company. Lexis and Westlaw provide comprehensive databases of primary and secondary authorities, as well as additional database products. Many attorneys subscribe to one or both of these services. Both are relatively expensive, generally assessing charges on a per minute basis, so they are usually available only to legal practitioners.

Lexis and Westlaw operate similarly. Users select a collection of information to search (organized as "files" within "libraries" on Lexis, and "databases" on Westlaw). Searches can be run using Boolean logical connectors or simple English questions (called Natural Language™ searching on Westlaw and Freestyle™ searching on Lexis), and the service will retrieve any documents in the selected database that match the requested search terms. McDonald (1987) describes more fully how these searches may be formulated. For example, a researcher interested in whether repressed memories of abuse would toll the Alabama statute of limitations could search the Alabama files for all cases involving repressed memories, which would locate *Travis v. Ziter*, 681 So.2d 1348 (Ala. 1996). In *Travis,* the Alabama Supreme Court held that the period of time in which memories of sexual abuse were repressed would not act as a period of "insanity" under Alabama law to stop the running of the statute of limitations, finding that there was not a scientific consensus about the validity of repressed memories. Similar searches in databases for other jurisdictions would reveal how courts in other states have decided the same question.

Computer-assisted legal research can also be conducted using CD-ROM forms of print material. West Publishing Company, for example, has published CD-ROM versions of many of its case reporters. Most legal CD-ROM products can be relatively expensive, but a number of smaller publishers have produced compilations of primary authority, such as U.S. Supreme Court decisions, at reasonable rates. Thus, for a reasonable fee, the practitioner can follow developing case law on scientific evidence, use of forensic psychological testimony in a variety of cases, or any other issue of interest to practitioners.

In addition, increasing amounts of primary authority can be found at sites on the Internet, much of it at no charge. As noted earlier, the full text of decisions of the U.S. Supreme Court are available on the Internet. Recent reported decisions of the U.S. Courts of Appeals are also available on the Internet, as are decisions from a growing number of state courts. The full text of federal statutes and regulations, as well as many state codes, are also available online. Due to copyright restrictions, many of the editorial enhancements found in printed materials, such as summaries or headnotes added by private publishers, are not available on the Internet. As with most features of the Internet, legal research sites are rapidly evolving, and more sophisticated research tools may be available in the near future. The locations of the source material change too frequently to be listed here, but most Internet search engines (such as Yahoo!, Lycos, and others) will catalogue many of the sites where sources of legal authority may be found and can provide the most up-to-date information.

CONCLUSION

The key to legal research is persistence and, above all, patience. The researcher interested in obtaining more detailed instruction should consult the materials identified in the References appended to this chapter. For example, Cohen (1992) provides an overview of legal research with more detailed research strategies offered by Corbin (1979), Jacobstein (1994), Roberts (1986), and *West's Law Finder* (1991). The reader interested in electronically based services can consult Evans (1974), Grossman (1994), Hazelton (1993), and Leith (1991), and further explanation of legal research terms can be found in the *Legal Research*

Dictionary (Legal Information Services, 1987). The maze of the law can be difficult to navigate, but the dedicated researcher can be successful.

REFERENCES

Black's law dictionary (6th ed.). (1990). St. Paul, MN: West.

Cohen, M. L. (1992). *Legal research in a nutshell.* St. Paul, MN: West.

Corbin, J. B. (1979). *Find the law in the law library: A guide to legal research.* Chicago: American Library Association.

Eddmonds v. Peters, 93 F.3d 1307 (7th Cir. 1996).

Evans, J. H. (1979). *Law on the net.* Berkeley, CA: Nolo Press.

Grossman, G. S. (Ed.). (1994). *Legal research: Historical foundations of the electronic age.* New York: Oxford University Press.

Harris v. Forklift Systems, Inc., 510 U.S. 17 (1993).

Hazelton, P. A. (1993). *Computer assisted legal research: The basics.* St. Paul, MN: West.

Jacobstein, J. M. (1994). *Fundamentals of legal research* (6th ed.). Westbury, NY: Foundation Press.

The legal research dictionary: From advance sheets to pocket parts. (1987). Newton Highlands, MA: Legal Information Services.

Leith, P. (1991). *The computerized lawyer: A guide to the use of computers in the legal profession.* London; New York: Springer-Verlag.

McDonald, A. L. (1987). *Communicating with legal databases: Terms and abbreviations for the legal researcher.* New York: Neal-Schuman.

McLaughlin, J. M. (1997). *Weinstein's federal evidence: Commentary on the rules of evidence for the United States Courts.* New York: Matthew-Bender.

Olson, K. C. (1988). *Practical approaches to legal research.* New York: Haworth Press.

Price, M. O. (1989). *Effective legal research.* Boston: Little, Brown.

Rabidue v. Osceola Refining Co., 805 F.2d 611 (6th Cir. 1986).

Roberts, B. K. (1986). *Legal research guide: Patterns and practice.* Charlottesville, VA: Michie.

Statsky, W. C. (1975). *Legislation analysis: How to use statutes and regulations.* St. Paul, MN: West.

Travis v. Ziter, 681 So.2d 1348 (Ala. 1996).

Wagner v. Roche Laboratories, 77 Ohio St. 3d 116, 671 N.E.2d 252 (1996).

Weissenberger, G. (1996). *Weissenberger's Ohio evidence.* Cincinnati: Anderson.

West's law finder: A legal research manual. (1991). St. Paul, MN: West.

Wooten v. Houston County Health Care Authority, 681 So.2d 147 (Ala. Civ. App. 1995).

Wren, C. G., & Wren, J. R. (1983). *The legal research manual: A game plan for legal research and analysis.* Madison, WI: Adams & Ambrose.

Wren, C. G., & Wren, J. R. (1988). *Computer assisted legal research.* Madison, WI: Adams & Ambrose.

PART TWO

APPLYING PSYCHOLOGY TO CIVIL PROCEEDINGS

CHAPTER 4

Mediating Domestic Law Issues

KATHRYN D. HESS and PAUL BRINSON

DAILY WE are exposed to the issues surrounding our domestic laws. One cannot read a newspaper or magazine or view a television news broadcast without seeing both discussion of "family values," the 1990s code word for family law public policy, and the results of those policies impinging on family members. For example, one local news page of the *Atlanta Journal/Atlanta Constitution* contained three stories (Good & Davis, 1997; Payne, 1997; Sibley, 1997). All three dealt with domestic law issues. The first, "Broken Family Suffers Loss," describes a three-year-long, two-state custody fight resulting in the death of a 14-year-old by falling or jumping from a moving car to avoid returning to the home of the current custodial parent. Following the death, the custody fight continued over where the burial would occur (Good & Davis, 1997, p. C3)! "DeKalb Court, Schools Differ on Youth's Guilt" deals with the difference in the school's zero-tolerance policies and the county court's rules of evidence and their impact on a 17-year-old high school student (Sibley, 1997, p. C3). The third article deals with aggravated assault charges for a 10-year-old boy following a stabbing of his 12-year-old brother for accusing him of "tormenting" his 4-year-old sister (Payne, 1997, p. C3). Similarly, on a daily basis, psychological practitioners deal with a plethora of domestic law issues.

Today's family is not the same as the family of the 1950s or 1970s. Elrod and Spector (1996), in summarizing the 1990 U.S. Census Bureau Report, note that not only are people waiting until later to marry, but fewer people are choosing to marry, with 30% of the households being composed of single dwellers. Nearly half of all marriages end in divorce, although, at last, the percentage is slightly dropping. Thirty percent of U.S. children live in single-parent families, and nearly as many (27%) are born to a mother who never married. Teenage mothers account for 9% of U.S. births. Violent juvenile crime continues to grow and is heavily represented by products of divorced, single-parent, and teenage parent families.

This chapter provides practitioners with a general working knowledge of domestic and juvenile laws and an understanding of the issues and values around which these laws and procedures evolved, without which a clinician cannot practice in domestic issues. We focus on specific issues of interest to the clinician in dealing with marriage, divorce, child custody, differences in adult and juvenile court systems, and domestic violence. This chapter provides a practical framework upon which a clinician can develop an evaluation and a treatment plan or testimony. Finally, the chapter provides the psychologist with both a knowledge base and an agenda to develop domestic and family policy.

HOW THE DOMESTIC COURTS FUNCTION

Increasingly, the architects of our most intimate family life are no longer family and kinship ties but rather federal legislative statutes and the domestic courts (Elrod, 1995). Through their judgments, domestic courts often define what parents a child has and knows, as well as the most intimate social context and value system in which a child is to develop. Parental or custodial rights may be terminated and family relationships extensively restructured on the premise that the judge or various experts know best how a family should function, although in many cases, experience has amply demonstrated that satisfactory family functioning cannot be dictated. In recognition of the fallacy of expert omniscience, domestic courts have become increasingly reluctant to intervene in ongoing family relationships any more than necessary to resolve the issues at hand; rather, the courts are encouraging families to reorganize themselves. Acknowledging the domestic court's conservative view toward intervention in domestic matters, it is incumbent on the clinician to formulate opinions and responses in conservative terms, sensitive to his or her personal biases and recognizing the family's essential right to self-determination.

Society generally recognizes the family's right to self-determination, but a breakdown in the family structure or function can trigger court involvement. In the event that the requisite threshold of disruption occurs, the courts will intervene to mediate the family's difficulties. In these cases, the court's intervention is usually intended to minimize the disruption of the ongoing functions of the family, and the court is generally willing to allow families the opportunity to resolve their differences through negotiation and on their own terms. In the event the family members are unable or unwilling to negotiate an agreement, the court will provide a final decision, which is presumably consistent with the values of the broader community. The goals of domestic jurisprudence are to achieve efficiency, harmony, and balance in the family order.

Mermin (1982) suggests a number of important services offered to society and the family by domestic jurisprudence. These services include (a) the definition of a status in society including minority, marriage, legitimacy, domains of responsibility, or immunity from responsibility; (b) the settlement of domestic disputes through arbitration or negotiation and as a final authority in reaching a decision; (c) the maintenance of order through policing, protection, and definition of the relationships among family members; (d) the protection of the family against the exercise of excessive or unfair government power; and (e) assurances that family members enjoy the minimum decencies of life, such as economic protection, preservation of social status, and maintenance of the individual's physical and psychological well-being.

The domestic or chancery court has protection as its central purpose (Paulsen, Wadlington, & Goebel, 1974). The court has traditionally executed its responsibility through a determination of fault or failure to fulfill contractual marital responsibilities, agreements for custody and visitation following the dissolution of a marriage, and provision for the support and maintenance of those deemed unable to support themselves. With the formation of the juvenile court system in the United States in the late 19th century, the state extended its responsibility to the actions of delinquent children and their subsequent rehabilitation. More recently, the domestic courts have begun to intervene in support of children's relationships with grandparents and other significant family members. Important progress has been made in the intervention and development of policy regarding abused and neglected children, the termination of parental rights, abortion, and foster or adoptive placement.

The courts typically respect community standards and continuation of family relationships in their application of testimony and subsequent judgments. Recent domestic court actions tend to embrace expeditious decisions on behalf of any minors involved rather than finding fault among the litigants. The court's attention has become increasingly directed toward remedies that provide an economic foundation for protecting children and others unable to provide for themselves (Aldous, 1997; Mermin, 1982). Issues of child abuse and maltreatment are exceptions to this trend and indicate that psychological and sociological factors are also frequent considerations in arriving at judgments.

The domestic court is permitted broad dispositional powers and procedural limitations, especially in regard to its treatment of juveniles. In fulfillment of his or her responsibility, the domestic court judge, more often than a judge in other courts, enlists the advice of professionals from other disciplines in identifying problems, recommending courses of action, and interpreting facts presented to the court. It is into this dynamic arena for the resolution of some of life's most intense problems that a psychologist may be asked to offer professional input.

CLINICAL CONTRIBUTIONS TO DOMESTIC COURT

The development of the family court and juvenile justice system over the past 150 years has paralleled the growth in influence of psychologists and the social sciences. Indeed, the juvenile justice system was initiated through the cooperative efforts of social workers and the court system. The primary purposes of the juvenile justice system were the rehabilitation of juvenile offenders and the identification of children in need of care. These tasks are heavily invested in psychological theory, particularly as it concerns etiology of the problems. Thus, the clinician in domestic court finds clinical and judicial purposes closely tied in helping realize the potential of the family to function in its own behalf.

In the past, input from the social sciences to the domestic court has primarily been limited to clinical input (Goldzband, 1983; Underwager & Wakefield, 1992), frequently reflecting the judgment and personal bias of the psychologist rather than scientific fact. Recent flagrant abuses by mental health professionals, centered around charges of abuse in childcare facilities, raised questions about the expert's role (Wakefield & Underwager, 1992). As *Daubert* replaces the *Frye* standard for admissability of evidence or expert testimony, the nature of psychological evidence should become more empirically oriented (Bala, 1994a, 1994b; Hess, Chapter 19, this volume).

On the other hand, the domestic courts have done little to solicit empirical input from psychologists on domestic issues. Melton (1984) pointed out that Chief Justice Burger cited "common sense and intuition" as his primary authority on domestic issues. The reliance of the court on common sense and intuition is not altogether surprising in light of the court's support for the "reasonable man hypothesis" and "rule of reason" concepts. Melton points out that the use of intuition and unsupportable clinical lore represents a major threat to the application of empirical information in the courtroom because the legal system traditionally relies on previous commentary as a basis for current decisions.

With these points in mind, the question then becomes: Do psychologists have knowledge to offer domestic jurisprudence that goes beyond common sense and clinical lore? The answer is yes, depending on the context (Melton, 1984). By the same token, the question should be asked as to whether the court is ready or willing to accept information that may be at variance with commonly or traditionally held beliefs.

If the psychologist's influence is to be felt in the domestic courtroom, it is incumbent on him or her to have a clear understanding of the questions at hand and to formulate responses with an eye to their social, legal, and scientific implications.

GUIDELINES FOR THE PSYCHOLOGIST IN DOMESTIC COURT

The American Psychological Association (APA, 1994) has developed guidelines for child custody evaluations in divorce procedures based on their *Ethical Principles of Psychologists and Code of Conduct* (APA, 1992). Although these are not intended to be exhaustive or mandatory, they are intended to promote proficiency in conducting evaluations and will be discussed further in the custody section of this chapter. Additionally, child custody guidelines were developed in the 1980s by at least six states and should be consulted by psychologists in those states (APA, 1992). Guidelines to aid in determining specific standards of practice for psychological services in the courtroom have been developed by the Committee on Ethical Guidelines for Forensic Psychologists (1991). An examination of the standards developed by the American Psychological Association regarding professional practice should also serve to assist clinicians in their participation in domestic legal issues (*Standards for Providers of Psychological Services,* APA, 1977; "Specialty Guidelines for the Delivery of Services," APA, 1981; *Standards for Educational and Psychological Testing,* APA, 1985; "Ethical Principles of Psychologists and Code of Conduct," APA, 1992; *Record Keeping Guidelines,* APA, 1993). Following these general guidelines, reports and testimony to the court should be conservative, comprehensive, and concise and should demonstrate a sensitivity to the complex emotional, psychological, and personal rights of all individuals and family members involved. Clinicians need to remember that they are not called upon by the court to render a decision, but rather to offer an evaluation and interpretation of the psychological issues presented as relevant to the questions before the court.

Contributions by Blau (1984a, 1984b, 1985), Grisso (1986), Hess (1985), Melton, Petrila, Poythress, and Slobogin (1987), Shapiro (1984), I. B. Weiner (1985; Chapter 18, in this volume), and Ziskin (1981) are useful in developing forensic reports and courtroom testimony.

TRADITIONAL AND CONSTITUTIONAL PRINCIPLES RELATED TO DOMESTIC JURISPRUDENCE

PHILOSOPHICAL UNDERPINNINGS OF DOMESTIC COURT

Although the traditional goal of the domestic court has been to protect and support the integrity of the family unit, the role of the contemporary domestic court has shifted significantly in the past 150 years. Domestic jurisprudence relied on common law concepts of the family as the basis for decisions in domestic proceedings. More recently, drawing upon the philosophies of John Locke and John Stuart Mill regarding the proper relationship of the government to the governed and the intrinsic nature of man, the courts have shifted toward preserving individual liberties and establishing responsibilities among family members.

Simultaneously, the Industrial Revolution, changing concepts regarding the roles of women, children, and families, and efforts to establish a more pluralistic democracy mark changes in domestic law. As society became more integrated with a philosophical and economic stake in the child, changes occurred in the role of education, in equal participation in social institutions, and in perception, from seeing children as under the dominion of their parents to seeing the family as a socializing agent of the greater society. One effect of these changes is the decreased reliance on common law theory and the increase in statutory provisions.

PRINCIPLES GOVERNING THE DOMESTIC COURT

Broadly speaking, the principles and doctrines governing the domestic court are categorized in three areas: jurisdiction, procedures, and disposition. Issues of jurisdiction relate to the basis under which the court is empowered to act in a given circumstance. Procedures reflect the judicial processes, such as giving testimony, and serve as the vehicle for offering the protection of individual rights from undue state interference. The third area, disposition, refers to the range of alternatives the court has at its disposal to implement its decisions. Similarities and differences in the contractual nature of the domestic court and the rehabilitative nature of the juvenile justice system will be explored.

Several themes thread themselves throughout the operation of the courts, including the doctrine of *parens patriae;* the natural right to marry; the civil and contractual nature of marriage; issues of minority, competency, and responsibility; the best interests of the child doctrine; and the tender years doctrine.

Jurisdiction

The domestic court system falls under the responsibility of the individual states, as it is not expressly provided for in the Constitution. The existence of the domestic court is well rooted in the English common law and the doctrine of *parens patriae*. The contemporary domestic courts are the direct descendants of the English Chauncery Court or "Common Court" and have responsibility for the resolution of disputes rising out of a marriage or issues involving the care or behavior of minor children.

Although the federal courts traditionally avoided becoming involved in domestic issues, decisions such as *In re Gault* (1967) and legislation such as the Uniform Marriage and Divorce Act (UMDA, 1979), the Uniform Services Former Spouses Protection Act (USFSPA, 1990), the Civil Service Retirement Spouse Equity Act (CSRSEA, 1984), the Child Support Recovery Act (CSRA, 1992), the Uniform Child Custody Jurisdiction Act (UCCJA, 1979), the Parental Kidnapping Prevention Act (PKPA, 1980), the International Parental Kidnapping Crime Act (IPKCA, 1993), and the Family and Medical Leave Act (FMLA, 1993) indicate the growing federal role in domestic issues. The increased federal activity has primarily centered around constitutional issues of due process and rights to privacy. The UMDA, the UCCJA, and the PKPA are federal responses to the growing problems of interstate disputes regarding marriage, child custody, and the removal of children by noncustodial parents. These acts are essentially recommended statutory legislation which individual states are encouraged to enact in an effort to create a uniform set of laws regarding marriage, child custody, and the interstate transportation of children of disputed custody. On an international level, the Hague Conference on Private International Law adopted the Hague International Child Abduction Convention (1980) and the Hague Convention on the Protection of Children and Cooperation in Respect of Intercountry Adoption (1993), and is currently working on a Convention on the Protection of Minors, a revision of the 1961 Hague Convention concerning jurisdiction and law regarding minors.

Many have argued for the removal of domestic issues from the court system and for greater use of the less adversarial administrative processes such as arbitration, conciliation, mediation, or education; however, there has been little change in the domestic court's jurisdictional rights. On the contrary, the courts have vigorously defended their jurisdiction as the final arbiter of domestic issues.

In contrast to the extensive common law basis for the jurisdiction of the domestic court, the juvenile justice system is a relatively novel judicial program. Although the juvenile justice system clearly falls under the precepts of the *parens patriae* concept, the system, as it operates in the United States, developed out of attempts to wed social and psychological thought with the judicial process, and to operate in the interests of the children brought before the court.

The *parens patriae* origins of the juvenile courts cast issues as more civil than criminal in nature. Consequently, the juvenile court is not bound by many of the due process issues, rules of evidence, and right to representation that govern adults in criminal courts. From its inception, the juvenile court was intended to be rehabilitative in purpose and to focus on correcting the circumstances antecedent to the child's appearance before the court. The procedures in juvenile court are generally informal and closed to public observation, and they invest broad discretionary powers in the juvenile court judge.

Procedures

Procedures within domestic jurisprudence, exclusive of the juvenile court, are similar to other jurisdictions (civil or criminal), facilitating the presentation and illustration of relevant facts while protecting the rights of the individuals from undue government intrusion. The domestic court follows such standard evidentiary rules in the presentation of testimony as due process procedures, rights of appeal, and other procedures protected by the Constitution or by precedent. To the uninitiated, procedural limits frequently appear arbitrary or intended to unnecessarily extend legal proceedings, thereby raising financial and emotional costs. However, specific procedures have evolved over the centuries as the primary vehicle for protecting the basic rights granted by the Constitution or legislation, allowing the court to function as fairly as possible. Foster (1964) points out that well-defined legal procedures represent the vanguard of protection for individual freedoms, defining in practice the rights of individuals while assuring the facts relevant to interests of the opposing parties and society.

Because the juvenile court system attempts to provide guidance and rehabilitation for the child rather than to assess responsibility and punishment, state courts have often held that the procedural safeguards enjoyed by adults are unnecessary to protect the interests of the child. The reasoning is that under the *parens patriae* doctrine, the court is charged with protecting the interests of the child; therefore, there is presumed to be no conflict of interest between the needs of the state and the needs of the minor in question.

Because the state's needs and the child's needs are presumed to be the same, procedures in juvenile court are relatively unstructured, informal, and directed toward the clinical needs of the children it serves as opposed to being more procedure bound. The unstructured nature of the procedures of the juvenile court has been justified by the need to protect children from the stress of traditional court procedures as well as to shield their juvenile records from others such as adult criminal justice system agents.

These claims of sealed records may be more rhetoric than fact because the integrity and ultimate secrecy of the facts surrounding a juvenile case are typically left to the discretion of the presiding judge. It should also be noted that police jurisdictions, social welfare agencies, and other public agencies frequently maintain records regarding juveniles under their care—records that may be solicited by other governmental or social agencies at a later date.

Disposition

The court is granted the authority to take whatever action is necessary to protect vulnerable family members and to place a child in circumstances that the court feels are most favorable for the well-being of the child, provided the child's due process rights are protected. In fulfillment of this role, the court assumes or assigns custody or guardianship of the children involved, establishes responsibilities, and makes judgments regarding financial arrangements for the interests of the children and other family members.

The court is further vested with the power to encourage parental participation with the child through the assignment of custody and visitation and in programs such as counseling or therapy which are intended to contribute positively to the overall well-being of the child in question. If necessary, the court also has the power to terminate parental rights if, in the court's opinion, the present living conditions are a threat to the life or well-being of the child. In the disposition of a case, the clinician can be of particular service to the court by evaluating workable possibilities and suggesting alternatives that foster the reorganization of the family.

The Psychologist's Role

In each of these areas, jurisdiction, procedures, and disposition, the court may call on the advice of expert witnesses such as social workers and psychologists. The psychologist may be asked to assess the present living conditions and emotional atmosphere within the home, the competency of a minor, the legitimate religious beliefs of a parent refusing medical treatment of a child's illness, the suitability of prospective parents or children for adoption or foster placement, grounds for termination of parental rights, determination for treatment as a juvenile or an adult in a criminal case, or the ability of parents to act in the best interest of their children.

THEMES IN FAMILY LAW

In addition to the *parens patriae* concept, other themes are woven throughout family law. These include the natural, basic right of all people to marry (*Loving v. Virginia*, 1967), the contractual or partnership nature of marriage, and competency or fitness as a parent. Also included are concepts about the nature and competency of minor children, responsibility or dependency, the best interests of the child doctrine, and concepts regarding the natural relationship and obligations existing between parents and their children. Most of these legal concepts have their origins in Roman law, common law, or ecclesiastical doctrines regarding the nature and purpose of marriage and the proper relationship between husbands and wives or between parents and their children. Collectively, these themes contribute to the normative model family, its character, and the proper relationships among family members.

PARENS PATRIAE

The doctrine of *parens patriae* is central to domestic law. This doctrine, passed down from Roman law and adopted into English common law in about the 11th century, presumes the state as protector and trustee for those persons determined unable to act in their own behalf. Under *parens patriae*, the state represented by the courts is responsible for securing the property rights of minor children and other classes presumed incompetent to administer their own affairs against possible loss through the incapacity of the child's natural parents or guardians to protect their interests (Mack, 1925). Under common law, this threshold is presumed to have been crossed when the family is presented to the court as disrupted and unable to continue as an intact unit.

Can the state's ability to guard the child's interest exceed the parent's ability? The court typically presumes that the natural parent-child bonds in an intact family are sufficiently strong to assure the protection of a minor's interest. The implicit shift in thought—that in a disrupted family the natural bonds between parent and child no longer exert sufficient force of responsibility to assure the protection of the child's interest—is presumptive at best. By the same token, one must question the court' s ability to balance the demands of the general public against the needs of the child in question. These sets of needs are mutually exclusive and represent possible conflicts of interest. It stretches the limits of reason to assume that the interests of the larger society are synonymous with the interests of the individual, yet this is precisely the task before the juvenile judge. Some jurisdictions have addressed this problem by providing for a guardian ad litem. The court appoints a competent neutral party (e.g., an attorney or psychologist) to the ad litem (during the interim) role who is competent to pursue the minor's interests, thus freeing the court from a conflict of interest.

Implicit within the *parens patriae* doctrine is the assumption that in matters concerning children, the court is the guardian of the well-being of any minor children involved. In fulfilling this role, the court is presumed to act in the best interests of the child and as such cannot be in a conflict of interest with the child's interests. As it is the presumption that the wishes of the court are for the child's best interest, there has been a reluctance on behalf of the domestic courts to delegate their jurisdiction in matters involving children. Although the court is forbidden to delegate this responsibility to outside agencies, it can through its broad discretionary powers employ a wide range of means to achieve its goals, including requesting intervention and input from psychologists.

COMPETENCY, RESPONSIBILITY, DEPENDENCY, AND THE BEST INTERESTS OF THE CHILD DOCTRINE

Children have been viewed traditionally by the courts as dependent and incapable of making sound independent judgments. They are treated differently from adults in almost all cases: statutory law, representation in court, treatment in juvenile court, and issues of parental responsibility for the child. The court recognizes the natural bond between the parent and child and in almost all but the most extreme circumstances strives to maintain and support the parent-child relationship. The best interest of the child doctrine implies that the responsibility of the court is first to protect the interests of the child. Just as there are possible conflicts of interest when considering the rights of parents and the rights of children, so too there are serious questions about whether or not the interests of the child are synonymous with the court's interest. Under the *parens patriae* concept, the court has been put into the final role of mediating the needs of the social order and the needs of the child. Clearly, these needs are not always the same.

Under English common law, children under the age of majority are considered incapable of sound independent judgment and therefore must look to their parents or guardian for direction and decision making. Thus, the normative model presupposes "an intact family system, characterized by dependent children, who rely on their parents for support, care, nurture and protection" (Weithorn, 1982, p. 86). This relationship among family members transcends individual needs and possible conflicts of interest. English common law presupposes that the interests of the children are consonant with the interests of their parents, who will execute their trust to the benefit of their children. This model of mutual responsibility and the inalienable right of parents to execute this responsibility has been repeatedly supported in court.

What exactly is the nature of the legal concept of minority and of competence and, logically, at what point does a child become competent to make his or her own decisions? There are no simple answers to the second portion of the question, but the courts have laid down a fairly clear framework for determining competence. According to one court's reasoning, competence represents "the capacity for individual choice" (*Ginsberg v. N.Y.*, 1968). Although this description may not appear to be particularly illuminating, implicit within it is the understanding that "individual choice" requires an understanding on the part of the individual of the possible consequences of various alternative choices.

In her investigation into children's decision-making competence, Weithorn (1982) defines competence as "an individual's skills, abilities, knowledge or experience or a capacity to perform in a certain manner" (p. 89). We question the assumption that all persons less than 18 years of age are incompetent to make decisions regarding their welfare; however, states have strongly supported parents' rights to provide consent or refusal for actions of their children (Weithorn, 1982). This right to privacy in decision making on behalf of children has repeatedly been supported through the decisions in the courts (*Parham v. J.L. & J.R.*, 1979; *Prince v. Massachusetts*, 1944; *Wisconsin v. Yoder*, 1972).

THE CONTRACTUAL NATURE OF MARRIAGE

Marriage is recognized under common law as a contract or civil partnership in which each member of the marriage is granted certain rights and charged with responsibilities, either implied or stated. Because marriage, as the fundamental family unit, is of vital importance to society, the state takes an active and continuing role in defining the expectations and relationships between marital partners and family members. Consistent with its esteemed social status, marriage is protected and regulated by statutes in virtually all jurisdictions (Kuchler, 1978).

Several specific conditions have been presumed to be implicit within the marital contract. The court recognizes marriage as a singular relationship between a man and a woman, and though not all jurisdictions specifically limit marriage to heterosexual unions, all cases that have come before the court have restricted marriage to individuals of the opposite sex. In all jurisdictions, the courts have defined marriage between men and women of certain blood relationships as incestuous and therefore prohibited. Although statutes in all jurisdictions prohibit incestuous marriages, they differ as to what degree of consanguinity constitutes incest.

As a contract, marriage is generally subject to limits similar to other contracts, including age limits, the competency of the parties to enter into the contract, statutes relating to fraud and full disclosure, and the freedom of choice for individuals to enter into marriage. In the absence of satisfactory fulfillment of these provisions, the marriage is subject to being voided, annulled, or dissolved under existing divorce statutes.

Marriage laws are currently in a state of flux. Some jurisdictions are considering legalizing same-sex relationships and reducing premarital requirements, others are attempting to modify divorce rates by making it more difficult to get married or to obtain a divorce. Louisiana established a two-tiered system of marriage licenses in 1997. The regular marriage license allows the couple a no-fault divorce after a six-month separation, whereas a covenant marriage license requires premarital counseling and either a two-year separation or proof of abuse, adultery, or felony prior to divorce (Goodman, 1997). In 1995, Alabama eliminated blood tests and other health tests and removed residency requirements (Maclean, 1997). The marriage and couples therapist must know the current statues where he or she is practicing.

FAMILY LAW ISSUES

INDIVIDUAL RIGHTS, FAMILY RIGHTS, AND THE PROFESSIONAL CONSULTANT

Philosophers, theologians, psychologists, legal theorists, and the public at large have generally recognized the legitimacy of differing statuses for groups and their subsequent differential treatment rights, depending on their present status. For example, married persons and single persons are treated differently for tax purposes, adults and minors are treated differently in terms of ability to make binding contracts, and mentally competent and mentally incompetent individuals have differing legal responsibilities. Prior to the mid-19th century, domestic decisions were generally based on civil precepts of property, with children as chattel and men as sole proprietors of the family's wealth and relationships.

With the advent of the Civil War and the equality provisions of the Fourteenth Amendment, the issue of different treatment for individuals of differing status became a problem for the courts. Problems that have been manifest in recent legal and social history include broad issues such as civil rights, women's rights, and abortion. Contributing to the complexity of the problem has been the parallel development of individual psychology in the late 19th century. Drawing upon the perspective of the individual and his or her development, the courts have also begun to weigh issues of rights to custody, individuals' and children's rights, the natural bonds among family members, and the proper developmental environment for children. Domestic rulings involving individuals of differing status implicitly address questions regarding the competency of parents to act in the interests of their children or the child's ability to act in his or her own behalf, a presumption elevating the child to equal status with the parents.

The implicit position of the court in a divorce and custody suit is that the marital disruption places the child at risk, and the court must assure that the interests of children are protected. Under the mantle of *parens patriae* and guided by the best interests of the child doctrine, the court acts to ensure the interests of any children involved. In the past, this action has resulted in the court's radically restructuring parent-child relationships through custody, visitation, and support. In apparent recognition of the court's inability to dictate family relationships in all cases, several alternative arrangements have been developed, such as joint custody and protection of rights to visitation for the noncustodial parent.

MARITAL AND FAMILY PRIVACY

Several landmark cases have served to define and support the concept of marital and family privacy and parents' rights to control over their children (e.g., *Pierce v. Society of Sisters,* 1925). English common law viewed husband and wife as "being of one body"; consequently, there developed presumptions regarding the sacredness of the marital unit and subsequent need for protection from undue public interference. In the case of *Griswold v. State of Connecticut* (1965), Justice Douglas, drawing on specified provisions from the Fourteenth Amendment prohibiting undue governmental interference, stated:

> Specific guarantees in the Bill of Rights have penumbras, formed by emanations from those guarantees that give them life and substance. . . . Various guarantees create zones of privacy. . . . We deal with a right of privacy older than the Bill of Rights—older than our political parties, older than our school system. Marriage is a coming together for better or for worse, hopefully enduring and intimate to the degree of being sacred. It is an association that promotes a way of life, not causes. (p. 4)

The specifics of the *Griswold* case affirm the right for married couples to use contraceptives, but its more important impact is to acknowledge realms of married life as so sacred and private that the state may not intrude.

Children are generally protected under the same rights to privacy as adults, although in some cases the courts have gone further, finding that under certain circumstances, the child's right to privacy may be superior to the interests of their parents (*Planned Parenthood v. Danforth,* 1976). The support for children's rights to privacy has been particularly evident in cases where children have attempted to avail themselves of community resources such as contraception (*Carey v. Population Serv. Intn'l.,* 1972), family planning (*Planned Parenthood v. Danforth,* 1976), and drug abuse programs and psychological testing (*Merriken v. Cressman,* 1973).

Stanton (1982) points out that when the question arises as to who controls the rights to privacy, the family or the children, the courts have generally supported a family-based theory of privacy and integrity over the individual and autonomous rights of children. Notable exceptions have occurred in situations where children, either by their actions or petition, demonstrate competency in making their own decisions (*Planned Parenthood v. Danforth,* 1976).

The courts have generally recognized a number of areas of family life as so intimate that they are protected by provisions of the Constitution and the Bill of Rights. Specifically, the courts have ruled in favor of marital privacy in areas including abortion (*Roe v. Wade*, 1973), procreation (*Skinner v. State of Oklahoma*, 1942), the marital couple's right to use contraception (*Eisendtadt v. Baird*, 1967; *Griswold v. State of Connecticut*, 1965), and family relationships, rearing and educating children (*Pierce v. Society of Sisters*, 1925; *Whalen v. Row*, 1977; *Planned Parenthood of Southeastern Pennsylvania v. Casey*, 1990).

Privileged Communication among Family Members

Privileged communication refers to the common law or statutory rights granted to specified individuals that preserve communications from being compelled in testimony. Privileged communication is permitted in specified circumstances because the disclosure of designated information would frustrate a relationship that society has determined to be worthy of fostering and preserving. Communications between spouses enjoy the status of privileged communication, and, consequently, marital partners cannot be compelled to provide testimony regarding private communications between them; on the other hand, marital partners are not foreclosed from giving testimony if they should so elect. The pivotal issue regarding privileged communications within the family is the necessarily narrow conditions that define private communications.

Although the privacy of communications between parents and their children has generally been supported by the courts, there is no common law provision granting privileged communication to family members beyond the spouses. The defense of privacy of communication among family members has typically fallen under the scope of rights to privacy rather than of privileged communication (see *In re A & M*, 1978) (Stanton, 1982). This becomes relevant in a case where a child, under no coercion, discloses a parent's drug abuse to the authorities.

A significant issue facing the clinician arises out of the common law provisions necessary to assure the status of privileged communication. Under common law, for a communication to be considered private, it must occur only between parties involved. A third party such as a child or other family member being present or information relayed between parties such as child-parent-therapist may invalidate the provisions necessary for privileged communication. Because the statutes regarding privileged communication are derived through the state legislatures, clinicians should become familiar with their local statutes to assure their clients the extent and nature of the protection available under the scope of privileged communication. In particular, some jurisdictions provide that all competent and relevant evidence, unless specifically excluded by privilege, may become compelled testimony.

Marriage

Marriage is a social institution, universally recognized across all cultures, although it may take various forms in different parts of the world. In Western cultures, marriage has been primarily governed by religious precepts. The early church held that marriage was a sacrament, ordained by God and consummated by His hand. Ecclesiastical doctrine specified the nature and conditions necessary for the marital contract, including who could marry, minimum ages for marriage, the need for mutual consent, the purpose for marriage (procreation), and the conditions under which a marriage could be voided. These early doctrines, specified in the *Casti Connubi* and other church proclamations, were adopted with some statutory modification into English common law and the Anglican Church upon its formation by Henry III.

In England, the church maintained control over marriage until 1857, when jurisdiction was transferred to the statutory domestic courts. The transfer of jurisdiction from the ecclesiastical courts to domestic courts did not promote much change in the law regarding marriage. Indeed, the legislation effecting the transfer of authority stipulated that the courts base their decisions on precedents formulated in the ecclesiastical courts. In continental Europe, the Protestant clergy rejected the concept of marriage as a religious sacrament, insisting that it be honored as a contract based on civil law.

In the United States, marriage has always been considered a civil contract with special statutory status governed by the domestic courts. All jurisdictions in the United States accept marriages performed by recognized clergy, and some jurisdictions recognize common law marriages, although the latter are viewed with increasing skepticism. The civil foundation for marriage in the United States should not imply the absence of religious influences; on the contrary, the civil statutes governing marriage reflect the adoption of virtues originating in traditional religious thought, only adopted and administered by the civil courts.

In the United States, jurisdiction over marriage rests with the various states; consequently, over the years a wide range of legislation governing marriage has developed. These laws, particularly those concerning divorce and child custody, have frequently conflicted with one another, causing confusion of jurisdiction when decisions in one state's jurisdiction are argued in another state. In an effort to reduce the number of conflicting statutes, the federal government has proposed several comprehensive laws for implementation in various states, including the aforementioned UMDA, UCCJA, FMLA, USFSPA, CSRSEA, and PKPA statutes.

Although the Constitution does not deal specifically with marriage, the Supreme Court recognized in *Meyer v. Nebraska* (1923) that the right "to marry, establish a home and bring up children" was an essential part of the liberty guaranteed by the Fourteenth Amendment. This judgment was strengthened in *Skinner v. State of Oklahoma* (1942), in which the Supreme Court extended its view on the right to marry, saying, "Marriage is one of the 'basic rights of man,' fundamental to our very existence and survival, therefore the state cannot force sterilization since a basic premise of marriage is procreation."

Marriage has generally been viewed as a contract, relation, or condition existing between one man and one woman. In the case of *Reynolds v. United States* (1878), the court held that polygamy is not legal, although it may be permitted by religious institutions. Marriage is a contract for life that may only be terminated by the court following a formal hearing of the facts presented for divorce (*Popham v. Duncan,* 1930). Consistent with this concept of marriage for life, marriage cannot be performed for a period of time or in degrees of involvement. Thus, all privileges accorded the marital status are enjoyed by marital couples. Laws and statutes regarding same-sex marriages are under review in a number of states. Hawaii, for example has clarified its marriage licensing statutes to apply only to male-female couples (Elrod, 1995). Some states and cities are offering benefits to domestic partners that used to be reserved to marital couples, but the U.S. House of Representatives, for instance, has refused to fund the District of Columbia's Domestic Partners Ordinance.

When persons planning to marry enter into antenuptial agreements regarding a broad range of property issues, the court retains the privilege of examination to verify that certain minimal provisions of disclosure, consideration, and support have been given. Individuals may not contract away the legitimate power of the court to rule in marital issues (*Popham v. Duncan*, 1930). Thus, it might be said that marriage is a partnership between a man, a woman, and the state, with the state being the senior partner in the contract.

The state, through its statutory provisions for marriage, stipulates the antecedent conditions necessary for a valid marriage to take place. These qualifications to marry generally include minimum ages, general physical and mental conditions, presence of voluntary consent, absence of a presently valid marriage, and limitations on consanguinity.

Dissolution of Marriage—Void and Voidable

Marriages are considered either void, voidable, or valid and may be dissolved through annulment, divorce, or death of a spouse. Specific conditions necessary for each action to dissolve a marriage are generally specified in individual state codes regarding marriage and divorce.

A void marriage is one that is forbidden by common law or statute, or would have been forbidden had the facts been known at the time of the marriage. Some marriages are void from the outset and are never recognized. Other marriages may be voidable, but are not considered void until some protest is made regarding the validity of the marriage. A marriage may be void for a number of reasons, including presence of a currently valid marriage, consanguinity or other relationships specified by statute, and, more pertinent to clinicians, violations of the presumptions governing contracts such as incompetency, consent to the marriage under duress, or failure to provide full disclosure of relevant facts or medical condition prior to the marriage.

Voidable marriages generally require a petition to the court to effect an annulment. A marriage may be voidable for a number of reasons, usually reasons that violate conditions of status or the basic conditions necessary for a valid marital contract. Violations of the premises of a valid contract include incompetency or failure to understand the nature and implications of the marital contract; marriage below minimum age requirements; duress; failure to disclose material information that may be relevant to the basis or purpose of the marriage; and presence of a medical or psychiatric condition such as venereal disease, impotency, or genetic disorder that would incapacitate the individual from fulfilling the implied obligations of the marital contract.

Physical or mental difficulties having an onset following the marriage are not considered a basis for annulment. Individuals who are mentally retarded may be permitted to marry provided they are competent to give consent to the marriage and the cause of their difficulties are unlikely to be genetically transmitted. The presence of a mental disorder (e.g., schizophrenia) is not necessarily a condition for voiding a marriage. For example, the court found that though it was understood between the parties that the defendant had a history of mental illness, the disorder was in a state of remission at the time of entering into the marital agreement; therefore, the contract was valid (Krause, 1977, p. 321).

A number of other conditions have been found to be a satisfactory basis for nullifying a marriage. Impotency, regardless of cause, physical or psychological, is considered a basis for nullifying a marriage (Krause, 1977). In another case, intoxication was found as a basis for nullifying a marriage on the grounds of incapacity to consent to a binding agreement, thus illustrating the need for knowledgeable consent for a contract to be binding (*Parken v. Saileau*, 1968). In specific regard to the medical or psychological bases for annulment, the courts have held that the condition in question must have existed prior to the marriage and been concealed from the marital spouse.

Annulment

Annulment is a legal process that terminates and invalidates a void or voidable marriage. The major difference between an annulment and a divorce is that an annulment is retroactive to the inception of the marriage, and a divorce is effective from the date of the decree forward, a point laden with important implications for inheritance. Consequently, the partners or heirs in an annulled marriage may have substantially different rights than in a marriage ended by a divorce.

Generally, for an annulment to be granted, the contested circumstances must have existed at the initiation of the marriage and have been concealed from the spouse. Annulment usually does not provide for permanent alimony or support obligations, although temporary support provisions may be granted, depending on the local statutes. The grounds for an annulment are similar to grounds for a divorce and include impotency, fraud, dare or jest, prior existing marriage, mental incapacity, and duress. Defenses to an annulment include continuing to live with the person after learning of grounds for annulment, antenuptial knowledge of the contested condition, and res judicata, or expiration of the statute of limitations.

Divorce

Divorce is the most common form for dissolution of a marriage and represents the legal termination of a valid marriage. Divorce must be concluded under the auspices of the court following a formal hearing. This degree of formality is necessary because the state is presumed to have a vital interest in the marriage. Further, it is presumed that the material interests of the estranged couple and any children of the marriage are at risk (Strickman, 1982). Divorce stands in marked contrast to the relatively informal procedural requirements for initiating a marriage. The procedural differences in treatment of marriage and divorce arise out of differing perceptions regarding the interests of the parties involved. In the case of marriage, it is presumed that the parties define their interests as similar and not conflictual, whereas in the case of divorce, the parties define their interests as different and unresolvably in conflict, thus a state of risk exists.

Under common law, prior to granting a divorce, some basis or fault had to be demonstrated in justification of the divorce. These grounds were typically presented as breaches of the implicit provisions of the marital contract, including adultery, desertion, mental cruelty or inhumane treatment, abuse, insanity, drug addiction, and gross neglect, all of which could call for psychological expertise in presenting to a court. During the 1970s and 1980s, there was a shift in focus from fault finding to expeditious decisions regarding marital property, support, and custodial issues, and most states enacted no-fault divorce statutes, which permit a divorce without proof of wrongdoing. In the 1990s, some states have begun a return to "fault" divorces and increased time required to live apart (Goodman, 1997; T. Walker, 1992a).

There are several important points to consider regarding no-fault divorce statutes. In particular, note the conditions necessary to justify the divorce action. These conditions include a determination of complete incompatibility of temperament, a determination of an irretrievable breakdown of the marriage, and an unwillingness to reconcile differences between the estranged spouses. Generally, the court will accept statements from the parties in testimony of the necessary conditions, and the divorce will be granted forthwith.

The courts have attempted to objectify the decision-making process in no-fault divorces by defining the phrases "incompatibility of temperament," "irretrievable breakdown in the marriage," and "failure to reconcile." For example, in *Phillips v. Phillips* (1973), the court stated that incompatibility refers to conflicts in personalities and disposition so deep as to be irreconcilable and render it impossible for the parties to continue a normal marital relationship with each other. And in the case of *Rikard v. Rikard* (1980), reconciliation is defined as a resumption of marital cohabitation in the fullest sense of living together as husband and wife, having sexual relations, and, where possible, joint domicile. The intentions of the parties must be to resume their married life entirely and not merely to enjoy each other's company temporarily, for limited purposes, or as a trial reconciliation. The length of their cohabitation is not material in determining whether there has been a reconciliation sufficient to deny the cause of action in the divorce.

In the event that the divorce is contested, a number of actions may invalidate claims of an irretrievable breakdown in the marriage. For example, should the spouses continue actions traditionally reserved for married couples, such as cohabitation or continued sexual relations, the court may justifiably question the basis for granting a no-fault divorce. In some jurisdictions, the courts have reserved the option to recommend counseling or mediation in an attempt to clarify the present state and condition of the marriage prior to granting a no-fault divorce. The clinician involved in marital counseling and likely to be drawn into the courtroom to testify must be informed about the law; for example, therapeutic recommendations such as graduated sexual or other relations could have legal impact in the marriage or divorce outcome. There is no stipulation for the clinician to be held harmless.

For a determination of custody, the divorcing spouses implicitly state that they are unable to resolve their differences and therefore submit their problem to the court for a decision. On the other hand, does the fact that a family seeks a divorce necessarily imply that the conflicts are unresolvable? The court's general agreement to go along with negotiated agreements worked out between the divorce attorneys for the division of property, custody arrangements, and the provisions for support indicates that the courts recognize the right of the families to decide for themselves how to best carry their family forward following divorce. The court decides only when no agreement can be reached.

Alternative Dispute Resolution

Beginning in the 1980s, developments in the psychological and legal literature regarding divorce promoted several novel approaches to negotiating divorce and conflict resolution. These approaches have been variously called conciliation, mediation, arbitration, and parent education depending on the specific goal and circumstances under which they are employed. The goal of these approaches to negotiation is to facilitate communication and increased understanding between the estranged parties. Negotiation is favored as an alternative because it is rooted in the concepts of individual choice and the family's right to effect their own resolution to their differences. Further, many advocates of these negotiating strategies suggest that negotiated settlements are likely to be less expensive, more permanent, and reduce the stress of divorce and family reorganization on all family members, particularly children.

In an effort to understand the possibilities and drawbacks of negotiated settlements, we must first specify the goals, procedures, and responsibilities of the various participants. Although conciliation and mediation are appropriate for couples both with and without children, this discussion will assume that children are likely to be present and a matter for consideration.

Conciliation.   The goal of formal conciliation processes is the reorganization and preservation of the marital unit. Conciliation may be initiated at any point in the negotiating process from the first recognition of difficulty through the first several weeks following the filling of a divorce petition. In the event that a conciliation is brought about, the marriage is reaffirmed and the court ceases action in the matter; in this sense, conciliation is similar to marital therapy in its goals and methods (Sprenkle & Storm, 1983).

As an aspect of the court's support for marriage, conciliation programs have been adopted by many jurisdictions as a prerequisite or adjunctive process to petitions for a divorce. In these cases, the courts often employ staff clinicians and social workers to meet with the divorcing couple and assess the likelihood of a reconciliation.

Mediation.   Divorce mediation is intended to be a nonadversarial means of conflict resolution in contested areas of the divorce action such as financial, property, and custodial issues. The goal of mediation is to forge an agreement that fairly meets the needs of all the parties, thereby avoiding litigation. Mediation is an attempt to arrive at a mutually satisfactory agreement regarding property and custodial issues, thereby encouraging a family to arrive at their own solution to the conflicting issues surrounding divorce. The assumption is that a settlement in which the parties have taken an active role is more likely to be successful in resolving differences and encourages the development of a successful foundation for the resolution of postdivorce differences.

A satisfactory divorce is the presumed outcome from the mediation process. On this point, mediation stands in marked contrast to the conciliation process, where the goal is the reaffirmation of the marriage. In both conciliation and mediation, the family members are encouraged to articulate their differences and reorganize their roles toward each other (Foster & Freed, 1983; Irving, 1980).

Arbitration. Arbitration is a negotiating strategy in which the parties agree to present their case to a neutral third party, who then renders a decision that is binding on both parties to implement. Arbitration is most closely aligned with traditional jurisprudence in which the neutral judge renders a binding verdict. Arbitration is sometimes useful in issues such as temporary child or spousal support. Not all states, however, have accepted the use of arbitration, and some have ruled that the rulings may be overturned if not in the best interests of the child (Elrod, 1995). In all three of the above approaches, the divorcing couple is permitted the opportunity to appeal for a court judgment should they disagree with the negotiated settlement.

Parent Education Programs. The most recent trend for family courts is education programming for separated and divorcing parents, established as a result of state legislation or court rules. The first court affiliated programs began in the 1970s, and their numbers grew in the early 1990s as either a form of premediation orientation or as a voluntary or court-mandated parent education program. In 1996, there were more than 560 programs in more than 40 states, and they seemed to be evolving into a distinct field of practice (Salem, Schepard, & Schlissel, 1996). The programs are offered by family courts, private and public mental health agencies, community-based agencies, and educational institutions. Presenters come from varied backgrounds, though often, due to the emotionally laden content, mental health professionals are group facilitators. Most programs emphasize (a) postdivorce reactions of parents, (b) postdivorce reactions of children, (c) children's developmental needs, and (d) the benefit of cooperative postdivorce parenting (Braver, Salem, Pearson, & DeLusé, 1996; for further information, see the special issue on parent education in divorce and separation by *Family and Conciliation Courts Review,* McIsaac, 1996).

Problems Associated with Alternative Dispute Resolutions

The role of peacemaker is attractive, yet divorce mediation represents an area of intervention that creates complex ethical questions. Contributing to this complexity is the espoused role of the mediator, a neutral third party with ambiguous purpose, methods, and ethical limits. A number of significant questions have been addressed by members of the psychological and legal community as well as by the consumers of mediation services, the divorcing couples.

Becker (1996) discusses the ethical conflicts deriving from the role of lawyer-mediator, such as fraudulent contracts and disclosure of confidential information that arise from the relationships of the mediator and the family members.

If the mediator is a nonlawyer, the question arises whether the mediator is engaging in unauthorized practice of law (Girdner, 1985b, 1986). Regardless of the professional orientation of the mediator, Girdner (1985a) and Manocherian (1985) have written on the difficulty of determining who the mediator represents: mother, father, or child. Goldzband (1982, 1983) and Payne and Overend (1990) have focused on how best to determine what is fair and equitable to all parties.

In a review of divorce therapy outcome research, Sprenkle and Storm (1983) surveyed 22 studies covering the areas of mediation and conciliation divorce groups, separation techniques, and marriage counseling with divorce as an unintended outcome. They concluded that among couples who resolved their differences regarding child custody, mediation facilitated high rates of pretrial agreements, high levels of satisfaction with their mediated agreements as compared with resolutions imposed by courts, a reduction in the amount of litigation following final order, an increase in joint custody arrangement, and a decrease in expenses frequently associated with court resolutions of custodial differences. They found that conditions that favored the mediation efforts included a moderate level of conflict between divorcing parties and acceptance of both parties of the divorce, the absence of third parties involving themselves in the dispute, a willingness by both parties to communicate, the absence of money as a major issue, and the acceptance and support by the opposing attorneys of the mediation process.

In discussing theories behind the divorce and the mediation process, Kaslow (1983, 1984a, 1984b) suggests that both the family and the individuals be assessed in the following areas prior to a clinical intervention such as conciliation or mediation: (a) individual development, including cognitive, emotional, chronological, and economic issues; (b) family development, including duration of the marriage, developmental levels of the children in the family, the nature of the couple's relationship including conflict and adjustment in the family; and (c) present status of the marriage and conflict resolution abilities, including perceptions of the marriage, perceptions of divorce actions to date, perceptions of default, and desires for reconciliation. From these factors and the couple's specified goals regarding the marriage outcome, Kaslow believes the counselor or mediator can determine how best to proceed with the couple in the conciliation or mediation efforts.

CUSTODY

Custody issues have been explored extensively in both legal and psychological literature in the past decade. Standards for conducting custody evaluations have been developed (APA, 1994). *Family Law Quarterly* has presented an annual review of federal and state changes in family law since 1992 (T. Walker, 1992b) and has published special issues on topics such as custody and working with mental health professionals (American Bar Association, 1995).

A clinician may be asked to serve as a consultant to the court in several types of custody disputes. The first example is a private dispute between the parents or between a parent and other family member or third party following a divorce. In these cases, the court is involved because there was a breakdown in the ability to solve the custody issue among the parties. A second kind of dispute involves issues such as assisted conception, surrogate parents, and unwed fathers contesting adoptions. In the third type of custody issue, the parties involve the parent and the state (usually the Division of Child Welfare or Department of Human Resources) in cases where there has been an allegation of parental abuse or neglect and may involve the attenuation or termination of parental rights.

As of 1997, all states have enacted a version of the UCCJA and nearly all have adopted some version of the PKPA making child abduction by a noncustodial parent a felony (Elrod & Spector, 1996, p. 754). The Hague Convention on International Child Abduction is useful in returning children to their country of habitual residence for resolution of any custody dispute (Silberman, 1994).

The UCCJA (1979) provides a uniform framework around which custodial issues may be developed, thereby encouraging consistency in rulings across jurisdictions. In establishing criteria for determination of custody, the UCCJA suggests the application of the following: (a) the age and sex of the child; (b) the wishes of the child as to his or her custodian; (c) the interactions and interrelationships of the child with parents, siblings, and significant others; (d) the child's adjustment to home, school, and community; and (e) the mental and physical health of all parties involved.

STANDARDS FOR A DETERMINATION OF CUSTODY

In divorces prior to the late 1800s, fathers almost always retained custody of their children. However, with the shift in family work patterns, mothers were presumed to be more satisfactory caretakers for young children, particularly children under the age of 6 or 7 years. The presumption in favor of mothers retaining custody became formalized in the tender years doctrine. The tender years doctrine was supported by theories of personality development that discounted the influence of the father in favor of the child's relationship with the mother during the formative tender years. The influence of these mother-centered theories is exemplified in the research of John Bowlby, who, as late as the 1950s, made the statement that there was no point in investigating the father-child relationship because it was of no consequence to the development of children (Bowlby, 1969). Indeed, typical studies of father-child interaction in the period prior to the late 1960s involved questionnaires given to mothers who were asked to describe the relationships between fathers and their children (Bowlby, 1969).

More recent research has indicated that fathers and mothers are equally capable of fulfilling the needs of their children (Lamb, 1996). Changing attitudes about child rearing coupled with the movement of women into the full-time workforce outside of the home culminated in changes in family law that have encouraged the development of a variety of custodial arrangements. In 1996, the U.S. Census Bureau reported five times more single mothers than single fathers with custody of children under the age of 18; however, in the United States, single-father families are growing at the rate of 10% per year (Milbank, 1997). Two recent controversial cases involved mothers who worked or attended school. In the first, a Washington, D.C., lawyer working long hours lost custody to her unemployed husband (Clay, 1995). In a Michigan case (*Ireland v. Smith*, 1994), a teenage mother temporarily lost custody when the child's father petitioned that his mother would watch the child while he worked, rather than placing the child in child care while the child's mother attended college classes.

Since the 1980s, much has been written on the role of psychology in custody disputes and the assessment of parenting (Brodzinsky, 1993; Clark, 1995; Heilbrun, 1995; Jameson, Erhenberg, & Hunter, 1997; Roseby, 1995; Stahl, 1994; Weithorn, 1987; Zarski, Knight, & Zarski, 1985). The American Psychological Association (1994) developed 16 guidelines for child custody evaluations. The first three focus on the purpose: (a) that the primary purpose of a custody evaluation is to assess the best psychological interests of the child, (b) that the child's well-being and interests are paramount, and (c) that the focus is on the needs of the child, the parenting capacity, and the resulting fit. The next four focus on preparing for the evaluation: (d) the role of the psychologist is that of an objective impartial professional expert; (e) the psychologist has obtained specialized competence in the areas needed; (f) the psychologist recognizes personal and societal biases and strives to overcome such biases; and (g) the psychologist avoids multiple relationships. The third section of guidelines concerns conducting the evaluation: (h) the scope of the evaluation, (i) informed consents, (j) information to the participants regarding limits of confidentiality and disclosure of information, (k) use of multiple methods of data gathering, (l) conservative interpretation of the assessment data, (m) limits of opinions, (n) recommendations based on the best interests of the child, (o) clarification of financial arrangements, and (p) record keeping.

Morris (1997) notes that participation in custody evaluations may lead to malpractice claims and ethical complaints filed against the evaluator. This is partially due to the nature of the evaluations (parents unhappy with final custody arrangements) and partially to the number of ethical standards that have direct relevance to the conduct of the evaluations.

There is no disagreement that the best interests of the child are the heart of custody determination, but there is variation in how best to assess the child's best interest and in court guidelines for children of different ages. Ackerman and Ackerman (1997) surveyed 201 psychologists who had participated in at least ten custody evaluations. All of the respondents preferred to be retained by the court or jointly by both attorneys. Almost all respondents used testing as part of their assessment procedure and tended to administer four to five tests per person being evaluated. Heinze and Grisso (1996) reviewed five "tests" that are currently used in assessing parenting capacity. These measures use a variety of methods: observation of parents, parental preferences of the child, stress levels of parents, and child abuse potential of parents. As can be seen from the variety of assessments used, no one "test" currently available would be appropriate in all custody evaluations. In addition to intelligence measures and projective techniques, some of the newer techniques used include Ackerman-Schoendorf Scales for Parent Evaluation of Custody (AS-PECT) (Ackerman & Schoendorf, 1992), Bricklin Perceptual Scales (Bricklin, 1984), Parent-Child Relationship Inventory (Gerard, 1994), and the Parenting Stress Index (Abidin, 1990).

Types of Custody Arrangements

Currently, custody arrangements tend to fall into one of four patterns: sole custody, divided custody, split custody, and joint custody. Sole custody is the most commonly approved form of custody upon the dissolution of a marriage. In this form, custody is awarded to one parent with visitation rights to the noncustodial parent. The noncustodian may by informal agreement have authority over some decisions concerning the child, but the ultimate control and legal responsibility remain with the custodial parent. Noncustodial parents often experience feelings of loss of their children similar to bereavement, and the custodial parents often feel overwhelmed, overburdened, and trapped by the responsibility. Hyde (1984) points out that it is difficult for a mother to establish a career, to earn a living for her family, to become financially independent, and to establish a social life as well as provide the child care normally provided by two parents. Perhaps the most negative indictment of sole custody is that it tends to indicate to a child that one parent is right and one is wrong regarding divorce and custody.

Divided or alternating custody allows each parent to have the child for a part of the year, exercising full control over the child while the child is in his or her custody and having visitation rights for the period of time when the child is in the custody of the other parent. Critics of divided custody generally believe that it creates confusion for the child with regard to authority and that shifting the child from home to home results in an unstable environment with lack of permanent associations for the child.

Split custody occurs when custody of one or more of the children is awarded to one parent with the remaining children being awarded to the other. As this arrangement may tend to further disrupt the family unit, it is not generally approved at this time unless there are compelling circumstances to indicate that it would be in the best interest of the children.

The fourth type of custody is joint or shared custody, which is defined as a sharing of legal or physical custody by both parents so as to assure the access of the child to both separated or divorced parents in a frequent and continuing manner. There seems to be increasing support for joint custody in those cases where there is a willingness of both parties to carry out such a plan. There have been a number of arguments for and against joint custody, ranging from the futility of attempting to make Solomonic decisions, to the likelihood of continuing strife between the parents, to the opportunity of preserving the functional integrity of the various parent-child relationships; however, the goal is not to arrive at one state of law applicable to everyone. Rather, the goal is to develop a repertoire of custodial arrangements that might be applied to foster the best interests of the children and to encourage continued relationships between the parents and child as well as with the broader social support network of the child.

A large number of psychologists and practitioners in domestic legal issues encourage placement of a child with the parent who seems most likely to encourage and foster the continued contact between the child and the noncustodial parent. Indeed, the California statutes favoring joint custody also provide that in the event sole custody is determined to be in the child's best interest, the placement should be made with the parent who evidences a willingness to share residential time as well as decision making with the child (Foster & Freed, 1983).

B. A. Weiner (1985) noted that in the past decade there were numerous changes in family law in response to the changing role of women, increased interest in parenting on the part of fathers, and interest in the rights of the children caught as unwitting third parties in the conflict. This trend has continued. Elrod and Spector (1996) in an annual review of family law noted that 1994–1995 was a year in which children's issues of child custody and support dominated the arena of family law on national, state, and local levels, indicating the unsettled state of affairs in determining optimal custody policy.

EFFECTS OF DIVORCE ON CHILDREN

The past 40 years have shown a dramatic increase in the number of children affected by divorce. Each year, more than one million children in the United States experience the divorce of their parents (U.S. Bureau of the Census, 1997, p. 106). Though these families have been studied since the early 1970s regarding the effects of divorce, the earlier studies tended to focus on the effect of divorce on clinical cases. More recently, families not in the clinical population have also been studied, leading to slightly different findings.

Early studies of divorced families revealed that a number of changes were generally common to these families. Typically, divorced families experienced lowered economic stability, higher levels of interpersonal stress, loyalty conflicts, and an increased reliance on external support systems such as relatives and institutional and social service providers to aid in meeting familial needs. In addition, children frequently experienced major shifts in the amount and quality of parental contact available to them from both the custodial and noncustodial parents. Although the detrimental effects of these shifts in circumstances are often ameliorated by the second or third year following the divorce (Hetherington, 1979; Hetherington, Cox, & Cox, 1979; Wallerstein & Kelly, 1980), the family may develop chronically inadequate means of meeting their needs. Some of the research suggested that these adjustment problems decrease significantly with time and assistance from external sources.

Generally, the most pervasive changes found in the early studies of children from divorced families were disruptions in their academic achievement and social relationships. Research indicated that although divorced families were generally stabilized by the second or third year following the divorce, the performance of children from divorced families continues to lag behind children from intact families (Lamb, 1977). Atkeson, Forehand, and Richard (1982) further cite the parents' personal adjustment and the postdivorce relationship between parents and between parents and their children as material factors affecting the child's adjustment.

As samples of children experiencing divorce became more representative of all children experiencing divorce, fewer negative consequences were found than in the earlier studies. Amato and Keith (1991b) performed a metanalysis of 92 comparative studies of children living in divorced single-parent families and children in continuously intact families. In general, they found that children from divorced families were less well adjusted than their intact family counterparts but that the differences were small, with the most recent studies finding even smaller differences between groups. Amato and Keith found only moderate support for theories regarding the effect of parental absence and economic disadvantage, but the effect of continued family conflict was strongly supported. Thus, it appears that although all three affect a child's postdivorce adjustment and are necessary for understanding the ways divorce affects children, it may be that continued parental conflict maintains the impairment of children of divorce. In fact, children of divorced families that have low levels of conflict do better than children in high-conflict, intact families.

Cherlin et al. (1991) found that there was little difference in adjustment of postdivorce 11-year-olds if the adjustment five years earlier, prior to the divorce, was held constant. A longitudinal study by Chase-Lansdale, Cherlin, and Kiernan (1995) found long-term negative effects when the participants were 23 years of age, effects that were not displayed when they were 11 years of age. There may be some stressors in late adolescence or early adulthood that are not revealed by the cross-sectional studies.

A review of the literature of adult children of divorce supports the view that parental divorce has lasting implications for their achievement level and quality of life (Amato & Keith, 1991a). It seems certain that we do not yet know all of the parameters for maximizing a successful adjustment following divorce, but it does seem that an important factor promoting the success of the child's postdivorce adjustment is the quality of the relationship that develops between the child and the divorced parents.

A large body of research indicates that the circumstances that foster the most positive social, intellectual, and moral development are high levels of contact with both parents, provided the parents are able to minimize their personal conflicts (Kurdek & Berg, 1983; Kurdek, Blisk, & Siesky, 1981; Wallerstein & Kelly, 1980). By the same token, no research supports the presumption that the child benefits from minimizing contact with the noncustodial parent, except in cases where the family is continually disrupted by verbal and/or physical conflict. In these cases, exposure to continued conflict is detrimental to the child's well-being in both divorced and intact families (Amato & Keith, 1991b).

Finally, parents should be supported in their efforts to initiate independent lifestyles that recognize their status as functional parents. The stabilization process may be expected to take from two to five years depending on the level of conflict, economic changes, and development of a viable social network outside of the marriage. It is unreasonable to assume that interruption of parental contact with the children of the marriage will encourage a reorganization and stabilization including the children. Both parents need the active support of the court and broader social system during the process of reorganization.

In recognition of the need for stability and contact with both parents, the courts should discourage modifications of custodial arrangements that further limit contact with both parents without demonstration of substantial cause.

STEPPARENTS AND STEPFAMILIES

Because 75% of divorced mothers and 83% of divorced fathers remarry within five years, most children who experience divorce will also experience the remarriage of at least one of their parents (Fine, 1997). Under common law and current domestic law, stepparents do not enjoy the same privileges regarding stepchildren as do birth parents. Much recent legislation has been directed toward considering on a case-by-case basis visitation rights of divorcing stepparents, as well as grandparents and other persons such as second cousins who had functioned as de facto parents. Questions about the current law in a particular state should be referred to lawyers practicing in that state.

Typically, the remarriage of a person paying child support or alimony does not change the individual's obligation for paying either. The court assumes that the person marries with a full understanding of these obligations. Further, child support and alimony may not be discharged under bankruptcy proceedings. Whether or not the support payments are affected by pensions or retirement savings is currently being decided in the courts. Alimony will customarily stop if the receiver should remarry. Although women have typically been the recipients of alimony, recent court decisions have awarded men alimony. Other arrangements reflect a shift toward remedial alimony, or alimony that continues for a period while the recipient is retrained for employment so that the recipient can support himself or herself in the interim. In the past, the marriage of the individual receiving alimony was the criterion under which alimony would stop, resulting in many women living with men outside of marriage so as not to terminate the alimony payments. Recent court decisions have somewhat changed the criteria for cessation of alimony payments by including the condition of residing with another man for a period as sufficient reason to stop payments.

Visitation is a right rather than an obligation and needs to be considered when either of the divorced parents remarries. Many problems between divorced spouses do not arise until one or the other remarries. The unmarried former spouse may react with jealousy and anger and, if that person has custody, may prevent the other former spouse from seeing the children. By the same token, the new stepparent confused about his or her role with the stepchildren or resentful of the continued influence of the former spouse may agitate the status quo that had been achieved between the divorced couple.

The noncustodial parent may react to the marriage of a former spouse by a cessation of visitation or support payments. The clinician should be aware of the potential problems with the advent of a marriage within the divorced family, be aware of the legal responsibilities associated with the children, and be prepared to counsel clients accordingly in an effort to reestablish a balance within the new family structure.

BLENDED FAMILIES

The blended family may be defined as a family involving children from prior marriages as well as from the current marriage and involving several sets of interacting parents. Premarital counseling to address the financial and emotional shifts resulting from blending families may be useful in avoiding some of the destructive stress associated with joining two and three families. In some cases, it might be helpful for the clinician to work with all of the parties, former spouses and new family members, to facilitate the adjustment of all families concerned.

Fine and Kurdek (1992) note that just as they affect intact and single-parent families, the parenting practices and family climate affect children's adjustment in stepfamilies. A finding unique to stepfamilies, however, is that parents develop more positive relationships with their stepchildren when they do not initially assume an active role in discipline but rather wait until a trusting relationship has developed.

An important area for consideration in working with blended families is the issue of discipline and the rights of the stepparent with regard to his or her stepchildren. Typically, custodial and noncustodial parents have the right and responsibility to invoke appropriate disciplinary procedures when dealing with children and are protected from abuse or liability statutes so long as their behavior and discipline fall within the broad disciplinary mores of the greater community. In addition, birth parents have rights with regard to visitation and contact with their children that are substantially different from rights for stepparents and other persons significant to the child.

Stepparents have no disciplinary or visitation rights regarding a stepchild; their status is essentially that of any other nonfamily member. The result of this condition is that should a stepparent threaten or harm a stepchild, a reasonable parental act may turn into an assault or battery, subjecting the stepparent to both civil and criminal liability. Likewise, reasonable touching by a biological parent to medicate or inspect a tender area, when done by a stepparent might be taken out of context and viewed as sexual assault or fondling (Bernstein & Haberman, 1981). On the other hand, a stepparent who has adopted a stepchild would be accorded the full rights of the birth parents.

In the event of the failure of the blended family, it is important to consider that contracts between parents or between parents and stepparents regarding the care and custody of children might well be held invalid, as the parents may not contract away the right of the court to rule on a custodial issue.

Bonding in the Stepfamily

Stepparents' fears about establishing a sound "parental" relationship with their stepchildren may be complicated by their limited rights of access to that child in the event of a divorce. As many laws stand now, in the event of a subsequent divorce within a blended family, the stepparent or foster parent would enjoy no rights toward the former spouse's children. A petition to the court to continue contact with the child following the divorce would be unsupportable under extant law. This condition would also hold true in most states in the event of the death of a spouse, in that the children would likely be remanded to the surviving biological parent. Texas has given stepparents standing to seek custody if a child's birth parent dies (Elrod, 1995).

This issue becomes doubly complicated in the case of multiple sets of children: mine, yours, and ours. Since this issue of the rights of stepparents toward their stepchildren has become a significant litigation issue, there has been some movement recognizing the possible relationships between stepparents and children. "Psychological parentage" represents the pivotal issue promulgated by Goldstein, Freud, and Solnit (1979) and is a substantial factor in determining the best interests of the child. Again, as this issue is currently in a state of flux, a good working relationship with a family lawyer in the party's jurisdiction is necessary to stay abreast of the changes.

ADOPTION

Adoption issues center on consent to adoption, eligibility to adopt, and effects of adoption. The "Baby Jessica" (*In re Clausen*, 1993) and "Baby Richard" (*In re Kirchner*, 1995) cases are two of the more visible cases that have granted biological fathers custody even though the children had been in adoptive families for several years. Both cases involved the need for "consent" from biological parents. Some states have established laws narrowing the time frame for unwed fathers to show their commitment by requiring support for the mother during pregnancy or by their maintaining a relationship with the child. In cases where the fathers have abandoned their parental rights or not maintained a relationship, or where conception resulted from a rape, courts have allowed adoption without the biological father's consent. Some of these cases can be quite complex, and case law is now being established on those cases where the biological parents differ in the sequence of events or degree of relationships, or where two or more states or countries are involved. "Baby Sam," which involved numerous versions of the facts surrounding prenatal events as well as the state having jurisdiction, involved appeals on jurisdiction prior to addressing the custody issue (Associated Press, 1997).

A California appeals court has ruled that people who contract to create a child through new technology become the child's legal parents and are responsible for child support (Davis, 1998). The contractual parents, who divorced before her birth, had arranged for the creation of Jaycee, the child of anonymous sperm and egg donors, and had arranged for her to be implanted and carried to term by a surrogate mother. This ruling sends the message that people cannot create babies without accepting the consequences and supports those who want to be declared parents but fear that the courts will find surrogates or sperm or egg donors legal parents of the children they arranged to create. This case will be observed closely by other state courts and legislatures and likely result in new laws.

Who can adopt is also being challenged. A Florida case is questioning the statute that bars homosexual partners from adopting (*Cox v. Florida Department of Health and Rehabilitation Services*, 1995). The District of Columbia has found that homosexual partners may jointly adopt a child previously adopted by one of the partners (*In re M.M.D.*, 1995). Other cases such as whether lesbian partners may adopt a child conceived by artificial insemination are currently being filed.

"Open" adoptions have been recognized by the New York State Supreme Court (*In re Gerald*, 1995); these allow a parent to include visitation and communication rights in the document surrendering the child if the adopting parents agree. Indiana has also allowed postadoption visitation (Ind. Code Ann., 1964).

Adoption may affect grandparents' rights. In a Tennessee case, adoption by a stepfather terminated the visitation right of the paternal grandparents. Although historically grandparents have lacked legal standing, all 50 states have passed some type of grandparent visitation act; the Grandparents for Children's Rights organization estimates more than 250 calls weekly from grandparents concerned about access to their grandchildren (Singhania, 1997). As in other areas, the courts come into play only when family members are unable to resolve the relationships on their own.

National and state courts have been active in adoptions in the 1990s. The Uniform Adoption Act (UAA, 1995) distinguished between different types of adoptions: agency, independent, or stepparent. UAA also set standardized procedures for consents and relinquishments, including a 30-day claim period following a proposed adoption for biological fathers, eight days for a birth mother to change her mind, evaluation of all prospective parents, and open adoptions (Elrod, 1995). As a result of UAA, many states are reevaluating their adoption statues for in-state and interstate adoptions.

In May 1993, the Hague Conference on Private International Law proposed the Convention on Protection of Children and Cooperation in Respect of Intercountry Adoption. The Convention endorsed intercountry adoptions, created rules of procedure and recognition of international adoption decrees, and established a central agency in each country to evaluate the suitability of adoptive parents and children. We await the results of this effort.

DOMESTIC VIOLENCE

Family violence as discussed in this chapter includes spouse abuse, parent abuse, child abuse, and incestuous relationships. Although domestic violence seems to have been present in both Eastern and Western cultures since recorded time, the amount of attention being paid to it in the 1980s and 1990s has increased dramatically. Similarly, the legal system, in recognizing the convergence of family problems and criminal behavior, is developing new strategies for coping with abuse.

The U.S. Department of Justice, Bureau of Justice Statistics (1986) report on the rates of family violence finds that when family violence occurs, about 88% of the violent behaviors are assaults, 10% are robberies, and 2% are rapes. They report that more than half of all violent crimes committed by relatives involve spouses or ex-spouses and that three-fourths of the spousal attacks involve individuals who are divorced or separated. About one-fourth of persons violently victimized by a spouse or ex-spouse report a series of similar victimizations within the previous six months, a higher rate of previous victimizations than any other class of victims of violent crimes. They report that about six million people, or 3.2% of all Americans are victims of violent crimes each year. Although men are three times more likely than women to be victimized by violent strangers, women are three times more likely than men to be victimized by family members (U.S. Department of Justice, 1986). A decade later, the Bureau of Justice Statistics, comparing victim-offender relationships, finds that 47% of all violent crime, 66% of sexual assault, and 49% of physical assault is between relatives or acquaintances, and notes that husbands or boyfriends killed 28% of female murder victims (U.S. Department of Justice, 1996).

Incidence of domestic violence tends to be cyclical. Widom (1989) discussed the intergenerational patterns and the variety of forms the abuses can take over the life cycle of the family. Kaufman and Zigler (1987) reviewed the literature on intergenerational violence and concluded that the best estimate was a rate of about 30%, which is considerably higher than the 2% to 4% rate found in the general population. Although this chapter separates them, spouse and child abuse are believed to be variations of family violence rather than individual entities.

SPOUSE ABUSE

Over the past 20 years, numerous books have been written on the etiology of spouse abuse (Dobash & Dobash, 1979; Gelles & Straus, 1988; Martin, 1976; Moore, 1979; Straus, Gelles, & Steinmetz, 1980; L. Walker, 1979). Domestic violence has been explored from a variety of views, such as psychoanalytic, sociological, economic, and spousal interaction. Initial research consisted of surveys identifying the prevalence, extent, and types of violence; more recent studies have focused on interpersonal variables. These include women's new status at the societal level, marital inequality, violence (Yllo, 1984), the effect of domestic violence legislation on police intervention disposition (Bell, 1985), and the effects on mental and physical health of the women and children (Campbell & Lewandowski, 1997; Follette, Polusny, Bechtle, & Naugle, 1996). Initially, there was difficulty obtaining accurate statistics on all areas of domestic violence due to both unreliable record keeping from many sources of statistics and differences in defining the issue. The police tend to define domestic violence by its effect, legal systems by degree of severity, and social science researchers by degree of acceptance within the community. After 20 years of empirical research, estimates of the number of women abused by their partners each year range from 2.1 million (Langan & Innes, 1986) to more than 8 million (Straus, 1991, as cited in Hirschel, Hutchison, & Dean, 1992). Obviously, we have not resolved even the incidence rates, so other parametric and causal questions also remain unsolved.

Treatment and Reduction of Domestic Violence

As the police change their role in investigating and disposing of family disputes, there is a need for consultation in areas such as defusing violence, problem resolution, mediation, and appropriate referral, as well as in basic inservice information identifying abuse and the characteristics of the abused and the abusers. Bell (1984), Brown (1984), Dutton (1984), and Loving (1980) describe early attempts by various communities to provide more appropriate police services. Hirschel et al. (1992) discuss the effectiveness of several possible police responses: providing advice to the couple, separating the couple, issuing a citation to the offender, and arresting the offender.

A second avenue for input in the legal system is through the courts. Both judges and lawyers are becoming increasingly aware of the issues involved in the battered wife syndrome (Duryee, 1995; Frazier & Borgida, 1985; "Special Issue on Domestic Violence," 1995; L. Walker, 1984) and are accepting exculpatory testimony of expert witnesses in cases where the victims have fought back and incurred assault or homicide charges. Consultation with lawyers is important in helping them understand the apparent inconsistencies in abused women's behavior, such as the fear of filing for divorce from a battering spouse, or leaving and returning to an abusive situation several times, or returning to request alimony and/or child support. Continuing changes in statutes encourage changes in police and court interventions.

Treatment of both the abused and the abuser often begins with legal interventions. In many families, the first step to resolving the abuse is contacting a crisis hotline or shelter where information regarding local legal alternatives is provided. For the abuser, the first contact may follow as a result of a legal intervention or at the suggestion of a divorce judge or lawyer. Treatment approaches may include individual, group, or marital sessions. L. Walker (1979) discussed the use of individual sessions for both partners in an abusive situation. Neidig (1984), working with military families, has developed a treatment program for couples. Bograd (1984) examined the biases that may arise from family systems approaches and the implications these biases have on joint treatment. Menard and Salius (1990) discussed the judicial response to violence. Bourne (1995) and Gottlieb (1995) discussed the ethical and legal issues in the management of domestic violence.

The Violence Against Women Act (VAWA, 1994), a part of the 1994 crime bill, attempts to have crimes against women considered in the same manner as those motivated by religious, racial, or political bias. VAWA also provides for a national telephone hotline to assist victims and requires states to recognize protection orders of other states (Klein, 1995). Some states are not yet in compliance with VAWA.

CHILD ABUSE

In 1874, the Society for Prevention of Cruelty to Children (SPCC) was established as an appendage to the American Society for the Prevention of Cruelty to Animals and came to be a determining force in obtaining child protective laws. Presently, although there is no official definition of maltreatment, all states have had child abuse and neglect protection laws since the 1960s. The Juvenile Justice Standards Project (1981) is the first set of legal definitions that explicitly state that harm to a child, not the characteristics of the abuser (individuals having poor parenting skills) or the acts of mistreatment (physical force or neglect), should serve as the determining factor in defining child abuse and neglect.

Kempe's recognition of the battered child syndrome sparked the public's attention to the issue (C. Kempe, Silverman, Steele, Droemueller, & Silverman, 1962). The practitioner needs to be familiar with the developments concerning the etiology, treatment, and prognosis in the intervening three decades (Belsky, 1993; Dubowitz, Black, Starr, & Zuravin, 1993; Melton & Barry, 1994; Milner, 1991; Starr & Wolfe, 1991).

The American Psychological Association (1996), because of the prevalence and effects of abuse on cognitive, emotional, and social development, has developed a guide for including information on child abuse and child neglect in graduate professional training. The guide contains information about: (a) the prevalence of child abuse and neglect, (b) the consequences of abuse and neglect, (c) theories about the development of abusive and neglectful behaviors in adults, (d) the recognition and referral of abused and neglected children and adults, (e) the responses to abuse and neglect (child protection system, legal involvement, and mental health interventions), and (f) the prevention of child abuse and neglect. It also provides resources on ethical issues, involvement with other professionals, assessment of victims and their families, and interventions with both victims and perpetrators for trainees in clinical, counseling, and school psychology.

Clinicians are often called on to testify as expert witnesses regarding child abuse and neglect; they also are called on as material witnesses concerning abuse or neglect by parents or others when their clients are involved in litigation. Barth and Sullivan (1985) provide information on obtaining evidence that is useful in court cases when one is called as a material or fact witness rather than as an expert witness. The former involves presenting observations rather than opinions that have been derived from observations. Such a case may occur when the clinician (or teacher or physician or school bus driver) observes fresh welts or bruises, a child sent out in snowstorms inadequately clothed, or acts of violence. Sagatun (1991) addresses the admissibility of expert testimony on child abuse and child sexual abuse. A qualified expert may discuss the characteristics of an abused child, the characteristics of a class of victims, and observed behavior of the child in question, but the testimony can be offered only after someone has challenged the assertion that the child has been abused. Sattler (1997) provides comprehensive guidelines for assessment and clinical and forensic report writing in child maltreatment cases.

Children are victims of abuse from a variety of sources. Physical abuse, neglect, and sexual abuse may occur as a direct action of parents, siblings, and extended family. Professionals may come into contact with an abused child through many different avenues. Reporting laws have made it mandatory for citizens, including psychologists, to report suspected abuse. Surveys of licensed psychologists have revealed that the laws are not adhered to 100% of the time. Brosig and Kalichman (1992a), reviewing earlier literature, found that between 30% and 40% of practicing psychologists are noncompliant. Furthermore, they found that the wording of the law affected likelihood to report in that the psychologists were more likely to report when the legal requirements were clear and specific (Brosig & Kalichman, 1992b). Professionals were less likely to report when they did not feel that they had enough evidence. In cases involving clients, some practitioners are concerned that reporting may harm the therapeutic relationship. It is important to maintain trust between therapist and client in order to continue the therapy after the necessary break in confidentiality.

Institutional as well as intrafamilial abuse is too often the outcome for child victims who are removed from their family's neglect or abuse and are placed in a foster care system only to be further abused. Keeping children in foster care for prolonged periods can be considered an abuse per se (Davidson, 1983).

The Adoption Assistance and Child Welfare Act of 1980 was designed to provide funding for services that would facilitate a speedy return of children to their parents or to assist in the adoption of those who were not able to return to their family of origin.

CHILD SEXUAL ABUSE

Child sexual abuse (CSA) is defined by Browne and Finkelhor (1986) as any forced or coerced sexual behavior imposed on a child and/or sexual activity between a child and a much older person, whether or not obvious coercion is involved. Prevalence has been estimated to be between 15% to 33% in females in the general population, rising to 35% to 75% in clinical populations, and from 13% to 16% for males in the general population, and 13% to 23% in a male clinical population (Polusny & Follette, 1995). Finkelhor (1979), studying the incidence of incest and child abuse through a survey of students, reported findings that most sexual victimization of children was incestuous in nature.

The 1980s and 1990s saw a flood of research (with a wide range of populations and methodological problems) on the effects of sexual abuse. Beyond the scope of this chapter to cover in detail, reviews by Browne and Finkelhor (1986) and Polusny and Follette (1995) survey the research to date. They have identified initial reactions of fear, anxiety, depression, anger, hostility, and inappropriate sexual behavior and long-term effects for both females and males. Higher levels of general psychological distress include depression and anxiety disorders, suicidal behaviors, self-mutilation, somatic complaints, and substance abuse. A practitioner working with either a child or adult survivor needs to be proficient in the etiology, treatment, and legal resources for dealing with incest and sexual abuse and would find Briere (1991); Burgess, Groth, Holstrom, and Sgroi (1978); Finkelhor (1990); Kempe and Kempe (1984); Kendall-Tackett, Williams, and Finkelhor (1993); Kuehule (1996); and Milner (1992) useful references.

Following the disclosure of CSA, the child finds that the trauma is not over. Generally, the child and family then come into contact with a number of institutions, such as child protective services, medical institutions, law enforcement, social service agencies, and court systems that may not be responsive to the child's psychological needs. Wakefield and Underwager (1992) focus on ways interviews with children can be biased unknowingly by the interviewers (interrogators) who are trying to elicit as much information as possible from the child in anticipation of adjudication. Concerning the veracity of child witnesses in sexual abuse cases, Meyer and Geis (1994) write that rather than discussing the virtues and demerits of anatomically correct dolls and the suggestibility of children, that we research how to determine which children are invalid witnesses.

The question of what kinds of expert testimony will be allowed is still unanswered. *In re Amber* (1987) a trial court found that a child had been abused based on a psychologist's testimony regarding the alleged victim's play with anatomically correct dolls. Because it needed to but did not meet the *Frye* test (see Chapter 19, this volume), the appellate court excluded the testimony and reversed the trial court judgment (Sagatun, 1991). Perhaps in the next ten years some of these issues will be resolved.

CONCLUSION

We have surveyed a number of issues involving current domestic law and provided references for further study. Although much has been accomplished in improving the statutes ensuring the rights of individuals and families, it is apparent that the job has just begun. The clinician must be aware of changes in the literature, in the availability of local resources, and of local, state, and national legal and policy developments.

Psychological findings have influenced policy, legislation, and police training. Psychological research on parenting, bonding, effects of various custodial arrangements, and violent behavior have become part of clinical training and practice. Through the collaborative efforts of lawyers and psychologists, we can continue to profoundly and beneficially affect the lives of our most vulnerable fellow humans.

REFERENCES

Abidin, R. R. (1990). *Parenting Stress Index* (3rd ed.). Odessa, FL: Psychological Assessment Resources, Inc.

Ackerman, M. J., & Ackerman, M. C. (1997). Custody evaluation practices: A survey of experienced professionals (revisited). *Professional Psychology: Research and Practice, 28*, 137–145.

Ackerman, M. J., & Schoendorf, K. (1992). *Ackerman–Schoendorf Scales for Parent Evaluation of Custody (ASPECT)*. Los Angeles: Western Psychological Services.

Adoption Assistance and Child Welfare Act of 1980, P.L. 96-272.

Aldous, J. (1997). The political process and the failure of the child labor amendment. *Journal of Family Issues, 18*, 71–91.

Amato, P. R., & Keith, B. (1991a). Parental divorce and adult well being. *Journal of Marriage and Family, 53*, 43–58.

Amato, P. R., & Keith, B. (1991b). Parental divorce and the well being of children: A meta analysis. *Psychological Bulletin, 110*, 26–46.

American Bar Association. (1995, Spring). Special symposium on working with mental health professionals. *Family Law Quarterly, 29*.

American Psychological Association. (1977). *Standards for providers of psychological services* (Rev.). Washington, DC: Author.

American Psychological Association. (1981). Specialty guidelines for the delivery of services by counseling psychologists. *American Psychologist, 36*, 652–663.

American Psychological Association. (1992). Ethical principles of psychologists and code of conduct. *American Psychologist, 47*, 1597–1611.

American Psychological Association. (1993). *Record keeping guidelines*. Washington, DC: Author.

American Psychological Association. (1994). Guidelines for child custody evaluations in divorce proceedings. *American Psychologist, 49*, 677–680.

American Psychological Association. (1996). *Agenda for including information in child abuse and neglect in graduate and professional education and training*. American Psychological Association Public Interest Directorate. Washington, DC: Author.

American Psychological Association, American Educational Research Association, & National Council on Measurement in Education. (1985). *Standards for educational and psychological testing.* Washington, DC: Author.

Associated Press. (1997, November 10). Alabama couple wins round in interstate custody fight. *Montgomery Advertiser*, 5B.

Atkeson, B. M., Forehand, R. L., & Richard, K. M. (1982). The effect of divorce on children. In B. B. Lahey & A. E. Kaldin (Eds.), *Advances in clinical child psychology* (Vol. 5). New York: Plenum Press.

Bala, N. (1994a). Children, psychiatrists and the courts: Understanding the ambivalence of the legal profession. *Canadian Journal of Psychiatry, 39*, 526–530.

Bala, N. (1994b). Children, psychiatrists and the courts: Understanding the ambivalence of the legal profession: II. *Canadian Journal of Psychiatry, 39*, 531–539.

Barth, R. P., & Schleske, D. (1985). Comprehensive sexual abuse treatment programs and reports of sexual abuse. *Children and Youth Services Review, 7*, 285–298.

Barth, R. P., & Sullivan, R. (1985). Competent evidence in behalf of children. *Social Work, 30*, 130–136.

Becker, L. (1996). Ethical concerns in negotiating family law agreements. *Family Law Quarterly, 30*, 587–659.

Bell, D. J. (1984). The police response to domestic violence: An exploratory study. *Police Studies: The International Review of Police Development, 7*, 23–30.

Bell, D. J. (1985). Domestic violence: Victimization, police intervention. and disposition. *Journal of Criminal Justice, 13*, 525–534.

Belsky, J. (1993). Etiology of child maltreatment: A developmental analysis. *Psychological Bulletin, 114*, 413–434.

Bernstein, B. E., & Haberman, B. G. (1981). Lawyer and counselor as a team: Problem awareness in the blended family. *Child Welfare, 60*, 211–219.

Blau, T. H. (1984a). Expert testimony. In R. Corsini (Ed.), *Encyclopedia of psychology.* New York: Wiley.

Blau, T. H. (1984b). *The psychologist as expert witness.* New York: Wiley.

Blau, T. H. (1985). The psychologist as expert in the courts. *Clinical Psychologist, 38*, 76.

Bograd, M. (1984). Family systems approaches to wife batterings: A feminist critique. *American Journal of Orthopsychiatry, 54*, 558–568.

Bourne, R. (1995). Ethical and legal dilemmas in the management of family violence. *Ethics & Behavior, 5*, 261–271.

Bowlby, J. (1969). *Attachment.* New York: Basic Books.

Braver, S. L., Salem, P., Pearson, J., & DeLusé, S. R. (1996). Content of divorce programs: Result of a survey. *Family and Conciliation Courts Review 34*, 41–59.

Bricklin, B. (1984). *Brickin Perceptual Scales.* Furlong, PA: Village.

Briere, J. (Ed.). (1991). *Treating victims of child sexual abuse.* New York: Jossey-Bass.

Brodzinsky, D. M. (1993). On the use and misuse of psychological testing in child custody evaluations. *Professional Psychology: Research and Practice, 24*, 213–219.

Brosig, C. L., & Kalichman, S. C. (1992a). Clinicians' reporting of suspected child abuse: A review of the empirical literature. *Clinical Psychology Review, 12*, 155–168.

Brosig, C. L., & Kalichman, S. C. (1992b). Child abuse reporting decisions: Effects of statutory wording of reporting requirements. *Professional Psychology Research and Practice, 23*, 486–492.

Brown, S. E. (1984). Police responses to wife beating: Neglect of a crime of violence. *Journal of Criminal Justice, 12*, 277–288.

Browne, A., & Finkelhor, D. (1986). Impact of child sexual abuse. *Psychological Bulletin, 99*, 66–77.

Burgess, A. W., Groth, A. N., Holstrom, L. L., & Sgroi, S. M. (1978). *Sexual assault of children and adolescents.* Lexington, MA: Lexington.

Campbell, J. C., & Lewandowski, L. A. (1997). Mental and physical health effects of intimate partner violence on women and children. *Psychiatric Clinics of North America, 20,* 353–374.

Carey v. Population Services International, 438 U.S. 678 (1972).

Chase-Lansdale, P. L., Cherlin, A. J., & Kiernan, K. E. (1995). The long-term effects of parental divorce on the mental health of young adults: A developmental perspective. *Child Development, 66,* 1614–1634.

Cherlin, A. J., Furstenberg, F. F., Jr., Chase-Lansdale, P. L., Kiernan, K. E., Robbins, P. K., Morrison, D. R., & Teitlee, J. O. (1991). Longitudinal studies of the effects of divorce on children in Great Britain and the United States. *Science, 252,* 1386–1389.

Child Support Recovery Act, 18 U.S.C.A. § 228 (1992).

Civil Service Retirement Spouse Equity Act, 5 CFR 831 (1984).

Clark, B. K. (1995). Acting in the best interests of the child: Essential components of a child custody evaluation. *Family Law Quarterly, 29,* 19–38.

Clay, R. A. (1995, December). Courts reshape image of "the good mother." *APA Monitor,* p. 31.

Committee on Ethical Guidelines for Forensic Psychologists. (1991). Specialty guidelines for forensic psychologists. *Law and Human Behavior, 6,* 655–665.

Cox v. Florida Department of Health and Rehabilitation Services, 656 So. 2nd 902 (Fla., 1995).

Davis, A. (1998, March 11). Artificial-reproduction arrangers are ruled child's legal parents. *Wall Street Journal,* B9.

Davidson, H. A. (1983, December). Children's rights: Emerging trends for the 1980s. *Trial,* pp. 44–48.

Dobash, R. E., & Dobash, R. (1979). *Violence against wives.* New York: Free Press.

Dubowitz, H., Black, M., Starr, R., & Zuravin, S. (1993). *A conceptual definition of child neglect: Foundations for a new national strategy.* New York: Guilford Press.

Duryee, M. A. (1995). Guidelines for family court services intervention when there are allegations of domestic violence: Domestic violence [Special issue]. *Family and Conciliation Courts Review, 33,* 79–86.

Dutton, D. C. (1984). Interventions into the problem of wife assault: Therapeutic policy and research implications. *Canadian Journal of Behavioral Science, 16,* 281–297.

Eisendtadt v. Baird, 405 U.S. 438, 453 (1967).

Elrod, L. D. (1995). A review of the year in family law. *Family Law Quarterly, 28,* 541–557.

Elrod, L. D., & Spector, R. G. (1996). A review of the year in family law: Children's issues take spotlight. *Family Law Quarterly, 29,* 741–769.

Family and Medical Leave Act (FMLA), 29 U.S.C. §§ 2601 et seq. (1993).

Fine, M. A. (1997). Helping children cope with marital conflict, divorce, and remarriage. *In Session: Psychotherapy in Practice, 3,* 55–67.

Fine, M. A., & Kurdek, L. A. (1992). The adjustment of adolescents in stepfather and stepmother families. *Journal of Marriage and the Family, 54,* 725–736.

Finkelhor, D. (1979). *Sexually victimized children.* New York: Free Press.

Finkelhor, D. (1990). Early and longterm effects of child sexual abuse: An update. *Professional Psychology: Research and Practice, 21,* 325–330.

Follette, V. M., Polusny, M. A., Bechtle, A. E., & Naugle, A. E. (1996). Cumulative trauma: The impact of child sexual abuse, adult sexual assault, and spouse abuse. *Journal of Traumatic Stress, 9,* 25–35.

Foster, H. H. (1964). Social work, the law, and social action. *Social Casework, 45,* 383–386.

Foster, H. H., & Freed, D. J. (1983). Child custody and the adversary process: Forum convenient? *Family Law Quarterly, 17*, 133–150.

Frazier, P., & Borgida, E. (1985). Rape trauma syndrome evidence in court. *American Psychologist, 40*, 984–993.

Gelles, R. J., & Straus, M. A. (1988). *Intimate violence.* New York: Simon & Schuster.

Gerard, A. B. (1994). *Parent-Child Relationship Inventory (PCRI): Manual.* Los Angeles, CA: Western Psychological Services.

Ginsberg v. N.Y., 390 U.S. 629, 649-50 (1968).

Girdner, L. K. (1985a). Adjudication and mediation: A comparison of custody decision-making processes involving third parties. *Journal of Divorce, 8*, 33–47.

Girdner, L. K. (1985b). Strategies of conflict: Custody litigation in the United States. *Journal of Divorce, 9*, 1–15.

Girdner, L. K. (1986). Child custody determination. In E. Seidman & J. Rappaport (Eds.), *Redefining social problems* (pp. 165–183). New York: Plenum Press.

Goldstein, J., Freud, A., & Solnit, A. J. (1979). *Beyond the best interest of the child.* New York: Free Press.

Goldzband, M. G. (1982). *Consulting in child custody: An introduction to the ugliest litigation for mental health professionals.* Lexington, MA: Lexington.

Goldzband, M. G. (1983). Current trends affecting family law and child custody. *Psychiatric Clinics of North America, 6*, 683–693.

Good, J. B., & Davis J. (1997, July 26). Broken family suffers another loss. *The Atlanta Journal/The Atlanta Constitution*, p. C3.

Goodman, E. (1997, August 12). When people get married they believe theirs will last. *Montgomery Advertiser*, p. A6.

Gottlieb, M. C. (1995). Family violence and family systems: Who is the patient? *Ethics & Behavior, 5*, 273–277.

Grisso, T. (1986). *Evaluating competencies: Forensic assessments and instruments.* New York: Plenum Press.

Griswold v. State of Connecticut, 381 U.S. 479, 85 S. Ct. 1678. 14 L.Ed.2d 510 (1965).

Hauge Convention on the Protection of Children and Cooperation in Respect of Inter-country Adoption. (1993, May 29). The Hauge Conference on private international law, final act of the seventeenth session.

Hauge International Child Abduction Convention S. Treaty Doc. No 11, 99th Cong., 1st Sess., Reprinted in 19 I.L.M. 1501 (1980).

Heilbrun, K. (1995). Child custody evaluation: Critically assessing mental health experts and psychological tests. *Family Law Quarterly, 29*, 63–78.

Heinze, M. C., & Grisso, T. (1996). Review of instruments assessing parenting capacities used in child custody evaluations. *Behavioral Sciences and the Law, 14*, 293–313.

Hess, A. K. (1985). The psychologist as expert witness: A guide to the courtroom arena. *Clinical Psychologist, 38*, 75–76.

Hetherington, E. M. (1979). Divorce: A child's perspective. *American Psychologist, 34*, 851–858.

Hetherington, E. M., Cox, M., & Cox, R. (1979). Play and social interaction in children following divorce. *Journal of Social Issues, 35*, 26–49.

Hirschel, J. D., Hutchison, I. W., & Dean, C. W. (1992). The failure of arrest to deter spouse abuse. *Journal of Research in Crime and Delinquency, 29*, 7–33.

Hyde, L. M. (1984). Child custody in divorce. *Juvenile and Family Court Journal.* Reno, NV: National Council of Juvenile Family Count Judges.

Ind. Code Ann. § 31-3-1-13 (1994).

In re A & M, No. 61 A.D. 2d 426, 403 (New York State, 2d. 375, 381, 1978).

In re Amber B. 191 Cal. App. 3d 682, 236 Cal. Rptr 623 (1987).

In re Clausen, 505 N.W.2d 575 (Mich. 1993).

In re Gault, 387 U.S. 1 (1967).

In re Gerald (Cindy W.), 625 N.Y.S. 2d 509 (App. Div. 1995).

In re Kirchner, 649 N.E.2d 324 (Ill. 1995).

In re M.M.D., 662 A.2d 837 (D.C. Ct. App. 1995).

International Parental Kidnapping Crime Act, Pub.L. No. 103-173 (1993).

Ireland v. Smith, Michigan Cir. Ct., Macomb County June 27,1994 Docket no. 93-385.

Irving, H. H. (1980). *Divorce mediation: A rational alterative to the adversary systems.* New York: Universe.

Jameson, B. J., Ehrenberg, M. F., & Hunter, M. A. (1997). Psychologists' rating of the best-interest-of-the-child custody and access criterion: A family system assessment model. *Professional Psychology: Research and Practice, 28,* 253–262.

Juvenile Justice Standards Project, Institute of Judicial Administration, American Bar Association. (1981). *Standards relating to abuse and neglect.* Cambridge, MA: Ballinger.

Kaslow, F. W. (1983). Stages and techniques of divorce therapy. In P. A. Keller & L. G. Ritt (Eds.), *Innovations in clinical practice: A sourcebook: II.* Sarasota, FL: Professional Resource Exchange.

Kaslow, F. W. (1984a). Divorce: An evolutionary process of change in the family system. *Journal of Divorce, 7,* 21–40.

Kaslow, F. W. (1984b). Divorce mediation and its emotional impact on the couple and their children. *American Journal of Family Therapy, 12,* 58–64.

Kaufman, J., & Zigler, E. (1987). Do abused children become abusive parents? *American Journal of Orthopsychiatry, 57,* 186–192.

Kempe, C. H., Silverman, F., Steele, B., Droemueller, W., & Silverman, H. (1962). The battered child syndrome. *Journal of the American Medical Association, 181,* 17–24.

Kempe, R., & Kempe, C. (1984). *The common secret: Sexual abuse of children and adolescents.* New York: Freeman.

Kendall-Tackett, K. A., Williams, L. M., & Finkelhor, D. (1993). Impact of sexual abuse in children: A review and synthesis of recent empirical studies *Psychological Bulletin, 113,* 164–180.

Klein, C. F. (1995). Full faith and credit: Interstate enforcement of protection orders under the Violence Against Women Act of 1994. *Family Law Quarterly, 29,* 253–271.

Krause, H. D. (1977). *Family law in a nutshell.* St. Paul, MN: West.

Kuchler, F. W. (1978). *Law of engagement and marriage.* Dobbs Ferry, NY: Oceana.

Kuehule, K. (1996). *Assessing allegations of child sexual abuse.* Sarasota FL: Professional Resource Press.

Kurdek, L. A., & Berg, B. (1983). Correlates of children's adjustments to their parents' divorces. In L. A. Kurdek (Ed.), *Children and divorce.* San Francisco: Jossey-Bass.

Kurdek, L. A., Blisk, D., & Siesky, A. E. (1981). Correlates of children's long-term adjustment to their parents' divorce. *Developmental Psychology, 17,* 565–579.

Lamb, M. E. (1977). The effects of divorce on children's personality development. *Journal of Divorce, 1,* 163–174.

Lamb, M. E. (Ed.). (1996). *The role of the father in child development* (3rd ed.). New York: Wiley.

Langan, P., & Innes, C. (1986). *U.S. Bureau of Justice statistics special report: Preventing domestic violence against women.* Washington, DC: U.S. Bureau of Justice Statistics.

Loving, N. (1980). *Responding to spouse abuse and wife beating.* Washington, DC: Policy Executive Research Forum.

Loving v. Virginia, 388 U.S. 1 (1967).

Mack, J. W. (1925). The chauncery procedure in the juvenile court. In J. Addams, C. J. Herrick, A. L. Jacoby, & others (Eds.), *The child, the clinic, and the court: A group of papers* (pp. 310–319). New York: New Republic.

Maclean, J. F. (1997, November 4). Area, state figures show popularity of matrimony. *Montgomery Advertiser*, A1–2.

Manocherian, J. (1985). Family mediation: A descriptive case study. *Journal of Divorce, 8*, 97–118.

Martin, D. (1976). *Battered wives.* San Francisco, CA: Glide.

McIsaac, H. (Ed.). (1996). Parent education in divorce and separation [Special issue]. *Family and Conciliation Courts Review, 34*(1).

Melton, G. B. (1984). Developmental psychology and the law: The state of the art. *Journal of Family Law, 22*, 445–482.

Melton, G. B., & Barry, F. (1994). *Protecting children from abuse and neglect: Foundations for a new national strategy.* New York: Guilford Press.

Melton, G. B., Petrila, J., Poythress, N. G., & Slobogin, C. (1987). *Psychological evaluations for the courts: A handbook for mental health professionals and lawyers.* New York: Guilford Press.

Menard, A. E., & Salius, A. J. (1990). Judicial response to family violence: The importance of message. Mediation and spouse abuse [Special issue]. *Mediation Quarterly, 7*, 293–302.

Mermin, S. (1982). *Law and the legal system.* Boston: Little, Brown.

Merrikcn v. Cressman, 354 F. Supp. 913 (E.D. Penn. 1973).

Meyer, J. F., & Geis, G. (1994). Psychological research on child witnesses in sexual abuse cases: Fine answers to mostly wrong questions. *Child and Adolescent Social Work Journal, 11*, 209–220.

Meyer v. Nebraska, 262 U.S. 390 (1923).

Milbank, D. (1997, October 3). More dads raise families without mom. *The Wall Street Journal*, p. B1.

Milner, J. S. (Ed.). (1991). Physical child abuse [Special issue]. *Criminal Justice and Behavior, 18.*

Milner, J. S. (Ed.). (1992). Sexual child abuse [Special issue]. *Criminal Justice and Behavior, 19.*

Moore, D. M. (1979). *Battered women.* Beverly Hills, CA: Sage.

Morris, R. J. (1997). Child custody evaluations: A risky business. *Register Report, 23*, 6–7.

Neidig, P. H. (1984). *Spouse abuse: A treatment program for couples.* Champaign, IL: Research Press.

Parental Kidnapping Prevention Act of 1980, P.L. 61 1.

Parham v. J.L. & J.R., 422 U.S. 584 (1979).

Parken v. Saileau, 213 So. 2d. 190 (1968).

Paulsen, M. G., Wadlington, W., & Goebel, J. (1974). *Cases and other material on domestic relations* (2nd ed.). Mineola, NY: The Foundation.

Payne, D. (1997, July 26). 10 year old charged after brother stabbed. *The Atlanta Journal/The Atlanta Constitution*, p. C3.

Payne, J. D., & Overend, E. (1990). Divorce mediation: Process and strategies: An overview. *Family and Conciliation Courts Review, 28*, 27–34.

Phillips v. Phillips, 274 So. 2d. 71 (1973).

Pierce, R., & Pierce, L. H. (1985). The sexually abused child: A comparison of male and female victims. *Child Abuse and Neglect, 9*, 191–199.

Pierce v. Society of Sisters, 268 U.S. 510 (1925).

Planned Parenthood v. Danforth, 423 U.S. 52, 75 (1976).

Planned Parenthood of Southeastern Pennsylvania v. Casey 744 F. Supp. 1323 (E.D. Pa. 1990).

Polusny, M. A., & Follette, V. M. (1995). Long term correlates of child sexual abuse: Theory and review of the empirical literature. *Applied and Preventive Psychology: Current Scientific Perspectives, 4*, 143–166.

Popham v. Duncan, 87 Colo. 149, 285 p. 757, 70 A.L.R. 824 (1930).

Prince v. Massachusetts, 321 U.S. 158 (1944).

Rikard v. Rikard, 378 So. 2d (1980).

Roe v. Wade, 409 U.S. 817 (1973).

Roseby, V. (1995). Uses of psychological testing in a child focused approach to child custody evaluations. *Family Law Quarterly, 29*, 97–110.

Sagatun, I. J. (1991). Expert witnesses in child abuse cases. *Behavioral Science and the Law, 9*, 201–215.

Salem, P., Schepard, A., & Schlissel, S. W. (1996). Parent education as a distinct field of practice: The agenda for the future. *Family and Conciliation Courts Review, 34*, 9–22.

Sattler, J. M. (1997). *Clinical and forensic interviewing of children and families.* San Diego, CA: Jerome Sattler.

Shapiro, D. L. (1984). *Psychological evaluation and expert testimony.* New York: Van Nostrand-Reinhold.

Sibley, C. (1997, July 26). Dekalb court, schools differ on youth's guilt. *The Atlanta Journal/The Atlanta Constitution*, p. C3.

Silberman L. (1994). Hauge convention on international child abduction: A brief overveiw and case law analysis. *Family Law Quarterly, 28*, 9–34.

Singhania, L. (1997, November 3). Laws back grandparents who sue their children for visitation rights. *Montgomery Advertiser*, 6E.

Skinner v. State of Oklahoma, 316 U.S. 535, 541, 62 S.Ct. 1100, 1113. 86 L.Ed. 1655 (1942).

Special issue on domestic violence. (1995). *Family Law Quarterly, 29*(2).

Sprenkle, D. H., & Storm, C. L. (1983). Divorce therapy outcome research: A substantium and methodological review. *Journal of Marital and Family Therapy, 9*, 239–258.

Stahl, P. M. (1994). *Conducting child custody evaluations: A comprehensive guide.* Thousand Oaks, CA.: Sage.

Stanton, A. M. (1982). Child-parent privilege for confidential communications: An examination and proposal. *Family Law Quarterly, 16*, 1–67.

Starr, R. H., & Wolfe, D. A. (Eds.). (1991). *The effect of child abuse and neglect: Issues and research.* New York: Guilford Press.

Straus, M. A., Gelles, R., & Steinmetz, S. K. (1980). *Behind closed doors: Violence in the American family.* Garden City, NY: Anchor.

Strickman, L. P. (1982). Marriage, divorce and the Constitution. *Family Law Quarterly, 15*, 259–348.

Underwager, R., & Wakefield, H. (1992). Poor psychology produces poor law. *Law and Human Behavior, 16*, 233–243.

Uniform Adoption Act, 9 U.L.A. 1 (West Supp. 1995).

Uniform Child Custody Jurisdiction Act, 9 UCA III (1979).

Uniform Marriage and Divorce Act, 402, 9A UCA 197-198 (1979).

Uniform Services Former Spouses Protection Act, DL 101-510 (1990).

United States Bureau of the Census. (1997). *Statistical abstract of the United States: 1997* (117th ed.). Washington, DC: Author.

U.S. Department of Justice, Bureau of Justice Statistics. (1986). *Crime and justice facts.* Washington, DC: Author.

U.S. Department of Justice, Bureau of Justice Statistics. (1996, April). Criminal victimization 1994. *Bureau of Justice Statistics Bulletin.* Washington, DC: Author.

Violence Against Women Act, 18 U.S.C.A § 2265 1994 Pub.L. No.103-322, Title IV, 108 Stat. 1902-55.

Wakefield,H., & Underwager, R. (1992). Assessing credibility of children's testimony in ritual sexual abuse allegations. *Issues in Child Abuse Accusations, 4,* 32–44.

Walker, L. E. (1979). *The battered woman.* New York: Harper & Row.

Walker, L. E. (1984). *The battered woman syndrome.* New York: Springer.

Walker, T. B. (1992a). Family law in the fifty states: An overview. *Family Law Quarterly, 25,* 417–520.

Walker, T. B. (Ed.). (1992b). Anniversary issue: Twenty-five years of the Family Law Quarterly. *Family Law Quarterly, 25.*

Wallerstein, J. S., & Kelly, J. B. (1980). *Surviving the breakup: How children and parents cope with divorce.* New York: Basic Books.

Weiner, B. A. (1985). An overview of child custody laws. *Hospital and Community Psychiatry, 36,* 838–843.

Weiner, I. B. (1985). Preparing forensic reports and testimony. *Clinical Psychologist, 38,* 78–80.

Weithorn, L. A. (1982). Developmental factors and competence to make informed treatment decisions. *Child and Youth Services, 4,* 85–100.

Weithorn, L. A. (Ed.). (1987). *Psychology and child custody determinations.* Lincoln: University of Nebraska Press.

Whalen v. Row, 429 U.S. 589, 599 (1977).

Widom, C. S. (1989, April 14). The cycle of violence. *Science, 244,* 160–166.

Wisconsin v. Yoder, 406 U.S. (1972).

Yllo, K. (1984). The status of women, marital equality, and violence against wives. *Journal of Family Issues, 5,* 307–320.

Zarski, L. P., Knight, R., & Zarski, J. J. (1985). Child custody disputes: A review of legal and clinical resolution methods. *International Journal of Family Therapy, 7,* 96–106.

Ziskin, J. (1981). *Coping with psychiatric and psychological testimony* (2 Vols., 3rd ed.). Marina Del Rey, CA: Law and Psychology.

CHAPTER 5

Personality Assessment in Personal Injury Litigation

JAMES N. BUTCHER and KATHRYN B. MILLER

PSYCHOLOGISTS ARE increasingly becoming involved in personal injury litigation cases as expert witnesses. Their expanded involvement in the courtroom comes, in part, from the increased number of cases that incorporate a mental health or "pain and suffering" component to damage claims. It has also resulted from maturation of the field of psychological assessment: many attorneys understand that psychologists now use objective evaluation methods that can provide valuable testimony about the mental health status of litigants.

REQUIREMENTS OF THE EXPERT WITNESS

THE ADVERSARIAL CONTEXT OF PERSONAL INJURY ASSESSMENTS

Most psychologists involved in personal injury assessments are persons originally trained in clinical, counseling, or neuropsychology, who entered the field as a "helping" professional. Their venturing into forensic assessment, with its high potential for challenge, represents a different type of psychological assessment context than most are accustomed to. They may find themselves, at times, consulting or providing test interpretations that actually work against the wishes and intent of the individuals being tested. Psychologists who wander afield from the relatively safe environment of clinical assessment may find the often confrontive nature of legal challenge in forensic assessment quite difficult, particularly if their academic background is spotty or incomplete or if they employ assessment methods that cannot withstand the harsh scrutiny of sharp cross-examination. Expert witnesses need to assure that they have the

We would like to thank Steven Rouse for assisting us with data reported in this chapter. We would also like to thank Linda Fresquez for assisting us with typing.

necessary expertise for personal injury litigation consultation and need to employ the most objective methods available in their assessments.

Appropriate Background for Personal Injury Case Expertise

Educational Requirements

It is extremely important for the psychologist to demonstrate appropriate educational background that provides sufficient focus for using psychological tests in forensic settings. A doctoral degree in a mental health field is a minimum requirement; for example, a PhD or PsyD in clinical, counseling, or health psychology with an appropriate clinical internship is desirable. This educational background should be taken in academic programs that are approved by the American Psychological Association. The psychologist should also be able to demonstrate that he or she holds appropriate licensure, often a requirement for purchasing psychological tests (American Psychological Association, 1986).

Experience Requirements

The proposed expert witness should be able to demonstrate work-related experiences in health or mental health settings pertinent to the case, for example, mental health centers, hospitals, rehabilitation, or neuropsychology settings. For example, if the case being tried is one that involves alleged physical injury, the psychologist should have substantial professional experience evaluating similar cases in a medical setting; if the case being tried involves assessing posttraumatic symptoms, the psychologist should have relevant experience evaluating or treating individuals in crisis or posttraumatic situations.

Expertise in Procedures Being Employed

To be a credible witness, the psychologist needs to demonstrate expertise in the techniques being used to assess the litigant. A history of graduate-level coursework in the psychological procedures being used is important. It is also desirable for the psychologist to demonstrate extensive current experience through postdoctoral professional experiences, continuing education experience, teaching graduate courses, or publishing relevant research articles in peer-reviewed resources. Ultimately, each case will determine which, if any, of the experts submitted by counsel will be allowed to testify.

Documentation of Expertise

It is valuable for the forensic practitioner to be able to document expertise in testifying about psychological procedures used in the case. Prior testimony, having been admitted by other courts to testify in similar cases, can serve to establish one as a qualified expert. It is important for psychologists to keep a record of previous cases in which they have testified in personal injury litigation.

MEASURING INSTRUMENTS IN FORENSIC ASSESSMENT

Most psychologists testifying in personal injury cases employ procedures that can be objectively interpreted because of the need to defend one's conclusions in an adversarial environment. Any psychological test used should be psychometrically structured to allow for appropriate discriminations in forensic assessment. For example, in the case of a clinical procedure, the test should be able to make a clear differentiation between persons with mental health problems and those who are not psychologically disturbed. A psychological test like the Millon Clinical Multiaxial Inventory (MCMI) cannot be appropriately used in forensic assessment because it does not provide norms that allow for the discrimination between patients and normals (Hess, 1998). All persons who are administered the test are assumed to have psychological problems as assessed by the test. The results are therefore considered to be biased toward "finding" problems in the client (Otto & Butcher, 1995).

The most widely used and objective method of evaluating a litigant's mental health status in court cases is the Minnesota Multiphasic Personality Inventory (MMPI-2) (Lubin, Larsen, & Matarazzo, 1984; Watkins, Campbell, Niebirding, & Hallmark, 1995). It is also the most widely used instrument in forensic assessment (Borum & Grisso, 1995; Keilen & Bloom, 1986; Lees-Haley, Smith, Williams, & Dunn, 1995) and in personality-clinical research (Butcher & Rouse, 1996). The MMPI-2 is a paper-and-pencil questionnaire comprising 567 symptoms, beliefs, and attitudes that reflect potential mental health problems in test takers who respond frankly to the items. The MMPI was originally developed in the 1940s as an objective measure of personality and symptomatic behavior. Since that time, an extensive amount of empirical research has been published documenting and detailing the meaning of the empirical scales of the inventory.[1]

When the MMPI was revised in 1989, the MMPI Re-standardization Committee took efforts to maintain the continuity of the original clinical scales because of their rich database. The traditional scales are essentially the same in the MMPI-2 as in the original instrument. The MMPI Committee also developed a number of new measures for the revised test that provide information with respect to other clinical problem areas such as substance abuse and marital problems.

The inventory contains a number of measures that address test-taking attitudes, perhaps the most important factor to evaluate in individuals being assessed in forensic settings. In court cases, litigants often possess the motivation to present themselves in a particular way, to either appear free of psychological disturbance or severely disabled and deserving of compensation. Any psychological assessment procedure, if it is to shed light on the test taker, needs to have a means of appraising the varying motivations of litigants. The revised version of the inventory contains several indexes to assess clients' self-presentation styles. These will be addressed later in this chapter.

ISSUES IN THE ASSESSMENT OF
PERSONAL INJURY CLAIMANTS

Research on the impact of psychological factors in the manifestation of physical illness has yielded varying results depending on the specific area studied. We review current research on the role that personality factors play in the presentation and maintenance of physical symptoms. As in any MMPI-2-based assessment, the way the individual presents himself or herself is a crucial consideration for interpretation. A valid, interpretable protocol is necessary for an appropriate personality and symptomatic appraisal. Some individuals involved in personal injury cases who wish to be viewed as psychologically disabled may present an extreme and hardly credible set of mental health symptoms (Butcher, 1997a, 1997b). This type of profile, however, is not consistent with valid profiles. Research on disability determination cases typically does not find extremely exaggerated MMPI-2 profiles but instead shows F scale elevations clearly within an interpretable range (Flamer & Birch, 1992; Long, Nelson, & Butcher, 1995).

LOW BACK INJURY AND PAIN

Low back pain (LBP) is one of the most costly problems in the American workplace. Billions of dollars are lost each year through worker's compensation claims around LBP and lost earnings. Of particular concern are the statistics suggesting that the longer someone is out of work, the lower his or her probability of returning to work, even over short periods (Gallagher et al., 1989). These statistics have led researchers to suggest that LBP sufferers should return to work as soon as possible after pain onset to prevent the development of a more chronic form.

In a review of the literature, Love and Peck (1987) concluded that the MMPI is not useful in determining the etiology of LBP. All LBP patients generally score higher on Hypochondrasis (Hs) and Hysteria (Hy), typically known as the conversion V profile. However, they suggest that LBP patients differ in important ways on the MMPI, which may reflect their affective and behavioral response to their pain as well as their response to different forms of treatment. They found that low ego strength or elevated Paranoid (Pa) or Schizophrenia (Sc) scales were predictors of poor outcome in a pain management program. These elevated scores may represent a subgroup with greater premorbid psychological problems (such as externalization of blame) and complaints of physical problems that predict poor response to treatment.

Gallagher et al. (1989) found that psychosocial as opposed to physical symptoms predicted return-to-work six months after initial assessment in a combined sample of clinic patients and applicants for Social Security Administration compensation. Significant predictors of return-to-work status were length of time out of work, ease of changing occupations, score on the MMPI Hy scale, locus of health control, and ability to perform daily tasks. Gatchel, Polatin, and Mayer (1995) also found that score on the MMPI Hy scale, as well as self-reported pain and disability and litigation status were important in differentiating those who returned to work within one year from those who did not. In this follow-up study, severity of initial low back injury and physical demands of the job were not found to be predictive of subsequent return-to-work status.

The most effective way to determine the relative contributions of premorbid personality characteristics and postinjury factors in the manifestation of back pain is to conduct prospective studies. Fordyce, Bigos, Batti'e, and Fisher (1992) assessed 3,020 industrial employees using a variety of instruments including the MMPI. The workers were followed for an average of three years, during which time 117 employees reported back injury. Initial score on the MMPI Hy scale was a significant predictor of later back injury. In particular, the lassitude/malaise, denial of social anxiety, and need for affection Harris Lingoes scales from the Hy scale were found to be predictive. In general, psychological variables had greater predictive power than biomechanical variables, suggesting that emotional or psychological factors may play a key role in the development of physical symptoms. In another prospective study, depression predicted application for early retirement in a six-month follow-up of 111 patients with acute back pain (Hasenbring, Marienfeld, Kuhlendahl, & Soyka, 1994). Overall, there appears to be an interaction between psychological factors and LBP such that those who are more depressed and more likely to respond to psychological problems physically have a greater likelihood of developing and maintaining chronic back pain.

HEAD INJURY

Head injury is a particularly difficult area to assess because symptoms commonly associated with it are often considered pathological in other contexts. Standard indicators of malingering such as F and Fp need to be evaluated differently when assessing a head injury case because individuals may elevate these scales when reporting valid symptoms. Alfano, Neilson, Paniak, and Finlayson (1992) conducted a profile analysis of 103 patients judged by a neurosurgical team to have moderate to severe closed-head injuries (CHI). Overall, the subjects showed elevations on all MMPI clinical scales except Si. The most frequent two-point code for men was 8-2, and the most frequent two-point code for women was 1-3. Because of these valid elevations produced in CHI cases, Gass proposed an MMPI-2 CHI correction factor (Gass & Wald, in press). This 15-item correction factor reflects the physical and cognitive symptoms frequently seen in CHI patients. These items load most heavily on the Pt and Sc scales. In a cross-validation study, Gass and Wald found that this correction factor discriminated 54 closed-head trauma individuals from 2,600 normals. None of the closed-head trauma individuals were involved in litigation, nor did they have any premorbid history of psychiatric disorders or alcohol dependence. For information related to frequency of various MMPI-2 codes in patients with head injury, Putnam, Kurtz, Millis, and Adams (1995) should be consulted.

POSTTRAUMATIC STRESS DISORDER

Emotional damage or distress is increasingly being claimed by litigators against defendants such as employers. Specifically, people may claim that they have developed posttraumatic stress disorder (PTSD) as a result of harassment, difficult work conditions, or an accident. This poses a problem for attorneys because it is extremely difficult to determine the change in a person's emotional functioning without any premorbid data. Lack of premorbid data precludes determining a causal relationship between the event and current functioning because it is unknown whether or not the person had preexisting emotional problems. Blanchard et al. (1996) looked at the development of PTSD after a motor vehicle accident (MVA) and found that 70% of the people who developed PTSD symptoms within four months of the accident could be predicted using four variables: prior major depression, extent of physical injury sustained, fear of dying in the accident, and the initiation of litigation. Mayou, Bryant, and Duthie (1993), however, did not find that premorbid psychopathology, baseline depression, or neuroticism was predictive of the later development of PTSD after an MVA. Other investigations have found that attributional or coping style is important in moderating the effects of stress on the individual (Hovanitz & Kozora, 1989; McCormick, Taber, & Krudelback, 1989).

There has been debate in the literature as to whether the MMPI accurately assesses PTSD as opposed to a more general form of emotional distress (Miller, Goldberg, & Streiner, 1995). The MMPI posttraumatic stress scales, PK and PS, were originally designed using veteran samples. Some studies have found that Keane's subscale (PK) does not well discriminate PTSD veterans from non-PTSD veterans (Silver & Salamone-Genovese, 1991; Vanderploeg, Sison, & Hickling, 1987); other studies suggest better discrimination (Keane, Malloy, & Fairbank, 1984; Munley, Bains, Bloem, & Busby, 1995). Studies assessing the efficacy of the MMPI PTSD scale in civilian populations have also found mixed results. Neal et al. (1994), using a sample of 70 civilians in the United Kingdom, concluded that the MMPI PTSD scale was useful in quantifying PTSD symptom severity, but cautioned against using it as a dichotomous indicator of PTSD. Flamer and Birch (1992) found that even in civilian trauma cases, the PTSD scale was elevated in genuine trauma cases when compared against chronic pain and mental health patients. Overall, high elevations on the PK scale should be interpreted with caution because they may indicate PTSD or they may indicate more chronic mental health problems.

FACTORS TO CONSIDER WHEN CONDUCTING PERSONALITY ASSESSMENTS WITH THE MMPI-2

In forensic settings, it is difficult to determine whether an individual claiming problems as a result of an injury or stressful experience or exposure to toxic substance is manifesting symptoms consistent with such injuries or whether other factors such as psychological adjustment are also contributing to his or her problems. In these situations, the professionals involved may be asked to render an opinion or evaluate:

1. Whether there is a possibility that the individual's physical complaints are due to actual organic changes.
2. Whether the symptoms of disability result from a psychological disorder such as traumatic reaction to stress or "traumatic neurosis."
3. Whether the pattern of symptoms may be neither physical nor "psychological," but are instead contrived to gain compensation or to obtain special services or considerations such as job transfer or reduced workload. It has been noted that malingering is difficult to determine without direct objective evidence (Marcus, 1983).

Psychological evaluation may prove valuable in appraising personality factors contributing to an individual's symptom pattern or appraising the dynamics of an individual's response to an acquired physical disability. However, psychological evaluations in disability determinations have some inherent limitations. It is not possible to determine, on the basis of the MMPI-2, or any psychological test for that matter, whether a claimant's injuries are actually based on organic conditions or derive from personality factors. It is also not possible to determine, with confidence, on the basis of a psychological test alone whether the patient is malingering. It is not possible to establish with any degree of certainty the nature of an individual's premorbid personality and its influence on current functioning unless psychological testing was conducted at an earlier point in time prior to the present disability. There are no foolproof ways of detecting premorbid personality or preinjury functioning with only present-time measurement.

Nevertheless, psychological testing can be of value in disability determinations in a number of ways. If the psychological tests provide, as the MMPI-2 does, scales that measure response attitudes, the individual's cooperation with the assessment, and "believability," then the results can be reliably assessed. Psychological assessment instruments, if they are objectively derived and validated, can provide a comparison of the client's symptomatic status with that of numerous other cases. Psychological testing can also provide some indication of the severity and long-term stability of the individual's problems.

In assessing the behavior of litigants in personal injury assessments, a psychologist needs to be aware of a number of factors that could impact the evaluation.

ATTORNEY BRIEFINGS PRIOR TO TEST ADMINISTRATION

One of the most problematic factors encountered in forensic assessment is the tendency of many attorneys to guide their clients through a desired strategy for responding to psychological test items. MMPI-2 interpretation is based on the assumption that standard administration procedures have been followed and the client has received the same instructions as the normative sample. Some attorneys may try to aid their clients in producing a desired clinical pattern, for example, to emphasize a problem area while not getting tripped up by the validity indicators. When conducting assessments of clients who possibly have been coached, it is important to determine the extent and nature of the information they were provided about the testing. The assessment psychologist should ask the client what he or she has been told and forensic testing reports should reflect a discussion of any likely response sets so that those employing the report will be aware of potentially test-spoiling conditions.

IMPORTANCE OF ASSESSING PROFILES AGAINST POPULATION BASE RATES

In interpreting MMPI-2 patterns for a given population, it is often useful to determine what "typical" or modal profiles exist in similar samples. For example, among samples of alcoholic patients, the most frequent profiles contain Pd scale elevations, and among chronic pain samples, the dominant profile pattern usually involves the 1-3 code. Knowing, for example, that a client's profile deviates substantially from the base rate might provide interpretive insights about the client. Several studies have described extensive base rate information that can be employed to provide an appropriate context for forensic MMPI-2 profile interpretation (Ben-Porath, McNulty, Watt, & McCormick, 1997; Butcher, 1997a, 1997b; Long et al., 1995; Putnam et al., 1995). The frequency data are made available in the National Computer System's computer-based interpretive program (the Minnesota Report) for forensic settings (Butcher, 1997b).

Butcher (1997b) examined the major self-presentation styles of personal injury litigants by grouping profiles according to the following categories: the defensive claimant, the exaggerated problem presentation, and the honest self-portrayal. He then developed base rate information for this sample (*N* = 157) of personal injury litigants and presented profile frequency information for different response styles. It was not possible to group cases into actual versus feigned records or type of personal injury because only the profiles were available for evaluation. Therefore, the group mean profiles of all cases were divided into groups based on whether the validity pattern reflected an essentially normal response approach, a highly defensive protocol, or a highly exaggerated pattern.

The three group mean profiles shown in Figures 5.1–5.3 are informative. The first profile (the clearly valid cases) shows a clear pattern of somatic symptoms in the context of a validity pattern that is credible. The second profile (the defensive records) shows a presentation of self as experiencing somatic problems but in a context of problem denial or claiming of excessive virtue. The third profile presents a rather different pattern, one in which the individual is

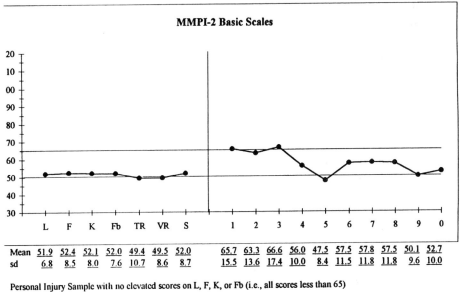

Figure 5.1   Personal Injury Claimants with Essentially Valid MMPI-2 Validity Scale Profiles.

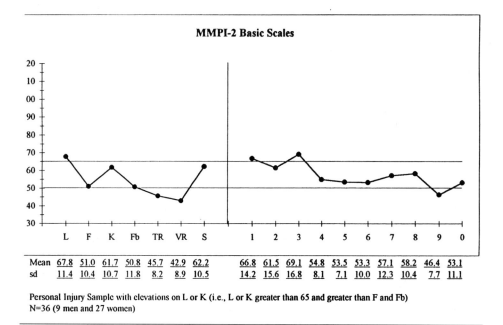

Figure 5.2   Personal Injury Claimants with a "Fake-Good" Validity Scale Configuration.

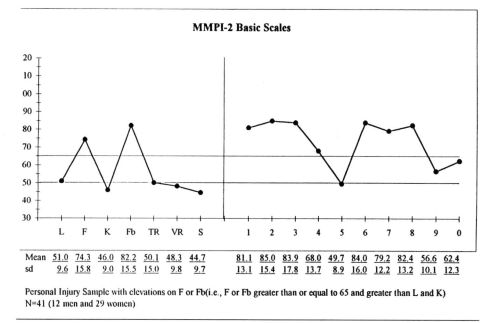

Figure 5.3   Personal Injury Litigants with an Exaggerated Symptom Presentation on the MMPI-2 Validity Scales.

likely to be exaggerating symptoms. In this pattern, the litigant is asserting great psychological disability and symptoms of distress but in the context of an exaggerated or low credible response pattern.

IMPORTANCE OF ASSESSING PRIOR MENTAL HEALTH HISTORY

For cases in which a litigant alleges mental health problems as a result of an accident or circumstance such as workplace harassment, it is assumed that the individual was not experiencing mental health problems prior to the incident. The veracity of the claim rests upon whether the incident actually occurred and whether it was powerful enough to have caused the alleged mental health problems. The defense (usually a corporation or an insurance carrier) may attempt to establish that the alleged injury likely existed prior to the incident and therefore the claimed damages could not have been the sole responsibility of the defendant. Efforts to establish the existence of prior mental health problems can involve procedures such as obtaining preaccident medical records or psychological testing or having witnesses testify that the problems actually preceded the alleged incident. At times, it may be possible for the defense attorneys to obtain records such as an MMPI-2 that had been administered when the client was in marital therapy or seeking mental heath services for other reasons. In such cases, it may be possible to learn whether or not the client's mental health problems resulted from the claimed incident. The following case illustrates the value of obtaining mental health records for problems that actually occurred before the accident in question.

CASE EXAMPLE

Ms. X, age 35, alleged that she had suffered psychological and neurological damage as a result of an incident in which she claimed to have been injured when a rental car with a stuck accelerator chased her around a rental car lot. Witnesses testified that she was not actually hit by the car. Attorneys for the plaintiff introduced into evidence a psychological evaluation conducted after the incident that suggested she had suffered irreparable damage because of the incident and was experiencing severe mental health problems as a result. She claimed to be so impaired cognitively that she could not even perform simple mental tasks such as reading bedtime stories to her children. Her MMPI-2 profile (shown in Figure 5.4) suggested that she was experiencing substantial mental health problems in the context of a valid but somewhat exaggerated test performance.

Psychological testing conducted prior to the incident, however, indicated that the mental health disability that she claimed actually preceded her so-called accident. Ms. X had actually been evaluated about one month prior to the incident as part of a different lawsuit in which she was allegedly rear-ended by a garbage truck. She had litigation pending from this incident as well. The MMPI-2 evaluation in this earlier litigation showed that she was experiencing a pattern of severe emotional disturbance *at the time* the second accident occurred (see MMPI-2 pattern in Figure 5.5). The jury in this case found for the defense.

MMPI-2

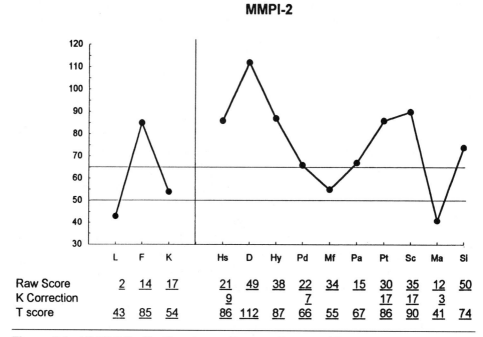

	L	F	K		Hs	D	Hy	Pd	Mf	Pa	Pt	Sc	Ma	Si
Raw Score	2	14	17		21	49	38	22	34	15	30	35	12	50
K Correction					9			7			17	17	3	
T score	43	85	54		86	112	87	66	55	67	86	90	41	74

Figure 5.4   MMPI-2 Profile Showing an Extreme Pattern of Psychological Symptoms.

MMPI-2

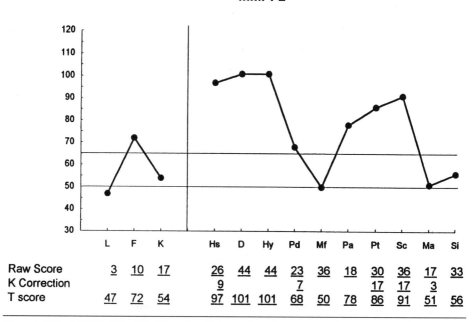

	L	F	K		Hs	D	Hy	Pd	Mf	Pa	Pt	Sc	Ma	Si
Raw Score	3	10	17		26	44	44	23	36	18	30	36	17	33
K Correction					9			7			17	17	3	
T score	47	72	54		97	101	101	68	50	78	86	91	51	56

Figure 5.5   MMPI-2 Profile Showing Severe Psychological Adjustment Problems.

They did not believe that the incident in the rental car lot had caused the mental damages that the plaintiff claimed, in large part because the problems preexisted the incident.

ANALYSIS OF POSTACCIDENT ADJUSTMENT

Attorneys might attempt to clarify the extent of psychological damage to litigants by conducting postaccident assessments. For instance, a defense team might conduct a psychological evaluation at different points after the incident to determine whether the client is showing physical or psychological symptoms consistent with the claimed disability. The MMPI-2 can be helpful in making this determination. Extreme elevations on F, Fb, or Fp are signals that the individual is not selectively responding to symptoms but is instead indiscriminantly exaggerating symptoms. For example, the MMPI profile shown in Figure 5.6 illustrates this problem. The litigant claimed disabling ear damage after a sudden change in cabin pressure, which occurred when an aircraft was descending. As shown in Figure 5.6, the litigant produced a highly exaggerated *F* scale score, greater than a *T* of 80, and a clinical profile that showed no selective responding. Unlike most genuine patients, he responded in the clinical range across all of the traditional MMPI clinical scales; all clinical scale scores were *T* > 70. He showed no specific pattern of symptoms as one would find in clients who are accurately reporting their internal states. Instead, the litigant simply endorsed all or most symptoms without specificity.

Clients who are alleging posttraumatic stress from interpersonal situations such as workplace harassment may also tend to exaggerate and present

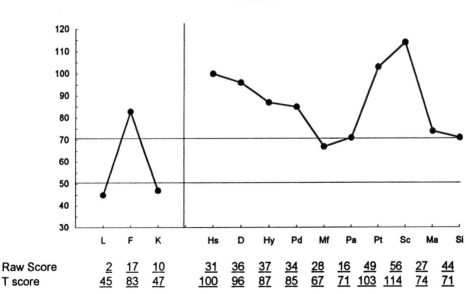

MMPI

		L	F	K		Hs	D	Hy	Pd	Mf	Pa	Pt	Sc	Ma	Si
Raw Score		2	17	10		31	36	37	34	28	16	49	56	27	44
T score		45	83	47		100	96	87	85	67	71	103	114	74	71

Figure 5.6 Extreme Symptom Claiming on the Original MMPI without Differential Symptom Endorsement.

an extreme pattern of symptoms that they believe reflect their anguish and "disability," but which appear on the testing to be extreme, even malingered, because they are not a specific symptom review. The profile shown in Figure 5.7 clearly shows this feigned traumatic distress in a case where the litigant alleged PTSD after being fired from his job for sexually harassing several women.

Clients who are experiencing genuine PTSD tend to present more specific psychological symptoms with a credible validity pattern. A woman who filed a suit against the owner of the apartment building in which she was living produced the MMPI-2 profile shown in Figure 5.8. A few months earlier, she had experienced a traumatizing sexual assault because the apartment compound's security system had been breached. After the sexual assault, she experienced considerable PTSD symptoms, as noted by the elevation on scales 2 and 7 of the MMPI-2.

ASSESSMENT OF MALINGERING

Because of the potential financial reward, individuals involved in litigation are frequently motivated to exaggerate symptoms or personality characteristics in either a positive or negative direction on the MMPI. For instance, people alleging industry-related back pain may want to simultaneously make their physical symptoms look worse than they are while making their mental health look better than it actually is. An advantage of using the MMPI-2 is that it has several validity indicators designed to detect instances of exaggeration and defensiveness. The success of both the standard validity scales (F, Fb, L, K) and additional scales (F-K, Fp, S, Mp) at detecting malingerers has been widely reviewed in the literature, both in forensic settings and in analogue studies using college

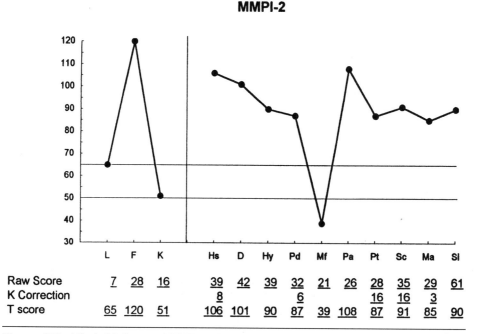

	L	F	K		Hs	D	Hy	Pd	Mf	Pa	Pt	Sc	Ma	Sl
Raw Score	7	28	16		39	42	39	32	21	26	28	35	29	61
K Correction					8			6			16	16	3	
T score	65	120	51		106	101	90	87	39	108	87	91	85	90

Figure 5.7   Likely Malingered MMPI-2 Profile.

MMPI-2

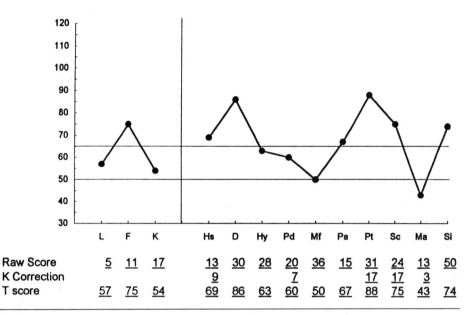

	L	F	K		Hs	D	Hy	Pd	Mf	Pa	Pt	Sc	Ma	Si
Raw Score	5	11	17		13	30	28	20	36	15	31	24	13	50
K Correction					9			7			17	17	3	
T score	57	75	54		69	86	63	60	50	67	88	75	43	74

Figure 5.8   MMPI-2 Profile of a Woman Who Was Raped in Her Apartment When the Security Had Been Breached.

students. It is important for a forensic psychologist to know the strengths and limitations of the MMPI-2 validity indicators at detecting malingering.

DETECTION OF SYMPTOM EXAGGERATION, OR
FAKING-BAD ON THE MMPI-2

The "fake-bad" literature suggests that the validity indicators are usually effective at distinguishing malingerers from nonmalingerers. The most effective validity scales, however, may vary according to the sample characteristics and diagnosis. Graham, Watts, and Timbrook (1991) assessed the ability of the MMPI-2 to discriminate honest versus faking-bad college samples and college students faking-bad versus psychiatric patients. They found that the F, Fb, and F-K scales were successful at discriminating between these groups, although the cutoff scores varied depending upon the comparison groups. Psychiatric patients required higher cutoff scores to distinguish them from faking-bad college students than in the other condition. A cutoff score of $F > 18$ maximally discriminated between the college samples, whereas a cutoff score of $F > 27$ for men and $F > 29$ for women was most effective in discriminating the psychiatric sample from the faking-bad college students.

Studies asking clinical populations to either answer honestly or fake-bad have generally found that the standard validity scales accurately distinguish the two groups. Rogers, Sewell, and Ustad (1995) assessed which validity indicators discriminated between honest and fake-bad outpatient samples and what cutoff scores were optimal. They concluded that $F > 29$ most effectively distinguished between the groups, with a hit rate of 90.5%, followed by $Fp > 9$ and $F-K > 18$, with hit rates of 86.9% and 83.4%, respectively. Berry et al. (1996) obtained similar results with a different outpatient sample: $F > 29$, $Fp > 9$, and $F-K > 18$ resulting in hit rates of 92.9%, 91.5%, and 85.9%, respectively.

Similar results have been found with more severe populations. Bagby, Buis, and Nicholson (1995) asked two inpatient hospital populations, totaling 288 people, to either fake-good or fake-bad and 344 college students to respond honestly. The F scale emerged as the most effective detector of faking-bad profiles. Although the Ds-r2 and O-S index also significantly discriminated between the honest and fake-bad responders, the authors cautioned against using these scales because they did not add incremental value to the faking-bad prediction. Schretlen, Wilkins, Van Gorp, and Bobholz (1992) paid prison inmates to fake-bad on a battery of psychological tests including the MMPI. They found that the MMPI F-K scale, combined with the sum of the first five Bender Gestalt scores and the Malingering Scale Vocabulary subtest, optimally discriminated the faking versus honest groups. The authors concluded that a battery of psychological tests is preferable to one test to detect faking because individuals have difficulty consistently faking a response across tests. Multiple tests allow the investigator to discern subtle discrepancies or inconsistencies in responses.

In addition to determining the effects of general symptom exaggeration on the MMPI, studies have also sought to determine the effects of specific types of information on the validity indicators. Information about specific disorders such as schizophrenia, major depression, and PTSD have been supplied to normal adult populations to see if their faking of these disorders can be detected. Subjects have also received information about the validity indicators to see if that improves their ability to reliably fake disorders. Cramer (1995), using psychology students, found that students given specific information about either major depression or paranoid schizophrenia produced more valid profiles than individuals told simply to fake either disorder without any additional information. Although the informed versus uninformed groups produced significantly different profiles, the F and Fb validity indicators were still able to discriminate these groups from authentic responders. Wetter, Baer, Berry, Robinson, and Sumpter (1993) found similar results when comparing the profiles of adults asked to fake either PTSD or paranoid schizophrenia with psychiatric patients diagnosed with those disorders. Even though fakers were given specific information about the disorders and monetary incentives to produce valid profiles, their MMPI profiles were significantly different than those of the psychiatric groups. The F, Fb, F-K, and Ds validity indicators successfully discriminated between the groups, with hit rates varying between 73% and 95%.

An interesting study by Rogers, Bagby, and Chakraborty (1993) sought to discriminate which information is most effective for fakers: specific information about schizophrenia, information about the validity scales, or a combination of both. They compared the MMPI-2 profiles of these three groups with an uncoached group and a schizophrenic inpatient sample. They found that individuals given specific information about the validity indicators were more effective at faking profiles than any of the other groups. Of particular concern was the inability of the standard validity scales (F, Fb, and F-K) to accurately distinguish these individuals from the psychiatric sample.

The overreporting of symptoms has also been studied in relation to head injuries. In a comprehensive review of the literature, Berry and Butcher (1997) analyzed the effectiveness of the MMPI-2 in detecting feigned head injury. Overall, they found most support for the use of the F scale in detecting overreporting, with the F-K, Ds/Ds2, and Fb scales also receiving some support. F scale T scores above 80 may be indicative of an exaggerated profile, and T scores above 90 should definitely raise suspicions. An additional complicating factor in assessing feigned head injury is that individuals may not universally feign symptoms; for instance, they may feign cognitive symptoms but not psychological symptoms. Therefore, these two domains should be viewed independently, without assuming that feigning in one invariably leads to feigning in the other.

Detection of Symptom Underreporting, or Faking-Good on the MMPI-2

Individuals involved in personal injury litigation may be motivated to downplay any preexisting psychological problems while exaggerating symptoms caused from the alleged accident. They want to portray themselves in the best light possible to convince people that their problems are real. The validity indicators on the MMPI are also designed to detect these faking-good individuals.

The standard validity scales L and K as well as some newer scales, positive malingering (Mp), social desirability (Sd), and S, have been found to effectively discriminate those who underreport symptoms from honest responders. Baer, Wetter, and Berry (1992) conducted a meta-analysis of 25 studies assessing the ability of the MMPI to detect underreporting of symptoms. The optimal cutoff scores used to discriminate those underreporting symptoms compared to those answering honestly varied among studies. Overall, however, the mean effects for the L, K, and L + K scales averaged approximately 1.0, suggesting a difference of about 1 standard deviation between the underreporters and honest reporters. The mean effects for the Mp and Sd scales were 1.59 and 1.60, respectively. Bagby et al. (1995) also found that the Mp and L scales effectively discriminated between those college students told to fake-good versus those given standard instructions.

A relatively new scale currently being evaluated for its success in detecting those motivated to fake-good is the superlative self-presentation scale (S). This scale has five different factors: belief in human goodness, serenity, contentment with life, patience and denial of irritability and anger, and denial of moral flaws. The S scale effectively distinguished between the MMPIs of male pilots seeking a job with a major airline and the MMPI-2 restandardization sample. People with high S scores reported fewer clinical problems and presented fewer negative personality traits than normals (Butcher & Han, 1993). Baer, Wetter, Nichols, Greene, and Berry (1995) applied the S scale to a sample of participants told to either fake-good or answer in the standard manner.

They found that the S scale and Wiggin's social desirability scale (Wsd) added incremental validity above and beyond the L and K scales to the detection of faking-good responders. In conducting regression analyses on the data, the L and K scales did not add any predictive power beyond that of the S and Wsd scales. The authors concluded that the S and Wsd scales may be the most effective scales for detecting underreporting of symptoms. These data, of course, must be interpreted with caution until subsequent studies replicate the results. However, they do suggest that the S scale shows promise as a method for detecting underreporting of psychopathology.

Although many studies have advocated the success of the obvious-subtle scales in detecting both faking-good and faking-bad, they have not been included in this review because of their questionable validity. The "subtle" items on some of the MMPI clinical scales were included largely as a result of chance and do not relate significantly to external criteria. That is, these "subtle" items are essentially an artifact of empirical scale construction and were originally included on the clinical scales as a result of incomplete cross-validation (see discussion in Pope, Butcher, & Seelen, 1993). Although some investigators have attempted to employ these subtle measures as indices of test validity (Greene, 1991; Weiner, 1948), these items have been pretty well discredited (Nelson, 1987; Weed, Ben-Porath, & Butcher, 1990) and have been dropped from the test publisher's list of recommended MMPI-2 scales. Therefore, we recommend against using the obvious-subtle scales as a method for discriminating between malingerers and honest responders.

THE EFFECTS OF LITIGATION ON THE PERSONAL INJURY CLAIMANT

MMPI PROFILES OF LITIGANTS

When personality profiles of pending disability claimants are studied, the response pattern appears to be more exaggerated and generally more pathological than in the general population (Pollack & Grainey, 1984; Sternbach, Wolf, Murphy, & Akeson, 1973). Whether these differences reflect an element of "acuteness" versus chronicity or a trend toward excessive symptom claiming to emphasize perceived disability is not known. Most of the MMPI research involving work compensation cases, however, reflects this increased level of psychological symptoms. Work compensation claimants have been studied descriptively by a number of authors. In cases where physical injury is believed to be involved, the MMPI profile of worker's compensation cases usually involves extreme scale elevations on Hs, D, and Hy (Hersch & Alexander, 1990; Repko & Cooper, 1983; Shaffer, Nussbaum, & Little, 1972). The vague physical symptoms associated with these code types are likely to be of psychological origin or at least exacerbated by psychological conditions rather than purely physical.

Regardless of the type of claim being made, personal injury litigants generally display elevations on the clinical scales of the MMPI. Gandolfo (1995) compared worker's compensation claimants alleging harassment versus those making a claim for something other than harassment. He found similar elevated profiles with regard to scales 1, 2, 3, 7, and 8 between the groups. The main difference was that harassment claimants also elevated scale 6, indicating that they felt angry, mistreated, and suspicious, which is consistent with their claims of harassment. Overall, however, their MMPI profile patterns resembled those of other worker's compensation claimants. Similarly, Snibbe, Peterson, and Sosner (1980) found that worker's compensation applicants had generally similar and rather disturbed MMPI profiles (with high elevations on scales F, 1, 2, 3, 4, and 8), regardless of the reason for the claim (psychiatric, low back pain, or head injury).

The Impact of Litigation on Treatment Outcome

Historically, people have referred to "compensation neurosis" or "litigation neurosis" as if they were conditions that people had until litigation was settled. Inherent in these terms is the assumption that a claimant's behavior is somehow changed during the course of litigation and that it miraculously improves when litigation terminates. Unfortunately, the belief in this pattern of behavior has led some pain clinics to deny treatment to those clients involved in litigation, with the assumption that they would be difficult clients and not make great improvements during litigation. This denial of treatment shortly after an accident may actually do more harm to the client than the involvement in litigation.

Literature reviews have found that litigation status does not appear to consistently impact treatment outcome regardless of the type of injury the person claimed: neck injury, low back injury, head injury, or chronic pain (Evans, 1994; Mendelson, 1982, 1995). In fact, Evans concluded that one of the greatest predictors of successful outcome was the inclusion of psychological services in the treatment plan. It was also important that individuals received immediate intervention, with the goal of returning them to work as quickly as possible, even if their work functioning was at a lower level than before. Binder, Trimble, and Mc-Niel (1991) assessed individuals one and two years after litigation settlement and found significantly less psychiatric impairment among individuals who had shorter durations between injury and settlement, suggesting that rapid settlement was most beneficial to the mental health of the litigants. Mendelson (1995) studied a group of 264 subjects who had not yet returned to work at the time of litigation settlement. The subjects were a heterogeneous group whose claims included industrial, automobile, and other accidents. A follow-up study at a mean of 23.1 months after litigation settlement, found that 75% of the subjects remained unemployed. Contrary to the compensation neurosis hypothesis, these data suggest that the majority of individuals not working at the end of litigation will also not be working two years later. In general, the longer people are out of work, the less likely they are to return. This may be one way the process of litigation impacts people's functioning. Litigation may prevent them from receiving immediate treatment and prevent them from returning to work promptly, both of which are negatively correlated with long-term outcome.

Evans (1994) surveyed personal injury patients involved in automobile accidents about their impression of the most difficult stressor related to the accident at 1, 3, 4, 12, 18, and 24 months postaccident. After the first month, 78% reported that their medical symptoms were the most stressful. Surprisingly, at 6 months and each time period thereafter, the most frequent stressful event reported was the uncooperativeness of medical insurance carriers in promptly paying medical bills. By 24 months, nearly all respondents reported that failure of the insurance companies to honor financial obligations was the greatest stressor remaining from their accident. Of particular interest is their finding from a subgroup of the patients that 97% of the people whose insurance carriers paid their bills promptly (within 30 days) had returned to work, compared to only 4% of the subgroup whose insurance carriers were taking more than 90 days to make payments. These results indicate that there may be myriad factors impacting any individual's return to work after an accident.

Most previous studies have focused on the characteristics of the individual, such as premorbid psychopathology and personality, which contribute to postaccident functioning. Although these individual factors certainly play a role in the course of the individual's recovery, it is also likely that they interact with external factors. As the above studies found, the legal and insurance systems are not designed to maximize an individual's recovery. The excessive paperwork and delays associated with these systems are likely to contribute to litigants' stress and thereby detrimentally impact their long-term recovery.

CONCLUSION

Currently, worker's compensation and personal injury litigation are multibillion dollar businesses involving legal, medical, psychological, industrial, union, insurance, and government personnel in increasingly heated opposition. Concern over fraud and claim exaggeration has increased as economic retrenchment and policy liberalization have increased incentives for claims falsification. In addition, conditions that are difficult to verify, such as psychological and stress-induced disability, are increasingly being claimed in compensation cases. Consequently, psychological professionals are being asked to make determinations about possible exaggeration, malingering, and exacerbation of physical problems claimed by litigants.

The psychologist faced with such evaluations may be asked to assess whether a plaintiff's complaints are possibly due to stress or malingering. Clearly, no foolproof method of determining such distinctions is available at this time. However, by selecting the most objective, valid, and reliable tests appropriate to the complaints, conducting thorough interviews, and carefully recording case notes and test reports, clinicians can be helpful in clarifying the extent to which psychological factors may be involved in personal injury cases.

Assessment for court testimony poses some unique challenges to the psychologist, which require consideration of a variety of factors. One of the most significant is the extent to which the client has been coached by an attorney. Attorney coaching is likely to produce invalid profiles, which are exaggerated in either a positive or negative direction. Most research has found that, even with coaching, the MMPI-2 validity indicators are still able to detect malingering. There is some indication, however, that explicit knowledge about the validity indicators can reduce their effectiveness. For detecting exaggeration or overreporting of symptoms, the F, Fb, and F-K scales are most effective; in addition, the new Fp scale has shown some promising results. For detecting underreporting of symptoms, the L and K standard validity indicators are effective. Recent studies have also found the Mp scale and the relatively new S scale to be effective at detecting faking-good profiles. More research is needed, however, to confirm these preliminary findings.

Despite considerable research and debate, assessment of malingering on the MMPI-2 is often inconclusive. Researchers have hypothesized that elevated scores on the Hs, D, and Hy scales are indicative of psychological contributions to physical ailments at the very least and possibly malingering. Psychological contributions are posited to result in more chronic and exaggerated forms of physical problems. But though this hypothesis appears to be true in a general sense, it should be interpreted with caution because there are instances when nonmalingerers also elevate these scales; for instance, most individuals with LBP or a head injury elevate these scales above average. Therefore, the classic conversion V profile (with elevated Hs and Hy scales) cannot automatically be interpreted as a malingered profile. The psychologist must incorporate all relevant data, including premorbid personality functioning, type of injury, and validity scale indices to make a determination about the likelihood of malingering.

Personality assessment in personal injury cases is a growing field in need of more research on the true psychological sequelae to injury. To date, research has largely focused on the differences between those who are obviously malingering their symptoms and the actual symptoms of real sufferers. Continued research should attempt to build on and refine our knowledge about malingered symptoms using valid, objective, standardized instruments, such as the MMPI-2. This will ultimately allow psychologists to provide more accurate testimony on the personality characteristics and motivation of litigants.

NOTE

1. In cases where the original MMPI had been administered it would be necessary to rescore the answer sheet to plot the raw scores on the MMPI-2 norms. To accomplish this, the psychologist needs to delete the 13 items on the original validity and clinical scales that were dropped from the inventory when the test was revised in 1989. The new raw scores can then be plotted on an MMPI-2 profile sheet to obtain the new profile. Only the traditional MMPI invalidity and clinical scale scores can be obtained in this rescoring method.

REFERENCES

Alfano, D. P., Neilson, P. M., Paniak, C. E., & Finlayson, M. A. J. (1992). The MMPI and closed-head injury. *The Clinical Neuropsychologist, 6*(2), 134–142.

American Psychological Association. (1986). *American Psychological Association guidelines for computer-based tests and interpretations.* Washington, DC: Author.

Baer, R. A., Wetter, M. W., & Berry, D. T. R. (1992). Detection of underreporting of psychopathology on the MMPI: A meta-analysis. *Clinical Psychology Review, 12,* 509–525.

Baer, R. A., Wetter, M. W., Nichols, D. S., Greene, R., & Berry, D. T. R. (1995). Sensitivity of MMPI-2 validity scales to underreporting of symptoms. *Psychological Assessment, 7*(4), 419–423.

Bagby, R. M., Buis, T., & Nicholson, R. A. (1995). Relative effectiveness of the standard validity scales in detecting fake-bad and fake-good responding: Replication and extension. *Psychological Assessment, 7*(1), 84–92.

Ben-Porath, Y. S., McNulty, J. L., Watt, M., & McCormick, R. A. (1997). Unpublished data from a substance abuse program at the Cleveland VAMC.

Berry, D. T. R., Adams, J. J., Borden, J. W., Clark, C. D., Thacker, S. R., Burger, T. L., Wetter, M. W., & Baer, R. A. (1996). Detection of a cry for help in the MMPI-2: An analog investigation. *Journal of Personality Assessment, 67*(1), 26–35.

Berry, D. T. R., & Butcher, J. N. (1997). Detection of feigning of head injury symptoms on the MMPI-2. In C. Reynolds (Ed.), *Detection of malingering in head injury litigation* (pp. 209–239). New York: Plenum Press.

Binder, R. L., Trimble, M. R., & McNiel, D. E. (1991). The course of psychological symptoms after resolution of lawsuits. *Journal of Psychiatry, 148*(8), 1073–1075.

Blanchard, E. B., Hickling, E. J., Taylor, A. E., Loos, W. R., Forneris, C. A., & Jaccard, J. (1996). Who develops PTSD from motor vehicle accidents? *Behavioral Research and Therapy, 34*(1), 1–10.

Borum, R., & Grisso, T. (1995). Psychological test use in criminal forensic evaluations. *Professional Psychology: Research and Practice, 26*, 465–473.

Butcher, J. N. (1997a). *Base-rate information for the personal injury samples in the Minnesota forensic study.* Unpublished study.

Butcher, J. N. (1997b). *User's guide to the Minnesota Report: Forensic system.* Minneapolis, MN: National Computer Systems.

Butcher, J. N. (1997c). Frequency of MMPI-2 scores in forensic evaluations. *MMPI-2 News & Profiles.*

Butcher, J. N., & Han, K. (1993). Development of an MMPI-2 scale to assess the presentation of self in a superlative manner: The S scale. In J. N. Butcher & C. D. Spielberger (Eds.), *Advances in personality assessment* (Vol. 10, pp. 25–50). Hillsdale, NJ: Erlbaum.

Butcher, J. N., & Rouse, S. (1996). Clinical personality assessment. *Annual Review of Psychology, 47*, 87–111.

Cramer, K. M. (1995). The effects of description clarity and disorder type on MMPI-2 fake-bad validity indices. *Journal of Clinical Psychology, 51*(6), 831–839.

Evans, R. W. (1994). The effects of litigation on treatment outcome with personal injury patients. *American Journal of Forensic Psychology, 12*(4), 19–34.

Flamer, S., & Birch, W. (1992, May). *Differential diagnosis of post-traumatic stress disorder in injured workers: Evaluating the MMPI-2.* Paper presented at the 27th annual Symposium on Recent Developments in the Use of the MMPI (MMPI-2), Minneapolis, MN.

Fordyce, W. E., Bigos, S. J., Batti'e, M. C., & Fisher, L. D. (1992). MMPI scale 3 as a predictor of back injury report: What does it tell us? *Clinical Journal of Pain, 8*, 222–226.

Gallagher, R. M., Rauh, V., Haugh, L. D., Milhous, R., Callas, P. W., Langelier, R., McClallen, J. M., & Frymoyer, J. (1989). Determinants of return-to-work among low back pain patients. *Pain, 39*, 55–67.

Gandolfo, R. (1995). MMPI-2 profiles of worker's compensation claimants who present with complaints of harassment. *Journal of Clinical Psychology, 51*(5), 711–715.

Gass, C. S., & Wald, H. S. (in press). MMPI-2 interpretation and closed-head trauma: cross-validation of a correction factor.

Gatchel, R. J., Polatin, P. B., & Mayer, T. G. (1995). The dominant role of psychosocial risk factors in the development of chronic low back pain disability. *Spine, 20*(24), 2702–2709.

Graham, J. R., Watts, D., & Timbrook, R. E. (1991). Detecting fake-good and fake-bad MMPI-2 profiles. *Journal of Personality Assessment, 57*(2), 264–277.

Greene, R. L. (1991). *MMPI-2/MMPI: An interpretive manual.* Boston: Allyn & Bacon.

Hasenbring, M., Marienfeld, G., Kuhlendahl, D., & Soyka, D. (1994). Risk factors of chronicity in lumbar disc patients: A prospective investigation of biologic, psychologic, and social predictors of therapy outcome, *Spine, 19*(24), 2759–2765.

Hersch, P. D., & Alexander, R. W. (1990). MMPI profile patterns of emotional disability claimants. *Journal of Clinical Psychology, 46*(6), 798–799.

Hess, A. K. (1998). Review of the Millon Clinical Multiaxial Inventory-III. *Mental Measurements Yearbook.* Lincoln: University of Nebraska Press.

Hovanitz, C. A., & Kozora, E. (1989). Life stress and clinically elevated MMPI scales: Gender differences in the moderating influence of coping. *Journal of Clinical Psychology, 45,* 766–777.

Keane, T. M., Malloy, P. F., & Fairbank, J. A. (1984). Empirical development of an MMPI subscale for assessment combat related posttraumatic stress disorder. *Journal of Consulting and Clinical Psychology, 52,* 888–891.

Keilen, W. G., & Bloom, L. J. (1986). Child custody evaluation practices: A survey of experienced professionals. *Professional Psychology: Research and Practice, 17,* 338–346.

Lees-Haley, P. R., Smith, H. H., Williams, C. W., & Dunn, J. T. (1995). Forensic neuropsychological test usage: An empirical survey. *Archives of Clinical Neuropsychology, 11,* 45–51.

Long, B., Nelson, O., & Butcher, J. N. (1995, March). *The MMPI-2 in workplace sexual harassment discrimination cases.* Paper given at the 30th annual Symposium on Recent Developments in the Use of the MMPI-2, St. Petersburg, FL.

Love, A. W., & Peck, C. L. (1987). The MMPI and Psychological factors in chronic low back pain: A review. *Pain, 28,* 1–12.

Lubin, B., Larsen, R. M., & Matarazzo, J. D. (1984). Patterns of psychological test usage in the United States: 1935–1982. *American Psychologist, 39,* 451–454.

Marcus, E. H. (1983, Spring). Causation in psychiatry: Realities and speculations. *Medical Trial Technical Quarterly, 29,* 424–433.

Mayou, R., Bryant, B., & Duthie, R. (1993). Psychiatric consequences of road traffic accidents. *British Medical Journal, 307,* 647–651.

McCormick, R. A., Taber, J. I., & Krudelback, N. (1989). The relationship between attributional style and posttraumatic stress disorder in addicted patients. *Journal of Traumatic Stress, 2,* 477–487.

Mendelson, G. (1982). Not cured by a verdict. *Medical Journal of Australia, 2,* 132–134.

Mendelson, G. (1995). Compensation neurosis revisited: Outcome studies of the effects of litigation. *Journal of Psychosomatic Research, 39*(6), 695–706.

Miller, H. R., Goldberg, J. O., & Streiner, D. L. (1995). What's in a name? The MMPI-2 PTSD scales. *Journal of Clinical Psychology, 51*(5), 626–631.

Munley, P. H., Bains, D. S., Bloem, W. D., & Busby, R. M. (1995). Post-traumatic stress disorder and the MMPI-2. *Journal of Traumatic Stress, 8*(1), 171–178.

Neal, L. A., Busuttil, W., Rollins, J., Herepath, R., Strike, P., & Turnbull, G. (1994). Convergent validity of measures of post-traumatic stress disorder in a mixed military and civilian population. *Journal of Traumatic Stress, 7*(3), 447–455.

Nelson, L. (1987). Measuring depression in a clinical population using the MMPI. *Journal of Consulting and Clinical Psychology, 35,* 788–790.

Otto, R., & Butcher, J. N. (1995). Computer-assisted psychological assessment in child custody evaluations. *Family Law Quarterly, 29,* 79–96.

Pollack, D. R., & Grainey, T. F. (1984). A comparison of MMPI profiles for state and private disability insurance applicants. *Journal of Personality Assessment, 48*(2), 121–125.

Pope, K. S., Butcher, J. N., & Seelen, J. (1993). *MMPI/MMPI-2/MMPI-A in court: Assessment, testimony, and cross-examination for expert witnesses and attorneys.* Washington, DC: American Psychological Association.

Putnam, S. H., Kurtz, J. E., Millis, S. R., & Adams, K. M. (1995, March). *Prevalence and correlates of MMPI-2 codetypes in patients with traumatic brain injury.* Paper given at the 30th annual Symposium on Research Developments in the Use of the MMPI-2, St. Petersburg, FL.

Repko, G. R., & Cooper, R. (1983). A study of the average workers' compensation case. *Journal of Clinical Psychology, 39,* 287–295.

Rogers, R., Bagby, R. M., & Chakraborty, D. (1993). Feigning schizophrenic disorders on the MMPI-2: Detection of coached simulators. *Journal of Personality Assessment, 60*(2), 215–226.

Rogers, R., Sewell, K. W., & Ustad, K. L. (1995). Feigning among chronic outpatients on the MMPI-2: A systematic examination of fake-bad indicators. *Psychological Assessment, 2*(1), 81–89.

Schretlen, D., Wilkins, S. S., Van Gorp, W. G., & Bobholz, J. H. (1992). Cross-validation of a psychological test battery to detect faked insanity. *Psychological Assessment, 4*(1), 77–83.

Shaffer, J. W., Nussbaum, K., & Little, J. M. (1972). MMPI profiles of disability insurance claimants. *American Journal of Psychiatry, 129*(4), 64–67.

Silver, S. M., & Salamone-Genovese, L. (1991). A study of the MMPI clinical and research scales for post-traumatic stress disorder diagnostic utility. *Journal of Traumatic Stress, 4*(4), 533–548.

Snibbe, J. R., Peterson, P. J., & Sosner, B. (1980). Study of psychological characteristics of a worker's compensation sample using the MMPI and Millon Clinical Multiaxial Inventory. *Psychological Reports, 47,* 959–966.

Sternbach, R. A., Wolf, S. R., Murphy, R. W., & Akeson, W. H. (1973). Traits of pain patients: The low back "loser." *Psychosomatics, 14,* 226–229.

Vanderploeg, R. D., Sison, G. F., & Hickling, E. J. (1987). A reevaluation of the use of the MMPI in the assessment of combat-related posttraumatic stress disorder. *Journal of Personality Assessment, 51,* 140–150.

Watkins, C. E., Campbell, V. L., Niebirding, R., & Hallmark, R. (1995). Contemporary practice of psychological assessment by clinical psychologists. *Professional Psychology, 26,* 54–60.

Weed, N., Ben-Porath, Y. S., & Butcher, J. N. (1990). Failure of the Weiner-Harmon MMPI subtle scales as predictors of psychopathology and as validity indicators. *Psychological Assessment: A Journal of Consulting and Clinical Psychology, 2,* 281–283.

Weiner, D. (1948). Subtle and obvious keys for the Minnesota Multiphasic Personality Inventory. *Journal of Consulting Psychology, 12,* 164–170.

Wetter, M. W., Baer, D. T. R., Berry, D., Robinson, L. H., & Sumpter, J. (1993). MMPI-2 profiles of motivated fakers given specific symptom information: A comparison to matched patients. *Psychological Assessment, 5*(3), 317–323.

CHAPTER 6

Assessing Educational Disabilities

DANIEL J. RESCHLY

ASSESSMENT OF educational disabilities has become a major and sometimes controversial responsibility of psychologists in the United States. Although many kinds of psychologists may be involved with the educationally disabled, the approximately 21,000 to 23,000 school psychologists in the United States have psychoeducational assessment with this population as one of their primary activities. This chapter discusses the nature of assessment of educational disabilities with attention devoted to legal influences, procedures mandated by law as well as those suggested by best professional practices, and current problems and controversies.

Assessment of educational disabilities has been prominent in school psychology since the earliest days of this specialty of professional psychology. Arnold Gesell, often credited as being the first school psychologist, was hired by the Connecticut State Department of Education in 1913 to examine school-age children suspected of being mentally retarded (Fagan & Delugach, 1984; Fagan & Wise, 1994). Throughout this century, special education services for disabled students has expanded gradually, as have school psychological services. By 1970, there were at least some school psychologists in every state and a number of states had well-developed school psychological services with ratios as low as 2,000 students for each psychologist.

Special education legislation was the key factor in establishing psychological services in schools. Some states did not provide school programs for the disabled and there were few psychologists in those states. Other states provided relatively high levels of funding to local districts for provision of services to the disabled, which usually led to employment of school psychologists (Fagan, 1987a, 1987b, 1992; Kicklighter, 1976); however, up to about 1975, the development of school psychology was gradual and uneven.

The need for assessment of educational disabilities has expanded dramatically since 1975 because of mandatory special education legislation at the state

127

and federal levels, which led to a substantial increase in numbers of school psychologists in virtually every state. The current national ratio of students to psychologists is approximately 1,800:1, a twofold improvement over the ratios in the 1970s (Lund, Reschly, & Martin, 1998). The assessment of educational disabilities now involves the expenditure of hundreds of millions of dollars each year for services to the 4.6 million school-age children classified as disabled and in need of special education, that is, about 11% of children and youth age 5 to 17 (U.S. Department of Education, 1996). In short, assessment of educational disabilities is an enormous enterprise.

DECISION MAKING AND DISABILITY CLASSIFICATION

Psychoeducational assessment with students suspected of or classified as disabled occurs within the context of a complex classification system and is related to two fundamental kinds of decisions. The decisions to be made are quite similar to diagnostic decision making in other areas of psychology such as clinical or counseling psychology, but the classification system may not resemble other classification systems. This chapter clarifies the fundamental decisions to be made and the context within which those decisions are made.

Disability classification is based on a combination of diagnostic constructs that have evolved throughout the past century. It is not a pure classification system in the sense of a set of consistent principles or uniform underlying bases (Hobbs, 1975; Reschly, 1996). J. Mercer (1979) described two fundamentally different approaches to diagnosis of handicapping conditions: the medical model and a social system model (see Table 6.1).

Table 6.1
Comparison of Medical and Social System Models of Disabilities

Characteristic	Medical Model	Social System Model
Definition of problem	Biological anomaly	Discrepancies between expected and observed behavior in specific context
Focus of initial diagnosis	Focus on cause with purpose of curing or compensating for the underlying disorder	Eliminate symptoms through direct educational treatment or behavioral interventions
Assessor	Typically, medical professionals in preschool years	During school-age years by professionals in education or psychology
Incidence	Low (about 1% of school-age population)	High (about 10% of school-age population)
Prognosis	Life-long disabilities	Disabilities recognized officially during school years
Cultural status	Cross-cultural	Culturally specific context
Comprehensiveness	Usually affects performance in most roles in most contexts	May affect one or a few roles in a few contexts

Medical Model

The term medical model is perhaps unfortunate in that it suggests that the assumptions and approaches to problems are typical of how processionals in medicine solve problems. Kauffman and Hallahan (1974) pointed out large differences in the concept of medical model as used in the social sciences and the approach to solving problems actually used in medicine. Therefore, the model should be seen as a heuristic device and not taken literally as indicative of practices in medicine.

The most important characteristics of the medical model for the purposes of this chapter are that abnormal patterns of behavior or development are attributed to an identifiable underlying biological pathology. The etiology or cause, direct or indirect, of deviant behavior is seen as stemming from biological anomalies. Other important characteristics of the medical model are that it is cross-cultural—that is, the same underlying biological abnormalities cause approximately the same deficits in behavior regardless of the social class or cultural group that might be involved. The medical model is seen as a deficit model, and the underlying biological anomaly is seen as an inherent part of the individual.

Social System Model

In contrast to the medical model, the social system model uses an ecological perspective (J. Mercer, 1979; Reschly, 1996). Deviant behavior or abnormal patterns of development are seen not as inherent characteristics of the individual, but rather as reflecting a discrepancy between what the individual has learned in a cultural context and the expectations for normal behavior in a specific social role and social setting. Classification of certain patterns of behavior as being disabled involves application of social norms within a particular social setting to observed patterns of behavior. The norms or expectations for behavior are determined by the larger society. The social system model suggests a complex interaction among the individual's learned patterns of behavior, the social setting in which a specific behavior is judged, the social role in which the individual is engaged, and the expectations for the behavior. In this model, social and cultural factors are extremely important because they determine: (a) the behaviors learned by the individual, (b) the expectations for behavior in a specific role or setting, and (c) the standards used to judge the appropriateness of behaviors.

To illustrate the distinction between social system and medical model disabilities, it is useful to consider the following examples. Most children with a specific learning disability (SLD) have difficulties with reading. Often, there is no evidence of other difficulties at school, in the home, or in the community. Would a youngster with that pattern of development be regarded as disabled in a society that did not have compulsory school attendance and strong expectations for the acquisition of literacy skills between the ages of 5 and 17? On the other hand, a youngster with cerebral palsy, which usually involves easily observed muscular difficulties, would likely be regarded as disabled regardless of the time, place, or nature of society. In a real sense, social system model disabilities are created by the demands we place on children and youth in a complex, rapidly changing, technologically sophisticated society. To attribute the etiology of these disabilities to societal expectations does not, however, make them any less real or any less serious for individuals involved.

DISTRIBUTION OF DISABILITIES AND MODELS OF DISABILITIES

The prevalence of disabilities in the 13 categories recognized in federal legislation is summarized in Table 6.2. Several important trends are revealed in these prevalence data. First, the vast majority of the students with disabilities are in the categories of SLD (accounting for over 50%), followed by speech-language (SL), mental retardation (MR), and seriously emotionally disturbed (SED). These four disabilities account for over 90% of the students with disabilities in U.S. schools. Students with disabilities in the other nine categories account for less than 10% of the population with disabilities.

Virtually all students with disabilities in three of the four high-incidence categories (SLD, SL, SED) have disabilities that are mild in degree and that are best explained by the social system model of deviance. Approximately half of the students with MR have mild or social system model forms of disability; the other half of the MR population and virtually all of the students in the nine disability categories denoted as "other" in Table 6.2 have medical model kinds of disabilities.

This distinction between models and the disability distribution characteristics have vast significance for psychological assessment and for the legal controversies over educational programming for students with disabilities. The principal legal issue with medical model disabilities is not diagnosis, usually done by medical personnel prior to school entrance, but rather, appropriate programming, the degree to which students with these disabilities should be integrated with regular education students, and the relative benefits of different educational programs or placements. These issues often involve extreme psychological assessment challenges.

The primary legal issues and assessment challenges with social system model disabilities are: (a) whether or not a specific youngster ought to be

Table 6.2
Number and Proportion of Population of Students with Disabilities (by Category)

Category	Number	Percent of Disabled	Percent of Population	Range among States
SLD	2,316,884	51.1	5.27	2.73 (GA) to 9.23 (MA)
SL	1,003,190	22.1	2.28	1.16 (HI) to 3.88 (NJ)
MR	488,673	10.8	1.11	0.30 (NJ) to 3.14 (AL)
SED	391,064	8.6	0.89	0.05 (MS) to 2.05 (CT)
Other*	334,078	7.4	0.76	
Total	4,533,889	100.0	10.31	6.86 (HI) to 14.90 (MA)

Source: U.S. Department of Education, 1995, pp. A6–A9, A34–A37. Includes multiple disabilities, deaf, hard of hearing, orthopedic impairments, other health impairments, visual impairments, deaf-blindness, autism, and traumatic brain injury.

classified as disabled, typically using psychological and educational tests; (b) which of the mildly disabling categories is most appropriate, and (c) whether overrepresentation of minority students in particular mildly handicapping classifications such as SLD, MR, or SED constitutes discrimination (Reschly, 1979, 1996).

ELIGIBILITY DECISIONS

Classification-placement decisions involve the application of federal and state laws that establish a two-pronged criterion for eligibility: Can the student be classified as disabled? and Does the student need special education or related services (e.g., counseling) to receive an appropriate education? Affirmative answers to these questions make the child eligible for important legal protections and, typically, the expenditure of markedly increased monies for special education and related services (Parrish & Chambers, 1996). Eligibility decisions have high-stakes consequences that are important to the individual, family, school, and community. The guidelines for eligibility decisions and the implications for psychological assessment will be considered after a discussion of the legal sources of those guidelines.

LAYERS OF LEGAL INFLUENCE

Legal influences on assessment of educational disabilities emanate from several levels and a variety of sources. Litigation involving assessment questions has been highly influential on legislation, which in turn has provided the basis for additional litigation. Through this dynamic process, a wide variety of requirements for assessment has gradually evolved (Bersoff, 1982a; Prasse, 1995; Reschly, 1983; Reschly & Bersoff, 1999).

A recurring cycle of litigation, then legislation, then further litigation was first described by Bersoff (1982a). That cycle continues today and can be expected to continue into the future. The general sequence has been litigation in the federal courts, followed by legislation at the state and federal level, and then further litigation in the courts based on that legislation. Two types of litigation have been particularly important to psychological assessment of students with disabilities: the right to an education and placement bias.

RIGHT TO EDUCATION: PRE-1975 LITIGATION

Although a number of court cases dealing with testing and educational assessment issues appeared before 1970 (see Bersoff, 1979), major cases dealing directly with individual assessment of students with disabilities did not appear until then. Two cases in the federal district courts (*Mills v. Board of Education*, 1972; *PARC v. Commonwealth of Pennsylvania*, 1972) established the rights of disabled students to educational services. Prior to these landmark cases, many disabled students were either excluded entirely from the public schools by local, district, and state policies or were provided educational services that were not individually tailored to their unique needs. The plaintiffs in these cases—advocacy groups formed by parents of students who had medical model disabilities—asked federal district courts to apply the Fourteenth Amendment concepts of equal protection and due process and to force the states to provide appropriate educational services to *all* students. The courts agreed with the parental claims, deciding that exclusion of disabled students from public schools constituted a violation of the concept of equal protection of the laws and the concept of due process. Further discussion of the early legal cases can be found in Bersoff (1982a), Reschly (1988), and Reschly and Bersoff (1999).

The major impact of these cases was the advancement of the rights of students with disabilities to educational services and to due process protections in educational decisions made about them. These court precedents in 1972 were used by parent advocacy groups throughout the United States in efforts to convince state legislatures to pass mandatory special education legislation. In fact, virtually every state passed such mandates between 1972 and 1975, largely in response to the court precedents. Thus, the litigation establishing the rights of students with disabilities to appropriate educational services and guaranteed due process protections in decision making were the crucial steps leading to the enormous expansion of services for persons with disabilities and the accompanying upsurge in demands for assessment services.

PLACEMENT BIAS: PRE-1975 LITIGATION

A second kind of case also applying the concepts of equal protection and due process but advocating fewer, rather than more, special education services appeared in the federal district courts at about the same time. Cases alleging discriminatory assessment practices and improper special education placement and programming were destined to have a profound influence on subsequent legislation and on assessment of students with disabilities. Three cases (*Diana v. State Board of Education,* 1970; *Guadalupe Organization v. Tempe Elementary School District No. 3,* 1972; *Larry P. v. Riles,* 1972, 1974) were filed on behalf of minority students placed in mild mental retardation (MMR) special class programs, a social system kind of disability. In the three districts involved—Monterey County, California, in *Diana;* Tempe, Arizona, in *Guadalupe;* and San Francisco in *Larry P.*—minority students were placed in programs for persons with MMR at about 1.5 to 3 times the rate of placement for nonminority students. Plaintiffs claimed this overrepresentation pointed to a denial of equal protection of the laws and that the procedures whereby students were referred, evaluated, and placed violated fundamental principles of due process.

The *Diana* and *Guadalupe* cases, involving bilingual Hispanic and Native American students, were settled by consent decrees that established a number of safeguards in the classification-placement process, including determination of primary language, assessment instruments administered using procedures consistent with the student's primary language, reliance on nonverbal rather than verbal ability measures with language-minority children, greater reliance on adaptive behavior measures, and due process protections. The outcomes of these cases were highly influential on state and federal legislation. Some of the phrases that appeared in the *Diana* and *Guadalupe* consent decrees appear verbatim in the rules and regulations accompanying state and federal legislation passed in the mid-1970s (e.g., *Education of the Handicapped Act*, 1975; Reschly, 1979).

The *Larry P.* case was somewhat different, in that the primary language of the home was not a central issue. The plaintiffs were black students and intelligence tests became the central issue in the case. *Larry P.* resulted in injunctions in 1972 and 1974, restraining, first, the San Francisco Unified School District and, later, the entire state of California, from using IQ tests with black students.

There is a clear irony in the pre-1975 litigation. In one type of case, school districts were cited by the federal courts for violation of equal protection and due process rights because special education services were *not* provided (*Mills*, 1972; *PARC*, 1972); in the other, the same constitutional principles were the basis for ruling that special education with minority students was used *excessively* (*Diana*, 1970; *Guadalupe*, 1972; *Larry P.*, 1972, 1974). Different types of disabilities were involved—a critical feature often ignored in commentaries on the cases. The right to education cases involved medical model disabilities, whereas the placement bias cases involved social system disabilities such as MMR. Although the cases seem very different, the same general principles emerged from both: Classification-placement decisions must be made using a process that ensures accountability and fairness, and different treatment (either placement or nonplacement) must be justified. These principles continue to have enormous impact on the practice of psychological assessment.

STATE AND FEDERAL LEGISLATION

State legislatures passed mandatory special education bills in every state by the mid-1970s. Students with disabilities had to be served by the public schools, and the educational programs had to meet certain standards. Generally, the legislation provided state monies for these programs, thus alleviating part of the burden of providing expensive special education and related services incurred by local districts. Rather than attempting further discussion of state legislative mandates, the key principles in a subsequent federal law with which all states now comply will be discussed. This federal law also incorporated the major principles from the pre-1975 litigation.

The federal Education of the Handicapped Act (EHA) (1975), reauthorized in 1991 and 1997 as the Individuals with Disabilities Education Act (IDEA), provides federal monies to assist state and local agencies in educating students with disabilities. To qualify for this assistance, the educational services for disabled students must meet the following requirements.

Free, Appropriate Education

The first and most important of the general principles was the right of all students with disabilities to free, appropriate, publicly supported education (FAPE). Subsequent interpretation of EHA-IDEA by the courts has established that this right truly does apply to all students, even those who have no apparent learning ability (*Timothy W. v. Rochester*, 1988, 1989). The effect of this principle is that many more students are now diagnosed as disabled and provided special education services and that students with more severe disabilities, previously excluded from public schools, are present in school settings where they receive a full range of assessment and programming services. The implications for assessment of the FAPE principle were a greatly increased need for individual psychoeducational assessment services as well as the need for specialized skills not previously emphasized in graduate programs, for example, assessment of communication skills with autism or the contingencies maintaining severe self-injurious behaviors.

Least Restrictive Environment

A second important EHA-IDEA principle is least restrictive environment (LRE): "That to the maximum extent appropriate, children with disabilities . . . are educated with children who are non-disabled. That special classes, separate schooling or other removal of children with disabilities from the regular educational environment occurs only when the nature or severity of the disability is such that education in regular classes with the use of supplementary aids and services cannot be achieved satisfactorily" (*IDEA*, 1991, at 550). LRE had the effect of greater integration of students with disabilities with general education students and greatly increasing the complexity of psychological assessment. It is important to note that neither the law nor any court pronounces a full inclusion requirement mandating that all students with disabilities be educated in general education environments. To determine whether a student with a disability can be placed by the school outside of the general education classroom in a more restrictive setting such as a special class, the following criteria were established by the courts: (a) the educational benefits available to the child in a regular classroom supplemented with appropriate aids and services, as compared to the educational benefits of a more restrictive special education placement; (b) the nonacademic benefits to the handicapped child of interaction with nonhandicapped children; (c) the effect of the presence of the handicapped child on the teacher and other children in the regular classroom; and (d) the costs of supplementary aids and services necessary to mainstream the handicapped child in the regular classroom setting (*Board of Education v. Holland*, 1992, 1994).

The courts also have required that LRE decisions be data-based, establishing the need for more behavioral assessment through observation of natural environments to determine the effects of a student with a disability on other students and the degree to which that student profits from being in the general education environment.

Individualized Education Program

Students with disabilities also were guaranteed an individualized educational program (IEP) that was to be reviewed annually and modified as appropriate. The emphasis on greater individualization increased demands for criterion-referenced assessment, leading to clear specification of strengths and weaknesses and the development of assessment information useful in designing and evaluating instructional interventions and psychological treatments.

Due Process

The due process protections established in the courts, then mandated in state and federal legislation, guaranteed the rights of children with disabilities (in the case of minor children, their parents or guardians) to: (a) receive advance notice of decisions a school is contemplating, (b) receive information in an understandable form, (c) be told the reasons the decision is contemplated, (d) be told who is making the decision, and (e) refuse to permit the school to make decisions with which they disagree. Complex hearing procedures are available to schools and to parents to resolve disputes.

Children with disabilities or, depending on age, their parents, have access to nearly everything a psychologist might do as part of the assessment of educational disabilities, including the right to examine test protocols. These rights mean that the work of psychologists can be scrutinized by parents and their legal advocates and challenged in a legal proceeding. These legal rights of children and parents can establish legal and ethical dilemmas for psychologists, who in IDEA are mandated to share their findings, including the documents and procedures used to produce the findings. Other legal requirements mandate that they conform to laws regarding the nondisclosure of copyrighted materials such as test protocols and to ethical principles concerned with maintaining test security and confidentiality of information. Easy resolutions to these dilemmas do not exist. Psychologists must study the available ethical codes as well as materials from professional associations on the resolution of such dilemmas (American Psychological Association, 1994; National Association of School Psychologists, 1994).

Protection in Evaluation Procedures

The EHA-IDEA legal principles that have the greatest influence on assessment appear in the Protection in Evaluation Procedures Provisions (PEP). The PEP section of IDEA federal regulations is relatively brief and is reprinted in its entirety in Table 6.3.

Subsection 530, General, requires the State Department of Education to monitor implementation of the regulations that follow. This section also includes the highly significant provision forbidding racial or cultural discrimination in testing and evaluation materials and procedures used to evaluate and place students as disabled. This sweeping generalization forbidding discrimination is difficult to implement because there is no definition of discrimination nor criteria to define discriminatory practices that might be applied to assessment processes, assessment procedures, or placement outcomes (Reschly, 1979; Reschly & Bersoff, 1999). The meaning of the nondiscrimination clause is the subject of continuing litigation to be discussed in a subsequent section.

Subsection 531, Preplacement Evaluation, requires a thorough individual evaluation of the child's educational needs prior to placement, focusing on specific educational needs.

Subsection 532, Evaluation Procedures, contains a number of crucial, but somewhat ambiguous, requirements concerning assessment. Each of these requirements might be interpreted differently by various persons involved with assessment of students with disabilities. For example, when is it clearly not

Table 6.3
IDEA Protection in Evaluation Procedures Provisions *(34 CFR 300)*

§ *300.530 General.* (a) Each State educational agency shall insure that each public agency establishes and implements procedures which meet the requirements of §§ 121.1-530–300.534. (b) Testing and evaluation materials and procedures used for the purposes of evaluation and placement of disabled children must be selected and administered so as not to be racially or culturally discriminatory (20 U.S.C. 1412(5)©).

§ *300.531 Preplacement evaluation.* Before any action is taken with respect to the initial placement of a disabled child in a special education program, a full and individual evaluation of the child's educational needs must be conducted in accordance with the requirements of § 300.532 (20 U.S.C. 1412(5)©).

§ *300.532 Evaluation procedures.* State and local educational agencies shall insure, at a minimum, that:

(a) Tests and other evaluation materials

   (1) Are provided and administered in the child's native language or other mode of communication, unless it is clearly not feasible to do so;

   (2) Have been validated for the specific purpose for which they are used; and

   (3) Are administered by trained personnel in conformance with the instructions provided by their producer;

(b) Tests and other evaluation materials include those tailored to assess specific areas of educational need and not merely those which are designed to provide a single intelligence quotient;

(c) Tests are selected and administered so as best to ensure that when a test is administered to a child with impaired . . . sensory, manual, or speaking skills, the test results accurately reflect the child's aptitude or achievement level or whatever other factors the test purports to measure, rather than reflecting the child's impaired sensory, manual, or speaking skills (except where those skills are the factors which the test purports to measure);

(d) No single procedure is used as the sole criterion for determining an appropriate educational program for a child;

(e) The evaluation is made by a multidisciplinary team or group of persons including at least one teacher or other specialist with knowledge in the area of suspected disability; and

(f) The child is assessed in all areas related to the suspected disability including, where appropriate, health, vision, hearing, social and emotional status, general intelligence, academic performance, communicative status, and motor abilities (20 U.S.C. 1412(5)©).

§ *300.533 Placement procedures.*

(a) In interpreting evaluation data and in making placement decisions each agency shall

   (1) Draw upon information from a variety of sources, including aptitude and achievement tests, teacher recommendation, physical condition, social or cultural background, and adaptive behavior;

   (2) Insure that information obtained from all of these sources is documented and carefully considered;

   (3) Insure that the placement decision is made by a group of persons, including persons knowledgeable about the child, the meaning of the evaluation data, and the placement options; and

Table 6.3 (Continued)

---

(4) Insure that the placement decision is made in conformity with the least restrictive environment rules in §§ 300.550–300.554.

(b) If a determination is made that a child is disabled and needs special education and related services, an individualized education program must be developed for the child in accordance with §§ 300.340–300.349 of Subpart C (20 U.S.C. 1412(5)©; 1414(a)(5)).

§ 300.534 Reevaluation. Each State and local educational agency shall insure:

(a) That each disabled child's individualized education program is reviewed in accordance with §§ 300.340–300.349 of Subpart C, and

(b) That an evaluation of the child, based on procedures which meet the requirements under § 300.532, is conducted every three years or more frequently if conditions warrant or if the child's parents or teacher requests an evaluation (20 U.S.C. 1412(5)).

Source: Individuals with Disabilities Education Act (1997) 34 Code of Federal Regulations 300.

feasible to administer an evaluation procedure in a child's native language? Does this mean that bilingual examiners have to be provided for all non-English-speaking students suspected of being disabled? What alternatives should be applied if it is impossible to provide an examiner fluent in the child's language? Is translation of test items acceptable, despite the many problems in semantics associated with direct translations? What does "validated for the specific purpose" mean with respect to educational and psychological tests? Is a predictive validity coefficient of 0.5 or 0.7 sufficient? Moreover, how stringently should specific purposes be interpreted? For example, does an ability test have to be normed for blind children in order to meet the specific purposes requirement?

Other provisions in this subsection that are particularly important in legal proceedings include the requirement of trained personnel, the concept of educational need rather than a single general intelligence quotient, test results accurately reflecting the child's aptitude or achievement rather than the effects of a sensory impairment or physical disability, multidisciplinary team decision making, and multifactored assessment. It should be noted that the multifactored assessment domains are to be assessed "where appropriate." This provision has sometimes been misinterpreted as indicating that all students must be assessed in all of the areas. This is clearly not the case, as some of the areas listed may not be related to the suspected disability and would, therefore, not be a required part of the preplacement evaluation.

The *placement procedures* are discussed in *Subsection 533,* with a number of requirements designed to ensure that evaluation data are interpreted properly and considered carefully in the placement decisions. There is emphasis on careful consideration of a variety of sources of information, group decision making, and consideration of different placement options.

Reevaluation of students classified as disabled and placed in a special education program is required every three years according to *Subsection 534* of EHA and IDEA (1991). The reevaluation requirement has been revised in the IDEA

(1997) statute, but, because the regulations are currently being drafted, it is impossible to determine how much of a change in practice will occur.

A virtual revolution in assessment of the disabled has occurred over the past two decades, and conceptions of best practices continue to evolve (Thomas & Grimes, 1995). Numerous legal requirements have been established where relatively little legal influence existed previously. Many of these requirements, as noted before, are ambiguous and subject to different interpretations. The general effect, however, is clear. General principles governing assessment of students with disabilities are now firmly established. Due process regulations ensure the rights of children and parents to carefully monitor and challenge the assessment services provided by psychologists and other professionals. The meaning of these provisions is in a continuing process of clarification through further litigation.

POST-1975 LITIGATION

Over the past 25 years, the right to education and placement bias litigation has continued. Nearly all of the right to education cases involve issues of FAPE. The touchstone case regarding FAPE is *Board of Education v. Rowley* (1982), where "appropriateness" was defined as "reasonable educational benefit" rather than ideal, most effective, or best educational program. The assessment data indicating that the plaintiff, Amy Rowley, a deaf youngster, was achieving at or above grade level in all of her school subjects were a key factor in the court's determination that an "appropriate" education in this instance did not require the employment by the district of a sign language interpreter. The concept of appropriate has been further elaborated in numerous cases since 1982.

Placement Bias Cases

A second major kind of litigation, based primarily on the EHA-IDEA principle of nondiscrimination, continues to be refined in the federal courts and in other legal and quasi-legal processes. The two most fundamental issues in the placement bias litigation over the past two decades have been: (a) the appropriateness of conventional measures of intelligence with black students, and (b) the acceptability of disproportionate placement of minority students in programs for students with MMR. Both of these questions are adjudicated under the nondiscrimination clause in the PEP section of federal regulations (IDEA, 1991). In *Larry P. v. Riles* (1979), Judge Peckham ruled that IQ tests were biased against black students and that IQ test use was primarily responsible for the overrepresentation of black students in special classes for the mildly retarded. Peckham then banned the use of IQ tests if the outcome of such testing was a diagnosis of MMR and placement in special education programs that he regarded as "dead-end" and inferior.

Federal court judges reached different conclusions on essentially the same set of facts in *PASE v. Hannon* (1980), *Marshall v. Georgia* (1984, 1985), *S-1 v. Turlington* (1986). In these cases, patterns of black student overrepresentation in MMR and the use of IQ tests were permitted because defendant schools convinced the courts that rigorous due process protections were carefully implemented, IQ tests were used with a wide variety of other measures that were more important than IQ in determining diagnosis and placement decisions, multidisciplinary teams of professionals and parents made the decisions, special education was a last resort as a means to cope with chronic and severe achievement deficits, and the special education programs expanded opportunities for academic and social development.

The concept of fairness adopted by the court had a profound impact on the decisions in the placement bias trials. In *Larry P.,* the court at least implicitly adopted an equal results definition of fairness, meaning that the same outcomes have to be achieved for all sociocultural groups. If necessary to produce equal outcomes, differential treatment of individuals has to be implemented in this conception of fairness, for example, use of different assessment procedures or different classification criteria, as in the *Larry P.* decision. The inherent problem with equal results notions of fairness is that they almost inevitably require differential treatment of individuals with the same behaviors, depending on their sociocultural characteristics.

The main alternative to an equal results definition is equal treatment, which requires that all individuals with similar characteristics be treated in the same way regardless of race, ethnicity, social class, or gender. Equal treatment allows disproportionate outcomes by race, ethnicity, social class, or gender as long as individuals are treated in comparable ways. The inherent weakness of equal treatment is that long-standing patterns of disproportionate outcomes continue to exist, including, for example, differential placement of students by race in special education or admission to professional schools and universities.

After prevailing with the Ninth Circuit in 1984, the *Larry P.* plaintiffs sought an expanded injunction against the use of IQ tests because, in their view, school psychologists and special educators were subverting the 1979 trial opinion by using IQ tests as part of the evaluation of the eligibility of black students for other disabilities, especially SLD. The original *Larry P.* (1979) opinion that enjoined the use of IQ tests was narrowly drawn: IQ tests were banned "for the identification of black E.M.R. [educable mentally retarded] children or their placement into E.M.R. classes . . . or a substantially equivalent category." In 1986, the 1979 opinion was markedly expanded to "the complete prohibition against using IQ tests for identifying or placing black pupils in special education . . . an IQ test may not be given to a black pupil even with parental consent. Moreover, when a school district receives records containing test protocols from other agencies . . . IQ scores contained in the records shall not become a part of the pupil's current school record. There are no special education related purposes for which IQ tests shall be administered to black students" (*Larry P.,* 1986, p. 4).

The 1986 injunction appears to be a classic case of violation of equal protection, for it meant that the California Department of Education (CDE) was ordered to establish different rules regarding the exercise of parental discretion and decision making depending on the race of the child. If the child was black, one set of rules applied; however, a different set of rules was established if the child was white. It was an astonishing, even stunning turn of events in a case that had been, originally in 1972, decided on the basis of a school district's violation of equal protection of the law. How Judge Peckham was led into making what seems to be an obvious and egregious error is not apparent from the original injunction or the correction that soon was made in another suit that continued the *Larry P.* saga into the 1990s (*Crawford v. Honig,* 1988, 1992).

In May 1988, *Crawford v. Honig* was filed in district court as a class action suit against the California Department of Education on behalf of black students whose parents were prevented by the 1986 *Larry P.* injunction from making decisions about IQ testing in preplacement evaluations of their children, a right exercised by parents of white children. The case was recognized immediately as directly relevant to the *Larry P.* issues and remanded to Judge Peckham. In 1992, Peckham rescinded the 1986 expanded injunction on due process grounds because the members of the Crawford plaintiff class, black children who may be diagnosed as SLD using IQ tests, were not represented in the original *Larry P.* plaintiff class or at the 1986 proceeding that produced the expanded injunction. Judge Peckham in 1992 described the 1979 opinion as "clearly limited to the use of IQ tests in the assessment and placement of African-American students in dead end programs such as MMR. . . . Despite the Defendants' attempts to characterize the court's 1979 order as a referendum on the discriminatory nature of IQ testing, this court's review of the decision reveals that the decision was largely concerned with the harm to African-American children resulting from improper placement in dead-end educational programs" (*Crawford* and *Larry P.,* 1992, pp. 15, 23).

SUMMARY

Since 1979, there have been four trials in the federal district courts on issues related to overrepresentation of African American children in special education programs. The judicial scoreboard is 3 to 1; that is, defendant school districts and state departments of education have prevailed in three of the trials. The only trial in which plaintiffs prevailed was *Larry P.* Two of the trial opinions were upheld when appealed to U.S. Circuit Courts of Appeal (*Larry P.,* 1984; *Marshall* [a.k.a., *Georgia State Conferences of NAACP*], 1985). The circuit court results are 1 to 1. The Ninth Circuit affirmed the *Larry P.* trial opinion banning IQ tests for the narrow purpose of classifying black children as MMR, and the Eleventh Circuit affirmed the *Marshall* trial court opinion that permitted African American overrepresentation in special education MMR programs and the use of IQ tests with black children. Neither case was appealed to the U.S. Supreme Court; therefore, it is likely that these contradictory circuit court opinions will not be resolved by a higher court opinion. Unlike the legal concept of "appropriate education" that was defined by a Supreme Court opinion, the legal meaning of "nondiscrimination" in the context of assessment of students with disabilities is likely to remain elusive and ambiguous.

Although a number of authors have focused primarily on the IQ testing aspects of the litigation (e. g., Bersoff, 1982a, 1982b; Elliott, 1987; Reschly, 1980), a better understanding is gained by focusing on the implicit issues in these cases that motivated the plaintiffs and the central role of treatment outcomes in shaping judicial opinions (Reschly, Kicklighter, & McKee, 1988a, 1988b, 1988c). Moreover, the late Judge Peckham's final commentary on the *Larry P.* issues clearly indicated that his concern was primarily with the effectiveness of educational programs rather than the narrow issue of test bias.

Although no litigation before the federal courts currently is dealing with nondiscrimination claims in special education, there has been a significant increase in interest in overrepresentation concerns in the 1990s. The federal Office of Civil Rights (OCR), an arm of the Department of Education, has been especially active in asserting discrimination in the classification and placement of minority children in special education programs. A recent commentary by an OCR official claimed that these examples of discrimination were identified in investigations of school districts: "(1) more minority students are placed in overly restrictive placements, (2) differential use of IQ scores with instances of IQ tests being the de facto sole instrument for determining eligibility with minority students, but a full multifactored assessment was carried out with nonminority students, and (3) differential application of prereferral strategies on the basis of race" ("OCR Investigations Cast a Wide Net," 1995, p. 7).

Clearly, the same concerns about psychological assessment of students with disabilities still exist and require continued attention to ensure that professional practices meet at least the equal treatment criterion of fairness. It should be noted, however, that the OCR claims are not based on rigorous equal treatment studies of the special education assessment and placement decisions of black and white students. The few rigorous studies that exist indicate that equal treatment criteria are met in current assessment services with black and white students suspected of being disabled or who are disabled (*Coalition to Save Our Children v. State Board of Education*, 1995; Reschly & Kicklighter, 1985; Reschly & Ward, 1991). One reason that additional studies on equal treatment have not been published is the extreme difficulty in gaining access to appropriate data sets due to the reluctance of local and state educational agencies to undergo such scrutiny. This reluctance, in itself, may be cause for concern.

DIAGNOSTIC CONSTRUCTS AND CLASSIFICATION CRITERIA

The diagnostic constructs, that is, the areas in which a student can be classified as disabled, are specified to varying degrees in federal and state law. The *Diagnostic and Statistical Manual of Mental Disorders* (American Psychiatric Association, 1994), the controlling diagnostic system in most clinical and counseling practice, is largely irrelevant to classification of disabilities in educational settings. The federal IDEA (1991, 1997) includes conceptual definitions of disabling conditions. The federal conceptual definitions are rather general with few specific classification criteria or rules to guide decisions. More specific criteria to guide the assessment process and decisions about eligibility typically are provided at the state level in a document usually called something like *State of _____ Rules of Special Education*. In all of the placement bias litigation, professional decision making in relation to state rules was examined rather than conformance to the general federal definitions.

States have considerable freedom in formulating diagnostic constructs and classification criteria concerning educational disabilities. Terminology varies considerably among states and is frequently dissimilar to the federal terminology. For example, all states have a special education diagnostic category that is comparable in meaning and purpose to the federal SLD category. The terminology, however, varies considerably, with some states using a term such as neurologically impaired. Moreover, the classification criteria also vary significantly. According to C. Mercer, King-Sears, and Mercer (1990), approximately 80% of states require a severe discrepancy between ability and achievement as part of the SLD classification criteria. This apparent uniformity is, however, ephemeral because of the widely differing ways to determine whether or not a specific child meets the criteria for a severe discrepancy. In one state, known to the author, the discrepancy must be at least 1 standard deviation in standard score points. In another, a 2 standard deviation discrepancy is required. For these and other reasons, classification and eligibility decisions about a specific child may vary depending on the state he or she is in as well as other complex factors. These variations are most likely to affect social system model disabilities such as SLD. Knowledge of state special education rules is essential in the assessment of students with disabilities. Further information on state rules as well as classification guidelines usually can be obtained from the division of special education of the state department of education.

SYSTEM REFORM TRENDS AND ASSESSMENT IMPLICATIONS

Increasing evidence suggests that significant reforms are needed in the current system of delivering educational and psychological services to students with disabilities (Reschly & Ysseldyke, 1995). Thorough discussion of problems in the current system, such as the absence of documented benefits of special education programs, heavy reliance on assessment measures such as IQ tests that have little treatment validity, the use of nonfunctional and stigmatizing categories such as MR, and overrepresentation of minority students, are beyond the scope of this chapter. The reform trends, however, have vast implications for the assessment of educational disabilities and require significant changes in the contributions of psychologists.

A major shift to a focus on *outcomes* rather than intervention inputs or processes is apparent in the reform literature. An outcomes orientation has been applied to analyses of overrepresentation of minority students in special education (Reschly, 1979; Reschly & Tilly, 1993). Greater attention to documentation of outcomes is pervasive in general and special education (Ysseldyke, Thurlow, & Bruininks, 1992). In the future, the usefulness of assessment activities with students with disabilities will be judged by the degree to which they are related to producing positive outcomes. Assessment practices that merely document the existence of the problem increasingly will be viewed as limited and irrelevant. Those that are useful in formulating treatment goals, monitoring progress, and evaluating outcomes increasingly will be used as part of the future delivery system.

Assessment for the purpose of developing interventions is increasingly emphasized in the reform literature (Ysseldyke et al., 1997). Problem solving with students with disabilities requires behavioral definitions of presenting problems, direct measures of behaviors in natural settings, design of interventions, monitoring progress with intervention revisions as necessary, and evaluating outcomes. All are more consistent with the experimental tradition in psychology as well as the short-run empiricism described by Cronbach (1975) as a promising replacement for interventions guided by aptitude by treatment interactions. Problem solving depends heavily on curriculum-based and behavioral assessment measures that are developed and applied in the natural settings of classrooms, playgrounds, homes, and communities.

Significant advances in assessment technology permit greater emphasis on measures functionally related to interventions. Most of these advances can be classified as behavioral assessment procedures (Shapiro & Kratochwill, 1988). The knowledge base for practice has improved substantially with the development of curriculum-based assessment, which fosters a close relationship between assessment and treatment (Deno, 1985; Howell, Fox, & Morehead, 1993; Shapiro, 1989; Shinn, 1989). Advances in the assessment of instructional environments provides further technological support to academic and behavioral interventions (Christenson, Ysseldyke, & Thurlow, 1989; Ysseldyke & Christenson, 1987a, 1987b, 1993; Ysseldyke, Christenson, & Kovaleski, 1994; Ysseldyke & Marston, 1990). Parallel advances in behavioral assessment of social and emotional phenomena have led to equally substantial improvements in practice in these areas (Alessi & Kaye, 1983; Shapiro & Kratochwill, 1988). Technologically sophisticated assessment methods, for example, the Ecobehavioral Assessment Systems Software (EBASS) (Greenwood, Carta, Kamps, Terry, & Delquadri, 1994), have been developed to aid in the detailed collection of observational data in classrooms.

The assessment technology to support practice guided by an outcomes criterion is now available for the first time in the history of assessment of students with disabilities. Behavioral assessment measures also can be used in decisions about eligibility for various special programs and in decisions about placement (Gresham, 1985, 1991; Shinn, Tindal, & Stein, 1988). It appears that virtually the same students will be identified as needing specialized instruction and social-emotional interventions using behavioral assessment procedures; however, the behavioral assessment procedures yield information useful for intervention planning and evaluation as well as eligibility determination.

INSTRUCTIONAL DESIGN

Behavior assessment and instructional analysis are inextricably related in functional assessment of academic behaviors. The marriage of instructional design principles (e.g., Englemann & Carnine, 1982) with behavioral intervention technologies has produced impressive outcomes for students (Becker & Carnine, 1980). Meta-analysis evidence indicates that interventions driven by behavioral assessment of social or emotional domains or curriculum-based assessment of academic skills domains have effect sizes that are two to three times the effect sizes associated with traditional, largely norm-referenced, standardized assessment practices (Kavale, 1990). These superior results likely will create the dynamics for assessment practices to change rapidly in the late 1990s and early 2000s. Use of this knowledge base produces results that are potentially markedly superior to traditional special education programs or instruction based on matching teaching methods to presumed strengths in cognitive style, information processing, or neuropsychological status.

BEHAVIOR CHANGE

Behavior change principles are well established (Stoner, Shinn, & Walker, 1991; Sulzer-Azaroff & Mayer, 1991). In addition, characteristics of effective schools and effective teaching are well represented in the school psychology literature (e.g., Bickel, 1990). There is a solid knowledge base for alternative approaches to assessment and intervention; however, the assessment services and special education for most children and youth with disabilities do not apply all, or even most, of this knowledge base.

One of the main themes in system reform is improved application of the available knowledge on assessment and producing closer links between assessment and interventions (Ikeda, Tilly, Stumme, Volmer, & Allison, 1996). Improved application of this knowledge base will be facilitated by the movement toward noncategorical classification and integration of diverse programs intended to serve children and youth (Reschly & Ysseldyke, 1995). Reductions in the amount of time devoted to standardized testing to determine eligibility will permit greater opportunities for school psychologists to be involved in new roles related to functional assessment and interventions.

The continuing education needs of psychologists who provide assessment services to students with disabilities have, arguably, never been greater. Much of what is in current programs regarding standardized, norm-referenced assessment is of declining importance. Preservice and continuing education opportunities to acquire the new set of skills are expanding but, to date, are inadequate to meet the needs of personnel in systems undergoing rapid changes. Meeting these continuing education needs is one of the greatest current challenges to university graduate programs and to professional associations.

The traditional training of psychologists continues to provide a solid foundation for the competencies needed in the delivery system of the future. The focus on learning; on knowledge of normal and exceptional patterns of development; on sensitivity to cultural differences; on measurement, assessment, and counseling methods; and on relationship skills is unique among professionals in schools involved with providing assessment and intervention services to students with disabilities. These foundation competencies need to be supplemented with skills in functional assessment and effective interventions that are crucial to improved assessment of children with disabilities.

PSYCHOLOGICAL TESTIMONY IN LEGAL PROCEEDINGS

Use of psychoeducational assessment in legal or quasi-legal proceedings such as due process hearings has usually been restricted to the testimony of expert witnesses or examination of the results from standardized tests. It is crucial to note that typical school psychology practitioners meet the criteria for court recognition as expert witnesses. Moreover, most psychologists will appear one or more times in their careers as expert witnesses in an administrative hearing or in court. Although testimony on standardized test results are acceptable kinds of evidence, their impact often is diminished by attacks on the tests and the nearly inevitable appearance of contradictory testimony from other experts representing the other side. Furthermore, the highly inferential court testimony that psychologists sometimes provide in court is quite vulnerable to impeachment during cross-examination (Faust & Ziskin, 1988; Ziskin & Faust, 1988).

Psychologists often experience frustration in attempting to explain complex patterns of behavior with imprecise, but intricate, diagnostic constructs and complicated classification criteria. Explanations of these matters in legal proceedings can be particularly trying when cross-examination may be devoted to undermining the salience and credibility of the testimony. Sattler's (1982) account of his experiences in *Larry P.* is an excellent illustration of this problem.

Although sound testimony from genuine experts is probably essential and irreplaceable, this testimony can be significantly enhanced if supported by a variety of more tangible forms of evidence. In the *S-1 v. Turlington* (1986) trial, a videotape was shown in which black and white regular education students of approximately average ability were contrasted with black and white students classified as MMR and placed in special education programs. The children were about 10 years old. Each child was shown in a brief interview and then asked to perform common, everyday cognitive skills such as telling time, performing simple computations, and reading a brief passage. Differences among these students were not apparent in the interview or from casual observation. However, dramatic differences among the students on these relatively simple cognitive tasks were obvious to everyone in the court. The critical differences between disabled and nondisabled were exemplified far better by the videotape than any expert witness using protocols from standardized tests, normal curve distributions, and deviation IQ scores could ever have shown. The videotape provided a means whereby far more tangible examples of the basic issue in the litigation could be presented. Similar uses of videotape would seem appropriate and desirable in due process hearings and civil court proceedings concerning disabled students.

In addition to videotape, a variety of other kinds of evidence such as audiotape, samples of daily work, observation protocols, and interview schedules can be used to support expert testimony. A major problem with some of the previous placement bias cases—*Larry P.* and *PASE*—is the relatively sparse use of these alternative kinds of evidence, which left federal district court judges with the unenviable tasks of determining item bias and whether certain students were truly retarded. Psychologists can best serve the courts by presenting tangible evidence that reflects the basic phenomena rather than relying only on testimony.

CONCLUSION

Legal influences on school psychology and other professions associated with assessment of educational disabilities have expanded enormously over the past two decades. Further influence through the gradual evolution of case law and the enactment of legislation should be anticipated. The uneasy relationship between the courts and psychologists and the occasional misuse and distortion of psychological evidence by the courts requires substantial additional efforts toward mutual understanding. Greater appreciation on the part of psychologists for the essential role of the courts in determining the educational rights of students with disabilities is needed as well as greater understanding by the courts of the strengths and limitations of psychoeducational assessment. Better assessment can produce better evidence, which, in turn, will improve legal decisions that affect the lives of children and youth.

REFERENCES

Alessi, G., & Kaye, J. (1983). *Behavioral assessment for school psychologists.* Washington, DC: National Association of School Psychologists.

American Psychiatric Association. (1994). *Diagnostic and statistical manual of mental disorders* (4th ed.). Washington, DC: Author.

American Psychological Association. (1992). Ethical principles of psychologists and code of conduct. *American Psychologist, 47,* 1597–1611.

Becker, W. C., & Carnine, D. W. (1980). Direct instruction: An effective approach to educational intervention with the disadvantaged and low performers. In B. B. Lahey & A. K. Kazdin (Eds.), *Advances in clinical and child psychology* (Vol. 3, pp. 429–473). New York: Plenum Press.

Bersoff, D. N. (1979). Regarding psychologists testing: Legal regulation of psychological assessment on public schools. *Maryland Law Review, 39,* 27–120.

Bersoff, D. N. (1982a). The legal regulation of school psychology. In C. R. Reynolds & T. B. Gutkin (Eds.), *The handbook of school psychology* (pp. 1043–1074). New York: Wiley.

Bersoff, D. N. (1982b). Larry P. and PASE: Judicial report cards of the validity of individual intelligence tests. In T. Kratochwill (Ed.), *Advances in school psychology* (Vol. 2, pp. 61–95). Hillsdale, NJ: Erlbaum.

Bickel, W. E. (1990). The effective schools literature: Implications for research and practice. In T. B. Gutkin & C. R. Reynolds (Eds.), *The handbook of school psychology* (2nd ed., pp. 847–867). New York: Wiley.

Board of Education v. Holland, 786 F. Supp. 874 (E.D. CA 1992) (9th Cir. 1994).

Board of Education v. Rowley, 102 S. Ct. 3034 (1982).

Christenson, S. L., Ysseldyke, J. E., & Thurlow, M. L. (1989). Critical instructional factors for students with mild handicaps. *Remedial and Special Education, 10,* 21–31.

Coalition to Save Our Children v. State Board of Education (1995), Civil Action Nos. 56-1816–1822-SLR, U.S. District Court for the District of Delaware.

Crawford et al. v. Honig, No. C-89-0014 RFP U.S. District Court, Northern District of California, Complaint for Declaratory Judgment, May 1988; Order, September 29, 1989; Memorandum and Order, August 31, 1992.

Cronbach, L. J. (1975). Beyond the two disciplines of scientific psychology. *American Psychologist, 30,* 116–127.

Deno, S. L. (1985). Curriculum-based measurement: The emerging alternative. *Exceptional Children, 52,* 219–232.

Diana vs. State Board of Education, No. C-70-37 RFP U.S. District Court, Northern District of California, Consent Decree, February 3, 1970.

Education of the Handicapped Act. (1975). P.L. 94-142, 20 U.S.C. 1400-1485, 34 CFR-300.

Elliott, R. (1987). *Litigating intelligence.* Dover, MA: Auburn House.

Englemann, S., & Carnine, D. (1982). *Theory of instruction: Principles and applications.* New York: Irvington.

Fagan, T. K. (1987a). Gesell: The first school psychologist: Part I. The road to Connecticut. *School Psychology Review, 16,* 103–107.

Fagan, T. K. (1987b). Gesell: The first school psychologist: Part II. Practice and significance. *School Psychology Review, 16,* 399–409.

Fagan, T. K. (1992). Compulsory schooling, child study, clinical psychology, and special education: Origins of school psychology. *American Psychologist, 47,* 236–243.

Fagan, T. K., & Delugach, F. J. (1984). Literary origins of the term, "school psychologist." *School Psychology Review, 13,* 216–220.

Fagan, T. K., & Wise, P. S. (1994). *School psychology: Past, present, and future.* White Plains, NY: Longmans.

Faust, D., & Ziskin, J. (1988). The expert witness in psychology and psychiatry. *Science, 241,* 31–35.

Greenwood, C. R., Carta, J. J., Kamps, K., Terry, B., & Delquadri, J. (1994). Development and validation of standard classroom observation systems for school practitioners: Ecobehavioral Assessment Systems Software (EBASS). *Exceptional Children, 61,* 197–209.

Gresham, F. M. (1985). Behavior disorder assessment: Conceptual, definitional, and practical considerations. *School Psychology Review, 14,* 495–509.

Gresham, F. M. (1991). Conceptualizing behavior disorders in terms of resistance to intervention. *School Psychology Review, 20,* 23–36.

Guadalupe Organization v. Tempe Elementary School District No. 3, No. 71–435 (D. Ariz., January 24, 1972) (consent decree).

Hobbs, N. (Ed.). (1975). *Issues in the classification of children* (Vols. 1 & 2). San Francisco: Jossey-Bass.

Howell, K. W., Fox, S. L., & Morehead, M. K. (1993). *Curriculum-based evaluation teaching and decision making* (2nd ed.). Columbus, OH: Merrill.

Ikeda, M. J., Tilly, W. D., III, Stumme, J., Volmer, L., & Allison, R. (1996). Agency-wide implementation of problem solving consultation: Foundations, current implementation, and future directions. *School Psychology Quarterly, 11,* 228–243.

Individuals with Disabilities Education Act, (1990, 1997), 20 U.S.C. Chapter 33, Sections 1400–1485 (Statute).

Individuals with Disabilities Education Act, (1991), 34 C.F.R. 300 (Regulations).

Individuals with Disabilities Education Act, (1997), 20 U.S.C. 1400 et. Seq. (Statute).

Kauffman, J. M., & Hallahan, D. (1974). The medical model and the science of special education. *Exceptional Children, 41,* 97–102.

Kavale, K. (1990). The effectiveness of special education. In T. B. Gutkin & C. R. Reynolds (Eds.), *The handbook of school psychology* (2nd ed., pp. 868–898). New York: Wiley.

Kicklighter, R. H. (1976). School psychology in the US: A quantitative survey. *Journal of School Psychology, 14,* 151–156.

Larry P. v. Riles (1972, 1974, 1979, 1984, 1986, 1992), 343 F. Supp. 1306 (N.D. Cal. 1972) (preliminary injunction); aff'd 502 F. 2d 963 (9th cir. 1974); 495 F. Supp. 926 (N.D. Cal. 1979) (decision on merits); aff'd (9th cir. no. 80-427 Jan. 23, 1984). Order modifying judgment, C-71-2270 RFP, September 25, 1986. Memorandum and Order, August 31, 1992, aff'd F. (9th Cir. 1994).

Lund, A. R., Reschly, D. J., & Martin, L. M. (1998). School psychology personnel needs: Correlates of current patterns and historical trends. *School Psychology Review, 27*, 106–120.

Marshall et al. v. Georgia (1984, 1985). U.S. District Court for the Southern District of Georgia, CV482-233, June 28, 1984; Affirmed (11th Cir. No. 84-8771, Oct. 29, 1985). (Appealed as NAACP v. Georgia). Note: the court of appeals decision was published as Georgia State Conference of Branches of NAACP v. State of Georgia.

Mercer, C. D., King-Sears, P., & Mercer, A. R. (1990). Learning disabilities definitions and criteria used by state education departments. *Learning Disability Quarterly, 13*, 141–152.

Mercer, J. (1979). In defense of racially and culturally nondiscriminatory assessment. *School Psychology Digest, 8*, 89–115.

Mills v. Board of Education, 348 F. Supp. 866 (D.D.C. 1972).

National Association of School Psychologists. (1994). *Professional conduct manual: Principles for professional ethics and standards for the provision of school psychological services.* Washington DC: National Association of School Psychologists.

OCR Investigations Cast A Wide Net. (1995). *Urban Perspectives, 2*(1), p. 7.

(PARC) Pennsylvania Association for Retarded Children v. Commonwealth of Pennsylvania, 343 F. Supp. 279 (E.D. Pa. 1972). (PARC).

Parrish, T. B., & Chambers, J. G. (1996). Financing special education. *The Futures of Children: Special Education for Students with Disabilities, 6*(1), 121–138.

(PASE) Parents in Action on Special Education v. Joseph P. Hannon. U.S. District Court, Northern District of Illinois, Eastern Division, No. 74 (3586), July 1980.

Prasse, D. P. (1995). School psychology and the law. In A. Thomas & J. Grimes (Eds.), *Best practices in school psychology III* (3rd ed., pp. 41–50). Washington, DC: National Association of School Psychologists.

Reschly, D. J. (1979). Nonbiased assessment. In G. Phye & D. Reschly (Eds.), *School psychology: Perspectives and issues* (pp. 215–253). New York: Academic Press.

Reschly, D. J. (1980). Psychological evidence in the *Larry P.* opinion: A case of right problem-wrong solution. *School Psychology Review, 9*, 123–135.

Reschly, D. J. (1983). Legal issues in psychoeducational assessment. In G. Hynd (Ed.), *The school psychologist: Contemporary perspectives* (pp. 67–93). Syracuse, NY: Syracuse University Press.

Reschly, D. J. (1988). Alternative delivery systems: Legal and ethical issues. In J. L. Graden, J. E. Zins, & M. J. Curtis (Eds.), *Alternative educational delivery systems: Enhancing instructional options for all students* (pp. 525–552). Washington, DC: National Association of School Psychologists.

Reschly, D. J. (1996). Identification and assessment of children with disabilities. *The Future of Children: Special Education for Children with Disabilities, 6*(1), 40–53.

Reschly, D. J., & Bersoff, D. N. (1999). Law and school psychology. In T. B. Gutkin & C. R. Reynolds (Eds.) *The handbook of school psychology* (3rd ed.). New York: Wiley.

Reschly, D. J., & Kicklighter, R. H. (1985). *Comparison of black and white EMR students from Marshall vs. Georgia.* Paper presented at the annual convention of the American Psychological Association, Los Angeles, ERIC ED 271 911.

Reschly, D. J., Kicklighter, R. H., & McKee, P. (1988a). Recent placement litigation: Part I. Regular education grouping: Comparison of *Marshall* (1984, 1985) and *Hobson* (1967, 1969). *School Psychology Review, 17*, 7–19.

Reschly, D. J., Kicklighter, R. H., & McKee, P. (1988b). Recent placement litigation: Part II. Minority EMR overrepresentation: Comparison of *Larry P.* (1979, 1984, 1986) with *Marshall* (1984, 1985) and *S-1* (1986). *School Psychology Review, 17,* 20–36.

Reschly, D. J., Kicklighter, R. H., & McKee, P. (1988c). Recent placement litigation: Part III. Analysis of differences in *Larry P., Marshall,* and *S-I* and implications for future practices. *School Psychology Review, 17,* 37–48.

Reschly, D. J., & Tilly, W. D. (1993). The WHY of system reform. *Communique, 22*(1), 1, 4–6.

Reschly, D. J., & Ward, S. M. (1991). Use of adaptive measures and overrepresentation of black students in programs for students with mild mental retardation. *American Journal of Mental Retardation, 96,* 257–268.

Reschly, D. J., & Ysseldyke, J. E. (1995). School psychology paradigm shift. In A. Thomas & J. Grimes (Eds.), *Best practices in school psychology* (3rd ed.), (Vol. 3, pp. 17–31). Washington DC: National Association of School Psychologists.

S-1 v. Turlington, Preliminary Injunction, U.S. District Court, Southern District of Florida, Case No. 79-8020-Civ-CA WPB, June 15, 1979. Affirmed United States Court of Appeals, 5th Circuit, January 26, 1981, 635 F 2d 342 (1981). Trial on Merits, May 19–June 4, 1986. Order on Motion to Dismiss, No. 79-8020-Civ-Atkins, U.S. District Court, Southern District of Florida, October 9, 1986.

Sattler, J. (1982). The psychologist in court: Personal reflections of one expert witness in the case of *Larry P. School Psychology Review, 11,* 306–319.

Shapiro, E. S. (Ed.). (1989). *Academic skills problems: Direct assessment and intervention.* New York: Guilford Press.

Shapiro, E. S., & Kratochwill, T. R. (Eds.). (1988). *Behavioral assessment in schools: Conceptual foundations and practical applications.* New York: Guilford Press.

Shinn, M. R. (Ed.). (1989). *Curriculum-based measurement: Assessing special children.* New York: Guilford Press.

Shinn, M. R., Tindal, G. A., & Stein, S. (1988). Curriculum-based measurement and the identification of mildly handicapped students. *Professional School Psychology, 3,* 69–85.

Stoner, G., Shinn, M. R., & Walker, H. M. (1991). *Interventions for achievement and behavior problems.* Washington DC: National Association of School Psychologists.

Sulzer-Azaroff, B., & Mayer, G. R. (1991). *Behavior analysis for lasting change.* Fort Worth, TX: Holt, Rinehart and Winston.

Thomas, A., & Grimes, J. (Eds.). (1995). *Best practices in school psychology III.* Washington DC: National Association of School Psychologists.

Timothy W. v. Rochester, Sch. Dist., IDELR, 559:480 (D.N.H., 1988, Case No. C-84-733-L); IDELR 441:393 (1st Cir., 1989, Case No. 88-1847).

United States Department of Education. (1995). *Seventeenth annual report to Congress on the implementation of the Education of the Individuals with Disabilities Education Act.* Washington, DC: Office of Special Education and Rehabilitation Services, Author.

United States Department of Education. (1996). *Eighteenth annual report to Congress on the implementation of the Education of the Individuals with Disabilities Education Act.* Washington, DC: Office of Special Education and Rehabilitation Services, Author.

Ysseldyke, J. E., & Christenson, S. L. (1987a). *The instructional environment scale.* Austin, TX: Pro-Ed.

Ysseldyke, J. E., & Christenson, S. L. (1987b). Evaluating students' instructional environments. *Remedial and Special Education, 8,* 17–24.

Ysseldyke, J. E., & Christenson, S. L. (1993). *The instructional environment system-II.* Longmont, CO: SOPRIS West.

Ysseldyke, J. E., Christenson, S. L., & Kovaleski, J. (1994). Identifying students' instructional needs in the context of classroom and home environments. *Teaching Exceptional Children, 26*(3), 37–41.

Ysseldyke, J. E., Dawson, P., Lehr, C., Reschly, D., Reynolds, M., & Telzrow, C. (1997). *School psychology: A blueprint for training and practice II.* Bethesda, MD: National Association of School Psychologists.

Ysseldyke, J. E., & Marston, D. (1990). The need of assessment information to plan instructional interventions: A review of the research. In T. B. Gutkin & C. R. Reynolds (Eds.), *The handbook of school psychology* (2nd ed., pp. 661–682). New York: Wiley.

Ysseldyke, J. E., Thurlow, M. L., & Bruininks, R. H. (1992). Expected educational outcomes for students with disabilities. *Remedial and Special Education, 13*(6), 19–30.

Ziskin, J., & Faust, D. (1988). *Coping with psychiatric and psychological testimony* (Vols. 1–3, 4th ed.). Los Angeles: Law and Psychology Press.

CHAPTER 7

Civil Competency

RALPH SLOVENKO

LAWYERS CALL doctors incompetent. Chief Justice Warren Burger called lawyers incompetent. Everywhere there seems to be incompetence, even in the ranks of professionals, and the laws on licensing and certification are not reassuring.

In his now famous Peter principle, Laurence J. Peter wrote that in a hierarchy, employees tend to rise to their level of incompetence (Peter & Hull, 1969). Peter observed that employees start off competent, then rise, through promotion, to a position where they are not competent to perform the job. In other words, cream rises until it sours. Peter later wrote that this principle applies to all or at least most professions (*The Peter Prescription*, 1972).

There are various techniques to protect competence. Israeli kibbutzniks rotate jobs every three or four years. General Motors inaugurated a series of work rules for its Saturn plant in Tennessee to enhance morale and productivity. Instead of performing a single repetitive task, employees work together in self-directing teams of 6 to 15 people; each team is responsible for large sections of the car, and its members have the latitude to reach a consensus on how to divide and rotate job assignments. The workers receive a salary instead of an hourly wage, their pay directly based on performance (Alexander, 1985).

It can be difficult to determine whether incompetence lies with the person, with others, or with the system. The legal standard for measuring incompetence is related to vocational, social, educational, and other circumstances. Even if millions of people behave foolishly, the behavior is still foolish, but we tend to approve it. Custom or state of the art can be a measure of competency or negligence. Thus, in *Stepakoff v. Kantar* (1985), where it was alleged that the psychiatrist's negligence led to the patient's suicide, the court held that the psychiatrist was required to exercise only the care and skill customarily exercised by an average qualified psychiatrist. In a malpractice (professional negligence) action, the complainant is obliged as a matter of law to call as an expert witness a member of the profession (or one familiar with the profession) to testify as to the standard of care of the profession.

Webster's defines competency as "the quality or state of being functionally adequate or of having sufficient knowledge, judgment, skill, or strength (as for a particular day or in a particular respect)." Competency depends on the activity or the task. In a dialogue in Richard Condon's *Prizzi's Honor*, a novel turned into a celebrated film, Charley (a mafia hit man), wondering whether he can trust a woman he thinks he loves, asks, "Do I ice her? Do I marry her?" Replies girlfriend Maerose, "Just because she's a thief and a hitter don't mean she ain't a good woman in all other departments."

Competency as a legal concept refers to one's ability to perform an act or choose in a certain situation. Its connotation is contextual, relating to the specific task to be accomplished or decision to be made. Therefore, incompetency in one area does not necessarily imply incompetency in another. For example, in an Ontario case, a 78-year-old man was found competent to marry though lacking in testamentary capacity (*In re McElroy*, 1978). The criteria for determining competency vary according to the purpose to be served. Depending on the context, competency may mean the legal capacity to serve as a professional, to testify in court, to make a will, or to make a decision to accept or refuse medical treatment (Glass, 1997).

COMPETENCY OF A PROFESSIONAL

The word "profession" comes from the Latin *profiteri*, "to profess," meaning to make a public dedication to the ideals and practices associated with a learned calling. Professionalism involves several elements: fidelity to ethics and integrity as a meaningful commitment, service with competence and dedication, meaningful education, and civility.

Every professional organization, in one way or another, must face up to the incompetency of a member. Expulsion or discipline of a member may be based either on emotional instability or on professional misconduct. However, the degree of proof necessary to justify loss of membership or suspension varies from state to state and from profession to profession. In some states, professional misconduct must be shown by a preponderance of the evidence, in others, by clear and convincing evidence. Seldom does a malpractice suit trigger a hearing by a disciplinary board. Negligence as established in litigation is not equated with incompetency to practice nor even with a presumption of incompetency. Seldom is mental or emotional instability a sufficient ground for disciplinary action. Generally, acts or omissions, which themselves would be ground for discipline, bring to light mental or emotional problems. Often, the issue of mental instability is raised in mitigation of the wrongful conduct. In a few cases, however, the petition for suspension is based on a rule that provides for the suspension of individuals who are mentally or emotionally unstable.[1]

In the case of lawyer competency in criminal cases, until the 1970s, the prevailing standard of effective assistance of counsel was the mockery-of-justice test, under which representation was considered ineffective or incompetent only when it was so poor as to "reduce the trial to a farce" or render it a "mockery of justice." Under this test, lawyers could appear in court drunk or could fall asleep during trial and still not be found ineffective. (Disciplinary action, however, could be brought against an attorney for appearing in court intoxicated.) The test required "such a minimal level of performance from counsel" that it was called "a mockery of the Sixth Amendment" (Bazelon, 1973, p. 20). It was feared that honoring such claims would force trial judges to intervene whenever a possible error was being committed, lead appellate courts to second-guess defense tactics with the benefit of hindsight, make lawyers more reluctant to accept court assignments, and encourage lawyers with desperate cases to commit errors deliberately. In the early 1970s, the Supreme Court approached the issue of ineffective counsel in terms of whether counsel fell "within the range of competence demanded of attorneys in criminal cases" (*McMann v. Richardson*, 1970). The Supreme Court subsequently ruled that reversal of a conviction will only be required when the defendant shows that the attorney acted improperly in a way that directly and adversely affected the result at trial (*Strickland v. Washington*, 1984).

A status report from the American Bar Association asserts that 13 of every 100 students who graduate from an accredited law school show signs of drug or alcohol dependency. A report by the National Transportation Safety Board cites alcohol use as a common denominator in fatal commercial aviation accidents. In a survey of 9,600 physicians, 8% admitted to having abused or been dependent upon alcohol or other drugs during their lives. A report by the American Nurses Association links 68% of all state board actions against nurses to substance abuse (Coombs, 1997).

The Louisiana Court of Appeal in *Hidding v. Williams* (1991) ruled that a physician's failure to disclose his chronic alcohol abuse vitiated the patient's consent to surgery. There was a poor outcome, but no evidence that the physician was under the influence of alcohol at the time of surgery, or that his hands trembled, or that the care fell below acceptable standards. Nonetheless, the court said, "Because this condition creates a material risk associated with the surgeon's ability to perform, which if disclosed would have obliged the patient to have elected another course of treatment, the fact-finder's conclusion that non-disclosure is a violation of the informed consent doctrine is entirely correct" (p. 470). It is a risk about which the patient should have been informed (Slovenko, 1994).

COMPETENCY OF A WITNESS

As a general rule, in civil or criminal cases, every adult witness is presumed competent to testify unless it can be shown that the witness does not have personal knowledge of the matters about which he or she is to testify, that he or she does not have the ability to recall the subject matter, or that he or she does not understand the duty to testify truthfully (Rule 601). Any objection to the competency of a witness must be raised at the time the party is presented as a witness; absent objection at that time, the claim of incompetency is waived.

Generally, the decision whether or not to hold a competency hearing is a matter entirely within the discretion of the trial judge. A witness may be found competent despite the fact that in another case he or she may have been found criminally insane or incompetent to stand trial. In these or other cases, a psychiatrist or psychologist may be called to testify whether the witness has sufficient memory, understands the oath, and has the ability to communicate (Slovenko, 1995). Among the considerations to be taken into account in deciding whether to order a psychiatric examination, many courts include protection of privacy and not deterring complaints and law suits of certain kinds. As one court put it, "It is unpleasant enough to have to testify in a public trial subject to cross-examination the results of which will be spread on the record in open court to disqualify you, or at least to spice up your cross-examination" (*United States v. Gutman,* 1984).

The rule that allows an individual deemed insane to testify assumes that jurors are capable of evaluating a witness's testimony. "If a lunatic takes the stand and babbles gibberish, the jury will ignore it and the defendant will not be harmed," said the court in *Gutman.* In this case, the witness had been hospitalized 13 months earlier and was described as "highly depressed" with "some psychiatric thought disorder in addition to the difficulty he has in organizing and being relevant." This witness for the state was again hospitalized some two months after testifying. The court listed several factors in its decision not to order an examination of the witness's ability to testify: (a) protection of the witness's privacy interests, (b) potential for harassment of witnesses, (c) the possibility that a mental exam will hamper law enforcement by deterring potential witnesses from coming forward, (d) whether the witness was a key to the case, and (e) are substantial indications that the witness is suffering from a mental abnormality at the time of trial.

It has long been established that age alone is not determinative of testimonial competency (Myers, 1993). The issue of competency of a child witness to testify came before the U.S. Supreme Court in 1895 in an oft-cited case, *Wheeler v. United States.* The question was whether the five-year-old son of a murder victim could testify. The homicide took place on June 12, 1894; the case was tried on December 21 of that year. (In those days, trials took place soon after the event.) In reply to questions put to him on his voir dire, the boy said that he knew the difference between the truth and a lie, that if he told a lie the bad man would get him, and that he was going to tell the truth. When asked what they would do with him in court if he told a lie, he replied that they would put him in jail. He also said that his mother had told him that morning to "tell no lie," and when asked what the clerk had said to him when he was told to hold up his hand, he answered, "Don't you tell no story." He was asked about his residence, his relationship to the deceased, and whether he had ever been to school, to which he responded in the negative. The Supreme Court said:

> That the boy was not by reason of his youth, as a matter of law, absolutely disqualified as a witness, is clear. While no one would think of calling as a witness an infant only two or three years old, there is no precise age which determines the question of competency. This depends on the capacity and intelligence of the child, his appreciation of the difference between truth and falsehood, as well as of his duty to tell the former. The decision of this question rests primarily with the trial judge, who sees the proposed witness, notices his manner, his apparent possession or lack of intelligence, and may resort to any examination which will tend to disclose his capacity and intelligence as well as his understanding of the

obligations of an oath. As many of these matters cannot be photographed into the record, the decision of the trial judge will not be disturbed on review unless from that which is preserved it is clear that it was erroneous. . . . [T]he boy was intelligent, understood the difference between truth and falsehood, and the consequences of telling the latter, and also what was required by the oath which he had taken. At any rate, the contrary does not appear. Of course, care must be taken by the trial judge, especially where, as in this case, the question is one of life or death. On the other hand to exclude from the witness stand one who shows himself capable of understanding the difference between truth and false-hood, and who does not appear to have been simply taught to tell a story, would sometimes result in staying the hand of justice. (pp. 524–525)

In early law, a child or adult could be automatically barred from testifying because of insufficient religious training. Wigmore, the leading authority on evidence, in 1935 recommended that there be no requirement of competency of a child witness (Wigmore, 1979). He argued against the qualifying of witnesses by judges because of the judiciary's lack of expertise in this area. He argued for permitting children to testify and allowing the jury or judge to assess the over-all credibility of the testimony. Although Wigmore's view has not been en-tirely adopted, numerous studies support the competency of child witnesses. However, lawyers do not like to put children on the stand and usually will do so only if their testimony is necessary. Jurors usually want medical evidence to corroborate a child's story of sexual abuse (Survey, 1997).

Psychological research confirms the popular view that children are more sub-ject to suggestion than adults, but Elizabeth Loftus and Graham Davies (1984) observe, "Perhaps age alone is the wrong focus for these studies. Whether chil-dren are more susceptible to suggestive information than adults probably de-pends on the interaction of age with other factors. If an event is understandable and interesting to both children and adults, and if their memory for it is still equally strong, age differences in suggestibility may not be found. But if the event is not encoded well to begin with, or if a delay weakens the child's mem-ory relative to an adult's, then age differences may emerge." To obtain accurate information from young children, the danger of suggestion must be taken into account as well as the fact that children have greater communication difficulties than adults and are often in need of assistance in this regard.

At common law it was presumed that a child under age 14 was not competent. At present there is no fixed age below which a witness is deemed incompetent, although children under age 10 or 14 are routinely examined by the court. As it is generally understood, the question in each case is whether the witness under-stands the obligations of the oath and has sufficient intelligence to give evi-dence. Age is considered along with the child's understanding of all the facts and circumstances of the case. It is often essential that the child have an under-standing of the obligation of an oath and the obligation to tell the truth. For these purposes, it is generally sufficient if the child knows it is wrong to lie and that lying will be punished. In this regard, it was significant in *State v. Green* (1976) that a child witness said he would be spanked if he lied.

The level of suggestibility of a witness is an important factor in determining competence. Of particular concern is the nature of certain kinds of evidence. For instance, sex offense cases are particularly difficult when they involve children or individuals with a mental disability. Recently, considerable attention has been paid to the subject of children as witnesses in sexual abuse cases. In some jurisdictions, legislation has specifically addressed the question of competency of children in such cases. For example, a Colorado statute provides: "The following persons shall not be witnesses: . . . (b) (I) Children under ten years of age who appear incapable of receiving just impressions of the facts respecting which they are examined or of relating them truly. (II) This proscription does not apply to a child under ten years of age, in any civil or criminal proceeding for child abuse, sexual abuse, sexual assault, or incest, when the child is able to describe or relate in language appropriate for a child of that age the events or facts respecting which the child is examined" (Colo. Stat., 1995). This statute was interpreted to render a child competent even though the child did not know the difference between telling the truth and lying (*People v. District Court*, 1990). In some jurisdictions in sex offense cases, corroboration of the minor's allegations is required as a matter of law (Margolick, 1984; Melton, 1981; see also Press, 1985; Renshaw, 1985).

The vast majority of the literature on suggestibility shows that young children (under age 7) are susceptible to an experimenter's suggestion and that resistance to suggestion increases with age (Yarmey, 1984). Under the law of evidence, the courts recognize that leading questions are undesirable; courts make an exception in the case of children, yet it is the child witness who is probably most easily misled by a suggestive question. Children are especially suggestible and compliant with parents and those adults whom they seek to please and protect. Thus, the child's suggestibility very much depends on the examiner. On cross-examination, attorneys ask questions that confuse the child; they confuse adults, too. Children tend to speak and think slowly, and the adult world gets impatient with them; they take longer to understand questions and to give answers. An adult may try to elicit a story that makes sense from one point of view. Children may have only one word for an object; they may not know the meaning of words such as penis, vagina, and anus. They may not have the same sense of time and chronology as adults, thus confusing lunch and dinner, for example.

In the judicial process, children are perceived as highly suggestible and susceptible to the influence of others and prone to fantasy (Cashmore & Bussey, 1996). By and large, judges and juries view the testimony of child witnesses with suspicion (Goodman, Golding, Helgeson, Haith, & Michelli, 1987). Over 60% of juries and over 80% of health professionals believe children are unreliable. Children fidget, their voices drop, they look down or away, and this can be interpreted as their not telling the truth or being less effective. For security, a child may hug a doll while testifying, and that action may impugn credibility (see Goodman & Michelli, 1981).

The competency of elderly witnesses has also been questioned. Research shows the elderly experience a decline in episodic memory (which affects specific events like what happened at yesterday's meeting) but not in implicit memory (which affects the large variety of mental activities that occur spontaneously, without having to make an intentional effort, like driving a car) or semantic memory (the overall store of information and experience people accumulate over a lifetime). The elderly also tend to suffer from source amnesia, when they know something but cannot remember when or where they learned it (Goleman, 1990).

COMPETENCY TO MAKE A WILL

A will or testament is a legal document describing a person's wishes regarding the disposition of his or her property upon the person's death. At the time of the making of the will, testator's must have "testamentary capacity," which means the capacity to understand and remember the nature and extent of their property, the persons who are the natural objects of their bounty, and the disposition that they desire to make of the property. It is not necessary that a person desiring to make a will have the capacity to make a contract and do business generally or to engage in complex and intricate business matters (*Petterson v. Imbsen*, 1923). A guardian may not make a will for a ward, but the fact that a guardian was appointed does not of itself invalidate a will for lack of testamentary capacity (*Matter of Lanning*, 1997).

Making a will actually requires only minimal competency, for it is an easy task. Moreover, whereas the terms of the disposition in the will are the testator's, the actual writing of the will is usually done by a lawyer. Though estate planning is complex, the formalities in making a will are simple. Even a considerable degree of eccentricity will not incapacitate a person in making a will. However, despite the language of courts upholding freedom of testation, the testamentary capacity concept has been used at times to undo the testamentary act in furthering society's interests in family maintenance. But generally speaking, a will is difficult to overturn.

Usually, the only way a disappointed heir can contest a will is on the grounds of a lack of testamentary capacity at the time of the making of the will or on the grounds that the testator was susceptible, because of mental condition, to undue influence or duress in the making of the will. These challenges most frequently focus on some sort of bodily disease or infirmity, alcohol or drug use, or cerebral arteriosclerosis. To establish either capacity or incapacity or undue influence, psychiatric testimony is usually presented. A presumption of undue influence arises when the beneficiary actively participated in the preparation and execution of the will and unduly profited from it (*In re Estate of Anders*, 1975).

A person who is addicted to drugs or liquor does not lack testamentary capacity if he or she is lucid or sober when the will is made. One who contests the will must establish that the influence of the drugs or liquor negated the "calm judgment" that the law requires. That is, the burden of proof is on the contestant of the will to establish that the testator was not lucid at the time of the making of the will. It is a heavy and difficult burden. Proof of addiction alone, for example, is not sufficient to carry the burden. The contestant must affirmatively show that the testator was intoxicated, affecting lucidity, at the time the will was made (an early case illustrating this point is *Elkinton v. Brick*, 1888).

Proof that the testator suffered from an insane delusion when making the will may also be enough to render the act invalid. An insane delusion is defined as a belief in things that do not exist and that no rational mind would believe to exist. The subject matter of the delusion must have no foundation in fact, be unable to be dispelled by reason, and be the product of mental disorder or the product or offspring of a delusion. Delusional religious beliefs are a common source of litigation but do not generally affect capacity unless the mind of the believer assumes a chronic delusional state that controls and dictates the conduct of the testamentary act. A belief in witchcraft is not necessarily conclusive on the issue of insanity (*Rice v. Henderson*, 1954).

The effect of a lack of testamentary capacity is to invalidate the entire will. In general, one part of the will cannot be rejected for lack of capacity while another part, written at the same time, is acceptable as the decedent's will.[2] However, in cases where a part of the will is affected by an insane delusion, there is a growing trend to strike out that particular provision if in doing so there is no effect on the other parts of the will that are not a result of the delusion.

A will expresses a relationship between an individual and the people he or she loves or hates. As one author put it, "Perhaps more than any other human document [wills] reflect the character of the writer and reveal his relationship with family, friends, and the world at large. His nature, his prejudice, his interests, his eccentricities, and the full range of man's virtues and vices can be found in the pages of wills" (Menchin, 1963). A lawyer in Washington, D.C., provided the proper levity to an otherwise mundane legacy:

> As for my debts, just and unjust,
> And to many creditors who did me trust,
> I hereby direct my executor to tell
> Them all kindly to go to hell.
> Then posthumously in court we will fight:
> For litigation is a lawyer's delight.

COMPETENCY TO CONTRACT

An individual is usually considered competent to contract if he or she understands the nature of the contract and its consequences. If the individual is actually incompetent at the time of entering into the contract but has not been declared legally incompetent, the contract is usually considered voidable rather than void. That is, the impaired individual has the option of affirming the contract, but if he or she wishes to nullify it, court action will be necessary. The interests of commerce dictate preserving the validity of contracts, but at the same time, society has a *parens patriae* interest in protecting the welfare of impaired individuals. In the case of contracting for basic necessities—shelter, clothes, food, and medical services—the policy of protecting the mentally incompetent is less critical than in other cases because there is usually a fair trade in these matters.

A consumer is allowed to be greedy, stupid, and gullible, but is protected from fraud. Customers are smarter than ever, but good judgment is often overcome by greed or gullibility. While looking for good buys at an antique show situated on the grounds of an old farm, one woman commented, "One hundred years ago, they used to milk cows here. Now they milk people." U.S. law enforcement officials report that letter scams from Nigeria rake in $250 million a year from Americans. The Nigeria letter scams hook victims by playing on their greed or gullibility. In such cases, the legal concept of vice of consent (error or fraud) rather than contractual incompetency may come into play.

An individual unable to handle personal affairs with some degree of prudence may be adjudicated incompetent. A guardian or conservator (usually a family member or an attorney) is thereupon appointed to handle the person's affairs. Because the percentage of the U.S. population 80 years or older has tripled since 1950, there are more cases of impaired capacity, notably due to Alzheimer's disease. In January 1996, at the urging of the elderly, a comprehensive competency law went into effect in California; the Due Process in Competence Determinations Act requires clear and convincing evidence of inability to appreciate the consequences of one's acts before appointing a conservator.

In some states, the determination of incompetency is a blanket incompetency ruling, which deprives the individual of any contractual capacity, including (theoretically) even buying groceries. In other states, a determination of incompetency may be limited, for example, to the managing of business affairs (Note, 1959; Slovenko, 1973; Weihofen, 1966). In the ordinary course of events, a merchant would find it awkward and time-consuming to go to the courthouse to check on the legal status of every contracting party. People do not wear badges indicating competency; hence, one contracts at a risk.

For centuries there have been calls to simplify language in commercial transactions as well as in the law generally. (Napoleon simplified the civil code to make it understandable.) However, the devotion to archaic language is rooted in a desire for well-settled meaning, and the use of seemingly redundant terms stems from a prudent effort to cover every contingency. The informed consent form used by physicians and hospitals in medical care likewise tends to be boilerplate. In recent years, there has been a crescendo of voices calling for plain and readable language. Some legislatures have enacted "plain English" laws calling for simple language in contractual forms in sales, mortgages, and leases.

COMPETENCY REGARDING MEDICAL CARE

In the ordinary course of medical practice, the physician discusses the illness and proposed treatment with the patient. The informed consent form is usually distributed by the nurse or administrator shortly before the procedure is to take place. Researchers have noted that these consent forms are written at a level too difficult for most people to understand (Mariner & McArdle, 1985). To protect the patient's right to make a voluntary and knowledgeable (informed) decision about treatment, the law imposes a correlative duty on the physician to disclose the relevant risks and benefits that the patient might be expected not to know. Actually, the informed consent document is designed to provide evidence of consent rather than to help a patient make a decision about treatment. In any event, the document as evidence may backfire under the theory that "if contracting parties write at all they must write it all because the law presumes they wrote it all if and when they write at all."

Medical care providers may act in the absence of express consent if (a) the patient is unable to give consent (because unconscious, intoxicated, mentally ill, incompetent); (b) there is a risk of serious bodily harm if treatment is delayed; (c) a reasonable person would consent to treatment under the circumstances; and (d) this patient would consent to treatment under the circumstances. In general, the courts have upheld the ability of a competent adult to refuse medical treatment, even if that care is deemed necessary to save or sustain life. The New York Court of Appeals upheld the termination of respiratory capabilities by a patient who previously, while competent, had manifested a desire not to be placed on a respirator. The rule is more sparingly applied in the case of incompetent patients, however. In a companion case, the court refused to terminate treatment of a patient who had never been competent (*Matter of Storar*, 1981).

The doctrine of substituted judgment is often used as a method by which the court makes a decision for the incompetent person. Originally, in the appointment of a guardian, the doctrine was used as a method for authorizing the disposition of an incompetent's property. Then it came to be employed in deciding whether to authorize withholding medical treatment for persons deemed incompetent. The goal of the doctrine is to make the decision that incompetent persons would make were they capable. It is often put in language that emphasizes the best interests of the person affected. For instance, sterilization proceedings may be included in some jurisdictions under the broad equity powers of probate courts to act for incompetent persons. The rationale is that all persons have a privacy right to choose to be sterilized, and incompetent persons must be afforded a means for making such a decision. In general, however, a guardian's decision as to what is in the person's best interests is granted only on a showing of clear and convincing evidence.

Decisions concerning euthanasia or the termination of life-support systems raise even more serious questions about competency. Can one ever be competent to make a decision about death? The New York cases draw a distinction between competent and incompetent decisions about death, although it is difficult to explain the difference. Ernest Becker wrote in his book *The Denial of Death* (1973) that "the idea of death, the fear of it, haunts the human animal like nothing else, it is a mainspring of human activity—activity designed largely to avoid the fatality of death, to overcome it by denying in some way that it is the final destiny of man" (see Haber, 1982). Becker's thesis is that under no condition can one make a rational decision about one's own death; rather, one is always in extremis, hence non compos mentis on this matter.

Because individuals in medical care are often exceedingly vulnerable and dependent, the informed consent document is regarded much like a contract of adhesion—one that is looked upon with a great deal of circumspection. An adhesion contract is a contract heavily restrictive of one party and nonrestrictive of another; because of the grave inequality of bargaining power, doubts arise as to its representation as a voluntary and uncoerced agreement.

Relationships between patients—in business parlance, consumers—and physicians are becoming increasingly depersonalized. Health maintenance organizations (HMOs) and managed care corporations pose ethical dilemmas where profit and the provision of quality medical care are often in conflict. Then too, the physician's integrity is compromised by gifts from pharmaceutical companies (Anstett, 1997).

The U.S. Supreme Court has ruled that decisionally incompetent individuals cannot consent to voluntary hospitalization, as this requires informed consent (*Zinermon v. Burch,* 1990). They must be admitted by way of an involuntary commitment that affords them the procedural safeguards set out in the mental health code (Winick, 1997). In *Kennedy v. Schafer* (1995), the Eighth Circuit Court of Appeals considered whether the state's failure to supervise the patient adequately to protect her from harming herself amounted to a deprivation of her constitutional rights. Although the Fourteenth Amendment does not generally impose a duty on a state to protect its citizens, the state may incur an affirmative obligation to provide safe and humane conditions of confinement when it assumes custodial control over the care of an individual such as a prisoner or an involuntarily committed mentally ill or retarded patient. Because the individual in this case was voluntarily admitted to the state facility by her parents, the court held that she was not entitled to the same due process right to a safe and humane environment as would a patient under the same circumstances who had been involuntarily committed to the facility.

Involuntary commitment to a mental hospital of itself is neither a determination of incompetency nor a deprivation of civil or political rights. Hence, the status of a mental patient is or—should be—the same as that of any individual, and he or she should have all the rights listed in the mental patient's bill of rights without their enumeration. Identification of commitment with incompetency proceedings, which is still sometimes done in some jurisdictions, stems from the time when commitment spelled the end of an individual's contact with the outside world. The prevailing view today is that commitment, even without a competency hearing, entitles the hospital to use non-intrusive therapies in the case of a non-consenting patient.

COMPETENCY OF A MINOR TO CONSENT TO TREATMENT

Minors (typically under age 18) are not considered legally competent to act on their own. The consent, express or implied, of a parent or guardian is necessary to authorize treatment or services. Absent that consent, treatment in law regardless of the outcome constitutes a battery (if there is physical contact) or possibly negligence. To this general rule, however, there are a number of exceptions: (a) *parens patriae,* (b) emergencies, (c) emancipated minors, (d) mature minors, and (e) certain types of care.

The state, as *parens patriae* (father of the people), may protect the best interests of a minor in the face of parental refusal to consent to treatment deemed necessary to preserve the life or health of the minor. Under this authority, for example, the state can compel vaccination or fluoridation. And the state may override parental consent. Even with parental consent, sterilization or transplantation involving a minor is a procedure fraught with legal hazards, so court authorization is required or at least warranted (as in *Hart v. Brown*, 1972). Some states by legislation forbid a minor under 18 from getting a tattoo with or without parental permission. When a parent refuses on religious or other grounds to provide medical treatment for a child, courts are likely to grant an application to overrule the parent if the treatment is life threatening (*In re Sampson*, 1992), but not if it will only improve the child's comfort or appearance (*In re Green*, 1972). In the case of mental health hospitalization, the responsibility for the care and treatment of the patient becomes invested in the hospital or court, so a parent has no right of access to the minor's records (*In re J.C.G.*, 1976).

In an emergency where delay would produce serious risks for the minor, a physician may proceed with treatment without awaiting parental consent. Consent is implied from the emergency, defined as "a situation wherein, in competent medical judgment, the proposed surgical or medical treatment or procedures are immediately or imminently necessary and any delay occasioned by an attempt to obtain a consent would reasonably jeopardize the life, health or limb of the person affected, or would reasonably result in disfigurement or impairment of faculties" (Mo. Stat.). When the question arises, the courts give a broad interpretation to emergency. Thus, the treatment of a fracture was deemed an emergency, though it was not life-saving but done to stop pain and suffering (*Greenspan v. Slate*, 1953; *Sullivan v. Montgomery*, 1935). The Michigan Supreme Court (*Luka v. Lowrie*, 1912) had this to say about implied consent in emergency situations:

> The fact that surgeons are called upon daily, in all our large cities, to operate instantly in emergency cases in order that life may be preserved, should be considered. Many small children are injured upon the streets in large cities. To hold that a surgeon must wait until perhaps he may be able to secure the consent of the parents before giving to the injured one the benefit of his skill and learning, to the end that life may be preserved, would, we believe, result in the loss of many lives which might otherwise be saved. It is not to be presumed that competent surgeons will want only to operate, nor that they will fail to obtain the consent of parents to operations where such consent may be reasonably obtained in view of the exigency. Their work, however, is highly humane and very largely charitable in character, and no rule should be announced which would tend in the slightest degree to deprive sufferers of the benefit of their services.

An emancipated minor—a minor who is legally free from the care, custody, and control of his or her parents—may give a legally valid consent. By dint of certain legislation, pregnancy amounts to emancipation. Alabama's statute, for example, provides: "Any minor who is married, or having been married is divorced, or has borne a child may give effective consent to any legally authorized medical, dental, health or mental health services for himself, his child or for herself or her child" (Ala. Code, 1973).

Under the mature minor doctrine, a minor is permitted to consent to medical treatment if he or she is sufficiently mature to understand the nature of the procedure and its consequences and the alternatives to that treatment. But maturity is a matter of dispute. It is a behavioral test. One pediatrician suggested that any child who could get to the doctor's Greenwich Village office by subway from the Bronx was, in her eyes, an adult. The mature minor doctrine has found application in cases where the minor is at least 15 years of age, the treatment is for the benefit of the minor, and the procedure is something less than major or serious in nature. There is apparently only one case (*Bonner v. Moran*, 1941) where liability has been imposed on a doctor for treating a minor without parental consent. The operation in this case, however, was not for the benefit of the minor, a 15-year-old, but rather was a transplant operation for the benefit of a cousin (consent was by an aunt), yet the case has been cited or relied upon in discussions of the need for parental consent in every situation.

In recent years, ad hoc exceptions (characterized as "general medical emancipation" statutes) have been made to parents' authority to consent, usually to help deal with problems that have high social costs, such as venereal disease, drug or alcohol abuse, contraception, and pregnancy. Underlying psychodynamics may be identical among individuals showing different symptoms or behavior, but it is only the named symptom or behavior that opens the door to care or treatment without parental consent. Some states set a minimum age for consent in these treatments or procedures. Many people—for example, Eunice Kennedy Shriver ("Sex Values," 1981), who suggested that programs involving parents in their children's lives are more worthy of support than those that isolate them—argue that such services should not be provided without parental consent, notice, or consultation. In any event, a number of state statutes authorize minors to receive mental health treatment without parental consent. For example, an Illinois statute provides: "Any minor fourteen years of age or older may request and receive counseling services or psychotherapy on an outpatient basis. The consent of the parent, guardian, or person in loco parentis shall not be necessary to authorize outpatient counseling or psychotherapy" (Ill. Stat.).

The majority of states have enacted statutes permitting minors to consent without parental notice or consultation to receive treatment for venereal disease and drug or alcohol abuse, and to seek and receive counseling on and devices for contraception. In *Carey v. Populations Services* (1977), the Supreme Court upheld the right of minors to obtain contraceptives without parental consent. In the wake of that decision, the Sixth Circuit Court of Appeals in *Doe v. Irwin* (1980) ruled that contraceptives may be provided to minors also without the knowledge of their parents. A number of state statutes specifically provide that records concerning the treatment of a minor for venereal disease or the performance of an abortion shall not be released or in any manner be made available to the parent (N.Y. Public Health Law, 1977). However, in the event the minor is using a family insurance plan to pay for service, the parents may learn about it when they receive a benefit report from the insurer.

As a tangential observation, it may be noted that the Georgia Supreme Court ruled the state's seduction statute unconstitutional; the statute gave the parent of a daughter a cause of action against anyone who seduced the daughter. The court said the statute was outmoded, harking back to the time when parents "had property interests in the bodies of their children" (*Franklin v. Hill*, 1994).

The U.S. Supreme Court in 1976 in *Planned Parenthood of Missouri v. Danforth* ruled that a parent may not veto a minor's decision to have an abortion, but the Court went on to say, "We emphasize that our holding . . . does not suggest every minor, regardless of age or maturity, may give effective consent for termination of her pregnancy." This language might imply that immature or incompetent minors are required to obtain parental consent to abortion, even in the first trimester, just as they must for any other procedure. That issue came to the Supreme Court in 1979 in *Bellotti v. Baird*. In that case, the Court said that every minor has the right to go directly to a court without consulting her parents. Justice Powell said, "A pregnant minor is entitled in such a proceeding to show either: (1) that she is mature enough, well enough informed to make her abortion decision, in consultation with her physician, independently of her parents' wishes; or (2) that even if she is not able to make this decision independently, the desired abortion would be in her best interests."

In many contexts, the scope and application of a state constitutional right of privacy may be broader and more protective of privacy than the federal constitutional right of privacy as interpreted by the federal courts. After nearly a decade of legal battles and a crucial change in court membership, the California Supreme Court in 1997 struck down as a violation of privacy a law that would have required an unmarried minor either to obtain consent from one parent for an abortion or, as an alternative, to persuade a judge, in a confidential hearing, that she was mature enough to make the decision or that an abortion was in her best interests. The court said:

> [T]he statute denies a pregnant minor, who believes it is in her best interest to terminate her pregnancy rather than have a child at such a young age, control over her own destiny. In addition, the statutory requirement that the minor obtain parental consent or judicial authorization will delay the minor's access to a medically safe abortion in many instances, and thereby will increase, at least to some extent, the health risks posed by an abortion. Finally, in some instances, a minor who does not wish to continue her pregnancy but who is too frightened to tell her parents about her condition or go to court may be led by the statutory restrictions to attempt to terminate the pregnancy herself or seek a "back-alley abortion"— courses of conduct that in the past have produced truly tragic results—or, alternatively, to postpone action until it is too late to terminate her pregnancy, leaving her no choice but to bear an unwanted child. Of course, such consequences unquestionably would represent a most significant intrusion on the minor's protected privacy interest. (*American Academy of Pediatrics v. Lungren,* 1997)

The question has been raised whether a state may impose a requirement of parental notice (as opposed to consent or consultation) as a condition of a minor's receiving an abortion. Given notice, parents may be supportive and may dissuade their minor from having an abortion. Justice Stevens in *Bellotti* remarked in a footnote: "[Our previous decisions do not determine] the constitutionality of a statute which does no more than require notice to the parents, without affording them or any other third party an absolute veto." Two years later, in 1981, in *H. L. v. Matheson*, the Supreme Court by a 6–3 vote upheld a Utah parental notification law. The Court said: "A statute setting out a 'mere requirement of parental notice' does not violate the constitutional rights of an immature, dependent minor. The Utah statute gives neither parents nor judges a veto power over the minor's abortion decision." The Supreme Court's decision does not make parental notification mandatory nationwide but leaves it up to each state to decide whether to impose the requirement.

As a matter of practice, the procedure set out by the Court in *Bellotti* has been and continues to be ignored. Abortion clinics around the country are carrying out abortions on minors just as they are on adults. No path is beaten to the courthouse door for a determination of maturity or best interests. Should there be complications, however, the minor will usually find that a hospital will not admit her without parental consent. Emergency care in a clearly life-saving situation may be available, but even then the hospital (while administering such care) will as a matter of practice attempt to contact a parent or guardian.

What actually is the hazard in treating a minor without parental consent? In general, physicians and other therapists appear to be overly fearful in the care and treatment of minors, leading quite often to tragic results. Although the law defines an emergency broadly, many physicians and hospitals define it very narrowly. One publicized case (Ramos, 1981) involved a minor who split his lip and was spurting blood, but the doctor in the emergency room refused to suture it without parental consent. In actual fact, there has not been a reported case in any state since the aforementioned 1941 transplant case in which a physician or health facility has been held liable for treating a minor over age 15 without parental consent (Pilpel, 1972).

Parental consent is no insulation against liability in the case of faulty treatment. Consent protects from a charge of battery, but not from negligence or malpractice. In a case where the treatment measures up to acceptable standards of care but there is no parental consent or applicable exception, the parents may claim that their expenses for the support and maintenance of their child were increased by an unfavorable result of the treatment, but that is not likely.

CONCLUSION

In law, competency depends on the context and is defined in relation to a particular act: writing a will, entering into a contract, or testifying in court. Even then, it depends on the nature of the will or contract or type of case. Rarely is a person totally incompetent to carry out any type of act. Incompetency may be the symptom of an illness and, like other symptoms, may respond to treatment.

NOTES

1. "Validity and Application of Regulation Requiring Suspension of Disbarment of Attorney Because of Mental or Emotional Illness," 50 A.L.R.3d 1259.

2. "Partial Invalidity of a Will," 64 A.L.R.3d 261.

REFERENCES

Ala. Code title 22, §104 (16)(Supp. 1973).

Alexander, C. P. (1985, August 5). GM picks the winner. *Time*, p. 42.

American Academy of Pediatrics v. Lungren, 66 Cal. Rptr.2d 210, 940 P.2d 797 (1997).

Anstett, P. (1997, August 19). Prescription for trouble. *Detroit Free Press*, p. 6-F.

Bazelon, D. (1973). The defective assistance of counsel. *University of Cincinnati Law Review, 42*, 1.

Becker, E. (1973). *The denial of death.* New York: Free Press.

Bellotti v. Baird, 428 U.S. 132 (1979).

Bonner v. Moran, 75 U.S. App. D.C. 156, 126 F.2d 121 (1941).

Carey v. Population Services International, 431 U.S. 678 (1977).

Cashmore, J., & Bussey, K. (1996). Judicial perceptions of child witness competence. *Law and Human Behavior, 20,* 313.

Colo. Stat. §13-90-106 (1995).

Coombs, R. H. (1997). *Drug-impaired professionals.* Cambridge, MA: Harvard University Press.

Doe v. Irwin, 615 F.2d 1162 (6th Cir. 1980).

Elkinton v. Brick, 44 N.J. Eq. 154, 15 Atl. 391 (1888).

Franklin v. Hill, 264 Ga. 302, 444 S.E.2d 778 (1994).

Glass, K. C. (1997). Redefining definitions and devising instruments: Two decades of assessing mental competence. *International Journal of Law and Psychiatry, 20,* 5.

Goleman, D. (1990, March 27). Studies offer fresh clues to memory. *New York Times,* p. C-1.

Goodman, G. S., Golding, J. M., Helgeson, V. S., Haith, M. M., & Michelli, J. (1987). When a child takes the stand/jurors' perceptions of children's eyewitness testimony. *Law and Human Behavior, 11,* 27.

Goodman, G. S., & Michelli, J. A. (1981, November). Would you believe a child witness? *Psychology Today,* p. 82.

Greenspan v. Slate, 12 N.J. 426, 97 A.2d 390 (1953).

Haber, H. G. (1982). In re *Storar:* Euthanasia for incompetent patients, a proposed model. *Pace Law Review, 3,* 351.

Hart v. Brown, 29 Conn. Sup. 368, 289 A.2d 386 (1972).

Hidding v. Williams, 578 So.2d 1192 (La. App. 1991).

H. L. v. Matheson, 450 U.S. 398 (1981).

Ill. Stat. ch. 91 1/2, §3-5016(a).

In re Estate of Anders, 226 N.W.2d 170 (S.D. 1975).

In re Green, 448 Pa. 338, 292 A.2d 387 (1972).

In re J.C.G., 144 N.J. Super. 579, 366 A.2d 733 (1976).

In re Lanning, 565 N.W.2d 794 (S.D. 1997).

In re McElroy (1978), 93 D.L.R. (3d) 522.

In re Sampson, 29 N.Y.2d 900, 328 N.Y.S.2d 686, 278 N.E.2d 918 (1972).

In re Storar, 52 N.Y.2d 363, 420 N.E.2d 64, 438 N.Y.S.2d 266 (1981).

Kennedy v. Schafer, 71 F.3d 292 (8th Cir. 1995).

Loftus, E., & Davies, G. M. (1984). Distortions in the memory of children. *Journal of Social Issues, 40,* 51.

Luka v. Lowrie, 171 Mich. 122, 136 N.W. 1106 (1912).

Margolick, D. (1984, September 22). The corroboration requirement in prosecuting sexual abuse. *New York Times,* p. 13.

Mariner, W. K., & McArdle, P. A. (1985). Consent forms, readability, and comprehension: The need for new assessment tools. *Law, Medicine and Health Care, 13,* 68.

McMann v. Richardson, 397 U.S. 759 (1970).

Melton, G. B. (1981). Children's competency to testify. *Law and Human Behavior, 5,* 73.

Menchin, R. S. (1963). *The last caprice.* New York: Simon & Schuster.

Mo. Stat. title 28, sec. 431,063.

Myers, J. E. B. (1993). The competence of young children to testify in legal proceedings. *Behavioral Sciences and the Law, 11,* 121.

N.Y. Public Health Law ch. 763 (McKinney 1977).

Note. (1959). Mental illness and the law of contracts. *Michigan Law Review, 57,* 1020.

People v. District Court, 791 P.2d 682 (Colo. 1990).

Peter, L. J. (1972). *The Peter prescription.* New York: Morrow.

Peter, L. J., & Hull, R. (1969). *The Peter principle.* New York: Morrow.

Petterson v. Imbsen, 46 S.D. 540, 194 N.W. 842 (1923).

Pilpel, H. (1972). Minor's rights to medical care. *Albany Law Review, 36,* 462.

Planned Parenthood of Missouri v. Danforth, 428 U.S. 52 (1976).

Press, A. (1985, February 18). The youngest witness: Is there a "witch hunt" mentality in sex-abuse cases? *Newsweek,* p. 72.

Ramos, S. (1981, January 22). Insuring medical aid if parents are away. *New York Times,* p. 15.

Renshaw, D. C. (1985, July). When sex abuse is falsely charged. *Medical Aspects of Human Sexuality,* p. 116.

Rice v. Henderson, 140 W. Va. 284, 83 S.E.2d 762 (1954).

Rule 601, Federal Rules of Evidence.

Sex values for teens. (1981, March 1). *New York Times,* p. E-21.

Slovenko, R. (1973). *Psychiatry and law.* Boston: Little, Brown.

Slovenko, R. (1994). Informed consent: Information about the doctor. *International Journal of Medicine & Law, 13,* 467.

Slovenko, R. (1995). *Psychiatry and criminal culpability.* New York: Wiley.

State v. Green, 267 S.C. 599, 230 S.E.2d 618 (1976).

Stepakoff v. Kantar, 393 Mass. 836, 473 N.E.2d 1131 (1985).

Strickland v. Washington, 104 S. Ct. 2052 (1984).

Sullivan v. Montgomery, 155 Misc. 418, 279 N.Y.S. 575 (1935).

Survey. (1997, July 3). Lawyers find children can make very difficult witnesses. *Detroit Legal News,* p. 1.

United States v. Gutman, 725 F.2d 417 at 420 (7th Cir. 1984).

United States v. Lightly, 677 F.2d 1027 (4th Cir. 1982).

United States v. Odom, 736 F.2d 104 (4th Cir. 1984).

Weihofen, H. (1966). Mental incompetence to contract or convey. *Southern California Law Review, 39,* 211.

Wheeler v. United States, 159 U.S. 523 (1895).

Wigmore, J. (1979). *Evidence* (Rev. ed.). Boston: Little, Brown.

Winick, B. J. (1997). *The right to refuse mental health treatment.* Washington, DC: American Psychological Association.

Yarmey, A. D. (1984). Age as a factor in eyewitness memory. In G. L. Wells & E. F. Loftus (Eds.), *Eyewitness testimony/psychological perspectives* (p. 142). New York: Cambridge University Press.

Zinermon v. Burch, 494 U.S. 113 (1990).

PART THREE

APPLYING PSYCHOLOGY TO CRIMINAL PROCEEDINGS

CHAPTER 8

Dangerousness Risk Assessments: Research, Legal, and Clinical Considerations

THOMAS R. LITWACK and LOUIS B. SCHLESINGER

IN A variety of contexts, our legal system allows and even calls for assessments of the "dangerousness" of certain individuals—that is, assessments of the probability, or *risk*, that those individuals will cause certain types of harm under particular conditions within varying periods of time (*Schall v. Martin*, 1984; Shah, 1978). Such assessments can significantly affect the lives of those individuals (*Barefoot v. Estelle*, 1983; *United States v. Salerno*, 1987) and, if a serious proclivity toward violence goes undetected, very possibly other individuals—that is, potential victims—as well (Monahan, 1993; Schlesinger, 1996, p. 314). Mental health professionals are often called upon, and may even be obliged, to participate in these decisions (*Addington v. Texas*, 1979; *Tarasoff v. Regents of the University of California*, 1976). As Borum (1996) has recently observed: "The assessment and the management of violence risk are critical issues, not just for psychologists and psychiatrists in forensic settings but for all practicing clinicians. Despite a long-standing controversy about the ability of mental health professionals to predict violence, the courts continue to rely on them for advice on these issues and in many cases have imposed on them a legal duty to take action when they know or should know that a patient poses a risk of serious danger to others" (p. 954).

This chapter addresses, primarily, assessments of dangerousness concerning mentally disordered individuals possibly at risk for violence in the community.

The authors wish to thank Alexander Brooks, Steve Hart, Dale McNiel, and Renate Wack for their helpful comments regarding earlier drafts of this chapter. The authors would also like to thank Randy Borum, Steve Hart, Dale McNiel, John Monahan, Ed Mulvey, Marnie Rice, Richard Rogers, Jeffrey Swanson, Randall Salekin, and Chris Webster for generously providing articles, materials, information, and insights that were very useful in the preparation of this chapter.

First, we review the most prominent research published through 1997 regarding such assessments. Then we survey some recent developments in the law that bear upon determining when individuals may legally be deprived of their liberty based upon assessments of dangerousness. Finally, we consider some of the primary factors and procedures that leading forensic clinicians, and our own experience, suggest should be a part of proper and comprehensive clinical assessments of dangerousness.

THE RESEARCH

Introduction

The first comprehensive review of the research literature regarding assessments of dangerousness was Monahan's *Predicting Violent Behavior: An Assessment of Clinical Techniques,* which appeared in 1981. (An earlier review by Dix, 1980, was also quite useful.) Monahan updated his 1981 review in another prominent article published in 1984 (see also Wettstein, 1984). We (Litwack & Schlesinger, 1987) reviewed the research literature through 1985 for the first edition of this volume and arrived at conclusions somewhat different from Monahan's. Some years later, Litwack, Kirschner, and Wack (1993) reviewed the relevant studies published during 1985–1990 and concluded, echoing both Monahan and Litwack and Schlesinger, that "research . . . had *not* negated the possibility that clinical evaluations of dangerousness *can* have a unique and useful role to play in making determinations of dangerousness that our society has decided should be made" (p. 269).

Readers are referred to these works for more complete reviews of the research literature prior to 1990 than space allows for here. In addition, since 1990 there have been fairly extensive reviews of the research literature by Borum (1996), Brooks (1992), Monahan (1996, 1997), Monahan and Steadman (1994), Otto (1992, 1994), Bjørkly (1995), and Mossman (1994a). (Regarding Otto's 1992 review, see also Hart, Webster, & Menzies, 1993, and Mossman, 1994b.)

We nevertheless review certain earlier signal studies because of their continuing notoriety and because they illustrate important points regarding studies of assessments of dangerousness in general. Then we review three major research studies published in recent years, and one study, the MacArthur Violence Risk Assessment Study (Steadman et al., 1994), that is ongoing, to evaluate the current state of research concerning assessments of dangerousness. First, however, a historical overview may be in order.

It has often been asserted, most notably by Supreme Court Justice Harry Blackmun and two concurring Justices in their dissenting opinion in the case of *Barefoot v. Estelle* (1983), that research has shown that predictions of violence by mental health professionals are wrong at least two times out of three. Even more negative statements about the validity and legitimacy of such predictions have characterized academic and professional discussions of the issue. Indeed, as will be seen shortly, there have been prominent statements to the effect that mental health professionals have no ability whatsoever to assess future dangerousness.

We briefly review some of these assertions before going on to explain that: (a) despite advances in research methodology, it remains the case that "we know very little about how accurately violent behavior can be predicted in many circumstances" (Monahan, 1981, p. 37); (b) given this lack of knowledge, it has certainly *not* been demonstrated that "predictions of violence" by mental health professionals are wrong at least two times out of three (or that mental health professionals have no ability to predict future violence); (c) in any event, the test for clinicians should not be how well they can "predict" violence but, rather, how well they can assess the *risk* of engaging in violent behavior that a patient poses; (d) although actuarially based risk assessment schemes or findings should certainly be consulted when they are relevant and available (and cost-effective to use), often such assistance will *not* exist when dangerousness assessments are called for; and (e) in any event, there are good reasons to believe (even if it has not yet been demonstrated) that knowledgable clinicians can often make important, unique, and even crucial contributions to many assessments of dangerousness.

Monahan, in his 1981 monograph, provided a good overview of the distinctions, and commonalities, between actuarial and clinical approaches to assessment (pp. 95–128). We define the distinction as follows: "Actuarial" risk assessments are based on *previously demonstrated and validated associations* between various specified, well-defined, and measurable predictor variables (e.g., age and history of arrests) and the probability that certain types of individuals (e.g., released mentally disordered offenders) will commit a certain type of harmful behavior (e.g., serious violence against others) in certain circumstances (e.g., in the community) within a certain time frame (e.g., within the next two years). That is, an actuarial assessment of dangerousness is an assessment of the probability of occurrence of a certain type of violent behavior by a certain type of individual in certain circumstances within a certain time frame that has been arrived at by determining the relationships that have existed in the past between certain individual and/or situational characteristics (regarding similar individuals) and violence. "Clinical" risk assessments may take into account the same, or similar, "predictive" data (e.g., age and history of arrests), but clinical assessors arrive at conclusions primarily through reasoning (hopefully, logical reasoning) regarding the data rather than by applying mechanical formulas; and clinical assessors may and do take into account whatever available (or obtainable) data they deem relevant to their assessment, including data that can only be obtained through clinical methods (e.g., a patient's fantasies or level of insight regarding the causes of past transgressions). Thus, although clinicians undoubtedly vary in their knowledge of which factors to consider when evaluating dangerousness, and in their ability to properly assess and weigh those factors, we do not accept the notion, suggested by others (e.g., Grove & Meehl, 1996), that clinical judgments are merely "subjective" or "impressionistic."

Historical Viewpoints

In one of the first reviews of the then existing research literature, Dershowitz (1969) concluded that "for every correct psychiatric prediction of violence there are numerous erroneous predictions. That is, among *every group* of inmates presently confined on the basis of psychiatric predictions of violence, there are *only a few* who would . . . actually engage in violence if released" (p. 47; emphasis added). Not long after, the editors of the *Harvard Law Review* went so far as to conclude that "The difficulty of predicting the type and severity of an individual's anticipated antisocial conduct creates grave doubts as to the constitutional validity and the wisdom of present statutes authorizing police power commitments" ("Developments in the Law," 1974, p. 1245).

Similar conclusions were echoed by a task force of the American Psychological Association (1978) that proposed: "It does appear from reading the research that the validity of psychological predictions of dangerous behavior, at least in the sentencing and release situation . . . , is extremely poor, so poor that one could oppose their use on the strictly empirical grounds that psychologists are not professionally competent to make such judgements" (p. 1110). In 1974, a task force of the American Psychiatric Association determined that "the state of the art regarding predictions of violence is very unsatisfactory. The ability of psychiatrists or/and other professionals to reliably predict future violence is unproved" (p. 30). And, in the same year, a widely cited law review article that reviewed the relevant literature stated that "psychiatrists cannot tell us which persons are potentially dangerous" (Ennis & Litwack, 1974, p. 749).

Even more dramatically, based on their own studies, two of the most prominent researchers in the field, Cocozza and Steadman (1978), concluded that "*no* [psychiatric] expertise [to predict dangerous behavior] exists and . . . the attempt to apply this supposed knowledge to predict who will be dangerous results in *complete failure*" (p. 274; emphasis added). Indeed, Megargee (1981), another leading observer of the field at the time, went so far as to say that the "identification of the potentially violent individual with sufficient accuracy to warrant preventative detention . . . is an *impossible* quest" (p. 181; emphasis added).

Questions about such negative conclusions concerning professional assessments of dangerousness began to arise when Monahan (1981) advocated a more open-minded stance: "Empirically, it is much less clear to me now than it once was that relatively accurate prediction is impossible under all circumstances. . . . [M]ost existing research in this area leaves something to be desired. . . . I believe a more judicious assessment of the research to date is that *we know very little about how accurately violent behavior may be predicted under many circumstances*" (p. 37). Nevertheless, in 1984, Monahan still maintained that studies had "demonstrated that clinical predictions of violent behavior among institutionalized mentally disordered people are accurate at best one-third of the time" and that "more studies concluding that psychiatrists and psychologists are relatively inaccurate clinical predictors of whether mentally disordered offenders who have been institutionalized for lengthy periods of time will offend once more are not needed. There are so many nails now in that coffin that I propose we declare the issue officially dead" (p. 13). And as recently as 1993 (April 6, p. C1), *The New York Times* featured a report of a newly published, prominent study of assessments of dangerousness by mental health professionals under the headline "Who Will Turn Violent? Hospitals Have to *Guess*" (emphasis added).

That study (Lidz, Mulvey, & Gardner, 1993; to be discussed in detail below) it-self concluded that, though "clinical judgment has been undervalued in previous research," nevertheless, "clinicians are relatively inaccurate predictors of vio-lence" (p. 1010). Still, this study did provide evidence that clinicians did signifi-cantly better than chance in assessing dangerousness. Taken together with Otto's 1992 review of earlier studies, which concluded that such studies demon-strated that "mental health professionals have some ability to predict dangerous behavior" (p. 127), many statements can now be found in the literature that are far more positive and optimistic about the ability of mental health professionals to assess dangerousness—at least when aided by actuarial instruments—than was formerly the case. For example, in 1994, Webster, Harris, Rice, Cormier, and Quinsey proposed a comprehensive system for assessing dangerousness regard-ing mentally disordered offenders which relies on both actuarial and clinical data ("The Violence Prediction Scheme"); and they concluded the presentation of their system with the observation that "[t]here is every reason to suppose that, collectively, we can become increasingly adept at isolating the absence and pres-ence of risk and of attenuating serious violence of the kind that arises in con-junction with mental disorder" (p. 66). Even more recent volumes (Campbell, 1995a, 1995b; Webster & Jackson, 1997) have confidently proposed guidelines for assessing the risk of spousal assault, sexual violence, and violence in general. In-deed, as we shall see, although clinicians can take heart at the newfound (if still somewhat grudging) respect within the research community for clinical insights and methods, the ideological pendulum may now have swung too far in the di-rection of *overestimating* the *proven* utility of actuarial instruments, and even clinical judgments, in assessing dangerousness.

EARLIER INFLUENTIAL STUDIES

Kozol, Boucher, and Garofalo (1972)

The most widely cited study for the often stated proposition that predictions of violence by mental health professionals are wrong at least two times out of three, even when based on a known history of violence and extensive clinical examinations, is a study by Kozol, Boucher, and Garofalo (1972). A close ex-amination of this study reveals, however, that it does *not* justify any such conclusion. Rather, this study illustrates how cautious one should be before drawing firm conclusions from most, if not all, studies of assessments of dangerousness.

From clinical examinations, extensive life histories, and psychological tests, a team of mental health professionals evaluated 592 males convicted of as-saultive offenses (usually sexual in nature) and sentenced to a special facility for continued evaluation and treatment. Of these men, 386 were eventually di-agnosed as *not* dangerous by the evaluating team and eventually released. In addition, 49 men diagnosed as still dangerous were also released by judicial or parole authorities *against the advice* of the professional staff.

The released individuals were followed up in the community. At the end of the follow-up period of up to five years, 8% of the patients considered by the evaluating teams to be *nondangerous* were found to have committed a serious assaultive crime. By contrast, 34.7% of the patients viewed as dangerous by clinicians, but nevertheless released, were discovered to have committed a serious crime.

On the surface, the clinicians studied here did appear to do much better than chance in their evaluations because the recidivism rate of offender patients released against the advice of the evaluating teams was much higher than the recidivism rate of patients evaluated to be no longer dangerous. However, it appears from the report that the evaluees deemed dangerous but nevertheless released were, on average, at risk for recidivism in the community for a significantly longer period than those released after clinical judgments of nondangerousness. Thus, it cannot be definitively concluded from this study that the clinicians at issue demonstrated at least *some* unique ability to assess dangerousness. But, for the reasons that follow, neither can it be legitimately concluded from this study that "predictions of violence" by mental health professionals are wrong at least two-thirds of the time.

To begin with, Kozol, Boucher, and Garofalo reported subsequently (1973) that at least 14 of their 49 patients diagnosed as dangerous and yet released were patients who had been committed and studied during the early years of their program and who would *not* have been diagnosed as dangerous in the latter years of their study (when, presumably, diagnostic techniques and judgments were more refined). Thus, Kozol et al. may eventually have developed a diagnostic system that was able to predict, with at least 50% accuracy, which of their sample of patients would be dangerous if released.

Second, the recidivism rate reported by Kozol et al. (1972, 1973) for the patients deemed dangerous—be it 35% or 50%—may have been far less than the actual recidivism rate. Hall (1982) has pointed out that there is good reason to believe that only 20% of serious crimes lead to an arrest. Thus, many seeming false positives (especially among individuals with a history of serious violence) may, in fact, be undiscovered true positives.

Third, and very important, the 49 patients released despite clinical judgments of dangerousness were *not a representative sample* of patients judged to be dangerous by the clinicians in this study, much less of other samples of seemingly dangerous individuals. Because these 49 individuals were released by judicial or parole authorities *against professional advice,* they were almost certainly "borderline" patients—in terms of their dangerousness—who presented much evidence of being no longer dangerous (despite some evidence to the contrary). Why else would they have been released? Presumably, therefore, if the far larger number of patients diagnosed as dangerous by the teams and *not* released *had been* released, their rate of recidivism—and the apparent accuracy of the clinical assessments of dangerousness—might have been far higher than it appeared to be for the "borderline" patients. Thus, this study simply does *not* demonstrate that "predictions of violence" by mental health professionals are likely to be wrong two-thirds of the time regardless of the sample of individuals being evaluated (Litwack, 1996; Litwack et al., 1993, pp. 251–252), the circumstances involved, or the confidence of the evaluators in their judgments (McNiel, Sandberg, & Binder, 1997).

Finally—and this is a crucial point—the judgments of dangerousness at issue in this study, *like most judgments of dangerousness,* were never "predictions of violence" to begin with. The patients supposedly "predicted" to be violent were actually, and more conservatively, simply *"not recommended* for release" (p. 390)—and clinical concerns regarding a patient's potential dangerousness that lead to a conclusion that the patient cannot be recommended for release do not equate with a "prediction" that a patient will definitely be violent if released (Mulvey & Lidz, 1995). That is, a clinical judgment that a patient is "dangerous"—even a judgment that an individual is sufficiently dangerous to warrant confinement—is rarely, if ever, a prediction that a patient unquestionably *will* be violent if at liberty or, at least, if unsupervised. Rather, almost always, it is (only) a judgment that the assessee poses a *significant* risk of acting violently in certain circumstances (though perhaps a sufficiently serious risk of causing sufficiently serious harm to warrant preventive detention or some other preventive action).

Indeed, in forensic settings, patients with histories of *serious* violence may well be deemed still "dangerous" by clinicians *and judges* if it is merely *questionable* whether or not they would again be seriously violent if released (Litwack, 1996, pp. 108–115; Litwack et al., 1993, pp. 262–265). Thus, if a patient deemed by a clinician to be too dangerous to be recommended for release is nevertheless released and does not recidivate, it is simply incorrect to conclude that the clinician made a prediction that turned out to be wrong. To the contrary, although the clinician may have concluded that the patient posed too great a risk of causing serious harm to *recommend* the patient for release, the clinician may also have concluded that the patient might well not recidivate.

The Baxstrom and Dixon Studies

The Baxstrom studies (Steadman & Cocozza, 1974) and the similar Dixon study (Thornberry & Jacoby, 1979) concerned hundreds of individuals (usually convicted offenders) confined for many years in hospitals for the "criminally insane" because, supposedly, they were considered to be too dangerous to be released to civil mental hospitals, much less to the community. Yet, as a result of judicial decisions, these patients were nevertheless transferred to civil hospitals. Follow-up studies determined that only a small percentage of these supposedly dangerous individuals had to be returned to secure facilities from civil facilities, and that only a small minority of patients ultimately released to the community were rearrested for violent offenses. (The great majority of the Baxstrom patients, many of whom were quite elderly, did require continued confinement in civil facilities. Of the 65% of Thornberry and Jacoby's sample who were ultimately discharged, 11% were rearrested for violent offenses.)

The findings of these studies indicate that in the not very distant past many mentally ill individuals have been needlessly and wrongfully confined in unduly restrictive facilities because of erroneous assumptions and/or claims that they were too dangerous to live in less restrictive conditions. But it is equally clear that the determinations of dangerousness upon which the unnecessarily severe confinements reviewed in these studies were grounded were *not* based on careful, individualized assessments but on what have been described as "administrative decisions" (*Baxstrom v. Herold*, 1966, n.3), "global assessments" (Steadman & Cocozza, 1980, p. 212), and "political predictions" (Thornberry & Jacoby, 1979, p. 26). Indeed, after reviewing the Dixon study, Litwack (1996) pointed out that "once even a semblance of an individualized examination was performed . . . on the Dixon patients, only a distinct minority were still deemed to be dangerous" (p. 118).

Assessments of Dangerousness Based on Threats of Violence

Most studies of assessments of dangerousness do not specify whether any of the assessees evaluated for dangerousness were threatening violence at the time. Therefore, these studies are simply irrelevant to determining how well mental health professionals can assess dangerousness regarding individuals (particularly psychotic individuals) who *are* threatening to commit violence. By contrast, MacDonald (1963, 1967) studied the postrelease behavior of a cohort of patients hospitalized because they had made threats to kill. Of 77 such patients about whom follow-up information was obtainable, 3 had later taken the lives of others, and 4 had committed suicide. However, *since all the individuals in MacDonald's cohort were hospitalized—and presumably treated—it is impossible to know how many would have acted violently without the imposition of hospitalization.* Most likely, though, the patients in MacDonald's cohort would not have been released unless they apparently no longer had active intentions to kill.

MacDonald's study raises an important question: How can we determine what percentage of mentally ill people who are threatening to kill will actually do so without refraining from confining such individuals even when it appears, to mental health professionals, that their threats should be taken seriously? The answer is, of course: *We can't!* That is, more generally, ethical and legal constraints make it impossible to determine the actual dangerousness of many of those individuals who are most definitely believed to be dangerous by mental health professionals.

RECENT AND ONGOING STUDIES

1. Menzies and Webster (1995) and Menzies, Webster, McMain, Staley, and Scaglione (1994) have reported on a large-scale follow-up study of a set of clinical and actuarial assessments of dangerousness that were also evaluated in earlier studies (see Litwack et al., 1993, pp. 253–255, for a critique of the earlier studies). In brief, 162 accused persons who were evaluated at a forensic clinic *primarily for competency to stand trial or for their current need for inpatient psychiatric treatment* were also "evaluated" for dangerousness through the application of certain actuarial instruments and by asking the clinicians making the competency/mental health assessments to rate the assessees according to the assessors' global view of the patient's "dangerousness to others in [the] future" (Menzies & Webster, 1995, p. 768). After a six-year follow-up involving an extensive record review, a few items measured via actuarial instruments (relatively young age, employment status, and rated hostility) were somewhat predictive of in-hospital violence; neither the actuarial instruments nor clinical ratings were at all predictive of community violence.

However, the clinical assessments were very brief and the criteria for determining dangerousness very vague. There is no evidence that the subject population had a history of repetitive or serious violence. (Indeed, only 19.9% of the assessees were currently charged with a violent offense of *any* degree of seriousness.) Clinicians were not asked to assess future dangerousness in light of the intervention of treatment or the lack thereof. And no attempt was made to assess the subject's likely future circumstances in the community.

In short, the clinical evaluations studied here were *irrelevant* to actual clinical practice. Although emergency room mental health clinicians may well have to make dangerousness assessments based on a brief evaluation and minimal information, determinations that a patient is dangerous in such circumstances are *very short-term* assessments—typically a determination that the patient poses a serious threat of violence within the next 48 or 72 hours if not hospitalized. (And because such assessments concern the patient's risk of violence *in the community* if not properly treated, if a patient hospitalized on the basis of such an assessment is *not* violent in the hospital, that in no way invalidates the original assessment.) Some forensic patients (e.g., insanity acquittees) *are* typically assessed for long-term dangerousness but, if proper practice is followed, only after considerable information is accumulated regarding the patients' histories, after the patients are observed on the ward and in treatment for lengthy periods of time, and after extensive consideration is given to the circumstances the patients likely would face in less restrictive settings.

2. Lidz et al. (1993) published a study on dangerousness assessments that was deemed by Monahan in 1996 to be, until that time, "surely the most sophisticated study published on the clinical prediction of violence" (p. 111). That study concluded that mental health professionals *can* do better than chance in evaluating dangerousness. It was also noteworthy for determining postassessment patient violence in the community not solely from official records but also via community interviews with the patients and significant collaterals (Mulvey & Lidz, 1993; Mulvey, Shaw, & Lidz, 1994). Still, a close examination of this study demonstrates how difficult it is to study assessments of dangerousness in a way that does justice to the issues involved.

Pairs of clinicians were asked to independently rate hundreds of psychiatric emergency department patients on a scale from 1 to 5 regarding the patients' "potential . . . violence toward others during the next 6 months." Patients who received a summed rating of at least 3 out of a possible score of 10 were included in the "predicted violent" group. Each of these patients was then matched for sex, race, and age with another emergency room patient who had elicited less staff concern about future violence to others.

Ultimately, 357 matched pairs were followed up for six months after their discharge from the hospital. Violent incidents were reported in 36% of the comparison cases and 53% of the predicted cases, a statistically significant difference. Even when the patients' preadmission history of violence was controlled for, the clinicians still did statistically better than chance, leading the authors to conclude that "this study . . . show[s] that clinical judgment has been undervalued in previous research" (Lidz et al., 1993, p. 1010). However, because a significant percentage of the patients who did act violently in the community were not identified as dangerous by the clinicians (the measure of the "sensitivity" of the clinical judgments), and because a considerable percentage of patients who did not act violently in the community were in the predicted violent group (the measure of the "specificity" of the judgments), the authors also concluded that "the low sensitivity and specificity of these judgments show that clinicians are relatively inaccurate predictors of violence" (p. 1010).

In fact, the picture is more complex and less definitive. To begin with, the clinicians in this study were not predicting violence but, rather, rating their patients' *potential* for violence. It is simply incorrect to conclude that a patient who elicits some clinical concern regarding future dangerousness (e.g., summed ratings of 3 or 4 out of a possible 10) has been predicted to be violent (cf. Mulvey & Lidz, 1995). Lidz et al. (1993) did find that patients about whom clinicians expressed serious concern—those who had a summed score of 6 or above—were no more likely to commit violence than patients regarding whom the clinicians had expressed some, but less, concern. But a high clinical rating regarding "potential violence" does not necessarily mean a judgment that the patient is very likely to commit violence. Such a concern may rather reflect a judgment that the patient is at risk for committing serious violence, even if the risk of occurrence is not high. And the studied judgments were made prior to hospitalization and/or treatment, which may well have modified the original assessments.

On the other hand, even though the clinicians in this study did demonstrate a better than chance ability to assess future dangerousness, because the clinicians' judgments were not compared with judgments by laypersons, the study did not demonstrate that mental health professionals have any *special* ability to assess dangerousness. And this study certainly does not demonstrate (nor does it refute the idea) that psychiatric emergency room clinicians have sufficient ability to assess future dangerousness to justify emergency commitments based on their assessments of dangerousness. This is because the follow-up measures and analysis, however much a step forward from past efforts, did not assess a crucial variable: whether the patients' violence in the community, when it occurred, was sufficiently serious, and occurred sufficiently soon after their return to the community, that it would have justified continued confinement had it been foreseen! Even if clinicians can do better than chance when they assess dangerousness, that is a far cry from determining that they can assess dangerousness sufficiently well to justify depriving a person of his or her liberty based on such an assessment.

[Zeiss, Tanke, Fenn, and Yesavage (1996) found that psychiatric inpatients deemed in need of *recommitment* following a brief initial commitment on the grounds of dangerousness exhibited more violence after their eventual release than committed patients who were not deemed in need of recommitment, leading the authors to conclude that "practicing clinicians were able to identify a subset of psychiatric inpatients who were likely to commit future acts of violence" (p. 251). However, the differences in the rates of recidivism for the two groups did not begin to appear until *one year after release*; it took over a year and a half after release for a majority of the recommitted patients to commit a known assault; and the postrelease violence was "not generally of a serious nature" (p. 251).]

As will be discussed in more detail in our section on the law, "clear and convincing evidence" of dangerousness is required to justify an extended civil commitment (*Addington v. Texas*, 1979). That a clinical determination of dangerousness can be shown likely to be somewhat better than a random judgment (i.e., better than chance) does not render that judgment, in itself, "clear and convincing evidence" of dangerousness. To put it another way, statistical significance may not amount to legal significance.

Responding in some degree to this concern, Gardner, Lidz, Mulvey, and Shaw (1996a), in a follow-up analysis of the data compiled from the previously discussed study, compared actuarial and clinical "predictions" of future violence for their accuracy in predicting *any* community violence versus predicting *serious* community violence. Actuarial predictions had lower rates of false-positive and false-negative errors than the clinical "predictions" for *any* violence. But the actuarial instruments were not superior to clinical judgments in predicting *serious* violence—the issue of practical concern.

Even more important, *data regarding three of the most important variables in the actuarial prediction equation were collected from patients, not in the emergency room, but in the community after their discharge from the hospital.* These variables were the patient's score on the hostility subscale of the Brief Symptom Inventory (BSI), the patient's recent history of drug abuse, and the patient's recent history of violence. Gardner, Lidz, Mulvey, and Shaw (1996b) reported that a simple decision tree relying on these three variables (a BSI hostility score greater than 2, more than three prior violent acts, and heavy drug use) and age less than 18 predicted future violence as well as a regression-based method using those and other variables. However, it is questionable, at best, whether the data required for the decision tree could be validly and reliably collected in the emergency room, given patients' clinical conditions (and other practical considerations) at that time. At the very least, therefore, it has not been demonstrated by these studies that actuarial methods are superior to clinical methods in determining which patients evaluated in psychiatric emergency rooms should or should not be hospitalized involuntarily. To the contrary, *because the clinicians in Gardner et al.'s studies did as well as the actuarial scheme in predicting future serious violence, and since there is every reason to believe that the necessary actuarial data would not have been nearly as valid if collected in the emergency room (if it could have been collected there at all), to date there is every reason to suppose that clinicians are superior to actuarial methods in determining short-term serious dangerousness—the only decision that is actually called for!—regarding individuals brought for evaluation to psychiatric emergency rooms.*

3. In a series of articles (see especially Harris, Rice, & Quinsey, 1993; Rice & Harris, 1995, 1997), Rice et al. and various coauthors have reported on an extensive attempt to derive an actuarial scheme for assessing future dangerousness regarding mentally disordered offenders. The results of their efforts have led, in turn, to the development of The Violence Prediction Scheme (Webster et al., 1994), which combines the "statistical prediction instrument" that was derived (the Violence Risk Assessment Guide or VRAG) with clinical considerations to form what is probably the most comprehensive (and best

validated) tool to date for assessing the future dangerousness of mentally disordered offenders.

The VRAG

Harris et al. (1993) obtained important information from the files of 618 mentally disordered offenders released from secure confinement, followed them up for an average of 7 years (later for 10 years), and then determined how the variables they had measured rated to recidivism. They found that the best predictor of subsequent recidivism, or lack thereof, was the subject's score on the Psychopathy Checklist–Revised version (PCL-R; Hare, 1991), the score having been derived from file data. Also contributing to the final regression equation were separation from a parent before the age of 16, never having been married, elementary school maladjustment, and failure on prior conditional release, among other factors (12 in all). The PCL-R score correlated .34 with recidivism; the final regression equation correlated .459 with recidivism.

However, these correlations were derived for any subsequent violent offense, including "simple" assaults; most of the violent failures were "fairly minor" (Rice & Harris, 1995, p. 744); and the correlations were derived for any violent offense over a seven-year period at risk. These factors significantly limit the legal utility of the VRAG. Even if it could be predicted with relative certainty that a subject who scored high on the VRAG would commit a simple assault within the next seven years, it is very questionable if that would justify the subject's continued detention on either moral or economic grounds. (Serious recidivism was considered to be more than one common assault, armed robbery without victim injury, or any more serious instance of violent behavior [Marnie Rice, personal communication, February 25, 1997]).

Even when only severe violent recidivism was considered, and even over a mean of 10 years, the VRAG performed equally well in that the *relative* likelihood of offending was equally well predicted by the VRAG score. But, granting that the VRAG "can be used to assign persons from different but similar populations to *relative* risk categories with some confidence" (Webster et al., 1994, p. 64; emphasis in original), the crucial legal issue may be not how well a test differentiates the relative degrees of risk posed by members of a group of previous offenders being considered for release, but how well the test determines the *specific* degree of risk posed by individual offenders—in terms of their likelihood of recidivism, the likely imminence of their recidivism if they fail, and, not least, the probable, or even plausible, severity of their violence if they fail (Villeneuve & Quinsey, 1995, pp. 408–409).

The VRAG has been cross-validated and applies equally well to determining the relative risk of violent recidivism (but not specifically sexual recidivism) among released sex offenders (Rice & Harris, 1997). In *Doe v. Poritz* (1995), the Supreme Court of New Jersey ruled that in determining the level of community notification justified upon a sex offender's release from confinement, "the [absolute] probability of reoffense on the part of moderate- or high-risk offenders is not the issue . . . but rather the relatively greater risk of reoffense compared either to the low-risk or the moderate risk offender class" (622 A.2d at 384). Still, given the absence of evidence that high VRAG scores are strongly correlated with the commission of *serious* violence within a few years after release from secure confinement, it remains questionable whether the VRAG should be used for individualized assessment to determine that a potential releasee should be confined—although it should also be noted that individuals scoring very high on the VRAG in Harris et al.'s 1993 study were virtually certain to recidivate with at least some violence within seven years (Harris et al., 1993); and nearly 50% of offenders considered to be sexually deviant psychopaths were discovered to have recidivated with some violence within a year of release from secure detention (Rice & Harris, 1997).

On the other hand, the VRAG appears to be a useful determinant of when offenders who have been mentally disordered are *safe* to be released from secure confinement. Extrapolating slightly from the data provided by Harris et al. (1993, p. 327) and Webster et al. (1994, p. 34), it can be seen that study subjects who scored in the lower half of all subjects on the VRAG had an average recidivism rate of only slightly over 10% *after an average of seven years at risk*. Taking into account the additional fact that most of that recidivism was due to fairly minor violence, it seems fair to conclude that mentally disordered offenders falling within that range on the VRAG (and deemed by clinicians suitable for release from secure confinement) almost certainly do not require secure detention to protect the public (though they may still require nonsecure hospitalization or intensive community supervision; Webster et al., 1994, p. 65).

However, as the authors of the VRAG fully recognized, it can legitimately be used only regarding members of populations similar to those in the study populations. Thus, the VRAG cannot be definitively used to estimate the risk of recidivism of mentally disordered offenders committed to mental institutions but *not* approved for release by legal authorities. For example, a history of homicide was *negatively* related to recidivism in the studied sample, but it might well be positively related to recidivism in the sample of patients who were seriously mentally disturbed and not released (Litwack et al., 1993, pp. 251–252). And VRAG scores do not take into account the potential seriousness of the possible recidivism of, for example, sex offenders (Furr, 1993).

Moreover, obtaining the primary component of the VRAG—the PCL-R score—requires considerable effort and technical expertise, even when it is obtained from file data (Harris et al., 1993). And there is some question whether the PCL-R is equally predictive with female patients and minority group members (Kosson, Smith, & Newman, 1990; Salekin, Rogers, Ustad, & Sewell, 1998). On the other hand, if the PCL-R was scored by trained assessors based on a clinical interview as well as file data, it might prove to be an even better predictor of recidivism than it was found to be by Harris and Rice and their coinvestigators (Serin, 1996).

The PCL-R appears to be among the most robust predictors of recidivism, even over and above criminal history (Salekin, Rogers, & Sewell, 1996; see also Furr, 1993; Serin & Amos, 1995). For recent reviews, see Hare (1996); Hare and Hart (1992); Hart and Hare (1996, 1997a); Hart, Hare, and Forth (1994); Gacono and Hutton (1994); and Serin (1996); see also Heilbrun (1996), who reported that psychopathy as measured by instruments other than the PCL-R also predicted recidivism better than criminal history. It should be noted, however, that, apart from the question of the generalizability of the PCL-R as a predictive instrument, and apart from whatever practical problems may be entailed in deriving valid PCL-R scores in many situations, a crucial issue concerning the PCL-R is the question of what PCL-R scores—from 0 to 40—can most legitimately be used as cutoff scores for prediction purposes (Salekin et al., 1996, pp. 206–207). There is also the question of which aspects of the PCL-R are most predictive, and whether the PCL-R sufficiently weighs the variable of childhood antisocial behavior to best determine psychopathy and to be a maximally effective predictor (Rice, 1997; personal communication, February 25, 1997).

As noted, correlations between VRAG scores and recidivism were not obtained for forensic patients deemed unsuitable for release from secure confinement by the ultimate authorities. A subsidiary finding of a study by Quinsey and Maguire (1986) makes clear, however, that serious attention should be paid to clinical judgments that a long-term forensic patient remains seriously dangerous and in need of continued secure confinement. Quinsey and Maguire reported this finding as follows:

> It has been argued . . . that a group of patients who are passed over repeatedly for release under conditions of indeterminate confinement will eventually come to contain a very high proportion of truly dangerous persons if only a proportion of the clinical assessments have any validity at all. . . . [A] group of 28 long-term patients [who were] assigned maximal dangerousness ratings . . . should, according to this argument, be a very dangerous group of individuals. Of these individuals, 20 were [ultimately released] or transferred to a less secure facility; of these, 6 [were] returned to [the maximum security institution] from less secure institutions . . . and 6 others were convicted of new offenses. Of these latter, one committed a serious sexual assault on a child using a weapon, one received life imprisonment for a series of aggressive sexual crimes against children, one received life for a sadistic rape, two were given life for attempted murder, and one was convicted of mischief and theft. Given the very short follow-up period [for these patients], these results unambiguously confirm the dangerousness of this group. (p. 168; cf the long-term forensic patients described by Litwack, 1996)

Litwack et al. (1993) observed as part of their review of the entire study: "One wonders how dangerous these patients would have been had they been released [to the community] when they were still 'assigned maximally dangerous ratings'! [Moreover,] Quinsey and Maguire did not provide an explanation of why these patients were released. It would be instructive to know. Were they confined under sentences that expired? Did judges release or transfer them against clinical advice? Or did the clinicians ultimately lose sight of the patients' dangerousness? And . . . are there lessons to be learned [from these outcomes] for future assessments of dangerousness? These are [among] the types of questions . . . that future studies of assessments of dangerousness should focus upon" (pp. 251–252). (Regarding why these patients were released, the answer, apparently, is that all the above reasons applied to one or more of the cases. Personal communication from Vernon Quinsey via Marnie Rice, February 25, 1997.)

The Violence Prediction Scheme

In recognition of the idea that clinical considerations and judgments have a legitimate and potentially important role to play in risk assessments even when relevant actuarial predictive schemes are available, the Violence Prediction Scheme (Webster et al., 1994) integrates the VRAG with a clinically determined ASSESS-LIST to arrive at rather comprehensively based conclusions regarding risk assessment. The term ASSESS-LIST is a mnemonic device indicating 10 items "often considered important by experienced forensic clinicians" in assessing dangerousness (p. 48). The items recommended for consideration are: **A**ntecedent history (e.g., witnessed family violence, was an abuse victim, failed on release); **S**elf-presentation (e.g., insight, prosocial attitudes, impulsivity); **S**ocial and psychosocial adjustment (e.g., social skills, coping skills); **E**xpectations and plans (i.e., whether or not realistic); **S**ymptoms; **S**upervision (availability, compliance with medication); **L**ife factors (e.g., age, marital status); **I**nstitutional behavior; **S**exual adjustment; and **T**reatment progress.

Webster et al. (1994) conclude that, when validated and relevant actuarial data are available, "[i]f adjustments [to actuarial assessments] are made conservatively and only because of factors that a clinician believes, on good evidence, to be related to the likelihood of violent recidivism in an individual case, predictive accuracy may be optimized" (p. 57).* Regarding "actuarial" assessment instruments, Borum (1996) has observed that, "At a minimum, these devices can serve as a checklist for clinicians to ensure that essential areas of inquiry are recalled and evaluated. At best, they may be able to provide hard actuarial data on the probability of violence among people (and environments) with a given set of characteristics, circumstances, or both" (p. 948). This appears to be particularly true of the Violence Prediction Scheme.

Webster, Douglas, Eaves, and Hart (1997) have also developed the HCR-20 (second version), which is intended to be a more broadly applicable guide to risk assessment than the Violence Prediction Scheme, though the HCR-20 focuses on many of the variables that are central to the Violence Prediction Scheme. The HCR-20 calls for the assessment of 20 variables that have been shown to be risk factors for future violence: 10 historical variables, 5 clinical variables (lack of insight, negative attitudes, current symptoms of mental disorder, impulsivity, nonresponsiveness to treatment), and 5 risk management variables. Although the HCR-20 has only begun to be tested for its utility, it appears to have high face validity at least as a checklist for areas to be considered and evaluated in many, if not most, assessments of dangerousness.

4. The MacArthur Violence Risk Assessment Study, an ongoing research project described in detail by Steadman et al. (1994), may provide important new information to aid in dangerousness risk assessments. In this project, which constitutes an attempt to rectify methodological inadequacies of previous studies (Monahan & Steadman, 1994), hundreds of civilly committed individuals from three geographically diverse sites will be evaluated, while hospitalized and with the aid of specially designed assessment instruments, to determine their levels of impulsivity, anger, psychopathy, and delusions; their social support (or lack thereof) in the community will also be evaluated. After

their release, the patients will be closely followed up in the community, in part by regular interviews of both patients and significant others ("collaterals"), to determine the degree of their violent behavior in the community (Mulvey & Lidz, 1993). An attempt will then be made to determine if there is any connection between patients' scores on the specialized assessment instruments and their levels of recidivism in the community.

Although the results of this study may prove to be useful, its limitations must also be recognized. First, the study will have little to say about the legitimacy of the commitment decisions themselves or, more generally, the validity of clinical assessments leading to confinement rather than release. The patients will be assessed sometime after their initial confinements and (with rare exceptions, perhaps) released with clinical agreement (or at least acquiescence). Hence, the study will have far more to say about whether the specially designed instruments can be useful in avoiding premature releases (false negatives) than it will have to say about the legitimacy of commitment decisions (or avoiding false positives).

Second, the study will concern itself with a patient group that, in general, does not have a history of serious violence. The subject sample will be civil committees, not convicted offenders or insanity acquittees, and it is likely that there will be few members of the study population with high (or even relatively high) psychopathy scores. Therefore, even if the specialized instruments do not prove useful in assessing dangerousness with this population, that does not mean they would not be useful with a more violence-prone population, or that other variables that could be assessed (e.g., the patient's likely compliance with medication and other treatment recommendations) would not be successful predictors with this population.

Third, it remains to be seen whether postrelease patient violence in the community will be delineated with sufficient specificity regarding its seriousness and imminence after release so that, if there are significant relationships between scores on the specialized instruments and recidivism, the predictive equations derived will have practical meaning and utility for psychiatric and judicial commitment decisions. (For recommendations for future research concerning assessments of dangerousness, see Monahan, 1996, p. 115; Monahan & Steadman, 1994.)

OVERALL OBSERVATIONS

1. As we shall see in more detail below, progress is being made in defining and validating variables that are risk factors for violence. Based on such findings, actuarial schemes are being developed that may prove quite useful in making dangerousness risk assessments in certain cases. Nevertheless, two related points must be kept in mind. First, the most important and most certain clinical assessments of dangerousness cannot be tested for their "accuracy" without releasing from confinement precisely those individuals who most clearly pose a serious risk of committing serious violence if released. No number of studies showing a high rate of false positives for "predictions" made regarding marginally dangerous individuals (e.g., Kozol et al., 1972), or regarding

patients without a serious history of violence (e.g., Mulvey & Lidz, 1993), can change this essential fact. Second, and similarly, it is unlikely that we will ever have meaningful objective data to inform us about the statistical risk of violence of confineable individuals because if such individuals are confined it will be impossible to determine their base rate for violence (if not confined), or to validate the possible predictive power of various combinations of actuarial variables regarding such individuals (Litwack, 1993; but see Fagan & Guggenheim, 1996, for an interesting study of the validity of judicial assessments of dangerousness regarding juveniles that were released against judicial advice).

This chapter will not review the extensive and increasingly rich literature on the assessment of potential inpatient violence. For recent findings and reviews, see, for example, Ball et al. (1994); Bjørkly (1995, 1996); Hill, Rogers, and Bickford (1996); McNiel and Binder (1994a, 1994b, 1995); and Shaffer, Waters, and Adams (1994). It should be noted, however, that attempts to validate predictors for in-hospital violence also may run into the problem that, within the hospital, extra managerial efforts to reduce the risk of violence will be devoted to seemingly dangerous individuals.

One group of possibly dangerous individuals regarding whom possibly useful risk assessment equations can be developed is convicted offenders who are released from prison once their sentences have expired or for other legal reasons, even if they are still considered to be dangerous (but not civilly committable) by various professionals or authorities. Approximately half the population studied by Harris et al. (1993) came from such a group (somewhat mentally disordered offenders who were psychiatrically evaluated after their convictions but who were nonetheless sent to prison to serve their sentences). It must be noted, however, that unless such offenders are in mandated treatment programs, it is not possible to compare the utility of any derived actuarial assessment instruments with meaningful clinical judgments (i.e., clinical judgments that are based on in-depth interviews with the offenders as well as other relevant information).

2. The focus on false positive and false negative rates that has dominated much of the discussion regarding the legitimacy of clinical assessments of dangerousness is fundamentally misplaced—as has been the argument that false positive rates are too high to justify detentions based on such assessments. As noted earlier, an assessment that a person is "dangerous" (and even in need of confinement) is not necessarily (or even usually) a prediction that the person will become violent unless certain steps are taken. Rather, it is usually only a conclusion that the person poses a certain risk of a certain degree of violence that (it is recognized in many cases) may or may not eventuate depending on not wholly foreseeable future circumstances. Thus, Mulvey and Lidz (1995) recommend that assessments of dangerousness be reconceptualized in terms of "clinical concerns" about possible future violence.

Similarly, a clinical decision, or recommendation, to release a hospitalized patient does not mean that a prediction has been made that the patient will no longer be violent. Rather, it usually represents a judgment that, taking into account the perceived risk of future violence and the patient's legitimate liberty interests (and perhaps other factors as well, such as population pressures in the institution), the risk is one that should be taken. Indeed, as also noted above, even if it was foreseeable, based on the patient's history, that a patient would be likely to commit additional acts of relatively minor violence some months in the future, a clinical and/or judicial decision might well be reasonably made to release the patient. If such a patient did later act violently—as was expected!—should the patient be considered a false negative?

In recent years, Mossman (1994a, 1994b) and others (e.g., Rice & Harris, 1995) have advocated the use of receiver operating characteristics (ROC) analysis as a means for portraying the accuracy of dangerousness assessments. This analytic tool may well allow researchers to better evaluate the relative validity and utility of various assessments tools or techniques. However, ROC analyses can be as misleading as false positive and false negative rates if such analyses view and rate assessments as if they were predictions. Moreover, it is not clear that ROC analyses can adequately take into account different time periods involved in reoffending (as can survival curves), or whether ROC analyses can adequately take into account the relative seriousness of different instances of recidivism.

3. In short, actuarial assessments of dangerousness have yet to be proven to be superior to clinical assessments in many important contexts. Mossman (1994a) surveyed a large number of studies of "violence prediction" and concluded that the average accuracy of long-term (one-year) "predictions" of violence was greater for actuarial methods than for clinical methods. (He found no difference between the two methods for short-term "predictions.") However, the actuarial and clinical studies he surveyed were generally not studies of alternative means of assessment for the same populations (see also Litwack et al., 1993, pp. 256–260). And because clinical determinations of dangerousness are often not predictions of violence, it is far from clear how the relative "validity" of clinical and actuarial assessments of dangerousness can best be measured.

Therefore, the issue of the relative merits of clinical versus actuarial assessments needs to be approached much more open-mindedly and broad-mindedly than has often been the case (cf. e.g., Grisso & Appelbaum, 1992; Miller & Morris, 1988). When truly relevant and meaningful actuarial data are available, it may well be the case that actuarial schemes will usually predict the occurrence or nonoccurrence of an event (e.g., an act of violence) with greater accuracy than clinical judgment (Grove & Meehl, 1996). However, as we have discussed, there are no validated actuarial bases for determining dangerousness in many circumstances. And actuarial predictions may not sufficiently specify the possible severity or temporal closeness of predicted violence to be meaningful for use in actual decision making.

4. Moreover, the distinction between actuarial and clinical assessments is blurring to the point where there is often no meaningful distinction between the two. For example, good clinical assessment routinely takes into account such actuarial predictors as a history of violence; conversely, the most powerful actuarial predictor in recent studies—the PCL-R score—is, in significant part, a *clinical* variable. Even when it is derived from file data, obtaining a PCL-R score requires considerable training, effort, and expertise; also, an evaluator must make a clinical judgment regarding the extent to which the evaluee manifests such traits as superficial charm, a grandiose sense of self-worth, a lack of remorse or empathy, and conning and being manipulative. That is, obtaining a PCL-R score, even

from file data, is not simply a "mechanical" operation (cf. Grove & Meehl, 1996). Ideally, according to Hart and Hare (1997b), "psychopathy should be assessed using expert observer (i.e., clinical) ratings. The ratings should be based on a review of case history materials . . . supplemented with interviews or behavioral observations whenever possible."

Accordingly, for example, it is meaningless to speak of the VRAG as an actuarial instrument free of clinical input. Indeed, *the VRAG has its predictive power in large part because it takes "clinical" variables and assessments into account.* Thus, bearing in mind Monahan's admonition that "[f]ocusing on a limited number of relevant and valid predictor items . . . is more important than an exhaustive examination that yields much irrelevant and ultimately confusing information" (1981, p. 126), the upshot is simply that assessors of dangerousness should be willing to consider all apparently relevant and useful (and cost-effective) sources of information in making their assessments without unnecessarily limiting themselves to either "actuarial" or "clinical" data (Webster et al., 1994).

5. The question remains, however: How can the legitimacy and utility of clinical assessments of dangerousness best be evaluated if clinical determinations of dangerousness, and/or clinical recommendations of confinement or release, cannot properly be viewed as predictions and if, in any event, many assessments of dangerousness cannot be tested without releasing possibly very dangerous individuals? There may be no easy answer to this question, but Mulvey and Lidz's observation in 1985 may still be apt:

> [I]t is only by knowing "how" the process [of dangerousness assessment] occurs that we can determine both the potential and strategy for improvement in [such assessments]. . . . Detailed description of these decisions as they actually occur (using either participant observation or coded transcripts) could provide a systematic way to limit [the] presently broad range of potential explanatory variables by isolating those case, clinician, and context variables that appear most central to the decision-making process. In short, the initial stage of description, so critical to the development of grounded theory, has been largely sidestepped in research on the prediction of dangerousness. It is necessary to go back to basics and to do the work that ideally would have been the first step to systematic inquiry. (pp. 215–216)

In part in response to Mulvey and Lidz's call, Litwack (1996) observed and described in some detail the individualized bases for assessments of dangerousness regarding each patient among a representative sample of insanity acquittees confined, on the ground of their dangerousness, in a forensic hospital. To the best of our knowledge, however, there are no other such reports in the entire literature on assessments of dangerousness. For example (to the best of our knowledge), there has not been a single description of the precise bases for commitment decisions on the grounds of dangerousness regarding a representative sample of patients evaluated in psychiatric emergency rooms, or a representative sample of patients recommitted after their emergency commitments. (See, however, Segal, Watson, Goldfinger, & Averbuck, 1988, for an analysis of the perceived indicators of dangerousness that *generally* characterized a sample of emergency civil committees.) Pfohl, 1978, observed a large number of assessments of dangerousness regarding inmates of a hospital for the "criminally insane," and described a number of biases that he believed seriously infected many of those assessments. However, Pfohl provided no data regarding the frequency of the alleged lapses in diagnostic objectivity, and he did not describe a representative sample of the evaluations he studied in any detail.

6. Recent years have seen the publication of a number of empirical studies that have provided data suggesting that certain variables should be considered risk factors for future violence. That is, the presence of these factors indicates that the individual involved poses a significantly greater risk of acting violently than similarly situated individuals who do not exhibit the risk factors. Of course, the presence of even the best validated risk factors does not necessarily indicate that the person exhibiting such factors is *likely* to be seriously (or even minimally) violent in the future, or that preventive action should be taken. Also, certain putative risk factors need to be studied further to confirm their status as risk factors, to better determine their temporal relationship to violence, and/or to determine the extent to which they are risk factors independent of other, often co-occurring risk factors (see, e.g., Dinwiddie & Yutzy, 1993; Swanson, Borum, Swartz, & Hiday, 1997; Swanson, Borum, Swartz, & Monahan, 1996; Swanson et al., 1997). Nevertheless, and in no particular order, we will briefly list here certain variables that have recently received empirical support for their status as risk factors for violence and that may be of particular interest to practicing clinicians:

- Active psychotic symptoms + substance abuse + a history of violence or current hostile attitudes (Swanson et al., 1996, 1997a, 1997b; Torrey, 1994)
- Delusions of being threatened or controlled by outside forces ("threat/ control override [TCO] symptoms") (Link & Stueve, 1994; Link, Monahan, Stueve, & Cullen, 1997)
- The presence of delusional beliefs about significant others and specific personal targets, especially that a significant other has been replaced by an imposter (Nestor, Haycock, Doiron, Kelly, & Kelly, 1995; Silva, Leong, Garza-Trevino, & Le-Grand, 1994a; Silva, Leong, Weinstock, & Kaushal, 1994b; Silva, Leong, Weinstock, & Klein, 1995; but cf. Dinwiddie & Yutzy, 1993)
- Command hallucinations to commit violence when the hallucinated voice is identified and/or when there is also a delusion related to the hallucination (Junginger, 1995), or when the content of the hallucinations include references to self-harm (Kasper, Rogers, & Adams, 1996)
- Erotomania with multiple delusional objects and a history of serious antisocial behavior unrelated to delusions (Menzies, Fedoroff, Green, & Isaacson, 1995)
- Recent and currently active narcissistic injury, isolation of affect or grossly inappropriate affect, threatening or provocative behavior which is usually minimized by the patient, and the availability of a weapon (Schulte, Hall, & Crosby, 1994)

7. After reviewing the research literature for the first edition of this volume, we determined (paraphrasing somewhat) that there was no research that contradicted the following, we believe common sense, conclusions:

a. When an individual has clearly exhibited a recent history of repeated violence, it is reasonable to assume that that individual poses a serious risk of acting violently again in the foreseeable future unless there has been a significant change in the attitudes or circumstances that led to violence, repeatedly, in the recent past.

b. Even when an individual's history of violence is a somewhat distant history of serious violence, which led to a continuing confinement, it can reasonably be assumed that that individual remains at risk for violence, if released from confinement, if it can be shown that he or she maintains the same complex of attitudes and personality traits (and physical abilities) that led to violence in the past and that, if released, the individual would confront circumstances quite similar to those that led to violence in the past.

c. Serious dangerousness may reasonably be said to exist when psychotic individuals make serious threats or statements of intention to commit violence (at least in the absence of evidence that such threats have frequently been made in the past *without* resulting violence).

d. Even in the absence of a history or threats of violence, there may be occasions when an individual is so clearly *on the brink* of violence that a determination of dangerousness—and preventive action based on that determination—is justified (e.g., when an individual is experiencing command hallucinations to do harm and doubts that he or she can resist the commands; or, perhaps, in the case of an individual who sat incessantly at a window with a loaded rifle because of paranoid fears that his home was about to be attacked).

e. Although mental health professionals have yet to demonstrate any special ability not shared equally by lay persons to assess dangerousness, they may well yet demonstrate such an ability, at least in certain circumstances. At least, they may well possess special techniques or knowledge, or abilities to articulate the meaning of their findings, that can meaningfully and legitimately aid in making determinations of dangerousness.

Writing ten years after the publication of those conclusions, we believe they are still accurate, or at least unchallenged by actual research findings.

THE LAW

In this section, we briefly review certain important legal developments concerning assessments of dangerousness by mental health professionals.

ASSESSMENTS OF DANGEROUSNESS AND THE SUPREME COURT

Despite qualms expressed by various professional organizations and legal commentators and some of their own brethren (all well summarized by Faigman, Kaye, Saks, & Sanders, 1997, pp. 283–295), the Supreme Court of the United States has been receptive to assessments of dangerousness (and even predictions of violence) by mental health professionals in a variety of circumstances. Most notably, perhaps (and perhaps most notoriously), in *Barefoot v.*

Estelle (1983), by a 6–3 vote, the Supreme Court upheld the constitutionality of a sentence of death that was based, in part, on the prediction of a testifying psychiatrist that the "probability" that the defendant would commit additional crimes of violence in prison if not executed was "one hundred percent and absolute" (*Texas v. Barefoot*, Record at 2131; quoted by Appelbaum, 1984, at p. 169).

Although mindful of the questions that existed regarding the validity of predictions of violence by mental health professionals, in *Barefoot* (1983) the majority opined that such questions could adequately be dealt with by the trier of fact: "We are not persuaded," stated the Court, "that such testimony is almost entirely unreliable [i.e., invalid] and that the factfinder and the adversary system will not be competent to uncover, recognize and take due account of its shortcomings" (463 U.S. at 899). In *Schall v. Martin* (1984), the Supreme Court observed that "from a legal point of view there is nothing inherently unattainable about a prediction of future criminal conduct" and that the Court had "specifically rejected the contention, based on . . . sociological data . . . , 'that it is impossible to predict future violent behavior'" (467 U.S. at 278–279).

The Supreme Court has more recently ruled, in *Daubert v. Merrell Dow Pharmaceuticals* (1993), that under the Federal Rules of Civil Procedure, which govern civil trials in federal court, witnesses should be allowed to testify as experts only if the subject of their testimony was "scientific knowledge," and that "in order to qualify as 'scientific knowledge,' an inference or assertion must be derived by the scientific method" (113 S. Ct. 2795). The court added, "This entails a preliminary assessment of whether the reasoning or methodology underlying the testimony is valid" and that "[o]rdinarily, a key question to be answered in determining whether a theory or technique is scientific knowledge that will assist the trier of fact will be whether it can be (and has been) tested" (*id.* at 2796).

Given that mental health professionals have yet to demonstrate that they have any special ability to assess dangerousness, and given that they have yet to demonstrate that they can do better than chance in a variety of situations, it could be argued that mental health professionals should not be allowed to testify as experts under the *Daubert* standard. However, (a) historically, the Supreme Court has been receptive to professional assessments of dangerousness; (b) in almost any case in which such assessments are made they will be based, at least in part, on validated risk factors (e.g., a history of violence); (c) mental health professionals could well make the point that they cannot validate their expertise in many circumstances without releasing dangerous individuals; (d) throughout our society, mental health professionals are expected by the law to make professional assessments of dangerousness when patients pose a serious risk of harm to others (see, e.g., *Tarasoff v. Regents of the University of California* (1976); (e) the Supreme Court also stated in *Daubert* that, still, "[w]idespread acceptance can be an important factor in ruling particular evidence admissible" (*id.* at 2797), and clinical assessments of dangerousness are widely accepted by the clinical community and increasingly by the academic community; and (f) if nothing else, it is likely that mental health professionals will be better able than laypersons to articulate, highlight, and analyze the factors that go into a dangerousness risk assessment (cf. Litwack, Gerber, & Fenster, 1980). Given all this, it is highly unlikely that the *Daubert* decision will affect the admissibility of professional assessments of dangerousness in federal courts or in states that follow the *Daubert* decision.

CIVIL COMMITMENT DECISIONS

In *Addington v. Texas* (1979), the Supreme Court ruled that individuals could be involuntarily committed to a mental hospital for an extended period of time only if there was "clear and convincing evidence" that they met a constitutionally legitimate legal standard for confinement. Therefore, to the extent that dangerousness as well as mental illness is required by law to justify an extended commitment, *Addington* requires that such dangerousness be proven by clear and convincing evidence (i.e., more than a preponderance of the evidence but less evidence than is required for proof beyond a reasonable doubt). The Court in *Addington* also observed that "[w]hether the individual is mentally ill and dangerous to either himself or others and is in need of confined therapy turns on the meaning of the facts *which must be interpreted by expert psychiatrists and psychologists*" (441 U.S. at 429; emphasis added).

There are two points to note about the *Addington* decision. First, it applied only to extended confinements; therefore, presumably (and as is current practice), less than clear and convincing evidence of mental illness and dangerousness could justify a relatively brief commitment for the purpose of further evaluation. Second, it is important to recognize that the requirement of clear and convincing evidence of dangerousness, when it exists, is not a requirement of proof that the individual is more likely than not to be violent if not hospitalized. Rather, it is a requirement for clear and convincing evidence of enough risk of enough harm to justify the confinement at issue (see, e.g., *Rogers v. Okin*, 1980).

Indeed, in a 1990 decision, the Ninth Circuit Federal Court of Appeals ruled that "a finding of [a] 'substantial risk' [of violence sufficient to justify an extended civil commitment] may be based on any activity that evinces a *genuine possibility* of future harm to persons or property" (*U.S. v. Sahhar*, 917 F.2d at 1207; emphasis added). The court of appeals also rejected the notion that, to be constitutional, a civil commitment must be based on a recent overt act or threat of violence. Rather, the court stated, "Whether [worrisome] activity occurred recently is but one factor . . . to consider in weighing the evidence" (*id.* at 1207; see also *U.S. v. Evanoff*, 8th Cir., 1993).

The decision in the *Sahhar* case is emblematic of a trend that has occurred in recent years away from the strict standards for civil commitments that were established in some jurisdictions in the 1970s toward more flexible and perhaps more realistic criteria. This trend can be seen by comparing more recent decisions with the rulings in *Lessard v. Schmidt* (1972), an often cited federal court decision of a generation ago that strictly limited the government's power to civilly commit mentally ill individuals. In *Lessard,* the court ruled that a commitment could be justified only by proof of "an extreme likelihood that if the person is not confined he will do immediate harm to himself or others." The Lessard court further held that determinations of dangerousness had to be "based upon a finding of a recent overt act, attempt, or threat to do substantial harm to oneself or another" (349 F. Supp. 1078).

In addition to rejecting the notion that violence must be likely and/or based on a recent overt act or threat to justify a commitment, other recent court decisions have rejected the notion that future dangerousness must be "imminent" to justify confinement. For example, in 1991, the Supreme Court of Massachusetts held that, "to the degree that the anticipated harm is serious . . . some lessening of a requirement of imminence seems justified" (*Commonwealth v. Rosenberg*, 573 N.E. 2d at 958). In *Seltzer v. Hogue* (1993), a New York State Appellate Court upheld the continued confinement of a mentally ill person who in the past had "invariably" became violent following his release from hospitalization, even though he had not been "imminently" violent upon release. Thus, Litwack (1993) concluded: "it appears that as the earlier abuses of the civil commitment system (see, e.g., *O'Connor v. Donaldson*, 1975) are supplanted in judicial and public concern by concern about potential violence by mentally ill persons who perhaps could not be committed under a strict reading of earlier and more libertarian oriented decisions, the judicial pendulum is swinging toward a greater willingness to allow civil commitments to protect the public from potential danger, and to allow that danger to be assessed broadly, rather than by rigid, impractical rules" (p. 363). Moreover, it should be pointed out, the Supreme Court has ruled that insanity acquittees may be required to prove that they are no longer dangerous before being released from confinement (*Jones v. United States*, 1983). And in the case of *In re George L.* (1995), the New York Court of Appeals observed that "compliance or lack of dangerousness in a facility does not necessarily mean that an individual does not suffer from a dangerous mental disorder" (624 N.Y.S. 2d at 103).

Of course, it is ultimately for the courts, rather than clinicians, to decide when mentally disordered individuals pose a sufficient risk of causing sufficient harm to justify depriving them of their liberty. But emergency room clinicians must themselves make such decisions regarding emergency admissions, and judges frequently look to clinicians for their input and insights before making their decisions. Therefore, before clinicians deem a patient dangerous for commitment purposes, they should be mindful of the fact that they are, indeed, making a risk assessment—and that, just as a sufficient risk (rather than a certainty) of future violence may justify a patient's confinement, so, too, a patient's right to liberty should be weighed in the balance. (For an excellent discussion of the justifications for confining sex offenders on the grounds of their dangerousness, see Brooks, 1992; regarding Canadian law, see Douglas, Macfarlane, & Webster, 1996.)

THE *TARASOFF* CASE AND THE DUTY TO PROTECT

In the well-known case of *Tarasoff v. Regents of the University of California* (1976), the Supreme Court of California ruled: "once a therapist does in fact determine, or under applicable professional standards reasonably should have determined, that a patient poses a serious danger of violence to others, he bears a duty to exercise reasonable care to protect the foreseeable victim of that danger" (17 Cal. 3d at 439). The *Tarasoff* ruling has been followed in most states (though with significant variations from state to state); as Monahan (1993) observed in a seminal article, "[i]n jurisdictions in which appellate courts [or legislatures] have not yet ruled on the question, the prudent clinical is well advised to proceed under the assumption that some version of *Tarasoff* liability will be imposed. . . . The duty to protect, in short, is now a fact of professional life for nearly all American clinicians and, potentially, for clinical researchers as well" (p. 242).

The case law, research, and voluminous commentary that has followed from the *Tarasoff* decision cannot be reviewed here, nor the various laws (and/or professional regulations) defining *Tarasoff*-like duties that have been adopted in many states, nor the differing responsibilities held by inpatient and outpatient clinicians. (But, for recent examples of relevant research and judicial analyses, see Binder & McNiel, 1996, and *Fraser v. U.S.,* 1996.) Suffice it to say that, clearly, one component of the duty to protect is the duty to conduct a professionally adequate risk assessment when such an assessment is called for. The next section reviews current thinking regarding the major components of professional risk assessments of dangerousness.

THE CLINICAL ASSESSMENT OF DANGEROUSNESS

In his 1981 monograph, Monahan listed 14 important "questions for the clinician [to consider] in predicting violent behavior." In 1972, Kozol et al. similarly presented an excellent (and somewhat different) list of questions for clinicians to consider when assessing dangerousness. (Later, Prins, 1996, pp. 54–56, and Webster & Polvi, 1995, also provided very thoughtful lists of such questions that can serve as excellent reminders and guides for clinicians.) Still, when we reviewed the clinical literature on assessing dangerousness for the first edition of this volume, it seemed that, even with these earlier contributions, there was a relative lack of published guidance on the topic in comparison to its importance (although there were also a number of useful British contributions, e.g., from Scott, 1977, and Cox, 1982).

Recent years, however, have seen the publication of many useful guides to the clinical assessment of dangerousness in a variety of situations, including contributions by Appelbaum and Gutheil (1991), Boer, Wilson, Gauthier, and Hart (1997), Borum, Swartz, and Swanson (1996), Bednar, Bednar, Lambert, and Waite (1991), Beck (1990), Campbell (1995a, 1995b), Hall (1987), Kropp and Hart (1997), Lion (1987), Madden (1987), Lewis (1987), McNiel (1998), Monahan (1993), Pollack, McBain, and Webster (1989), Pollack and Webster (1990), Prins (1988, 1996), Saunders (1995), Tardiff (1996), Wack (1993), and Webster et al. (1994, 1997). (And see Meloy, 1989, for a good account of general principles of forensic evaluation.)

We cannot recount here all of the suggestions made by all of these authors. Rather, in what follows, we attempt to highlight what we believe to be some of the primary themes and ideas that flow from the literature regarding the clinical assessment of dangerousness. (The important subject of the assessment of possibly relevant organic factors will not be covered here. But see, in that regard, Lewis, 1987; Lion, 1987; McNiel, 1998; and Tardiff, 1996.)

It is important first to make the obvious observation that what would be an adequate or proper assessment of dangerousness depends crucially on the circumstances. Emergency room clinicians do not have the information, or the time available to gather information, that clinicians typically have in long-term forensic facilities. Clinicians in private practice may understandably be hesitant about asking a potentially dangerous client possibly stressful questions, or challenging the client in certain ways, because of reasonable fears for their own safety. (Tardiff has emphasized that "[t]he safety of the therapist is a prime consideration, because even a feeling that one is unsafe will impair evaluation and treatment," 1996, p. 117; see also Beck, 1990, pp. 198–199, and Borum et al., 1996, p. 211.) Therefore, the suggestions that follow should all be considered with the understanding that clinicians cannot be expected to do more than is reasonable under the circumstances.

FOUR BASIC POINTS

At the risk of oversimplification, it appears that four key themes consistently emerge from both the professional literature and court decisions regarding what a reasonably competent assessment of dangerousness entails when circumstances suggest that a dangerousness assessment is in order. That is, virtually all experienced commentators emphasize these themes. When *Tarasoff* liability has been imposed upon clinicians (at least in reported cases), it has usually been because of the failure of the clinician to abide by one or more of these themes (see, e.g., *Peck v. the Counseling Service of Addison County*, 1985; Monahan, 1993). Again, these themes can be discussed only briefly here.

1. *All reasonable efforts should be made to obtain details of the patient's past history of violence and response to treatment for violence.* For any reasonably comprehensive assessment, "[t]he painstaking assembling of facts and the checking of information from a variety of sources are essential" (Prins, 1988, p. 600). As Scott (1977) has observed: "Before factors can be considered, they must be gathered. It is patience, thoroughness and persistence in this process, rather than diagnostic or interviewing brilliance, that produces results. In this sense the telephone, written requests for records, and the checking of information against other informants are the important diagnostic devices [and can also be used to check the veracity of the patient's own accounts]" (p. 129).

Kozol et al. (1972) emphasized that an offender's versions of events should be "compared with the victim's version [and other sources of information]. . . . Our most serious errors in diagnosis," they wrote, "have been made when we ignored the details in the description of the assault" (p. 384). Tardiff (1996, p. 62) emphasized that it is also important to determine the *intended* injury. And when a patient's level of dangerousness depends crucially on his or her willingness to take prescribed medications (and/or to avoid abusing substances), the patient's history of treatment compliance is also important to consider.

2. *Clinicians must be alert to their own tendencies to avoid, deny, or wishfully minimize violent (or violence-related) themes and affects; and—consistent with the clinician's safety—if necessary for an informed judgment, ultimately the patient should be asked direct questions about his or her history of, and inclinations toward, violent behavior.* Kozol et al. (1972) observed that "[t]he problem for the examiner is to elicit information relevant to [dangerousness], and this can best be done by

informality and astute indirection" (p. 383). Ultimately, however, if necessary to obtain the relevant information, patients being assessed for dangerousness should be asked direct and specific questions about their history of violence (as both perpetrator and victim), fantasies of violence, level of anger, plans to commit violence, familiarity with and access to weapons, techniques of self-control and stress management (and how successful or unsuccessful those techniques have been in the past), motivation for self-control, empathy toward others (especially potential victims), and their insight into the nature, causes, and seriousness of their problems with violence. One should also inquire into the presence of substance abuse and possible organically based dyscontrol syndromes.

When patients appear to be at risk for violence, they should be asked if they are thinking of harming anyone and, if so, how they have dealt with such thoughts and feelings in the past (Beck, 1990, p. 194). Appelbaum and Gutheil (1991) suggest that it is often useful to ask the following question: "Have you ever, for any reason, accidentally or otherwise, caused death or serious injury to another human being?" Borum et al. (1996) suggest: "Are you the sort of person who has trouble controlling your temper?" "Have you found yourself hitting people or damaging things when you are angry?" Monahan (1993) has observed:

> Directly asking patients about violent behavior and possible indices of violent behavior (e.g., arrest or hospitalization as "dangerous to others") is surely the easiest and quickest way to obtain this essential information. Open-ended questions such as "What is the most violent thing you have ever done?" or "What is the closest you have ever come to being violent?" may be useful probes, as might "Do you ever worry that you might physically hurt somebody?" The obvious problem, of course, is that patients may lie or distort their history or their current thoughts. . . . Quite often, however, patients are remarkably forthcoming about violence. (p. 244; see also Mulvey et al., 1994)

Even when a risk assessment is not the focus of an evaluation, it would seem that any comprehensive mental health assessment should include posing such questions.

McNiel (1998) suggests that it can be useful to ask patients experiencing TCO ("threat/control override") symptoms what they would do if they came into contact with those they perceive as tormenting or persecuting them. He also observes that "[o]ne approach to facilitating patients' self-disclosure about their violent behavior is to precede such questions by inquiring about whether that patient has been the victim of such behavior" (p. 97). Borum et al. (1996) suggest that questions about a patient's history of and inclinations toward violence "should be asked as neutrally as possible, as if inquiring about routine symptoms" (p. 212).

Even when patients distort, deny, or minimize their history of violence, comparing the patient's account with what can be derived from records and conversations with significant others, including past victims, can provide useful information. So can questioning the patient about noteworthy discrepancies. And it is important to assess the reasons for a patient's minimization or denial of significant violent actions in the past.

3. *Consider the circumstances the evaluee may well be facing in the future (if not kept in secure confinement).* Are these circumstances similar to those that have led to violence in the past (e.g., a discordant family situation), or are these

circumstances that have reduced the risk of violence in the past (e.g., a support-ive family environment or social network)? If the former, does the evaluee demonstrate a meaningful understanding of how he or she can avoid violence in similar circumstances? Has the evaluee demonstrated a commitment to avoid-ing violence? (In general, it is worth noting Lion's 1987 observation that an "[a]ppearance of tranquility in a [recently] violent person can be deceptive. Dis-charging the patient can be an error when the problem has not been really re-solved. The clinician must consider whether anything has really changed," p. 5.)

4. *When in doubt, consult.* Simply put, it is both ethically and legally advisable to obtain a second, knowledgeable opinion about what to do when it is uncertain whether a patient poses a serious risk of causing serious harm to another person (or self) or when one's course of action is not clear (Monahan, 1993, pp. 245–246). Moreover, assessments of dangerousness are more likely to be correct when they are arrived at by more than one clinician (McNiel & Binder, 1993; Werner, Rose, & Yesavage, 1990; see also Schwartz & Pinsker, 1987, regarding the possible use of outside evaluators to mediate disputes between staff members or between staff members and patients regarding assessments of dangerousness).

MORE COMPREHENSIVE DANGEROUSNESS ASSESSMENTS

In addition to the preceding points, which apply to some degree to all assess-ments of dangerousness, a number of experienced forensic clinicians have written about the requirements for comprehensive dangerousness assessments regarding individuals who have been seriously violent in the past and who are currently being assessed for dangerousness in institutional settings or who are under supervision in outpatient settings. Some of the major points regarding comprehensive assessments that emerge from these writings, and from our own experience, follow.

1. *As the violent history of the assessee becomes more distant in time, more efforts may be required to accurately reconstruct the details of the assessee's history of violence, but such efforts should be made. All potential sources of meaningful information regard-ing the assessee's former violence, current behavior, and mental status should be consid-ered* (Mullen, 1992, p. 314; Prins, 1996, p. 57; Scott, 1977, p. 138; Webster & Polvi, 1995, pp. 1380, 1386; Wiest, 1981, p. 274). It is necessary to understand as well as possible not only the details of previous violent acts (Pollack & Webster, 1990, p. 495; Wiest, 1981, p. 273), but also the offender's behavior *before and after* those acts (Wack, 1993, p. 281) and what were the triggers (including unconscious trig-gers) for the patient's violence (Glasser, 1996).

2. *It is often sensible to have patients assessed by clinicians not attached to the pa-tient's ward before final decisions or recommendations are made.* Treating clinicians, and ward staff in general, may become so invested in believing that particular patients under their care have made adequate progress; or may so want to avoid disrupting the relative equilibrium achieved by a formerly more disorganized patient; or may so want to support the aspirations of a well-liked patient, that they avoid seeing negative signs and avoid confronting the patient with diffi-cult but necessary questions (Prins, 1988, pp. 608–609; 1996, p. 54). Conversely, a patient who is uncooperative, independent, or challenging toward staff may

be viewed as more dangerous than he or she really is. Therefore, except in obvious cases perhaps, a more detached evaluator may be called for.

3. *When inpatients pose a possible risk of serious violence, recommendations for release should not be made without subjecting the patient to a stress interview regarding the sources of his or her previous violence and/or what the patient needs to do to avoid violence in the future.* Borum et al. (1996) observed: "Many potentially violent patients can and will appear calm and non-threatening when not challenged, frustrated, or irritated. The clinician needs to be able to gingerly increase the frustration or challenge in the interview to test the frustration tolerance and impulse control of the patient without precipitating a dangerous outburst. A highly structured, unchallenging interview can dull the examiner into underestimating the violent potential of the patient" (p. 211).

In certain circumstances, with certain patients, we would make the point even more strongly: Sometimes it is precisely the question or challenge that *will* precipitate a "dangerous outburst" that must be posed (although, as Borum et al., 1996, emphasize, always in conditions of safety for the clinician). Indeed, sometimes the clinician's inner sense that certain areas should be avoided lest the patient become overly disturbed is the best guide to determining what areas require further exploration (Glasser, 1996, p. 279).

Of course, there is no legitimate reason to provoke a patient needlessly. Thus, there may be no reason to subject a patient to a stress interview if it is clear from other information that less secure supervision is not in order in any event. But when a patient with a history of serious violence is being considered for transfer to a less secure setting, it is hard to imagine concluding that transfer is in order without at least determining how the patient reacts to stressful questions regarding the circumstances he or she is likely to face in a new setting. If a patient's stability in the community is dependent on regularly taking prescribed psychiatric medication, the depth of the patient's understanding of the need for medication, and the patient's commitment to taking that medication, must be tested via challenging questions. (It is well for the clinician to remember that no question or challenge he or she might pose is likely to be as stressful to the patient as reality itself; and that, regardless of the patient's expressed wishes, it does the patient no favor to transfer him or her to a less secure, and probably more stressful, setting, only to have the patient regress into violent or otherwise seriously disturbed behavior.)

Still, because of their understandable desire to retain a therapeutic and supportive stance with the patient—and because of their perhaps justifiable fear of retaliation from a frustrated and/or provoked patient—it may be unrealistic to expect ward clinicians to conduct the necessary stress interview with certain patients. Thus, once again, it may be advisable, even necessary, in certain cases to have an assessment performed by an off-ward evaluator. But this possibility raises an additional potential problem: *To conduct an adequate stress interview, the assessor must be knowledgeable beforehand about the particular vulnerabilities of the patient.* Thus, in order to conduct a thorough stress interview, the clinician must first be thoroughly informed about what has triggered violence or regressions in the patient in the past. Indeed, it cannot be overemphasized that comprehensive dangerousness evaluations can be accomplished only if the assessor is first well versed about the patient's history. It has often been said of legal trial practice that "preparation is the key to cross-examination." Equally so, **preparation is the key to a fully satisfactory dangerousness evaluation.**

4. *Group therapy may be a useful assessment tool, both to discover underlying feelings and concerns and to evaluate whether a previously violent offender still lacks genuine empathy for others.* Cox (1982) observed:

> The mercurial flashpoint(s) of a dynamic group [may] provide [a] disclosure of the patient's inner world [before the patient] had time to reflect upon the consequences. The dynamics of the situation are far removed from those of a formal assessment session, in which [the patient] may well be asking himself about the wisdom of making a particular reply to a question. . . . [The] spontaneity [of the group] offers us insight into ways in which the patient deals with unknown situations. . . .
>
> [Moreover], a patient who is in a therapeutic group with its spontaneously evolving, unpredictable emotional life, tending to mobilize disclosure potential may, for the first time, declare within such a group that [there] is unfinished business which preoccupies him. (pp. 83, 87)

5. *Determining the patient's level of insight regarding the genesis and dynamics of his or her previous violence—and his or her need to comply with treatment recommendations—can provide important information regarding the patient's vulnerability to regression in response to stress.* To the extent that an individual's violence in the past stemmed from and was a defense against psychic pain, evidence that the individual can now confront and appropriately deal with such feelings is a positive prognostic sign—although it must equally be born in mind that insight is no guarantee against regression and that some offenders, particularly psychopathic and compulsive offenders, may well be able to give the appearance of having considerable insight into their past difficulties while still retaining their most deep-seated and most dangerous pathologies (Cox, 1982). However, if the patient cannot achieve a meaningful (i.e., seemingly accurate and affect-laden) understanding of the psychological forces, defects, and vulnerabilities that led to his or her previous violence—or how to realistically deal with such problems in the future—that would suggest that the patient is still unable to deal with these forces without special assistance (e.g., close supervision and/or medication).

Moreover, as Meloy (1987) has observed, it is important to determine the patient's level of insight regarding his or her "thoughts and feelings before, during, and after previous violent acts. . . . The unwillingness or inability to evoke memories of intrapsychic experience concurrent with violent behavior is a poor prognostic indicator, and suggests a borderline personality organization with either psychopathic or histrionic traits, respectively. If the patient is able to evoke his thought-affect experience, its evaluation as a catalytic or non-catalytic event in relation to violence should be determined and clinically documented. The assessment of aggressive thought-affect complexes when actual violence did not occur is also critical to prevent systematic bias in the direction of overpredicting violence" (p. 41).

6. *When a patient's history of violence has been, at least in part, in response to delusions or fantasies, it is important to search for the continued (even if hidden) existence of delusions, fantasies, or preoccupations related to violence* (Meloy, 1988; Webster et al., 1994, p. 56). Both extended interviews and projective tests may be useful in this regard, as might monitoring and examining the patient's behavior and activities for signs that he or she is still preoccupied with concerns that led to violence in the past. Indeed, when evaluating inpatients, staff who regularly observe and speak with the evaluee may provide crucial information about the patient's preoccupations that may not be forthcoming in formal interviews. In any event, it

should be noted that *the discovery of unspoken delusions, fantasies, or preoccupations related to violence—and determining how a patient currently responds to stress—cannot be accomplished by actuarial methods.*

7. *A comprehensive dangerousness assessment should include an evaluation of the patient's level of self-esteem and susceptibility to narcissistic injury, as well as his or her ability to relate to other people well enough to maintain self-esteem and to tolerate personal losses, should they occur.* Cox's 1982 observation on the subject is noteworthy: "I have rarely seen a patient from any diagnostic category in whom self-esteem regulation was not closely related in one way or another to his core psychopathology and, ipso facto, to his deviant behavior. . . . The recovery of lost self esteem, or the establishment of hitherto negligible or precarious self esteem, features repeatedly in psychiatric histories [of violent individuals], ranging from those of the inadequate recidivist to the catastrophic homicidal activity of a patient with previously overcontrolled personality characteristics, or the psychotically disturbed patient, . . . or to the narcissistic psychopath's intense delight that everyone was looking for him when he was on the run" (p. 82).

Thus, indications that a patient remains highly susceptible to overwhelming feelings of worthlessness or emptiness should be worrisome signs (Wishnie, 1977), even if the patient understands having these feeling and that they led to violence in the past. Similarly, the persistence of severe interpersonal difficulties may suggest that the patient has yet to overcome a major source of low self-esteem, and that away from a protective environment the patient will be vulnerable to suffering from loneliness and rejection.

Schulte et al. (1994) have described a group of violent or potentially violent individuals whose dangerousness was intimately related to their susceptibility to narcissistic injury. Lion (1987, p. 11) has suggested that "[p]atients' vulnerability to object loss can often be obtained from their histories." Madden (1987, p. 61) observed that "violent behavior is [often] a screen that . . . serves to protect a fragile individual who is very afraid." Therefore, he suggests, a good question for the assessor to consider is: "What makes the patient afraid?" (cf. Estroff, Zimmer, Lachicotte, & Benoit, 1994; Swanson et al., 1997).

8. *An assessment of the patient's capacity for empathy may be crucial.* Kozol et al. (1972) observed: "The essence of dangerousness appears to be a paucity of feeling-concern for others. . . . The potential for injuring another is compounded when this lack of concern is coupled with anger" (p. 379). (Of course, while lack of empathy is a risk factor for recidivism, some patients without empathy do learn to control or moderate their aggressive impulses out of self-interest and with the help of treatment. When a patient's previous violence has stemmed from the combination of psychopathic character pathology and either substance abuse or a psychotic episode, successful treatment of the patient's substance-abusing tendencies and/or, if necessary, the patient's vulnerability to psychotic episodes can significantly reduce the risk of recidivism even if the character pathology remains.)

In evaluating an offender's level of empathy, stress interviews, group therapy, and projective testing may be useful (Revitch & Schlesinger, 1978, pp. 142–144; 1981, pp. 24–46). Serious consideration should also be given to administering the PCL-R to help clarify an assessee's proclivity toward antisocial behavior. It should be kept in mind, however, that only very high PCL-R scores (generally > 29 out of a possible 40) are a good sign of the existence of the "taxon" of psychopathy (Harris, Rice, & Quinsey, 1994; Rice, 1997); and only low scores indicate a low risk of recidivism. Midrange scores seem to be of little predictive value.

9. *Patients with a history of serious violence on supervised outpatient status should be monitored closely for signs of regression toward violent behavior.* According to Lion (1987), "Good follow-up is the key to good assessment in all aspects of medicine, particularly with patients who are prone to impulsiveness and aggressiveness. The clinician needs to ascertain whether a particular patient seeks help in times of stress. . . . [Moreover,] the existence of violence in the thoughts and lives of [potentially dangerous] patients must be monitored as closely as depression" (pp. 15–16). Wack (1993) has described in detail many of the requirements for a comprehensive risk assessment regarding forensic patients on conditional release status. And it is worth noting Prins's (1996) observation that "the price that supervisors pay for ensuring the liberty of the [patient] to live safely in the community is that of 'eternal vigilance.' Supervisors must therefore be willing to ask 'unthinkable' and 'unaskable' questions if they are to engage effectively in this work" (p. 60).

10. *When evaluating individuals who belong to a class of offenders (or potential offenders) regarding whom specialized risk assessment instruments have been developed, consideration should be given to employing those instruments.* For example, the Violence Prediction Scheme (Webster et al., 1994) can be usefully employed regarding a fairly wide range of mentally disordered offenders. And specialized assessment instruments and/or guides have been developed to be applied to sex offenders, child abusers, and spouse abusers and batterers (see, e.g., Boer et al., 1997; Campbell, 1995a, 1995b; Kropp & Hart, 1997; Webster & Jackson, 1997).

AVOIDING ASSESSMENT ERRORS

A number of commentators have suggested that assessments of dangerousness can be improved if assessors avoid making errors that have frequently been observed to pertain to dangerousness evaluations (see, e.g., Ennis & Litwack, 1974, pp. 719–734; Hall, 1987; Monahan, 1981, pp. 57–65; Pfohl, 1978; Webster & Menzies, 1989; Webster & Polvi, 1995). Some relevant recommendations for avoiding common errors follow.

1. *Make judgments based on adequate information.* Dietz observed that "[t]he most remediable error in the clinical prediction of crime is the making of a prediction without sufficient data to provide a basis for informed judgment" (quoted in Pollack & Webster, 1990, p. 495). In certain cases, it is essential to review available victim statements, police reports, trial transcripts, or recordings of prior confessions (Mullen, 1992, p. 314; Scott, 1977, p. 138). But it is equally important to fully evaluate an offender's ability and desire to avoid violence in the future. In any event, all pertinent information should be reviewed—and reviewed for accuracy—as circumstances permit and/or require. Webster and Polvi (1995) made the important point that "[i]f this review is undertaken early in the assessment, as it should be, it may be possible to arrange for the recovery of missing items of information" (p. 1380).

2. *Focus on those variables that are most relevant to determining dangerousness and the specific question regarding dangerousness that is at issue.*

3. *Always consider the nature of the situations the offender is likely to be in if released from his or her current level of confinement or supervision; and whether the offender's previous violence was due more to circumstances that have now changed or can change than to "dispositional variables or personal traits"* (Monahan, 1981, p. 64; Pfohl, 1978, p. 212). Of course, in almost all cases, the offender's previous violence will be due to some combination of personal and situational factors. The task of the evaluator is to weigh how those factors interacted in the past and the chances of similar interactions in the future.

4. *Recognize one's own legitimate doubts regarding an assessee's dangerousness, and legitimate disagreements between evaluators and among staff, to avoid unjustifiably confident determinations of dangerousness (in either direction).* Avoid adopting a judgmental perspective, advocating a cause, or aligning oneself too closely with the patient's wishes and desires. Be open to information that contradicts one's initial, or even stated, opinion. Indeed, as Appelbaum and Gutheil (1991, p. 350) have stressed, it is useful, and probably ethically required, in many forensic evaluations to imagine that one was retained as an expert by the "other side of the case," and to imagine how one's evaluation or conclusions might be different if that were so.

5. *Be as knowledgeable as possible about documented risk factors for violence and look for risk factors.* For example, in emergency room contexts, it will often be appropriate to question patients regarding the possible presence of TCO symptoms. In most contexts in which a dangerousness evaluation is required, it will be necessary to inquire about the possibility of substance abuse.

6. *Be careful not to underestimate the potential for violence in female patients who have a history of violence.* Although it is true that, on the whole in our society, women have a much lower rate of violence than men, recent research indicates that women who evidence risk factors for violence are about as likely as men to commit violence (Newhill, Mulvey, & Lidz, 1995), and that, relative to their estimations regarding men, clinicians tend to underestimate the risk of future violence by such women (Coontz, Lidz, & Mulvey, 1994; McNiel & Binder, 1995). As Taylor and Monahan (1996) observed, factors that mitigate against risk in a general offender population (e.g., female gender, non-young age) may not necessarily mitigate against risk among people with serious mental disorders.

7. *Consider base rate information or actuarial assessments, if reasonably obtainable and relevant, regarding the statistical likelihood that patients similar to the one being evaluated will act violently if preventive action is not taken.* Indeed, in his 1981 monograph, Monahan stated that "knowledge of the appropriate base rate is the most important single piece of information necessary to make an accurate prediction" (p. 60). The base rate of violence for a given group is the proportion of people *in that group* who would commit violence under certain circumstances within a given time period (pp. 59, 66). Actuarial assessments of dangerousness, if validated and useful, in a sense provide the base rates of violence (or at least of detected violence) for individuals who obtain various scores, or various combinations of (perhaps weighted) subscores, on the actuarial index.

Monahan (1981) also recognized, as we have repeatedly noted, that "[i]n many circumstances [meaningful] base rates are neither available nor readily obtainable" (p. 152). However, when a confined individual being considered for release appears to belong to a class of offenders with a low rate of recidivism (e.g., offenders like those studied by Harris et al., 1993, who have low PCL-R scores), clinicians should certainly question recommending retention (on the grounds of dangerousness) unless they can explain why this individual is likely to be different from the class of offenders to which he or she appears to belong. Conversely, *when a patient appears to belong to a class of individuals with a high rate of serious recidivism, even if the patient also appears to be no longer dangerous (e.g., based on behavior in the institution), caution should be exercised before concluding that the patient poses a substantially lesser threat of recidivism than other members of that class.*

TWO SPECIAL PROBLEMS: CATATHYMIC OFFENDERS AND COMPULSIVE OFFENDERS

Catathymic Offenders

The concept of the catathymic crisis has recently been reviewed at length by Schlesinger (1996). Hans W. Maier (1912) introduced the concept of catathymia, which he conceived of as a psychological process or reaction activated by a strong and tenacious affect connected to an underlying complex of ideas that overwhelms the individual's psychological homeostasis and disrupts logical thinking. Wertham (1937, 1978) was the first to refocus the concept to explain certain otherwise inexplicable acts of violence committed by an individual who has had a long-term relationship with the victim. In contrast, however, Satten, Menninger, and Mayman (1960) used the concept of the catathymic crisis to describe sudden murderous acts triggered by an individual who the perpetrator has just met, "when the victim to be is unconsciously perceived as a key figure in some past traumatic configuration. [The] behavior, or even the mere presence, of this figure adds a stress to the unstable balance of forces, which results in a sudden extreme discharge of violence, similar to the explosion that takes place when a percussion cap ignites a charge of dynamite" (p. 52).

Revitch (1964) described a condition that he termed "catathymic attacks," which consisted of seemingly unprovoked explosions of rage followed often by partial amnesia for the event. (Many, but not all, of Revitch's cases were seen in a female prison population.) More recently, Meloy (1992) and Wilson, Daly, and Daniele (1995) have described catathymic-like violence stemming from various disorders of attachment.

Revitch (1977) and Revitch and Schlesinger (1978, 1981, 1989), following both Satten et al. (1960) and Wertham (1937), defined two types of catathymic processes leading to violence: the acute and the chronic. The acute process involves a sudden act of violence triggered by a sudden overwhelming affect. Many times, the perpetrator of the assault cannot give a logical explanation for the act. In many, but not all, cases, he or she only partially recalls it. The clinician, too, may be hard-pressed to understand what triggered the violent episode.

In addition to Satten and his colleagues, other writers have described and discussed sudden explosive murders without apparent motive (e.g., Blackman, Weiss, & Lambert, 1963). Ruotolo (1968) described cases of sudden murder triggered by an injury to the pride system. Karpman (1935) contended that unresolved oedipal conflicts could generate such outbursts.

Wertham (1937, 1978) described the clinical development of the *chronic* catathymic crisis as involving certain stages. First, a traumatic experience creates in the individual an unresolvable inner conflict that produces extreme emotional tension. The individual then comes to believe that an external situation is responsible for his or her inner tension, and thinking becomes more and more egocentric and disturbed. Eventually, the patient decides that a violent act, against another or self, is the only way out. The individual may struggle against the urge to commit violence, but if the extreme emotional tension persists, the act may well be carried out. If it is, the act is typically followed by a period of relief from emotional tension and perhaps even calmness and superficial normality. On the other hand, suicide may follow the eventual murder if the catathymic tension is not completely discharged after the violent event.

Revitch and Schlesinger (1981, 1989) divided the chronic catathymic process into three stages: incubation, violent act, and relief. The incubation state, they noted, may last from several days to even a year. The offender often views the violence he or she is considering (as a means of discharging unbearable tension) as ego-alien or unreal. The offender may even inform friends, therapists, or clergy of his or her thoughts. Unfortunately, the offender's warnings are often ignored or misunderstood.

Revitch and Schlesinger (1981) reported that the most common type of catathymic murder occurs within the framework of an ego-threatening relationship that may activate "(a) [a feeling of] sexual inadequacy or an intensification of unresolved incestuous or homosexual conflicts; (b) [possibly] a transfer of negative emotions to the victim from another subject, so that the victim has only a symbolic significance for the offender; and (c) a feeling of helplessness and confusion" (p. 128). As these feelings come to the surface and disrupt logical thinking, the future victim often pulls back from the relationship with the offender, thereby creating more anger, conflict, and disorganization. However, it is the conflicts engendered by the relationship itself that primarily disrupt the offender's psychological integration and lead to violence.

Depression (most commonly), disorganized thinking, and/or obsessive rumination often characterize the incubation period. After the violent act, it often seems ego-alien to the perpetrator and has a dreamlike quality. Also important for diagnostic purposes (if only after the fact) is that, in spite of the relief that often results, there is hardly any evidence of rage or anger against the victims. On the contrary, they are typically remembered with sympathy. Thus, catathymic violence, in such cases, is not primarily an act of revenge but a means of securing liberation from a deep-seated conflict.

Implications for Risk Assessment.   Acute catathymic episodes are essentially unpredictable. However, many chronic catathymic homicides and attacks possibly could have been prevented if the existence of a building catathymic crisis had been recognized and treated with sufficient urgency. Many chronic catathymic processes present themselves initially as cases of depression, but if there is any reason to suspect that the patient is considering a violent solution to his or her problem, further inquiry must be made.

An important sign that should alert the clinician to a serious risk of catathymic violence is an indication that the patient has come to the conclusion that the only way out of the state of built-up frustration, tension, and depression is to commit an act of violence. If such an idea is not reported directly by the patient, the examiner should question the patient carefully to see if such an idea has ever occurred to him or her. The clinician should not be overly concerned that questioning in such a direct fashion will implant such an idea; on the contrary, it is often experienced by prospective offenders as comforting to know that someone, at least, understands their plight and the depth of their inner disturbance. "When patients are seriously violent, their actions are rarely entirely ego-syntonic or conflict free. The [mental health professional] is most likely to prevent future violence if he or she treats the proposed violence as a therapeutic issue. This means discuss it with the patient. Discussion is not a substitute for action, when action is judged to be necessary. But, whatever one does or contemplates, one should try to involve the patient in a discussion of the issue and the proposed course of action" (Beck, 1990, p. 194).

In some cases, however, the catathymic patient's growing obsession with violence may not be recognized at all because warning signs are ignored and/or because of a failure to elicit sufficient information from the client—perhaps because the clinician is uncomfortable with or frightened by violent ideation. As Kutzer and Lion (1984) observed, "[t]he biggest obstacle to assessment is the clinician's denial" (p. 71). However, eliciting the patient's feelings is only a first step in evaluation and treatment. Some cases of catathymic violence probably could have been prevented if the perpetrator's stated concerns about losing control were taken sufficiently seriously—that is, if it was recognized that the patient's preoccupation with violence was the outgrowth of a severe and building catathymic crisis, or if it was recognized that treatment was not yet defusing the crisis. It is important to bear in mind that the mere fact that the patient is expressing concerns about violence does not necessarily mean that he or she is discharging the underlying tension.

If the clinician is uncertain of the patient's intentions or stability, further examination is necessary to help uncover an underlying delusion, a still-building catathymic process, or a serious ego-syntonic idea to commit violence. If drugs or alcohol are involved or if the individual is experiencing severe stress, the risk of violence increases. In some cases, hospitalization should be encouraged, if for no other reason than to temporarily defuse the situation (cf. Schulte et al., 1994, p. 621). And it should be noted that the chronic catathymic process can be repeated even after a long prison term if the underlying dynamics that led to the violence initially have not been resolved.

Compulsive Offenders

Some individuals experience an extreme internal pressure to commit an act of violence, illegal sexual contact, or some other criminal act that may lead to violence. Such cases have been described in the literature as far back as 1886 by Krafft-Ebing (1934) and more recently by Revitch and Schlesinger (1989) and Myers, Reccoppa, Burton, and McElroy (1993).

Compulsive offenses may be committed in a specific, ritualistic manner, or they may be more diffuse (Revitch & Schlesinger, 1981). Fantasies of violence may precede the act by many years. Once the violence begins, however, repetition is usually frequent and at close intervals (although in some cases, many years elapse between crimes). Schlesinger and Revitch (1983) report that many compulsive acts of violence have an underlying basis in sexual conflicts. The sexual dynamics may be overt, as in cases of rape or sex murder; or they may be covert, as in some break-in and entries, so that the sexual dynamics can be elicited only through careful clinical examination and with the aid of psychological tests (Schlesinger & Kutash, 1981).

Compulsive offenders rarely reveal their intention to act violently. They are mostly introverted, isolated, schizoid individuals who harbor intense fantasies of a violent nature but do not share these fantasies with others. Fantasy may serve as a "substitute for action," but it may also "prepare the way" for action (Beres, 1961). On the other hand, in the case of some potentially compulsive offenders, their sexual conflicts—including hostility to women, preoccupation with maternal sexual conduct, overt or covert incestuous preoccupations, guilt over and rejection of sex as impure, or feelings of sexual inferiority—may be discernible before a history of serious violence emerges.

Implications for Risk Assessment.   The following signs, when seen in considerable combination, should alert the clinician to the possible development of an underlying compulsive syndrome and the possibility of severe dangerousness, even if the individual has no history of violence and has not directly expressed any intent to commit violence:

1. A history of mistreatment of women, or fantasies of assaulting women
2. Breaking and entering committed alone and under bizarre circumstances
3. Fetishism for female underclothing or destruction of them
4. Expressions of hatred, contempt, or fear of women
5. Dislike for cats or actual violence against cats or other animals
6. Violent and primitive fantasy life
7. Confusion of sexual identity, as elicited on projective tests
8. Sexual inhibitions and moral preoccupation with sexual conduct
9. Feelings of isolation and blurring of reality boundaries

Even prior to any evidence of acting out of violence, when presented with a case exhibiting the above signs, mental health professionals should seriously consider taking preventive action to protect potential victims. Such action might include (a) immediate involvement of the patient in individual psychotherapy, together with close monitoring of the patient's behavior by responsible family members; (b) encouraging the patient to accept voluntary hospitalization if violence appears imminent; (c) perhaps warning any individual whom the patient has identified as a potential victim. (Seemingly successful psychotherapeutic interventions in some cases have been described by Schlesinger & Revitch, 1990; and Kristainsson, 1995, has reported on the potential utility of pharmacotherapy, together with other interventions, with chronic psychopaths.)

Individuals who have a history of serious violence of a seemingly compulsive nature are obviously powerfully disposed to violence and may well act violently again even after lengthy prison terms or hospital stays. Indeed, there are numerous accounts of individuals who committed bizarre murders after having served lengthy prison sentences for similar homicides (e.g., Guttmacher, 1963; Kozol et al., 1972; Schlesinger & Revitch, 1990). High intelligence, good adjustment in prison, and a good work record are useless prognostic indicators when a dangerous sexually motivated compulsion is present.

Careful examination of the patient's fantasy life is thus particularly important when a compulsive process is suspected (whether or not the patient has yet acted violently). Especially in cases of gynocide and sexual assault, there is frequently a history of sadistic fantasies. To elicit such dangerous fantasies, there is no substitute for a thorough, unhurried interview. Some projective psychological tests, most notably the thematic techniques, may also be helpful.

Often, however, the patient will not reveal such fantasies, even though he or she is harboring them. Moreover, compulsive offenders may sometimes evidence considerable insight into their condition and yet retain their compulsive tendencies. Thus, compulsive offenders who have been in confinement for some period of time may evidence few signs of continued dangerousness, and their continued dangerousness may easily escape detection, especially if insufficient weight is given to the details of their compulsive history. Given the severity of the compulsive disorder, however—especially when there is a history of repeated violence or violence mixed with sexual impulses—extreme caution should be exercised before any presumption of nondangerousness is arrived at in such cases.

CONCLUSION

The field of dangerousness risk assessments has made considerable strides in recent years in terms of (a) advances in research methodology; (b) the development of the PCL-R and its validation as an instrument that can significantly contribute to assessments of dangerousness; (c) the identification of a number of validated risk factors for violence; (d) the development of actuarial risk assessment instruments; and (e) the explication of guidelines for clinical assessments (Webster & Jackson, 1997). However, further and more refined developments are necessary in each of these areas. In particular, supposed risk factors for violence, and actuarial risk assessment schemes that derive from them, must be studied for their association with various degrees of violence over various time periods if they are to be of maximum practical utility and legal relevance. Clinical assessments of dangerousness need to be monitored and described more extensively and more precisely to better determine the degree to which they follow the relevant guidelines recommended in the literature (and if not, why not?), and the degree to which clinical judgments of dangerousness are based on facts and logic rather than on mere intuition or idiosyncratic presumptions.

A hopeful sign for the future is that the advantages and limits of both actuarial and clinical methods of risk assessment are increasingly being recognized throughout the field. Indeed, in recent years, there has been a refreshing absence from the literature of the polemical and unjustified attacks on clinical assessments that characterized many earlier writings.* However, there remains, among academic observers, a strong preference for actuarial assessments that is neither realistic (because validated and legally useful actuarial means of assessment are not, and may never be, available regarding many important risk assessments) nor justified by actual data (because actuarial risk assessment formulas have yet to be proven to be superior to many of the risk assessments that clinicians actually make). On the other hand, there is now a widespread recognition that both actuarial and clinical contributions can be useful in making dangerousness risk assessments, at least in many cases.

NOTE

More recently, Quinsey, Harris, Rice, & Cormier (1998) have called for "the complete replacement of existing practice with actuarial methods" (p. 171). But it remains questionable whether truly relevant and/or cost effective actuarial assessment schemes will be available for all necessary evaluations of dangerousness.

REFERENCES

Addington v. Texas, 441 U.S. 418 (1979).

American Psychiatric Association. (1974). *Clinical aspects of the violent individual.* Washington, DC: American Psychiatric Association.

American Psychological Association. (1978). Report of the task force on the role of psychology in the criminal justice system. *American Psychologist, 33,* 1099–1113.

Appelbaum, P. S. (1984). Hypothetical, psychiatric testimony, and the death sentence. *Bulletin of the American Academy of Psychiatry and the Law, 12,* 169–177.

Appelbaum, P. S., & Gutheil, T. G. (1991). *Clinical handbook of psychiatry and the law* (2nd ed.). Baltimore: Williams & Wilkins.

Ball, E. M., Young, D., Dotson, L. A., Brothers, L. T., & Robbins, D. (1994). Factors associated with dangerous behavior in forensic inpatients: Results from a pilot study. *Bulletin of the American Academy of Psychiatry and the Law, 22*(4), 605–620.

Barefoot v. Estelle, 463 U.S. 880 (1983).

Baxstrom v. Herold, 383 U.S. 107 (1966).

Beck, J. C. (1990). Clinical aspects of the duty to warn or protect. In R. Simon (Ed.), *Review of clinical psychiatry and the law* (Vol. 1, pp. 191–204). Washington, DC: American Psychiatric Press.

Bednar, R. L., Bednar, S. C., Lambert, M. J., & Waite, D. R. (1991). *Psychotherapy with high risk clients: Legal and professional standards.* Pacific Grove, CA: Brooks/Cole.

Beres, D. (1961). Perception, imagination, and reality. *International Journal of Psychoanalysis, 41,* 327–334.

Binder, R. L., & McNiel, D. E. (1996). Application of the Tarasoff ruling and its effect on the victims and the therapeutic relationship. *Psychiatric Services, 47*(11), 1212–1215.

Bjørkly, S. (1995). Prediction of aggression in psychiatric patients: A review of prospective prediction studies. *Clinical Psychology Review, 15,* 475–502.

Bjørkly, S. (1996). Report form for aggressive episodes: Preliminary report. *Perceptual and Motor Skills, 83,* 1139–1152.

Blackman, N., Weiss, M. M. A., & Lambert, J. W. (1963). The sudden murderer. *Archives of General Psychiatry, 8,* 289–294.

Boer, D. P., Wilson, R. J., Gauthier, C. M., & Hart, S. D. (1997). Assessing risk for sexual violence: Guidelines for clinical practice. In C. D. Webster & M. A. Jackson (Eds.), *Impulsivity: Perspectives, principles, and practice.* New York: Guilford Press.

Borum, R. (1996). Improving the clinical practice of violence risk assessment: Technology, guidelines, and training. *American Psychologist, 51,* 945–956.

Borum, R., Swartz, M., & Swanson, J. (1996, July). Assessing and managing violence risk in clinical practice. *Journal of Practicing Psychiatry and Behavioral Health*, 205–215.

Brooks, A. D. (1992). The constitutionality and morality of civilly committing violent sexual predators. *University of Puget Sound Law Review, 15*, 709–754.

Campbell, J. C. (Ed.). (1995a). *Assessing dangerousness: Violence by sexual offenders, batterers, and child abusers*. Thousand Oaks, CA: Sage.

Campbell, J. C. (1995b). Prediction of homicide by battered women. In J. C. Campbell (Ed.), *Assessing dangerousness: Violence by sexual offfenders, batterers, and child abusers*. Thousand Oaks, CA: Sage.

Cocozza, J. J., & Steadman, H. J. (1978). Prediction in psychiatry: An example of misplaced confidence in experts. *Social Problems, 25*, 265–276.

Commonwealth v. Rosenberg, 410 Mass 347, 573 N.E.2d 949 (1991).

Coontz, P. D., Lidz, C. W., & Mulvey, E. P. (1994). Gender and the assessment of dangerousness in the psychiatric emergency room. *International Journal of Law and Psychiatry, 17*(4), 369–376.

Cox, M. (1982). The psychotherapist as assessor of dangerousness. In J. R. Hamilton & H. Freeman (Eds.), *Dangerousness: Psychiatric assessment and management* (pp. 81–87). London: Gaskell.

Daubert v. Merrell Dow Pharmaceuticals, Inc., 113 S. Ct. 2786 (1993).

Dershowitz, A. (1969, February). The psychiatrist's power in civil commitment. *Psychology Today*, p. 47.

Developments in the law: Civil commitment of the mentally ill. (1974). *Harvard Law Review, 87*, 1190–1406.

Dinwiddie, S. H., & Yutzy, S. (1993). Dangerous delusions? Misidentification syndromes and professional negligence. *Bulletin of the American Academy of Psychiatry and the Law, 21*(4), 513–521.

Dix, G. E. (1980). Clinical evaluation of the "dangerousness" of "normal" criminal defendants. *Virginia Law Review, 66*, 523–581.

Doe v. Poritz, 142 N.J. 1; 662 A.2d 367 (1995).

Douglas, K. S., Macfarlane, E., & Webster, C. D. (1996). Predicting dangerousness in the contemporary Canadian mental health and criminal justice systems. *Canada's Mental Health, 43*(3), 4–10.

Drukteinis, A. M. (1992). Serial murder—The heart of darkness. *Contemporary Psychiatry, 22*, 532–538.

Ennis, B. J., & Litwack, T. R. (1974). Psychiatry and the presumption of expertise: Flipping coins in the courtroom. *California Law Review, 62*, 693–752.

Estroff, S. E., Zimmer, C., Lachicotte, W. S., & Benoit, M. L. S. (1994). The influence of social networks and social support on violence by persons with serious mental illness. *Hospital and Community Psychiatry, 45*(7), 669–679.

Fagan, J., & Guggenheim. (1996). Preventive detention and the judicial prediction of dangerousness for juveniles: A natural experiment. *Journal of Criminal Law and Criminology, 86*(2), 415–448.

Faigman, D., Kaye, D., Saks, M., & Sanders, J. (1997). *Modern scientific evidence: The law and science of expert testimony*. St. Paul, MN: West.

Fraser v. U.S., 674 A.2d 811 (Conn., 1996).

Furr, K. D. (1993). Prediction of sexual or violent recidivism among sexual offenders. *Annals of Sex Research, 6*, 271–286.

Gacono, C. B., & Hutton, H. E. (1994). Suggestions for the clinical and forensic use of the Hare Psychopathology Checklist–Revised (PCL–R). *International Journal of Law and Psychiatry, 17*(3), 303–317.

Gardner, W., Lidz, C. W., Mulvey, E. P., & Shaw, E. C. (1996a). A comparison of actuarial methods for identifying repetitively violent patients with mental illness. *Law and Human Behavior, 20*(1), 35–48.

Gardner, W., Lidz, C. W., Mulvey, E. P., & Shaw, E. C. (1996b). Clinical versus actuarial predictions of violence in patients with mental illness. *Journal of Consulting and Clinical Psychology, 64*(3), 602–609.

Glasser, M. (1996). The management of dangerousness: The psychoanalytic contribution. *Journal of Forensic Psychiatry, 7*(2), 271–283.

Grisso, T., & Appelbaum, P. S. (1992). Is it unethical to offer predictions of future violence? *Law and Human Behavior, 16*(6), 621–633.

Grove, W. M., & Meehl, P. E. (1996). Comparative efficiency of informal (subjective, impressionistic) and formal (mechanical, algorithmic) prediction procedures: The clinical-statistical controversy. *Psychology, Public Policy, and Law, 2*(2), 293–323.

Guttmacher, M. (1963). Dangerous offenders. *Crime and Delinquency, 9,* 381–390.

Hall, H. V. (1982). Dangerous predictions and the maligned forensic professional: Suggestions for detecting distortions of true basal violence. *Criminal Justice and Behavior, 9,* 3–12.

Hall, H. V. (1987). *Violence prediction: Guidelines for the forensic practitioner.* Springfield, IL: Thomas.

Hare, R. D. (1991). *Manual for the Hare Psychopathy Checklist–Revised.* Toronto: Multi-Health Systems.

Hare, R. D. (1996). Psychopathy: A clinical construct whose time has come. *Criminal Justice and Behavior, 23,* 25–54.

Hare, R. D., & Hart, S. D. (1992). Psychopathy, mental disorder and crime. In S. Hodgins (Ed.), *Mental disorder and crime* (pp. 104–115). Newbury Park, CA: Sage.

Harris, G. T., Rice, M. E., & Quinsey, V. L. (1993). Violent recidivism of mentally disordered offenders: The development of a statistical prediction instrument. *Criminal Justice and Behavior, 20,* 315–335.

Harris, G. T., Rice, M. E., & Quinsey, V. L. (1994). Psychopathy as a taxon: Evidence that psychopaths are a discrete class. *Journal of Consulting and Clinical Psychology, 62*(2), 387–397.

Hart, S. D., & Hare, R. D. (1996). Psychopathy and risk assessment. *Current Opinion in Psychiatry, 9,* 380–383.

Hart, S. D., & Hare, R. D. (1997a). Psychopathy: Assessment and association with criminal conduct. In D. M. Stoff, J. Brieling, & J. Maser (Eds.), *Handbook of antisocial behavior* (pp. 22–35). New York: Wiley.

Hart, S. D., & Hare, R. D. (1997b). The association between psychopathy and narcissism: Theoretical views and empirical evidence. In E. Ronningstam (Ed.), *Disorders of narcissism: Theoretical, empirical, and clinical implications* (pp. 415–436). Washington, DC: American Psychiatric Press.

Hart, S. D., Hare, R. D., & Forth, A. E. (1994). Psychopathy as a risk marker for violence: Development and validation of a screening version of the revised Psychopathy Checklist. In J. Monahan & H. J. Steadman (Eds.), *Violence and mental disorder.* Chicago: University of Chicago Press.

Hart, S. D., Webster, C. D., & Menzies, R. J. (1993). A note on portraying the accuracy of violence predictions. *Law and Human Behavior, 17*(6), 695–700.

Heilbrun, A. B. (1996). *Criminal dangerousness and the risk of violence.* Lanham, MD: University Press of America.

Hill, C. D., Rogers, R., & Bickford. (1996). Predicting aggressive and socially disruptive behavior in a maximum security forensic psychiatric hospital. *Journal of Forensic Sciences, 41*(1), 56–59.

Hillbrand, M. (1995). Aggression against self and aggression against others in violent psychiatric patients. *Journal of Consulting and Clinical Psychology, 63*(4), 668–671.

In re George L., 85 N.Y.2d 295, 624 N.Y.S.2d 99, 648 N.E.2d 475 (1995).

Jones v. United States, 463 U.S. 354 (1983).

Junginger, J. (1995). Command hallucinations and the prediction of dangerousness. *Psychiatric Services, 46*(9), 911–914.

Karpman. (1935). *The individual criminal.* Washington, DC: Nervous and Mental Disease.

Kasper, M. E., Rogers, R., & Adams, P. A. (1996). Dangerousness and command hallucinations: An investigation of psychotic inpatients. *Bulletin of the American Academy of Psychiatry and Law, 24*(2), 219–224.

Kosson, D. S., Smith, S. S., & Newman, J. P. (1990). Evaluating the construct validity of psychopathy in black and white inmates: Three preliminary studies. *Journal of Abnormal Psychology, 99*(3), 250–259.

Kozol, H. L., Boucher, R. J., & Garofalo, R. F. (1972). The diagnosis and treatment of dangerousness. *Crime and Delinquency, 19,* 371–392.

Kozol, H. L., Boucher, R. J., & Garofalo, R. F. (1973). Dangerousness: A reply to Monahan. *Crime and Delinquency, 19,* 554–555.

Krafft-Ebing, R. von. (1934). *Psychopathia sexualis* (F. J. Redman, Trans.). Brooklyn, NY: Physicians and Surgeons Book.

Kristainsson, M. (1995). Incurable psychopaths? *Bulletin of the American Academy of Psychiatry and Law, 23*(4), 555–562.

Kropp, P. R., & Hart, S. D. (1997). Assessing risk for violence in wife assaulters: The spousal risk assessment guide. In C. D. Webster & M. A. Jackson (Eds.), *Impulsivity: Perspectives, principles, and practice.* New York: Guilford Press.

Kutzer, D., & Lion, J. R. (1984). The violent patient: Assessment and intervention. In S. Saunders, A. M. Anderson, C. A. Hart, & G. M. Rubenstein (Eds.), *Violent individuals and families: A handbook for practitioners* (pp. 69–86). Springfield, IL: Thomas.

Lessard v. Schmidt, 349 F. Supp. 1078 (1972); vacated on other grounds, 414 U.S. 473 (1974).

Lewis, D. O. (1987). Special diagnostic and treatment issues concerning violent juveniles. In L. Roth (Ed.), *Clinical treatment of the violent person* (pp. 138–155). New York: Guilford Press.

Lidz, C. W., Mulvey, E. P., & Gardner, W. (1993). The accuracy of predictions of violence to others. *Journal of the American Medical Association, 269,* 1007–1011.

Link, B. G., Monahan, J., Stueve, A., & Cullen, F. T. (1997). *Real in their consequences: A sociological approach to understanding the association between psychotic symptoms and violence.* Paper prepared for publication.

Link, B. G., & Stueve, A. (1994). Psychotic symptoms and the violent/illegal behavior of mental patient compared to community controls. In J. Monahan & H. J. Steadman (Eds.), *Violence and mental disorder.* Chicago: University of Chicago Press.

Lion, J. R. (1987). Clinical assessment of violent patients. In L. Roth (Ed.), *Clinical treatment of the violent person* (pp. 1–19). New York: Guilford Press.

Litwack, T. R. (1993). On the ethics of dangerousness assessments. *Law and Human Behavior, 17,* 479–482.

Litwack, T. R. (1994). Assessments of dangerousness: Legal, research, and clinical developments. *Administration and Policy in Mental Health, 21*(5), 361–377.

Litwack, T. R. (1996). "Dangerous" patients: A survey of one forensic facility and review of the issue. *Aggression and Violent Behavior, 1*(2), 97–122.

Litwack, T. R., Gerber, G. L., & Fenster, C. A. (1980). The proper role of psychology in child custody disputes. *Journal of Family Law, 18,* 269–300.

Litwack, T. R., Kirschner, S. M., & Wack, R. C. (1993). The assessment of dangerousness and predictions of violence: Recent research and future prospects. *Psychiatric Quarterly, 64,* 245–273.

Litwack, T. R., & Schlesinger, L. B. (1987). Assessing and predicting violence: Research, law, and applications. In I. B. Weiner & A. K. Hess (Eds.), *Handbook of forensic psychology* (pp. 205–207). New York: Wiley.

MacDonald, J. M. (1963). The threat to kill. *American Journal of Psychiatry, 120,* 125–130.

MacDonald, J. M. (1967). Homicidal threats. *American Journal of Psychiatry, 124,* 475–482.

Madden, D. J. (1987). Psychotherapeutic approaches in the treatment of violent persons. In L. Roth (Ed.), *Clinical treatment of the violent person* (pp. 54–75). New York: Guilford Press.

Maier, H. W. (1912). Katathyme wahnbildung und paranoia. *Zietschrift für die Gesamte Nurologie und Psychiatrie, 13,* 555–610.

Malmquist, C. P. (1995). Depression and homicidal violence. *International Journal of Law and Psychiatry, 18*(2), 145–162.

McNiel, D. E. (1998). Empirically-based clinical evaluation and management of the potentially violent patient. In P. M. Kleespies (Ed.), *Emergencies in mental health practice: Evaluation and management* (pp. 95–116). New York: Guilford Press.

McNiel, D. E., & Binder, R. L. (1993, August 22). *Inter-rater agreement: A strategy for improving violence risk assessment.* Paper presented at the annual convention of the American Psychological Association, Toronto, Ontario.

McNiel, D. E., & Binder, R. L. (1994a). The relationship between acute psychiatric symptoms, diagnosis, and short-term risk of violence. *Hospital and Community Psychiatry, 45*(2), 133–137.

McNiel, D. E., & Binder, R. L. (1994b). Screening for risk of inpatient violence: Validation of an actuarial tool. *Law and Human Behavior, 18*(5), 579–586.

McNiel, D. E., & Binder, R. L. (1995). Correlates of accuracy in the assessment of psychiatric inpatients' risk of violence. *American Journal of Psychiatry, 152*(6), 901–906.

McNiel, D. E., Sandberg, D. A., & Binder, R. L. (1997, August). *The relationship between confidence and accuracy in violence risk assessment.* Paper presented at the annual convention of the American Psychological Association, Chicago.

Megargee, E. I. (1981). Methodological problems in the prediction of violence. In J. R. Hays, T. K. Roberts, & K. S. Solway (Eds.), *Violence and the violent individual* (pp. 179–191). New York: Spectrum.

Meloy, J. R. (1987). The prediction of violence in outpatient psychotherapy. *American Journal of Psychotherapy, 41,* 38–45.

Meloy, J. R. (1988). Violence and homicidal behavior in primitive mental states. *Journal of the American Academy of Psychoanalysis, 16*(3), 381–394.

Meloy, J. R. (1989). The forensic interview. In R. J. Craig (Ed.), *Clinical and diagnostic interviewing* (pp. 322–343). Northvale, NJ: Jason Aronson.

Meloy, J. R. (1992). *Violent attachments.* Northvale, NJ: Jason Aronson.

Menzies, R., Fedoroff, J. P., Green, C. M., & Isaacson, K. (1995). Prediction of dangerous behavior in male erotomania. *British Journal of Psychiatry, 166,* 529–536.

Menzies, R., & Webster, C. D. (1995). Construction and validation of risk assessments in a six-year follow-up of forensic patients: A tridimensional analysis. *Journal of Consulting and Clinical Psychology, 63*(5), 766–778.

Menzies, R., Webster, C. D., McMain, S., Staley, S., & Scaglione, R. (1994). The dimensions of dangerousness revisited: Assessing forensic predictions about violence. *Law and Human Behavior, 18*(1), 1–29.

Miller, M., & Morris, N. (1988). Predictions of dangerousness: An argument for limited use. *Violence and Victims, 3*(4), 263–283.

Monahan, J. (1981). *Predicting violent behavior: An assessment of clinical techniques.* Beverly Hills, CA: Sage.

Monahan, J. (1984). The prediction of violence behavior: Toward a second generation of theory and policy. *American Journal of Psychiatry, 141,* 10–15.

Monahan, J. (1993). Limiting therapist exposure to Tarasoff Liability. *American Psychologist, 48,* 242–250.

Monahan, J. (1996). Violence prediction: The past twenty years and the next twenty years. *Criminal Justice and Behavior, 23*(1), 107–120.

Monahan, J. (1997). The scientific status of research on clinical and actuarial predictions of violence. In D. Faigman, D. Kaye, M. Saks, & J. Sanders (Eds.), *Modern scientific evidence: The law and science of expert testimony.* St. Paul, MN: West.

Monahan, J., & Steadman, H. J. (1994). Toward a rejuvenation of risk assessment research. In J. Monahan & H. J. Steadman (Eds.), *Violence and mental disorder: Developments in risk assessment.* Chicago: University of Chicago Press.

Mossman, D. (1994a). Assessing predictions of violence: Being accurate about accuracy. *Journal of Consulting and Clinical Psychology, 62*(4), 783–792.

Mossman, D. (1994b). Further comments on portraying the accuracy of violence predictions. *Law and Human Behavior, 18*(5), 587–593.

Mullen, P. E. (1992). The clinical prediction of dangerousness. In D. J. Kavanagh (Ed.), *Schizophrenia: An overview and practical handbook* (pp. 309–319). London: Chapman Hall.

Mulvey, E. P., & Lidz, C. W. (1985). Back to basics: A critical analysis of dangerousness research in a new legal environment. *Law and Human Behavior, 9*(2), 209–219.

Mulvey, E. P., & Lidz, C. W. (1993). Measuring patient violence in dangerousness research. *Law and Human Behavior, 17,* 277–288.

Mulvey, E. P., & Lidz, C. W. (1995). Conditional prediction: A model for research on dangerousness to others in a new era. *International Journal of Law and Psychiatry, 18*(2), 129–143.

Mulvey, E. P., Shaw, E., & Lidz, C. W. (1994). Editorial: Why use multiple sources in research on patient violence in the community? *Criminal Behaviour and Mental Health, 4,* 253–258.

Myers, W. C., Reccoppa, L., Burton, K., & McElroy, R. (1993). Malignant sex and aggression: An overview of serial sexual homicide. *Bulletin of the American Academy of Psychiatry and the Law, 21,* 435–451.

Nestor, P. G., Haycock, J., Doiron, S., Kelly, J., & Kelly, D. (1995). Lethal violence and psychosis: A clinical profile. *Bulletin of the American Academy of Psychiatry and Law, 23*(3), 331–341.

Newhill, C. E., Mulvey, E. P., & Lidz, C. W. (1995). Characteristics of violence in the community by female patients seen in a psychiatric emergency service. *Psychiatric Services, 46*(8), 785–789.

O'Connor v. Donaldson, 422 U.S. 563 (1975).

Otto, R. K. (1992). Prediction of dangerous behavior: A review and analysis of second generation research. *Forensic Reports, 5,* 103–133.

Otto, R. K. (1994). On the ability of mental health professionals to "Predict dangerousness": A commentary and interpretation of the "dangerousness" literature. *Law and Psychology Review, 18,* 43–68.

Peck v. The Counseling Service of Addison County, 499 A.2d 422 (Vt., 1985).

Pfohl, S. J. (1978). *Predicting dangerousness.* Lexington, MA: Lexington Books/Heath.

Pollack, N., McBain, I., & Webster, C. (1989). Clinical decision making and the assessment of dangerousness. In K. Howells & C. R. Hollen (Eds.), *Clinical approaches to violence.* New York: Wiley.

Pollack, N., & Webster, C. (1990). The clinical assessment of dangerousness. In R. Bluglass & P. Bowden (Eds.), *Principles and practice of forensic psychiatry.* London: Churchill Livingstone.

Prins, H. (1988). Dangerous clients: Further observations on the limitation of mayhem. *British Journal of Social Work, 18,* 593–609.

Prins, H. (1996). Risk assessment and management in criminal justice and psychiatry. *Journal of Forensic Psychiatry, 7*(1), 42–62.

Quinsey, V., Harris, G. T., Rice, M. E., & Cormier, C. A. (1998). *Violent Offenders: Appraising and Managing Risk.* Washington, DC: American Psychological Association.

Quinsey, V., & Maguire, A. (1986). Maximum security psychiatric patients: Actuarial and clinical predictions of dangerousness. *Journal of Interpersonal Violence, 1*(2), 143–171.

Revitch, E. (1964). Paroxysmal manifestations of non-epileptic origin: Catathymic attacks. *Diseases of the Nervous System, 25,* 662–669.

Revitch, E. (1977). Classification of offenders for prognostic and dispositional evaluation. *Bulletin of the American Academy of Psychiatry and Law, 5,* 1–11.

Revitch, E., & Schlesinger, L. B. (1978). Murder: Evaluation, classification, and prediction. In I. L. Kutash, S. B. Kutash, & L. B. Schlesinger (Eds.), *Violence: Perspectives on murder and aggression* (pp. 138–164). San Francisco: Jossey-Bass.

Revitch, E., & Schlesinger, L. B. (1981). *Psychopathology of homicide.* Springfield, IL: Thomas.

Revitch, E., & Schlesinger, L. B. (1989). *Sex murder and sex aggression: Phenomenology, psychopathology, psychodynamics, and prediction.* Springfield, IL: Thomas.

Rice, M. E. (1997). Violent offender research and implications for the criminal justice system. *American Psychologist, 52*(4), 414–423.

Rice, M. E., & Harris, G. T. (1995). Violent recidivism: Assessing predictive validity. *Journal of Consulting and Clinical Psychology, 63,* 737–748.

Rice, M. E., & Harris, G. T. (1997). Cross-validation and extension of the violence risk appraisal guide for child molesters and rapists. *Law and Human Behavior, 21*(2), 231–241.

Rogers v. Okin, 634 F.2d 650 (1st Cir.) (1980).

Rogers, R., Sewell, K. W., Ross, M., Ustad, K., & Williams, A. (1994). Determinants of dangerousness in forensic patients: An archival study. *Journal of Forensic Sciences, 40*(1), 74–77.

Ruotolo, A. (1968). Dynamics of sudden murder. *American Journal of Psychoanalysis, 26,* 162–176.

Salekin, R. T., Rogers, R., & Sewell, K. W. (1996). A review and meta-analysis of the Psychopathy Checklist and Psychopathy Checklist–Revised: Predictive validity of dangerousness. *Clinical Psychology: Science and Practice, 3*(3), 203–215.

Salekin, R. T., Rogers, R., Ustad, K. L., & Sewell, K. W. (1997). Female psychopathy and recidivism. *Law and Human Behavior, 22*(1), 109–128.

Satten, J., Menninger, K., & Mayman, M. (1960). Murder without apparent motive. A study in personality disintigration. *American Journal of Psychiatry, 117,* 48–53.

Saunders, D. G. (1995). Prediction of wife assault. In J. C. Campbell (Ed.), *Assessing dangerousness: Violence by sexual offenders, batterers, and child abusers.* Thousand Oaks, CA: Sage.

Schall v. Martin, 467 U.S. 253 (1984).

Schlesinger, L. B. (1996). The catathymic crisis (1912–present): A review and clinical study. *Aggression and Violent Behavior, 1,* 307–316.

Schlesinger, L. B., & Kutash, I. L. (1981). The criminal fantasy technique: A comparison of sex offenders and substance abusers. *Journal of Clinical Psychology, 37,* 210–218.

Schlesinger, L. B., & Revitch, E. (1983). Sexual dynamics in homicide and assault. In L. B. Schlesinger & E. Revitch (Eds.), *Sexual dynamics of antisocial behavior* (pp. 206–227). Springfield, IL: Thomas.

Schlesinger, L. B., & Revitch, E. (1990). Outpatient treatment of the sex murderer and potential sex murderer. *Journal of Offender Counseling, Services and Rehabilitation, 15,* 163–178.

Schulte, H. M., Hall, M. J., & Crosby, R. (1994). Violence in patients with narcissistic personality pathology: Observations of a clinical series. *American Journal of Psychotherapy, 48*(4), 610–623.

Schwartz, H. I., & Pinsker, H. (1987). Mediating retention or release of the potentially dangerous patient. *Hospital and Community Psychiatry, 38*(1), 75–77.

Scott, P. D. (1977). Assessing dangerousness in criminals. *British Journal of Psychiatry, 131,* 127–142.

Segal, S. P., Watson, M. A., Goldfinger, S. M., & Averbuck, D. S. (1988). Civil commitment in the psychiatric emergency room: III. Disposition as a function of mental disorder and dangerousness indicators. *Archives of General Psychiatry, 45,* 759–763.

Seltzer v. Hogue, 594 N.Y.S.2d 781 (1993).

Serin, R. C. (1996). Violent recidivism in criminal psychopaths. *Law and Human Behavior, 20*(2), 207–217.

Serin, R. C., & Amos, N. L. (1995). The role of psychopathy in the assessment of dangerousness. *International Journal of Law and Psychiatry, 18,* 231–238.

Shaffer, C. E., Waters, W. F., & Adams, S. G. (1994). *Journal of Consulting and Clinical Psychology, 62*(5), 1064–1068.

Shah, S. A. (1978). Dangerousness: A paradigm for exploring some issues in law and psychology. *American Psychologist, 33,* 224–238.

Silva, J. A., Leong, G. B., Garza-Trevino, E. S., & Le-Grand, J. (1994). A cognitive model of dangerous delusional misidentification syndromes. *Journal of Forensic Sciences, 39*(6), 1455–1467.

Silva, J. A., Leong, G. B., Weinstock, P. S., & Kaushal, K. (1994). Delusional misidentification syndromes and dangerousness. *Psychopathology, 27,* 215–219.

Silva, J. A., Leong, G. B., Weinstock, R., & Klein, R. L. (1995). Psychiatric factors associated with dangerous mis-identification delusions. *Bulletin of the American Academy of Psychiatry and Law, 23*(1), 53–61.

Steadman, H. J., & Cocozza, J. (1974). *Careers of the criminally insane.* Lexington, MA: D. C. Heath & Company.

Steadman, H. J., & Cocozza, J. (1980). The prediction of dangerousness—Baxstrom: A case study. In G. Cooke (Ed.), *The role of the forensic psychologist* (pp. 204–215). Springfield, IL: Thomas.

Steadman, H. J., Monahan, J., Appelbaum, P. S., Grisso, T. A., Mulvey, E. P., Roth, L., Robbins, P. C., & Klassen, D. (1994). Designing a new generation of risk assessment research. In J. Monahan & H. Steadman (Eds.), *Violence and mental disorder: Developments in risk assessment.* Chicago: University of Chicago Press.

Swanson, J., Estroff, S., Swartz, M., Borum, R., Lachicotte, W., Zimmer, C., & Wagner, R. (1997). *Psychiatry.*

Swanson, J. W., Borum, R., Swartz, M., & Hiday. (1997). *Characteristics of violent events among people with severe mental disorder.* Paper submitted for publication.

Swanson, J. W., Borum, R., Swartz, M., & Monahan, J. (1996). Psychotic symptoms and disorders and the risk of violent behavior in the community. *Criminal Behaviour and Mental Health, 6,* 309–328.

Tarasoff v. Regents of the University of California, 17 Cal. 3d 425, 551 P.2d 334 (1976).

Tardiff, K. (1996). *Concise guide to assessment and management of violent patients* (2nd ed.). Washington, DC: American Psychiatric Press.

Taylor, P. J., & Monahan, J. (1996). Commentary: Dangerous patients or dangerous diseases. *British Medical Journal, 312,* 967–969.

Thornberry, T. P., & Jacoby, J. E. (1979). *The criminally insane: A community follow-up of mentally ill offenders.* Chicago: University of Chicago Press.

Torrey, E. F. (1994). Violent behavior by individuals with serious mental illness. *Hospital and Community Psychiatry, 45*(7), 653–662.

United States v. Evanoff, 10 F.3d 559 (8th Cir.) (1993).

United States v. Sahhar, 917 F.2d 1197 (1990); *cert. denied,* 111 S. Ct. 1591 (1991).

United States v. Salerno, 481 U.S. 739 (1987).

Villeneuve, D. B., & Quinsey, V. L. (1995). Predictors of general and violent recidivism among mentally disordered inmates. *Criminal Justice and Behavior, 22*(4), 397–410.

Wack, R. C. (1993). The ongoing risk assessment in the treatment of forensic patients on conditional release status. *Psychiatric Quarterly, 64,* 275–293.

Webster, C. D., Douglas, K. S., Eaves, D., & Hart, S. D. (1997). *The HCR-20 Scheme: The assessment of dangerousness and risk (Version 2).* Burnaby, BC: Mental Health, Law, and Policy Institute, Simon Fraser University.

Webster, C. D., Harris, G. T., Rice, M. E., Cormier, C., & Quinsey, V. L. (1994). *The Violence Prediction Scheme: Assessing dangerousness in high risk men.* Toronto, ON: University of Toronto.

Webster, C. D., & Jackson, M. A. (1997). *Impulsivity: Perspectives, principles, and practice.* New York: Guilford Press.

Webster, C. D., & Menzies, R. J. (1989). The clinical prediction of dangerousness. In D. N. Weisstaub (Ed.), *Law and mental health: International perspectives* (Vol. 3). Toronto, ON: Pergamon Press.

Webster, C. D., & Polvi, N. H. (1995). Challenging assessments of dangerousness & risk. In J. Ziskin (Ed.), *Coping with psychiatric and psychological testimony* (5th ed.). Los Angeles: Law and Psychology Press.

Werner, P. D., & Meloy, J. R. (1992). Decision making about dangerousness in releasing patients from long term hospitalization. *Journal of Psychiatry and Law, Spring,* 35–47.

Werner, P. D., Rose, T. L., & Yesavage, J. A. (1990). Aspects of consensus in clinical predictions of violence. *Journal of Clinical Psychology, 46*(4), 534–538.

Wertham, F. (1937). The catathymic crisis: A clinical entity. *Archives of Neurology and Psychiatry, 37,* 974–977.

Wertham, F. (1978). The catathymic crisis. In I. L. Kutash, S. B. Kutash, & L. B. Schlesinger (Eds.), *Violence: Perspective on murder and aggression.* San Francisco: Jossey-Bass.

Wettstein, R. M. (1984). The prediction of violent behavior and the duty to protect third parties. *Behavioral Sciences and the Law, 2,* 291–317.

Who will turn violent? Hospitals have to guess. (1993, April 6). *The New York Times,* p. C1.

Wiest, J. (1981). Treatment of violent offenders. *Clinical Social Work Journal, 9,* 271–281.

Wilson, M., Daly, M., & Daniele, A. (1995). Familicide: The killing of spouse and children. *Aggressive Behavior, 21,* 275–291.

Wishnie, H. (1977). *The impulsive personality.* New York: Plenum Press.

Zeiss, R. A., Tanke, E. D., Fenn, H. H., & Yesavage, J. A. (1996). Dangerousness commitments: Indices of future violence potential? *Bulletin of the American Academy of Psychiatry and Law, 24*(2), 247–253.

CHAPTER 9

Evaluating Eyewitness Testimony in Adults and Children

GAIL S. GOODMAN, ALLISON D. REDLICH, JIANJIAN QIN, SIMONA
GHETTI, KIMBERLY S. TYDA, JENNIFER M. SCHAAF, and ANNETTE HAHN

HOW ACCURATE is eyewitness testimony? Part of our fascination with this question derives from the fact that people's fate may hang on human memory, which is known to be fallible. Innocent people accused of serious crimes through eyewitness reports face false imprisonment, financial ruin, and loss of reputation. And not only can the fate of the accused rest on witness accuracy, but so may the fate of the victim; for instance, if an accurate victim is not believed, the victim may endure further assaults by the perpetrator and disillusionment with the legal system. Nevertheless, our courts necessarily rely on witness testimony, making its study of substantial practical importance. It is also of profound theoretical significance. Research on eyewitness testimony informs theories of memory and has led to new insights about the workings of the human mind. Given the crucial nature of these issues, it is not surprising that the study of eyewitness memory is an active and at times controversial endeavor.

Courts currently show a surprising inclination to permit psychologists to educate judges and jurors about eyewitness testimony. In educating the court, psychologists may testify as expert witnesses about relevant research findings or provide an evaluation of a specific witness. In either case, a firm grounding in current knowledge about eyewitness reports is essential.

In this chapter, we examine issues and research findings of importance to psychologists who serve as expert witnesses on eyewitness testimony. The literature in this field is extensive; rather than reviewing it all, we focus on key issues. (For more in-depth coverage, several recent books and review articles on specific eyewitness memory issues are available: e.g., Goodman, Emery, & Haugaard, 1997; Sporer, Malpass, & Koehnken, 1996; Thompson et al., 1997.) Our goal is to present a more balanced view than is common in discussions of eyewitness testimony. Most research in this area and consequently most reviews focus on the inaccuracies of human memory. In contrast, we present evidence relevant to both accuracies and inaccuracies. We also review research literature on both adult and child witnesses.

We first discuss factors known to affect memory acquisition, storage, and retention. While doing so, we discuss research on eyewitness memory and identification generally, for adults and children. We next address a number of special topics of particular importance to expert witnesses who testify about eyewitness memory. These topics include face recognition, individual differences in eyewitness memory ability, "repressed/recovered memory," memory in abuse victims, and child and elderly witnesses. Our discussion of special topics adds to the more general discussion of research on memory and identification presented first. We close with a discussion of ecological validity, that is, the generalizability of research findings to actual forensic situations, and with a few comments on the role of expert witnesses who educate the court about eyewitness testimony in children and adults.

HUMAN MEMORY

The scientific study of eyewitness testimony capitalizes on a simple fact: An objective record of the original event is available against which to evaluate the witness's report. Without this, the validity of a witness's statements cannot be determined. For actual crimes, the availability of an objective record is extremely unlikely. There is usually no definitive way to know whether the witness's report—even a detailed one given with great confidence—is correct or not. Many clinical discussions of memory for traumatic events, although valuable as sources of anecdotal information, are problematic because no objective record is available. In contrast, scientific studies of eyewitness testimony, although sometimes lacking in ecological validity (i.e., in the realisticness and trauma of real crime), provide many replicable findings that can be helpful in evaluating a witness's report.

When a record of the original event is available, one finds that memory is not perfect. Eyewitness reports contain accuracies but inaccuracies as well. The presence of accuracies and inaccuracies is consistent with theories of memory that emphasize its reconstructive nature (e.g., Bartlett, 1932; E. Loftus, 1979a). A reconstructive approach proposes that memory is not like a videotape recorder that stores all information encountered. Instead, forgetting may occur, and human memory becomes an amalgamation of what actually happened (the main source of accuracies) and what a person intuits, hears, or infers must have happened, sometimes inaccurately (one source of inaccuracies).

The reconstructive view of memory is generally accepted among psychologists who study human memory and eyewitness testimony. But an important debate exists about whether memory for events can change irreversibly (as implied by the reconstructive view) or whether memories are more permanent (see Alba & Hasher, 1983; McCloskey & Egeth, 1983). Under the latter view, "forgetting" does not occur, but retrieval failures do. That is, the original memory is retained but cannot be retrieved unless the right retrieval cue can be found. Without attempting to resolve this controversy here, we take the view that, for all practical purposes, memories may be permanently lost or changed because retrieval conditions may not be found—if they indeed exist—that can provide the cues needed to unleash the "true" memory.

According to a reconstructive approach, memory can be divided into three stages: acquisition, retention, and retrieval. Acquisition refers to the encoding of information into memory. Retention refers to the storage of information over time. Retrieval refers to the witness's ability to access what has been retained. Many factors, to be reviewed here, affect each of these stages and consequently affect witnesses' reports.

When a complex event such as a crime occurs (the encoding stage), it is impossible to attend to all of it, much less remember every detail of the incident. Instead, people form a general interpretation of the event (e.g., "I'm being robbed") and encode what they can based on what seems most important, novel, and salient to them at the time (e.g., "He has a gun"). If a detail is only glimpsed but not thoroughly examined, a witness's expectations may distort what is seen; for example, a stick in an assailant's hand might be encoded as a gun. Thus, even at this early stage, a totally complete and accurate representation of the event is unlikely to be stored. During the retention stage, the interpretation of the event may be retained relatively well, but details may be readily forgotten or undergo further change and distortion. One source of memory change is misleading postevent information offered by other witnesses or interviewers (E. Loftus, 1979a). Finally, during the retrieval stage, when a witness tries to communicate his or her memory of what happened, the conditions of retrieval will have an important influence on what is remembered.

When psychologists testify in courts of law about eyewitness testimony, they often begin by explaining that memory can be divided into the three stages just described. We have therefore organized this chapter by first discussing factors that affect these three stages.

ACQUISITION

When a crime takes place, many factors affect how well a witness can encode the event. The crime (e.g., a mugging) may last only a few seconds, occur once, and be violent. On the other hand, the crime (e.g., incest) might last minutes or hours, take place repeatedly, and be committed with minimal force. Factors such as these will affect how well the witness can encode and later remember what happened.

Temporal Factors

A number of temporal factors influence a witness's ability to encode an event. One of the most significant is the length of time a witness has to view it. In general, the longer the exposure, the more accurate the witness's testimony (Clifford & Richards, 1977; Ellis, Davies, & Shepherd, 1977; Gross & Hayne, 1996; Laughery, Alexander, & Lane, 1971; McKelvie, 1988). This principle is well-known from the general field of memory research (see Klatzky, 1980; G. Loftus & Loftus, 1976).

Although longer exposures lead to increased accuracy, the duration of an event must often be judged by the witness's report. This can be problematic because there is a human tendency to overestimate the duration of criminal events (Buckhout, 1974; C. Johnson & Scott, 1976; Marshall, 1966). Time markers may serve as aids for reporting durations, however. If the witness was watching a half-hour TV show during the time of a robbery, that show can be used to help gauge how long the event lasted or the approximate time that it occurred. Similarly, people also show a systematic error in underestimating how long ago events occurred, and landmarks (e.g., the witness's birthday, presidential elections) can help date when an incident took place (E. Loftus & Marburger, 1983). Interestingly, such telescoping of memory is not as problematic for events in which individuals have participated (Betz & Skowronski, 1997).

Although exposure duration constrains encoding, the type of information processing a witness performs during the exposure period is also important. For example, laboratory studies indicate that, given the same exposure period, people who engage in deeper processing (e.g., semantic judgments, such as those about a person's personality) are later more likely to recognize the person's face than are people who engage in more shallow processing (e.g., structural judgments, such as focusing on a specific facial feature) (Baddeley, 1979; Bloom & Mudd, 1991; Bower & Karlin, 1974; McKelvie, 1985; Winograd, 1981; but see Wells & Hryciw, 1984). However, these effects need to be replicated in field research to ensure their generalizability to actual eyewitness situations that find their way into the legal system.

How frequently an event was experienced is another temporal factor likely to affect eyewitness reports. Traditional laboratory studies indicate that the more frequently an item is experienced, the better it is retained (e.g., Ebbinghaus, 1885/1964). Also, as one might expect, the more often a person is seen, the easier it is to identify him or her (Sanders & Warnick, 1979). But one difference between laboratory and real-life events is that, whereas the former can be repeated in an identical fashion, no two real-life events will be identical. Also, real-life events are more complicated and detailed than stimuli used in traditional laboratory studies; although the gist of repeated events may be remembered quite well, details may begin to blur. For instance, children who are victims of incest or repeated sexual assault are not always able to remember the details of each incident or whether a certain act occurred during the first or fifteenth assault. Such examples are consistent with results of studies of repeated, realistic incidents, which indicate that as an event recurs, it may become difficult to remember exactly when a specific detail or act was experienced (Fivush, 1984; Fivush, Hudson, & Nelson, 1984; K. Nelson & Gruendel, 1981), even though what is recalled is quite accurate.

Although some crimes do reoccur, many criminal events are novel, if not startling, one-time incidents. For these kinds of events, memory—even children's memory—can be quite accurate and fairly detailed (e.g., Baker-Ward, Gordon, Ornstein, Larus, & Clubb, 1993; Fivush, 1984; Linton, 1982; Peterson & Bell, 1996; Rudy & Goodman, 1991; Saywitz, Goodman, Nicholas, & Moan, 1991). However, many factors impinge on the person's memory for one-time and repeated events, making it impossible to base predictions of memory accuracy simply on how often an event was experienced.

The Core Event versus Peripheral Detail

Crime witnesses are most likely to encode and remember what is often called the core event, for example, that they experienced a robbery, a kidnapping, or a sexual assault. As part of the core event, actions are more likely to be encoded and retained than are peripheral details or the culprit's physical features. This trend holds for stressful as well as nonstressful events and for adult and child witnesses. For example, Christianson and Loftus (1991) examined adults' memories after viewing a thematic series of slides. The content of one critical slide in the middle of the series was varied as either emotional or neutral. Their findings indicate that when the critical slide was emotional, participants were better at remembering a central than a peripheral detail. Clifford and Scott (1978) also reported that adults who had just viewed a videotape of a violent incident (physical assault) or a nonviolent incident (verbal exchange) recalled more about the assailants' actions than about their physical appearance. A similar pattern is also found with children; for example, central actions of stressful and nonstressful events tend to be remembered relatively well by children (e.g., Davies, Tarrant, & Flin, 1989; Goodman, Hirschman, Hepps, & Rudy, 1991; see also Pear & Wyatt, 1914).

The interpretation of an event can influence memory. Interpretations at the time of encoding and/or retrieval can affect the information that is retrieved, so that a witness who thought a visitor was a real estate agent versus a potential thief would probably remember different information (Anderson & Pichert, 1978; Zadny & Gerard, 1974). Sometimes, however, a witness will misinterpret the core event or important parts of it. Not surprisingly, such witnesses are less likely to provide accurate reports. Buckhout's (1974) adult participants, who viewed a videotape of a card game and a subsequent assault, were later asked to recall what happened. Witnesses who misinterpreted the attack recalled the events less accurately than those who interpreted it correctly.

In addition to remembering actions that occurred, witnesses may recall many other features of an event that are important to police investigation or courtroom testimony. For example, a license plate number or what the culprit was wearing may be crucial bits of evidence. Because attention is selective, it may be impossible for the witness to encode all of the relevant information. The most salient details are likely to be best attended and retained (Marquis, Marshall, & Oskamp, 1972). A gun pointed at the witness, for example, is likely to be better attended to than the color of the culprit's shirt. For some reason, the upper part of the face (e.g., eyes and nose) appears to be more salient than the lower part (e.g., mouth and chin; Laughery et al., 1971). However, if a witness intentionally focuses attention on a specific detail with the goal of remembering it, presumably that strategy aids subsequent memory.

People often assume that someone who can provide testimony about peripheral detail must have been paying close attention to the central events as well or must have an exceptional memory. But a person's testimony can be accurate about central issues without including peripheral detail, and vice versa. Wells and Leippe (1981) reported a negative correlation between the ability to recognize a confederate and the ability to recall unimportant details. Adults in the experiment watched a man steal a calculator. Those who attended to the culprit's face and later recognized him accurately were less likely to remember minor details about the room. Unfortunately, jurors are often impressed by memory for peripheral detail and may be less willing to believe a witness who cannot remember such information.

Expectations

A person's expectations can either enhance or impede accurate perception and memory. When an event is predictable, expectations support rapid encoding and recall of it. A study by Zadny and Gerard (1974) exemplified this point. They asked adults to observe a skit involving a student registering for classes. The adults were led to believe that the student was either a chemistry, psychology, or music major, and the student carried items relevant to all three of these fields. Those biased to believe that the student was a chemistry major recalled proportionally more chemistry-related items than those biased to believe the student was a psychology or music major; adults in the latter two groups recalled more psychology and music-related items, respectively. The authors concluded that biasing information affected the encoding stage because subjects who were biased *after* viewing the event recalled items relevant to all three majors.

Expectations can also lead to inaccuracies. Accurate recall of expected information can be accompanied by "memory" of expected information not actually encountered (Bartlett, 1932; Graesser, 1981; Holst & Pezdek, 1992; List, 1986). Expectations may be used to confirm the presence of expected information but at the same time to supersede detailed analysis, so that a person might remember seeing a car, for example, but be unable to say what it looked like (Friedman, 1979). Expectations may also bias an observer so that he or she fails to notice detail that seems irrelevant or fails to match his or her encoding scheme, as when supporters of a football team see all the infractions made by the other side but not those made by their own team (Hastorf & Cantril, 1954). Moreover, stereotypical expectations can bias eyewitness reports in both adults (Chen & Geiselman, 1993; but see Treadway & McCloskey, 1989) and children (Leichtman & Ceci, 1995).

Expectations are especially likely to lead to inaccuracies when an event is viewed under ambiguous, fast-moving circumstances. For example, hunting accidents often occur when a hunter's expectations lead to the misperception of a person as prey (E. Loftus, 1979a; Sommer, 1959). Laboratory studies also confirm the important role expectations play in biasing perceptions and memory when ambiguous information is quickly viewed (e.g., Bruner & Postman, 1949). When longer processing time is possible, however, expectations can increase the attention paid to unexpected details. Expected information serves this function because it defines what is unexpected. To interpret the unexpected event, attention may quickly shift to detailed encoding of the novel event (Friedman, 1979; G. Loftus & Mackworth, 1978). As a consequence, unexpected information may later be recognized with heightened accuracy (Friedman, 1979; Graesser, 1981; Maki, 1990).

Violence and Stress

Many criminal events are violent in nature and therefore traumatic or, because of their potential for violence, cause witnesses anxiety. Some researchers adopt field research methods in which they analyze police reports of actual crimes or interview witnesses of actual crimes. Although such research is rich in ecological validity, typically the studies suffer from low internal validity (e.g., a plethora of confounded variables, a small number of subjects). Other researchers conduct laboratory-based studies in which witnesses' emotional responses to and memories of more standardized incidents (e.g., stressful medical procedures, slide-depicted or staged violent events) are examined. Overall, controversy exists over the effects of stress on memory. In particular, questions arise concerning how well laboratory researchers have been able to mimic the levels of stress induced by criminal events and how well field researchers have pinned down cause-effect relations. For both types of research, the extent to which findings can be generalized to witnesses in specific real-life crimes can be questioned (Deffenbacher, 1983; Egeth & McCloskey, 1984; Tollestrup, Turtle, & Yuille, 1994).

Results from field studies tend to show that witnesses can retain information about stressful events well, although findings may depend on the type of stressful event experienced and whether or not it is thought and talked about later. In one study, Bidrose and Goodman (in press) analyzed eyewitness reports of four child sexual abuse victims. The girls, who ranged in age from 8 to 15 years at time of interview, had been photographed and audiotaped during sexual acts with adult males, so that an objective record of many of the sexual assaults was available. In reports to the police and to the courts, substantial accuracy was maintained. Other studies on memory in adult rape victims (Koss, Tromp, & Tharan, 1995; Tromp, Koss, Figueredo, & Tharan, 1995) suggest that memories for such experiences contain more central than peripheral details, are reasonably accurate and well-retained for long periods, but are not completely indelible. When memories for rape were compared to memories for other unpleasant intense experiences, the most powerful discriminator from other unpleasant memories was the degree to which memories for rape were less well-remembered, being less clear and vivid, more emotionally intense, less meaningfully ordered, and less thought and talked about.

Other studies have concentrated on bystander witnesses or comparisons of bystander and victim witnesses to nonsexual events. Yuille and Cutshall (1986) interviewed 13 witnesses who had observed a shooting incident in which one person was killed and a second seriously wounded. The interviews took place four to five months after the incident, and the information witnesses provided was compared to their original reports to the police made within two days of the incident. The results showed high accuracy in witnesses' accounts after the four- to five-month delay. Although some errors occurred (e.g., regarding age, height, and weight estimations), the amount or accuracy of recall changed little over a five-month period. Moreover, witnesses' self-reported stress level at the time of the incident appeared to have no negative effects on subsequent memory. In another study, Christianson and Hubinette (1993) interviewed 58 witnesses (victims and bystanders) about their memory for and emotional reactions to robberies after 4- to 15-month intervals. They found that witnesses' recollections of actual robberies (e.g., action, weapon, clothing) were highly consistent with information originally obtained in the police reports. However, witnesses' recollection of dates and other information, such as times, was not as consistent. Although the victims' self-reported stress levels did not significantly differ from those of bystander witnesses, victims' reports were more accurate.

Another type of field research—or at least nonlaboratory research—concerns the "flashbulb memory" phenomenon (R. Brown & Kulik, 1977). Flashbulb memory refers to the type of memories people often report following experiences of highly charged emotional events (e.g., the assassination of President Kennedy or the explosion of the space shuttle *Challenger*). These memories appear to contain vivid and durable information about specific circumstances surrounding the events, such as the time of day, the location, the ongoing activities, the clothes the person was wearing, and his or her affective experiences (Bohannon, 1988; Bohannon & Symons, 1993). Furthermore, higher levels of emotional responses at the time of the event appear to be associated with better recollection of the flashbulb circumstances (Bohannon, 1992; Christianson, 1989). To account for the flashbulb memory phenomenon, some proposed a special "Now print!" neuropsychological mechanism that "freezes" the exact details of a scene in memory (Brown & Kulik, 1977). Others have argued that special memory mechanisms for traumatic memories are not necessary at all (Hembrooke & Ceci, 1995). Evidence suggests that flashbulb memories can be accurate or at least more accurate than memory for mundane events (Christianson, 1989; McGaugh, 1995), but they are not immune from forgetting or distortion (Christianson, 1989, 1992; McCloskey, Wible, & Cohen, 1988; Neisser & Harsch, 1993). In summary, studies based on field methods indicate that stress at the time of the event does not impair witnesses' memory for central details directly associated with the stressful experiences (Yuille & Tollestrup, 1992).

Laboratory-based studies yield a somewhat more complex picture of the relation between stress and memory. Some studies reveal an impairing impact of stress on adults' and children's reports (e.g., E. Loftus & Burns, 1982; Merritt, Ornstein, & Spicker, 1994; Peters, 1991; Qin, Eisen, et al., 1997). For example, in the study by Loftus and Burns, participants were asked to view a film depicting a bank robbery. At the end of the film, the robbers, chased by guards, turn and shoot. In the nonviolent version, no one is hit. In the violent version, a bullet hits a young boy in the face. The boy covers his face in pain as he falls to the ground bleeding. Participants who viewed the violent version remembered less about the film than those who saw the nonviolent version. However, it can be argued that only participants' memory for details that were not directly associated with the shooting was impaired. Their memories of the central information (e.g., the shooting and the boy falling to the ground bleeding) may be well retained. Moreover, a number of the studies indicate errors of omission rather than commission as a result of stress (e.g., Qin, Eisen, et al., 1997).

Yet other laboratory research points to an enhancing relation between stress and memory (e.g., Goodman, Hirschman, Hepps, Rudy, 1991) or fail to uncover any relation at all between stress and memory (Baker-Ward et al., 1993; Goodman, Bottoms, Schwartz-Kenney, & Rudy, 1991; Howe, Courage, & Peterson, 1995; Peterson & Bell, 1996), or find both positive and negative effects within the same study (Quas et al., in press). Goodman and colleagues (Goodman, Hirschman, et al., 1991) found positive effects; they examined children's memory for doctor visits during which they received an inoculation. When the memories about the doctor visits were compared for children who exhibited greater versus less distress, more distressed children evinced better recall and less suggestibility. Similarly, Quas et al. report that children who were more stressed during a medical procedure were less suggestible. However, the same children also reported less information in free recall and doll reenactment than less stressed children, perhaps because they did not want to talk about or demonstrate the stressful and somewhat embarrassing medical procedure. Peterson and Bell also found mixed results. Children of 2 to 13 years of age were interviewed about their memories for a traumatic injury that brought them to a hospital for emergency treatment. The interviews were conducted a few days and six months after the injury. Their findings indicated that children at all ages provided a considerable amount of information about the injury. Interestingly, although they found that distress during hospital treatment decreased recall, children's distress at time of injury did not affect the amount or accuracy of their recall of the incident.

A widely cited explanation for the relation between stress and memory is Easterbrook's cue-utilization hypothesis (1959). Easterbrook proposed that arousal has the effect of limiting the range of attention and hence the number of cues that can be used in solving a task. Under moderate levels of stress, attention narrows to include only salient or immediately relevant cues; peripheral or less important cues go unattended. Performance is usually heightened under such conditions because potentially distracting, irrelevant cues are ignored, and processing focuses only on relevant cues. Under high levels of arousal, however, the range of attention is further narrowed so that even some relevant cues are ignored, causing performance to decline. The attentional narrowing proposed by Easterbrook received equivocal support in studies of adults, with the exception that memory for central information appears to remain strong despite high levels of stress (see Christianson, 1992, for a detailed review). Several studies of children did not find the type of interaction (i.e., interaction between type of information and stress ratings) that would be expected if Easterbrook's hypothesis is accurate (e.g., Goodman, Hirschman, et al., 1991; Peterson & Bell, 1996; Vandermaas, Hess, & Baker-Ward, 1993).

The phenomenon called "weapon focus" may fit reasonably well with Easterbrook's (1959) hypothesis. Weapons are one source of stress in many criminal situations. It has been proposed that when a weapon is in view, attention becomes focused on it, resulting in less attention directed at the culprit's face. Evidence for such a weapon focus was found in several laboratory studies (e.g., C. Johnson & Scott, 1976; E. Loftus, Loftus, & Messo, 1987; Maass & Kohnken, 1989). In research by Loftus et al., participants watched a series of slides depicting an event in a fast-food restaurant. Half of the participants saw a customer point a gun at the cashier, whereas the other half saw him hand the cashier a check. Participants' eye movements were recorded while they were viewing the slides. In addition, their memories of the slides were examined. The results showed that participants' eyes fixed more and also longer on the gun than on the check. Participants' memory in the weapon condition was also poorer than the memory of those in the check condition. However, several field studies on weapon focus yield a different picture (e.g., Tollestrup et al., 1994; Yuille & Cutshall, 1986). For example, in a study based on police reports of a robbery, eyewitnesses to crimes involving a weapon provided more information about clothing and physical appearance details compared to those involved in a robbery without a weapon (Tollestrup et al., 1994). Furthermore, the presence of a weapon did not affect the accuracy of witnesses' reports, although the presence of a weapon did have a detrimental effect on witnesses' ability to recognize the person who held the weapon. Tollestrup et al. speculated that perhaps descriptions are more vigorously pursued from eyewitnesses of crimes involving a weapon, but the type or quality of information encoded was not useful at subsequent identification tasks.

The mixed findings across different studies of stress and memory have prompted researchers to search for factors that might mediate the relation between stress and memory. Within the child eyewitness memory literature, several individual-difference variables, including parent-child interaction style (Goodman, Quas, Batterman-Faunce, Riddlesberger, & Kuhn, 1994), children's temperament (Merritt et al., 1994), and children's physiological reactivity (Stein & Boyce, 1995), have been identified as potentially important in affecting children's stress levels during the event and their memory performance later. For example, Goodman et al. (1994) interviewed 3- to 10-year-olds about a stressful medical procedure, voiding cystourethrogram fluoroscopy (VCUG), involving urethral catheterization. Results indicated that children whose mothers were emotionally supportive were less stressed during the VCUG and also evidenced better memory several weeks later. In the study by Merritt et al., children who scored higher on adaptability and approach-withdrawal tendencies were less upset during the medical procedure and also evinced more complete recall than children who scored lower on these two temperament indices.

In summary, the relation between stress and memory is likely to be a complex one. Whether stress has a negative impact on memory may partly depend on the type of information (e.g., central versus peripheral) being tested. It may also be mediated by individual-difference variables. Even if the stress involved in many criminal events does inhibit memory, which is still open to debate, this does not mean that witnesses to traumatic incidents will remember nothing or that what they do remember will be fraught with error. It may simply mean that their memories will be relatively limited. What they do remember might still be quite accurate.

Conclusion

Because attention is limited, people cannot encode everything about real-life events, particularly those as complex as most crimes. We have reviewed the ways temporal factors affect encoding and how attention is most likely to focus on central, salient information. Our expectations can distort what is encoded, though they usually do not, and violent events may lead to reduced memories for peripheral information, although memories for central information (e.g., the action, the weapon) may still be largely accurate. Acquisition factors influence what is encoded, which in turn determines what can be stored and retained.

RETENTION

Retention is the second stage of memory. During the retention interval, encoded information may be affected by various forces. The length of time that passes between an event and its attempted report may lead to forgetting. In addition, information acquired during the retention interval can, under some circumstances, distort the original memory (or at least the witness's report of it). We examine some of the factors that can lead to such malleability of memory and also discuss conditions that make memory relatively resistant to change.

Delay

One of the most replicable findings of memory research is that forgetting increases with time. Ebbinghaus's (1885/1964) famous "forgetting curve" represented the fact that the rate of forgetting of nonsense syllables is steepest during the first few postexposure minutes and then levels off. Forgetting also occurs for real-life events, but the rate at which information is lost varies considerably (see Ellis, 1981, and Shepherd, 1983, for reviews). Memory for highly familiar information may decline quite slowly. For example, in a study by Bahrick, Bahrick, and Wittlinger (1975), recognition memory for pictures of high school classmates remained almost perfect after 35 years and was still quite accurate after an average delay of 45 years. Even studies that involve recognition of strangers do not always find a decline in accuracy, at least over the delay intervals tested. In a review of seven roughly comparable eyewitness identification experiments that employed delays ranging from an immediate to a five-month interval, Shepherd found no clear relation between delay and correct recognitions or incorrect choices. These findings led Shepherd to conclude that, at least for face recognition, other factors such as amount of attention received by the target during encoding may be more important than delay.

With sufficiently long delays, people almost invariably forget some of what was originally encoded. Although the gist of an event may be remembered indefinitely, more specific information (e.g., exactly what the suspect looked like or exactly how the event unfolded) tends to become lost. Examples are not hard to find. When adults were exposed to an irate stranger for 45 seconds, their ability to later pick him out of a video lineup dropped considerably over time, from 65% of the adults providing correct recognitions after a one-week delay to only 10% correct recognitions after an 11-month delay (Shepherd, 1983, Experiment 2). Even when the number of correct recognitions does not decline with time, the number of false recognitions of innocent people can increase dramatically. In the American justice system, false recognition of an innocent person is considered more grievous than failing to identify a true culprit, making false recognition an error of substantial import.

Studies examining the effect of delay on memory recall with children have found results similar to studies conducted with adults. As with adults, there are circumstances in which length of delay does not significantly influence accuracy of memory reports, particularly for personally salient events. In a study conducted by Baker-Ward et al. (1993), children aged 3, 5, and 7 years did not evidence significant forgetting over a period of varying delays (1, 3, or 6 weeks). Although 3- and 5-year-olds showed some forgetting, after the 6-week delay, recall for reported features was (arguably) impressive, especially given the children's young ages: 65% for the 3-year-olds and 75% for the 5-year-olds. With longer delays (e.g., 1–6 years), forgetting in children increases (Goodman, Bottoms, et al., 1991; Quas et al., in press). In fact, there is evidence to suggest that forgetting occurs more quickly in children than in adults (Brainerd, Reyna, Howe, & Kingma, 1991; Flin, Boon, Knox, & Bull, 1992).

In some studies, recall after a delay has been improved by the use of cues. For instance, Pipe, Gee, and Wilson (1993) found that the introduction of object and verbal cues into memory interviews was more effective in increasing the amount of information reported at a 10-week delay in comparison to a 10-day delay. Specifically, 5- to 6-year-old children, after interacting with an unfamiliar magician, were interviewed at the two time delays. At the 10-day delay, most information was reported in the free recall portion of the interview before the introduction of cues. At the 10-week delay, however, cues, particularly object cues, were effective at accessing details not reported during free recall. Unfortunately, the introduction of some forms of cuing (e.g., dolls and toy props) can also lead to increased errors, especially in young children (e.g., Goodman, Quas, Batterman-Faunce, Riddleberger, & Kuhn, 1997). Thus, the introduction of cues during forensic interviews may be an important addition, but caution is warranted. In any case, it seems that for both children and adults, forgetting of salient aspects of real-life events does not necessarily occur as rapidly as the typical Ebbinghaus forgetting curve for nonsense syllables might imply.

An important factor that may affect the relation between delay and accuracy in memory is repeated questioning. Often, before witnesses give testimony in the courtroom, they are questioned several times by police officers, attorneys, and so forth. Some studies have found a positive relation between the number of interviews (conducted at differing time intervals) and accuracy in remembering (e.g., Goodman, Bottoms, et al., 1991; Scrivner & Safer, 1988). Repeated interviewing appears to keep memories alive and helps inoculate against forgetting. Nevertheless, with repeated misleading questioning, the potential for increases in inaccuracies exists (Warren & Lane, 1995). Warren and Lane recommend interviewing witnesses as soon as possible after an event to inoculate against forgetting and decrease susceptibility to suggestibility. However, often in rape and child abuse cases, for example, victims cannot be interviewed until months or even years have passed since the time of the experience(s), because the crime may not be disclosed before then.

Malleability of Memory

In evaluating studies of eyewitness testimony, it is important to pay special attention to whether memory merely fades over time or whether inaccuracies begin to appear in witnesses' reports. One source of inaccuracies is misleading

postevent information. This information can be introduced during the retention interval in various ways: through discussions held by witnesses after a
criminal event, through questioning by police and attorneys, through exposure to newspaper articles and television news, and even through one's own
thoughts and dreams. Although studies of memory malleability often involve both retention and retrieval factors, we focus on memory malleability
in this section on retention.

E. Loftus (1975, 1977, 1979a) has demonstrated that, through the use of misleading questioning, witnesses can be made to report such things as barns that
were not seen (Loftus, 1975), an assailant with curly hair whose hair was in fact
straight (E. Loftus & Greene, 1980), broken glass in car accidents that in reality
involved no broken glass (E. Loftus & Palmer, 1974), incorrect colors of objects
(E. Loftus, 1977), and changes in the frequency of one's own headache pain
(E. Loftus, 1979a). Misleading questions are especially effective in altering eyewitness reports when the questions are complex and therefore direct witnesses'
attention away from the misleading detail. The relatively simple question "Did
you see the stop sign?" falsely presupposes information but directs adults' attention to the presupposition, so fewer adults are misled (Johnson, 1979, as cited
in E. Loftus & Ketcham, 1983). Timing is also important in evaluating the effects
of misleading questioning. The greatest distortion occurs when misleading information is introduced after a delay and just before the final memory test, instead of right after the initial event (E. Loftus, 1979a). Because of the delay,
memory may fade to the point where witnesses do not notice that the misleading
information is incorrect.

Another way to add postevent information to witnesses' reports is to use
verbs of different strengths when asking questions. E. Loftus and Palmer (1974)
found that adults who were exposed to stronger verbs in earlier questioning
(i.e., "About how fast were the two cars going when they *smashed* into each
other?" as compared to when *hit* is used) were more likely to report the presence of broken glass at the accident scene in a later memory test, even though
none was present in the film that depicted the accident. Because smashing and
broken glass are both associated with severe accidents, the adults apparently
inferred that broken glass must have been present and incorporated this inference into their reports (see also Christiaansen, Sweeney, & Ochalek, 1983). Even
more subtle changes in the wording of a question can significantly alter a witness's report. If a witness is asked, "Did you see *the* stop sign?" a yes response
(even though a stop sign had not been seen) is more likely than if the witness is
asked, "Did you see *a* stop sign?" (E. Loftus & Zanni, 1975).

Misleading information is most likely to be accepted if the source of the communication is of high status or appears to be unbiased (Bregman & McAllister,
1982; Ceci, Ross, & Toglia, 1987; Dodd & Bradshaw, 1980; E. Loftus, 1980). Thus,
if a person involved in a car accident claimed that the accident occurred in front
of a yield sign instead of a stop sign, witnesses would presumably be less likely
to change their reports than if a police officer made the same claim. The police
officer would be both high in status and relatively unbiased.

Although the effects of misleading information on eyewitness reports have
been clearly established and seem to be more easily obtained in young children

than adults (Ceci et al., 1987; but see Zaragoza, 1991), it is important to note that the majority of these demonstrations involve peripheral detail (Yuille, 1980). It is more difficult to change a witness's report about central information (Dritsas & Hamilton, as cited in E. Loftus, 1979a; see also Loftus, 1979b), information with high memory strength (Marquis et al., 1972; Read & Bruce, 1984), and negative information with high personal significance (Bruck, Ceci, & Hembrooke, 1998). However, if a person's memory is weak enough, for example, because of a long time interval between encoding and retrieval, it is possible that reports might even change for more central information. It is only recently that studies have shown that under certain conditions adults and children can be led to report entirely fictitious events that never actually occurred (e.g., Hyman, Husband, & Billings, 1995; Leichtman & Ceci, 1995). Such "implanted memories" may depend in part on the plausibility of the events suggested (Pezdek, Finger, & Hodge, 1997). Similarly, in a study with children, Pezdek and Roe (1997) found that it is easier to obtain memory malleability effects about a plausible change in an action that did occur than to suggest an entirely new action that did not occur.

Originally, Loftus (1979a) interpreted misinformation effects as indicating that a witness's memory can become distorted and, perhaps, irreversibly changed. However, other researchers argue that memory distortion, such as the misinformation effect, can occur without suggestions affecting a person's ability to remember the original event (McCloskey & Zaragoza, 1985; Zaragoza & Koshmider, 1989; Zaragoza, McCloskey, & Jamis, 1987). For example, misinformation effects can occur because of retrieval competition between the suggested information and event information (e.g., participants remember both the original and misleading information, but the misleading information is stronger in memory because it is more recent and thus more accessible; Belli, 1989; Bowers & Bekerian, 1984), "gap-filling" tendencies, in which use of suggested information fills in a memory gap (e.g., participants fail to encode part of the original event and thus fill in the gap in their memory with the suggested information; McCloskey & Zaragoza, 1985), or the power of demand characteristics (e.g., social influence factors that lead participants to agree with the interviewers' suggestion even though the participants remember the original event accurately; McCloskey & Zaragoza, 1985). In their study, McCloskey and Zaragoza varied Loftus's procedure by including on the final memory test the item originally seen (e.g., a hammer) and an item neither seen nor suggested (e.g., a wrench). If the suggested item (e.g., a screwdriver) had erased the witnesses' original memory, then witnesses should only be able to guess when forced to make a choice between the original and a new item. Instead, witnesses exposed to misleading information remember the original item about as well as witnesses who were not exposed to misleading information. Thus, it appears that misleading questioning does not necessarily erase a witness's memory.

Another possible mechanism for misinformation effects involves errors in source monitoring (M. Johnson, Hastroudi, & Lindsay, 1993), the process by which people make judgments about when, where, and how a memory was acquired. The model was developed on the basis of a series of studies by Marcia Johnson and her colleagues (Johnson, 1988; Johnson & Raye, 1981; Johnson,

Foley, Suengas, & Raye, 1988), which concerned the processes involved in distinguishing memories of actual events and memories of prior imaginings and fantasies (i.e., reality monitoring). This line of research has yielded evidence that failure of source monitoring (i.e., misremembering the postevent suggested information as the original information) plays a role in at least some memory distortions following misleading postevent information (e.g., Belli, Lindsay, Gales, & McCarthy, 1994; D. Lindsay, 1990; Lindsay & Johnson, 1989; Zaragoza & Lane, 1994). Evidence suggests that when people make errors regarding the source of their memory, they become susceptible to various other kinds of memory distortions and illusions. For example, in a study by Jacoby, Kelley, Brown, and Jasechko (1989), participants who had been exposed to a nonfamous name would later call that name famous if they did not remember that they had seen the name in a previous experimental session after a long delay. The name may have seemed like a familiar one when it was exposed a second time, but because participants failed to recall the source of their knowledge they mistakenly attributed the name's familiarity to the fame of the nonfamous person. This result highlights the fact that people often make inferences and attributions concerning the source of retrieved knowledge, and that these source attributions are prone to error.

Developmental differences in source monitoring may also render young children more susceptible to misinformation effects than are older children and adults. Studies suggest that compared to older children and adults, younger children are less able to accurately monitor the source of suggested information (Ackil & Zaragoza, 1995), perform worse at remembering sources of actions they actually performed versus actions they only imagined themselves performing (Parker, 1995), and are more vulnerable to the effects of source similarity (D. Lindsay, Johnson, & Kwon, 1991). In a series of studies, Lindsay et al. demonstrated that although both children and adults are more likely to confuse sources when sources are highly similar, source monitoring improves during the preschool and childhood years.

Recent studies generally point to the multimechanism nature of memory distortion, that is, a confluence of all or several of the above mechanisms. However, at least under certain conditions, such as long retention intervals, memory impairment (i.e., actual memory change) may occur as the result of misinformation (Belli et al., 1994; Belli, Windschitl, McCarthy, & Winfrey, 1992).

Resistance to Misleading Information

Are there ways to induce resistance to suggestibility and make reports more tamper-resistant? As expected, warning people about the possible presence of misinformation helps ward off the ill effects. If a witness is told, for example, "Some of the questions you were asked may have contained incorrect information. Please answer the questions now only on the basis of what you actually experienced during the incident," or if the witness has been educated about the effects of leading questions, he or she may edit from memory much of the incorrect information (Christiaansen & Ochalek, 1983; Read & Bruce, 1984; see Greene, Flynne, & Loftus, 1982). A general warning may have a similar effect. In a study by Warren, Hulse-Trotter, and Tubbs (1991), half of the participants in each of three age groups (7-year-olds, 12-year-olds, and adults) received warnings that the questions they were to be asked were tricky or difficult and that they should answer only what they confidently remembered. Warnings significantly reduced the effect of misleading questions across all age groups. It seems that the more explicit the warning, the more likely it will be effective (e.g., Hasher, Attig, & Alba, 1981). It is also helpful to provide at least one of the warnings immediately before the witness's report. In this case, the warning can be given as long as 45 minutes after the misleading information and still be effective (Christiaansen & Ochalek, 1983).

Because adults are more resistant to blatant than to subtle misinformation, exposure to blatant misinformation can serve as a warning. If we suggested to a witness that a purple gorilla had been present at the crime scene, the witness would be unlikely to incorporate that information into his or her eyewitness report (see Ornstein et al., 1992, for children's acceptance of blatant misinformation). Interestingly, blatantly misleading information has an alerting effect, so that people reject more subtle misinformation as well (E. Loftus, 1979b). The beneficial effects on subtle misinformation are present, however, only when both kinds of misleading information are presented at the same time, not when the blatant misleading information is delayed.

Witnesses' commitment to their initial report may also make memory more resistant to change, as shown by Bregman and McAllister (1982). They asked adults to view a videotaped car accident and, afterward, to fill out a questionnaire concerning what had happened. Those in the commitment condition were requested to sign their name on the questionnaire before turning it in. After all of the adults were subsequently exposed to misleading information, the committed ones were less likely to change their reports. However, commitment can also make people commit to their earlier mistakes.

Finally, witnesses may be better able to overcome the effects of misleading information if the order of questioning matches the original input sequence. In Loftus's studies, adults view a criminal incident, are subjected to misleading information, and then are questioned about what originally happened. If the final memory test consists of questions presented in random order, the predicted distortions emerge: a subset of adults incorporate misleading information into their reports. But if the questions on the memory test are given in an order that matches the original event sequence, the effect can disappear (Bowers & Bekerian, 1983; see Bekerian & Bowers, 1984). Unfortunately, in real criminal investigations, the original order will often be unknown, making it difficult to decide how best to order the questions.

Conclusion

In sum, memory can suffer during the retention interval because of both forgetting and contamination by postevent information. This decline in quantity and accuracy of report is not inevitable, however. It depends in part on the kind of information encoded: central, familiar, or well-encoded information is more resistant to forgetting and distortion than is more peripheral, less familiar, or poorly encoded information. It also depends on the credibility and status of the source of misinformation: high-status and unbiased sources are more likely to produce change. It depends on whether warnings were given and whether witnesses committed themselves to an earlier report. As will be seen later, it may also depend on the interviewing technique used and certain individual difference factors.

RETRIEVAL

During retrieval, the information that was encoded and then retained is brought back into the open or at least back into consciousness. Typical retrieval situations for witnesses include reporting to the police, viewing lineups, recounting to friends and mental health professionals, and testifying in court. We will review the ways in which accuracy and completeness of testimony can depend on the interviewing techniques used and the retrieval environment. We will also examine the relation between witnesses' confidence in their memory and the accuracy of their statements.

Interviewing Techniques

Ideally, testimony should be accurate and rich in detail. Unfortunately, there is often a trade-off between accuracy and completeness. Interviewing techniques that yield the highest accuracy also yield the least complete testimony; whereas techniques that yield more detailed reports also yield the most inaccuracies (Cady, 1924; Dent & Stephenson, 1979; Lipton, 1977; Marquis et al., 1972). For example, Marquis et al. presented a film showing a woman being knocked down by a car in a parking lot and an ensuing struggle between the woman's companion and the driver of the car. Afterward, the experimenters interviewed the adult witnesses using the following techniques: free recall, in which the adults were asked to report everything they could remember about the movie; open-ended questions that probed for general and specific information; multiple-choice questions that mentioned several alternative answers; and leading questions that suggested the answer (e.g., "There were cars in the area" or "The events you saw took place in the street, didn't they?"). Marquis et al. found that for easy items that had been recalled with high probability in a pretest, type of question made little difference: accuracy and completeness were high regardless of question type. But for difficult items, question type did matter: Free recall yielded perfect accuracy but the least complete testimony; multiple-choice and leading questions produced the most complete but also the least accurate report; and open-ended questions fell between these extremes. (We can speculate that the leading questions may have produced inaccuracies because the adults suspected that the interviewer was trying to mislead them; Goodman & Reed, 1986).

Given these results, and those on misinformation effects, the best way to interview a witness would seem to be first to elicit free recall (e.g., "Tell me what happened"), followed by open-ended and then more specific questions. Multiple-choice and misleading questions should be avoided. In this way, both accuracy and completeness can be encouraged (for a review, E. Loftus, Greene, & Doyle, 1989; Snee & Lush, 1941). However, forensic situations may not be as straightforward as laboratory experiments, with many pragmatic and social factors involved that are not typically at work in the laboratory.

This is perhaps particularly true when the witness is a child. Even 3- and 4-year-old children can be proportionally as accurate in free recall as older children and adults (Goodman & Reed, 1986; Leippe, Romanczyk, & Manion, 1991). Testimony from younger children is less complete than from older children and adults, but younger children can provide more details when specific questions are asked, although specific and misleading questions can also increase error rates (e.g., Bruck, Ceci, Francouer, & Barr, 1995; Hutcheson, Baxter, Telfer, & Warden, 1995). Nevertheless, when children (5 years old and up) are interviewed with free recall questions about events that have a sexual meaning, they often make omission errors, that is, not reporting something that actually happened, rather than commission errors, that is, reporting something that actually did not happen (e.g., Saywitz et al., 1991). Thus, free recall may be less than completely satisfactory as a forensic tool when sensitive information is at issue.

Despite the obvious importance of eyewitness information in criminal investigation, there is currently no established policy or training in the United States on how to conduct an effective interview (McGough, 1997), as there is in the United Kingdom, at least for children. This may be because it is unclear that research has uncovered the optimal interviewing techniques for all witnesses in all situations. Fortunately, several authors have focused their research on evaluating the effectiveness of various types of interviews (e.g., Sternberg, Lamb, et al., 1996) and on creating models of interviewing techniques (e.g., Geiselman & Fisher, 1989; Yuille, 1988). As part of this effort, Sternberg et al. (1996) performed detailed psycholinguistic analyses of transcripts of interviews conducted with children who were alleged victims of sexual abuse. Their aim was to investigate the relation between interviewer utterances and the length and richness of children's responses to these utterances. As expected, facilitative utterances (i.e., invitational, nonsuggestive encouragements to continue talking) elicited responses that were three times longer and almost three times richer in detail than responses following directive utterances (in which the interviewer asks the child to focus attention on something the child had mentioned earlier), leading utterances (in which the interviewer asks the child to focus attention on something he or she had not mentioned earlier), and suggestive utterances (for which a particular response is expected). Nevertheless, invitational utterances were rare (2.2%); thus, the effects of increased employment of such utterances is unknown.

In another study (Lamb et al., 1997), the effect of different styles in the introductory phase of the interview (rapport building) on the accuracy and completeness of children's reports was investigated. The interviews started by requiring children to report information about the same content areas (child's family, school or kindergarten activities, and a recent holiday). That information was elicited in two ways: in one condition, interviewers used open-ended probes; in the other condition, they employed more directive probes. After this introductory phase, the interview continued in the same way under both conditions. Results showed that children in the open-ended rapport-building phase provided three times as many details as children in the directive rapport-building phase. Moreover, this trend persisted throughout the whole interview.

An example of model interviews is the cognitive interview (CI) (Fisher & Geiselman, 1992; Geiselman & Fisher, 1989; Geiselman, Saywitz, & Bornstein, 1993), which can be used with both adults and older children to obtain extensive and accurate reports of events (e.g., McCauley & Fisher, 1995). Based on general principles of memory retrieval, cognition, and communication, its instructions require that witnesses: (a) reconstruct mentally the personal and environmental context at the time of the crucial event; (b) report everything, including partial information, even though it may be considered unimportant; and (c) recount the event in a variety of orders and from a variety of perspectives. Furthermore, witnesses are given specific directions to facilitate the recall of details, conversations, and names.

Although advantages of the CI seem to be consistently found with adults, (e.g., Fisher & Geiselman, 1992), it is not as well established with children. For example, Milne, Bull, Koehnken, and Memon (1995) used a revised version of the CI with children age 8 to 10 years. They compared the effect of the CI to a standard interview (SI), during which children did not receive the specific instructions of CI, but did answer the same questions. Children in the CI condition did not recall more than the ones in the SI conditions during the first free recall phase of the interview. In the CI condition, the recall was richer in the questioning phase that followed. Children gave more details in the content categories of person and actions. On the other hand, recall in the CI condition contained significantly more incorrect recall and confabulations than recall in the SI, even though across all recall categories there was no significant error difference. Memon, Cronin, Eaves, and Bull (1993) hypothesized that some children cannot understand and effectively use CI instructions, which would account for inconsistent results with children and underline the need to take into consideration the cognitive and linguistic capabilities of an individual child.

Another example of an interviewing technique is the stepwise method (Yuille, 1988; Yuille, Hunter, Joffe, & Zaparniuk, 1993), which has been recommended for use with children. Through a progressive "funnel" approach to the forensic topic of concern, the stepwise interview aims to maximize the quality and quantity of information from the child. In addition, it is supposed to minimize the stress of the investigation and the contaminant effects of repeated interviews. A similar approach has been proposed in the Memorandum of Good Practice for British Courts (Bull, 1995). Although such interviewing techniques appear promising, there is still no gold-standard interview that is widely agreed to be the best choice for all or even a subset of witnesses.

Interviewing Considerations: Timing and Atmosphere

The question often arises whether it is best to interview a witness immediately after a stressful event or wait until the stress subsides. Unfortunately there is little scientific research on this important retrieval issue. Several studies of recall of arousal-producing words or events indicate that memory improves over time (Butters, 1970; Kleinsmith & Kaplan, 1963; Scrivner & Safer, 1988), but the finding is not always replicated. Some of these studies involve repeated interviewing and find that new information is accessed across interviews. When such hypermnesia is examined by asking for repeated recall of stressful criminal events, increases in the reporting of accurate information are at times accompanied by increases in the reporting of inaccuracies, nullifying the beneficial effect (Buckhout, 1974). An explanation of this phenomenon could come from the possibility that when arousing stimuli are experienced during the retention interval, hypermnesia is inhibited (Shaw, Bekerian, & McCubbin, 1995). In any case, even when witnesses recall significantly more new information across attempts, without the nullifying effect of inaccuracies, the amount often does not exceed how much is forgotten (Turtle & Yuille, 1994).

The retrieval atmosphere is also important. Whenever a witness is approached by the police, there may be social pressure to identify someone or give a lengthy report. As Buckhout (1974) pointed out, the police would hardly bother to have a witness come in for an identification unless they have a suspect in mind. High-status interviewers tend to elicit longer reports from lower-status individuals, but high-status interviewers also produce greater misinformation effects should they introduce false postevent suggestions (Ceci et al., 1987; Marquis et al., 1972). When a retrieval atmosphere is intimidating, one might expect a drop in accuracy. An intense police interrogation and hostile cross-examination in court may constitute atmospheres of particular intimidation. One of the few studies to investigate hostile versus friendly interviewers surprisingly found no difference in accuracy or quantity of report with adults (Marquis et al., 1972), although intimidating interviewers can increase errors in children's reports (Carter, Bottoms, & Levine, 1996: Goodman, Bottoms, et al., 1991). In a number of situations, an intimidated child witness can be expected to be less accurate. When forced to identify an assailant by touching him or her (as was done in England), accuracy suffers (Dent, 1977). The retrieval atmosphere has been studied in particular for children's testimony, and several studies have shown that social support promotes better performance in terms of children's accuracy and resistance to suggestion (Carter et al., 1996; Goodman, Bottoms, et al., 1991; Moston, 1992; Dezwirek-Sas, 1992).

Context Reinstatement

The extent to which the retrieval environment matches the encoding situation is an important determinant of a person's ability to provide accurate and complete eyewitness testimony (see Tulving, 1983, for a theoretical account). The more cues shared at acquisition and retrieval, the better retrieval will be. This fact has important implications for interviewers because it implies that testimony may be greatly enhanced as more and more retrieval cues can be found. Several kinds of contextual cues exist, including both environmental and emotional cues, and there is no evidence that a particular kind of cue is superior to another in improving retrieval performance (e.g., see Cutler & Penrod, 1988), probably because the effects of context reinstatement interact with other variables (Cutler & Penrod, 1988; McSpadden, Schooler, & Loftus, 1988).

The use of guided memory procedures can provide additional cues. Malpass and Devine (1981b) used such procedures to enhance eyewitness identification of adult witnesses who had viewed a staged vandalism five months earlier.

Adults were helped to visualize the classroom where the incident took place, their position in it, the suspect, the vandalism itself, and their reaction to it. When then presented with a photo lineup that included the culprit, 60% of the witnesses were correct in their identifications. In comparison, only 40% of the witnesses who were not given the guided memory task correctly identified him. The guided memory procedure did not lead to more false identifications or false rejections of the culprit. However, more recently, McSpadden et al. (1988) provided evidence against the enhancing effect of guided memory, and E. Loftus (1994) points to the risk, entailed in using visualization together with other kinds of "memory work," of contribution to creating false memories.

Context reinstatement may explain why it is easier to identify someone from a live lineup than from a photo lineup (Egan, Pittner, & Goldstein, 1977). Because witnesses view criminals in the flesh, it is easier for them to identify the person when he or she again stands before them. In fact, context reinstatement may be a problem for the ecological validity of eyewitness testimony research that presents assailants on slides and videotape and tests memory using the same medium. Because context reinstatement effects will be strong, the rate of correct identifications may be atypically high compared to real-life crime investigations where the assailant is first seen live and then identified via photographs (Maass & Brigham, 1982).

Context reinstatement seems to be effective in facilitating children's event recall (Price & Goodman, 1990). Furthermore, Pipe, Gee, and Wilson (1993) found that children's report is improved more by cues related to specific activities than by environmental context cues. However, as pointed out earlier in this chapter, props and toys as cues can also lead to more errors in younger children's reports.

Confidence and Accuracy

At retrieval, some witnesses will seem quite confident of their statements; others will not. A large number of studies shows that confidence is highly related to jurors' perception of the credibility of a witness, regardless of whether the witness is an adult (e.g., Cutler & Penrod, 1989b; Cutler, Penrod, & Dexter, 1990; Penrod & Cutler, 1995, for a review) or a child (Goodman et al., 1998; Leippe, Manion, & Romanczyk, 1992). Are confident witnesses more accurate?

When Deffenbacher (1980) reviewed the extant literature about 20 years ago, he found 22 independent experiments that indicated a significant positive correlation between confidence and accuracy. At the same time, 21 studies found nonsignificant or even negative correlations between confidence and accuracy. Deffenbacher attempted to resolve these contradictory results by examining the conditions under which witnesses encoded, stored, and retrieved the crucial information. He found that when these conditions were optimal, a positive correlation between confidence and accuracy typically emerged; when they were not, no relation or a negative relation existed. Given that confidence and accuracy are often uncorrelated, Deffenbacher concluded that "the judicial system should cease and desist from reliance on eyewitness confidence as an index of eyewitness accuracy" (p. 258).

The optimality hypothesis has been challenged and not always supported (Egeth & McCloskey, 1984; Stephenson, 1984; Wells, Rydell, & Seelau, 1993). Research shows that the relation between accuracy and confidence can be affected by several factors (e.g., Brigham, 1990; Cutler & Penrod, 1989a). One factor is the type of eyewitness task adults are supposed to accomplish. For instance, the majority of the research about the confidence-accuracy relation has been conducted on eyewitness identifications (e.g., Wells, Ferguson, & Lindsay, 1981), whereas fewer studies have concerned the relation between accuracy of memories for staged events, such as simulated crimes, and confidence about those memories. Of the latter type, the few studies that exist (e.g., Perfect, Watson, & Wagstaff, 1993; Smith, Kassin, & Ellsworth, 1989; Stephenson, 1984) obtained contradictory results. For instance, the correlation between confidence and accuracy found by Stephenson ranged from .53 to .64, whereas the correlation in Smith et al.'s study ranged from .14 to .17. Robinson and Johnson (1996) explained those differences by pointing out that the confidence ratings referred to memories that were tested differently, that is, through recognition (Smith et al., 1989) versus recall (Stephenson, 1984). In Robinson and Johnson's study, indeed, the confidence-accuracy correlation was significantly higher in the recall condition than the recognition condition. These results have implications for the criminal justice system: it is important to know whether there are tasks in which accuracy and confidence are consistently and positively related.

Conclusion

The retrieval context plays a crucial role in forensic interviews. Research on the optimal forensic interview to be used in a specific situation (e.g., with child victim/witness in sexual assault cases) is currently underway. In principle, retrieval cues can serve a useful role, but misleading retrieval cues raise the specter of suggestibility, as was discussed earlier in the section on memory malleability. Intimidation of witnesses, especially children, can lead to increased error. More research is needed on the best ways to interview adult and child witnesses, especially when traumatic events are involved.

SPECIAL ISSUES

We now turn to a number of special issues in the study of eyewitness memory. We focus on issues that have received considerable attention in recent years, such as face recognition, "repressed/recovered" memories, eyewitness memory in abuse victims, individual differences in eyewitness ability, the elderly as witnesses, use of anatomically detailed dolls, children's suggestibility, and children's testimony in court.

FACE RECOGNITION

As reviewed above, the ability to recognize an unfamiliar face varies considerably depending on the conditions of encoding, retention, and retrieval. Additional factors such as the fairness of identification procedures used by authorities must also be considered (see Chance & Goldstein, 1984; Malpass,

1996; Narby, Cutler, & Penrod, 1996; Wells, 1993, for reviews). Although we have already examined many of the factors that affect eyewitness identification (e.g., encoding opportunity, delay interval), it is worthwhile here to consider several topics specific to face recognition (see Sporer et al., 1996, for a review).

Cross-Racial Identification

The majority of studies and meta-analyses to date indicate that cross-race identifications are more difficult than same-race identifications (Bothwell, Brigham, & Malpass, 1989; Chance, Goldstein, & McBride, 1975; Feinman & Entwisle, 1976; Luce, 1974; Malpass & Kravitz, 1969; Malpass, Lavigueur, & Weldon, 1973; Shapiro & Penrod, 1986; see Chance & Goldstein, 1996; R. Lindsay & Wells, 1983, for reviews). More specifically, these studies show that it is more difficult for members of one race (e.g., Caucasian) to recognize someone from a different race (e.g., African American). One study indicates that the effect increases with age of the witness, at least into adulthood (Goldstein & Chance, 1980; see Lee, Goodman, & Barry, 1998); other research shows that the effect is likely to be at least partly a function of meaningful experience with members of different races (Brigham, Maass, Snyder, & Spaulding, 1982; Chance, Goldstein, & Anderson, 1986; Platz & Hosch, 1988).

Lineup Fairness

Imagine that you have witnessed a crime, and a week later the police ask you to view a photo lineup of three men. It turns out that two of them are suspects in the crime. If you were randomly guessing when attempting the identification, what would be the chances of selecting one of the two men? The chances are high (66% if you feel you must make a choice, and 50% if you include "none" as an option). What if your instructions included biased statements such as "We have reason to believe that the culprit is in today's lineup?" What if you were allowed to see that only one lineup member arrived in handcuffs? Most defense attorneys would assert that such lineups were unfair.

Psychologists have devised several ways to evaluate the fairness of a lineup (Brigham, Ready, & Spier, 1990; Doob & Kirshenbaum, 1973; Malpass & Devine, 1983). It is generally acknowledged that the functional size of a lineup (i.e., the number of viable lineup members) may be much smaller than the nominal size (i.e., the number of members present). If the foils are dissimilar from the suspect, the suspect may be easily picked out by mock witnesses, that is, people who were not present at the crime but who have heard a description of the suspect. An extreme example of this would be if a witness described the perpetrator as a Caucasian man and a lineup of six people was presented: one Caucasian and five African Americans. Importantly, the similarity of the foils to the suspect is not the only variable to consider in creating a fair lineup. If the foils are more similar to the suspect than they are to each other, the suspect may stand out in the lineup (Laughery, Jensen, & Wogalter, 1988; Wogalter, Marwitz, & Leonard, 1992). Photo arrays may provide greater opportunity for selection of appropriate foils (Cutler, Berman, Penrod, & Fisher, 1994). However, if a photo array is used, care must be taken to match the pose and expression of the photos presented (Buckhout, 1974).

Sequential lineups, in which persons or photographs of persons are presented one at a time, may have advantages over traditional lineup procedures because they discourage witnesses from simply choosing the lineup member most similar to their memory of the suspect (R. Lindsay & Wells, 1985). A sequential lineup is especially effective when witnesses are unaware of the total number of persons to be presented (R. Lindsay, Lea, & Fulford, 1991).

Another identification procedure is the showup, in which a single suspect is presented to a witness. Though this procedure has long been criticized as too leading, recent research indicates that it may not be as biasing as previously thought. Indeed, a witness may be more likely to indicate that the suspect is not present in a showup than in a lineup (Gonzalez, Ellsworth, & Pembroke, 1993; see Yarmey, Yarmey, & Yarmey, 1996).

Unconscious Transference

Sometimes a face is recognized by a witness, but the witness is unsure or incorrectly identifies the circumstances under which it was first seen. If a face in a lineup looks familiar to the witness, he or she may identify that person as the culprit, even if that person was really an innocent bystander to the crime or someone encountered at a completely different time. This is called unconscious transference, and has led to mistaken identification in actual cases (Buckhout, 1984; Houts, 1963). Although this phenomenon has some experimental support (E. Brown, Deffenbacher, & Sturgill, 1977; E. Loftus, 1976), recent studies indicate that it is not easy to recreate the phenomenon in the laboratory. Read, Tollestrup, Hammersley, McFadzen, and Christensen (1990) found little evidence of unconscious transference across five studies. Ross, Ceci, Dunning, and Toglia (1994) found that what appeared to be unconscious transference was in reality a by-product of adults' confusion: many incorrectly believed at the time of the incident that the assailant and a bystander were the same person. Interestingly, in a recent study comparing child (5 to 8 years old) and adult witnesses, unconscious transference effects were found for adults but not for children (Ross et al., 1998).

Interference

Seeing other faces does not always result in unconscious transference, but it may still affect retrieval. Searching through mug shots, for example, may make it harder to identify the face of a suspect because the intervening faces may interfere with memory (Laughery et al., 1971). Suppose that a witness views many mug shots after the crime and selects no one. Then a lineup that includes a face from the mug shots is presented, and the face seen before is selected. It is difficult to know whether this selection was made based on the familiarity of having seen the face in the mug shots or because that person was the culprit. Viewing mug shots may also be detrimental because it could cause the witness to develop a negative response set, responding no to faces even if they have been seen previously. The commitment effect, mentioned earlier, represents another danger. An incorrect identification made in the presence of others stands relatively little chance of being altered at a later time, even if the correct option becomes available (Brigham & Cairns, 1988; Gorenstein & Ellsworth, 1980).

Disguises

Sometimes even familiar people can be difficult to recognize because their appearance has changed with a new hairstyle, weight fluctuation, or simply the passage of years. These differences between initial appearance and subsequent identification exacerbate difficulties that witnesses have in identifying criminals. Criminals can capitalize on and extend these difficulties through the use of disguises (Shapiro & Penrod, 1986). Changes in clothing, pose, and expression have all been found to decrease identification accuracy (Davies & Milne, 1982; Sporer, 1993a; Wogalter & Laughery, 1987). Upper facial features and hair seem to have particular significance, and disguises that cover them (such as a hat) or distort them (such as glasses) may be especially effective (Cutler, Penrod, & Martens, 1987; Patterson & Baddeley, 1977; Sporer, 1993b). Similarly, a disguised voice makes voice recognition more difficult (see Clifford, 1983; Read & Craik, 1995).

Training

Obviously, it would be advantageous if people could be trained to become better witnesses. Training studies indicate that it is possible to improve adults' ability to recognize other-race faces through a variety of techniques (Elliott, Wills, & Goldstein, 1973; Lavrakas, Buri, & Mayznere, 1976; Malpass et al., 1973), but it is more difficult to improve recognition of same-race faces. In any case, it is not clear how long training effects last (Lavrakas et al., 1976).

Psychologists have investigated whether police are more accurate in recognition of culprits or in recalling events. Two findings emerge. One is that police officers are more likely than civilians to "see" criminal events in ambiguous circumstances (Tickner & Poulton, 1975; Verinis & Walker, 1970). The second is that police are generally no better than civilians in recognizing faces (Billig & Milner, 1976) but may remember more information about specific details, such as license plate numbers, dress, and physical appearance, especially if given sufficient time to encode these features (Clifford & Richards, 1977). Thus, training can be helpful but not always as helpful as might be hoped.

There is evidence to indicate that older children may benefit from training on photo identification tasks. In general, children have a more difficult time with target-absent photo lineups and often do not seem to understand that the person of interest (i.e., the perpetrator) may not be present in the photo lineup. When 5- to 7-year-old children received practice trials on target-present and target-absent photo lineups, their accuracy on a subsequent lineup identification task was higher than that of children who did not receive the training (Goodman, Bottoms, Schwartz-Kenney, & Rudy, 1991). However, the use of practice trials did not improve photo lineup accuracy for 3- to 4-year-olds, indicating that this type of training may not be effective for very young children.

INDIVIDUAL DIFFERENCES

Can we predict who, at a given age, is likely to provide accurate testimony? The answer at this time appears to be no, although a few individual difference measures seem to hold promise.

Intelligence and Cognitive Abilities

Are more intelligent witnesses more accurate witnesses? The relation between intelligence and eyewitness testimony has been examined in numerous studies employing a variety of intelligence measures: standardized intelligence tests, achievement tests, digit span, social intelligence tests, and verbal fluency (Chance & Goldstein, 1984; Feinman & Entwisle, 1976; Gilliland & Burke, 1926; Goetze, 1980; Goldstein & Chance, 1964; Goodman, Hirshman, et al., 1991; Gudjonsson, 1984, 1987; Howells, 1938; Kaess & Witryol, 1955; King, 1984; Powers, Andriks, & Loftus, 1979). For normal adults, no consistent relation between intelligence and accuracy has been found. The two tasks—eyewitness reports and intelligence tests—seem to tap quite different abilities.

Specifically in regard to suggestibility, there have been mixed results regarding the relation between intelligence and susceptibility to suggestion (Clare & Gudjonsson, 1993, 1995; Gudjonsson, 1987, 1988; Powers et al., 1979). According to Gudjonsson (1988), it may be that only below-average intelligence is associated with increases in suggestibility and memory impairment.

Metamemory (beliefs regarding how memory functions and one's own memory capabilities) is another cognitive individual difference factor that may influence suggestibility and memory performance in both children and adults (Henry & Norman, 1996; O'Sullivan & Howe, 1995). For instance, over-confidence in one's memory abilities may negatively impact adults' and children's vulnerability to suggestion (Tousant, 1984, as cited in Loftus et al., 1992). Additional cognitively related factors thought possibly to influence children's memory and suggestibility include language capabilities (Carter et al., 1996), source-monitoring abilities (Ceci, Loftus, Leichtman, & Bruck, 1994), and imaginativeness (Shyamalan, Lamb, & Sheldrick, 1995).

Eidetic imagery and visual imagery are two other cognitive abilities that are sometimes mentioned as possibly related to eyewitness accuracy. There is little reason to believe that either of these can be used to predict accurate testimony (Chance & Goldstein, 1984; Clifford & Bull, 1978; M. Courtois & Mueller, 1981), although some measures of facial recognition abilities show predictive power concerning adults' accuracy on lineup tasks (Hosch, 1994; Hosch, Bothwell, Sporer, & Saucedo, 1990, 1991).

Thus, it appears that certain cognitive abilities (low intelligence, face recognition ability) may be helpful when assessing eyewitness testimony. However, these certainly should not be used as single determinants of accuracy. Given the limited and contradictory information currently available for cognitive factors such as intelligence (in the normal range), metamemory, eidetic imagery, and visual imagery, reliance on these factors to predict accuracy is probably unwarranted.

Cognitive Style, Personality Measures, and Attitudes

Inconsistent findings typically emerge when one attempts to predict the accuracy of a witness's report from measures of cognitive style or personality. For example, field dependence-independence has been found to correlate with eyewitness accuracy in some studies but not in others (Hoffman & Kagan, 1977; Hosch, 1994; Lavrakas et al., 1976; Marin, Holmes, Guth, & Kovac, 1979; Messick & Damarin, 1964; Witkin, Dyk, Faterson, Goodenough, & Karp, 1974; see Clifford & Bull, 1978, for a review). Measures of extroversion-introversion, reflection-impulsivity, level of compliance, attitudes toward certain groups, and self-monitoring have met a similar fate (Brigham & Barkowitz, 1978; Gudjonsson, 1990, 1991; Hosch & Cooper, 1981; Hunt, 1928; Hyman & Billings, 1995; King, 1984; Shepherd, 1981; Trouve & Libkuman, 1992; Ward & Loftus, 1985). For most of these measures and others (e.g., need for approval; Schill, 1966), little research has been conducted, so firm conclusions are premature.

Gender

Do males or females make better witnesses? Given the available research, the best answer to this question is that males and females sometimes notice and remember different things, but one group is not better than the other. Powers et al. (1979) asked adults to view a videotape showing a male and female who happen upon a confrontation in a parking lot. A day later, the adults were exposed to misleading information and then asked questions about the original event. Females were more accurate and resistant to suggestion about female-oriented details, whereas men were more accurate and resistant to suggestion about male-oriented details.

There may be two exceptions to the general similarity of male and female witnesses. First, several experiments investigating gender differences for face recognition and for person memory have produced evidence favoring female superiority (Yarmey, 1993; see Shepherd, 1981, for a review). Most of these studies are traditional laboratory experiments, however, which differ in important ways from real-life criminal events. Second, if an event is violent, female bystander witnesses may be at a slight disadvantage on eyewitness tasks (Clifford & Scott, 1978; C. Johnson & Scott, 1976). It has been hypothesized that in comparison to males, females may feel more fear and less efficacy when experiencing a violent situation.

Anxiety

Earlier, we reviewed evidence, pro and con, relevant to the claim that memory is relatively poor for stressful events. In a similar vein, it has been proposed that people who are highly anxious may retain less than their calmer counterparts, perhaps because anxious people are preoccupied with task-irrelevant processing, such as noticing their own feelings of nervousness. Siegel and Loftus (1978) measured adults' anxiety levels and self-preoccupation. The adults then viewed slides of a purse-snatching incident; immediately after viewing the slides, the adults completed a questionnaire designed to determine eyewitness accuracy. The more anxious and self-preoccupied adults performed more poorly on the questionnaire than those who scored lower on the anxiety and self-preoccupation measures. Similar results were obtained by Dobson and Markham (1992), with high-anxiety witnesses exhibiting poorer recognition memory than low-anxiety witnesses for a series of slides depicting a purse-snatching incident. However, these differences in accuracy between high- and low-anxiety adults were present only when the task contained anxiety-inducing instructions. It is suggested that low-anxiety adults may perform better under stressful than nonstressful conditions. Thus, the accuracy of an eyewitness's performance may be based on an interaction between individual and situational factors. Other studies, though not always as representative of eyewitness tasks, have produced somewhat more ambiguous but generally similar results (Buckhout, Alper, Chern, Silverberg, & Slomovits, 1974; Mueller, Bailis, & Goldstein, 1979; Nowicki, Winograd, & Millard, 1979; Zanni & Offerman, 1978).

RECOVERED MEMORIES OF CHILDHOOD ABUSE

In the past few years, few topics have been as controversial as "repressed" memory of traumatic experiences, especially of child sexual abuse. In the 1980s, there was a sudden surge of claims of recovery of repressed memories of childhood sexual abuse (CSA), which motivated researchers to question the validity of such claims (D. Lindsay & Read, 1994; E. Loftus, 1993). Freud (1915/1957) proposed that when a person encounters a traumatic event, such as CSA, the person may engage in an unconscious process of forcing the traumatic memory out of conscious awareness. In other words, according to Freud, memories of traumatic events can be repressed. Although the repressed memory is not consciously accessible to the person, it may express itself indirectly through dreams, flashbacks, or psychological difficulties. It is believed that repressed memories of traumatic events can be recovered under certain conditions (e.g., during psychotherapy).

The validity of recovered memories of CSA, especially those recovered during the process of psychotherapy, remains under heated debate (Alpert & Brown, 1996; Berliner & Williams, 1994; Harvey & Herman, 1994; D. Lindsay & Read, 1994; E. Loftus, 1993; Read & Lindsay, 1994). Those who question the validity of such memories contend that most, if not all, of the factors known to increase memory distortion in laboratory studies are also present in some types of psychotherapy sessions. These factors include experiencing repeated exposure to suggestions from a trusted authority; believing in the plausibility of suggested information (e.g., hidden memories); having strong motivation for memory recovery; searching for long-ago, thus often vague, memories; and using techniques that enhance imagery and lower response criterion (e.g., guided visualization, age regression, hypnosis). Although memory recovery techniques may help genuine survivors of childhood abuse retrieve memories, many argue that such techniques impose a substantial danger of creating false memories in vulnerable adults who do not have an abuse history (D. Lindsay & Read, 1994; E. Loftus, 1993; Ornstein, Ceci, & Loftus, 1996a, 1996b; Read & Lindsay, 1994).

Those who believe in the validity of recovered memories argue that a significant proportion of adult survivors of CSA can forget their earlier abuse experiences (Briere & Conte, 1993; Harvey & Herman, 1994; Herman & Schatzow, 1987; Williams, 1994) and that recovering and dealing with memories of CSA is an integral part of psychotherapy (C. Courtois, 1992; Herman, 1992; Olio,

1994). In addition, proponents of recovered memories argue that laboratory research on suggestibility and memory distortion has only limited generalizability to therapeutic situations and that the risk of implanting false memories of CSA in clients who do not have such a history is minimal (Alpert, Brown, & Courtois, 1996a, 1996b; Berliner & Williams, 1994; L. Brown, 1996; Olio, 1994; Pezdek, 1994).

Several related but distinct questions are involved in the recovered memory controversy. One question is whether memories of traumatic events can be repressed or otherwise lost from consciousness. There exists a large body of published case studies and clinical reports on functional amnesias, in which emotionally traumatic events can produce extensive amnesia for much or all of a patient's personal past (see Spiegel, 1995). Although these cases typically involve situations in which a single traumatic experience produced retrograde amnesia for both traumatic and nontraumatic events, they nevertheless show that traumatic memories can be excluded from conscious awareness.

In addition, the results from a number of recent studies of adults' memories of CSA clearly indicate that forgetting or nonreport of CSA in not uncommon (Briere & Conte, 1993; Herman & Schatzow, 1987; E. Loftus, Polonsky, et al., 1994; Widom & Morris, 1997; Williams, 1994). For example, in a prospective study conducted by Williams, 129 women were interviewed who had documented incidents of abuse 17 years earlier. These women were asked questions about childhood experiences with sex, but were not directly asked about the documented abuse incident. Williams found that 38% of the women failed to report the documented abuse. Also using a prospective methodology, Widom and Morris (1997) recently found that underreport of CSA is common among adults with documented histories of CSA.

Although researchers generally agree that traumatic memories of CSA can become lost, the mechanisms for such memory loss are far from clear (Alpert, Brown, et al., 1996; D. Lindsay & Read, 1994; E. Loftus, 1993). Amnesia of CSA may occur either because of special defense mechanisms, such as repression or dissociation (Berliner & Williams, 1994; Briere & Conte, 1993; Herman & Schatzow, 1987), or because of normal memory processes that apply to both traumatic and nontraumatic events, such as decay, interference, inhibition, and intentional or unintentional failure to rehearse an event (D. Lindsay & Read, 1994; Ornstein et al., 1996a). To date, available studies do not provide evidence to distinguish among these possibilities. In summary, although researchers agree that victims of childhood trauma may fail to disclose their abuse experiences, researchers are not sure about the exact cause of victims' failure to report.

Another question in the debate concerns whether lost memories can be accurately recovered. Evidence on this question is far from definitive. There are several clinical reports in which patients' recovered abuse memories have been objectively verified and appeared credible (e.g., Martinez-Taboas, 1996; Nash, 1994). In a few notable legal cases, the accused perpetrator corroborated the recovered memory of abuse (Horn, 1993). Attempts have also been made to evaluate corroborative evidence for adults who reported the loss of childhood abuse memories (e.g., Chu, Frey, Ganzel, & Matthews, 1995; Dalenberg, 1996; Herman

& Schatzow, 1987; Williams, 1995). For example, Herman and Schatzow reported that 74% of the patients in their study were able to obtain corroborations from another source (e.g., family members or the perpetrator), although they did not specify what percentage of the patients with severe memory loss had obtained corroboration. Despite these results, controversy exists regarding whether the reported studies have demonstrated the veracity of recovered memories. Certain methodological limitations (e.g., the memory loss and the corroboration are often based on participants' self-reports) preclude a definitive conclusion. In addition, currently there is no solid evidence that people can forget and then recover years of repeated, horrific abuse of the kind that is sometimes described in repressed memory cases (e.g., satanic ritual abuse; Ofshe & Watters, 1994; Qin, Goodman, Bottoms, & Shaver, 1998).

Can an entire false memory of childhood abuse be created in individuals who never experienced the alleged abuse? A number of former patients of psychotherapy have come to believe that their recovered memories of CSA were false (e.g., deRivera, 1997; Lief & Fetkewicz, 1995; E. Nelson & Simpson, 1994; Pasley, 1994). Although subjective experience itself cannot be taken as definitive evidence of false memory (Berliner & Williams, 1994; Harvey & Herman, 1994), the existence of these cases nevertheless suggests the possibility of false memory formation (Qin, Tyda, & Goodman, 1997). However, currently no hard empirical evidence to demonstrate the phenomenon unequivocally is available (Pope, 1996). Direct experimental demonstration is out of the question because of ethical considerations. Nevertheless, findings that suggest the possibility are abundant. Aside from evidence that memory distortion about certain details of events can occur as a result of suggestion (see Ceci & Bruck, 1993; D. Lindsay & Read, 1994, for reviews), a number of studies conducted in recent years demonstrate that, under certain conditions, a significant minority of adults can provide detailed reports of recollections about events that did not occur in their childhood (e.g., Hyman et al., 1995; Hyman & Pentland, 1996; E. Loftus & Pickrell, 1995; see Pezdek, 1994; Pezdek et al., 1997). For example, in a study conducted by Loftus and colleagues, participants were led to believe that several specific events had happened to them when they were around 5 years old; one event (being lost in a shopping mall) had not actually happened. Participants were asked to work on remembering the events and provide details of the events in two interviews. As a result, 6 out of 24 participants claimed that they had fully or partially remembered the false event. Comparable results have been obtained by several researchers using a similar paradigm (Hyman & Billings, 1995; Hyman et al., 1995; Hyman & Pentland, 1996). However, limitations on ecological validity raise doubts about the extent the findings from these studies can be generalized to the memory recovery processes within psychotherapy (e.g., Alpert et al., 1996a; L. Brown, 1996).

In summary, there is currently no definitive answer to many of the questions involved in the repressed memory debate. On the one hand, studies show that real victims of childhood abuse may at times fail to report the abuse, may forget the abuse for periods of time, and may then remember it again. On the other hand, there is accumulating evidence that false memories can be created in a minority of adults under certain conditions. Without independent corroborative evidence, we cannot be certain which of these two phenomena is the most frequent or how to definitively differentiate between true and false memories.

MEMORY IN ABUSE VICTIMS

The debate about repressed and recovered memory raises the issue of memory in abuse victims more generally. Abuse and neglect are associated, at least under certain circumstances, with detrimental effects on several areas of children's emotional and cognitive development (see Cicchetti & Toth, 1995, for a review) and thus may influence children's memory and suggestibility as well. A history of maltreatment may also lead to the development of dissociative and posttraumatic stress disorder (PTSD) symptoms (Putnam, 1993; van der Kolk & Fisler, 1995). These dissociative and PTSD symptoms may further influence memory. In one study investigating maltreated children's memory, children who scored higher on measures of dissociation and lower on a measure of global adaptive functioning (GAF) tended to exhibit poorer memory for a personally experienced stressful event (Eisen, Goodman, Qin, & Davis, 1998; Qin, Eisen, et al., 1997).

Research on individuals with histories of severe abuse or other traumatic events indicates that these memory deficiencies may continue into adulthood (Bremner, Randall, Scott, Capelli, et al., 1995). Recently, Bremner and colleagues (Bremner, Krystal, Southwick, & Charney, 1995) reported decrements in explicit memory abilities in adults who experienced traumatizing events, such as Vietnam veterans (Bremner, Southwick, Johnson, Yehuda, & Cahrney, 1993) and prisoners of the Korean war (Sutker, Winstead, Galina, & Allain, 1991). One might expect similar trends for adults who experienced severe and prolonged child abuse. Although the presence of an abuse history may be a factor to consider for both children and adults, scientifically based knowledge about the effects of abuse on eyewitness memory is just beginning to accumulate.

THE CHILD WITNESS

Although we have reviewed much of the research on children's eyewitness memory already, a number of issues that are either unique to or particularly important regarding child witnesses are dealt with next. Increased reporting of crimes against children (e.g., sexual assault and child physical abuse) has brought more and more children into contact with the legal system. As a result, in recent years, research on the eyewitness abilities of children has blossomed (see Melton et al., 1995; Goodman, Emery, et al., 1997, for reviews) and has helped spawn modifications in the legal system's response to children. We have already noted that children recall less than adults in free recall but can be more suggestible than adults when an interviewer turns to more specific and leading questioning, and that children tend to be more prone than adults to false identifications on target-absent lineups. Here we focus on three issues of special interest: children's suggestibility when repeatedly interviewed, children's use of anatomically detailed dolls, and children's eyewitness testimony in court.

Children's Suggestibility When Repeatedly Interviewed

Children are, at least under some circumstances, more suggestible than adults (see Ceci & Bruck, 1993; Goodman, Emery, & Haugaard, 1997, for reviews). Some of these circumstances seem to be the same as those that lead to heightened suggestibility in adults: a relatively weak memory and a high-status interviewer (Ceci et al., 1987; Goodman, 1984; E. Loftus, 1979a). When children's memory is equivalent in strength to adults', age differences in suggestibility are less likely to occur and may even be reversed (Duncan, Whitney, & Kunen, 1982). Although 3-year-olds have been found to be more suggestible than older children and adults generally, they are still capable of resisting some false suggestions.

Repeated nonmisleading interviewing helps maintain accurate memory (Brainerd & Ornstein, 1991), but repeated misleading questioning can have an adverse effect on preschoolers' eyewitness reports. For example, in a study by Leichtman and Ceci (1995), 3- to 4-year-old and 5- to 6-year-old children were led to believe a man (Sam Stone) was clumsy (pre-event stereotype). After observing a nonclumsy Sam Stone in their classroom, the children were then interviewed four times over the course of several weeks with highly suggestive misleading questions (postevent suggestion). In a fifth and final interview, children were interviewed by a new interviewer who asked about what happened. Approximately 46% of the 3- to 4-year-olds and 30% of the 5- to 6-year-olds spontaneously reported that Sam Stone ripped a book and/or soiled a teddy bear, when in fact he had not. When follow-up probes were asked, 72% of the 3- to 4-year-olds and approximately 33% of the 5- to 6-year-olds claimed that Sam Stone had committed these acts. However, these percentages decreased for both age groups when children were asked if they really saw Sam Stone perform these acts, and then dropped even lower when gently challenged if Sam Stone really had ripped a book and/or soiled a teddy bear. Additionally, one should be aware that these children received both a pre-event stereotype and postevent suggestions. Children in the control condition and children who received either the pre- or postsuggestion performed better (see also Poole & Lindsay, 1995). In contrast to findings emphasizing children's suggestibility, in one- or two-time neutral interviews that include misleading questions, although age differences emerge, children's false reports to abuse-related questions are surprisingly low (Rudy & Goodman, 1991; Tobey & Goodman, 1992). Although it seems likely that repeated misleading suggestions can contribute to false memory formation in children (and adults), including contributing to false memories of traumatic events, it is less clear that researchers have adequately pinpointed the conditions under which false memories of CSA are formed.

Anatomically Detailed Dolls

One controversial interviewing technique for children in forensic investigations of sexual abuse involves the use of anatomically detailed (AD) dolls (see Everson & Boat, 1994; Koocher et al., 1995, for reviews). Some propose that these special dolls aid children's reporting of sexual experiences, particularly embarrassing details or ones for which children may not have the words. In contrast, others propose that the dolls are highly suggestive and may lead to false accusations and permanently altered memories.

In support of the dolls' use, some empirical studies have found increased reporting of genital contact when such contact had occurred (e.g., Goodman, Quas, et al., 1997; Saywitz et al., 1991). For example, in Goodman, Quas, et al.'s study, 3- to 10-year-olds who experienced genital touch during a medical procedure were later asked a free recall question about what happened and then to describe and demonstrate the medical procedure with AD dolls. Regardless of age, children were more likely to disclose genital touch with the AD dolls than in free recall. In Saywitz et al.'s study of children who received either a medical checkup involving a genital exam or a scoliosis exam, most children affirmed genital touch only when the interviewer asked specific questions about genital contact and pointed to the genital area of an AD doll. It must also be noted, however, that a few of the children who did not have the genital exam falsely assented to the leading questions. Specifically, 8% (three children) falsely claimed vaginal or anal touch when asked the AD doll-assisted specific questions. Thus, results from the Saywitz et al. study point to the potential benefits as well as the delicateness of AD doll use.

Using a similar procedure to the Saywitz et al. (1991) study, Bruck, Ceci, Francouer, and Renick (1995) found that for 2- to 3-year-olds, AD doll-aided questions did not elicit additional accurate information compared to children's demonstrations on their own bodies. Moreover, some of the children demonstrated sexualized play (e.g., inserting fingers or objects into genital openings), which prompted the authors to conclude that AD dolls should not be used in forensic abuse investigations.

To date, several guidelines regarding the use of AD dolls have been recommended. These guidelines suggest that (a) the dolls should not be used as a diagnostic test to claim that a child has or has not been abused; (b) interpersonal factors such as age, cultural background, and socioeconomic status should be considered when using the dolls; and (c) professionals using AD dolls should have received sufficient training on proper investigative techniques. Overall, although there is evidence to suggest that clinical and forensic professionals who conduct abuse interviews with children use AD dolls frequently (Conte, Sorenson, Fogarty, & Rosa, 1991), questions about the effects of AD dolls on children's disclosures of true abuse versus errors of false report have not been fully addressed in scientific research.

Children's Eyewitness Testimony in the Courtroom

In the United States and numerous other countries, children's eyewitness accuracy in the courtroom is of major concern (Spencer & Flin, 1990). It is feared that the stress of courtroom confrontation may interfere with children's ability to communicate accurately and fully to triers of fact, a fear supported by research findings (Goodman et al., 1992). Several reforms to empower and protect child witnesses, and that hopefully help ensure that accurate statements are introduced into evidence, have been suggested and implemented in the past decade (Davies & Westcott, 1995), including testimony via closed-circuit television, videotaped testimony, and more liberal introduction of out-of-court statements via hearsay exceptions. Although such techniques may help relieve children's stress, in the eyes of jurors, the impact and credibility of children's testimony can suffer when such innovations are employed (Goodman, Myers, & Redlich, 1997; Goodman, Tobey, et al., 1998).

When children must take the stand in court and confront the accused, a significant problem regarding their accuracy derives from attorneys' questioning styles. Unfortunately, it is not a rare occurrence for children to be asked questions in "legalese," that is, complex questions with convoluted sentence formations, such as double negatives and dual-part questions. Children have difficulty comprehending and answering these types of questions in comparison with more direct and developmentally appropriate questions (e.g., Carter et al., 1996; Perry et al., 1995). Unfortunately, few states require that children be asked questions in a developmentally appropriate manner (Walker, 1997).

In summary, the courts grapple with the dilemma of ensuring defendants' rights while accommodating child witnesses' special needs. In recent years, there have been attempts to implement courtroom reforms to foster children's eyewitness accuracy and even to spare them the need to testify, but the reforms have often met with legal challenge and with reductions in the perceived credibility of children's eyewitness accounts. When children testify in the traditional manner, attorneys' use of legalese is likely to be an important contributor to children's errors. Courts need to be educated that questioning of children, in and out of court, must be developmentally appropriate to ensure their eyewitness accuracy.

The Elderly Witness

When the first edition of this handbook was published, relatively little research existed on the testimony of elderly witnesses. Ten years later, the same dearth exists. Research generally finds that the elderly, compared to younger adults, recall less about events (Yarmey, 1984, 1996), tend to make more memory errors (E. Loftus & Doyle, 1987), and have more difficulty recognizing faces shown from one viewpoint (Deffenbacher, 1991). In a study by Yarmey (1993), 18- to 65-year-olds were approached by a young adult female investigator inquiring about directions. A couple of minutes later, the adults were asked to describe the woman and identify her from one of a series of eyewitness identification measures (e.g., single photograph or a 6-person voice lineup). Yarmey found that age significantly affected description accuracy: young adults (18–29) were significantly better than middle-age adults (30–44), who, in turn, were significantly better than older adults (45–65) in description accuracy. Age did not influence accuracy on any of the identification measures.

When the eyewitness performance of the elderly is compared to that of children, results are equivocal: the elderly are sometimes more suggestible than children but sometimes less suggestible (Coxon & Valentine, 1997; Loftus, Levidow, & Duensing, 1992). Similar to children, older individuals, in some instances, may have more difficulty remembering sources of information and may be more vulnerable to suggestion than younger adults (Coxon & Valentine, 1997; D. Lindsay, 1994). For example, in a standard Loftus misinformation paradigm (see above), older adults ($M = 70.4$ years) were more susceptible to misleading suggestions and were more confident that their incorrect answers were correct, than were younger adults ($M = 34.9$ years) (Cohen & Faulkner, 1989, Experiment 2). However, it must be noted that findings of impaired performance for elderly witnesses do not hold for all elderly persons. That is, some older people's memory abilities do not decline with advancing age and may match those of younger adults (E. Loftus & Doyle, 1987). In conclusion, more studies are needed before we will know whether conditions exist under which the elderly perform comparably to other adult witnesses. Additionally, studies examining individual differences in the elderly's memory capacities are needed. R. Lindsay (1985, as cited in Yarmey, 1996) sums up the problems posed by elderly eyewitness testimony: "It is unclear how useful knowledge of a small difference in accuracy will be. If an elderly eyewitness is 10% less likely than a middle-aged eyewitness to make a correct identification, how can this information be used? Surely the elderly eyewitness will not be prevented from giving evidence. Should the trier of fact give less weight to an identification obtained from an elderly witness? Perhaps . . ." (p. 524).

ECOLOGICAL VALIDITY

In this chapter, we have reviewed a wealth of research on eyewitness testimony, most of it based on scientific, laboratory studies. One frequently asked question about research on eyewitness testimony concerns ecological validity: How much do findings from the laboratory generalize to forensic situations? For example, how much do research participants who know that their testimony has no serious consequences act like real-life eyewitnesses? Some studies have tried to create conditions more similar to actual legal situations (Brigham et al., 1982; Malpass & Devine, 1981c; Murray & Wells, 1982), with some surprising results. For example, it might be argued that the rate of false identification in eyewitness research is often high because participants know that their responses will not result in arrest; in real life, witnesses might be more cautious. Yet, when a realistic vandalism was staged and adults led to believe that the suspect would go to jail, they attempted more identifications (83%) than did those who thought "he would get a good talking to" (26%); the two groups did not differ overall in the number of errors committed (Malpass & Devine, 1981c). Yuille and Wells (1991) assert that the criterion of ecological validity is fulfilled if the results can be extended to the real situation, which requires researchers to show that the two contexts (the experimental setting and the criminal and/or forensic situation) elicit the same cognitive, social, and emotional processes. Over the years, researchers have gone to great lengths to try to make their studies of eyewitness testimony as ecologically valid as possible. However, ethical considerations limit the degree of ecological validity that can be achieved while still maintaining rigorous scientific control of variables and adequate internal validity. Thus, although the study of eyewitness testimony has come a long way and has produced many replicable, forensically important results, there may always be questions about the generalizability of the results.

THE PSYCHOLOGIST AS EXPERT WITNESS

Having completed our review of the literature, we would like to comment briefly on the role of the expert witness on eyewitness testimony. Psychologists may be asked to provide expert testimony to the courts about the eyewitness abilities of children or adults. When psychologists testify, they typically describe the findings of relevant studies, as we have done in this chapter. Expert testimony by psychologists has, at times, been criticized for bias or exceeding scientifically verifiable bounds (e.g., Lyon, 1995; Mason, 1991). The courts require only that the admission of expert opinion leads marginally to a better understanding of the evidence in a case (Melton, 1994), and thus the legal standards for expert testimony are surprisingly low. Expert witnesses must keep in mind that professional ethical standards may be much higher. Clearly, given that the fate of the accused and of the victim—and of one's discipline—may be seriously affected by expert testimony, the decision to testify in court as an expert witness is a serious one.

In most states, the Federal Rules of Evidence (FRE) frame the admissibility of expert evidence, especially in criminal proceedings. In addition to the FRE, the U.S. Supreme Court's decision in *Daubert v. Merrell Dow Pharmaceuticals* (1993) has resulted in new standards. The *Daubert* decision emphasizes the reliability of expert information (e.g., Is the knowledge reasonably relied on in the field of science? Are the methods falsifiable?), the relevance of the information (e.g., Are the findings generalizable to the situation at hand?), and legal sufficiency (e.g., Is the testimony more probative than prejudicial?). The *Daubert* decision specifies that the judge should predetermine if scientific evidence to be admitted through expert testimony is scientifically valid and that it will assist the trier of fact to understand or determine a fact at issue. Generally, the judge has broad discretion in qualifying an expert and admitting his or her testimony. Decisions concerning the application of the *Daubert* standards to expert testimony on eyewitness memory are beginning to be made. For instance, in a recent U. S. Eighth Circuit Court of Appeals decision (*United States v. Rouse*, 1996), the justices decided that research on children's suggestibility met the standards set in *Daubert*.

Regarding expert testimony in court, professionals generally are not permitted to testify as to the credibility of a particular witness (e.g., *State v. Milbradt*, 1988). For instance, opinions that a victim's testimony is accurate and that the person has been victimized have been criticized as opinions of credibility. Many psychological commentators argue that psychologists should not testify in court as to the "ultimate legal issue" (Melton & Limber, 1989, see Myers et al., 1989). Experts who testify about eyewitness memory should be mindful of such restrictions and controversies.

CONCLUSION

Research on the psychology of testimony began about 100 years ago, and research on human memory began even earlier. Looking at the many years of accumulated research, we know that eyewitness testimony can be far from perfect, and we have identified many of the factors that affect eyewitness reports. We still have more to learn about the accuracies and inaccuracies of human memory. In particular, more realistic and ecologically valid yet scientifically sound research is needed. Nevertheless, professionals who study eyewitness memory can provide valuable information to the courts.

REFERENCES

Ackil, J. K., & Zaragoza, M. S. (1995). Developmental differences in eyewitness suggestibility and memory for source. *Journal of Experimental Child Psychology, 60,* 57–83.

Alba, J. W., & Hasher, L. (1983). Is memory schematic? *Psychological Bulletin, 93,* 203–231.

Alpert, J. L., Brown, L. S., Ceci, S. J., Courtois, C. A., Loftus, E. F., & Ornstein, P. A. (1996). *Final conclusions of the APA working group on investigation of memories of childhood abuse* (pp. 1–14). Washington DC: American Psychological Association.

Alpert, J. L., Brown, L. S., & Courtois, C. A. (1996a). Symptomatic clients and memories of childhood abuse: What the trauma and child sexual abuse literature tells us. *American psychological association working group on investigation of memories of childhood abuse final report* (pp. 15–105). Washington DC: American Psychological Association.

Alpert, J. L., Brown, L. S., & Courtois, C. A. (1996b). Response to "Adult recollections of childhood abuse: Cognitive and development perspectives." *American psychological association working group on investigation of memories of childhood abuse final report* (pp. 198–220). Washington DC: American Psychological Association.

Anderson, R. C., & Pichert, J. W. (1978). Recall of previously unrecallable information following a shift in perspective. *Journal of Verbal Learning and Verbal Behavior, 17,* 1–12.

Baddeley, A. D. (1979). Applied cognitive and cognitive applied psychology: The case of face recognition. In L. G. Nilsson (Ed.), *Perspectives on memory research.* Hillsdale, NJ: Erlbaum.

Bahrick, H. P., Bahrick, P. O., & Wittlinger, R. P. (1975). Fifty years of memory for names and faces: A cross-sectional approach. *Journal of Experimental Psychology: General, 104,* 54–75.

Baker-Ward, L., Gordon, B. N., Ornstein, P. A., Larus, D. M., & Clubb, P. A. (1993). Young children's long-term retention of a pediatric examination. *Child Development, 64,* 1519–1533.

Bartlett, F. C. (1932). *Remembering.* Cambridge, England: Cambridge University Press.

Belli, R. F. (1989). Influences of misleading postevent information: Misinformation interference and acceptance. *Journal of Experimental Psychology: General, 118,* 72–85.

Belli, R. F., Lindsay, D. S., Gales, M. S., & McCarthy, T. T. (1994). Memory impairment and source misattribution in postevent misinformation experiments with short retention intervals. *Memory and Cognition, 22,* 40–54.

Belli, R. F., Windschitl, P. D., McCarthy, T. T., & Winfrey, S. E. (1992). Detecting memory impairment with a modified test procedure: Manipulating retention interval with centrally presented event items. *Journal of Experimental Psychology: Learning, Memory, & Cognition, 18,* 356–367.

Berkerian, D. A., & Bowers, J. M. (1983). Eyewitness testimony: Were we mislead? *Journal of Experimental Psychology: Learning, Memory, & Cognition, 9,* 139–145.

Berliner, L., & Williams, L. M. (1994). Memories of child sexual abuse: A response to Lindsay and Read. *Applied Cognitive Psychology, 8,* 379–388.

Betz, A. L., & Skowronski, J. J. (1997). Self-events and other events: Temporal dating and event memory. *Memory and Cognition, 25,* 701–714.

Bidrose, S., & Goodman, G. S. (in press). Testimony and evidence: A scientific case study of memory for child sexual abuse. *Applied Cognitive Psychology.*

Billig, M., & Milner, D. (1976). A spade is a spade in the eyes of the law. *Psychology Today, 2,* 13–15, 62.

Bloom, L. C., & Mudd, S. A. (1991). Depth of processing approach to face recognition: A test of two theories. *Journal of Experimental Psychology: Learning, Memory, & Cognition, 17,* 556–565.

Bohannon, J. N. (1988). Flashbulb memories for the space shuttle disaster: A tale of two theories. *Cognition, 29,* 179–196.

Bohannon, J. N. (1992). Arousal and memory: Quantity and consistency over the years. In E. Winograd & U. Neisser (Eds.), *Affect and accuracy in recall: The problem of "flashbulb" memories* (pp. 65–91). New York: Cambridge University Press.

Bohannon, J. N., & Symons, V. L. (1993). Flashbulb memories: Confidence, consistency, and quantity. In E. Winograd & U. Neisser (Eds.), *Affect and accuracy in recall: Studies of "flashbulb" memories* (pp. 65–91). New York: Cambridge University Press.

Bothwell, R. K., Brigham, J. C., & Malpass, R. S. (1989). Cross-racial identification. *Personality and Social Psychology Bulletin, 15,* 19–25.

Bothwell, R. K., Brigham, J. C., & Pigott, M. A. (1987). An exploratory study of personality differences in eyewitness memory. *Journal of Social Behavior and Personality, 2,* 335–343.

Bower, G. H., & Karlin, M. B. (1974). Depth of processing pictures of faces and recognition memory. *Journal of Experimental Psychology, 103,* 751–757.

Bowers, J. M., & Bekerian, D. A. (1984). When will postevent information distort eyewitness testimony? *Journal of Applied Psychology, 69,* 466–472.

Brainerd, C. J., & Ornstein, P. A. (1991). Children's memory for witnessed events: The developmental backdrop. In J. Doris (Ed.), *The suggestibility of children's recollections* (pp. 10–20). Washington, DC: American Psychological Association.

Brainerd, C. J., Reyna, V., Howe, M., & Kingma, J. (1991). The development of forgetting and reminiscence. *Monographs of Society for Research in Child Development, 55*(Serial No. 222).

Bregman, N. J., & McAllister, H. A. (1982). Eyewitness testimony: The role of commitment in increasing reliability. *Social Psychology Quarterly, 45,* 466–472.

Bremner, J. D., Krystal, J. H., Southwick, S. M., & Charney, D. S. (1995). Functional neuroanatomical correlates of the effects of stress on memory. *Journal of Traumatic Stress, 8,* 527–553.

Bremner, J. D., Randall, P., Scott, T. W., Capelli, S., et al. (1995). Deficits in short-term memory in adult survivors of childhood abuse. *Psychiatry Research, 59,* 97–107.

Bremner, J. D., Southwick, S. M., Johnson, D. R., Yehuda, R., & Charney, D. S. (1993). Childhood physical abuse and combat-related posttraumatic stress disorder in Vietnam veterans. *American Journal of Psychiatry, 150,* 235–239.

Briere, J., & Conte, J. (1993). Self-reported amnesia for abuse in adults molested as children. *Journal of Traumatic Stress, 6,* 21–31.

Brigham, J. C. (1990). Target person distinctiveness and attractiveness as moderator variables in the confidence-accuracy relationship in eyewitness identifications. *Basic & Applied Social Psychology, 11,* 101–115.

Brigham, J. C., & Barkowitz, P. (1978). Do "they all look alike"? The effect of race, sex, experience, and attitudes on the ability to recognize faces. *Journal of Applied Psychology, 8,* 306–318.

Brigham, J. C., & Cairns, D. L. (1988). The effect of mugshot inspections on eyewitness identification accuracy. *Journal of Applied Social Psychology, 18,* 1394–1410.

Brigham, J. C., Maass, A., Snyder, L. D., & Spaulding, K. (1982). Accuracy of eyewitness identifications in a field setting. *Journal of Personality and Social Psychology, 42,* 673–681.

Brigham, J. C., Ready, D. J., & Spier, S. A. (1990). Standards for evaluating the fairness of photograph lineups. *Basic & Applied Social Psychology, 11,* 149–163.

Brown, E., Deffenbacher, K., & Sturgill, W. (1977). Memory for faces and circumstances of encounter. *Journal of Applied Psychology, 62,* 311–318.

Brown, L. S. (1996). On the construction of truth and falsity: Whose memory, whose history. In K. Pezdek & W. P. Banks (Eds.), *The recovered memory/false memory debate* (pp. 341–353). San Diego, CA: Academic Press.

Brown, R., & Kulik, J. (1977). Falshbulb memories. *Cognition, 5,* 73–99.

Bruck, M., Ceci, S. J., Francouer, E., & Barr, R. (1995). "I hardly cried when I got my shot": Influencing children's reports about a visit to their pediatrician. *Child Development, 66,* 193–208.

Bruck, M., Ceci, S. J., Francouer, E., & Renick, A. (1995). Anatomically detailed dolls do not facilitate preschoolers' reports of pediatric examination involving genital touching. *Journal of Experimental Psychology: Applied, 1,* 95–109.

Bruck, M., Ceci, S. J., & Hembrooke, H. (1998). Reliability and credibility of young children's reports: From research to policy and practice. *American Psychologist, 53,* 136–151.

Bruner, J. S., & Postman, L. (1949). Perception, cognition, and behavior. *Journal of Personality, 18,* 14–31.

Buckhout, R. (1974). Eyewitness testimony. *Scientific American, 231,* 23–31.

Buckhout, R. (1984). Double mistaken identification in Dallas: Texas v. Lenell Geter and Anthony Williams. *Social Action and the Law, 10,* 3–11.

Buckhout, R., Alper, A., Chern, S., Silverberg, G., & Slomovits, M. (1974). Determinants of eyewitness performance on a lineup. *Bulletin of the Psychonomic Society, 4,* 191–192.

Bull, R. (1995). Good practice for video recorded interviews with child witnesses for use in criminal proceedings. In G. Davies, S. Lloyd-Bostock, M. McMurran, & C. Wilson (Eds.), *Psychology, law, and criminal justice: International developments in research and practice* (pp. 100–117). Berlin, Germany: Walter de Gruyter.

Butters, M. J. (1970). Differential recall of paired associates as a function of arousal and concreteness-imagery levels. *Journal of Experimental Psychology, 84,* 252–256.

Cady, H. M. (1924). On the psychology of testimony. *American Journal of Psychology, 35,* 110–112.

Cahill, L., & McGaugh, J. L. (1995). A novel demonstration of enhanced memory associated with emotional arousal. *Consciousness & Cognition: An International Journal, 4,* 410–421.

Carter, C. A., Bottoms, B. L., & Levine, M. (1996). Linguistic and socioemotional influences on the accuracy of children's reports. *Law and Human Behavior, 20,* 335–358.

Ceci, S. J., & Bruck, M. (1993). Suggestibility of the child witness: A historical review and synthesis. *Psychological Bulletin, 113,* 403–439.

Ceci, S. J., Loftus, E. F., Leichtman, M. D., & Bruck, M. (1994). The possible role of source misattributions in the creation of false beliefs among preschoolers. *International Journal of Clinical and Experimental Hypnosis, 42,* 304–320.

Ceci, S. J., Ross, D. F., & Toglia, M. P. (1987). Suggestibility of children's memory: Psycholegal implications. *Journal of Experimental Psychology: General, 116,* 38–49.

Chance, J. E., & Goldstein, A. G. (1996). The other-race effect and eyewitness identification. In S. L. Sporer, R. S. Malpass, & G. Koehnken (Eds.), *Psychological issues in eyewitness identification* (pp. 153–176). Mahwah, NJ: Erlbaum.

Chance, J. E., & Goldstein, A. G. (1984). Face-recognition memory: Implications for children's eyewitness testimony. *Journal of Social Issues, 40,* 69–86.

Chance, J. E., Goldstein, A. G., & Anderson, B. (1986). Recognition memory for infant faces: An analog of the other-race effect. *Bulletin of the Psychonomic Society, 24,* 257–260.

Chance, J. E., Goldstein, A. G., & McBride, L. (1975). Differential experience and recognition memory for faces. *Journal of Social Psychology, 97,* 243–253.

Chen, Y. E., & Geiselman, R. E. (1993). Effects of ethnic stereotyping and ethnically-related cognitive biases on eyewitness recollections of height. *American Journal of Forensic Psychology, 11,* 13–19.

Christiaansen, R. E., & Ochalek, K. (1983). Editing misleading information from memory: Evidence for the coexistence of original and postevent information. *Memory and Cognition, 11,* 467–475.

Christiaansen, R. E., Sweeney, J. D., & Ochalek, K. (1983). Influencing eyewitness descriptions. *Law and Human Behavior, 7,* 59–65.

Christianson, S. A. (1989). Flashbulb memories: Special, but no so special. *Memory and Cognition, 17,* 435–443.

Christianson, S. A. (1992). Emotional stress and eyewitness memory: A critical review. *Psychological Bulletin, 112,* 284–309.

Christianson, S. A., & Hubinette, B. (1993). Hands up: A study of witnesses' emotional reactions and memories associated with bank robberies. *Applied Cognitive Psychology, 7,* 365–379.

Christianson, S. A., & Loftus, E. F. (1991). Remembering emotional events: The fate of detailed information. *Cognition and Emotion, 5,* 81–108.

Chu, J. A., Frey, L. M., Ganzel, B. L., & Matthews, J. A. (1995). *The nature and validity of memories of childhood abuse.* Unpublished manuscript.

Cicchetti, D., & Toth, S. L. (1995). A developmental psychopathology perspective on child abuse and neglect. *Journal of the American Academy of Child and Adolescent Psychiatry, 34,* 541–565.

Clare, I. C. H., & Gudjonsson, G. H. (1993). Interrogative suggestibility, confabulation, and acquiescence in people with mild learning disabilities (mental handicap): Implications for reliability during police interrogations. *British Journal of Clinical Psychology, 32,* 295–301.

Clare, I. C. H., & Gudjonsson, G. H. (1995). The vulnerability of suspects with intellectual disabilities during police interviews: A review and experimental study of decision-making. *Mental Handicap Research, 8,* 110–128.

Clifford, B. R. (1983). Memory for voices: The feasibility and quality of earwitness evidence. In S. Lloyd-Bostock & B. R. Clifford (Eds.), *Evaluating witness evidence* (pp. 189–218). Chichester, England: Wiley.

Clifford, B. R., & Bull, R. (1978). *The psychology of person identification.* London: Routledge & Kegan Paul.

Clifford, B. R., & Richards, V. J. (1977). Comparison of recall by policemen and civilians under conditions of long and short durations of exposure. *Perceptual and Motor Skills, 45,* 503–512.

Clifford, B. R., & Scott, J. (1978). Individual and situational factors in eyewitness testimony. *Journal of Applied Psychology, 63,* 352–359.

Cohen, G., & Faulkner, D. (1989). Age differences in source forgetting: Effects on reality monitoring and on eyewitness testimony. *Psychology and Aging, 4,* 10–17.

Conte, J. R., Sorenson, E., Fogarty, L., & Rosa, J. (1991). Evaluating children's reports of sexual abuse: Results from a survey of professionals. *American Journal of Orthopsychiatry, 61*, 428–437.

Courtois, C. A. (1992). The memory retrieval process in incest survivor therapy. *Journal of Child Sexual Abuse, 1*, 15–31.

Courtois, M. R., & Mueller, J. H. (1981). Target and distractor typicality in facial recognition. *Journal of Applied Psychology, 66*, 639–645.

Coxon, P., & Valentine, T. (1997). The effects of the age of eyewitnesses on the accuracy and suggestibility of their testimony. *Applied Cognitive Psychology, 11*, 415–430.

Cutler, B. L., Berman, G. L., Penrod, S., & Fisher, R. P. (1994). Conceptual, practical, and empirical issues associated with eyewitness identification test media. In D. F. Ross, J. D. Read, & M. P. Toglia (Eds.), *Adult eyewitness testimony: Current trends and developments*. New York: Cambridge University Press.

Cutler, B. L., & Penrod, S. D. (1988). Improving the reliability of eyewitness identification: Lineup construction and presentation. *Journal of Applied Psychology, 71*, 281–290.

Cutler, B. L., & Penrod, S. D. (1989a). Forensically relevant moderators of the relation between eyewitness identification accuracy and confidence. *Journal of Applied Psychology, 74*, 650–652.

Cutler, B. L., & Penrod, S. D. (1989b). Moderators of the confidence-accuracy correlation in face recognition: The role of information processing and base-rates. *Applied Cognitive Psychology, 3*, 95–107.

Cutler, B. L., Penrod, S. D., & Dexter, H. R. (1990). Juror sensitivity to eyewitness identification evidence. *Law & Human Behavior, 14*, 185–191.

Cutler, B. L., Penrod, S. D., & Martens, T. K. (1987). Improving the reliability of eyewitness identification: Putting context into context. *Journal of Applied Psychology, 72*, 629–637.

Dalenberg, C. J. (1996). Accuracy, timing and circumstances of disclosure in therapy of recovered and continuous memories of abuse. *Journal of Psychiatry & Law, 24*, 229–275.

Daubert v. Merrell Dow Pharmaceuticals, 509 U.S. 579 (1993).

Davies, G. M., & Milne, A. (1982). Recognizing faces in and out of context. *Current Psychological Research, 2*, 235–246.

Davies, G., Tarrant, A., & Flin, R. (1989). Close encounters of the witness kind: Children's memory for a simulated health inspection. *British Journal of Psychology, 80*, 415–429.

Davies, G., & Westcott, H. (1995). The child witness in the courtroom: Empowerment or protection? In M. S. Zaragoza, J. R. Graham, G. N. C. Hall, R. Hirschman, & Y. S. Ben-Porath (Eds.), *Memory and testimony in the child witness* (pp. 199–213). Thousand Oaks, CA: Sage.

Deffenbacher, K. A. (1980). Eyewitness accuracy and confidence: Can we infer anything about their relationship? *Law & Human Behavior, 4*, 243–260.

Deffenbacher, K. A. (1983). The influence of arousal on reliability of testimony. In S. Lloyd-Bostock & B. R. Clifford (Eds.), *Evaluating witness evidence* (pp. 235–254). Chichester, England: Wiley.

Deffenbacher, K. A. (1991). A maturing of research on the behaviour of eyewitnesses. *Applied Cognitive Psychology, 5*, 377–402.

Dent, H. R. (1977). Stress as a factor influencing person recognition in identification parades. *Bulletin of the British Psychological Society, 30*, 339–340.

Dent, H. R., & Stephenson, G. M. (1979). An experimental study of the effectiveness of different techniques of questioning child witnesses. *British Journal of Social & Clinical Psychology, 18*, 41–51.

deRivera, J. (1997). The construction of false memory syndrome: The experience of re-tractors. *Psychological Inquiry, 8,* 271–292.

Dezwirek-Sas, L. (1992). Empowering child witnesses for sexual abuse prosecution. In H. Dent & R. Flin (Eds.), *Children as witnesses* (pp. 181–199). Chichester, England: Wiley.

Dobson, M., & Markham, R. (1992). Individual differences in anxiety level and eyewit-ness memory. *Journal of General Psychology, 119,* 343–350.

Dodd, D. H., & Bradshaw, J. M. (1980). Leading questions and memory: Pragmatic con-straints. *Journal of Verbal Learning and Verbal Behavior, 19,* 695–704.

Doob, A. N., & Kirshenbaum, H. (1973). Bias in police lineups—Partial remembering. *Journal of Police Science and Administration, 1,* 287–293.

Duncan, E. M., Whitney, P., & Kunen, S. (1982). Integration of visual and verbal infor-mation in children's memories. *Child Development, 53,* 1215–1233.

Easterbrook, J. A. (1959). The effect of emotion on the utilization and organization of behavior. *Psychology Review, 66,* 183–201.

Ebbinghaus, H. E. (1964). *Memory: A contribution to experimental psychology.* New York: Dover. (Original work published 1885)

Egan, D., Pittner, M., & Goldstein, A. G. (1977). Eyewitness identification: Photographs vs. live models. *Law and Human Behavior, 1,* 199–206.

Egeth, H. E., & McCloskey, M. (1984). The jury is still out: A reply to Deffenbacher. *American Psychologist, 39,* 1068–1069.

Eisen, M. L., Goodman, G. S., Qin, J., & Davis, S. (1998). Memory and suggestibility in maltreated children: New research relevant to evaluating allegations of abuse. In S. Lynn & K. McConky (Eds.), *Truth in memory* (pp. 163–189). New York: Guil-ford Press.

Elliott, E. S., Wills, E. J., & Goldstein, A. G. (1973). The effects of discrimination train-ing on the recognition of white and oriental faces. *Bulletin of the Psychonomic Society, 2,* 71–73.

Ellis, H. D. (1981). Practical aspects of face memory. In G. L. Wells & E. F. Loftus (Eds.), *Eyewitness testimony* (pp. 12–37). Cambridge, England: Cambridge Univer-sity Press.

Ellis, H. D., Davies, G. M., & Shepherd, J. W. (1977). Experimental studies of face iden-tification. *National Journal of Criminal Defense, 3,* 219–234.

Everson, M. D., & Boat, B. W. (1994). Putting the anatomical doll controversy in per-spective: An examination of the major uses and criticisms of the dolls in child sex-ual abuse evaluations. *Child Abuse & Neglect, 18,* 113–129.

Feinman, S., & Entwisle, D. R. (1976). Children's ability to recognize other children's faces. *Child Development, 47,* 506–510.

Fisher, R. P., & Geiselman, R. E. (1992). *Memory-enhancing techniques for investigative in-terviewing: The cognitive interview.* Springfield, IL: Thomas.

Fivush, R. (1984). Learning about school: The development of kindergatners' school scripts. *Child development, 55,* 1697–1709.

Fivush, R., Hudson, J., & Nelson, K. (1984). Children's long-term memory for a novel event: An exploratory study. *Merrill-Palmer Quarterly, 30,* 303–316.

Flin, R., Boon, J., Knox, A., & Bull, R. (1992). The effect of a five-month delay on chil-dren's and adults' eyewitness memory. *British Journal of Psychology, 83,* 323–336.

Freud, S. (1957). Repression. In J. Strachey (Ed. & Trans.), *The standard edition of the complete psychological works of Sigmund Freud* (Vol. 14, pp. 146–158). London: Hogarth Press. (Original work published 1915)

Friedman, A. (1979). Framing pictures: The role of default knowledge in automized encoding and memory for gist. *Journal of Experimental Psychology: General, 108,* 315–355.

Geiselman, R. E., & Fisher, R. P. (1989). The cognitive interview technique for victims and witnesses of crime. In D. C. Raskin (Ed.), *Psychological methods in criminal investigation and evidence* (pp. 191–215). New York: Springer.

Geiselman, R. E., Saywitz, K. J., & Bornstein, G. K. (1993). Effects of cognitive questioning techniques on children's recall performance. In G. S. Goodman & B. L. Bottoms (Eds.), *Child victims, child witnesses: Understanding and improving testimony* (pp. 71–93). New York: Guilford Press.

Gilliland, A., & Burke, R. (1926). A measure of sociability. *Journal of Applied Psychology, 10,* 315–326.

Goetze, H. (1980). *The effect of age and method of interview on the accuracy and completeness of eyewitness accounts.* Unpublished dissertation, Hofstra University, New York.

Goldstein, A. G., & Chance, J. E. (1964). Recognition of children's faces. *Child Development, 35,* 129–136.

Goldstein, A. G., & Chance, J. E. (1980). Memory for faces and schema theory. *Journal of Psychology, 105,* 47–59.

Gonzalez, R., Ellsworth, P. C., & Pembroke, M. (1993). Response biases in lineups and showups. *Journal of Personality and Social Psychology, 64,* 525–537.

Goodman, G. S. (Ed.). (1984). The child witness: Conclusions and future directions for research and legal practice. *Journal of Social Issues, 40,* 157–175.

Goodman, G. S., Bottoms, B. L., Schwartz-Kenney, B. M., & Rudy, L. (1991). Children's testimony about a stressful event: Improving children's reports. *Journal of Narrative & Life History,* 69–99.

Goodman, G. S., Emery, R. E., & Haugaard, J. J. (1997). Developmental psychology and law: Divorce, child maltreatment, foster care, and adoption. In I. Sigel & A. Renninger (Eds.), *Handbook of child psychology: Vol. 4. Child psychology in practice* (5th ed., pp. 775–874). New York: Wiley.

Goodman, G. S., Hirschman, J. E., Hepps, D., & Rudy, L. (1991). Children's memory for stressful events. *Merrill-Palmer Quarterly, 37,* 109–157.

Goodman, G. S., Myers, J. E. B., & Redlich, A. D. (1997). *Children's evidence: Effects of hearsay on jurors' decisions in child sexual abuse cases.* Paper presented at the International Conference on Applied Psychology, San Francisco.

Goodman, G. S., Pyle-Taub, E., Jones, D. P. H., England, P., Port, L. P., Rudy, L., & Prado, L. (1992). Emotional effects of criminal court testimony on child sexual assault victims. *Monographs of the Society for Research in Child Development, 57*(Serial No. 229).

Goodman, G. S., Quas, J. A., Batterman-Faunce, J. M., Riddlesberger, M. M., & Kuhn, J. (1994). Predictors of accurate and inaccurate memories of traumatic events experienced in childhood. *Consciousness and Cognition, 3,* 269–294.

Goodman, G. S., Quas, J. A., Batterman-Faunce, J. M., Riddlesberger, M., & Kuhn, J. (1997). Children's reactions to and memory for a stressful experience: Influences of age, knowledge, anatomical dolls, and parental attachment. *Applied Developmental Sciences, 1,* 54–75.

Goodman, G. S., & Reed, (1986). Age differences in eyewitness testimony. *Law and Human Behavior, 10,* 317–332.

Goodman, G. S., Tobey, A. E., Batterman-Faunce, J. M., Orcutt, H., Thomas, S., & Shapiro, C. (1998). Face-to-face confrontation: Effects of closed-circuit technology on children's eyewitness testimony and jurors' decisions. *Law and Human Behavior, 22,* 165–203.

Gorenstein, G. W., & Ellsworth, P. D. (1980). Effect of choosing an incorrect photograph on a later identification by an eyewitness. *Journal of Applied Psychology, 665,* 616–622.

Graesser, A. (1981). *Prose comprehension beyond the world.* New York: Springer.

Greene, E., Flynne, M. B., & Loftus, E. F. (1982). Inducing resistance to misleading information. *Journal of Verbal Learning and Verbal Behavior, 21*, 207–219.

Gross, J., & Hayne, H. (1996). Eyewitness identification by 5- to 6-year-old children. *Law and Human Behavior, 20*, 359–373.

Gudjonsson, G. H. (1984). A new scale of interrogative suggestibility. *Personality and Individual Differences, 5*, 303–314.

Gudjonsson, G. H. (1987). The relationship between memory and suggestibility. *Social Behavior, 2*, 29–33.

Gudjonsson, G. H. (1988). The relationship of intelligence and memory to interrogative suggestibility: The importance of range effects. *British Journal of Clinical Psychology, 27*, 185–187.

Gudjonsson, G. H. (1990). The relationship of intellectual skills to suggestibility, compliance and acquiescence. *Personality and Individual Differences, 11*, 227–231.

Gudjonsson, G. H. (1991). The effects of intelligence and memory on group differences in suggestibility and compliance. *Personality and Individual Differences, 12*, 503–505.

Harvey, M. R., & Herman, J. L. (1994). Amnesia, partial amnesia, and delayed recall among adult survivors of childhood trauma. *Consciousness and Cognition, 3*, 295–306.

Hasher, L., Attig, M. S., & Alba, J. W. (1981). I knew it all along: Or did I? *Journal of Verbal Learning and Verbal Behavior, 20*, 86–96.

Hastorf, A. H., & Cantril, H. (1954). They saw a game: A case study. *Journal of Abnormal and Social Psychology, 49*, 129–234.

Hembrooke, H., & Ceci, S. J. (1995). Traumatic memories: Do we need to invoke special mechanisms? *Consciousness & Cognition: An International Journal, 4*, 75–82.

Henry, L. A., & Norman, T. (1996). The relationships between memory performance, use of simple memory strategies and metamemory in young children. *International Journal of Behavioral Development, 19*, 177–199.

Herman, J. L. (1992). *Trauma and recovery.* New York: Basic Books.

Herman, J. L., & Schatzow, E. (1987). Recovery and verification of memories of childhood sexual trauma. *Psychoanalytic Psychology, 4*, 1–14.

Hoffman, C., & Kagan, S. (1977). Field dependence and facial recognition. *Perceptual and Motor Skills, 44*, 119–124.

Holst, V. F., & Pezdek, K. (1992). Scripts for typical crimes and their effects on memory for eyewitness testimony. *Applied Cognitive Psychology, 6*, 573–587.

Horn, M. (1993, November 29). Memories, lost and found. *U.S. News and World Report*, 52–63.

Hosch, H. (1994). Individual differences in personality and eyewitness identification. In F. Ross, J. D. Read, & M. P. Toglia (Eds.), *Adult eyewitness testimony: Current trends and developments* (pp. 328–347). New York: Cambridge University Press.

Hosch, H. M., Bothwell, R. K., Sporer, S. L., & Saucedo, C. (1990). *The accuracy of witness' choice: Facial recognition ability, reaction time, and confidence.* Southwestern Psychological Association, Houston, TX.

Hosch, H. M., Bothwell, R. K., Sporer, S. L., & Saucedo, C. (1991). *Assessing eyewitness identification accuracy.* Southwestern Psychological Association, New Orleans, LA.

Hosch, H. M., & Cooper, D. S. (1981). *Victimization and self-monitoring as determinants of eyewitness accuracy.* Unpublished manuscript, University of Texas at El Paso.

Houts, M. (1963). *From evidence to guilt.* Springfield, IL: Thomas.

Howe, M. L., Courage, M. L., & Peterson, C. (1995). Intrusions in preschoolers' recall traumatic childhood events. *Psychonomic Bulletin and Review, 2*, 130–134.

Howells, T. H. (1938). A study of ability to recognize faces. *Journal of Abnormal and Social Psychology, 33*, 124–127.

Hunt, T. (1928). The measurement of social intelligence. *Journal of Applied Psychology, 12,* 317–333.

Hutcheson, G. D., Baxter, J. S., Telfer, K., & Warden, D. (1995). Child witness statement quality: Question type and errors of omission. *Law & Human Behavior, 19,* 631–648.

Hyman, I. E., & Billings, F. J. (1995). *Individual differences and the creation of false childhood memories.* Manuscript in preparation.

Hyman, I. E., Jr., Husband, T. H., & Billings, F. J. (1995). False memories of childhood experiences. *Applied Cognitive Psychology, 9,* 181–197.

Hyman, I. E., & Pentland, J. (1996). The role of mental imagery in the creation of false childhood memories. *Journal of Memory and Language, 35,* 101–117.

Jacoby, L. L., Kelley, C. M., Brown, J., & Jasechko, J. (1989). Becoming famous overnight: Limits on the ability to avoid unconscious influences of the past. *Journal of Personality and Social Psychology, 56,* 326–338.

Johnson, C., & Scott, B. (1976). *Eyewitness testimony and suspect identifications as a function of arousal, sex of witness, and scheduling of interrogation.* Paper presented at the meeting of the American Psychological Association, Washington, DC.

Johnson, M. K. (1988). Reality monitoring: An experimental phenomenological approach. *Journal of Experimental Psychology: General, 117,* 390–394.

Johnson, M. K., Foley, M. A., Suengas, A. G., & Raye, C. L. (1988). Phenomenal characteristics of memories for perceived and imagined autobiographical events. *Journal of Experimental Psychology: General, 117,* 371–376.

Johnson, M. K., Hastroudi, S., & Lindsay, D. S. (1993). Source monitoring. *Psychological Bulletin, 114,* 3–28.

Johnson, M. K., & Raye, C. L. (1981). Reality monitoring. *Psychological Review, 88,* 67–85.

Kaess, W. A., & Witryol, S. L. (1955). Memory for names and faces: A characteristic of social intelligence. *Journal of Applied Psychology, 39,* 457–462.

King, M. A. (1984). *An investigation of the eyewitness abilities of children.* Unpublished doctoral dissertation, University of British Columbia.

Klatzky, R. L. (1980). *Human memory* (2nd ed.). San Francisco: Freeman.

Kleinsmith, L. J., & Kaplan, S. (1963). Paired associated learning as a function of arousal and interpolated interval. *Journal of Experimental Psychology, 65,* 190–193.

Koocher, G. P., Goodman, G. S., White, C. S., Friedrich, W. N., Sivan, A. B., & Reynolds, C. R. (1995). Psychological science and the use of anatomically detailed dolls in child sexual-abuse assessments. *Psychological Bulletin, 118,* 199–222.

Koss, M. P., Tromp, S., & Tharan, M. (1995). Traumatic memories: Empirical foundation, forensic, and clinical implications. *Clinical Psychology: Science & Practice, 2,* 111–132.

Lamb, M., Hershkowitz, I., Sternberg, K. J., Esplin, P. W., Hovav, M., Manor, T., & Yudilevitch, L. (1996). Effects of investigative style on Israeli children's responses. *International Journal of Behavioral Development, 19,* 627–637.

Laughery, K. R., Alexander, J. F., & Lane, A. B. (1971). Recognition of human faces: Effects of target exposure time, target position, pose position, and type of photograph. *Journal of Applied Psychology, 51,* 477–483.

Laughery, K. R., Jensen, D. G., & Wogalter, M. S. (1988). Response bias with prototypic faces. In M. M. Gruneberg, R. Sykes, & P. Morris (Eds.), *Practical aspects of memory: Current research and issues* (pp. 157–162). Chichester, England: Wiley.

Lavrakas, P., Buri, J., & Mayznere, M. (1976). A perspective on the recognition of other-race faces. *Perception and Psychophysics, 20,* 475–481.

Lee, J., Goodman, G. S., & Barry, S. (1998). *Cross-racial identification: A developmental study.* Manuscript in preparation.

Leichtman, M. D., & Ceci, S. J. (1995). The effects of stereotypes and suggestions on preschoolers' reports. *Developmental Psychology, 31,* 568–578.

Leippe, M. R., Manion, A. P., & Romanczyk, A. (1992). Eyewitness persuasion: How and how well do fact finders judge the accuracy of adults' and children's memory reports? *Journal of Personality & Social Psychology, 63,* 181–197.

Leippe, M. R., Romanczyk, A., & Manion, A. P. (1991). Eyewitness memory for a touching experience: Accuracy differences between child and adult witnesses. *Journal of Applied Psychology, 76,* 367–379.

Lief, H. I., & Fetkewicz, J. (1995). Retractors of false memories: The evolution of pseudomemories. *Journal of Psychiatry & Law, XXIII,* 411–435.

Lindsay, D. S. (1990). Misleading suggestions can impair eyewitnesses' ability to remember event details. *Journal of Experimental Psychology: Learning, Memory, and Cognition, 16,* 1077–1083.

Lindsay, D. S. (1994). Memory source monitoring and eyewitness testimony. In D. F. Ross, J. D. Read, & M. P. Toglia (Eds.), *Adult eyewitness testimony: Current trends and developments* (pp. 27–55). Cambridge, England: Cambridge University Press.

Lindsay, D. S., & Johnson, M. K. (1989). The eyewitness suggestibility effect and memory for source. *Memory and Cognition, 17,* 349–358.

Lindsay, D. S., Johnson, M. K., & Kwon, P. (1991). Developmental changes in memory source monitoring. *Journal of Experimental Child Psychology, 52,* 297–318.

Lindsay, D. S., & Read, J. D. (1994). Psychotherapy and memories of childhood sexual abuse: A cognitive perspective. *Applied Cognitive Psychology, 8,* 281–338.

Lindsay, R. C. L. (1985). Issues and policy in eyewitness identification: Psychological perspectives. *Criminal Reports, 47,* 252–269.

Lindsay, R. C. L., Lea, J. A., & Fulford, J. A. (1991). Sequential lineup presentation: Technique matters. *Journal of Applied Psychology, 76,* 741–745.

Lindsay, R. C. L., & Wells, G. L. (1983). What do we really know about cross-race eyewitness identification? In S. Lloyd-Bostock & B. R. Clifford (Eds.), *Evaluating witness evidence* (pp. 219–233). Chichester, England: Wiley.

Lindsay, R. C. L., & Wells, G. L. (1985). Improving eyewitness identifications from lineups: Simultaneous versus sequential lineup presentation. *Journal of Applied Psychology, 70,* 556–564.

Linton, M. (1982). Transformations of memory in everyday life. In U. Neisser (Ed.), *Memory observed* (pp. 77–91). San Francisco: Freeman.

Lipton, J. P. (1977). On the psychology of eyewitness testimony. *Journal of Applied Psychology, 62,* 90–95.

List, J. A. (1986). Age and schematic differences in the reliability of eyewitness testimony. *Developmental Psychology, 22,* 50–57.

Loftus, E. F. (1975). Leading questions and the eyewitness report. *Cognitive Psychology, 7,* 560–572.

Loftus, E. F. (1976). Unconscious transference in eyewitness identification. *Law and Psychology Review, 2,* 93–98.

Loftus, E. F. (1977). Shifting human color memory. *Memory and Cognition, 5,* 696–699.

Loftus, E. F. (1979a). *Eyewitness testimony.* Cambridge, MA: Harvard University Press.

Loftus, E. F. (1979b). Reactions to blatantly contradictory information. *Memory and Cognition, 7,* 368–374.

Loftus, E. F. (1980). Impact of expert psychological testimony on the unreliability of eyewitness identification. *Journal of Applied Psychology, 65,* 9–15.

Loftus, E. F. (1993). The reality of repressed memories. *American Psychologist, 48,* 518–537.

Loftus, E. F. (1994). The repressed memory controversy. *American Psychologist, 49,* 443–445.

Loftus, E. F., & Burns, T. E. (1982). Mental shock can produce retrograde amnesia. *Memory and Cognition, 10,* 318–323.

Loftus, E. F., & Doyle, J. M. (1987). *Eyewitness testimony: Civil and criminal.* New York: Kluwer Law Book.

Loftus, E. F., & Greene, E. (1980). Warning: Even memory for faces may be contagious. *Law and Human Behavior, 4,* 323–334.

Loftus, E. F., Greene, E. L., & Doyle, J. M. (1989). The psychology of eyewitness testimony. In D. C. Raskin (Ed.), *Psychological methods in criminal investigation and evidence* (pp. 3–45). New York: Springer.

Loftus, E. F., & Ketcham, K. E. (1983). The maleability of eyewitness accounts. In S. Lloyd-Bostock & B. R. Clifford (Eds.), *Evaluating witness evidence* (pp. 159–171). Chichester, England: Wiley.

Loftus, E. F., Levidow, B., & Duensing, S. (1992). Who remembers best? Individual differences in memory for events that occurred in a science museum. *Applied Cognitive Psychology, 6,* 93–107.

Loftus, E. F., Loftus, G. R., & Messo, J. (1987). Some facts about "weapon focus." *Law & Human Behavior, 11,* 55–62.

Loftus, E. F., & Marburger, W. (1983). Since the eruption of Mt. St. Helens, has anyone beaten you up? Improving the accuracy of retrospective reports with landmark events. *Memory and Cognition, 11,* 114–120.

Loftus, E. F., & Palmer. J. C. (1974). Reconstruction of automobile destruction: An example of the interaction between language and memory. *Journal of Verbal Learning and Verbal Behavior, 13,* 585–589.

Loftus, E. F., & Pickrell, J. E. (1995). The formation of false memories. *Psychiatric Annals, 25,* 720–725.

Loftus, E. F., Polonsky, S., & Fullilove, M. T. (1994). Memories of childhood sexual abuse: Remembering and repressing. *Psychology of Women Quarterly, 18,* 67–84.

Loftus, E. F., & Zanni, G. (1975). Eyewitness testimony: The influence of the wording of a question. *Bulletin of the Psychnomonic Society, 5,* 86–88.

Loftus, G. R., & Loftus, E. F. (1976). *Human memory: The processing of information.* Hillsdale, NJ: Erlbaum.

Loftus, G. R., & Mackworth, N. H. (1978). Cognitive determinants of fixation location during picture viewing. *Journal of Experimental Psychology: Human Perception and Performance, 4,* 565–572.

Luce, T. S. (1974). *The role of experience in inter-racial recognition.* Paper presented at the annual meeting of the American Psychological Association, New Orleans.

Lyon, T. (1995). False allegations and false denials in child sexual abuse. *Psychology, Public Policy, and Law, 1,* 429–437.

Maass, A., & Brigham, J. C. (1982). Eyewitness identifications: The role of attention and encoding specificity. *Personality & Social Psychology Bulletin, 8,* 54–59.

Maass, A., & Kohnken, G. (1989). Eyewitness identification: Simulating the "weapon effect." *Law & Human Behavior, 13,* 397–408.

Maki, R. H. (1990). Memory for script actions: Effects of relevance and detail expectancy. *Memory and Cognition, 18,* 5–14.

Malpass, R. S. (1996). Enhancing eyewitness memory. In S. L. Sporer, R. S. Malpass, & G. Koehnken (Eds.), *Psychological issues in eyewitness identification* (pp. 177–203). Mahwah, NJ: Erlbaum.

Malpass, R. S., & Devine, P. G. (1981a). Eyewitness identification: Lineup instructions and the absence of the offender. *Journal of Applied Psychology, 66,* 482–489.

Malpass, R. S., & Devine, P. G. (1981b). Guided memory in eyewitness identification. *Journal of Applied Psychology, 66,* 343–350.

Malpass, R. S., & Devine, P. G. (1981c). Realism and eyewitness identification research. *Law and Human Behavior, 4,* 347–358.

Malpass, R. S., & Devine, P. G. (1983). Measuring the fairness of eyewitness identification lineups. In S. M. A. Lloyd-Bostock & B. R. Clifford (Eds.), *Evaluating witness evidence* (pp. 81–102). Chichester, England: Wiley.

Malpass, R. S., & Kravitz, J. (1969). Recognition for faces of own and other race. *Journal of Personality and Social Psychology, 13,* 330–334.

Malpass, R. S., Lavigueur, H., & Weldon, D. E. (1973). Verbal and visual training in face recognition. *Perception and Psychophysics, 14,* 285–292.

Marin, B. V., Holmes, D. L., Guth, M., & Kovac, P. (1979). The potential of children as eyewitnesses: A comparison of children and adults on eyewitness tasks. *Law and Human Behavior, 3,* 295–305.

Marquis, K. H., Marshall, J., & Oskamp, S. (1972). Testimony validity as a function of question form, atmosphere, and item difficulty. *Journal of Applied Social Psychology, 2,* 167–186.

Marshall, G. R. (1966). The organization of verbal material in free recall: The effects of patterns of associative overlap on clustering. *Dissertation Abstracts, 26,* 6171.

Martinez-Taboas, A. (1996). Repressed memories: Some clinical data contributing toward its elucidation. *American Journal of Psychotherapy, 50,* 217–230.

Mason, M. A. (1991). A judicial dilemma: Expert witness testimony in child sexual abuse cases. *Journal of Psychiatry and the Law, 19,* 185–219.

McCauley, M. R., & Fisher, R. P. (1995). Enhancing children's eyewitness testimony with the Cognitive Interview. In G. Davies, S. Lloyd-Bostock, M. McMurran, & C. Wilson (Eds.), *Psychology, law, and criminal justice: International developments in research and practice* (pp. 127–134). Berlin, Germany: De Gruyter.

McCloskey, M., & Egeth, H. E. (1983). Eyewitness identification: What can a psychologist tell a jury? *American Psychologist, 38,* 550–563.

McCloskey, M., Wible, C. G., & Cohen, N. J. (1988). Is there a special flashbulb-memory mechanism? *Journal of Experimental Psychology: General, 117,* 171–181.

McCloskey, M., & Zaragoza, M. (1985). Misleading postevent information and memory for events: Arguments and evidence against memory impairment hypotheses. *Journal of Experimental Psychology: General, 114,* 1–16.

McGaugh, J. L. (1995). Emotional activation, neuromodulatory systems, and memory. In D. L. Schacter (Ed.), *Memory distortions: How minds, brains, and societies reconstruct the past* (pp. 255–273). Cambridge, MA: Harvard University Press.

McGough, L. S. (1997). Achieving real reform: The case for American interviewing protocols. In M. S. Steward, D. S. Steward, L. Farquhar, J. E. B. Myers, M. Reinhart, J. Walker, N. Joye, J. Driskill, & J. Morgan (Eds.), *Interviewing young children about body touch and handling* (pp. 188–203). *Monographs of the Society for Research in Child Development, 61*(Serial No. 248).

McKelvie, S. J. (1985). Effect of depth of processing on recognition memory for normal and inverted photographs of faces. *Perceptual and Motor Skills, 60,* 503–508.

McKelvie, S. J. (1988). The role of spectacles in facial memory: A replication and extension. *Perceptual and Motor Skills, 66,* 651–658.

McSpadden, M. D., Schooler, J. W., & Loftus, E. F. (1988). Here today, gone tomorrow: The appearance and disappearance of context effects. In G. M. Davies & D. M. Thomson (Eds.), *Memory in context: Context in memory* (pp. 215–229). Chichester, England: Wiley.

Melton, G. B. (1994). Expert opinions: "Not for cosmic understanding." In B. D. Sales & G. R. VandenBos (Eds.), *Psychology in litigation and legislation. Master lectures in psychology* (pp. 59–99). Washington, DC: American Psychological Association.

Melton, G. B., Goodman, G. S., Kalichman, S. C., Levine, M., Saywitz, K. J., & Koocher, G. P. (1995). Empirical research on child maltreatment and the law. *Journal of Clinical Child Psychology, 24,* 47–77.

Melton, G. B., & Limber, S. (1989). Psychologists' involvement in cases of child maltreatment: Limits of role and expertise. *American Psychologist, 44,* 1225–1233.

Memon, A., Cronin, O., Eaves, R., & Bull, R. (1993). The cognitive interview and child witnesses. *Issues in Criminological and Legal Psychology, 20,* 3–9.

Merritt, K. A., Ornstein, P. A., & Spicker, B. (1994). Children's memory for a salient medical procedure: Implications for testimony. *Pediatrics, 94,* 17–23.

Messick, S., & Damarin, F. (1964). Cognitive styles and memory for faces. *Journal of Abnormal and Social Psychology, 69,* 313–318.

Milne, R., Bull, R., Koehnken, G., & Memon, A. (1995). The cognitive interview and suggestibility. *Issues in Criminological and Legal Psychology, 22,* 21–27.

Moston, S. (1992). Social support and children's eyewitness testimony. In H. Dent & R. Flin (Eds.), *Children as witnesses* (pp. 33–46). Chichester, England: Wiley.

Mueller, J. H., Bailis, K. L., & Goldstein, A. G. (1979). Anxiety and orienting tasks in picture recognition. *Bulletin of the Psychonomic Society, 13,* 145–148.

Murray, D. M., & Wells, G. L. (1982). Does knowledge that a crime was staged affect eyewitness performance? *Journal of Applied Social Psychology, 12,* 42–53.

Myers, J. E. B., Bays, J., Becker, J., Berliner, L., Corwin, D., & Saywitz, K. J. (1989). Expert testimony in child sexual abuse litigation. *Nebraska Law Review, 68,* 1–145.

Narby, D. J., Cutler, B. L., & Penrod, S. D. (1996). The effects of witness, target, and situational factors on eyewitness identifications. In S. L. Sporer, R. S. Malpass, & G. Koehnken (Eds.), *Psychological issues in eyewitness identification* (pp. 23–52). Mahwah, NJ: Erlbaum.

Nash, M. R. (1994). Memory distortion and sexual trauma: The problem of false negatives and false positives. *International Journal of Clinical and Experimental Hypnosis, 42,* 346–362.

Neisser, U., & Harsch, N. (1993). Phantom flashbulbs: False recollections of hearing the news about Challenger. In E. Winograd & U. Neisser (Eds.), *Affect and accuracy in recall: Studies of "flashbulb" memories* (pp. 9–31). New York: Cambridge University Press.

Nelson, E. L., & Simpson, P. (1994). First glimpse: An initial examination of subjects who have rejected their recovered visualizations as false memories. *Issues in Child Abuse Accusations, 6,* 123–133.

Nelson, K., & Gruendel, J. (1981). Generalized event representations: Basic building blocks of cognitive development. In A. Brown & M. Lamb (Eds.), *Advances in developmental psychology* (Vol. 1). Hillsdale, NJ: Erlbaum.

Nowicki, S., Winograd, E., & Millard, B. A. (1979). Memory for faces: A social learning analysis. *Journal of Research in Personality, 13,* 460–468.

Ofshe, R. J., & Watters, E. (1994). *Making monsters: False memories, psychotherapy, and sexual hysteria.* New York: Scribner.

Olio, K. A. (1994). Truth in memory. *American Psychologist, 49,* 442–443.

Ornstein, P. A., Ceci, S. J., & Loftus, E. F. (1996a). Adult recollections of childhood abuse: Cognitive and developmental perspectives. *American Psychological Association working group on investigation of memories of childhood abuse final report* (pp. 150–197). Washington, DC: American Psychological Association.

Ornstein, P. A., Ceci, S. J., & Loftus, E. F. (1996b). More on the repressed memory debate: A rejoinder to Alpert, Brown, and Courtois. *American Psychological Association working group on investigation of memories of childhood abuse final report* (pp. 221–240). Washington, DC: American Psychological Association.

Ornstein, P. A., Gordon, B. N., & Larus, D. M. (1992). Children's memory for a personally experienced event: Implications for testimony. *Applied Cognitive Psychology, 6,* 49–60.

O'Sullivan, J. T., & Howe, M. L. (1995). Metamemory and memory construction. *Consciousness and Cognition, 4,* 104–110.

Parker, J. F. (1995). Age differences in source monitoring of performed and imagined actions on immediate and delayed tests. *Journal of Experimental Child Psychology, 60,* 84–101.

Pasley, L. (1994). Misplaced trust: A first-person account of how my therapist created false memories. *Skeptic, 2,* 62–67.

Patterson, K. E., & Baddeley, A. D. (1977). When face recognition fails. *Journal of Experimental Psychology: Human Learning and Memory, 3,* 406–417.

Pear, T. H., & Wyatt, S. (1914). The Testimony of normal and mentally defective children. *British Journal of Psychology, 3,* 388–419.

Penrod, S. D., & Cutler, B. L. (1995). Witness confidence and witness accuracy: Assessing their forensic relation. *Psychology, Public Policy, & Law, 1,* 817–845.

Perfect, T. J., Watson, E. L., & Wagstaff, G. F. (1993). Accuracy of confidence ratings associated with general knowledge and eyewitness memory. *Journal of Applied Psychology, 78,* 144–147.

Perry, N. W., McAuliff, B. D., Tam, P., Claycomb, L., Dostal, C., & Flanagan, C. (1995). When lawyers question children: Is justice served? *Law and Human Behavior, 19,* 609–629.

Peters, D. P. (1991). The influence of stress and arousal on the child witness. In J. Doris (Ed.), *The suggestibility of children's recollections* (pp. 60–76). Washington, DC: American Psychological Association.

Peterson, C., & Bell, M. (1996). Children's memory for traumatic injury. *Child Development, 67,* 3045–3070.

Pezdek, K. (1994). The illusion of illusory memory. *Applied Cognitive Psychology, 8,* 339–350.

Pezdek, K., Finger, K., & Hodge, D. (1997). Planting false childhood memories: The role of event plausability. *Psychological Science, 8,* 437–441.

Pezdek, K., & Roe, C. (1997). The suggestibility of children's memory for being touched: Planting, erasing, and changing memories. *Law and Human Behavior, 21,* 95–106.

Pipe, M. E., Gee, S., & Wilson, C. (1993). Cues, props, and context: Do they facilitate children's event reports? In G. S. Goodman & B. L. Bottoms (Eds.), *Child victims, child witnesses: Understanding and improving testimony* (pp. 25–45). New York: Guilford Press.

Platz, S. J., & Hosch, H. M. (1988). Cross racial/ethnic eyewitness identification: A field study. *Journal of Applied Social Psychology, 18,* 972–984.

Poole, D. A., & Lindsay, D. S. (1995). Interviewing preschoolers: Effects of nonsuggestive techniques, parental coaching, and leading questions on reports of nonexperienced events. *Journal of Experimental Child Psychology, 60,* 129–154.

Pope, K. S. (1996). Memory, abuse, and science: Questioning claims about the false memory syndrome epidemic. *American Psychologist, 51,* 957–974.

Powers, P. A., Andriks, J. L., & Loftus, E. F. (1979). Eyewitness accounts of females and males. *Journal of Applied Psychology, 64,* 339–347.

Price, D. W., & Goodman, G. S. (1990). Visiting the wizard: Children's memory for a recurring event. *Child Development, 61,* 664–680.

Putnam, F. W. (1993). Dissociative disorders in children: Behavioral profiles and problems. *Child Abuse and Neglect, 17,* 39–45.

Qin, J. J., Eisen, M. L., Goodman, G. S., Davis, S. L., Hutchins, D., & Tyda, K. S. (1997, April). The impact of dissociation and trauma on maltreated children's memory of stressful events. In J. A. Quas & G. S. Goodman (Chairs), *Individual differences in children's memory and suggestibility: New research findings and directions.* Symposium presented at the Society for Research in Child Development Biennial Meeting, Washington, DC.

Qin, J. J., Goodman, G. S., Bottoms, B. L., & Shaver, P. R. (1998). Repressed memories of ritualistic and religion-related child abuse. In S. Lynn & K. M. McConkey (Eds.), *Truth in memory* (pp. 260–283). New York: Guilford Press.

Qin, J. J., Tyda, K., & Goodman, G. S. (1997). Retractors' experiences: What we can and cannot conclude. *Psychological Inquiry, 8,* 312–317.

Quas, J. A., Goodman, G. S., Bidrose, S., Pipe, M. E., Craw, S., & Ablin, D. S. (in press). Emotion and memory: Children's long-term remembering, forgetting, and suggestibility. *Journal of Experimental Child Psychology.*

Read, J. D., & Bruce, D. (1984). On the external validity of questioning effects in eyewitness testimony. *International Review of Applied Psychology, 33,* 33–49.

Read, J. D., & Craik, F. I. M. (1995). Earwitness identification: Some influences on voice recognition. *Journal of Experimental Psychology: Applied, 1,* 6–18.

Read, J. D., & Lindsay, D. S. (1994). Moving toward a middle ground on the "false memory debate": Reply to commentaries on Lindsay and Read. *Applied Cognitive Psychology, 8,* 407–435.

Read, J. D., Tollestrup, P., Hammersley, R., McFadzen, E., & Christensen, A. (1990). The unconscious transference effect: Are innocent bystanders ever misidentified? *Applied Cognitive Psychology, 4,* 3–31.

Robinson, M. D., & Johnson, J. T. (1996). Recall memory, recognition memory, and the eyewitness confidence-accuracy correlation. *Journal of Applied Psychology, 5,* 587–594.

Ross, D. F., Ceci, S. J., Dunning, D., & Toglia, M. P. (1994). Unconscious transference and mistaken identity: When a witness misidentifies a familiar but innocent person. *Journal of Applied Psychology, 79,* 918–930.

Ross, D. F., Hoffman, R., Warren, A., Burlingham, A., Marsil, D., & Lindsay, R. C. L. (1998, March). *Unconscious transference and mistaken identity in children: Are children more or less susceptible than adults to misidentifying a familiar but innocent person from a lineup?* Paper presented at the American Psychology-Law Society Meetings, Redondo Beach, CA.

Rudy, L., & Goodman, G. S. (1991). Effects of participation on children's reports: Implications for children's testimony. *Developmental Psychology, 27,* 527–538.

Sanders, G. S., & Warnick, D. (1979). Some conditions maximizing eyewitness accuracy: A learning/memory model. *Basic and Applied Social Psychology, 2,* 67–69.

Saywitz, K. J., Goodman, G. S., Nicholas, E., & Moan, S. F. (1991). Children's memories of a physical examination involving genital touch: Implications for reports of child sexual abuse. *Journal of Consulting and Clinical Psychology, 59,* 682–691.

Schill, T. (1966). Effects of approval motivation and varying conditions of verbal reinforcement on incidental memory for faces. *Psychological Reports, 19,* 55–60.

Scrivner, E., & Safer, M. A. (1988). Eyewitnesses show hypermnesia for details about a violent event. *Journal of Applied Psychology, 73,* 371–377.

Shapiro, P. N., & Penrod, S. D. (1986). Meta-analysis of facial identification studies. *Psychological Bulletin, 100,* 139–156.

Shaw, G. A., Bekerian, D. A., & McCubbin, J. A. (1995). Effects of videotaped violence on hypermnesia for imaginally encoded concrete and abstract words. *Perceptual & Motor Skills, 80,* 467–477.

Shepherd, J. W. (1981). Social factors in face recognition. In G. Davies, H. Ellis, & J. Shepherd (Eds.), *Perceiving and remembering faces* (pp. 55–79). London: Academic Press.

Shepherd, J. W. (1983). Identification after long delays. In S. Llyod-Bostock & B. R. Clifford (Eds.), *Evaluating witness evidence* (pp. 173–187). Chichester, England: Wiley.

Shyamalan, B., Lamb, S., & Sheldrick, R. (1995, August). *The effects of repeated questioning on preschoolers' reports.* Poster presented at the American Psychological Association Convention, New York.

Siegel, J. M., & Loftus, E. F. (1978). Impact of anxiety and life stress upon eyewitness testimony. *Bulletin of the Psychnomic Society, 12,* 479–480.

Smith, V. L., Kassin, S. M., & Ellsworth, P. C. (1989). Eyewitness accuracy and confidence: Within- versus between-subjects correlations. *Journal of Applied Psychology, 74,* 356–359.

Snee, T., & Lush, D. (1941). Interaction of the narrative and interrogatory methods of obtaining testimony. *Journal of Psychology, 11,* 229–230.

Sommer, R. (1959). The new look on the witness stand. *Canadian Psychologist, 8,* 94–99.

Spencer, J. R., & Flin, R. (1990). *The evidence of children: The law and the psychology.* Great Britain: Blackstone Press.

Spiegel, D. (1995). Hypnosis and suggestion. In D. L. Schacter, J. T. Coyle, G. D. Fishcback, M. Mesulam, & L. E. Sullivan (Eds.), *Memory distortion* (pp. 129–149). Cambridge, MA: Harvard University Press.

Sporer, S. L. (1993a). Clothing as a contestual cue in facial recognition. *German Journal of Psychology, 17,* 183–199.

Sporer, S. L. (1993b). Eyewitness identification accuracy, confidence, and decision times in simultaneous and sequential lineups. *Journal of Applied Psychology, 78,* 22–33.

Sporer, S. L., Malpass, R. S., & Koehnken, G. (1996). *Psychological issues in eyewitness identification.* Mahwah, NJ: Erlbaum.

State v. Milbradt, 756 P.2d 620 (Or. 1988).

Stein, N., & Boyce, T. (1995, April). The role of physiological reactivity in attending to, remembering, and responding to an emotional event. In G. Goodman & L. Baker-Ward (Chairs), *Children's memory for emotional and traumatic events.* Symposium conducted at the Society for Research in Child Development Meetings, Indianapolis.

Stephenson, G. M. (1984). Accuracy and confidence in testimony: A critical review and some fresh evidence. In D. J. Mueller, D. E. Blackman, & A. J. Chapman (Eds.), *Psychology and law* (pp. 229–248). Chichester, England: Wiley.

Sternberg, K. J., Lamb, M. E., Hershkowitz, I., Esplin, P. W., Redlich, A., & Sunshine, N. (1996). The relation between investigative utterance types and the informativeness of child witnesses. *Applied Developmental Psychology, 17,* 439–451.

Sutker, P. B., Winstead, D. K., Galina, Z. H., & Allain, A. N. (1991). Cognitive deficits and psychopathology among former prisoners of war and combat veterans of the Korean conflict. *American Journal of Psychiatry, 148,* 67–72.

Thompson, C. P., Herrmann, D. J., Bruce, D., & Read, J. D. (Eds.). (1998). *Autobiographical memory: Theoretical and applied perspectives.* Mahwah, NJ: Erlbaum.

Tickner, A., & Poulton, E. (1975). Watching for people and actions. *Ergonomics, 18,* 35–51.

Tobey, A. E., & Goodman, G. S. (1992). Children's eyewitness memory: Effects of participation and forensic context. *Child Abuse and Neglect, 16,* 779–796.

Tollestrup, P. A., Turtle, J. W., & Yuille, J. C. (1994). Actual victims and witnesses to robbery and fraud: An archival analysis. In D. F. Ross, J. D. Read, & M. P. Toglia (Eds.), *Adult eyewitness testimony: Current trends and developments* (pp. 144–160). London: Cambridge University Press.

Treadway, M., & McCloskey, M. (1989). Effects of racial stereotypes on eyewitness performance: Implications of the real and the rumoured Allport and Postman studies. *Applied Cognitive Psychology, 3,* 53–63.

Tromp, S., Koss, M. P., Figueredo, A. J., & Tharan, M. (1995). Are rape memories different? A comparison of rape, other unpleasant, and pleasant memories among employed women. *Journal of Traumatic Stress, 8,* 607–627.

Trouve, R. J., & Libkuman, T. M. (1992). Eyewitness performance of personality types as a function of induced arousal. *American Journal of Psychology, 105,* 417–433.

Tulving, E. (1983). *Elements of episodic memory.* Oxford, England: Clarendon Press.

Turtle, J. W., & Yuille, J. C. (1994). Lost but not forgotten details: Repeated eyewitness recall leads to reminiscence but not hypermnesia. *Journal of Applied Psychology, 79,* 260–271.

United States v. Rouse, 100 F. 3d 360 (8th Cir. 1996).

van der Kolk, B. A., & Fisler, R. E. (1995). Dissociation and the fragmentary nature of traumatic memories: Overview and exploratory study. *Journal of Traumatic Stress, 8,* 505–525.

Vandermaas, M. O., Hess, T. M., & Baker-Ward, L. (1993). Does anxiety affect children's reports of memory for a stressful event? *Applied Cognitive Psychology, 7,* 109–127.

Verinis, J. S., & Walker, V. (1970). Policeman and the recall of criminal details. *Journal of Social Psychology, 81,* 217–221.

Walker, N. E. (1997, April). Should we question how we question children during child abuse investigations. In M. Bruck & H. A. Hembrooke (Chairs), *Beyond suggestibility: Interviews, interviewers, and the information they elicit from children.* Washington, DC: Society for Research in Child Development.

Ward, R. A., & Loftus, E. F. (1985). Eyewitness performance in different psychological types. *Journal of General Psychology, 112,* 191–200.

Warren, A., Hulse-Trotter, K., & Tubbs, E. C. (1991). Inducing resistance to suggestibility in children. *Law and Human Behavior, 15,* 273–285.

Warren, A. R., & Lane, P. (1995). Effects of timing and type of questioning on eyewitness accuracy and suggestibility. In M. S. Zaragoza, J. R. Graham, G. N. C. Hall, R. Hirschman, & Y. S. Ben-Porath (Eds.), *Memory and testimony in the child witness. Applied psychology: Individual, social, and community issues* (pp. 44–60). Thousand Oaks, CA: Sage.

Wells, G. L. (1993). What do we know about eyewitness identification? *American Psychologist, 48,* 553–571.

Wells, G. L., Ferguson, T. J., & Lindsay, R. C. (1981). The tractability of eyewitness confidence and its implications for triers of fact. *Journal of Applied Psychology, 66,* 688–696.

Wells, G. L., & Hryciw, B. (1984). Memory for faces: Encoding and retrieval operations. *Memory and Cognition, 12,* 338–344.

Wells, G. L., & Leippe, M. R. (1981). How do triers of fact infer the accuracy of eyewitness identifications? Memory of peripheral detail can be misleading. *Journal of Applied Psychology, 66,* 682–687.

Wells, G. L., Rydell, S. M., & Seelau, E. P. (1993). The selection of distractors for eyewitness lineups. *Journal of Applied Psychology, 78,* 835–844.

Widom, C. S., & Morris, S. (1997). Accuracy of adult recollections of childhood victimization: Part II. Child sexual abuse. *Psychological Assessment, 9,* 34–46.

Williams, L. M. (1994). Recall of childhood trauma: A prospective study of women's memories of child sexual abuse. *Journal of Consulting and Clinical Psychology, 62,* 1167–1185.

Williams, L. M. (1995). Recovered memories of abuse in women with documented child sexual victimization histories. *Journal of Traumatic Stress, 8,* 649–673.

Winograd, E. (1981). Elaboration and distinctiveness in memory for faces. *Journal of Experimental Psychology: Human Learning and Memory, 7,* 181–190.

Witkin, H., Dyk, R., Faterson, H., Goodenough, D., & Karp, S. (1974). *Psychological differentiation: Studies in development.* Hillsdale, NJ: Erlbaum.

Wogalter, M. S., & Laughery, K. R. (1987). Face recognition: Effects of study to test maintenance and change of photographic mode and pose. *Applied Cognitive Psychology, 1,* 241–253.

Wogalter, M. S., Marwitz, D. B., & Leonard, D. C. (1992). Suggestiveness in photospread lineups: Similarity induces distinctiveness. *Applied Cognitive Psychology, 6,* 443–453.

Yarmey, A. D. (1984). Age as a factor in eyewitness memory. In G. L. Wells & E. F. Loftus (Eds.), *Eyewitness testimony* (pp. 142–154). Cambridge, England: Cambridge University Press.

Yarmey, A. D. (1993). Adult age and gender differences in eyewitness recall in field settings. *Journal of Applied Social Psychology, 23,* 1921–1932.

Yarmey, A. D. (1996). The elderly witness. In S. L. Sporer, R. S. Malpass, & G. Koehnken (Eds.), *Psychological issues in eyewitness identification* (pp. 259–278). Mahwah, NJ: Erlbaum.

Yarmey, A. D., Yarmey, M. J., & Yarmey, A. L. (1996). Accuracy of eyewitness identifications in showups and lineups. *Law and Human Behavior, 20,* 459–477.

Yuille, J. C. (1980). A critical examination of the psychological and practical implications of eyewitness research. *Law and Human Behavior, 4,* 335–345.

Yuille, J. C. (1988). The systematic assessment of children's testimony. *Canadian Psychology, 29,* 247–262.

Yuille, J. C., & Cutshall, J. L. (1986). A case study of eyewitness of a crime. *Journal of Applied Psychology, 71,* 291–301.

Yuille, J. C., Hunter, R., Joffe, R., & Zaparniuk, J. (1993). Interviewing children in sexual abuse cases. In G. S. Goodman & B. L. Bottoms (Eds.), *Child victims, child witnesses: Understanding and improving testimony.* New York: Guilford Press.

Yuille, J. C., & Tollestrup, P. A. (1992). A model of the diverse effects of emotion on eyewitness memory. In S. A. Christianson (Ed.), *The handbook of emotion and memory: Research and theory* (pp. 201–215). Hillsdale, NJ: Erlbaum.

Yuille, J. C., & Wells, G. L. (1991). Concerns about the application of research findings: The issue of ecological validity. In J. Doris (Ed.), *The suggestibility of children's recollections* (pp. 118–128). Washington, DC: American Psychological Association.

Zadny, J., & Gerard, H. B. (1974). Attribution intentions and information selectivity. *Journal of Experimental Social Psychology, 10,* 34–52.

Zanni, G. R., & Offerman, J. T. (1978). Eyewitness testimony: An exploration of question wording upon recall as a function of neuroticism. *Perceptual and Motor Skills, 46,* 163–166.

Zaragoza, M. S. (1991). Preschool children's susceptibility to memory impairment. In J. Doris (Ed.), *The suggestibility of children's recollections* (pp. 27–39). Washington, DC: American Psychological Association.

Zaragoza, M. S., & Koshmider, J. W. (1989). Misled subjects may know more than their performance implies. *Journal of Experimental Psychology: Learning, Memory, and Cognition, 15,* 246–255.

Zaragoza, M. S., & Lane, S. M. (1994). Source misattributions and the suggestibility of eyewitness memory. *Journal of Experimental Psychology: Learning, Memory, and Cognition, 20,* 934–945.

Zaragoza, M. S., McCloskey, M., & Jamis, M. (1987). Misleading postevent information and recall of the original event: Further evidence against the memory impairment hypothesis. *Journal of Experimental Psychology: Learning, Memory, and Cognition, 13,* 36–44.

CHAPTER 10

Assessing and Aiding
Civil Jury Competence

JENNIFER K. ROBBENNOLT, STEVEN PENROD, and LARRY HEUER

IN A recent article entitled "Juries: They May Be Broken, but We Can Fix Them," Supreme Court Justice Sandra Day O'Connor (1997) observed: "Juries usually do their job very well. . . . But juries also have the ability to disappoint us, sometimes to the point of forcing us to question whether we should have jury trials at all. One of this country's great observers of human nature, Mark Twain, once complained that juries had become 'the most ingenious and infallible agency for defeating justice that human wisdom could contrive'" (p. 20). O'Connor and Twain have respectable company in their criticism of the jury. During the 1996 presidential campaign, candidate Robert Dole observed: "The legal guardrails that protected our society . . . have in many places been knocked down, even dismantled, often by the very judges and juries who have been entrusted with the sacred duty of upholding the law" (quoted in Tackett, 1996, p. 1). Richard A. Posner (1995), Federal Court of Appeals judge and former University of Chicago law professor, has sounded similar notes of concern about jury decision making: "In recent years, a series of highly publicized criminal trials in which obviously guilty defendants were acquitted by juries . . . has made the American jury a controversial institution. Civil juries have rendered some astonishing verdicts as well, ladling out billions in other people's money with insouciance and attracting a drumbeat of criticism from the business community" (p. 14).

In recent years, the civil jury in particular has come under attack. In civil cases, juries are asked to determine whether the defendant is liable, to award damages intended to compensate the plaintiff for injuries (compensatory damages), and, sometimes, to award damages intended to punish the defendant for engaging in egregious conduct and deter the defendant and others from engaging in such conduct in the future (punitive damages). Large jury verdicts—

such as the $2.7 million verdict against McDonald's when a customer was burned by hot coffee; the $5.5 million punitive damage award against Capital Cities, ABC, and two ABC employees as punishment against tactics used in an investigative report on *Prime Time Live*; and the $3.5 billion punitive damage verdict in a Louisiana railway fire case (Broder, 1997; Kozinski, 1995; Mifflin, 1997)—have caused some to conclude that juries are not an effective mechanism for awarding damages. In particular, critics of the civil jury contend that juries are arbitrary, capricious, and unprincipled in the manner in which they award damages, particularly punitive damages (e.g., Frank, 1949; Quayle, 1992). Policymakers advocating jury reform argue that civil juries are incompetent to decide the cases before them, biased in favor of plaintiffs, and overgenerous. In addition, they contend that huge damage awards given by juries have fueled a "litigation crisis" and have contributed to crippling delays in the civil justice system (Daniels, 1989). Justice O'Connor, dissenting in *Pacific Mutual Life Ins. Co. v. Haslip* (1991), commented, "[r]ecent years . . . have witnessed an explosion in the frequency and size of punitive damages awards" (p. 1066). Large damage verdicts stir incredible controversy and are typically the objects of substantial media attention.

In this chapter, we consider the two themes advanced by Justice O'Connor in the title of her recent commentary. We consider evidence on the question of just how "broken" the civil jury is, focusing particularly on research that examines the factors that do influence jury decision making and decision-making processes in civil cases. Then we consider a set of studies that have evaluated two of the mechanisms that have been advanced as "fixes" for jury problems: juror note taking and juror questioning of witnesses.

CIVIL JURY DECISION MAKING

Despite the focus on a few highly publicized cases, the empirical studies that have examined the overall pattern of punitive damage awards have generally found that punitive damages are awarded infrequently (though they remain a threat in a great many cases), are typically not extremely large (though exceptions secure substantial media attention), and are rarely collected in the amounts awarded by juries (though these reductions are not as extensively reported in the media as are the original awards) (e.g., Daniels & Martin, 1990; Landes & Posner, 1986; Peterson, Sarma, & Shanley, 1987; Rustad, 1991; United States General Accounting Office, 1989). For example, the $2.7 million verdict against McDonald's was reduced to $640,000, and the $5.5 million punitive damages verdict in the Food Lion case was reduced to $315,000.

In fact, there is little evidence of a civil justice system "out of control." However, there are aspects of jury-determined damages that are cause for some concern. Studies have found a large degree of unpredictability in jury-determined damage awards, such that juries may award differing amounts for seemingly similar injuries (studies reviewed in Saks, 1992). Thus, although the overall amount of damages awarded by juries is not out of control, there is large variability in awards made by juries. Moreover, studies have found that juries tend to overcompensate plaintiffs with relatively small losses, but tend to undercompensate plaintiffs with relatively large losses (Conrad & Bernstein, 1964; King & Smith, 1988).

LEGAL REFORM EFFORTS

Over the past decade, the U.S. Supreme Court has had occasion to rule on the constitutionality of large punitive damage awards five times (*BMW of North America v. Gore*, 1996; *Browning-Ferris Ind. v. Kelco Disposal, Inc.*, 1989; *Honda Motor Co. v. Oberg*, 1994; *Pacific Mutual Life Ins. Co. v. Haslip*, 1991; *TXO Production Corp. v. Alliance Resources Corp.*, 1993). The Court has held that the traditional method of awarding punitive damages—that is, the determination of the appropriateness and amount of punitive damages by a jury and subsequent review by both trial and appellate courts—is not "so inherently unfair as to deny due process and be *per se* unconstitutional" but has been willing to consider whether specific jury awards were excessive (*Pacific Mutual Life Ins. Co. v. Haslip*, 1991, p. 1043). In 1996, the Court, for the first time, did find a punitive damage award constitutionally excessive (*BMW of North America v. Gore*, 1996). However, in practice, the Court has left the responsibility for regulating punitive damage awards to the individual states.

Thus, advocates of tort reform have pursued nonjudicial avenues in attempts to restrain what they perceive as out-of-control damage awards, turning to the state and federal legislatures. Already a number of states have enacted and implemented a variety of measures that are aimed either at restricting the incidence and/or the amount of damage awards or at providing structure to the jury decision-making task (Hurd & Zollers, 1994). For example, a number of states have limited the amount of money that may be awarded either for noneconomic compensatory damages (e.g., pain and suffering) or for punitive damages (Hurd & Zollers, 1994). Similarly, a number of states have begun to require the jury to be more certain in their damages decision before they may award punitive damages. Thus, many states require juries to conclude that the evidence is "clear and convincing" that punitive damages are appropriately awarded, rather than that the "preponderance of the evidence" indicates that punitive damages ought to be awarded (e.g., Alaska Statutes, 1994; South Carolina Code Annotated, 1993). Other reforms attempt to better guide juries in making their damage award decisions. Many commentators argue that the instructions juries are given to guide them in their decisions regarding the imposition of punitive damages are insufficient (American College of Trial Lawyers [ACTL], 1989). The recently promulgated final draft of the Model Punitive Damages Act (1996) suggests a number of factors for the trier of fact to consider in determining the amount of a punitive award. The factors include the nature of the defendant's wrongful conduct and its effects, any monies paid out by the defendant that arose from the wrongful conduct, the profit obtained by the defendant through the wrongful conduct, compliance or noncompliance with applicable agency standards and/or any remedial measures taken or not taken by the defendant, and the effects of the award on innocent persons.

Other reform efforts would take the punitive damages decision out of the hands of the jury altogether. A few states have decided to allow judges to assess the amount of punitive damages to be awarded rather than juries (e.g., Connecticut General Statutes Annotated, 1987; Kansas Statutes Annotated, 1994). These types of reforms are usually justified by arguments that judges are less susceptible to bias and prejudice and are more qualified, through training and experience, to carry out such an important task (Koenig & Rustad, 1993; Sharkey, 1996). However, Owen (1994) notes that even judges can harbor prejudices and argues that compromise among jurors may result in more balance. These reforms raise the dual questions of how juries make decisions in civil cases and whether their decision-making processes signal serious problems.

JURY DECISION-MAKING PROCESSES

There has been limited research focusing on the process by which juries make their damage awards (e.g., Greene, 1989; MacCoun, 1993a). Relatively little is known about the strategies or cognitive processes used by jurors in determining damages (Goodman, Greene, & Loftus, 1989).

There is some empirical support for a number of possibilities that have been advanced as methods by which jurors assess damage amounts. An example is the story-teller model, which proposes that jurors combine the evidence presented into a narrative story; they then choose the verdict option that fits best with the story (MacCoun, 1993a). Specifically regarding damage awards, one hypothesis is that jurors anchor on an initial value and then adjust this value as they become aware of more and more new facts; this is termed anchoring and adjustment (Chapman & Bornstein, 1996; Hinsz & Indahl, 1995). Some interviewed jurors have reported that they arrived at their compensatory damage award by deciding upon an amount for each component of damages and then summing to get a total award amount (Goodman et al., 1989). However, an experimental study by Goodman et al. found that 27% of jury-eligible adults asked to read written vignettes and to award damages reported arriving at their damage award merely by "picking a fair number," rather than engaging in any calculations that would be required by the additive or anchoring and adjustment methods.

Although most empirical research that has examined how damages are awarded has looked at the damage awards of individual jurors, a recent study by Davis and colleagues examined the damage awards of juries following deliberation (Davis, Au, Hulbert, Chen, & Zarnoth, 1997). Davis et al. found that the mean damage awards of 6-person and 12-person juries did not differ significantly from the damage awards of individual jurors. However, 12-person juries awarded smaller amounts in damages than did 6-person juries. In addition, they found that, though a model based on the mean of the individual group members' initial damage awards did not result in a statistically significant fit to the observed group damage award decisions, a model based on the median of the closest members resulted in an acceptable fit. These results suggest that decisions by juries are not generally different from the decisions that would be made by individual jurors, however, the processes engaged in by juries do not approximate that of a simple mean but result in awards that are similar to the median of the jurors' initial judgments.

It is likely that the processes jurors use to arrive at punitive damage awards are somewhat different from those they use to calculate compensatory awards (Greene, 1989). First, juries are likely to have less information available to make a determination about punitive damages. Second, the "determination to punish or to deter is decidedly different from the decision to compensate, because it is motivated by different concerns" (Greene, 1989, p. 246). The more normative decisions about punitive damages may be guided less by the evidence presented than are decisions about compensatory damages. Third, the determination of an amount of punitive damages may be more of a process of negotiation than is the more calculation-oriented determination of compensatory damages. Interviews with jurors provide some evidence that final punitive damage awards represent a compromise between high and low amounts advocated by different factions of the jury. In addition, Greene notes that many punitive damage awards are rounded numbers (e.g., $1 million or $500,000), suggesting that minute calculations are likely not taking place.

INFLUENCES ON JURY DECISIONS

Outcome Severity

One factor thought to be an important consideration in the awarding of damages is the severity of the outcome to the plaintiff (see *BMW of North America v. Gore*, 1996). However, the expected relationship between injury severity and damage award is complex. Compensatory damages should logically be greater when the injuries and other damages are more severe because the resulting medical bills, lost wages, pain and suffering are increased. However, this is not necessarily the case with punitive damages. Punitive damages are not aimed at compensating the plaintiff and making him or her whole, as are compensatory damages, but are to punish and deter the defendant. In fact, many have argued that punitive damages ought to be scaled to the heinousness of the offense and *not* to the magnitude of the harm (Galanter & Luban, 1993). Nonetheless, in *TXO* (1993), the U.S. Supreme Court concluded that punitive damages ought to have some reasonable relationship to compensatory damage.

Social psychologists have found that judgments about responsibility for an event are influenced by the severity of the consequences of the accident. Walster (1966) found that participants judged a person's behavior as being more responsible for an accident when the accident was severe than when the accident was inconsequential. This effect did not seem to be due to a perception that the actor was more careless when the accident was severe, but instead, to the use of a more strict standard against which the behavior was compared when the consequences of that behavior were more severe.

The notion that as the severity of the outcome of an action increases, the responsibility attributed to the actor increases has been termed "defensive attribution." Fiske and Taylor (1991) explain defensive attribution: "[A]s the consequences of an action become more severe, they become more unpleasant, and the notion that they might be accidental becomes less tolerable: the fear that the same thing might involve the self becomes a realistic possibility.

Seeing the actions as avoidable and blaming a person for their occurrence makes the actions more predictable and hence avoidable by the self" (p. 85).

However, some attempts to replicate Walster's (1966) original findings have not been successful. For example, Shaver (1970) did not find the predicted differences in the attributions of responsibility for minor and severe accidents. Similarly, Thomas and Parpal (1987) did not find an effect of the severity of the consequences of an action on ratings of responsibility. It has been suggested that whether a relationship between outcome severity and judgment of responsibility is found depends on the personal and situational similarity between the study participants and the accident victim/plaintiff (Burger, 1981). Thus, our current understanding of the relationship between outcome severity and judgments of responsibility is incomplete at best.

The relationship between outcome severity and judgment has also been investigated as it relates to the awarding of damages. Several studies have shown that more compensatory damages are awarded when injuries are more severe. In a study of 8,231 medical malpractice cases, Taragin and colleagues (Taragin, Willett, Wilczek, Trout, & Carson, 1992) found that both the likelihood that a plaintiff would obtain a payment and the amount of that payment (either settlement or jury verdict) increased with the severity of the injury. Similarly, Peterson (1984) found that damage awards in general were affected by the level of severity of the plaintiff's injuries. In a recent study, Wissler, Evans, Hart, Morry, and Saks (1997) found that pain and suffering awards were strongly influenced by information about the nature, characteristics, and consequences of the injury.

The evidence with respect to the influence of injury severity on punitive damages is mixed. In a sample of product liability cases, Rustad (1992) found that both the likelihood that a plaintiff would be awarded punitive damages and the likelihood that he or she would actually collect them were correlated with how severely the plaintiff had been injured. However, given the correlational nature of Rustad's study, it is difficult to draw any precise conclusions. Cather, Greene, and Durham (1996) investigated the influence of the severity of the injury to the plaintiff on the amounts of compensatory and punitive damages awarded by jury-eligible adults in response to written vignettes. They found that overall damage awards in a personal injury case were higher when the plaintiff was more severely injured than when the plaintiff was only mildly injured, but did not find this relationship in other types of cases (product liability and insurance bad faith cases). When they examined punitive damages in particular, they did not find significant differences in the amounts awarded to severely injured and mildly injured plaintiffs.

The extent of the actual injury suffered by the plaintiff is not the only important factor related to the severity of the harm inflicted by the defendant. Equally important are the injuries that potentially could have resulted from the defendant's conduct. The Court, in *TXO* (1993), recognized that the relationship between injury severity and punitive damages was not absolute and could not be quantified in a numerical ratio. The Court cited a common example of circumstances in which punitive damages many times the compensatory damages would be appropriate: "For instance, a man wildly fires a gun into a crowd. By sheer chance, no one is injured and the only damage is to a $10 pair of glasses. A jury reasonably could find only $10 in compensatory damages, but thousands of dollars in punitive damages to teach a duty of care. We would allow a jury to impose substantial punitive damages in order to discourage future bad acts" (p. 459). The Court determined that it was appropriate to take into account the harm that could have potentially occurred due to the defendant's actions as well as the harm that did indeed occur, and to take into account the "possible harm to other victims that might have resulted if similar future behavior were not deterred" (p. 460). This approach to the relationship between the severity of the injury to the plaintiff and the punitive damage award was maintained in *BMW* (1996), where the Court found that an important guide for the review of punitive damage awards is the ratio of the award to the "harm or potential harm" caused by the defendant.

Karlovac and Darley (1988) noted that in determining an actor's negligence, the legal system takes into account not only the severity of the actual outcome, but also "the severity of all the harms that *could* foreseeably have eventuated from a risky action" (p. 289). In a series of studies, Karlovac and Darley investigated the influence of the severity of the potential harms risked by an actor on the judgments of participants. Using undergraduate participants and tape-recorded stories accompanied by slides, they examined the effect on judgments of varying the degree of the maximum possible harm that could have resulted from an actor's risky action. Karlovac and Darley found that judgments of negligence were influenced by the severity of the harm risked. Moreover, they found that judgments of the degree of punishment that was perceived as appropriate were also determined by the severity of the harm risked.

Defendant's Wealth

A second factor thought by some to be influential in juror determinations of damages is the wealth of the defendant. Because the purpose of compensatory damages is to "make the plaintiff whole," that is, to compensate the plaintiff for his or her losses, the wealth of the defendant ought to play no role in the amount of compensatory damages awarded. However, the purposes of punitive damages are different from those of compensatory damages. Punitive damages are intended to punish the defendant and to deter the defendant and others from engaging in similar behavior in the future. To punish or deter a wealthy defendant, the amount of punitive damages awarded must be sufficient to make an impact on the defendant (Simpson, 1996; see also Abraham & Jeffries, 1989; Arlen, 1992). Although the U.S. Supreme Court has not directly addressed the question of the relevance of the defendant's wealth, it has referred to the "financial position" of the defendant as a factor that could be taken into account and has approved of standards for reviewing jury awards of punitive damages that have included wealth as a factor (*Pacific Mutual Life Ins. Co. v. Haslip*, 1991; *TXO Production Corp. v. Alliance Resources Corp.*, 1993).

Hans and Ermann (1989), using written vignettes, found that their 201 student respondents were able to differentiate between the financial resources available to Mr. Jones and to the Jones Corporation and awarded a plaintiff suing the corporation more compensation than a plaintiff suing an individual. However, regression analysis indicated that there was not a consistent effect of the presumed resources of the defendant on awards. Rather, awards were more strongly linked to judgments about the defendant's recklessness, with participants attributing more recklessness to the corporation than to the individual.

A recent study attempted to delineate the distinction between the impact of a corporate identity on juror decisions and the impact of the defendant's wealth. Using written case materials, MacCoun (1996; see also MacCoun, 1993b) found that jury-eligible adults treated corporations differently than individual defendants, such that larger compensatory damage awards were assessed against the corporate defendant than against the wealthy individual defendant. However, MacCoun found that the compensatory damages awarded against the wealthy individual were no greater than those awarded against the poor individual.

Thus, it appears that there is little evidence for a "deep-pocket" effect, at least in terms of the impact of the wealth of the defendant on compensatory damage awards. This is as it should be; as noted above, the wealth of the defendant does not impact the extent of the plaintiff's damages nor the amount of money it ought to take to compensate the plaintiff. In contrast, wealth *should* influence punitive damage awards. However, none of the studies discussed examined the influence of the defendant's wealth on *punitive* damage awards. It remains to be seen whether decision makers can distinguish between the purposes of compensatory and of punitive damages and use information about the defendant's wealth to inform decisions about punitive damages but refrain from using such information in making decisions about compensatory damages.

Reprehensibility of the Defendant's Acts

Discussions of what factors ought to influence punitive damage awards invariably note that the nature and reprehensibility of the conduct complained of are relevant (Owen, 1994). Indeed, punitive damages may not be awarded at all unless the defendant's conduct is "outrageous, because of the defendant's evil motive or his reckless indifference to the rights of others" (Prosser & Keeton, 1984). Prosser and Keeton have noted that for punitive damages to be awarded there "must be circumstances of aggravation or outrage, such as spite or 'malice,' or a fraudulent or evil motive on the part of the defendant, or such a conscious and deliberate disregard of the interests of others that the conduct may be called wilful or wanton" (pp. 9–10). One of the guideposts identified by the U.S. Supreme Court in *BMW* (1996) was the degree of reprehensibility of the defendant's conduct. The Court noted that the reprehensibility of the defendant's conduct was "[p]erhaps the most important indicium of the reasonableness of a punitive damages award" because that award should reflect the "enormity" of the defendant's offense.

Cather et al. (1996) explored the influence of the reprehensibility of the defendant's conduct on compensatory and punitive damage awards. They utilized an experimental design using written vignettes and 80 jury-eligible adults. Overall (across compensatory and punitive damages), they found that participants awarded more damages in response to the high-reprehensibility scenarios than they did in response to the low-reprehensibility scenarios. In particular, however, they found that the punitive damage awards in the high-reprehensibility conditions were higher than the punitive damage awards in the low-reprehensibility condition, but that there was no significant difference in the amount of compensatory damages awarded in the high- and low-reprehensibility conditions. A problem with the reprehensibility manipulations used in the Cather et al. study is that the low-reprehensibility condition may not have amounted to even simple negligence let alone sufficient reprehensibility to justify a punitive damage award (e.g., in the low-reprehensibility condition for a product liability case, the defendant manufacturer had conducted considerable safety research and had been notified of only a few similar incidents). Because punitive damages may only be awarded when the defendant's conduct is wilful and wanton, this type of manipulation is unrealistic, as the jurors would not be allowed to award punitive damages under the conditions detailed in the low-reprehensibility conditions. More instructive would be whether jurors make the finer distinctions required of them when judging the behavior of defendants, all of whom have engaged in reprehensible conduct, but of varying degrees. In another study using 768 jury-eligible adults and an audiotaped trial, Horowitz and Bordens (1990) found that the reprehensibility of the defendant manufacturer's conduct (operationalized as the length of time the defendant was aware of the harmful effects of its product) was not correlated with compensatory damages, but was significantly correlated with punitive damage awards.

Individual Characteristics of Decision Makers

A variety of individual difference variables have been explored to determine their relationship to legal judgments (see Ford, 1986; Litigation Sciences, 1993). In general, demographic variables such as age, gender, and social class have proven to be of limited value in predicting judgments. However, some personality and attitudinal variables have proven somewhat more useful. Ellsworth (1993) and colleagues attempted to determine which components of the juror decision process are influenced by juror attitudes. Ellsworth notes that legal decisions are inherently imprecise and require the decision maker to resolve numerous ambiguities and to engage in a great deal of interpretation. Thus, there is ample room for juror attitudes to influence juror decisions. Ellsworth proposed that attitudes might influence verdicts in three distinct ways: (a) attitudes may influence jurors' evaluation of the credibility of witnesses; (b) the inferences drawn by jurors, which are based in part on the jurors' attitudes, may influence the jurors' construction of a narrative summary of the evidence; (c) attitudes may influence the manner in which jurors apply the judge's instructions regarding the law to the facts as they have constructed them. Ellsworth found support for the conclusion that attitudes influence verdicts in all three ways.

In their investigation of attitudes toward the police and toward due process, Casper, Benedict, and Perry (1989) hypothesized that attitudes might influence damage awards in a civil rights action through their role in shaping the processing of the testimony to which they are exposed. They found that attitudes operated to influence damage awards to some extent through their influence on jurors' interpretation of trial testimony, but that the attitudes also retained an independent effect on awards.

It has been noted that those attitudes that are most predictive are those that are specifically related to the decision to be made (Kassin & Wrightsman, 1988). For example, Kassin and Wrightsman (1983) found that their juror bias scale (JBS), which measured mock jurors' attitudes toward legal issues, was somewhat more predictive of juror verdicts than were measures of more general attitudes. When attempting to predict and understand juror awards of damages, it is likely that knowledge of juror attitudes toward the civil litigation system would be particularly useful. It seems plausible that jurors' attitudes toward the number and nature of the lawsuits filed and toward the role and functioning of the civil jury would influence their determinations of damage awards. A series of studies by Hans and Lofquist (1992, 1994) investigated jurors' attitudes toward civil litigation. They found that jurors in actual tort cases had strong negative views of both the frequency and legitimacy of civil lawsuits and believed that civil damage awards were too high. However, jurors also agreed that jurors generally do a good job and found their own jury experience to be positive. Hans and Lofquist found that their seven-item scale measuring juror attitudes toward civil litigation comprised two separate factors, one measuring attitudes toward the worth of civil litigation and a second measuring beliefs about the abilities of civil juries. Moreover, they found a significant correlation between jury members' average scores on the civil litigation scale and the jury's damage award, such that the more strongly the jurors believed there was a litigation crisis, the lower the damages awarded.

Other researchers have investigated the relationship between various measures of attitudes toward the civil litigation system and legal decisions and have found similar results. In telephone interviews, Moran, Cutler, and De Lisa (1994) found that attitudes toward tort reform predicted verdicts in both civil and criminal fictional cases. Similarly, Greene, Goodman, and Loftus (1991) found that the scores of jury-eligible adults on a scale measuring attitudes toward tort reform and damages (e.g., whether there is an insurance crisis, the influence of media on attitudes about civil lawsuits, and beliefs about attorney credibility and damage requests) were significantly correlated with damage awards, such that those with more favorable attitudes toward tort reform gave lower damage awards. In addition, they found a significant correlation between participants' estimates of the frequency of large damage awards and the amount of damages they awarded. Moreover, they found that such attitudinal measures were more reliable predictors than were demographic variables.

Jurors versus Judges

Clearly, many people believe that judges engage in qualitatively different kinds of decision making than jurors. For example, in his concurrence in *BMW of North America v. Gore* (1996), Justice Breyer noted that one cannot "expect jurors to interpret law like judges, who work within a discipline and hierarchical organization that normally promotes roughly uniform interpretation and application of the law." However, there is a paucity of research regarding the comparison between the decision making of jurors and the decision making of judges. The existing research suggests that there are far fewer differences in the decision making of jurors and judges than is commonly thought.

One of the earliest comparisons of judges and jurors was conducted by Kalven and Zeisel (1966; Kalven, 1964); they asked judges to report, for cases tried before them, how the jury decided the case and how they would have decided it had it been a bench trial. Across 4,000 civil cases, they found that judges and juries agreed 78% of the time as to the liability of defendants. In terms of the amount of damage awards, they found that when both the judge and jury decided in favor of the plaintiff, juries would have awarded more damages 52% of the time and judges would have awarded more damages 39% of the time, with approximate agreement in 9% of the cases. On the average, Kalven and Zeisel found that juries awarded 20% more in damages than judges would have awarded.

Recent research suggests that judges and lay jurors are similar in a number of aspects of decision making. For example, Landsman and Rakos (1994) found that judges' and jurors' liability decisions and perceptions of the trial were similarly affected by exposure to potentially biasing, but inadmissible, evidence. Interestingly, Landsman and Rakos found that although the effect of the biasing information was the same on judges and jurors, the jurors appeared to be more sensitive to their cognitive limitations in disregarding the evidence than were the judges. Howe and Loftus (1992) found that though students found higher levels of blameworthiness overall, judges and students were similarly influenced by the outcome of an offense and by the level of intention of the perpetrator.

In the first large-scale comparison of plaintiff win rates and recoveries in actual civil cases tried before juries and judges, Clermont and Eisenberg (1992) found that plaintiffs actually enjoy greater success in front of judges in three major categories of torts: product liability, medical malpractice, and motor vehicle cases. Only in marine and Federal Employers' Liability Act (FELA) cases was there a significantly higher win rate in front of juries than in front of judges. The pattern of similarities and differences in the amount of damages awarded was less clear. In some types of cases, judges awarded more in damages; in others, juries awarded more. It is not clear whether any of these differences were statistically significant. These findings suggest that judges and jurors may be differentially similar in decision making, depending on the type of case with which they are faced; however, there is no way to tell whether the cases that ended up before judges and juries were at all similar within each case type. There may be factors other than the identity of the fact finder that influenced the results in these cases.

In a set of experimental studies, Vidmar (1995) explored the assumptions that experienced legal professionals would produce lower and less variable pain and suffering awards than would juries. Vidmar found that the mean juror award was not significantly different from the mean award given by legal professionals; however, the jurors' awards were more variable than were those given by the legal professionals. Vidmar notes, however, that even the awards made by the legal professionals were highly variable, ranging from $22,000 to $82,000. Thus, "the awarding of noneconomic damages is a pretty subjective process even for trained experienced legal professionals" (p. 226). Further analysis was conducted by constructing randomly constituted juries from the pool of participants and assigning a damage award to each jury based on the median award given by its members. Using this method did not result in mean damage awards that were any different from the awards given by the legal professionals; however, the juries yielded awards that were less variable than those given by the legal professionals. This reduced variability is to be expected from "statistical juries" constructed in this manner and may not accurately reflect what might occur in actual jury deliberations. Interestingly, Vidmar used an actual case that had been tried before an arbitration panel, so it was possible to compare the damage awards made by the participants in the study to the actual award. The arbitration panel gave a total award of $58,300, the legal professionals gave a median award of $57,000, and the jurors gave a median award of $47,850. The differences among these awards were not statistically significant. Jurors and legal professionals also did not differ in their perceptions of the case or in the self-reported reasoning behind their awards.

Little is known about the relative decision making of judges and jurors. What we do know suggests that they may engage in decision-making processes that are quite similar; however, even this conclusion is preliminary at best. In particular, there is a notable lack of research exploring the similarities and differences in the processes by which judges and jurors determine damage awards.

SUMMARY

On balance, existing research on jury decision making in civil cases suggests that the process is, if not perfect, at least orderly. Jurors seem to give systematic consideration to factors such as the severity of outcomes and the reprehensibility of the alleged acts and do not seriously misuse information about a defendant's wealth. Furthermore, the decisions of juries seem to stack up reasonably well against the decisions of other, arguably more expert, decision makers. But these conclusions must be qualified, for the body of scientific research upon which they are based is not large. Most of the research on civil jury decision making is of quite recent vintage, and it is easy to imagine that our understanding of these processes will be much richer in another decade.

AIDS TO JURY DECISION MAKING

Although our survey of research on jury decision making in civil cases suggests that the civil jury is probably not as "broken" as some critics would like us to believe, many jury critics have nonetheless been quite inventive in advancing recommendations for jury aids. For instance, Justice O'Connor in her 1997 article recommended: "In my view, the first level for reform is in the courtroom. . . . Jurors should be allowed, and encouraged, to take notes at trial. I frankly cannot understand the resistance to this practice. . . . Taking notes is a way for a person to make sense of the information being received . . . and perhaps most importantly for the juror, to take an active, rather than a passive, part in what is going on" (pp. 23–24). Attorney Kenneth Adamo (1996) recommends: "Let Them Take Notes. . . . Allowing note-taking is almost de rigueur if juror comprehension and interest are to be maximized. . . . Allow the Jury to Ask Questions. . . . [I]f you want an interested and knowledgeable jury, especially as trial proceeds, you need to provide for juror questions" (pp. 354–355). Jason Scully (1996) writes: "With more guidance and increased comprehension, jurors may be able to fulfill their role as accurate decision-makers . . . improved trial techniques include . . . allowing jurors to take notes [and] allowing juror questions" (p. 648). Among the recommendations in the final report of the Blue Ribbon Commission on Jury System Improvement for the State of California (J. Clark Kelso, 1996) are: "adopt a Rule of Court which requires the trial court to inform jurors of their right to take written notes [and] . . . adopt a [rule] recommending that judges permit jurors to submit written questions to the court which, subject to the discretion of the trial judge and the rules of evidence, may be asked of witnesses who are still on the stand" (p. 1504). Abramson (1994) and Adler (1994), in their recent volumes on the jury, also advocated use of these procedures and drew approval from Judge Posner: "For complex modern cases, both Abramson and Adler propose a series of reforms to make the jury's task easier: allowing jurors to take notes and ask questions" (Posner, 1995, p. 16).

Despite the enthusiasm for jury note taking and juror questioning of witnesses expressed by such authorities as Justice O'Connor and the California commission, it turns out that these procedures are rather controversial and not universally endorsed. Arguments for and against note taking and questioning have been advanced by the courts, legal scholars, and social scientists alike, and the debate over these procedures is far from new. Appellate decisions concerning juror questions date back to 1825 and decisions about note taking to at least 1900. Furthermore, contemporary commentary is also abundant. Although many appellate courts have addressed these issues, there is no clear consensus on their advantages and disadvantages. There is some consensus on how the procedures should be evaluated, at least insofar as the same criteria appear repeatedly across cases. Unfortunately, the appellate judges writing these decisions draw upon their own experiences as the principal evidence concerning the strengths and weaknesses of the methods. Of course, until recently, there was little in the way of systematic evidence about the impact of the procedures for judges to rely on.

Although late to the scene, the social science community has generated some discussion and research on notes and questions (reviewed below) in the past quarter century. Until recently though, the empirical research was sparse and suffered from methodological limitations. First, some studies were conducted in laboratories; despite the advantages of internal validity conferred by laboratory methods, such studies can be weak on external validity, generalizability, and acceptance by legal policymakers. Second, some field research relied on very small sample sizes, further reducing the reliability and generalizability of results. Third, field studies generally did not employ random assignment of trials, thus threatening the internal validity of conclusions. Fourth, most field studies suffered from selection biases (of unknown magnitude) because participating judges appeared to favor the studied procedures. Fifth, most research was based exclusively on juror reactions and did not consider the perspectives of judges and lawyers who might be concerned about aspects of the procedures that would not concern jurors.

In our discussion, we focus on the results from two courtroom field experiments (reported in detail in Heuer & Penrod, 1988, 1989, 1994a, 1994b) that examine the consequences of permitting jurors to direct questions to witnesses during trials and to take notes. These studies largely avoid the problems alluded to above; the studies use random assignment of cases, employ large sample sizes, seek to minimize selection bias, and draw data from multiple sources. Data for the first experiment were obtained from 550 jurors, 29 judges (sitting in 63 different trials), and 95 lawyers—all of whom participated in the same 67 Wisconsin state court trials. Data for the second experiment included 75 civil and 85 criminal trials in courtrooms from 33 states; data were supplied by 1,229 jurors, 103 judges, and 220 lawyers.

The procedures in the experiments were similar and included approximately equal numbers of criminal and civil trials. In both studies, judges received packets of materials, including (a) instructions about the combination of questioning and note taking procedures they were to employ in their next jury trial; (b) suggestions about how to administer the procedures; and (c) questionnaires to be completed by the judge, the jurors, and the lawyers at the conclusion of the trial. All respondents were questioned about demographic information and asked their general evaluations of the trial, the trial participants, and the experimental procedures. Judges and lawyers were asked to complete questionnaires while the jury was deliberating. In most trials, questionnaires were completed before participants left the courtroom.

JUROR QUESTIONS

In an early review of the case law on jury questions, Purver (1970) noted that most courts concluded that the procedure is not improper but is a matter within the discretion of the trial judge. However, courts disagreed about whether juror questions should be encouraged or discouraged. In recent years, there have been a large number of federal and state court decisions regarding the propriety of juror question asking, and many courts have only recently addressed the question for the first time (e.g., *State v. Graves*, 1995; *Williams v. Commonwealth*, 1997). However, the general conclusion remains the same as that advanced by Purver: many courts are reluctant to encourage or to discourage juror questions. Some jurisdictions discourage the procedure; Texas has even prohibited juror questions (Wolff, 1990). On the other hand, some states provide for juror questions by state law (e.g., *Lawson v. State*, 1996) and others by court rule (e.g., *Cohee v. State*, 1997; *State v. Greer*, 1997).

Overall, appellate decisions reflect some disagreement among judges regarding the propriety of this procedure, but it is not difficult to find recent cases in which courts advise caution. The Second Circuit (*United States v. Douglas*, 1996) takes a firmly skeptical view: "In three recent cases, we have considered the issue of juror questioning of witnesses. . . . All three decisions expressed varying degrees of disapproval of juror questioning, though only *Ajmal* concluded that the questioning that occurred warranted reversal of the conviction. *Ajmal*, 67 F.3d at 15." In *United States v. Ajmal*, the Court chastised: "The district court's decision to invite juror questioning was not necessitated by the factual intricacies of this banal drug conspiracy, nor was it prompted by the urging of the jurors themselves. . . . Not surprisingly, the jurors took extensive advantage of this opportunity to question witnesses, including Ajmal himself. Such questioning tainted the trial process" (pp. 14–15). The Seventh Circuit in *United States v. Feinberg* (1996) also expressed reservations: "Whether to permit jurors to ask questions is a decision best left to the discretion of the district judge. . . . However, implicit in his exercise of discretion is an obligation to weigh the potential benefit to the jurors against the potential harm to the parties, especially when one of those parties is a criminal defendant. . . . In the vast majority of cases the risks outweigh the benefits" (p. 336).

Prior Research

There is some research discussing the potential advantages and disadvantages of juror questions. In addition to the Purver (1970) piece (which has been updated with cases through 1995), particularly thorough discussions of the impact of juror questions can be found in McLaughlin (1982), Wolff (1990), and in the Eighth Circuit opinion in *United States v. Johnson* (1989). On the empirical side, there was relatively little research on question effects prior to the Heuer and Penrod studies. A field study by Sand and Reiss (1985) allowed jurors in 26 trials to submit questions to the judge to be asked of witnesses. Unfortunately, there was no nonquestion control group. A pilot field experiment in Dane County, Wisconsin, by Penrod, Linz, and Rios (1984) used criminal trials in one courtroom that were randomly assigned to question-asking versus no-question conditions. Trials in the no-question control group were supplemented with trials from a second courtroom in which questions were not permitted (for a total of 31 trials), which created a partial confound between judges and question asking.

Proponents and critics of jury questions have advanced a number of proposals for questioning procedures and advanced numerous hypotheses about the impact of juror questions. These ideas guided the development of the Heuer and Penrod procedures and dependent measures. A number of courts have stated their preference about the procedures to be employed if juror questions are permitted. In *United States v. Polowichak* (1986), the court disapproved allowing juror questions within the hearing of other jurors and suggested that the district court require jurors to submit questions in writing, without revealing the question to other jurors, at which point the court could pose the question after determining that the question was proper. Similar procedures have been approved in recent state and federal cases such as *State v. Greer* (1997), *State v. Alexander* (1997), *United States v. Stierwalt* (1994), *United States v. Bush* (1995), *United States v. Feinberg* (1996) (where the court disapproved permitting jurors to ask their questions orally but did not overturn the defendant's conviction because the jury asked only "innocuous" questions), and *Commonwealth v. Urena* (1994). Courts and commentators have also suggested that both attorneys be allowed to make any objections to a juror's written question at a bench conference and that the judge's ruling on these objections be made outside the hearing of the jury (Dann, 1996; *DeBenedetto v. Goodyear*, 1985; *State v. Howard*, 1987).

In the Heuer and Penrod studies, for trials randomly assigned to permit juror questions, judges received instructions much like those outlined above and generally followed the recommendations. In trials assigned not to include juror questions, judges were asked to disallow direct questions to witnesses. In the Wisconsin study, jurors were permitted to pose questions in 33 trials and asked a total of 88 questions (2.3 questions per trial). Two-thirds were directed to prosecution witnesses and one-third to defense witnesses.[1] Fifteen of the 88 questions drew objections from the prosecution, the defense attorney, or both. They displayed considerable agreement about which were objectionable, both attorneys typically objecting to the same questions.

In the national study, questions were permitted in 71 trials, though questions were posed in only 51 (a finding that suggests jurors do not necessarily act on their license). Not counting questions submitted but not asked (due to lawyer objections or screening by the judges), jurors asked an average of 4.4 questions per criminal trial (median = 1.3) and 5.1 questions per civil trial (median = 1.8). In both civil and criminal trials, questions were asked at the rate of about one question per two hours of trial time (the median was only .25 questions per hour, with a modal rate of 0.0).

In the national study, the majority of jury questions were directed to prosecution or plaintiff witnesses (79% in civil trials, 77% in criminal trials). Though this may suggest some disparity in the rate of questions directed to opposing sides, when the amount of time prosecution and defense witnesses spent on the stand is considered, the rate is fairly evenly distributed; questions were submitted to prosecution witnesses at a rate of approximately .7 questions per hour of testimony, compared with a rate of approximately .5 per hour for defense witnesses. Twenty-four percent of the jurors' questions were objected to by one or both attorneys. As in the Wisconsin study, the attorneys in trials in the national study largely agreed about which questions were objectionable: 44% of the questions objected to were challenged by both lawyers. Defense attorneys reported that 81% of their objections were sustained, compared to 79% for prosecutors.

Evaluation of Major Possible Advantages of Juror Questions

Do Juror Questions Promote Juror Understanding of the Evidence and Issues? Scully (1996) argued: "[One] method of improving juror understanding is to allow the jurors to ask questions of expert witnesses. This would be helpful because an expert may overlook information that the jurors believe is crucial to making a decision" (pp. 650–651). In *Williams v. Commonwealth* (1997), the court similarly observed: "[A] juror may, and often does, ask a very pertinent and helpful question in furtherance of the investigation [citation omitted]" (p. 155). Similar arguments have been advanced by courts in *Ratton v. Busby* (1959), *Schaefer v. St. Louis & Suburban R. Co.* (1895), and *Krause v. State* (1942).

Heuer and Penrod's findings generally support the proposition that juror questions enhance juror understanding. In the Wisconsin cases, jurors permitted to ask questions were more satisfied that the questioning of witnesses had been thorough, seldom believed that a witness needed to be further questioned, and were more convinced that they had sufficient information to reach a responsible verdict. In the national study, jurors in question-asking trials were asked how helpful their questions were for clarifying the evidence, clarifying the law, and getting to the truth; overall, the answers indicated modest but positive appraisals. Jurors in trials in which questions were permitted also indicated they were somewhat better informed by the evidence and more confident that they had sufficient information to reach a responsible verdict.

Do Juror Questions Help Jurors Get to the Truth?   Some advocates of juror questions believe they can do more than aid understanding. The Supreme Judicial Court of Massachusetts observed in *Commonwealth v. Urena* (1994): "Indeed, there are asserted benefits to juror questioning of witnesses, such as the opportunity for jurors to more fully understand the evidence, . . . enhanced attentiveness of jurors, and furtherance of the truth-seeking ideal" (p. 1205). McLaughlin (1982) observed, "Rather than an indifferent battle of legal minds with jurors as mere spectators, a trial is above all a search for truth . . . while justice is blind, jurors need not also be" (pp. 697–698). In *State v. Kendall* (1907), the court held there was nothing improper in a juror asking a question with the apparent purpose of discovering the truth. The court pointed out that jurors usually ask pertinent questions that help in advancing the investigation. In other cases (e.g., *Hudson v. Markum*, 1997; *Louisville Bridge & Terminal Co. v. Brown*, 1925; *State v. Graves*, 1995; *United States v. Callahan*, 1979; *United States v. Thompson*, 1996; *White v. Little*, 1928), courts have observed that juror questions might aid the jury in finding the truth.

Heuer and Penrod's findings do not offer much support for this proposition. In both the Wisconsin and national studies, judges and attorneys were asked whether they believed juror questions helped get to the truth. Their answers indicated that they did not expect juror questions to help get to the truth, and after participating in a trial in which questions were permitted, they reported that the questions were not very helpful.

Do Juror Questions Increase Juror, Attorney, or Judge Satisfaction with the Trial or the Verdict?   As Judge B. Michael Dann (1996) put it, "The more active jurors are at trial, the more attentive they are to the proceedings. And juror satisfaction with the whole experience is enhanced" (p. 6). Jurors' overall satisfaction with their trials was assessed in both the Wisconsin and the national studies. In both, the conclusion was that jurors were quite satisfied with their experiences and their assessments were not influenced by the availability or use of juror questions. Jurors' satisfaction with their verdict and attitudes toward jury service were similarly unaffected by their opportunity to ask questions. The lawyers and judges in the national trial were also asked how satisfied they were with the jury's verdict. Overall, lawyers and judges indicated that they were reasonably satisfied (with judges somewhat more satisfied than attorneys); these assessments were also not influenced by the presence or absence of juror questions.

Do Juror Questions Alert Counsel to Issues That Require Further Development?   In *United States v. Callahan* (1979), the court observed: "If a juror is unclear as to a point in the proof, it makes good common sense to allow a question to be asked about it. If nothing else, the question should alert trial counsel that a particular factual issue may need more extensive development" (p. 1086). In both of Heuer and Penrod's studies, lawyers and judges were asked whether questions had signaled juror confusion about the law or the evidence. In both, lawyers and judges expected juror questions to provide useful information about the jury's thinking, but after participating in a trial in which questions were allowed, judges and lawyers agreed that questions did not yield these benefits.

Evaluation of Possible Disadvantages of Juror Questions

When Jurors Are Allowed to Ask Questions, Do They Become Advocates Rather Than Neutrals?   In *United States v. Johnson* (1989), Chief Judge Donald Lay observed: "The fundamental problem with juror questions lies in the gross distortion of the adversary system and the misconception of the role of the jury as a neutral factfinder in the adversary process. . . . [T]he neutrality and objectivity of the juror must be sacrosanct" (p. 713). The Second Circuit raised the same concern in several recent cases, including *United States v. Thompson* (1996) and *United States v. Bush* (1995), where it said: "Although we reaffirm . . . that juror questioning of witnesses lies within the trial judge's discretion, we strongly discourage its use. The most troubling concern is that the practice risks turning jurors into advocates, compromising their neutrality" (p. 515). McLaughlin (1982) described this phenomenon as the "12 angry men syndrome," in which jurors lose their objectivity and begin to deliver accusatorial questions to the witness.

Heuer and Penrod examined several types of evidence that indirectly address this concern. One was the pattern of jury decisions. The verdict pattern in the national study indicated that jury questions did not have a significant effect on the verdicts. Heuer and Penrod also asked the judges what their preferred verdict would have been in those trials. This allowed them to examine the rate of judge and jury agreement. The agreement rate was not affected by juror questions: judges and jurors agreed on the verdict in 69% of the cases. Although the agreement was slightly higher in cases in which questions were permitted (74% versus 65%), this difference was not statistically significant. In addition, there was no evidence that either lawyer was perceived less favorably as a result of the questioning procedure (a result that might be expected if jurors lost their neutrality). In fact, attorneys on both sides were perceived somewhat more favorably in trials where questions were permitted.

Do Jurors Ask Improper Questions?   One concern of trial attorneys is that jurors, because they are untutored in the law, will ask impermissible questions and should therefore be discouraged from asking any question at all. Chief Judge Donald Lay in *United States v. Johnson* (1989) observed: "because lay jurors will not understand the rules of evidence, they may well ask impermissible questions, such as those directed at the defendant's character" (p. 713). The court in *Day v. Kilgore* (1994) expressed the concern this way: "[Q]uestions from a jury, untrained in the rules of evidence, may be improper or may solicit information that is either irrelevant or outside of the evidence presented" (p. 518). Examples of jurors asking classically impermissible questions can be found in the case law. For example, in *Maggart v. Bell* (1931), one juror asked the defendant whether he was covered by accident insurance.

Despite these sorts of reservations, Heuer and Penrod found that although jurors do not know the rules of evidence, they nonetheless ask appropriate questions. In the Wisconsin study, both lawyers and judges reported that they did not expect juror questions to be inappropriate or inept, and they did not find them to be so. Lawyers and judges in the national study who participated in a trial with juror questions reported that improper questions were not a problem.

Do Juror Questions Interfere with Attorney Trial Strategies?   Attorneys in the Wisconsin study were also asked whether juror questions brought up information that they had deliberately omitted. This question was asked because preliminary questioning of trial attorneys revealed a fear that juror questions would play havoc with attorney trial strategies: "'trials should continue to be what parties deem to present to jurors,' not an extended search by those jurors for an underlying truth," as one attorney quoted by Tripoli (1997, pp. 104–105) put it. However, attorneys who participated in trials in which questions were permitted reported this was not a problem.

Are Trial Counsel Reluctant to Object to Inappropriate Juror Questions?   Numerous courts have refused to reverse when counsel did not object, during trial, to permitting jurors to ask questions (e.g., *Chicago Hanson Cab Co. v. Havelick*, 1869) or to improper juror questions (e.g., *Louisville Bridge & Terminal Co. v. Brown*, 1925). In considering whether counsel should be *required* to object to improper juror questions in order to preserve the point for appeal, the court in *State v. Sickles* (1926) asked whether this standard was appropriate when objections raise the risk of offending the juror. In *Day v. Kilgore* (1994), the South Carolina Supreme Court expressed the concern and noted the actions of its brethren in Texas: "When either the judge or the jury departs from their assigned roles, the lawyer is confronted with the dilemma of whether to object and risk alienating the judge or jury, or remain silent and risk waiving the issue for appeal purposes. . . . Confronted with a barrage of appeals where the jury departed from its normal role of passive listeners, the Texas Supreme Court issued an absolute prohibition on the procedure [*Morrison v. State*, 845 S.W.2d 882 (Tex.1992)]" (pp. 517–518).

Heuer and Penrod's studies show that lawyers are not immobilized by such fears. In the national and Wisconsin studies, lawyers objected to 20% and 17%, respectively, of questions submitted by jurors. In the national study, lawyers objected to at least one question in 40% of the trials in which at least one question was asked. Of course, Heuer and Penrod's practice of suggesting that jurors submit questions in writing (a procedure now formally adopted in some jurisdictions) so that attorneys may object in private offered some protection to an objecting attorney. Furthermore, if an objection was sustained, judges were asked to explain the ruling to the jury to minimize the possibility that jurors would draw an adverse inference.

General Conclusions about Juror Questioning of Witnesses

- Jury questioning promotes juror understanding of the facts and issues.
- Juror questions do not clearly help get to the truth.
- Juror questions do not alert trial counsel that issues require more extensive development.

- Juror questions do not increase participants' satisfaction with the trial, the judge, and the verdict.
- Jurors do not become advocates rather than neutrals.
- Although jurors do not know the rules of evidence, they ask appropriate questions.
- Juror questions do not interfere with attorney trial strategies.
- Counsel are not reluctant to object to inappropriate juror questions.

JUROR NOTE TAKING

The courts have frequently considered the merits of permitting jurors to take notes during trials (an exhaustive, 50,000-word review of the case law can be found in Larsen, 1996). Traditionally, courts were cool to the idea because juror literacy was far from uniform and there were reservations about allowing some jurors to rely on memory and others on notes. As the court in *Sligar v. Bartlett* (1996) observed: "The common law rule grew from a suspicion that a 'lettered' juror would be revered, and thus excessively persuasive to the other jurors who could not read or write. To guard against this notetaking was prohibited" (p. 1385).

The illiteracy objection has largely disappeared (but see *State v. Triplett*, 1992, for a contemporary expression of concern on this matter), but there are other objections to note taking and the courts in many jurisdictions have not resolved fully their stance on the question. Thus, it is possible to find recent decisions such as the one in *United States v. Darden* (1995) that take a disapproving or cautious approach: "Note taking by jurors is not a favored procedure. As we have stated, trial courts are properly concerned that the juror with the most detailed notes, whether accurate or not, may dominate jury deliberations" (p. 1537). In contrast, it is also possible to find recent decisions such as that in *Crum v. State* (1997) that take a neutral to approving stance on note taking: "The decision to allow jurors to take notes and consult them during deliberation is within the sound discretion of the trial judge" (p. 15).

Prior Research

Several studies have examined the advantages and disadvantages of juror note taking. The research methods employed in these studies have varied widely. The studies include a field study by Flango (1980), who assigned one civil trial and one criminal trial to a note-taking condition and compared them to two non-note-taking control trials. A field study by Sand and Reiss (1985) permitted jurors to take notes in 14 criminal and 18 civil trials. Neither of these field studies used random assignment of cases. At the other end of the methodological spectrum is a laboratory study by Hastie (1983), who randomly assigned six-person simulated juries to note-taking or non-note-taking conditions, presented them a videotape of an actual armed robbery trial, and had them deliberate to a verdict. Rosenhan, Eisner, and Robinson (1994) also conducted a laboratory experiment in which 144 jury-eligible college students and jurors were randomly assigned to note-taking or no-notes conditions, viewed a 75-minute videotaped simulation of a civil trial, and were tested for recall and comprehension of trial material immediately after the trial. Of course, the two Heuer and Penrod field experiments described earlier also manipulated the opportunity for jurors to take notes.

Note-Taking Procedures

In Heuer and Penrod studies, when a trial was assigned to the note-taking condition, judges were asked to permit jurors to take notes during all phases of the trial and to instruct the jurors about this permission as soon as practicable after the jury was impaneled. Judges were also provided suggested instructions about note taking. In trials assigned to the non-note-taking condition, judges were asked to bar notes.

Across Heuer and Penrod's two studies, juror note taking was allowed in 135 trials. When jurors were given the opportunity to take notes, most did so (66% in the Wisconsin study; 87% in the national study), but they did not take extensive notes. In the Wisconsin study, where trials lasted an average of 2.3 days, jurors took an average of 5.4 pages of notes. In the national study, the juror averages for civil trials (which lasted an average of nearly 10 days) were 14.4 pages of notes and for criminal trials (which lasted an average of nearly 6 days), 7.1 pages. In the national study, Heuer and Penrod estimated that jurors in both types of trials took an average of .6 pages of notes per hour of trial time.

Evaluation of Possible Advantages of Juror Note Taking

Does Juror Note Taking Serve as a Memory Aid? Some earlier studies (e.g., Flango, 1980; Sand & Reiss, 1985) reported that jurors found the note-taking procedure helpful as a memory aid, and courts (e.g., *Marbley v. State*, 1984; *Reece v. Simpson*, 1983; *State v. Trujillo*, 1994; *U.S. v. Carlisi*, 1940) have endorsed this seemingly reasonable proposition, arguing that there is no reason why notes should not be made by jurors, given that judges and lawyers make notes and given the possibility that notes might aid memory and enable them to consider the evidence more intelligently. In *Densen v. Stanley* (1919), the court concluded that note taking can assist the jurors in arriving at a correct and fair verdict. As the Oklahoma Court of Criminal Appeals (*Cohee v. State*, 1997) recently observed: "We find that jurors may benefit from notes in several ways: (1) jurors may follow the proceedings more closely and pay more attention as they take notes for later use; (2) jurors' memories may be more easily and reliably refreshed during deliberations; (3) jurors may make fewer requests to have portions of trial transcript read back during deliberations; and (4) the ability to use their notes may result in increased juror morale and satisfaction" (p. 2).

In both of Heuer and Penrod's studies, jurors were asked a variety of questions about their recall of the evidence. In the Wisconsin study, jurors even completed a multiple-choice test of their understanding of the judge's instructions. Heuer and Penrod's conclusion from both studies was that there was no evidence to suggest note taking produced better recall. Although we believe the evidence from the Heuer and Penrod field studies is more compelling than findings from prior, but weaker, field research, it is still difficult to argue that there is no memory advantage to juror note taking. As in the other field studies, the measures used by Heuer and Penrod may not have been sufficiently sensitive to detect memory benefits; Heuer and Penrod relied on quite general measures of recall rather than measures tailored to the facts of each case.

In assessing memory enhancement effects, the benefits of experiments in controlled environments (e.g., mock trials) are clear: they are much more powerful test settings because such studies can easily control the content of the trial, can vary the complexity of the trial, and can directly measure juror performance as a function of the opportunity to take notes. The Rosenhan et al. (1994) laboratory experiment on note taking did test jurors' recall and comprehension. Jurors were asked questions tailored to the particular case they had observed and they had their notes available for reference while answering the questions. On a measure of recall, note takers outperformed non-note-takers by a modest but significant margin. The authors report that 7 of the 10 highest scores on the recall measure were attained by note takers, whereas 8 of the 10 lowest scores were attained by non-note-takers. Among note takers, the authors found a positive relation between the quantity of notes taken and recall and between the degree of organization in notes and recall. The authors found no effect for notes on jurors' verdict preferences.

Does Note Taking Increase Juror Satisfaction with the Trial or the Verdict?   Dann (1996) concurs with the Oklahoma court in *Cohee* that note taking can have a salutary effect on jurors: "The more active jurors are at trial, the more attentive they are to the proceedings. And juror satisfaction with the whole experience is enhanced" (p. 6). In the Wisconsin experiment, Heuer and Penrod detected a slight increase in juror satisfaction with trials, but the finding was not replicated in the national experiment, nor did note taking influence jurors' verdict confidence in the national study. Of course, jurors were already quite satisfied with their verdicts and the procedures in their trials (on 9-point scales with higher scores indicating greater satisfaction, jurors' mean satisfaction with the verdict was 7, and their mean satisfaction with the trial procedure was 7.2), so there may be a ceiling effect in operation.

Evaluation of Possible Disadvantages of Juror Note Taking

Do Jurors' Notes Produce a Distorted Record of the Case?   According to the majority in *Thornton v. Weaber* (1955), jurors are unable to distinguish important from unimportant evidence and will therefore miss the important evidentiary points while noting the unimportant ones. These biased notes will, according to this analysis, then distort the jurors' evaluation of the trial evidence. (Similarly, the defendant in *State v. Triplett* (1992) argued—unsuccessfully—that juror notes had distorted the evidence.) In *United States v. Davis* (1900), the court considered whether it was appropriate for a judge, upon noticing that two jurors had occasionally taken notes, to direct them to discontinue and turn their notes over to the marshal. In ruling that note taking was improper, the appeals court stated, "Without corrupt purpose, his notes may be inaccurate, or meager or careless, and loosely deficient, partial, and altogether incomplete" (p. 839). This critique suggests that juror note taking will interfere with the accurate transmission of information from the courtroom to the deliberation room.

In both of Heuer and Penrod's studies, they concluded that notes tended to be a fair and accurate record of the trial proceedings. With respect to the most important trial outcome, Heuer and Penrod found no evidence that verdicts were affected by note taking. Heuer and Penrod also asked jurors whether their notes tended to be valuable records of the trial or mostly doodles, and they reported that they were considerably more likely to be accurate records. More impressive, perhaps, are the comments from one of the participating judges in this experiment, who was initially quite skeptical about jurors' note-taking abilities. Upon reviewing the notes from eight trials, his report included the following comments: "Approximately one-third of all the jurors . . . took surprisingly detailed notes. The notes were so clearly written and organized that I had little trouble determining what went on in the case. . . . Many of the notes were extremely articulate and well organized. I concluded that jurors have far better note-taking capacity than I had realized" (Barland, 1985, p. 1).

Is Note Taking Distracting?   In *Fischer v. Fischer* (1966), the court concluded that jurors should not be allowed to take notes because poor note takers are likely to be distracted. A similar argument was made more recently in *Matthews v. Commonwealth Edison Co.* (1995): "[U]nless a case is complex note taking by jurors is unwarranted and may even interfere with the jurors' ability to observe the witness and attend the testimony" (p. 7). Hastie (1983) similarly suggested that note takers might be distracted from assessing witness credibility. Flango (1980) suggests that note takers may distract non-note-takers or themselves by doodling. McLaughlin (1982) suggests that jurors, while making notes on a trivial point, will miss important evidence. The majority in *Thornton v. Weaber* (1955, and Flango, 1980) similarly suggested that note takers could not keep pace with the trial and would therefore miss important points. Jurors in note-taking trials in both Heuer and Penrod experiments overwhelmingly reported that the trial did not proceed too quickly for them to keep pace with the proceedings; 85% of the jurors in the Wisconsin study, and 87% of the jurors in the national study said this was not a problem. In both studies, note takers and non-note-takers in note-taking trials agreed that they were not distracted by note takers. In the Wisconsin study, the judges and attorneys said they neither expected nor found note taking to be distracting.

Do Note Takers Have an Undue Influence over Non-Note-Takers?   Several decisions have expressed concern that more prolific note takers might have inappropriate influence on other jurors. The court in *Fischer v. Fischer* (1966) concluded that jurors should not be allowed to take notes because skilled note takers will gain a marked influential advantage over other jurors. In *Thornton v. Weaber* (1955), the court cleverly speculated that note takers might have more influence because they might seem more alert and informed than non-note-takers. In *United States v. Davis* (1900), the court speculated that a juror who can refer to notes could have undue influence in conflicts of memory.

In both of Heuer and Penrod's studies, note takers and non-note-takers agreed that note takers should not and did not have an advantage over non-note-takers during deliberations. In addition, in the Wisconsin experiment, Heuer and Penrod found no evidence that better-educated jurors participated more in the jury's deliberations when aided by trial notes.

Do Juror Notes Favor One Side or the Other?   Flango (1980) suggested that note taking might favor the prosecution or plaintiff if jurors take notes early in the trial but lose their enthusiasm and take fewer notes later in the trial. Neither of the Heuer and Penrod studies found jurors to be more diligent note takers during earlier phases of a trial. In the Wisconsin study, jurors in note-taking trials did report slightly less favorable impressions of the defense attorney, but the effect was small and the pattern was not reproduced in the national study. As noted earlier, the national study also revealed no effect of note taking on verdicts. Overall, the clear conclusion is that note taking does not favor either the prosecution or the defense.

Does Juror Note Taking Consume Too Much Trial Time?   Several appellate decisions have indicated that note taking is acceptable only if it does not require substantial court time (e.g., *Tift v. Towns*, 1879; *Cahill v. Baltimore*, 1916). Hastie (1983) speculated that note taking might lengthen jury deliberations as jurors try to resolve discrepancies in their notes. However, Hastie's study came to the same conclusion as Heuer and Penrod's: in neither study was deliberation time affected by juror note taking. In the Wisconsin study, the jurors in note-taking trials did not report any increase in the difficulty of agreeing on the meaning of the law or on the application of the judge's instructions to trial facts or in acrimonious debate. The jurors in the national study indicated that very little deliberation time was devoted to discussions of notes (the median estimate was 1%; the mode was 0%).

General Conclusions about Juror Notes

- Juror notes probably are a minor memory aid.
- Juror note taking does not increase juror satisfaction with the trial, the judge, or the verdict.
- Juror notes do not produce a distorted view of the case.
- Note takers can keep pace with the trial.
- Note-taking jurors do not distract other jurors.
- Note takers do not have an undue influence over non-note-takers.
- Juror note taking does not favor either the prosecution or the defense.
- Juror note taking does not consume too much time.

CONCLUSIONS FROM COURTROOM EXPERIMENTS

With the exception of the finding that juror questions promote juror understanding and alleviate their doubts about the trial evidence, and some evidence that notes can aid juror recall of trial evidence, the findings reveal relatively little support for the possible advantages of note taking and questions. However, the findings are also overwhelmingly unsupportive of claims about possible harmful consequences. In short, the results of the courtroom experiments suggest that the effects of these procedures are quite innocuous—which is not to say that they cannot pose problems in rare instances. Despite the weak support for juror questions and notes, these procedures deserve consideration as a way to assist jurors with their often complicated task.

Commentators, scholars, attorneys, and judges have long complained about jury performance. It is noteworthy that both criticism and jury reforms have been advanced despite the lack of relevant systematic data. This situation is beginning to change as studies such as those discussed in this chapter provide new insights into the strengths and weaknesses of jury decision making and allow us to identify procedural reforms and decision aids that will optimize jury performance.

NOTE

1. Throughout this chapter, the word "prosecutor" is used to refer to both the prosecuting and plaintiff's attorneys.

REFERENCES

Abraham, K. S., & Jeffries, J. C. (1989). Punitive damages and the rule of law: The role of defendant's wealth. *Journal of Legal Studies, 18,* 415–425.

Abramson, J. (1994). *We, the jury: The jury system and the ideal of democracy.* New York: Basic Books.

Adamo, K. R. (1996). Reforming jury practice in patent cases: Suggestions towards learning to love using an eighteenth century system while approaching the twenty-first century. *Journal of the Patent and Trademark Office Society, 78,* 345–358.

Adler, S. J. (1994). *The jury: Trial and error in the American courtroom.* New York: Times Books.

Alaska Stat. § 09.17.020 (1994).

American College of Trial Lawyers (ACTL). (1989). *Report on punitive damages of the committee on special problems in the administration of justice.*

Arlen, J. H. (1992). Should defendants' wealth matter? *Journal of Legal Studies, 21,* 413–429.

Barland, T. (1985, January 10). Letter addressed to the Executive Secretary of the Judicial Council of Wisconsin.

BMW of North America, Inc. v. Gore, 517 U.S. 559 (1996).

Broder, J. M. (1997, September 10). Stares of lawyerly disbelief at a huge civil award. *New York Times,* p. C1.

Browning-Ferris Ind. v. Kelco Disposal, Inc., 492 U.S. 257 (1989).

Burger, J. M. (1981). Motivational biases in the attribution of responsibility for an accident: A meta-analysis of the defensive attribution hypothesis. *Psychological Bulletin, 90,* 496–512.

Cahill v. Baltimore, 129 Md. 17, 98 A. 235 (1916).

Casper, J. D., Benedict, K., & Perry, J. L. (1989). Juror decision making, attitudes, and the hindsight bias. *Law and Human Behavior, 13,* 291–310.

Cather, C., Greene, E., & Durham, R. (1996). Plaintiff injury and defendant reprehensibility: Implications for compensatory and punitive damage awards. *Law and Human Behavior, 20,* 189–205.

Chapman, G. E., & Bornstein, B. H. (1996). The more you ask for, the more you get: Anchoring in personal injury verdicts. *Applied Cognitive Psychology, 10,* 519–540.

Chicago Hanson Cab Co. v. Havelick, 131 Ill. 179, 22 N.E. 797 (1869).

Clermont, K. M., & Eisenberg, T. (1992). Trial by jury or judge: Transcending empiricism. *Cornell Law Review, 77*, 1124–1177.

Cohee v. State, 942 P.2d 211 (Okla. 1997).

Connecticut General Statutes Annotated, § 52-40 (West, 1987).

Conrad, A. F., & Bernstein, H. (1964). *Automobile accident costs and payments: Studies in the economics of injury reparations.* Ann Arbor: University of Michigan Press.

Commonwealth v. Urena, 417 Mass. 692, 632 N.E.2d 1200 (1994).

Crum v. State, W.L. 13162, (Tex. App. Hous. (14 Dist.) 1997).

Daniels, S. (1989). The question of jury competence and the politics of civil justice reform: Symbols, rhetoric, and agenda-building. *Law & Contemporary Problems, 52*, 269–298.

Daniels, S., & Martin, J. (1990). Myth and reality in punitive damages. *Minnesota Law Review, 75*, 1–64.

Dann, B. M. (1996). Free the jury. *Litigation, 23*, 5–6, 64–66.

Davis, J. H., Au, W. T., Hulbert, L., Chen, X., & Zarnoth, P. (1997). Effects of group size and procedural influence on consensual judgments of quantity: The example of damage awards and mock civil juries. *Journal of Personality and Social Psychology, 73*, 703–718.

Day v. Kilgore, 444 S.E.2d 515 (1994).

DeBenedetto v. Goodyear, 754 F.2d 512, 80 A.L.R. Fed. 879 (1985).

Densen v. Stanley, 17 Ala. App. 198, 84 So. 770 (1919).

Ellsworth, P. C. (1993). Some steps between attitudes and verdicts. In R. Hastie (Ed.), *Inside the juror: The psychology of juror decision making* (pp. 42–64). Cambridge, England: Cambridge University Press.

Fischer v. Fischer, 31 Wis. 2d 293, 142 N.W.2d 857 (1966).

Fiske, S. T., & Taylor, S. E. (1991). *Social cognition.* New York: McGraw-Hill.

Flango, V. E. (1980). Would jurors do a better job if they could take notes? *Judicature, 63*, 436–443.

Ford, M. C. (1986). The role of extralegal factors in jury verdicts. *Justice System Journal, 11*, 16–39.

Frank, J. (1949). *Courts on trial.* Princeton: Princeton University Press.

Galanter, M., & Luban, D. (1993). Poetic justice: Punitive damages and legal pluralism. *American University Law Review, 42*, 1393–1463.

Goodman, J., Greene, E., & Loftus, E. F. (1989). Runaway verdicts or reasoned determinations: Mock juror strategies in awarding damages. *Jurimetrics, 29*, 285–309.

Greene, E. (1989). On juries and damage awards: The process of decision making. *Law and Contemporary Problems, 52*, 225–246.

Greene, E., Goodman, J., & Loftus, E. F. (1991). Jurors' attitudes about civil litigation and the size of damage awards. *American University Law Review, 40*, 805–820.

Hans, V. P., & Ermann, M. D. (1989). Responses to corporate versus individual wrongdoing. *Law and Human Behavior, 13*, 151–166.

Hans, V. P., & Lofquist, W. S. (1992). Jurors' judgments of business liability in tort cases: Implications for the litigation explosion debate. *Law and Society Review, 26*, 85–115.

Hans, V. P., & Lofquist, W. S. (1994). Perceptions of civil justice: The litigation crisis attitudes of civil jurors. *Behavioral Science and the Law, 12*, 181–196.

Hastie, R. (1983). *Final report to the National Institute for Law Enforcement and Criminal Justice.* Unpublished manuscript, Northwestern University.

Heuer, L., & Penrod, S. D. (1988). Increasing jurors' participation in trials: A field experiment with jury note taking and question asking. *Law and Human Behavior, 12,* 409–430.

Heuer, L., & Penrod, S. D. (1989). Instructing jurors: A field experiment with written and preliminary instructions. *Law and Human Behavior, 13,* 231–261.

Heuer, L., & Penrod, S. D. (1994a). Juror note taking and question asking during trial: A national field experiment. *Law and Human Behavior, 18,* 121–150.

Heuer, L., & Penrod, S. D. (1994b). Trial complexity: A field investigation of its meaning and its effects. *Law and Human Behavior, 18,* 29–52.

Hinsz, V. B., & Indahl, K. E. (1995). Assimilation to anchors for damage awards in a mock civil trial. *Journal of Applied Social Psychology, 25,* 991–1026.

Honda Motor Co. v. Oberg, 512 U.S. 415 (1994).

Horowitz, I. A., & Bordens, K. S. (1990). An experimental investigation of procedural issues in complex tort trials. *Law and Human Behavior, 14,* 269–285.

Howe, E. S., & Loftus, T. C. (1992). Integration of intention and outcome information by students and circuit court judges: Design economy and individual differences. *Journal of Applied Social Psychology, 22,* 102–116.

Hudson v. Markum, 948 S.W.2d 1 (1997).

Hurd, S. N., & Zollers, F. E. (1994). State punitive damages statutes: A proposed alternative. *Journal of Legislation, 20,* 191–212.

Kalven, H. (1964). The dignity of the civil jury. *Virginia Law Review, 50,* 1055–1075.

Kalven, H., & Zeisel, H. (1966). *The American jury.* Boston: Little, Brown.

Kansas Statutes Annotated § 60-3701 (1994).

Karlovac, M., & Darley, J. M. (1988). Attribution of responsibility for accidents: A negligence law analogy. *Social Cognition, 6,* 287–318.

Kassin, S. M., & Wrightsman, L. S. (1983). The construction and validation of a juror bias scale. *Journal of Research in Personality, 17,* 423–442.

Kassin, S. M., & Wrightsman, L. S. (1988). *The American jury on trial: Psychological perspectives.* Bristol, PA: Hemisphere.

Kelso, J. C. (1996). Final report of the blue ribbon commission on jury system improvement. *Hastings Law Journal, 47,* 1433–1592.

King, E. M., & Smith, J. P. (1988). *Economic loss and compensation in aviation accidents.* Santa Monica, CA: RAND.

Koenig, T., & Rustad, M. (1993). The quiet revolution revisited: An empirical study of the impact of state tort reform of punitive damages in products liability. *Justice System Journal, 16,* 21–44.

Kozinski, A. (1995, January 19). The case of punitive damages v. Democracy. *The Wall Street Journal,* p. A19.

Krause v. State, 132 P.2d 179 (1942).

Landes, W. M., & Posner, R. A. (1986, September/October). New light on punitive damages. *Regulation, 10,* 33–36, 54.

Landsman, S., & Rakos, R. F. (1994). A preliminary inquiry into the effects of potentially biasing information on judges and jurors in civil litigation. *Behavioral Science and the Law, 12,* 113–126.

Larsen, S. (1996). Taking and use of trial notes by jury. *American Law Reports, 36,* 1–254.

Lawson v. State, 664 N.E.2d 773 (1996).

Louisville Bridge & Terminal Co. v. Brown, 211 Ky. 176, 277 S.W. 320 (1925).

Litigation Sciences. (1993). Psychological characteristics of punitive damage jurors. In *Jury Research* at 59. (PLI Corp. Law and Prac. Course Handbook Series No. 833) Practising Law Institute.

Marbley v. State, 461 N.E.2d 110 (1984).

MacCoun, R. J. (1993a). Inside the black box: What empirical research tells us about decision making by civil juries. In R. E. Litan (Ed.), *Verdict: Assessing the civil jury system* (p. 137). Washington, DC: Brookings Institution.

MacCoun, R. J. (1993b). *Is there a "deep-pocket" bias in the tort system?: The concern over biases against deep-pocket defendants* (Issue paper). Santa Monica, CA: RAND: Institute for Civil Justice.

MacCoun, R. J. (1996). Differential treatment of corporate defendants by juries: An examination of the "deep-pockets" hypothesis. *Law and Society Review, 30,* 121–161.

Maggart v. Bell, 116 Cal. App. 306, 2 P.2d 516 (1931).

Matthews v. Commonwealth Edison Co., W.L. 478820 (1995).

McLaughlin, M. A. (1982). Questions to witnesses and note taking by the jury as aids in understanding complex litigation. *New England Law Review, 18,* 687–713.

Mifflin, L. (1997, August 30). Judge pares $5.5 million award to grocery chain for ABC report. *New York Times,* p. A1.

Model Punitive Damages Act (1996).

Moran, G., Cutler, B. L., & De Lisa, A. (1994). Attitudes toward tort reform, scientific jury selection, and juror bias: Verdict inclination in criminal and civil trials. *Law and Psychology Review, 18,* 309–328.

Morrison v. State, 845 S.W.2d 882 (Tex. 1992).

O'Connor, S. D. (1997). Juries: They may be broken, but we can fix them. *Federal Lawyer, 44,* 20–25.

Oberg v. Honda Motor Co., 320 Or. 544, 888 P.2d 8 (1995).

Owen, D. G. (1994). A punitive damages overview: Functions, problems and reform. *Villanova Law Review, 39,* 363–413.

Pacific Mutual Life Ins. Co. v. Haslip, 498 U.S. 1306 (1991).

Penrod, S., Linz, D., & Rios, P. A. (1984). *Allowing jurors to ask questions in the courtroom: A field experiment.* Unpublished manuscript, University of Wisconsin–Madison.

Peterson, M., Sarma, S., & Shanley, M. (1987). *Punitive damages: Empirical findings.* Santa Monica, CA: RAND: The Institute for Civil Justice.

Peterson, M. A. (1984). *Compensation of injuries: Civil jury verdicts in Cook county.* Santa Monica, CA: RAND: The Institute for Civil Justice.

Posner, R. A. (1995, March 1). Juries on trial. *Commentary, 99,* 49.

Prosser, W. L., & Keeton, P. (1984). *Prosser and Keeton of the law of torts* (5th ed.). St. Paul, MN: West.

Purver, J. M. (1970). Propriety of jurors asking questions in open court during course of trial. *American Law Reports, 3rd Series, 31,* 872–892.

Quayle, D. (1992). Civil justice reform. *American University Law Review, 41,* 559–569.

Ratton v. Busby, 230 Ark. 667, 326 S.W.2d 889 (1959).

Reece v. Simpson, 437 So.2d 68 (1983).

Rosenhan, D. L., Eisner, S. L., & Robinson, R. J. (1994). Note taking can aid juror recall. *Law and Human Behavior, 18,* 53–61.

Rustad, M. (1991). *Demystifying punitive damages in products liability cases: A survey of a quarter century of trial verdicts.* Papers of the Roscoe Pound Found.

Rustad, M. (1992). In defense of punitive damages in products liability: Testing tort anecdotes with empirical data. *Iowa Law Review, 78,* 1–88.

Rustad, M., & Koenig, T. (1993a). The historical continuity of punitive damage awards: Reforming the tort reformers. *American University Law Review, 42,* 1269–1333.

Rustad, M., & Koenig, T. (1993b). The Supreme Court and junk social science: Selective distortion in amicus briefs. *North Carolina Law Review, 72,* 91–162.

Saks, M. J. (1992). Do we really know anything about the behavior of the tort litigation system—And why not? *University of Pennsylvania Law Review, 140,* 1147–1289.

Sand, L. B., & Reiss, S. A. (1985). A report on seven experiments conducted by district court judges in the second circuit. *New York University Law Review, 60,* 423–497.

Schaefer v. St. Louis & Suburban R. Co., 128 Mo. 64, 30 S.W. 331 (1895).

Scully, J. (1996). Markman and Hilton Davis, the Federal circuit strikes an awkward balance: The roles of the judge and jury in patent infringement suits. *Hastings Communications and Entertainment Law Journal, 18,* 631–655.

Sharkey, L. M. (1996). Judge or jury: Who should assess punitive damages? *University of Cincinnati Law Review, 64,* 1089–1139.

Shaver, K. G. (1970). Defensive attribution: Effects of severity and relevance on the responsibility assigned for an accident. *Journal of Personality and Social Psychology, 14,* 101–113.

Simpson, J. T. (1996). Discovery of net worth in bifurcated punitive damages cases: A suggested approach after Transportation Insurance Co. v. Moriel. *Southern Texas Law Review, 37,* 193–229.

Sligar v. Bartlett, 916 P.2d 1383 (1996).

South Carolina Code Annotated. § 15-33-135 (Law Co-op. 1993).

State v. Alexander, 1997 W.L. 116903 (1997).

State v. Graves, 274 Mont. 264, 907 P.2d 963 (1995).

State v. Greer, 1997 W.L. 728112 (1997).

State v. Howard, 320 N.C. 718, 360 S.E.2d 790, 794 (1987).

State v. Kendall, 143 N.C. 659, 57 S.E. 340 (1907).

State v. Sickles, 220 Mo. App. 290, 286 S.W. 432 (1926).

State v. Triplett, 421 S.E.2d 511 (1992).

State v. Trujillo, 869 S.W.2d 844 (1994).

Sylvester, J. R. (1990). Your Honor, may I ask a question?: The inherent dangers of allowing jurors to question witnesses. *7 Cooley Law Review, 213,* 217–221.

Tackett, M. (1996, April 20). Doles fires a salvo at Clinton judges. *Chicago Tribune,* p. 1.

Taragin, M. I., Willett, L. R., Wilczek, A. P., Trout, R., & Carson, J. L. (1992). The influence of standard of care and severity of injury on the resolution of medical malpractice claims. *Annals of Internal Medicine, 117,* 780–784.

Thomas, E. A. C., & Parpal, M. (1987). Liability as a function of plaintiff and defendant fault. *Journal of Personality and Social Psychology, 53,* 843–857.

Thornton v. Weaber, 380 Pa. 590, 112 A.2d 344 (1955).

Tift v. Towns, 63 Ga. 237 (1879).

Tripoli, L. (1997). Precipice of change . . . Professional groups urge striking changes in trial. *Inside Litigation, 3,* 1–6.

TXO Production Corp. v. Alliance Resources Corp., 509 U.S. 443 (1993).

United States General Accounting Office. (1989). *Product liability: Verdicts and case resolution in five states.* Washington, DC: Author.

United States v. Ajmal, 67 F.3d 12 (2d Cir. 1995).

United States v. Bush, 47 F.3d 511 (1995).

United States v. Carlisi, D.C. N.Y., 32 F. Supp. 479 (1940).

United States v. Callahan, 588 F.2d 1078 (1979).

United States v. Darden, 70 F.3d 1507 (8th Cir. 1995).

United States v. Davis, C.C. Tenn., 103 F. 457, *aff'd* C.A.6, 107 F. 753 (1900).

United States v. Douglas, 81 F.3d 324 (1996).

United States v. Feinberg, 89 F.3d 333 (1996).

United States v. Johnson, 892 F.2d 707 (1989).

United States v. Polowichak, 783 F.2d 410 (1986).

United States v. Stierwalt, 16 F.3d 282 (1994).

United States v. Thompson, 76 F.3d 442 (1996).

Vidmar, N. (1995). *Medical malpractice and the American jury: Confronting the myths about jury incompetence, deep pockets, and outrageous damage awards.* Ann Arbor: University of Michigan Press.

Walster, E. (1966). Assignment of responsibility for an accident. *Journal of Personality and Social Psychology, 3,* 73–79.

Watkins v. State, 216 Tenn. 545, 393 S.W.2d 141 (1965).

Weinstein, J. B. (1991). *Scientific evidence in complex litigation.* ALI-ABA Course—C607 ALI-ABA 709.

White v. Little, 131 Okla. 3123, 268 P. 221 (1928).

Williams v. Commonwealth, 484 S.E.2d 153 (1997).

Wissler, R. L., Evans, D. L., Hart, A. J., Morry, M. M., & Saks, M. J. (1997). Explaining "pain and suffering" awards: The role of injury characteristics and fault attributions. *Law and Human Behavior, 21,* 181–207.

Wolff, M. A. (1990). Juror questions a survey of theory and use. *Missouri Law Review, 55,* 817–873.

CHAPTER 11

Recommending Probation and Parole

ALFRED B. HEILBRUN

PSYCHOLOGISTS AND other mental health professionals are asked to play a role at every stage of the criminal justice system as the problems of dealing effectively with increasing crime and protection of an alarmed citizenry call out for solution. Police seek guidance on the behavioral attributes of unknown perpetrators to assist in their capture. The courts enlist professional input in determining culpability or readiness to stand trial in those accused of a crime. Prisons make use of professional experts (or their wares) in planning the conditions of incarceration that would best satisfy the requirements of court mandate, security, and rehabilitation of the prisoner.

The focus in this chapter is on the role of the mental health professional in general and the psychologist in particular during the final stage of our system of justice—the decision concerning whether convicted offenders shall be returned to society under some provisional status or be made to serve or continue their sentences in prison. This decision could allow the lawbreaker to avoid a prison sentence altogether (probation) or could determine a fractional amount of the court sentence that a criminal is required to spend in prison (parole). My emphasis will be on the practitioner's role in determining parole and probation status and the factors governing professional intervention. Accordingly, other important considerations relating to history and legal development of these conditional processes as well as broader contemporary issues will be ignored; the reader interested in a more general background discussion of parole and probation is referred to Vetter (1987).

The choice of probation rather than a prison term is most frequently based on factors distinguishing the novice offender who presents less danger to the community from the more dangerous criminal who often demonstrates a history of prior crimes. Misdemeanors rather than felonies, first-offense status, and the relative youthfulness of the offender argue for more lenient assignment to

303

probation. Puzzling exceptions to these determinants of choice are to be found if you examine criminal histories in sufficient number, but the philosophy of adjudication seems generally clear: Identify less serious offenders who should be more readily deterred from future criminality; do not commit them to a prison, where they could be unfavorably influenced by contact with more hardened inmates, but keep them under supervision in the community. In addition, there is also the economic factor to consider. The cost to society of incarcerating a criminal is many times that required to maintain someone on probation.

It is at this stage of choosing between prison and probation or of deciding the timing and conditions of parole that psychologists can play their most responsible role. I am not arguing that recommendations influencing probation and parole are necessarily any more important in the individual case than the psychologist's contributions to police work, courtroom proceedings, or institutional management of prisoners. However, there is a higher proportion of cases at the final stage of the criminal justice process in which assistance from a professional could serve a vital purpose. Decisions concerning probation and parole are required for most convicted criminals, so it is not only the occasional perplexing case that may call for professional input. Dealing with the sheer volume of choices to be made presents special problems as well. Accordingly, professionals have the opportunity to contribute to probation/parole decisions in two ways. They must be prepared to provide on request a detailed assessment for the extraordinary case, the clinical consultant role. At the same time, they should be able to devise screening procedures whereby all criminals awaiting a decision can be evaluated in an economic, uncomplicated way without reliance on further outside consultation.

That the psychologist can serve as a consultant in the individual parole or probation case and as a specialist in devising systems of outcome prediction having general applicability to criminal populations is hardly a revelation. What is less obvious is that psychologists have a unique opportunity to expand their assistance to responsible officials by integrating these contributions. Integration could provide a widely applicable psychological basis for assisting a definitive decision regarding probation or parole on the one hand, and alerting officials to the need for further individual consultation on the other.

The central concern of this chapter is whether a workable system of risk assessment and outcome prediction can be proposed, given today's understanding of criminal behavior and technology of psychological measurement. Before addressing this question, however, there are several preliminary considerations that require attention. First, several unresolved issues concerning the prediction of probation and parole outcome will be reviewed. Next, an overview of studies relating to prediction of performance on parole and probation may testify to our progress in surmounting these problems. Then we shall consider some research findings from my own laboratory bearing upon criminal dangerousness as a basis for predicting future lawlessness, especially violent behavior. Finally, I will return to the central concern of this chapter by proposing a system of risk assessment and recommendation for both parole and probation based on the dangerousness variable. The proposed system will be geared to balance the practical requirements of volume facing a judge or parole board and the need to identify specific cases in which decision making would profit from more intensive professional assistance.

ISSUES IN RISK ASSESSMENT

The value of recommendations by mental health professionals regarding probation or parole following criminal conviction hinges primarily upon the ability to make valid predictions regarding future antisocial conduct of the offender. The challenge, then, seems straightforward enough. Measurement technology must be improved and individual professional skills sharpened until a rigorous standard of accuracy is achieved. Despite the obvious nature and critical importance of the challenge, a major breakthrough is not evident in the ability to identify those who will engage in future misconduct, especially violence.

This section on issues relating to risk assessment will do what comes easiest: elaborate the problems that prevent us from doing what we are trained to do as effectively as we would like. However, this litany of gloom will be accompanied by suggestions concerning how the problems can be confronted or at least sidestepped to improve our predictions regarding parole and probation outcome. From this point on, the parole decision will be emphasized as the judgment point at which professional input may be utilized, as my own work and research experience resides entirely in that domain.

POLITICAL AND PHILOSOPHICAL ISSUES IN RISK ASSESSMENT

As previous discussions of sentencing (Melton, Petrila, Poythress, & Slobogin, 1987) and probation and parole (Vetter, 1987) have made clear, people are sent to prison with different goals and differing philosophies of sentencing and release in mind. There are four major views regarding incarceration. Because these are not mutually exclusive and may not be articulated in any given case, it is not always clear what should be accomplished by incarcerating a given prisoner or what the parameters of release should be. Furthermore, as the winds of social concern and responsive political posturing shift, the priorities for the varying goals of imprisonment may change. The importance associated with predicting criminal misconduct through risk assessment varies considerably depending on which philosophy of incarceration is invoked.

Most reasons for sending offenders to prison favor requiring them to serve their entire sentence, therefore arguing against parole and obviating the need for assessment of future risk. Determinant sentencing that necessitated spending the full prison sentence accorded for a particular crime would best serve the purpose of *deterrence*. Whatever preventive effects criminal penalties have on potential antisocial conduct in others would be greater if it were known that time in prison would not be attenuated by parole.

Criminals are also sent to prison as a *punishment* for their offenses. The public's sense of fairness, justice, and retribution calls for offenders to suffer commensurate with the seriousness of their crimes. If punishment is given priority and assuming that a just sentence has been handed down, there seems to be no rationale for subsequently paroling the criminal, thereby decreasing severity.

Criminals can be sent to prison as a form of *isolation* so that the public is protected for a period of time from the risk of further harm by a proven criminal. If protection from the specific person who has demonstrated dangerous behavior is warranted, certainly the longer this safeguard is in place the better.

Given these philosophies of incarceration favoring prisoners' serving their full sentences, it is little wonder that the parole system is currently under fire in many states. The only important goal for imprisonment that embraces a system of parole is *rehabilitation* of the criminal that will preclude further crime. On the assumption that there is something wrong and modifiable in the person who commits a crime, the philosophy of rehabilitation invites indeterminate sentencing that makes length of imprisonment contingent in some measure upon how far modification has progressed. Risk assessment assumes paramount importance as a way of determining whether and when rehabilitative efforts have rendered the prisoner safe for a return to society. Parole is considered with regard to readiness; deterrence, protection by isolation, and deserved punishment tend to be ignored.

Perhaps one of the reasons that parole has survived the arguments against it is that the value of parole has little to do with what people feel incarceration is supposed to accomplish. For one thing, the economic burden of requiring all prisoners to serve their full sentences would be staggering. For another, the prospect of gaining earlier release contributes to the manageability of prisoners and to safety of prison personnel, who must deal with the burgeoning numbers of proven antisocial men and women. In addition, though prisoner constraint and cooperation may be thinly veiled attempts to impress prison and parole officials and to shorten time in prison, sometimes constructive behavior, no matter what its motivation, contributes in some subtle way to the rehabilitation of antisocial criminals.

THE ISSUE OF PREDICTORS IN RISK ASSESSMENT

The extent to which future misconduct can be predicted is contingent upon what is available in the way of predictive constructs, how well these constructs submit to reliable measurement, and the realistic restrictions on assessment procedures in an overtaxed criminal justice system. One important controversy regarding predictive variables concerns whether future dangerous behavior should be predicted in light of the characteristics of the individual, the future situations in which the individual will be found, or some combination of person and situation. The limited prediction of violence reported in the literature, especially the emphasis on individual personality to the exclusion of situational variables, was sharply criticized a generation ago by several influential psychologists (Cocozza & Steadman, 1976; Monahan, 1981; Shah, 1978). Some complex interaction of person and situation was deemed to be more promising.

Without being able to specify the relative importance of the individual's personality makeup or environmental determination from one case of criminal conduct to the next, the controversy may come down to sheer practicality. What is available that can serve as the basis for prediction? Current individual characteristics present themselves for assessment at the time predictions are to be made; future situational determinants are at best a matter of speculation. The risk assessor may be able to establish general factors in the social and physical environment that are likely to pertain for a given individual: racial affiliation, socioeconomic status, rural versus urban living, viable social relationships. However, the specific situations that may arise to interact with personality and invite criminal behavior are far less certain than these general factors.

We know that some prediction is possible from current known qualities of the individual. It must be demonstrated that by adding speculation about future situations, accuracy is going to improve. For those of us who expressed confidence in prediction of violence from individual characteristics, it is encouraging to note that the reservations of the 1970s and 1980s concerning this unilateral emphasis seem to have abated somewhat as mental health status (Monahan, 1992) and a broader assortment of personality and psychiatric variables (Monahan & Steadman, 1994) have been identified as predictors.

Another controversy that has waged since Meehl's (1954) influential treatise on clinical and statistical prediction is whether prediction based on clinical integration of information or on actuarial statements represents a more valid procedure. In the current context, the question becomes whether risk assessment based on expert informed opinion regarding future misconduct on parole is more profitable in terms of hits and misses than normative tables or more sophisticated mechanical procedures that reflect degree of risk. The verdict in 1954 favored the use of actuarial prediction, and 40 more years of research have not altered that conclusion (Grove & Meehl, 1996). I take the position that a system of assessment involving both strategies of prediction may be necessary when parole decisions must be reached in large numbers. Use tables to assist in decisions where they are most powerful, toward their extremes; very high scores and very low scores lend themselves to more clear-cut predictions, especially if you are considering dichotomous outcomes such as presence or absence of future violence. Use clinical consultation in those cases when the tables are more equivocal, in the middle range where problems of discrimination around the midpoint are encountered. Hopefully, the more intensive but time-consuming assessment can disclose unique aspects of risk and answer more refined questions that will prove valuable when actuarial tables falter.

Finally, there is the issue concerning what type of predictive factors are more valuable in anticipating future criminality. Correlates of the behavior to be predicted are often preferred, perhaps because they are more accessible, rather than factors that are arguably more dynamically integral to criminal behavior. Let us say that future violence is the target of prediction. Several demographic variables have been linked to violent criminality: age, gender, social-economic status (Swanson, Holzer, Ganju, & Jono, 1990), to mention only a few. Although these can be used to predict future violence, it would be difficult to contend that being young, poor, or male make you act violently. Rather, there are characteristics associated with being young (impulsiveness), poor (diminished value structure), or male (physical aggressiveness) that may directly mediate violent conduct. There is likely some advantage in identifying factors that are more intrinsic to the dynamics of violent criminality as far as power of prediction goes. If, for example, it is the greater likelihood of impulsive behavior in the young that qualifies age as a predictor of violence, it would make more sense to measure impulsiveness directly and introduce it as the predictor. Doing so would allow individual differences in impulsivity, even among the young, to be minimized as a source of predictive error.

There is another advantage to selecting dynamic variables for prediction rather than statistical correlates, often demographic in nature. Correlates of violence such as gender and social status tend to be categorical and static, and age changes slowly. Consequently, there is limited opportunity to measure change over time. Individual traits that are dynamically linked to violence itself are more likely to reflect changes, should they occur, and allow for a better reading on current risk status.

THE ISSUE OF BASE RATE IN PREDICTION

Another legacy from Meehl's (Meehl & Rosen, 1955) early contributions to understanding psychological prediction is the emphasis on base rate of the event to be predicted. Although crime in general and violent crime in particular are popularly depicted in the American media as approaching epidemic proportions, they still represent exceptional events rather than the rule. Most people are not convicted of crimes in their lifetimes, and even fewer prove to be violent in a criminal sense. That judicially processed crimes, no matter how much attention they receive, are low-base-rate (infrequent) events ties in with our problems in assessing risk. For example, the risk of violent criminality for an individual in the short term, such as during parole, is associated with a base rate for violence of only about 12%. At least, this is so in the parole samples I have drawn in the state of Georgia (A. Heilbrun, 1996).

The prediction problem posed by low (or high) base rates is that the optimal rate for predicting an event is 50% (Meehl & Rosen, 1955). As the base rate drops for the event being predicted, errors of overprediction (false positives) become a serious matter: far too many are considered serious risks for violence but fail to behave violently. In the case of violence on parole, assuming no future violence for anyone being released becomes a compelling alternative to overpredicting the low-base-rate event in which many prisoners are inaccurately projected as posing such a danger. At least you would be right in a high percentage of the cases if you always predicted no violence, although abandoning the risk of future violence as a consideration in judging suitability for parole would probably attract criticism concerning insensitivity to public safety.

Some of the resolutions to the low-base-rate problem in prediction qualify as obvious but unrealistic. One would be to choose populations for our predictions that have higher base rates for the particular event in question. Using violence as our example, this would argue for limiting prediction to people with an established history of aggressive crime. As I have found, however, even if you restrict yourself to criminals with a record of past violence, the base rate for violence on parole does not reach a substantial figure anywhere close to the optimal 50% figure. The second possibility is to devise or identify more powerful predictors of violence that will work despite a low base rate. This, of course, is what we have been trying to do—without remarkable success.

There are other resolutions to the base-rate problem that may be less obvious and deserve attention. One represents a merger of the two discussed previously: develop a more powerful extreme in generating predictions by employing several variables in combination or for successive screening so that future violence is being forecast for only that fraction of a population about whom we can be more certain. Kozol, Boucher, and Garofalo (1972) reported some success using this strategy, for example, when they designated only 11% of their sex offenders as dangerous and found that 35% of subsequent offenses were committed by this group. One problem is immediately evident in this approach. The small percentage of sex offenders identified as dangerous and for whom recidivism would be predicted raises a concern about how much we can limit our predictions as a way of improving the hit-miss ratio for a low-base-rate event.

It is also possible to improve prediction accuracy for a low-base-rate criminal event by extending the period of time we track the individuals that have been assessed. Studies of parole and probation, mine included, have been guilty of examining the conduct of criminals released from prison or retained on probation in the community for a relatively short period of time. Although this may be convenient to the logistics of investigation, it results in a less accurate representation of parole or probation failure or success. Some have clearly succeeded, when success is understood as a discharge from conditional status; others have clearly failed when technical violation or criminal recidivism results in a return to prison. A third group, sometimes considered successful, may be continuing on parole or probation at the time of the study. This indeterminate group must inevitably include some who will ultimately succeed on parole and others who will fail. If everyone were tracked to a final determination, the base rate for parolee crime in general and violence in particular would increase and assessment of risk would be given a better chance at success.

OVERVIEW OF RESEARCH ON PAROLE
AND PROBATION PREDICTION

Given the problems that confront risk assessment and the effort to predict future misconduct on parole and probation, it may be of interest to examine the research literature to weigh our progress. A substantial number of studies conducted in the 1960s and 1970s (see below) were concerned with the nature of prior offenses and whether success or failure on parole could be predicted from past criminal behavior. The parole risk for the prisoner who had committed a nonviolent property offense versus those who had engaged in a violent crime against a person was a popular basis for comparison, actually dating back to much earlier investigations (Tibbitts, 1931–1932; Vold, 1931; Warner, 1923). The consensual finding identified violent prisoners as better parole prospects. That the more dangerous offender proved to be a safer risk attracted explanation in terms of the one-time-only situational nature of violent crimes like murder that left the criminal generally prepared to meet social expectations (Stanton, 1969). However, another view of this evidence (A. Heilbrun, 1978) explained the seeming advantage of violent criminals in terms of research methodology. The studies were not following the parolees for a sufficient period of time to gain a reliable picture of the relative parole risk of nonviolent and violent offenders. As examples, evidence of lower risk on parole for men convicted of violent rather than nonviolent crime was cited for tracking periods of 6 months (Gottfredson, Ballard, & O'Leary, 1966; A. Heilbrun, Knopf, & Bruner, 1976), 12 months (Fildes & Gottfredson, 1972; Gottfredson, Neithercutt, Nuffield, & O'Leary, 1973; Neithercutt, 1972; Wenk, Gottfredson, & Radwin, 1970), and 24 months (Babst & Mannering, 1965).

The importance of the tracking period in parole outcome studies of violent and nonviolent offenders was considered in the 1978 Heilbrun paper by selecting more than 1,500 male felons from the files of the Georgia Board of Pardons and Paroles. The selection was random except for the requirements that parole outcome had to be final—successful discharge or unsuccessful revocation and return to prison—and that a roughly equivalent number of violent and nonviolent cases would be selected for analysis. The differences in parole outcome between violent and nonviolent offenders disappeared once success or failure was clearly established in every case. The dangerousness of prior crime did not have a bearing on the person's parole prospects.

Loeber and Dishion (1983) completed an exhaustive review of studies concerning the prediction of male delinquency that had been reported during the same period of the 1960s and 1970s. Most relevant to the present discussion are the predictors of recidivism among delinquents, as probation decisions are likely to hinge upon whether offenders might recidivate if they remain free on probation rather than being incarcerated. The reviewers established a rank order for predicting recidivism among delinquents based on an index reflecting relative improvement over chance. The best five predictors in decreasing order of efficiency were (a) stealing, lying, or truancy; (b) child problem behavior; (c) criminality or antisocial behavior of family members; (d) prior delinquency; and (e) socioeconomic status. Recidivism was more likely, then, if the delinquent showed a history of problem behavior, broadly defined, or grew up in settings conducive to antisocial behavior. Translated into probation terms, greater risk would be inferred as problems and disruptive setting conditions reflect unfavorably upon the psychological assets of delinquents.

Melton et al. (1987, pp. 165–207) summarized a number of later studies reported in the 1970s and 1980s that clearly portray the problems of predicting dangerous behavior. They focused specifically on the prediction of violent criminality, emphasizing the problem of false-positive predictive errors (in which the risk of violence is thought to be great in those who do not behave violently following release from an institution). Studies reported gross overprediction of violence when parole cases were considered, when the criminally insane were tracked, or when sex criminals were the object of study.

I might add, as an aside, that too much emphasis can be placed on the overprediction of violence for criminals released from prison on parole as a type of miscalculation. The priority assigned to false-positive errors or false-negative errors should depend on the implications of being wrong. Overconcern regarding the risk of violence on the part of parole officials means that many prisoners would be unduly delayed in their release or, if released, would be placed under closer surveillance and stricter prohibitions than are necessary. On the other hand, false-negative errors, the failure to identify the person who demonstrates violence on parole as a serious risk, is an even worse problem from a community perspective. Both types of predictive errors have a cost and merit our concern; priority depends on whose rights are deemed to be paramount.

A review of more recent studies of probation and parole outcome offers a blend of "something old" and "something new." Statistical prediction again was found to be superior to clinical prediction in a study of recidivism on parole (Hassin, 1986), and past violence proved to be a fallible basis for predicting future conduct (Clannon & Jew, 1985), as was true in the earlier survey (A. Heilbrun, 1978). Evidence for the validity of several new sources of prediction in probation outcome was reported, including the Client Management Classification System (Harris, 1994), the Lifestyle Criminality Screening Form (Walters, Revella, & Baltrusaitus, 1994), the Level of Supervision Inventory (Andrews, Kiessling, Robinson, & Mickus, 1986), moral development theory (Van Voorhis, 1985) and social control theory (Lindquist, Smusz, & Doerner, 1985), the Manchester predictor (Wilkinson, 1994), a rating scale based on presentence investigation (Liberton, Silverman, & Blount, 1992), and the Case Classification System (Schauer, 1990).

Parole-outcome studies revealed a similar diversity in predictive measures that seemed promising: a family-problems index (Fendrick, 1991), a progress-assessment system (Shawver, Clanon, Kurdys, & Friedman, 1985), and Hare's Psychopathy Checklist (Hart, Kropp, & Hare, 1988; Serin, Peters, & Barbaree, 1990). It seems safe to conclude from these more recent studies of parole and probation risk assessment that there are many available approaches to predicting outcome, but none as yet offers a satisfactory solution to the problems of false-positive and false-negative errors.

CRIMINAL DANGEROUSNESS AS A PREDICTOR

My own efforts to develop a construct that could be used to improve the understanding and prediction of criminal behavior, especially violence, began with the description of a two-factor index of dangerousness (A. Heilbrun, 1979). I shall describe the origins of the construct and report evidence validating the construct and its measurements as succinctly as possible. A more extended discussion is available elsewhere (A. Heilbrun, 1996). Once this has been done, we can return to the business at hand in the next section as the criminal dangerousness construct is evaluated exclusively as a predictor of parole outcome and long-term criminal conduct.

I chose to adopt the more reactionary view in the 1970s that criminal dangerousness could be understood as an enduring characteristic of the individual rather than as a description of the criminal behavior restricted to a particular situation. The latter can be recognized as an extension of the interactional viewpoint that assigns considerable weight to situational demands in criminal conduct. In my view, the person brought the potential for dangerous conduct into any given situation and continued to harbor the same predisposition after the situation came to an end and before another one arose that could serve as a trigger. This represented an effort to conceptualize dangerousness in classical personality terms. In addition to proposing dangerousness as an enduring predisposition, I also departed from a unitary-trait or single-category approach to understanding and prediction of criminal activity. Two broad personality variables, encompassing social values on the one hand, and cognitive status on the other hand, were to serve as a basis for understanding dangerous criminal behavior but only as they interact with each other.

THE PROPOSED CONSTRUCT OF CRIMINAL DANGEROUSNESS

The original set of personality markers underlying dangerousness proposed in 1979 included psychopathic personality and cognitive competence. Antisociality, defined in terms of the relative absence of prosocial values and presence of antisocial values, subsequently replaced the psychopathy term. The failure to keep behavior within the moral and legal boundaries of society conveyed by antisociality was the critical feature in the original proposal, and psychopathy introduced too much surplus meaning into the dangerousness construct. Cognitive competence, a term borrowed from Mischel (1973), refers to the cognitive qualities that contribute to effective thinking (e.g., judgment, reasoning, planning) and otherwise reflect competent social transaction (e.g., extroversion, social insight). It was proposed that the individual who is highly antisocial and is limited in cognitive competence presents the most serious risk of harming victims through criminal activity in general and violence in particular. Thus, it is the collaboration of both antisociality and cognitive deficit that represents the upper extreme of criminal dangerousness and threatens greater harm to crime victims. If the individual is neither antisocial nor cognitively deficient, the risk of serious harm to victims should be low. Those who demonstrate one of the critical factors but not the other were assumed to fall in some intermediate position on the dangerousness dimension.

The rationale underlying the proposed interface between antisociality and cognitive limitation went like this: A person with an antisocial value system will lack a deterrent to misconduct that keeps most people out of serious conflict with the law. As antisociality increases, the risk that criminal conduct will occur goes up. Further, if the person lacks the cognitive qualities that go into effective thinking, the crimes that are committed will tend to be poorly planned and executed. The victims of these crimes will be put in greater jeopardy by unintentional and unnecessary confrontations that can turn property crimes into violence. Even if criminal-victim confrontation is part of an intended crime, the cognitive limitations of the dangerous offender make it more likely that the criminal transaction will escalate in violence. With diminished capabilities of the criminal come decisions that are impulsive, poorly reasoned, illogical, insightless, or otherwise unrealistic, and criminal situations that get out of hand.

In theory, there is no reason why this rationale cannot be reversed to anticipate the same possible endangerment of victims. Incompetent cognition could contribute to more frequent criminal acts, and antisociality of the criminal could put the victim of an ongoing crime at greater risk. It is probably the case that both antisociality and cognitive incompetence work in unison to increase the frequency of criminal activity and to enhance the risk of violence for the victims of these crimes. Dangerousness, then, was expected to predict both the general criminal bent of the individual and, at its extreme, the risk of serious violence to the victims of these crimes.

THE MEASUREMENT OF ANTISOCIALITY AND COGNITIVE COMPETENCE AND QUANTIFICATION OF THEIR INTERACTION

The measurement of antisociality and cognitive competence has represented a compromise between clear specification of variables under study and the pragmatics of studying large numbers of prisoners, which requires using what is available in the way of relevant information. Antisociality estimates were based on ratings of case history information for those criminals drawn from the parole board files. The diagnostic criteria for antisocial personality disorder (Feighner et al., 1972) were used to generate ratings in nine areas relevant to antisocial conduct and summarized in the criminal's social history. When the prisoners under investigation had been drawn from a pool of men referred for parole assessment, antisociality was gauged by personality scales: the Psychopathic Deviate (*Pd*) scale from the Minnesota Multiphasic Personality Inventory (MMPI) (Hathaway & McKinley, 1951) and the Socialization scale (*So*) from the California Psychological Inventory (CPI) (Gough, 1957). The scales were used in tandem (*Pd-So*) to bolster the power of measurement. Gauging by consistency of the evidence, it is clear that the indices based on ratings and on psychometric scales are interchangeable measures of antisocial personality.

Evidence of cognitive status was taken from the IQ score of the Culture Fair (Cattell & Cattell, 1958), used by the Georgia Department of Corrections to assess mental ability. An intelligence test as a measure of cognitive competence falls short of a battery of sophisticated procedures that could be developed to assess cognitive qualities such as judgment, reasoning, planning, social insight, and the like. However, a low IQ would certainly imply limitations in these higher-order mental processes, just as a high IQ would suggest more competent cognitive development.

As it was proposed that antisociality and cognitive deficiencies work interactively to determine risk for criminal activity in general and for violence in particular, a multiplicative index has been used to reflect their combined strength. The antisociality scores for a given sample of prisoners are transformed into standard *T* scores with a mean of 50 and a standard deviation of 10. Intelligence quotients are transformed in the same way, with lower IQs receiving higher standard scores. Transformed scores for each prisoner are multiplied so that 2500 represents the hypothetical average of the criminal dangerousness scores for any given sample; scores above that level signal a relatively higher risk of crime and violence, and scores below 2500 reflect lower risk. As scores become more extreme at the higher end of the dimension, both the severity of the crime at risk and its probability of occurrence are presumed to increase correspondingly. Conversely, decreasing scores on the lower end convey the risk of less serious crimes and lower probability of occurrence.

Validation of the Criminal Dangerousness Index

Before returning to the question of whether an index of dangerousness, conceived and quantified as described, can contribute to parole prediction, one more question concerning the variable should be answered. Does the evidence regarding how the dangerousness index relates to criminal behavior and violence support its validity?

Several approaches to validate the dangerousness index have been taken, with retrospective analysis of prior criminal activity being central. Relating dangerousness to past criminal convictions can tell us whether the severity of harm to the victim implied by a high dangerousness score corresponds to the harm actually confirmed in a prisoner's criminal history. To do this with any degree of precision, three assumptions were made in ordering types of crimes. First, aggressive crimes against people (violence) were accepted as more harmful than nonviolent crimes against property; this seems to be a matter of general agreement. The second assumption was that violent crimes themselves can be ordered in terms of the physical and psychological harm to the victim. The severity table used by the Georgia Board of Pardons and Paroles served as the arbiter of harm conveyed by types of criminal violence. Third, it was assumed that any one type of violent crime, whatever its place on the severity table, can be broken down into degrees of harm to the victim (and dangerousness of the criminal) by examining the circumstances of each offense.

Table 11.1 includes the average dangerousness scores for men at varying levels of crime severity, with each subsequent comparison intended as a more serious challenge to demonstrating index validity. The top rows report the dangerousness of men in the broadest categories of crime—those who have most recently been sent to prison for violent crimes as opposed to nonviolent offenders with no violent crimes in their history. Past violence was associated with significantly higher dangerousness scores, as would be expected. (Statistical significance here and in all other comparisons reported as showing a difference refer to at least the 5% level of confidence.)

Categorical comparisons restricted to violent offenders only are reported next in both an initial and replication sample. High-severity violence refers to the act of murder. Intermediate-severity violence includes crimes that involve intent and physical (including sexual) aggression toward the victim or the threat of such violence (e.g., rape, voluntary manslaughter, assault, robbery). Low-severity violence lacks intent (e.g., involuntary manslaughter, vehicular homicide) or represents more passive types of sex offenses (e.g., peeping Tom, exhibitionism, child molestation). Criminals examined in this way fell into predictable order of dangerousness as far as severity of violence is concerned, with the differences in both the initial and replication samples varying reliably. Separating violent offenders in this way also makes it clear

Table 11.1
Criminal Dangerousness of Categories and Types of Criminals
Varying in Level of Harm to the Victims

Category and/or Type of Crime	Mean Dangerousness Score
Violent (*N* = 504)	2543.89
Nonviolent (*N* = 101)	2327.29
Violence	
High severity (*N* = 77)	2660.99
Intermediate severity (*N* = 104)	2504.07
Low severity (*N* = 94)	2351.93
Violence (replication)	
High severity (*N* = 100)	2746.63
Intermediate severity (*N* = 301)	2528.93
Low severity (*N* = 103)	2327.29
Violent sex offenses only	
Rape (*N* = 77)	2844.93
Child molestation (*N* = 161)	2333.97
Incest (*N* = 47)	2377.57
Within specific violent crimes	
Heterosexual child molesters (*N* = 138)	2457.13
Homosexual child molesters (*N* = 23)	1945.04
More brutal rapists (*N* = 70)	2680.37
Less brutal rapists (*N* = 72)	2329.67
Death-penalty murderers (*N* = 109)	2658.50
Life-sentence murderers (*N* = 134)	2360.83

Source: Adapted from A. Heilbrun (1996).

why the comparison between violent and nonviolent criminals did not result in a more robust difference. Many men who are categorized as violent but whose crimes lack physical aggressiveness or intent do not register very high on the dangerousness dimension.

The next set of comparisons in Table 11.1 narrows the scope of within-violence analysis to sexual crimes alone and only those involving physical contact with the victim. This time, men who victimize women (rape) were compared with others who target children outside of their families (child molestation) or within the family (incest). The singular elevation in dangerousness of rapists and the significant, almost identical, drop in dangerousness when either type of offender against children is considered correspond to the more aggressive nature of rape and greater potential for serious harm to adult sex victims than to victimized children.

Finally, the most difficult discriminations attempted for the dangerousness index involve within-crime analyses in which men committing a specific violent act but doing so in a particularly aggressive or brutal fashion were compared with others convicted of the same crime but judged from the criminal circumstances to be less abusive in their conduct. Looking at the bottom set of comparisons in Table 11.1 involving discrimination within specific violent crimes, it can be seen that even a low-severity display of violence like child molestation can be broken down by dangerousness. Heterosexual offenders present a greater danger to their victims than the especially passive homosexual men who victimize boys. Rape as mid-severity violence, subdivided by ratings of brutality shown to their victims, also fell in line with prediction. Rapists rated as more brutal turned out to be more dangerous.

Discrimination at the high-severity end of violence is reported last. Murderers who were sentenced to be executed for their crimes, frequently because of the heinous nature of their acts and lack of mitigating circumstances, were compared to others who had been given a life sentence. The dangerousness score successfully distinguished between these two brands of murderers.

DANGEROUSNESS, LONG-TERM PREDICTION OF CRIME AND VIOLENCE, AND PREDICTION OF PAROLE OUTCOME

Now that the basic discrimination evidence based on criminal history has been shown to validate the dangerousness index, we can return to the issue of risk assessment for future events. The first data to be considered bear upon the long-range prediction of criminal conduct. This, along with evidence regarding parole prediction, will provide a more direct examination of the index as it would be used by the forensic professional—as a prospective risk-assessment tool.

A study reported by A. Heilbrun (1996) monitored the long-term criminal behavior of 248 prisoners after they were released from prison and following risk assessment. The data clearly showed that the dangerousness index was capable of distinguishing between better and poorer risks over the 3 to 21 years the men were tracked, although the ability to surpass base rates for failure (recidivism) and success (nonrecidivism) was contingent on considering only the extremes of the score distribution. The upper and lower quartiles of dangerousness scores proved to be effective ranges for predicting both recidivism and nonrecidivism. Although this was determined empirically, it is exactly what would be anticipated theoretically based on the specifications of the two-factor interactive model. Given uncorrelated scores, only about one prisoner out of four should show both attributes of dangerousness, high antisociality and low cognitive competence, using sample midpoints as cutting scores. The upper quartile of dangerousness scores mirrors this 25% figure. Similarly, only about one in four should combine both determinants of low risk, low antisociality and high cognitive competence. The lower dangerousness quartile would include those who combine both benign qualities.

The 248 men demonstrated a 62% base rate for criminal recidivism of any type following risk assessment and release from prison. Those in the highest quartile (HQ) of sample dangerousness scores recidivated in 83% of the cases, well above base rate. Lowest-quartile (LQ) prisoners were convicted of further crime 48% of the time, substantially below base rate. The high-intermediate quartile (HIQ) and low-intermediate quartile (LIQ) figures were similar to each other and both fell at or near base rate: 57% and 62% recidivists, respectively. Multiple recidivism, conviction for more than one crime following release from prison, was found in about 42% of the men who were followed. The HQ group included 57% multiple recidivists compared to only 26% of the LQ group. The intervening quartiles provided near base rate figures (38%–46%).

As far as benefiting society, the most important prediction concerns future conviction for a violent crime. Violence was demonstrated by 23% of the sample over the tracking period, with the following percentages within the four quartiles of criminal dangerousness scores: HQ = 44%, HIQ = 21%, LIQ = 16%, and LQ = 10%. The pattern of results, verified as significant by nonparametric statistics, remains the same whether we are considering criminal recidivism, multiple recidivism, or future violence. Men in the top quartile of scores, those who are clearly dangerous according to theory, are serious risks for crime in general or violence if followed long enough. Those in the lowest quartile are fairly safe bets when it comes to committing future crime and violence, as theory would require. Dangerousness scores falling between these extremes offer no improvement over base rate in assessing risk.

Demonstrating that the dangerousness index allows long-term prediction of future criminal recidivism in general, multiple recidivism, and violent crime when used at quartile extremes bodes well for prediction of shorter-term parole outcome. Three additional bodies of evidence (A. Heilbrun, 1996) bearing directly upon the effectiveness of the dangerousness index in parole risk assessment support this conclusion, although each study offers its own unique slant. One study examined parole performance for 313 male sex offenders. Like other samples to follow, four quartiles of dangerousness scores were formed and ability to predict parole failure by quartile status was determined. Failing parole was defined by a return to prison because of criminal recidivism or technical violation of conditions. The LQ group included only 9% who failed, well below the 23% base rate; the inclusion of 38% parole failures in the HQ group exceeded base rate. The 15% and 27% figures for LIQ and HIQ departed modestly from the overall parole failure rate. Variation among these failure frequencies was verified statistically.

The second sample is noteworthy, because it provides evidence on parole risk assessment in women prisoners, a less-studied group relative to their male counterparts. Any thought that women might be generally more docile as parole candidates, thus making prediction of parole failure more difficult, proved groundless. A 23% failure base rate in the sample of 98 women prisoners turned out to be identical to the figure obtained for the male sex offenders. Prediction from the dangerousness index was even more powerful for the women than for the men, with a 4% failure rate for LQ women and a 57% rate for HQ women. The intermediate quartiles included 16%–21% women who failed on parole. Differences among the quartile rates proved to be reliable.

The third sample of 200 male prisoners that was examined did not demonstrate an overall relationship between dangerousness and prediction of parole failure without further refinement, but these data provide a useful lesson regarding parole risk-assessment instruments. It is likely that prediction of parole failure ran into trouble in this analysis because of the relatively low base rate of 13% for the sample. When the same sample was considered for efficacy of predicting parole success (discharge) from the dangerousness score, a more favorable basis for prediction was revealed. Success had a 54% base rate, close to the optimal figure for prediction. (The two base rates do not sum to 100% because of the indeterminate cases that were included in the sample.) Given a more advantageous base rate, the dangerousness index proved to be a reliable predictor. LQ men succeeded in 67% of the cases, whereas HQ prisoners had only a 33% success rate. Success on parole for intermediate quartiles fell between 56% and 62%. The lesson here is that under certain circumstances, an instrument may be successful in predicting one type of parole outcome but not another.

As was noted earlier in the chapter, studies that evaluate parole risk-assessment instruments without following all subjects through to final determination of discharge or revocation are likely to include some who have avoided a return to prison up to a point in time but eventually will fail. Such studies may underestimate the power of a risk-assessment device by creating false-positive cases (i.e., those predicted to fail on parole but who do not) by ignoring signs that warn of eventual parole failure. This methodological limitation could have contributed to the results of the study reported in the previous paragraph, because about a third of the parolees were not followed to final determination.

The next question, of course, is whether poor parole adjustment that may put someone in jeopardy of revocation is itself predictable from the dangerousness index. To check this, raters who reviewed files to establish parole status across these outcome studies were asked to consider the parolees with yet indeterminate outcomes and to distinguish between those for whom no problems on parole were recorded and those for whom problems on parole were a matter of record. When 28 troubled parolees were collected from the three samples, they proved significantly more dangerous ($M = 2700.68$) than 112 others who remained on parole without any problems being cited ($M = 2330.51$). Accordingly, the dangerousness index is not only capable of predicting clear-cut extremes in parole outcome, success versus failure, but shows promise of anticipating more subtle variations in parole adjustment.

A COMPREHENSIVE PROGRAM FOR ASSESSING RISK AND COUNTERACTION

Having attempted to make the case for criminal dangerousness as an individual-difference personality construct and a two-factor index as a measure, I use this final section to recommend how the index might be introduced into a broad program of parole risk assessment. Any risk-assessment instrument could be substituted for the index of dangerousness in this proposed plan as long as it demonstrated (a) the same psychometric properties, especially prediction efficacy that exceeds base rate at both ends of the score dimension, and (b) reasonable logistics that do not exceed the resources of space, time, and personnel that would be expected within the criminal justice system.

PRELIMINARY RISK ASSESSMENT

There is considerable value in initiating the assessment of dangerousness as soon as the criminal enters prison. One reason is that highly dangerous prisoners, as defined by the index, tend to accommodate poorly to prison regulations, and those who are at the low-dangerousness end of the dimension demonstrate a record of prison conduct relatively free of disciplinary problems (Heilbrun & Heilbrun, 1985). Establishing the risk of prison misconduct, especially violence, at the outset could alert prison staff to potential trouble and allow for counteractive steps to be taken. The value of early assessment and counteraction goes beyond improving institutional tranquility. It also might prevent highly dangerous prisoners, who appear to be destined for future parole problems in the years ahead, from continuing their antisocial ways despite the restraint, surveillance, and disciplinary code of a prison. Prosocial accommodation to regulations by the dangerous criminals should begin as soon as possible during incarceration, no matter what their motivation for conformity may be. Abiding by the rules could prove to be an instructive experience for the prisoner.

A second reason for obtaining an early assessment of dangerousness is that it would allow time for basic intervention to improve the gross cognitive limitations suggested by restricted IQ and to modify the deviant values of the antisocial personality. The opportunity to correct these flaws is never going to be better than in prison, where prisoners are under strict control, ample time is usually available, and motivation can be influenced by the common desire for release. Required, of course, are the means of improving cognitive skills like reasoning, planning, judgment, social insight, and impulse control as well as modifying values in low-IQ individuals; these prisoners will possess only limited ability to improve. The means referred to here include standardized procedures for measuring facets of cognition and value that will allow specific deficits to be identified as well as retraining techniques that will improve the dangerous criminal's ability to utilize higher mental processes. I realize this has a pie-in-the-sky ring to it. However, there seems to be no reason in principle why individual assessment and training of cognitive functions and values cannot be put on the same footing as present prison programs that take criminal and social history as a guide and introduce prisoners into sex offender, substance-abuse, anger-management, and other programs intended to modify dangerous personal qualities. I am aware of no formal programs in prisons geared to achieve these diagnostic and training goals; perhaps the case has not been made forcefully enough to warrant such efforts.

Proposing early measurement of dangerousness (or any other risk-provoking attributes) as a way of attenuating future problems may seem to exceed what would be generally regarded as parole risk assessment. Nevertheless, this suggestion helps to emphasize my opinion that professional consultation in the process of parole and probation decision making should go beyond the standard practice of generating a risk estimate and identifying potential dangers that may lie ahead when a given criminal is being considered.

In the same spirit of expanded responsibilities, standard consultation requested when parole is being considered should include an assessment of "needs and solutions" (K. Heilbrun, 1996), so that what may present a problem for the parolee or probationer is clearer, as well as what can be done to avert the problem. The early appraisal of dangerousness is a way of getting a head start on counteracting some of the most pressing needs in social accommodation for the highly dangerous criminal and doing so under conditions of control and reinforcement not available after release.

STANDARD RISK ASSESSMENT FOR MAKING PAROLE RECOMMENDATIONS

Parole consultation in the individual case, once the prisoner is eligible for release, may be requested because some feature of the case, such as the alarming nature of past criminal offenses or current mental status, raises special concern for the parole board. At other times, judicial ruling at the time of sentencing requires a special preparole assessment.

Individual consultation, for whatever reason requested, can only be made available for a small fraction of the prisoners that are considered for parole. That is why I believe an assessment program should be made available to parole boards that makes allowance for recommendations based on both statistical tables and individual case study. This allows a much broader coverage of service that begins with readily available actuarial predictions of parole outcome for all candidates. Intensive assessment of risk in spot cases can be requested when predictions from statistical tables become murky, aspects of the crime remain controversial, or assessment of needs and counteractive measures is of special interest. All that would be needed for the actuarial table of dangerousness scores is the routine collection of intelligence measures and the gathering of case history data necessary for antisociality ratings on prisoners entering a prison system. Such information is commonly made available by the early processing of prisoners. Norms specific to gender and region could be rapidly established for the multiplicative dangerousness scores that result. The quartile-extremes method that worked well in long-range prediction of crime and violence as well as predicting parole failure or success is a place to start in establishing parameters of risk, although more elaborate statistical procedures could be explored.

A high dangerousness score in the upper quartile should be sufficient to sound an alarm so that a compelling reason to grant parole would be required or at least special safeguards would be invoked if parole is granted. A low dangerousness score, suggesting a very limited chance of failure, might tip the scale so that parole would be denied only if some extraordinary factor argued against it. In other words, the dangerousness score could help set the tone of discussion in as high as 50% of the cases under parole consideration without requiring further forensic consultation.

Individual case consultation to the parole board might be of greater value within this broad assessment program when actuarial scores do not allow a definitive statement regarding the risk imposed by dangerousness—that is, in the intermediate quartiles. Such consultation generally takes the form of a clinical assessment in which the information from many sources is integrated into a set of observations relevant to a prisoner's projected adjustment on parole. How many sources of information will be utilized by the consultant is a matter of assessment style as well as the logistical restraint associated with evaluation within a prison setting in which ordinary conditions of time and material may be curtailed. Suggestions regarding how clinical assessment in the prisons culminates in parole recommendations are based on my own experience in the Georgia system.

Given a referral for parole evaluation, four governing principles of clinical assessment are worth keeping in mind. First, as far as possible, be sure that all observations regarding the prisoner are relevant to parole adjustment. Any conclusion that is not related or readily relatable in some way to future success or failure in the community is worse than superfluous, for it may serve as a springboard for misinterpretation by decision makers not trained to make psychological leaps of inference. Second, provide some counteractive measures for the problems and limitations of the prisoner whenever possible; problems are commonplace in parole assessments, but solutions, whether to be implemented in prison or out, will challenge your role as an expert. Third, do not feel compelled to come up with explicit "parole" or "do not parole" recommendations. Boards are constituted to make those decisions; the assessor's responsibility is to provide additional behavioral considerations that will assist them. Finally, try to overcome the temptation to shade your observations toward the likelihood of failure. Although we are not dealing with many winners of model-citizen awards, more parolees are successfully discharged from parole than returned to prison following revocation. Recognize psychological strengths in the prisoner when they can be found, and do not ignore any other factors that would contribute to prosocial conformity outside of prison, such as family support.

These general caveats behind us, the next consideration is the sources of information that may prove useful for a parole assessment. Having multiple sources not only broadens our knowledge about the prisoner but helps to counteract the fallible nature of such information because they allow for cross-checks on factualness. If the same behavior is suggested by some combination of social history, criminal circumstances, prison record, psychological tests, and performance in the interview, it is especially deserving of attention. Having various threads of information also allows for integration across sources and for more comprehensive formulations that would be lacking if assessment depended too much on a single source, such as interview or psychological testing alone.

Five types of available information about the prisoner can feed into a useful set of recommendations, beginning with two relating to developmental background. A *social history* (plus standard demographic data) offers a glimpse of the family conditions under which prisoners developed and their record of success or failure in developmental areas marking social competence (e.g., level of educational attainment, military service, job performance, marital history, incidence of drug or alcohol dependency). Past ability to meet social commitments and to avoid the pitfalls of chemical dependency say something about the psychological resources that will be available should the prisoner once again be exposed to the demands of community life. Of course, these are static properties and must be considered in light of more recent evidence regarding psychological resources.

Criminal history complements the social information, in that it adds another bellwether of social competence. A history featuring an arrest record beginning at puberty, institutional experience in youth detention centers, and criminal recidivism extending into the adult years can be considered as another marker of social incompetence—an inability to meet society's code of conduct. Evidence of violence within the criminal history is an obvious warning sign, but an analysis of the prisoner's criminality should not be overlooked. Criminal circumstances of the most recent crime(s) may reveal psychological evidence of dangerousness in the guise of brutality, poor judgment, impulsiveness, or transactional incompetence. Progression in denial or acceptance of responsibility for criminal acts also can be established by comparing the initial version prisoners gave to the police, statements before the court, and current declarations when interviewed. A straightforward admission of guilt and acceptance of responsibility, or at least progress in that direction, may be as close to remorse as one can expect.

The *prison file* for the offender represents a different kind of background source that takes assessment beyond past social development and criminal history to the prisoner's adjustment while incarcerated. Although it may be tempting to avoid the often ponderous prison file as a source of information, it does contain a potentially valuable record of actual behavior that will usually stretch over a number of years up to the present. Files should include evaluations of performance on details and other activities, the types of self-help programs completed by the prisoner and intended to modify risk-provoking characteristics, efforts toward educational upgrading or acquisition of work skills, disciplinary reports, parole reviews, and changes in security status. If you are patient enough, counseling notes that chronicle contacts with the prisoner can reflect attitude changes, constructive or otherwise. Of importance in some cases, the file may make reference to deviant behavior that signals some form of serious psychological disorder. Prisons, even with mental health units, are not geared to operate as sophisticated psychiatric settings, but it is difficult to imagine substantial deviance going undetected given the extensive surveillance found there. The cases where this information would be most valuable are those in which mental status was at issue before incarceration. A comparison between current impression (interview, tests), recent or not-so-recent past reflected in the file, and preincarceration evidence may allow you to specify psychological change for the better or worse over time.

Psychological tests offer a fourth source of information valuable for parole assessment. Which particular tests is a matter of professional preference and assessment constraints. The battery I prefer includes an up-to-date retest on the intelligence measure used by the Georgia prison system. A current estimate of intelligence is quite important, as adjustment problems in general and crime in particular are frequently a matter of unintelligent choices. An achievement test is part of the battery for two reasons. Basic skill levels provide some insight into the learning effectiveness of the prisoner when compared to the extent of formal schooling and efforts at prison upgrading. Whether a sixth-grade reading level has been attained on achievement tests also determines whether self-administered personality tests can be used. When they can, scores on the MMPI and the CPI have proven to be quite informative. The former offers another way of detecting psychological disorders, and the CPI provides a broad-ranging normal personality profile. Perhaps needless to add, these inventories plus the IQ score offer an updated estimate of criminal dangerousness. Anyone familiar with the responses to objective personality tests by prisoners in parole assessment settings will know that prisoners are systematically guarded in their self-presentation. Yet both instruments contain validity scales to signal blatant faking, and the MMPI includes a correction for guardedness. After many years of reading personality test profiles for parole assessment, I have found that most can be interpreted, and the prisoner's effort to dissimulate can be compensated by a modest intuitive correction.

The *interview* probably qualifies as the standard assessment instrument of the forensic expert called upon to make recommendations for parole. It can make a real contribution as long as the information generated is kept in proper perspective. The interview is probably least useful when it comes to distinguishing fact from fiction. Prisoners, who assign excessive importance to the assessor's opinions, usually do not want to say anything that dims their prospects for release and often introduce statements that are blatantly self-enhancing. That does not mean that the substance of statements should be disregarded, but if something sounds important, try to verify it. The interview is probably most useful as a basis for firsthand observation of the prisoner's verbal and transactional behavior. Mental status can be gauged from the coherence, relevance, spontaneity, and logic of spoken communication. Interpersonal style may be evident in the way the prisoner relates to the assessor, although this is often interwoven with uncharacteristic displays of deference.

It should not pass without notice that the interview is the only source of information of those discussed that is interactive. The assessor is free to influence the type and timing of information that will become available. This can be advantageous, although the risk of biased observation is present given the special circumstances of an interview where so much power and authority is invested in the clinician.

RECOMMENDATIONS FOR PROBATION

Even though the dangerousness index has not been tested for probation-outcome prediction, there is no obvious reason why it should not be effective. The same factors that promote criminal conduct (antisociality) and poor planning and faulty execution of the crimes (cognitive deficits) should be as relevant to the potential probationer as to the more seasoned criminal in prison. Measurement procedures would remain the same. Given that the dangerousness index is shown to be effective at the quartile extremes, much the same general system of probation assessment could be advised as was recommended for parole. That is, seriously consider incarcerating the most dangerous (top quartile) rather than extending probation, or at least impose conditions involving close monitoring and concerted efforts at intervention. The least dangerous (bottom quartile) should respond well to more relaxed conditions of probation. Recommendations based on more complete evaluations can be sought in selected cases for those who fall between.

REFERENCES

Andrews, D. A., Kiessling, J. J., Robinson, D., & Mickus, S. (1986). The risk principle of case classification: An outcome evaluation with young adult probationers. *Canadian Journal of Criminology, 28,* 377–384.

Babst, D. V., & Mannering, J. W. (1965). Probation versus imprisonment for similar types of offenders: A comparison by subsequent violations. *Journal of Research in Crime and Delinquency, 2,* 60–71.

Cattell, R. B., & Cattell, A. K. S. (1958). *IPAT Culture Free Intelligence Test.* Champaign, IL: Institute of Personality and Ability Testing.

Clannon, T. L., & Jew, C. (1985). Predictions from assessments of violent offenders under stress: A fifteen-year experience. *Criminal Justice and Behavior, 12,* 485–499.

Cocozza, J., & Steadman, H. (1976). The failure of psychiatric predictions of dangerousness: Clear and convincing evidence. *Rutgers Law Review, 29,* 1084–1101.

Feighner, J. P., Robins, E., Guze, S. B., Woodruff, R. A., Winokur, G., & Munoz, R. (1972). Diagnostic criteria for use in psychiatric research. *Archives of General Psychiatry, 26,* 57–63.

Fendrick, M. (1991). Institutionalization and parole behavior: Assessing the influence of individual and family characteristics. *Journal of Community Psychology, 19,* 109–122.

Fildes, R., & Gottfredson, D. M. (1972). Cluster analysis in a parolee sample. *Crime and Delinquency, 9,* 2–11.

Gottfredson, D. M., Ballard, K. B., Jr., & O'Leary, V. (1966). Uniform parole reports: A feasibility study. *Journal of Research in Crime and Delinquency, 3,* 97–111.

Gottfredson, D. M., Neithercutt, M. G., Nuffield, J., & O'Leary, V. (1973). *Four thousand lifetimes: A study of time served and parole outcomes.* National Council on Crime and Delinquency Monograph. Davis, CA.

Gough, H. G. (1957). *Manual for the California psychological inventory.* Palo Alto, CA: Consulting Psychologists Press.

Grove, W. M., & Meehl, P. E. (1996). Comparative efficiency of informal (subjective, impressionistic) and formal (mechanical, algorithmic) prediction procedures: The clinical-statistical controversy. *Psychology, Public Policy, and Law, 2,* 293–323.

Harris, P. M. (1994). Client management classification and prediction of probation outcome. *Crime and Delinquency, 40,* 154–174.

Hart, S. D., Kropp, P. R., & Hare, R. D. (1988). Performance of male psychopaths following conditional release from prison. *Journal of Consulting & Clinical Psychology, 56,* 227–232.

Hassin, Y. (1986). Two models for predicting recidivism: Clinical versus statistical. *British Journal of Criminology, 26,* 270–286.

Hathaway, S. R., & McKinley, J. C. (1951). *Manual for the Minnesota multiphasic personality inventory* (Rev. ed.). Minneapolis: University of Minnesota Press.

Heilbrun, A. B. (1978). Race, criminal violence, and length of parole. *British Journal of Criminology, 18,* 53–61.

Heilbrun, A. B. (1979). Psychopathy and violent crime. *Journal of Consulting and Clinical Psychology, 47,* 509–516.

Heilbrun, A. B. (1996). *Criminal dangerousness and the risk of violence.* Lanham, MD: University Press of America.

Heilbrun, A. B., & Heilbrun, M. R. (1985). Psychopathy and dangerousness: Comparison, integration and extension of two psychopathic typologies. *British Journal of Clinical Psychology, 24,* 181–195.

Heilbrun, A. B., Knopf, I. J., & Bruner, P. (1976). Criminal impulsivity and violence and subsequent parole outcome. *British Journal of Criminology, 16,* 367–377.

Heilbrun, K. S. (1996). *Prediction versus control models relevant to risk assessment: The importance of legal decision-making context.* Division 41 presidential address, 1996 convention of the American Psychological Association, Toronto, Canada.

Kozol, H., Boucher, R., & Garofalo, R. (1972). The diagnosis and treatment of dangerousness. *Crime and Delinquency, 18,* 371–392.

Liberton, M., Silverman, M., & Blount, W. R. (1992). Predicting probation success for the first-time offender. *International Journal of Offender Therapy & Comparative Criminology, 36,* 335–347.

Lindquist, C. A., Smusz, T. D., & Doerner, W. (1985). Causes of conformity: An application of control theory to adult misdemeanant probationers. *International Journal of Offender Therapy & Comparative Criminology, 29,* 1–14.

Loeber, R., & Dishion, T. (1983). Early predictors of male delinquency: A review. *Psychological Bulletin, 94,* 68–99.

Meehl, P. E. (1954). *Clinical versus statistical prediction: A theoretical analysis and a review of the evidence.* Minneapolis: University of Minnesota Press.

Meehl, P. E., & Rosen, A. (1955). Antecedent probability and the efficacy of psychometric signs, patterns, or cutting scores. *Psychological Bulletin, 52,* 194–216.

Melton, G. B., Petrila, J., Poythress, N. G., & Slobogin, C. (1987). *Psychological evaluations for the courts: A handbook for mental health professionals and lawyers.* New York: Guilford Press.

Mischel, W. (1973). Toward a cognitive social learning reconceptualization of personality. *Psychological Review, 80,* 252–283.

Monahan, J. (1981). *Predicting violent behavior: An assessment of clinical techniques.* Beverly Hills, CA: Sage.

Monahan, J. (1992). Mental disorders and violent behavior: Attitudes and evidence. *American Psychologist, 47,* 511–521.

Monahan, J., & Steadman, H. J. (Eds.). (1994). *Violence and mental disorder: Developments in risk assessment.* Chicago: University of Chicago Press.

Neithercutt, M. G. (1972). Parole violation patterns and commitment offense. *Journal of Research in Crime and Delinquency, 9,* 87–98.

Schauer, E. J. (1990). A validation of the Case Classification System in Texas probation: A replication study. *Dissertation Abstracts International, 51*(4A), 1397–1398.

Serin, R. C., Peters, R. D., & Barbaree, H. E. (1990). Predictors of psychopathy and release outcome in a criminal population. *Psychological Assessment, 2,* 419–422.

Shah, S. A. (1978). Dangerousness: A paradigm for exploring some issues in law and psychology. *American Psychologist, 33,* 224–238.

Shawver, L., Clanon, T. L., Kurdys, D., & Friedman, H. (1985). Predicting and improving parole success with PAS. *Federal Probation, 49,* 34–37.

Stanton, J. M. (1969). Murderers on parole. *Crime and Delinquency, 15,* 149–155.

Swanson, J., Holzer, C., Ganju, V., & Jono, R. (1990). Violence and psychiatric disorder in the community: Evidence from the Epidemiological Catchment Area surveys. *Hospital and Community Psychiatry, 41,* 761–770.

Tibbitts, C. (1931–1932). Success or failure on parole can be predicted: A study of the records of 3000 youths paroled from the Illinois State Reformatory. *Journal of Criminal Law and Criminology, 22,* 11–50.

Van Voorhis, P. (1985). Restitution outcome and probationers' assessments of restitution: The effects of moral development. *Criminal Justice and Behavior, 12,* 259–287.

Vetter, H. J. (1987). Recommending probation and parole. In I. B. Weiner & A. K. Hess (Eds.), *Handbook of forensic psychology* (pp. 319–351). New York: Wiley.

Vold, G. B. (1931). *Prediction methods and parole.* Minneapolis: The Sociological Press.

Walters, G. D., Revella, L., & Baltrusaitis, W. J. (1994). Predicting parole/probation out-come with the aid of the Lifestyle Criminality Screening Form. *Psychological Assessment, 2,* 313–316.

Warner, S. C. (1923). Determining parole from the Massachusetts Reformatory. *Journal of Criminal Law and Criminology, 14,* 172–207.

Wenk, E. A., Gottfredson, D. M., & Radwin, M. S. (1970). A modern information system for uniform parole reports data. *Journal of Research in Crime and Delinquency, 7,* 58–70.

Wilkinson, J. (1994). Using a reconviction predictor to make sense of reconviction rates in the probation service. *British Journal of Social Work, 24,* 461–475.

CHAPTER 12

Defining and Assessing
Competency to Stand Trial

RONALD ROESCH, PATRICIA A. ZAPF,
STEPHEN L. GOLDING, and JENNIFER L. SKEEM

COMPETENCY TO stand trial is a concept of jurisprudence allowing the postpone-
ment of criminal proceedings for those defendants who are considered unable
to participate in their defense on account of mental or physical disorder or retardation. Because trial competency issues are raised substantially more often
than the insanity defense, psychologists involved in forensic assessment and
consultation are likely to have frequent experience with it. It is estimated that
between 25,000 and 39,000 competency evaluations are conducted in the United
States annually (Hoge et al., 1997; Steadman & Hartstone, 1983). Stated somewhat differently, between 2% and 8% of all felony defendants are referred for
competency evaluations (Bonnie, 1992; Golding, 1993; Hoge, Bonnie, Poythress,
& Monahan, 1992). Given a steady increase in felony arrest rates, the rate of
competency referrals is increasingly steadily as well. In this chapter, we present
an overview of competency laws, research, and methods of assessment with the
aim of providing forensic psychologists with the basic information they need to
conduct competency evaluations. We do not believe, however, that this chapter
will sufficiently prepare a novice forensic psychologist to carry out such evaluations. As we make clear, the issues surrounding a competency determination
are highly complex. An evaluator needs not only a high level of clinical knowledge and skills but also considerable knowledge of the legal system.

We urge the reader interested in pursuing work in the competency area to
supplement this chapter with other materials (e.g., Bonnie, 1992, 1993; Grisso,
1992; Melton, Petrila, Poythress, & Slobogin, 1987; Ogloff, Wallace, & Otto, 1991;
Roesch, Hart, & Zapf, 1996; Roesch, Ogloff, & Golding, 1993; Winick, 1995, 1996),
as well as workshops and other forms of continuing education. Also, *Specialty*

Guidelines for Forensic Psychologists (Committee on Ethical Guidelines for Forensic Psychologists, 1991) contains important practice standards for competency evaluations.

DEFINING COMPETENCY

Provisions allowing for a delay of trial because a defendant is incompetent to proceed have long been a part of the legal due process. English common law allowed for an arraignment, trial, judgment, or execution of an alleged capital offender to be stayed if he or she "be(came) absolutely mad" (Hale, 1736, cited in Silten & Tullis, 1977, p. 1053). Over time, statutes have been created in the United States and Canada that have further defined and extended the common law practice (see S. Davis, 1994; Rogers & Mitchell, 1991; Verdun-Jones, 1981; Webster, Menzies, & Jackson, 1982, for reviews of Canadian competency law and practice). The modern standard in U.S. law was established in *Dusky v. United States* (1960). Although the exact wording varies, all states use a variant of the *Dusky* standard to define competency (Favole, 1983). In *Dusky*, the Supreme Court held: "It is not enough for the district judge to find that 'the defendant is oriented to time and place and has some recollection of events,' but that the test must be whether he has sufficient present ability to consult with his lawyer with a reasonable degree of rational understanding—and whether he has a rational as well as factual understanding of the proceedings against him" (p. 402).

Although the concept of competency to stand trial has been long established in law, its definition, as exemplified by the ambiguities of *Dusky*, has never been explicit. What is meant by "sufficient present ability?" How does one determine whether a defendant "has a rational as well as factual understanding?" To be sure, some courts (e.g., *Wieter v. Settle*, 1961) and legislatures (e.g., Utah Code Annotated, 1994) have provided some direction to evaluators in the form of articulated *Dusky* standards (discussed below), but the typical forensic evaluation is left largely unguided except by a common principle, in most published cases, that evaluators cannot reach a finding of incompetency independent of the facts of the legal case (an issue we will return to later).

The problems in defining and assessing competency lead to a broad range of interpretations of the *Dusky* standard. Because the courts and legislatures have given mental health professionals a large share of the responsibility for defining and evaluating competency, it should not be surprising to find that mental status issues such as presence or absence of psychosis have played a dominant role (historically at least) in the findings of evaluators. In fact, evaluators initially involved in assessing competency seemed to equate psychosis with incompetency (Cooke, 1969; McGarry, 1965; Roesch & Golding, 1980). Furthermore, evaluators in the past rarely took into account the specific demands of a defendant's case. Early evaluators were employed typically in state mental hospital settings (the site of the majority of competency evaluations at that time) and had no training either in the assessment of competency or in matters of law. As a consequence, the evaluations were based on the same standard mental status examinations that had been used with other patients in the hospital. If psychological tests were used at all, they were used as a diagnostic tool to determine presence or absence of psychosis.

Over the past 20 years, these entrenched practices have been challenged and changed. Thus, research provided evidence that the presence of psychosis was not sufficient by itself for a finding of incompetency (Roesch & Golding, 1980), and modern empirical studies of competency reports demonstrate that evaluators rarely make that simple conceptual error (Heilbrun & Collins, 1995; Nicholson, LaFortune, Norwood, & Roach, 1995; Skeem, Golding, Cohn, & Berge, 1997). However, although forensic evaluators today typically have more training than in the past, most states still do not require forensic evaluator training (Farkas, DeLeon, & Newman, 1997), and examiners are usually only "occasional experts" (Grisso, 1987).

The specific psycholegal abilities required of a defendant are the most important aspect of assessing fitness. The contextual nature of competence has been explored by researchers in the area. Some researchers and scholars have argued that competence should be considered within the context in which it is to be used. For example, the abilities required by the defendant in his or her specific case should be taken into account when assessing competence. This contextual perspective was summarized by Golding and Roesch (1988) as follows: "Mere presence of severe disturbance (a psychopathological criterion) is only a threshold issue—it must be further demonstrated that such severe disturbance in *this* defendant, facing *these* charges, *in light of existing* evidence, anticipating the substantial effort of a *particular* attorney with a *relationship of known characteristics,* results in the defendant being unable to rationally assist the attorney or to comprehend the nature of the proceedings and their likely outcome" (p. 79). The importance of a contextual determination of specific psycholegal abilities has been repeatedly demonstrated by empirical findings that assessed competencies in one area of functioning are rarely homogeneous with competencies in other areas of functioning (Bonnie, 1992; Golding & Roesch, 1988; Grisso, Appelbaum, Mulvey, & Fletcher, 1995; Skeem et al., 1997).

Recent Supreme Court decisions in both the United States and Canada, however, have confused this issue by finding that the standard by which competency is to be judged is not context-specific. In *R. v. Whittle* (1994), the Supreme Court of Canada ruled that there is to be only one standard for competency regardless of the specific abilities to be performed by an accused. The Court concluded that there is no difference in the essential abilities needed among making active choices about waiving counsel, making decisions at trial, confessing, or pleading guilty. The Court ruled that different standards of competency should not be applied for different aspects of criminal proceedings and that the test to be used is one of "limited cognitive capacity" (p. 567) in each of these circumstances. However, unlike *Godinez v. Moran* (1993), the forensic examiners had actually evaluated Mr. Whittle in these specific contexts, regardless of whether or not the standard to be applied was the same or different as a function of the context.

In *Godinez v. Moran* (1993), the U.S. Supreme Court held similarly that the standard for the various types of competency (i.e., competency to plead guilty, to waive counsel, to stand trial) should be considered the same. Justice Thomas wrote for the majority:

> The standard adopted by the Ninth Circuit is whether a defendant who seeks to plead guilty or waive counsel has the capacity for "reasoned choice" among the alternatives available to him. How this standard is different from (much less higher than) the *Dusky* standard—whether the defendant has a "rational understanding" of the proceedings—is not readily apparent to us. . . . While the decision to plead guilty is undeniably a profound one, it is no more complicated than the sum total of decisions that a defendant may be called upon to make during the course of a trial. . . . Nor do we think that a defendant who waives his right to the assistance of counsel must be more competent than the defendant who does not, since there is no reason to believe that the decision to waive counsel requires an appreciably higher level of mental functioning than the decision to waive other constitutional rights. (p. 2686)

In his dissent, Justice Blackmun noted that the "majority's analysis is contrary to both common sense and long-standing case law" (*Godinez v. Moran*, 1993, p. 2691). He reasoned that competency cannot be considered in a vacuum, separate from its specific legal context. Justice Blackmun argued that "competency for one purpose does not necessarily translate to competency for another purpose" (p. 2694) and noted that prior Supreme Court cases have "required competency evaluations to be specifically tailored to the context and purpose of a proceeding" (p. 2694). What is egregiously missing from the majority's opinion in *Godinez*, however, is the fact that, unlike Whittle, Moran's competency to waive counsel or plead guilty to death penalty murder charges was never assessed by the forensic examiners, regardless of which standard (rational choice or rational understanding) was employed.

The *Godinez* holding has been subsequently criticized by legal scholars (Perlin, 1996) and courts alike. In the words of the Third Circuit Court of Appeals, "This difficult case presents us with a window through which to view the real-world effects of the Supreme Court's decision in *Godinez v. Moran*, and it is not a pretty sight" (*Government of the Virgin Islands v. Charles*, 1995, p. 401). The problem is not whether or not the standards for various psycholegal competencies are higher, different, or the same, but rather, more fundamentally, whether or not the defendant has been examined with respect to these issues in the first place.

Standards of competence are one area of inquiry, whereas the conceptualization of competence is another. Some researchers and scholars have provided reconceptualizations of competence to stand trial. Winick (1985, 1995) persuasively argued that in some circumstances it may be in the best interests of the defendant to proceed with a trial, even if he or she is incompetent. Winick postulated that this could take the form of a provisional trial wherein the support of the defense attorney would serve to ensure protection of the defendant. This would allow the defendant to proceed with his or her case while maintaining decorum in the courtroom and without violating the defendant's constitutional rights. As well, Bonnie (1992, 1993) has provided a reformulation of competence to stand trial. Bonnie proposed a distinction between two types of competencies: competence to assist counsel and decisional competence. He argued that defendants found incompetent to assist counsel would be barred from proceeding until they were restored to competence. Defendants found decisionally incompetent, on the other hand, may be able to proceed in certain cases where his or her lawyer is able to present a defense.

The past 15 years have also seen the development of better training programs for professionals in forensic psychology and psychiatry. Many graduate psychology programs and law schools cooperate to provide instruction in psychology as well as law, and a number of departments of psychology include forensic psychology as an area of expertise (Bersoff et al., 1997; Roesch, Grisso, & Poythress, 1986).

Another major change has been the shift in the location of competency assessments. Roesch and Golding (1980) argued that inpatient evaluation, which was the common practice until recently, is unnecessary in all but perhaps a small percentage of cases, as most determinations of competency can easily be made on the basis of brief screening interviews (to be discussed later in this chapter). Community-based settings, including jails and mental health centers (see Fitzgerald, Peszke, & Goodwin, 1978; Melton, Weithorn, & Slobogin, 1985; Ogloff & Roesch, 1992; Roesch & Ogloff, 1996), appear to be increasingly used to conduct evaluations. In 1994, Grisso and his colleagues published the results of a national survey they had conducted to determine the organization of pretrial forensic evaluation services in the United States (Grisso, Coccozza, Steadman, Fisher, & Greer, 1994). These researchers concluded that "the traditional use of centrally located, inpatient facilities for obtaining pretrial evaluations survives in only a minority of states, having been replaced by other models that employ various types of outpatient approaches" (p. 388). One compelling reason for this shift is cost. Laben, Kashgarian, Nessa, and Spencer (1977) estimated that the cost of the community-based evaluations they conducted in Tennessee was one-third the cost of the typical mental hospital evaluation (see also Fitzgerald et al., 1978). In 1985, Winick estimated that in excess of $185 million was spent each year on competency evaluation and treatment in the United States; in 1996, he estimated that these costs could be two to three times as high as they were in 1985.

The widespread use of screening instruments would serve to lower these rising costs, as the majority of individuals, for whom incompetence clearly is not an issue, would be screened out. Only those defendants whom the screening instrument has identified as potentially incompetent would then be sent on for a more formal assessment of competence. Screening instruments can be administered in outpatient settings as well as in local jails or courthouses, thereby also serving to eliminate the unnecessary detention of clearly competent individuals.

Base rates for competency referrals (from 2% to 8% of felony arrests) and for incompetency determinations (from 7% to 60%) vary widely across jurisdictions and evaluation settings (Nicholson & Kugler, 1991; Skeem et al., 1997). This occurs for a number of reasons, including variations in examiner training and use of forensically relevant evaluation procedures (Skeem et al., 1997), the availability of pretrial mental health services, the nature of the referral system, inadequate treatment services for the chronically mentally ill and a criminalization of their conduct, and the extent to which judges scrutinize bona fide doubt about a defendant's competency before granting evaluation petitions (Golding, 1992). Nevertheless, the modal jurisdiction typically finds only 20% of those referred incompetent to proceed with their trial. Precise data are not available, but conservatively, half of those found competent presented little or no reason for doubting their competency and could have been detected by adequate screening procedures. This is true in the United States as well as in other countries. Zapf and Roesch (1998) investigated the rate of (in)competence in individuals remanded to an inpatient setting for an assessment of fitness to stand trial in Canada. Their results indicate that only 11% of the remands were unfit to stand trial and, further, that with the use of a brief screening interview, 82% of the remands could have been screened out at some earlier time as they were clearly fit to stand trial (Zapf & Roesch, 1997). Many of the assessment procedures we describe later in this chapter are either explicitly designed for screening or could easily be adapted for use in such settings.

A major change in the past few decades has been the development of a number of instruments specifically designed for assessing competence. This work was pioneered by McGarry and his colleagues (see Lipsitt, Lelos, & McGarry, 1971; McGarry, 1965; McGarry & Curran, 1973). Their work was the starting point for a more sophisticated and systematic approach to the assessment of competency. In 1986, Grisso coined the term "forensic assessment instrument" (FAI) to refer to instruments that provide frameworks for conducting forensic assessments. FAIs are typically semistructured elicitation procedures and lack the characteristics of many traditional psychological tests. However, they serve to make forensic assessments more systematic. These instruments help evaluators to collect important and relevant information and to follow the decision-making process that is required under the law. Since the time that the term was coined, a number of assessment instruments have been developed that are designed to work in this way, and it appears that the use of FAIs has been slowly increasing (Borum & Grisso, 1995; see Skeem et al.'s 1997 finding that few occasional experts use such devices). This trend is encouraging, because empirical data suggest that trained examiners using FAIs achieve the highest levels of interexaminer and examiner-adjudication agreement (Golding, Roesch, & Schreiber, 1984; Nicholson & Kugler, 1991; Skeem et al., 1997). Before turning to a review of assessment methods, we provide a brief overview of the legal procedures involved in competency questions.

OVERVIEW OF PROCEDURES

Laws regarding competency vary from state to state, although most jurisdictions follow procedures similar to the overview we describe in this section. Clinicians should consult their own statute for the specific law and procedure applicable in each state.

The issue of competency may be raised at any point in the adjudication process (Golding & Roesch, 1988). If a court determines that a bona fide doubt exists as to a defendant's competency, it must consider this issue formally (*Drope v. Missouri*, 1975; *Pate v. Robinson*, 1966), usually after a forensic evaluation, which can take place in the jail, an outpatient facility, or in an institutional setting.

One legal issue that may concern evaluators is whether information obtained in a competency evaluation can be used against a defendant during the guilt phase of a trial or at sentencing. Some concerns have been raised about possible self-incrimination (Berry, 1973; Pizzi, 1977), but all jurisdictions in the United States and Canada provide either statutorily or through case law that information obtained in a competency evaluation cannot be introduced on the issue of guilt unless the defendant places his or her mental state into evidence at either trial or sentencing hearings (*Estelle v. Smith,* 1981; Golding & Roesch, 1988).

Once a competency evaluation has been completed and the written report submitted (see Melton et al., 1987; Petrella & Poythress, 1983; Skeem et al., 1997, for a discussion of the content of these reports), the court may schedule a hearing. However, if both the defense and the prosecution accept the findings and recommendations in the report, a hearing does not have to take place. It is likely that in the majority of states, a formal hearing is not held for most cases. If a hearing is held, the evaluators may be asked to testify, but most hearings are quite brief and usually only the written report of an evaluator is used. In fact, the majority of hearings last only a few minutes and are held simply to confirm the findings of evaluators (Steadman, 1979). The ultimate decision about competency rests with the court, which is not bound by the evaluators' recommendations (e.g., *North Dakota v. Heger,* 1982). In most cases, however, the court accepts the recommendations of the evaluators (Hart & Hare, 1992; Steadman, 1979; Williams & Miller, 1981).

At this point, defendants found competent proceed with their case. For defendants found incompetent, either trials are postponed until competency is regained or the charges are dismissed, usually without prejudice. The disposition of incompetent defendants is perhaps the most problematic area of the competency procedures. Until the case of *Jackson v. Indiana* (1972), virtually all states allowed the automatic and indefinite commitment of incompetent defendants. In *Jackson,* the U.S. Supreme Court held that a defendant committed solely on the basis of incompetency "cannot be held more than the reasonable period of time necessary to determine whether there is a substantial probability that he will attain that capacity in the foreseeable future" (p. 738). The Supreme Court did not specify how long a period of time would be reasonable, nor did it indicate how progress toward the goal of regaining competency could be assessed.

The *Jackson* decision led to revisions in state statutes to provide for alternatives to commitment as well as limits on the length of commitment (Roesch & Golding, 1980). The length of confinement varies from state to state, with some states having specific time limits (e.g., 18 months); other states base length of treatment on a proportion of the length of sentence that would have been given if the defendant had been convicted.

Once defendants are found incompetent, they may have only limited rights to refuse treatment (see Winick, 1983, for a review). Medication is the most common form of treatment, although some jurisdictions have established treatment programs designed to increase understanding of the legal process (e.g., Pendleton, 1980; Webster, Jenson, Stermac, Gardner, & Slomen, 1985) or that confront problems that hinder a defendant's ability to participate in the defense (D. Davis, 1985; Siegel & Elwork, 1990).

This brief overview of competency procedures is intended to provide a basic understanding of the process. For a more complete discussion of the legal issues as well as a review of empirical research on the various aspects of the competency procedures, the reader is referred to reviews by Golding and Roesch (1988), Nicholson and Kugler (1991), Roesch et al. (1993), and Winick (1996).

ASSESSING COMPETENCY

Though there has been some confusion over the definition of competency, there nevertheless appears to be generally good agreement among evaluators about whether a defendant is competent or not. The few studies of reliability that have been completed report that pairs of evaluators agree in 80% or more of the cases (Goldstein & Stone, 1977; Poythress & Stock, 1980; Roesch & Golding, 1980; Skeem et al., 1997). When evaluators are highly trained and use semistructured competence assessment instruments, even higher rates of agreement have been reported (Golding et al., 1984; Nicholson & Kugler, 1991).

When base rates of findings of competency are considered, however, these high levels of agreement are less impressive, and they do not suggest that evaluators are necessarily in agreement about the criteria for a determination of competency. Without even directly assessing a group of defendants, a psychologist could achieve high levels of agreement with an examining clinician simply by calling all defendants competent (base rate decision). Because in most jurisdictions, approximately 80% of all referred defendants are competent (for reasons discussed later in this chapter), the psychologist and the examiner would have modest agreement even making no decisions at all. (Though the problem of base rates can be corrected through the use of certain statistics such as Kappa, the studies reporting reliability usually have small samples overall and consequently very few incompetent defendants.) Most disturbing, Skeem and colleagues (1997) demonstrated that examiner agreement on specific psycholegal deficits (as opposed to overall competency) averaged only 25% across a series of competency domains. It is the more difficult decisions, involving cases where competency is truly a serious question, that are of concern. How reliable are decisions about these cases? To date, no study has accumulated enough of these cases to answer this question.

Of course, high levels of reliability do not ensure that valid decisions are being made. For example, two evaluators could agree that the presence of psychosis automatically leads to a finding of incompetency; as long as the evaluators are in agreement about their criteria for determining psychosis, the reliability of their final judgments about competency will be high. As we suggest throughout this chapter, it is quite possible that the criteria used by too many evaluators inappropriately rely on traditional mental status issues without considering the functional aspects of a particular defendant's case.

Validity is, of course, difficult to assess because of the criterion problem. Criterion-related validity is usually assessed by examining concurrent validity and predictive validity (Messick, 1980). Predictive validity is impossible to assess fully because only defendants who are considered competent are allowed to proceed. It is feasible to look at the predictive validity of decisions about competent defendants, but not possible, of course, to assess the decisions about incompetent defendants, as they are referred for treatment and judicial proceedings are suspended. Concurrent validity is also difficult to determine because it does not make sense to look simply at correlations with other measures (e.g., diagnosis, intelligence) if one adopts a functional, case by case, assessment of a defendant's competency. For these reasons, then, there is no "correct" decision against which to compare judgments.

As we have indicated, the courts usually accept mental health judgments about competency. Does this mean that the judgments are valid? Not necessarily, because courts often accept the evaluator's definition of competency and his or her conclusions without review, leading to very high levels of examiner-judge agreement (Hart & Hare, 1992; Skeem et al., 1997). We have argued (Roesch & Golding, 1980) that the only way of assessing the validity of decisions about incompetency is to allow defendants who are believed to be incompetent to proceed with a trial anyway. This could be a provisional trial (on the Illinois model) in which assessment of a defendant's performance could continue. If a defendant was unable to participate, then the trial could be stopped; if a verdict had already been reached and the defendant was convicted, the verdict could be set aside.

We suspect that in a significant percentage of trials, alleged incompetent defendants will be able to participate. In addition to the obvious advantages to defendants, the use of a provisional trial could provide valuable information about what should be expected of a defendant in certain judicial proceedings (e.g., the ability to testify, identify witnesses, describe events, evaluate the testimony of other witnesses). Short of a provisional trial, it may be possible to address the validity issue by having independent experts evaluate the information provided by evaluators and other collateral information sources. We have used this technique in our research and will discuss this later in the chapter. In the next section, we review various methods for assessing competency.

THE FUNCTIONAL EVALUATION APPROACH

We believe the most reasonable approach to the assessment of competency is based on a functional evaluation of a defendant's ability matched to the contextualized demands of the case. An assessment of the mental status of a defendant is important, but it is not sufficient as a method of evaluating competency. Rather, the mental status information must be related to the specific demands of the legal case, as has been suggested by legal decisions such as the ones involving amnesia. As in the case of psychosis, a defendant with amnesia is not per se incompetent to stand trial, as has been held in a number of cases (e.g., *Ritchie v. Indiana,* 1984; *Wilson v. United States,* 1968). In *Missouri v. Davis* (1983), the defendant had memory problems due to brain damage. Nevertheless, the Missouri Supreme Court held that amnesia by itself was not a sufficient reason to bar the trial of an otherwise competent defendant. In *Montana v. Austed* (1982), the court held that the bulk of the evidence against the defendant was physical and not affected by amnesia. Finally, in a Maryland decision (*Morrow v. Maryland,* 1982), the court held that, because of the potential for fraud, amnesia does not justify a finding of incompetence. The court also stated that everyone has amnesia to some degree because the passage of time erodes memory. These decisions are of interest because they support the view that evaluators cannot reach a finding of incompetency independent of the facts of the legal case, an issue we will return to later. Similarly, a defendant may be psychotic and still be found competent to stand trial if the symptoms do not impair the defendant's functional ability to consult with his or her attorney and otherwise rationally participate in the legal process.

Some cases are more complex than others and may, as a result, require different types of psycholegal abilities. Thus, it may be that the same defendant is competent for one type of legal proceeding but not for others. In certain cases, a defendant may be required to testify. In this instance, a defendant who is likely to withdraw in a catatonic-like state may be incompetent. But the same defendant may be able to proceed if the attorney intends to plea bargain (the way the vast majority of all criminal cases are handled).

The functional approach is illustrated in the famous amnesia case of *Wilson v. United States* (1968). In that decision, the Court of Appeals held that six factors should be considered in determining whether a defendant's amnesia impaired the ability to stand trial:

1. The extent to which the amnesia affected the defendant's ability to consult with and assist his lawyer
2. The extent to which the amnesia affected the defendant's ability to testify in his own behalf
3. The extent to which the evidence in suit could be extrinsically reconstructed in view of the defendant's amnesia; such evidence would include evidence relating to the crime itself as well as any reasonable possible alibi.
4. The extent to which the Government assisted the defendant and his counsel in that reconstruction
5. The strength of the prosecution's case; most important here will be whether the Government's case is such as to negate all reasonable hypotheses of innocence. If there is any substantial possibility that the accused could, but for his amnesia, establish an alibi or other defense, it should be presumed that he would have been able to do so.
6. Any other facts and circumstances which would indicate whether or not the defendant had a fair trial (*Wilson v. United States,* 1968, pp. 463–464)

One could substitute any symptom for amnesia in the above quote. If this were done, the evaluation of competency would certainly be one based on a determination of the manner in which a defendant's incapacity may have an effect on the legal proceedings. In fact, some states, such as Florida, see Winick, 1983, and Utah, 1994, already specify that the evaluators must relate a defendant's mental condition to clearly defined legal factors, such as the defendant's appreciation of the charges, the range and nature of possible penalties, and capacity to disclose to attorney pertinent facts surrounding the alleged offense (see Winick, 1983). Utah's statute goes the furthest in this direction, specifying the most comprehensive range of psycholegal abilities to be addressed by evaluators (including the iatrogenic effects of medication and decisional competencies) and also requiring judges to identify specifically which psycholegal abilities are impaired when a defendant is found incompetent.

The assessment of competency requires consideration of both mental status as well as psycholegal abilities. Unfortunately, current data indicate that evaluators often do not address an appropriate range of psycholegal abilities and most often do not tie their psychopathological observations to their psycholegal conclusions (Skeem et al., 1997). We now turn to a review of the history of competency assessment methods.

MEASURES OF COMPETENCY

Prior to the 1960s, there were no standard methods for assessing competency. One of the first was a checklist developed by Robey (1965), which focuses on court process issues such as understanding the legal process. Another early procedure used a checklist and a set of interview questions devised by Bukatman, Foy, and DeGrazia (1971). Neither of these early measures was used often (Schreiber, 1978). By far the greatest impact on competency assessment came first from the seminal work of A. Louis McGarry and his colleagues at Harvard Medical School's Laboratory of Community Psychiatry. McGarry, a psychiatrist, was involved in the development of two measures: the Competency Screening Test (CST) and the Competency Assessment Instrument (CAI). We will discuss these measures in addition to a number of other measures that have since been developed.

The Competency Screening Test

The CST was created by Lipsitt et al. (1971) as a screening measure to identify clearly competent defendants and thus minimize the need for lengthy inpatient evaluations. Such a screening process was considered important because the vast majority of defendants referred for evaluations are competent. The reason is that many other factors influence referrals, including the use of the evaluation commitment as a method for denying bail, as a tactical maneuver to delay a trial, as a way of providing a basis for a reduction in charges or sentences, and as a means of getting defendants who are seen as in need of mental health treatment out of the jails and into the hospitals (Dickey, 1980; Golding, 1992; Menzies, Webster, Butler, & Turner, 1980; Roesch & Golding, 1985; Teplin, 1984).

The CST, however, has not often been used as a screening device. Many evaluators have not chosen the CST because of various validity considerations. The scoring method has been criticized (Brakel, 1974; Roesch & Golding, 1980) because of its idealized perception of the criminal justice system; certain responses may actually reflect a sense of powerlessness in controlling one's outcome in the legal system and may be based on past experiences with the legal system.

The CST has been examined in a number of studies. It has high levels of inter-rater reliability in terms of scoring the incomplete sentence format (Randolph, Hicks, & Mason, 1981), but studies comparing classification based on CST cutoff scores and hospital evaluation decisions reveal that it has a high false-positive rate, that is, it tends to identify many individuals as incompetent who are later determined to be competent in hospital evaluations (Lipsitt et al., 1971; Nottingham & Mattson, 1981; Randolph et al., 1981; Shatin, 1979).

The results of these studies lead one to give a mixed review of the CST. Although it appears that the CST is a reliable instrument, serious questions can be raised about its usefulness as a screening device because of the potential for misclassifying possibly incompetent defendants. At this point, it is not possible to recommend that it be used as a sole method of screening defendants.

The Competency Assessment Instrument

The most important measure developed by McGarry, the CAI contains 13 items related to legal issues. It has served as the basis for subsequent forensic assessment instruments. The items include "appraisal of available legal defenses," "quality of relating to attorney," and "capacity to disclose pertinent facts." Each item is scored on a 1 to 5 scale, ranging from "total incapacity" to "no incapacity." The CAI manual contains clinical examples of levels of incapacity as well as suggested interview questions.

The CAI has been used in a number of jurisdictions, although perhaps more as an interview structuring device than in the two-stage screening manner (with the CST), as originally intended by McGarry (see Laben et al., 1977; Schreiber, 1978). Unfortunately, there are few studies reporting either reliability or validity data. We used the CAI in a North Carolina study (Roesch & Golding, 1980). Thirty interviews conducted by pairs of interviewers yielded item percent agreement ranging from 68.8% to 96.7%, with a median of 81.2%. The interviewers were in agreement on the competency status of 29 of the 30 defendants (26 competent, 3 incompetent). The interviewers' decisions were in concordance with the more lengthy hospital evaluation decisions in 27 of 30 cases, or 90%. In subsequent studies (Golding et al., 1984; others summarized Nicholson & Kugler, 1991), the CAI has shown high levels of *trained* interexaminer agreement and examiner-outcome agreement. Obviously, the CAI appears to hold promise as both a screening device and a full-blown interview. Its primary disadvantage, discussed below, is in the range of psycholegal abilities articulated and its lack of focus on the nexus of psychopathology and psycholegal impairment.

The Interdisciplinary Fitness Interview

The IFI is designed to assess both the legal and psychopathological aspects of competency (Golding et al., 1984). The original IFI comprised three major sections: (a) legal issues (5 items); (b) psychopathological issues (11 items); and (c) overall evaluation (4 items). The three items in the consensual judgment section reflect postassessment resolution of differences among judges.

Each of the general items represents an organizing scheme for more specific subareas that have been seen to influence competency decisions. For example, six subareas are subsumed under the broad "capacity to appreciate," which forms the core of item 1. These are (a) appreciating the nature of the state's criminal allegation; (b) ability to provide a reasonable account of one's behavior prior to, during, and subsequent to the alleged crime; (c) ability to provide an account of relevant others during the same time period; (d) ability to provide relevant information about one's own state of mind at the time of the alleged crime, including intentions, feelings, and cognitions; (e) ability to provide information about the behavior of the police during apprehension, arrest, and interrogation; and (f) projected ability to provide feedback to an attorney about the veracity of witness testimony during trial, if a trial is likely to be involved. Note, however, in line with the open-textured nature of the competency construct, that a complete enumeration is not possible; rather, an attempt is made to summarize the general lay of the land, allowing for specifics to be a matter of personal judgment.

The IFI was designed so that evaluators would have to consider both legal and mental status issues, but neither in isolation. The format of the IFI requires evaluators to relate their observations to the specific demands of the legal situation. For each item, evaluators are asked to rate the degree of incapacity of the defendant, as well as to give the item a score to indicate the influence that the incapacity might have on the overall decision about competency. Thus, a defendant may receive a score indicating the presence of hallucinations (item 10) but receive a low-weight score because the evaluator has determined that the presence of hallucinations would not have much effect on the conduct of the legal case. Another defendant with the same symptom may receive a high-weight score because the hallucinations are considered to be more of a potential problem during the legal proceedings.

A training manual for use of the IFI has been developed as a guide for evaluators. For each item, the manual provides a set of suggested questions and follow-up probes and also gives clinical guidance for the handling of typical problems.

Golding et al. (1984) used the IFI in a study of pretrial defendants in the Boston area who were referred by court clinics to a state mental hospital for competency evaluation. They were interviewed by teams composed of a lawyer and either a psychologist or a social worker. The interviews were conducted jointly, but each evaluator independently completed the IFI rating form. The results demonstrated that judgments about competency can be made in a reliable manner by lawyers and mental health evaluators; they were in agreement on 97% of their final determinations of competency. By type of decision, the interviewers found 58 defendants to be competent, 17 incompetent, and disagreed on the remaining 2 cases.

The IFI has recently been revised (Golding, 1993) to reflect changes in constitutional law and the adoption by many states of "articulated" competency standards (e.g., Utah, 1994). In its current form, the Interdisciplinary Fitness Interview–Revised taps 31 relatively specific psycholegal abilities organized into 11 global domains. The IFI-R was developed on the original model used by Golding et al. (1984), but was altered to reflect a decade of experience, numerous court opinions, and the accumulated professional literature on competency assessments. For example, it specifically addresses the issue of the iatrogenic effects of psychotropic medications (*Riggins v. Nevada*, 1992), a defendant's decisional competency to engage in rational choice about trial strategies, proceeding *pro se* or pleading guilty (see discussion of *Godinez v. Moran, 1993,* above), and competency to confess. It was developed to mirror Utah's new articulated competency code, which mandates that examiners address its 11 global domains. Although it has not yet been empirically studied, a revised and comprehensive training manual is available (Golding, 1993).

Golding et al. (1984) also commented on one of the research problems inherent in studies of competency assessment. Because most defendants are competent (77% in the above study), it is difficult to obtain a sufficiently large sample of incompetent defendants. It is clear to us that decisions about most defendants referred for competency evaluations are straightforward; that is, they are competent to stand trial, a finding that is evident regardless of the method of assessment. The potential value of the IFI-R or other structured assessment methods, we believe, is in assessing defendants whose competency is truly questionable.

The Fitness Interview Test

The FIT (Roesch, Webster, & Eaves, 1984) was originally created in 1984 to assess fitness to stand trial in Canada. It has since been extensively revised, and the current version is referred to as the Fitness Interview Test (Revised edition) (Roesch, Zapf, Eaves, & Webster, 1994). The FIT focuses on the psycholegal abilities of the individual. The scoring system has been changed to a 3-point scale, with a score of 2 meaning definite or serious impairment, 1 meaning possible or mild impairment, and 0 meaning no impairment. As well, the items on the FIT were developed to parallel the standards for fitness that were established in section 2 of the 1992 revision of the *Criminal Code of Canada.*

The FIT takes approximately 30 minutes to administer and consists of a structured interview that covers three main areas: (a) the ability to understand the nature or object of the proceedings, or factual knowledge of criminal procedure; (b) the ability to understand the possible consequences of the proceedings, or the appreciation of personal involvement in and importance of the proceedings; and (c) the ability to communicate with counsel, or to participate in the defense. Each of these three sections is broken down into specific questions that tap into different areas involved in fitness to stand trial. The first section assesses the defendant's understanding of the arrest process, the nature and severity of current charges, the role of key players, legal processes, pleas, and court procedure. The second section assesses the defendant's appreciation of the range and nature of possible penalties, appraisal of available legal defenses, and appraisal of likely outcome. The final section assesses the defendant's capacity to communicate facts to the lawyer, relate to the lawyer, plan legal strategy, engage in his or her own defense, challenge prosecution witnesses, testify relevantly, and manage courtroom behavior.

Recent research indicates that the FIT demonstrates excellent utility as a screening instrument (Zapf & Roesch, 1997). In this study, results of the FIT and an institution-based fitness assessment were compared for 57 defendants remanded to an inpatient psychiatric institution for an evaluation of fitness. The FIT correctly predicted fitness status (i.e., fit or unfit) for 49 of the 57 individuals. The remaining 8 individuals were judged to be unfit by the FIT and fit as a result of the inpatient assessment. This was to be expected, as a screening instrument should overestimate the rate of unfitness without making any false-negative errors. There was 100% agreement between the FIT and the institution-based assessment for those individuals deemed fit to stand trial.

The Georgia Court Competency Test

The GCCT was originally developed by Wildman et al. (1978) and has since gone through a number of revisions (see Bagby, Nicholson, Rogers, & Nussbaum, 1992; Johnson & Mullet, 1987; Nicholson, Briggs, & Robertson, 1988; Wildman, White, & Brandenburg, 1990). The original version consisted of 17 items; the revised version, referred to as the Mississippi State Hospital Revision (GCCT-MSH), consists of 21 items. The first 7 items of the GCCT-MSH require the defendant to visually identify the location of certain participants in the courtroom. This is followed by questions related to the function of certain individuals in the courtroom, the charges that the defendant is facing, and his or her relationship with the lawyer.

Recent research on the GCCT-MSH has indicated that this instrument displays high levels of reliability and validity (Nicholson, Robertson, Johnson, & Jensen, 1988). Three factors have been identified by Nicholson, Briggs, et al. (1988): courtroom layout, general legal knowledge, and specific legal knowledge. These same three factors were later replicated by Bagby et al. (1992). It was later suggested that this three-factor solution may be appropriate only for defendants who have been ordered to undergo assessment at the pretrial stage (Ustad, Rogers, Sewell, & Guarnaccia, 1996). These researchers indicated that a two-factor solution (legal knowledge and courtroom layout) may be more appropriate for defendants who have been adjudicated incompetent and who are undergoing inpatient treatment to restore competence. The major drawback of the GCCT-MSH is that it focuses on foundational competencies and relatively ignores the more important decisional competencies stressed in the IFI and FIT approaches (Bonnie, 1992).

The MacArthur Competence Assessment Tool–Criminal Adjudication

The MacCAT-CA (Bonnie, Hoge, Monahan, & Poythress, 1996) was developed as part of the MacArthur Network on Mental Health and the Law. This instrument is currently being released only for research purposes. It was developed from a number of research instruments (see Hoge et al., 1997, for a complete discussion of its development) and assesses three main abilities: understanding, reasoning, and appreciation.

The MacCAT-CA consists of 22 items and takes approximately 30 minutes to administer. The basis of the items is a short story about two men who get into a fight; one is subsequently charged with a criminal offense. The first 8 items assess the individual's understanding of the legal system; most of these items consist of two parts. The defendant's understanding is first assessed and, if it is unsatisfactory or appears to be questionable, the information is then disclosed to the defendant and his or her understanding is again assessed. This allows the evaluator to determine whether or not the individual is able to learn disclosed information. The next 8 items assess the individual's reasoning skills by asking which of two disclosed facts would be most relevant to the case. Finally, the last 6 items assess the individual's appreciation of his or her own circumstances. A large study is currently underway to determine national norms for the MacCAT-CA.

Other Specialized Assessment Instruments

In recent years, there has been a move toward the development of competence assessment instruments for specialized populations of defendants. We will not go into detail about these specialized instruments here, but the reader should be aware that they exist. Everington (1990) has developed an instrument designed to assess competence with mentally retarded defendants called the Competence Assessment for Standing Trial for Defendants with Mental Retardation (CAST-MR). Recent research on the CAST-MR has indicated that this instrument shows good reliability and validity (Everington & Dunn, 1995). Other researchers have focused their efforts on another special population, juvenile defendants (see Cooper, 1995; Cowden & McKee, 1995). Research in this area has indicated a negative correlation between age and competency status; that is, younger defendants are more likely to be found incompetent (Cooper, 1995; Cowden & McKee, 1995).

GUIDELINES FOR EVALUATORS

We conclude our chapter with a discussion of several issues to which an examiner must pay special attention when conducting an evaluation of competency (see, generally, Committee on Ethical Guidelines for Forensic Psychologists, 1991). Even before seeing a defendant face-to-face, it is good clinical practice to speak with both the defense and prosecuting attorneys to determine as accurately as possible why the fitness issue was raised, what evidence was offered, and what sort of trial and dispositional alternatives are being considered by both sides.

All indications of prior mental health contacts should be pursued *before* the interview takes place, so that the examiner has as complete a set of mental health records as possible. Similarly, complete police reports of the alleged crime are necessary and a past criminal history record helpful, particularly if the defendant has cycled through the criminal justice and mental health systems several times. Obviously, if the defendant is an inpatient, observational records should be consulted, as well as all routine psychological test data. Finally, the examiner should maintain an accurate record of when, where, and how information about the defendant was made available, as well as a date and time record of all contacts with the defendant, attorneys, and other mental health professionals. These records are invaluable at later stages if legal tactics designed to confuse or mislead a witness are attempted.

Having prepared for an examination in this fashion, one can conduct an efficient and comprehensive interview in a short period of time. Most delays in conducting an evaluation and most time spent in inpatient status can thus be avoided, and a more relevant examination conducted, if these steps are taken.

Prior to the interview, the defendant should be fully informed about any limitations on the interview's confidentiality. The possibility of recording the interview should be discussed, although permission should also be obtained from the defendant's attorney.

The examiner should be aware of any aspects of the interview and the resulting report that are covered by statute or accepted practice within the jurisdiction. As an example of the former, some states require *Miranda*-like warnings that inform the defendant of the limitations of confidentiality that may apply. Similarly, other states dictate the form of the report to the court, and an examiner's report may be excluded if it does not comply with the required format.

In *People v. Harris* (1983), for example, a psychiatrist's report (that the defendant was competent) was excluded and the defendant's subsequent conviction was reversed because the opinion was presented in conclusory terms and failed to give the clinical facts and reasons upon which it was based, thus precluding the trier of fact from independently assessing the weight to be given such an opinion. The current competency statutes in Illinois (as in Florida and Utah) are in many ways models of this developing trend. They require the examiner to address the facts upon which the conclusion is based, to explain how the conclusion was reached, to describe the defendant's mental and physical disabilities and how these impair the ability to understand the proceedings and assist in the defense, to discuss the likelihood that the defendant will respond to a specified course of treatment, and to explain procedures that would be employed to compensate for the defendant's disabilities, if any. We applaud this sort of specification and urge examiners to adopt the practice, even if it is not mandated in their own jurisdiction.

The conduct of a competency evaluation and the reports prepared for court should therefore be in complete accord with both the spirit and the letter of contemporary legal standards. The examiner must therefore be thoroughly acquainted with the legal literature and in some sense anticipate developments in one's practice. For example, *Estelle v. Smith* (1981) clearly prohibits the introduction of material obtained under court-ordered competency proceedings at a critical (guilt or sentencing) stage of trial. Many states mirror this in their statutes but nevertheless do not regulate the common practice of requesting competency and sanity evaluations at the same time, often resulting in a combined report. We believe this practice is unfortunate and recommend that separate interviews, with distinct reports, be prepared. A trier of fact is required to separate these issues, yet it is cognitively almost impossible to do so when the reports are combined. A defendant who is clearly psychotic and "legally insane" at the time of an assault may respond rapidly to treatment upon arrest and be just as nonpsychotic and "legally fit" when actually examined. Caution and fairness dictate keeping the reports separate so that the two issues can be considered independently by the courts.

CONCLUSION

This chapter touches upon only a small selection of the vast amount of research and writing on competence to stand trial. The purpose of this chapter was only to give a brief overview of competency law, research, and assessment. For a comprehensive review of the recent empirical research on competence to stand trial, the reader is referred to Grisso (1992) and Cooper and Grisso (1996). These authors review the research on the evaluation of competence in two 5-year intervals (1986–1990 and 1991–1995). As well, Nicholson and Kugler (1991) conducted a meta-analysis using 30 studies and over 8,000 defendants that provides a quantitative review of the comparative research on competence. These references as well as those listed in the introductory paragraph of this chapter will provide the reader with a more in-depth understanding of competency to stand trial.

REFERENCES

Bagby, R. M., Nicholson, R. A., Rogers, R., & Nussbaum, D. (1992). Domains of competency to stand trial: A factor analytic study. *Law and Human Behavior, 16,* 491–507.

Berry, F. D., Jr. (1973). Self-incrimination and the compulsory mental examination: A proposal. *Arizona Law Review, 15,* 919–950.

Bersoff, D., Goodman-Delahunty, J., Grisso, J. T., Hans, V. P., Roesch, R., & Poythress, N. G. (1997). Training in psychology and law: Models from the Villanova conference. *American Psychologist, 52,* 1301–1310.

Bonnie, R. J. (1992). The competence of criminal defendants: A theoretical reformulation. *Behavioral Sciences and the Law, 10,* 291–316.

Bonnie, R. J. (1993). The competence of criminal defendants: Beyond Dusky and Drope. *University of Miami Law Review, 47,* 539–601.

Bonnie, R. J., Hoge, S. K., Monahan, J., & Poythress, N. G. (1996). *The MacArthur Competence Assessment Tool—Criminal adjudication.* Unpublished manuscript.

Borum, R., & Grisso, T. (1995). Psychological test use in criminal forensic evaluations. *Professional Psychology: Research and Practice, 26,* 465–473.

Brakel, S. J. (1974). Presumption, bias, and incompetency in the criminal process. *Wisconsin Law Review, 1974,* 1105–1130.

Bukatman, B. A., Foy, J. L., & DeGrazia, E. (1971). What is competency to stand trial? *American Journal of Psychiatry, 127,* 1225–1229.

Chernoff, P. A., & Schaffer, W. G. (1972). Defending the mentally ill: Ethical quicksand. *American Criminal Law Review, 10,* 505–531.

Committee on Ethical Guidelines for Forensic Psychologists. (1991). Specialty guidelines for forensic psychologists. *Law and Human Behavior, 15,* 655–665.

Cooke, G. (1969). The court study unit: Patient characteristics and differences between patients judged competent and incompetent. *Journal of Clinical Psychology, 25,* 140–143.

Cooper, D. K. (1995). Juvenile competency to stand trial: The effects of age and presentation of factual information in the attainment of competency in juveniles. *Dissertation Abstracts International, 56*(10-B), 5761.

Cooper, D. K., & Grisso, T. (1996, August). *Five-year research update (1991–1995): Evaluations for competence to stand trial.* Paper presented at the American Psychological Association Convention, Toronto, Ontario, Canada.

Cowden, V. L., & McKee, G. R. (1995). Competency to stand trial in juvenile delinquency proceedings–cognitive maturity and the attorney-client relationship. *University of Louisville Journal of Family Law, 33,* 629–660.

Davis, D. L. (1985). Treatment planning for the patient who is incompetent to stand trial. *Hospital and Community Psychiatry, 36,* 268–271.

Davis, S. (1994). Fitness to stand trial in Canada in light of the recent Criminal Code amendments. *International Journal of Law and Psychiatry, 17,* 319–329.

Dickey, W. (1980). Incompetency and the nondangerous mentally ill client. *Criminal Law Bulletin, 16,* 22–40.

Drope v. Missouri, 420 U.S. 162 (1975).

Dusky v. United States, 362 U.S. 402 (1960).

Estelle v. Smith, 49 U.S. L.W. 4490 (1981).

Everington, C. T. (1990). The competence assessment for standing trial for defendants with mental retardation (CAST-MR): A validation study. *Criminal Justice and Behavior, 17*(2), 147–168.

Everington, C., & Dunn, C. (1995). A second validation study of the competence assessment for standing trial for defendants with mental retardation (CAST-MR). *Criminal Justice and Behavior, 22,* 44–59.

Farkas, G., DeLeon, P., & Newman, R. (1997). Sanity examiner certification: An evolving national agenda. *Professional Psychology: Research & Practice, 28,* 73–76.

Favole, R. J. (1983). Mental disability in the American criminal process: A four issue survey. In J. Monahan & H. J. Steadman (Eds.), *Mentally disordered offenders: Perspectives from law and social science* (pp. 247–295). New York: Plenum Press.

Fitzgerald, J. F., Peszke, M. A., & Goodwin, R. C. (1978). Competency evaluations in Connecticut. *Hospital and Community Psychiatry, 29,* 450–453.

Godinez v. Moran, 113 St. C. 2680 (1993).

Golding, S. L. (1992). Studies of incompetent defendants: Research and social policy implications. *Forensic Reports, 5,* 77–83.

Golding, S. L. (1993). *Interdisciplinary Fitness Interview–Revised: A training manual.* State of Utah Division of Mental Health.

Golding, S. L., Roesch, R., & Schreiber, J. (1984). Assessment and conceptualization of competency to stand trial: Preliminary data on the Interdisciplinary Fitness Interview. *Law and Human Behavior, 8,* 321–334.

Golding, S. L., & Roesch, R. (1988). Competency for adjudication: An international analysis. In D. N. Weisstub (Ed.), *Law and mental health: International perspectives* (Vol. 4, pp. 73–109). New York: Pergamon Press.

Goldstein, R. L., & Stone, M. (1977). When doctors disagree: Differing views on competency. *Bulletin of the American Academy of Psychiatry and the Law, 5,* 90–97.

Golten, R. J. (1972). Role of defense counsel in the criminal commitment process. *American Criminal Law Review, 10,* 385–430.

Government of the Virgin Islands v. Charles, 72 F.3d 401 (3rd Cir., 1995).

Grisso, T. (1986). *Evaluating competencies: Forensic assessments and instruments.* New York: Plenum Press.

Grisso, T. (1987). The economic and scientific future of forensic psychological assessment. *American Psychologist, 42,* 831–839.

Grisso, T. (1992). Five-year research update (1986–1990): Evaluations for competence to stand trial. *Behavioral Sciences and the Law, 10,* 353–369.

Grisso, T., Appelbaum, P., Mulvey, E., & Fletcher, K. (1995). The MacArthur treatment competence study II: Measures of abilities related to competence to consent to treatment. *Law & Human Behavior, 19,* 127–148.

Grisso, T., Coccozza, J. J., Steadman, H. J., Fisher, W. H., & Greer, A. (1994). The organization of pretrial forensic evaluation services: A national profile. *Law and Human Behavior, 18,* 377–393.

Hart, S. D., & Hare, R. D. (1992). Predicting fitness for trial: The relative power of demographic, criminal and clinical variables. *Forensic Reports, 5,* 53–65.

Heilbrun, K., & Collins, S. (1995). Evaluations of trial competency and mental state at time of offense: Report characteristics. *Professional Psychology: Research and Practice, 26*, 61–67.

Hoge, S. K., Bonnie, R. J., Poythress, N., & Monahan, J. (1992). Attorney-client decision-making in criminal cases: Client competence and participation as perceived by their attorneys. *Behavioral Sciences and the Law, 10*, 385–394.

Hoge, S. K., Bonnie, R. J., Poythress, N., Monahan, J., Eisenberg, M., & Feucht-Haviar, T. (1997). The MacArthur Adjudicative Competence Study: Development and validation of a research instrument. *Law and Human Behavior, 21*, 141–179.

Jackson v. Indiana, 406 U.S. 715 (1972).

Johnson, W. G., & Mullett, N. (1987). Georgia Court Competency Test–R. In M. Hersen & A. S. Bellack (Eds.), *Dictionary of behavioral assessment techniques.* New York: Pergamon Press.

Kaufman, H. (1972). Evaluating competency: Are constitutional deprivations necessary? *American Criminal Law Review, 10*, 465–504.

Laben, J. K., Kashgarian, M., Nessa, D. B., & Spencer, L. D. (1977). Reform from the inside: Mental health center evaluations of competency to stand trial. *Journal of Clinical Psychology, 5*, 52–62.

Lewin, T. H. (1969). Incompetency to stand trial: Legal and ethical aspects of an abused doctrine. *Law and Social Order, 2*, 233–285.

Lipsitt, P. D., Lelos, D., & McGarry, A. L. (1971). Competency for trial: A screening instrument. *American Journal of Psychiatry, 128*, 105–109.

McGarry, A. L. (1965). Competency for trial and due process via the state hospital. *American Journal of Psychiatry, 122*, 623–631.

McGarry, A. L., & Curran, W. J. (1973). *Competency to stand trial and mental illness.* Rockville, MD: National Institute of Mental Health.

Melton, G. B., Petrila, J., Poythress, N. G., & Slobogin, C. (1987). *Psychological evaluations for the courts: A handbook for mental health professionals and lawyers.* New York: Guilford Press.

Melton, G. B., Weithorn, L. A., & Slobogin, L. A. (1985). *Community mental health centers and the courts: An evaluation of community-based forensic services.* Lincoln: University of Nebraska Press.

Menzies, R. J., Webster, C. D., Butler, B. T., & Turner, R. C. (1980). The outcome of forensic psychiatric assessment: A study of remands in six Canadian cities. *Criminal Justice and Behavior, 7*, 471–480.

Messick, S. (1980). Test validity and the ethics of assessment. *American Psychologist, 35*, 1012–1027.

Missouri v. Davis, 653 S.W. 2d. 167 (Mo. Sup. Ct. 1983).

Montana v. Austed, 641 P. 2d. 1373 (Mont. Sup. Ct. 1982).

Morrow v. Maryland, 443 A. 2d. 108 (Md. Ct. App. 1982).

Nicholson, R., LaFortune, K., Norwood, S., & Roach, R. (1995, August). *Pretrial competency evaluations in Oklahoma: Report characteristics and consumer satisfaction.* Paper presented at the American Psychological Association Convention, New York.

Nicholson, R. A., Briggs, S. R., & Robertson, H. C. (1988). Instruments for assessing competency to stand trial: How do they work? *Professional Psychology: Research & Practice, 19*, 383–394.

Nicholson, R. A., & Kugler, K. E. (1991). Competent and incompetent criminal defendants: A quantitative review of comparative research. *Psychological Bulletin, 109*, 355–370.

Nicholson, R. A., Robertson, H. C., Johnson, W. G., & Jensen, G. (1988). A comparison of instruments for assessing competency to stand trial. *Law and Human Behavior, 12*, 313–321.

North Dakota v. Heger, 326 N.W.2d 855 (1982).

Nottingham, E. J., & Mattson, R. E. (1981). A validation study of the competency screening test. *Law and Human Behavior, 5,* 329–336.

Ogloff, J. R. P., & Roesch, R. (1992). Using community mental health centers to provide comprehensive mental health services to jails. In J. R. P. Ogloff (Ed.), *Psychology and law: The broadening of the discipline* (pp. 241–260). Durham, NC: Carolina Academic Press.

Ogloff, J. R. P., Wallace, D. H., & Otto, R. K. (1991). Competencies in the criminal process. In D. K. Kagehiro & W. S. Laufer (Eds.), *Handbook of psychology and law* (pp. 343–360). New York: Springer-Verlag.

Pate v. Robinson, 383 U.S. 375 (1966).

Pendleton, L. (1980). Treatment of persons found incompetent to stand trial. *American Journal of Psychiatry, 137,* 1098–1100.

People v. Harris, 133 Ill. App. 3d. 633 (1983).

Perlin, M. L. (1996). "Dignity was the first to leave": Godinez v. Moran, Colin Ferguson, and the trial of mentally disabled criminal defendants. *Behavioral Sciences and the Law, 14,* 61–81.

Petrella, R. C., & Poythress, N. G. (1983). The quality of forensic evaluations: An interdisciplinary study. *Journal of Consulting and Clinical Psychology, 51,* 76–85.

Pizzi, W. T. (1977). Competency to stand trial in federal courts: Conceptual and constitutional problems. *University of Chicago Law Review, 45,* 20–71.

Poythress, N. G., & Stock, H. V. (1980). Competency to stand trial: A historical review and some new data. *Psychiatry and Law, 8,* 131–146.

Randolph, J. J., Hicks, T., & Mason, D. (1981). The Competency Screening Test: A replication and extension. *Criminal Justice and Behavior, 8,* 471–482.

Regina v. Whittle, 2 S.C.R. 914 (1994).

Riggins v. Nevada, 112 S. Ct. 1810 (1992).

Ritchie v. Indiana, 468 N.E. 2d. 1369 (Ind. Sup. Ct. 1984).

Robey, A. (1965). Criteria for competency to stand trial: A checklist for psychiatrists. *American Journal of Psychiatry, 122,* 616–623.

Roesch, R., & Golding, S. L. (1980). *Competency to stand trial.* Urbana: University of Illinois Press.

Roesch, R., & Golding, S. L. (1985). The impact of deinstitutionalization. In D. P. Farrington & J. Gunn (Eds.), *Current research in forensic psychiatry and psychology* (pp. 209–239). New York: Wiley.

Roesch, R., Grisso, T., & Poythress, N. G., Jr. (1986). Training programs, courses, and workshops in psychology and law. In M. F. Kaplan (Ed.), *The impact of social psychology on procedural justice* (pp. 83–108). Springfield, IL.: Thomas.

Roesch, R., Hart, S. D., & Zapf, P. (1996). Conceptualizing and assessing competency to stand trial: Implications and applications of the MacArthur Treatment Competence Model. *Psychology, Public Policy, and Law, 2,* 96–113.

Roesch, R., & Ogloff, J. R. P. (1996). Settings for providing civil and criminal mental health services. In B. D. Sales & S. A. Shah (Eds.), *Mental health and law: Research, policy and services* (pp. 191–218). Durham, NC: Carolina Academic Press.

Roesch, R., Ogloff, J. R. P., & Golding, S. L. (1993). Competency to stand trial: Legal and clinical issues. *Applied and Preventative Psychology, 2,* 43–51.

Roesch, R., Webster, C. D., & Eaves, D. (1984). *The Fitness Interview Test: A method for assessing fitness to stand trial.* Toronto: University of Toronto Centre of Criminology.

Roesch, R., Zapf, P. A., Eaves, D. & Webster, C. D. (1998). *The Fitness Interview Test* (Rev. ed.). Burnaby, BC: Mental Health, Law, & Policy Institute, Simon Fraser University.

Rogers, R. R., & Mitchell, C. N. (1991). *Mental health experts and the criminal courts.* Scarborough, Ontario: Carswell.

Schreiber, J. (1978). Assessing competency to stand trial: A case study of technology diffusion in four states. *Bulletin of the American Academy of Psychiatry and the Law, 6,* 439–457.

Shatin, L. (1979). Brief form of the Competency Screening Test for mental competence to stand trial. *Journal of Clinical Psychology, 35,* 464–467.

Siegel, A. M., & Elwork, A. (1990). Treating incompetence to stand trial. *Law and Human Behavior, 14,* 57–65.

Silten, P. R., & Tullis, R. (1977). Mental competency in criminal proceedings. *Hastings Law Journal, 28,* 1053–1074.

Skeem, J. L., Golding, S. L., Cohn, N. B., & Berge, G. (1997). *The logic and reliability of evaluations of competence to stand trial.* Manuscript submitted for publication.

Steadman, H. J. (1979). *Beating a rap?: Defendants found incompetent to stand trial.* Chicago: University of Chicago Press.

Steadman, H. J., & Hartstone, E. (1983). Defendants incompetent to stand trial. In J. Monahan & H. J. Steadman (Eds.), *Mentally disordered offenders: Perspectives from law and social science* (pp. 39–62). New York: Plenum Press.

Teplin, L. (1984). Criminalizing mental disorder: The comparative arrest rate of the mentally ill. *American Psychologist, 39,* 794–803.

Utah Code Annotated § 77-15-1 *et seq.* (1994).

Ustad, K. L., Rogers, R., Sewell, K. W., & Guarnaccia, C. A. (1996). Restoration of competency to stand trial: Assessment with the Georgia Court Competency Test and the Competency Screening Test. *Law and Human Behavior, 20,* 131–146.

Verdun-Jones, S. N. (1981). The doctrine of fitness to stand trial in Canada: The forked tongue of social control. *International Journal of Law and Psychiatry, 4,* 363–389.

Webster, C. D., Jenson, F. A. S., Stermac, L., Gardner, K., & Slomen, D. (1985). Psychoeducational programmes for forensic psychiatric patients. *Canadian Psychology, 26,* 50–53.

Webster, C. D., Menzies, R. J., & Jackson, M. A. (1982). *Clinical assessment before trial.* Toronto: Butterworths.

Wieter v. Settle, 193 F. Supp. 318 (W.D. Mo. 1961).

Williams, W., & Miller, K. K. (1981). The processing and disposition of incompetent mentally ill offenders. *Law and Human Behavior, 5,* 245–261.

Wildman, R. W., Batchelor, E. S., Thompson, L., Nelson, F. R., Moore, J. T., Patterson, M. E., & deLaosa, M. (1978). *The Georgia Court Competency Test: An attempt to develop a rapid, quantitative measure of fitness for trial.* Unpublished manuscript, Forensic Services Division, Central State Hospital, Milledgeville, GA.

Wildman, R. W., II, White, P. A., & Brandenburg, C. A. (1990). The Georgia Court Competency Test: The base rate problem. *Perceptual and Motor Skills, 70,* 1055–1058.

Wilson v. United States, 391 F.2d. 460 (1968).

Winick, B. J. (1983). Incompetency to stand trial: Developments in the law. In J. Monahan & H. J. Steadman (Eds.), *Mentally disordered offenders* (pp. 3–38). New York: Plenum Press.

Winick, B. J. (1985). Restructuring competency to stand trial. *UCLA Law Review, 32,* 921–985.

Winick, B. J. (1995). Reforming incompetency to stand trial and plead guilty: A restated proposal and a response to Professor Bonnie. *Journal of Criminal Law and Criminology, 85,* 571–624.

Winick, B. J. (1996). Incompetency to proceed in the criminal process: Past, present, and future. In D. B. Wexler & B. J. Winick (Eds.), *Law in a therapeutic key: Developments in therapeutic jurisprudence* (pp. 77–111). Durham, NC: Carolina Academic Press.

Zapf, P. A., & Roesch, R. (1997). Assessing fitness to stand trial: A comparison of institution-based evaluations and a brief screening interview. *Canadian Journal of Community Mental Health, 16,* 53–66.

Zapf, P. A., & Roesch, R. (1998). Fitness to stand trial: Characteristics of remands in Canada since the 1992 Criminal Code amendments. *Canadian Journal of Psychiatry, 43,* 287–293.

CHAPTER 13

Specific Intent and Diminished Capacity

CHARLES R. CLARK

CASE EXAMPLES

CASE EXAMPLE 1: ASSAULT WITH INTENT TO COMMIT MURDER

A MIDDLE-AGED white male with a long history of alcoholism was charged with assault with intent to commit murder on a police officer at the man's home in a trailer park. Neighbors of the defendant reported that he had been drinking heavily during the day and was visibly drunk and verbally obnoxious. They warned him that they would call the police, and before he managed to get back into his trailer (by crawling through a hole he made in the screen door, because he could not manage to unlatch the door), the defendant reportedly declared that he would shoot any police officer who tried to arrest him. It was the better part of an hour before police responded to the neighbors' complaints. Police got no answer when they repeatedly knocked on his door and called for him. Finally, while the police were still on the scene, a gun was fired from inside the defendant's trailer, apparently directed at the police. No one was hurt and the defendant was arrested. Defense raised the issue of diminished capacity, focusing on whether the defendant was capable of intending to kill a police officer at the time he shot his gun.

CASE EXAMPLE 2: INVOLUNTARY MANSLAUGHTER WITH A MOTOR VEHICLE

A Native American male with a history of epilepsy was charged with two counts of involuntary manslaughter with a motor vehicle along with failure to stop at a serious or aggravated personal injury accident. His seizure disorder had never been fully controlled by medication, and he had been restricted from driving. He

350

indicated that despite this, he sometimes did drive his mother's car. On one prior occasion he had an apparent seizure while driving and ran the car into a parked vehicle at low speed; that collision did not cause any injuries and he was not prosecuted. On this second occasion, however, the defendant, who reported no memory for the incident, was driving some miles over the speed limit in a residential area when he drove onto the curb and struck a sign before striking a group of people further on. The collision killed two young children and injured their mother and grandfather. After this collision, the car driven by the defendant continued on until it was stopped by a tree. Witnesses reported that once the car was stopped, the rear wheels of the car continued to spin, indicating that the driver was still depressing the accelerator. A witness related that on approaching him the defendant had a dazed appearance and was not responsive to what the excited and angry witness shouted at him. The bystanders and others ran to the aid of the victims, some distance down the street. While they were being attended to, and some time after the collision, the defendant was observed to get out of his vehicle, inspect the damage to it, get back in, and drive away. The question of diminished capacity was raised in his defense, including the question of whether the defendant had been conscious of what he had done at the time he left the scene of the accident.

Case Example 3: Arson

An African American man was accused of arson in his apartment building. Allegedly, he woke a neighbor early one morning, crying that his apartment was on fire. By the time police and firefighters responded, the fire was extinguished. It appeared to have originated on the top of the defendant's gas stove, which was scorched and where a number of burned papers were found. Some of the carpet adjacent to the stove had been charred as well. The neighbors reported that the defendant, who had been in mental health treatment in the community for some years but who had apparently stopped taking his medication, had been behaving bizarrely. He reportedly walked in the hall nude and talked to himself. He had recently complained that he could not light his stove and that he needed help to cook dinner for his wife, although he was unmarried and had never been seen with a woman. He had reportedly disassembled the gas connection to his stove the day before the fire, and the neighbors had detected a smell of gas before they called a gas company repairman, who reconnected it. On the basis of this report, police arrested the defendant. While in custody he acted strangely. He proclaimed, "My purpose is to bring the church to the third heaven," and he said that the police had been sent by Lucifer. He stated that he was hearing the voice of God, and he seemed to be responding to internal stimulation. At one point during the interview he reportedly pulled an apple from his pants and yelled, "Women don't need a penis to ovulate!" On examination later, he adamantly denied ever intending to set a fire. He reported that he awoke to the smell of gas in his apartment and that he thought the pilot light had gone out and tried to light it with a twist of paper. Defense raised the question of both insanity and diminished capacity, the latter issue involving the question of whether the defendant had been capable of forming the intent for arson.

Case Example 4: Premeditated Murder and
Assault with Intent to Kill

An African American man was charged with the premeditated murders of his union local president and a committeeman, and with assault with intent to kill in the shooting of two other union committeemen, all of them white. The defendant was a former union committeeman closely allied to the former president, who had been on the losing side of a prolonged leadership conflict within the union local. The defendant entered the union headquarters on a Saturday morning and after reportedly voicing some perfunctory greetings, he found one of his rivals, whom he had accused of being central to the ouster of the former governing caucus, and shot him in the head with a handgun. He briefly pursued another man who fled the building before proceeding to the office where the president and other committeemen were meeting. In rapid succession, he shot and killed the president and shot the other two men, one in the head and one in the chest, before turning and leaving the office. One of the wounded men escaped outside and was pursued by the defendant before the man fell; he reported that the defendant leveled his gun at him, but then left without firing another shot. The defendant surrendered peaceably, and identified himself as the shooter: "It's me, I shot 'em." The defense of diminished capacity was raised in his trial. Although he had no history of mental disorder, a version of the "Black Rage" defense (see Grier & Cobbs, 1968) was cited in explanation for his acts, supported by arguments that the defendant had suffered from racial prejudice and discrimination, and that he had identified the victims as perpetrators of racist policy and practice within the union.

Case Example 5: Premeditated Murder

A 19-year-old white male was accused of the premeditated murder some three years before of a 15-year-old girl. She had claimed that she was pregnant by him and had refused to consider an abortion. After the girl disappeared, suspicion fell on the defendant, but he passed a lie detector test and charges were not brought. Finally, a girlfriend of the defendant reported that he had revealed to her that he had accidentally killed the girl and had buried her in a remote location. Following this lead, police discovered the girl's body in a shallow grave in a wooded area by a lake on a farm owned by the defendant's cousin. Confronted with this evidence, he admitted killing her, but he claimed that though he had thought of killing her the day before the death and had even dug the grave, in the event it was an accident. He had gone with her to the remote location where he had dug the grave, he said, but only to talk about what needed to be done. He claimed that after digging the grave he had calmed down and had given up the idea of killing her, and that he had returned with her to this site only because it was a good place to talk. He been sitting and holding her, he said, discussing her pregnancy and their future, when she bit his arm when he playfully wrapped it around her face. In twisting away from her, he said, she wound up dead; he thought he had broken her neck. Though the death was an accident, he reported that he concealed her body in the grave he had dug, filling it in with the shovel he had left on the site. He later reported no memory for the burial itself, but he claimed he assumed that he had been the one who did that. It was the position of defense at trial that the defendant had diminished capacity. In addition to his claim not to have acted on the intent he admitted having formed, evidence was offered that although he was not aware of it, he was a victim of sexual abuse as a preschooler at a daycare center that had been the focus of a highly publicized prosecution about 10 years before. It was suggested that the killing was a reenactment of threatening "games" the abusive staff members of the preschool had subjected the children to, one of which allegedly involved a burial.

* * *

To differing extents, these case scenarios all raise questions, some more plausible than others, of the extent to which a defendant to criminal charges should be considered guilty. Each defendant's mental state is clearly at issue, even if there are also questions about just what the defendants did. But though they bear a superficial resemblance to claims of insanity, they are fundamentally different. Only one of the cases involves a claim that at the time of the alleged offense the defendant was suffering from a severe mental disorder such as psychosis. Others involve claims of intoxication, epilepsy, or the effects of unusual stress and trauma, conditions that would not ordinarily come under the ambit of the insanity defense. For the clinician who examines a defendant for whom the diminished capacity or related intoxication defense has been raised, it is critical to understand the distinctions among these approaches to examining mental state at the time of an offense and the insanity defense. Unfortunately, the law and the legal history of these alternatives to the insanity defense is less than entirely coherent. Moreover, as has been pointed out before (Clark, 1982), the concept of diminished capacity may make more sense from a legal perspective than from a psychological perspective. It involves, to an extent that exceeds that of other psycholegal entities like insanity, prescientific conceptualizations of intentionality. In asking psychologists and psychiatrists to offer opinions about a defendant's ability to form the intent necessary for conviction, the law assumes that its constructs have genuine psychological content open to clinical investigation. That this assumption may be unwarranted in at least some cases in which diminished capacity is raised will become evident from a view of the development of the approach in the United States and the sorts of practical issues that arise in forensic evaluations of defendants.

ACTUS REUS AND MENS REA

It is a hallmark of Anglo-American law that two elements must be present in order for criminal guilt to be established: a wrongful deed or *actus reus* and a criminal intent or wicked state of mind, the *mens rea*. Both of these basic elements, indeed all of the elements of the crime charged, must be established beyond a reasonable doubt (*In re Winship*, 1970).

The person who unwillingly performs an illegal act, whether consciously or unconsciously, is not guilty of the offense. But though volition may be seen as being a mental construct—and it is explicitly included in irresistible impulse and American Law Institute tests of insanity—it is different from diminished capacity approaches and ordinarily involves no mental health examination. Put differently, and as will be discussed further, volition has not typically been seen as relevant to the question of diminished capacity. The store clerk forced at gunpoint to tie up other employees and open a safe for a robber is not guilty, just as a somnambulist who exposes himself by walking outside unclothed is not guilty of a crime. The element of *actus reus,* although always open to question and never assumed in a criminal conviction, is seldom open to a specifically mental health defense. Except in some cases of the insanity defense, questions of voluntariness ordinarily pertain to the issue of *actus reus* and not *mens rea.* The so-called automaton defense, for instance, in which the defendant asserts a lack of volition and often a lack of consciousness as well, attacks the prosecution claim that there was an *actus reus* (Melton, Petrila, Poythress, & Slobogin, 1997).

It is in respect to the question of whether a defendant formed *mens rea* that forensic psychologists are most likely to be asked to provide expert opinions. As discussed in the chapter on criminal responsibility, legal insanity may be seen to negate *mens rea* or mental guilt altogether, in a global way. The individual who meets any of the various tests of insanity is said to be not guilty, not because no illegal act was committed but because the actor lacked the requisite state of mind, for example, the capacity to appreciate the wrongfulness of conduct. Although insanity can be encompassed under the rubric of *mens rea,* some scholars would contend that sanity is not an "element" of the offense, at least not one that needs to be proven by the prosecution. Rather, in this view, a defendant is legally insane and not culpable even if he or she formed the "intent" required for conviction (Steadman et al., 1993). The entire concept of *mens rea* has changed over time, from a term encompassing the concept of blameworthiness to one that simply denotes the intent to cause a defined act (Steadman et al., 1993).

In contrast to the wholesale negation of mental guilt and therefore criminal responsibility implicit in the insanity defense, diminished capacity considers *mens rea* in a piecemeal fashion, as one or another discreet act of intent. In theory, if not in practice at some times and in some places, diminished capacity does not lead to outright acquittal of any criminal wrongdoing or any general exculpation, but rather to a finding that a person was not capable of forming intent for a particular crime that is charged. What would follow, in theory, is a conviction for some lesser included offense. Additionally, not all crimes are susceptible to this partial defense approach.

Central to the diminished capacity approach are the distinctions made in the law between crimes involving general intent and those involving specific intent. Only specific intent crimes are open to a diminished capacity approach. Confusingly, diminished capacity is often referred to as a *mens rea* defense, although strictly speaking, *mens rea* itself includes general intent as well as the more global moral blameworthiness involved in the concept of criminal responsibility or insanity. To add to the confusion, there is no universal agreement as to which crimes involve specific as opposed to general intent. The development of the law in this regard has been viewed as more a matter of expediency than the logical result of legal theory (Dix, 1971).

Finally, the essential logic behind diminished capacity or *mens rea* defenses is identical to that of the so-called intoxication defense, which is also based in the distinction between general and specific intent. In practice, diminished capacity and intoxication defenses may be indistinguishable. In one investigation of sequential pretrial referrals to Michigan's centralized diagnostic center, the Center for Forensic Psychiatry, ostensibly for opinions on insanity and/or diminished capacity, it was found (Clark, 1988) that most (77%) of those defendants for whom diminished capacity was raised as a defense reported substance abuse at the time of the offense, in significant contrast to those for whom insanity but not diminished capacity was raised, of whom only 39% claimed substance abuse. Because of the substantial similarity of its conceptual base to diminished capacity defenses, the intoxication defense as it involves a claim of incapacity to form intent will not be treated separately here. For a broader discussion of other ways in which intoxication or addiction may affect the grading of responsibility or findings of guilt, see Melton et al. (1997).

GENERAL AND SPECIFIC INTENT

In rough outline, the distinctions between general and specific intent follow a ranking of criminal culpability that is perhaps best illustrated by the American Law Institute Model Penal Code (1962), which included the recommendation that a defendant's level of culpability should be measured by an examination of mental state with respect to all elements of the offense (p. 24). Liability was proposed to be assigned depending on whether the offender acted purposely, knowingly, recklessly, or negligently. Purposeful intent, the highest level of criminal intent, was posited to occur when the offender has the conscious object of committing the act or causing a result. Intent that is knowing involves an awareness by the perpetrator of the nature of the criminal conduct or its circumstances. By contrast, a reckless intent occurs when the offender consciously disregards the substantial and unjustifiable risks involved in the conduct, and a negligent intent exists when the actor should have been aware of the risk and failed to be so (p. 21). The term "willfulness," which occurs in a number of statute designations of crimes, was proposed as an intent element corresponding to knowing intent (p. 22). In respect to the Model Penal Code hierarchy, specific intent, which involves the imputation of some positive subjective mental state, unlike negligence and possibly recklessness as well, most closely corresponds to purposeful and knowing intent (Melton et al., 1997). The drafters of the Model Penal Code proposed that negligence in any case roughly corresponds to the common law requirement of general intent (American Law Institute, p. 23).

In theory, specific intent may be viewed as a higher-order or more seriously criminal purpose than general intent; another way to understand the distinction is that general intent crimes are seen as those involving the simple intent to commit the illegal act itself, although that illegal act may be quite serious, such as a killing or rape. Persons convicted of general intent crimes should have been conscious of their actions and the expected results (Melton et al., 1997). By contrast, specific intent crimes usually require the intent to achieve some additional result beyond the consequences of the general intent crime itself. Thus, in some jurisdictions, a person who illegally breaks into a house is guilty of a general intent crime only, whereas breaking and entering with the further intent of committing larceny would always be viewed as a specific intent offense. Similarly, a sexual assault would be a general intent crime in some jurisdictions, whereas breaking and entering with intent to rape, or assault with intent to rape, would be specific intent offenses. In the solitary case of first-degree murder, specific intent consists of the elements of premeditation and deliberation, supposedly higher or more demanding elements than the mere intent to kill or malice aforethought.

Although, with the exception of first-degree murder, the specific intent offense may entail the actual accomplishment of some effect beyond that of the general intent crime, it need not do so. The would-be rapist may be stopped before he actually perpetrates the rape, for instance. Paradoxically, therefore, an assault or a burglary with intent to commit a rape that was never accomplished might be a more serious offense than the rape itself. This would seem to be an exception of the general prohibition against criminal sanctions for evil thoughts alone, an instance in which a conviction is possible when the actual act or *actus reus* is nothing more than would have been needed for a general intent offense, and in which there is no separate *actus reus* corresponding to the higher and further specific intent. Whether the further specific intent results in a completed act or not, the specific intent crime is always one that is graded as more serious, in regard to the possible penalty, for example, than an included general intent offense. It is more serious specifically because of the enormity of the act intended.

In some jurisdictions, any crime that by statute incorporates an explicit intent, for example, assault with intent to commit murder, is on that account a specific intent offense. Crimes of larceny are typically viewed as specific intent offenses regardless of their circumstances or the nature of what is stolen. Larceny involves not merely the unlawful taking of another's property, an act that may be nothing more than a general intent offense or even a misdemeanor, as in many cases of joyriding or the unauthorized use of a vehicle; larceny is unlawfully taking that property with the further intent of carrying it away, converting it to one's own use, or otherwise depriving the owner of it (Black, 1979, pp. 792–793).

In any jurisdiction in which diminished capacity or *mens rea* defenses are permitted, the highest degree of homicide, usually called first-degree murder, is considered a specific intent crime. In fact, as seen in the discussion of legal developments in this area, much of the focus of case law in respect to diminished capacity has been on murder. In this instance, the specific intent elements are viewed as premeditation and deliberation. These elements, operationally unitary (both must be present for a first-degree murder to have occurred), are subject to somewhat different constructions in various jurisdictions, but generally refer respectively to plotting, contriving, planning, or thinking about the killing beforehand, and weighing and examining the reasons for and against a contemplated act or course of conduct, acts, or means (Black, 1979, p. 384). With temporary exceptions only in California, as discussed below, what is usually called second-degree murder, which requires malice aforethought but not premeditation and deliberation, has been considered a general intent offense that is not susceptible to a diminished capacity or *mens rea* approach. Despite its intuitive connotations of evil intent, the concept of malice survives in law as a mental element that is simply a term of art, a shorthand designation for one of a number of mental elements that would satisfy the requirements for a murder conviction, as opposed to a conviction of the lesser offenses of manslaughter or negligent homicide (Morse, 1979, 1984). The malice required for a second-degree murder conviction could involve the intent to kill, but it could also involve no more than the intent to cause great bodily harm, the willful and wanton disregard of risk to life, or simply the commission of another felony during which a homicide occurs (LaFave & Scott, 1972).

To recapitulate, the specific intent offenses that are potentially open to a diminished capacity or *mens rea* defense are somewhat arbitrarily determined, but include at least premeditated and deliberated murder, larcenies, and those offenses designated as explicitly incorporating some further intent.

ELABORATION OF DIMINISHED CAPACITY DOCTRINE IN CALIFORNIA

It is always theoretically possible for defendants charged with crimes, particularly murder, to claim that they had been incapable of forming premeditation, deliberation, or some other specific intent. These claims have always been rare and, perhaps even more than in the case of insanity pleas, they have rarely been successful. Legal developments in California in regard to this issue made the defense at least more frequent, if in general no more successful.

The ways in which *mens rea* doctrine evolved prior to the development of modern psychology, with its ramifying and complex explanations for human behavior and motivation, resulted in what many mental health professionals might look upon as a barren, jejune, skeletal, and primitive conceptualization of intent. Case law in this area did not invite deeper explorations of the dynamics of intentional conduct, such as its developmental origins or its expression of unconscious drives, or from a behavioral perspective, the individual's learning history. The law did not evince any interest in considering broader affective issues in gauging whether a person was capable of criminal intent. As stated above, volitional factors—the objective or subjective freedom of the individual to form intent and purpose—were not recognized as germane to *mens rea*. Aside from those jurisdictions that employed an insanity standard with a volitional prong, incorporating some variation of an irresistible impulse test, considerations of volition were judged relevant, if at all, only to the question of whether the *actus reus* took place (Bonnie & Slobogin, 1980). Conduct that was compelled in some manner might deserve to be excused in some instances, but not because intentionality, conceived of as a rather purely cognitive process, had not been present or possible. In one view, the lack of volition in committing a crime negated not *mens rea* but rather the *actus reus:* there was no criminal act that required explanation or exculpation (Dix, 1971; Erlinder, 1983). It followed from this strictly limited view of *mens rea* as an abstractly cognitive function that the defense of diminished capacity, on the few occasions it might have been raised, would have involved little need for expert witnesses.

All of this changed over the course of about a quarter-century in California. The changes wrought there and copied elsewhere eventually met a backlash of public outrage engendered by the deeply unpopular results that diminished capacity and an expansive view of the role of psychological factors in crime produced in certain notorious cases. However, the effects of these changes continue to resonate in jurisdictions throughout America.

California, as was the case with several other states, dealt with the dilemma of protecting the rights of the accused to avoid self-incrimination when the accused was also raising the insanity defense—an affirmative defense requiring the commission of the deed—by bifurcating the trial into a guilt phase and an insanity phase. Thus, a determination would be made that the defendant was the one who committed an act before it would be determined if the defendant was culpable, or criminally responsible. However, a determination of guilt intrinsically involves a determination that not only the *actus reus* but also the *mens rea* occurred. Because insanity theoretically negates *mens rea*, there is a natural question of how evidence of mental abnormality can be excluded from trial at the guilt phase. If guilt as well as criminal responsibility is in this sense mental as well as physical, expert testimony about mental disorder ought to be permitted at the guilt phase. This was the conclusion reached by the California Supreme Court in a 1949 landmark decision *(People v. Wells)*.

Wells was a convict serving a sentence in a California penitentiary when he allegedly assaulted a prison guard. As this was a capital offense at the time, namely, assault with malice aforethought, at the guilt phase of the trial, Wells's defense tried to introduce evidence on the question of whether he had entertained malice. Defense experts intended to testify that Wells was under tension resulting from fears for his own safety at the time he assaulted the guard. This testimony was ruled inadmissible. On appeal of Wells's conviction, the State Supreme Court ultimately held that evidence of Wells's claimed abnormality was material to the question of his guilt and that it had been an error by the trial court to exclude this evidence from the guilt phase.

By breaching the separation between considerations of guilt and culpability, *Wells* influenced the further course of diminished capacity law in California. The real impetus to introduce more frequent and explicit considerations of mental state into determinations of guilt, rather than reserving them solely for determinations of legal insanity, involved what was perceived as the inadequacy of the insanity test itself (Morse, 1979). At the time, California was using the century-old M'Naghten Rule (1843), which holds that to establish insanity, it must be proven that at the time of the act, and as a result of mental disease or defect, the individual did not know the nature and quality of the act he or she was doing or did not know he or she was doing what was wrong. This seemingly all-or-nothing, black-or-white, and wholly cognitive test of insanity seemed to some to make no allowance for other important mental considerations, such as volition, the ability to resist committing an act disturbed individuals might recognize as wrong but that their mental illness impelled them to do. It was felt that the M'Naghten standard for insanity was too narrow a test to provide a just and humane result in many cases of obviously disordered individuals. The expansion of diminished capacity doctrine into areas it had never gone before, in California or elsewhere, seemed to fill the gap. As the court admitted in *People v. Henderson* (1963), diminished capacity became the means by which the courts could ameliorate the harshness of the M'Naghten standard that had been imposed by the legislature; the approach came to be seen as the ameliorative defense. Its first application came in the case of *People v. Gorshen* (1959).

Nicholas Gorshen was a Russian immigrant and a longshoreman. He came to work one day in an intoxicated condition and was sent home by his foreman. He took offense and fought with the man before he went home. He then got a gun, came back to the docks, and shot his foreman dead in front of witnesses, including police officers. In his trial for first-degree murder, the noted psychiatrist Bernard Diamond testified in Gorshen's behalf that he was a long-standing schizophrenic who had been hallucinating for years. When his foreman told him to leave work, Diamond testified, Gorshen's precarious psychological equilibrium was threatened, and he viewed the demand as an attack on his manhood. As a result, Diamond offered, Gorshen had been compelled to retaliate against the source of the threat. Diamond did not dispute Gorshen's own admission that he had consciously intended to shoot his foreman, but he testified that in any case, Gorshen did not possess the mental state required for malice aforethought or anything implying intention, premeditation, or deliberation.

No testimony rebutting Diamond's testimony that Gorshen was schizophrenic was offered, but Gorshen was determined by the judge in a bench trial to be sane under the M'Naghten standard, and he was found guilty of first-degree murder. On appeal, the California Supreme Court affirmed Gorshen's conviction but added that the expert testimony that Gorshen would have been incapable of the malice required for murder—testimony considered but rejected by the trial court—had been properly admitted at trial. The court declined to provide a clear definition of what malice consisted of, but by its ruling it appeared in effect to approve what amounted to a redefinition of malice that had been offered by the expert witness, one that called for a volitional component (Dix, 1971) heretofore absent not only from the concept of malice but from the insanity test. The California Supreme Court held that malice existed when an individual commits an act intentionally and of his or her own free will, rather than as a result of an abnormal compulsion. The way to a larger consideration of subjective psychological factors in guilt determinations could be discerned. If traditional *mens rea* concepts such as insanity and malice did not permit relevant expert testimony on mental abnormality, those intent elements might be so construed as to permit the judge or jury to weigh the defendant's ability to morally assess or control his conduct (Morse, 1979). This process was evidently at work in the next significant case of this type considered by the court, *People v. Wolff* (1964).

Dennis Wolff, charged with murder, was if anything more obviously disturbed than was Gorshen, yet like him he did not seem to qualify for an insanity verdict using the M'Naghten standard. Wolff was only 15 years old when he allegedly developed a plan to kidnap girls and bring them home for sexual purposes. For the plan to work, however, he needed to get his mother out of the way. After one failed attempt, he succeeded in this by beating her to death with an ax handle. At his trial, expert testimony was heard that Wolff was a schizophrenic and that he was legally insane, but the jury convicted him of first-degree murder.

As in the Gorshen case five years earlier, the California Supreme Court on appeal upheld the jury's finding that Wolff was sane, but it held that he had not been capable of the mental processes needed to commit first-degree murder, namely, premeditation. It was plain that Wolff had carefully planned the homicide and had applied considerable thought to it. However, the court held that more was required for premeditation that Wolff, psychotic as he was, had been capable of. The defendant must have been able, the court ruled, to "maturely and meaningfully" reflect on the enormity of the offense contemplated. Accordingly, the court found that Wolff was guilty of only second-degree murder.

In essence, the court had declared that it was not enough that the defendant engaged in what might resemble commonsense conceptions of premeditation and deliberation. Rather, the "quantum of his moral turpitude and depravity" needed to be ascertained. At issue was not the simple apparent fact of intent, but rather the quality of whatever intent was formed. Though *mens rea* might otherwise be apparent, it could be negated by a finding that the defendant was morally incapable of true intent. This naturally begged the question of just what the real element looked like, but it opened the door to an expanded consideration of expert testimony on the issue. The growing trend seemed to validate the hope that Bernard Diamond, the defense expert in *Gorshen*, had expressed, namely, that diminished capacity might become a vehicle for the introduction of a richer, expanded view of the role that mental health issues play in criminal behavior (Diamond, 1961). With this new approach, he wrote, society could no longer evade its obligations to provide the defendant with therapeutic help, for the defendant would now officially be labeled sick and the courts would have publicly acknowledged the need for treatment. Indeed, as time went on and new developments took place, diminished capacity was viewed as having developed into a "finely honed instrument" for the defense (Bird & Vanderet, 1972). Defense attorneys could imagine how such factors as the stress of being a prisoner could be introduced to mitigate guilt (Marx, 1977).

In the decade following *Wolff,* an expanded view of intent elements continued in California. *People v. Conley* (1966) applied the *Wolff* logic regarding premeditation to the question of malice aforethought. William Conley allegedly had been drinking heavily for a number of days when he killed his estranged lover and her husband. He claimed later that he had no intention to kill anyone and no memory of having done so. Expert testimony was heard to the effect that the amount of alcohol Conley had consumed would have impaired the judgment of an ordinary person. A psychologist testified that in fact Conley was in a dissociative state at the time of the homicides and could not function normally. Arguing that diminished capacity could negate the malice aforethought required for murder, the defense requested that the jury also be instructed that it might find Conley guilty of voluntary manslaughter; this motion was denied, and the jury returned a two-count conviction of first-degree murder.

On appeal, the California Supreme Court reversed Conley's convictions because of the trial court's denial of manslaughter instructions. What amounted to the redefinition of malice that had started in *Wells* and continued in *Gorshen* was then elaborated upon. For malice to have been present, the court held, the person must have been able to comprehend his duty to govern his actions in accord with the duty imposed by law. This refinement of malice stood in sharp contrast to more traditional formulations. Although still and ostensibly cast in terms of *mens rea,* malice under *Conley* actually became a mini-insanity test, a cognitive-affective version of the M'Naghten standard (Morse, 1979). In the process, diminished capacity seemed to have succeeded to some extent to ameliorate the perceived harshness and strictures of the insanity test.

In 1973, in *People v. Cantrell,* the California Supreme Court ruled that irresistible impulse, not recognized in California as a test of legal insanity, could not serve as a complete defense to a crime. For just that reason, the court held, however, that a defendant claiming diminished capacity must be permitted at the guilt phase of trial to show by competent evidence that the act alleged was a result of an irresistible impulse that had been caused by mental disease. Such testimony, the court held, could bear on issues of intent to kill and malice aforethought.

The continued recognition of a role for volition that was evident in *Conley* and *Cantrell* reached a new point in *People v. Poddar* (1974). Prosenjit Poddar may be familiar to many as the killer of Tatiana Tarasoff and the subject of the leading case on the duty of therapists to protect third parties endangered by their patients, *Tarasoff vs. Regents of the University of California* (1976). Poddar was an Indian naval architecture student who was rejected by Tarasoff, a fellow student to whom he had formed an attachment. After a period of despondency and emotional distress, during which he reportedly disclosed to a university counseling psychologist that he intended to kill his girlfriend when she returned from abroad, Poddar fatally stabbed Tarasoff after shooting at her with a pellet gun. At trial, expert witnesses presented Poddar as schizophrenic, although this testimony was rebutted by prosecution. The jury failed to find Poddar legally insane, and instead convicted him of first-degree murder. Citing its rulings in *Conley* and *Cantrell,* however, the California Supreme Court overturned the conviction and ruled that Poddar could be convicted at most of voluntary manslaughter unless it could be established that he was both aware of his duty to act within the law and was not incapable of so doing.

Sweeping aside what was thought to be a bar against using a *mens rea* or diminished capacity approach as a complete defense to a crime, the California Supreme Court ruled in *People v. Wetmore* (1978) that evidence of mental disorder could be used at the guilt phase of trial to negate any mental element even if outright acquittal might result. Wetmore, a chronic psychiatric patient, was charged with burglary after he broke into an apartment with what he claimed was the belief that the apartment was his. As in many other cases of burglary, or breaking and entering with larcenous intent, if the intent to commit larceny could be negated, there might be no lesser included felony of which the defendant could be convicted.

Denouement: An End to California's Version of Diminished Capacity

In retrospect, such significant changes in the way mental guilt was assessed could not have gone unchallenged. Public outrage at the logical results of the expanded or enriched diminished capacity doctrine the California Supreme Court brought about especially galvanized opposition and contributed to its repeal. As is apparent from the closely contemporaneous events regarding the insanity defense after John Hinckley's 1982 acquittal by reason of insanity for his attempt to assassinate President Ronald Reagan, larger social trends were also involved in the retrogressive changes.

Certainly, the new view of diminished capacity had its critics even before worst came to worst. Dix (1971) detailed a variety of objections that had been raised to this approach. Among them were fears that the successful use of diminished capacity would yield shorter prison terms for convicted criminals, endangering the public, and that some individuals would win outright acquittal by means of this defense with no protection for society, even the psychiatric hospitalization mandated for those found legally insane. In a prescient manner, he further cited fears by some that the issues involved in the new diminished capacity defense were too complex for juries to understand and that by default, the question would be turned over to expert witnesses, whose testimony would be admitted on this issue despite its unreliability. Echoing this concern, Morse (1979) asserted that California's diminished capacity approach had not provided any clear standards for judges and juries to apply. It was unclear from the *Wolff* decision, for instance, just how to determine whether a murderer's premeditation and deliberation was mature and meaningful.

The growing and crucial role of the psychiatric expert witness in determinations of diminished capacity was in many ways the crux of the problem seen by critics of the expanded diminished capacity defense. Dix (1971) complained that the admission of expert testimony on this issue was an error. The *Wells* decision, he held, leaped from a finding that evidence of psychological abnormality had some logical relevance to the question of guilt to a conclusion that such evidence was thereby admissible. A critical analysis of the way psychiatric testimony was actually used in these cases, Dix offered, indicated that the testimony never actually addressed the question of whether or not some state of mind required for imposition of criminal liability was absent, but instead supported an entirely different claim, namely, that both the defendant's actions and state of mind were the result of unconscious influences. In the view of Dix and others, citing psychological abnormality as a way of disproving intent was a legal fiction that simply permitted a psychological explanation for the behavior to be presented in court. Dix saw this as placing the psychiatric expert witness in an unfair position, playing a ritualistic role in the proceedings and mouthing the magic words that would permit the court to mitigate the defendant's guilt.

Arenella (1977) viewed the California developments similarly. The *Wolff* decision, he held, shifted the focus away from the question of whether a defendant actually entertained the requisite intent to the question of how and why the defendant entertained it. In this manner, diminished capacity, ostensibly an investigation of a defendant's capacity for intent, had become a disguised version of diminished responsibility, a different project entirely. Where diminished responsibility is used, as in Europe, mental abnormality simply mitigates or reduces the level of culpability of a criminal, but it does not do so by seeking to disprove the defendant's ability to form some intent element. If the diminished capacity were employed honestly, as the *mens rea* doctrine it purported to be, Arenella argued, it would involve only evidence that actually had a bearing on whether requisite intent was missing, and it would rarely serve any purpose not already served by the insanity defense.

Morse (1979, 1984) agreed that diminished capacity had come to be treated as diminished responsibility. Indeed, he pointed out, there is no easy way for psychiatric testimony that is strictly confined to questions of *mens rea* to rule out or negate the capacity of the defendant to form those intent elements. Morse (1984) saw no danger in a strictly applied *mens rea* approach to diminished capacity, which was unlikely to benefit the defendant in any case. Correctly anticipating the rulings by federal courts in the coming decade, Morse asserted that a strict *mens rea* defense, challenging the prosecution's claim that all requisite intent elements were present at the time of a crime, is constitutionally protected.

It is not apparent, of course, that the essential rationale behind the progressive expansion of diminished capacity doctrine in California was the provision of greater and more comprehensive psychiatric or psychological explanations for criminal behavior. Nor is it apparent that the increased involvement of mental health experts in court proceedings was seen as desirable, although that was occurring during this time in respect to a variety of legal issues. The apparent rationale for the expanded diminished capacity approach was the perception that existing statutes inadequately considered the influence of mental abnormality, and that the harshness of the M'Naghten insanity standard in particular needed to be ameliorated. To the extent that the California diminished capacity approach was based on this perceived need, it was deprived of a rationale when the California Supreme Court in *People v. Drew* (1974) bypassed the legislature and ruled that the American Law Institute Model Penal Code insanity test (ALI, 1962) could be used. Despite its perception that M'Naghten was inadequate, the court had previously been unwilling to invade the province of the legislature and set a judicial test of insanity, and its rulings from *Gorshen* on seemed aimed at avoiding any need to do so. The ALI insanity standard differs from M'Naghten to two ways: it permits a volitional as well as a cognitive test of culpability, and its advisedly ambiguous use of the terms "substantial" and "appreciate" grants considerable discretion in determining whether a particular defendant was insane. Under the ALI standard, Gorshen, Wolff, Poddar, and even Conley might have been found legally insane, obviating the need for appellate redefinition of *mens rea* requirements. With the *Drew* decision, the continued relevance of the diminished capacity ameliorative defense was called into question (Waddell, 1979). But that by itself did not bring about the demise of the approach. It was a defense that had outgrown its original mission and that had clearly taken on a life of its own. Then, with the Dan White murder trial, the diminished capacity defense went from being well-known to lawyers to being notorious, and deeply troubling to the public. It is unlikely to be a coincidence that this reaction also took place during a time of general questioning of the expanded use of the insanity test itself, questioning that after the Hinckley trial in 1982 culminated in an unprecedented wave of insanity reform legislation in Congress and in state legislatures around the country.

Daniel White was 32 years old when he shot and killed San Francisco mayor George Moscone and an openly homosexual city supervisor, Harvey Milk, on November 27, 1978. As reported later by a defense psychiatric expert (Blinder, 1981–1982), White was one of one of eight children of a firefighter and was himself a firefighter and a former police officer when he decided to run for a post as a city supervisor in 1977. After a hard-fought campaign, he was elected to represent his working-class district, but he encountered personal financial problems. After resigning in early November 1978, he reconsidered and asked Mayor Moscone to reappoint him to the supervisor post. Reportedly, Moscone first promised White his support and then withdrew it. On the morning of November 27, White went to City Hall with a loaded handgun and ten extra rounds of ammunition. He avoided security personnel and metal detectors by entering City Hall through a window. White confronted the mayor and shot him four times before reloading his gun. He then encountered Harvey Milk, whom he believed had been involved in the mayor's decision not to reappoint him. White shot Milk five times, then left the building and ultimately surrendered to the police.

Many questioned the remarkable outcome of Dan White's murder trial and how it could be that the killings of two prominent local political figures resulted in a jury verdict only of voluntary manslaughter. There were suggestions (Szasz, 1981–1982) of a politically motivated collusion between the defense and the surprisingly ineffective prosecution, as well as the influence of antihomosexual prejudice. In any event, the ostensible justification for the jury finding seemed to be provided by expert witness testimony on diminished capacity.

The press seized on a point in the trial when defense expert Dr. Martin Blinder testified that White was a manic-depressive whose depressive episodes, one of which he said led to the homicides, were exacerbated by his bingeing on "junk food–Twinkies, cupcakes, and Cokes" (Szasz, 1981–1982). Diminished capacity was immediately ridiculed by reporters as the "Twinkie Defense," although the actual effect on the jury of this part of the testimony is uncertain. The jury did get to hear from several defense experts that White had been incapable of forming the intent elements required for first-degree murder or even second-degree murder.

Dr. Donald Lunde was asked by a defense attorney if there had been premeditation in White's act of killing, despite the evidence that in various ways White had at least prepared to commit homicide. Echoing the language of the *Wolff* decision 15 years earlier, Lunde testified in response that not only had White not premeditated and deliberated the killings, but because of his mental condition— which he presented as severe depression and a compulsive personality—White was not capable of any sort of mature and meaningful reflection (Szasz, 1981–1982). Dr. George Solomon, also testifying for defense, similarly testified that to reasonable medical certainty, White had lacked the capacity to maturely and meaningfully premeditate and deliberate (Solomon, 1981–1982). Echoing the language of *Conley,* Lunde testified about the question of malice, declaring that the last thing White was capable of doing was thinking clearly about his "obligations to society, other people, the law and so on" (Szasz, 1981–1982). Blinder asserted that premeditation and deliberation both require "reasonably clear thinking," and that at the time of the offense White "no longer had his wits about him" (Blinder, 1981–1982).

As a footnote to this case, Dan White was sentenced to the maximum term of confinement for voluntary manslaughter and was released on parole when he became eligible in 1984. He quietly returned to San Francisco, where he committed suicide in October 1985.

INSANITY DEFENSE REFORM AND THE FATE OF DIMINISHED CAPACITY

The controversy raised by the Dan White trial contributed to efforts to abolish the diminished capacity defense in California. The verdict was widely viewed as an outrage and an offense to common sense. Closely contemporaneous with the White trial, the California Supreme Court observed in the *Wetmore* case (1978), as discussed above, that diminished capacity could conceivably result in outright acquittal when the crime charged, such as burglary in *Wetmore,* permitted no lesser included felony. The court in *Wetmore* indicated the need for legislative clarification of diminished capacity procedures (Morse & Cohen, 1982). What was ultimately received was a legislative repudiation of the entire diminished capacity approach pioneered by the court.

California Senate Bill 54 (1981) reversed judicial redefinitions of intent elements and in effect codified more traditional unadorned forms of premeditation and deliberation and of malice. The legislature determined that it would no longer be necessary to prove that the defendant maturely and meaningfully reflected on the depravity of an act in order to find that a killing was done with premeditation and deliberation, and a finding of malice would no longer require proof of awareness by the defendant of an obligation to act within the body of laws governing society. In a related development, California Senate Bill 590 (1981) seemed to restrict the scope of expert testimony in criminal cases by indicating that psychiatrists and psychologists are not presumed to be able to determine sanity or insanity. Finally, a California ballot initiative, Proposition 8, entitled "The Victims' Bill of Rights," was approved by California voters in 1982 and "abolished" diminished capacity as a defense at trial (Kraus, 1983); it replaced the ALI insanity standard with a modified, restrictive M'Naghten test (Steadman et al., 1993).

The Hinckley trial, which resulted in the acquittal by reason of insanity of a would-be assassin of an American president, may well be the defining moment in the 20th-century treatment of mental disorder at the time of offense, uncannily similar in its impact to Daniel M'Naghten's acquittal 140 years before, after his attempt to assassinate the prime minister of Great Britain. In both cases, an acquittal at trial resulted in public outrage and restrictive reform. The Dan White trial in a smaller way was a defining moment in the brief and more parochial history of diminished capacity in California, seeming to many to exemplify all that was wrong with a liberal consideration of mental abnormality in adjudicating guilt for criminal acts. Still, it is apparent that at least with respect to diminished capacity and insanity reform measures, larger social forces were at work. Efforts to rescind what was viewed as an overly generous treatment of mentally disordered offenders in California were already in train by the time White committed his homicides, just as similar efforts were afoot in other states before Hinckley shot President Reagan.

A get-tough attitude in California had already yielded changes in sentencing procedures and provisions for the commitment of insanity acquittees by 1978, and these had already begun to yield results. Indeed, a downturn in the numbers of insanity pleas in California preceded the return of the M'Naghten standard to that state and reflected the changes already implemented that made insanity a less attractive defense option (Steadman et al., 1993). That the shift in California from the ALI test to M'Naughten did not produce any demonstrable effects in either the rate of insanity pleas or the rate of success for those pleas (Steadman et al., 1993) suggests that any notion that the strictures of the M'Naghten standard needed to be ameliorated, by an expanded diminished capacity doctrine or by a liberalized insanity test, was mistaken.

In any event, diminished capacity was tarred with the same brush as insanity during the wave of reform legislation that took place in the late 1970s and early 1980s. Aside from the decisive repudiation in California of its unique approach to diminished capacity, what may have been the strongest blow to an expanded *mens rea* rationale of diminished capacity as diminished responsibility was delivered by IDRA, the federal Insanity Defense Reform Act (1984), which responded most immediately to the Hinckley case.

Along with its elimination of the volitional prong of the ALI insanity test then in use in federal courts, its modification of the cognitive prong, its shifting of the burden of proof from prosecution to defense, and its requirement that insanity be proven by clear and convincing evidence, IDRA (1984) sought to eliminate the diminished capacity defense. After delineating the conditions under which a severe mental disease or defect could result in the affirmative defense of insanity, Congress determined that "Mental disease or defect does not otherwise constitute a defense."

In conjunction with the passage of IDRA in 1984, the Federal Rules of Evidence were revised to restrict the scope of expert testimony in respect to mental conditions. The revised rule provides that "No expert witness testifying with respect to the mental state or condition of a defendant in a criminal case may state an opinion or inference as to whether the defendant did or did not have the mental state or condition constituting an element of the crime charged or of a defense thereto." It provides that "Such ultimate issues are matters for the trier of fact alone" (Federal Rules of Evidence, 704 (b)). This restriction in the role of the expert clearly applies both to insanity and other issues such as diminished capacity. It was intended to limit testimony by expert witnesses to the presentation and explanation of their diagnoses, such as whether the defendant had a severe mental disease or defect, and what the characteristics of such a condition, if any, may have been (Senate Report, 1984).

Given subsequent federal court rulings, it would appear that Congress actually failed to do more than eliminate the possibility of an affirmative California-style diminished responsibility defense and that, as Morse (1984) asserted, the *mens rea* diminished capacity partial defense is constitutionally protected from legislative reform.

In *U.S. v. Frisbee* (1985), a U.S. District Court in California found that a defendant could submit psychiatric testimony in support of his contention that he did not have the specific intent required for first-degree murder. The defendant was reportedly a chronic alcohol abuser who suffered from periodic blackouts or seizures and from amnesia. However, the court also held that the experts could not state an opinion or inference as to whether the defendant did or did not form a specific intent to kill at the time of the murder. The court opined that the IDRA provision—that, aside from insanity, mental disease or defect does not constitute a defense—was not intended to limit the admissibility of evidence negating specific intent as such. Rather, it held that this provision was aimed at eliminating any affirmative defense other than insanity in which mental abnormality is offered in exculpation, as an excuse for an offense. The court drew the distinction between the often confused defense of diminished capacity, which is properly understood to involve the negation of intent elements, and diminished responsibility, which simply mitigates guilt. Citing *Frisbee* and the Senate Report on the change of the Federal Rules of Evidence, the District of Columbia District Court in *U.S. v. Gold* (1987) found that the reform measures did not preclude defense-offered testimony on the capacity of the defendant to formulate specific intent.

In a similar way, the Third Circuit Court of Appeals in *U.S. v. Pohlot* (1987) overturned a district court ruling that prevented a defendant from introducing any evidence of mental abnormality. It held that both the wording and the legislative history of the IDRA "leave no doubt that Congress intended . . . to bar only alternative 'affirmative defenses' that 'excuse' misconduct not evidence that disproves an element of the crime itself," and that admitting psychiatric evidence to negate *mens rea* does not constitute a defense but only negates an element of the offense, and that it therefore is not barred *(Pohlot)*. The court drew the distinction between diminished capacity, focusing on the presence of intent elements, and diminished responsibility, which it identified with California case law. It presented *mens rea* as an element that is generally satisfied by any showing of purposeful activity, regardless of its psychological origins, and stated that testimony about explanations for the behavior may mislead the jury. In this case, while affirming the right of the defendant to present expert testimony on the question of *mens rea,* seemingly both in respect to the actual presence of absence of intent and the defendant's capacity to formulate it, the court barred testimony concerning the defendant's subconscious motivation in attempting to hire a professional killer to murder his wife, testimony that would not go to the strict question of *mens rea.* Regarding evidence of the defendant's meaningful understanding of his actions and their consequences, the court wrote, "We often act intending to accomplish the immediate goal of our activity, while not fully appreciating the consequences of our acts. But purposeful activity is all the law requires" *(Pohlot).*

A similar conclusion was reached the following year by the Ninth Circuit Court of Appeals in *U.S. v. Twine* (1988). Agreeing with the courts in *Frisbee, Gold,* and *Pohlot,* it held that the IDRA did not abolish the diminished capacity defense as such. However, after finding that the district court judge had considered and was unpersuaded by the defendant's diminished capacity defense, it affirmed Twine's conviction for making telephone and mail threats to kidnap and injure. The Sixth Circuit followed suit in *U.S. v. Newman* (1989), which focused on a defendant's claim that alcoholism produced a chronic brain syndrome that precluded the formulation of sufficient *mens rea* for a crime of transporting stolen property. While upholding the defendant's conviction, the court in that case held that both insanity and diminished capacity are permissible defenses under IDRA.

The following year, the Eleventh Circuit Court of Appeals made the same finding in vacating a conviction for drug offenses in *U.S. v. Cameron* (1990). It held that despite a "semantic war of labels," both Congress and the courts had recognized a distinction between evidence of psychological impairment that supports an affirmative defense and evidence that simply negates an element of the offense charged. Testimony that helps the trier of fact determine the defendant's specific state of mind with regard to actions at the time the alleged offense was committed does not constitute an affirmative defense, but instead goes to the question of whether the prosecution had met its burden of proving all of the essential elements of the crime *(Cameron).* Continuing this unbroken chain of findings, the District of Columbia Circuit Court reached a similar conclusion in *U.S. v. Childress* (1995), where a psychologist had been prevented at trial from presenting testimony that the defendant, facing drug conspiracy charges, was effectively retarded. The court held that though the trial court would need to determine whether the intended expert testimony was sufficiently grounded in science to warrant its use in the courtroom, psychological testimony would be otherwise admissible if it was directed not at an affirmative excuse for illegal conduct but rather at the question of whether the defendant entertained the specific intent alleged, namely, the conspiratorial understanding and purpose *(Childress).*

As suggested in *Childress,* it is one thing for the courts to acknowledge the legal viability of expert testimony on the question of whether the defendant was able to form specific intent or actually did so, and another to find a sound scientific basis for any such testimony. It is the point of the discussion below that in fact it is a most difficult task to marshal the clinical evidence needed to support an opinion that a defendant actually had diminished capacity. As Morse declared (1984), if the *mens rea* approach is applied strictly and is not simply a vehicle for a proposed excuse, it is unlikely to be of any benefit to the defendant who seeks to use it. It was knowledge of this truth that informed the "abolition" of the insanity defense in several states during the reform era of the past 20 years and replaced it with a *mens rea* defense. If the provision of a *mens rea* defense as a substitute for insanity was meant to comfort anyone concerned about the impact of mental illness, *mens rea* must be seen as cold comfort indeed.

It is curious that all three of the states that did away with the insanity defense—Montana in 1979, Idaho in 1982, and Utah in 1983—are states with small populations in which the insanity defense was seldom used. None of them was ever obliged to face large numbers of insanity acquitees or make provisions for their care and the safety of the community in regard to them. The thrust of the abolition reform, however, was to reduce the number of acquittals by reason of insanity. Perhaps with problems of such a small scope it could have been anticipated that any change might not necessarily be a change in the direction desired. Indeed, in Utah, a study of acquittals due to mental state at time of offense indicated that there were as many in the two years following abolition of the traditional insanity defense—seven—as there were during the nine years preceding the reform (Heinbecker, 1986, cited in Steadman et al., 1993). This is not to suggest that any possible confusion in Utah or the other states has resulted in a more liberal climate for recognizing the impact of mental disorder on criminal conduct. Robert Howell (personal communication, March 4, 1997), a psychologist involved in the legislative debate over Utah's reformed code, related that very grossly disordered offenders who easily might have been acquitted by reason of insanity in another jurisdiction are now routinely unable to avoid conviction.

From the review of Montana's experience by Steadman and his colleagues (Steadman et al. 1993), abolition of insanity has not led to any great success in using the substituted *mens rea* variant. In the six years after reform, only five persons in the seven Montana counties studied successfully won acquittal on the basis of their mental state at the time of the crime, although rates at which defendants entered criminal responsibility pleas were not affected. Steadman and his colleagues discovered that another avenue for mentally disordered defendants may have not found. Prior to reform, most of those defendants who had been found incompetent to stand trial were later adjudicated legally insane. With that no longer possible, the vast majority of those found incompetent after reform had their charges dismissed or deferred; many of those individuals were civilly committed to the same hospital as those who had been found not guilty by reason of insanity. Thus, the investigators found, a different legal provision was being used to produce nearly identical results.

To summarize, the general trend in the United States in the direction of restricting the use of mental state evidence in criminal cases has led to the curtailment of testimony that serves to explain an offender's mental state, yet it has left intact, in some places as the only option, a defendant's freedom to introduce evidence that would negate intent. However, a primary objective of the reforms seems to have been the elimination of considerations of individual psychology in the determination of guilt. Consequently, the history of these reforms provides little guidance to anyone hoping to translate terms used by behavioral science into terms relevant to the law on *mens rea*.

FORENSIC EVALUATIONS OF DIMINISHED CAPACITY AND *MENS REA*

The forensic psychologist who is asked to offer an opinion on the question of a defendant's capacity to formulate the specific intent for an alleged offense is, to an extent far exceeding cases in which insanity is at issue, hard put to offer anything relevant and material. The expert can, and many do, explore the extent to which defendants' mental abnormality, if they have any—and some can certainly be discerned, especially if they did the offenses—affected their awareness of what they were doing, their moral evaluation of it, their anticipation of the full array of its effects, and the various alternatives they had to acting this way. The expert can, in other words, use the diminished capacity issue as the analogue of an insanity defense, substituting some relatively minor mental abnormality for the severe mental disease or defect required for insanity, seeking exculpation by explanation. If no settled mental abnormality is apparent, the psychologist can advert to intoxication or even to stress; if feasible, the perpetrator's ability to control himself or herself may be called into question. In one case encountered by the author, a narcotics addict was accused of robbing a convenience store along with a companion. The defense attorney argued that the defendant was unable to form the intent for armed robbery because of his intoxication (he had been drinking alcohol) and need for narcotics (that, he said, was why he robbed the place) and because of the stress produced by conflict with his wife that morning.

It must be apparent from the foregoing review of the history of diminished capacity and *mens rea* law that this approach to demonstrating an inability to form requisite intent is irrelevant to the issues as the law has defined them. Since the death of diminished capacity as diminished responsibility in California, there is no jurisdiction that actually invites an expert witness to hazard a guess as to what psychological elements true criminal intent ought to involve, or what character flaws, attitudes, and emotional or chemical states can spoil what would otherwise constitute perfect requisite *mens rea*.

Theoretically bootless as such an approach certainly is, experience amply demonstrates that some experts have not been at all deterred from engaging in it by the simple absence of any legal provision allowing expert witnesses to redefine criminal intent and infusing it with the sort of psychological meaning they may feel is lacking in traditional *mens rea* concepts. Perhaps the inordinately arcane nature of *mens rea* doctrine leads to confusion among lawyers and judges as to what the appropriate scope of expert testimony ought to be and results in their conflation of diminished capacity and diminished responsibility. Then, too, many lawyers may have their own reasons to encourage expert testimony that involves a broad exploration of human motivation and psychological dynamics even if it does not actually address the question of whether specific intent was or could have been formed. From the defense point of view at least, diminished capacity can serve as a vehicle for introducing humanizing truths and myths about the defendant, information that could not otherwise come before the jury and that the law holds ought not to be considered.

As a practical matter, if any testimony on diminished capacity is admissible, it is difficult to disqualify expert witnesses from testifying in regard to technically irrelevant issues about intent, providing the testimony is cloaked in the proper language of intent. The retrenchment of the law during the past two decades of retrogressive reform must have some effect on the scope of expert testimony, but in this area, it is most unlikely that expert witnesses can be forced to conform their conduct to the requirements of the law and confine their analyses only to the strict questions of *mens rea*.

This is not to say that those experts who do wish to confine themselves to speaking of intent strictly in the terms laid down by the law often have much to say. The meagerness of expert contributions to the resolution of questions of intent may itself have much to do with the disinclination of many experts to remain in the restricted role ordained by the reformed statutes and by case law. The question of the capacity for intent is only theoretically, and not actually, separate from the question of whether intent was formed. This is the dilemma that the forensic psychologist faces in examining a defendant in regard to diminished capacity: a psychological examination cannot ordinarily lead to a conclusion that a defendant lacked the capacity to formulate intent for an offense the defendant appears to have committed.

In many instances, unless the expert undertakes to redefine what "real" specific intent is—as in the case of the *Wolff* court's declaring that premeditation and deliberation in murder must involve mature and meaningful reflection on the enormity of the offense contemplated—there is not much left to be said. There is a fundamental difference between a question of whether intent was or could have been formed on the one hand, and a question of the quality and characteristics of whatever intent was formed on the other. The expert who wishes to address the former issue is not often helped by addressing the latter. Understanding that a defendant was depressed and that the intent she formed to smother her child and relieve him of the sufferings of this world may explain how and why the killing took place, and it may contribute to an opinion on insanity, but it does not provide an answer to the question of whether she premeditated or deliberated a murder. From the point of view of the law's minimal and cognitive construction of intent, the answer to that question may come ready to hand, but will not call for any sophisticated analysis of the killer's psychology. In most instances, if the defendant engaged in planning or preparation, and especially if he or she announced an intention to kill, it will be difficult from a behavioral science viewpoint to refute a prosecution claim that the defendant not only could but did premeditate and deliberate the killing. By comparison, competent opinion testimony on the issue of insanity in the usual case is a great deal easier. It is easier to demonstrate that as a result of mental disease or defect a defendant lacked the capacity to appreciate the wrongfulness of the conduct, for instance, than to demonstrate that a mental condition, however severe it is, prevented the defendant from doing what he or she seems to have done. Insanity does not invite the expert witness or anyone else to determine what precise offense was committed: insanity is an affirmative defense in which an exculpating excuse is offered for an offense that itself is not contested. Yet, this is what a positive opinion in respect to diminished capacity implies: Because the defendant could not or did not form the requisite intent elements for it, whatever crime was committed could not have been the one charged.

The dilemma of the expert witness may be illustrated by a case similar to that of *Conley* involving a 40-year-old woman charged with two counts of first-degree murder. She was an alcoholic who had been divorced but never entirely separated from her alcoholic husband; he owned a bar. For nearly 24 hours before the slayings, she had been drinking with her ex-husband and his girlfriend in his tavern. Talk turned to the daughter the defendant shared with her ex-husband, the defendant's fitness as a mother, and whether it was right that she should retain custody of the child. Drunk and angry, the defendant left, drove home, and returned to the bar with a loaded shotgun in the trunk of her car. Once back inside, she resumed her hot exchange with her ex-husband's girlfriend, during which she was heard to threaten the woman's life. The defendant then left the bar again, telling a barmaid on her way out to "hit the floor" when she came back, and telling her that she would not like what she was going to do. The defendant presently returned to the locked door of the bar with the shotgun, and when her ex-husband and his girlfriend opened the door for her she fatally shot both of them in rapid succession. She then fled to her apartment, hid the shotgun, told her boyfriend to deny that she had been gone, and passed out.

It may certainly be asked whether any crime would have been committed but for the defendant's drunkenness, and even whether she would have been so drunk if she had not been an alcoholic. But these are not the questions that must be answered in respect to the diminished capacity question that was raised at trial. It may be a fair question whether the defendant was guilty of first-degree murder, specifically whether anyone as thoroughly intoxicated as she was should be held to have engaged in true premeditation and deliberation. But it is not apparent how a psychologist could answer that question, or at least do so any more validly than could a layperson. The ultimate answer would seem to draw more on value judgments—sympathy for the victim or mercy for the defendant—than on psychology as such. From the law's point of view, what looks like premeditation and deliberation, even if they are infused with alcohol, may be taken to be actual premeditation and deliberation. The jury in this instance agreed with the prosecutor that they were, and the defendant was convicted of first-degree murder.

What is the candid expert witness left to say when diminished capacity is raised? There may be several options, depending on the circumstances of the offenses and the findings on examination.

First, although genuine cases of diminished capacity should not be expected to occur often, some individuals truly lack the capacity to form requisite intent and therefore they must not have formed it. Because larceny, a specific intent crime, necessitates an understanding of the concept of property, some individuals may be so mentally retarded or otherwise limited cognitively that they are simply incapable of larceny. Such an individual walking off with goods not his or her own may not have formed any intent to commit larceny because of an inability to comprehend the essential notion of property. Similarly, it is possible to provide competent testimony to the effect that an individual is so demented as to be incapable of planning his or her next step, much less premeditating and deliberating murder.

Though they are theoretically possible, there are reasons why these sorts of diminished capacity cases are seldom encountered in practice. First of all, substantially retarded individuals who seem to be acting like thieves are unlikely to be charged with larceny. If they are, someone in a position to gate them into the mental health or criminal justice systems, including the police, district attorney, and arraigning magistrate, is likely to have formed the impression that they were not so intellectually impaired to begin with. Second, those who most clearly have diminished capacity in the sense that they have gross cognitive impairment are as unlikely to commit specific intent offenses as they are unlikely to engage in any other sophisticated, purposeful, and goal-directed behavior.

Still, it is possible that in other more subtle ways a defendant may evidence diminished capacity in the sense of having been incapable of formulating the specific intent. In the first case scenario at the head of the chapter, some of the evidence for the assault with intent to murder with which the drunk was charged when he fired a shot in the direction of the police was his reported threat beforehand that he would shoot any police officer who came to arrest him. But given the length of time that elapsed between the threat and the gunshot, together with his gross intoxication, it is at least possible that in the event the act of assault was not informed by his previously formed intent, and even that he was incapable of remembering what he said or what he intended to do by the time the police actually came. He reported, plausibly enough, no memory at all for the incident. He had a reported history of numerous alcoholic blackouts, which are commonly understood to involve an inability for short-term memory to be encoded into long-term storage. The time elapsed between the threat and the shot may well have exceeded the span of his short-term storage and thus would have prevented him from keeping his plan in mind. Naturally, as interesting at this analysis may be, it goes more to the question of whether the defendant's prior statement was proof of his intent to kill than to the greater question of whether at the time he took the shot, drunk or not, he did intend to kill the police.

The second case scenario, of the epileptic hit-and-run driver, also appears to afford the forensic examiner a limited opportunity to explore capacity for intent. The prosecutor in that case believed that one of the crimes charged, leaving the scene of a personal-injury accident, must be a specific intent offense as it required knowledge by the subject that he had caused personal injury to others. It appeared likely that the defendant had one of his characteristic seizures at the time of the accident. From the vivid reports of witnesses, particularly one man who encountered and observed the defendant just after the fatal collision, the defendant may have been experiencing postictal clouding of consciousness prior to driving off. It is not implausible that he did not comprehend the witness who demanded to know if he understood what he had just done; he appeared dazed and unresponsive. Postictal confusion may have prevented him from understanding what had just happened. He would not have remembered it if he had been in a seizure at the time of the collision, and he did not come back, or even look toward the crowd gathered around the people he had struck down, some distance behind him, before he eventually drove away. Again, as in the case of the first scenario, as engaging as such speculation might be, it has limited application to the larger issues. The prosecution agreed to drop the charge in question, but that left the defendant facing two more serious general intent homicide charges for which his epilepsy was, if anything, an aggravating factor, because he drove a vehicle when he knew he was restricted by his condition from doing so and had even had a prior accident produced by a seizure.

Second, in some instances, it is easier to offer testimony that pertains to the actuality of intent rather than to the capacity for intent. These are cases in which a consideration of the defendant's psychology and the circumstances of the alleged offense suggests a plausible factual alternative to the crime alleged.

A case in point involved a man without any prior criminal history who had been charged with breaking and entering a department store with intent to commit larceny. He claimed that he had entered the store late at night solely to find some anticonvulsant medication he was afraid he had dropped there the day before. On examination, he appeared to be rigidly obsessive and hypochondriacally preoccupied; he had a history of mild neurological impairment. Over the years, he had persistently worried about the health of his daughter and of children in general. The day before the break-in, he claimed, he had been in the department store cafeteria and had dropped a vial containing his pills on the floor. He thought he had recovered all of the pills, but he worried later that a number were missing. He became worried that some child would come into the cafeteria, would find and pick up the pills, and would be harmed by them. He resolved to get back into the store and search for his pills. He tried to contact security officers in the now-closed store without success. He assumed that if he called the police, they would simply tell him to wait until morning, but he worried that if he did it would be too late. Finally, with mounting anxiety, he forced a door open, and a silent alarm brought the police, who found him in the store and arrested him. He had no merchandise or other stolen property in his possession. Police reported that an ice machine in the cafeteria had been moved aside. In this case, it is not likely that, despite his history and presentation, the defendant could be said to have been incapable of larceny, unless the meaning of the term were reinterpreted to mean something more than it has ordinarily been understood to mean. The real question in this case, however, is not whether the defendant could have formed the intent to commit larceny, but whether he did so.

Naturally, because the issue cast in this light necessarily involves a judgment of what occurred in fact, it must be answered in the final analysis by the trier of fact. However, this is a case in which the results of a psychological evaluation lent plausibility to an alternative explanation for the behavior in question, one that, if true, would mean that even if he had entered the store illegally and might be subject to sanctions for that, he was not guilty of breaking and entering with intent to commit larceny.

It is unclear the extent to which expert testimony bearing on the actuality of intent rather than capacity for intent would be admissible. In Michigan, for example, appellate decisions seem to indicate that the only question that can be considered in this regard is whether the defendant was incapable of forming specific intent, not whether he did or not (*People v. Savoie,* 1984). The issue is unclear in federal jurisdictions. For example, the Third Circuit in *Pohlot* (1987), in noting that "evidence of mental abnormality may help indicate lack of mens rea even when a defendant is legally sane," appeared to suggest that such testimony would be acceptable. On the other hand, the revised Federal Rules of Evidence (Rule 704 (b)) appears to preclude such testimony in declaring that "No expert witness . . . may state an opinion or inference as to whether the defendant did or did not have the mental state or condition constituting an element of the crime charged or of a defense thereto." The rule identifies these as the "ultimate issues" that are matters for the trier of fact alone.

The forensic psychologist faced with this issue in an actual case must understand the admissibility of opinion testimony in that jurisdiction concerning actuality of intent. It is not recommended in any case that the expert offer an opinion on the "ultimate issue" and testify in effect that it is his or her opinion that the defendant is guilty or is not guilty. Opinions of this type exceed the scope of other expert psychological opinions, such as whether a defendant is competent to stand trial or meets the criteria to be considered legally insane, and should be objectionable to psychologists if not to the law. However, there are occasions when the contributions an expert can make to the judge or jury's determination of whether a defendant did or did not form specific intent are valuable. On other occasions, of course, when the defendant is denying forming the intent in fact, the expert is unlikely to shed much light on the defendant's claim to innocence. The third vignette at the head of the chapter is a case in point. The defendant, charged with arson, maintained that the fire was an accident. Evidence of his mental disorder may contribute plausibility to his claim that he accidentally set off the fire when he woke to the smell of gas in his apartment and tried to relight his stove's pilot light. A judge or jury might reasonably conclude that someone would need to be crazy to light a match in an apartment filled with gas, and take evidence of his disorder into consideration in deciding whether he had formed the intent to commit arson in fact. But the psychologist in that case is not in a position to provide evidence about the probability that the defendant, in denying the alleged intent, was telling the truth. This limitation is likely to apply to the majority of cases in which a defendant denies forming intent.

Third, in a great many cases in which diminished capacity is at issue, testimony directly relevant to either capacity for intent or actuality of intent will not be possible. The fourth and fifth cases at the start of the chapter are examples of this. In these instances, though the contributions of the forensic examiner are sought, it is seldom possible to offer testimony other than that there is no good or plausible reason to conclude that the defendant was not capable of forming intent; that the defendant was capable of engaging in conscious, goal-directed behavior; and even that the behavior of the defendant alleged is not consistent with loss of consciousness, planfulness, or direction. Most cases in which a defendant appears to have met the criteria for legal insanity fall into this category. Because of the different approaches the two defenses take to the issue of *mens rea,* it will typically be easier to demonstrate that, for example, a defendant lacked substantial capacity to appreciate the wrongfulness of conduct than that the defendant could not have formed specific intent.

In some of these cases, the defense may not be so much interested in eliciting an opinion on capacity for intent as such, but in describing and even explaining the defendant's conduct to the judge or jury. If that is the point, the forensic psychologist may have much to contribute. The danger here lies in the possibility that the psychologist will conflate explanation and exculpation, and testify that because the defendant's intentions and conduct may be understood in terms of his or her psychology, they do not meet criteria for requisite intent. This sort of testimony would recapitulate the diminished capacity as diminished responsibility approach taken in California prior to reforms there, and it should be understood as such. As long as the law defines intent as it does, as a skeletal cognitive affair, testimony of this sort may be misleading to the jury even if it is permitted by the court. Psychologists and psychiatrists are not in a position to define what requisite legal intent must involve, or even what sorts of mental or emotional disorders preclude it. Inevitably, expert testimony cast in this way involves an arrogant or even magical claim by the expert—for example, that though it may appear that the defendant premeditated and deliberated a homicide because he thought about it, planned it, and even announced his intentions, he actually could not have formed such intent because of mental abnormality. If there is testimony that a masked armed robber was incapable of forming the intent for armed robbery because of his psychological problems, the jury is simply left to ask in that case, "Who was that masked man?" Psychologists often have a great deal to offer in terms of delineating data within their purview concerning a defendant and his or her behavior. But psychologists are not capable of transubstantiation or alchemy, transforming what the law may consider to be requisite intent into something else because of assumptions about what sorts of mental factors must enter into a genuine criminal act.

CONCLUSION

The history of diminished capacity and *mens rea* conceptualizations indicate a potential for contributions to be made by forensic psychologists and psychiatrists to the resolution of questions of intent. The conceptualizations of intent embodied by the law's approach to criminal liability, however, sharply limit the extent to which psychological and psychiatric expert testimony will actually be relevant to the ultimate issue to be determined by the trier of fact.

REFERENCES

American Law Institute. (1962). Model Penal Code, Proposed official draft.

Arenella, P. (1977). The diminished capacity and diminished responsibility defenses: Two children of a doomed marriage. *Columbia Law Review, 77,* 827–865.

Bird, R. E., & Vanderet, R. C. (1972). Diminished capacity. In R. M. Cipes (Ed.), *Criminal defense techniques.* New York: Binder.

Blinder, M. (1981–1982). My psychiatric examination of Dan White. *American Journal of Forensic Psychiatry, 2,* 12–27.

Black, H. C. (1979). *Black's Law Dictionary* (5th ed.). St. Paul, MN: West.

Bonnie, R., & Slobogin, C. (1980). The role of mental health professionals in the criminal justice process: The case for informed speculation. *Virginia Law Review, 43,* 427–522.

California Senate Bill No. 54. (1981). Amending §§ 21, 22, 26, 188, and 189 of the California Penal Code, and adding §§ 28 and 29.

California Senate Bill No. 590. (1981). Amending § 1027 of the California Penal Code.

Clark, C. R. (1982). Clinical limits of expert testimony on diminished capacity. *International Journal of Law and Psychiatry, 5,* 155–170.

Clark, C. R. (1988). *Diminished capacity in Michigan: Factors associated with forensic evaluation referrals.* Paper presented at American Psychology-Law Society Conference, Miami Beach.

Diamond, B. (1961). Criminal responsibility of the mentally ill. *Stanford Law Review, 14,* 59–86.

Dix, G. E. (1971). Psychological abnormality as a factor in grading criminal liability: Diminished capacity, diminished responsibility, and the like. *Journal of Criminal Law, Criminology, and Police Science, 62,* 313–334.

Erlinder, C. P. (1983). Post-traumatic stress disorder, Vietnam veterans and the law: A challenge to effective representation. *Behavioral Sciences and the Law, 1,* 25–50.

Federal Rules of Evidence, FRE 704(b), amended by Comprehensive Crime Control Act of 1984, Pub.L. No. 98-473.

Grier, W. H., & Cobbs, P. M. (1968). *Black rage.* New York: Basic Books.

Heinbecker, P. (1986). Two year's experience under Utah's mens rea insanity law. *Bulletin of the American Academy of Psychiatry and Law, 14*(2), 185–191.

In re Winship, 397 U.S. 358, 364 (1970).

Insanity Defense Reform Act of 1984, P.Law 98-473, 18 U.S.C. § 17.

Kraus, F. R. (1983). The relevance of innocence: Proposition 8 and the diminished capacity defense. *California Law Review, 71,* 1197–1215.

LaFave, W., & Scott, A., Jr. (1972). *Handbook of criminal law.* St. Paul, MN: West.

Marx, M. L. (1977). Prison conditions and diminished capacity—A proposed defense. *Santa Clara Law Reporter, 17,* 855–883.

Melton, G. B., Petrila, J., Poythress, N. G., & Slobogin, C. (1997). *Psychological evaluations for the courts: A handbook for mental health professionals and lawyers* (2nd ed.). New York: Guilford Press.

M'Naghten's Case, 10 Cl. & F. 200, 8 Eng. Rep. 718 (H.L. 1843).

Morse, S. J. (1979). Diminished capacity: A moral and legal conundrum. *International Journal of Law and Psychiatry, 2,* 271–298.

Morse, S. J. (1984). Undiminished confusion in diminished capacity. *Journal of Criminal Law and Criminology, 75,* 1–55.

Morse, S. J., & Cohen, E. (1982, June). Diminishing diminished capacity in California. *California Lawyer,* 24–26.

People v. Cantrell, 8 Cal. 3d 672, 504 P.2d 1256, 105 Cal. Rptr. 792 (1973).

People v. Conley, 64 Cal. 2d 310, 411 P.2d 911, 49 Cal. Rptr. 815 (1966).

People v. Drew, 22 Cal. 3d 333, 583 P.2d 1318, 149 Cal. Rptr. 910 (1974).

People v. Gorshen, 51 Cal. 2d 716, 336 P.2d 492 (1959).

People v. Henderson, 60 Cal. 2d 482, 386 P.2d 677 (1963).

People v. Poddar, 10 Cal. 3d 750, 518 P.2d 342, 111 Cal. Rptr. 910 (1974).

People v. Savoie, 419 Mich. 118 (1984).

People v. Wells, 33 Cal. 2d 330, 202 P.2d 53 (1949).

People v. Wetmore, 22 Cal. 3d 318, 583 P.2d 1308, 149 Cal. Rptr. 264 (1978).

People v. Wolff, 61 Cal. 2d 795, 394 P.2d 959, 40 Cal. Rptr. 271 (1964).

Senate Report No. 225. (1984). 98th Cong., 2d Sess. 230, reprinted in U.S. Code Cong. & Ad. News 3182, 3412.

Solomon, G. F. (1981–1982). Comments on the case of Dan White. *American Journal of Forensic Psychiatry, 2,* 22–26.

Steadman, H. J., McGreevy, M. A., Morrissey, J. P., Callahan, L. A., Robbins, P. C., & Cirincione, C. (1993). *Before and after Hinckley: Evaluating insanity defense reform.* New York: Guilford Press.

Szasz, T. (1981–1982). The political use of psychiatry—The case of Dan White. *American Journal of Forensic Psychiatry, 2,* 1–11.

Tarasoff v. Regents of the University of California, 551 P.2d 334 (1976).

U.S. v. Cameron, 907 F.2d 1051 (11th Cir. 1990).

U.S. v. Childress, 58 F.3d 693 (D.C. Cir. 1995).

U.S. v. Frisbee, 623 F. Supp. 1217 (D.C. Cal. 1985).

U.S. v. Gold, 661 F. Supp. 1127 (D.D.C. 1987).

U.S. v. Newman, 889 F.2d 88 (6th Cir. 1989).

U.S. v. Pohlot, 827 F.2d 889 (3rd Cir. 1987).

U.S. v. Twine, 853 F.2d 676 (9th Cir. 1988).

Waddell, C. W. (1979). Diminished capacity and California's new insanity test. *Pacific Law Journal, 10,* 751–771.

CHAPTER 14

The Assessment of Criminal Responsibility: Current Controversies

STEPHEN L. GOLDING, JENNIFER L. SKEEM,
RONALD ROESCH, and PATRICIA A. ZAPF

IN THE first edition of this *Handbook*, Golding and Roesch (1987) presented a review of current controversies in the adjudication of criminal responsibility by placing them in historical context. The original chapter focused on the legal, philosophical, and behavioral science evolution of concepts of *mens rea*, attempts to reform or abolish the insanity defense, the "guilty but mentally ill" verdict, and practice guidelines for the conduct of MSO (mental state at the time of offense) evaluations. A more research-oriented review of related issues, including juror decision making in criminal responsibility cases, attitudes toward the insanity defense, the recidivism of insanity acquittees, and the psychometric characteristics of methods of evaluating MSO, was published by Golding (1992). This chapter is written to build on both prior chapters and should be read in conjunction with them. Thus, no attempt is made to incorporate the prior and fuller discussions of certain issues. Rather, these issues, where relevant, are summarized and then expanded upon. The major foci of this chapter are: (a) insanity standards and the construal of criminal responsibility; (b) developments in the assessment of criminal responsibility; and (c) issues in the disposition of insanity acquittees.

INSANITY STANDARDS AND THE CONSTRUAL OF CRIMINAL RESPONSIBILITY

LEGAL DEVELOPMENTS

In the decade since our original review of the historical development of the insanity defense and its philosophical, legal, moral, and scientific roots (Golding

& Roesch, 1987), little has changed substantially in terms of the underlying jurisprudential logic of the defense, the jurisdictional variants of the defense, and criticisms of both. A variety of scholarly reviews of the development of the insanity defense that should be consulted include Eigen (1995), Golding and Roesch (1987), Gray (1972), Hermann (1983), Perlin (1994), Platt and Diamond (1965, 1966), R. Smith (1981), and Walker (1978).

We have summarized the moral and legal logic that underlies the insanity defense:

> In cognizing and regulating social interactions in terms of fundamental principles of "fairness" and "justice," we assume that all such social interactions, including the societal judgment of criminal or civil responsibility for certain classes of proscribed behavior, are based upon an ethical calculus that assigns individual blame, culpability, liability, punishability, and moral and criminal responsibility as a function of intentionality and mental capacity. The classical formulation of this moral presupposition is the legal maxim, *Actus non facit reum, nisi mens sit rea*, which translates freely into modern English as "An act is not legally cognizable as evil, and hence criminally punishable, unless it is committed by a person who has the capacity to cognize the act as evil[1] and then freely chooses to do it." (Golding & Roesch, 1987, p. 395)

The modern trend has been to narrow the historically broad interpretation of *mens rea*, which made it roughly synonymous with "culpable intentionality" (Stroud, 1914, p. 13), and to equate the narrowed interpretation with such phrases as proscribed conduct performed "intentionally," "recklessly," "knowingly," or "purposefully" (Wales, 1976). Another trend has been to give decision makers an "in-between" verdict, namely, "guilty but mentally ill" (which, in reality, is simply a guilty verdict with no guarantee of differences in sentencing, disposition, or mental health treatment (Bumby, 1993; Golding, 1992; Golding & Roesch, 1987). Finally, some states continue to experiment with varying levels of abolition.[2] Currently, the modal insanity defense criteria involve either the traditional American Law Institute formulation (with or without the "volitional" prong) or restricted versions of the traditional M'Naghten test.[3]

Controversy surrounding definitional and procedural aspects of the insanity defense has continued since the origins of the defense (see early reviews by Ballantine, 1919; Crotty, 1924; Guy, 1869; Keedy, 1917, 1920). In many respects, the changes in legal standards continue to revolve around the same "circle of argument" (Golding & Roesch, 1987), with little evidence that the ebb and flow of changes and argument is well understood empirically (Perlin, 1994).

In a comprehensive study of various "insanity defense reforms," Steadman and colleagues (1993) argued that, despite all the publicity surrounding reform, "Black letter law is altered, but actual practices are barely modified . . . alternatively, the consequences of reform can be far different than the intended outcomes" (p. 139). The unintended consequences of reforming NGRI (not guilty by reason of insanity) verdict options that appeared in some of their studied jurisdictions (there was wide variability) included an increase in "guilty but mentally ill" adjudications and an increased use of incompetency to stand trial for mentally ill offenders charged with serious crimes. Unfortunately, because the research did not code relevant, specific aspects of defendants' mental disorder (beyond diagnosis) or important crime scene characteristics, even the results from the jurisdictions that showed little or no effect (of reformed NGRI options) cannot be fully interpreted, because we do not know what *kinds* of NGRI verdicts remained unchanged and for whom. In the juror decision-making analogue literature (discussed below), the construal of these characteristics is pivotal to decision making under various standards and reforms. These two research traditions continue to address somewhat different issues. This is unfortunate because our own experience with respect to forensic cases is that the reforms do affect outcomes with respect to ultimate dispositions, recidivism, and cost (see "Issues in the Disposition of Insanity Acquittees" below).

The Empirical Characteristics of NGRI Verdicts

Research on the empirical realities of the adjudication of criminal responsibility has continued to demonstrate the same basic phenomena since earlier reviews (Golding, 1992; Pasewark, 1986). The research is primarily directed at describing the NGRI population in traditional demographic and diagnostic terms and at "demythologizing" public misconceptions of the insanity defense (see Silver, Circincione, & Steadman, 1994, for a review). Juror and judge decision making is "rational" and rather consistently identifies a group of individuals with common characteristics.[4] The defense is seldom raised (averaging, in a recent study, fewer than 1% of total felony indictments [Steadman et al., 1993]) and highly variable in its "success" rate,[5] with that rate modally being 25% of those who raise the issue. There is a high rate of agreement among forensic experts of similar levels of training, experience, and methodology and high levels of agreement between examiner opinions and judge/juror decisions.[6] NGRI verdicts are typically achieved as either a stipulation between defense and prosecution or bench trials and rarely involve contested "battles of experts" in front of jurors (Golding, 1992; Melton, Petrila, Poythress, & Slobogin, 1997; Silver et al., 1994) . Defendants who are "acquitted" as NGRI typically have major psychotic diagnoses and extensive mental health histories, often with prior civil commitments or prior findings of incompetency[7] (see Golding, 1992; Golding, Eaves, & Kowaz, 1989; Ogloff, Schweighofer, Turnbull, & Whittemore, 1992; Steadman et al., 1993).

Unfortunately, this type of sociodemographic research does not address the more theoretically interesting question: What types of mental disorder characteristics (beyond "psychosis") and what aspects of offense incident characteristics (planning, intentionality behaviors, reasonableness of motive) influence expert, judge, and/or juror decision making? Finkel (1995) and Roberts and Golding (1991) have argued and presented rather convincing data from analogue studies that jurors' individual construal of the case and particular defendant characteristics, along a set of dimensions,[8] are major determinants of mock decision making. It would be important for large-scale research on both examiner judgments and the verdicts reached by judges and the rare trial jury to examine what elements or factors are relied upon in reaching decisions. Research on interexaminer agreement (addressed elsewhere in this chapter) is not very useful because it focuses on global agreement. Recent research on the logic and structure of examiner decision making in competency evaluations (Skeem, Golding, Cohn, & Berge, in press) demonstrates high global agreement in ultimate conclusions, but very poor agreement in examiner logic, including defendants' particular abilities and incapacities. Logically, we would expect the same in NGRI evaluations. Similarly, we know of no empirical study of the crime characteristics that lead actual judicial decision makers or forensic examiners to conclude that the defendant lacked the legally or morally relevant mental state. This point is particularly critical because few examiners, in our experience, pay close attention to collateral reports or crime scene data with respect to its consistency with their inferences about a defendant's mental state (see "Third-Party Information" below, and Melton et al., 1997).

RESEARCH ON JURY DECISION MAKING

Although data on the reliability and validity of well-founded forensic criminal responsibility opinions (see Note 19) is encouraging, there are no modern studies[9] of actual jury or bench trials, expert testimony for and against the defendant's mental state, and case-specific factors that are weighed in accepting or rejecting an insanity claim. Logically, we can place some weight in surveys of attitudes toward insanity and insanity dispositions, and compare that to what is empirically known (Silver et al., 1994). Most of what we know is based on jury simulation studies.[10] Although there are problems that arise with this methodology, a careful analysis of analogue studies produces a rather consistent set of findings and implications.

The Role of Judicial Instruction

Jurors are expected to determine an appropriate verdict by conscientiously applying the law to a fair evaluation of the evidence (*Wainwright v. Witt*, 1985). As suggested above, the effect of specific language differences in legal standards for insanity has been intensely debated for over two centuries. The nature and outcome of these debates, however, have shown either weak or little practical influence on jurors as a main effect.[11] Research repeatedly demonstrates that mock jurors often do *not* apply judicial instruction on various legal definitions of insanity in rendering verdicts (Finkel 1989, 1991; Finkel, Shaw, Bercaw, & Kock, 1985; Ogloff, 1991; Ogloff et al., 1992; Simon, 1967). For example, the Insanity Defense Reform Act (IDRA) (1984) was formulated after Hinckley's acquittal to narrow the language of the American Law Institute standard (ALI, 1962), thereby curbing the number of insanity verdicts (by eliminating the volitional prong). In an analogue study, Finkel (1989) found *no* verdict differences among mock jurors who were given IDRA instructions, ALI instructions, or very narrow "wild beast" instructions (*Arnold's Case,* 1724; cited in N. Walker, 1978).

In fact, Finkel and others have found that it often makes no difference whether jurors are given *any* test or standard; mock jurors who receive no insanity definitions or who are told to use their "best lights" judgment to decide a case produce verdict patterns indistinguishable from those of mock jurors who receive various insanity test instructions[12] (Finkel, 1989; Finkel & Handel, 1988;

Ogloff, 1991). The fact that jurors determine whether a defendant is sane or insane *without* the guidance of legal instructions suggests that they rely on their own knowledge about insanity and other cognitive structures to make these decisions. It does not imply that they "nullify" instructions, rather that their own implicit theories of insanity guide their interpretation of the admittedly vague and nonspecific linguistic terms of insanity standards.

The Role of Jurors' Case-Relevant Attitudes and Conceptions of Insanity

Although the legal system implicitly assumes that people are blank slates who can apply the law in a wholly evidence-driven fashion, substantial research indicates that people have "knowledge structures" that reflect their life experiences and guide their behavior (Fiske, 1993; Schneider,1991). These knowledge structures include constructs such as attitudes, schemas, prototypes, and stereotypes, and appear highly relevant to legal decision making (see Moran, Cutler, & DeLisa, 1994; Pennington & Hastie, 1986; V. Smith, 1991; Stalans, 1993). Several sources of research, in various stages of development, suggest that individual differences in these structures are critical in understanding why jurors reach particular verdicts in insanity defense cases.

Jurors' Case-Relevant Attitudes.   The insanity defense is controversial and involves scientific as well as political-moral issues. Although public opinion polls and empirical studies often find support for the basic logic of the insanity defense, they consistently reveal powerful negative attitudes toward the defense (Cutler, Moran, & Narby, 1992; Ellsworth, Bukaty, Cowan, & Thompson, 1984; Hans, 1986; Hans & Slater, 1984; Homant & Kennedy, 1987; Jeffrey & Pasewark, 1983; Pasewark & Seidenzahl, 1979; Roberts & Golding, 1991). For example, Roberts, Golding, and Fincham (1987) found that, although 78% of their subjects believed that severe mental illness suggested impairment in one's capacity to make rational decisions and form criminal intent, 66% believed that insanity should *not* be allowed as a complete criminal defense. Across studies, results reflect a primary concern that the insanity defense is an easily abused "loophole" in the law that allows many guilty criminals to escape punishment (Silver et al., 1994). Additional concerns include beliefs that insanity is easily malingered[13] and that the public is poorly protected[14] from dangerous criminals who are adjudicated insane (Golding, 1992; see also Perlin, 1994, Chapter 5). Similarly, jurors' case-specific negative attitudes toward both mental health experts and individuals with severe mental illness appear relevant in their decision making in insanity defense cases (Cutler et al., 1992; Perlin, 1994; Skeem, 1997).

Many of the above concerns reflect inaccurate knowledge about the insanity defense. Such myths are not only prevalent but may also be inflexible. Jeffrey and Pasewark (1983) presented subjects with factual statistics on the frequency and success rate of the insanity defense. Approximately *half* of subjects maintained their opinion that the insanity defense was overused and abused despite having seen contradictory evidence. Especially troubling is the robust finding that these prevalent, potentially inflexible, negative attitudes toward the insanity defense exert considerable influence on mock jurors' verdicts in insanity cases (Bailis, Darley, Waxman, & Robinson, 1995; Cutler et al., 1992;

Ellsworth et al., 1984; Homant & Kennedy, 1987; Roberts et al., 1987; Robinson & Darley, 1995). For example, Roberts and Golding (1991) found that mock jurors' attitudes toward the insanity defense were *more* strongly associated with their verdicts than were the study design variables, which included manipulations of available verdict categories (insanity vs. insanity supplemented by guilty but mentally ill), and case facts (the relationship of the defendant's delusion to the crime and the planfulness of the crime). The most determinative dimension underlying these attitudes was jurors' belief in strict liability (versus a belief that mental state is relevant to a defendant's blameworthiness). In essence, then, jurors' verdicts may depend more on their attitudes and opinions than on case facts and court instruction.

Despite strong evidence on the biasing effect of negative attitudes toward the insanity defense on verdicts, bias may often go undetected based on limitations in current knowledge and legal procedures. First, despite abundant research on insanity defense attitudes, no validated measure of these attitudes has yet been developed.[15] Second, except in cases involving interracial violent crimes, capital punishment, or pretrial publicity, judges are accorded broad discretion in selecting the topics to be addressed during voir dire (Johnson & Haney, 1994; Sklansky, 1996). Although insanity defense cases arguably invoke equally powerful biases, the case law reflects a trend in which judges refuse to inquire about bias against the insanity defense or even allow the impanelment of jurors who express biases against the defense or against the mentally ill (Perlin, 1994). In our opinion, the voir dire process would ideally be reformed such that prospective jurors' case-relevant preconceptions and attitudes were routinely examined in insanity defense cases.

Jurors' Case Construals.   Additional lines of research suggest that jurors' views are critical. In addition to their case-specific attitudes, jurors' individual ways of interpreting evidence are related to their verdicts. Mock jurors draw *different* inferences about defendants' cognitive and volitional impairments when given *identical* case descriptions (Bailis et al., 1995; Roberts & Golding, 1991; Roberts et al., 1987; Roberts, Sargent, & Chan, 1993; Simon, 1967; Whittemore & Ogloff, 1995). These inferences, in turn, strongly predict their verdicts. For example, Roberts and Golding presented mock jurors with case vignettes in which they manipulated available verdict categories, the relationship of the defendant's paranoid delusion to the crime, and the planfulness of the crime. The attitude-related ways in which mock jurors interpreted the case evidence were the most powerful predictors of verdict choice. For example, individual differences in jurors' *perceptions* of the extent to which a defendant was mentally disordered, capable of rational behavior, capable of acting differently, or capable of understanding the wrongfulness of his (the defendants in the cases were male) behavior explained substantially more variance in verdicts than did the objective manipulation of case evidence.

Finkel and Handel (1989), using different methodology, also found that jurors actively construct the meaning of case information in rendering verdicts. They presented mock jurors with four vastly different case vignettes and asked them to render a verdict and explain the reasoning underlying their decisions. Using a rationally derived categorization scheme, they found that mock jurors cited multiple, rational reasons for their decisions in each case (the categorization scheme included, for example capacity-incapacity to make responsible choices, unimpaired-impaired awareness and perceptions, no motive–evil motive for criminal act). The pattern of the cited constructs or "reasons" systematically *differed* based on the verdict that mock jurors reached. In essence, then, jurors construed case information in complex, discriminating ways that were consistent with their verdict choices.

Similarly, Whittemore and Ogloff (1995) found that differences in mock jurors' *perceptions* of a defendant's mental state at the time of trial (MST) predicted their verdicts. Despite the authors' manipulation of the defendant's MST (symptom-free, neurotic, or psychotic), mock jurors differed in their perceptions of the extent to which given defendants were mentally disordered. When mock jurors' inferred that the defendant was psychotic at the time of the trial, they were more likely to deem him insane.

Jurors' Implicit Theories or Prototypes of Insanity. In essence, then, jurors *construct* the meaning of case information. These constructions or interpretations are more strongly associated with jurors' verdicts than with the case as objectively given and appear unaffected by judicial instruction. Based on these findings, several authors have argued that jurors render insanity verdicts by carefully resorting to their personal knowledge or implicit theories of insanity (Finkel & Handel, 1989; Roberts & Golding, 1991; Roberts et al., 1987). However, the nature of these theories and the process by which they affect verdicts remains unclear. The studies that have attempted to infer the nature of mock jurors' conceptions of insanity based on jurors' judgments about insanity-case vignettes have produced somewhat conflicting results in terms of the relative importance of various construal dimensions (Bailis et al., 1995; Finkel & Handel, 1989; Roberts et al., 1987; Robinson & Darley, 1995). To date, studies that *directly* analyze what people mean by "insane" in the context of an analysis of actual jury decisions are virtually nonexistent: "what everybody knows about insanity is perilously unchartered" (Perlin, 1994, p. 294).

Based on the above results, related results, and promising leads in general legal decision-making studies (V. Smith, 1991, 1993), some of us are currently investigating jurors' conceptions of insanity by applying a prototype theory of categorization (Skeem, 1997). Specifically, we wish to determine what jurors' conceptions of insanity are, the extent to which they differ across individuals, and the extent to which they influence construal of case information and verdicts. This type of research is also being pursued (using a different, story-oriented methodology) by Finkel (1995; Finkel & Groscup, 1997). Though the results are preliminary, Finkel and Groscup found that undergraduate subjects describe insanity cases as involving young defendants with a history of strain, mental disorder, violence, and abuse, who perpetrate various crimes (including murder), after various precipitating events (such as the loss of loved ones) on a stranger. For successful insanity cases, the defendant's motive is related to a grandiose delusion; for unsuccessful cases, revenge is the motive. What remains to be tested is the extent to which such prototypes differ among individuals and/or influence jurors' verdicts.

The Role of Insanity Case Facts.   Jurors' decisions are not determined solely by subjective factors. Although "individual differences in social-moral cognition" appear most critical in understanding jurors' verdicts, objective manipulation of case facts does have some impact on jurors' verdicts. For example, the level of a defendant's mental disorder and the planfulness and bizarreness of the crime are associated with jurors' verdicts (Roberts & Golding, 1991; Roberts et al., 1987). As noted earlier, the characteristics of insanity acquittees suggest that juror and judicial decision making is rational and relatively consistent.

FUTURE RESEARCH DIRECTIONS

Most of the studies reviewed in this section are analogue studies completed with undergraduate subjects. Further research is needed to discern whether these results generalize to jurors or jury-eligible adults and to actual cases in which, for instance, jury deliberation and other aspects of the more normal process take place (Simon, 1967). In a related sense, further research is needed with jurors or jury-eligible adults to determine whether undergraduates' attitudes, conceptions, and judgments adequately reflect their breadth and variability (Abbott, Hall, & Linville, 1993; MacCoun, 1989; cf. Roberts & Golding, 1991). Some of the analogue studies, like those in which case facts are manipulated, could be adapted and completed using "real" cases to illuminate critical factors in juror decision making. For instance, rather than studying the relative frequency among insanity acquittees and non-insanity acquittees of gross variables such as "psychotic" or "nonpsychotic," one might complete a more informative, finer-grained analysis of "case-texture" variables, including the type of motives, intents, defendants, victims, defendant-victim relationships, precipitating events, and offenses that discriminate between successful or unsuccessful insanity pleas (see Steury & Choinsky, 1995).

DEVELOPMENTS IN THE ASSESSMENT OF CRIMINAL RESPONSIBILITY

RCRAS AND SEMISTRUCTURED PROPOSALS

The Rogers Criminal Responsibility Assessment Scales (R-CRAS) (Rogers, Wasyliw, & Cavanaugh, 1984) were designed to quantify the elements of the ALI criteria for criminal nonresponsibility. Based on a comprehensive evaluation, the examiner rates a series of scales grouped into five areas: (a) reliability of report, (b) organicity, (c) psychopathology, (d) cognitive control, and (e) behavioral control. For example, the psychopathology section involves ratings of bizarre behavior, anxiety, amnesia, delusions, hallucinations, depressed or elevated mood, verbal coherence, and affective and thought disorder. In addition, there are a series of more global ratings on final judgments of insanity and impairment. Thus, the R-CRAS is an instrument that reflects relative importance assigned by examiners to the first-order elements of an insanity decision (e.g., the presence and relevance of psychopathology to MSO). It should be noted that these elements are fairly abstract psychological and legal terms (e.g., "delusions at the time of alleged crime") and do not necessarily represent the cues that are actually used by professional examiners in making their decisions. This is a major issue of contention between Rogers, Melton et al. (1997) and Golding (1992) in the evaluation of this instrument. Rogers believes it important to quantify the issue, although it would be unfair to assume that he does not recognize the value of more qualitative data (see Rogers & Ewing, 1992). Melton and Golding agree that quantification is essentially illusory at this stage in the development of evaluations of criminal responsibility. Both groups of authors agree, in large measure, on the domain of conceptual elements to be addressed.

Rogers has reported modest interrater reliabilities at the item level (average kappa = 0.58), with lower values (0.49) associated with the product question, (i.e., was the loss of control attributable to underlying psychopathological disturbance), one of the most frequent sources of disagreement in contested trials (Rogers, Wasyliw, & Cavanaugh, 1984). Final judgments with the R-CRAS also show reasonable levels of agreement between examiners and triers of fact (96% with respect to sanity, with lower levels of agreement on insanity [70%]; Rogers, Cavanaugh, Seman, & Harris, 1984). These findings are in general accord with the levels of agreement between clinicians and courts found in other studies of final judgment that use no formalized interviews or rating scales (Golding, 1992). Unfortunately, all studies in this area appear to use criterion-contaminated groups, in that the examination process is part of the judicial/criterial determination.

A number of proposals for semistructured protocols for examining MSO issues have been made (see, for example, Golding & Roesch, 1987; Melton et al., 1997; Ogloff, Roberts, & Roesch, 1993). They share in common an open-ended structure, with special attention to developing multisource data, identification of legally and psychologically relevant dimensions of the criminal responsibility evaluation, and disclosure of the logical links in an evaluator's reasoning. The need to develop such a comprehensive analysis is clear. These less-structured approaches have been shown to be empirically useful in various contexts (see Melton et al., 1997, for a review), but they have not been studied in the same fashion as the R-CRAS (previously discussed). The R-CRAS and less structured MSO evaluation techniques make their most important contributions by clarifying for the trier of fact the underlying bases for professional judgment (Golding, 1990, 1992), hence potentially highlighting the areas of disagreement so that expert testimony can be of more assistance to judge or juror. As argued elsewhere in this chapter, there is strong reason to believe that forensic examiners reach their generally high level of agreement in ultimate opinions by very different logical and empirically sustainable routes (see Skeem et al., in press, for an example in the context of competency evaluations). The critical issue remains the association between organic or psychopathological disturbance and control/moral judgment capacities; these devices are most useful when they serve the heuristic value of (a) highlighting the aspects of the defendant's psychological state that are relevant, (b) describing a purported relationship to control and judgment capacities, and (c) organizing known data about the empirical relationships between disorder and psychological capacities in various states and situations.

THE ROLE OF THIRD-PARTY AND CRIME SCENE INFORMATION

It is now a commonly accepted professional standard of practice that forensic evaluators seek to examine the consistency of mental health history and other archival data, along with details of the crime scene and witnesses' accounts of the defendant before, during, and after the alleged incident. This "consistency" examination is relevant to issues of malingering[16] and aids in supporting or challenging various psychological interpretations of the defendant's MSO. The importance of this aspect of a forensic examination at the time of the offense has been discussed by Golding (1992), Heilbrun, Rosenfeld, Warren, and Collins (1994), Melton et al. (1997), Ogloff et al. (1993), and Rogers (1997). It is beyond the scope of this chapter to discuss the relevance of so-called profiling, and it would be difficult to do so in light of the lack of empirical data of the reliability and validity of such techniques. Notwithstanding the lack of empiricism, the thrust behind the importance of crime scene evidence and collateral sources in supporting/challenging psychological interpretations of the defendant's MSO cannot be overemphasized. Although a forensic expert at trial should not mislead the trier of fact with respect to the degree of empirical support for this type of analysis, it is desirable to disclose the underlying data and logic of one's opinions, including the consistency (or lack thereof) of behavioral evidence with various psychological interpretations. A few examples will help develop this point.

Suppose a defense expert asserts that a young defendant, who killed a police officer with a rifle shot from the driver's side of a car in a high-speed chase following a "gas skip," was depressed, agitated, and suicidal and was trying to arrange a passive suicide ("death by cop"). The novelty of the assertion aside, the critical issue has to do with depression and its manifestations, along with the behavioral evidence. The evidence in support of the theory comes from the defendant's self-report, clinical interviews, and some self-report personality inventories. Close examination of the police reports and forensic evidence, however, reveals that the defendant fired several times, that his shots fit a tight pattern that targeted the police officer, and that he was trained in marksmanship. Further, the defendant was observed to duck when the police shot out his car's tires. Immediately after his arrest, and in the months following, (a) the defendant showed no behavioral indications of depression according to correctional officers' observations of his mood, interactions with others, facial expressions, sleep and appetite, or general demeanor; and (b) his letters from jail to several friends, relatives, and a girlfriend revealed no indications of depression, suicidality, or preoccupation with morbid themes, and had a considerable future orientation. Is there a direct scientific basis for integrating these data? Clearly not, but there is a basis for asserting that these data are inconsistent with the defense's claim, based partially on psychological data and knowledge of depression and partially on logical reasoning. It would obviously be an important task for future research to examine carefully, in representative populations, the link between behavioral manifestations of mental capacities and incapacities. It is in this sense that the development of more standardized protocols for crime scene analysis of behavioral data relevant to purported psychological states is warranted.

Suppose that a defendant charged with two murders has an expert who wishes to assert that the defendant was delusionally "inspired" to the murders by psychotic "revelations from God." The issue may be partially joined by a detailed examination of the defendant's phenomenological experience, the cultural context, and its consistency with the development of delusions versus overvalued ideas, as we discuss below.[17] Nevertheless, behavioral data and forensic evidence are also relevant: the fact that the written "revelation" at issue was edited by the defendant over time; that the name of "God's servant" who was to carry out the "removal" was first left blank, then filled in by the defendant; and that the defendant then allegedly performed the "removal" when the named person was deemed "undesirable." Additional data concern an attempt to flee the police, use of an alias, and a public statement, following arrest, that the revelation did not say "to kill" but rather "to remove" the victims. In conjunction with other psychological data, what does this suggest about the delusionality of the revelation and its *unmittlebar* characteristics (see Delusion section)? Again, the available data are indirect, but they are inconsistent with what is known about delusionally inspired behavior. Moreover, they are difficult to link logically to delusional as opposed to personally inspired motivation.[18]

Finally, consider an evaluation of a confession in which the police view of the confession's validity and the defendant's rationale for complying with police coercion are at issue. Close examination of the confession reveals that the defendant's statements about his position and the nature of his killing of the victim are inconsistent with his handedness, his claimed position vis-à-vis the victim, and the nature of the depression fractures to the victim's skull (see Melton et al., 1997, p. 238, for a similar type of confession case). Such evidence does not unequivocally point in a particular direction, but it is consistent with the nature of the defendant's mental state claims about the circumstances of the confession (that the police had given him the information and that he confessed, based on those details, to protect his wife, who he believed had committed the act and whose own inconsistent statements were also in dispute).

The thread that runs through these and other examples is that forensic evaluators need to pay close attention to crime scene data as well as to more traditional sources of third-party information (mental health records, witness statements, and the like). All such sources need to be integrated in as straightforward a manner as possible. Where limited scientific data exist to support the inference (e.g., descriptive studies of the characteristics of hallucinations or delusions), they should be referenced; where otherwise indicated, the evaluator's logical link analysis should be declared and scrutinized.

As Melton et al. (1997) note, the role of the forensic evaluator is not to "resolve conclusively all conflicting accounts about the case" (p. 50), but rather to conduct an evaluation that can be scrutinized in terms of all available evidence, both psychological and behavioral. The same issue often arises in neuropsychological evaluations in both civil and criminal contexts (Matarazzo, 1990). However, modern forensic standards of practice are to address the issue of the consistency of behavioral crime scene evidence with psycholegal formulations and to allow the trier of fact to make the determination of their significance, guided by whatever scientific evidence can be directly or indirectly adduced.

THE ROLE OF DELUSIONS IN ASSESSMENTS OF CRIMINAL RESPONSIBILITY

The nature and quality of a defendant's delusionality is central in determining the extent of impairment in MSO. Several issues are involved. In *contested* cases,[19] forensic examiners are particularly apt to encounter defendants with extreme or idiosyncratic beliefs about religion, politics, or personal identity, and a question of the delusionality of those beliefs will arise. Delusionality also enters the adjudicatory process when the issues of intentionality, compulsion, or the reasonableness of the defendant's conduct may be related to a delusion. Finally, delusionality is an important aspect of risk assessment with respect to release decisions.

Although there are surprisingly few studies on the frequency and nature of delusions among NGRI defendants, indirect data as well as experience suggest that delusionality is a vital issue. Delusions are highly prevalent among individuals who suffer from psychosis (Winters & Neale, 1983);[20] in turn, roughly 50% of those defendants who raise the insanity defense and 70% of insanity acquittees have psychotic diagnoses (Andreasen & Flaum, 1994; Cirincione, Steadman, & McGreevy, 1995; Ogloff et al., 1992; Rice & Harris, 1990; Taylor et al., 1994). Moreover, delusions are specifically and substantially related to violence (Taylor et al., 1994).

In an extensive analysis of case records, Häfner and Böker (1982) found that 70% of individuals with schizophrenia who were accused of homicide had delusional beliefs about their relationship to their victim. Similarly, in an interview study, Taylor (1985) found that 40% of psychotic defendants acted *directly* upon delusions during their offenses. The frequency of *nonpathological* but radical religious and/or political beliefs and the extent of the relationship between these beliefs and violence has not been systematically studied (Taylor et al., 1994). However, defendants whose criminal acts are related to such fervently held beliefs are clearly plausible candidates for mental state evaluations.

Distinguishing between radical beliefs and delusions is a difficult but critical task in assessing criminal responsibility.[21] Respecting the principles of autonomy and self-determination, our legal system holds responsible the extremist who chooses to act upon a radical system of beliefs, expressing her desires, values, and "personhood" through the crime (see Hermann, 1990). The basic moral logic of the insanity defense, however, excuses the mentally disordered individual who acts upon a pathological, uncontrollable belief system that distorts her sense of reality, thereby impairing her capacity for rational choice. Arguably, the same logic applies to delusions that would "justify" the actions.[22]

Notwithstanding the centrality of this issue in assessing criminal responsibility, there are relatively few data-oriented studies or professional practice standards available in the forensic literature to aid in assessing the delusionality of beliefs. In "grey area" cases, or cases in which defendants are neither clearly sane nor insane, the classification of beliefs as delusory is presumably a major source of disagreement among examiners. There is no bright line of de-marcation between extreme beliefs and delusions (Garety & Hemsley, 1994; Olt-manns, 1988). Moreover, religious and political belief systems, which reference nonphysical entities and events, are not scientifically testable; consequently, there is "no full standard of truth independent of what the [defendant] says" (Saks, 1991; Taylor et al., 1994, p. 167). For these reasons, in this section we re-view recent progress in defining and assessing delusions and their likely conse-quences. The purpose of this section is to introduce readers to the complex issues involved in assessing delusions and to aid clinicians in conducting in-formed assessments of defendants' beliefs in the context of insanity evalua-tions. Emphasis is placed on issues relevant to distinguishing between extreme religious or political beliefs and delusions.

Defining and Conceptualizing Delusions

The *DSM-IV* defines a delusion as follows: "A *false belief* based on incorrect infer-ence about external reality that is *firmly sustained* despite what almost everyone else believes and despite what constitutes incontrovertible and obvious proof or evidence to the contrary. The belief is *not one ordinarily accepted by other members of the person's culture or subculture* (e.g., it is not an article of religious faith). When a false belief involves a value judgment, it is regarded as a delusion only when the judgment is so extreme as to *defy credibility"* (American Psychiatric As-sociation, 1994, p. 765; emphasis added).

Although this "concise and handy" definition is adequate for most forensic and clinical purposes, its shortcomings are readily exposed when one attempts to delineate its boundaries (Sedler, 1995). As noted above, there is often no stan-dard of proof by which to assess the falsity of beliefs in many religious, political, and identity systems. Similarly, it is difficult to evaluate the incredibility or im-plausibility of beliefs: clinicians rarely agree upon the extent to which beliefs are bizarre (Flaum, Arndt, & Andreasen, 1991; Oltmanns, 1988; cf. Mojtabai & Nicholson, 1995; R. Spitzer, First, Kendler, & Stein, 1993). The degree of convic-tion with which a belief is held also does not clearly distinguish between delu-sional and nondelusional beliefs. Like delusional beliefs, nondelusional but highly valued beliefs are often held with great zeal and intensity even in the face of contradictory evidence. Moreover, most patients shift between periods in which they are certain about their delusions and periods in which they have par-tial or full insight (see Harrow, Rattenbury, & Stoll, 1988; Sacks, Carpenter, & Strauss, 1974).

These difficulties are "frequently compounded by ambiguity surrounding the presence or absence of cultural support for the person's belief" (Olt-manns, 1988, p. 3). It is difficult to determine the extent to which the nature of a belief, its experience, or its expression must deviate[23] from that accepted by a designated subgroup to classify as delusional. Clearly, examiners must have considerable knowledge of the social, religious, political, and even scientific context of a defendant's belief to adequately assess its delusionality (see Barn-house, 1986; Oltmanns, 1988). Failure to carefully consider patients' subcul-tural and religious background often results in misdiagnosis (see Lu, Lukoff, & Turner, 1994).

Most current attempts to systematically analyze delusions are based on the seminal work of Jaspers[24] (1963; see Garety & Hemsley, 1994; Mullen, 1979, 1985; Sedler, 1995). Jaspers arguably provides the most comprehensive, enduring, and clinically useful theory for distinguishing among various categories of delusional and nondelusional beliefs. A simplified summary of this theory focused on differentiating delusional from nondelusional beliefs per se is presented here (see C. Walker, 1991 for detail).

Jaspers argued that the criteria of conviction, imperviousness to counterargument, and impossibility or bizarreness were insufficient[25] external criteria that did not capture the essence of delusionality.[26] Rather, "overvalued beliefs," or even "delusion-like ideas"[27] could be distinguished from primary delusions, based on Jaspers's approach, by attention to three more fundamental criteria. First, primary delusions are distinguished from secondary delusions and beliefs that are merely overvalued based on the extent and nature of their "un-understandability."[28] Second, primary delusions are "unmediated"[29] by thought, analysis, deduction, or reflection, while overvalued ideas and secondary delusions reflect varying degrees of cognitive appraisal and inference. Third, primary delusions reflect a distinctive change in an individual's personality functioning;[30] that is, they are a distinct change in the totality of the individual's personal meanings and ways of construing the world.

An overvalued idea is understandable, the product of cognitive interpretation, and can be viewed in terms of an individual's personality, life experiences, and sociocultural background. Overvalued ideas are relatively easily understood "as exaggerations, diminutions, or combinations of phenomena which we ourselves experience" (Jaspers, 1963, quoted in C. Walker, 1991, p. 100). In contrast, a secondary delusion ("crazy idea") is *only* understandable in the sense that it emerges through one's process of reasoning about psychopathological experiences (e.g., based on the quiet voices and buzzing an individual occasionally hears, she arrives at the conclusion that she is a target of government surveillance). A primary delusion is *not* understandable because it originates in a direct, immediate experience of new meaning unmediated by thought and unconnected to the person's fundamental personality (e.g., one sees a "man in a brown coat . . . he is the dead Archduke," C. Walker, 1991, p. 99). Thus, whereas overvalued ideas have "clear precedent" in an individual's existing personality and meaningful life events, secondary delusions emerge from other psychopathological experiences, and primary delusions fundamentally change an individual's personality or "way of looking at the world" (C. Walker, 1991). Although Jaspers's classification has been subject to little empirical research and can be criticized for relying heavily on the subjective criterion of "understandability" (Mullen, 1985), his theory provides useful guidance in conceptualizing the key distinctions among delusions and overvalued ideas.

Since Jaspers's work, there has been a recent "emerging consensus that delusions are complex, multidimensional phenomena" (Taylor et al., 1994, p. 163). As demonstrated above, delusions cannot be fully defined by checklists of necessary and sufficient criteria (Oltmanns, 1988). Thus, researchers have begun to view delusions as beliefs that deviate "to a greater or lesser extent from normal beliefs along a number of dimensions" (Garety & Hemsley, 1994, p. 40). Based on this dimensional conception, several instruments have been developed to aid in assessing delusions (see Garety & Hemsley, 1994, Chapters 4–5; Harrow et al., 1988; Kendler, Glazer, & Morgenstern, 1983; Taylor et al., 1994). A particularly promising example of these instruments is described below.

Progress in Measuring and Assessing Delusions and Their Relation to Violence

Several instruments are available to *aid* in assessing whether beliefs are delusional, explore and describe their content, and determine their core dimensions and likely consequences. These instruments have promising psychometric characteristics and appear to be useful in forensic and risk-assessment contexts.

Determining Whether Beliefs Are Delusional. Traditional psychological tests such as the MMPI-2 or Rorschach, or newer instruments such as the Personality Assessment Inventory, are not "magic bullets" but can be useful sources of supplementary information to aid in determining the probability of delusional thinking. Delusions are highly prevalent among individuals with psychosis; in fact, "delusion has long been regarded as one of the central characteristics of psychosis or madness, and [usually] involves more than false and arbitrary ideas" (Andreasen & Flaum, 1994; Mullen, 1985, p. 17). Thus, profile patterns and clinical signs indicative of thought disorder or other manifestations of psychosis increase the likelihood that an extreme belief is pathological.[31] However, potentially delusional beliefs are complex phenomena that require *direct, specific* assessment focused on discerning the nature of the belief, the phenomenology and organization of experiences relevant to the belief, and the extent to which the belief and its expression are understandable based on the defendant's personality or sociocultural background. Thus, traditional psychological tests are relatively less important than detailed interviews of the defendant and knowledgeable others and careful reviews of relevant legal and mental health records (see below). The latter data are also necessary to address the core issue of the extent to which possibly delusional thinking is related to the defendant's MSO.

Several structured interviews have been developed to increase the reliability and validity of diagnoses and/or to improve the quality and comprehensiveness of clinical interviews (see Andreasen, Flaum, & Arndt, 1992; Luria & Guziec, 1981; Manchanda, Hirsch, & Barnes, 1989). The Present State Examination (PSE-9; Wing, Cooper, & Sartorius, 1974) is grounded in the phenomenological approach and was created primarily for the latter purpose. The most recent revision, PSE-10, is compatible with *DSM-III-R, DSM-IV,* and *ICD-10* diagnostic systems (Wing, 1996). The PSE is, in our opinion, the most comprehensive structured interview available to aid in assessing the delusionality of beliefs. The PSE is closely linked to Jaspers's approach, distinguishes between partial and full delusions, and includes detailed attention to the potential influence of the defendant's religious and political subculture on her beliefs. Moreover, at the heart of the PSE is a comprehensive symptom glossary which aids in making relatively fine distinctions with respect to each item.

Although data are apparently not yet available for the PSE-10, the PSE-9 demonstrates rates of agreement comparable to or exceeding those of other structured interviews (see Luria & Guziec, 1981; Manchanda & Hirsch, 1986).

The PSE-9 interrater reliability for delusions is excellent and comparable to that achieved with Andreasen's (1987) Comprehensive Assessment of Symptoms and History (CASH) and the anchored Brief Psychiatric Rating Scale (Andreasen et al., 1992; Gabbard et al., 1987; Lukoff, Liberman, & Nuechterlein, 1986; World Health Organization, 1979).

Exploring and Describing the Content of Possible Delusions.   The PSE provides definitions, sample inquiries, and rating points not only for assessing the basic delusionality of beliefs, but also for exploring what *kind* of potentially delusional ideas a defendant holds (e.g., grandiose, referential, persecutory, thought insertion). The CASH (Andreasen, 1987), a structured interview for assessing major mental illness, provides little guidance in defining basic delusionality, but covers a wider range of delusional content than the PSE. In addition to detailed definitions and probes for exploring specific kinds of delusions, the CASH includes an extensive rating system for various types of formal thought disorder (i.e., derailment, illogicality, pressure) and other positive and negative symptoms of schizophrenia. A comprehensive analysis of these symptoms can highlight sometimes subtle signs of psychosis. When defendants express themselves in a relatively disconnected fashion, this arguably increases the probability that their beliefs are delusional rather than merely eccentric.

Unfortunately, we could not find reliability data for the types of delusions where examiner (dis)agreement is of most interest for our purposes, namely, "grey area" religious and political delusions or overvalued ideas. Reliability for less nebulous types of delusions is, however, quite high when structured interviews are employed. For example, the PSE-9 has excellent rates of interrater reliability with respect to paranoid delusions (interclass $r = .93$), grandiose delusions ($r = .93$), and delusions of passivity ($r = .92$) (Amador, Strauss, Yale, & Gorman, 1991).

Determining the Contours or Dimensions of a Delusion.   As explained above, several leaders in the study of delusions have begun to conceptualize delusions as beliefs that differ from normal beliefs across various sets of dimensions, and have created assessment instruments to assess delusions as multidimensional phenomena. Pamela Taylor and colleagues (1994) have developed a sophisticated version of such an instrument, the Maudsley Assessment of Delusions Schedule (MADS). The MADS is a structured interview designed to reliably and validly assess key dimensions and possible consequences of an individual's "principal abnormal belief" (e.g., the belief the individual deems most important). This purpose is relevant to evaluations of criminal responsibility and disposition in that it emphasizes links between delusional dimensions and violence. Taylor and her colleagues suggest that clinicians use the MADS *after* they have administered the delusion subsection of the PSE to determine the delusionality of beliefs and identify their content. The key dimensions assessed by the MADS were derived from prior research and the MADS item-development studies. They include (a) conviction, (b) belief-maintenance factors (i.e., seeking evidence to support the belief, reaction to belief-challenging information), (c) affective impact of the belief, (d) preoccupation with the belief, (e) systematization of the belief, (f) idiosyncrasy of the belief, (g) insight, and (h) manner and degree of action on belief. Items related to the action dimension reflect three types of action on the basis of delusion: (a) aggression toward self or others; (b) defensive action such as withdrawal; and (c) no action or single, unobtrusive action (Wessely et al., 1993). The MADS has excellent interrater reliability (*M* kappa = .82), and good test-retest reliability (*M* kappa = .63) (Taylor et al., 1994).

Dimensions of Delusions Associated with Violence.   The MADS has been used to investigate the frequency of acting upon delusions and the characteristics of delusions that are associated with acting violently. Wessely et al. (1993; see also Taylor et al., 1994) found that, of 83 delusional patients studied over a *brief, 28-day* period, 60% reported having acted in some way on their delusions, but only 11% reported having acted violently toward themselves or others based on their delusions. The authors attempted to relate particular types of delusions to propensities toward general action and found that only persecutory delusions were particularly likely to be directly acted upon (violently *or* nonviolently). Two dimensions of delusions that are assessed by the MADS were related to *action in general:* belief-maintenance factors and affective impact (see Buchanan et al., 1993). Specifically, acting "on a delusion was associated with being aware of and having actively sought 'evidence' that supported [or refuted] the belief together with, paradoxically, some reduction in the conviction with which the belief was held on direct challenge. Acting was also associated with a range of affective changes (e.g., increase in [sadness], fear or anxiety) which the patient attributed to the belief" (Taylor et al., 1994, p. 176).

Other data on dimensions of psychotic belief also support the importance of assessing the nature and characteristics of delusionality thoroughly. Link and Stueve (1994) found that what they term "threat/control override symptoms" (thoughts and delusions about being harmed, having one's mind controlled, thought insertion, etc.) were a significant factor in accounting for community aggression and weapons use. Steury and Choinski (1995) also uncovered some interesting relationships in an elegant descriptive and correlational analysis of violent crime characteristics that distinguish mentally ill defendants from non-mentally-ill defendants. Compared with non-mentally-ill defendants, mentally ill defendants' crimes more often involved, for example, lack of apparent motive, delusional motive, relatively unplanned actions, more use of knives than guns, and no history of conflict or trouble with the victim, combined with a greater likelihood of arguing with the victim at the onset of the offense. Notably, mentally ill defendants' victims were less often strangers. These data, taken together with Taylor's work, obviously need replication in larger samples with careful attention to the complex dimensions of delusion. Nevertheless, they point the way for sophisticated forensic research on delusionality and its relationship to criminal responsibility (see Mulvey, 1994, for a similar analysis).

ISSUES IN THE DISPOSITION OF INSANITY ACQUITTEES

Inherent in an original decision to find a defendant NGRI is concern about the ultimate disposition of such acquittees. Jurors place a great deal of emphasis on this issue in their deliberations (see Golding, 1992). Further, a comparison of data on the rates and success of insanity pleas and the nature of insanity dispositions with data on public perceptions about these issues clearly reveals that the public overestimates the frequency and successfulness of the insanity plea and underestimates the nature and length of institutionalization following an insanity "acquittal" (Silver et al., 1994). Curiously, in *Shannon v. United States* (1994), the Supreme Court held that NGRI defendants have no right to a jury instruction that makes clear the post-"acquittal" commitment process, as such an instruction would violate the long-standing principle that a jury must base its verdict on the evidence before it. Although this may be "correct" jurisprudential theory, it violates commonsense justice, in that we have strong reasons to believe that jurors do pay attention to this issue and that their assumptions are incorrect (see above).[32]

THE ROLE OF DANGEROUSNESS, MAXIMUM SENTENCE, AND MENTAL ILLNESS

In *Jones v. United States* (1983), the Supreme Court of the United States affirmed that because an insanity acquittee was not guilty of a criminal offense, a principled and constitutional approach to the disposition of insanity acquittees must focus on the issues of mental disorder and its relationship to future dangerousness, not on the length of incarceration associated with the acquittee's underlying criminal conduct.[33] Also, to commit an insanity acquittee, the state must prove only by a preponderance of the evidence that the acquittee is mentally ill and dangerous. Implied in the decision is the assumption that the court may place a higher burden on the defendant to prove, in future release hearings, that she was no longer mentally ill and not at a high risk for future dangerous behavior. The assumption that the Court is comfortable with such asymmetries in the civil versus criminal commitment context is reinforced by their decisions in *Foucha v. Louisiana* (1992) and *Kansas v. Hendricks* (1997). In a complex decision, four justices in *Foucha* held Louisiana's broad NGRI commitment statute unconstitutional because it would allow continued confinement of insanity acquittees based on dangerousness alone. In contrast, four other justices (now in clear majority on the Court) would have allowed the commitment on the grounds that the NGRI verdict was sufficient to justify the continued commitment, especially in light of the vagaries of mental illness. In her determining vote, Justice O'Connor agreed that, as written, the broad Louisiana statute was unconstitutional, but the commitment could be constitutional "if, unlike the situation in this case, the nature and duration of detention were tailored to reflect pressing public safety concerns related to the acquittee's continuing dangerousness" (at 88–89). It is unfortunate that this critical decision was argued in the context of *Foucha*, whose original NGRI was based on a "drug induced psychosis" (which is an atypical ground for an insanity defense) and that his "lack of mental illness" at petitioned release was "antisocial personality disorder." Nevertheless, the trend of the Court is clearly in the direction of loose boundaries with respect to the criteria for mental illness *(Hendricks)* and the criteria for dangerousness in the postconviction/NGRI context.

One of the unappreciated consequences of an NGRI disposition is that the adjudicating court can maintain jurisdiction and control via monitoring programs, conditional release, and revocation for a virtual lifetime period if needed. As *Jones v. United States* (1983) made clear, the criterion for ultimate release is nondangerousness as well as relevant concern with the role of current mental illness.

Insofar as many insanity acquittees have significant lifelong psychopathological difficulties that are controlled only to a certain extent and are subject to fluctuations associated with variable dangerousness (Golding et al., 1989), systematic programs for trained professionals to monitor insanity acquittees' release makes a good deal of sense (Bloom, Williams, & Bigelow, 1991). Although little attention has been paid to this problem in the majority of jurisdictions, those jurisdictions that have implemented such systems uniformly report positive results. Well-known conditional release programs exist in British Columbia, California, Maryland, New York, Oregon, and several other states (Bloom et al., 1991; Golding et al., 1989; Griffin, Steadman, & Heilbrun, 1991; Heilbrun & Griffin, 1993; Heilbrun, Lawson, Spier, & Libby, 1994; McGreevy, Steadman, Dvoskin, & Dollard, 1991; Psychiatric Security Review Board, 1994; Silver & Tellefsen, 1991; Tellefsen, Cohen, Silver, & Dougherty, 1992; Wiederanders, 1992; Wilson, Tien, & Eaves, 1995). The coordination, control and training of community supervisors is critical to the success of these programs (Golding, 1991), especially with reference to ongoing monitoring of a supervisee's risk status (Wack, 1993).

Wiederanders (1992) followed a group of insanity acquittees who had been conditionally released with follow-up supervision under tightly controlled circumstances with a group of insanity acquittees that had been released because they reached their maximum sentences. The groups were obviously constituted nonrandomly, but Wiederanders demonstrates that they were substantially equal on known predictors of recidivism. The two groups were found to differ dramatically both in their frequency of failure of community tenure (5.8% vs. 27.3%) and in their rate of failure (faster for the unsupervised group). Wiederanders attributes such differences to the ability to monitor deterioration and to intervene earlier and in a preventative fashion. Results from all of the community supervision programs referenced previously are consistent with this conclusion. The empirical proposition, though not yet fully tested, makes clinical, legal, and social policy sense. If this population is known to be more difficult to treat (due to ineffectiveness of medication, medication refusal, fluctuating clinical/dangerousness course, etc.), then a balanced conditional release program, which errs on the side of false positives (revoking community tenure and reinstituting a higher level of supervision), is a rational system. It also appears to be an empirically justifiable system.

An unstudied aspect of the dispositional issue has to do with the ultimate costs and effectiveness of placing prototypic insanity acquittees in forensic treatment contexts versus placement in traditional correctional facilities. Although some data clearly support the monitored release of NGRI acquittees, the larger trend, in those states with either guilty but mentally ill or highly restricted (or nonexistent) insanity defenses, is to place such defendants in correctional environments for the majority of their sentence or institutionalization. Wiederanders (1992; Wiederanders & Choate, 1994) and Golding et al. (1989) have shown that articulated follow-up of insanity acquittees in the community is feasible and worthy of study. What we do not have is informative data on the differences between similar individuals "treated" in correctional versus forensic mental health contexts. We know of no empirical studies of this issue, but clearly they are now quite timely. With respect to mental health economics, the question is whether society eventually pays more or less for treating mentally disordered offenders in prison or in forensic mental health systems. Clearly, the cost per diem while initially incarcerated will favor prison over mental health system dispositions. However, the analysis also needs to include days institutionalized, days in the community at lower cost, and the likelihood and financial, emotional, and moral costs of recidivism. Again, we know of no direct data, but, on logical grounds, we propose that treated and supervised mentally ill and dangerous offenders would cost less, financially and emotionally, than prison-incarcerated mentally ill offenders who receive less mental health treatment and supervision.[34]

NOTES

1. For comprehensive and scholarly reviews of the history of the *mens rea* doctrine, see Sayre (1932), Stroud (1914), and Morse (1992). The problem is how to consider the conjunction of the proscribed behavior *(actus reus)* and an appropriate degree and type of intentionality and mental capacity *(mens rea)* in ascribing guilt or culpability.

2. "It is a defense . . . that the defendant, as a result of mental illness, lacked the mental state required as an element of the offense charged. Mental illness is not otherwise a defense" (Utah Annotated Code, § 76-2-305, 1997). Other states that follow the abolitionist approach are Montana and Idaho. Curiously, the essence of the American Law Institute standard for insanity appears as a mitigating condition at sentencing in all three abolitionist jurisdictions: "Evidence of mental condition shall be received, if offered, at the time of sentencing . . . the court shall consider such factors as . . . the capacity of the defendant to appreciate the wrongfulness of his conduct or to conform his conduct to the requirements of law at the time of the offense charged" (Idaho Code, Section 19-2523(1); see similar language in Section 46-14-312(a) of the Montana Code and Section 76–3-207(3)(d) of the Utah Code). This approach has consistently survived constitutional challenge (*State v. Korell*, 1984; *State v. Herrera & Sweezey*, 1995). Unfortunately, all courts hearing this abolitionist issue have effectively sidestepped the "ultimate justice" issue by observing that legislatures may, within their power, adopt such jurisprudential strategies, however unwise they may be.

3. These issues are reviewed in full in Golding (1992), Melton et al. (1997), and Perlin (1994). The abolitionist position still holds sway in Utah, Idaho, and Montana, where a restricted *mens rea* only defense is allowed. The traditional ALI "substantial incapacity to appreciate or inability to conform" criterion is now less common, and the reformed ALI/M'Naghten Rule (the traditional test, minus the volitional prong [discussed at length in Golding and Roesch, 1987]), common in federal and state statutes, are the modal view of NGRI criteria.

4. We later address studies of decision making with respect to their implications for what factors are weighed in decision making and the influence of jury instructions and insanity defense standards.

5. The "success" rates vary wildly in Silver's review, from 7% to 87%, averaging 26%. Unfortunately, as described above, no attempt was made to code clinical characteristics of the defendants beyond simple diagnosis, and there is a high likelihood of extreme jurisdictional differences in the types of clinical pictures presented. For earlier studies and summaries of success rates, see Janofsky, Vandewalle, and Rappeport (1989) and Pasewark (1986).

6. See references and comments at Note 19.

7. A detailed examination of a large NGRI cohort by Golding, Eaves, and Kowaz (1989) found that 78.7% had been previously hospitalized, with a mean of 4.11 hospitalizations; 43.4% of these prior admissions were for forensic reasons. Over half of the subjects with prior admissions were discharged within one year of their index offense, and 44.6% committed their index offense within six months of their last discharge.

8. Included in both these research traditions are dimensions such as (a) ability to think and reason rationally and clearly, (b) capacity to perceive and be aware without distortion, (c) capacity to choose courses of action, (d) rational motivation for actions, (e) ability to control thoughts, feelings, and behaviors, and (f) responsibility for altering one's mental state by intoxication, noncompliance with medication, and other factors.

9. See Simon (1967) for a review of first-generation work with more representative juror samples.

10. For an excellent review of the strengths and weaknesses of jury simulation studies, see Diamond (1997).

11. Roberts and Golding (1991) have consistently found effects for guilty but mentally ill (GBMI) alternatives, as have others. However, the effect, we believe, is largely mediated by juror construals, as they also argue.

12. As Diamond (1997) observes, many of the effects and their strength depend on the way the verdicts are formulated, the alternatives, existence of contextual effects, and so forth.

13. A proposition for which there is little empirical support. Although a review of the evidence on malingering is beyond the scope of this chapter, the issue is comprehensively addressed in R. Rogers (1997). A variety of increasingly sophisticated techniques are available. See also Gacono, Meloy, Sheppard, and Speth (1995) and Gothard, Viglione, Meloy, and Sherman (1995) for specific applications in insanity and incompetency populations. In practice, most issues of malingering are detected by inconsistencies with mental health records, witness statements, observations by ward or correctional personnel, and crime scene evidence, in addition to psychological test scores and other such data. See "Third-Party Information" below.

14. As analyzed in "Disposition of Insanity Acquittees," the public may be poorly served by dispositions that treat NGRI acquittees as criminal convicts rather than dangerously mentally ill individuals.

15. A number of attitudinal items are available but have not been extensively studied nor cross-validated (Golding, 1992). Skeem (1997) is trying to improve on the psychometric qualities of these prior scales.

16. This is especially true in the examination of amnesia (Rogers, 1997; Schachter, 1996; 1986a, 1986b; Taylor & Kopelman, 1984). There is a useful descriptive literature on the characteristics of amnesias under various circumstances, which is not definitive but which provides useful cues for examining the consistency of a defendant's claims.

17. In an actual case, the defendant described his revelatory experience in subculturally normative terms, that is, he prayed and asked for guidance from God about a

particular problem, awoke to find his mind "inspired" by God's revelation, and wrote out his revelation with the "ideas in his mind" controlling the content. He did not experience this as a hallucinatory phenomenon, did not experience any indications of mania, and experienced himself as choosing the words to use as he inspected his mind. The themes and emotional content of the revelation were consistent with his personal history and individual belief. He cautiously approached others in his close circle of like-minded friends with the details of the revelation.

18. The adult victim and intended victims had challenged his attempts to set up a subgroup based on his prophetic leadership; an infant victim was the only child of the adult victim, who would "spread her seed."

19. Research on the reliability of forensic judgments of insanity (summarized in Melton et al., 1997; Golding, 1992; Hoge & Grisso, 1992; Rogers & Ewing, 1992) reveals high rates of agreement among well-trained examiners using similar conceptual schemes. Careful reading of the studies reviewed also points indirectly to those types of cases likely to be contested: comorbidity with personality disorder; highly idiosyncratic and paranoid religious, political, or identity systems; intoxication or failure to take medications; and extremely bizarre conduct.

20. Particularly relevant to forensic assessments, they argue that delusions of reference, persecution, and control are particularly prevalent.

21. As may be seen in the competence literature, the courts and examiners regularly distinguish between radical beliefs and delusions, treating as rational and valid decisions and actions that express unconventional, extreme beliefs rather than delusions (Golding, 1993; Saks, 1991).

22. In Georgia, a defendant who cannot establish an insanity defense on the grounds of mental incapacity to distinguish right from wrong can nevertheless sustain an insanity defense on the grounds that the delusion "leads him to believe that his action is right, i.e. 'Justified' "*and that, under those circumstances, his actions would have been legally justifiable* (*Lawrence v. State*, 1995; materials in italics added for clarification).

23. Consider delusions versus idiosyncratic ideas in revelatory religions. What distinguishes a delusion from an idiosyncratic revelation? Vote of the church authorities? The number of persons who believe the revelation? What are the normative phenomenological experiences of "normal" recipients of revelation? These issues are troublesome and have not received empirical attention.

24. For an interesting historical analysis and critique of Jaspers, see Berrios (1991).

25. Interestingly, many modern and otherwise informative accounts of the problem of clinically assessing delusionality mistakenly refer to the external criteria as the essence of Jaspers's system (M. Spitzer, 1990).

26. "To say simply that a delusion is a mistaken idea which is firmly held by the patient and cannot be corrected gives only a superficial and incorrect answer to the problem" (Jaspers, 1963, p. 93).

27. *Wahnhafte Ideen*, literally "crazy-like ideas," as opposed to *Unsinn*, insane ideas.

28. Primary delusions are *unverständlich*, that is, "un-understandable." Unlike normal ideas, overvalued beliefs, and "crazy-like" ideas, they do not "emerge understandably from other psychic events and can(not) be traced back psychologically to certain affects, drives, desires and fears" (Jaspers, 1963, Professional Psychology: Research and Practice, 106–107).

29. Real delusional experience is *unmittlebar*, unmediated by thought processes. "Primary delusional experience is the direct, unmediated, intrusive knowledge of meaning . . . not considered interpretations, but meaning directly experienced" (Jaspers, 1963, Professional Psychology: Research and Practice, 99–100).

30. *Umwändlung der Persönlichkeit*.

31. This is an important direction for future research. Regrettably, most of the clinical literature on delusional disorder (*DSM* 297.1) does not include comprehensive assessment of thought disorder from a psychometric or language-analysis perspective. Thus, when criteria for delusionality are vague and there is no obvious clinical thought disorder or other schizophrenic or affective psychotic indicators, delusional disorder is often the subject of controversy in forensic applications.

32. In fairness, the *Shannon v. United States* (1994) majority would allow such instructions to counteract overt testimony by a witness or a prosecutor that the "defendant would go free," when this is not the jurisdictional rule. This reinforces our earlier comments about the importance of voir dire in NGRI juror selection.

33. Jones had stolen a coat from a department store. The Court presumes that any criminal act is presumptive of dangerousness, however counterintuitive that may be. Despite the legal standard's focus on mental disorder and its relationship to future dangerousness, the available empirical evidence strongly suggests a different view. Length of *initial* periods of hospitalization for NGRI acquittees has been found, in general, to be primarily determined by the nature of the individual's criminal offense (see Golding, 1992, for a review). In addition, though there is some variability in findings, NGRI acquittees are generally not institutionalized for periods of time that are significantly shorter than either unsuccessful NGRI pleaders or non-NGRI convictees (Silver, 1995). If anything, the trend is toward longer periods of incarceration.

34. Hafemeister and Petrila's (1994) excellent review of treatment of mentally disordered offenders suggests this direction, but there do not appear to be any empirical studies directly on point.

REFERENCES

Abbott, W., Hall, F., & Linville, E. (1993). *Jury research: A review and bibliography.* Philadelphia: American Bar Association.

Amador, X., Strauss, D., Yale, S., & Gorman, J. (1991). Awareness of illness in schizophrenia. *Schizophrenia Bulletin, 17,* 113–132.

American Law Institute. (1962). *Model penal code* § 4.01. Philadelphia: Author.

American Psychiatric Association. (1994). *Diagnostic and statistical manual of mental disorders* (4th ed.). Washington, DC: American Psychiatric Press.

Andreasen, N. (1987). *Comprehensive assessment of symptoms and history (CASH).* Iowa City, IA: Department of Psychiatry.

Andreasen, N., & Flaum, M. (1994). Characteristic symptoms of schizophrenia. In T. Widiger, A. Frances, H. Pincus, M. First, R. Ross, & W. Davis (Eds.), *DSM-IV sourcebook.* Washington, DC: American Psychiatric Association.

Andreasen, N., Flaum, M., & Arndt, S. (1992). The comprehensive assessment of symptoms and history (CASH): An instrument for assessing diagnosis and psychopathology. *Archives of General Psychiatry, 49,* 615–623.

Bailis, D., Darley, J., Waxman, T., & Robinson, P. (1995). Community standards of criminal liability and the insanity defense. *Law & Human Behavior, 19,* 425–446.

Ballantine, H. W. (1919). Criminal responsibility of the insane and feeble-minded. *Journal of the American Institute of Criminal Law and Criminology, 9,* 485–499.

Barnhouse, R. (1986). How to evaluate patients' religious ideation. In L. Robinson (Ed.), *Psychiatry and religion: Overlapping concerns.* Washington, DC: American Psychiatric Press.

Berrios, G. E. (1991). Delusions as "wrong beliefs": A conceptual history. *British Journal of Psychiatry, 159,* 6–13.

Bloom, J. D., Williams, M. H., & Bigelow, D. A. (1991). Monitored conditional release of persons found not guilty by reason of insanity. *American Journal of Psychiatry, 148,* 444–448.

Buchanan, A., Reed, A., Wessely, S., Garety, P., Taylor, P., Grubin, D., & Dunn, G. (1993). Acting on delusions: II. The phenomenological correlates of acting on delusions. *British Journal of Psychiatry, 163,* 77–81.

Bumby, K. M. (1993). Reviewing the guilty but mentally ill alternative: A case of the blind "pleading" the blind. *Journal of Psychiatry and Law, 21,* 191–220.

Cirincione, C., Steadman, H., & McGreevy, M. (1995). Rates of insanity acquittals and the factors associated with successful insanity pleas. *Bulletin of the American Academy of Psychiatry and Law, 23,* 399–409.

Crotty, H. D. (1924). The history of insanity as a defence to crime in English criminal law. *California Law Review, 12,* 105–123.

Cutler, B., Moran, G., & Narby, D. (1992). Jury selection in insanity defense cases. *Journal of Research in Personality, 26,* 165–182.

Diamond, S. S. (1997). Illuminations and shadows from jury simulations. *Law and Human Behavior, 21,* 561–572.

Eigen, J. P. (1995). *Witnessing insanity: Madness and mad-doctors in the English Court.* New Haven, CT: Yale University Press.

Ellsworth, P., Bukaty, R., Cowan, C., & Thompson, W. (1984). The death-qualified jury and the defense of insanity. *Law & Human Behavior, 8,* 81–93.

Finkel, N. (1989). The Insanity Defense Reform Act of 1984: Much ado about nothing. *Behavioral Sciences and the Law, 7,* 403–419.

Finkel, N. (1991). The insanity defense: A comparison of verdict schemas. *Law & Human Behavior, 15,* 533–555.

Finkel, N. (1995). *Commonsense justice: Jurors' notions of the law.* Cambridge, MA: Harvard University Press.

Finkel, N., & Groscup, J. (1997). Crime prototypes, objective versus subjective culpability, and a commonsense balance. *Law & Human Behavior, 21,* 209–230.

Finkel, N., & Handel, S. (1988). Jurors and insanity: Do test instructions instruct? *Forensic Reports, 1,* 65–79.

Finkel, N., & Handel, S. (1989). How jurors construe "insanity." *Law & Human Behavior, 13,* 41–59.

Finkel, N., Shaw, R., Bercaw, S., & Kock, J. (1985). Insanity defenses: From the jurors' perspective. *Law and Psychology Review, 9,* 77–92.

Fiske, S. (1993). Social cognition and social perception. *Annual Review of Psychology, 44,* 155–194.

Flaum, M., Arndt, S., & Andreasen, N. (1991). The reliability of "bizarre" delusions. *Comprehensive Psychiatry, 32,* 59–65.

Foucha v. Louisiana, 504 U.S. 71 (1992).

Gabbard, G., Coyne, L., Kennedy, L., Beasley, C., Deering, C., Schroder, P., Larson, J., & Cerney, M. (1987). Interrater reliability in the use of the Brief Psychiatric Rating Scale. *Bulletin of the Menninger Clinic, 51,* 519–531.

Gacono, C. B., Meloy, J. R., Sheppard, K., & Speth, E. (1995). A clinical investigation of malingering and psychopathy in hospitalized insanity acquittees. *Bulletin of the American Academy of Psychiatry and Law, 23,* 387–397.

Garety, P., & Hemsley, M. (1994). *Delusions: Investigations into the psychology of delusional reasoning.* New York: Oxford University Press.

Golding, S. L. (1990). Mental health professionals and the courts: The ethics of expertise. *International Journal of Law and Psychiatry, 13,* 281–307.

Golding, S. L. (1991). Increasing the coherence of forensic mental health services: An introduction. *Journal of Mental Health Administration, 18,* 175–177.

Golding, S. L. (1992). The adjudication of criminal responsibility: A review of theory and research. In D. Kagehiro & W. Laufer (Eds.), *Handbook of psychology and law* (pp. 230–250). New York: Springer-Verlag.

Golding, S. L. (1993). *Interdisciplinary Fitness Interview–Revised: Training manual.* Unpublished manuscript.

Golding, S. L., Eaves, D., & Kowaz, A. (1989). The assessment, treatment and community outcome of insanity acquittees: Forensic history and response to treatment. *International Journal of Law and Psychiatry, 12,* 149–179.

Golding, S. L., & Roesch, R. (1987). The assessment of criminal responsibility: A historical approach to a current controversy. In I. Weiner & A. Hess (Eds.), *Handbook of forensic psychology* (pp. 395–436). New York: Wiley.

Gothard, S., Viglione, D. J., Meloy, J. R., & Sherman, M. (1995). Detection of malingering in competency to stand trial evaluations. *Law and Human Behavior, 19,* 493–506.

Gray, S. (1972). The insanity defense: Historical development and contemporary relevance. *American Criminal Law Review, 10,* 559–583.

Griffin, P. A., Steadman, H. J., & Heilbrun, K. (1991). Designing conditional release systems for insanity acquittees. *Journal of Mental Health Administration, 18,* 231–241.

Guy, W. A. (1869). On insanity and crime; and on the plea of insanity in criminal cases. *Journal of the Royal Statistical Society, 32*(Series A), 159–191.

Hafemeister, T. L., & Petrila, J. (1994). Treating the mentally disordered offender: Society's uncertain, conflicted, and changing views. *Florida State University Law Review, 21,* 731–871.

Häfner, H., & Böker, W. (1982). *Crimes of Violence by mentally abnormal offenders* (H. Marshall, Trans.). Cambridge, England: Cambridge University Press.

Hans, V. (1986). An analysis of public attitudes toward the insanity defense. *Criminology, 24,* 383–414.

Hans, V., & Slater, D. (1983). John Hinckley, Jr. and the insanity defense: The public's verdict. *Public Opinion Quarterly, 47,* 202–212.

Hans, V., & Slater, D. (1984). "Plain crazy": Lay definitions of legal insanity. *International Journal of Law & Psychiatry, 7,* 105–114.

Harrow, M., Rattenbury, F., & Stoll, F. (1988). Schizophrenic delusions: An analysis of their persistence, of related premorbid ideas, and of three major dimensions. In T. Oltmanns & B. Maher (Eds.), *Delusional beliefs* (pp. 184–211). New York: Wiley.

Heilbrun, K., & Griffin, P. A. (1993). Community-based forensic treatment of insanity acquittees. *Law and Human Behavior, 16,* 133–150.

Heilbrun, K., Lawson, K., Spier, S., & Libby, J. (1994). Community placement for insanity acquittees: A preliminary study of residential programs and person-situation fit. *Bulletin of the American Academy of Psychiatry and Law, 22,* 551–560.

Heilbrun, K., Rosenfeld, B., Warren, J., & Collins, S. (1994). The use of third party information in forensic assessments: A two-state comparison. *Bulletin of the American Academy of Psychiatry and Law, 22,* 399–406.

Hermann, D. (1990). Autonomy, self-determination, the right of involuntarily committed persons to refuse treatment, and the use of substituted judgment in medication decisions involving incompetent persons. *International Journal of Law and Psychiatry, 13,* 361–385.

Hermann, D. H. J. (1983). *The insanity defense: Philosophical, historical, and legal perspectives.* Springfield, IL: Thomas.

Hoge, S. K., & Grisso, T. (1992). Accuracy and expert testimony. *Bulletin of the American Academy of Psychiatry and Law, 20,* 67–76.

Homant, R., & Kennedy, D. (1987). Subjective factors in clinicians' judgments of insanity: Comparison of a hypothetical case and an actual case. *Professional Psychology: Research and Practice, 5,* 439–446.

Idaho Code Annotated, Section 19-25234 (1997).

Insanity Defense Reform Act of 1984. Pub.L. 98-473, 18 U.S.C. Sec. 401-406 (1984).

Janofsky, J. S., Vandewalle, M. B., & Rappeport, J. R. (1989). Defendants pleading insanity: An analysis of outcome. *Bulletin of the American Academy of Psychiatry & Law, 17,* 203–211.

Jaspers, K. (1963). *General psychopathology* (J. Hoenig & M. Hamilton, Trans.). Manchester, England: Manchester University Press.

Jeffrey, R., & Pasewark, R. (1983). Altering opinions about the insanity plea. *Journal of Psychiatry & Law, 11,* 29–40.

Johnson, C., & Haney, C. (1994). Felony voir dire: An exploratory study of its content and effect. *Law & Human Behavior, 18,* 487–506.

Jones v. United States, 103 S.Ct. 3043 (1983).

Kansas v. Hendricks No. 95-1649/95-9075. 65 U.S.L.W. 4564 (1997).

Keedy, E. R. (1917). Insanity and criminal responsibility. *Harvard Law Review, 30,* 535–560, 724–738.

Keedy, E. R. (1920). Criminal responsibility of the insane—A reply to Professor Ballantine. *Journal of American Institute of Criminal Law and Criminology, 10,* 14–34.

Kendler, K., Glazer, W., & Morgenstern, H. (1983). Dimensions of delusional experience. *American Journal of Psychiatry, 140,* 466–469.

Lawrence v. State, 454 S.E.2d 446 (Sup. Ct. Georgia, 1995).

Link, B. G., & Stueve, A. (1994). Psychotic symptoms and the violent/illegal behavior of mental patients compared to community controls. In J. Monahan & H. Steadman (Eds.), *Violence and mental disorder: Developments in risk assessment* (pp. 137–159). Chicago: University of Chicago Press.

Lu, F., Lukoff, D., & Turner, R. (1994). Religious or spiritual problems. In T. Widiger, A. Frances, H. Pincus, M. First, R. Ross, & W. Davis (Eds.), *DSM-IV sourcebook.* Washington, DC: American Psychiatric Association.

Lukoff, D., Liberman, R., & Nuechterlein, K. (1986). Symptom monitoring in the rehabilitation of schizophrenic patients. *Schizophrenia Bulletin, 12,* 578–602.

Luria, R., & Guziec, R. (1981). Comparative description of the SADS and PSE. *Schizophrenia Bulletin, 7,* 248–257.

MacCoun, R. (1989). Experimental research on jury decision-making. *Science, 244,* 1046–1049.

Manchanda, R., & Hirsch, S. (1986). Rating scales for clinical studies on schizophrenia. In P. Bradley & S. Hirsch (Eds.), *The psychopharmacology and treatment of schizophrenia* (pp. 234–262). New York: Oxford Medical.

Manchanda, R., Hirsch, S., & Barnes, T. (1989). A review of rating scales for measuring symptom changes in schizophrenia research. In C. Thompson (Ed.), *The instruments of psychiatric research* (pp. 59–86). New York: Wiley.

Matarazzo, J. D. (1990). Psychological assessment versus psychological testing: Validation from Binet to the school, clinic, and courtroom. *American Psychologist, 45,* 999–1017.

McGreevy, M., Steadman, H. J., Dvoskin, J. A., & Dollard, N. (1991). New York State's system of managing insanity acquittees in the community. *Hospital and Community Psychiatry, 42,* 512–517.

Melton, G. B., Petrila, J., Poythress, N. G., & Slobogin, C. (1997). *Psychological evaluations for the courts: A handbook for mental health professionals and lawyers* (2nd ed.). New York: Guilford Press.

Mojtabai, R., & Nicholson, R. (1995). Interrater reliability of ratings of delusions and bizarre delusions. *American Journal of Psychiatry, 152,* 1804–1806.

Montana Code Annotated, Section 46-14-312(a) (1997).

Moran, G., Cutler, B., & DeLisa, A. (1994). Attitudes toward tort reform, scientific jury selection, and juror bias: Verdict inclination in criminal and civil trials. *Law & Psychology Review, 18,* 309–328.

Morse, S. J. (1992). The "guilty mind": Mens rea. In D. Kagehiro & W. Laufer (Eds.), *Handbook of psychology and law* (pp. 207–229). New York: Springer-Verlag.

Mullen, P. (1979). Phenomenology of disordered mental functions. In P. Hill, R. Murray, & A. Thorley (Eds.), *Essentials of postgraduate psychiatry* (pp. 36–40). London: Academic Press.

Mullen, P. (1985). The mental state and states of mind. In P. Hill, R. Murray, & A. Thorley (Eds.), *Essentials of postgraduate psychiatry* (2nd ed., pp. 17–21). London: Grune & Stratton.

Mulvey, E. P. (1994). Assessing the evidence of a link between mental illness and violence. *Hospital and Community Psychiatry, 45,* 663–668.

Ogloff, J. (1991). A comparison of insanity defense standards on juror decision making. *Law & Human Behavior, 15,* 509–531.

Ogloff, J., Schweighofer, A., Turnbull, S., & Whittemore, K. (1992). Empirical research regarding the insanity defense: How much do we really know? In J. Ogloff (Ed.), *Law and psychology: The broadening of the discipline* (pp. 171–207). Durham: Carolina Academic Press.

Ogloff, J. R., Roberts, C. F., & Roesch, R. (1993). The insanity defense: Legal standards and clinical assessment. *Applied and Preventative Psychology, 2,* 163–178.

Oltmanns, T. (1988). Approaches to the definition and study of delusions. In T. Oltmanns & B. Maher (Eds.), *Delusional beliefs* (pp. 3–11). New York: Wiley.

Pasewark, R. (1986). A review of research on the insanity defense. In S. A. Shah (Ed.), *The law and mental health. Annals of the American Academy of Political and Social Science, 484,* 100–114.

Pasewark, R., & Seidenzahl, D. (1979). Opinions concerning the insanity plea and criminality among patients. *Bulletin of the American Academy of Psychiatry and Law, 7,* 199–202.

Pennington, N., & Hastie, R. (1986). Evidence evaluation in complex decision making. *Journal of Personality and Social Psychology, 51,* 242–258.

Perlin, M. (1994). *The jurisprudence of the insanity defense.* Durham: Carolina Academic Press.

Platt, A. M., & Diamond, B. L. (1965). The origins and development of the "wild beast" concept of mental illness and its relation to theories of criminal responsibility. *Journal of the History of the Behavioral Sciences, 1,* 355–367.

Platt, A. M., & Diamond, B. L. (1966). The origins of the "right and wrong" test of criminal responsibility and its subsequent development in the United States: An historical survey. *California Law Review, 54,* 1227–1259.

Psychiatric Security Review Board. (1994). A model for management and treatment of insanity acquittees. *Hospital and Community Psychiatry, 45,* 1127–1131.

Rice, M., & Harris, G. (1990). The predictors of insanity acquittal. *International Journal of Law and Psychiatry, 13,* 217–224.

Roberts, C., & Golding, S. (1991). The social construction of criminal responsibility and insanity. *Law & Human Behavior, 15,* 349–376.

Roberts, C., Golding, S., & Fincham, F. (1987). Implicit theories of criminal responsibility: Decision making and the insanity defense. *Law & Human Behavior, 11,* 207–232.

Roberts, C., Sargent, E., & Chan, A. (1993). Verdict selection processes in insanity cases: Juror construals and the effects of guilty but mentally ill instructions. *Law & Human Behavior, 17,* 261–275.

Robinson, P., & Darley, D. (1995). *Justice, liability and blame: Community views and the criminal law.* San Francisco: Westview Press.

Rogers, R. (1997). *The clinical assessment of malingering and deception* (2nd ed.). New York: Guilford Press.

Rogers, R., Cavanaugh, J. L., Seman, W., & Harris, M. (1984). Legal outcome and clinical findings: A study of insanity evaluations. *Bulletin of the American Academy of Psychiatry and the Law, 12,* 75–83.

Rogers, R., & Ewing, C. P. (1992). The measurement of insanity: Debating the merits of the R-CRAS and its alternatives. *International Journal of Law and Psychiatry, 15,* 113–123.

Rogers, R., Wasyliw, O. E., & Cavanaugh, J. L. (1984). Evaluating insanity: A study of construct validity. *Law and Human Behavior, 8,* 293–303.

Sacks, M., Carpenter, W., & Strauss, J. (1974). Recovery from delusions: Three phases documented by patient's interpretation of research procedures. *Archives of General Psychiatry, 30,* 117–120.

Saks, E. (1991). Competency to refuse treatment. *North Carolina Law Review, 69,* 945–999.

Sayre, F. (1932). Mens re. *Harvard Law Review, 45,* 974–1026.

Schachter, D. L. (1986a). Amnesia and crime: How much do we really know? *American Psychologist, 41,* 286–295.

Schachter, D. L. (1986b). On the relation of genuine and simulated amnesia. *Behavioral Sciences and the Law, 4,* 47–64.

Schachter, D. L. (1996). *Searching for memory: The brain, the mind, and the past.* New York: Basic Books.

Schneider, D. (1991). Social cognition. *Annual Review of Psychology, 42,* 527–561.

Sedler, M. (1995). Understanding delusions. *Psychiatric Clinics of North America, 18,* 251–262.

Shannon v. United States, 114 S. Ct. 2419 (1994).

Silver, E. (1995). Punishment or treatment? Comparing the lengths of confinement of successful and unsuccessful insanity defendants. *Law and Human Behavior, 19,* 375–388.

Silver, E., Circincione, C., & Steadman, H. J. (1994). Demythologizing inaccurate perceptions of the insanity defense. *Law and Human Behavior, 18,* 63–70.

Silver, S. B., & Tellefsen, C. (1991). Administrative issues in the follow-up treatment of insanity acquittees. *Journal of Mental Health Administration, 18,* 242–252.

Simon, R. (1967). *The jury and the defense of insanity.* Boston: Little, Brown.

Skeem, J. (1997). *Understanding juror decision making and bias in insanity defense cases: The role of naïve conceptions and case-relevant attitudes regarding criminal insanity.* Unpublished doctoral prospectus, University of Utah.

Skeem, J. L., Golding, S. L., Cohn, N. B., & Berge, G. (in press). The logic and reliability of evaluations of competence to stand trial. *Law and Human Behavior.*

Sklansky, J. (1996). Right to a jury trial [Special issue: 25th Annual Review of Criminal Procedure]. *Georgetown Law Journal, 84,* 1139–1160.

Smith, R. (1981). *Trial by medicine: Insanity and responsibility in Victorian trials.* Edinburgh: Edinburgh University Press.

Smith, V. (1991). Prototypes in the courtroom: Lay representations of legal concepts. *Journal of Personality and Social Psychology, 76,* 220–228.

Smith, V. (1993). When prior knowledge and law collide: Helping jurors use the law. *Law & Human Behavior, 17*(5), 507–536.

Spitzer, M. (1990). On defining delusions. *Comprehensive Psychiatry, 31,* 377–397.

Spitzer, R., First, M., Kendler, K., & Stein, D. (1993). The reliability of three definitions of bizarre delusions. *American Journal of Psychiatry, 150,* 880–884.

Stalans, L. (1993). Citizens' crime stereotypes, biased recall and punishment preferences in abstract cases: The educative role of interpersonal sources. *Law & Human Behavior, 17,* 451–470.

State v. Herrera & Sweezey, 895 P.2d 359 (Utah, 1995).

State v. Korell, 690 P.2d 992 (Montana, 1984).

Steadman, H. J., McGreevy, M. A., Morrissey, J., Callahan, L. A., Robins, P. C., & Cirincione, C. (1993). *Before and after Hinckley: Evaluating insanity defense reform.* New York: Guilford Press.

Steury, E., & Choinski, M. (1995). "Normal" crimes and mental disorder: A two-group comparison of deadly and dangerous felonies. *International Journal of Law and Psychiatry, 18,* 183–207.

Stroud, D. A. (1914). *Mens rea or imputability under the laws of England.* London: Sweet & Maxwell.

Taylor, P. (1985). Motives for offending among violent and psychotic men. *British Journal of Psychiatry, 147,* 491–498.

Taylor, P., Garety, P., Buchanan, A., Reed, A., Wessely, S., Ray, K., Dunn, G., & Grubin, D. (1994). Delusions and violence. In J. Monahan & H. Steadman (Eds.), *Violence and mental disorder: Developments in risk assessment* (pp. 161–182). Chicago: University of Chicago Press.

Taylor, P. J., & Kopelman, M. D. (1984). Amnesia for criminal offences. *Psychological Medicine, 14,* 581–588.

Tellefsen, C., Cohen, M. I., Silver, S. B., & Dougherty, C. (1992). Predicting success on conditional release of insanity acquittees: Regionalized versus nonregionalized hospital patients. *Bulletin of the American Academy of Psychiatry and Law, 20,* 87–100.

Utah Code Annotated, Section 76-2-305(1) (1997).

Wack, R. (1993). The ongoing risk assessment in the treatment of forensic patients on conditional release status. *Psychiatric Quarterly, 64,* 275–293.

Wainwright v. Witt, 105 S.Ct. 844 (1985).

Wales, H. W. (1976). An analysis of the proposal to "abolish" the insanity defense in S. 1: Squeezing a lemon. *University of Pennsylvania Law Review, 124,* 687–712.

Walker, C. (1991). Delusion: What did Jaspers really say? *British Journal of Psychiatry, 159,* 94–103.

Walker, N. (1978). *Crime and insanity in England: Vol. I. The historical perspective.* Edinburgh: University of Edinburgh Press.

Wessely, S., Buchanan, A., Reed, A., Cutting, J., Everitt, B., Garety, P., & Taylor, P. (1993). Acting on delusions: I. Prevalence. *British Journal of Psychiatry, 163,* 69–76.

Whittemore, K., & Ogloff, J. (1995). Factors that influence jury decision making: Disposition instructions and mental state at the time of the trial. *Law & Human Behavior, 19,* 283–303.

Wiederanders, M. R. (1992). Recidivism of disordered offenders who were conditionally vs. unconditionally released. *Behavioral Sciences and the Law, 10,* 141–148.

Wiederanders, M. R., & Choate, P. A. (1994). Beyond recidivism: Measuring community adjustments of conditionally released insanity acquittees. *Psychological Assessment, 6,* 61–66.

Wilson, D., Tien, G., & Eaves, D. (1995). Increasing the community tenure of mentally disordered offenders: An assertive case management program. *International Journal of Law and Psychiatry, 18,* 61–69.

Wing, J. (1996). Scars and the PSE tradition. *Social Psychiatry and Psychiatric Epidemiology, 31,* 50–54.

Wing, J. K., Cooper, J. E., & Sartorius, N. (1974). *The description and classification of psychiatric symptoms: An instruction manual for the PSE and CATEGO system.* Cambridge, England: Cambridge University Press.

Winters, K. C., & Neale, J. M. (1983). Delusions and delusional thinking in psychotics: A review of the literature. *Clinical Psychology Review, 3,* 227–253.

World Health Organization. (1979). *Schizophrenia: An international follow-up study.* New York: Wiley.

CHAPTER 15

Forensic Psychology and Law Enforcement

JOHN T. SUPER

POLICING IN America and abroad has a history marked by periods of progress and stagnation. A review of modern law enforcement's development is beyond the scope of this chapter; a more thorough yet punctuated account of the history of policing is presented in *A History of Police Psychological Services* (Reese, 1987). Psychology's role in policing has a shorter yet similar history.

Psychology's presence has been seen and felt in several emergency service fields, including fire control, emergency medical, corrections, and law enforcement. Psychology's initial inroad into emergency services was in the arena of law enforcement. During the first quarter of the 20th century, Terman and Otis (1917) used psychological instruments (intelligence testing) in an attempt to identify capable police officer applicants. Gradually, psychological services have met with increasing acceptance by law enforcement personnel. This is in part reactionary and in part visionary. It is reactionary because some agency chiefs may use psychological services primarily to increase indemnity for themselves and their agency; it is visionary because some administrators perceive the usefulness of psychological services to assist the agency in pursuit of its mission statement. Psychological service provision is becoming more common at federal, state, and local levels. Moreover, preemployment psychological evaluation services are routinely provided for private sector security positions, including armed security officers and some nuclear power plant employees. Although several branches of emergency services utilize psychological services on a select basis, the address of this chapter will be limited to psychology's role in providing services to law enforcement agencies. For expedience, the provision of psychological services to law enforcement agencies will henceforth be referred to as police psychology. This chapter summarizes some of the current concepts and psychological services provided to law enforcement agencies, which moves beyond that contained in the aforenoted sources.

CONSULTANT PSYCHOLOGISTS
VS. STAFF PSYCHOLOGISTS

Historically, there have been two primary modes of service delivery for psychologists seeking to apply their trade in a law enforcement setting. This includes the consultant psychologist and the staff or in-house psychologist. The difference between the two is reflected less in the types of services they provide for an agency than in the relationship between the agency and the police psychologist. Consultant psychologists contract with a department to provide services; they generally do not receive benefits associated with being employees. The consultant psychologist has been and continues to be the principal point at which behavioral sciences and law enforcement merge. In a nationwide survey of police psychologists (Bartol, 1996), 26% of survey participants ($N = 152$) were employed as in-house or staff psychologists. Nearly three-quarters of his sample were employed as full- or part-time consultant psychologists. A staff psychologist is an employee of the agency and may be a sworn law enforcement officer; the position tends to be more viable for larger departments due to larger budgets and larger numbers of service recipients.

Advantages and disadvantages are associated with both the psychologist consultant and staff psychologist positions. Psychological consultants usually are in an existing practice with office space, insurance, and other requirements of an independent practice; they are usually housed external to the agency. Some of the benefits of a consulting psychologist include (a) greater opportunity for confidentiality, (b) greater perceived confidentiality by employees, and (c) increased autonomy to pursue outside activity. The benefits of a staff psychologist include (a) greater availability to prospective clientele, (b) increased access to potential research data, (c) greater opportunity to provide services at agency and organizational levels, and (d) greater opportunity to receive feedback regarding service provision. These benefits are not intended to be exhaustive; rather, they are major differences to be considered when determining the type of employment relationship a psychologist would like to have with an agency.

With the increasing use of in-house police psychologists, there is a concomitant increasing need for a type of policy and procedure manual usually referred to as General Orders (GOs). GOs are broadly defined rules of conduct and procedures that guide how law enforcement personnel operate. Although services provided by psychologists to law enforcement agencies continue to evolve, GOs may guide psychologists when requests for service provision are made that are beyond the scope of their experience. At the time of this writing, many departments that utilize behavioral sciences services do not have specifically designated roles or delegated job duties for psychologists. In a survey regarding GOs (Super & Blau, 1997), 76% of 25 targeted law enforcement departments responded after one follow-up contact. The departments were randomly selected from agencies represented by psychologists who attended the 1995 Federal Bureau of Investigation's Organizational Issues in Law Enforcement Conference. Of 19 responding agencies, 6 reported having Standard Operating Procedures (SOPs) or GOs specifically for a Behavioral Science Unit or a Psychological Services Section. SOPs, though allowing some flexibility, tend to be more specific and therefore more restrictive then GOs. SOPs are not routinely distributed agencywide; they tend to focus on conduct and procedures employed by psychologists. GOs are distributed agencywide, and most agencies require all employees to read them. Behavioral science GOs should broadly define services and limits thereof to employees; they should be constructed to maintain parity of purpose and style with other agency GOs. Psychological services for law enforcement has reached a stage of development that makes construction of GOs viable and helpful. A model set of GOs is presented in Appendix A.

There have been several books devoted to police psychology (Blau, 1994; Chandler, 1990; Reiser, 1972). The references from this point forward will primarily utilize data published between the late 1980s and the time this chapter was written. For the interested reader, a list of resources most likely to contain articles germane to the field of police psychology is presented in Appendix B.

Services offered by police psychologists to law enforcement agencies are generally categorized into one of two broad categories: organizational services and employee assistance services.

ORGANIZATIONAL SERVICES

The types of psychological services offered to law enforcement agencies are varied and evolving. In this section, attention to topic areas will be proportionate to the time invested threat by police psychologists.

Organizational functions can be more easily conceptualized if viewed as a type of service with several branches. One branch involves management consultation and interagency consultation. Preemployment psychological assessment services, fitness-for-duty evaluations, special unit evaluations, hostage negotiation team consultations, deadly force incident evaluations, and field consultation make up a second branch of organizational services. A third branch includes investigative-type activities such as serial crime profiling, psychological autopsies, investigative hypnosis, and cognitive interviewing. A fourth branch of organizational services is training, which may include stress-reduction seminars, peer counselor training, and academy instruction.

Bergen, Aceto, and Chadziewicz (1992) reviewed job satisfaction and employment activities of six police psychologists or groups of police psychologists. Although a small sample size was used, this study was remarkable as it was the first to categorize time spent in various activities by police psychologists. Five of the six respondents reported psychological testing represented a portion of their job duties; four of the six reported engaging officer counseling, training, organizational development, personality and criminal profiling, and family counseling as a part of their employment activities. The study's participants do not appear to be representative of police psychologists, in that most police psychologists engage no personality or criminal profiling. Investigative job duties represent, at most, a small percentage of what the average police psychologist does. Bergen et al. indicated that approximately 37% of the psychologist's time was utilized in counseling, 32% in selection and screening activities, 11% in training, 10% in organizational development, and 9% in other types of activities, which include personality and criminal profiling. Bartol (1996) surveyed a mix of full-time in-house, full-time consultant, and part-time consultant police psychologists regarding average monthly percentage of time spent in various activities. Nearly 35% of the respondents' time, during the course of a month, was engaged in preemployment screening activities while about 27% of the time was used to provide counseling or treatment for agency personnel or their family members. Only 8.5% of the time was used for research and development or consultation with management. Even less time (5.4%) was devoted to investigative types of activities, such as profiling of offenders, forensic hypnosis, and handwriting analysis.

CONSULTATION TO MANAGEMENT

Management consultation tends to be the cornerstone of organizational services. Management consultations are most likely to result in administrative decisions with agencywide implications. For example, in 1990, this author participated in a project with an agency's chief deputy to explore the benefits and detriments of 12-hour work shifts. This consultation was initiated by a chief deputy making a request for a research project. A literature review was completed which yielded factory workers' reactions to 12-hour shifts and the number of industrial accidents noted between groups of workers in various shifts. This research lead to the agency being the first in the area to convert to 12-hour work shifts. Initially, there was considerable skepticism and concern voiced by deputies that fatigue near the end of the shift may increase their probability of injury. The deputies, however, acclimated well to the new shift and reported having greater opportunity to pursue personal and leisure activities. Further, the fears of increased motor vehicle accidents, injuries, and stress-related disorders were not realized. From this data, a decision was made that affected every employee. Clearly, this demonstrates the impact a psychologist may have on law enforcement agencies through management consultation.

Consultation to management is an excellent means whereby intervention or prevention can be made on an agencywide basis. This is perhaps no better exemplified than in the area of strategic planning. Strategic planning involves setting realistic goals and objectives, developing a plan of action to attain them, implementing the plan of action, evaluating the goals and the plan, and modifying the goals and/or plan of action, if needed. The purpose of strategic planning is to improve an agency's relative standing in an area or industry regarding a targeted variable. Examples of target variables include decreasing employee attrition, increasing employee morale, increasing the efficiency of dispatchers, or modifying management policy to better reflect society's evolving needs and standards. The use and utility of strategic planning has been well documented in industrial, organizational, and management fields. Although introduced a dozen years ago, the professional psychologist's contributions to strategic planning has not been fully embraced by many law enforcement departments. Recent efforts to explain the purpose of strategic planning and how psychologists may contribute to the welfare of the agency through participation in the strategic planning process have been made by Wells and Blau (1994).

Hostage Negotiation Consultation

The use of trained hostage negotiators has increased since the 1970s (Blau, 1994). Historically, the primary role of negotiator has been and continues to be to stall the hostage-taker or barricaded subject from acting impulsively. Psychological techniques can be used by negotiators to defuse explosive situations. The negotiator can employ psychological principles such as reinforcement and demonstration of empathy and understanding when attempting to develop a positive relationship with the perpetrator. Many hostage-takers or barracaders develop an oppositional or adversarial relationship with law enforcement personnel for which psychological expertise may be useful.

Barracaders are individuals who "hole up" in a home or location and may threaten suicide; hostage-takers are generally involved in a criminal act with at least one other person who is initially involved against his or her consent. Frequently, the motivation of the barracader is attention, suicide, or both; the motivation of a hostage-taker may be to secure some kind of transportation, finances, or other demands. The approaches hostage negotiators take with barracaders and hostage-takers may appear different, but both essentially involve delaying acts of aggression and minimizing violence or impulsivity. Time is essentially the ally of the law enforcement agency, as the agency tends to have greater access to resources.

Traditionally, the hostage negotiation team has little to do with command decisions, which are usually controlled by ranking personnel who have direct access to a tactical response team and the hostage negotiation team. H. Russell and Beigel (1989) have identified types of hostage situations, and Noesner and Dolan (1992) have identified guidelines for training officers who may be first responders to the scene and may act as initial negotiators. McMains (1988) has identified several roles that a psychologist may take in negotiations: professional, consultant, and participant observer. The role of participant observer is what most lay individuals consider the primary role of a psychologist in hostage negotiations. The participant observer responds to the scene along with other members of the team, which may include a primary and secondary negotiator, several communication specialists, and one or more supervisors. The negotiators establish dialogue with the subject. The communications specialists gather intelligence and make necessary contacts to implement tactical decisions (i.e., having the power turned off in a building). The supervisors provide consent for tactical decisions and may have indirect involvement in the negotiation through the secondary negotiator. The participant observer psychologist generally has indirect access to the negotiation through the secondary negotiator. Contact is generally in writing and may include suggested areas of inquiry or positive reinforcement for the negotiators if they are making progress. Psychologists may participate in a negotiation by assessing and identifying various needs of the perpetrator or developing approaches by which the negotiator may establish or build upon a relationship with the hostage-taker or barracader. Psychologists may serve the negotiators in any way that may be of assistance to them: from providing coffee and getting a coat, to scripting different approaches the negotiator may use. Generally, the psychologist is not and arguably should not be the primary negotiator. In fact, the psychologist may not be the best negotiator when compared with well-trained veteran law enforcement personnel (Borum, 1988).

The Stockholm Syndrome or Hostage Identification Syndrome (U.S. Department of State, 1988) refers to hostages identifying with the hostage-takers and forming a psychological bond with them. Spending a considerable amount of time with the hostage-taker in less than adequate environmental surroundings (no heat, no lights) may result in the hostage feeling sorry for the hostage-taker and viewing him or her as an underdog or martyr. Although this phenomenon was first identified in Sweden, it has been noted with some regularity elsewhere. From one perspective, the syndrome can be viewed as promoting the survival of the hostage by establishing a relationship with the aggressor. If taken to extremes, however, it could thwart law enforcement efforts and endanger the safety of the hostage. The first negotiation to which this author provided consultation occurred when an individual entered a restaurant and took several employees hostage, maintaining them overnight. At one point early the next morning, after approximately eight hours of being with the hostage-taker, one of the employees had moved out of sight of the hostage-taker, but rather than run to the beckoning police officers, who were standing nearby, the hostage hurried back to the hostage-taker. The Stockholm Syndrome may result in long-term effects that may require psychological follow-up services—not only for the hostages, but also for bewildered law enforcement personnel.

PREEMPLOYMENT PSYCHOLOGICAL EVALUATIONS

Preemployment evaluations are the most frequently requested psychological service provided to law enforcement agencies. At a minimum, most preemployment psychological evaluations involve objective personality measures and a clinical interview; many clinicians also routinely include a cognitive measure in preemployment testing batteries. Guidelines for preemployment psychological evaluations have been produced and are in the process of being refined by psychologists working in association with the International Association of Chiefs of Police; proposed modifications were not available at the time of this writing. The original guidelines have been reprinted elsewhere (Blau, 1994). Sample reports, interview formats, and commonly used instruments for preemployment psychological evaluations of law enforcement personnel have been presented for review by Blau.

Due to the volume of preemployment psychological evaluations conducted by psychologists and because results bear directly on an applicants' employment status, this service has the potential to be challenged in courts and regulated by law more than other services provided by police psychologists. Important legal considerations include the Americans with Disabilities Act of 1990 (ADA, 1991), translated to more functional language by the Equal Employment Opportunity Commission (EEOC, 1991). This act modified the temporal sequencing of preemployment psychological evaluations: under the

ADA, during the preemployment stage of the selection process, employers cannot inquire whether an individual has a disability. ADA language indicates that even unintentional screening out of individuals or a class of individuals with disabilities cannot be done by an employer unless the employer demonstrates that the criteria, as illustrated in the job description, relate to the position for which the individual with the disability is applying and is consistent with business necessity. These strictures are perceived by some authors as resulting in greater stress and liability for psychologists performing preemployment psychological evaluations for law enforcement officers; however, although the law has been in place since 1991, empirical evidence regarding a psychologist's liability is still undetermined. The purpose of the ADA is to prevent persons with disabilities from being excluded for employment unless their disability renders them unable to perform specified job duties in a satisfactory manner. Further, agencies are required to make reasonable accommodations for persons with disabilities, though a precise definition of reasonable accommodation continues to be grist for legal arenas and is likely to vary depending on the size of the agency and its resources.

Using personality tests that may be overly personally intrusive was raised in the case of *Soroka v. Dayton Hudson Corporation* (1992). Target Department Stores had used a combination of the original Minnesota Multiphasic Personality Inventory (MMPI) (Hathaway & McKinley, 1983) and the California Psychological Inventory (CPI) (Gough, 1986) to screen prospective applicants for store security positions. The court enjoined the Dayton Hudson Corporation in a civil case for invasion of privacy issues regarding questions contained in the hybrid screening instrument. This decision appears to be tangentially related to preemployment psychological evaluations for criminal justice system employees. The court, however, acknowledged differences between security officers for private entities and applicants for public safety positions such as police officers and correctional officers. Although *Soroka* does not appear to vacate the ruling of *McKenna v. Fargo* (1978), where courts upheld the use of psychological testing for firefighter applicants to determine their ability to withstand psychological pressures inherent to the job, *Soroka* sets the stage for increased challenges. Based in part on this information, many psychologists applauded the release of the MMPI-2 (Hathaway & McKinley, 1989), which sanitized the test of many objectionable items. The reader is referred to Super (1997b) for a select review of relevant case law and ethical considerations as applicable to preemployment psychological evaluations.

Select ethical issues specific to preemployment evaluations merit examination. The first involves General Standard 1.21 of The APA Ethical Principles of Psychologists and Code of Conduct, which addresses a psychologist's role in provision of services: "When a psychologist agrees to provide services to a person or entity at the request of a third party, the psychologist clarifies to the extent feasible, at the outset of the service, the nature of the relationship with each party. This clarification includes the role of psychologist (such as therapist, organizational consultant, diagnostician, or expert witness), the probable uses of the services provided or the information obtained, and the fact that there may be limits to confidentiality" (APA, 1992, p. 1602). When conducting preemployment psychological evaluations, it should be made clear to the applicant that the agency is the primary client. The APA lends support to this position under General Standard 2.09 (APA, 1992, p. 1604), which indicates that the psychologist is to inform the parties in advance of who is the client and the manner in which testing data may be used. General Standard 2.09 also addresses when an explanation of results shall be made; for some types of evaluations (e.g., preemployment or security screenings and forensic evaluations), results may not be interpreted to the individual undergoing examination. This, however, is not recommended as rationale for a carte blanche denial of feedback for preemployment psychological evaluations; rather, a systematic approach should be utilized to provide applicants feedback when requested. It is highly recommended that information included in the report should be relevant and tied to the purpose for which the report is being prepared. This is likely to decrease the probability of objectionable content being included, which can be grounds for a legal challenge.

Psychological testing instruments have been developed specifically for preemployment psychological evaluations. The Inwald Personality Inventory (IPI) (Inwald, 1980, 1982) and several other tests are commonly used in the field of law enforcement for preemployment psychological evaluations. In 1991, Shusman and Inwald administered the MMPI and the IPI to a group of 246 male correctional officers. They followed the correctional officers' careers for approximately three and a half years. The authors determined that the greatest percentage of officers who were correctly classified regarding number of absences, latenesses, and disciplinary interviews were derived from discriminant function analysis using both the IPI and the MMPI in combination.

Inwald and Brockwell (1991) used the IPI and the MMPI to predict global job performance of 307 government security hirees after 9 to 12 months on the job. Again, the greatest prediction accuracy was derived when using discriminant function equations of both tests in combination. When global performance categories in this study were reduced to two groups, successful versus unsuccessful, the IPI and MMPI had a true classification rate of 77.2%. Scogin, Schumacher, Gardner, and Chaplin (1995) studied the relationship between IPI and MMPI scores and job performance in 69 officers. Criterion variables included verbal reprimands, written reprimands, vehicular reprimands, citizen complaints, any negative indicators, and positive recognitions. Discriminant function equations provided incremental validity to the hiring process to predict negative criterion variables.

A singular match between personality type and police officer performance has not been found and probably does not exist. Lorr and Strack (1994) used archival data of two groups of 275 police candidates and found no fewer than three distinct personality profiles in both samples. Even from a generalist's prospective, however, Hogan, Hogan, and Roberts (1996) indicated well-structured measures of normal personality tend to be valid predictions for most occupations.

Many studies demonstrate that psychological testing of personality and behavioral factors provides utility in the hiring process. Some studies, however, using personality assessment to predict job performance measures do not reveal promising results. Mullins and McMains (1995) attempted to predict academy standing for a group of 64 recruits. The authors concluded that the MMPI was unsuccessful in predicting criterion variables. This, however, is not unusual. A more appropriate predictor variable for this study would have been a measure of cognitive ability.

Sarchione, Cuttler, and Nelson-Gray (1995) attempted to use the CPI to predict groups of officers who received disciplinary action. The officers scored significantly lower than the standardization sample on the responsibility, self-control, socialization, tolerance, sense of well-being, and flexibility scales; and higher on the police performance effectiveness index, and the social maturity index.

Although paper-and-pencil objective personality tests such as the Minnesota Multiphasic Personality Inventory-2 (MMPI-2), the Inwald Personality Inventory, (IPI), the California Psychological Inventory (CPI), and the Sixteen Personality Factor Questionnaire (16 PF) (Catell, Eber, & Tatsuoka, 1970) have been used with regularity to assess prospective law enforcement officers, other tests have gained research attention. The national Police Officers Selection Test (POST) was used in a series of seven validity studies (Rafilson & Sison, 1996). The POST is an entry-level examination of arithmetic, reading, grammar, and incident report writing skills developed using critical incident techniques (Flanagan, 1964).

Officers' response style when taking preemployment psychological tests has also received more research attention. This has gone beyond the use of traditional validity scales or indices used to assess dissimulation. There has been at least one study that has attempted to identify response distortion and to enumerate steps whereby distortion may be identified and corrected (Christiansen, Goffin, Johnston, & Rothstein, 1994). Perhaps the most specific recent attempt to study dissimulation on preemployment testing was by Borum and Stock (1993). Using the MMPI and the IPI, they looked at differences between those applicants who were identified as being deceptive and those for whom no deception was indicated. The Ego Strength Scale Minus K Correction Scale (ES – K) index from the MMPI demonstrated a highly significant difference between the two groups.

Methods other than paper-and-pencil tests have also been getting increased attention. The Behavioral-Personnel Assessment Device (B-PAD) (Rand, 1987; Young, 1992) requires applicants to review a number of policing scenarios and answering questions based on what they have viewed. Alternative forms of selecting law enforcement officers include assessment centers (Bromley, 1995; Coulton & Feild, 1995) and situational interviews (Gabris & Rock, 1991). A method that may hold promise and can be used during FTO or possibly during academy training focuses on peer assessment (Schumacher, Scogin, Howland, & McGee, 1992).

Research involving assessment of minority individuals has also received increased attention. Hiatt and Hargrave's (1994) research revealed, at most, trivial differences in selection rates or ratings of job performance between gay and lesbian and heterosexual law enforcement applicants. Ethnic differences have also been studied using the MMPI-2 (Timbrook & Graham, 1994).

Cognitive testing continues to be an important component in many law enforcement agencies' preselection process. In science, there occurs a phenomenon similar to an intangible pendulum that swings on a continuum between opposing methods of practice, schools of thought, and the like. In the late 1980s and the early 1990s, the pendulum appears to have swung toward political justification and away from scientific justification regarding preemployment psychological evaluations for law enforcement officer applicants. Although political and scientific needs are both important in the area of preemployment evaluation and selection of applicants, much more concern and emphasis was placed on decreasing adverse impact than was placed on increasing the incremental validity and utility of psychological measures used to assess applicants. This position was influenced in part by the ADA and the Civil Rights Act of 1991. A well-reasoned challenge to the position has been made by Gottfredson (1996). She reviewed a preemployment testing battery used for a large county law enforcement agency which was nearly sanitized of cognitive measures in an attempt to reduce disparate impact. Other researchers have also vocally criticized reducing the validity of a measure as a means for decreasing disparate impact (C. Russell, 1996; Schmidt, 1996). There are some researchers who strive for the best of both worlds, the political and scientific. It appears that the best way to increase validity and decrease disparate impact is to use measures of cognitive ability in conjunction with research-validated personality measures to assess applicants (Hunter & Schmidt, 1996).

For individuals who have not had experience in the field of preemployment psychological evaluations, Table 15.1 represents a logical progression of the process. Because of recent legal challenges to psychologists conducting preemployment evaluations (*Soroka v. Dayton Hudson Corporation*, 1992) and with

Table 15.1
Steps in Preemployment Psychological Evaluation

---

1. Obtain a copy of the preemployment psychological evaluation guidelines. Be aware of the new preemployment psychological evaluation guidelines under revision.

2. Prior to testing, make sure the applicant provides informed consent (Janik, 1994). Depending on the nature of the tests, they may have to be administered after a conditional offer of employment has been made (ADA, 1991).

3. Administer test.

4. Score test.

5. Gather relevant available data.

6. Review data.

7. Interview applicant.

8. Identify convergent data patterns among history obtained through available record review, information provided by applicant through interview, and psychological testing data.

9. Provide recommendation in the form of a suitability rating.

10. Be prepared for an appeal.

---

more agencies pursuing accreditation, having an appeal process in place is a prudent tactical practice. A sample appeal process is presented in Table 15.2. According to the Commission on Accreditation for Law Enforcement Agencies, Inc. (CALEA), applicants who are not selected for employment should have an appeal process they may invoke. A checklist can be affixed to the file folder of the applicant which will detail whether an appeal process was initiated and at which step it was vacated if not taken through to fruition. A sample checklist is presented in Appendix C. This systematic approach involves an initial inquiry, initial letter, follow-up inquiry, postselection interview, and appeal process, which includes a second and possibly third evaluation.

There are several important intangible points when attempting to provide psychological services to law enforcement agencies. One police psychologist, who at last count was providing services for approximately 142 law enforcement agencies, believes developing a liaison with a contact person in the department is important. For consulting psychologists, it is important to form a liaison with an individual with as high a ranking as possible. Down the line, such a relationship will probably help avoid pitfalls in terms of access to records and receipt of remuneration for services rendered. For the staff psychologist, it is important to form a liaison with the director of human resources. The Behavioral Science Unit will frequently work in concert with this director when conducting preemployment psychological evaluations. This is likely to decrease the probability of pitfalls. Many police psychologists conduct preemployment psychological evaluations over a two-day period. The applicant is tested on the first day; the tests

Table 15.2
Preemployment Psychological Evaluation Appeal Process

If an applicant is in disagreement with the final rating regarding psychological suitability for employment, he or she may engage in an appeal process much like the following:

1. At the applicant's expense, he or she can choose an independent evaluator, a psychologist or psychiatrist experienced in preemployment evaluations of criminal justice system employees, for reevaluation to determine fitness for employment as a law enforcement or correctional officer. The cost of the evaluation shall be paid by the contesting applicant.

2. To maximize the second evaluation's objectivity, the original test data or reports shall not be forwarded to the independent evaluator.

3. Independent evaluation results shall be marked "confidential" and forwarded directly to the initial evaluator.

4. If new information generated by the independent evaluation contraindicates the initial psychological preemployment assessment, the applicant may petition for a third evaluation by an agency-appointed psychologist. The initial evaluator, the director of personnel, and the bureau chief will determine whether to allow or deny a third psychological evaluation.

5. If a third evaluation is conducted by an agency-designated psychologist or psychiatrist and is in agreement with that of the independent evaluator's, the agency will continue the application process for the applicant based on the newly generated information.

6. If the applicant is not accepted for employment at the agency after a third evaluation, the decision is final and the applicant may reapply in one year.

are scored and an applicant interview is conducted on the second day. One of the common problems many in-house psychologists experience is the personnel office neglecting to inform applicants of the two-day process for the psychological evaluations. This results in scheduling difficulties and time delays, which may seem catastrophic when viewed by an overworked hiring board and understaffed agency. These types of difficulties are most likely to be overcome with a good working relationship with the director of human resources.

Estimates vary on the cost of training law enforcement personnel. Ash, Siora, and Britton (1990) indicated that it costs between $10,000 and $20,000 to train each officer. A cost analysis by this author (Super, 1996) indicated that a midsize department with an in-house academy spends approximately $15,000 for training and processing from the time an applicant contacts the agency's human resource department until he or she initiates field training. Hence, the use of preemployment psychological evaluations makes good fiscal sense if evaluators can screen out unsuitable applicants and select suitable ones.

FITNESS-FOR-DUTY EVALUATIONS

Fitness-for-duty evaluations (FFDEs) are generally more involved than preemployment psychological evaluations. The typical FFDE consists of informed consent, clinical interview, collateral interviews, psychological testing, and indepth record review. FFDEs are requested much less frequently than preemployment psychological evaluations.

It is incumbent upon the police psychologist not to engage FFDEs for inappropriate reasons. FFDE guidelines have been established by psychologists working in concert with the International Association of Chiefs of Police. At this time, however, like preemployment psychological evaluation guidelines, they are under revision. As a general rule, it is recommended that requests or authorization for FFDEs be made to the psychologist from the agency's chief ranking officer or a designee. This serves several purposes: decreasing the probability of inappropriate or frivolous referrals for FFDEs, increasing availability to personnel records, and increasing access to department employees for collateral interviews. If the agency's chief ranking officer requests and appoints the police psychologist to conduct a fitness for duty evaluation, obstacles such as chain of command become less of an issue when conducting collateral interviews. When the agency's chief officer or designee requests a FFDE, the police psychologist has the opportunity to work in various agency bureaus and has access to interviews with several levels of management without violating organizational structure.

The best method for determining an officer's fitness for duty is use of multiple sources and convergent data patterns (Ostrov, Nowicki, & Beazley, 1987). There is no particular psychological testing pattern indicative of nonfitness for duty. This is not surprising, given that officers may be psychologically unfit for duty for a number of reasons.

Conducting FFDEs tends to require more time than preemployment psychological evaluations. It is recommended that the reports be concise and address the specific questions raised. Information contained in the FFDE report should include reason for referral, relevant background information, behavior observations, mental status examination, test results, summary, and conclusions. Just as forensic assessment should avoid diagnosis in the areas of competency and mental state at the time of offense, this author is of the opinion that perfunctory diagnostic impression not be included. Excluding such diagnosis is likely to mitigate against inappropriate use of testing results, also, it is less likely to stigmatize officers as "unfit" who later are determined fit to return to duty. Several authors have addressed logistical and methodological aspects of FFDEs (Ostrov et al., 1987; Saxe-Clifford, 1986; Stone, 1990). For review of relevant law and ethical considerations as they apply to FFDEs, the reader is referred to Super (1997b).

An important aspect of mandatory psychological evaluations is informed consent. Clearly, if an officer is compelled to undergo a psychological evaluation, it is imperative that he or she understand the limits of confidentiality and the purpose of the evaluation. It is recommended that informed consent be in written form and include the signature of a witness after the officer has been given the opportunity to make inquiry regarding the contents of the informed consent form. This act is likely to provide increased protection for the psychologist should the FFDE results be discordant to the opinion of the evaluatee. Finally, an appeal process similar to that for preemployment psychological evaluations is likely to reduce the probability of being enjoined in a law suit or being investigated by the state regulating department. Serafino (1990) addressed the importance of using simple and understandable language on informed consent forms. It was recommended that "statement of understanding" be used as a title for consent forms to decrease the appearance of the adversarial-type nature of the evaluation. A practice that this author uses, consistent with that of Serafino, involves release of records. Release of the FFDE to an outside agency should be done only with a signed release from both the officer undergoing the evaluation and a representative designated by the chief of the agency to release the agency's confidential or legal documents.

SPECIAL UNIT EVALUATIONS

Psychological assessment can be used by promotional boards to aid in decision-making and for appointment to special units. Special units within law enforcement includes Special Weapons and Tactics (SWAT), Tactical Responses Teams (TRT), and Hostage Negotiation Teams (HNT). Super (1995) completed a validity study to identify tests that may be used to predict successful SWAT/TRT personnel performance. Thirty-four active part-time SWAT personnel with a minimum of one year of SWAT experience from two medium-size law enforcement agencies served as subjects. Each participant was given a battery of psychological tests (excluding traditional tests of psychopathology, as each participant had been exposed to these tests prior to appointment as an emergency service employee and did not evidence psychopathological profiles). Tests included the Wonderlic Personnel Test, the CPI, and the Fundamental

Interpersonal Relations Organizational-Behavior (FIRO-B). SWAT team personnel tended to be of average intellect. They are likely to be described as task-focused, productive, ambitious, and responsible. In the second part of this study, senior SWAT team members and commanders selected the 10 best SWAT officers and the 10 least best SWAT officers of the 34 participants. Several CPI scales yielded significantly different mean scores, after correction for experiment-wise error, between those officers rated best and those officers rated least best. The best SWAT personnel were described as more self-disciplined, conscientious, adherent to rules, comfortable accepting rules, conforming, and helpful.

Preappointment personality assessment has been studied for hostage negotiators, and use of psychological testing for selection of hostage negotiators has received increased attention over the course of the past two decades (Getty & Elam, 1988). Allen, Fraser, and Inwald (1991) used psychological testing to identify personality characteristics correlated with successful performance of police hostage negotiators.

There is a serious need for rigorous research regarding psychological assessment and special unit appointments. It is recommended that such research follow the evaluative procedures as described by Dwyer, Prien, and Bernard (1990), which include predictive validity research and cross-validation follow-up.

RESEARCH

Validational studies for preemployment and fitness-for-duty evaluations continue to be an area of research interest for police psychologists. The importance of psychological testing validity cannot be overemphasized for such evaluations. There are several types of validity. Particularly important for preemployment psychological evaluations is predictive validity, a type of criterion-related validity generally using some measure to predict another measure taken at a later time. It is incumbent upon researchers and practitioners to validate tests and procedures they use to demonstrate their ability to select the most appropriate applicants or to screen out those applicants who are likely to be problematic. A recent validation study conducted by Super (1997c) attempted to predict Officer Certification Examination (OCE) results with a cognitive measure (Wonderlic, 1983). Pass-fail standing on the OCE, a comprehensive examination covering academy material, was used as the criterion variable. Because the OCE involves centralized testing, it is likely to increase parity of applicants graduating from local academies regarding their understanding of academy curriculum, as they are required to demonstrate proficiency of course content under standardized testing conditions. Super (1997c) found 89% of the subjects in the initial sample were correctly classified ($N = 55$) using a discriminant function equation with the Wonderlic Personnel Test, 96% of the cross-validation sample ($N = 29$) were correctly classified.

A common assumption among individuals performing preemployment psychological evaluations for law enforcement personnel is that individuals with higher levels of intellect are more likely to have difficulties on the job, possibly stemming from boredom. This author has not reviewed data that support this position. To the contrary, at least one study found that individuals who scored higher on tests of intellect tend to require less time to respond to calls and possess greater map-reading efficiency (Kovach, Surrette, & Aamodt, 1988).

Mixed findings have resulted when personality measurement instruments have been used in an attempt either to identify those individuals who may exhibit poor performance or to identify those individuals possessing characteristics likely to result in good performance. This increases the need and importance of local normative studies. In a study by Blau, Super, and Brady (1993), approximately 80% of officers rated best and least best were correctly identified using scales from the original MMPI. It should be noted, however, that all the officers were currently employed as detention officers, patrol officers, or detectives; hence, this was not a true predictive validational study but a concurrent validational study. Super, Blau, Wells, and Murdock (1993) engaged a predictive analysis to determine which personality aspects discriminate between best and least best correctional officers based on interviews with seasoned and senior administrators. The sample included 32 subjects. Results indicated that the Correctional Officers Interest Blank (Gough & Aumack, 1982) differentiated those officers rated best from those officers rated least best at the $p < .05$ level of statistical significance. The MMPI, the 16 PF, and the FIRO-B (Schutz, 1966) failed to differentiate between the groups in this study.

Research is the foundation on which psychological services are based, and the importance of research in newer areas of psychological application cannot be overemphasized. Although a complete review of the research literature is beyond the scope of this text, authors such as Holbrook, White, and Hutt (1994), who have researched the relationship between shift work, law enforcement behavior, and sleep hygiene, bear noting.

INVESTIGATIVE SERVICES

Many individuals entering or aspiring to enter the field of police psychology routinely identify investigative services as what police psychologists do, a misperception promulgated and glamorized by several recent movies and television programs. Investigative services include serial crime profiling, psychological autopsies, investigative hypnosis, and handwriting analysis. But as noted (Bartol, 1996), little of a police psychologist's time is generally used in these types of activities.

Serial Crime Profiling

Serial crime profiling is used to derive psychological data about an individual from a methodological study of a crime scene. The purpose of profiling is to provide information to investigators that may increase the likelihood of perpetrator apprehension and arrest. Horn (1988) described criminal personality profiling as an attempt to provide likely behavioral and personality characteristics of the perpetrator. Profiling has been used anecdotally and unofficially for several decades. In the 1980s, Federal Bureau of Investigations agents attempted to systematize profiling. Profiling is most effective when used to identify behavioral and personality characteristics of individuals committing repeat offenses. Douglas, Ressler, Burgess, and Hartman (1986) described organized versus disorganized offenders. Organized offenders were described as intelligent, methodical, angry, and depressed; disorganized offenders were more likely to be described as coming from a family with an unstable income, being treated punitively as a child, being frightened, being confused, living alone, and having known the victim. The Federal Bureau of Investigations has been integral in developing profile patterns of serial murderers and serial rapists (Hazelwood & Warren, 1989).

Horn (1988) described seven steps of psychological profiling: (a) evaluation of the criminal act, (b) comprehensive analysis of the crime scene, (c) comprehensive analysis of the victim, (d) thorough review of preliminary police reports, (e) review of medical examiner's autopsy (for homicide cases), (f) development of a profile with offender characteristics, and (g) investigation of leads that may be generated based on the profile. An additional step of follow-up and data collection is recommended to refine profiling; validational data tend to be sparse and much needed.

Tetem (1989) reported that investigations were significantly enhanced by psychological profiling in 77% of the 193 cases reviewed. Pinizzotto and Finkel (1990) found profiles generated by professional profilers contained more information to help in identifying possible offenders than profiles generated by police detectives, untrained clinical psychologists, and undergraduate students. In conclusion, profiling is, at best, a tool that can be utilized by law enforcement to assist well-trained investigators in developing new leads. Profiling continues to be more art than science.

Psychological Autopsy

Blau (1994) traced the origins of psychological autopsies to insurance companies that were attempting to determine whether deaths of consumers were by suicide or other means. The purpose of a psychological autopsy is to increase our understanding of the mind-set of an individual posthumously. Psychological autopsies involve studying records generated by or for the individual within a one- to three-month period prior to their expiration. Interviews may be conducted with the spouse, other relatives, friends, work cohorts, clergy, physicians, and neighbors. From this, a profile is constructed of the individual's mental state prior to death. Psychological profiling is frequently used to determine whether a deceased individual exhibited behavioral and dispositional correlates of a prototypic suicide completer. This procedure is rarely used by law enforcement, public defenders, or state attorneys unless there is a question as to whether an individual may have died by suicide or homicide, natural causes, or other. Like most other forensic evaluations, psychological autopsies are best performed and most likely to yield valid results if convergent data patterns from multiple sources emerge.

Although some case law allowing the admissibility of testimony based on psychological autopsy has been favorable for the expert (*Evans v. Provident Life and Accident Insurance Co.*, 1982), uncertainty continues to abound regarding admissibility under the Federal Rules of Evidence. At the current state of scientific development, this uncertainty is appropriate.

Investigative Hypnosis

The American Psychological Association's Division of Psychological Hypnosis (1993) has described hypnosis as a procedure that seems to involve changes in sensations, perceptions, thoughts, behaviors, and feelings. Spiegel and Spiegel (1987) have described hypnosis as a shift in one's concentration which may reduce one's peripheral awareness and increase the ability to focus. Kirsch and Lynn (1995) described a number of points psychological science has revealed about hypnosis: (a) hypnosis is not equivalent to gullibility or mental weakness; (b) hypnosis is not synonymous with or even related to sleep; (c) hypnosis is more dependent on the characteristics of the individual being hypnotized than on the hypnotist's skill; (d) persons maintain their ability to regulate their behavior during hypnosis; (e) persons can monitor events in their surroundings during hypnosis; (f) spontaneous posthypnotic amnesia seldom occurs; (g) hypnosis increases one's suggestibility to a minor degree; (h) hypnosis is not dangerous when practiced by trained professionals; (i) most hypnotized persons are not faking; (j) hypnosis does not increase memory accuracy; and (k) hypnosis does not foster literal reexperience of childhood events.

At worst, investigative hypnosis by poorly or undertrained individuals may result in creation of false memories or seeding of information that may mislead investigators. At best, hypnosis may decrease outside distractions, increase concentration and focus, and allow an individual to provide investigators with leads that may further an investigation. It has been recommended by the Society for Clinical and Experimental Hypnosis that only trained and licensed psychologists or psychiatrists, without affiliation with the investigating law enforcement agency, conduct investigative hypnosis.

To minimize the probability of implanting memories, the professional conducting the hypnosis should not be informed about the case. This double-blind type approach will decrease the probability of contamination of the hypnotist's analysis of the case facts. A thorough interview should be conducted by detectives prior to investigative hypnosis to gain as much information as possible. Once under hypnosis, the subject is generally asked to free-associate about a specific set of questions submitted by the team of hypnotist and detectives. Like most forensic procedures, informed consent must be given prior to hypnotic induction. Under hypnosis, after the individual gives account of the incident, follow-up probes may be made to derive further information. During these follow-up probes, the professional should be cautious not to contaminate information provided by the witness. Techniques to solicit more information during hypnosis include slow motion and stop action. Information obtained through hypnosis is not used to form a case. Rather, like profiling, information obtained through hypnosis may provide investigative leads. Individual states vary as to what type of hypnotic evidence is admissible in court.

From a law enforcement perspective, and to decrease the probability of legal friction stemming from investigative hypnosis, the method is best used as an investigative tool. There has been case law against the use of hypnosis in the court (*People v. Shirley*, 1982). Admissibility of hypnotically refreshed memory has even been addressed by the U.S. Supreme Court (*Leyra v. Denno*,

1954). To minimize problems inherent with hypnosis, Kline (1986) recommends the following steps:

1. Only qualified mental health professionals should conduct the investigation.
2. A professional should be independent of a law enforcement agency.
3. A prehypnotic interview with the subject should be conducted by detectives regarding facts of the case.
4. All aspects, including the prehypnotic interview and the examination itself, should be recorded.
5. Outside influences should be reduced and only the hypnotist and the subject should be present during the actual hypnosis.

Other methods have been developed to help witnesses recall information they may have difficulty retrieving. One such technique has been referred to as cognitive interviewing (Geiselman, Fisher, MacKinnon, & Holland, 1985; Geiselmen, Fisher, Raymond, Jurkevich, & Warhaftig, 1987); it has not received the same criticisms as hypnosis, including the possibility of memory creation.

A cognitive interview begins with open-ended questions by the investigator. Cognitive interviewing techniques attempt to solicit more information from the interviewee than that gleaned by conventional techniques. Specific cognitive interview techniques are applied after the free recall of the event and include reinstating the context of the event, recalling the event in different sequence, and attempting to view the event from different perspectives. Reinstatement of the context attempts to place the individual in a frame of mind that is similar to his or her state of mind on the day of the incident. This is done by having the interviewee vividly describe events occurring immediately prior to the act in question. It may require the interviewee to reinstate the context of the entire day leading up to the incident. Cognitive interviewing attempts to reestablish, in vitro, the environment, the mood, the setting, and the various sensations and feelings that may have been experienced by the interviewee.

A second technique frequently used in cognitive interviewing is modifying the sequence of events. By changing the sequence of events and compartmentalizing aspects of the incident, information that the witness may deem unimportant but that can be germane to the case may be recalled. The interviewer may have the witness stop the action at a particular point in the recall and describe the still picture of the incident. The event can be recalled out of sequence or in reverse order.

The technique of changing perspective attempts to have the witness describe the incident through another person's eyes, possibly one who was standing in a different position from the witness. Other information retrieval techniques involve asking witnesses to isolate specified physical characteristics, sounds, or perceptions to retrieve information they may deem nonrelevant. Cognitive interviewing appears to be a viable alternative to hypnosis when interviewing witnesses or victims of crime. Whether cognitive interviews are susceptible to some of the shortcomings noted with investigative hypnosis remains to be seen.

TRAINING

Training is a cornerstone of organizational services and can have agencywide implications. A psychologist, strategically placed to provide training services to agency personnel, can increase his or her utility to the agency exponentially. Some areas in which psychologists may train agency personnel include academy instruction, stress reduction, and peer counselor training. Academy instruction on topics such as interviewing mentally disturbed citizens, suicide intervention and prevention, sensitivity training, multicultural training, human diversity training, and many other areas are routinely taught by psychologists. Academy instruction can expose many individuals to services provided by a psychologist. It is often an underutilized area of service provision.

Stress-reduction seminars are best used preventatively rather than as an intervention. The effects of stress on agency personnel can include diminution of work quality, somatization, marital problems, and alcohol use (DeAngelis, 1993; Goleman, 1992; Madamba, 1986; Pendergrass & Ostrov, 1986). Sources of stress in the workplace include shift work, management style, and, although to a lesser extent, the dangerousness inherent in the job. Secondary stress prevention may involve administrative changes via management consultation. A tertiary system to address stress involves treating stress through brief counseling, relaxation training, and health and wellness consultation.

Peer counseling training has had mixed acceptance at various agencies. Some agencies report successful programs, several others have not reported positive results. In fact, several agencies have disbanded peer counseling programs. Klyver (1986) described a successful peer counseling program with the Los Angeles Police Department. In 1983, there were 200 peer counselors who had worked with several thousand individuals providing thousands of hours of counseling. Issues addressed included family relationships, alcohol and drug abuse, and financial problems.

EMPLOYEE ASSISTANCE

The primary distinction between organizational services and employee assistance services is who is viewed and treated as the client. The agency is generally deemed the client for organizational services, and the individual officer or family member is generally viewed as the client for employee assistance services. Confidentiality must be afforded the individual(s) being treated. Employee assistance services include individual counseling, group counseling, critical incident counseling, family consultation, referral services, health and wellness programming, smoking cessation, and psychological evaluation. This is by no means an exhaustive list of employee assistance services that can be offered to law enforcement agencies by police psychologists. Various articles have addressed family counseling and stress prevention/intervention for law enforcement officers and their spouses. An international conference sponsored by the Federal Bureau of Investigations in 1994, *Law Enforcement Families Issues and Answers*, spawned a plethora of articles on theories, methods, and procedures to provide psychological services to law enforcement officers and their families. The importance of timely counseling as an intervention cannot be overstated for a law enforcement officer who has been involved in a traumatic incident. The probability of exposure to an event that may lead to an acute stress disorder or a posttraumatic stress disorder *(DSM-IV)* tends to be higher for law enforcement officers when compared with many other professions.

The concept of confidentiality tends to have more face validity for a psychologist consultant than a staff psychologist. For psychologists who are employed in-house, issues regarding confidentiality are more likely to be questioned and viewed with distrust. It is vitally important that a clear-cut policy regarding confidentiality be established and that it be sanctioned by the agency's chief officer. This is likely to decrease the officers' perception that receipt of psychological services may result in embarrassment or possible loss of standing within the department.

As noted earlier in this chapter, a psychologist who conducts FFDEs should not provide psychological counseling to employees. Just as certainly, psychologists who have conducted psychological counseling should not conduct FFDEs for individuals. Even in small, isolated departments, it would behoove the department to solicit and sponsor external service provision to avoid the above conflicts.

White (1987) surveyed 366 municipal, county, and state police agencies in the United States. Approximately 58% of the agencies provided in-house counseling services, 82% used outside consultant mental health services, and approximately 50% used a combination of in-house and consultant mental health services. The first in-house counseling program was established in 1943 in Portland, Oregon; consultant mental health counseling services were first provided in the early 1950s to the metropolitan police department in Washington, D.C. Agencies without access to consultant mental health professionals or in-house counseling programs generally are resigned to use hospital-based programs or drug and alcohol rehabilitation centers. As a rule of thumb, the larger the agency, the more likely it is to have access to consultant mental health professionals or on-staff mental health professionals.

Girodo (1991) indicated that officers working undercover are most likely to be in need of mental health services. Nevertheless, most agencies offering consultant or in-house psychological services programs attempt to make available mental health provision to all agency employees and to members of their immediate family. Mental health services to families is important. In one survey, 75% of the spouses of police officers reported stress from their mate's employment (DeAngelis, 1991).

This author has often been approached by law enforcement officers in a dejected state saying, "My wife and I are fighting, my kid is flunking school, and I can't do a thing about it." In cases such as this, the discourse between the officer and his or her spouse may be a symptom of external stressors. If external stressors and pressures can be lessened or modified, tensions between the couple may diminuate. Some agencies with psychological services sections are not averse to providing psychological evaluations for children. In some school districts where school psychologists are several months behind in testing, the psychological evaluation provided by the police psychologist can be used to assist in determining an appropriate school placement for a child.

LIMITATIONS

The nature and type of services provided by police psychologists are dynamic and evolving. This, however, can result in police psychologists being placed in the uncomfortable position of refusing legitimate service requests. Requests for employee assistance or organizational services that are beyond the scope of psychology as a science or beyond the psychologist's expertise are likely to be made during the course of the police psychologist's tenure. It may be tempting to say "yes" to build or improve upon an established liaison with agency personnel. Ethically, however, and for the sake of the projected relationship between the police psychologist and administrators, the psychologist is bound to provide only those services for which he or she is trained, educated, or experienced. It behooves a psychologist to recognize limits and set boundaries. This may require provision of referral services for individuals who may be experiencing difficulties with which the police psychologist has limited expertise, or it may require more hours of service provision than the police psychologist has available. At this point, having a referral network in place allows for continuity of care and is likely to be the best course of action.

All police psychologists should ensure that individuals and the organization that will utilize their services understand how to access services. This information may be disseminated through a flier that goes out with the paychecks listing times, telephone numbers, and places of service provision that can be directly accessed by department personnel. Organizational service requests generally occur if the psychologist participates in staff meetings.

There is no golden key to unlock all the doors within a law enforcement agency. Rather, hard work, dedication, and, to a certain extent, assimilation and accommodation of police experience is necessary for a successful program. At this time, there are several organizations in which psychologists may participate to learn more about police psychology. These groups include the Council of Police Psychological Services, the Society of Police and Criminal Psychologists, the International Association of Chiefs of Police, and Division 18 of the American Psychological Association.

APPENDIX A
Behavioral Science Unit General Order

1.0 Purpose

    1.1 Establishment of guidelines. This General Order establishes guidelines for the Behavioral Science Unit and for service provision. Law enforcement involves a broad range of situations and circumstances requiring understanding and modifying of human behavior. The Behavioral Science Unit may assist employees or the organization in psychological matters.

    1.2 All services provided by the Behavioral Science Unit shall be in compliance with the American Psychological Association's Ethical Principles of Psychologists, Code of Conduct, the Specialty Guidelines of Forensic Psychologists, and Florida State Statutes 415, 491, 490, and 90.

2.0 Rules and Procedures. There are two general types of services provided through the Behavioral Science Unit. Those include Human Resource Services and Organizational Services.

    2.1 Human Resource Services include individual counseling, group counseling, stress reduction counseling, referral services, liaison services for EAP [Employee Assistance Program] mental health counseling, and referral for ministerial or chaplain services.

        2.1.1 Employees or their respective family members are considered clients when receiving Human Resource Services. All information conveyed to Behavioral Science Unit's staff members under these conditions shall be confidential and privileged in accordance with the referenced Florida statutes and professional ethical guidelines.

            2.1.1.1 All information revealed to the psychologist, with the exception of 1) immediate threat of harm to self or others, or 2) abuse or neglect of children, handicapped persons, or the elderly shall remain confidential. Notwithstanding the above exceptions, information shall not be released to anyone without the expressed and written permission of the client or in response to a court order.

        2.1.2 Service provision shall consist mainly of short-term psychological intervention. Services provided by the Behavioral Science Unit staff will be at no cost to the employee.

            2.1.2.1 If reasonable time and consideration can not be provided for persons seeking Human Resource Services, they may be placed on a waiting list or referred for external service provision. For the latter, co-payments and deductibles may apply and are the responsibility of the service recipient.

        2.1.3 Service may be initiated by contacting the Behavioral Science Unit at extension ____ .

        2.1.4 Inquiry shall not be made by any ranking or non-ranking member of the Manatee County Sheriff's Office regarding information conveyed to a Behavioral Science Unit staff member.

        2.1.5 If human resource services are provided by an external consultant to a MCSO employee or their family, the external consultant shall be precluded from engaging specified organizational services involving that employee as outlined in sections 2.2.2, 2.2.3, and 2.2.4 of this General Order.

    2.2 Organizational Services. Organizational services include but are not limited to fitness-for-duty evaluations, pre-employment psychological evaluations, pre-appointment SWAT evaluations, pre-appointment Emergency Services Team evaluation, intra-agency consultations, training, program development, management consultation, and research.

2.2.1 Organizational services may be provided by the Behavioral Science Unit staff or external consultants. Unless indicated, the agency shall be designated as the client for organization services. This means that confidentiality and privilege are held by the agency or by an appointed representative thereof.

2.2.2 Mandatory fitness-for-duty evaluations shall not be conducted by the Behavioral Science Unit staff. Such evaluations will be conducted external to the agency. All requests for fitness-for-duty evaluations must come from the agency's chief administrator or designee. A fitness-for-duty evaluation is not to be requested as a disciplinary action. The purpose of a fitness-for-duty evaluation is to determine if an individual is psychologically fit to carry out specific job duties and if not fit, to determine recommendations which may result in eventual fitness. Behavioral Science Unit staff can consult with the agency's chief administrator or designee as to the appropriateness of fitness-for-duty evaluations and referral issues to be addressed.

    2.2.2.1 The deputy causing the discharge of the firearm shall be examined by a MCSO-approved psychologist to determine if the deputy's emotional state permits them continued privileges to carry a firearm. If the psychologist diagnoses the deputy as being in an emotional state which precludes safely carrying a firearm, the deputy shall be removed from line-duty and placed on inside-duty pending a decision by the Sheriff/designee in the matter, unless such action has already been taken. If the psychologist diagnoses the deputy as being in an emotional state which does not preclude carrying a firearm, the deputy shall be allowed to continue line-duty and carry a firearm, unless administratively suspended from duty.

    2.2.2.2 A Behavioral Science Unit staff member shall be available to review the contents of a Fitness For Duty Evaluation with the requesting party.

    2.2.2.3 The Behavioral Science Unit shall provide custodial services for externally conducted Fitness For Duty Evaluation reports or related material.

2.2.3 Examinations. Candidates for SWAT shall be subject to a psychological fitness examination.

    2.2.3.1 Pre-appointment SWAT evaluations shall not be conducted by a Behavioral Science Unit psychologist. Behavioral Science Unit staff shall be available to the SWAT Commander to assist with evaluation referrals.

    2.2.3.2 After successfully completing all initial requirements to become a SWAT member, and prior to full acceptance, the candidate shall be given a psychological examination by a licensed psychologist or psychiatrist. The examination shall be at the expense of the MCSO. Thereafter, such examinations shall be given only when deemed necessary by the Chief of the Enforcement Bureau and the SWAT Commander.

    2.2.3.3 A Behavioral Science Unit staff member shall be available to review the report with the Chief of the Enforcement Bureau and the SWAT commander.

    2.2.3.4 The psychological evaluation materials and reports shall be maintained in the Behavioral Science Unit.

2.2.4 Examinations. Candidates for the Emergency Services Team shall be subject to a pre-appointment psychological examination.

2.2.4.1 Preappointment Emergency Services Team evaluations shall not be conducted by a Behavioral Science Unit psychologist. Behavioral Science Unit staff shall be available to the Emergency Services Team Commander to assist in evaluation referrals.

2.2.4.2 The candidate shall be given a psychological examination by a licensed psychologist or psychiatrist after successfully completing all initial requirements to become a member of the Emergency Services Team. The examination shall be at the expense of the MCSO. Thereafter, such examinations shall be given only when deemed necessary by the Chief of the Enforcement Bureau and the Emergency Services Team Commander.

2.2.4.3 A Behavioral Science Unit staff member shall be available to review the report with the Chief of the Enforcement Bureau and the Emergency Services Team Commander.

2.2.4.4 The psychological test materials and reports shall be maintained in the Behavioral Science Unit.

2.2.5 Preemployment Psychological Examination. Prior to appointment to probationary status, each selected candidate for a certified law enforcement/correctional officer position shall be examined by a licensed psychologist to evaluate job related characteristics. The psychological screening shall be conducted after said applicant has been given a conditional offer of employment.

2.2.5.1 Preemployment psychological evaluations may be conducted by Behavioral Science Unit staff. Requests for preemployment psychological evaluations shall be made to the Behavioral Science Unit by the Director of the Personnel Section.

2.2.5.2 Raw data and results of these examinations shall be maintained on file in the Behavioral Science Unit. A copy of each candidate's psychological report shall be provided to the Personnel Section and shall be maintained with strict confidentiality in locked files not accessible to the public or unauthorized personnel.

2.2.6 Due to inherent stress in the criminal justice system, all applicants for noncertified positions who have a history of mental health diagnosis, psychiatric hospitalization, Baker Act or psychotropic medication prescription shall be required to undergo a psychological evaluation. The examination shall be conducted by a licensed psychologist. Record maintenance and examination requests shall be in accordance with sections 2.2.5.1 and 2.2.5.2 of this General Order.

2.2.7 Preemployment intellectual screenings shall be conducted by Behavioral Science Unit staff. Record maintenance and examination requests shall be in accordance with sections 2.2.5.1 and 2.2.5.2 of this General Order.

2.2.8 The Behavioral Science Unit staff may provide intra-agency consultations, training, program development and research.

2.2.8.1 Intra-agency consultation on matters regarding human behavior can be scheduled by department supervisors. On a limited basis, specific areas of psychological science can be researched by the Behavioral Science Unit staff.

2.2.8.2 Document familiarization—All supervisors shall be aware of the existence of infectious disease/bloodborne pathogen documents, as reference material, located in the Behavioral Science Unit.

2.2.8.3 Training services are offered through the Behavioral Science Unit on such issues as stress reduction, smoking cessation, and post-traumatic stress.

    2.2.8.3.1 Requests for teaching services can be made to the Behavioral Science Unit by the Training Director. Services may include academy instruction, FTO/CTO [Field Training Officer/Correctional Training Officer] instruction, or inservice training.

2.2.8.4 In special cases, investigative services can be provided by the Behavioral Science Unit (serial crime profiling, psychological autopsy, and investigative hypnosis).

2.2.9 Organizational/Human Resource Services is a blend of human resource and organizational services. This area of service provision includes Traumatic Incident Counseling.

    2.2.9.1 Although organizational in nature, Traumatic Incident Counseling shall be an exception whereby the individual receiving services shall be the holder of confidentiality. Service provision inquiries shall neither be confirmed nor denied without the expressed, written consent of the employee(s). The exception to confidentiality shall be as outlined in section 2.1.1.1 of this General Order.

    2.2.9.2 Traumatic Incident group services should be requested by the Scene Commander or the Emergency Services Commander.

        2.2.9.2.1 Traumatic events may include death or injury of an officer in the line-of-duty, death or severe injury of a citizen, severe child injury or any situation in which a Scene Commander or Emergency Services Commander opines that prolonged and/or severe emotional trauma may have occurred.

        2.2.9.2.2 The Behavioral Science Unit staff will determine if individual, group or combined services involving one or more sessions with agency members of varying job assignments are appropriate.

        2.2.9.2.3 All persons involved in or with a traumatic incident, to include law enforcement officers, correctional officers, special team members and communication specialists, shall be included in the Traumatic Incident Service process. The Scene Commander or Emergency Services Commander shall contact immediate supervisors of affected personnel which then shall notify affected employees to attend Traumatic Incident Counseling. The designated time and place of the service shall be determined jointly by the Scene Commander and Behavioral Science Unit staff.

    2.2.9.3 Individual traumatic counseling services shall be provided within similar framework as the group services.

        2.2.9.3.1 Individual follow-up services may be appropriate following group Traumatic Incident Counseling. Follow-up services may be provided by Behavioral Science Unit staff, EAP, a peer counselor, or clergy. This may be coordinated through the Behavioral Science Unit.

Source: Super (1997).

APPENDIX B
Journal Titles Relevant to Police Psychology

Journal Title	Publishers
1. *Behavioral Science*	American Psychological Association, (202) 336-5500
2. *Behavioral Sciences and the Law*	John Wiley & Sons, Inc., (212) 850-6000
3. *Bulletin of the American Academy of Psychiatry and the Law*	American Academy of Psychiatry, (860) 242-5450
4. *Crime and Delinquency*	Sage Publications, (805) 499-0721
5. *C. J. Management & Training Aid Digest*	Washington Crime News Services, (800) 422-9267 or (703) 573-1600
6. *Criminal Justice and Behavior*	Sage Publications, (805) 499-0721
7. *Criminal Justice Periodicals Index*	UMI Company, (800) 521-0600 or 313) 761-4700
8. *Criminology*	American Society of Criminology, (614) 292-9207
9. *Forensic Reports**	Hemisphere Publishing Corporation, (800) 821-8312 or (215) 785-5800
10. *Journal of Criminal Justice*	Elsevier Science Ltd., (212) 633-3950
11. *Journal of Criminal Justice & Behavior*	Sage Publications, (805) 499-0721
12. *Journal of Criminal Law & Criminology*	Northwestern University School of Law, (312) 503-8467
13. *Journal of Personality & Social Psychology*	American Psychological Association, (202) 336-5500
14. *Journal of Police and Criminal Psychology*	Society of Police & Criminal Psychologists, (512) 245-2174
15. *Journal of Police Science & Administration**	International Association of Chiefs of Police, (301) 948-0922
16. *Journal of Traumatic Stress*	Plenum Publishing Corporation, (212) 620-8000
17. *Law and Human Behavior*	Plenum Publishing Corporation, (212) 620-8000
18. *Law Enforcement News*	John Jay College of Criminal Justice, (212) 237-8442
19. *Personnel Psychology*	Personnel Psychology Incorporated, (419) 352-1562
20. *The Police Chief*	International Association of Chiefs of Police, (301) 948-0922

* Not currently in print.

APPENDIX C
Processing Form

Name: _____ Date: _____

Social Security Number: _____

Step/Procedure	Disposition/Notes	Date
1. Presented for evaluation	Yes No	_____
1a. Rescheduled	Yes No	_____
2. Presented for interview	Yes No	_____
2a. Rescheduled	Yes No	_____
3. Report to personnel	_____	_____
4. Initial applicant inquiry	_____	_____
5. Letter to applicant	_____	_____
6. Follow-up applicant inquiry	_____	_____
7. Applicant postselection interview (discuss appeal process)	_____	_____
8. Applicant letter of appeal received	_____	_____
9. Receipt of independent psychological evaluation	_____	_____
10. Bureau chief/Personnel director meeting	_____	_____
11. Third evaluation	Yes No	_____
12. Appeal process results	Hired Not Hired	_____

Comments: _____

_____

_____

REFERENCES

Allen, S. W., Fraser, S. L., & Inwald, R. (1991, April). *Assessment of personality characteristics related to successful hostage negotiators and their resistance to posttraumatic stress disorder.* In J. T. Reese, J. M. Horn, & C. Dunning (Eds.), *Critical incidents in policing* (pp. 1–7). Washington, DC: U.S. Department of Justice, Federal Bureau of Investigations.

American Psychiatric Association. (1994). *Diagnostic and statistical manual of mental disorders* (4th ed.). Washington, DC: American Psychiatric Association.

American Psychological Association. (1992). Ethical principles of psychologists and code of conduct. *American Psychologist, 47*(12), 1597–1611.

American Psychological Association, Division of Psychological Hypnosis. (1993). Hypnosis. *Psychological Hypnosis, 2*(3).

Americans with Disabilities Act of 1990, Pub.L. No. 101-336, S2, 104 Stat. 328 (1991).

Ash, P., Siora, K., & Britton, C. (1990). Police agency officer selection practices. *Journal of Police Science and Administration, 17*(4), 258–269.

Bartol, C. R. (1996). Police psychology then, now, and beyond. *Criminal Justice and Behavior, 23*(1), 70–89.

Bergen, G. T., Aceto, R. T., & Chadziewicz, M. M. (1992). Job satisfaction of police psychologists. *Criminal Justice and Behavior, 19*(3), 314–329.

Blau, T. H. (1994). *Psychological services for law enforcement.* New York: Wiley.

Blau, T. H., Super, J. T., & Brady, L. (1993). The MMPI good cop/bad cop profile in dentifying dysfunctional law enforcement personnel. *Journal of Police and Criminal Psychology, 9*(1), 2–4.

Bromley, M. (1995). Evaluating the use of the assessment center model for entry level police officer selection in a medium sized police agency. *Journal of Police and Criminal Psychology, 10*(4), 33–40.

Borum, W. R. (1988). A comparative study of negotiator effectiveness with "mentally disturbed hostage-taker" scenarios. *Journal of Police and Criminal Psychology, 4*, 17–20.

Borum, R., & Stock, H. V. (1993). Detection of deception in law enforcement applicants: A preliminary investigation. *Law and Behavior, 17*(2), 157–166.

Catell, R., Eber, H., & Tatsuoka, M. (1970). *Handbook for the 16 personality factor questionnaire (16PF).* Champaign, IL: Institute for Personality and Ability Testing.

Chandler, J. (1990). *Modern police psychology for law enforcement and human behavior professionals.* Springfiled, IL: Thomas.

Christiansen, N. D., Goffin, R. D., Johnston, N. G., & Rothstein, M. G. (1994). Correcting the 16 PF for faking: Effects on criterion-related validity and individual hiring decision. *Personnel Psychology, 47*, 847–860.

Coulton, G. F., & Feild, H. S. (1995). Using assessment centers in selecting entry-level police officers: Extravagance or justified expense. *Public Personnel Management, 24*(2), 223–254.

DeAngelis, T. (1991). Police stress takes its toll on family life. *APA Monitor, 22*(7), 38.

DeAngelis, T. (1993). Workplace stress battles fought all over the world. *APA Monitor, 24*(1), 22.

Douglas, J., Ressler, R., Burgess, A., & Hartman, C. (1986). Criminal profiling from crime scene analysis. *Behavioral Sciences and the Law, 4*(4), 401–421.

Dwyer, W. O., Prien, E. P., & Bernard, J. L. (1990). Psychological screening of law enforcement officers: A case for job relatedness. *Journal of Police Science and Administration, 17*(3), 176–182.

EEOC Equal Employment Opportunity for Individuals with Disabilities: Final Rule, 55(44) Fed. Reg. (1991).

Evans v. Provident Life and Accident Insurance Co., Kan. Ct. App. 64, 689 (1982).

Flanagan, J. C. (1964). The critical incident technique. *Psychological Bulletin, 51,* 327–358.

Gabris, G. T., & Rock, S. M. (1991). Situational interviews and job performance: The results in one public agency. *Public Personnel Management, 20*(4), 469–483.

Geiselman, R. E., Fisher, R. P., MacKinnon, D. P., & Holland, H. L. (1985). Eyewitness memory enhancement in the police interview: Cognitive retrieval mnemonics versus hypnosis. *Journal of Applied Psychology, 70*(2), 403.

Geiselman, R. E., Fisher, R. P., Raymond, D. S., Jurkevich, L. M., & Warhaftig, M. L. (1987). Enhancing eyewitness memory: Refining the cognitive interview. *Journal of Police Science and Administration, 15*(4), 292.

Getty, V. S., & Elam, J. D. (1988). Identifying characteristics of hostage negotiators and using personality data to develop a selection model. In J. Reeve & J. Horn (Eds.), *Police psychology: Operational assistance* (pp. 159–171). Washington, DC: U.S. Government Press.

Girodo, M. (1991). Symptomatic reactions to undercover work. *Journal of Nervous and Mental Disease, 179*(10), 626–630.

Goleman, D. (1992, December). New light on how stress erodes health. *New York Times Science Times,* p. B5.

Gottfredson, L. S. (1996). Racially gerrymandering the content of police tests to satisfy the U.S. justice department: A case study. *Psychology, Public Policy, and Law, 2*(3/4), 418–446.

Gough, H. G. (1986). *The California psychological inventory.* Palo Alto, CA: Consulting Psychologists Press.

Gough, H. G., & Aumack, F. L. (1982). *Correctional officers' interest blank.* Palo Alto, CA: Consulting Psychologists Press.

Hathaway, S. R., & McKinley, J. C. (1983). *Minnesota multiphasic personality inventory manual for administration and scoring.* Minneapolis: University of Minnesota Press.

Hathaway, S. R., & McKinley, J. C. (1989). *Minnesota multiphasic personality inventory–2 manual for administration and scoring.* Minneapolis: University of Minnesota Press.

Hazelwood, R., & Warren, J. (1989). The serial rapist: His characteristics and victims. *FBI Law Enforcement Bulletin, 58*(2), 18–25.

Hiatt, D., & Hargrave, G. E. (1994). Psychological assessment of gay and lesbian law enforcement applicants. *Journal of Personality Assessment, 63*(1), 80–88.

Hogan, R., Hogan, J., & Roberts, B. W. (1996). Personality measurement and employment decisions: Questions and answers. *American Psychologists, 51*(5), 469–477.

Holbrook, M. I., White, M. H., & Hutt, M. J. (1994). Increasing awareness of sleep hygiene in rotating shift workers: Arming law enforcement officers against impaired performance. *Perceptual and Motor Skills, 79*(1), 520–522.

Horn, J. (1988). Criminal personality profiling. In J. Reese & J. Horn (Eds.), *Police psychology: Operational assistance* (pp. 211–224). Washington, DC: U.S. Government Printing Office, Federal Bureau of Investigation.

Hunter, J. E., & Schmidt, F. L. (1996). Intelligence and job performance: Economic and social implications. *Psychology, Public Policy, and Law, 2*(3/4), 447–472.

Inwald, R. E. (1980). *Inwald personality inventory.* New York: Hilson Research.

Inwald, R. E. (1982). *Inwald personality inventory technical manual.* Kew Gardents, NY: Hilson Research.

Inwald, R. E., & Brockwell, A. L. (1991). Predicting the performance of government security personnel with the IPI and MMPI. *Journal of Personality Assessment, 56*(3), 522–535.

Janik, J. (1994). Considerations in administering psychological pre-selection procedures to law enforcement applicants. *Journal of Police and Criminal Psychology, 10*(2),
32–34.

Kirsch, I., & Lynn, S. J. (1995). The altered state of hypnosis: Changes in the theoretical
landscape. *American Psychologist, 50*(10), 846–858.

Kline, M. (1986). Hypnosis in police work. In W. Bailey (Ed.), *The encyclopedia of police
science.* New York: Garland.

Klyver, N. (1986). L.A.P.D.'s peer-counseling program after three years. In J. Reese &
H. Goldstein (Eds.), *Psychological services for law enforcement.* Washington, DC: U.S.
Government Printing Office.

Kovach, R. C., Surrette, M. A., & Aamodt, M. G. (1988). Following informal street
maps: Effects of map design. *Environment and Behavior, 20*(6), 683–699.

Leyra v. Denno, 347 U.S. 556 (1954).

Lorr, M., & Strack, S. (1994). Personality profiles of police candidates. *Journal of Clinical
Psychology, 50*(2), 200–207.

Madamba, H. (1986). The relationship between stress and marital relationships of police
officers. In J. Reese & H. Goldstein (Eds.), *Psychological services for law enforcement.*
Washington, DC: Superintendent of Documents.

McKenna v. Fargo, 451 F. Supp. 1355 (1978).

McMains, M. (1988). Psychologists' roles in hostage negotiations. In J. Reese & J. Horn
(Eds.), *Police psychology: Operational assistance* (pp. 281–317). Washington, DC: U.S.
Government Printing Office, Federal Bureau of Investigation.

Mullins, W. C., & McMains, M. (1995). Predicting patrol officer performance from a
psychological assessment battery: A predictive validity study. *Journal of Police and
Criminal Psychology, 10*(4), 15–25.

Noesner, G., & Dolan, J. (1992). First responder negotiation training. *FBI Law Enforcement Bulletin, 61*(8), 1–4.

Ostrov, E., Nowicki, D. E., & Beazley, J. P. (1987, February). Mandatory police evaluations: The Chicago model. *The Police Chief,* pp. 30–35.

Pendergrass, V., & Ostrov, N. (1986). Correlates of alcohol use by police personnel. In
J. Reese & H. Goldstein (Eds.), *Psychological services for law enforcement.* Washington,
DC: Superintendent of Documents.

People v. Shirley, 50 U.S.P.L.W. 2579 (1982).

Pinizzotto, A., & Finkel, N. (1990). Criminal personality profiling: An outcome and
process study. *Law and Human Behavior, 14*(3), 215–233.

Rafilson, F., & Sison, R. (1996). Seven criterion-related validity studies conducted with
the national police officer selection test. *Psychological Reports, 78,* 163–176.

Rand, R. R. (1987). Behavioral police assessment device: The development and validation
of an interactive, pre-employment, job related, video psychological test. *Dissertation
Abstracts International, 48*(3-A), 610–611.

Reese, J. T. (1987). *A history of police psychological services.* Washington, DC: U.S. Government Printing Office.

Reiser, M. (1972). *The police department psychologist.* Springfiled, IL: Thomas.

Russell, C. J. (1996). *The nassau county police case: Impressions.* Unpublished manuscript,
University of Oklahoma. (Available at www.ipmaac.org/nassau/)

Russell, H., & Beigel, A. (1989). *Understanding human behavior for effective police work*
(2nd ed.). New York: Basic Books.

Sarchione, C. D., Cuttler, M. J., & Nelson-Gray, R. O. (1995). *Personality constructs, the CPI,
and job difficulties in police officers.* Paper presented at the 103rd annual APA Convention, New York.

Saxe-Clifford, S. (1986, February). The fitness for duty evaluation: Establishing policy.
The Police Chief, 38–39.

Schmidt, F. L. (1996, December 10). New police test will be a disaster [Letter to the editor]. *Wall Street Journal*, p. A23.

Schumacher, J. E., Scogin, F., Howland, K., & McGee, J. (1992). The relation of peer assessment to future law enforcement performance. *Criminal Justice and Behavior,* *19*(3), 286–293.

Schutz, W. (1966). *The interpersonal underworld: FIRO.* Palo Alto, CA: Science and Behavior Books.

Scogin, F., Schumacher, J., Gardner, J., & Chaplin, W. (1995). Predictive validity of psychological testing in law enforcement settings. *Professional Psychology: Research and Practice, 26*(1), 68–71.

Serafino, G. F. (1990). Informed consent for police officers undergoing psychological evaluation. *Journal of Police and Criminal Psychology, 6*(1), 2–5.

Shusman, E. J., & Inwald, R. E. (1991). A longitudinal validation study of correctional officer job performance as predicted by the IPI and MMPI. *Journal of Criminal Justice, 19,* 173–180.

Soroka v. Dayton Hudson Corporation, 822 P. 2d 1327 (1992).

Spiegel, H., & Spiegel, D. (1987). Forensic uses of hypnosis. In I. Weinder & R. A. Hess (Eds.), *Handbook of forensic psychology.* New York: Wiley.

Stone, A. V. (1990, February). Psychological fitness for duty evaluation. *The Police Chief,* 39–53.

Super, J. T. (1995). Psychological characteristics of successful SWAT/tactical response team personnel. *Journal of Police and Criminal Psychology,* 60–63.

Super, J. T. (1996). Intelligence testing as a predictor of officer certification examination performance. In J. T. Reese & R. M. Solomon (Eds.), *Organizational issues in law enforcement* (pp. 259–265). Washington, DC: U.S. Government Printing Office.

Super, J. T. (1997a). Select legal and ethical aspects of pre-employment psychological evaluations. *Journal of Police & Criminal Psychology, 12*(2), 1–6.

Super, J. T. (1997b). Select legal and ethical aspects of fitness for duty evaluations. *Journal of Criminal Justice, 25*(3), 223–229.

Super, J. T. (1997c). Intelligence testing and officer certification examination standing. *Journal of Criminal Justice, 25*(1), 43–47.

Super, J. T., & Blau, T. H. (1997). Survey of psychological services general orders in law enforcement. *Journal of Police & Criminal Psychology, 12*(1), 7–12.

Super, J. T., Blau, T. H., Wells, C. B., & Murdock, N. (1993). Using psychological tests to discriminate between best and least best correctional officers. *Journal of Criminal Justice, 21*(2), 143–150.

Terman, L. M., & Otis, A. (1917). A trial of mental and pedagogical tests in civil service examination for policemen and firemen. *Journal of Applied Psychology, 1,* 17–29.

Tetem, H. (1989). Offender profiling. In W. Bailey (Ed.), *The encyclopedia of police science.* New York: Garland.

Timbrook, R. E., & Graham, J. R. (1994). Ethnic differences on the MMPI-2? *Psychological Assessment, 6*(3), 212–217.

United States Department of State, Bureau of Diplomatic Security. (1988). *Hostage taking: Preparation, avoidance, and survival.* Washington, DC: U.S. Government Printing Office.

Wells, C. B., & Blau, T. H. (1994, January). Strategic planning: Management style of the future. *The Police Chief,* 48–49.

Wonderlic, E. F. (1983). *Wonderlic personnel test manual.* Northfield, IL: Wonderlic and Associates.

Young, T. (1992). *Use of the behavioral police assessment device in the selection of law enforcement officers.* Doctoral dissertation, the Professional School of Psychology. (University Microfilms No. LD02540).

CHAPTER 16

Polygraph ("Lie Detector") Testing: The State of the Art

WILLIAM G. IACONO and CHRISTOPHER J. PATRICK

POLYGRAPHERS, INCLUDING those with scientific training, claim that polygraph tests have greater than 90% accuracy, that this claim is supported by the scientific literature, that their techniques are based on sound scientific principles, and that scientists agree with these claims (e.g., Raskin, Honts, & Kircher, 1997a). They further argue that these techniques have great evidentiary value and advocate using them in criminal and civil court proceedings as well as to screen out undesirable employees (e.g., Horvath, 1985, 1993; Raskin et al., 1997a). In this chapter, we critically examine the empirical literature and arguments used to support these claims.

APPLICATIONS

Polygraph tests are typically used in circumstances where the question at hand cannot be easily resolved by the available evidence. When the investigation of a known suspect by a law enforcement agency reaches an evidentiary dead end, police may rely on a polygraph test as the means of last resort to resolve the case. Sometimes those who fail these tests, pressured to own up to their misdeeds, confess, thereby providing the police with incriminating evidence they otherwise would not have. Polygraph tests are used by insurance agencies to verify the claims of those insured; by defense attorneys to confirm their client's stories; in family court to help resolve charges of misbehavior parents level at each other in their effort to obtain custody of their children; by the police to verify victims' charges; by controversial people in the public eye, like Anita Hill and Mark Fuhrman, who wish to sway public opinion in their favor by advertising the fact that they passed a "lie detector"; by the government to protect national security by requiring those with access to classified information to pass tests confirming that they have not made unauthorized disclosures; and even by those running fishing contests to verify that winners actually followed contest rules rather than purchasing their lunker from the local supermarket.

The Employee Polygraph Protection Act (EPPA) of 1988 (Public Law 100-347) eliminated much of the most widespread application of polygraph testing, the periodic screening of employees to verify their good behavior and the preemployment screening of potential hires to see if they possess the qualities desired by the employer. However, the government exempted itself from coverage by this law. The result has been more widespread use of polygraph tests by the government for these purposes (Honts, 1991; Horvath, 1993). Horvath (1993), in a survey of the practices of over 600 large city police departments, noted that more than 67,000 applicants for law enforcement positions take these tests each year, with 22% rejected as a consequence of polygraph test outcome. There are over two dozen federal agencies that routinely use polygraph tests, including the Central Intelligence Agency, Department of Defense, Federal Bureau of Investigation, National Security Agency, U.S. Army, and U.S. Air Force, and most of these use the polygraph as both an investigative and screening tool.

THE POLYGRAPH AND THE POLYGRAPHER

Field polygraphs are briefcase-size instruments capable of monitoring the autonomic responses elicited by the subject's answers to test questions. Expandable pneumatic belts positioned around the upper thorax and abdomen provide two separate recordings of the chest movements associated with inspiration and expiration. Changes in skin resistance (the galvanic skin response or GSR) are detected by electrodes attached to the fingertips. For the "cardio" channel, a partly inflated blood pressure cuff attached to the arm reflects relative changes in blood pressure and provides an index of pulse. These signals are amplified and fed to motorized ink pens that reproduce them on moving chart paper. Although this instrument is relatively simple, it is nonetheless adequate for the intended purpose. Patrick and Iacono (1991a) demonstrated that a field polygraph produces records of physiological reactivity that are comparable to those obtained by sophisticated laboratory equipment.

Modern polygraphic recording has become computerized. Various options are available, one of the most common consisting of a laptop computer, a coupling unit that provides for amplification of the physiological signals and their conversion to digital form, and a printer. With such an arrangement, there is no need for the traditional polygraph instrument or a chart record of the physiological activity. The adequacy of the recordings can be determined online using the computer monitor, and the digitally stored data can be plotted with a printer, producing a continuous record or "chart" in much the same manner that a conventional instrument would. With currently available software, it is possible to have the computer render the verdict in the form of a probability statement as to the likelihood the person was truthful when responding to the questions. Because this software is sold commercially, the nature of the algorithms and data used to justify the probability statements is proprietary. Little is known about their validity.

Training in polygraphy is provided by free-standing polygraph schools, most of which are accredited by the American Polygraph Association. The most prestigious of these is at the Department of Defense Polygraph Institute (DoDPI; formerly the U.S. Army Military Police School). This school offers a one-semester, intensive, hands-on course in polygraphy that covers the various techniques and interview practices employed by examiners. This school also has an in-house research program staffed by doctoral-level psychologists, some of whom share in the teaching of students with polygraph examiners and law enforcement agents. Graduates of the program are typically apprenticed to practicing examiners before becoming fully certified to administer tests on their own. DoDPI offers training for many state and city police departments and most federal government agencies, including the military police, the FBI, the IRS, and all of the government security agencies (except the CIA, which trains its own examiners). DoDPI represents the best training the profession of polygraphy has to offer. Most accredited schools do not offer as rigorous a program as DoDPI; not all practicing polygraph examiners are graduates of approved schools; and because polygraphy is not regulated in most states, polygraphers are not necessarily licensed to practice their trade.

TYPES OF TESTS

The polygraph itself is not capable of detecting lies, and there is no pattern of physiological response that is unique to lying. Because of this, all polygraph tests involve asking different types of questions, with differential responding to those pertinent to the issue at hand determining the test outcome. The four classes of tests currently used in field applications are reviewed below.

SPECIFIC INCIDENT INVESTIGATIONS

The Control Question Test

The so-called control question test (CQT) remains the technique of choice among polygraphers who conduct specific incident investigations like those concerned with known criminal acts. The CQT typically consists of about 10 questions. The two types of question that are important to the determination of guilt or innocence are referred to as relevant and control questions. The relevant questions deal directly with the incident under investigation (e.g., Did you shoot Bill Birditsman on the night of March 18?). Control items cover past behaviors that one might associate with "the kind of person" who is capable of killing (e.g., Before the age of 24, did you ever deliberately hurt someone you were close to?). It is assumed that guilty suspects will be more concerned with the relevant than with the control questions. The reverse pattern is expected with innocent people.

The typical CQT consists of a pretest interview (lasting from about 30 minutes to perhaps two hours in some cases) followed by the administration of at least three "charts" (i.e., three separate presentations of the question sequence while the subject's physiological responses are monitored). The positions of control and relevant questions are usually varied from chart to chart to minimize habituation, with each relevant question paired with a control item in the question sequence. The latter practice is known as the zone of comparison (ZOC) procedure. Developed by Backster (1962), the ZOC format has gained favor because it compensates for variations in subject reactivity during the test and also provides for more objective chart analysis. After the collection of the physiological data, the CQT interrogation is brought to a close with the posttest interview. At this point, the polygrapher announces the verdict and attempts to elicit confessions from those who fail.

The pretest phase of the CQT is critical to the successful administration of the test. It is during this interview that the polygrapher attempts to create the circumstances that lead the innocent person to be more disturbed by the possibly trivial issues raised by the control items than by the relevant questions that have to do with the matter under investigation. A common criticism of the CQT is that it is biased against truthful persons because the relevant questions may be just as arousing to innocent suspects, who may view their freedom or livelihood as dependent on their physiological response to these items, as they are to the guilty (Lykken, 1974). To reduce the likelihood of this occurrence, polygraphers use the pretest interview to focus the subject's "psychological set" on the control questions if the examinee is innocent or on the relevant questions if he or she is guilty. Two tactics are used to accomplish this objective.

The first is to convince the subject that lies will be detected. One way to achieve this goal is to demonstrate that the polygraph can detect a known lie. In a typical scenario the examiner connects the subject to the polygraph and says, "I'm going to ask you to pick a number from 1 to 10, write it down, and then show it to me. Both of us will know which number you've picked. After that, I will say a number and ask you if it is yours. I want you to answer 'no' to each number I say, including the one you picked." The polygrapher then records the subject's responses to each number and announces afterward that the largest reaction occurred when the subject lied; if this were indeed the case, the examiner may point it out on the chart. If it were not the case, the examiner may say that it was anyway or mechanically alter the subject's response to the target number to create the impression that it elicited a clearly detectable reaction. Some achieve the desired result by having the subject pick a card from a stacked deck and then relying on the physiological record to "determine" which one he or she picked. Some variant of this type of demonstration procedure, often called a stim test, is used routinely by most polygraphers.

A second tactic for establishing the correct psychological set is to continually emphasize the importance of being truthful at all times. No distinction is made between the relevant and the control questions regarding the burden of truthfulness. Consequently, innocent individuals are led to believe that lying to control questions will lead to a failed test outcome. How it is that they should reach this conclusion is explained for a case of theft by one of polygraphy's leading proponents, David Raskin (1989), as follows:

Since this is a matter of a theft, I need to ask you some general questions about yourself in order to assess your basic honesty and trustworthiness. I need to make sure that you have never done anything of a similar nature in the past and that you are not the type of person who would do something like stealing that ring and then would lie about it. . . . So if I ask you, "Before the age of 23, did you ever lie to get out of trouble?" you could answer that no, couldn't you? Most subjects initially answer no to the control questions. If the subject answers yes, the examiner asks for an explanation. . . . [and] leads the subject to believe that admissions will cause the examiner to form the opinion that the subject is dishonest and therefore guilty. This discourages admissions and maximizes the likelihood that the negative answer is untruthful. However, the manner of introducing and explaining the control questions also causes the subject to believe that deceptive answers to them will result in strong physiological reactions during the test and will lead the examiner to conclude that the subject was deceptive with respect to the relevant issues concerning the theft. In fact, the converse is true. Stronger reactions to the control questions will be interpreted as indicating that the subject's denials to the relevant questions are truthful. (pp. 254–255)

Before Backster's (1962) introduction of the numerically quantified ZOC, CQTs were globally evaluated (Reid & Inbau, 1977). With global scoring, all the information available to the examiner is used to make the diagnosis. Hence, in addition to the physiological data, the plausibility of the subject's account of the facts, his or her demeanor during the examination, and information from the investigative file may all figure into the evaluation.

With numerical scoring, which is now favored by most polygraphers, the examiner is specifically trained to ignore all the ancillary data and base the decision exclusively on the physiological recordings. Adjacent control/relevant item responses are compared for each separate physiological channel. A score from $+1$ to $+3$ is assigned if the response to the control item is larger, with the magnitude of the score determined by how large a difference is observed. Likewise, a score from -1 to -3 is assigned if the relevant member of the question pair elicited the stronger response. A total score is obtained by summing these values over all channels and charts, with a negative score less than -5 prompting a deceptive verdict, a positive score exceeding $+5$ a truthful verdict, and scores between -5 and $+5$ considered inconclusive and therefore warranting further testing. In our experience with government examiners, about 10% of CQTs end with inconclusive outcomes.

Both global and numerical chart evaluation have high interscorer reliability. Studies in which examiners blind to case facts evaluate the original examiners' charts typically report reliabilities around .90 (e.g., Honts, 1996; Horvath, 1977; Patrick & Iacono, 1991b). The retest reliability of polygraph testing has not been evaluated. The absence of such data is unfortunate because often questions about the possible increment in validity gained by retesting a defendant arise in legal proceedings.

Directed Lie Test

The directed lie test (DLT) is often considered a subtype of the CQT. The chief difference lies in the nature of the control questions. For a DLT, the "probable lie" control questions of the CQT are replaced with "directed lie" questions.

Directed lies are statements that the subject admits involve a lie before the test begins. In fact, the polygrapher specifically instructs the subject to answer the question deceptively and to think of a particular time when he or she has done whatever the directed lie question covers. Examples of directed lies are "Have you ever done something that hurt or upset someone?" or "Have you ever made even one mistake?" As with the CQT, guilty subjects are expected to respond more strongly to the relevant questions, and innocent subjects should react more strongly to the directed lies.

Guilty Knowledge Test

An alternative to the CQT for specific incident investigations is the guilty knowledge test (GKT; Lykken, 1959, 1960). Rather than asking directly whether the examinee was responsible for the crime under investigation, the GKT probes for knowledge indicative of guilt details regarding a crime or incident that only the person who did it would know about. (The GKT has also been called the "concealed knowledge test," but this more generic term is problematic because it implies unnecessarily that guilty knowledge is effortfully hidden.) The GKT consists of a series of questions about the crime posed in multiple-choice format. Each question asks about one specific detail of the crime and is followed by a series of alternative answers, including the correct answer as well as other plausible but incorrect options. An example of a GKT question concerning one detail of a homicide is as follows: "If you were the one who beat Donna Fisbee to death, then you will know what was used to kill her. Was she beaten with: (a) a brick? (b) a crowbar? (c) a pipe? (d) a baseball bat? (e) a hammer?" When presented with a question of this type, the true culprit would be expected to emit a larger physiological reaction to the correct alternative, whereas an innocent person, knowing nothing about the incident, would respond more or less at random.

The simple premise underlying the GKT is that a person will exhibit larger orienting reactions to key information only if he or she recognizes it as distinctive or important. The GKT tests for knowledge of information rather than for deceptiveness, and the irrelevant alternatives are true controls rather than pseudo-controls. In the CQT, deceptiveness is inferred from a pattern of enhanced reactions to relevant questions, but the possibility that innocent concern rather than deception is responsible for this outcome can never be ruled out. A pattern of consistent reactions to critical items on a GKT can (within a small, estimable probability) mean only that the examinee possesses guilty knowledge. On a GKT question with 5 alternative answers, the odds that an innocent person with no knowledge of the crime would react most intensely to the key (relevant) alternative are 1 in 5. On a GKT including 10 such questions, the odds are vanishingly small (< 1 in 10,000,000) that an innocent person would react differentially to the key alternative on each and every test question.

The first study of the GKT (Lykken, 1959) and most others conducted since have utilized peripheral response measures, most commonly skin resistance or skin conductance, as indices of stimulus orienting. More recently, event-related brain potentials (ERPs)—in particular, the P300 component of the ERP—have been utilized to detect deception within a GKT format. This approach relies on the fact that the amplitude of the P300 increases in inverse relationship to the probability of occurrence of a stimulus, with P300s larger for more rarely occurring ("oddball") stimuli. In a P300 GKT procedure, the crime-relevant keys comprise the rare stimuli. When these keys are interspersed with the crime-irrelevant multiple-choice alternatives, to the person without guilty knowledge, none of the alternatives is "odd," so none elicits a P300. For the guilty person, the set of crime-relevant keys are recognized as special, and because they are far fewer in number than the set of irrelevant alternatives, they elicit a P300.

EMPLOYEE SCREENING TEST: THE RELEVANT/(IR)RELEVANT TEST

Up until a decade ago, the type of polygraph examination administered most frequently in the United States was the employment screening polygraph test. This type of test was used by businesses to weed out prospective hires with criminal tendencies or substance abuse problems (preemployment polygraph test), or to identify current employees engaged in theft, sabotage, or other activities detrimental to the business (periodic screening test). By the late 1980s, as many as 2 million examinations of this type were administered annually within the private sector (O'Bannon, Goldinger, & Appleby, 1989).

However, following a vigorous debate, much of which was focused on issues of intrusiveness and infringement of personal rights associated with polygraph testing, Congress enacted the EPPA, thereby banning private employers from requiring or even requesting applicants to undergo polygraph tests as a condition of employment. The EPPA covers not only the polygraph but any "mechanical or electrical device" used to render an opinion as to honesty or dishonesty. It also prohibits random testing of current employees and limits the use of the polygraph in specific investigations of job-related wrongdoing. Violations may result in federal fines of up to $10,000 and constitute grounds for civil litigation. Some types of private sector jobs and industries (i.e., government contractors, security companies, and pharmaceutical manufacturers) are exempt from the act. The main effect of the EPPA has been to limit the use of the polygraph for employee screening to government employers, including police departments and national defense and security agencies.

In contrast to specific incident tests, screening examinations contain relevant questions of the form "Have you ever . . . ?" or "During the period in question, did you . . . ?" Because appropriate controls for these broad sorts of questions cannot be constructed, examiners use the relevant/irrelevant (R/I) test format for pre- and postemployment screening. Apropos its name, the R/I test includes only two types of items: relevant questions concerning matters of interest (e.g., drug use, criminal behavior, and loyalty) and innocuous or irrelevant questions (also called norms). The latter include items like "Is your last name Birditsman?" and "Is today Sunday?"

The R/I screening test can be distinguished from the traditional R/I test, which was developed in 1917 by William Marston and was subsequently refined by John Larson (1921) for use in criminal investigations. In this type of test, relevant questions were each preceded and followed by an irrelevant question, with an evocative item unrelated to the crime in question presented at the end of the test to establish the examinee's ability to respond (Lykken, 1981). Consistently greater reactions to the relevant items of the test were interpreted as evidence of deceptiveness. However, because of the obvious confound posed by the differential potency of the two categories of test questions, the traditional R/I examination has been roundly criticized. For purposes of employment screening, polygraph examiners now commonly use a variant of the R/I procedure that might more appropriately be called the relevant/relevant (R/R) technique.

In a screening test of this type, three or more question sequences are typically presented covering the same topics, but with the form of the questions and their order varied. Fewer irrelevant items are included in the test, and they are included mainly to provide a "rest period or return to baseline" rather than a norm for comparison purposes. The test can more accurately be characterized as a polygraph-assisted interview where the development of questions is guided both by the polygrapher's impressions of the examinee's truthfulness as well as the comparative reactions to the various relevant items: "The cardinal rule in chart interpretation is, any change from normal requires an explanation" (Ferguson, 1966, p. 161). If the subject shows persistently strong reactions to one or more content areas in relation to the rest, the examiner concludes that the subject lied or was particularly sensitive about these issues for some hidden reason. In this case, the examiner will probe the examinee for an explanation of what might have provoked these responses and will administer additional question sequences focusing on these specific issues. Examinees who are adept at "explaining away" their reactions are thus likely to avoid incrimination. Thurber (1981) reported that among applicants for a police training academy, those who scored highest on a questionnaire measure of impression management were most likely to pass a polygraph screening test.

The preemployment polygraph test is used to determine whether a job candidate is the kind of person who is likely to be a bad employment risk. Questions are typically asked concerning the individual's employment history, job commitment, record of job-related misconduct, health problems, and problems with drugs or alcohol. The type of screening test conducted most frequently by national security organizations is the periodic or aperiodic screening test. Periodic screening tests are conducted at regular intervals to determine whether existing employees have been honest in their work and whether they remain loyal to the agency. Aperiodic screenings, as the term suggests, are conducted less frequently and with minimal advance warning. Besides being more economical, this practice is thought to produce a more powerful deterrent to malfeasance. The knowledge that they may be asked to submit to a polygraph test at any time is believed to dissuade existing employees from engaging in misconduct. In effect, the polygraph establishes a climate of fear in which employees are presumably less inclined to be dishonest because they fear detection (Samuels, 1983).

In security-sensitive positions, continued confidentiality and propriety are the primary issues of concern on screening examinations. Within the U.S. Department of Defense, for example, close to two-thirds of the 12,548 polygraph tests conducted during the year 1996 were administered in the context of the agency's Counterintelligence-Scope Polygraph (CSP) program, which was implemented to deter and detect espionage, sabotage, and terrorism by employees and contractors (United States Department of Defense, 1996). The CSP screening examination contains questions that ask whether the examinee has ever engaged in spying or sabotage or knows anyone involved in such activities; has ever sold or handed over classified information to unauthorized parties or been asked to do so or knows anyone who has done so; or has engaged in any unauthorized contact with foreign government agents. According to Defense Department policy, if an employee declines to take a polygraph screening test, he or she may forfeit or be denied access to classified materials and potentially be moved to another position of equal pay and responsibility, but with lower security authorization.

DETERMINING VALIDITY

The conclusions that are drawn about the accuracy of polygraph tests are determined in part by the range and quality of evidence that a reviewer is willing to consider. Because there are so many studies that touch on the accuracy issue, and because much of the research conducted in this field is not carried out by scientists or published in scientific, peer-reviewed journals, we preface our evaluation of the literature with a summary of the important methodological issues that a serious investigation of polygraph validity must address.

EVALUATION OF POLYGRAPH CHARTS

As indicated previously, polygraphers reach conclusions using either a global approach to chart interpretation or semi-objective numerical scoring. Because both approaches are still currently taught and used, studies of polygraph accuracy should examine both practices.

Regardless of the procedure used to score the charts, the field examiner normally has been exposed to extrapolygraphic cues such as the case facts, the behavior of the suspect during the examination, and sometimes a confession from the examinee. For an investigation to provide a useful estimate of the accuracy of the psychophysiological test, the original examiner's charts must be reinterpreted by "blind" evaluators who have no knowledge of the suspect or case facts. Even though those trained in numerical scoring are specifically taught to ignore extrapolygraphic cues, Patrick and Iacono (1991b) showed that they nevertheless did attend to them in their field study of Royal Canadian Mounted Police (RCMP) polygraph practices.

RCMP examiners are trained at the Royal Canadian Police College, Canada's version of DoDPI. These polygraphers are taught numerical scoring and disdain the global approach. To determine if these examiners were indeed uninfluenced by extrapolygraphic cues, we compared the examiners' verdicts contained in their written reports with the verdicts they should have obtained given their own numerical scores for 276 examinations. For 59 subjects, the examiners contradicted the conclusions dictated by their own numerical scores by offering written verdicts that were not supported by the charts. It is of considerable interest that in 93% of these cases, they offered written opinions favoring the truthfulness of the subjects by assigning inconclusive verdicts to charts numerically scored deceptive and truthful verdicts to charts numerically scored inconclusive. These charts were blindly rescored by different examiners. By comparing these blind scores to the original scores, it was possible to determine if the original examiners were more likely to generate numerical scores indicating truthfulness than the blind examiners. This was indeed the case (Iacono, 1999), suggesting that the numerical scoring of the original examiners was also influenced by their belief that suspects were more likely to be innocent than was indicated by the physiological data.

The final interesting observation to emerge from these analyses was that the original examiner's written opinion regarding truthfulness was more likely to be accurate than his numerical score or the blind examiners' rescores. For subjects who were identified as innocent because someone else confessed to the crime covered by the CQT they took, the original examiners were correct 90% of the time, compared to a 70% hit rate for their numerical scores and a 55% hit rate for the blind scorers.

Collectively, these findings have a number of interesting implications. First, they indicate that examiners are indeed influenced by extrapolygraphic data, and that these data affect both their ultimate decisions and their numerical scores. Second, they suggest that at some level, the examiners are aware that the psychophysiological assessment is biased against the innocent, so they tend not to trust numerical scores that do not indicate truthfulness. And third, they indicate that examiners can improve their accuracy when they rely on case facts and other extraneous information rather than basing their decisions entirely on the polygraph chart tracings. One may be tempted to use such data to argue that blind chart scoring underestimates the accuracy of polygraph verdicts, yet it is critical to keep in mind that the only reason the CQT is seen as having probative value is because it is assumed that the psychophysiological part of the assessment provides a scientifically valid method for detecting liars. No court of law would accept as evidence the opinion of a human "truth verifier," a skilled interviewer who can use the available evidence to reach a correct judgment. The fact that these data show that the original examiner is more accurate when he or she overrides the charts speaks to the invalidity of the psychophysiological test when used to determine truthfulness.

FIELD VS. LABORATORY INVESTIGATIONS

Polygraph studies can be divided into two broad categories, depending on the circumstances under which the test is administered. Field studies, like our study with the RCMP discussed above, involve real-life cases and circumstances. The subjects are actual criminal suspects. Laboratory studies require naive volunteers to simulate criminal behavior by enacting a mock crime. The latter approach provides unambiguous criteria for establishing ground truth but cannot be used to establish the accuracy of the procedure because the motivational and emotional concerns of the subjects are too dissimilar from those involved in real-life examinations. Unlike those faced with an actual criminal investigation, guilty subjects in the laboratory have little incentive to try and "beat" the test, and both guilty and innocent subjects have little to fear if they are diagnosed deceptive. Administering the CQT to laboratory subjects is especially likely to lead to overestimates of accuracy for the innocent. Innocent subjects can reasonably be expected to respond more strongly to the potentially embarrassing control questions concerning their personal integrity and honesty than to the relevant questions dealing with a simulated crime they carried out only to satisfy experimental requirements. On the other hand, laboratory research does permit more efficient investigation of the influence of "extra-guilt" variables and the relative merits of different testing procedures.

It is interesting to note that two laboratory studies that used mock circumstances designed to approximate some of those found in real life produced error rates that were very different from those of typical studies. Patrick and Iacono (1989) used prison inmates who were led to believe that failing a CQT could possibly lead to reprisals from other inmates who were counting on them to appear innocent on their tests. Forman and McCauley (1986) had their participants choose to be either innocent or guilty, the latter choice leading to a larger monetary reward if they passed the CQT. In these two studies, the average accuracy for the CQT was 73%, considerably lower than the 88% reported for laboratory studies without such verisimilitude (Kircher, Horowitz, & Raskin, 1988). Although these studies raise hopes that laboratory manipulations approximating real life may be possible, because there are so many differences between the two situations, it is unlikely that any laboratory study will successfully simulate all the aspects of a real-life investigation. By illustrating that simple improvements to the experimental protocol can produce profound shifts in hit rates, these reports do, however, point out the difficulty in relying on a typical mock crime study to estimate real-life accuracy.

Laboratory studies of the GKT are also likely to overestimate its accuracy, more so for guilty than innocent individuals. Well-designed laboratory experiments construct a scenario in which guilty participants must attend to details of the crime that the examiner expects perpetrators to know, and which can be used to construct the GKT. In real life, a criminal may not attend to the aspects of a crime that an investigator views as salient, and many details may be forgotten. On the other hand, if a person does remember the details of a real-life crime, these should evoke greater physiological reactions, thereby making it easier to detect the guilty.

Unfortunately, The GKT is not used to any significant extent by field polygraph examiners in the United States or Canada, a surprising state of affairs considering its unique advantages. There appear to be two reasons for this. The first is that the CQT is much easier to construct than the GKT, and there is a prevailing belief among field examiners that it is virtually infallible (Patrick & Iacono, 1991b). The second is that to construct a GKT, there must be salient details of the crime that are known only to the perpetrator. Not all crimes meet this criterion. For example, alleged sexual assaults in which the question of force versus consent is the only issue to be resolved by the polygraph test would not be amenable to a GKT. Podlesny (1993; Podlesny, Nimmich, & Budowle, 1995) reviewed case facts from criminal investigations referred to the FBI polygraph unit and concluded that only a small proportion of these cases (5–13%) were amenable to a GKT. However, a limitation of this work (acknowledged by the author) is that the crimes investigated by the FBI—that is, federal offenses, which do not ordinarily include crimes such as burglary, assault, and homicide—are not representative of the types of cases handled by local police forces. A more important limitation is that these case files were not prepared with the understanding that they should contain information suitable for the development of GKT items. The best information for a GKT item would not necessarily be useful as evidence. For instance, the decor of a room where a murder was committed may be irrelevant as evidence but a highly useful source of GKT material. As Iacono and Lykken (1997c) noted, a review of police files prior to the discovery of the evidentiary value of fingerprints would probably turn up few cases where fingerprint evidence would have been available. A further issue even in cases where a GKT would be applicable is that the key information must not be revealed to innocent suspects (although see Bradley & Rettinger, 1992). This is a significant problem in North America, where details of a crime often appear in the popular press soon after an investigation begins. However, the fact that the GKT is used routinely by police in countries such as Japan (Yamamura & Miyata, 1990) and Israel (Elaad, 1990) suggests that these obstacles are not insurmountable.

Unfortunately, only the CQT has been subject to extensive evaluation using field investigations. For this reason, in addressing the validity of the CQT, we focus on what we have learned from the field studies conducted to date. There are no field studies of the employee screening test and only two of the GKT, facts that limit our ability to use field studies to evaluate these techniques.

Problems Establishing Ground Truth

The advantage of field investigations, that they are based on actual crimes, is also a significant drawback because prima facie evidence of innocence or guilt is often lacking. One unsatisfactory procedure to deal with this problem involves relying on judicial outcomes to establish ground truth. This approach is compromised by the following problems: (a) some people are falsely convicted of crimes; (b) for practical reasons, some innocent individuals will plead guilty to crimes they did not commit; (c) because of legal technicalities that prevent the admission of evidence and the notion that one must be proved guilty beyond a reasonable doubt, many guilty defendants will escape conviction; and (d) the judicial decision may not be independent of the polygraph test results if these results influenced the proceedings.

Another method for operationalizing ground truth is to rely on confessions to identify the culpable and clear the innocent. Although occasionally confessions are false, and those who confess may differ in important ways from those who do not, the major problem with this strategy concerns the likelihood that the confession is not independent of the original polygraph examiner's assessment. For reasons that are unrelated to test accuracy, confessions are associated almost exclusively with charts that indicate a deceptive outcome. When this occurs, the verified cases included in a validity study will be biased in favor of demonstrating high accuracy for the technique.

To make this point clear, consider the following example. Ten women are suspects in a criminal investigation. A polygrapher tests them one by one until a deceptive outcome is obtained, say on the sixth suspect tested. (Under these circumstances, the remaining four women typically would not be tested unless the crime was believed to involve more than one perpetrator.) According to usual practice, the examiner then attempts to extract a confession from the sixth suspect. If the examinee fails to confess, her guilt or innocence cannot be confirmed. It is possible that the polygrapher committed two errors in testing these six cases: the person with the deceptive chart may have been innocent, and one of those tested before her could have been guilty. In the absence of confession-backed verification, however, the polygraph records from these six cases will never be included as part of a sample in a validity study. On the other hand, if the sixth suspect does confess, these six charts, all of which confirm the original examiner's assessment, will be included. The resulting sample of cases would consist entirely of charts the original examiner judged correctly and would never include cases in which an error was made. As Iacono (1991) has shown, if polygraph testing actually had no-better-than-chance accuracy, by basing validity studies on confession-verified charts selected in this manner, a study could misleadingly conclude that the technique was virtually infallible. Given how cases are selected in confession studies of validity, it should not be surprising that field validity studies typically report that the original examiner was 100% correct (or nearly so; see Raskin, Honts, & Kircher, 1997b) for the cases chosen for study. The case selection method assures this result.

Another approach to establishing ground truth is to use panels composed of legal experts to review case facts, disregarding technicalities related to evidentiary rules. If the panel members can reach a consensus, their decision can serve as the ground truth criterion. This approach has been tried in two studies (Bersh, 1969; Barland & Raskin, 1976), both of which are methodologically flawed. The panels in Bersh were given the results of the polygraph tests as well as posttest confessions that followed failed tests as part of the case files they reviewed, thus confounding the polygraph outcomes with their verdicts. In Barland and Raskin (1976), the panel had difficulty reaching consensus in many of the cases, the case data have been characterized by the authors as inadequate (Barland, 1982; Raskin, 1986), and panel decisions were also confounded by the panelists being given confessions that followed failed tests as part of the case record.

Because the panel approach need not be limited by the flaws of these two studies, Dohm and Iacono (1993) carried out an investigation to determine if there was promise in this method for establishing ground truth. Their study addressed two questions: Can panels reliably make ground truth determinations from case files that have the polygraph data, including confessions following failed tests, removed from them? and Can panels make accurate decisions? Dohm and Iacono investigated how well three different six-member panels composed of lay persons, attorneys, or police officers could pick the guilty party by reviewing case file data. All the cases used in this study were from military criminal investigations, and all included a confession that was elicited after one of the suspects failed a CQT. In addition, all had multiple suspects. In a study such as this, it was important to avoid one-suspect case files that would necessarily lead panelists to conclude that the only individual investigated was most likely guilty. As the files were selected because someone confessed, relying on one-suspect case files would serve to inflate the accuracy of the panels. In every case, two judges who reviewed the case files before their being given to the panels verified by consensus that the confessions were to the charges contained in the CQT relevant questions. With respect to the first question posed above, the reliability of decision making did not differ as a function of panel composition; the overall panel reliability was about .75. Because polygraphers assert their tests are over 90% accurate, to avoid the criticism that a mismatch between the panel's determination of ground truth and the polygraph verdict was due to inconsistency in panel deliberations, much higher panel reliability would be desirable. With respect to the second question, the panels did a poor job identifying correctly the suspect who confessed, hitting on the correct individual less than 25% of the time. Hence, the panel approach to determining ground truth was neither especially reliable nor valid. Unless there is a convincing demonstration that the panel approach can overcome these serious liabilities, it would be inadvisable to rely on panels to establish ground truth.

Obtaining Independent Evidence of Guilt and Innocence

Using judicial outcomes, confessions, and panel decisions to determine ground truth are all unacceptable options. Of the three, confessions hold the greatest appeal as a potential criterion because they provide the least ambiguous indication of guilt. However, as noted above, confessions that are elicited because someone failed a polygraph test cannot be used to verify that test because the confession was not independent of test outcome. Confessions that arise outside the context of the polygraph examination do not suffer from this problem and could be used to establish ground truth.

Iacono and Lykken (1997a; Iacono, 1999) have outlined how a field study of CQT validity could be executed that would accomplish this result. To eliminate the contamination that arises when confessions are used to establish ground truth, an adequate field study would require that a law enforcement agency administer polygraph tests to all willing criminal suspects brought in for questioning but without posttest interrogation of the suspects and without scoring the charts or communicating the test results to anyone. The charts would be sealed and stored awaiting resolution of the case. At the time a case was to be closed, an independent panel would review the available evidence to see if it could be used to verify the issues covered by the CQT relevant questions presented to suspects. In this manner, the ground truth criterion, which could still be confession-based (because now whatever confession arose would have been independent of the results of the sealed polygraph exam), would be obtained independently of the outcome of the CQT. The polygraph charts from those cases where the panel was unanimous in its determination of who was guilty and innocent (cases where the confession was retracted, contradicted by other evidence, or was otherwise unconvincing could be discarded by the panel) would then be scored blindly and compared with the criterion judgments. Practical concerns, such as those focused on suspects' rights, would have to be addressed before such a project could be launched. Moreover, because police polygraphers already are convinced that the CQT has near-perfect validity and there is no indication that the use of polygraphy by law enforcement agencies will be restricted, police agencies are unlikely to cooperate with such a project. However, as long as no study such as this exists, it will not be possible to determine the field accuracy of any polygraph technique.

WHAT CAN BE CONCLUDED ABOUT POLYGRAPH VALIDITY

The literature relevant to the validity of polygraph testing has been reviewed repeatedly in the past decade. Consequently, there are many sources the interested reader can turn to for insights and perspective that extend the review presented below (Abrams, 1989; Bashore & Rapp, 1993; Ben-Shakar & Furedy, 1990; Furedy & Heselgrave, 1988; Honts & Quick, 1996; Honts, Raskin, & Kircher, 1997; Iacono, 1995, 1999; Iacono & Lykken, 1997a, 1997b, 1997c; Iacono & Patrick, 1988, 1997; Lykken, 1998; Raskin, Honts, & Kircher, 1997a, 1997b; Saxe, 1991, 1994).

CONTROL QUESTION TEST

In the first edition of this book, we (Iacono & Patrick, 1987) reviewed all of the field studies available at that time. Ignoring the investigations that used panels to establish ground truth, these studies fell into two distinct groups. One set, conducted by proponents of polygraphy, was published in police trade journals. These investigations all reported high accuracy for the CQT (about 90% for both criterion-innocent and -guilty subjects). The other set, consisting of investigations published in peer reviewed scientific journals, reported much lower accuracy (about 57% and 76%, respectively, for criterion-innocent and guilty subjects). Both sets of studies had serious methodological shortcomings in that they either failed to specify how ground truth was determined or selected cases because a confession followed a "deception indicated" polygraph test. For the reasons we have stated above as well as in our 1987 review, none of these investigations is adequate for evaluating polygraph test accuracy. In this section, we focus on field studies since 1987 that deal with CQT validity.

The most important new study was that of Patrick and Iacono (1991b). In this RCMP field study involving over 400 cases, we attempted to circumvent the confession-bias confound by reviewing police files for evidence of ground truth that was collected outside of the context of the polygraph examination (e.g., a confession by someone who did not take a polygraph test, a statement that no crime was committed because items believed stolen were actually misplaced). Independent evidence of ground truth was uncovered for 24 criterion-innocent suspects and one criterion-guilty suspect. The fact that it was easier to come by independent evidence of the innocence rather than the guilt of someone taking a CQT stemmed from how the police use polygraph tests to assist their investigations. Already noted was the fact that polygraph tests are typically administered in cases where the evidence is ambiguous and the police have exhaustively explored available leads to no avail. When a case reaches this point, the investigating officer is hoping that polygraph testing will help close out the case. Ideally, the suspect will fail and confess, thus giving the investigating officer incriminating evidence that can be used to prosecute the suspect. However, if the suspect merely fails, with no new evidentiary leads to follow, the case is effectively closed, with the police concluding that the individual who failed is guilty. On the other hand, if the suspect passes, the case is often left open, and the search for new suspects and evidence continues.

For those independently confirmed as innocent by Patrick and Iacono (1991b), the blind rescoring of their polygraph charts produced a hit rate of 57%. Because chance accuracy is 50%, this result indicates the CQT has little better than chance accuracy with the innocent. It also indicates that innocent people are indeed often more disturbed by relevant than control questions. Because only one criterion-guilty person was identified in this investigation, it was not possible to estimate the accuracy of the CQT with persons independently confirmed as guilty.

Although there are no scientifically credible data regarding the accuracy of the CQT with guilty people, there is good reason to doubt the validity of truthful polygraph verdicts. Honts, Raskin, and Kircher (1994) showed that with less than a half hour of instruction regarding CQT theory and how to recognize control and relevant questions, a substantial majority of guilty subjects in a mock crime study could learn to escape detection by augmenting their autonomic responses to control questions. They were able to do this using both physical and mental countermeasures such as biting the tongue or subtracting 7 serially from a number over 200 when the control question was asked. Moreover, experienced examiners were unable to identify those subjects who employed countermeasures successfully.

There are several field studies of CQT accuracy besides that of Patrick and Iacono (1991) that have emerged in the past decade (Honts, 1996; Honts & Raskin, 1988; Raskin, Kircher, Honts, & Horowitz, 1988). All three of these studies are affected by the confession-bias confound and thus cannot be used to estimate field validity. The study by Raskin et al. was an improvement over the typical confession study, in that evidence corroborating the confession was also required to establish ground truth. However, although this additional requirement increases confidence in the legitimacy of the confession, it does not circumvent the confession-bias confound because the corroborating information could not have been obtained without the confession following the failed CQT.

The Directed Lie Test

Little is known about the validity of the DLT. Although one field study involving the DLT has been published (Honts & Raskin, 1988), only a single directed lie question was used, and this question was embedded in a conventional CQT, making it difficult to determine how the polygraph tests would have fared had directed lie controls been used exclusively. The DLT is likely to be especially susceptible to countermeasures. When the examiner introduces the directed lies to the subject, they are explained as questions designed to elicit a response pattern indicative of lying. Hence, their purpose is made transparent to subjects who may understand that a strong response to these questions will help them pass the test. An additional problem with directed lies is that the examiner has no idea what issues are covered by the directed lies and how strong an emotional response they are capable of eliciting. For instance, if the directed lie was "Have you ever done something that you later regretted?" and the subject had killed someone in a drunk driving incident, might not the emotions elicited by the directed lie be stronger autonomic responses than the material covered by a relevant question related to theft, fraud, and so on?

THE GUILTY KNOWLEDGE TEST

Of the three classes of polygraph tests considered in this review, only the GKT is spurned by practicing polygraphers. Because of this, there is little data available from real-life GKT applications that can be used to evaluate its validity. Laboratory demonstrations of simulated crimes have shown the GKT to be highly accurate. A comprehensive review of mock-crime investigations conducted between 1959 and 1987 (Iacono & Patrick, 1988) revealed mean hit rates of 82% and 95% for guilty and innocent participants, respectively. The GKT was 100% accurate in classifying innocent subjects in 6 of 11 studies. All but two of these laboratory experiments found that false-negative errors were more common than false-positive, indicating that the GKT may be biased in favor of guilty suspects. Other more recent reviews have reported similar results and conclusions (Ben-Shakar & Furedy, 1990; Lykken, 1998; Raskin et al., 1997a).

GKT studies in which ERPs have served as the dependent measure have been similarly impressive in their classification accuracy. Farwell and Donchin (1986; see also Farwell & Donchin, 1991) reported perfect classification of "guilty" and "innocent" subjects based on a comparison of their P300 reactions to relevant and irrelevant items of information. High rates of detection have subsequently been reported in work by Peter Rosenfeld and colleagues (Johnson & Rosenfeld, 1992; Rosenfeld, Angell, Johnson, & Qian, 1991; Rosenfeld et al., 1988; Rosenfeld, Nasman, Whalen, Cantwell, & Mazzeri, 1987), and John Allen and colleagues (Allen & Iacono, 1997; Allen, Iacono, & Danielson, 1992; van Hoof, Brunia, & Allen, 1996). Other investigators have also successfully applied ERP paradigms to detection deception (e.g., Boaz, Perry, Raney, Fieschler, & Shuman, 1991). Because the P300 is more directly linked to cognitive and memory processes involved in recognition of previously learned material (Allen et al., 1992; Bashore & Rapp, 1993), it offers a potentially more sensitive and conceptually informative approach to the detection of guilty knowledge.

Because the test is virtually never used in North America, no field studies of the GKT have yet been conducted here. However, two studies have been reported by investigators in Israel. Elaad (1990) examined skin resistance tracings from the GKT records of 50 innocent and 48 guilty criminal suspects, tested by examiners from the Israel Police Scientific Interrogation Unit, whose criterion status had been established via confession. The GKT was administered in all cases following the CQT, and included from one to six questions ($M = 2.04$) repeated from two to four times ($M = 3.28$). Using blind chart evaluation and predefined score classification criteria (cf. Lykken, 1959) and excluding inconclusives, 98% of the innocent and 42% of the guilty examinees were correctly classified. Using score classification criteria that optimized discriminability, 94% of the innocent and 65% of the guilty suspects were correctly classified.

In a follow-up investigation, Elaad, Ginton, and Jungman (1992) examined both respiration and skin resistance response records from confession-verified innocent and guilty polygraph examinees ($N = 40$ per group). As in the initial study, polygraph tests were conducted by Israeli police examiners, and in all but one case the GKT was administered following a standard CQT. GKTs included from one to six questions ($M = 1.80$) repeated from two to four times ($M = 3.25$). Using blind chart evaluations and a priori score classification criteria, decisions based on skin resistance scores alone (excluding inconclusives) were 97% accurate for innocent suspects and 53% accurate for guilty suspects. When decisions were based on a combination of both skin resistance and respiration response scores, the hit rates for innocent and guilty examinees were 94% and 75%, respectively.

The results of these two studies indicate, consistent with a substantial body of laboratory research, that the GKT is highly accurate with innocent suspects. These data also suggest that the GKT may have a substantial false-negative error rate in real-life cases. However, there are two prominent methodological weaknesses in these studies that constrain the conclusions that can be drawn. The first is that the GKTs in these studies contained an average of only two questions. This compromises test sensitivity because it lowers the odds that information uniquely salient to the perpetrator would be represented on the test. Relevant to this, the laboratory GKT study that produced the lowest hit rate for guilty participants reported to date (45%) was one in which a highly abbreviated three-item GKT was used (Forman & McCauley, 1986).

A further problem is that the GKTs in these field studies were (with just one exception) administered as an addendum to a full-length CQT. The physiological response habituation resulting from repeated presentations of the accusatory relevant and control questions on the initial test would almost certainly have the effect of diminishing response differentiation between critical and noncritical GKT items among guilty examinees. In fact, O'Toole, Yuille, Patrick, and Iacono (1994) demonstrated precisely this effect in an analogue study involving administration of both CQT and GKT examinations. Compounding this problem is the fact that the GKT question sets in the Elaad et al. studies were presented repeatedly to examinees (i.e., an average of three times). Empirical research has consistently demonstrated that when an examinee is administered the same GKT repeatedly, accuracy diminishes with each repetition (Balloun & Holmes, 1978; Lieblich, Naftali, Shmueli, & Kugelmass, 1974; Orne, Thackray, & Paskewitz, 1972).

How susceptible is the GKT to countermeasures? Lykken (1960) suggested that any response pattern that deviates significantly from random can serve as a flag that countermeasures have been used to conceal guilt. For example, examinees who deliberately augmented their reactions to one irrelevant alternative on each test question could still give themselves away by consistently exhibiting their second largest response to the relevant alternative. Similarly, a response pattern in which reactions to relevant alternatives were consistently the smallest would be statistically aberrant and suggestive of distortion.

Honts, Devitt, Winbush, and Kircher (1996) recently questioned this perspective. In this study, 40 college students were administered a GKT concerning a burglary of a residence that 30 of them had witnessed on videotape. Countermeasure participants were given instructions in how to augment their reactions to noncritical GKT alternatives by pressing their toes on the floor or counting backwards by seven. Using various procedures to contrast responses to key and foil alternatives for the five GKT questions, the authors reported that detectability was diminished for guilty individuals who used countermeasures, in particular those who employed physical countermeasures. The authors concluded that the GKT "has no special immunity to the effects of countermeasures" (p. 84).

However, Lykken's (1960) point was not that the GKT is immune to dissimulation, but rather that efforts to distort the test result are potentially detectable via a probabilistic analysis of the overall distribution of test responses. A significant weakness in the Honts et al. study is that the GKT procedure included a mere 5 questions, as opposed to 25 in the Lykken study, precluding the type of distributional analysis that Lykken performed. Acknowledging this problem, the authors attempted to deal with it by performing a bootstrap statistical analysis to simulate "what likely would have occurred if we had 25 [GKT] series for analyses" (p. 89). However, the bootstrap statistical technique (cf. Simon, 1992) depends critically on the assumption that the test sample (i.e., 5-question GKT in this study) is a random sample of the larger population data set (i.e., 25-question GKT)—a highly questionable assumption in this instance, considering factors (e.g., habituation, practice) that could systematically affect patterns of responding over the course of a more extended question set. Consequently, this study—although predictably showing that "guilty" examinees can simulate a "truthful" pattern of responding on a GKT—does not present a serious challenge to Lykken's earlier demonstration that the dissimulation effort itself is potentially detectable.

GKTs based on brain electrophysiology may provide the surest protection against countermeasures. It is easy to figure out how to manipulate autonomic reactions, but how does one enhance a brain potential? Because the brain response of interest is registered within a few hundred milliseconds, before it is possible to react behaviorally, it would be difficult to alter one's response to a GKT key without also affecting the response to the irrelevant alternatives (Iacono, 1999).

EMPLOYEE SCREENING

Because almost everyone recognizes that the R/I test is biased against the innocent (a fact borne out by a recent study by Horowitz, Kircher, Honts, & Raskin, 1997), it has been replaced by the CQT for specific incident investigations. However, the variant of this procedure that was referred to earlier as the R/R test is widely used by the government for employee screening. In view of its importance to national security and its impact on the civil rights of government workers, it is surprising how little empirical evidence exists concerning the validity of this technique. No published validation studies have appeared to date in scientific journals.

Although the R/R test appears more credible on its face than the traditional R/I test, its premises and implementation have also been challenged. Heightened reactions to certain specific questions may occur for reasons other than deceptiveness due to, for example, indignation about being asked that question; exposure to some related issue through the media; or knowledge of someone else who has engaged in the sort of activity covered by that question. Moreover, there is no reason to assume that enhanced reactions to an evocative question will subside once the examinee has offered an explanation for those enhanced reactions to the examiner. In fact, the CQT rests on the opposing assumption that truthful subjects will remain worried about control questions even after these items have been modified to accommodate their admissions. These criticisms give rise to the concern that like its R/I counterpart, the R/R technique is likely to be associated with a high false-positive error rate. In fact, however, as the R/R test is applied by government agents, the false-negative error rate seems to be a much more substantial concern.

Historically, the base rate of deceptive outcomes on Defense Department screening examinations has been very low. Honts (1991), aggregating agency data for the years 1986–1989, reported that of the 31,085 cases in which conclusive opinions were rendered, only 167 (0.4%) yielded deceptive outcomes. In 129 of these cases, the examinee subsequently admitted to engaging in activities that could potentially have accounted for the positive test result. In 1996, a total of 7,933 screening examinations yielded conclusive opinions, with deceptive outcomes obtained in 163 cases (2%). Most of these cases were considered to be resolved as a function of relatively minor admissions by examinees that did not result in further adjudication (U.S. Department of Defense, 1996).

Two interesting points emerge from these statistics. First, the rate of positive (deceptive) outcomes for these polygraph screening tests has historically been low. Even if all of these tests were false positives (and there is no evidence this was so), the false-positive error rate would be trivial (at most 2%). Second, a greater number of deceptive outcomes was obtained during the year 1996 than in the years 1986–1989 combined, a period involving nearly four times as many examinations. It seems likely that this shift is connected at least indirectly to two high-profile espionage cases that came to light during the 1990s.

In February 1994, following a year-long investigation, career CIA officer Aldrich J. Ames was arrested for selling classified information to the former Soviet Union and to Russia over a period of almost nine years, activities that irreparably damaged a number of CIA operations and led to the deaths of at least 10 U.S. agents stationed undercover in the former Soviet Union (Weiner, 1994). The case was an embarrassment to the CIA because Ames had gone undetected for so long despite obvious indiscretions on his part (e.g., drunkenness, absenteeism, spending sprees), and to CIA polygraph examiners because they had cleared him on polygraph screening tests conducted in 1986 and 1991 when Ames was engaged in selling secrets to operatives in Moscow. The failure of the polygraph in the Ames case could be one instance in which an "undersocialized type" succeeded in passing a polygraph test by offering the examiner plausible but innocuous explanations for incriminating responses rather than admitting guilt. Indeed, Ames commented to reporters that passing a polygraph test merely requires "confidence and a friendly relationship with the examiner . . . rapport, where you smile and you make him think you like him" (Burns, 1994, p. 3A).

In November 1996, Harold J. Nicholson, a branch chief in the CIA's counterterrorism center, was charged with transmitting national secrets to Russia over a two-year period in exchange for cash payments totaling approximately $120,000. Although his crimes were not considered to be as damaging as those of Ames, the discovery of Nicholson's treachery rocked the U.S. intelligence community because he was the highest-ranking CIA official ever accused of espionage and prior to his apprehension had been considered a rising star in the agency (Smith & Hall, 1996). Following a year-long investigation, Nicholson was arrested in Washington as he prepared to board a connecting flight to New York, en route to what authorities believed was a scheduled meeting with Russian agents in Zurich. Of interest to the present discussion, CIA and FBI officials reported that suspicions about Nicholson's activities first arose after he failed a routine, espionage-related polygraph screening test in October 1995.

These two recent cases vividly illustrate the importance of polygraph screening procedures within federal government agencies and, particularly in the case of Ames, the serious damage that can result when these screening tests fail. The noted increase in the rate of "deceptive" outcomes in DoD screening tests during 1996 as compared to the years 1986–1989 could in part reflect heightened concerns about false-negative errors aroused by the Ames case. Of course, as the bias toward detecting perpetrators increases, the potential for false-positive errors increases accordingly. This is obviously a problem in the screening context, where the vast majority of examinees undergoing screening tests are likely to be innocent of any wrongdoing.

Research conducted at DoDPI offers some insight into why so few individuals fail polygraph screening tests. In their unpublished government report, Barland, Honts, and Barger (1989) described the results of a large analogue study that was designed to assess the validity of periodic espionage screening tests utilized by federal government agencies, including the Department of Defense, the National Security Agency, the CIA, the Military Intelligence division of the U.S. Army, and the Air Force Office of Special Investigations. Participants in the study were 207 Army personnel and civilian employees at the Ft. McClellan military base in Alabama. Forty-four of these participants went through complex espionage simulations in which they met with an agent purportedly engaged in espionage who recruited them to collaborate in this activity. Consequent to their recruitment, these "guilty" participants committed acts of mock espionage in which they copied or stole classified documents—that is, activities that periodic screening tests were designed to detect. Subsequently, all study participants underwent polygraph screening tests conducted by an experienced federal examiner. Examinees were advised that any admissions of criminal behavior or security violations could result in an internal investigation that might damage their careers.

The results of this study indicated a high rate of correct classification for innocent participants, but a very low hit rate for guilty participants. Excluding inconclusive decisions, 94% (105/112) of innocent participants were correctly classified based on original examiner evaluations; this hit rate climbed to 97% when 4 participants were excluded who, although innocent of the mock espionage, confessed to real-world security violations during the polygraph posttest. For guilty participants, the hit rate (excluding inconclusives) for original examiners was only 34%. Subsequently, Honts (1992) examined whether degree of experience in polygraph security testing played a role in these results and concluded that it did not; consistent with Barland et al. (1989), Honts found a very low hit rate (40%) for guilty participants whether screening tests were administered by examiners who conducted screening tests primarily, or by examiners who conducted specific-incident examinations almost exclusively.

The Barland et al. (1989) report thus confirmed what was evident from government data on the outcome of counterintelligence screening polygraph testing: the polygraph test employed by government agencies to screen for violations of national security is highly susceptible to false-negative errors. Of course, the findings of an unpublished analogue study should be interpreted with caution. However, the Barland et al. study—which involved procedures and motivational conditions that were quite realistic, and was conducted by government-employed investigators whose interests would (if anything) have been contrary to the results obtained—raises serious questions about the validity of the polygraph screening test. The high false-negative rate for this procedure could be related to several factors, but the most likely is related to the fact that the examiners in this study, who were unaware of the base rate of guilt (about 50%), were following the established field practice of passing almost everyone who took the test. Because periodic screening in real life is in a sense a fishing expedition in which the probability of a catch (i.e., the base rate of spying) is presumed to be very low, and because examiners are likely to be discouraged from falsely accusing innocent people, many of whom are high-ranking, well-educated and -trained government officials with many years of government service, testing and decision making practices in the screening context are likely to be biased toward finding few examinees deceptive (Barland et al., 1989; Honts, 1994).

Since the Barland et al. (1989) report was completed, a foreword has been added by the director of DoDPI (Michael H. Capps) which states that these findings have prompted the agency to develop "a new type of security examination which corrected the problem of false negative errors discovered in the research reported here." However, details of this revised procedure and relevant validational data were not publicly available at the time of this writing.

THE POLYGRAPH IN COURT

THE ADMISSION OF POLYGRAPH TESTIMONY

Polygraph tests often find their way into criminal court through one of two routes. One involves the stipulated test in which polygraph examinations are administered with the prior agreement of prosecuting and defense attorneys.

Often, the prosecution will agree to a stipulated test when the case against the defendant is weak. In these circumstances, if the suspect passes the test, the charges are dropped. If the test is failed, the prosecution reserves the right to submit the polygraph findings to the court. About half of U.S. states endorse the use of stipulated tests, but Canadian courts refuse them.

Another way that polygraph results may enter a courtroom is over the objection of the prosecution in cases where it can "advance the cause of the defense." This practice is allowed by law in New Mexico, provided the polygraph test administration satisfies certain standards. It is also a strategy increasingly adopted by defense attorneys who wish to determine if current circumstances favor the admission of polygraph tests. Often, a hearing is requested before a judge who is asked to determine if polygraph tests satisfy standards for scientific evidence in light of new laws and rulings and/or in light of recent developments in the field that may indicate polygraphy has been improved significantly since the last time the court considered admitting such evidence.

In 1924, in *Frye v. United States*, the U.S. Supreme Court established the rules for what constituted acceptable scientific evidence. In this case, James Frye was denied the opportunity to have considered as evidence the results of a polygraph test administered by William Marston, the "father" of modern polygraphy. Although the *Frye* ruling is no longer relevant to federal courts, it is still influential to the laws of many states that followed the *Frye* precedent of requiring "general acceptance" of a technique by the relevant scientific community before its results can be admitted as evidence. With the current federal criteria for scientific evidence, laid out in *Daubert v. Merrell Dow Pharmaceuticals* (1993), the general acceptance of a technique among scientists remains important along with other considerations, such as whether the technique is based on sound scientific principles and methods or has been the subject of scientific peer review. Hence, following motions submitted by defense attorneys, many courts hold hearings based on principles outlined in *Frye* or *Daubert* to determine if a defendant's passed polygraph test should be admitted as evidence (see Faigman, Kaye, Saks, & Sanders, 1997, for a more thorough review of the legal status of polygraph testing in the United States). Such hearings are now likely to be influenced by a recent Supreme Court ruling that dealt specifically with the admissibility of polygraph tests. In *U.S. v. Scheffer* (1998), the Court ruled that defendants in military court martial proceedings do not have a right to admit as evidence the results of exculpatory polygraph tests. Because the court noted in its decision that there is no consensus in the scientific community that polygraph evidence is valid, it is possible that *Scheffer* will reduce the likelihood that polygraph tests will be admitted as a result of *Frye* or *Daubert* hearings.

When a defense attorney arranges for a client to take a polygraph test, the results of the test are protected by attorney-client privilege. If the defendant fails the test, the results would not be divulged, because doing so would only serve to undermine the defendant's credibility. A test administered under these circumstances is considered to be "friendly." Such a test stands in contrast to an "adversarial" test administered by the police, the results of which would be known to the prosecution. Because fear of the consequences of being detected is considered to be important to the valid outcome of a test, and there appears to be less to lose and therefore less to fear with a friendly test, it seems likely that friendly tests would be easier to pass than adversarial tests. Moreover, because the defendant is paying the polygrapher with the hope of passing the test, the examiner is being pressured, at least by the defendant, to produce the desired outcome. In a procedure that is as subjective and unstandardized as the CQT, it is easy to imagine how subtle adjustments to the procedure could increase the likelihood of friendly tests being passed. Unfortunately, there are no data attesting to the validity of friendly tests. All the existing field studies deal with adversarial tests.

How Juries Evaluate Polygraph Evidence

An important issue surrounding the use of polygraph evidence in court is the weight that is likely to be attached to this evidence by juries. Because of the scientific and technical aura that surrounds the practice of polygraph testing—an aura enhanced by alternative names such as "psychophysiological detection of deception" and "forensic psychophysiology"—and because the polygraph appears to strike to the heart of the issue at hand (i.e., Is the defendant telling the truth?), concerns have been expressed that juries may assign excessive probative weight to this evidence. This argument has in fact been used successfully to exclude polygraph testimony in court (see e.g., *United States v. Alexander*, 1975).

A modest empirical literature exists on this topic. The results of more recent studies contrast quite markedly with those of older studies, which suggested that polygraph evidence could indeed be quite influential in affecting juror decision making. In a poll of jurors conducted after a criminal trial in which polygraph evidence was admitted, Forkusch (1939) reported that 5 of 10 respondents accepted the testimony of the polygraph expert "without question," and 6 respondents indicated that they considered the polygraph results conclusive. Koffler (1957) asked mock jurors to arrive at a verdict based on hypothetical case evidence, and then asked them to reassess their decision on the basis of new evidence indicating that the defendant had taken a polygraph test and failed. The majority (85%) of jurors changed their vote from innocent to guilty when presented with the polygraph outcome and advised that it was 99.5% accurate. However, in a similar study employing a similar methodology, Carlson, Pasano, and Januzzo (1977) reported that 25% of participants reversed their decision of innocent when presented with polygraph evidence purported to be 95% accurate.

Subsequently, Markwart and Lynch (1979) presented polygraph evidence to juror panels during the course of a mock trial and found a significant difference in the percentage of guilty verdicts when polygraph evidence was introduced that was unfavorable to the accused as opposed to when no polygraph evidence was introduced (66% vs. 12%). Cavoukian and Heselgrave (1980) found that when jurors rendered verdicts individually, based on written case scenarios, polygraph evidence favoring the defendant tended to reduce the number of guilty decisions, although this effect was mitigated by an instruction that the polygraph was only 80% accurate.

More recently, Spanos, Myers, DuBreuil, and Pawlak (1992) assessed the relative impact on juror decision making of polygraph evidence and eyewitness testimony in a mock trial context and reported that the former had minimal influence in comparison to the latter. Myers and Arbuthnot (1997) examined the impact of CQT and GKT polygraph testimony on individual and group juror decision making when a "deceptive" polygraph test outcome (described as "80–90% accurate") was presented in the context of a videotaped rape-murder trial simulation. These authors found that neither type of polygraph evidence influenced verdicts significantly in comparison with a no-polygraph control condition. Furthermore, jurors rated both types of polygraph testimony as less influential in their decision making than other forms of evidence presented during the trial (i.e., eyewitness testimony, forensic evidence, medical examiner testimony).

Thus, recent studies indicate that juries do not attach excessive weight to polygraph test evidence in reaching a verdict. The difference in findings between older and more recent research in this area could in part reflect differences in the methodologies used (e.g., polygraph evidence presented during the trial versus after a decision was made; videotaped versus written trial scenarios; polygraph characterized as somewhat fallible as opposed to virtually infallible). Whatever the case, the inconsistent findings and methodological limitations of these studies warrant considerable caution before generalizing these findings to juror decision making in real-life criminal cases. The artificial, analogue nature of most of this research (including of the more recent studies) is one obvious issue. Another is that in these studies, the polygraph evidence has typically been presented in conjunction with other kinds of evidence that appear to carry more probative weight for jurors (Myers & Arbuthnot, 1997). In real-life criminal investigations, the polygraph test tends to be invoked precisely when little or no other inculpatory evidence exists (Patrick & Iacono, 1991b), and it is in these instances that the polygraph test may carry the greatest weight in court. Consider a typical polygraph case where the outcome hinges largely on the credibility of a victim and an alleged rapist because the only issue concerns the use of force. If both witnesses' testimony was equally credible, but one boosted his or her claim to truth with a passed polygraph test, would the jury be swayed by the results of the polygraph? This is precisely the type of scenario that juries asked to consider polygraph evidence are likely to be confronted with. Future studies in this area should systematically investigate the influence of polygraph testimony as a function of variations in the extent and quality of other available trial evidence.

SCIENTIFIC OPINION

The opinion of scientists regarding polygraphy is obviously important. Conventional polygraph tests have a weak conceptual foundation. Moreover, serious methodological problems that are unlikely to be easily overcome make it unlikely that any line of research will yield findings that resolve concerns about accuracy. Given this state of affairs, there is considerable value in the broad-based sampling of the opinions of scientists with the background and expertise to evaluate polygraph tests. In addition, the courts in both *Frye* and again in *Daubert* have made the views of the scientific community about the general acceptance of a technique important to the determination of whether it can be used to develop evidence. Hence, those working in forensic settings have a natural interest in prevailing scientific opinion about the theory and accuracy of polygraph tests.

Three surveys (Amato, 1993; Gallup Organization, 1984; Iacono & Lykken, 1997d) of scientific opinion regarding polygraph techniques have been conducted to date (see Iacono & Lykken, 1997a, 1997d, for reviews). In this section, we focus on the report from Iacono and Lykken (1997d). Unlike the other surveys, that of Iacono and Lykken has the following features: (a) it is published in a peer reviewed scientific journal; (b) it covers the opinions of two different scientific organizations; (c) it specifically addresses the theory and accuracy of polygraph tests; (d) it focuses on the CQT, the evidentiary value of which is most frequently brought before courts; and (e) it is the only survey to be carried out since the Supreme Court's *Daubert* decision.

Iacono and Lykken (1997d) surveyed members of the Society for Psychophysiological Research (SPR) and Fellows of the American Psychological Association's (APA) Division 1 (General Psychology). Psychophysiology is the parent discipline from which polygraphy is derived, and SPR's journal, *Psychophysiology*, as well as its annual scientific meeting, often feature material on polygraphy. Members of SPR thus have specialized expertise and knowledge relevant to the evaluation of polygraph tests. Over 90% of a random sample of SPR members responded to the survey. Because it is the psychological and psychometric properties of polygraph tests that makes them controversial, it seemed appropriate to survey the distinguished group of APA Fellows to supplement the views of the SPR membership and determine the extent to which common opinions are shared widely among psychologists. Because the psychological factors that are important to polygraph test outcome are diverse, tapping many subareas of psychology (e.g., clinical, social, measurement, industrial-organizational, physiological), distinguished general psychologists seemed especially appropriate to survey. Seventy-four percent of APA Fellows participated in their survey.

Table 16.1 presents the results for questions asked in common to the membership of both organizations. The findings are consistent across groups, suggesting that the CQT is viewed as neither scientifically sound nor suitable as scientific evidence. APA Fellows were also unimpressed with the foundation for the directed lie variant of the CQT. Members of both groups saw the GKT as being based on sound scientific principles and theory. The contrast in the scientific credibility of the CQT and GKT is important because it indicates that respondents are not generally skeptical about detection of deception techniques, but have doubts that are specific to the CQT. Because the members of these two organizations answered these questions in highly similar fashion, it is reasonable to assume agreement for the questions listed in Table 16.2 that were unique to each group.

Proponents of the CQT claim that the accuracy of the CQT is over 90% for innocent and 95% for guilty people (e.g., Raskin et al., 1997a). As can be seen from the first two questions in Table 16.2, scientists are dubious of such claims.

Table 16.1
Scientific Opinion of Polygraph Accuracy

Questionnaire Item	Percent Who Agree	
	SPR	APA
1. CQT based on scientifically sound theory	36	30
2. DLT based on scientifically sound theory	NA	22
3. GKT based on scientifically sound theory	77	72
4. Would advocate admitting failed CQTs as evidence in court	24	20
5. Would advocate admitting passed CQTs as evidence in court	27	24
6. Reasonable to conclude that an individual who fails 8 out of 10 GKT items has guilty knowledge	72	75

Note: SPR = Society for Psychophysiological Research; APA = American Psychological Association; CQT = control question test; DLT = directed lie test; GKT = guilty knowledge test; NA = question not asked

The responses to items 3 and 4 indicate that to alleviate such doubts, scientists would require considerably better or more convincing evidence, ideally from field studies. The responses to items 5 and 6 reveal that APA Fellows believed that the CQT is neither a standardized nor objective procedure. The rest of the data in Table 16.2 indicate that survey respondents believe that friendly tests are easier to pass than adversarial tests and that countermeasures can be used effectively to defeat a CQT.

These survey data justify a strong conclusion: There is substantial skepticism among knowledgeable scientists about the CQT and the claims made by CQT proponents. With regard to the court's interest in prevailing scientific opinion of the validity and scientific foundation for the CQT, it is apparent from our data that CQT polygraphy is not generally accepted by the relevant scientific community.

CONCLUSION

Polygraph testing has thrived in North America despite the weak theoretical and empirical foundation for conventional detection deception techniques and in spite of widespread skepticism concerning their validity among scientists. This state of affairs exists for several reasons that derive from polygraphy's value as an investigative tool. First, there is no dispute about the utility of polygraph testing. The fact that many criminal suspects confess following failed tests provides a means to resolve many important criminal investigations that otherwise would go unprosecuted and unresolved. In employee screening, the admissions employees make about their alcohol use, sex lives, and colleagues' suspect behavior provide the government with what is considered to be valuable information that would be virtually impossible to obtain via any other (legal) means. As Jones and Sigall (1971) demonstrated, confessions and admissions are likely to follow polygraph tests as long as those taking them remain naïve and continue to believe in the validity claims of

Table 16.2
Scientific Opinion of CQT Polygraphy

Topic	Questionnaire Item	Group Asked	Mean Estimate/% Who Agree
Accuracy	1. CQT is at least 85% accurate:		
	a. in tests of guilty suspects	SPR	27
	b. in tests of innocent suspects	SPR	22
	2. Best estimate of CQT accuracy		
	a. with innocent suspects	APA	63
	b. with guilty suspects	APA	60
	3. Strong empirical evidence required before accuracy claims of proponents are believed	APA	93
	4. Reasonable for courts to give "substantial weight" to results of laboratory studies to estimate CQT validity in real life	SPR	17
Test Properties	5. The CQT can "accurately be called a standardized procedure"	APA	20
	6. The CQT is "relatively independent of differences among examiners in skill and subjective judgment"	APA	10
Friendly Tests	7. "Friendly" CQTs more likely to be passed than those taken under adversarial conditions	SPR	75
	8. If guilty, would take a "friendly" CQT	APA	72
	9. If innocent, would take an "adversarial" CQT	APA	35
Countermeasures	10. "CQT can be beaten by augmenting one's response to the control questions"	SPR	99
	11. Criminals and spies likely to beat a CQT	APA	92
	12. Confident could personally learn how to defeat a CQT	APA	75

Note: SPR = Society for Psychophysiological Research; APA = American Psychological Association; CQT = control question test

polygraphers. Second, the practice of polygraphy, rather than deriving from psychological science and relying on practioners with scientific training, has developed as a profession with almost no input or oversight from psychology. Given the consequences that polygraph tests have for those who are subject to them, it is most unfortunate that this important area of applied psychology has been governed almost exclusively by lay practioners.

For many decades, polygraph testing has been part of the fabric of our institutions of law enforcement and national security. Consequently, reliance on polygraphy as an investigative tool is unlikely to diminish in the future.

What remains uncertain is whether the CQT will become accepted as credible scientific evidence in court. As our review indicates, there is little evidence to support such use, and what evidence does exist, coupled with the obvious weaknesses in CQT theory, indicates that the CQT has little more than chance accuracy with innocent people and can be easily defeated by guilty people who learn to augment their responses to control questions. Certainly, the CQT fails to meet the standards for scientific evidence laid out by *Frye* and *Daubert*.

The GKT, by contrast, is scientifically sound. Unfortunately, well-designed field research with the GKT is needed. Absent such work, it would be premature to advocate the admissability of GKT evidence in court. The possibility that the GKT may be biased in favor of guilty people passing should not be seen as limiting its application any more than the absence of fingerprints on a murder weapon should be seen as a limitation of this type of evidence. Failing a properly constructed and administered GKT (see, e.g., Iacono, 1995; Iacono, Boisvenu, & Fleming, 1984; Lykken, 1981) has the potential to be very incriminating. Unlike the situation with the CQT, the logic of the GKT is simple to grasp. A jury does not need to be told that a defendant has failed a GKT or is lying. Instead, the jury can be told the defendant gave his or her largest response to, for example, 9 of 10 of the key alternatives on a 10-item GKT. We believe most reasonable people would find such evidence compelling if (a) the defendant could offer no satisfactory explanation for having the guilty knowledge (a good GKT would use as items only questions that the defendant denied knowledge of and could not "guess" the correct answer to); (b) the examiner, blind to which alternatives were the keys, could not have influenced the outcome of the test; and (c) 10 known-to-be-innocent individuals took the same test with none failing more than four items.

REFERENCES

Abrams, S. (1989). *The complete polygraph handbook.* Lexington, MA: Lexington Books.

Allen, J. J., & Iacono, W. G. (1997). A comparison of methods for the analysis of event-related potentials in deception detection. *Psychophysiology, 34,* 234–240.

Allen, J. J., Iacono, W. G., & Danielson, K. D. (1992). The identification of concealed memories using the event-related potential and implicit behavioral measures: A methodology for prediction in the face of individual differences. *Psychophysiology, 29,* 504–522.

Amato, S. L. (1993, November). *A survey of the Society for Psychophysiological Research regarding the polygraph: Opinions and interpretations.* Unpublished master's thesis, University of North Dakota.

Backster, C. (1962). Methods of strengthening our polygraph technique. *Police, 6,* 61–68.

Balloun, K., & Holmes, D. (1978). Effects of repeated examinations on the ability to detect guilt with a polygraphic examination: A laboratory experiment with a real crime. *Journal of Applied Psychology, 64,* 316–322.

Barland, G. H. (1982). On the accuracy of the polygraph: An evaluative review of Lykken's Tremor in the blood. *Polygraph, 11,* 258–272.

Barland, G. H., Honts, C. R., & Barger, S. D. (1989). *Studies of the accuracy of security screening polygraph examinations.* Fort McClellan, AL: Department of Defense Polygraph Institute.

Barland, G. H., & Raskin, D. C. (1976). *Validity and reliability of polygraph examinations of criminal suspects* (Report No. 76-1, Contract No. N1-99-0001). Washington, DC: National Institute of Justice, Department of Justice.

Bashore, T. R., & Rapp, P. E. (1993). Are there alternatives to traditional polygraph procedures? *Psychological Bulletin, 113*, 3–22.

Ben-Shakar, G., & Furedy, J. J. (1990). *Theories and applications in the detection of deception.* New York: Springer-Verlag.

Bersh, P. J. (1969). A validation study of polygraph examiner judgments. *Journal of Applied Psychology, 53*, 393–403.

Boaz, T. L., Perry, N. W., Raney, G., Fieschler, I. S., & Shuman, D. (1991). Detection of guilty knowledge with event related potentials. *Journal of Applied Psychology, 76*, 788–795.

Bradley, M. T., & Rettinger, J. (1992). Awareness of crime-relevant information and the guilty knowledge test. *Journal of Applied Psychology, 77*, 55–59.

Burns, R. (1994, May 2). Fallout from Ames case centers on how to fix CIA. *Tallahassee Democrat*, 3A–4A.

Carlson, S. C., Pasano, M. S., & Januzzo, J. A. (1977). The effect of lie detector evidence on jury deliberations: An empirical study. *Journal of Police Science & Adminstration, 5*, 148–154.

Cavoukian, A., & Heselgrave, R. J. (1980). The admissability of polygraph evidence in court: Some empirical findings. *Law and Human Behavior, 4*, 117–131.

Daubert v. Merrell Dow Pharmaceuticals, 113 C.Ct. 2786 (1993).

Dohm, T. E., & Iacono, W. G. (1993). *Design and pilot of a polygraph field validation study* (Technical Report No. 227). Minneapolis, MN: Personnel Decisions Research Institute.

Elaad, E. (1990). Detection of guilty knowledge in real-life criminal applications. *Journal of Applied Psychology, 75*, 521–529.

Elaad, E. (1997). Polygraph examiner awareness of crime-relevant information and the guilty knowledge test. *Law and Human Behavior, 21*, 107–120.

Elaad, E., Ginton, A., & Jungman, N. (1992). Detection measures in real-life criminal guilty knowledge tests. *Journal of Applied Psychology, 77*, 757–767.

Employee Polygraph Protection Act of 1988, Pub.L. 100-347, 102 Stat. 646, 29 U.S.C. 2001-2009.

Faigman, D. L., Kaye, D. H., Saks, M. J., & Sanders, J. (1997). The legal relevance of scientific research on polygraph tests. In D. L. Faigman, D. Kaye, M. J. Saks, & J. Sanders (Eds.), *Modern scientific evidence: The law and science of expert testimony* (pp. 554–564). St. Paul, MN: West.

Farwell, L. A., & Donchin, E. (1986). The "brain detector": P300 in the detection of deception. *Psychophysiology, 24*, 434.

Farwell, L. A., & Donchin, E. (1991). The truth will out: Interrogative polygraphy ("lie detection") with event related brain potentials. *Psychophysiology, 28*, 531–547.

Ferguson, R. J. (1966). *The polygraph in private industry.* Springfield, IL: Thomas.

Forkusch, M. D. (1939). The lie detector and the courts. *New York University Law Quarterly Review, 16*, 202–231.

Forman, R. F., & McCauley, C. (1986). Validity of the positive control test using the field practice model. *Journal of Applied Psychology, 71*, 691–698.

Frye v. United States, 293 F.1013 (1924).

Furedy, J. J., & Heselgrave, R. J. (1988). Validity of the lie detector: A psychophysiological perspective. *Criminal Justice & Behavior, 15*, 219–246.

Gallup Organization. (1984). Survey of members of the American Society for Psychophysiological Research concerning their opinion of polygraph test interpretation. *Polygraph, 13*, 153–165.

Honts, C. R. (1991). The emperor's new clothes: Application of polygraph tests in the American workplace. *Forensic Reports, 4,* 91–116.

Honts, C. R. (1992). Counterintelligence Scope Polygraph (CSP) test found to be poor discriminator. *Forensic Reports, 5,* 215–218.

Honts, C. R. (1994). Psychophysiological detection of deception. *Current Directions, 3,* 77–82.

Honts, C. R. (1996). Criterion development and validity of the CQT in field application. *Journal of General Psychology, 123,* 309–324.

Honts, C. R., Devitt, M. K., Winbush, M., & Kircher, J. C. (1996). Mental and physical countermeasures reduce the accuracy of the concealed knowledge test. *Psychophysiology, 33,* 84–92.

Honts, C. R., & Quick, B. D. (1996). The polygraph in 1995: Progress in science and the law. *North Dakota Law Review, 71,* 987–1020.

Honts, C. R., & Raskin, D. C. (1988). A field study of the validity of the directed lie control question. *Journal of Police Science & Administration, 16,* 56–61.

Honts, C. R., Raskin, D. C., & Kircher, J. C. (1994). Mental and physical countermeasures reduce the accuracy of polygraph tests. *Journal of Applied Psychology, 79,* 252–259.

Honts, C. R., Raskin, D. C., & Kircher, J. C. (1997). A rejoinder to Iacono and Lykken. In D. L. Faigman, D. Kaye, M. J. Saks, & J. Sanders (Eds.), *Modern scientific evidence: The law and science of expert testimony* (pp. 629–631). St. Paul, MN: West.

Horowitz, S. W., Kircher, J. C., Honts, C. R., & Raskin, D. C. (1997). The role of comparison questions in physiological detection of deception. *Psychophysiology, 34,* 108–115.

Horvath, F. (1977). The effect of selected variables on the interpretation of polygraph records. *Journal of Applied Psychology, 62,* 127–136.

Horvath, F. (1985). Job screening. *Society, 22,* 43–46.

Horvath, F. (1993). Polygraph screening of candidates for police work in large police agencies in the United States: A survey of practices, policies, and evaluative comments. *American Journal of Police, 12,* 67–86.

Iacono, W. G. (1991). Can we determine the accuracy of polygraph tests? In J. R. Jennings, P. K. Ackles, & M. G. H. Coles (Eds.), *Advances in psychophysiology* (Vol. 4, pp. 201–207). London: Jessica Kingsley.

Iacono, W. G. (1995). Offender testimony: Detection of deception and guilty knowledge. In N. Brewer & C. Wilson (Eds.), *Psychology and policing* (pp. 155–171). Hillsdale, NJ: Erlbaum.

Iacono, W. G. (1999). The detection of deception. In L. G. Tassinary, J. T. Cacioppo, & G. Berntson (Eds.), *Handbook of psychophysiology.* New York: Cambridge University Press.

Iacono, W. G., Boisvenu, G. A., & Fleming, J. A. (1984). The effects of diazepam and methylphenidate on the electrodermal detection of guilty knowledge. *Journal of Applied Psychology, 69,* 289–299.

Iacono, W. G., & Lykken, D. T. (1997a). The scientific status of research on polygraph techniques: The case against polygraph tests. In D. L. Faigman, D. Kaye, M. J. Saks, & J. Sanders (Eds.), *Modern scientific evidence: The law and science of expert testimony* (pp. 582–618). St. Paul, MN: West.

Iacono, W. G., & Lykken, D. T. (1997b). A response to professors Raskin, Honts, and Kircher. In D. L. Faigman, D. Kaye, M. J. Saks, & J. Sanders (Eds.), *Modern scientific evidence: The law and science of expert testimony* (pp. 627–629). St. Paul, MN: West.

Iacono, W. G., & Lykken, D. T. (1997c). A rejoinder to Raskin, Honts, and Kircher. In D. L. Faigman, D. Kaye, M. J. Saks, & J. Sanders (Eds.), *Modern scientific evidence: The law and science of expert testimony* (pp. 631–633). St. Paul, MN: West.

Iacono, W. G., & Lykken, D. T. (1997d). The validity of the lie detector: Two surveys of scientific opinion. *Journal of Applied Psychology, 82,* 426–433.

Iacono, W. G., & Patrick, C. J. (1987). What psychologists should know about lie detection. In I. B.Weiner & A. K. Hess (Eds.), *Handbook of forensic psychology.* New York: Wiley.

Iacono, W. G., & Patrick, C. J. (1988). Polygraphy techniques. In R. Rogers (Ed.), *Clinical assessment of malingering and deception* (pp. 205–233). New York: Guilford Press.

Iacono, W. G., & Patrick, C. J. (1997). Polygraph and integrity testing. In R. Rogers (Ed.), *Clinical assessment of malingering and deception* (2nd ed., pp. 252–281). New York: Guilford Press.

Johnson, M. M., & Rosenfeld, J. P. (1992). Oddball-evoked P300-based method of deception detection in the laboratory: II. Utilization of non-selective activation of relevant knowledge. *International Journal of Psychophysiology, 12,* 289–306.

Jones, E. E., & Sigall, H. (1971). The bogus pipeline: A new paradigm for measuring affect and attitude. *Psychological Bulletin, 76,* 349–364.

Kircher, J. C., Horowitz, S. W., & Raskin, D. C. (1988). Meta-analysis of mock crime studies of the control question polygraph technique. *Law & Human Behavior, 12,* 79–90.

Koffler, J. (1957). The lie detector: A critical appraisal of the technique as a potential undermining factor in the judicial process. *New York Law Forum, 3,* 123–158.

Kugelmass, S., & Lieblich, I. (1966). The effects of realistic stress and procedural interference in experimental lie detection. *Journal of Applied Psychology, 50,* 211–216.

Larson, J. A. (1921). Modification of the Marston deception test. *Journal of the American Institute of Criminal Law and Criminology, 12,* 391–399.

Lieblich, I., Naftali, G., Shmueli, J., & Kugelmass, S. (1974). Efficiency of GSR detection of information with repeated presentation of series of stimuli in two motivational states. *Journal of Applied Psychology, 59,* 113–115.

Lykken, D. T. (1959). The GSR in the detection of guilt. *Journal of Applied Psychology, 43,* 385–388.

Lykken, D. T. (1960). The validity of the guilty knowledge technique: The effects of faking. *Journal of Applied Psychology, 44,* 258–262.

Lykken, D. T. (1974). Psychology and the lie detector industry. *American Psychologist, 29,* 725–739.

Lykken, D. T. (1981). *A tremor in the blood: Uses and abuses of the lie detector.* New York: McGraw-Hill.

Lykken, D. T. (1988). Detection of guilty knowledge: A comment on Forman and McCauley. *Journal of Applied Psychology, 73,* 303–304.

Lykken, D. T. (1998). *A tremor in the blood: Uses and abuses of the lie detector* (2nd ed.). New York: Plenum Press.

Markwart, A., & Lynch, B. E. (1979). The effect of polygraph evidence on mock jury decision-making. *Journal of Police Science and Administration, 7,* 324–332.

Myers, B., & Arbuthnot, J. (1997). Polygraph testimony and juror judgments: A comparison of the guilty knowledge test and the control question test. *Journal of Applied Social Psychology, 27,* 1421–1437.

O'Bannon, R. M., Goldinger, L. A., & Appleby, G. S. (1989). *Honesty and integrity testing.* Atlanta, GA: Applied Information Resources.

Orne, M. T., Thackray, R. I., & Paskewitz, D. A. (1972). On the detection of deception: A model for the study of the physiological effects of psychological stimuli. In N. S. Greenfield & R. A. Sternbach (Eds.), *Handbook of psychophysiology* (pp. 743–785). New York: Holt, Rinehart and Winston.

O'Toole, D., Yuille, J. C., Patrick, C. J., & Iacono, W. G. (1994). Alcohol and the physiological detection of deception: Arousal and memory influences. *Psychophysiology, 31*, 253–263.

Patrick, C. J., & Iacono, W. G. (1989). Psychopathy, threat, and polygraph test accuracy. *Journal of Applied Psychology, 74*, 347–355.

Patrick, C. J., & Iacono, W. G. (1991a). A comparison of field and laboratory polygraphs in the detection of deception. *Psychophysiology, 28*, 632–638.

Patrick, C. J., & Iacono, W. G. (1991b). Validity of the control question polygraph test: The problem of sampling bias. *Journal of Applied Psychology, 76*, 229–238.

Podlesny, J. A. (1993). Is the guilty knowledge polygraph technique applicable in criminal investigations? A review of FBI case records. *Crime Laboratory Digest, 20*, 57–61.

Podlesny, J. A., Nimmich, K. W., & Budowle, B. (1995). *A lack of case facts restricts applicability of the guilty knowledge deception detection method in FBI criminal investigations* (U.S. Department of Justice Technical Report). FBI Forensic Research and Training Center, Quantico, VA.

Raskin, D. (1986). The polygraph in 1986: Scientific, professional and legal issues surrounding applications and acceptance of polygraph evidence. *Utah Law Review, 1*, 29–74.

Raskin, D. (1989). Polygraph techniques for the detection of deception. In D. Raskin (Ed.), *Psychological methods in criminal investigation and evidence* (pp. 247–296). New York: Springer.

Raskin, D. C., Barland, G. H., & Podlesny, J. A. (1978). *Validity and reliability of detection of deception.* Washington, DC: U.S. Government Printing Office.

Raskin, D. C., Honts, C. R., & Kircher, J. C. (1997a). The scientific status of research on polygraph techniques: The case for polygraph tests. In D. L. Faigman, D. Kaye, M. J. Saks, & J. Sanders (Eds.), *Modern scientific evidence: The law and science of expert testimony* (pp. 565–582). St. Paul, MN: West.

Raskin, D. C., Honts, C. R., & Kircher, J. C. (1997b). A response to professors Iacono and Lykken. In D. L. Faigman, D. Kaye, M. J. Saks, & J. Sanders (Eds.), *Modern scientific evidence: The law and science of expert testimony* (pp. 619–627). St. Paul, MN: West.

Raskin, D. C., Kircher, J. C., Honts, C. R., & Horowitz, S. W. (1988). *A study of the validity of polygraph examinations in criminal investigation. Final report to the National Institute of Justice.* Unpublished manuscript, Department of Psychology, University of Utah, Salt Lake City.

Reid, J. E., & Inbau, F. E. (1977). *Truth and deception: The polygraph ("lie detector") technique* (2nd ed.). Baltimore: Williams & Wilkins.

Rosenfeld, J. P., Angell, A., Johnson, M., & Qian, J. (1991). An ERP-based, control-question lie detector analog: Algorithms for discriminating effects within individuals' average waveforms. *Psychophysiology, 38*, 319–335.

Rosenfeld, J. P., Cantwell, B., Nasman, V. T., Wodjdac, V., Ivanov, S., & Mazzeri, L. (1988). A modified, event-related potential based guilty knowledge test. *International Journal of Neuroscience, 42*, 157–161.

Rosenfeld, J. P., Nasman, V. T., Whalen, R., Cantwell, B., & Mazzeri, L. (1987). Late vertex positivity in event-related potentials as a guilty knowledge indicator: A new method of lie detection. *Polygraph, 16*, 258–263.

Samuels, D. J. (1983). What if the lie detector lies? *Nation, 237*, 566–567.

Saxe, L. (1991). Science and the CQT polygraph: A theoretical critique. *Integrative Physiological & Behavioral Science, 26*, 223–231.

Saxe, L. (1994). Detection of deception: Polygraph and integrity tests. *Current Directions, 3*, 69–73.

Simon, J. (1992). *Resampling: The new statistics.* Belmont, CA: Duxbury Press.

Smith, R. J., & Hall, C. W. (1996, November 19). CIA officer charged with spying. *Washington Post*, A1.

Spanos, N. P., Myers, B., DuBreuil, S. C., & Pawlak, A. E. (1992). The effects of polygraphy and eyewitness testimony on the beliefs and decisions of mock jurors. *Imagination, Cognition, and Personality, 12*, 103–113.

Thurber, S. (1981). CPI variables in relation to the polygraph performance of police officer candidates. *Journal of Social Psychology, 113*, 145–146.

United States Department of Defense. (1996). *Department of Defense polygraph program: Annual polygraph report to Congress, fiscal year 1996*. Washington, DC: Author.

United States v. Alexander, 526 F.2d 161, 168 (8th Cir. 1975).

United States v. Scheffer, 1998 WL 141151 U.S.

van Hoof, J. C., Brunia, C. H. M., & Allen, C. J. (1996). Event-related potentials as indirect measures of recognition memory. *International Journal of Psychophysiology, 21*, 15–31.

Weiner, T. (1994, December 29). Director of C.I.A. to leave, ending troubled tenure. *New York Times*, A1.

Yamamura, T., & Miyata, Y. (1990). Development of the polygraph technique in Japan for detection of deception. *Forensic Science International, 44*, 257–271.

CHAPTER 17

Forensic Uses of Hypnosis

ALAN W. SCHEFLIN, HERBERT SPIEGEL, and DAVID SPIEGEL

LAW INTERACTS with hypnosis in five different ways: by (a) regulating who may practice hypnosis and under what conditions that practice may occur (the lay hypnotist issue); (b) deciding who bears responsibility when hypnosis is used for antisocial purposes; (c) determining whether a person may testify after hypnosis is used to refresh memory; (d) setting the appropriate standard of care therapists must use when hypnotizing patients; and (e) ruling on the use of various hypnotic techniques in courtroom advocacy by lawyers attempting to sway jurors and influence witnesses (Scheflin, 1998).

In this century, the primary forensic uses of hypnosis have been for the purpose of assisting victims, witnesses, and occasionally defendants in enhancing memory of a crime. Consequently, we will address the third and fourth issues, which are the only areas of interaction currently active and controversial. The use of hypnosis to refresh recollection has been subjected both to continued scientific debate and to considerable judicial controversy, which has culminated in over 800 appellate decisions affecting legal rights as well as clinical practice (Scheflin & Shapiro, 1989).

HISTORY

Some aspects of hypnosis can trace their history back to the most ancient of civilizations, but there is little evidence that hypnosis was used regularly before the 1880s to refresh the recollection of victims, witnesses, or culprits in criminal or civil cases. Although the first recorded instance of the use of hypnosis to refresh memory in court appears in 1846 (Gravitz, 1995), it was an isolated event that was not widely reported (see Appendix).

Medical professionals first began systematically to examine the relationship between hypnosis and memory for forensic purposes in the closing two decades

474

of the 19th century (Ellenberger, 1970). French and German hypnosis specialists were clearly aware of potential problems with hypnotically refreshed recollection. The current "false memory" debate is in fact a replay of a similar discussion 100 years ago. Albert Moll (1889/1958) noted that "retroactive hallucinations," his name for false memories, "are of great importance in law. They can be used to falsify testimony. People can be made to believe that they have witnessed certain scenes, or even crimes" (pp. 345–346).

The great French hypnosis pioneer, Hippolyte Bernheim (1891/1991), penned similar concerns: "I have shown how a false memory can cause *false testimony given in good faith,* and how examining magistrates can unwittingly cause false testimony by suggestion" (p. 92). Bernheim provided a dramatic example of his point by suggesting to a subject in trance that he had been awakened in the middle of the night by a raucous neighbor's singing and coughing. After the hypnosis, the subject not only reported the implanted incident of the loud neighbor, but also supplied details of the event not suggested by Bernheim, thereby adding confabulation to the false report.

Despite this recognition of the use of hypnosis to refresh recollection, and the potential dangers, there is little evidence that hypnosis regularly was used by police or others for memory refreshment of victims or witnesses of crimes. When police were tempted to use hypnosis, they sought to obtain confessions from criminal defendants. In 1893, Dutch police captured a vicious serial killer and sought to discover the location of the buried bodies of some of his victims. A statute prohibited hypnotically refreshed recollection from being introduced into evidence, but the Dutch police were concerned only with obtaining information about the crimes. When word of the police plans to hypnotize the killer became public, a multinational outcry forced them to back down ("Hypnotism and the Law," 1893).

There is also little evidence that courts were asked to address the issue of the admissibility into evidence of hypnotically refreshed recollection. Although several European countries in the late 1800s and early 1900s conducted major trials involving hypnosis, none of these trials appears to concern hypnosis and memory (Harris, 1989). Instead, the issue usually involved alleged hypnotic seduction or the use of hypnosis to produce antisocial criminal conduct in others (Laurence & Perry, 1988). Indeed, when hypnosis was in the news in the last decade of the past century, as it frequently was, the story was almost always about the power of hypnosis to override a person's will. As noted by Brodie-Innes (1891): "Recently the public mind has been startled by accounts of strange new powers, with mysterious and unknown possibilities, and by alarming hints of crimes of an entirely new class, more obscure, more terrible, and more difficult of detection than any yet known to medical jurisprudence" (p. 51).

Publicity in the 1880s and 1890s about the possibility of using hypnosis to induce criminal conduct had its influence on lawyers. As one legal author ("Hypnotism in Criminal Defense," 1894) observed in 1894, insanity was a favored plea of criminal suspects, but "today hypnotism is the fashionable defense" (p. 249).

Also in 1894, George DuMaurier published his international blockbuster, *Trilby.* Whereas detectives then were fortunate enough to be immortalized in fiction by the brilliant Arthur Conan Doyle, creator of Sherlock Holmes, hypnosis had the misfortune to be tainted with the evil genius Svengali.

Appellate courts in the United States, from the early 1800s to 1968, addressed hypnosis issues in only 50 cases or so (Scheflin & Shapiro, 1989). Not more than two or three of these cases involved investigative hypnosis and memory. Every state court adhered to the brief statement by the California Supreme Court in *People v. Ebanks* (1897) quoting the trial judge's comment that "the law of the United States does not recognize hypnotism" (p. 1053). Despite the fact that the court was referring to a minor evidentiary point (Brown, Scheflin, & Hammond, 1998), the court's broad language had the consequence that hypnosis was not recognized as a defense in criminal cases and hypnotically refreshed recollection was not admitted into evidence in any case.

After hypnosis received official professional approval as a therapeutic procedure, first by the British Medical Association (1955) and then by the American Medical Association (1958) and the American Psychiatric Association (1961), police departments began to express a renewed interest in it to help solve crimes. Lay hypnotists openly began training police officials in the 1950s, and some professionals began assisting the police in conducting hypnotic interviews (Arons, 1967).

The Three Legal Rules Governing Hypnotically Refreshed Memory

The police use of hypnosis for memory recovery was of investigative value, but courts still refused to hear the testimony of previously hypnotized witnesses. In 1968, a Maryland court in *Harding v. State* opened the door for the first time in America to hypnotically refreshed recollection. The court reasoned that refreshing memory with hypnosis was no different than refreshing memory any other way. Besides, the court noted, cross-examination and the availability of experts allowed sufficient challenge to hypnotically refreshed testimony.

In a realistic sense, forensic hypnosis is born in 1968 with the *Harding* court's "open admissibility" rule. Thus, forensic hypnosis, except for the relatively brief discussions at the end of the past century, is only 30 years old. Those 30 years, however, have been tumultuous.

The first ten years, however, were relatively quiet. During the 1968–1978 time frame, every court in the United States that addressed the issue of hypnotically refreshed recollection adopted *Harding*'s "open admissibility" ruling. In 1978, however, the Ninth Circuit Federal Court of Appeals in *United States v. Adams* sounded a warning that the use of hypnosis to refresh memory may contain special dangers. That warning led to the development of two rules, each of which restricted the admission of hypnotically refreshed testimony.

The most restrictive rule, known as the per se exclusion rule because it automatically prohibits hypnotically refreshed testimony in all cases, was first adopted in 1980 by the Minnesota Supreme Court in *State v. Mack,* and then by the California Supreme Court in its influential decision in *People v. Shirley* (1982). These courts concluded that hypnosis lacked reliability, created undue suggestibility, increased confidence in the accuracy of false memories, and led to confabulated testimony. Furthermore, because of the increased confidence in inaccurate recall, subjects could not effectively be cross-examined.

In between the *Mack* and *Shirley* cases, in time and in decision, the New Jersey Supreme Court in 1981 rejected the wide-open *Harding* ruling and the completely closed per se rule of *Mack*. Instead, the New Jersey justices in *State v. Hurd* (1981) permitted hypnotically refreshed recollection to be admissible in court provided certain guidelines had been followed. This third approach, after the opposite open admissibility and per se exclusion rulings, became known as the "admissibility with safeguards" test or the "totality of the circumstances" test.

The main difference between the per se exclusion rule and the totality of the circumstances test is the former's rejection of every case in which hypnosis has been performed, compared to the latter's requirement that every case have a pretrial hearing to determine if the hypnosis sessions were likely to be unduly suggestive (Scheflin, 1994a, 1994b).

In per se states, a witness or victim may give a statement, which must be recorded, to the police. If hypnosis is later used on this witness or victim, the testimony will be restricted to a recitation of what had been previously stated and recorded before hypnosis was used. The per se exclusion rule not only bars testimony that is recalled during and/or after the hypnosis session, but it also prevents the subject from making a posthypnotic identification of the defendant (McConkey & Sheehan, 1995).

The totality of the circumstances test, on the other hand, mandates that the judge before trial evaluates how the hypnosis session was conducted. If rigorous guidelines have been met and the judge concludes that the hypnosis did not taint the reliability of the testimony, posthypnotic recall testimony is admissible into evidence.

With the articulation of these three tests, courts in each state and in the federal system simply had to pick and choose which approach they preferred. We have already noted that approximately 50 appellate cases were reported from the 1800s to 1968. By contrast, from 1968 to the present, more than 800 appellate cases involving hypnosis, almost all of which concern hypnotically refreshed recollection, have been decided. As Sheehan (1996) has observed in a recent review of the past decade of hypnosis research, forensic hypnosis, which was barely mentioned by Kihlstrom (1985) in his review of trends in hypnosis research, now has become one of the fastest growing areas of specialization.

In 1987, the U.S. Supreme Court held that the per se exclusion rule could not automatically be applied to defendants in criminal cases because it would violate their Sixth Amendment constitutional rights (*Rock v. Arkansas*, 1987).

THE PRESENT

Only two or three states appear to follow the permissive open admissibility rule of *Harding*, and no commentator has endorsed it. The overwhelming majority of states now follow the per se exclusion rule, with perhaps one-third of the states, and the federal courts (*Borawick v. Shay*, 1995), adopting the totality of the circumstances test.

In states that follow the per se exclusion rule, there is only a very minor role left for forensic hypnosis: developing investigative leads to solve crimes. Because the posthypnotic testimony is inadmissible, police are likely to want to do the hypnosis themselves. Thus, if forensic hypnosis is to have a future, two things must occur. First, the prevailing science must support the benefits over risks of using hypnosis; second, the states adopting the per se exclusion rule must be persuaded to shift to a case-by-case analysis. How likely are these prospects?

HYPNOSIS: A DEFINITION

Controversy and intense disagreement have been an important part of the history of forensic applications of hypnosis because hypnosis has often been mystified and because it deals with issues of crucial importance to the law (i.e., will, choice, responsibility, and awareness). Hypnosis remains an area of theoretical, if not frequently practical, importance in relation to the more common and thorny issues of criminal and civil responsibility related to psychiatric illness.

Hypnosis is a complex alteration in consciousness that can be understood as attentive, receptive concentration characterized by parallel, or dissociated, awareness. This shift in concentration may result in intense absorbing perceptual experiences but is always controllable and reversible. It may involve sensitivity to internal cues in self-hypnosis. The interaction between focal attention and peripheral awareness is a constant theme in human consciousness, but with hypnosis there appears to be a relative diminution of peripheral awareness to facilitate the enhancement of focal concentration (Spiegel, 1994). Although at no time does peripheral awareness disappear entirely, its suspension allows for the relative suspension of critical judgment, or suggestibility, often observed in particular in highly hypnotizable individuals. People in a trance tend to focus on what to do rather than why they are doing it. They are capable of experiencing vivid sensory alterations such as tingling, lightness, or heaviness in extremities, alterations in motor control (e.g., letting an arm float up in the air with a feeling that they cannot control it, although, in fact, they can). They also experience changes in temporal orientation, such as reliving the past as though it were the present, and dissociation (e.g., feeling a part of the body or a part of their awareness as being separate from the rest).

The everyday experience most analogous to the hypnotic experience is that of becoming so absorbed in a good novel, movie, or play that one enters the imaginary world and temporarily suspends awareness of the real one. Laboratory research has, in fact, shown that highly hypnotizable individuals are more likely to have these hypnoticlike (Shor, Orne, & O'Connell, 1962) or absorbing (Tellegen & Atkinson, 1974) experiences. Research in the laboratory and the clinic over the past several decades has demonstrated that hypnotizability is a stable and measurable trait (Hilgard, 1965; Spiegel & Spiegel, 1978), as stable during the adult life span as intelligence (Morgan, Johnson, & Hilgard, 1974; Piccione, Hilgard, &

Zimbardo, 1989). It is at its peak during the human life cycle in late childhood (Morgan & Hilgard, 1973) and declines gradually throughout adolescence and the adult life span into senescence (Stern, Spiegel, & Nee, 1978–1979). Approximately one-fourth of a psychiatric outpatient population was found not to be hypnotizable, and only 5 to 10% can be considered highly hypnotizable (Spiegel & Spiegel, 1978). Thus, some people are not at all hypnotizable, a few are extremely hypnotizable, and the majority of the population has some moderate capacity to experience hypnosis. Hypnotizability tests provide a series of instructions after hypnotic induction and then assess the number of items that the subjects are capable of experiencing, such as sensory and motor alterations, temporal reorientation, and vividness of imagery.

The intense absorption and ability to dissociate information at the periphery of awareness typical of the hypnotic state contribute to the increase in suggestibility also associated with it. Hypnotized individuals are not unable to resist suggestion, but are less likely to because of their absorption in the focal instruction and their ability to dissociate temporal context, awareness of prior life experiences, and evaluation of the person providing the instructions. Thus, hypnotized individuals are more likely to go along with instructions than they would ordinarily be and are less likely to critically judge them, at least until later on (Spiegel, 1994; Spiegel & Spiegel, 1984a, 1987).

The phenomenon of hypnotic suggestibility has lent a special mystification to the field of hypnosis, and there has been no small amount of it in the forensic setting. The dramatic and compelling examples of previously amnesic material unearthed with hypnosis, especially in a traumatized witness or victim, led to hopes that hypnosis could be used as a kind of "truth serum" and that the material elicited with it had some higher order of veracity than ordinary memories. The limitations of this approach have been documented at least as far back as Freud's famous and still controversial recantation of his original theory of the etiology of neuroses. Along with Breuer, he used hypnosis to help patients with hysterical symptoms relive early events that had led to the formation of the symptoms. He initially uncovered material suggesting that at least one of their parents or close relatives had sexually abused these patients. He later revised his theory, though not necessarily his beliefs (Breuer & Freud, 1955; Masson, 1992), reinterpreting these memories as fantasies produced by the patient. It is clear that at the very least the sensitivity of the hypnotized person's relatedness to his or her environment makes it critically important to take into account any pressure being applied to provide certain kinds of information (McConkey & Sheehan, 1995). Even in the best of cases, it is possible for a subject to come up with material that is responsive to internal needs or external factors rather than the truth. Recently, a number of reports have emerged illustrating either self-serving and feigned stories elicited under hypnosis (Orne, 1979; Spiegel & Spiegel, 1984b), or an artificially induced experimental confabulation in a highly hypnotizable subject instructed to stick by an invented story (Spiegel, 1980). Thus, it is clear from the clinical literature that it is possible for hypnotized individuals to come up with compelling stories that are not necessarily true.

FORENSIC EXPERIENCE WITH HYPNOSIS

Hypnosis with Defendants

In several cases, hypnosis has been abused in an effort to obtain information from a defendant about a crime (Scheflin & Shapiro, 1989). In *Leyra v. Denno* (1954), hypnosis was used in an attempt to coerce a confession from Leyra, who was accused of killing his parents. After hours of intense interrogation shortly after the murders, a doctor offered to treat Leyra for a headache. The doctor hypnotized Leyra and told him that he might as well confess to the murders and assured his patient that he would see to it that the police would "go easy" on him. Leyra confessed to the doctor. Shortly after this, he was taken to the front of the police station and in the presence of his business partner repeated the confession. He was found guilty and sentenced to the electric chair, but this conviction was reversed on appeal with the reasoning that the confession had been coerced using hypnosis. At the next trial, he was found guilty, this time on the basis of his second confession made in front of his business partner. This conviction went all the way to the U.S. Supreme Court and, on a split decision, a new trial was ordered. The majority opinion, written by Justice Black, held that the second confession should be considered part of a continuum clearly related to the first confession and thereby similarly coerced. By the time a third trial was undertaken, the remaining evidence was largely circumstantial and inadequate. Despite this, Leyra was again found guilty, but, because of the sparse evidence, the case was reversed on appeal. Leyra was eventually freed of all charges because of a coercive misuse of hypnosis to elicit a confession, and no one else has ever been convicted of the crime.

Orne reports the opposite kind of problem in the case of *State v. Papp* (1978) (Orne, 1979). A defendant who claimed amnesia for parts of the crime underwent hypnosis. His performance during hypnotic age regression suggested his own exoneration. Expert witnesses for the prosecution testified, however, that his behavior was typical of someone simulating, rather than experiencing, hypnosis. On the strength of this testimony, the hypnosis session was interpreted as self-serving and was not introduced in court. In another case, *People v. Ritchie* (1977), Orne reports that a defendant undergoing hypnosis implicated his wife rather than himself, but the court eventually decided to exclude the hypnotic evidence.

On the other hand, Mutter (1984, 1990) has reported cases where hypnosis with the defendant produced exonerating statements that were later independently corroborated. Indeed, *Rock v. Arkansas* (1987) is just such a case.

The law is clear that hypnosis may be used with criminal defendants, but only with their informed consent. The Sixth Amendment prohibits an automatic exclusion rule regarding posthypnotic testimony.

Hypnosis with Witnesses and Victims

The greatest interest in the use of hypnosis with victims and witnesses of crime remains in those cases in which the person was emotionally or physically traumatized by the criminal activity and adopted a defensive repression or denial in response (Putnam, 1979). Such individuals claim no memory for some or all of the events, and this amnesia cannot be accounted for on the basis of head injury or intoxication. Such amnesic syndromes are recognized in the *DSM-IV* as dissociative amnesia and as components of acute stress disorder and posttraumatic stress disorder (American Psychiatric Association, 1994). Traumatic amnesias may be reversible using hypnosis, usually accompanied by the experience of strong emotion. Indeed, the greater accessibility of these memories when the emotion can be experienced and, it is hoped, controlled by hypnosis is explained (Butler & Spiegel, 1997) by the theory of state-dependent memory (Bower, 1981). This research demonstrates that people are better able to remember the content of material when they are in the same emotional state while trying to recall it that they were in when the material was learned. Often, traumatized individuals avoid thinking about the content of the trauma because it naturally elicits the painful emotions of helplessness, fear, and rage that they experienced during the event. There is some agreement in the field that such spontaneously elicited memories, coming as a complete reversal of a previous amnesia and without suggestion regarding the details, deserve serious attention (Orne, 1979). Nonetheless, such memories cannot be presumed automatically free of either internal or external contamination.

In *State v. Hurd* (1981), where the New Jersey Supreme Court adopted the admissibility with safeguards rule, a woman awoke to find herself being stabbed repeatedly in the neck. She had no memory of any perceptions prior to the knife approaching her neck. She was hypnotized in the presence of the police, and the conventional screen technique (Spiegel & Spiegel, 1978) was used in an effort to elicit clues regarding her assailant. During this trance experience she spontaneously abreacted with a great deal of emotion, crying, and shouting while reliving the assault. She gave descriptive information about the assailant but initially refused to identify him. When asked whether it was, in fact, her ex-husband, she tearfully assented that it was. After the trance she expressed some dismay at this new information and said that she had somehow known who it was but had not wanted to admit it to herself. Unfortunately, the police case ended rather than began at this point, and no additional corroborative information was obtained. The victim's previous posttraumatic stress disorder, which included insomnia, nightmares, irritability, and reduced ability to function, was reversed after the hypnotic abreaction. The court ruled, however, that in the absence of additional corroboration it was possible that the information she produced under hypnosis was the result of suggestion or some self-serving memory. Therefore, the charges ultimately were dropped. The legal standard of "beyond a reasonable doubt" requires substantial corroboration of hypnotically elicited memories.

In recent years, it has become more common to use hypnosis to refresh recollection not subject to traumatic repression. The most widely cited of these approaches (Reiser, 1980) has been adopted by police departments around the country to refresh or improve previously existing recall in situations in which little or no trauma may be involved. Hypnotized subjects are told that their memories are analogous to a videotape and that the use of hypnosis can help them provide additional details of which they are unaware. This approach may have the unfortunate effect of encouraging subjects to come up with fantasies that are reported as memories (confabulation), or to develop an artificial sense of certainty about the veracity of their memory because the memory survived a hypnotic interrogation (concreting). Indeed, in one case, a police officer told a subject in trance that she could "lift the mask of the bank robber in order to see his face."

One important case that epitomized the extreme in terms of the abuse of hypnosis, and also of a legal overreaction to such abuse, is the California case of *People v. Shirley* (1982), which adopted the per se exclusion rule (Spiegel, 1987). Donald Lee Shirley was indicted for rape and convicted largely by the testimony of his victim. The two had met earlier that evening in a local bar and returned to the victim's home. Both had been drinking a good deal and subsequently engaged in sexual activities. The defendant then left to get some beer from his own apartment. She sat at home and made no effort to contact the police. He returned with the beer, a friend came to visit, and shortly thereafter the defendant left. After talking for some time with her friend, the victim decided that she had been raped and called the police.

Because of her intoxication, her memory of the facts of the case was extremely poor, and a number of inconsistencies in her repeated descriptions of the events were evident. Indeed, the victim was unable to tell a consistent, coherent story. The night before she was to testify at the trial, she was hypnotized by one of the prosecutors and her testimony conveniently became more consistent. This led to the defendant's conviction and to a reversal by the Supreme Court of California.

In its lengthy opinion, the court relied heavily on Diamond's (1980) argument that whenever a witness is subjected to hypnosis, the dangers of confabulation, making up new information reported as memory, or concreting, a false sense of confidence on the part of the witness, are so serious that the witness should be precluded from testifying. This, in fact, was the way the court ruled.

The *Shirley* opinion initially held that any witness or victim who had been hypnotized for forensic purposes would not be allowed to testify *at all* regarding *any* of the facts of the case. Thus, this initial ruling disqualified the witness, not just the posthypnotic testimony. It went far beyond the prevailing belief that the product of hypnotic interrogation should not be admitted and excluded the witnesses themselves. However, the Supreme Court of California modified its *Shirley* ruling to indicate that any memories that had been recorded before the hypnosis session would be admissible; any new information remembered during or after the hypnosis was excluded. *Shirley* was also modified to be inapplicable to defendants, a ruling that predates the *Rock v. Arkansas* opinion by five years.

It is clear that a witness who has been hypnotized will be subject at least to challenge by opposing counsel. At the same time, there are a number of problems with this per se ruling, one of which is that a nonhypnotizable person who is subjected to a hypnotic ceremony will not experience hypnosis, yet may be denied the opportunity to testify on the basis of presumably having been hypnotized. This is a situation in which the measurement of hypnotizability is extremely important. Because it is clear that hypnotizability is a stable and measurable trait, and because people vary in their hypnotic capacity from no responsivity to very high, it is important to take into account hypnotic responsivity and the nature of the attempt at a hypnotic ceremony to determine whether hypnosis has indeed occurred. The California Supreme Court accepted this argument in *People v. Caro* (1988), where David Spiegel was able to show that the witness was not hypnotizable despite police efforts to create a trance. The court held that the witness could testify fully because hypnosis had not in fact occurred despite the attempts to employ it.

FORENSIC HYPNOSIS RULES AS A THREAT TO THERAPY

Hypnosis currently is under siege in the therapeutic setting on two fronts. First, per se rules serve as a threat to therapists using hypnosis without informed consent forms, because the therapist may be depriving the patient of the ability to testify in court (Scheflin, 1993). Second, hypnosis is still a major target of the false memory advocates who continue to make several mistakes about it: (a) they attribute to hypnosis what is really the malleability of memory; (b) they argue, without proof, that hypnosis always contaminates memory despite the fact that the courts are filled with cases where the hypnosis did not alter the prehypnotic recall, or where the hypnotic recollections were verified independently; (c) they move from the premise that hypnosis involves suggestion, to the conclusion that the hypnotic session must inevitably be *unduly* suggestive or mostly the product of suggestion (fantasy); and (d) they argue that hypnosis is always an exercise in fantasy and imagination and therefore cannot result in historically accurate recollection.

STUDIES OF HYPNOTIC MEMORY ENHANCEMENT

The experimental literature has attempted to answer some of the questions of the effectiveness of hypnosis on improving recall, but has been limited by the strained analogy between the laboratory and the forensic setting. The literature has shown convincingly that there is no enhancement of recall of nonsense material by hypnosis (Barber & Calverley, 1966; Dhanens & Lundy, 1975; Rosenhan & London, 1963), and that there is no enhancement of the *recognition* of meaningful material (Timm, 1981).

The more interesting, and more significant, area has been the study of enhancement of *recall* of meaningful material. A number of earlier studies indicate greater recall of meaningful material under hypnosis, but the price paid is an increase in incorrect recall and an increased sense of confidence not justified by the ratio of incorrect to correct new material. It should be noted that few of these studies have attempted to control response bias. This is important because it is clear that repeated trials, even without hypnosis, can result in an increase in the reporting of new correct and incorrect information (Erdelyi, 1970, 1996). Indeed, the proportion of correct-incorrect responses is similar in hypnosis and nonhypnosis recall conditions; there is simply more productivity in the hypnosis condition (Dywan & Bowers, 1983). This study is particularly interesting because it demonstrates that low hypnotizables in the hypnotic condition perform no differently from high or low hypnotizables who are not hypnotized. It was only the high hypnotizables in the hypnosis condition who showed an increase in productivity as well as confidence. However, even with this group, no follow-ups were conducted to determine whether the reports were actually believed to be memories.

It is important to remember that the concept of confabulation is originally derived from the description of Korsakov's psychosis, in which a severe thiamine (a vitamin) deficiency results in obliteration of the ability to record and retrieve short-term memory. When such patients are asked a simple memory question, they will tend to confabulate or make up an answer, so that it *appears* that they have a memory when they do not. This use of the term *confabulation* is instructive because it reminds one that confabulation consists of both the construction of a pseudomemory and the deficiency or absence of an original memory. It is easier to confabulate in a situation in which there is no real memory to be pushed aside, as occurred in the *Shirley* case, where real memories were obliterated by an alcoholic blackout.

A number of other limitations exist in the possible analogy between laboratory and forensic settings. The usual problem in the court is deciding the effect of hypnosis on a witness months or years after the event occurs. All but one of the analogue studies that demonstrated hypnotic effects on content or confidence did so during a hypnotic session or immediately after it. These effects, although statistically significant, are usually not large. Given the general difficulty in maintaining actively sought behavioral change caused by hypnosis over a follow-up period of months or years, it is at best speculative to assume that a hypnotic effect demonstrated in the laboratory within the first few hours of hypnotic interrogation will last months or years afterward.

One interesting study by Laurence and Perry (1983) shows that hypnotized individuals, told that they heard something while they were sleeping, which in fact they did not hear, tended to report as real memories this hypnotically induced memory seven days later. This is identical to the experiment conducted by Bernheim a century ago and by Orne in 1982 (Barnes, 1982). It is also reminiscent of the "honest liar" experiment reported by Spiegel (1980). But even in the Laurence and Perry study, only a minority of the highly hypnotizable subjects continued after seven days to report pseudomemories for the peripheral details tested in the experiment, although the effect was significant. However, this study, and others based on it, were reviewed by McCann and Sheehan (1988), who pointed out that the results did not suggest great concern about hypnotically implanted pseudomemories. There is little empirical evidence to demonstrate that the effects of hypnosis on hypnotizable individuals last for months or years required by the legal process.

Second, even in experiments that attempt to replicate the kind of emotional arousal that may occur in rape or assault, in a staged mock assassination (Timm, 1981), or in a gory film (Putnam, 1979), such artificial settings cannot reproduce the sense of fear, pain, and helplessness that real victims and witnesses may experience during a crime. Thus, the intertwined roles of emotion and content in memory retrieval cannot be adequately replicated in a laboratory.

Third, motivational issues are clearly important in testimony. It is very different for a college student to attempt to recall information to perform in an experiment than for a witness to provide information that may lead to someone's incarceration. These motivational factors are crucial, especially when they affect the response criterion (i.e., the willingness of the subject to report something as a memory); it cannot be assumed that factors that influence the response criterion in a laboratory experiment are the same as those that affect a witness's willingness to testify. Finally, none of these laboratory studies deals with the kind of traumatic stress, global amnesia for an event, and its spontaneous recovery by hypnosis that may occur in the clinical forensic setting.

The Council on Scientific Affairs of the American Medical Association convened a panel to prepare a report on the scientific status of refreshing recollection by the use of hypnosis. This report was approved by the House of Delegates for publication in the *Journal of the American Medical Association* (American Medical Association, 1985). The eight-member panel concluded that there is no evidence that hypnosis enhances recall of meaningless material or any kind of recognition memory, such as a photo identification lineup. When hypnosis has been used to facilitate recall of meaningful past events, it has elicited a mixture of accurate and inaccurate information that cannot be disentangled without external corroboration. Furthermore, the hypnotic ceremony may enhance confidence in memory without enhancing accuracy. However, hypnosis may be especially useful in situations in which witnesses or victims have been traumatized and suffer from amnesia. Guidelines recommended for such use included careful efforts to elicit the best memory prior to hypnosis, precautions against suggesting specific responses or the need to produce new information, tape recording of all contact between the hypnotist and the witness, and an assessment of the witness's hypnotic responsiveness.

Two recent books have contained thorough reviews of the hypnosis and memory literature. The first (Hammond et al., 1995), issued by the American Society of Clinical Hypnosis, contains a complete and detailed set of guidelines that must be followed in forensic hypnosis settings. This book received the Arthur Shapiro Award from the Society for Clinical and Experimental Hypnosis as the finest book on hypnosis published that year. The second book (Brown et al., 1998) is even more thorough in analyzing the current scientific literature. Both books conclude that (a) when proper guidelines are followed, hypnosis may be effective in retrieving otherwise unavailable information, and (b) court concerns with confabulation and concreting address the nature of memory itself, not properly conducted hypnosis.

MEASUREMENT OF HYPNOTIZABILITY

When hypnosis is to be employed in the forensic setting, the hypnotizability of the subject should be tested using one of the standardized hypnotizability scales, such as the Hypnotic Induction Profile (HIP) (Spiegel & Spiegel, 1978), the Stanford Hypnotic Susceptibility Scales (SHSS) (Weitzenhoffer & Hilgard, 1959), the Stanford Hypnotic Clinical Scale (SHCS) (Hilgard & Hilgard, 1975), or the Barber Creative Imagination Scale (BCIS) (Barber & Wilson, 1978–1979) to document the subject's degree of hypnotic responsivity, if any. Indeed, if a subject fails to demonstrate any hypnotic responsivity on formal testing, the person conducting the session would be well advised to forgo any further hypnotic ceremonies because the subject is unlikely to respond and the problems inherent with the appearance of having induced hypnosis can be avoided.

At the other end of the spectrum, the problems of confabulation and an artificial sense of confidence noted by Diamond (1980) and the California Supreme Court (*People v. Shirley*, 1982) are especially applicable to the small subgroup of the population who measure as highly hypnotizable, *whether or not hypnosis formally has been used.* An intense, structured, and leading police interrogation, or a carefully orchestrated preparation for testimony by an attorney, could theoretically have the same effect that a formal hypnotic ceremony could have, thus resulting in a false confession (Connery, 1977). Factors that can influence eyewitness testimony and the vulnerability of witnesses to being led by examiners using hypnosis should be viewed as part of the same continuum (Gudjonsson, 1992). Indeed, one issue often overlooked in the forensic setting is that of individual differences. On the basis of experience with hypnosis, some individuals are clearly more malleable and vulnerable to exploitation of this kind than others, whether or not a formal trance is induced. This issue is especially important in the area of coerced confessions (Spiegel & Spiegel, 1984b).

The main point is that a highly hypnotizable individual in a coercive setting is excessively vulnerable to manipulation, even without the formal use of hypnotic techniques. Furthermore, some of the experimental literature supports this view, indicating that high hypnotizability may be an equal or more important factor than the formal use of the hypnotic ceremony (Zelig & Beidleman, 1981). However, Dywan and Bowers (1983) argue that both high hypnotizability and a formal induction of hypnosis are necessary to produce an alteration in the recall of information. In any event, it is clear from clinical experience that hypnoticlike events may occur even when a formal hypnotic induction ceremony has not occurred. For that reason, hypnosis can never be excluded from the legal setting (Beahrs, 1988)—even if everyone agreed that exclusion was a good idea. Thus, there is important value in measuring hypnotic responsivity in the forensic setting. Forensic examiners and clinicians should show sensitivity to the possibility that hypnoticlike events may occur in coercive settings. Highly hypnotizable people are especially vulnerable to their environments, even to the extent of abandoning their own enlightened self-interests.

THE FUTURE

Since the late 1980s, evidence has been mounting that the current state of the legal rules concerning hypnosis with memory is unscientific and unfair. The harsh rigidity of the per se rule, and the alleged scientific justifications for it, have been the subject of modern challenges.

FACTUAL PROBLEMS WITH THE PER SE RULE

Scheflin (1994a, 1994b) has criticized the per se exclusion rule on several factual grounds.

Sexual Seduction

Under the per se rule, an unethical hypnotist who uses trance to facilitate seduction will have committed the perfect crime: the subject-victim will be unable to testify because all the memories are posthypnotic. Today, even the supporters of the per se rule have acknowledged in print that an exception must be made for illegal or unethical conduct committed while the subject was in trance (Giannelli, 1995).

Time Delays

Suppose an individual is hypnotized and has no new memories. Five years later, with no intervening hypnosis, additional memories surface. Is the witness disqualified to testify in regard to them simply because of the hypnosis five years earlier? Is there any time limit after which the memories cannot be attributed to the hypnosis?

Self-Hypnosis

Suppose a subject is taught self-hypnosis and practices the technique regularly. Are all memories now contaminated?

Audiotapes

The market is flooded with "self-hypnosis/subliminal message" audiotapes. Does listening to such a tape disqualify a person from testifying?

Therapeutic Hypnosis

Suppose a patient arrives at therapy and the therapist decides hypnosis would be beneficial. During the trance, memories, which were not the subject of the hypnosis, are revealed. Should the per se rule disqualify the witness from testifying about them? If so, the patient may then sue the therapist for taking away the patient's legal rights without informed consent. Modern commentators (Brown et al., 1998; Hammond et al., 1995; Scheflin, 1993) urge the use of informed consent forms in this situation to protect therapists and their patients.

SCIENTIFIC PROBLEMS WITH THE PER SE RULE

When the American Medical Association issued its 1985 report, little solid research had been done from which valid conclusions could safely be drawn (Kihlstrom, 1985). McCann and Sheehan (1988) found only three studies, all of them either seriously flawed or highly exaggerated in their conclusions concerning the ease of hypnotically implanting false memories. Frischholz (1996) has presented an effective critique of the AMA report, noticing that the report uses an outmoded definition of hypnosis and relies mostly on memory research using nonsense material in laboratory settings.

One of the major problems with the AMA report is the failure to recognize the distinction between memory and hypnotically assisted memory. Precisely the same contaminations the experts cautioned against—confabulation, undue self-confidence, increased responsiveness to suggestion and/or social influences and demand characteristics—may be produced in memory without hypnosis, as memory researchers have repeatedly demonstrated (Brown et al., 1998). Sheehan (1996) is correct in observing, "an important conclusion that has emerged from the literature is that memory contamination is a function of memory and influence and not a danger specific to the use of hypnosis" (p. 13).

For forensic hypnosis to have a future, indeed, for forensic hypnosis to have the right to have a future, the science must show that when hypnotic procedures are used carefully, memory contamination is not inevitable.

Despite the impressive quantity and quality of studies since 1985, the AMA recently reaffirmed its 1985 report without a single citation to the current scientific literature (American Medical Association, 1994). Four members of the original eight-member committee that drafted the AMA report now conclude that it no longer states the prevailing science.

CURRENT SCIENTIFIC OPINION

After almost a decade of silence, there is a strong recent shift in scientific opinion about the value of hypnosis with memory. Unlike the earlier negative views, which were not supported by careful research, the current favorable opinion concerning hypnosis with memory is based on a substantial body of significant research. In analyzing this research, much of which has appeared after 1985, it is highly significant that *every* recent major work on forensic hypnosis has advocated the replacement of the per se exclusion rule with the totality of the circumstances test (Brown et al., 1998; Hammond et al., 1995; McConkey & Sheehan, 1995; Scheflin & Shapiro, 1989). Only Orne and his associates maintain a minority negative view (Karlin, 1997; Karlin & Orne, 1996, 1997; Perry, Orne, London, & Orne, 1996), but their opinion has been strenuously challenged (Scheflin, 1996, 1997).

In a recent paper, Lynn and Kirsch (1996) reach an important conclusion: "False memories can be created with or without hypnosis, and the role of hypnosis in their creation is likely to be quite small. . . . Hypnosis does not reliably produce more false memories than are produced in a variety of nonhypnotic situations in which misleading information is conveyed to participants" (p. 151). Furthermore, according to Lynn and Kirsch, "The role of hypnosis in enhancing confidence in false memories is also exaggerated" (p. 152). As Sheehan (1996) has recently noted, the consensus "appears to be that, 'the courts must decide on a case by case basis the admissibility of hypnotically recalled material'" (p. 13, quoting Scheflin, 1994a). Wagstaff (1996), one of Britain's foremost forensic experts, described his experience as an expert in a case where the police used hypnosis. In his report, Wagstaff concluded: "But I would argue that, instead of a blanket rejection of anything said by the witness in such cases, we must judge each case individually. Perhaps we might more usefully ask, what might be the effect of this *particular* hypnosis session, on *particular* statements, made by this *particular* witness?" (p. 189).

FUNDAMENTAL FAIRNESS

Consider the following case (Scheflin, 1997). A 4-year-old girl went to her mother and said "Daddy's touching me in my private parts." The mother had a breakdown and was hospitalized. The child, now in the custody of Daddy, learned not to talk about this—look what happened to Mommy when she was told. Several years pass and the molestation continued. Medical records of the child were consistent with molesting, but the child would not talk when asked. After a year of therapy, hypnosis was used and the child talked about the molesting. New York courts would not admit her posthypnotic testimony despite the fact that there was independent medical corroborating evidence that she was molested. Without her evidence, there was no proof that Daddy was the molester. Daddy retained custody.

Where is the justice in telling that little girl that the courts will not hear her story?

Fundamental fairness demands that each case be heard on its own merits, at least at a preliminary hearing where the quality of the evidence can be judicially assessed. The per se rule prohibits posthypnotic memories from being admitted into evidence even though it can be shown that the hypnosis procedures were scrupulously neutral and that the memories can be independently corroborated as true.

Although the per se exclusion rule might be defended on the grounds that it saves money to avoid hearings, trading judicial economy for a lesser form of justice is a poor bargain. Furthermore, because most trials have preliminary hearings anyway, the cost savings, if any, would not be substantial.

SCIENCE AND THE SUPREME COURT

Even if science and fundamental fairness fail to sway courts, a recent development in the U.S. Supreme Court is likely to force states to reevaluate their per se exclusion rule. In the *Daubert v. Merrell Dow Pharmaceuticals, Inc.* (1993) case, the Court changed the test for the admissibility of scientific evidence in all federal courts. More than half the states have now adopted this new approach, which favors the introduction of relevant evidence and which makes the judge, not the scientific community, the gatekeeper to determine whether expert testimony is scientific. Because the new test is built on flexibility, several courts have held that per se exclusion rules are no longer defensible. In two cases involving polygraphs, the U.S. Court of Appeals for the Fifth Circuit held that evidence obtained from a lie detector cannot automatically be excluded (*United States v. Pettigrew*, 1996; *United States v. Posado*, 1995). In another polygraph case, the Ninth Circuit in *United States v. Cordoba* (1996) held that its per se exclusion rule against the admission of polygraph evidence was "effectively overruled" by the "flexible inquiry assigned to the trial judge by *Daubert*." The court further noted that other per se rules were equally as vulnerable to abolition and had already been overthrown.

More directly on this point, in *Rowland v. Commonwealth* (1995), a stepmother saw her stepson shoot her and her daughter. The stepmother's physician diagnosed her as having posttraumatic stress disorder and he recommended she see Dr. William Wester, a psychologist. Wester agreed with the diagnosis and decided to treat her with hypnosis. Before beginning the hypnosis treatment, Wester took complete statements from the stepmother about the shooting incident. The first statement was audiotaped and the second statement was videotaped. Following the videotaping, Wester used hypnosis for the first time. The stepmother's statement while in trance was virtually identical to her recorded prehypnotic statements. The defendant requested that all testimony from the stepmother be suppressed, but the trial judge ruled otherwise. The defendant on appeal argued for a rule of per se inadmissibility. In a 4–3 decision, the Supreme Court of Kentucky held that a per se inadmissibility rule was no longer appropriate and might violate *Daubert.*

In May 1997, the U.S. Supreme Court, in *United States v. Scheffer,* agreed to decide the issue of whether per se exclusion rules in polygraph cases violate a criminal defendant's Sixth Amendment constitutional right to present a defense. *Scheffer* thus appears before the Court in the same posture as the *Rock v. Arkansas* (1987) case did with hypnosis.

Although commentators predicted that the Supreme Court would abolish per se exclusion rules (Fried, 1997), the Court's opinion reached the opposite result with minimal mention of *Daubert* and *Rock.* Whether the Court would also uphold the per se exclusion rule in hypnosis cases cannot be predicted because first, the Court emphasized that it was ruling in a case involving a rule of evidence established by the president in military cases. Thus, the rule might not be supportable in non-military criminal courts. Second, the majority noted that the evidence in hypnosis cases generally involves primary factual testimony, while in polygraph cases the evidence is secondary because it is designed to support the credibility of the person who takes the polygraph test, and thus does not recite crucial facts that might never be heard from others. Finally, some of the justices recognized a "tension" between the reasoning of *Scheffer* and the purpose of *Daubert.* They warned that "some later case might present a more compelling case for the introduction" of such polygraph testimony. There was also considerable disagreement in the several opinions concerning whether the factual underpinnings of the majority's rejection of the reliability of polygraphs evidence was itself accurate. Certainly, the final chapter is not yet written on the viability of the per se exclusion rule in hypnosis cases. It will be interesting to see whether the federal and state courts that abolished their per se rules will now reinstate them.

Two Recent Attacks on Hypnosis

Within the past few years, two new attacks on hypnosis with memory have surfaced. First, even when hypnosis is not being utilized directly, its contaminating effects occur with techniques that are actually "disguised" hypnosis.

According to Perry (1995), disguised techniques, which are prevalent in stage hypnosis shows, have been picked up and used by "recovered memory" therapists, who have added their "New Age ideology which argues that insight into the cause of symptoms leads to their alleviation" (p. 196). Does Perry doubt that this may be true?

Disguised hypnosis is any use of guided imagery, relaxation, or imagination. Perry writes about a student who discussed with her mother whether she should participate in a hypnosis experiment. On the morning of the experiment, the mother said that maybe the daughter should not participate because "you might never come out of it." This acted as a prehypnotic suggestion and the student had great difficulty coming out of the trance. Spiegel (1997), however, would classify the mother's behavior as a nocebo, a negative message that inhibits healing, operating in a similar fashion to the effect of positive expectation for treatment known as a placebo. Thus, according to this attack, *even therapists who do not use hypnosis are using hypnosis.*

The second attack argues that hypnotic consequences may affect people who are not responsive to hypnotic suggestion. In two recent articles, Orne and colleagues (Orne, Whitehouse, Dinges, & Orne, 1996; Orne, Whitehouse, Orne, & Dinges, 1996), based on retrospective analyses of earlier research, argued that low and medium hypnotizables are vulnerable to contamination from the inherently corrupting influence of hypnosis. Thus, *even those who are not affected by hypnosis are affected by hypnosis.* Brown et al. (1998) carefully analyze and reject this attack based on methodological flaws in the Orne research design.

No court has yet dealt with these recent attacks on the impact of hypnosis on memory.

CONCLUSION

In summary, hypnosis is a naturally occurring phenomenon, an extreme form of concentration with intensity of focus and relative suspension of peripheral awareness. It may be formally applied in certain limited circumstances to reverse amnesias, especially those related to traumatic events. It may also occur spontaneously under duress. Hypnosis can be a useful tool in the forensic setting, but may also create difficulties. The measurement of hypnotic responsivity can be useful in determining to what degree such problems are likely to have occurred. Hypnosis is no shortcut or replacement for standard forensic investigative procedures, but it may be of great help in special circumstances, especially when trauma has occurred and there is accompanying functional amnesia or when the possible uncovering of even a small amount of new information would lead to the discovery of important additional evidence. When hypnosis is used for forensic purposes, strict guidelines must be scrupulously followed.

Hypnotic phenomena are naturally occurring and intertwined with traumatic experience, which is the day-to-day fare of both criminal and civil law. They are not easily disentangled, and even if banishment of hypnosis were possible, it would not solve problems of the reliability of memory so important to the conduct of justice. Better that hypnotic phenomena should be understood and employed wisely and temperately. The current state of the law of forensic hypnosis may appear quite odd (Scheflin, 1997):

> According to the Karlin and Orne position supporting the *per se* exclusion rule for hypnotized witnesses, a person who has been lobotomized can testify in court, a person who has received massive electroshock treatments can testify in court, a person who has taken enormous dosages of mind-altering psychiatric drugs or psychedelics can testify in court, a person who has suffered substantial organic brain damage can testify in court; but a person who had been competently hypnotized by an experienced licensed professional who carefully followed strict guidelines to avoid undue suggestions, cannot testify in court. (p. 160)

Whether this position should continue to prevail will be the challenge of the future.

APPENDIX
Significant Dates in the History of Forensic Hypnosis

1846	First recorded use of hypnosis in court.
1889	Moll discusses "retroactive hallucinations" with hypnosis in the legal arena.
1891	Bernheim conducts experiments with hypnotically implanted false beliefs.
1897	California Supreme Court declares that "the law of the United States does not recognize hypnotism" *(Ebanks).*
1955	The British Medical Association becomes the first professional organization to endorse the medical use of hypnosis.
1958	The American Medical Association officially approves hypnosis as a therapeutic procedure.
1961	The American Psychiatric Association endorses hypnosis as a therapeutic procedure.
1967	Herbert Spiegel makes a film, *Fact or Fiction,* demonstrating hypnotic alteration of memories.
1968	A Maryland court becomes the first in the country to permit hypnotically refreshed recollection to be admitted into evidence *(Harding).*
1977	Orne files an affidavit in a California case suggesting that certain guidelines be followed to avoid hypnotic contamination of memory.
1978	A federal court for the first time raises the possibility that the use of hypnosis with memory may create dangers *(Adams).*
1980	The Minnesota Supreme Court decides that a per se exclusion rule must be applied in cases where hypnosis is used to refresh recollection *(Mack).*
1980	Diamond publishes an influential law review article in the *California Law Review* arguing that hypnosis inevitably contaminates memory and should not be used for memory retrieval.
1981	Between the extreme open-admissibility and per se exclusion rules, the New Jersey Supreme Court adopts a middle position (admissibility with safeguards or totality of the circumstances), permitting the admission of hypnotically refreshed recollection provided certain guidelines had been followed *(Hurd).*
1982	The California Supreme Court holds that a previously hypnotized witness is disqualified from testifying *(Shirley).*
1982	Orne conducts an important experiment for a BBC-TV documentary suggesting that it is easy to implant false memories with hypnosis.
1983	Laurence and Perry publish a research study suggesting it is easy to implant false memories with hypnosis.
1985	The American Medical Association publishes a Council on Scientific Affairs Report, *Scientific Status of Refreshing Recollection by the Use of Hypnosis,* which is critical of the use of hypnosis with memory.
1985	The California legislature passes legislation adopting a per se exclusion rule in criminal cases involving hypnotically refreshed memory.
1985	The U.S. Supreme Court decides that a per se exclusion rule is unconstitutional when applied to criminal defendants *(Rock).*
1986	The first repressed memory case is decided by an appellate court *(Tyson).*
1989	Publication of Scheflin and Shapiro, *Trance on Trial* (Guilford).
1989	Publication of an important paper by McCann and Sheehan raising serious questions about the research supporting the position that it is easy to implant false memories with hypnosis.

1992   The False Memory Syndrome Foundation is established.

1993   The U.S. Supreme Court adopts a new rule concerning the admissibility of scientific evidence *(Daubert)*.

1994   Scheflin publishes a detailed attack on the per se exclusion rule, citing (a) cases of sexual seduction, (b) civil cases, (c) self-help hypnosis cases, (d) hypnosis audiotape cases, (e) false confession cases, (f) time delay cases, and (g) therapeutic hypnosis cases.

1995   McConkey and Sheehan publish *Hypnosis, Memory, and Behavior in Criminal Investigation* (Guilford), advocating the totality of the circumstances test, providing guidelines for the use of hypnosis with memory, and suggesting a closer inquiry into the motivations of those seeking hypnosis to refresh their recollections.

1995   The American Society of Clinical Hypnosis publishes its *Clinical Hypnosis and Memory: Guidelines for Clinicians and for Forensic Hypnosis* (ASCH Press). ASCH favors the totality of the circumstances test in the courts.

1995   Frischholz delivers a paper at the annual meeting of Society for Clinical and Experimental Hypnosis (SCEH), seriously challenging the conclusions reached by the 1985 AMA report. Half of the original AMA committee now agree with this paper.

1995   The Second Circuit Court of Appeals decides that the totality of the circumstances test governs the admissibility of hypnotically refreshed recollection in federal courts *(Borawick)*.

1996   The Supreme Court decides not to review the *Borawick* case, thus leaving its ruling adopting the totality of the circumstances test as the law in federal courts.

1996   A thorough debate on whether courts should favor the per se exclusion rule or the totality of the circumstances test begins with the publication in the *Cultic Studies Journal* of a paper by Karlin and Orne, favoring exclusion and a paper by Scheflin favoring admission with safeguards.

1996   Two additional attacks surface against hypnosis. First, it is argued that many procedures, such as relaxation, guided imagery, visualization, etc., are "disguised" hypnosis. Second, it is argued that even low hypnotizables are adversely affected by the use of hypnosis with memory.

1997   The debate between Karlin & Orne and Scheflin continues in the *Cultic Studies Journal*.

1998   A complete review and analysis of the hypnosis and memory literature is published by Brown, Scheflin, and Hammond, *Memory, Trauma Treatment, and the Law* (Norton).

REFERENCES

American Medical Association. (1958, September 13). Council on mental health, medical use of hypnosis. *Journal of the American Medical Association, 168,* 186–189.

American Medical Association. (1985). Council on scientific affairs, scientific status of refreshing recollection by the use of hypnosis. *Journal of the American Medical Association, 253,* 1918–1923.

American Medical Association. (1994). *Council on scientific affairs, memories of childhood abuse* (CSA Report 5-A-94).

American Psychiatric Association. (1994). *Diagnostic and statistical manual of mental disorders* (4th ed.). Washington, DC: American Psychiatric Association.

Arons, H. (1967). *Hypnosis in criminal investigation.* Springfield, IL: Thomas.

Barber, T. X., & Calverley, D. S. (1966). Effects of recall of hypnotic induction, motivational suggestions, and suggested regression: A methodological and experimental analysis. *Journal of Abnormal Psychology, 71,* 169–180.

Barber, T. X., & Wilson, S. C. (1978–1979). The Barber Suggestibility Scale and the Creative Imagination Scale: Experimental and clinical applications. *American Journal of Clinical Hypnosis, 21,* 84–96.

Barnes, M. (Producer and Director). (1982). *Hypnosis on trial.* Television documentary. London, England: British Broadcasting Company.

Beahrs, J. O. (1988). Hypnosis cannot be fully nor reliably excluded from the courtroom. *American Journal of Clinical Hypnosis, 31,* 18–27.

Bernheim, H. (1991/1980). *New studies in hypnotism* (R. S. Sandor, Trans.). New York: International Universities Press. (Original work published in 1891)

Borawick v. Shay, 68 F.3d 597 (2nd Cir. (Conn.)) (1995); *cert. denied,* 116 S.Ct. 1869, 134 L.Ed.2d 966 (1996).

Bower, G. H. (1981). Mood and memory. *American Psychologist, 36,* 129–148.

Breuer, J., & Freud, S. (1955). In J. Strachey (Ed. & Trans.), *The standard edition of the complete psychological works of Sigmund Freud* (Vol. 2, pp. 183–251). London: Hogarth Press.

British Medical Association. (1955, April 23). Supplementary annual report of council, 1954–1995. *British Medical Journal,* (Suppl.), 190–193.

Brodie-Innes, J. W. (1891). Legal aspects of hypnotism. *Juridical Review, 3,* 51–61.

Brown, D., Scheflin, A. W., & Hammond, D. C. (1998). *Memory, trauma treatment, and the law.* New York: Norton.

Butler, L., & Spiegel, D. (1997). Trauma and memory. In L. Dickstein, M. Riba, & J. Oldham (Eds.), *Repressed memories* (pp. 13–53). Washington, DC: American Psychiatric Association Press.

Connery, D. S. (1977). *Guilty until proven innocent.* New York: Putnam.

Daubert v. Merrell Dow Pharmaceuticals, Inc., 509 U.S. 579, 113 S.Ct 2786, 125 L.Ed. 2d 469 (1993).

Dhanens, T. P., & Lundy, R. M. (1975). Hypnotic and waking suggestions and recall. *International Journal of Clinical and Experimental Hypnosis, 23,* 68–79.

Diamond, B. L. (1980). Inherent problems in the use of pretrial hypnosis on a prospective witness. *California Law Review, 68,* 313–349.

DuMaurier, G. (1894). *Trilby.* New York: Harper & Row.

Dywan, J., & Bowers, K. S. (1983). The use of hypnosis to enhance recall. *Science, 222,* 184–185.

Ellenberger, H. F. (1970). *Discovery of the unconscious: The history and evolution of dynamic psychiatry.* New York: Basic Books.

Erdelyi, M. H. (1970). Recovery of unavailable perceptual input. *Cognitive Psychology, 1,* 99–113.

Erdelyi, M. H. (1996). *The recovery of unconscious memories: Hypermnesia and reminiscence.* Chicago: University of Chicago Press.

Fried, R. (1997, May 20). Supreme Court to rule on use of polygraph tests. *The Court TV Recorder.*

Frischholz, E. J. (1996, November 11). *Latest developments in forensic hypnosis and memory.* Paper presented at the 47th annual Workshops and Scientific Program of the Society for Clinical and Experimental Hypnosis, Tampa, FL.

Giannelli, P. C. (1995). The admissibility of hypnotic evidence in U.S. courts. *International Journal of Clinical and Experimental Hypnosis, 43,* 212–233.

Gravitz, M. A. (1995, April). First admission (1846) of hypnotic testimony in court. *American Journal of Clinical Hypnosis, 37*(4), 326–330.

Gudjonsson, G. H. (1992). *The psychology of interrogations, confessions and testimony.* New York: Wiley.

Hammond, D. C., Garver, R. B., Mutter, C. B., Crasilneck, H. B., Frischholz, E., Gravitz, M. A., Hibler, N. S., Olson, J., Scheflin, A. W., Spiegel, H., & Wester, W. (1995). *Clinical hypnosis and memory: Guidelines for clinicians and for forensic hypnosis.* Des Plaines, IL: American Society of Clinical Hypnosis Press.

Harding v. State, 5 Md.App. 230, 246 A.2d 302 (1968), *cert. denied,* Harding v. Maryland, 395 U.S. 949, 89 S.Ct. 2030, 23 L.Ed.2d 468 (1969).

Harris, R. (1989). *Murder and madness: Medicine, law, and society in the fin de siecle.* Oxford, England: Clarendon Press.

Hilgard, E. R. (1965). *Hypnotic susceptibility.* New York: Harcourt, Brace, & World.

Hilgard, E. R., & Hilgard, J. R. (1975). *Hypnosis in the relief of pain.* Los Altos, CA: Kaufmann.

Hypnotism in criminal defence. (1894). *The Barrister,* pp. 249–251.

Hypnotism and the law. (1893, October 14). *Law Times,* p. 500.

Karlin, R. A. (1997). Illusory safeguards: Legitimizing distortion in recall with guidelines for forensic hypnosis: Two case reports. *International Journal of Clinical & Experimental Hypnosis, 45*(1), 18–40.

Karlin, R. A., & Orne, M. T. (1996). Commentary on *Borawick v. Shay:* Hypnosis, social influence, incestuous child abuse, and satanic ritual abuse: The Iatrogenic creation of horrific memories for the remote past. *Cultic Studies Journal, 13*(1), 42–94.

Karlin, R. A., & Orne, M. T. (1997). Hypnosis and the iatrogenic creation of memory: On the need for a *per se* exclusion of testimony based on hypnotically influenced recall. *Cultic Studies Journal, 14*(2), 172–206.

Kihlstrom, J. F. (1985). Hypnosis. *Annual Review of Psychology, 36,* 385–418.

Laurence, J.-R., & Perry, C. (1983). Hypnotically created memory among highly hypnotizable subjects. *Science, 222,* 523–524.

Laurence, J.-R., & Perry, C. (1988). *Hypnosis, will, and memory: A psycho-legal history.* New York: Guilford Press.

Leyra v. Denno, 347 U.S. 556, 74 S.Ct. 716, 98 L.Ed. 948 (1954).

Lynn, S. J., & Kirsch, I. I. (1996). Alleged alien abductions: False memories, hypnosis, and fantasy proneness. *Psychological Inquiry, 7*(2), 151–155.

Masson, J. M. (1992). *The assault on truth: Freud's suppression of the seduction theory* (Rev. ed.). New York: Harper Perennial.

McCann, T., & Sheehan, P. W. (1988). Hypnotically induced pseudomemories—Sampling their conditions among hypnotizable subjects. *Journal of Personality & Social Psychology, 54,* 339–346.

McConkey, K. M., & Sheehan, P. W. (1995). *Hypnosis, memory, and behavior in criminal investigation.* New York: Guilford Press.

Moll, A. (1958). *The study of hypnosis.* New York: Julian Press. (Original work published in 1889)

Morgan, A. H., & Hilgard, E. R. (1973). Age differences in susceptibility to hypnosis. *International Journal of Clinical and Experimental Hypnosis, 21,* 78–85.

Morgan, A. H., Johnson, D. L., & Hilgard, E. R. (1974). The stability of hypnotic susceptibility: A longitudinal study. *International Journal of Clinical and Experimental Hypnosis, 22,* 249–257.

Mutter, C. B. (1984). The use of hypnosis with defendants. *American Journal of Clinical Hypnosis, 27,* 42–51.

Mutter, C. B. (1990). The use of hypnosis with defendants: Does it really work? *American Journal of Clinical Hypnosis, 32,* 257–262.

Orne, M. T. (1979). The use and misuse of hypnosis in court. *International Journal of Clinical and Experimental Hypnosis, 27,* 311–341.

Orne, M. T., Whitehouse, W. G., Dinges, D. F., & Orne, E. C. (1996). Memory liabilities associated with hypnosis: Does low hypnotizability confer immunity? *International Journal of Clinical and Experimental Hypnosis, 44,* 354–367.

Orne, M. T., Whitehouse, W. G., Orne, E. C., & Dinges, D. F. (1996). "Memories" of anomalous and traumatic autobiographical experiences: Validation and consolidation of fantasy through hypnosis. *Psychological Inquiry, 7*(2), 168–172.

People v. Caro, 46 Cal.3d 1035, 251 Cal.Rptr. 757, 761 P.2d 680 (1988).

People v. Ebanks, 117 Cal. 652, 49 P. 1049, 40 L.R.A. 269 (1897).

People v. Ritchie, No. C-36932. Super.Ct. Orange Co., California, April 7, 1977, unrep. (1977).

People v. Shirley, 31 Cal.3d 18, 723 P.2d 1354, 181 Cal.Rptr. 243 (1982), *stay denied,* California v. Shirley, 458 U.S. 1125, 103 S.Ct. 13, 73 L.Ed. 2d 1400 (1982), *cert. denied,* California v. Shirley, 459 U.S. 860, 103 S.Ct. 133, 74 L.Ed. 2d 114.

Perry, C. (1995). The false memory syndrome (FMS) and "disguised" hypnosis. *Hypnos, 22,* 189–197.

Perry, C., Orne, M. T., London, R. W., & Orne, E. C. (1996). Rethinking per se exclusions of hypnotically elicited recall as legal testimony. *International Journal of Clinical and Experimental Hypnosis, 44,* 66–80.

Piccione, C., Hilgard, E. R., & Zimbardo, P. G. (1989). On the degree of stability of measured hypnotizability over a 25-year period. *Journal of Personality and Social Psychology, 56*(2), 289–295.

Putnam, W. H. (1979). Hypnosis and distortions in eyewitness memory. *International Journal of Clinical and Experimental Hypnosis, 27,* 437–448.

Reiser, M. (1980). *Handbook of investigative hypnosis.* Los Angeles: LEHI.

Rock v. Arkansas, 483 U.S.44, 107 S.Ct. 2704, 97 L.Ed. 2d 37 (1987).

Rosenhan, D., & London, P. (1963). Hypnosis in the unhypnotizable: A study in rote learning. *Journal of Experimental Psychology, 65,* 30–34.

Rowland v. Commonwealth, 901 S.W.2d 871 (Ky.Sup.Ct.) (1995).

Scheflin, A. W. (1993, August). Avoiding malpractice liability. *American Society of Clinical Hypnosis Newsletter, 34*(1), 6.

Scheflin, A. W. (1994a). Forensic hypnosis: Unanswered questions. *Australian Journal of Clinical and Experimental Hypnosis, 22,* 23–34.

Scheflin, A. W. (1994b). Forensic hypnosis and the law: The current situation in the United States. In B. J. Evans & R. O. Stanley (Eds.), *Hypnosis and the law: Principles and practice* (pp. 25–48). Heideleberg, Victoria, Australia: Australian Society of Hypnosis.

Scheflin, A. W. (1996). Commentary on *Borawick v. Shay:* The fate of hypnotically retrieved memories. *Cultic Studies Journal, 13*(1), 26–41.

Scheflin, A. W. (1997). False memory and Buridan's ass: A response to Karlin and Orne (1996). *Cultic Studies Journal, 14*(2), 207–289.

Scheflin, A. W. (1998). Ethics and hypnosis: A preliminary inquiry into hypnotic advocacy. In W. Matthews & J. Edgette (Eds.), *Current thinking and research in brief therapy: Solutions, strategies, narratives* (Vol. 2, pp. 307–328). New York: Taylor & Francis.

Scheflin, A. W., & Shapiro, L. (1989). *Trance on trial.* New York: Guilford Press.

Sheehan, P. W. (1996, August 17). *Contemporary trends in hypnosis research.* State-of-the-Art Address presented at the 26th International Congress of Psychology, Montreal, Canada.

Shor, R. E., Orne, M. T., & O'Connell, D. B. (1962). Validation and cross-validation of a scale of self-reported personal experiences which predicts hypnotizability. *Journal of Psychology, 53,* 55–75.

Spiegel, D. (1987). The *Shirley* decision: The cure is worse than the disease. In R. W. Rieber (Ed.), *Advances in forensic psychology and psychiatry* (Vol. 2, pp. 101–118). Norwood, NJ: ABLEX.

Spiegel, D. (1994). Hypnosis. In R. E. Hales, S. C. Yudofsky, & J. A. Talbott (Eds.), *American Psychiatric Press textbook of psychiatry* (2nd ed., pp. 1115–1142). Washington, DC: American Psychiatric Press.

Spiegel, D., & Spiegel, H. (1984a). *Hypnosis: The psychosocial therapies* (Part 2, pp. 701–737). American Psychiatric Association Committee on Psychiatric Therapies.

Spiegel, D., & Spiegel, H. (1984b). Uses of hypnosis in evaluating malingering and deception. *Behavioral Sciences and the Law, 2*(1), 51–65.

Spiegel, H. (1980). Hypnosis and evidence: Help or hindrance? *Annals of New York Academy of Science, 347,* 73–85.

Spiegel, H. (1997). Nocebo: The power of suggestibility. *Preventive Medicine, 26*(5), 616–621.

Spiegel, H., & Spiegel, D. (1978). *Trance and treatment: Clinical uses of hypnosis.* New York: Basic Books.

State v. Hurd, 86 N.J. 525, 432 A.2d 86 (1981).

State v. Mack, 292 N.W.2d 764 (Minn.) (1980).

State v. Papp, (1978). No. 78-02-00229. C.P. Summit Co., Ohio; Lorain Co. No. 16862, March 23, 1978; unrep.; app'd U.S.Sup.Ct. No. 79-5091, *cert. denied* October 27, 1979.

Stern, D. B., Spiegel, H., & Nee, J. C. (1978–1979). The Hypnotic Induction Profile: Normative observations, reliability and validity. *American Journal of Clinical Hypnosis, 31,* 109–132.

Tellegen, A., & Atkinson, G. (1974). Openness to absorbing and self-altering experiences ("absorption"), a trait related to hypnotic susceptibility. *Journal of Abnormal Psychology, 83,* 268–277.

Timm, H. W. (1981). The effect of forensic hypnosis techniques on eyewitness recall and recognition. *Journal of Police Science and Administration, 9,* 188–194.

United States v. Adams, 581 F.2d 193 (9th Cir. 1978), *cert. denied,* 439 U.S. 1006 (1970).

United States v. Cordoba, 104 F.3d 225 (9th Cir.) (1996).

United States v. Pettigrew, 77 F.3d 1500 (5th Cir.) (1996).

United States v. Posado, 57 F.3d 428 (5th Cir.) (1995).

United States v. Scheffer, United States Supreme Court Docket No. 96-1133 (1997).

Wagstaff, G. F. (1996). Should "hypnotized" witnesses be banned from testifying in court? Hypnosis and the M50 murder case. *Contemporary Hypnosis, 13,* 186–190.

Weitzenhoffer, A. M., & Hilgard, E. R. (1959). *Stanford Hypnotic Susceptibility Scales: Forms A and B.* Palo Alto, CA: Consulting Psychologists Press.

Zelig, M., & Beidleman, W. B. (1981). The investigative use of hypnosis: A word of caution. *International Journal of Clinical and Experimental Hypnosis, 24,* 401–412.

PART FOUR

COMMUNICATING EXPERT OPINIONS

CHAPTER 18

Writing Forensic Reports

IRVING B. WEINER

EFFECTIVE CONSULTATION flows from effective communication. Applied psychologists have usually learned this lesson well from their training and professional experience. They know that their opinions and recommendations are valuable only to the extent that they can be meaningfully conveyed to others.

No matter how sharply they have honed their communications skills as consultants in other contexts, however, most psychologists must learn some new ground rules when they enter the forensic area. As helping professionals, they have been accustomed to working solely on behalf of persons involved in their cases and not knowingly to anyone's disadvantage. The administration of civil and criminal justice marches to a different drummer, however, known as the *adversarial system.* As exemplified by typical courtroom proceedings, the adversarial system pits verbal combatants against each other to produce a winner and a loser. Clinicians provide help in their cases, to the best of their ability; lawyers win or lose their cases. They air opposing views before the bench, and the arguments that hold sway result in a judgment that gratifies some parties to the case and dismays others.

The adversarial system calls on attorneys to promote the interests of their clients while intentionally trying to prevent opposing attorneys' clients from keeping or getting something they want to have, such as a sum of money or an adjudication of innocence. The concerns of the judge rest not with who gets what or which party feels better or worse, but rather with safeguarding due process and strict adherence to the rules of evidence. Impartial judicial oversight ensures a full and equal hearing before the bench—every person's "day in court"—whatever the outcome. The familiar statue of the blindfolded goddess of justice, allowing the scales to balance where they will, vividly portrays this feature of the judicial process (see Barrett & Morris, 1993).

Given the nature of the adversarial system, psychologists beginning in forensic work are likely to be what Brodsky and Robey (1972) described many years ago as "courtroom-unfamiliar." As one step in becoming effective consultants, they need to familiarize themselves with the adversarial system and become comfortable with offering opinions that may contribute to severe penalties and crushing disappointments on the losing side of a case.

In addition, psychologists undertaking forensic consulting must learn to deal with *impersonal clients*. Forensic clients are not individuals seeking service directly on their own behalf. In some cases, they are an entity, such as a court seeking advice, a prosecutor's office seeking a conviction, or a company seeking to defend itself against charges of negligence or malfeasance. In other cases, they are attorneys acting on behalf of a person they are representing in a litigation. Forensic psychologists usually have some direct contact with the plaintiff or defendant in a case on which they are consulting, especially for purposes of conducting a formal evaluation. However, this will not be the person with whom they make arrangements for the evaluation or discuss the nature and import of their findings; instead, such matters are discussed with the entity or attorney who constitutes the psychologist's client.

The general implications of identifying impersonal clients accurately and working with them appropriately are elaborated by Monahan (1980) in a monograph with which all forensic psychologists should be conversant. The present chapter addresses specific implications of working within the adversarial system and with impersonal clients for the writing of forensic reports. Especially important in this regard are decisions concerning whether a report should be written at all and, if so, how it should be focused. After discussing guidelines for making such decisions, the chapter concludes with some suggestions for writing forensic reports in a clear, relevant, informative, and defensible manner.

DECIDING WHETHER A REPORT SHOULD BE WRITTEN

Deciding whether to write a report may seem to be a frivolous consideration; psychologists are accustomed, after all, to writing reports as a necessary and expected culmination of providing consultative services. In forensic work, however, the inevitability of a written report is tempered by rules concerning the nature of evidence. Expert opinions become evidence not when they are formulated in a consultant's mind, but only when they are stated orally under oath or written down, whether in formal reports that are voluntarily submitted in evidence or informal notes that are subpoenaed during a discovery process. For this reason, attorneys typically advise persons involved in litigation to think whatever they like but write down only what they are prepared to justify in testimony. An exception in this regard involves written communications to an attorney in anticipation of a trial, which may be considered part of the attorney's work product and are not required to be disclosed. With respect to formal statements of the psychologist's findings and opinions, however, the decision whether to write a report should be made in light of the preferences of the client and certain ethical principles and professional realities that govern the practice of law and psychology.

Forensic clients differ in the kinds of information they want to have. Judges seeking help in reaching a decision usually want as much relevant information as possible and are interested in any opinion, whatever its implications, that can guide their actions. Hence, in court-ordered consultations a written report will typically be expected, and a thorough elaboration of the nature and significance of the psychologist's findings will be welcome.

By contrast, attorneys trying a case are seeking to enter in evidence only opinions that will strengthen the plea being made on behalf of their client. If the consultant's conclusions would be damaging to their case, attorneys may prefer not to have a report written. The following three cases, each of a type common in the practice of forensic psychology, illustrate circumstances in which the attorney expressed such a preference.

CASE EXAMPLES

Case Example 1: Mr. A

Mr. A was a 33-year-old systems analyst who had undergone surgery in connection with an accurately diagnosed medical condition. Apparently as a consequence of some careless surgical procedures, he had suffered some unanticipated postoperative complications. Although not permanently disabling, these complications had prolonged Mr. A's recovery, delayed his return to work, and required him to undergo a physical rehabilitation program. His attorney believed that medical malpractice could be demonstrated and that Mr. A was entitled to compensatory and punitive damages. He believed further that his client must have suffered psychological as well as physical distress, thus warranting a larger award than if his iatrogenic problems were only physical.

The psychologist's evaluation suggested that Mr. A was an emotionally resourceful individual who was coping effectively with his unfortunate medical situation. Compared to most people with his illness who had required surgery, he seemed to be adjusting well psychologically. He was, in fact, the kind of patient one hopes to see on a rehabilitation service, for whom an optimistic prognosis for full recovery without emotional setbacks seems likely. As a compassionate individual, the attorney was pleased to receive an oral report to this effect. As Mr. A's representative in a personal injury suit, however, he recognized that the psychologist's opinion, if introduced as evidence, would be more likely to reduce than increase the amount of the damages that would be awarded. Hence, he did not request a written report.

Case Example 2: Mr. B

An attorney sought a psychologist's opinion while preparing to defend Mr. B, a 37-year-old elementary school teacher accused of sexually molesting several girls in his fifth-grade class. Mr. B had allegedly fondled these girls during class sessions by reaching into their underclothes while he was sitting at his desk and they approached him to ask a question or turn in an assignment. Aside from doubting that his client would have committed such acts so publicly, the attorney was puzzled by the manner in which the complaints had emerged. The initial allegation of molestation was made by just one girl, who spoke to her parents about it. Later, after this girl's parents had talked with the school principal and the police had been called in to investigate, several other girls in Mr. B's class told their parents that they too had been fondled by him.

Interestingly, reports from the school indicated that the girl who had complained first was socially popular and a leader among her peers. Also of note was the impression of several interviewers that none of the girls seemed particularly upset while talking about having been molested; instead, they told their stories as if they were pleased and proud about them. As for Mr. B, he had for many years been a highly admired teacher in this school, known especially for a warm and caring attitude toward his students.

The attorney wondered whether there was any reason to think that a group of girls who had in fact not been molested would say that they had been. Some possibilities will come quickly to the minds of psychologists familiar with the romantic fantasies and peer-group interactions that commonly characterize prepubescent development in 10 and 11-year-old girls.

Consider, for example, the possibility of a young girl first fantasizing about an appealing, perhaps paternal male teacher making a sexual overture toward her and then fabricating such a story as a way of feeling attractive and grown-up and impressing her parents and peers in certain ways. Consider further the possibility of other girls in the class, having heard this story from a popular trendsetter, claiming, "He did it to me too." This is the well-known stuff of which mass hysteria is made, as described in such classical papers as "The Phantom Anesthetist of Matoon" (Johnson, 1945) and in the recounting of the Salem witch trials (Starkey, 1949).

In mentioning these possibilities to the attorney, the psychologist indicated that they constituted clinical formulations and could not be substantiated with solid empirical evidence. Having a possible explanation that child specialists would find plausible is quite a different matter from having a line of defense that will stand up in court. The psychologist advised the attorney that many of the compelling speculations in this case, if offered in testimony, could be made to look foolish under skillful cross-examination and might thereby detract from other aspects of the defense he was building. Hence, a report was not written.

CASE EXAMPLE 3: MR. C

This third illustration, because of publicity surrounding it, must be presented in bare outline only. An attorney representing Mr. C, a young man charged with a serious crime, was planning to file a plea of incompetence to stand trial. He had been struck by his client's strange and disturbed behavior and expected that a formal psychological examination would provide corroborating evidence of incompetency. On the basis of his examination, the psychologist concluded that the young man was indeed "acting" strangely—that he was, in fact, malingering. When he conveyed this opinion to the attorney in a telephone conversation, the attorney indicated that the psychologist would be paid for his time but would not be asked to submit a report.

ETHICAL PRINCIPLES AND PROFESSIONAL REALITIES

For psychologists unfamiliar with forensic consulting, the preceding three illustrations of being in effect dismissed from a case prior to preparing a written report could raise some disturbing questions about proper practice. One might be especially concerned about Case 3, in which the psychologist provided an expert opinion that an accused felon was attempting to fake psychological disturbance. How could the attorney ignore these findings and continue building a case for incompetency, and should the psychologist allow this to happen? The answers to these questions touch on some ethical and realistic considerations in the practice of law and psychology.

The Quality of Expert Opinions

To prepare themselves for sometimes unenthusiastic responses to their opinions, forensic consultants need to remain sufficiently humble to recognize that they may at times be in error, or at least not possessed of all the answers. Clinicians must appreciate in particular that their skill and judgment do not transcend all of the imperfections in their assessment tools. As Shapiro (1991, Chapter 4) reminds forensic consultants: Expert psychological opinions are not statements of fact, but only reasonable conclusions based on the information that is available and has been carefully analyzed.

The psychologist in Case 3 was reasonably certain that the defendant was malingering but would not have been prepared to testify that he was absolutely certain—nor indeed should he have been, given the difficulty of establishing malingering with absolute certainty (see Maloney, 1985, Chapter 12; Rogers, 1988). From the attorney's point of view, then, the opinion concerning malingering could be taken as a possibility, but not as the only one. The attorney might also have had in hand information unknown to the psychologist, perhaps even another expert opinion, that in his view argued against malingering.

Like the imperfections of assessment methods, the existence of multiple, contradictory expert opinions brings a sobering measure of reality into forensic consulting. One expert's opinion is neither the only nor the last word. There are no obligations that would have prevented the attorney in Case 3 from listening to the psychologist's opinion concerning malingering and then turning to a new consultant, or perhaps a string of consultants, until a qualified psychologist was found in whose opinion the defendant was truly incapable of understanding the proceedings against him and consulting effectively with his attorney, that is, incompetent to stand trial as defined by the *Dusky* standard (see Chapter 14; see also Grisso, 1988; Roesch, Ogloff, & Golding, 1993).

Learning of such an outcome, the first consultant could feel strongly that this last expert lacked sufficient experience or diagnostic acumen to recognize a clear case of malingering. However, the court in such a case would ordinarily accept a licensed psychologist with some experience in assessing competence in criminal defendants as qualified to offer such opinions; hence, assuming this last expert was thus credentialed, the court would be unlikely to pass further on his or her professional skills. To be sure, issues of competency and criminal responsibility typically feature expert witness testimony on both sides of the case, and arguments may ensue concerning which of several qualified professionals are best qualified to give reliable testimony. The point remains, however, that it is entirely appropriate and consistent with prevailing practice for attorneys to challenge or reject the opinions of a consultant they have retained and to seek other consultants whose opinions will serve better to support their case.

Considerations in Practicing Law

Instead of questioning the quality of expert opinions that fail to meet their needs, attorneys may decide on the basis of a consultant's opinion to change their approach to a case or even discontinue working on it. For example, becoming convinced that a client in a criminal case has been faking emotional disturbance, is lying about his or her guilt, or has in other ways behaved in a reprehensible manner may lead an attorney to decline to represent that person further or, if court-appointed, to ask to be excused from the case.

Yet our system of criminal justice entitles everyone to a defense, no matter how barbarous the offense, how despicable the alleged offender, or how guilty the accused appears to be. Regardless of how many attorneys choose not to represent certain kinds of clients, every defendant in a criminal case will in the end be represented by a member of the bar. Furthermore, this eventually retained or appointed attorney will be ethically responsible for presenting the strongest possible case on behalf of the defendant. A weak or half-hearted defense of a defendant whom an attorney regards as being guilty or having few redeemable qualities can result in the attorney's appearing inept or unethical in the eyes of the legal community. Ineffective or unprepared trial lawyers may even risk being publicly chastened by the bench for having done a poor job in their client's behalf. Moreover, a decision reached in such an instance could well be reversed on appeal to a higher court by virtue of the defendant's having had ineffective counsel.

In addition to preventing such negative consequences, a strong case presented on behalf of a client considered difficult to defend can enhance an attorney's professional reputation. Hence, trial attorneys may enjoy or even seek out opportunities to take on challenging cases and construct convincing briefs in them, especially in trials that capture media attention. Such recent media events as the O. J. Simpson and McVeigh murder trials are cases in point.

Forensic psychologists need to appreciate these realistic motivations for attorneys to continue quite properly to build cases that expert consultants think are flawed. Moreover, there are instances in which attorneys have no choice but to continue with a case, regardless of reservations about the worthiness of the client or the weight of the evidence. For example, defense attorneys appointed by the court are in fact rarely given an option to withdraw from the case and can expect the court to be especially intolerant of a lackluster effort on their part. Likewise, prosecuting attorneys may be assigned cases by the office for which they work, without begin given much latitude to choose which ones they would prefer to try. These various considerations provide ample basis for conscientious and ethical attorneys to decline to have their consultants furnish evidence that would be damaging to their case.

Considerations in Practicing Psychology

Turning now to the second troublesome question raised by Case 3, how can the psychologist allow pertinent information in effect to be suppressed? Being reasonably certain from his data that the accused was malingering psychosis, how could he sit silently while a competency hearing was taking place? To make matters worse, suppose that daily newspaper accounts of the hearing were predicting that the defendant would be found incompetent to stand trial because of emotional disturbance and be sent for treatment.

Psychologists struggling with this kind of question need to recognize that their dismay derives from their professional experience with the case conference model. In the case conference model, all relevant information is sought and a wide range of opinions is considered in arriving at a diagnostic formulation and treatment plan. This model is seldom approximated in forensic consultation, except when the client is the court. Then, as noted earlier, any testimony will be welcome that helps the court decide on a disposition.

For attorneys, however, who in conformance with the adversarial system are pleading just one side of a case, welcome testimony comprises only evidence that supports their arguments. If expert opinions exist that would support the other side of the case, it is up to opposing counsel to find and produce them. Confronted with such realities on cases in which they have consulted, psychologists may experience disappointment, anger, or perhaps even a sense of outrage. They may feel that, in situations such as Case 3, their findings should be brought to light to prevent a malingering criminal from escaping justice. They may become tempted to call the prosecuting attorney or the judge and volunteer their opinion, or to inform the media that critical information concerning the case is being suppressed.

Except in extraordinary circumstances, responsible psychologists must resist any such temptations. To do otherwise would abuse the defendant's right to confidentiality and violate the Ethical Principles of Psychologists and Code of Conduct adopted by the American Psychological Association:

> Psychologists have a primary obligation and take reasonable precautions to respect the confidentiality rights of those with whom they work or consult, recognizing that confidentiality may be established by law, institutional rules, or professional or scientific relationships. . . . Psychologists disclose confidential information without the consent of the individual only as mandated by law for a valid purpose, such as (1) to provide deeded professional services to the patient or the individual or organizational client, (2) to obtain appropriate professional consultation, (3) to protect the patient or client or others from harm, and (4) to obtain payment for services, in which case disclosure is limited to the minimum that is necessary to achieve the purpose. (American Psychological Association, 1992, p. 1606)

Finally with respect to deciding whether a report should be written following a forensic consultation, psychologists should be sufficiently aware of applicable case and statutory law and the implications of their findings to advise their attorney clients concerning whether a report is likely to be helpful to them. In addition to being much appreciated, informed opinions of this kind can even result in attorneys requesting a report of findings that would appear to weaken their position, as in the following case.

CASE EXAMPLE 4: MS. D

An attorney representing Ms. D requested an evaluation of the extent to which she was suffering from posttraumatic stress disorder or any other psychological problems as a consequence of an automobile accident in which she had been involved. On the basis of ample historical data, a detailed clinical interview, and examination with a comprehensive battery of psychological tests, the psychologist concluded that this woman was not displaying any emotional difficulties or behavior problems attributable to the accident. Discussing his impressions in an informal conversation with his attorney client, the psychologist stated flatly, "I don't think I can help you."

Surprisingly, however, the attorney responded that he could put these negative findings to good use. He went on to say that Ms. D had been pressing him to seek compensation for psychic damage and disability as well as for her well-documented physical injuries. A strong written statement from the psychologist concerning his negative findings would help him convince her to drop this part of her claim, he said, thereby sparing him from having to pursue a weak part of his case and allowing him to focus on the strong part. A written report was accordingly prepared.

DETERMINING THE FOCUS OF FORENSIC REPORTS

Once a decision has been made that a report will be written, the forensic psychologist must then decide what to say in this report. Now is the time to keep in mind that whatever is written down is discoverable and may become entered in evidence. Moreover, when psychologists are called to testify in a legal proceeding, their testimony on direct examination will ordinarily be based on their written report, which means that everything in the report will be subject to question on cross-examination. As a basic principle, then, forensic psychologists should limit their written reports to statements they will feel comfortable about having read aloud in the courtroom and to conclusions they will feel able to defend against reasonable challenge.

Beyond this preliminary consideration, the appropriate focus of forensic reports varies from one case to the next in relation to the needs of the client. As in providing other kinds of psychological services, forensic consultants should be guided by the familiar principle of giving clients what they want, within appropriate limits dictated by their professional judgment and ethical standards. This guideline does *not* imply that psychologists should provide attorneys whatever opinions or conclusions they would like to have in order to strengthen their case.

Meeting the client's needs refers to providing the desired services, not the desired findings.

Reports should accordingly focus on matters of concern to the client without including all of the psychological observations that could be made about a person or situation being evaluated. This aspect of focusing forensic reports is embodied in the American Psychological Association (1992) Code of Conduct as follows: "In order to minimize intrusions on privacy, psychologists include in written and oral reports, consultations, and the like, only information germane to the purpose for which the communication is made" (p. 1606). More specific guidelines in this regard appear in the Specialty Guidelines for Forensic Psychologists: "With respect to evidence of any type, forensic psychologists avoid offering information from their investigations or evaluations that does not bear directly upon the legal purpose of their professional services and is not critical as support for their product, evidence, or testimony, except where such disclosure is required by law" (Committee on Ethical Guidelines for Forensic Psychologists, 1991, p. 662).

As a further note concerning propriety in this regard, it is helpful to distinguish between acts of commission and acts of omission in writing reports. Regarding commission, forensic psychologists should under no circumstances compromise their integrity by knowingly making inaccurate or misleading statements. Regarding omission, on the other hand, it is rarely warranted or necessary to answer questions that the client has not asked. Forensic reports focused within the limits described thus far will nevertheless vary in breadth as a function of the nature of the case and the line of attack or defense the client is intending to pursue.

Providing Narrowly Focused Consultations

In some forensic cases, the questions being asked by the client call for fairly limited data collection and a rather narrowly focused written report. The following two cases illustrate such circumstances.

CASE EXAMPLES

Case Example 5: WAIS-R and Shipley Institute of Living Scale

A young man accused of burglarizing some homes in his neighborhood had signed a confession. His attorney felt that he had been frightened into signing a confession that he was incapable of understanding. The psychologist asked to assess this possibility administered the Wechsler Adult Intelligence Scale–Revised (WAIS-R) and the Shipley Institute of Living Scale. The accused appeared unfamiliar with many of the vocabulary items in these two tests, including several that are listed in the Thorndike-Lorge index as being more frequently used than some of the key words in the confession he had signed. The psychologist's report consisted of stating this finding and indicating its implications for a reasonably certain conclusion that the young man did not fully understand the text of his confession.

CASE EXAMPLE 6: *DSM-IV*

An attorney preparing to plead diminished capacity in defending a man charged with attempted murder had received some discrepant reports from several consultants concerning her client's mental status. As one stop in trying to resolve this discrepancy, she asked a psychologist experienced in the Rorschach assessment of schizophrenia if he would review the defendant's Rorschach protocol and answer two questions: Was the record taken properly, and is it consistent with a *DSM-IV* diagnosis of schizophrenia? In the consultant's opinion the answers to these two questions were yes and no, respectively, and this is what was communicated to the attorney in a relatively brief and narrowly focused report.

These examples of narrowly focused forensic consultations may appear to incorporate some undesirable clinical practices. In the first place, the psychologists in both cases based their opinion on just one or two specialized tests, whereas psychodiagnostic assessment as commonly practiced involves a multifaceted test battery. Second, in Case 6, the psychologist conducted a blind analysis of the test protocol without seeing the subject or knowing anything about him except his age and sex. Most clinicians regard such blind analysis as appropriate only for didactic or research purposes; in practice, most clinicians agree, diagnoses should be made by them, not by their tests, and only following thoughtful integration of test findings with relevant information about a subject's history and circumstances.

Psychologists concerned about such matters might be understandably reluctant to provide the narrow kind of consultation requested in Cases 5 and 6. From the perspective of attorneys attempting to muster bits of evidence in support of their case, however, the request in both cases for a narrowly focused consultation is entirely appropriate. It was accordingly appropriate for the psychologists to respond just to the questions being raised, provided that they felt confident of their ability to do so. Moreover, submitting a narrowly focused report did not prevent the psychologist in Case 6 from also assuming an educative function and pointing out to the attorney that an informed psychodiagnostic opinion concerning the subject's mental status would have to be based on an integrated utilization of a test battery and contextual information, not just blind evaluation of a single test protocol.

BROADENING THE FOCUS OF FORENSIC CONSULTATION

Although instances of narrowly focused consultations are important to identify and put in perspective, they seldom occur in the practice of most forensic psychologists. Instead, consultative requests are likely to require attention to multiple sources of information in the preparation of reports. Even when psychologists are consulted primarily as experts in psychological test evaluation, they should conduct themselves as broadly knowledgeable mental health professionals who integrate interview data, background information, and test findings into comprehensive opinions and conclusions concerning the case. Psychologists who testify on the basis of a written report that deals solely with test findings and must plead ignorance when asked about other elements of the case are poorly prepared to present themselves effectively. They weaken their client's arguments by being exposed as an expert who has only a superficial grasp of the case, and they demean their own professional status by failing to present themselves as anything more than a tester.

Adequate attention to the context of a forensic case does not always call for extensive data collection or record review, however. Sometimes just a few bits of background information suffice for preparing an effectively focused report, as in the following case.

CASE EXAMPLE 7: MR. E

Mr. E was a 34-year-old man who had suffered a closed head injury in an accident for which there was alleged liability. He had been rehabilitated on a neurological service to the point where he was considered to have achieved his maximum recovery. His attorney wanted to establish how much permanent loss of function remained as a consequence of the accident. A WAIS-R, administered as part of an extensive test battery, yielded a Full-Scale Intelligence Quotient (IQ) of 103.

Although no preaccident WAIS-R IQ was on record in Mr. E's case to provide a baseline, his record revealed that he had received a PhD in chemical engineering from a prestigious university and had had a successful career up to the time of his accident. This fact alone, given the considerable unlikelihood of such prior accomplishment by a person with an IQ of 103, established a solid basis for arguing that at least some loss of mental capacity could be attributed to the accident, probably too much to allow him to resume his career. The written report was accordingly focused on these particular findings.

Turning to more general guidelines in determining the scope of a report, the previously noted difference between the typical expectations of attorneys and those of judges influence the amount of information a forensic consultant gathers and reports. To recapitulate this difference, attorneys are operating as adversaries on their clients' behalf and are interested in expert opinions that support the case they are making, whereas judges are neutral to both sides of a case and interested in as many relevant opinions as they can obtain. Hence, reports prepared for attorneys will ordinarily be more limited in scope and more narrowly focused on conclusions pointing in one particular direction than reports prepared for the court. The breadth of the psychologist's focus will additionally be influenced by the *time frame* of the inquiry, with specific respect to whether attention must be paid to present, past, or future circumstances.

Addressing Present Circumstances

When forensic psychological opinions must address primarily the present status of a plaintiff or defendant, the data that need to be collected are relatively limited, and the task of interpreting them is relatively uncomplicated. As previously noted, for example, questions of whether defendants are competent to stand trial concern mainly whether they are currently able to understand the charges against them and participate effectively in their defense. Consultants may struggle with translating these legal criteria of competency into psychological terms, and they may encounter cases of marginal competency that are difficult to call one way or the other. Whatever the difficulty of the task in these evaluations, however, the critical data for determining a defendant's present functioning capacity will be available from currently obtainable interview, test, and observational data.

Assessment of personal injury also focuses mainly on current mental or emotional state and functioning capacity. Evaluations of allegedly reactive psychological conditions or loss of functioning capacity are a bit more complicated than determining competency, because current capacity must ordinarily be compared to some baseline of previous functioning, prior to an allegedly harmful incident. In most cases, verifiable records of past events provide a baseline for such comparisons. These records may comprise previously obtained intelligence, neuropsychological, or personality test findings; documentation of a claimant's educational and occupational history (as in Case 7); clinicians' and hospital notes concerning prior medical problems and mental health services; and testimony from relatives and long-time acquaintances concerning earlier patterns of behavior and adjustment.

Addressing Past Circumstances

Opinions that must address the past status of an individual ordinarily require more extensive data collection than present status evaluations and a more broadly focused report in which the conclusions are less certain. The most commonly encountered cases of this kind involve questions of criminal responsibility. As elaborated in Chapter 15, criminal responsibility is determined by the nature of a defendant's mental state at the time of an offense and the extent to which this mental state contributed to the commission of the offense. Efforts to establish a prior mental state and its likely consequences require forensic psychologists to seek out information and confront uncertainties that stretch their capacities well beyond the relatively modest demands of conducting a present status evaluation.

For example, suppose an adult male defendant whose attorney is pleading him not guilty by reason of insanity to a felonious assault committed three months earlier shows substantial evidence on psychological examination of a long-standing schizophrenic disorder. This may constitute good reason to believe that the accused was in all likelihood significantly psychologically disturbed three months earlier and probably long before that. Even if uncontested, however, this conclusion would not necessarily demonstrate that the defendant's disorder was responsible for his having committed his offense.

Case Example 8: Daniel Lee Young

Just prior to the 1984 Summer Olympics in Los Angeles, a man named Daniel Lee Young drove his car recklessly onto a crowded sidewalk, killing one pedestrian and injuring 54 others. In his subsequent trial, he was identified as having a chronic paranoid schizophrenic disorder. It was nevertheless found that his schizophrenia was not a contributing factor in his homicidal and assaultive behavior. He was considered to have been legally sane at the time of the crime and was sentenced to a prison term of 106 years and 4 months to life on one count of first-degree murder and 48 counts of attempted murder.

Suppose, as a contrasting example, that an offender pleading temporary insanity or diminished capacity presently appears to be so psychologically capable and well-functioning as to make it doubtful that he or she was seriously disturbed just a few months earlier, when the crime was committed. Could it nevertheless be argued that any person, no matter how well-functioning at the moment, could fall prey to an acute psychotic or dissociative episode during a period of duress? Or, on the other hand, could it be concluded from currently obtained interview and test data that a defendant is not the kind of person who is likely to show psychotic or dissociative reactions to stress? Neither conclusion, whatever its psychological justification, would carry much evidentiary weight, unless it could be convincingly amplified with respect to the nature and amount of stress the defendant was actually likely to have been experiencing prior to the criminal act and how he or she was actually behaving just before and while committing it.

With this in mind, forensic psychologists addressing questions of criminal responsibility need to investigate carefully and report clearly the events leading up to and occurring during the commission of a crime. The defendant's own recollections, the police arrest report, and statements given by eyewitnesses and other informants should be integrated with current personality evaluations to yield informed opinions concerning whether the stresses in a defendant's life and his or her behavior while committing a crime seem consistent with applicable criteria for reduced criminal responsibility (see Blau, 1984, Chapter 7; Shapiro, 1991, Chapter 3).

Addressing Future Circumstances

In three other types of forensic cases the questions being asked challenge psychologists not to reconstruct the past, but to predict the future. Two of these types of cases involve requests for aid in sentencing convicted criminal offenders, sometimes with respect to whether they should initially be sent to prison or placed on probation, and at other times with respect to whether an offender in prison should be given parole. As noted in Chapter 12, being able to answer such questions effectively depends on being able first to find answers to certain other questions, such as how likely an offender is to commit further crimes, especially violent ones; how responsive the person will be to counseling, psychotherapy, job training, or other rehabilitative efforts attempted outside of prison; and how adequate the available services are for providing the kinds of nonprison interventions that offer promise of a successful outcome.

These are usually difficult matters to ascertain on the basis of currently available information, and forensic reports concerned with them must typically be more complicated, detailed, and tentative than reports concerned with present functioning alone. To extrapolate accurately from current assessment data to future expectations bearing on the advisability of probation or parole, forensic consultants need to muster whatever clinical and empirical knowledge can be obtained concerning recidivism, violence risk, treatment response, and available resources and relate this information to the case at hand.

The other type of forensic case that touches on future circumstances involves consulting with respect to custody and visitation rights in families of divorce. What arrangements will be in the best interests of the children? Which parent will provide them better care and supervision? When and in what circumstances should the noncustodial parent have access to them? Like estimating the advisability of probation or parole, these child care questions are difficult to answer from presently available data.

Among other demands faced by forensic psychologists in such cases, their examination must with few exceptions extend to all members of the family who will be affected by a custody decision, including both parents, all dependent children, and other significant figures in the home or in the child's life. Should a remarried parent be seeking to gain primary residential custody, the stepparent may also need to be evaluated. In addition, to lend some reasonable certainty to their efforts to predict the future, psychologists offering opinions in custody cases need to draw on relevant research findings and clinical wisdom concerning developmental aspects of child-parent relationships and the impact of divorce on children and their parents (see Folberg, 1991; Hetherington & Arasteh, 1988; Hodges, 1991; see also Chapter 4).

ON BEING CLEAR, RELEVANT, INFORMATIVE, AND DEFENSIBLE

The present chapter has indicated to this point that writing useful and effective forensic reports requires psychologists to have a good grasp of the legal and behavioral issues surrounding a case, then determine what kinds of information will best help to resolve these issues, and next gather and evaluate such information. Once these tasks are accomplished, what remains is for consultants to express their impressions and conclusions in a clear, relevant, informative, and defensible manner.

BEING CLEAR

Forensic consultants should ordinarily begin their reports by indicating the sources of information they have utilized. When, where, for what reason, and in what fashion were parties to the case directly evaluated? What records were examined, such as depositions, police reports, medical charts, and school or military files? What collateral persons were questioned and for what purpose? To what extent were other discussions, reviews of psychological literature, or examinations of case law undertaken to further the consultant's knowledge and understanding of the case? Explicit answers to such questions in the introduction to a forensic report promote clarity by minimizing uncertainty concerning the basis on which consultants have formed the opinions to be stated in their report.

In proceeding to state their findings and conclusions, forensic psychologists should strive to write in ordinary English and to limit their use of technical jargon. As previously mentioned, a written report may be gone over word for word by opposing counsel during a deposition or read aloud in its entirety in the courtroom. Some attorneys may even prefer on direct examination to have a consultant's report entered verbatim, to avoid having imprecise or poorly worded statements slip into an extemporaneous presentation. Hence, consultants should not plan on writing a formal, somewhat technical report for the record and then giving their courtroom testimony in an informal, conversational manner that is easy to follow and understand. Instead, the written report itself should be as clear and conversational as the psychologist can make it. This means using unstilted and uncomplicated language that will be comfortable for consultants to repeat on the witness stand and comprehensible to their audience and that will give little opportunity for cross-examining attorneys to badger them with questions about what they mean.

Along with using ordinary language in reports, except where technical terms such as a formal diagnosis may be required, forensic psychologists should concentrate on writing about the *people* they have evaluated, rather than about psychological processes. A statement such as "Coping capacities are good" does not communicate as clearly as "Ms. F has good capacities to cope with stressful experiences without becoming unduly upset by them." When psychologists fail to guard adequately against being murky, impersonal descriptions of psychological processes often go hand in hand with jargon. Compare, for example, "Much castration anxiety is present" with "This man gives evidence of being more fearful than most people of being harmed physically." Sometimes, consultants may not realize that certain expressions commonly used by professionals are not generally understood by the public. For example, "Reality testing is poor" reads better as "Mr. G's reality testing is poor" but even better as "Mr. G often fails to see things the way most people do and consequently tends to show what most people would regard as poor judgment." Harvey (1997) has elaborated several such recommendations for improving the readability of psychological reports.

BEING RELEVANT

As in responding to consultation requests in other areas of practice, psychologists achieve relevance in forensic reports by addressing and attempting to answer the referral question. Being relevant means omitting much of what could be said about an individual's personality characteristics and probable ways of responding in various kinds of circumstances, and instead providing a distillate of those features of the individual that bear directly on the issues in the case and the client's questions about them.

But what are the client's questions? To some extent, relevance is achieved by adhering to the previously noted ethical guidelines concerning appropriately focused forensic reports. However, to translate this concept into practice—and thereby conduct an adequate evaluation and write a relevant report—forensic psychologists need to be pursuing some specifically stated question, such as whether an accused is competent to stand trial or an allegedly brain-injured person has suffered demonstrable loss of intellectual or cognitive function. If no such question has been framed, one must be elicited from the client by asking,

"Why do you want to have this person evaluated?" or "What is it that you would like to learn from me?"

In addition to identifying what information to obtain and how best to organize and report it, specific referral questions also help psychologists anticipate at least in part how well they will be able to respond to consultative requests. Expectations concerning how useful or how powerful the psychological data will be can often be shared with clients to good effect. For example, alerting an attorney that evaluations of possible future behavior generate less certain results than evaluations of present status can enhance the effectiveness of an eventual report by minimizing any unwarranted expectations on the attorney's part. Cases 2 and 4 presented earlier also illustrate how working with a clear referral question can make it possible to provide a relevant consultation based on the anticipated impact of one's impressions.

Forensic psychologists can increase the relevance of their consultations further by drawing on familiarity with statutory and case law applicable to a case in the particular jurisdiction in which it is being processed. Cognizance of applicable legal standards is an ethical responsibility in forensic practice (Committee on Ethical Guidelines for Forensic Psychologists, 1991, p. 658), and judicious integration of such knowledge into a report, especially with respect to appropriate terminology, will usually enhance its relevance.

Thus, for example, psychologists preparing reports in personal injury cases should address in specific terms the issue of proximate cause as spelled out in tort law, and those preparing reports in custody cases should devote specific attention to the best interests of the child doctrine, which is a prominent theme in family law (see Chapter 4). The differing criteria employed in various state and federal jurisdictions for what constitute mitigating mental circumstances in criminal behavior also illustrate the necessity to adequate legal knowledge (see Chapter 13; see also Ogloff, Roberts, & Roesch, 1993; Shapiro, 1991, Chapter 2). To express a relevant opinion concerning criminal responsibility, forensic psychologists must appreciate how their findings fit with applicable ways of defining it and express themselves accordingly. In a jurisdiction in which the M'Naghten Rule applies, for example, the utility of the consultant's report is enhanced by the following kind of statement:

> Mr. H frequently has difficulty perceiving events in his life realistically, and as a result, he often misjudges how his behavior affects other people. The severity of this problem and strong indications that he has had it for a long time make it reasonable to think that he was not fully capable of appreciating the wrongfulness of his actions at the time of the crime. Significantly in this regard, when asked directly if he thought he was doing anything wrong, he said, "I had every right to do it."

BEING INFORMATIVE

Like clinical reports, forensic reports should be written in an informative manner that educates the nonpsychologist reader. This informational objective can usually be achieved by relating psychological data and impressions to benchmarks that the audience will recognize. For example, a statement that a subject has received a WAIS-R Full-Scale IQ of 100 communicates adequately to other psychologists about the person's overall IQ level but becomes intelligible to most people only when amplified with some educational information, such as that the WAIS-R is currently the most widely used measure of adult intelligence and comprises several subtests sampling different kinds of abilities; that, although there is some error of measurement associated with a WAIS-R IQ, an obtained score of 100 means that there is a 95% probability that the subject's true IQ is between 95 and 105; and that about half of all people receive an IQ score higher than 100 on this test and half a lower score.

Similarly, with respect to impressions of psychological disorder, consultants should indicate, as done in Case 6, how the findings compare with the diagnostic criteria of widely used nomenclatures, for example, "The way this person is thinking and feeling, as reflected in the interview and test findings, is consistent with a *DSM-IV* diagnosis of Major Depressive Disorder."

In some instances, consultants may usefully summarize in textbook fashion a set of circumstances that point to a particular conclusion. For example, a psychologist consulting on a criminal case in which the court was considering a suspended sentence wrote the following informative opinion: "I am concerned about having this man return without supervision to his previous place of residence. Being a white male in his late 50s, who would be living alone in a run-down section of town, and who has previously attempted to take his own life, he would be in a very high risk group for suicidal behavior." An informative educational approach of this kind, in a report that is easy to understand and speaks explicitly to the issues at hand, promotes effective communication. Combined with good judgment concerning when reports should be written and how narrowly or broadly they should be focused, skills in being clear, relevant, and informative in their writing of reports contribute substantially to psychologists providing effective forensic consultation. Finally, it seems in order to suggest some ways in which forensic reports can be written to enhance their defensibility in the face of challenge.

BEING DEFENSIBLE

Unlike clinical reports, which are typically either praised or ignored but are rarely demeaned, at least not publicly, forensic reports are fair game to opposing counsels whose proper task and duty to their client calls for them to challenge and poke holes in what the psychologist has written, as publicly and embarrassingly as they can. Accordingly, forensic psychologists should be motivated to spare themselves as much such grief as they can by writing reports that say what needs to be said in as defensible a manner as possible. Elsewhere (Weiner, 1995), I have elaborated various ways in which psychologists can minimize their legal and ethical jeopardies in conducting personality assessments. With specific respect to writing forensic reports, the remainder of this chapter identifies four considerations that can help consultants avoid potential pitfalls in giving expert witness testimony.

First, when offering conclusions about people they have evaluated, forensic psychologists can keep to more solid ground by describing how the subjects resemble certain types of people who have had certain kinds of experiences, rather than by categorizing them as being a particular type of person who has had a particular kind of experience. The following examples illustrate the difference between describing and categorizing people: "This woman shows many features in common with people who have a stress disorder subsequent to a traumatic experience" versus "This woman has a posttraumatic stress disorder"; "Often children with the kinds of personality characteristics I found in Suzie have not had the benefit of receiving much nurturance from their parents" versus "Suzie has not been adequately nurtured by her parents"; "Mr. I's attitudes and dispositions closely resemble those often seen in persons who act violently toward others" versus "Mr. I is likely to act violently toward others." The second parts of each of the preceding illustrations seldom cause problems for their authors when they appear in clinical reports as statements of what the psychologist believes. In forensic reports, however, they expose consultants to difficult questions concerning how they know for sure that people have these conditions, and whether they were actually present to observe whether these events occurred. By describing rather than categorizing, psychologists can blunt the thrust of such challenges. Thus, in the example of Suzie, the consultant who describes does not say that she was adequately nurtured by her parents, but only that she shows characteristics in common with children who have not been adequately nurtured.

Second, in similar fashion, relative statements about people usually create fewer difficulties for forensic consultants than absolute statements. In this instance, there is some interprofessional convergence between psychologists' familiarity with uncertainty and attorneys' attention to such matters as "reasonable certainty" and "preponderance of evidence." Statements about persons examined in forensic cases that are couched in terms of conditions they are more or less likely to have, behavior they probably showed in the past or will be inclined to show in the future, and reasonable alternative implications of both for the legal issues in a case will typically stand the consultant in good stead. Likewise, statements that paint people in relative terms as being more or less likely than other people to show certain characteristics invite fewer challenges than pictures painted only in black and white. Thus, for example, it is much easier to justify having written "Ms. J is more self-centered than most people" than "Ms. J is a very self-centered person."

Third, consistent with what psychologists know about the imperfect nature of their assessment tools and about false-negative findings, forensic psychologists should avoid writing statements that rule out conditions or events. The fact that conditions (e.g., some disorder) or events (e.g., having committed child abuse) are not suggested by a psychologist's data does not eliminate the possibility of their existing. To minimize their exposure to being challenged and possibly embarrassed as a result of having overstated the findings, forensic psychologists should lay the stress in their reports on what their findings demonstrate as probably being present (e.g., "There is substantial indication in the available data that Mr. K is a psychologically stable, well-organized, and capable person"; "The evidence at hand suggests that Ms. L is quite depressed and possibly suicidal at the present time").

On those occasions when reporting of negative findings seems definitely called for or is mandated, consultants can still protect themselves by exercising caution in drawing conclusions from these findings, as in writing the following: "Although it is not possible on the basis of the test findings to rule out closed-head injury, the data obtained in the examination do not contain any evidence of neuropsychological impairment."

Fourth and finally, forensic psychologists are well advised to avoid including illustrative test responses in their reports. Knowledgeable examiners are often tempted to illustrate their points with such test responses as critical items from the MMPI-2 and rich content themes from the Rorschach. Including such examples typically does more harm than good in a forensic context, however, because they open the door to questions about what individual test responses mean. Once a foot is in this door, cross-examining attorneys can easily make most psychologists and their tests look foolish. All they need to do is pick out and pick on a few subtle items from the MMPI-2 and some subtle indices of cognitive slippage from the Rorschach and ask for justification of the scale placement or interpretation assigned to them. The correct answer in the courtroom to questions of what individual responses mean is that they mean nothing at all by themselves; only when test items are considered in relation to each other and combined into various multiple-item scales and configurations do they provide a basis for valid interpretations. Psychologists who have already assigned significance to individual responses in their reports are in a poor position to give this answer, and the effectiveness of what they have written may be reduced by challenges they could otherwise have avoided.

REFERENCES

American Psychological Association. (1992). Ethical principles of psychologists and code of conduct. *American Psychologist, 47,* 1597–1611.

Barrett, G. V., & Morris, S. B. (1993). The American Psychological Association's amicus curiae brief in Price Waterhouse v. Hopkins: The values of science versus the values of the law. *Law and Human Behavior, 17,* 201–216.

Blau, T. H. (1984). *The psychologist as expert witness.* New York: Wiley.

Brodsky, S. L., & Robey, A. (1972). On becoming an expert witness: Issues of orientation and effectiveness. *Professional Psychology, 3,* 173–176.

Committee on Ethical Guidelines for Forensic Psychologists. (1991). Specialty guidelines for forensic psychologists. *Law and Human Behavior, 15,* 655–665.

Folberg, J. (Ed.). (1991). *Joint custody and shared parenting* (2nd ed.). New York: Guilford Press.

Grisso, T. (1988). *Competency to stand trial evaluations: A manual for practice.* Sarasota, FL: Professional Resource Exchange.

Harvey, V. S. (1997). Improving the readability of psychological reports. *Professional Psychology, 28,* 271–274.

Hetherington, E. M., & Arasteh, J. D. (Eds.). (1988). *Impact of divorce, single parenting, and stepparenting on children.* Hillsdale, NJ: Erlbaum.

Hodges, W. F. (1991). *Interventions for children of divorce* (2nd ed.). New York: Wiley.

Johnson, D. M. (1945). The "phantom anesthetist" of Mattoon: A field study of mass hysteria. *Journal of Abnormal and Social Psychology, 40,* 175–186.

Maloney, M. P. (1985). *A clinician's guide to forensic psychological assessment.* New York: Free Press.

Monahan, J. (Ed.). (1980). *Who is the client?* Washington, DC: American Psychological Association.

Ogloff, J. R. P., Roberts, C. F., & Roesch, R. (1993). The insanity defense: Legal standards and clinical assessment. *Journal of Applied and Preventive Psychology, 2,* 163–178.

Roesch, R., Ogloff, J. R. P., & Golding, S. L. (1993). Competency to stand trial: Legal and clinical issues. *Journal of Applied and Preventive Psychology, 2,* 43–51.

Rogers, R. (Ed.). (1988). *Clinical assessment of malingering and deception.* New York: Guilford Press.

Shapiro, D. L. (1991). *Forensic psychological assessment.* Boston: Allyn & Bacon.

Starkey, M. L. (1949). *The devil in Massachusetts.* New York: Knopf.

Weiner, I. B. (1995). How to anticipate ethical and legal challenges in personality assessments. In J. Butcher (Ed.), *Clinical personality assessment: Practical applications* (pp. 95–103). New York: Oxford University Press.

CHAPTER 19

Serving as an Expert Witness

ALLEN K. HESS

WE ARE becoming both a more litigious society and a society that seeks psychological understanding of problems ranging from the spiritual to the legal. The practitioner who used to deal with the legal system a few times in a career now regularly faces clients with varying degrees of legal difficulties that may have prompted them to seek the psychologist's services. In fact, a small but increasing component of many practices consists of forensic consultations with attorneys. Often, attorneys ask the consulting psychologist to provide expert witness testimony regarding child custody, civil or criminal competence, insanity, witness credibility, and personality and behavioral propensities. Besides the traditional clinical and applied areas, many areas of experimental psychology have been applied to legal issues (Erickson & Simon, 1997; Hess, 1987). Redmount (1965) proposed that psychologists may be useful in certifying the competence of people drafting wills, in assessing damage in accident cases (e.g., assessing "brain damage," emotional disorder, and pain), in establishing testimonial reliability, in determining trademark cases, in resolving domestic relations issues, and in defining standards of normative conduct.

The role of the expert witness is not a new one for psychologists. Sporer (1997) notes psychological arguments cited in Brauer in 1841 to limit testimony by women and children, the experiments reported by Binet in 1900 regarding the influence of various types of suggestive questions on the error rate in schoolchildren's answers, and the work by Stern in 1902 regarding the psychology of testimony. Blau (1984) cites the work of Goldofski in 1904, Jaffe in 1903, and Lobstien in 1904 among early expert witnesses. Yet, serving as an expert witness is a role that only recently occupies increasing numbers of psychologists and great amounts of their time and interest. This chapter provides a brief

This chapter has been substantively and stylistically enhanced by the caring commentary of Kathryn D. Hess, Robert Van Der Velde, Steven Walfish, Irving B. Weiner, and Peter Zachar, for which the author is grateful.

historical account of the legal basis for expert witness testimony, shows what sorts of questions should concern the psychologist when first invited to work with an attorney on a case, suggests strategies for developing the forensic case, and presents a strategy for appearing in court.

A BRIEF HISTORICAL INTRODUCTION

In 1486, two Dominican monks, Johann Sprenger and Heinrich Kraemer, spurred by Pope Innocent VIII's call to attack witchcraft and the Devil (who appeared in mentally ill, female, and Jewish forms in disproportionate numbers), wrote a divinely inspired text. The *Malleus Malificarum*, or Witches' Hammer, allowed the more inquisitionally minded (Millon, 1969) to prove the existence of witchcraft, to describe signs and symptoms of the condition, and to specify the legal form of examining and sentencing more than 100,000 of the accused for the next 200 years, well into the "Enlightenment." This early appearance of the expert witness and, by the way, manualized assessment and treatment procedures, should sensitize the psychologist about the responsibility of serving as an expert witness (and to manualized practice).

Juries were originally composed of people who had firsthand knowledge of the events before the court. By the mid-1850s there was a shift toward our current lay juror system. This shift, coupled with the increasingly complex and specialized knowledge that was developing during the Enlightenment and the Industrial Revolution, created the need for the judicial decision maker with increasing frequency to call upon those possessing specialized knowledge to visit the courtroom. The jury and adversary systems did not and have not ceded authority to others; however, faced with questions such as determining *mens rea*, the capacity to form evil intent, as in the case of the assassination of Sir Robert Peel's secretary by David M'Naghten in 1842, the courts called on experts to provide an understanding of knowledge beyond that of the court. There were fewer professions then, the chief ones being engineering, law, medicine, and the ministry. Thus, the question of who was an expert did not have the importance that it has now.

FRYE, JENKINS, THE FEDERAL RULES OF EVIDENCE, AND DAUBERT

During the 1920s, interest in truth-and-lie-detection devices took several forms. Marston's interest in and popularizing of the lie detector led him to adorn his comic book character, Wonder Woman, with a lie-detecting bracelet in her efforts to save us from criminals. Marston's interest also led to the lie detector's entering the courtroom. This case served as the whetstone for the courts to sharpen their definition of expert testimony in the *Frye* test. *Frye v. United States* (1923) held that between experimental and well-recognized scientific principles or discoveries lies a twilight zone, and that "the thing from which the deduction is made [by the expert witness] must be sufficiently established to have gained general acceptance in the particular field in which it belongs" (Blau, 1984, p. 5). In *Frye*, the lie detector did not meet the standard. After the *Frye* test, times were quiet until the success of the Clarks, who used children's choice of black or white dolls as playmates to illustrate the devaluation of black children, presumably as a function of segregated school systems. The Clarks served as amici curiae in the *Brown v. Board of Education* (1954) case that first led to the integration of our schools and then our other political and social institutions (also see Chapter 1).

The psychologist as an expert witness in what was termed psychiatric matters appeared in *Jenkins v. United States* (1962), in which the court held that "the determination of a psychologist's competence to render an expert opinion based on his findings as to presence or absence of mental disease or defect must depend upon the nature and extent of his knowledge. It does not depend upon his claim to the title 'psychologist.' And that determination, after hearing, must be left in each case to traditional discretion of trial court subject to appellate review" (Blau, 1984, p. 346). The *Jenkins* court defined the expert witness as:

> qualified to testify because he has firsthand knowledge that the jury does not have of the situation or transaction at issue. The expert has something different to contribute. This is the power to draw inferences from the facts that a jury would not be competent to draw. To warrant the use of expert testimony, then, two elements are required. First, the subject of the inference must be so distinctively beyond the ken of the average layman. Second, the witness must have such skill, knowledge or experience in that field or calling as to make it appear that his opinion of inference will probably aid the trier of fact in his search for truth. The knowledge may in some fields be derived from reading alone, in some from practice alone, or as is more commonly the case, from both. (Beis, 1984, p. 234)

The Supreme Court codified and Congress legislated the Federal Rules of Evidence (FRE) in 1975. Similar but not always identical rules have been adopted to govern proceedings in most state courts. The FRE or a facsimile governs nonjury cases, criminal and civil cases, worker's compensation cases, and proceedings in probate court whether a judge or a magistrate presides. The FRE are followed, but in a relaxed manner, in arenas such as grand jury proceedings, extradition proceedings, preliminary hearings in criminal cases, sentencing or probation hearings, issuing search or arrest warrants or criminal summonses, or contempt proceedings, because these latter events are considered nonadversarial (Bailey, 1995). FRE 702 holds that "If scientific, technical, or other specialized knowledge will assist the trier of fact to understand the evidence or to determine a fact in issue, a witness qualified as an expert by knowledge, skill, experience, training, or education, may testify thereto in the form of an opinion or otherwise." FRE 702 establishes that the expert's purpose is to help the trier of fact (the judge or jury) understand technical evidence. The judge will rule on the introduction of an expert witness to the extent that the judge sees the untrained layperson has need for the expert's enlightenment. The expert may qualify on the basis of specialized degrees and courses, practical experience, specific training, or a particular skill or knowledge. Thus, a manager of a gravel pit possessing only an eighth-grade education but who worked for 20 years to become pit boss may be the best person to determine whether particular gravel could have stuck in the grooves of a tire, causing an automobile to lose traction. Naturally, a highway department engineer who attended workshops on surface friction might be in a position by virtue of education and training to help determine whether the road material was adequate to prevent skids. The judge rules on the qualifications of the expert relevant to the issue at hand (Green & Nesson, 1984).

Rule 703 states, "The facts or data in the particular case upon which an expert bases an opinion of inference may be those perceived by or made known to him at or before the hearing. If of a type reasonably relied upon by experts in the particular field in forming opinions or inferences upon the subject, the facts or data need not be admissible in evidence." Rule 703 reflects the liberal thrust of the FRE in removing "the common law requirement that experts base their opinions on matters within their personal knowledge or matters already admitted into evidence" (L. Perrin, 1997, p. 939). Rule 703 allows for three sources of data: firsthand observation by the witness, as in an examination of a patient; presentation of evidence at trial, which may have been presented by another witness or by the hypothetical question; and information from sources other than the expert's direct perception, such as hospital records, nurse, police, or family reports, public opinion surveys, or computer-generated psychological test profiles and reports. The balance here is between opening the door to hearsay, as in the case of public opinion surveys where all the data is thirdhand, and the use of an accepted technique "of a type reasonably relied upon by experts in the particular field."

Rule 704 establishes that "Testimony in the form of an opinion of inference otherwise admissible is not objectionable because it embraces an ultimate issue to be decided by the trier of fact." Previous to this rule, experts had to engage in circumlocutions when approaching the issue the jury or judge needed to decide. Thus, the expert might say a person's test results showed an intelligence level that did not allow for the understanding of any but the simplest arithmetical calculations, as in simple adding or subtraction, and that test results showed the person to be unduly suggestible. If the case involved the person's signing a will that disadvantaged loved ones, the expert could all but conclude for the jury that the person was not competent by skill or independence of judgment but could not say so to the jury. Now the expert can. In effect, Rule 704 lets the attorney dispense with laying the predicates by hypothetical questions that had been used so the expert witness's opinion about the ultimate issue could be heard by the court. However, judges may still determine that the fact finder should not be unduly influenced by an expert if the opinion is more emotional or inflammatory than factual or probative.

Rule 705 states, "The expert may testify in terms of opinion or inference and give his reasons therefor without prior disclosure of the underlying facts or data, unless the court requires otherwise. The experts may in any event be required to disclose the underlying facts or data on cross-examination." Though it may not appear so on the surface, the effect of this rule is to obviate the need for the hypothetical question, consistent with Rule 704. (Before leaving the FRE, the interested reader may want to examine Article V concerning privilege and Article VIII concerning hearsay.)

The next major change in defining expert witness testimony came almost two decades later with the *Daubert* case. *Daubert v. Merrell Dow Pharmaceuticals* (1993) arose when Benedictin was taken by pregnant mothers for morning sickness;

subsequently, their children were born with limb reduction birth defects. Both sides produced expert witnesses. The appeal to the Supreme Court resulted in the Court's replacing the seven-decade-old *Frye* standard that called for scientific evidence to have "general acceptance" in a field or be based on a corpus of knowledge. The Court recognized FRE 702 as governing whether the evidence met the two-prong test of "scientific knowledge that will assist the trier of fact to understand the evidence or determine a fact in issue." Rather than a general acceptance test only, *Daubert* shifts the judgment of scientific knowledge to the trier of fact with four criteria: testability of a theory or technique, rooted in Karl Popper's criterion of the falsifiability of a theory; the degree to which theory or techniques have been subject to peer review such as publication; the known or potential error rate of a technique; and general acceptance by the relevant scientific community (the Frye test).

The Court considered whether *Daubert* would cause a "free-for-all" with its more liberal rules but expressed confidence that through vigorous cross-examination, presentation of contrary evidence, and careful instruction on the burden of proof, the jury would be able to sort out the evidence. Because experts can be persuasive and misleading, the judge must rule between the prejudicial and the probative value of the testimony exercising more control over experts than over lay witnesses (Weinstein cited in *Daubert v. Merrell Dow*, 1993). Debate rages on such issues as whether *Daubert* liberates science so that noncanonical theories and findings can appear in court or whether it abets "junk science," whether it will help or confuse judges and juries, and whether it allows for the fact finder to hear all the evidence or allows the clever attorney to welcome through the back door dubious findings and those with no foundation. The reader interested in *Daubert* and its implications can consult an emerging literature (cf. Gless, 1995; Goodman-Delahunty, 1997; L. Perrin, 1997).

The next development involved the role of the judge as gatekeeper regarding admitting an expert's testimony into evidence. Joiner (*General Electric Co. v. Joiner*, 1997) was an electrician who had to make repairs with his hands and arms immersed in fluids containing polychlorinated biphenyls (PCBs). PCBs were banned by Congress in 1978 as hazardous to human health. Joiner contracted small cell cancer and sued the manufacturers of PCBs, including the General Electric Co. Expert witnesses on behalf of Joiner introduced animal research that was excluded by the district court judge because the evidence "did not rise above 'subjective belief or unsupported speculation.'" The Supreme Court reviewed the case and found that the appropriate standard for reviewing the judge's rulings concerning the admissability of scientific evidence is the "abuse of discretion" standard. That is, a judge must ignore logic, settled law, relevance, or reliability to have abused his or her discretion. Changing from *Frye* to *Daubert* did not diminish the judge's gatekeeping role regarding expert evidence.

The effects of *Daubert* regarding the use of expert evidence will be determined as cases filter through courts. Though *Daubert* is determinative in federal jurisdictions, how it will be adopted by state courts is an evolving process. *Daubert* appears more liberal than *Frye*. In the court's language, it appears more liberal in that it includes *Frye's* general acceptance as one criterion—"Finally, general acceptance can yet have a bearing on the inquiry" (*Daubert v. Merrell Dow*, 1993)—though not necessarily the dispositive or determining criterion as in *Frye*. Yet some have argued that *Daubert* will be more restrictive. Goodman-Delahunty and Foote (1995) might be reading *Daubert* as requiring all four criteria when they argue that "The *Daubert* decision imposes what we believe is a higher standard upon the testimony of forensic psychologists than did the *Frye* 'general acceptance' standard . . . the emphasis in *Daubert* is on requirements for validity and reliability which may be more technically stringent than a general acceptance test, particularly the requirement that the methods be "falsifiable" (p. 198). Reed (1996) finds that the unprepared expert witness will have a tougher time in court, and the prepared witness finds *Daubert* more liberal than *Frye*. His reasoning is based on *Chapple v. Granger* (1994), where the court found a fixed neuropsychological battery more compelling than the flexible battery. This prompted Reitan, developer of the battery named for him, to lament that courts, not psychologists, appear to be deciding on the scientific merit of psychological tests. County Court Judge Gless (1995) focuses on the added burden of *Daubert* on judges who need to sharpen their performance in judging the soundness of scientific evidence. The next few years will tell to what extent *Daubert* is adopted by state courts, how *Daubert* will affect evidence, and how *Daubert* will need modification.

Meehl has been the beacon for psychology as an empirical science for a half century. It should surprise no one that Meehl is as dogged in his attacks on fuzzy-thinking clinicians in this millennial time as he has been since the late 1940s. For example, Meehl (1997) states, "Since clinical experience consist of anecdotal impressions by practitioners, it is unavoidably a mixture of truth, half-truths, and falsehoods. The scientific method is the only known way to distinguish these, and it is both unscholarly and unethical for psychologists who deal with other persons' health, careers, money, freedom, and even life itself to pretend that clinical experience suffices and that quantitative research on diagnostic and therapeutic procedures is not needed" (p. 91). Grove and Meehl (1996) revisit issues Meehl raised almost a half century ago (Meehl, 1954) and conclude with even greater confidence in the superiority of formal (statistical) over informal (clinical) prediction procedures. Any forensic psychologist unfamiliar with Meehl's arguments flirts with malpractice. Nonetheless, future inquiry as to the difference between nomothetic arguments and the need for a particular decision in a particular case may help the forensic psychologist. Thus, there may be a 70% chance of rain, but the individual is faced with a discrete decision: to carry or leave at home the umbrella. Practical ethics (Pepper, 1942) may require us to use legal criteria (a preponderance of evidence or 51%) rather than statistical significance (95% or the vaunted $p < .05$). This raises parallel questions concerning the definitions of "scientific" and "expert."

While the term scientific is being carefully defined by courts and philosophers of science and law, and while psychology is continually debating over its scientific nature in the face of the rapidly increasing number of practitioners, the scientific testimony many psychologists are rendering may be less scientific than expert. In Florida, a famous restaurant with a multimillion-dollar wine cellar burned (Stevens, 1997). The insurance company claimed most of the expensive wines were undamaged; the restaurant owners claimed damage. Both sides brought in wine tasters. Chemists who are nomothetic scientists would have been useless. It is exactly the subjective, clinical impressions of these expert tasters that helped the sides to settle the case. So it may be with psychologists as clinicians. But this raises the question of whether the expert witness is basing his or her testimony on scientific or subjective grounds, and whether any science applied to the individual case is artful practice.

Brown (1997) raises another set of issues when she challenges us to use the role of the expert witness subversively. She specifically enjoins psychologists to fight for social justice and debrides the notion that "forensic psychologists should have no values about where they work and what they do and that such a 'values-free' stance will translate into objectivity. By stating that (a) all psychologists have values and (b) I know what mine are and am willing to tell anyone and be cognizant of the effects of those values on my work, I was clearly in violation of that creeping norm of valuelessness by even thinking about social justice as a context for my work in the justice system" (p. 450).

The final issue discussed here is related to most of the above-mentioned questions: To what extent are psychologists purveying "junk science" when they help construct various abuse syndromes? A recent mutation is the "reactive attachment disorder": a parent adopts a child whose history may not be known or who comes with a history of abuse; when the child has trouble relating with the parent, the parent subsequently kills the child, claiming stress due to the child's detachment. Are we pandering to lethal narcissistic personalities by providing them with this defense? Unlike defense attorneys, who may be assigned by the courts, psychologists do not have to provide defenses to clients.

THE OPENING

Problems that arise in forensic cases most probably will be traceable to a neglected issue or incorrect decision during the first telephone call between the consulting psychologist and the attorney or client. What may seem to be an inconsequential issue that should be handled easily and early in the relationship could grow into a major problem if left unattended. Professional psychologists involved in forensic cases will be successful if they consider the following.

WHO CALLS YOU?

The psychologist's performance in the legal arena is not solely a function of how well or poorly he or she testifies, but is highly dependent upon the attorney or legal team who retains the services of the psychologist. It is hard to overemphasize the skills, ability, understanding, and attitudes of the attorney. The psychologist must depend on the attorney's ability to understand and use the psychologist's findings, and the attorney's strategy and questions are the vehicles by which the psychologist brings forth findings in depositions and in the courtroom.

The typical case begins with a telephone call from an attorney. The attorney's manner allows the psychologist to see how the attorney creates a first impression with others, such as a jury. The attorney usually will describe the issues in the case, providing a basis for assessing the conceptual and oratorical skills of the attorney. Then the attorney will state the services he or she seeks from the psychologist in the case. This allows the psychologist to see (a) the degree to which the attorney understands psychological approaches, including the kinds of questions psychologists can and cannot answer, and the time it may take to perform the requested services; (b) the construct system the attorney is using in both the legal and psychological domains; and (c) the degree to which the attorney is interested in finding the answer to a question or merely wants to hire an expert opinion to support the case, often termed a "hired gun" (M. Singer & Nievod, 1987). Hired guns will mouth the words and opinions the attorney thinks will be beneficial to the client, no matter what the truth or probative value the opinions might have. Serving as a hired gun will not serve the truth, will quickly erode the psychologist's reputation, can result in legal and ethical actions against the psychologist, and is simply professionally unfulfilling.

When feeling pressure about how his or her testimony will be greeted by the attorney, the psychologist may find comfort in the American Bar Association's Standard 3-3.2 for prosecutors and Standard 4-4.4 for defense attorneys. Both use the same language in defining the lawyer's relations with the expert witness: "(a) A prosecutor [lawyer] who engages an expert for an opinion should respect the independence of the expert and should not seek to dictate the formation of the expert's opinion on the subject. To the extent necessary, the prosecutor should explain to the expert his or her role in the trial as an impartial expert called to aid the fact finders and the manner in which the examination of witnesses is conducted." And "(b) It is unprofessional conduct for a prosecutor [lawyer] to pay an excessive fee for the purpose of influencing the expert's testimony or to fix the amount of the fee contingent upon the testimony the expert will give or the result in the case" (*Selected Statutes, Rules and Standards on the Legal Profession*, 1984, p. 165 for prosecutors and p. 179 for defense attorneys).

The attorney's description of the case at hand typically opens the way for an interchange between the psychologist and the attorney. The psychologist may ask about the pertinent facts in the case and the theory the attorney is using to support the complaint or the defense. This allows the psychologist to assess the way the attorney conceives and presents the issues in the case, the degree to which the attorney understand the capabilities of and the limits to psychology, and how the attorney will regard the psychologist's questions and opinions both now and as the case proceeds. Understanding some of the issues in the case, at least those involving psychology, the psychologist may offer a few suggestions about how he or she may help in the case. The degree to which the attorney is able and willing to understand the psychological theory and procedures is an indicator of whether the attorney is seeking the expert counsel of a psychologist or merely seeking to retain a hired gun. The psychologist can err here by getting too specific about the psychological aspects of the case.

Some of these issues may arise in the context of the first telephone conversation. If they do not, they should be broached soon afterward. It is critical to see the role the attorney has in mind for the psychologist and the way the attorney regards psychology and the psychologist, both generally and specifically.

DOES THE PSYCHOLOGIST HAVE THE PERSONAL SKILLS FOR COURTROOM TESTIMONY?

When working with an attorney leads to courtroom testimony, the psychologist must assess his or her own personal skills. Depending on his or her personality structure, the psychologist may have to deal with one or both of two perilous attitudes: being utterly skeptical about what psychology could possibly contribute to the case, and being conflict-avoidant, in which case, the psychologist will find cross-examination excruciating. Courtroom combat is not for the fainthearted, the conflict-avoidant personality type, nor for those who simply like to argue but cannot cope with an attorney's attack without retaliating. The psychologist on the witness stand can expect rough treatment from opposing counsel. If the psychologist questions the worth of psychology in the case at hand or does not enjoy verbal combat, he or she may best serve the case and profession by declining forensic referrals.

The psychologist interested in self-assessment regarding courtroom attitude or personality may benefit from reading Ziskin and Faust (1994). They unremittingly attack psychological testimony, claiming that such testimony does not belong in the court. Their arguments provide a good measure for the reader to see whether he or she can withstand such an attack. C. C. Wang, originally trained in law, left that profession to become an artist and art connoisseur; he explained his decision: "I hated [the law]. I like everything beautiful and peaceful. I don't want to fight with people" (Lawrence, 1997, p. A-16). He correctly described courtroom litigation and wisely chose an immensely successful career creating and collecting art.

Psychologists should critically examine themselves for potential biases. The psychologist who testified only for defendants or only for plaintiffs in case after case should reveal this bias to the attorney. Similarly, any ethical, professional, or legal charges that have been raised about the psychologist should be revealed, or the psychologist should politely decline involvement in the case. For example, an attorney needed an expert witness in a complex drug case. He was delighted to have secured the services of a psychiatrist lawyer who was the head of mental health services in a major state penal facility. In the car, after the attorney met him at the airport, the expert mentioned that he was under indictment for running an illicit drug ring in the state prison. The attorney made a U-turn and deposited him at the airport. The attorney told me this story to explain why he asked whether I had been or was currently charged with any crime when he retained me to replace the other expert.

DOES THE PSYCHOLOGIST HAVE THE KNOWLEDGE BASE AND EXPERTISE TO ADDRESS THE ISSUES IN THE CASE?

Familiarity with the American Psychological Association Code of Ethical Conduct (APA, 1992) and with Specialty Guidelines for Forensic Psychologists

(Committee on Ethical Guidelines for Forensic Psychologists, 1991) will serve psychologists well in determining the boundaries of their competence to provide the requested service. For the psychologist involved with jail or prison cases, knowledge of the *Standards for Psychological Services in Jails and Prisons* (American Association of Correctional Psychologists, 1980) and the various standards for correctional facilities are important. Professionals using psychological tests and measurements need to practice in accord with the *Standards for Educational and Psychological Tests* (APA, 1985).

A doctoral degree does not confer a blanket level of expertise, the emanations from which will enlighten any case. In fact, the psychologist should judiciously weigh his or her training, education, and experience, including research, publications, and clinical placements and internships, against the case's issues. This assessment should guide the psychologist's decision to accept or decline involvement in the case. Lack of competence in the case's issues can trigger ethics complaints and malpractice law suits (see Chapter 24). For example, a cognitive psychologist may be the most appropriate expert witness in a case that involves whether two logos are discriminably different to the target consumer groups or whether one company infringed on another company's trademark. The same cognitive psychologist may not have the knowledge of developmental psychology that would help to determine whether a child witness had the requisite skills to have accurately encoded, stored, and retrieved information about a crime. The psychologist should send a curriculum vitae to the attorney, then have a frank discussion with the attorney about how the psychologist will contribute to the case. This helps guard against later charges of incompetence and misrepresentation.

Clear communication early in the case about the scientific basis of any testimony is crucial. Dawes (1994) is dubious about the basis of the science of clinical psychology and is scandalized by the lack of articulation between the science and the practice of clinical psychology. Before a clinical psychologist accepts a case, he or she should analyze the issues of the case with the extant psychology knowledge base, using Dawes as a skeptical companion. The psychologist should be able to respond affirmatively to the questions Dawes raises if he or she intends to use the base of scientific psychology as a foundation for testifying.

WHAT LEGAL KNOWLEDGE DOES THE PSYCHOLOGIST NEED?

The main contribution the psychologist can make is based on his or her knowledge of psychology. A case may involve diagnostic acumen in determining mental state, or it may involve knowledge of developmental psychology and parenting skills. A case concerning liability regarding the appropriate size, appearance, and placement of highway signs to minimize accidents could even call upon knowledge of cognitive and perceptual psychology. The psychologist need not know law as a lawyer must know the law. The psychologist need not know the exceptions to the hearsay rule, and the exceptions to these exceptions. In fact, the psychologist who knows a fair amount of law may be tempted to step into the role of legal consultant, causing role conflict, or to function as a pseudo-counselor (in the words of a colleague, to have "delusions of legal grandeur").

Nonetheless, psychologists will be more effective if they understand the legal theories into which their testimony will be fitted. Thus, the psychologist in a custody case should know that the "best interests of the child" is a term of art (a technical rather than colloquial term) for the attorney; it has specific meanings, so that the injudicious use of this term can color the outcome of the case. Likewise, the term "insanity" has different meanings in different jurisdictions. The psychologist may not know the legal terms of art at the beginning of the case; however, such knowledge is necessary to serve the case well. The necessity to learn about legal terms and theory provides an opportunity for the attorney and psychologist to educate each other and determine how well they work together.

Does the Psychologist Have the Time to Devote to the Case?

When working with attorneys and courts, psychologists will confront seemingly impossible deadlines that could compromise their services. They need to be clear about what can and cannot be provided in the time frame available. Often, an evaluation will be requested later in a case than it should have been, with an impending hearing date earlier than the psychologist would prefer. The psychologist needs to determine the pertinent dates in the case, the time needed to provide the services requested, and the degree to which competent professional services can be provided in the time allotted. Forensic work is time consuming and can be inconvenient, with hearings and conferences called at inopportune times and with witnesses who may be available only when the psychologist has other commitments. The psychologist may hurry to meet these demands only to learn that the case has been continued for weeks or even months; then more record review and preparation of materials already mastered will be required. When considering the time a case will require, the psychologist should be aware that *the three most important aspects of expert testimony are preparation, preparation, and preparation.* There is no recorded instance of a psychologist getting in trouble by overpreparing for a case. However, insufficient preparation can be humiliating. A psychologist should be aware that he or she will have to devote significant amounts of time to properly present a case.

What Role Do the Attorney and Psychologist Envision for the Psychologist?

The traditional role of the psychologist in the legal arena has been as an expert witness, but the use of psychological research in the *Brown v. Board of Education* case in 1954 saw the inclusion of the psychologist on the legal team as a consultant. Standard 7-1.1 of the ABA Criminal Justice Mental Health Standards (1989) describes three roles for mental health professionals: (a) the scientific and evaluative roles, (b) the consultant role, and (c) the treatment or rehabilitation role. At an early stage, the attorney and psychologist will determine which role the psychologist will assume. To what degree is the psychologist called upon to function in an expert witness versus a consultant role? To what degree can the attorney accept the psychologist as a consultant? Most important, is the case best served by the psychologist in the expert witness role, the consultant role, or a mixture of the two? Realistically, there is no pure expert or consultant role; however, the consultant role can predispose the psychologist to identify with the client's cause and lead to a loss of objectivity, as shown when the psychologist uses "we" and becomes overly tied to the case's outcome (R. Singer, 1995).

The psychologist must be mindful that the client may view the psychologist in the third or therapeutic role, a situation that can lead to conflict; for example, despite being warned of the limits to privilege and confidentiality, the client may relate to the psychologist as if the psychologist were serving as a psychotherapist (G. Perrin & Sales, 1994). Being held in police custody can shake a person. The detainee under police interrogation can feel an alliance with the psychologist who is the first friendly face the detainee sees, and can interpret a relationship as therapeutic rather than as part of the investigation. The psychologist may intentionally use reflexive empathy, or "communicating the 'quality of felt awareness' of the experience of another person," as opposed to receptive empathy, or "the perception and understanding of the experiences of another person" (Shuman, 1993, p. 298). Such a strategy may maneuver the client to reveal more information than is in his or her best interest to disclose, raising serious ethical and legal questions. Some practitioners hold that, once warned of his or her rights against self-incrimination, any method is fair in eliciting as much information as possible, even if it involves manipulating the interviewee's vulnerabilities. Others maintain that there is a duty to the welfare of the interviewee that his or her vulnerabilities not be exploited. Two questions arise: how to differentiate the clinical and forensic psychology roles, and whether the interviewee or the person hiring the psychologist has sole claim to the psychologist's allegiance. Given an interviewee who cannot monitor the situation for his or her own interests, the ethical psychologist may alert appropriate parties to the case that the interviewee needs assistance, be it psychological or legal. Ethical professional psychologists should try to define the role or roles they will play and be aware of any shift in the roles as the case proceeds.

Greenberg and Shuman (1997) raise questions about the inherent conflict between the therapeutic and forensic roles in which the psychologist may become enmeshed. If the therapist is a witness as to fact, therapist-client privilege may become an important question; this conundrum arises in marital cases when one party files for divorce intending to use grounds established though the course of marital therapy. In such a situation, the therapist should decline becoming an expert witness, thus avoiding a potential role conflict. On the other hand, the expert witness should not engage a party to the case in psychotherapy subsequent to the case. The peril here involves hopelessly confounding the transference, or client's perception of the therapist, as well as compromising subsequent legal events such as an appeal or a countersuit.

How Will a Shift to the Consultant Role Be Managed?

The expert, according to FRE 702 "will assist the trier of fact to understand the evidence or determine a fact in issue" or is supposed to help a judge or jury to understand a technical, esoteric body of knowledge that the judge or jury cannot otherwise be expected to understand. In this role, the expert can collect and examine data, then render an opinion on the technical issues relevant to the case.

As mentioned, the role of a psychological consultant to a lawyer has developed recently and received less attention than the expert witness role. Psychologists since *Brown v. Board of Education* (1954) have been increasingly involved in amicus curiae, or friend of the court cases and in indigent cases as provided for in FRE 706. Forensic psychological consultation accelerated considerably with the emphasis on applying social psychology to jury selection. The expert and consultant roles can be seen as being on a continuum. Because an attorney necessarily must consult with the expert on the issues, findings, and deposition and courtroom presentations, even the expert serves to some minimal extent as a consultant. Yet, there are significant differences between the roles, perhaps the principal difference being emotional commitment. Simply put, the expert's commitment should be to the truth, whereas the consultant's commitment may be to the cause or issue at hand; for example, the psychologists involved with the jury selection in the Chicago 7 trial were committed to the protest against the Vietnam War and committed to the civil rights movement of the 1960s. The consultant's efforts can become collaborative to the extent that the psychologist uses the pronoun "we" and may form countertransferences, or personally based emotional allegiances on the professional's part, to the attorney and clients identified with the cause (R. Singer, 1995). Identifying with and supporting political and social causes raises ethical concerns, but this identification may be consonant with aspects of the consultant role. However, when the psychologist as an expert witness identifies with the cause of the attorney's client, the expert's role is compromised and psychological science is in danger of being sold, rightfully provoking the criticism that experts are hired guns. This complex issue is addressed again below. Suffice it to say that at the outset, the psychologist needs to be aware of the type of role the lawyer intends the psychologist to fill and of the emotions and allegiances the psychologist both brings to the case and develops as the case progresses.

Who Is the Attorney?

Because a practicing psychologist's core professional identity and reputation are based on performing a service professionally and successfully, and because the psychologist's performance is dependent in part on the attorney, it is important to assess the attorney's reputation when considering accepting a forensic referral. The psychologist involved in forensic work can learn of attorney's character and abilities by following cases in the media, visiting courtrooms, calling upon a few trusted colleagues for their opinions, and trusting experience if he or she worked with the attorney on a prior case.

The attorney's reputation is not conclusive in determining how he or she may work now. For example, a psychologist worked with an attorney who was excellent in using psychological assessment to exclude incriminating statements his client made to police investigators. The psychologist's testimony was used adeptly to show how the client did not have the requisite mental capacity to understand his *Miranda* warning. Later, the psychologist welcomed the attorney's invitation to work on another case, one concerning self-defense. The attorney seemed distracted and was vague in articulating the theory of defense he intended to use and how the psychologist's testimony would help. He deferred scheduling conferences to review test results, abruptly left in the middle of the only pretrial conference he scheduled, and used the psychological evidence poorly in court. The client lost the homicide case. Several months later, the psychologist read in the newspapers that the attorney lost his license shortly after the case due to drug use. Because the psychologist's performance is dependent on the competence and character of the attorney in charge of the case, an assessment of the attorney's character and competence is highly recommended.

Who Are the Opposing Parties, the Opposing Parties' Attorneys, and the Judge?

As soon as the psychologist picks up the telephone, he or she must determine whether the case is one on which he or she is already working. As the conversation proceeds, and the attorney presents the main aspects of the case, the psychologist should ask who are the parties in the case, who are the attorneys that will be working on both sides of the case, and who is the judge. If the psychologist has been retained by the other side, he or she can politely decline the case without revealing that he or she is working on the case, end the phone call quickly but gracefully, and report the contact to the attorney who has retained the psychologist. Deleray (1988) reports a case in which an attorney called upon a psychologist to review records and give an opinion in a child custody case. The psychologist complied. Some time later, one of the psychologist's psychotherapy clients began to talk about a lawsuit. It became clear to the psychologist that the attorney who had retained the psychologist's consulting services was the counsel for the party opposing the psychologist's psychotherapy client. The psychologist was serving competing parties and in quite a role conflict. These conflicts are preventable by determining who the involved parties are before proceeding.

The psychologist should reveal to the attorney any social, political, financial, or other relationships that he or she may have with anyone involved in the case. Such relationships include instances where there is any possibility of conflicting interests or relationships that may cast the psychologist's testimony in a biased light. These relationships extend to those the psychologist's family might have with a party or with the party's relatives or friends. A relationship does not necessarily prevent the psychologist's involvement in a case. Both the psychologist and the attorney must weigh the degree to which there are any interests that can compromise the psychologist's ability to keep a confidence or to work without competing motives, or whether the psychologist will appear to others to have such a conflict and thereby compromise his or her testimony. By raising such questions at this point, major problems can be averted, and the attorney can gain confidence in the psychologist's awareness of ethical and legal concerns.

Naturally, the smaller the town, the more likely people will relate to each other in various roles (Schank & Skovholt, 1997; Sonne, 1994). There are three seemingly ironclad principles that are tested to their limits in small communities: confidentiality, competence, and conflicting interests. It is easier to follow these principles in urban centers; however, in a town of a few thousand people, it may be impossible to have attorneys, parties in the case, bailiff and clerks, and jurors who are not someone's Little League coach, schoolteacher, or banker. It remains the responsibility of the psychologist to avoid ethical dilemmas, but consultation with the attorney regarding how the law may view conflicting interests and with esteemed colleagues who are experienced in legal and ethical issues will help avoid problems.

Note that if the psychologist who seeks consultation reveals information sufficient to identify the parties in the case, the professional providing consultation to the psychologist may feel ethically compelled to intervene. This would usurp the psychologist's decision making. Consultation regarding ethics should be conducted in a way that gives the consultant enough information to help clarify ethical and professional issues but not enough to take the decision making from the psychologist who is seeking the consultation. For example, a clinician may not be sure whether to report a child abuse case because of uncertainties in the clinical data. The clinician may seek consultation and, in sharing the data, may find that the colleague has a lower threshold regarding reporting the possibility of child abuse and feels compelled to report the case to authorities. The colleague, responding to his or her own perceived duty, has usurped the clinician's decision making and duty of confidentiality and privilege to the client.

Who, besides the Attorney, May Call the Psychologist?

A variety of people may seek a psychologist's assistance to help resolve their legal troubles. Asking them to have their attorney call is advisable, so the psychologist can determine that his or her involvement in a case will be welcomed by the attorney and be consistent with whatever legal strategy is being considered. For example, a father called to ask the psychologist to schedule time to test his 15-year-old son, who was visiting Alabama from North Carolina over the winter holidays. The father revealed that the son had been diagnosed with bipolar disorder by a psychiatrist retained by the mother. A custody hearing was scheduled for the next month in North Carolina and the father wanted to show how the son regressed under the mother's care, with the hope that this presumed regression would result in his gaining child custody. The psychologist suggested to the father that he contact his attorney in North Carolina to determine whether (a) the father's strategy was consistent with the attorney's strategy, (b) a psychologist in the attorney's locale and the case's venue may have an existing working relationship with the attorney and the court, and (c) a psychologist who lived where the son and attorney lived might be more suitable for several reasons; such a psychologist can see the son for several sessions separated in time, providing a better diagnostic picture and incurring fewer travel expenses for the father.

Another example illustrates the potential for role conflict once the psychologist is working on a case. A third-year law student in a clerkship in the district attorney's office sought to interview the psychologist posing as a student who was researching a term paper on the role of the psychologist as an expert witness. It became readily apparent that the intern was trying to gather data to impugn the psychologist's credentials. The psychologist abruptly ended the interview, made verbatim notes of the discussion, and called the attorney who had retained him. A few weeks later, the clerk was seated at the district attorney's side during the psychologist's qualification as an expert witness and during his testimony. The district attorney's office tried to subvert the discovery process and put the psychologist in a role conflict, one that pitted being helpful to a "student" against that of the psychologist's revealing information only through the process of discovery.

WHO REFERRED THE PSYCHOLOGIST TO THE ATTORNEY?

The question of the referral source allows the psychologist to learn about possible unstated expectations that the caller may harbor. The person who referred the psychologist undoubtedly did so as a function of prior contacts and will have described the psychologist's skills, abilities, and character to the caller. Knowing the referral source may help clarify the caller's expectations. Second, it is good to know the type of informal referral network operating in one's professional milieu so one can anticipate future referrals. Finally, if the psychologist had a particular fee structure or other working relationship with the referral source, the psychologist can prevent potential misunderstandings with the caller by clarifying the current terms of employment.

WHO PAYS THE PSYCHOLOGIST?

The most satisfactory financial arrangement is through a written agreement with the attorney. Attorneys are likely to understand that a professional will bill for time spent on the telephone, scoring test protocols, writing reports, researching, and preparing for court. Also, this arrangement allows the attorney to have privilege regarding the psychologist because the attorney is then the client of the psychologist. If the attorney's client owned privilege, the psychologist could be placed in a position in which the client could invoke privilege; then the psychologist would be at risk for violating the client's privilege by communicating with the attorney unless a signed waiver is obtained beforehand. Without exception, the psychologist should tell individuals who seek the psychologist's forensic services to have their attorney contact the psychologist.

If the psychologist is involved with the client before a forensic contact arises, perhaps in a marital or child psychotherapy case, the relationship operating before the forensic involvement would be the controlling, regnant relationship; although the psychotherapist may be an expert in other contexts, he or she would be restricted to a factual witness role. Accepting an expert or consultant witness role would complicate the case at the least and subject the psychologist to role conflict and its deleterious consequences. The pressures to serve the psychotherapy client may come from one or another of the patients, the attorneys, or the psychologist's sense of obligation or identification to the psychotherapy client. For example, in a custody case, the psychologist may empathize with the parent or the child who is caught in a legal vise constructed by the other spouse or a parent. Nonetheless, the expert witness role may be best served by an independent psychologist, not the one providing clinical services to the client. As Monahan (1980) advises, know who your client is and what role to play.

How Does the Psychologist Determine and Bill Fees?

Some psychologists are copying attorneys by asking for retainers, which is a reasonable practice. However, a psychologist should never copy the attorney's practice of working on a contingent fee basis. The Specialty Guidelines for Forensic Psychologists states in IV. B that "forensic psychologists do not provide professional services to parties to a legal proceeding on the basis of 'contingent fees,' when those services involve the offering of expert testimony to a court or administrative body, or when they call upon the psychologist to make affirmations or representations intended to be relied on by third parties" (Committee on Ethical Guidelines for Forensic Psychologists, 1991).The conflict of interest and the appearance of such a conflict for the expert witness is inescapable in a contingent fee arrangement. This arrangement means the psychologist is or appears to be working to win the case to garner a paycheck rather than providing the court or jury with unbiased scientific guidance that the expert witness role demands.

Psychologists should find out about the prevailing local and regional fee schedules and the degree of specialization called for in the case, realistically assess their own expertise and level of experience, then set up their own fee schedule. Blau (1984) presents forms for the forensic practitioner for both billing and record keeping purposes. The psychologist should bill promptly and periodically. Thus, the psychologist who has tested an attorney's client may want to furnish a bill for services along with the report if there is no set arrangement for services beyond the testing and report. Failure to be accurate and timely in billing can present problems. In a pair of related cases, the attorneys, who were not known for their integrity, and the psychologist had an understanding that the psychologist would bill when the cases were concluded. The two attorneys kept telling the psychologist, who had provided case reviews and reports, that the psychologist would soon be called for the next hearing. They never informed the psychologist when the case and appeals were exhausted. More than a year later, the psychologist found out in a law reporter that the appeal had been lost. The attorneys had little incentive to call the psychologist because they would be paying the fee from their pocket, not from a client's award.

What Records Should the Psychologist Keep, and Where Should the Records Be Kept?

The record begins with the first telephone call or conversation. Keep records of all meetings, with dates and times and the parties attending the meetings. This should include the times a person joined a meeting or left a meeting in progress or left for a break or telephone call. This allows the psychologist to know what information others may or may not have. All clinical notes taken and test protocols collected as part of a forensic practitioner's interviews, interventions, or assessments form part of the case's record. The expert witness in deposition and court often is asked when certain facts were made known, by whom, and in what context. Notes become invaluable when a case is heard months after meetings have occurred.

A brief set of guidelines for record keeping is available (APA, 1993), and samples of various record forms can be found in Blau (1984). One's record keeping practices need to be in substantial compliance with any state statutes that may have been developed. Good practice includes keeping the records in a secure place with access limited to staff working on the case. The staff, who are covered under the cloak of the licensed psychologist's privilege, should know how to safeguard clinical and forensic materials.

A corrections dictum holds that if it is not documented, it did not occur. One can use recall or oral testimony, but written records are so much more reliable, substantial, and difficult to dispute. In one case, a company asked a psychologist to perform a fitness-to-return-to-duty evaluation of an employee who was described by coworkers and supervisors as paranoic and dangerous. The psychologist called the employee, explained the limits of confidentiality, the purpose of the examination, and the fact that, though the company hired the psychologist, the psychologist's opinions were not predetermined. The employee scheduled a meeting later in the week. Five minutes after the appointment time, the employee called to cancel the appointment. The record of the attempted evaluation forms part of the evidence the company intends to use in the coming years when the case comes to trial.

The psychologist needs to understand that his or her notes in the clinical arena may be seen as helpful and even necessary in providing clinical services to the client. In the legal arena, the notes, test data, and testing and research protocols are governed by the rules of evidence in the court's jurisdiction. Subject to certain privileges, the entirety of the records in the case can be discovered (Committee on Legal Issues, 1996). The psychologist is advised to consult closely with the attorney concerning communications and conveyance of case materials to the courts or any third party.

THE MIDGAME

Almost three decades ago, when I was an assistant professor, there were no forensic psychology programs or workshops, few journal articles, and no psychology and law journals. The only place to learn about the courts was by going to court. I regularly visited the courtroom one morning a week for a number of months. In court, one could actually see how decisions were made, how witnesses impeached their own cause, how attorneys either muffed their opportunities or brilliantly parlayed them into a winning hand for their clients. The rhythms of the court were felt in the marrow of one's bones. The psychologist wishing to become courtwise now can read books, take courses, subscribe to psychology and law journals, attend workshops, and watch the steady diet of televised court trials, proceedings, and legal analysts deluging the airwaves.

Notwithstanding this fare, I am convinced none of these resources replaces the real-time experience of watching a witness under direct examination and undergoing a skilled attorney's cross-examination, watching the judge make rulings and the jury's studied inscrutability—in short, attending court. What happens before the trial is the subject of this section.

GATHERING DATA

Securing Records

After agreeing to serve as an expert witness, the courtwise psychologist will want all the records regarding the case, including the attorney's information, the opposing attorney's evidence, and other records that can bear on psychological aspects of the case (e.g., employment and medical records). The psychologist will want access to parties whom the psychologist needs to assess for a complete evaluation. The attorney has an interest in seeing that the psychologist's expertise is fully exercised or the whole point of contracting for the psychologist's service is compromised. The attorney may say he or she has tried to obtain records or access to informants under the other side's control but has been stymied; the psychologist's reply should be that the attorney needs to relay the psychologist's request nonetheless. If the requested materials are then sent, the psychologist has been useful to the attorney; if the materials are not sent, then at trial the attorney can bring into evidence the lack of a forthcoming attitude by the other side.

If the attorney says he or she read the records and can provide a synopsis, saving time for all and money for the client, the psychologist should request all records nonetheless. In one case, the psychologist read a stack of mental health records in a jail suicide case that was two to three inches thick. Wading through hundreds of pages of charts, the psychologist noticed that the tone of the psychologist's and social worker's entries in the record changed two days before the inmate committed suicide, from being cursory and matter-of-fact to becoming highly detailed and correct in grammar, form, and content. The copy had a suspicious shadow. The psychologist asked the attorney to examine the original sheets because something seemed irregular. The attorney discovered that the records were pasted over the usual cursory and boilerplate entries and had been doctored.

In another case, a teenager accused her father of prolonged incest, describing specific sodomy practices. The relevant hospital records seemed to the attorney to be in good shape; however, the psychologist realized that some of the claimed sexual activities and some of her claimed symptoms had been described in clinical, highly specific terms by members of her psychotherapy group. She had listened but had not participated in the discussions. Other aspects of her personality fit this pattern; for example, schoolmates described her speaking about her classmates' experiences and boyfriends as her own. By examining progress notes of the therapy group and the police and child care worker's reports, the factitious nature of the patient's complaints became obvious. Psychologists read reports with a different set of lenses than do attorneys and should not gainsay the skills they bring to the case.

Scheduling Sessions with Sources

The psychologist should develop a plan with the attorney to determine whom the psychologist needs to interview or test, the reasons for the session, and the order of people to be interviewed or tested. This allows the attorney to learn the psychologist's reasoning and should help inform the attorney's evolving strategy. Just as in the search for relevant records, the psychologist should ask to assess those reasonably involved in a case, even if it is unlikely that the parties will agree to meet with the psychologist. When the psychologist is asked in court how well he or she prepared the case, the psychologist can name who he or she tested (or met with in whatever fact-finding procedure is pertinent to the case). When asked whether the psychologist tested the opposing attorney's client, the psychologist can say that he or she asked the attorney who retained the psychologist to request such a meeting, but the attorney reported that such attempts were rebuffed. This tack should be taken only with the approval of the attorney retaining the psychologist, because under certain circumstances, such a denial of a request to be examined is prejudicial unless the issue is brought up by the attorney representing the party refusing the examination.

In one case, four children were caught in a bitter, bizarre divorce dispute. A mother who, according to her hospital records, her psychiatrist, and her family's accounts of her behavior, had a longstanding bipolar disorder, wanted to retain custody of her children to keep them from the husband's family. She frequently abandoned her children and endangered them with high-speed vehicle rides. She walked the children on railway tracks for 15-minute periods, exclaiming to the children that if God did not want them to die, the train would not come down the track. The psychologist asked that he examine her with a battery of psychological tests. The request was denied. Plenty of ancillary evidence was available, but the unavailability of the mother for testing belied her attorney's plaint that they had operated openly and in good faith.

Constructing the Forensic Psychology Record

The courtwise psychologist will note the time, date, and duration of all telephone calls, the parties on the telephone, and whether the call was recorded and by whom. Similarly, a record of all meetings with the parties and particulars should be kept. Once the attorney retains the psychologist and so informs the court, records, test protocols, electronic recordings, and notes are subject to discovery. The meetings with the attorney retaining the psychologist are probable exceptions to this practice because there are communications concerning case strategy that may be part of the work product privilege, a part of the attorney-client privilege (McCormick, Elliott, & Sutton, 1981; Rothstein, 1981). The meetings are probably discoverable, although the contents of the meeting are probably privileged, though the law in this area changes rapidly.

In developing the evidentiary materials, the interviews, review of records, review of pertinent literature, test protocols and interpretations, the courtwise psychologist will review the judicial instructions the judge will give the jury. The psychologist who practices in a particular jurisdiction, be it federal, state, or municipal, should consider adding to his or her library the set of instruc-tions the judges use to tell the jury what the specific elements of the charges are that they are to use in their determinations. The responsible psychologist will use the instructions to help determine the strategy and the data needed to address the issues raised in the instructions. The attorney should be able to provide the psychologist with jury instructions that he or she expects the court to use.

The courtwise psychologist will keep records, test protocols, reports, and other materials indexed in a way that allows easy access to critical findings. The greater the amount of material, the greater the need to index. There is nothing so awkward as the expert witness saying, "I recall reading that person X said something like that. Wait a minute while I go through the records to see whether I can find what I am looking for."

Uninvited Contacts from Others

From time to time there will be an illicit contact from others. In all cases, im-mediately report the contact to the attorney who retained you and keep a record of the contact and the report to the attorney. A telephone log is indis-pensable, as are records of electronic mail. In one case, during a recess at a de-position regarding the rights of a student to special education, the attractive school administrator approached the student's expert witness and marveled at his brilliance. Playing with her necklace and skirt while licking her lips and fluttering her eyes, she said it sure would be nice to hire him as a consultant, given his skills and charm. She continued, saying that the school system and his children, who were students in the school system (was there a veiled threat of retaliation against his children?), sure could benefit from his services and the consultant fees that would be forthcoming. This blatant attempt to influ-ence (bribe? intimidate? seduce?) was witnessed by no one but reported to the young girl's attorney. The psychologist knew the ploy and responded to the school administrator as if she were a terrific person, saying they needed to talk after the case was settled because he was sure they could do a wonderful job together providing services to the school. When the deposition continued, he was not surprised at the hostile, pointed, and personal attack by the adminis-trator and her attorney. Of course, there was no consulting contact afterward.

Subpoenas

Expect to be subpoenaed. The subpoena is part of the discovery process. In preparing for a courtroom appearance, both sides want all the pertinent infor-mation they can secure; to do less is irresponsible and could subject an attorney to charges of ineffective counsel. Each side may make their experts available without a subpoena for discovery. The notion of last-minute surprise witnesses is largely a television fiction. Such witnesses would not allow for opposing counsel to fully discover the strengths and weaknesses of the witness and his or her testimony. This would not serve justice. M. Singer and Nievod (1987) point out that the court-naïve psychologist panics at being subpoenaed, but the court-wise psychologist reviews the request, calls the attorney retaining him or her, and understands what the attorney issuing the subpoena seeks. In areas where the attorney's need to discover conflicts with the psychologist's need to protect a client's confidential and even privileged information or the security of a psychological test, understanding the attorney's needs can result in a compromise by which the interest of the various parties are served. Divulging needed information that is not confidential or part of a confidential record rather than the wholesale revelation may be most appropriate. Also, divulging a third party's information, for example in records of family or group psychotherapy, may raise a host of issues about the third party's rights.

The Committee on Legal Issues (COLI) (APA, 1996) raises a set of helpful issues, beginning with whether the request for information carries the force of law. The client whose records are at issue should be informed about the requested material because he or she may have some claims against revealing the information. COLI suggests a number of ways to partially protect subpoenaed information, including revealing it only to another qualified psychologist retained by the adversary, limiting the information to the court's use by way of a seal or gag, and requesting that only relevant parts of the record be entered into the proceedings. The courtwise psychologist would do well to refer to the COLI suggestions. Regardless of the existence or success of the claim against a subpoena, the client, having been informed, can be psychologically prepared to encounter the impact of revealing the subpoenaed information. Thus, the psychologist would have acted in an ethical and caring manner. When the subpoena clashes with rights and privileges to the point that the conflict resists the negotiations suggested above, the court can provide guidance to the parties. From a legal perspective, the court provides protection from the legal consequences of revealing records. However, damages to the client's humanity and to the integrity of one's professional practice caused by revealing information are stresses for the psychologist to resolve. The ethical and caring psychologist earns, by way of experiencing moral angst, the generous forensic fees he or she charges.

Strategy Meeting

At some point, usually after data have been gathered, the attorney and expert witness should review and interpret the materials. The attorney may find the data unsupportive or even antithetical to his or her strategy. If the attorney does not like what was found, the attorney can pay the psychologist's fee up to that point, and not call the psychologist. An attorney may not like what the expert found, but the responsible attorney will want to hear the truth as the expert found it. To the extent that the attorney has not listed the psychologist on a witness roster, his or her work on the case may never be known if the other attorney does not ask about anyone who was consulted about the case. In one case, an attorney spoke with the psychologist for a few minutes on the telephone, sent him a check, and never called again. The attorney was assuring that the other side could not retain the psychologist in the case. Other than this instance, once attorneys retain the expert, they tend to use the expert.

The psychologist will review the data that support the attorney's theory of the case, the evidence that makes the theory vulnerable, and the data that may support an alternative and sometimes a stronger theory. For example, in a case of incestuous child sexual abuse, the alleged perpetrator took the child to a clinic on a number of occasions. He signed the clinic's consent forms, paid for the psychotherapy, and had gasoline receipts on clinic session dates from a service station near the clinic but distant from his home, verifying his taking the child to the clinic. This is inconsistent with a child abuse perpetrator. Though not conclusive in itself, the evidence was compelling; in the experience of several expert witnesses, there was never a case in which the perpetrator would take the victim to a clinic, risking and even inviting discovery of the crime. The attorney did not have the experience that would have allowed him to pursue this line of evidence, so the pretrial conference was vital in this case.

In this case, there were several expert witnesses. A productive strategy was developed about which expert would cover the various areas to be presented. Because the other side had several experts, it was decided that the academic department head would be the last witness. From this vantage, he could explain all the witnesses' testimonies for both sides. His role as a teacher, who could be above the fray or parade of experts and "hired guns," could give him the ability to complement the work of witnesses from both sides but point out limitations in their work in a way that used the expert testimony from both sides to bolster the theory the attorney proposed. Strategies based on social psychological findings regarding primacy and recency effects of a message and how arguments can be co-opted were relied upon to win this case.

At the pretrial meeting, one should learn about the personal style of the opposing attorneys and the judge. One judge was an avid fisherman. The attorney advised one-sentence answers instead of paragraph-long explanations, and where a sentence might otherwise work, he advised one-word answers. He told of the judge allotting just a few minutes per witness to clear his calendar to go fishing. This seemed to give justice short shrift, but this is the judge with whom both sides had to work. Appeals are expensive and need a basis; the judge had a federal lifetime appointment and was known as efficient and one who cleared his calendar. Better to know what one is facing and adjust to it than to fail gloriously and justly. At this point, one should learn what to expect of the attorneys who may be examining and cross-examining the expert witness. There is no way one can overestimate the value of predeposition and pretrial conferences.

The Deposition

Depositions are part of the process by which attorneys discover the other side's evidence so each side may prepare as complete a case presentation as possible in the interest of serving their respective clients and serving justice. Before a deposition, the wise psychologist and attorney will meet to decide strategy. Attorneys face a choice at this point. If they feel there is advantage in presenting a powerful case in the deposition, the witness may be quite detailed in revealing the evidence. In cases that seem sure to be tried, the witness should be responsive but need not be expansive. The witness should produce all legitimately requested evidence and honestly answer all questions, but the degree of detail offered by the expert witness can vary with the attorney's strategy. A good working relationship between the psychologist and the attorney involves an agreement on strategy and respect for the psychologist's position on telling the truth, the whole truth, and nothing but the truth. Any attorney not respecting this position is an attorney from whom the psychologist should part company (see the ABA Standards for prosecuting and defense attorneys, cited earlier). Nonetheless, the expert is not obliged to tell all, but only to be responsive to the specific question.

One example of negotiating the Scylla of revelation and the Charybdis of being spare in testimony involves a case concerning whether the conditions on death row were so abysmal as to violate the prisoners' rights to be free from cruel and unusual punishment. Over a three-day period, the psychologist hired by the state interviewed 12 death row prisoners, three life-without-parole inmates, three life-sentenced prisoners, and four guards (correctional officers) assigned to death row. The plaintiff's psychologist had spent a day and part of another interviewing eight prisoners. The state decided to let the plaintiff know all that their evidence consisted of and see about settling the case without a trial. The plaintiff's attorney hammered away at the state's psychologist. During such attacks, an expert witness may be induced to reveal more than is required, ignore data that conflict with evidence he or she developed, lose sight of the case strategy, or make statements beyond what the data support. In this case, the attorney wore down and the psychologist simply remained responsive to the attorney's questions without revealing more information than was asked.

One further feature of this case is worth noting. The psychologist found some extralegal punitive measures that the guards were taking on their own. He let the assistant attorney general know that if he were asked about using pitchforks to pin prisoners against the wall, among other practices, he would reveal what he found. Neither he nor the assistant attorney general should be put in a position to defend indefensible and abhorrent correctional practices. Why the plaintiff's expert witness did not ferret out the information about these practices is another matter. After some six hours of spirited deposition, the plaintiff's attorney asked, "Well, is there anything you did not say that is relevant and that you want to say or that I should know or should ask?" The psychologist replied, "I would be happy to answer any specific question that you may have." The deposition ended in the seventh hour. The case was settled without a trial shortly after the deposition.

Some may say the psychologist should have told about the guards' conduct, but the rules of engagement allow and even require vigorous, penetrating inquiry by the attorneys in discovery by which information is elicited. Stonewalling is inappropriate, unethical, and illegal. The truth, whole truth, and nothing but the truth are required of us in everyday life just as much as when we are under oath, as is the case on deposition and in court. But the rules require the attorney to ask specific questions and the deponent to be responsive, not to be a raconteur.

One must remember that the deposition should be treated as seriously as one treats the court appearance. The deposition is an extension of the court, and the oath plus the record are part of the judge's domain. Even if the setting is a hotel room and the attorneys are fairly casual, the deposition forms part of the court record. What the witness says on deposition can appear at the trial when the opposing attorney spots an inconsistency between what is said at the trial and on deposition. Thus, one should be just as practiced and careful in deposition as on trial.

In a case of jail suicide, five sets of defendants had about a dozen attorneys present. They were particularly critical of their opponent, who entered the room with an insult to those assembled. The psychologist who was retained by the county sheriff in charge of the jail was deposed in a particularly hostile way, starting with a withering review of his qualifications. After an unrelenting attack, he was asked where he had gained knowledge of a particular clinical technique. He replied, "Detroit." When the attorney asked, "Detroit, Michigan?" the expert sarcastically replied, "I am not a qualified geographer, so I cannot answer that definitively, but when I last checked, Detroit was some 70 miles north of Toledo, Ohio" to the guffaws of the dozen attorneys. Later, when the psychologist read the transcript of the deposition, the humor looked mean-spirited and prejudicial. Generally, humor ill befits the dignity of a competent expert witness. Be careful with humor. It can be useful, as is illustrated below, but use it with care.

When the deposition is taken, often the attorneys and the court reporter suggest that the witness stipulate or waive the right to review the transcription. This is rarely a good idea. There are several occasions when I caught errors in the transcription of test scores and of what for psychologists are technical terms though they may appear as common terms to nonpsychologists. The terms "cluster" and "factor" have specific meanings in statistical analysis, as do "base rate," "reliability," and "face validity" for the psychometrician, as do "observing ego" and "superego lacunae" for the psychoanalyst. The court reporter can misunderstand and misrecord technical terms, so waiving a proofreading of the transcript can result in a record of the psychologist's words that the psychologist did not say. The psychologist is then in the awkward position of having approved an incorrect transcript of his or her testimony that can be read back at trial.

THE END GAME: THE COURTROOM APPEARANCE

The Pretrial Meeting

If the case is straightforward and the attorney and psychologist have been in contact during the data-gathering stage, then the pretrial meeting should be a rehearsal of a set of important questions already reviewed in earlier conferences. These questions include what the psychologist found, how the findings may help the case, how the findings may be vulnerable on cross-examination, what information the judge or jury will already know and what information they will learn subsequent to the psychologist's testimony from other fact or expert witnesses, what is the examining style of the opposing counsel, and what style the judge affects. In a case with other expert witnesses, the conference will involve coordination of findings and developing a common strategy. If the psychologist and attorney work well together and the psychologist understands the attorney's theory and strategy, the psychologist may be able to suggest an order of presentation that will make the materials more effective. For example, in an incest case, several psychiatrists and psychologists testified for the prosecution about the extensive damage that seemed posttraumatic to them. The defense retained two psychologists, one of whom tested the members of the family except for the alleged victim. The other psychologist, who had impressive academic as well as clinical credentials, was used to explain how the mental health professionals' testimony fit together and could most parsimoniously and compellingly support a not guilty conclusion. He was used to tie up loose ends that the previous witnesses on both sides left dangling.

PREPARING MATERIALS

The expert witness should review all the materials to be used in court and have a copy of any other materials about which he or she may be questioned. For example, if a psychiatric report, hospital records, or another psychologist's test report may be at issue, the testifying psychologist should have a copy that he or she has reviewed beforehand. The expert witness should never examine a document for the first time on the stand. Being blindsided will result in a poor performance. Index and tabulate the materials that will be introduced and discussed in court. Fumbling through papers will detract from the psychologist's appearance.

The more material the psychologist can commit to memory, the more impressive will be the appearance. The expert witness should be thoroughly familiar with the tests and techniques employed. For example, when using the Wechsler or Stanford–Binet intelligence scales, I will review the psychometric properties of the instrument, including the most and the least reliable subtests; the literature that may qualify the client's results due to his or her age, gender, race, or ethnicity; and the standard error of differences in cases where subtest score differences may be an issue. Be sure no materials are included in what you bring to court that are not relevant to the case; on more than one occasion, expert witnesses have brought materials from another case to court, and their credibility suffered.

The expert witness should bring at least five copies of his or her curriculum vitae, one each for the judge, the court reporter, and each counsel to review during qualification of the witness. This helps the expert witness look prepared and evenhanded. One copy should be kept by the witness for reference when an attorney discusses a particular entry on the curriculum vitae. The expert witness should review the vitae before the trial, and a list of the clinician's pertinent clinical experiences should be given to the attorney at one of the pretrial meetings. For example, in a case concerning jail suicide, the psychologist listed the number of institutions that he visited and worked in and the number and type of inmates he interviewed, diagnosed, and treated. Similarly, he listed the number of times he was retained by the plaintiff and the defendant sides in similar cases so the attorney would know whether the psychologist was vulnerable to an attack as a plaintiff's or a defendant's witness. One psychologist on the jail suicide case, for philosophical and political reasons, has never been a defendant's witness in about 100 civil cases. If a witness has this kind of a skew in his or her history, the witness should be prepared to explain the apparent bias. As mentioned earlier, this should have been disclosed to the attorney when the attorney was first retaining the psychologist. The courtwise psychologist prepares questions for the attorney to ask in court so the psychologist's testimony will be focused for the specific case.

All that transpired so far occurred with the courtroom testimony in mind. Here is where the game is played out, where the people involved have their day in court, with oft-times dramatic and life-altering consequences in the balance.

Some Pragmatics about the Courtroom Appearance

There are workshops, articles, chapters, and books concerning pragmatics, gambits, and tricks attorneys use in confronting the other side's experts and an equal number of resources for the expert witness to counter these maneuvers with tricks of his or her own. This section provides a framework to understand the courtroom appearance and to make the psychologist's presentation effective.

The expert witness will usually be more at ease if he or she has visited the actual courtroom beforehand. Finding the location of the courthouse and courtroom and finding out about parking will avoid needless problems on the court day. The courtwise psychologist will become familiar with the acoustics, the lighting, the physical layout of the court, the position of the witness stand in relationship to the judge, jury, and counsel tables, and the spacing needed for people to see any visual aids that might be used. Walking around the room and the witness stand may avoid problems that one dignified expert witness experienced. She walked into the courtroom dressed in an elegantly understated suit, carried her briefcase with her as she ascended the three steps to the witness stand, gracefully sat in the chair, and, as she repositioned the chair, the back two legs went off the stand and she somersaulted backward into a heap.

Dressing for Court

The role of the expert witness is to present a set of findings clearly and persuasively. The highest-paid persuaders in our society are in the media. News anchors usually dress in a way that projects authority and honesty; like them, expert witnesses should consider wearing a dark blue or gray suit. Men should wear ties that are not garish and do not "make a statement." Women should consider a modest scarf or a simple necklace or lapel pin or brooch. Lapel pins that make partisan statements, political buttons, and showy jewelry should be avoided; they distract jurors at best and could antagonize them. Plaids, bow ties, umbrellas, and shoes that squeak can draw attention away from what the witness has to say and render him or her less effective. In recent years, shirts in formal situations often are colored, sometimes intensely, in contrast to what had been the court uniform for attorneys, the white shirt. Because judges may be slightly older and used to the respect that a white shirt or blouse implies, the expert cannot go wrong wearing a white shirt or blouse. These rules of thumb may be relaxed in the less formal family and child court settings and when the proceedings are in the judge's chambers, when the judge is more casually attired and when the parties are not antagonistic. Also, the expert witness should be aware of local customs; overdressing before a blue-collar jury can provoke resentment.

Court Decorum

Unless specifically instructed otherwise, the expert witness should not be in the courtroom during the trial except for his or her own appearance. Exceptions might include a case where the attorney wants the witness to observe a party to the case who was otherwise unavailable to the expert. Otherwise, the expert may be disqualified by violating FRE 615 or a variant of "The Rule." Rule 615 states: "At the request of a party the court shall order witnesses excluded so that they cannot hear the testimony of other witnesses, and it may make the order of its own motion. This rule does not authorize exclusion of (1) a party who is a natural person, or (2) an officer or employee of a party which is not a natural person designated as its representative by its attorney, or (3) a person whose presence is shown by a party to be essential to the presentation of his cause." This rule codifies a longstanding practice that discourages and exposes fabrication, inaccuracy, and collusion. If the expert attends the trial before and after the expert's appearance on the stand, his or her testimony could be influenced by hearing the other witnesses' testimony. Also jurors may infer that the expert does not have a busy practice and is personally invested in the case.

Before being seated, the expert is sworn in. Then the attorney retaining the expert will review the expert's credentials. At this point, the expert should have the copies of his or her curriculum vitae (in court, often called a résumé to avoid distancing from the jury) and be prepared to review education, training, experiences, skills, and specialized knowledge that make the witness important in understanding the issues in the case. This is not time for modesty, false or otherwise. Being neither boastful nor arrogant, given the expert witness worked hard to attain those credentials, he or she should be confident sharing them with the court. Occasionally, the other side's attorney may stipulate or agree to accept the expert without examining the credentials, but the retaining attorney often wants the judge and jury to hear all the outstanding accomplishments of this expert. From time to time, an expert may be limited in expertise. In one case concerning the understanding of the *Miranda* warning in an accused murderer with a 63 IQ and who had been drinking, the judge determined that the expert, though an instructor in the DUI (driving under the influence) school, did not have qualifications equal to clinical or research experience in giving people measured amounts of intoxicants and testing their cognitive functioning. However, as an instructor and practitioner of psychodiagnostics for 20 years, the witness was qualified to discuss the cognitive inability of the accused to understand *Miranda* with his level of intelligence, regardless of level of intoxication.

The presentation of evidence is generally ordered as follows: the plaintiff's or state's opening statement, the defendant's opening statement, the plaintiff's presentation of direct evidence and the cross-examination by the defendant's attorney, the defendant's presentation of direct evidence and the cross-examination by the state or plaintiff's attorney, the plaintiff's presentation of rebuttal evidence, the dependant's presentation of rebuttal evidence, the opening final argument by the state or plaintiff, the defendant's final argument, the closing final argument by the state or plaintiff, and the giving of instructions to the jury by the judge. The expert witness is typically involved in the presentation of direct evidence but may sometimes be recalled at the rebuttal stage. However, the expert can appear before the trial, too, in such events as a pretrial hearing to exclude evidence. In one case, the expert testified about the inability of a witness to identify the defendant due to the lighting conditions when the crime occurred; the witness further testified to the misuse of hypnosis and a tainted lineup procedure that virtually assured that the victim would identify the accused. With that evidence excluded by the judge, there was no other evidence upon which to proceed with the case.

The attorney retaining the expert will ask questions to place before the court the evidence reviewed in pretrial meetings. The effective expert articulates the evidence in terms of the legal standards that the judge will instruct the jury to follow when the jury deliberates. In a nonjury trial, the judge will refer to the legal standards in rendering a decision. This is the focal point of the attorneys' and the expert's efforts. The keys to success are to establish credibility, to teach, to tell a compelling story that integrates the facts, and to use words in almost a magical way that graphically illustrates the points, drawing the jurors into the story. The key for the expert to remember is that the jurors and judge want to make the right decision for the right reason.

Credibility is established by being retained in the first place (obviously, the attorney and his or her client value the expert, although jurors and judges may have a natural bias against the stereotype of the hired gun), by the review of credentials, and, most important, by the mastery of the materials presented clearly and compellingly. The effective expert listens to the questions carefully, formulates an answer consistent with the evidence gathered, and makes eye contact with the jury. No one likes a windbag, and the court has many witnesses and many cases, so the expert does not have the luxury of 50-minute blocks, as in college classes. However, it is a poor expert who tells the attorney or the court that an issue is complex. Perhaps the concepts of standard error or convergent validity or base rate or transference are complex issues. In one case, the expert was confronted with explaining why jailers should not have been alerted that the 25-year-old male with marital troubles and a few prior arrests, who was intoxicated and would be in jail for a day or two, was a suicide risk. The opposing counsel thundered that most jail suicides fit that pattern. The expert knew that the modal or most frequently occurring person in jail fit that pattern, making the profile of the suicidal inmate no different from the modal prisoner. The witness referred to a popular public service advertisement at that time, which claimed that the majority of traffic accidents occurred within 25 miles of one's home, so we should buckle our seat belts. However, what the ad did not say was that most of our driving occurs within 25 miles of home. Although we should buckle up in any event, the same faulty statistical reasoning was being applied in the case; that is, the majority of people in jail were about 25, male, intoxicated, had marital trouble, had one or two encounters with the law, and would be out in a day or two. Thus, there was no profile that the jailers could use to pick out this person as particularly suicidal. As the ad was mentioned, the jurors' heads bobbed in recognition, they carefully listened and understood the concept of base rates, and they rejected the claims of the victim's family. The key is to use 25-cent words to explain 25-dollar concepts. Berne's *Games People Play*

(1964) and Erikson's *Childhood and Society* (1950) are models in explaining complicated concepts simply. McElhaney (1997) advises avoiding words like *elucidate, illuminate, discern, explicate, and expound,* instead using *teach, tell, explain, help us understand, show us,* and *untangle.* Demonstrative words such as *show, see, watch, picture, view,* and *look at* will draw the listener into the expert's story.

Although speaking plainly will carry the day, the expert should avoid being too homey or down-to-earth. After all, the expert is in the courtroom because he or she has specialized knowledge to share. It is better to refer to technical terms, then explain them graphically. For example, when test results are presented, the opposing attorney may ask how these results can be relied upon, when the test has an error rate that could easily miss the "real IQ" by 5, 10, or even 15 points in either direction. The expert should explain that every measurement device has an error rate. For example, the local weather report may show that the temperature at the airport, at city hall, and in various parts of the city or town differ by a few degrees; taking the temperature yields a range of figures. So it is with human measurements. Our weight, blood sugar, cholesterol, and libido fluctuate, just as our intelligence and personality test scores vary. However, the scientific basis of psychology allows us to know the error range (the standard error of the instrument used). The expert can use a technical term that establishes expertise, but then should explain the term as the juror's favorite teacher would explain a new concept.

Attorneys will raise objections about qualifying the expert, about hearsay evidence, and about anything else they can contest. The courtwise expert will wait for the judge to hear the arguments and give direction to the witness. The expert witness need not be an attorney and know the vicissitudes of the hearsay rule to appreciate the drama. The hearsay rule is interesting and relevant to the psychologist. A good deal of our evidence is based on statements that are not the declarant's (the person declaring the statement in court) (Binder, 1975). The hearsay rule allows the mental health professional to use what otherwise would be hearsay to form a professional opinion. The expert is seen as having the experience and ability to determine the veracity of the statement; the experience and training of the expert adds more than just the weight of the data or statements that would accrue for the layperson (Binder, 1975). There are 40 exceptions to the hearsay rule. What gets admitted as evidence that will determine the trial's outcome may well hinge on the decisions made by a judge who has but seconds to decide on whether statements are hearsay. Legal knowledge is not necessary for expert witnesses, and certainly they should stay within their role and not participate in lawyerly deliberations; however, knowing the relevant procedural and substantive law makes the courtroom drama more meaningful and can help shape a more effective response by the expert witness.

Cross-Examination

An old legal adage goes, "If the attorney has the facts, pound on the facts. Lacking the facts, he or she should pound on the law. Lacking either, the attorney should pound the table." An opposing expert witness is an inviting target to pound, too. Attacking the expert is consistent with the opposing attorney's job to discredit testimony. There are a number of ways to attack testimony. The attorney may ask, "Doctor, are you aware of the many criticisms of the *DSM* (or intelligence and personality tests or violence prediction or psychotherapy or whatever procedure is the basis for testimony)?" If the expert answers no, then he or she is vulnerable for lacking knowledge of the literature. If the expert answers yes, then the witness is open to the question "Why in the world would you use a flawed technique in a case that could destroy people's lives?" To further confuse the expert, the attorney may use a double negative and a suggestive question, as in, "You are not telling us that you did not use the best devices available, are you?" The expert should answer, "Every technique is subject to criticism. It is that critical attitude by which we make progress in refining techniques. The techniques used in this case are reliable, and shed light on the issues we are facing" (if in fact this is true, and it should be true if the expert did his or her homework in reading the literature and selecting appropriate methodologies).

Misquoting deposition materials or using generalizations and vague terms are ways an attorney can lead a witness astray. The best tactic for the witness is to have the deposition at hand so the correct quote may be reread, and to answer vagueness with an open and specific response. Thus, in response to the query, "I would guess you are pretty confident in what you said today since you say you interviewed Mr. X for a long, long time," the appropriate response would be, "I interviewed Mr. X for two and a half hours, from 9:40 A.M. to 12:10 P.M. on March 23, 1998 and for another hour from 1:05 to 2:05 P.M. on the same date." The attorney can ask, "Would you agree that people lie? Now, you say you interviewed Mr. X for several hours. How do you know he did not lie to you?" Of course the witness would have to answer that people do lie. The witness should anticipate this sort of question. If the psychologist used techniques that have validity indicators, such as addressing questions with answers known to the interviewer, circular lines of questioning that ask similar questions at different points in the interview to determine consistency of responses, and psychometric instruments with dissimulation detection indices built in, then the witness can answer that precautions were taken to determine the truthfulness of the interviewee's responses.

A parallel line of inquiry may be phrased as "Doctor, have you ever made a mistake? How do you know you are not making a mistake today?" Of course, the expert will have made mistakes (if the expert says "No, I never made a mistake," then he or she will have lost credibility and appear arrogant). The appropriate response might be, "I am sure I have made errors. In this case, the evidence is correct. The scores reflect the intelligence (or whatever the issue is at hand) and the tests are consistent with each other and with the clinical interview materials, as we reviewed earlier today." In all cases, the expert should be forthcoming and say "I do not know" when he or she has no answer to a question. This is a stronger position than trying to bluff the attorney, who is skilled in forensics.

The list of trick questions goes on and is quite entertaining, but the best way to hone one's skills is to read Ziskin and Faust's *Coping with Psychiatric and Psychological Testimony* (1994). Their express purpose is to embarrass mental health professionals out of the courtroom. They provide an excellent compendium of ways of attacking expert psychological testimony. Years ago, I would read Ziskin the week before going to court because I knew that nothing the attorneys could throw at me would be the equal of Ziskin and none of the attorneys had read Ziskin. Now Ziskin and Faust, though still not commonly known, is on attorneys' reading lists. It is the vulnerable expert witness who does not hone his or her skills on Ziskin and Faust.

The attorney may insult the expert, his or her credentials, or the field of psychology. The expert should monitor his or her emotional reaction. If the expert's voice rises above the attorney's voice, the expert is losing. Juries can live with and even expect a vigorous argument from the attorneys, but the expert witness should not lose poise and the appearance of objectivity. It is curious how professionals trained not to react in kind to a patient's hostility will react to an attorney's attacks. Some witnesses will buckle under and meekly answer any way the attorney moves them. Others will respond hostilely. Both reactions are ineffective at the least. The judge is not insensitive nor are jurors stupid. The judge will let attacks proceed because both sides are entitled to make as vigorous a presentation of their case as possible. The most vicious cross-examination I have seen was in the Libby Zion case on *Court TV,* where Mr. Tom Moore screamed at expert and fact witness physician after physician. He usually broke the witnesses down within 15 to 30 seconds, with a few holding out for a minute or two. One cross-examining prosecuting attorney whispered to me, "Hess, Hess. Rudolf Hess, Nazi," in attempting to get me to lose my train of thought and my temper while presenting expert testimony. The best recourse for the witness is to take one's time, compose oneself, and answer any question in a factual way. If there is no question, then wait for one. If there seemed to be a question in the tirade, ask that it be repeated or restated.

We cannot cover every courtroom gambit, but the interested reader can refer to Blau (1984), Brodsky (1991), Merenbach and Stephen (1993), Matson (1994), and Wellman (1936), among other materials with court dialogue and gambits. Although it takes time, and *Court TV* is now available, nothing replaces the feel of being in court and witnessing the dialogue.

Humor

Humor is tricky. Generally, the gravity of the court and the issue preclude levity. Therefore, do not joke. However, in the tense atmosphere of a trial, the well-placed response can score points. After an intense cross-examination in a three-day-long child rape case, the attorney dismissed the expert witness with "Doctor, I think the jury has heard about as much psychological and psychiatric mumbo jumbo and jargon from all of you expert psychiatrists and psychologists that they can stomach." The psychologist responded in a soft tone, "I bet they heard about enough legal terms, too," at which point jury members nodded to the expert witness, started laughing, and stated, "Ain't that the truth," "We sure have," and "You said it." Apparently, the hostility toward the attorneys may have been greater than toward the mental health experts, or at least the jury felt the expert was in touch with the trial and their feelings.

But using humor can backfire. It can detract from the issues, can cast the witness as a smart aleck who may be seen as hostile, and can elicit sympathy for others whom the witness might not want portrayed sympathetically. The expert should be cautious in using humor, though its use can be devastatingly effective. In the case above, the attorney had been an unsympathetic and belittling person. The interchange came at the end of the presentation of evidence for both sides and before the final arguments. There was no chance for the attorney to respond effectively.

Leaving the Scene

The expert, having been dismissed by the judge after examination, cross-examination, and any redirect examination and recross-examination, should gather up any materials he or she brought to court that have not been attached, smile and nod to the judge for the courtesy of appearing in the court, smile and nod to the jury briefly for their attentiveness, and leave the courtroom. In certain circumstances, the expert may stop by the retaining counsel's table to see whether the witness should remain in the court building should he or she need to be recalled. As mentioned above, if the expert witness stays in the court, the jury may wonder about whether the witness has nothing else to do (whether practice is not thriving) and has an interest in the case beyond a professional one. Any query to the attorney about how the case is going can be made later; the attorney's job is not done because he or she still has the rest of the case to manage.

DOES THE PSYCHOLOGIST HAVE A ROLE IN THE COURTROOM?

The mental health expert witness has been described sardonically as "someone who wasn't there when it happened, but who for a fee will gladly imagine what it must have been like" (Sampson, 1993, p. 69). Wigmore (1909) satirized Munsterberg's grand claims for psychology's role in the courtroom and challenged psychology: "Whenever the Psychologist is ready for the Courts, the Courts are ready for him." But the past decades have demonstrated that psychology has contributions to make in the judicial arena. The psychologist can contribute to the welfare of individuals seeking justice and to our courts in providing assistance in understanding technical issues. In entering forensic practice, we must be sure that we are doing good and not just doing well for ourselves, as Bazelon (1973) criticized—that we are helping the court sort through increasingly complex technical and scientific information to seek truth. In doing so, we are fulfilling the command, "Justice, justice, thou shalt pursue" (Deuteronomy 16:20).

REFERENCES

American Association of Correctional Psychologists. (1980). Standards for psychological services in jails and prisons. *Criminal Justice and Behavior, 7*, 81–124.

American Bar Association. (1989). *ABA criminal justice mental health standards.* Washington, DC: Author.

American Psychological Association. (1985). *Standards for educational and psychological tests.* Washington, DC: Author.

American Psychological Association. (1992). Ethical principles of psychologists and code of conduct. *American Psychologist, 47*, 1597–1628.

American Psychological Association. (1993). Record keeping guidelines. *American Psychologist, 48,* 984–986.

Bailey, C. S. (1995). Hearsay changes under the proposed Alabama Rules of Evidence. *Journal of the Alabama Academy of Science, 66,* 137–147.

Bazelon, D. L. (1973). Psychologists in corrections—Are they doing good for the offender or well for themselves? In S. L. Brodsky (Ed.), *Psychologists in the criminal justice system* (pp. 149–154). Urbana: University of Illinois Press.

Beis, E. B. (1984). *Mental health and the law.* Rockville, MD: Aspen.

Berne, E. (1964). *Games people play.* New York: Grove Press.

Binder, D. F. (1975). *The hearsay handbook: The hearsay rule and its 40 exceptions.* New York: McGraw-Hill/Shephard's Citations.

Blau, T. H. (1984). *The psychologist as expert witness.* New York: Wiley.

Brown v. Board of Education, 347 U.S. 483 (1954).

Chapple v. Granger, 851 F. Supp. 1481 (E.D. Wash. 1994).

Brown, L. S. (1997). The private practice of subversion: The psychology of Tikkum Olam. *American Psychologist, 52,* 449–462.

Brodsky, S. L. (1991). *Testifying in court: Guidlines and maxims for the expert witness.* Washington, DC: American Psychological Association.

Committee on Ethical Guidelines for Forensic Psychologists. (1991). Specialty guidelines for forensic psychologists. *Law and Human Behavior, 15,* 655–665.

Committee on Legal Issues. (1996). Strategies for private practitioners coping with subpoenas of compelled testimony for client records or test data. *Professional Psychology, 27,* 245–251.

Daubert v. Merrell Dow Pharmaceuticals, 113 S. Ct. 2786 (1993).

Dawes, R. M. (1994). *House of cards: Psychology and psychotherapy built on myth.* New York: Free Press.

Deleray, J. E. (1988, Summer/Spring). The right choice! *Consulting Psychology Bulletin,* 9–10.

Erickson, R. J., & Simon, R. J. (1997). *The use of social science data in Supreme Court decisions.* Champaign: University of Illinois Press.

Erikson, E. H. (1950). *Childhood and society.* New York: Norton.

Frye v. United States, 293 Fed. 1013 (D.C. Cir. 1923).

General Electric Co. v. Joiner No. 96-188, decided December 15, 1997.

Gless, A. G. (1995). Some post-Daubert trial tribulations of a simple country judge: Behavioral science evidence in trial courts. *Behavioral Sciences and the Law, 13,* 261–291.

Goodman-Delahunty, J. (1997). Forensic psychological expertise in the wake of Daubert. *Law and Human Behavior, 21,* 121–140.

Goodman-Delahunty, J., & Foote, W. E. (1995). Compensation for pain, suffering and other psychological injuries: The impact of Daubert on employment discrimination claims. *Behavioral Sciences and the Law, 13,* 183–206.

Green, E. D., & Nesson, C. R. (1984). *Federal rules of evidence: With selected legislative history and new cases and problems.* Boston: Little, Brown.

Greenberg, S. A., & Shuman, D. W. (1997). Irreconcilable conflict between therapeutic and forensic roles. *Professional Psychology: Research and Practice, 28,* 50–57.

Grove, W. M., & Meehl, P. E. (1996). Comparative efficiency of informal (subjective, impressionistic) and formal (mechanical, algorithmic) prediction procedures: The clinical-statistical controversy. *Psychology, Public Policy, and Law, 2,* 293–323.

Hess, A. K. (1987). Dimensions of forensic psychology. In I. B. Weiner & A. K. Hess (Eds.), *The handbook of forensic psychology* (pp. 22–49). New York: Wiley.

Jenkins v. United States, 307 F.2d 637 (D.C. App. 1962).

Lawrence, L. (1997, July 24). C. C. Wang: The painter as supercollector. *The Wall Street Journal,* p. A-16.

Matson, J. V. (1994). *Effective expert witnessing* (2nd ed.). Boca Raton, FL: Lewis.

McCormick, C. T., Elliott, F. W., & Sutton, J. F., Jr. (1981). *Cases and materials on evidence* (5th ed.). St. Paul, MN: West.

McElhaney, J. W. (1997, May). Terms of enlightenment: Articulate expert witnesses help jurors visualize facts. *ABA Journal*, pp. 82–83.

Meehl, P. E. (1954). *Clinical versus statistical prediction: A theoretical analysis and a review of the evidence.* Minneapolis: University of Minnesota Press.

Meehl, P. E. (1997). Credentialed persons, credentialed knowledge. *Clinical Psychology: Science and Practice, 4,* 91–98.

Merenbach, D. G., & Stephen, A. (1993). *How to be an expert witness: Credibility in oral testimony.* Santa Barbara, CA: Fithian Press.

Millon, T. (1969). *Modern psychopathology.* Philadelphia: Saunders.

Monahan, J. (Ed.). (1980). *Who is the client?* Washington, DC: American Psychological Association.

Pepper, S. C. (1942). *World hypotheses.* Berkeley: University of California Press.

Perrin, G. I., & Sales, B. D. (1994). Forensic standards in the American Psychological Association's new ethics code. *Professional Psychology, 25,* 376–381.

Perrin, L. T. (1997). Expert witnesses under Rules 703 and 803(4) of the Federal Rules of Evidence: Separating the wheat from the chaff. *Indiana Law Journal, 72,* 939–1014.

Redmount, R. S. (1965). The use of psychologists in legal practice. *Practical Lawyer, 11,* 23–38.

Reed, J. E. (1996). Fixed vs. flexible neuropsychological test batteries under the Daubert standard for the admissibility of scientific evidence. *Behavioral Sciences and the Law, 14,* 315–322.

Rothstein, P. F. (1981). *Evidence in a nutshell: State and federal rules.* St. Paul, MN: West.

Sampson, K. (1993). The use and misuse of expert evidence in the courts. *Judicature, 77,* 68–76.

Schank, J. A., & Skovholt, T. M. (1997). Dual-relationship dilemmas of rural and small-community psychologists. *Professional Psychology, 28,* 44–49.

Selected statutes, rules and standards on the legal profession. (1984). St. Paul, MN: West.

Shuman, D. W. (1993). The uses of empathy in forensic examinations. *Ethics and Behavior, 3,* 289–302.

Singer, M. T., & Nievod, A. (1987). Consulting and testifying in court. In I. B. Weiner & A. K. Hess (Eds.), *The handbook of forensic psychology* (pp. 529–554). New York: Wiley.

Singer, R. (1995, August). Overcoming expert witness codependency. In A. M. Horton, Jr. (Chair.), *Forensic neuropsychology: Detecting malingering and coping with cross-examination.* Symposium conducted at the annual convention of the American Psychological Association, New York.

Sonne, J. L. (1994). Multiple relationships: Does the new ethics code answer the right questions? *Professional Psychology, 25,* 336–343.

Sporer, S. L. (1997). The origins of the psychology of testimony. In W. G. Bringmann, H. E. Luck, R. Miller, & C. E. Early (Eds.), *A pictorial history of psychology.* Carol Stream, IL: Quintessence.

Stevens, A. (1997, July 30). Thousands of bottles of wine on the wall, and they are a mess. *Wall Street Journal,* pp. A1, A8.

Wellman, F. L. (1936). *The art of cross-examination* (4th ed. revised and enlarged). New York: Macmillan.

Wigmore, J. (1909). Professor Munsterberg and the psychology of testimony: Being a report of the case of Cokestone v. Munsterberg. *Illinois Law Review, 3,* 399–445.

Ziskin, J., & Faust, D. (1994). *Coping with psychiatric and psychological testimony.* Beverly Hills, CA: Law and Psychology Press.

PART FIVE

INTERVENING WITH OFFENDERS

CHAPTER 20

Interventions: Punishment, Diversion, and Alternative Routes to Crime Prevention

JOAN McCORD

FOLK WISDOM has long maintained that misbehaving children become adolescent delinquents and adolescent delinquents become adult criminals. Recent studies in several cultures support this wisdom.

In London, among a group of working-class males, those who had been "troublesome" between the ages of 8 and 10 were most likely to be convicted for serious delinquent acts between the ages of 10 and 13, and an early conviction (along with poor family management practices) was an efficient predictor of later convictions—up to the age of 32 years (Farrington, 1986, 1995).

In Sweden, among males in a midsize community first studied in the third grade and traced to the age of 30, those who were aggressive at age 10 and hyperactive at 13 were the most likely to commit serious crimes both as adolescents and as adults (Magnusson, Klinteberg, & Stattin, 1992).

In Finland, especially among males, those considered to be aggressive at age 10 were also considered to be aggressive at age 14 and considered themselves aggressive at age 26. In addition, the males who had earlier been considered most aggressive were likely to have been arrested both for crimes and for alcohol abuse (Pulkkinen & Pitkanen, 1993).

In St. Louis, men who reported symptoms of conduct disorders in childhood were most likely to exhibit adult antisocial behavior and alcoholism (Robins & Ratcliff, 1979).

In Massachusetts, early misbehavior in school as well as parental rejection, poor family interactions, and little monitoring predicted subsequent serious criminal behavior (McCord, 1994).

Among children reared in an urban ghetto on the South Side of Chicago, aggressiveness in the first grade (together with low school attendance, frequent spanking, leaving home at an early age, and exposure to racial discrimination) predicted arrests for violent crimes as adults (McCord & Ensminger, 1997).

The evidence seems to support conflicting intervention strategies. On the one hand, if crime is a result of personality deficiencies or faulty socialization, reformative practices would be justified. On the other hand, if crime is an outgrowth of early aggressive behavior because society blames, condemns, and aggregates aggressive children, seemingly the best strategy for prevention would avoid setting in motion self-fulfilling prophecies.

Intervention strategies of the first type include attempts to correct personality problems, change socialization practices, educate, or deter through fear. Intervention strategies of the second type include diversion programs designed to avoid having youngsters perceived by themselves or others as "bad." Intervention strategies of both types can focus on correcting personality problems, changing socialization practices, and education. The differences between the two strategies are focused most sharply by contrasting the effects of punitive approaches with those of diversion.

This review first considers evidence about the effectiveness of punishment as a deterrent to crime. It then considers evidence about diversion as a deterrent. After showing that neither increases in punishments nor diversion programs show much promise for decreasing crime, the review considers evidence about effects of counseling programs. Again, the evidence is not encouraging. Finally, the review turns to evidence about effects of social manipulations and cognitive approaches. Preschool programs, educational and skills-training programs, and at least one postincarceration program seem to offer promising strategies for diverting the path leading from early misbehavior to crime.

PUNISHMENT AS PREVENTION

The view that fear of punishment reduces crime is as old as Western thought. Plato attributed to Protagoras the argument "He who desires to inflict rational punishment does not retaliate for a past wrong which cannot be undone; he has regard to the future, and is desirous that the man who is punished and he who sees him punished may be deterred from doing wrong again" (Plato, 324/1956). During the 18th century, Beccaria (1764/1963) and Bentham (1789/1988) placed this view at the foundation of criminology.

If fear of punishment deters crime, increasing sanctions should reduce criminality. So obvious had the link between pain and motivation appeared that its scientific scrutiny awaited the second half of the 20th century. Measures of the relationship between criminal activities and indices of the certainty and severity of punishment therefore offered promise for testing the role of hedonic calculations in motivations for crime.

Criminologists have bifurcated expected effects of punishment: those that influence the punished are considered to be specific deterrents; those that influence others who might commit crimes are considered to be general deterrents. As a specific deterrent, punishment is expected to prevent repetitions. When repetition occurs, theory suggests that punishment has been too lenient. This view has a deceptively obvious appearance. Yet, several studies show that severity of sanction is not monotonically related to rates of recidivism (e.g., Crowther, 1969; Glaser & Gordon, 1990; McCord, 1985; Sherman, 1992; Wolfgang, Figlio, & Sellin, 1972).

Possibly, criminals who receive long sentences learn to accept the procriminal values expressed by convicts (Glaser, 1969). Possibly, longer sentences increase resentment or decrease the socializing values that could control aggressive desires. Possibly, as the Opponent Process Theory suggests, punishments or the rewards of criminality acquire positive incentive value through time (Rosellini & Lashley, 1992; Solomon, 1980). Or, perhaps, punishments are irrelevant, serving only to endorse the image of "hardman" that many criminals find desirable (Katz, 1988).

Although severe punishments seem no more effective as crime deterrents than mild ones, the fear of pain continues to be thought of as an essential motivator. This belief may account for the widespread acceptance of a program in New Jersey that received publicity under the title Scared Straight (Heeren & Shichor, 1984; J. Miller & Hoelter, 1979). In that program, lifers dramatically showed young delinquents about life in prison. Despite its popularity, however, careful evaluations have shown the Scared Straight approach to be ineffective in preventing crime (Buchner & Chesney-Lind, 1983; R. Lewis, 1983).

If street crimes are committed by youngsters proving their courage, perhaps confirming the risks they are taking should not be expected to deter them. Perhaps, too, when people consider whether to commit a crime, they ignore potential sanctions. Although the latter hypothesis cannot be tested directly, Carroll (1982) tested it indirectly. He asked both offenders and nonoffenders to evaluate "crime opportunities" that varied in relation to amount of potential gain, severity of possible punishment, probability of gain, and probability of punishment. The results suggest that most people consider only one of the four features when evaluating opportunities. Participants in the study were, within the ranges considered, more likely to consider the amount or probability of gains than the amount or probability of punishment.

Effective punishments would seem to require that the individual at risk for punishment knows what would be punished. Studies of young children suggest that the timing of punishment as well as its regularity influence this knowledge (Bandura & Walters, 1963; Parke, 1969). The criminal justice system does not lend itself to providing clear and consistent signals for learning what society considers wrong. In an interesting discussion of this issue, Moffitt (1983) suggests that court delays, rewards for successfully executing crimes, and the sporadic nature of apprehension reduce the likelihood that legal sanctions can influence recidivism.

Fear of punishment could be ineffective in deterring further crime among criminals and nevertheless effectively reduce the probability that others would commit crimes. The Uniform Crime Reports seemed to provide a means for testing this general deterrence effect. In 1969, Tittle reported the results of an analysis of the Uniform Crime Reports for the years 1959 to 1963. He showed strong negative correlations between crime rates and his measure of the certainty of punishment, the ratio of convictions to crime rates. Using average length of sentence to measure severity, Tittle found a weak but positive correlation between severity of sanction and crime rate. Chiricos and Waldo (1970), however, reanalyzed the data and contested the conclusion that anything other than chance relationships between crime rates and either certainty or severity had been discovered.

A rash of studies followed. Many, like the one by Antunes and Hunt (1973), used data from the Uniform Crime Reports. Antunes and Hunt defined the ratio of prison admissions to crimes known to the police in the prior year as their measure of certainty. Median length of prison sentence provided their measures of severity. Using data for 1959 to 1960 as evidence of homicide, sex crimes, robbery, assault, burglary, larceny, and auto theft, they tested five linear models. Models predicting crime rates from certainty of punishment supported the hypothesis that a threat of punishment reduces crime. Models based on severity, however, suggested that increases in severity of punishment increased crime rates. As possible explanations for these increases, Antunes and Hunt suggested stigmatization, alienation, and a heightened sense of injustice.

Uses of official records of crime to study the effects of punishment have three major problems. First, official crime rates do not accurately measure crime. At a minimum, the records reflect behavior of victims, police, and judges as well as the behavior of criminals (Ebbesen & Konecni, 1982; Goldkamp & Gottfredson, 1985; M. Greenberg, Wilson, & Mills, 1982; McCord, 1997a). Second, correlational approaches to causality cannot uncover essential linkages between events. The direction and size of correlations between crime rates and other social factors depend on the statistical conditions under which the correlations are assessed (Greenberg & Kessler, 1982a). Third, motivation may have no relation to the reality being measured through official statistics. Motivation depends, at least in part, on how individuals perceive their opportunities. These problems and research generated in attempts to deal with them are discussed below.

Crime and clearance rates are used to assess police and prosecutor efficiency. Not surprisingly, they are subject to manipulation for political purposes. Nagin (1978) illustrated this by comparing recorded crimes, clearances, and clearance rates before and after a change of administration in New York City. His computations show that although the number of robberies cleared increased 9% between 1965 and 1966, the clearance rate declined 58% over that period of time. Police discretion and plea bargaining add further "noise" to what might appear to be objective measures of deterrence.

Researchers have used records of fatal automobile crashes as indirect measures of drunken driving. Ross (1982) used interrupted time series analyses to detect effects of changes in laws related to driving under the influence of alcohol. He reviewed effects of such changes in Norway, Sweden, Great Britain, Canada, Holland, France, New Zealand, Australia, Finland, and the United States. That review failed to show a reduction in accidents attributable to increasing the severity of punishment. In a more recent review of the effects of laws against drunk driving, Ross (1992) concluded: "The increasing popularity of mandatory jailing laws in the United States offers a broad and diverse field on which to look for deterrent impacts, and the findings are in general unfavorable" (p. 59). Increasing the perceived certainty of punishment (e.g., through campaigns to enforce laws against driving while intoxicated and checkpoints to identify the intoxicated), however, appears to have some deterrent value.

Changes in the social climate lead to changes in the law. These social changes may, of course, account for either presence or absence of apparent effects of changes in the law. Sadly, few studies have succeeded in providing adequate control groups and appropriate measures of crime (Sherman et al., 1997; Zimring, 1978). To avoid contamination among measures, one would like to manipulate threats of punishment experimentally, using random assignment or matched controls. Then, if crime could be measured accurately before and after the manipulation, it might be possible to discern effects of changes in celerity, certainty, or severity of punishment.

Among the problems encountered in learning how to prevent crime is convincing relevant authorities that they do not already know how best to handle crime. Sherman and Berk (1984), for example, planned a study of misdemeanor domestic violence in which police were expected to arrest, provide advice, or separate couples according to a random assignment. Only a few officers were willing to participate in the study and even those few sometimes failed to follow the random assignments.

Critical of correlational studies for their failure to produce reliable evidence, Cook (1977) cited "natural experiments" that tended to support a view that increasing the probability of punishment would decrease crime. Crimes decreased on New York subways during 1965 when police increased their presence. Also, crime rates remained constant in a precinct that increased police patrols by 40% while rising in the rest of the city. A 25% reduction in accidents followed closely upon advertisement of new rules regarding arrests for drunken driving embodied in the British Road Safety Act of 1967, as well.

After Chaiken (1978) discovered that police records inflated evidence of effectiveness of the patrolling policies on New York subways, Cook (1980) reviewed 11 studies based on natural experiments, concluding that they justify only modest claims. Acknowledging that identifying causal conditions in a nonexperimental setting can be extremely difficult, Cook suggested that police presence may increase the likelihood for people to report crimes.

D. Greenberg and Kessler (1982b) attempted the task of detecting a causal relationship between crime rates and clearance rates, as a measure of certainty, among 98 cities with populations over 25,000 in the United States. As in other studies, simple correlations based on cross-sectional rates produced evidence that could be interpreted as support for a deterrence hypothesis. Zero-order analyses showed negative correlations between clearance rates and murder, assault, robbery, and larceny. The data also suggested that crime rates might be influenced by population density, unemployment, and poverty. Because crime rates might be affecting clearance rates, Greenberg and Kessler also calculated two- and three-year lags between crime rates and clearance rates. Consistent effects from certainty of punishment disappeared when population, population density, unemployment, income, skewness of income, and proportion of households headed by women were taken into account.

Some of those who argue that fear of punishment will deter crime justifiably criticize the use of clearance rates to measure certainty and the use of changes in sentencing practices to measure severity. Fear depends on perceptions, and these measures of certainty and severity may be unrelated to perceived certainty or perceived severity of punishment.

Studies based on perceptions have typically asked people to estimate their likelihood for being caught and the severity of anticipated punishments. In one study, for example, students estimated penalties for two crimes: theft and smoking marijuana (Waldo & Chiricos, 1972). They also estimated the probability of arrest for these crimes. Then the students reported on their own thefts of less than $100 and their own use of marijuana. The students who reported smoking pot gave lower estimates of the likelihood for being caught and lower estimates of the likelihood for receiving a maximum penalty should they be caught. Students who reported having stolen also gave lower estimates of the likelihood for being arrested, but their estimates for penalties were not lower than those made by students who reported no thefts. The authors suggested that severity and certainty of punishment have a greater influence on crimes considered *mala prohibita* than on those considered *mala in se*.

Doubts that perceived penalties influenced use of marijuana were raised, however, when Meier and Johnson (1977) reported results from a national probability sample of adults over 18. In the national sample, those most likely to use marijuana were also likely to perceive punishment for its use as most severe. The data showed no relationship between perceived certainty of punishment and marijuana use.

Attempting to account for some of the inconsistencies and to specify more clearly how fear of punishment should influence crime, Grasmick and Bryjak (1980) explained the interactions that an adequate test would involve: Only if apprehension is viewed as a cost should one expect certainty of arrest to influence behavior, and only if arrest is perceived as reasonably likely should one expect estimates of severity to influence behavior. To test their refined propositions, Grasmick and Bryjak asked 400 randomly selected people to report whether they had participated in eight types of illegal activities: petty theft, theft of something worth at least $20, illegal gambling, intentional physical injury of another, income tax evasion, littering, illegal use of fireworks, and driving under the influence of alcohol. For each of these crimes, respondents estimated the probability that they would be arrested if they participated, estimated the chance they would be put in jail if arrested, and reported on the severity of problems that would be created by whatever punishment they considered a plausible consequence for participation.

As in the Meier and Johnson study, some of the evidence adduced by Grasmick and Bryjak seemed to show that more severe punishments increased criminal behavior: Those who gave larger estimates of the likelihood of being put in jail if arrested reported participating in more crimes. Analyses taking into account the severity of problems that would be encountered by probable punishments yielded a different picture. Among those whose scores for perceived certainty of punishment were in the highest quartile, subjective estimates of severity were significantly negatively correlated with participation. That is, the data supported the authors' interpretation that those who believed they were likely to be arrested if they committed crimes were influenced by their estimates of the effects of probable punishments. And, except for those who reported little anticipated inconvenience from the plausible outcome of arrest, criminal behavior appeared to be influenced by estimates of the certainty of punishment.

Estimates of the likelihood for punishment have been based on hypothetical situations in which respondents are asked to assume they have broken the law. Jensen and Stitt (1982) added a dimension to understanding such estimates by asking respondents to report the likelihood that they would commit certain types of crimes. High school students reported their past misbehavior, their probable future misbehavior, and the probabilities of punitive responses under hypothetical conditions of misbehavior. With prior misbehavior controlled statistically, perceived risk of punitive response was related to the students' hypothetical choice to use marijuana, to become drunk, to use more serious drugs, to truant, to participate in shoplifting, to commit vandalism, and to participate in burglary.

These studies of deterrence based on perceived penalties shared a bias that attributed reported behavior to expressed beliefs. Yet none of them could show whether the respondents' behavior had influenced their beliefs about punishment or whether their beliefs about punishment had influenced their behavior. Longitudinal studies could shed light on the direction of impact.

Reasoning that prior experience would affect estimates of punishment, Paternoster, Saltzman, Chiricos, and Waldo (1982a; Paternoster, Saltzman, Waldo, & Chiricos, 1982b) collected data from 300 college students at two interviews. During each interview, the students reported whether they had stolen something worth less than $10 and whether they had used marijuana or hashish during the prior year. Also during each interview, the students estimated the likelihood of being caught, being arrested, and being convicted for these acts. The investigators considered correlations between time-1 reports of behavior and time-2 perceptions of punishment to be experiential effects; they considered negative correlations between time-1 perceptions of punishment and time-2 reports of behavior to be deterrent effects. Correlations of the first type were stronger than those of the second. The authors concluded that experience influences judgments about punishment and that perceptions of punishment do not influence theft or drug use.

Bishop (1984), too, used a longitudinal design to study effects of perceived sanctions. More than 2,000 high school students responded to two questionnaires asking about participation in 13 types of crimes and about three types of constraints. As measures of the three types of constraints, students were asked to estimate the risk of legal sanctions, the risk of losing their friends if they got into trouble with the law, and the degree to which they believed in the rightness of the law. Bishop analyzed responses to the constraint questions from the first questionnaire as predictors of responses to the delinquent-involvement questions in the second questionnaire. Using multivariable linear regression, she found that all three types of constraints appeared to reduce criminality. Bishop interpreted the data as showing deterrent effects, but because she did not control for prior delinquency, the evidence does not distinguish experiential from deterrent effects.

Although not without problems, the studies based on subjective evaluations of penalties vindicated some of the assumptions of those utilitarians who believe that behavior is a consequence of attempts to maximize self-interest. These studies showed that a rational model of the relationship between perceived pain and intentional choice could give an account of some forms of criminal behavior. Yet, these studies failed to link actual punishments with motivations for crime. Unless subjective estimates of severity and certainty could be shown to be systematically related to objectively defined severity and certainty, a deterrent model of intervention would have no practical value.

In one of the few experimental studies of effects of punishment, Buikhuisen (1974) included measures of perception and an objective measure of illegal activity. Buikhuisen arranged to have an enforcement campaign against driving dangerous vehicles in one town. As a control, he arranged to have no enforcement campaign in a similar town. Using before and after measures based on random selection of automobiles, Buikhuisen discovered increased compliance with the law only in the town that had introduced the campaign of enforcement. There, a majority of both those who did and those who did not comply with the law were aware of the police campaign and knew of potential penalties. Those who disregarded the law were among the group most likely to appear in courts for other offences. They were younger, poorer, and less well-educated.

DIVERSION AS PREVENTION

During the first half of the 20th century, sociologists began to notice how frequently behavior could be conceived as the playing of roles assigned by associates (Cooley, 1902/1956; Mead, 1918; Tannenbaum, 1938; Thomas, 1923). This way of portraying behavior became known as Interaction Theory or Labeling Theory. To many, it seemed reasonable that actions of the criminal justice system provided a role that could lead to further criminal behavior (Ageton & Elliott, 1974; Becker, 1963; Erikson, 1962; Garfinkel, 1956; Kitsuse, 1962; Lemert, 1951; Schur, 1971). To avoid increasing crime through expectations imposed when a youngster was adjudicated delinquent, courts were urged to avoid using a stigmatizing label and police departments instituted a variety of "crime prevention" strategies that were designed to give children another chance.

Until recently, the belief that the probability for further delinquency was reduced by diverting youngsters away from the courts seemed too obvious to require evaluation. Indirectly, however, some of the studies that evaluated the deterrence model had also tested the theory that the criminal justice system increases crime through imposing expectations for misbehavior. Positive correlation between severity of sanction and crime rates could be interpreted as evidence of such a labeling process. Klein (1974) tested the theory more directly through looking at recidivism rates as a function of diversion from the criminal justice system.

In 1969, the proportions of arrested youths released by the police in Los Angeles County ranged from 2% to 82% in different departments. Klein selected the eight departments with the highest and the five departments with the lowest "diversion" rates. These 13 departments had roughly comparable recording procedures. Overall comparisons failed to show a pattern related to differences in diversion rates. When the delinquents were divided into first offenders and multiple offenders, however, a pattern emerged. For first offenders, those arrested in districts with high diversion rates were less likely to commit additional crimes during the two-year follow-up period. For multiple offenders, those arrested in districts with low diversion rates were less likely to commit additional crimes during the two-year follow-up period. On this evidence, it would be reasonable to conclude that a labeling effect is more likely to influence first-time offenders.

To test the generality of such a conclusion, McCord (1985) examined the criminal careers of 197 men who, as juveniles, had committed minor crimes that brought them to the attention of the police. In 1938, the police established a Crime Prevention Bureau to deflect juveniles from the courts. The Crime Prevention Bureau had processed and then released 163 of the juveniles at the time of their first encounter with the police; only 34 had been sent to court for a misdemeanor first offense. Comparison of those sent to court with those diverted through the Crime Prevention Bureau indicated neither racial nor social class bias. About half of both groups were from broken homes. Although both groups ranged in age from 7 to 17, those sent to court tended to be the older boys.

More than 30 years later, McCord gathered criminal records for the men. These records did not support the hypothesis that a court appearance would increase crime. Over half of the boys who had been "given a break" through the Crime Prevention Bureau (51%) were subsequently convicted for at least one Index crime. Fewer than a quarter (23%) of the 26 boys who had been convicted and fined, released, or placed on probation subsequently were convicted for any Index crimes. Of the 8 sent to reform school, 3 (38%) were later convicted for Index crimes. The diversion project had failed to decrease criminality. But the data also offered no support for a deterrence model.

Similar results were found when Glaser and Gordon (1990) retraced 1,121 people sentenced in 1984 for assault, burglary, drug crimes, driving under the influence, theft, and indecent exposure. They compared outcomes for those given probation only, probation with financial penalties, probation with jail time, and probation with jail time as well as financial penalties. For all the crimes studied, probation with fines resulted in fewer rearrests and revocations of probation than did probation alone or with jail time. This remained true even after taking into account effects of prior arrests, prior convictions, and prior drug problems.

A movement to avoid labeling by diverting youths from the juvenile courts became popular in the United States after World War II. Studies of these projects show that many of their clients would never have appeared on court dockets.

Typically, these studies report that the diversion programs tend to bring new groups of people into the criminal justice system. The Children and Young Persons' Act of 1969 reflected concern over possible effects from court processing in Great Britain. This act introduced cautioning, a formal warning procedure believed to be less serious and less stigmatizing than court processing. Farrington and Bennett (1981) studied effects of the new law by examining files of juveniles who had been younger than 15 when first arrested. Their sample included 202 who had been sent to court and 705 who had been issued a police caution. Disposition appeared to have been strongly influenced by age and seriousness of the offense. Even after statistically controlling effects of sex, age, race, social class, area, and seriousness of crime, those who received police cautions were less likely than those sent to court to have been rearrested during a 34-month follow-up period. Farrington and Bennett scrutinized the records of 47 cases to learn more about the delinquents. These records included information about family size, attitudes of the parents and the juvenile, academic performance, and school behavior. Analyses indicated that the juvenile's attitude predicted both disposition and rearrest. After statistically controlling effects of these attitudes, rearrest rates following cautions appeared to be greater than those following court appearance.

Probably the most coherent study of how labeling affects juveniles has come from the West and Farrington (1977) study of 411 youths reared in London. These youngsters had been interviewed about delinquent acts at ages 14–15, 16–17, and 18–19. When the youths turned 21, West and Farrington reviewed their court records. Farrington (1977) coordinated the court records with the self-reports of delinquency for the 383 youths who had been interviewed all three times. As measured through their own reports of crime, in agreement with the hypothesis of negative labeling effects, the convicted boys had actually committed more crimes.

To discover how the label of delinquent affected self-reported delinquency, Farrington matched 27 boys who had been first convicted between the ages of 14 and 16 to 27 boys who reported similar crimes at the age of 14 but had not been convicted. At age 16, the convicted group admitted to committing 84 more crimes. Their reports at age 16 included 251 crimes to which they had confessed at age 14 and an additional 65 crimes committed prior to age 14. At age 16, the unconvicted group confessed to 232 crimes they had previously acknowledged and added 43 to the earlier confessions. Because 41 of the 84 crimes that differentiated their self-reports at the age of 16 could be attributed to reporting errors, Farrington concluded that about half the effects of convictions were due to reduced concealment and half to increased criminal behavior.

The longitudinal study of London youths shows that effects of encounters with the court depend on the nature of these encounters. Delinquency reports of those first convicted between the ages of 18 and 21 showed practically no increase among those who had been fined as a penalty; among those who had been discharged without penalty, however, the self-reports showed marked increases (Farrington, Osborn, & West, 1978).

Data from several perspectives suggest that neither increasing the severity of punishment nor avoiding labeling youngsters has a beneficial influence on criminal behavior. In sum, the evidence has failed to support either punitive or diversionary strategies.

COUNSELING AS PREVENTION

Intervention programs have been designed with knowledge that delinquents typically have rejecting, aggressive parents (Dinitz, Scarpitti, & Reckless, 1962; Farrington, 1978; Glueck & Glueck, 1950; Gorman-Smith, Tolan, Zelli, & Huesmann, 1996; Hirschi, 1969; D. Lewis, Shanok, Pincus, & Glaser, 1979; McCord, 1979, 1991; Pulkkinen, 1983; Rutter, 1978). Not unreasonably, therefore, some programs have tried to provide substitutes for parental care.

One such project, The Cambridge-Somerville Youth Study, randomly assigned boys to either a treatment or a control group. The program included both "difficult" and "average" youngsters between the ages of 5 and 13. From 1939 to 1945, social workers tutored and counseled 253 boys from 232 families, assisting the boys and their families in a variety of ways (Powers & Witmer, 1951). In 1975, when the boys had become middle-aged men, their names and pseudonyms were checked through vital statistics, court and mental hospital records, and centers for treatment of alcoholism. When interviewed, many of the men in the treatment program recalled their counselors with affection and a majority believed the program had helped them lead better lives. Yet, when compared with their matched controls who had not received help through the program, those in the treatment group fared badly: they were more likely to have serious criminal records; to have been diagnosed manic-depressive, schizophrenic, or alcoholic; and to have died at a young age (McCord, 1978, 1992).

Other counseling programs, too, seem to have had detrimental effects. Adults who had received clinic treatment as children in St. Louis (Cass & Thomas, 1979) and in Hawaii (Werner & Smith, 1977) were less well-adjusted than their untreated peers. Discouragingly, Gersten, Langner, and Simcha-Fagan (1979) discovered that delinquents in New York were more likely to sustain delinquent activities if they had been referred for treatment. Because those referred for treatment had not been randomly selected, results of most of the negative evaluations have been treated as anomalies.

A handful of carefully designed evaluations of counseling programs suggest that such results may not be accidental. Many courts in the United States have volunteer programs to provide adult guidance to probationers. One of these, the Volunteers in Probation program, agreed to an evaluation in which consenting probationers were randomly assigned to the volunteer program or to a control group (Berger, Crowley, Gold, Gray, & Arnold, 1975). Two out of three (randomly selected) probationers received the special services of group counseling, individual counseling, and tutoring given by the volunteers. Those in the control group received the ordinary services of the court. Evaluations occurred after 6 months and again after 12 months.

Both self-reports and official records showed that participation in the program had iatrogenic effects. Those assigned to the control group and those who had been assigned to the volunteer program but had not participated in it decreased their rates of crime. Those who participated in the volunteer program, however, increased the number of crimes they reported and their records showed increases in the number of their police contacts.

Because of apparent deficiencies in the social skills of delinquents, many schools developed programs designed to increase self-confidence by giving students practice in discussing issues with well-adjusted peers. Typically, adult leaders guide the discussions. The programs have been called Positive Peer Culture, Peer Culture Development, and Peer Group Counseling as well as Guided Group Interaction. Gottfredson (1987) arranged to have students in public elementary and high schools randomly selected for inclusion in either the treatment or the control group of a Guided Group Interaction program. Overall, the results for elementary school children showed no effects. For the high school students, however, the Guided Group Interaction program tended to increase misbehavior and delinquency.

A spate of therapies have been devised in the attempt to reduce antisocial behavior. Reality therapy (Glasser, 1965) seems to be best known among them. Kaltenbach and Gazda (1975) claimed success for the approach in group practice; Yochelson and Samenow (1977) claimed success with hard-core criminals. Unfortunately, because the approach has not yet been used in a well-controlled study, conclusions about its effectiveness appear premature.

ENVIRONMENTAL MANIPULATIONS AS PREVENTION

Use of random assignment has permitted evaluation of several programs designed to affect criminality through manipulating the environment of people at high risk for crime. In one program (Reckless & Dinitz, 1972), educational environments were manipulated to provide "vulnerable" boys with programs designed to improve their self-esteem. Sixth-grade teachers in Columbus Ohio nominated "good" and "bad" boys. The latter were randomly assigned either to experimental or control classes in the seventh grade. The program lasted for three years. The experimental group received special help in reading; their discipline was based on "mutual respect"; and special lessons using role model techniques were introduced to teach them how to act. Ratings made by their teachers at the end of ninth grade suggested that the experimental boys were more cooperative, comfortable, honest, and less delinquent. However, no differences were found in the proportions who had police contacts or in the proportions committing serious Index offences. Nor were there differences in school performance, dropout rates, or school attendance.

Boys in the Ohio experiment designed by Reckless and Dinitz (1972) had been assigned to homogeneous groups of "bad" boys for their experimental treatment. Perhaps this feature of the experiment accounted for failure to show benefits—at least by objective measures. Klein (1971) discovered that programs providing gang members with group activities tended to be particularly damaging for 12- to 15-year-olds. Program activities increased cohesiveness of the gangs but also increased delinquency of the members. So clear was the evidence that Klein concluded that "there is good reason to doubt the desirability of continuing such programs or mounting new ones" (p. 119).

Dishion and Andrews (1995) used a random-assignment design to evaluate the impact of teaching techniques of family management and of focusing on peer relations and interactions. For the study, 83 boys and 75 girls, 10 to 14 years old, participated in 12 weekly 90-minute sessions focusing on their families, the teen interaction, both, or a self-directed change program. The two interventions with teen focus increased smoking and aggressive types of behavior (as measured by their teachers). Furthermore, my own research analyzing the source of harmful effects from the Cambridge-Somerville Youth Study indicates that aggregating misbehaving children may be particularly risky during early adolescence (McCord, 1997b).

The Department of Labor sponsored a program testing effects of altering the social environment (Lenihan, 1977). A randomly selected group of men were given $60 a week for 13 weeks after release from prison. The men eligible for this program had committed property crimes, were under 45 years of age, had spent less than three months on work release, had less than $400 in savings, and were not first-time offenders. After release, those who received money were more likely to help pay for household expenses and to help support their families. The money appeared to delay return to theft. Through the two years of the study, fewer men who received the $780 had been arrested for theft. The beneficial effects increased with increasing age and were most dramatic among the poorest risks: those discharged without parole and poorly educated. Reports by participants suggest that the money enabled them to buy clothes, helped them feel better, and allowed them time to find a decent job. Timing of the help may have been important to its effectiveness. Evidence from a pilot project conducted by A. Miller and Ohlin (1985) suggests that experiences after release have a greater impact on recidivism than either background or program experiences.

One of the most promising approaches to intervention combined educating mothers in skills related to child rearing with intellectual stimulation of their young children. In 1962, a project known both as High Scope and as The Perry Preschool Program began with a random assignment of children from low-income neighborhoods to either a preschool or a no-preschool group (Berrueta-Clement, Schweinhart, Barnett, Epstein, & Weikart, 1984). Home visits where parents were taught how to augment the school program were included in the interventions for the preschool group. The two groups have been traced both in school and as young adults. Those in the preschool program were more satisfied with their experiences in school and more likely to have graduated from high school. A higher proportion of those who attended preschool were employed and a higher proportion reported that they were self-supporting at age 19. The preschool program, including home visits, seems also to have reduced crime up to the age of 32: those in the program had significantly fewer arrests as juveniles and as adults. Criminal records showed that the intervention group had fewer adult felony arrests and that they were less likely to have been arrested more than four times (Schweinhart, Barnes, & Weikart, 1993).

Similar benefits have been shown when parent training has been combined with child training in early primary school (McCord, Tremblay, Vitaro, & Desmarais-Gervais, 1994; Tremblay, Pagani-Kurtz, Masse, Vitaro, & Pihl, 1995; Webster-Stratton & Hammond, 1997) and in the homes of 12- to 17-year-old delinquents (Borduin, Henggeler, Hanson, & Pruitt, 1995). Tremblay and his colleagues worked with Francophone boys in Montreal whose kindergarten teachers had identified them as among the most disruptive. A randomly selected group was assigned to a two-year treatment program in which the parents received training in family management and their children were assisted in improving their social skills. At the time of treatment, the boys were between the ages of 7 and 9. Treatment was evaluated against two control groups: one, a placebo, received attention through extensive biannual evaluations; the other received only whatever interventions were already available in the community. By age 15, the boys who had received treatment were more likely than those in either control group to be in regular school classes and less likely to have committed crimes. The program evaluated by Borduin and his colleagues attempted to empower parents by giving them skills to help address their adolescent's problems. Two hundred delinquents between the ages of 12 and 17 were randomly assigned to the treatment group or to a control group that was given individual counseling. A follow-up four years later indicated that the empowerment program was more successful: fewer had been arrested and they were less likely to have committed violent crimes.

A related approach that promises to have multiple benefits in terms of health, school performance, and employment as well as delinquency and crime has focused on intervention through home visits that help to educate mothers regarding child health and development while also providing educational stimulation to the infants. Although the children are still young, analyses have shown benefits in terms of behavior (Brooks-Gunn, Klebanov, Liaw, & Spiker, 1993).

An advantage of training parents in skills that improve their socializing practices is that the training may be beneficial to subsequent offspring. It is wise to remember, however, that many parent training programs fail. It is difficult to get parents who need help to participate in the programs and, even when they do participate, many return to their old habits after short periods of time. These difficulties seem to have been overcome by some promising programs that include home visits from the time the mother is pregnant through the first two years of the infant's life (Olds, Henderson, Tatelbaum, & Chamberlin, 1986; Olds & Kitzmann, 1990; Rauh, Achenbach, Nurcombe, Howell, & Teti, 1988).

COGNITIVE APPROACHES AS PREVENTION

Several short-term evaluations have provided evidence that teaching children special skills, even without parent training, may be a valuable tool to reducing their criminality. Guerra and Slaby (1990) taught incarcerated violent offenders that aggression was often counterproductive. As compared with both a group tutored in reading and mathematics who received the same amount of attention and a no-attention control, those who received the training regarding the counterproductivity of aggression were rated by their supervisors (who were blind regarding the treatment condition of those they rated) as less aggressive, impulsive, and inflexible.

Hudley and Graham (1993) taught unpopular, aggressive children how to recognize the intentions of others so that they would be less likely to attribute the intention to injure. They used role-playing techniques with nonaggressive, popular peers as teachers. Boys in fourth to sixth grades were assigned to one of three groups: the treatment group; a group having the same number of meetings, but these devoted to nonsocial problems; or a no-attention control group. Treatment lasted six weeks, with meetings two times a week. A month after treatment ended, an experimental session showed that the boys taught to recognize nonaggressive cues among their peers were less likely to complain about or criticize a partner whose actions frustrated them. Additionally, the teachers were more likely to recognize reduced aggressiveness among the boys trained to recognize nonaggressive cues.

Kazdin and colleagues (Kazdin, Esveldt-Dawson, French, & Unis, 1987) found that teaching problem-solving skills to hospitalized antisocial children between the ages of 7 and 13 was more effective in reducing dysfunctional behavior than was helping such children express themselves or than providing them with an equivalent amount of attention through games and talking. Although differences continued for a year posttreatment, few of the children maintained behavior within a normal range of problems.

Experiments have shown that training children to view television critically can reduce imitative aggression (Eron, 1986), and that academic tutoring can have social consequences for low-achieving children (Coie & Krehbiel, 1984). The results of experiments with such children indicate, however, that not all training in social skills is beneficial. In short, much remains to be learned regarding the types of training most likely to be beneficial in reducing aggressive, antisocial behavior.

SUMMARY

The evidence suggests that when a delinquent fails to receive penalties supporting the law, delinquency is likely to continue. Yet, the evidence does not show that serious penalties have more potent effects than mild penalties. It seems reasonable to interpret the receipt of penalties as a type of information from which youths can learn how society expects them to act.

Although a labeling effect seems to account for some criminal behavior, diversion programs have had only minor success. A recent intervention that may be particularly appropriate for reducing recidivism among juveniles has been developed from the work of Braithwaite (1989). Known both as reintegrative shaming and restorative justice, the program seeks to find a way for the guilty person to admit wrongdoing and yet to avoid being an outcast. The program is being evaluated through an experimental design in Canberra, Australia (Sherman & Strang, 1997).

Obviously, too little is known about how to produce socialized behavior. Counseling programs have typically been ineffective or damaging. Family training may be helpful, though keeping families in programs long enough to change parental behavior is a problem. Some, but not all, educational programs have had beneficial results. Those that seem effective should be replicated. New programs, designed for appropriate evaluation, should be started. Perhaps as a consequence, it will become possible to regard intervention as crime prevention.

REFERENCES

Ageton, S., & Elliott, D. S. (1974). The effects of legal processing on delinquent orientations. *Social Problems, 22,* 87–100.

Antunes, G., & Hunt, A. L. (1973). The impact of certainty and severity of punishment on levels of crime in American states: An extended analysis. *Journal of Criminal Law and Criminology, 64,* 489–493.

Bandura, A., & Walters, R. H. (1963). *Social learning and personality development.* New York: Holt, Rinehart and Winston.

Beccaria, C. B. (1963). *On crimes and punishments.* Indianapolis: Bobbs-Merrill. (Original work published in 1764)

Becker, H. S. (1963). *Outsiders.* Glencoe: Free Press.

Bentham, J. (1988). *The principles of morals and legislation.* Buffalo: Prometheus. (Original work published in 1789)

Berger, R. J., Crowley, J. E., Gold, M., Gray, J., & Arnold, M. S. (1975). *Experiment in a juvenile court: A study of a program of volunteers working with juvenile probationers.* Michigan: Institute for Social Research, University of Michigan.

Berrueta-Clement, J. R., Schweinhart, L. J., Barnett, W. S., Epstein, A. S., & Weikart, D. P. (1984). *Changed lives: The effects of the Perry preschool program on youths through age 19.* Ypsilanti, MI: High/Scope Press.

Bishop, D. M. (1984). Legal and extralegal barriers to delinquency. *Criminology, 22*(3), 403–419.

Borduin, C. M., Henggeler, S. W., Hanson, C. L., & Pruitt, J. A. (1995). Verbal problem solving in families of father-absent and father-present delinquent boys. *Child & Family Behavior Therapy, 7*(2), 51–63.

Braithwaite, J. (1981). The myth of social class and criminality reconsidered. *American Sociological Review, 46,* 36–57.

Braithwaite, J. (1989). *Crime, shame and reintegration.* Cambridge, England: Cambridge University Press.

Brooks-Gunn, J., Klebanov, P. K., Liaw, F. R., & Spiker, D. (1993). Enhancing the development of low-birthweight, premature infants: Changes in cognition and behavior over the first 3 years. *Child Development, 64*(3), 736–753.

Buchner, J. C., & Chesney-Lind, M. (1983). Dramatic cures for juvenile crime: An evaluation of a prisoner-run delinquency prevention program. *Criminal Justice and Behavior, 10*(2), 227–247.

Buikhuisen, W. (1974). General deterrence: Research and theory. *Abstracts on Criminology and Penology, 14*(3), 285–298.

Carroll, J. S. (1982). The decision to commit the crime. In J. Konecni & E. B. Ebbesen (Eds.), *The criminal justice system* (pp. 49–67). San Francisco: Freeman.

Cass, L. K., & Thomas, C. B. (1979). *Childhood pathology and later adjustment.* New York: Wiley.

Chaiken, J. M. (1978). What is known about deterrent effects of police activities. In J. A. Cramer (Ed.), *Preventing crime.* Beverly Hills, CA: Sage.

Chiricos, T. G., & Waldo, G. P. (1970). Punishment and crime: An examination of some empirical evidence. *Social Problems, 18*(2), 200–217.

Coie, J. D., & Krehbiel, G. (1984). Effects of academic tutoring on the social status of low-achieving, socially rejected children. *Child Development, 55,* 1465–1478.

Cook, P. J. (1977). Punishment and crime: A critique of current findings concerning the preventive effects of punishment. *Law and Contemporary Problems, 41,* 164–204.

Cook, P. J. (1980). The clearance rate as a measure of criminal justice system effectiveness. In E. Bittner & S. L. Messinger (Eds.), *Criminology review yearbook* (Vol. 2, pp. 669–676). Beverly Hills, CA: Sage.

Cooley, C. H. (1956). *Human Nature and the Social Order.* New York: Schocken. (Original work published in 1902)

Crowther, C. (1969). Crimes, penalties, and legislatures. *Annals of the American Academy of Political and Social Science, 381,* 147–158.

Dinitz, S., Scarpitti, F. R., & Reckless, W. C. (1962). Delinquency vulnerability: A cross group and longitudinal analysis. *American Sociological Review, 37*(4), 515–517.

Dishion, T. J., & Andrews, D. W. (1995). Preventing escalation in problem behaviors with high-risk young adolescents: Immediate and 1-year outcomes. *Journal of Consulting and Clinical Psychology, 63*(4), 538–548.

Ebbesen, E. B., & Konecni, V. J. (1982). Social psychology and the law: A decision-making approach to the criminal justice system. In J. Konecni & E. B. Ebbesen (Eds.), *The criminal justice system* (pp. 3–23). San Francisco: Freeman.

Erikson, K. T. (1962). Notes on the sociology of deviance. *Social Problems, 9*(3), 307–314.

Eron, L. D. (1986). Interventions to mitigate the psychological effects of media violence on aggressive behavior. *Journal of Social Issues, 42*(3), 155–169.

Farrington, D. P. (1977). The effects of public labelling. *British Journal of Criminology, 17,* 112–125.

Farrington, D. P. (1978). The family backgrounds of aggressive youths. In L. A. Hersov & M. Berger (Eds.), *Aggression and antisocial behaviour in childhood and adolescence* (pp. 73–93). Oxford, England: Pergamon Press.

Farrington, D. P. (1986). Stepping stones to adult criminal careers. In D. Olweus, J. Block, & M. Radke-Yarrow (Eds.), *Development of antisocial and prosocial behavior* (pp. 359–384). New York: Academic Press.

Farrington, D. P. (1995). The twelfth Jack Tizard memorial lecture: The development of offending and antisocial behavior from childhood: Key findings from the Cambridge study in delinquent development. *Journal of Child Psychology and Psychiatry, 36*(6), 929–964.

Farrington, D. P., & Bennett, T. (1981). Police cautioning of juveniles in London. *British Journal of Criminology, 21,* 123–135.

Farrington, D. P., Osborn, S. G., & West, D. J. (1978). The persistence of labeling effects. *British Journal of Criminology, 18,* 277–284.

Garfinkel, H. (1956). Conditions of successful degradation ceremonies. *American Journal of Sociology, 61,* 420–424.

Gersten, J. C., Langner, T. S., & Simcha-Fagan, O. (1979). Developmental patterns of types of behavioral disturbance and secondary prevention. *International Journal of Mental Health, 7,* 132–149.

Glaser, D. (1969). *The effectiveness of a prison and parole system.* New York: Bobbs-Merrill.

Glaser, D., & Gordon, M. A. (1990). Profitable penalties for lower level courts. *Judicature, 73*(5), 248–252.

Glasser, W. (1965). *Reality therapy.* New York: Harper & Row.

Glueck, S., & Glueck, E. T. (1950). *Unraveling juvenile delinquency.* New York: Commonwealth Fund.

Goldkamp, J. S., & Gottfredson, M. R. (1985). *Policy guidelines for bail.* Philadelphia: Temple University Press.

Gorman-Smith, D., Tolan, P. H., Zelli, A., & Huesmann, L. R. (1996). The relation of family functioning to violence among inner-city minority youths. *Journal of Family Psychology, 10*(2), 115–129.

Gottfredson, G. D. (1987). Peer group interventions to reduce the risk of delinquent behavior: A selective review and a new evaluation. *Criminology, 25*(3), 671–714.

Grasmick, H. G., & Bryjak, G. J. (1980). The deterrent effect of perceived severity of punishment. *Social Forces, 59*(2), 471–491.

Greenberg, D. F., & Kessler, R. C. (1982a). Model specification in dynamic analyses of crime deterrence. In J. Hagan (Ed.), *Deterrence reconsidered* (pp. 15–32). Beverly Hills, CA: Sage.

Greenberg, D. F., & Kessler, R. C. (1982b). The effect of arrests on crime: A multivariate panel analysis. *Social Forces, 60*(3), 771–790.

Greenberg, M. S., Wilson, C. E., & Mills, M. K. (1982). Victim decision-making: An experimental approach. In J. Konecni & E. B. Ebbesen (Eds.), *The criminal justice system* (pp. 73–94). San Francisco: Freeman.

Guerra, N. G., & Slaby, R. G. (1990). Cognitive mediators of aggression in adolescent offenders: 2. Intervention. *Developmental Psychology, 26*(2), 269–277.

Heeren, J., & Shichor, D. (1984). Mass media and delinquency prevention: The case of "Scared straight." *Deviant Behavior, 5*, 375–386.

Hirschi, T. (1969). *Causes of delinquency.* Berkeley: University of California Press.

Hudley, C., & Graham, S. (1993). An attributional intervention to reduce peer-directed aggression among African-American boys. *Child Development, 64*(1), 124–138.

Jensen, G. F., & Stitt, B. G. (1982). Words and misdeeds. In J. Hagan (Ed.), *Deterrence reconsidered* (pp. 33–54). Beverly Hills, CA: Sage.

Kaltenbach, R. F., & Gazda, G. M. (1975). Reality therapy in groups. In G. M. Gazda (Ed.), *Basic approaches to group psychotherapy and group counseling* (pp. 196–233). Springfield, IL: Thomas.

Katz, J. (1988). *Seductions of crimes.* New York: Basil Blackwell.

Kazdin, A. E., Esveldt-Dawson, K., French, N. H., & Unis, A. L. (1987). Problem-solving skills training and relationship therapy in the treatment of antisocial child behavior. *Journal of Consulting and Clinical Psychology, 55*(1), 76–85.

Kitsuse, J. I. (1962). Societal reaction to deviant behavior. *Social Problems, 9*, 247–256.

Klein, M. W. (1971). *Street gangs and street workers.* Englewood Cliffs, NJ: Prentice-Hall.

Klein, M. W. (1974). Labeling, deterrence and recidivism: A study of police dispositions of juvenile offenders. *Social Problems, 22*, 292–303.

Lemert, E. (1951). *Social pathology.* New York: McGraw-Hill.

Lenihan, K. J. (1977). *Unlocking the second gate: The role of financial assistance in reducing recidivism among ex-prisoners* (U.S. Department of Labor R & D Monograph 45). Washington, DC: U.S. Department of Labor.

Lewis, D. O., Shanok, S. S., Pincus, J., & Glaser, G. H. (1979). Violent juvenile delinquents. *Journal of the American Academy of Child Psychiatry, 18*, 307–319.

Lewis, R. V. (1983). Scared straight—California style. *Criminal Justice and Behavior, 10*(2), 284–289.

Magnusson, D., Klinteberg, F. B., & Stattin, H. (1992). Autonomic activity/reactivity, behavior and crime in a longitudinal perspective. In J. McCord (Ed.), *Facts, frameworks, and forecasts: Advances in criminological theory* (Vol. 3, pp. 287–318). New Brunswick: Transaction Press.

McCord, J. (1978). A thirty-year follow-up of treatment effects. *American Psychologist, 33*(3), 284–289.

McCord, J. (1979). Some child-rearing antecedents of criminal behavior in adult men. *Journal of Personality and Social Psychology, 37*, 1477–1486.

McCord, J. (1985). Deterrence and the light touch of the law. In D. P. Farrington & J. Gunn (Eds.), *Reactions to crime: The public, the police, courts, and prisons* (pp. 73–85). London: Wiley.

McCord, J. (1991). Family relationships, juvenile delinquency, and adult criminality. *Criminology, 29*(3), 397–417.

McCord, J. (1992). The Cambridge-Somerville Study: A pioneering longitudinal-experimental study of delinquency prevention. In J. McCord & R. E. Tremblay (Eds.), *Preventing antisocial behavior: Interventions from birth through adolescence* (pp. 196–206). New York: Guilford Press.

McCord, J. (1994). Family socialization and antisocial behavior: Searching for causal relationships in longitudinal research. In E. G. M. Weitekamp & H.-J. Kerner (Eds.), *Cross-national longitudinal research on human development and criminal behavior* (pp. 177–188). Dordrecht, the Netherlands: Kluwer.

McCord, J. (1997a). Placing American urban violence in context. In J. McCord (Ed.), *Violence and childhood in the inner city*. New York: Cambridge University Press.

McCord, J. (1997b, April 3–6). *Some unanticipated consequences of summer camps.* Paper presented at the Society for Research in Child Development Meeting, Washington, DC.

McCord, J., & Ensminger, M. E. (1997). Multiple risks and comorbidity in an African-American population. *Criminal Behaviour and Mental Health, 7*, 229–352.

McCord, J., Tremblay, R. E., Vitaro, F., & Desmarais-Gervais, L. (1994). Boys' disruptive behavior, school adjustment, and delinquency: The Montreal prevention experiment. *International Journal of Behavioral Development, 17*(4), 739–752.

Mead, G. H. (1918). The psychology of punitive justice. *American Journal of Sociology, 23*, 577–602.

Meier, R. F., & Johnson, W. T. (1977). Deterrence as social control: The legal and extralegal production of conformity. *American Sociological Review, 42*, 292–304.

Miller, A. D., & Ohlin, L. E. (1985). *Delinquency and community: Creating opportunities and controls.* Beverly Hills, CA: Sage.

Miller, J. G., & Hoelter, H. H. (1979). *Oversight on scared straight* (Prepared testimony). Washington, DC: U.S. Government Printing Office.

Moffitt, T. E. (1983). The learning theory model of punishment: Implications for delinquency deterrence. *Criminal Justice and Behavior, 10*(2), 131–158.

Nagin, D. (1978). General deterrence: A review of the empirical evidence. In A. Blumstein, J. Cohen, & D. Nagin (Eds.), *Deterrence and incapacitation: Estimating the effects of criminal sanctions on crime rates* (pp. 95–139). Washington, DC: National Academy of Sciences.

Olds, D. L., Henderson, C. R., Tatelbaum, R., & Chamberlin, R. (1986, January). Improving delivery of prenatal care and outcomes of pregnancy: A randomized trial of nurse home visitation. *Pediatrics, 77*(1), 16–28.

Olds, D. L., & Kitzmann, H. (1990, July). Can home visitation improve the health of women and children at environmental risk? *Pediatrics, 86*(1), 108–116.

Parke, R. D. (1969). Effectiveness of punishment as an interaction of intensity, timing, agent nurturance, and cognitive structuring. *Child Development, 40*, 213–235.

Paternoster, R., Saltzman, L. E., Chiricos, T. G., & Waldo, G. P. (1982). Perceived risk and deterrence: Methodological artifacts in perceptual deterrence research. *Journal of Criminal Law and Criminology, 73*(3), 1238–1258.

Paternoster, R., Saltzman, L. E., Waldo, G. P., & Chiricos, T. G. (1982). Causal ordering in deterrence research. In J. Hagan (Ed.), *Deterrence reconsidered* (pp. 55–70). Beverly Hills, CA: Sage.

Plato. (1956). *Protagoras* (B. Jowett, Trans.; revised by M. Ostwald). Indianapolis: Bobbs-Merrill. (Original work in 324)

Powers, E., & Witmer, H. (1951). *An experiment in the prevention of delinquency: The Cambridge-Somerville youth study.* New York: Columbia University Press.

Pulkkinen, L. (1983). Search for alternatives to aggression in Finland. In A. P. Goldstein & M. H. Segall (Eds.), *Aggression in global perspective* (pp. 104–144). Elmsford, NY: Pergamon Press.

Pulkkinen, L., & Pitkanen, T. (1993). Continuities in aggressive behavior from childhood to adulthood. *Aggressive Behavior, 19*(4), 249–263.

Rauh, V. A., Achenbach, T. M., Nurcombe, B., Howell, C. T., & Teti, D. M. (1988). Minimizing adverse effects of low birthweight: Four-year results of an early intervention program. *Child Development, 59,* 544–553.

Reckless, W. C., & Dinitz, S. (1972). *The prevention of juvenile delinquency: An experiment.* Columbus: Ohio State University Press.

Robins, L. N., & Ratcliff, K. S. (1979). Risk factors in the continuation of childhood antisocial behavior into adulthood. *International Journal of Mental Health, 7,* 96–116.

Rosellini, R. A., & Lashley, R. L. (1992). Opponent-process theory: Implications for criminality. In J. McCord (Ed.), *Facts, frameworks, and forecasts: Advances in criminological theory* (Vol. 3, pp. 47–62). New Brunswick: Transaction Press.

Ross, H. L. (1982). Interrupted time series studies of deterrence of drinking and driving. In J. Hagan (Ed.), *Deterrence reconsidered* (pp. 71–97). Beverly Hills, CA: Sage.

Ross, H. L. (1992). *Confronting drunk driving social policy for saving lives.* New Haven, CT: Yale University Press.

Rutter, M. (1978). Family, area and school influences in the genesis of conduct disorders. In L. A. Hersov & M. Berger (Eds.), *Aggression and anti-social behaviour in childhood and adolescence* (pp. 95–113). Oxford, England: Pergamon Press.

Schur, E. M. (1971). *Labeling deviant behavior: Its sociological implications.* New York: Harper & Row.

Schweinhart, L. J., Barnes, H. V., & Weikart, D. P. (1993). *Significant benefits: The High/Scope Perry Preschool Study through age 27.* Ypsilanti, MI: High/Scope Press.

Sherman, L. W. (1992). *Policing domestic violence: Experiments and dilemmas.* New York: Free Press.

Sherman, L. W., & Berk, R. A. (1984). The specific deterrent effects of arrest for domestic assault. *American Sociological Review, 49*(2), 261–272.

Sherman, L. W., Gottfredson, D., MacKenzie, D., Eck, J., Reuter, P., & Bushway, S. (1997). *Preventing crime: What works, what doesn't, what's promising.* A report to the United States Congress.

Sherman, L. W., & Strang, H. (1997, April 21st). *The right kind of shame for crime prevention.* RISE Working Papers.

Solomon, R. L. (1980). The opponent-process theory of acquired motivation: The costs of pleasure and the benefits of pain. *American Psychologist, 35*(8), 691–712.

Tannenbaum, F. (1938). *Crime and the community.* Boston: Ginn.

Thomas, W. I. (1923). *The unadjusted girl.* Boston: Little, Brown.

Tittle, C. R. (1969). Crime rates and legal sanctions. *Social Problems, 14,* 409–422.

Tremblay, R. E., Pagani-Kurtz, L., Masse, L. C., Vitaro, F., & Pihl, R. O. (1995). A bimodal preventive intervention for disruptive kindergarten boys: Its impact through mid-adolescence. *Journal of Consulting and Clinical Psychology, 63*(4), 560–568.

Waldo, G. P., & Chiricos, T. G. (1972). Perceived penal sanction and self-reported criminality: A neglected approach to deterrence research. *Social Problems, 19,* 522–540.

Webster-Stratton, C., & Hammond, M. (1997). Treating children with early-onset conduct problems: A comparison of child and parent training interventions. *Journal of Consulting and Clinical Psychology, 65*(1), 93–109.

Werner, E. E., & Smith, R. S. (1977). *Kauai's children come of age.* Honolulu: University Press of Hawaii.

West, D. J., & Farrington, D. P. (1977). *The delinquent way of life.* London: Heinemann.

Wolfgang, M. E., Figlio, R. M., & Sellin, T. (1972). *Delinquency in a birth cohort.* Chicago: University of Chicago Press.

Yochelson, S., & Samenow, S. E. (1977). *The criminal personality: II. The change process.* New York: Jason Aronson.

Zimring, F. E. (1978). Policy experiments in general deterrence: 1970–1975. In A. Blumstein, J. Cohen, & D. Nagin (Eds.), *Deterrence and incapacitation: Estimating the effects of criminal sanctions on crime rates* (pp. 140–186). Washington, DC: National Academy of Sciences.

CHAPTER 21

Practicing Psychology in Correctional Settings: Assessment, Treatment, and Substance Abuse Programs

MICHAEL A. MILAN, CHRISTOPHER E. CHIN, and QUANG XUAN NGUYEN

AS THE authors prepared this chapter and reflected on the changing manner in which psychotherapy has been depicted in the mental health literature in general and in the correctional psychology literature in particular over the past quarter century, we were struck by an apparent change in the profession's focus from individuals and the ways they may be treated to psychopathologies and the ways they should be treated. Though we support the movement toward the development of empirically validated therapies, we are concerned that in the rush to identify and specify the active ingredients of those therapies, the profession will lose its hard-earned appreciation of individual differences and of the art of engaging the individual client in the therapeutic relationship—the basis of both individual and group psychotherapy and psychosocial rehabilitation. We therefore provide a brief description of the changing demographics of the American prison population and comment on several issues involved in the assessment and treatment of individuals whose cultural backgrounds differ from those of the predominant members of the American middle class, individuals we believe are too often omitted in manualized treatment protocols.

We also provide a review of current substance abuse theory and treatment research, and a description of the essential components of substance abuse treatment programs that flow from that review. We do so for three reasons. First, the offense histories of today's prisoners (discussed in a subsequent section of this chapter) indicate that substance abuse and related sentencing guidelines may be the most important factors underlying the types of offenses committed and the growth of the prison population. Second, the manner in which substance abuse treatment procedures follow from substance abuse theory and research serves as a prototype for the development of treatment programs that address other problems experienced by prisoners. Third, the components of substance abuse treatment may well prove to be important in the treatment of these other problems. In addition, a discussion of substance abuse treatment allows us to share with the reader our observations from our work with probationers and parolees in the federal judicial system who are referred to us for treatment because of their substance use and abuse histories.

Many of the services psychologists provide to meet the needs of their clients in prison settings are the same as those provided by their colleagues working with other client populations. These routine services include the psychological assessment of prisoners as they enter the correctional system, throughout their stay, and as they are being considered for parole; the diagnosis and treatment of prisoners' mental disorders; and clinically relevant research that strives to improve the quality of the psychological services that are provided prisoners (Blackburn, 1993; Neitzel & Moss, 1972).

The services provided by psychologists in general are no less important in the prison setting than in the range of other settings in which psychologists work. However, the unique aspects of prison settings and imprisoned persons provide correctional psychologists with the opportunity to provide additional services that may be more imperative, if not more significant, in prisons than elsewhere (Milan & Evans, 1987). Some of these additional services involve bringing the psychological perspective to bear in efforts to attenuate or prevent the development of mental disorders in response to the stress, privation, and depersonalization of prison life (Toch, 1992); in efforts to develop and validate the effect of rehabilitation programs that meet the changing needs of a changing prison population; and in efforts to inform personnel decisions concerning the selection, assignment, retention, and advancement of correctional staff and administrators.

More specifically, correctional psychologists' potential contributions to the creation of a more humane prison environment may prove to be one of the most significant components of corrections professionals' efforts to ensure that prisoners are not harmed by the prison experience (Ayllon & Milan, 1979). In addition, correctional psychologists have important contributions to make to the development of rehabilitation programs for prisoners so that they will profit from their period of incarceration to the greatest degree possible (Milan & McKee, 1974). Correctional psychologists can also assist in the identification of rehabilitation needs, the design and delivery of rehabilitation services, and the formulation of educational and training practices that maximize acquisition and performance (Milan, 1988a).

The range of additional services that correctional psychologists may provide requires that they undertake what some might consider nontraditional activities more akin to those of community psychologists than clinical psychologists (Milan & Long, 1980). These services include consultation with academic and vocational instructors, education and supervision of master's- and bachelor's-level mental health staff, training of line correctional staff and their supervisors, collaboration with the administrative personnel of their institution, and even advocacy at the central office and legislative levels. In each of these activities, the expertise in the understanding of human behavior, thought, and emotion that correctional psychologists bring to the correctional profession should help to formulate practices and programs that foster improved adjustment and positive growth within a safe and humane prison environment (Milan, 1988b).

THE CHANGING COMPLEXION OF THE AMERICAN PRISON POPULATION

The efforts of correctional psychologists must be in accord with the needs and characteristics of the prison populations that they serve. During the past decade, American prisons have experienced a marked increase in the numbers of prisoners placed in their custody and a significant change in the characteristics of those prisoners (Mumola & Beck, 1997). The number of prisoners in the federal prison system increased from 40,223 at the end of 1985 to 105,544 at the end of 1996. During the same period, the number of prisoners in state prison systems increased from 462,284 to 1,076,625. These numbers, which do not include the prisoners of local jails, represent an overall increase of 234% in the total number of American prisoners since 1985. Jail inmates accounted for an additional 256,615 prisoners at the midpoint of 1985 and 518,492 at the midpoint of 1996, an increase of 202%.

Increases in the combined federal, state, and local incarceration rates are also considerably larger than would be expected by the increasing size of the American population alone. Between 1985 and 1996, the combined incarceration rates grew from 312 to 615 prisoners per 100,000 residents of the country. These numbers represent a 197% increase in the number of imprisoned adults, adjusted for the overall growth of the population of the country. The building of new prison beds, though a huge growth industry, has not been able to catch up with the increasing numbers of prisoners sentenced to those beds. At the end of 1996, the federal system was operating at 125% of capacity, and the state systems, on the average, were operating at 116% of capacity.

The characteristics of adult prison inmates have also changed during the past decade (Mumola & Beck, 1997). Members of minority groups became the majority of those incarcerated in federal and state prisons. For adult male minority group members, the shift in status from the minority to the majority of prison inmates occurred in 1992. By the end of 1995, federal and state prisons incarcerated 493,700 White males and 527,763 non-White males. White males had both the lowest incarceration rate (461 per 100,000 White males in the population) and the lowest rate of increase (187%) since 1985. Black males had the highest incarceration rate (an incredible 3,250 per 100,000 Black males), but the second highest rate of increase (208%). The incarceration rate for Hispanic males, who may be of any race, fell between those of White and Black males (1,174 per 100,000 Hispanic males), but their rate of increase (217%) was the highest of all identified imprisoned groups.

Unfortunately, trends for adult female prisoners have not been examined as closely as have trends for male prisoners. We do know, however, that adult female minority group members moved from being the minority to the majority of female prisoners in federal and state prisons in 1989, somewhat earlier than for their male counterparts. By the end of 1995, federal and state prisons incarcerated 31,700 White females and 32,200 non-White females. Between 1985 and 1995, the number of White females in federal and state prisons had increased by 294%, and the number of non-White female prisoners had increased by 305%.

CULTURAL DIVERSITY AND CORRECTIONAL PSYCHOLOGY

The analysis of the racial and ethnic characteristics of offenders over the past decade indicates not only that both the relative and absolute size of the male and female prison populations are considerably larger now than they were in the past, but also that an increasing larger proportion of those populations is composed of persons of diverse cultural backgrounds. Correctional psychologists must adjust their practices to better accommodate the characteristics of the prisoners they serve, as well as encourage and assist, through consultation and training, their fellow correctional professionals to do the same. The following material highlights some of the more important issues to be addressed in assessment and treatment with culturally diverse populations.

ASSESSMENT IN THE CULTURALLY DIVERSE ENVIRONMENT

Tanaka-Matsumi, Seiden, and Lam (1996) outline guidelines for assessment and treatment planning with clients of diverse cultural backgrounds. The first step is to determine the cultural background of clients and the degree to which they identify with that culture. This may be accomplished through interviews with the clients and, when possible, with colleagues familiar with that culture, family members, and significant others. The interviews may be supplemented with acculturation scales for specific populations, when available, that assess clients' language facilities, social support, and participation in ethnic and cultural activities.

The information gathered may alert correctional psychologists to the possibility of miscommunication and lack of understanding on the part of both psychologists and prisoners. The information may also provide a basis for determining whether psychologists may work with a prisoner unaided; with the consultation, support, or supervision of others, such as colleagues, translators, and the like; or make a referral to another professional or a paraprofessional who is better prepared, by dint of cultural background or training and experience, to work with the prisoner.

The correctional psychologists' knowledge of clients' cultural background plays an important role in the analysis of problems and needs. Okazaki and Sue (1995) noted that "Lack of research, training, or both in cross-cultural assessment often leads to misdiagnosis, overestimation, underestimation, or neglect of psychopathology, which in turn has grave consequences" (p. 373). Self-reports (descriptions) of problems and symptoms are often heavily influenced by cultural expectations and proscriptions (Draguns, 1990). Members of different cultures may describe the symptoms of the same disorder in different ways, or the symptoms of different disorders in the same way. Similarly, descriptions of thoughts, perceptions, and beliefs that might be indicative of a thought disorder or psychosis in members of the predominant culture may reflect the normal thought process of another culture, interpretations of events that are specific to another culture, metaphoric or idiomatic descriptions of problems of another culture, and the like.

TREATMENT IN THE CULTURALLY DIVERSE ENVIRONMENT

Clearly, sensitivity to cultural issues may prevent the damaging misdiagnosis of culturally appropriate patterns of adjustment as psychological problems when they do not exist, as well as the equally damaging failure to diagnose true problems that may be erroneously attributed to cultural differences that do not exist, or do not exist to the extent manifest in the client being assessed (Okazaki & Sue, 1995). In addition, the appreciation of cultural issues also aids in the determination of how intervention will proceed when psychological problems do exist and are to be addressed (Aponte, Rivers, & Wohl, 1995). This does not mean that new treatments must be developed for the various problems experienced by the various cultural groups, but that already validated treatments may be adjusted and provided in a manner that is appropriate for the cultural background of the recipients. Paniagua (1994) described some of these adjustments in his discussion of the assessment and treatment of Blacks, Hispanics (predominantly of Caribbean origin), Asians, and American Indians.

Organista and Muñoz (1996) emphasize the importance of following culturally sensitive relationship protocols when engaging Latinos in established treatment procedures. They suggest practicing *respeto* (respect) by formally addressing clients as Señor, Señora, or Señorita followed by their surnames, and *personalismo* (personalization) by devoting much of the early contacts to *palatica* (small talk) about shared backgrounds, experiences, and activities in order to develop *confianza* (trust) and the therapeutic alliance.

McNair (1996) describes cultural issues and their impact on the client that are particularly relevant for Black females. She notes that Black females are affected by, and must struggle against, both racism and sexism. Correctional psychologists who work with Black females should be sensitive to unreasonable expectations of strength that are held by Black women themselves and by others. These expectations are both a legacy of slavery's defeminization of Black females, who were required to work side-by-side with Black men, and an extension of the contemporary stereotype of Black women as the strong and domineering heads of a matriarchal family system. The strong value placed on the extended family in the Black culture also often results in Black females maintaining an intergenerational family network, with many members of the network frequently living in the same household. Correctional psychologists should be careful not to rush to the pejorative labeling of Black women's caretaking activities in the face of crises that flow from their strong family values as pathological, enabling, codependent, dysfunctional enmeshment, nonassertiveness, or the like.

ACCULTURATIVE STRESS AND CORRECTIONAL PRACTICES

Blacks, like so many members of other minority groups, must grapple with the "acculturative stress" (Anderson, 1991) that results from discrepancies in the values and beliefs of minority and majority cultures. The conflict between behaviors that are obligatory and appropriate within the context of a minority group culture and incompatible behaviors that are expected and required by the majority culture can engender regularly occurring discrimination experiences that degrade self-concept, self-esteem, and self-efficacy. These experiences can result in mistrust, hypervigilance, and overcompensation, to which correctional psychologists should be sensitive in the course of their activities.

Fudge (1996) sees degraded self-efficacy as a central problem with Black males, particularly those who engage in substance abuse, and advocates the development of a strong Black cultural identity to counteract the degrading and pathological effects of acculturative stress. This involves the development of an African-based perspective, in which the African origins of individuals are viewed as an asset and African ancestry becomes a source of strength, pride, and motivation. The process of developing this strong cultural identity, which is not dissimilar from the strong cultural identities of many other American groups, be they early or late arrivals on this continent, has been termed "nigrescence" (Cross, 1994). This process involves five predictable stages; correctional psychologists and other professionals should be aware of this process so that they may respond appropriately to its outward manifestations.

During the first stage of nigrescence (pre-encounter), individuals subscribe to the majority culture's views of their ethnic group and, by extension, themselves as conveyed in the media, interpersonal interactions, and the like. These are often negative and self-defeating. The second stage (encounter) is triggered by some naturally occurring or programmatic, impactful experience, situation, or event that prompts individuals to question their established beliefs concerning their cultural stereotypes and to begin the search for resolution. During the third stage (immersion), individuals actively work to reject the views of the majority culture and develop their own cultural identity. As individuals work through this stage, they may reject, condemn, and even attack the dominant culture and its practices.

The fourth stage of nigrescence (internalization) involves the confident incorporation of new beliefs and values about the minority culture. The new values provide the basis for a realistic appraisal of self-worth and a more reasoned, less dogmatic analysis of the values of the dominant culture and reaction to its practices. In the fifth and final stage (internalization-commitment), individuals extend their new cultural identity to their cultural group and engage in activities that enhance the quality of adjustment and life of its members, such as participating in prevention programs for at-risk youths or meals-on-wheels programs for impaired elderly.

Sensitivity to the cultural characteristics and issues that accompany the increasing diversity of the offender population, as well as the development of programs that address degrading and pathology-engendering effects of minority-majority conflict and discrimination, should be a constant concern of correctional psychologists. At the same time, however, correctional psychologists should not view these activities as an end in themselves; instead, in most instances, they are a necessary ingredient in the provision of additional psychological services that address mental health problems and contribute to the remediation or the rehabilitation needs of offenders. An informed approach to the development of rehabilitation programs should be based on an understanding of the offense profile of the prison population.

THE CHANGING NEEDS OF AMERICAN PRISONERS

The distribution of the types of offenses committed by prison inmates has changed dramatically during the past decade (Mumola & Beck, 1997). The three most common of the most serious offenses committed by prisoners of state prisons in 1985 were robbery (94,000 prisoners), burglary (74,500 prisoners), and murder (50,600 prisoners). The three most serious offenses in 1995 were violations of drug laws (224,900 prisoners, an incredible 478% increase during the 10-year period), robbery (134,800 prisoners, a 43% increase), and burglary (111,700 prisoners, a 50% increase). The three offenses with the greatest rates of increase between 1985 and 1995 were violations of drug laws, motor vehicle theft (a 256% increase to 22,400 prisoners), and rape and other sexual assaults (a 240% increase to 95,200 prisoners). In 1995, violations of drug laws were the single most common of the most serious offenses of White and Black prisoners alike, accounting for 86,100 (18%) of the White prisoners and 134,000 (27%) of the Black prisoners. These numbers represent a 306% increase for the White prisoners and a 707% increase for the Black prisoners since 1985.

The offense profile of incarcerated offenders suggests that rehabilitation programs addressing drug-related activities should be a top priority for correctional psychologists and their professional colleagues. A detailed analysis of substance abuse and criminal behavior provides more information about the issues to be addressed. The National Institute of Justice's Drug Use Forecasting Program reported that approximately 50% to 80% of arrested individuals were using substances at the time of their arrest (National Institute of Justice, 1992). Moreover, the Bureau of Justice Statistics reports that between 50% and 65% of annual jail admissions and federal and state prisoners are consistent users of illicit drugs (Lipton, 1994). Additional findings suggest that the prevalence of drug use is high not only among those incarcerated, but also among those on parole and probation (Prendergast, Hser, Chen, & Hsieh, 1992).

There is a growing body of data documenting the relation between drug use and crime. Increases in substance abuse have been shown to be associated with increases in criminal behavior (Falkin, Prendergast, & Anglin, 1994; Lipton, 1994). Moreover, one-third of the prisoner population satisfies the American Psychiatric Association's diagnostic criteria for substance dependency (Stewart, 1994). The individual, family, and societal costs of substance abuse, the large numbers of individuals incarcerated for drug and drug-related offenses, and the high rate of drug use within the criminal offender population make clear the need for the development and implementation of effective treatment programs within the criminal justice system.

Currently, the incarceration of substance-abusing offenders provides an opportunity to treat a population that would be unlikely otherwise to participate in substance abuse treatment (Lipton, 1994) or a range of other programs—such as anger control, anxiety management, conflict resolution, and esteem enhancement—that address problems that appear to characterize offender populations or contribute to criminal behavior. An important contribution of correctional psychologists is the evaluation of current approaches to a treatment or rehabilitation problem and the synthesis of effective practices into a program that is appropriate for the setting in which they work. The development of a substance abuse program is a case in point.

APPRAISAL OF CURRENT SUBSTANCE ABUSE TREATMENT PRACTICES

Although the offender population is clearly in need of substance abuse treatment programs, Peters, May, and Kearns (1992) found that such programs existed at fewer than one-third of this country's jails. Moreover, Falkin and Natarajan (1993) add that, by and large, the efficacy of the treatment programs that are provided to the offender population has not been adequately established. The majority of the programs in America (but certainly *not* elsewhere) have been based on the medical or "disease" model of addiction, which is currently the most popular conceptualization of drug dependency in the country (Peele, 1995). The disease model views drug dependency as a lifelong biological disorder. Recovery from the presumed disease of substance abuse typically involves the substance abuser's participation in some type of self-help program, which usually involves a 12-step approach, often in conjunction with an education regimen (Peele & Brodsky, 1991).

The popularity of the disease model of addiction can be attributed largely to Alcoholics Anonymous (AA) and similar programs, such as Narcotics Anonymous (NA) and Cocaine Anonymous (CA) (Le, Ingvarson, & Page, 1995). These 12-step programs provide drug-dependent individuals with increased support through peer group counseling and an appeal to a higher authority. Individuals who are recovering from substance abuse serve as role models by discussing their own recovery process and by providing encouragement to group members. Unfortunately, while the increased social support and related assistance the 12-step programs provide is most likely positive for group members, the more formal services of the helping professions and the potential benefits that they offer are usually ignored, if not actively discouraged.

Programs based on the disease model typically suggest that those who abuse harmful substances are "powerless" in the face of their disease; recovery involves surrendering themselves to a higher power (Le et al., 1995; Peele & Brodsky, 1991). This position raises many potential problems concerning self-efficacy. For instance, participants in programs advocating the disease model are taught that they are not responsible for the development of their "lifelong disease." As a result, participants may come to believe that they possess limited or no control over their behavior as it relates to their drug abuse, and relapse is interpreted as confirmatory evidence of their "powerlessness" (Peele, 1995).

Given these potentially iatrogenic implications of the disease model, it should not be surprising that the manner in which the disease model conceptualizes the causes and treatment of substance abuse has not been without its critics. These critics have called attention to the lack of adequate empirical evidence that confirms the proclaimed effectiveness of the disease model of AA and other 12-step programs (Lipton, 1994; Montgomery, Miller, & Tonigan, 1995).

Based on their review of the substance abuse literature, Peele and Brodsky (1991) concluded, "Every major tenet of the 'disease' view of addiction is refuted both by scientific research and by everyday observation" (p. 26). They also found that the majority of those who abuse harmful substances recover without any formal treatment whatsoever, which, in itself, argues against the disease model. Moreover, "recovered" alcoholics who attend 12-step programs, such as AA, were found to be less likely to continue their abstinence than those who "recover" on their own. Findings such as these call the rationale and efficacy of the disease model into question, as well as suggest that it does indeed result in iatrogenic effects.

Despite the lack of empirical support for the disease model of substance abuse and its treatment, and the potential for iatrogenic side effects that accompanies its advocacy, the disease model is undoubtedly the most commonly endorsed model of substance abuse by professionals and the lay public alike. The disease model is therefore likely to dominate substance abuse treatment programs for the foreseeable future. This is clearly another instance in which validity and efficacy are not best determined by public opinion polls, although acting on such polls may well contribute to politicians' reelections and administrators' reappointments. Nonetheless, the factors underlying the widespread acceptance of such a questionable model are beyond the scope of this chapter (see Peele, 1995, for a discussion of these factors). However, well-informed researchers, practitioners, and others who work with and study substance abuse in the criminal justice system should be encouraged to explore particularly promising, alternative treatment approaches that have been empirically investigated and supported by other countries, in other settings, and/or with other populations.

Unfortunately, the mental health professions do not play a formal role in the 12-step programs based on the disease model, although mental health professionals certainly do suspend their practitioner status and participate in such programs as recovering addicts. As a result, these programs are denied the benefits of the recent development of and support for more effective psychological methods of drug treatment (Crits-Christoph & Siqueland, 1996). The authors believe that psychologists have been enamored of the unsubstantiated, biologically oriented disease model of substance abuse and its treatment for far too long. We agree with Azrin, Donohue, Besalel, Acierno, and Kogan's (1994) convincing appeal to psychologists that they increase their efforts to develop, implement, evaluate, and disseminate their own psychologically based substance abuse treatment programs. We add that, in so doing, the needs of offenders, the challenges of offender rehabilitation, and the constraints imposed by imprisonment must not be overlooked.

THE DESIGN OF PRISON-BASED
SUBSTANCE ABUSE PROGRAMS

By and large, the psychologically based approaches that have shown the most promise in the treatment of substance abuse have been conducted in community settings rather than in prisons. The task of the correctional psychologist is to incorporate to the degree possible the key aspects of those programs in their own programs, and to advocate for the continuance and elaboration of those programs when offenders return to the community. As offenders strive to find a place in society following a period of imprisonment, they will likely encounter numerous threats to in-prison treatment gains that increase the likelihood of relapse. These transitional difficulties primarily involve community and social life, family structure and dynamics, and occupational attainment and career development (Stewart, 1994).

Our observations during our work with federal probationers and parolees have indicated that many offenders are ill-prepared to deal with these transitional issues, and that the difficulties they therefore experience make them particularly prone to substance abuse relapse or the renewal of illegal, drug-related activities. Relapse is always a threat in the substance abuse recovery process. It is therefore important that offenders' postrelease planning begin early during the period of incarceration to ensure that treatment efforts target all stages of the criminal justice system and involve comprehensive services that address not only offenders' drug problems directly, but also "their medical, psychological, social and practical deficits" (Lipton, 1994, p. 343).

Two behavioral and cognitive-behavioral approaches to substance abuse treatment in the community show promise for guiding the development of prison-based programs. These are the controlled drinking approach and the community-reinforcement model. Marlatt, Larimer, Baer, and Quigley (1993) have evaluated the controlled drinking approach to treatment and conclude that although somewhat controversial, it holds considerable promise for the treatment of at least some substance abusers. The controlled drinking approach is based on the harm-reduction model, which focuses on the incremental reduction of the harmful consequences that individuals experience as a result of their addictive behavior. In sharp contrast to the disease model, the harm-reduction model does not necessarily view total abstinence as the only acceptable goal for alcoholics; instead, it considers any decrease in substance use as progress, provided the decrease in usage corresponds to a reduction in harm associated with the addictive behavior.

Studies evaluating the controlled drinking approach have provided several predictors of success. For instance, regular employment, younger age, social support, shorter history of alcohol abuse, and psychological stability were shown to be associated with successful controlled drinking. In light of these correlates of successful treatment and this approach's focus on alcohol, it is clear that the effectiveness of the approach, although promising, must be replicated with a range of chronic, drug-dependent offenders before it can be accepted as an established and refined treatment modality for that population. Nonetheless, the data supporting the approach indicate that drinking in moderation, rather than total abstinence, as called for in the disease model, can be appropriate for at least some alcoholics.

COMMUNITY-REINFORCEMENT SUBSTANCE ABUSE TREATMENT

The community-reinforcement model of substance abuse treatment is a better-documented alternative to the controlled drinking approach for the treatment of several forms of substance abuse. This model, which includes the utilization of common behavioral and cognitive-behavioral techniques, was originally designed to treat clients with alcohol dependency (Hunt & Azrin, 1973). However, it has also been shown to be effective in the treatment of other types of drug addictions (e.g., cocaine) and includes many components that overlap with the relapse prevention strategies described by Marlatt and Gordon (1985). A thorough review of this model is therefore called for.

The community-reinforcement model conceptualizes alcohol and other drugs as both positive reinforcers and negative reinforcers. Their use can be positively reinforcing because it can produce pleasant subjective and/or physical feelings and promote social or peer acceptance in certain environments (e.g., parties). The use of alcohol and other drugs can also be negatively reinforcing, in that it can temporarily decrease negative subjective states (e.g., loneliness, work stress) and reduce aversive physical states (e.g., withdrawal symptoms). The "benefits" of alcohol and other drugs reinforce or strengthen substance abuse. Recognizing the reinforcing properties of alcohol and other drugs, the goal of community-reinforcement treatment is to enhance other areas of life, making these incompatible activities much more enjoyable, worthwhile, beneficial, and ultimately more reinforcing than the use of alcohol and other drugs (Hunt & Azrin, 1973).

With the recognition that the addictions are greatly influenced by clients' sociocultural environment, the community-reinforcement model capitalizes on the "natural deterrents of alcoholism" (Hunt & Azrin, 1973, p. 91) by rearranging clients' environmental contingencies. This involves the restructuring of "vocational, social, recreational and familial satisfactions" (p. 92). Unlike the disease model of substance abuse treatment, which emphasizes a "surrendering" of the individual to a higher power, the community-reinforcement model seeks to empower the clients by helping them develop and strengthen their own coping abilities and by helping them to improve the situations, events, and activities that naturally occur in their environment and throughout their life.

It is important to recognize that the community-reinforcement model does not represent a one-treatment-fits-all approach. Waltman (1995), in his review of the successful components of drug treatment programs, suggested that individualized and flexible treatment services are among the essential components in helping those who abuse harmful substances through the recovery process. Nonetheless, a number of components shared by programs based on the community-reinforcement model can be identified. In the following sections, we describe several of these components, provide specific examples of how they have been implemented, and discuss their relevance and applicability to the treatment of drug-addicted offenders within the prison system as well as in the community after release from prison.

STIMULUS CONTROL

Stimulus control involves assisting drug-dependent clients to identify persons, places, situations, and events that increase the likelihood of drug use and thus should be avoided. At the same time, clients should identify and participate in activities that are incompatible with substance use. For example, in their treatment of hospitalized alcoholics, Hunt and Azrin (1973) encouraged clients to participate socially with family, friends, and others where the use of alcohol would not be permitted. Clients were also counseled against interacting with individuals who also had difficulties with alcohol. To aid clients in meeting these requirements, an alcohol-free club was created in which clients were encouraged to come and socially interact with each other, significant others, friends, and guests. Participation in all club activities required sobriety. Consistent with the community-reinforcement model, this procedure enhanced clients' social life within the context of a drug-free environment.

In another illustration of stimulus control, Azrin, McMahon, et al. (1994) asked participants in their substance abuse program to construct two lists, a Risk list and a Safe list. The Risk list included persons, situations, and activities that could increase the likelihood of drug use; the Safe list included persons, situations, and activities that were incompatible with drug use. Safe list activities were scheduled daily, and time devoted to these activities was recorded on a daily planner. Of course, formulating a stimulus control plan is undoubtedly easier than following through on the plan. Therapists therefore assisted clients with the resolution of any problems encountered in their efforts to eliminate drug-using behavior by rearranging and improving their social environments.

Within the prison setting, stimulus control can be introduced and discussed as part of offenders' psychosocial training. This is particularly relevant for treatment participants who are approaching the end of their prison term and are getting ready to reintegrate into the community. Therapists should prepare participants by helping them identify drug-related situations that should be avoided when they are released from prison, as well as by helping them identify positive, nondrug-related situations.

Treatment should involve a discussion of how to avoid these "negative" situations and participate in "positive" ones, the identification of any foreseeable impediments to achieving these goals, ways to negotiate them, and the identification of all possible resources (e.g., family) offenders have for helping them achieve their goals. Finally, Lipton (1994) emphasized the importance of separating incarcerated offenders participating in a drug treatment program from the rest of the prison population. According to Lipton, minimizing interaction between treatment members and the rest of the prison population serves to "avoid the pervasive influence of the prisoner subculture and to neutralize the influence of the insidious prison code" (p. 338).

By working on these issues within the prison setting, a foundation of treatment (or training) is established that can be continued in the community after offenders are released from prison. As discussed previously, released offenders are likely to encounter high-risk situations and/or unforeseen impediments that may trigger relapse. The parole plan should therefore call for the continuation of the program initiated in the prison. Community workers should carefully observe whether offenders are achieving previously established goals, determine how they are negotiating previously identified obstacles, and provide services and resources that will help them achieve postrelease success.

URGE CONTROL

According to the conditioning model of relapse (Childress, McLellan, Ehrman, & O'Brien, 1988), drug cravings may be elicited when the recovering person is exposed to stimuli that were associated with drug use. Cravings and other physiological withdrawal symptoms are likely to contribute to recovering substance abusers' relapse, and an effective treatment program should include a procedure for controlling these internal motivational factors (Waltman, 1995). Whereas stimulus control techniques target external cues for drug use, urge control techniques attempt to "interrupt internal stimuli, (proprioceptive sensations, urges, thoughts, or incipient actions) associated with drug use and to then substitute competing internal and external stimuli" (Azrin, McMahon, et al., 1994, p. 859).

Azrin, McMahon, et al. (1994) developed the urge control procedure as a component of their behavioral treatment of drug abusers. First, clients were asked to identify and describe in detail a high-risk situation of substance use. Once the urge or thought to use was detected in the narrative, clients immediately initiated thought-stopping techniques. For instance, clients shouted "Stop!" or "No!" and then began reciting examples of the negative consequences of drug use. When the strength of the drug-related urge was reduced to an insignificant level, clients proceeded to self-relaxation techniques. Finally, clients were asked to visualize and describe themselves performing a reinforcing activity that competed with the unwanted urge. Following this process, the therapist reinforced clients for their performance and provided feedback and modeling for those steps in need of improvement.

Urge control procedures can be easily incorporated into the psychosocial skills training of substance-abusing offenders within the prison setting and in the community. These procedures can address triggers for relapse within both settings. Our anecdotal observations indicate that many offenders frequently fantasize about using drugs, particularly as the time of their release approaches. While in prison and after their release, offenders are likely to encounter numerous stimuli associated with previous drug use that can trigger internal cravings and relapse. Urge control techniques can be viewed as a method of enhancing offenders' internal resources for drug refusal, thereby increasing their repertoire of skills for achieving and maintaining abstinence.

FAMILY INVOLVEMENT

It is generally acknowledged that family and significant others represent an essential component of substance abusers' recovery process (Galanter, 1993; O'Farrell & Cowles, 1989; Waltman, 1995). The involvement of the family and significant others in the treatment process can significantly improve treatment prognosis. For example, Higgins, Budney, Bickel, and Badger (1994) report that cocaine-dependent individuals who had a significant other participate in their treatment program were approximately 20 times more likely to achieve abstinence than individuals who did not. Because of the important, positive impact that family and significant others can have on substance abusers' recovery process, Waltman (1995) suggested that all treatment programs should encourage their cooperation and participation.

In the community-reinforcement model, the family has a significant, active role in the recovery process of substance abusers. In fact, in their treatment of hospitalized alcoholics, Hunt and Azrin (1973) created synthetic or foster families for clients who did not have the benefits of partner or parental participation. Synthetic families consisted of relatives, employers, and others who had regular contact with the client and could assist in the treatment process. In Azrin, McMahon, et al.'s (1994) treatment program for substance abusers, family members who were unable to be physically present at treatment sessions with clients were encouraged to participate via speaker-phones. These practices can be extended to the prison setting.

Family members serve as the social and emotional support network for recovering clients, and they can also assist clients to achieve their treatment goals. As with stimulus and urge control, a focused discussion regarding the role of the family and significant others in the recovery process should be included as part of offenders' in-prison psychosocial training. Therapists should help clients identify all possible family members and significant others who will agree to assist them with reintegration efforts and established treatment goals. Therapists should help offenders in considering possible family reactions to their return, identifying potential conflicts that may be encountered, and exploring ways to strengthen familial relationships. This is particularly relevant for incarcerated offenders who commonly experience disrupted family structure and family dynamics. Finally, realistic expectations and goals for family participation in the treatment process should be explored and included in the parole plan.

CONTINGENCY CONTRACTING

Behavioral or contingency contracting represents "an operant technique that aims to reinforce desired behavior by controlling behavioral consequences delivered by external agents" (Waltman, 1995, p. 436). This procedure is commonly used in behavior therapy and is an integral part of the community-reinforcement approach to substance abuse treatment. Contingency contracting involves positive reinforcement that is contingent on completion of therapy assignments; participation in prosocial, nondrug-related activities;

and abstinence. Contingency contracting involves material and nonmaterial reinforcers delivered by therapists or others for desired behavior.

In the community-reinforcement model, the family and significant others provide the reinforcement. One of the major tasks for family members is to assist relatives who are recovering from substance abuse perform therapy assignments, such as stimulus and urge control procedures. This is typically accomplished through the development and implementation of behavioral or contingency contracts (Azrin, McMahon, et al., 1994).

The contract between clients and their families may be one of the most powerful components of the community-reinforcement model (Higgins et al., 1994). In their treatment of substance abusers, Azrin, McMahon, et al. (1994) helped clients negotiate behavioral contracts with family members. For example, clients agreed to perform household duties, find a job, complete therapy assignments, and abstain from drug use. In turn, family members agreed to reduce other household duties; engage in planned social events. In addition, some spouses also agreed to participate in enhanced, or more frequent, sexual interactions that were acceptable to them.

Reciprocal Relationship Counseling

If family members are to be effective partners in the treatment process, a strong relationship must exist between them and the recovering client. Relationship counseling in the community and, to the degree possible, in the prison is often necessary to enhance this relationship and facilitate contingency contracting. Reciprocal relationship counseling (Hunt & Azrin, 1973) is often used in the community-reinforcement model to strengthen family relationships (Azrin, McMahon, et al., 1994; Higgins et al., 1993; Higgins, Budney, Bickel, Foerg, et al., 1994). Originally intended for couples (Azrin et al., 1980; Azrin, Naster, & Jones, 1973), the community-reinforcement model extends the procedure to include clients' relatives and friends. Reciprocal relationship counseling generally involves a behavioral contracting process in which clients and their significant others identify behaviors and activities in which each agrees to engage to please the other if specified conditions are satisfied.

In their work with substance abusers, Hunt and Azrin (1973) used reciprocal relationship counseling to help couples identify several problem areas in their relationship, negotiate behaviors that each would agree to perform to improve the problem area, and specify the conditions under which the agreed upon behaviors would be performed. A typical condition specified by the partners of alcoholics was complete sobriety. Similarly, Higgins, Budney, Bickel, and Badger's (1994) use of the reciprocal relationship counseling procedure involved the development of contracts between clients and their significant other (not necessarily a spouse) in which mutual engagement in agreed upon positive activities was contingent on cocaine abstinence as indicated by urinalysis.

Reciprocal relationship counseling is beneficial for several reasons. First, it helps to enhance the relationship between individuals recovering from substance abuse and significant others by focusing on the identification and resolution of specific problem areas. Second, by strengthening this relationship, significant others can become more effective partners in the treatment process. Third, it promotes the recovering individual's participation in prosocial, nondrug-related activities and discourages drug use. Finally, it reinforces those who abuse harmful substances (and significant others) for being part of and maintaining positive familial and social relationships, thereby allowing these relationships to become more powerful natural deterrents to drug use.

SUPPLEMENTARY SERVICES

The treatment components described thus far have specifically targeted substance abuse, yet adjunctive components are also important in a treatment program in order to address those problems that are secondary to drug abuse but serve as potential triggers for relapse. These services can include academic preparation, financial counseling, medical assistance, parenting skills instruction, legal counseling, relaxation training, spiritual counseling, assertiveness training, nutritional education, and recreational activities (Waltman, 1995). According to Lipton (1994), because recidivism has been strongly associated with inadequate housing and employment, supplementary services addressing these two needs are critical. Improvements in vocational status and housing, as well as participation in recreational activities, are often essential to retain clients in treatment in the community (Higgins et al., 1991).

Vocational Counseling

Improving clients' vocational functioning is a major objective of the community-reinforcement model (Higgins et al., 1991). Using this approach in the treatment of alcoholism, Hunt and Azrin (1973) included a component designed to help clients obtain satisfactory employment. Unemployed clients were assisted with the following job-finding tasks: preparing résumés; contacting friends, relatives, and local employers to inquire about job leads; and applying and interviewing for available jobs. For example, role-play techniques were used to help prepare clients for their job interviews. Vocational services were also an integral part of Higgins et al.'s (1993) treatment of cocaine-dependent clients. In this study, clients were provided with alternative housing as well as vocational, academic, financial, and legal counseling. Azrin, McMahon, et al. (1994) added a highly structured Job Club component to their community-reinforcement program.

The Job Club was employed to assist clients to secure employment. Given the likelihood of vocational skill deficits and unemployment among released offenders, the application of vocational counseling to the treatment of this population is particularly important. Throughout imprisonment, offenders should receive vocational training to prepare them for job placement following release. During the final months of imprisonment, offenders should receive assistance in preparing résumés, identifying potential job openings, and practicing for job interviews. They should learn the proper way to explain their criminal history to their potential employer and then practice communicating this explanation. They should be provided with tips on how previous offenders were able to obtain sufficient employment to improve their chances of doing the same.

Upon release, offenders should immediately begin interviewing for positions and, when appropriate, employers should be informed about offenders' drug treatment and be asked to encourage their employees' continuance in the program (Waltman, 1995).

Housing and Recreation

Following release from prison, many offenders return to the environments in which their previous substance abuse occurred and so encounter various triggers for relapse. Housing is therefore an important factor to address. As the release date approaches, offenders should receive counseling regarding their housing options. Related to stimulus control, they should be informed of the risks of returning to their former communities and should be encouraged to relocate to recommended areas if possible. Obviously, their flexibility in relocating will depend on their success in finding gainful employment and the assistance of community counselors.

Creating a reinforcing social climate that overpowers any temptations to use substances is a basic tenet of the community-reinforcement model. To achieve this goal, this model strongly encourages participation in enjoyable recreational activities that are incompatible with drug use. In the Higgins et al. (1991) program, drug-dependent clients received counseling aimed at developing new recreational activities and rekindling interest in old activities in which clients engaged prior to their substance abuse. These activities served as positive reinforcers in contingency contracts. Although the applicability of this procedure is limited in prison-based treatment programs, prison therapists can assist offenders in creating a list of recreational activities in which they will engage following their release, and community counselors can then build on this foundation to better prevent relapse.

Effectiveness of the Community-Reinforcement Model

Supporting evidence for the efficacy of the community-reinforcement model in the treatment of substance abuse comes from a number of controlled outcome studies. As previously discussed, the model was originally implemented by Hunt and Azrin (1973) for the treatment of alcoholism. In their study, a program based on the model was compared to an existing hospital program based on the disease model of addiction. The results indicated that "the mean percent of time spent drinking, unemployed, away from home, and institutionalized was more than twice as high for the control group as for the community-reinforcement group" (p. 97).

In their treatment of 82 drug abusers, Azrin, McMahon, et al. (1994) compared a community-reinforcement program to a nonbehavioral, "supportive" treatment program that followed a group psychotherapy-type format. During the course of the program and at the end of a follow-up period, 37%, 54%, and 65% of the participants in the behaviorally based community-reinforcement program were drug-free at 2, 6, and 12 months, respectively. In contrast, only about 20% of the participants in the nonbehavioral program were drug-free at each of the three evaluation points. Not only did drug use decrease during the course of the behavioral program, but participation was also associated with improvements in other areas, including employment or school attendance, family relationships, depression, and alcohol use relative to the nonbehavioral program. Finally, the community-reinforcement program was effective across sex, age, education, marital status, and drug type. Azrin et al. (1996) followed participants in both programs for approximately another 9 months and concluded that the differential treatment effects were maintained.

In two controlled outcome studies involving the treatment of cocaine abusers, Higgins and colleagues (Higgins et al., 1991, 1993) compared a community-reinforcement program to a 12-step counseling program based on the disease model. In the first study of a 12-week program, Higgins et al. (1991) found that 85% of the participants in the community-reinforcement program completed treatment, whereas only 42% of the participants in the 12-step program did so. In addition, 77% of the participants in the behavioral program abstained from cocaine use for a period of 4 weeks and 46% achieved 8 weeks of abstinence. In comparison, only 25% of the participants in the 12-step program achieved 4 weeks of abstinence, and none achieved 8 weeks of abstinence. In the second study of a 28-week program, Higgins et al. (1993) found that 58% of participants in the community-reinforcement program completed treatment, but only 11% of the participants in the 12-step program did so. In addition, 68% of the participants in the behavioral program abstained from cocaine use for at least 8 weeks, and 42% abstained for 16 weeks. In contrast, only 11% of the participants in the 12-step program achieved abstinence for 8 weeks, and this dropped even further, to 5%, at 16 weeks.

CONCLUSION

The growing interest in and increased urgency for psychologically based drug rehabilitation services for juvenile and adult offenders are long-overdue responses to the drug epidemic plaguing the criminal justice system. Unfortunately, drug treatment programs for the offender population, particularly incarcerated offenders, have been scarce and the services provided have been limited. In recent years, there has been a noticeable increase in the development and implementation of a variety of drug treatment programs within the criminal justice system. However, outcome studies have yielded inconsistent support for the efficacy of the predominant types of programs.

There is a general consensus that an effective drug treatment program should be comprehensive and should address the specific needs of the offender population. According to Lipton (1994), "The complexity and changing nature of the drug abuse problem, as well as the level of our current knowledge about drug treatment in correctional settings, suggest that a period of experimentation with treatment interventions is needed, and that new techniques should be thoroughly evaluated" (p. 343). We agree, and although we have focused on behavioral and cognitive-behavioral procedures, we believe that the search for effective correctional programs should encompass all approaches and theoretical orientations with a reasonable expectation of success.

The evaluation of the efficacy of the community-reinforcement model of substance abuse treatment indicates that it is more effective than disease-model-oriented programs. The model represents a psychologically based method of drug treatment that has yielded promising results in the general population. The community-reinforcement model is appealing in that it encompasses etiology, maintenance, and recovery as well as relapse prevention in a parsimonious and coherent fashion. The challenge to correctional psychologists who wish to utilize the model is to retain its effective components while modifying them as called for by the unique requirements and constraints of the settings in which they work. Moreover, they must provide the services called for in a manner that is compatible with the needs and expectations of an increasingly diverse offender population.

America's substance abuse researchers and treatment providers have expressed the need for empirically validated treatment approaches. So it is ironic that the most popular and widely implemented forms of substance abuse treatment in this country are based on the disease model of addiction, a model that lacks convincing empirical support. Such is not the case in other countries that have all but abandoned the disease model in their programs (e.g., Peele, 1995). American correctional professionals in general and correctional psychologists in particular must bear the burden of bringing greater respect for empirical findings to the correctional decision-making process in this country if we are to escape the Dark Ages of prescientific psychologizing.

The thoughtful application of empirically validated psychological knowledge is particularly important when correctional decisions involve management, rehabilitation, and treatment issues that directly affect living conditions, psychological adjustment, recidivism, and relapse. Unfortunately, the ability of mental health professionals to influence correctional practices has too often been more hope than reality (e.g., Roth, 1980); for that reason, a redoubling of our efforts is called for. Perhaps this can be best accomplished by uniting with our colleagues in such professional organizations as the American Association for Correctional Psychology (an affiliate of the American Correctional Association), the American Psychology–Law Society (Division 41 of the American Psychological Association) and the American Academy of Forensic Psychology in a more concerted and focused effort to accomplish the changes called for.

As if accomplishing change within the justice system were not a sufficiently difficult task, it also appears that mental health professionals must expand their frame of reference and attempt to influence societal practices as well. As professionally difficult and politically incorrect as it may be to contemplate, however, the incidence of drug use in both the offender population and the general population in this country certainly suggests that our quarter-century-long war on drugs has failed, and that a drug-free society may well be more an impossible dream than a realistic possibility.

Drug prohibition has created a worldwide mega-industry. Until the enormous profits of the drug trade are eliminated, there is no reason to believe that sanctions, no matter how severe, will deter its upwardly mobile workers from replacing those who have been lost to the prison cells of the criminal justice system or the graveyards of competing drug entrepreneurs. Similarly, there is no reason to believe that legal sanctions, no matter how severe, will deter all, most, or even many current and future consumers of illicit drugs from at least their occasional use. The use of mind-altering substances has been a part of humankind's history from its very beginnings, and will undoubtedly continue to be so for so long as humans walk this and other planets.

Certainly, drug treatment programs, such as those that have been described herein, are necessary to free individuals from their addictions and dependencies. However, our denial of the realities of drug supply and demand have led to the adoption of policies and practices that may well have increased, rather than decreased, the harm that drugs cause our society. Our general refusal to allow needle exchange programs is only one case in point: How may users, partners of users, and children of users must be sacrificed to HIV infection and AIDS before we realize that its prohibition causes far more harm than would its wide-scale promotion?

Programs that are currently prohibited or restricted in this country but practiced with some success elsewhere must be considered if we are to minimize the harm that drugs cause our society in general and individuals in particular. One such program is the exchange of needles. Other programs to consider include the low-cost, nonprescription sale of syringes in pharmacies, increased reliance on methadone maintenance for those who have repeatedly failed in traditional drug treatment programs, and the supervised provision of heroin by prescription for those for whom all other alternatives have failed.

Perhaps more important, broad policy changes such as the legalization and regulation of some, many, or all drugs must also be considered. Contrary to popular opinion, advocates for the legalization and regulation of drugs in the same manner that alcohol is legal and regulated are not advocates for the wide-scale use of drugs. Instead, they seek to reduce the many harms caused by the illicit drug trade by reducing the profits that can be earned by trading in drugs, and they see the reduction in harm that will flow from legalization as far more significant than any increases in harm that it will engender.

Certainly, this country is not ready to adopt many, much less most or all, of the innovative possibilities that have been proven to reduce harm from drugs in other countries. Indeed, it may not be desirable to do so. However, it is certainly time to acknowledge that our current practice of "more of the same" has proven to be a failure. Given this reality, it is certainly time to work toward a new social climate in which the citizenry is willing to question their cherished beliefs about drugs and how to deal with them, and in which lawmakers are able to propose different approaches without the certainty that their political careers will come to an end. That social climate will not and cannot emerge until those who enforce the law, those who administer the criminal justice system, and those who provide therapeutic services to offenders set the occasion for a serious reconsideration of the way we think about and address drug use.

REFERENCES

Anderson, L. P. (1991). Acculturative stress: A theory of relevance to Black Americans. *Clinical Psychology Review, 11,* 685–702.

Aponte, J. F., Rivers, R. Y., & Wohl, J. (1995). *Psychological interventions and cultural diversity.* Needham Heights, MA: Allyn & Bacon.

Ayllon, T., & Milan, M. A. (with Roberts, M. S., & McKee, J. M.). (1979). *Correctional rehabilitation and managements: A psychological approach.* New York: Wiley.

Azrin, N. H., Acierno, R., Kogan, E. S., Donohue, B., Besalel, V. A., & McMahon, P. T. (1996). Follow-up results of supportive versus behavioral therapy for illicit drug use. *Behaviour Research and Therapy, 34,* 41–46.

Azrin, N. H., Besalel, V. A., Bechtel, R., Michalicek, A., Mancera, M., Carroll, D., Shuford, D., & Cox, J. (1980). Comparison of reciprocity and discussion-type counseling for marital problems. *American Journal of Family Therapy, 8,* 21–28.

Azrin, N. H., Donohue, B. C., Besalel, V. A., Acierno, R., & Kogan, E. S. (1994). A new role for psychology in the treatment of drug abuse. *Psychotherapy in Private Practice, 13,* 73–80.

Azrin, N. H., McMahon, P. T., Donohue, B., Besalel, V. A., Lapinski, K. J., Kogan, E. S., Acierno, R. E., & Galloway, E. (1994). Behavior therapy for drug abuse: A controlled treatment outcome study. *Behaviour Research and Therapy, 32,* 857–866.

Azrin, N. H., Naster, B. J., & Jones, R. (1973). Reciprocity counseling: A rapid learning-based procedure for marital counseling. *Behaviour Research and Therapy, 11,* 365–382.

Blackburn, R. (1993). *The psychology of criminal conduct: Theory, research and practice.* Chichester, England: Wiley.

Childress, A. R., McLellan, A. T., Ehrman, R., & O'Brien, C. P. (1988). Classically conditioned responses in opiod and cocaine dependence: A role in relapse? In B. A. Ray (Ed.), *Learning factors in substance abuse* (NIDA research monograph 84, pp. 25–43). Washington, DC: U.S. Government Printing Office.

Crits-Christoph, P., & Siqueland, L. (1996). Psychosocial treatment for drug abuse: Selected review and recommendations for national health care. *Archives of General Psychiatry, 53,* 749–756.

Cross, W. E. (1994). Nigrescence theory: Historical and explanatory notes. *Journal of Vocational Psychology, 44,* 119–123.

Draguns, J. D. (1990). Normal and abnormal behavior in cross-cultural perspective: Specifying the nature of their relationship. In J. J. Berman (Ed.), *Nebraska symposium on motivation: Vol. 37. Cross-cultural perspectives* (pp. 235–278). Lincoln: University of Nebraska Press.

Falkin, G. P., & Natarajan, M. (1993). *Evaluations of treatment programs for drug-dependent offenders.* New York: National Development and Research Institutes.

Falkin, G. P., Prendergast, M., & Anglin, M. D. (1994). Drug treatment in the criminal justice system. *Federal Probation, 58,* 31–36.

Fudge, R. C. (1996). The use of behavior therapy in the development of ethnic consciousness: A treatment model. *Cognitive and Behavioral Practice, 3,* 317–335.

Galanter, M. (1993). Network therapy for addiction: A model for office practice. *American Journal of Psychiatry, 150,* 28–36.

Higgins, S. T., Budney, A. J., Bickel, W. K., & Badger, G. J. (1994). Participation of significant others in outpatient behavioral treatment predicts greater cocaine abstinence. *American Journal of Drug Alcohol Abuse, 20,* 47–56.

Higgins, S. T., Budney, A. J., Bickel, W. K., Foerg, F. E., Donham, R., & Badger, G. J. (1994). Incentives improve outcome in outpatient behavioral treatment of cocaine dependence. *Archives of General Psychiatry, 51,* 568–576.

Higgins, S. T., Budney, A. J., Bickel, W. K., Hughes, J. R., Foerg, F., & Badger, G. (1993). Achieving initial cocaine abstinence with a behavioral approach. *American Journal of Psychiatry, 150,* 763–769.

Higgins, S. T., Delaney, D. D., Budney, A. J., Bickel, W. K., Hughes, J. R., Foerg, F., & Fenwick, J. W. (1991). A behavioral approach to achieving initial cocaine abstinence. *American Journal of Psychiatry, 148,* 1218–1224.

Hunt, G. M., & Azrin, N. H. (1973). A community-reinforcement approach to alcoholism. *Behaviour Research and Therapy, 11,* 91–104.

Le, C., Ingvarson, E. P., & Page, R. C. (1995). Alcoholics Anonymous and the counseling profession: Philosophies in conflict. *Journal of Counseling & Development, 73,* 603–609.

Lipton, D. S. (1994). The correctional opportunity: Pathways to drug treatment for offenders. *Journal of Drug Issues, 24,* 331–348.

Marlatt, G. A., & Gordon, J. R. (Eds.). (1985). *Relapse prevention.* New York: Guilford Press.

Marlatt, G. A., Larimer, M. E., Baer, J. S., & Quigley, L. A. (1993). Harm reduction for alcohol problems: Moving beyond the controlled drinking controversy. *Behavior Therapy, 24,* 461–504.

McNair, L. D. (1996). African American women and behavior therapy: Integrating theory, culture, and clinical practice. *Cognitive and Behavioral Practice, 3,* 337–349.

Milan, M. A. (1988a). Basic behavioral procedures in closed institutions. In E. K. Morris & C. J. Braukmann (Eds.), *Behavioral approaches to crime and delinquency: Application, research, and theory* (pp. 161–193). New York: Plenum Press.

Milan, M. A. (1988b). Token economy programs in closed institutions. In E. K. Morris & C. J. Braukmann (Eds.), *Behavioral approaches to crime and delinquency: Application, research, and theory* (pp. 195–222). New York: Plenum Press.

Milan, M. A., & Evans, J. H. (1987). Intervention with incarcerated offenders. In I. B. Weiner & A. K. Hess (Eds.), *Handbook of forensic psychology* (pp. 557–583). New York: Wiley.

Milan, M. A., & Long, C. K. (1980). Crime and delinquency: The last frontier? In D. Glenwick & L. Jason (Eds.), *Behavioral community psychology: Progress and prospects* (pp. 196–229). New York: Praeger.

Milan, M. A., & McKee, J. M. (1974). Behavior modification: Principles and applications in corrections. In D. Glaser (Ed.), *Handbook of criminology* (pp. 745–776). Chicago: Rand McNally.

Montgomery, H. A., Miller, W. R., & Tonigan, J. S. (1995). Does Alcoholics Anonymous involvement predict treatment outcome? *Journal of Substance Abuse Treatment, 12,* 241–246.

Mumola, C. J., & Beck, A. J. (1997). *Bureau of Justice Statistics Bulletin: Prisoners in 1996.* Washington, DC: U.S. Department of Justice.

National Institute of Justice. (1992). *Drug use forecasting–1991.* Washington, DC: National Institute of Justice.

Neitzel, M. T., & Moss, C. S. (1972). The role of the psychologist in the criminal justice system. *Professional Psychology, 3,* 259–270.

O'Farrell, T. J., & Cowles, K. S. (1989). Marital and family therapy. In R. K. Hester & W. R. Miller (Eds.), *Handbook of alcoholism treatment approaches: Effective alternatives* (pp. 183–205). New York: Pergamon Press.

Okazaki, S., & Sue, S. (1995). Methodological issues in assessment research with ethnic minorities. *Psychological Assessment, 7,* 367–375.

Organista, L. C., & Muñoz, R. F. (1996). Cognitive behavioral therapy with Latinos. *Cognitive and Behavioral Practice, 3,* 255–270.

Paniagua, F. A. (1994). *Assessing and treating culturally diverse clients: A practical guide.* Thousand Oaks, CA: Sage.

Peele, S. (1995). *Diseasing of America: How we allowed recovery zealots and the treatment industry to convince us we are out of control.* New York: Lexington Books.

Peele, S., & Brodsky, A. (1991). *The truth about addiction and recovery.* New York: Simon & Schuster.

Peters, R. H., May, R. L., & Kearns, W. D. (1992). Drug treatment in jails: Results of a nationwide survey. *Journal of Criminal Justice, 20,* 283–295.

Prendergast, M. L., Hser, Y. I., Chen, J., & Hsieh, J. (1992, November 4–7). *Drug treatment need among offender populations.* Paper presented at the annual meeting of the American Society of Criminology, New Orleans, LA.

Roth, L. (1980). Correctional psychiatry. In W. Curran, A. McGarry, & C. Retty (Eds.), *Modern legal medicine: Psychiatry and forensic science* (pp. 667–719). Philadelphia: Davis.

Stewart, S. D. (1994). Community-based drug treatment in the Federal Bureau of Prisons. *Federal Probation,* 24–28.

Tanaka-Matsumi, J., Seiden, D. Y., & Lam, K. N. (1996). The culturally informed functional assessment (CIFA) interview: A strategy for cross-cultural behavioral practice. *Cognitive and Behavioral Practice, 3,* 215–233.

Toch, H. (1992). *Mosaic of despair: Human breakdown in prison.* Washington, DC: American Psychological Association.

Waltman, D. (1995). Key ingredients to effective addictions treatment. *Journal of Substance Abuse Treatment, 12,* 429–439.

CHAPTER 22

Psychotherapy with Criminal Offenders

MAX J. MOBLEY

ONE OF the questions asked to test the intelligence of schoolchildren is, Why are criminals locked up? The answers given by Wechsler (1974) are clear (deterrence, protection for society, example to others, punishment or revenge, rehabilitation and segregation), but society itself seems much more conflicted about some of the reasons. It has been fairly clear that protection for society is a major reason, as demonstrated by the willingness to increase prison budgets at a rate higher than that of any other government institution.

Corrections has almost doubled the number of prison inmates during the past decade to 1,182,169 at the end of 1996 (Mumola & Beck, 1997). This number was managed by state systems operating 16% to 24% above capacity and the Federal Bureau of Prisons operating at 25% above capacity. Even this was not enough. Pressure on correctional systems continues, with the backup in jails due to overcrowding of prisons at 31,072, more than twice the number in 1987 (Camp & Camp, 1997). Crime rates have decreased modestly, suggesting that prisons may be successful in the goal of protecting society by incapacitating offenders. The acts of battery, theft, extortion, rape, and the like are at least contained behind the fences.

Most prisoners will be released at some point. Will corrections have achieved its cognate and "corrected" them? We have age working in our favor, as criminal behavior tends to burn out in middle age. We suspect that incarceration makes a stronger impression on the less psychopathic inmates that we hope we are getting as society increases its rate of incarceration. But how can we afford to keep people locked up until they are 40 years old? Can we keep casting a wider net, increasing the rate of incarceration? At some point, must we not do what corrections' name implies and correct?

The bottom-line standard for success in corrections has long been recidivism. The rate of felons returning to prison (new commitments with prior felonies) has not changed substantially from 32.3% in 1987 to 32.6% in 1997. This implies that twice as many people are returning to prison as was the case ten years ago. It appears that prison systems have not shown progress in their goals of primary and secondary deterrence. Yet construction continues, with almost 80,000 new beds under construction at the beginning of 1997. Corrections seems to be placing its emphasis on keeping offenders in institutions longer despite the emphasis in mental health practice toward deinstitutionalization.

Prison alone does not seem to have the desired effect of correcting behavior (Zamble & Porporino, 1990). What, then, can we say about prison's success in the goal of rehabilitation? Indicators of the success of treatment programs have increasingly appeared in the literature (see the special issue of *Criminal Justice and Behavior*, Gendreau, 1990). These successes have usually impacted a small segment of the inmate population and have had only small local impact on recidivism statistics, but they do provide valuable clues as to what works. Hope has not been lost. People continue to believe that our prisons should rehabilitate. F. Cullen, Skovon, Scott, and Burton (1990) found that, of people surveyed in two cities, the percentage indicating that the main emphasis of prisons should be rehabilitation was higher than for punishment or protection of society. This is less encouraging than it would first seem for correctional psychology, for it appears that most citizens define rehabilitation in terms of education and job preparation rather than psychotherapy.

Budgets in corrections have soared, but inmate cost per day has increased only about 20% in the past decade. As this only marginally tracks inflation, it is likely that programs have not increased and may have suffered in many systems. Priority is usually given to psychological treatment of the diagnosed mentally ill, about 4.2% of the correctional population in treatment on January 1, 1997, up almost a full percentage point since 1996. Chemical dependency treatment, which peaked at 200,980 in 1993, continued to involve about 13.6% of the inmate population at any given time in 1996. Increased emphasis on this area in the Byrne Formula Grants is likely to cause a resurgence in this type of treatment over the next few years. (The Edward Byrne Memorial State and Local Law Enforcement Assistance Formula Grant Program provides formula grants to states for a wide range of projects aimed at improving the functioning of the criminal justice system.) The growing treatment field in corrections has been sex offender treatment, which now involves 3.3% of the inmate population (C. Camp & Camp, 1997).

Where does this leave the considerable influx of psychologists, the result of consent decrees signed in the 1980s by many state departments of correction? It leaves us doing what is necessary (care of individuals with *DSM-IV* Axis I diagnoses), doing what shows promise of working (treatment of drug- and sex-related compulsions), and probing areas where we may help the offender develop controls over other specifically targeted behaviors that people fear from criminals. We have increasingly come to understand that prisoners differ in their motivation from the clients who usually seek mental health services; their clinical problems show more subtle thought distortion and striking disinhibition with much underlying personality disorder; and the settings in which we work are less supportive, warm, and empathic than the settings in which we trained and developed our skills.

This chapter is intended to provide the trained therapist with some insights into treatment of offenders. It begins with a discussion of estimates of treatment needs and then breaks down the tasks of the therapist into crisis intervention, long-term management, short-term therapy, and therapeutic programs. Each task is presented in terms of the characteristics of the client, therapist, and system that have a bearing on its success or failure.

MENTAL DISORDER IN OFFENDER POPULATIONS

How serious a problem is mental disorder in the offender population? In preparation for the first edition of this chapter about ten years ago, I asked administrators of mental health programs in several states to estimate the percentage of inmates in their systems who were "mentally disordered to the point of needing to be housed in special facilities." Their estimates showed considerable variation, ranging from less than 1% to 25% of the inmate population. Previously published estimates of psychiatric disorder have ranged from less than 5% (Petrich, 1976) to over 60% (Kal, 1977). Gibbs (1982) pointed out the problems related to sampling and inconsistent definitions that have contributed to the confusion.

Studies that have used standardized criteria, reviewed by Coid (1984), suggested that the prevalence of major psychosis was not more common among offenders than in the general population. Rates of mental retardation determined from screening tests have often been estimated to run three to five times the rates found by Denkowski and Denkowski (1985). These researchers found rates of mental retardation to be about 2% in state prison systems when more reliable individual batteries of tests were used. These findings contradict the opinion of many mental health professionals cited as early as 1972 by Abramson and more recently reviewed by Teplin (1983). These professionals speculated that mentally ill behavior has been "criminalized" and that many individuals who would formerly have been in mental hospitals are currently being dumped on "the system that cannot say no" (Levinson, 1984). This has almost certainly happened, but so has the reverse: psychologists and psychiatrists providing Get-out-of-Jail-Free cards to offenders they felt would be better diverted to the mental health system. Teplin (1984) cites National Institute of Mental Health statistics that show that between 1969 and 1980 the mental hospital inpatient census declined by 66%, and the average length of stay decreased by about 45% between 1969 and 1978. During an overlapping period, 1970 to 1980, the number of prisoners increased by about 61% (Travisono, 1984). The symmetry of these figures has suggested to some that the burden of caring for the chronically mentally ill may have shifted from mental health to the criminal justice system. The correlation here may also be largely coincidental. The rate of incarceration per 100,000 population has continued on about the same vector long after deinstitutionalization of mental hospitals was completed.

A study conducted in Ontario (Allodi, Kedward, & Robertson, 1977) did find an increased number and proportion of psychiatrically disordered individuals in jails during the period of reduction in hospital beds, although the jail census did not increase disproportionately. Many law enforcement officials will admit, off the record, that the needs of their communities may be better served by pressing criminal charges against individuals whom the community would prefer to do without than by taking them to a mental health facility. The individual may not be any more "cured" on release, but at least the sheriff and the community get a little longer breathing space.

An example from my experience is an individual who was received after several hospitalizations. His hospitalizations were usually short term, as his hypersexuality often placed other patients at risk. There was no problem making criminal charges against him because he tended to walk into other people's houses, undeterred by closed doors, helping himself to clothes and food. He had no income in prison but traded sexual favors for cookies, cigarettes, and pieces of paper on which he drew cryptic designs and wrote biblical quotes and words that had five letters. At times, he would get overloaded by the sexual demands of other inmates and become blatantly psychotic. This was usually easy to detect because he would not enter the office unless all recording devices and my briefcase, which he believed was a direct link to the FBI, had been removed. However, once stabilized, he adamantly refused medication. He did improve enough to make parole, but was back at the prison gate two days later, saying that he could not make it "out there." His mother called after about a week asking that he be let back in because she could not work and keep him from sexually abusing her other children while she was gone. She was informed that we could not take him back unless he committed a crime or violated probation. He was back a short time later for stealing a pair of pants from a clothesline. He flattened his time (completed his sentence without parole) and was discharged. He was not welcome back in his hometown. He drifted until he was struck and killed by a car while panhandling quarters by flagging down cars on a bridge.

This case is not intended to illustrate what happens to all mentally ill persons in prison, nor is it an isolated instance. The interface between correctional and community systems has often ranged from nonexistent to erratic, though correctional psychologists would benefit from visiting (networking) with community service providers. The situation has improved somewhat with the development of programs through state hospitals that provide supervised living arrangements for such individuals. The ability to mandate medications for such individuals has also improved after *Washington v. Harper* (1990).

Studies of arrests suggest that mentally disordered individuals are likely to find their way into the criminal justice system. Sosowsky's (1980) data suggest that mental status is causally related to the increased arrest rate. Teplin (1984) looked at individuals at the point of arrest and concluded that the mentally disordered had a significantly greater chance of being arrested than non-mentally disordered persons for similar offenses. A longitudinal study of a Swedish cohort (Crocker & Hodgins, 1997) suggests that noninstitutionalized mentally retarded individuals are more likely than members of the general population to be arrested for criminal acts. Given this apparently higher arrest rate, it is reasonable to hypothesize that the number of mentally disordered individuals in jails has probably also increased. The hypothesis is difficult to test, however, because information is not collected uniformly on representative samples nor analyzed to give proper epidemiological estimates (Gibbs, 1982). Best current estimates suggest that 6% to 7% of men (Teplin, 1994; Torrey et al., 1992) and a higher percentage of women (Teplin, 1996) in jail have severe mental illness.

Steadman and Ribner (1980) found that the percentage of inmates in a county jail who had prior inpatient hospitalization increased from 9% in 1968 to 12% in 1975. Although a prevalence increase of 3% sounds like only a bit more of a nuisance, the number of individuals in county jails also increased by 225% from 1968 to 1975; thus, the 3% increase in prevalence represented a 300% increase in the actual number of offenders with a history of prior inpatient hospitalization in the study.

However, the percentage or number of offenders with prior inpatient hospitalization does not provide a clear picture of mental disorder among incarcerated offenders. Often, hospitalization may be a legal maneuver rather than the treatment modality chosen by a mental health professional. Lawyers who have not had time to prepare their cases may request a court-ordered evaluation to get their clients out of jail and give themselves more time. Psychiatric assessment may be mandated by state law for certain felonies. Lacking a solid defense, a lawyer has little to lose by sending a client to the state hospital for a 30-day evaluation and hoping that the doctors can come up with something that the defense can use. Thus, many offenders with a prior history of hospitalization may never have been hospitalized for treatment of a mental disorder.

A clearer picture of psychopathology in prison populations is provided in a study by Collins and Schlenger (1983) comparing lifetime prevalence rate of *DSM-III* psychiatric disorders among male inmates of the North Carolina Department of Correction with rates for nonoffender samples from the Epidemiological Catchment Area Program sponsored by the National Institute of Mental Health. It is not surprising that the rate of antisocial personality diagnosis (28.9%) was 6 to 14 times higher than in the other samples. Alcohol abuse/dependence (49.5%) was 2 to 3 times higher; substance abuse/dependence (18.8%) was 2 to 23 times higher; schizophrenia (1%) and schizophreniform disorders (0.2%) were only marginally higher than the rates found in the other samples. Although manic episodes (1.1%) were only slightly higher among the offenders, major depressive episodes (5.3%) were more than twice as prevalent as among a nonincarcerated sample from the same state. Only anorexia nervosa, panic disorders, and somatization disorders were reported to affect a smaller percentage of incarcerated individuals. Overall, 70% of the incarcerated sample qualified for any diagnosis. Although this is approximately twice the rate for the nonincarcerated sample, the tendency of incarcerated samples to be drawn more heavily from the lower socioeconomic strata may account for a large part of the difference.

These percentages are important because they provide one type of needs assessment for treatment services. The percentages themselves can be argued. As Collins and Schlenger (1983) note, the prevalence of antisocial personality diagnosed by *DSM-III* rules in their study is lower than that found by James, Gregory, Jones, and Rundell (1980) using *DSM-III* criteria and lower than that diagnosed by judges in Hare (1983). In addition, there are great differences in the treatability of various disorders and the impact they have on the operations of correctional systems and vice versa.

One of the reasons given for a higher rate of mental disorder in prison (Toch, Adams, & Greene, 1987) is based on the assumption of a more restricted and self-defeating response repertoire of the mentally disordered, leading to punitive sanctions and more time served on their sentences. McCorkle (1995) tested this hypothesis and found that a history of being on psychiatric medications or previously hospitalized did not predict disciplinary infraction rate in prison. Some relationship was found between currently being on medication and disciplinary infraction rate, but only for females. Further, this effect was smaller than the effect of age on disciplinary infraction rate.

It does appear that a number of mentally disordered individuals do better in the predictable, structured environment of prisons. As Toch, Adams, and Grant (1989) note, prisons do seem to have beneficial effects for some offenders. Nevertheless, anyone who has worked in corrections has numerous horror stories of the inability of particular prisoner clients to adapt to incarceration. As noted above, over 3% of the mentally disordered are housed separately; this allows some behaviors that could be considered rule infractions to be treated as symptoms instead. This factor was not taken into account by McCorkle (1995).

Asking how large a problem the mentally disordered offender is to the correctional system is much like asking how big a problem a toothache is to an individual. If viewed as a percentage of the mass of a human body, a toothache is insignificant. However, a severe toothache can significantly reduce the functioning of the whole individual. The fact that hundreds of individuals are confined together greatly increases the impact of the problems of any one person on the others. This may well account for the tendency of correctional professionals, even mental health professionals, to overestimate the prevalence of mental disorders in correctional settings.

The seriousness of an individual's problem may also be exacerbated by incarceration. The individual is separated from previously established support systems. Methods of escaping from or dealing with problems that worked for the individual in the past may not be feasible in prison. The new stresses of adapting to the prison environment are added. The individual's self-confidence and ego strength are further undermined by concrete evidence of once again being a loser. In brief, treatment of emotional disorders is needed by a proportionately greater percentage of the population and is needed more intensely in a correctional setting than anywhere else outside a psychiatric hospital.

TYPES OF TREATMENT

Diagnosis seems to interact with the characteristics of the setting to produce four types of treatment for offenders: management, maintenance, outpatient, and programs. These types are outlined in Table 22.1 but are much more vague and interdependent than described. The typology is intended primarily to conceptualize the three-way interaction of therapist, client, and system.

Brodsky (1982) provides a similar description of program models for local jails; Steadman, McCarty, and Morrisey (1986) provide a conceptual guide to developing jail mental health services. Jail services will not be discussed separately in this chapter, but much of what is discussed is applicable. Differences relate primarily to the higher incidence of mental illness and drug withdrawal in jail, the higher risk of suicide in jail, the short length of many jail stays, and the fact that many smaller jails are largely unequipped to handle mentally disordered offenders.

Table 22.1
Therapy Tasks in a Correctional Setting

	Management	Maintnance	Outpatient	Programs
Problem type	Self-mutilation/ suicide Violence Posttrauma reactions Severe situational adjustment	Psychosis Mental retardation Major affective disorder Dementia Organic brain dysfunction	Impulse controls Fear passivity Family problems Adjustment problems Social skills	Chemical dependence Sex offender Criminal behavior
Referral source	Staff referral Intake monitoring Event involvement Self-referral	Intake evaluation History Age/medical status Event involvement	Self-referral Judge/lawyer/family Assessed program need Institutional history	Volunteers Assessed need Commitment order Lawyer/family request
Precipitated by	Stress/loss of control Loss of support system Victimization Terminal illness	Decompensation Bizarre behavior Inability to cope Danger to self or others	Anxiety/stress Depressive episode Family pressure Desire to self-improve	Hits bottom/arrests Admits problem Escape situation Desire to look good
Treatment goal	Crisis resolution Self-harm prevention Symptom reduction Plan support/ treatment	Stabilization Remission Reduce deterioration Improve coping	Increase options Skills/controls Reduce cognitive distortion Stabilize emotions	Cognitive control Relapse prevention Stop offending Lifelong plan
Duration	Hours to a few days, with possible referral to outpatient program	Days to years, depending on seriousness/brittleness of condition	6–15 individual or group sessions, or indefinite aftercare	30-day intensive, 6 to 12 months ongoing aftercare
Setting	Infirmary or hospital Mental health housing Lockdown areas	Mental health housing State hospital	Clinic/office Group room Any available space	Specialized housing

Management

Management usually means crisis management. Crises may occur concurrently with, or independently of, the other three treatment tasks. In prison settings, crises most commonly occur in conjunction with marital or child custody problems, failure to gain parole or setback in appeals or other legal action, disciplinary action that the individual considers unfair, threats by fellow inmates, sexual abuse or homosexual panic, or inability to tolerate conditions of incarceration, particularly punitive segregation. Management problems tend to subside with age and adaptation to incarceration as both stress effects and disciplinary problems decrease (Zamble, 1992).

Crises may also be manufactured to create an "out" when the individual has run up gambling debts, been labeled a snitch, provoked individuals willing to resort to violence, or in some way needs help and sees weakness or futility in asking for it directly. Such crises cannot simply be dismissed as malingering as they are associated with emotional states resulting from the crises mentioned above. Transient situational crises that are trivialized or ignored often lead to escalation of maladaptive behaviors. More clear-cut malingering occurs when the individual wants a cell change, wants to move to a more comfortable setting in a mental health program, or is trying to join an associate in a particular housing unit. It is necessary for the therapist to recall that instrumental behavior is labeled malingering when others find it offensive, and coping when others approve of that manner of manipulating the system. Whether poor coping evolves from mental disorder or poor judgment, the therapeutic task is to teach appropriate coping skills. Regardless of the source of the management task, there are factors in a correctional setting that often lead to rapid escalation.

An offender is made more vulnerable to crisis by the feeling of being alone. The family may be disrupted or dysfunctional, unable to visit, or may have given up on the offender. Inmates usually do not have friends in prison; rather, they have associates. These associates are usually viewed with only slightly more trust than the correctional officers. Associates may create or exacerbate a crisis by increasing pressure to react in a way that is consistent with convict code.

The very fact that a person is known as an offender suggests poor coping mechanisms. Experiences of having gone through several agencies, therapists, and programs that never "worked" only serve to "prove" to the offender the impossibility of getting "help." This tends to lead to demands for the therapist to "do me something." If this hooks into the therapist's own power or control needs, the therapist then becomes part of the problem.

Many offenders view admission of problems, expression of feelings other than anger, and compromise as signs of weakness that invite victimization and abuse. These beliefs and experiences further shut down options for dealing with the crisis.

Mental health workers employed by the correctional facility are likely to be thought of as part of the system. This may mean that the professional is seen by offenders as being on the wrong side of the we-they dichotomy and either not caring or likely to "snitch them off to the cops." Mental health workers may also be viewed as being there for the "crazies," making contact with them stigmatizing. Such views shut the inmate off from resources for dealing with the problem.

Management of Self-Destructive Behavior

Scarred wrists are a common sight in prison. The majority of these come from gestures intended to call attention to emotional pain or intended to obtain reassignment. But it is never safe to bet that any of these actions are solely "manipulative." Ivanoff (1992) found that psychiatric history and having a model for parasuicide were the strongest predictors of parasuicide in a sample of state prison inmates.

There were 117 suicides in American prisons in 1984. This rate (26.3 per 100,000) is more than twice the U.S. population rate (12.4 per 100,000) (G. Camp & Camp, 1985). The number of suicide deaths in prisons increased to 168 in 1996, though the prison population doubled; thus, the rate has actually dropped to about 22 per 100,000 (G. Camp & Camp, 1996). This is probably attributable to better training of staff and improved protocols for suicide prevention.

Suicide has traditionally been a bigger problem in jails than in prisons, with 293 suicides in 1983 (U.S. Dept. of Justice, 1984). This has led to production of a sizable volume of information and training aids; mentioned here are only a few examples. *Suicide in Jails* (National Institute of Corrections, 1983) provides information, training materials, and forms. A videotape training aid entitled *Suicide: The Silent Signals* is also available (National Sheriffs Association, 1984). A paper by Huggins (1985) was written to provide assistance to sheriffs. The second edition of *Training Curriculum on Suicide Detection and Prevention in Jails and Lockups* (National Center on Institutions and Alternatives [NCIA], 1988) provides intake screening forms and visual aids for training. A similar document (Hayes, 1995) available through the National Institute of Corrections (NIC) provides solid legal, practical, and statistical information on suicide. A more extensive treatment of the subject is *Suicide Behind Bars: Prediction and Prevention* (Lester & Danto, 1993). The American Correctional Association and the National Commission on Correctional Health Care have both issued standards on suicide prevention. Any policy written should heed these standards.

The techniques of crisis intervention taught to most psychologists and counselors (e.g., L. Cohen, Claiborn, & Specter, 1983) are usable in corrections settings if the therapist takes the characteristics of the environment into account. First, ensure that as little positive reinforcement as possible is given for self-destructive behavior. Inmates who feel that they have nothing else to bargain with may, in effect, hold themselves hostage. If their demands are acceded to, their threats against themselves are likely to increase. However, frustration of the use of suicidal gestures as a coping mechanism has its own risks; a gruesome demonstration of the offender's determination may follow.

Several years ago, adolescents at one unit began swallowing razor blades embedded in cheese or wrapped carefully in toilet paper; the blades could be swallowed without harm but still show up clearly on X-rays. The consulting physician, seeing a life-threatening situation, performed immediate surgery. When one of the inmates was presented for the fourth time for this surgery, the physician determined that he was at greater risk from repeated incisions through the abdominal wall than from the razor blade. The inmate was locked up, given a bed pan, and told to present evidence when he passed the razor blade. Vital signs were monitored regularly, but no trip to the hospital or other extra attention was provided. Subsequent cases were treated in much the same fashion without incident. The frequency of razor blade swallowing and, with it, the risk of death or serious injury declined drastically. In the boredom and perceived oppressiveness of incarceration, some individuals will go to great, and potentially fatal, lengths to produce a change in their circumstances.

This technique of nonintervention obviously raises some ethical and legal questions. It also illustrates the tightrope that therapists walk between suppressing dangerous behavior and seeming to withhold treatment. It is all too easy to engage in treatment that seems appropriate and effective at the time, but even minor attention from the media can produce shock and outrage in the community and lure lawyers into the arena.

Offenders accurately perceive that the correctional systems operate on management by crisis. Thus, they do not hesitate to manufacture a crisis when their needs are strong enough. This is not to say that any suicide attempt by an offender can safely be dismissed as manipulative. There is often an element of excitement in gambling with death that can turn a manipulative gesture into a lethal action. The real question involved is often, Does anybody care? An answer perceived by the offender to be in the negative can lead to either genuine despair or, among younger offenders in particular, see-what-you-made-me-do demonstrations. Finally, coping skills clearly need to be addressed whenever an offender sees suicidal threats or gestures as the method of choice in dealing with any stressful situation.

A second technique is precaution: Keep individuals prone to suicide around other people; this keeps the individual from obsessing about problems and prevents the privacy needed to carry out the suicidal act. However, in a correctional setting, other inmates may provide motivation, encouragement, and actual help in carrying out a suicide attempt. Fellow inmates have been known to provide pieces of glass, sharpened metal, hoarded medications, insecticides, syringes, and other potentially lethal objects to inmates who requested them for attempting suicide. They have even been known to cover for other inmates during a suicide attempt. Many have watched with interest and called other inmates to watch a suicide attempt, making no effort to notify anyone in authority. Asked what they did when a recent "suicide" was observed hanging from a knotted sheet, cell mates indicated that they had helped by pulling on his feet.

One individual, with no record of prior suicide attempts and no suicide threats, committed suicide by hanging himself. It was later found that other new commitments had discovered that he was very fearful of being abused or used sexually by other inmates. Although the inmate was in a single cell, the others played on his fears to the point that, apparently, death seemed preferable. He was a middle-aged white male with a history of depression and alcoholism, sentenced on a drug-related crime. His suicide generally fit the pattern described in an article by Hayes (1983) on jail suicides.

As in the case just described, most jail and prison suicides occur in single cells; therefore, it is essential to ensure continuous observation and appropriate interpersonal support. The therapist should train correctional officers, counselors, chaplains, and others that deal with the suicidal offender to ensure that a consistent plan is being consistently followed.

A third technique, the no-suicide contract, is a risky business. Many offenders with antisocial characteristics tend to place heavy emphasis on giving their word. Usually, a no-suicide contract is reliable if the individual is not psychotic and the therapist can get the offender's "convict word" (the promise offenders usually give to "cops" may be part of the cops-and-robbers game and carry no real obligation for them). It is usually worthwhile to spend some time exploring what an offender's word means to him or her. The other side of this is that anything the therapist seems willing to do is likely to be interpreted by the offender as a promise. A nonjudgmental "hmmm" can be read as agreement to comply with what the offender is requesting. Nothing destroys a therapist's credibility quicker than not doing what was "promised." It is therefore imperative that the therapist have a clear understanding of the available options within the system. This must be followed by clear verbalization of what the therapist has and has not agreed to do.

There is a tendency for a novel type of suicidal gesture to be copied by other inmates. Thus, a fourth technique is to have an action plan ready for a repetition after a novel suicidal gesture. This plan needs to be developed jointly with medical, security, and administrative staff to avoid confusion and missed signals.

Because the individuals most likely to be aware of situations leading up to crisis are the jailers or correctional officers, the fifth technique is preservice and inservice training of officers to recognize and properly respond to this type of crisis. Proper anticipation and early intervention can keep most problems from growing to crisis proportions. Otherwise, officers' responses may range from ignoring what they consider to be manipulation, to trying to make jokes to get the individual to see how ridiculous the situation is, to actually offering advice about how to "do it right." One officer who was busy unpacking some cleaning supplies was asked by an inmate porter assigned to help him if the inmate could use a piece of baling twine from one of the boxes to hang himself. The officer, thinking that the inmate was joking, said he thought it would do. A few minutes later, the officer was holding up the inmate waiting for someone to untie the twine from the stair railing.

Not all management cases involve suicidal ideation. Offenders tend to have an external locus of control that is further nurtured by the authoritarian and restrictive atmosphere of correctional facilities. This results in professionals being besieged with pleas for help, many of which are manifestations of learned helplessness and the manipulative tendencies of offenders. This can easily become a trap for any professional who needs to be needed and who finds it easier and more gratifying to "fix" problems about mail, classification, or the parole department than to confront dependency, teach problem solving, and risk being confronted for being uncaring and "just like the rest of them."

Management of Violent Behavior

Mental health workers may also be called on to manage the violent, disruptive, acting-out individual. There are several subtypes of what Toch (1982) calls the DDIs (disturbed disruptive inmates). Some are clearly mentally disordered individuals in a manic or schizophrenic episode. Some tend to be limited intellectually, or at least in their repertoire of responses, and see no option other than to fight back against any limits. Some do "crazy" things to earn admiration, be left alone, mess with the guards, or for a variety of objectives that are neither clearly seen nor articulated. Some simply appear to take pleasure in disrupting the system. Regardless of cause, dysfunctional behavior is being presented for analysis and treatment.

The mentally disordered individuals can usually be handled well by clinically trained staff. There may be an element of fear in their agitation, which is exacerbated and converted to anger by orders and threats and allayed by calm reassurance that the situation is under control and the therapist is neither anxious nor afraid. Once they have been given a chance to talk over whatever precipitated the outburst and given a clear idea of what will happen next, they usually cooperate.

I was once called to a city jail where a manic individual was housed following arrest for alleged parole violation. The individual had seriously damaged the steel fixtures of his cell and was so loud and convincing in his threats that six parole officers, the city police, and transport officers from the department of correction had chosen discretion as the better part of valor. The parolee was known to have fears about being beaten and was quite good at standing off authority figures with his ferocity and tremendous strength. But after being told twice about the sequence of events he could expect and given the assurance that I would stay with him until he was returned to prison, he submitted to handcuffing and transport.

It takes some experience to recognize when it is time to talk and when it is time to step back and let security do their job. I have used (and violated) this rule of thumb: If the offender keeps me talking while making no concessions for more than 15 minutes in a cell-extraction situation, I am probably being used and should step back.

Occasionally, correctional psychologists will encounter individuals whose lack of social control and verbal skills have required physical intervention to keep them from hurting themselves or someone else. Often, these individuals have either slipped through the cracks in the mental health system or the developmental disabilities system or have been ejected from these systems as too dangerous to staff. Where do developmentally disabled persons get sent when their sexually aggressive and destructive behaviors are so extreme that they endanger staff and other clients in a residential treatment setting? Usually back to their families, who have had no success in controlling them either. After a brief stay, they tend to get arrested and come to the department of correction. In my experience, some of these "offenders" regressed to infantile tactics such as holding their breath, biting themselves, banging their arms or heads, and lying on the floor kicking and screaming. They tended to recycle an anger-producing event for hours, keeping others upset with their temper tantrums. Though these behaviors are usually self-limiting, ignoring these outbursts may not work in a setting where their behavior can produce severe agitation in others who share their confinement. One such individual developed a pattern of spitting at, throwing urine on, and physically attacking the officers assigned to meet his needs. In addition, he would scream and kick the door of his cell for much of the night, falling asleep out of exhaustion in the early morning. At some point, his screaming began to affect the mental stability of the other offenders. The officers were so angered by his abuse that they feared losing control and hurting him. At that point, "danger to self and others" takes on a new dimension. The ethical question of using medication in the absence of a treatable illness wanes in importance. The inmate slept for some hours after an injection of Thorazine and awoke calm and puzzled over why everybody had been so upset.

Inmates who "intentionally" do "crazy" things tax the resources and skills of the entire system. The inmate who forgoes personal hygiene and engages in bizarre behavior to make himself unattractive as a sex object may be indistinguishable to most officers from the chronic schizophrenic. Although correctional officers tend to be highly skilled at spotting mentally disordered behavior, effective management of instrumental "crazy" behavior may take considerable explanation and inservice training. It is also essential that the correctional psychologist work with the system to help avoid the establishment of contingencies that reinforce "crazy" behavior. An inmate who injected saliva into his foot, knowing that one of his peers lost a leg with the same technique, is definitely viewed as abnormal by officers and administration. Yet, when mental health staff talked to him, he stated that he did it because he did not want to work. Asked why he did not simply refuse to turn out to work, he replied that he did not want to get sent to punitive segregation. His past experience showed that the disciplinary report usually got lost in the urgency of responding to his medical needs. Thus, instead of going to punitive isolation, he spent a week in the hospital and two or three more weeks in the department's aftercare facility.

Security staff are justifiably nervous when dealing with inmates who are willing to use their own bodies as weapons. Mental health staff are justifiably reluctant to reinforce such behavior by removing inmates from the circumstances that they were trying to escape. Correctional officers tend to see behavior that differs from their norms as "crazy." Psychologists may see the same behavior as being manipulative and kick it back to security as a management problem in an effort not to reinforce the "crazy" behavior with attention. This creates a dilemma for security personnel, who are liable for charges of negligence or failure to protect if they ignore the "crazy" behavior. The therapist may be seen as sidestepping obligations to the system to avoid dealing with a frightening or undesirable client. In other words, management problems must be handled cooperatively; neither security nor treatment staff have the skills and resources to handle them alone.

It is easy to avoid setting up groups and programs for violent offenders. After all, "violence" is not defined as a mental disorder in *DSM-IV*. It usually appears to be a manifestation or symptom of an Axis II disorder. The toughness aspect of the violent usually precludes any interest in therapy. Past treatment has shown little consistent effect. And the offenders can hurt you. But the problem is not going away. There were marked increases in prison violence in 1994 and 1995, including homicides and prison riots and disturbances (G. Camp & Camp, 1996). There were 13,724 assaults on staff in 1996; the average number of inmate-on-staff assaults per agency has risen from 220 to 327 in the past five years. Inmate-to-inmate violence is far more prevalent, with 29,540 assaults and 70 inmate homicides in 1996 (C. Camp & Camp, 1997). The statistics on inmate-to-inmate violence probably grossly underestimate the true prevalence. Most inmates try not to report assaults for fear of making themselves the targets of further and often escalated violence.

There are increasing numbers of people making the effort to reduce violence behind bars, and more and more materials are being developed. Tate et al. (1995) provide a good review of efforts with violent juveniles. The American Correctional Association markets a program that evolved from *Cage Your Rage* (M. Cullen, 1992) that includes a leader's guide, an offender workbook in English and Spanish, and videotapes. Roth (1987) edited a book that provides an overview of assessment and various modalities of treatment of violent behavior. Sonkin (1995) provides counselors with a guide to cognitive behavior approach to treating violent individuals. Cullen and Freeman-Longo (1996) provide treatment materials applying the techniques of relapse prevention to anger control.

The traditional correctional reaction to violence is to return violence or lock the offender in a smaller, tighter cage. If psychotherapists are to make a difference, here is fertile ground.

Posttraumatic Stress Management

Cuttings and killings in prison most often center around sexual matters, gang matters, snitching, debt collection, and drug deals, or otherwise being "dis'd" (disrespected). Anyone who is dis'd and does not respond effectively is "not a man," which translates into being a potential victim. According to convict code, if you are a man and want to have respect, you have to react; more often than not, a therapist only sees the aftermath of crises generated in this fashion.

Another primary source of trauma is sexual. Being "hit on" or harassed for sexual favors can be highly traumatic. Often, this is a power play (as are most rapes) rather than an invitation to sexual satisfaction. Targets are most often young, slightly built, "pretty white boys." Aggressors tend to be black individuals who were not homosexual on the street. Most male rapes are not reported, though individuals detected in consensual sexual behavior often cry rape. This is a messy and unclear area that is too often dodged as a security or medical problem by therapists. The aftermath of rape can be devastating to self-esteem and confidence in one's own masculinity. This can lead to isolation from family and girlfriends, depression, and, in occasional instances, suicide attempts. It may be helpful to establish a protocol of interviewing any offender who has been involved in a sexual or violent incident that comes to official attention. Few offenders seek counseling after such trauma. However, a devastating psychological aftermath and a dangerous cycle of retribution may be avoided if the mental health staff team up with the medical staff in dealing with these incidents.

There has always been a need for counseling of individuals facing terminal illness. The percentage of the inmate population over age 50 has increased from 4.9% in 1990 to 6.8% in 1996. Death from natural causes, other than AIDS related, accounted for 58.8% of deaths in 1996. Another 28.6% of deaths were related to AIDS impairment of the immune system (C. Camp & Camp, 1997). Thus, counseling related to terminal illness has gained importance.

MAINTENANCE

As discussed earlier, psychosis and mental retardation appear to be somewhat more prevalent among offender populations than in the community. As in the broader community, many of these individuals are able to integrate themselves into the prison community; they may require special education and additional supervision and structure. Others cannot reach a level of adaptive behavior that allows them to be on their own in either the community or the correctional facility.

All departments of correction and the larger jails now have either mental health areas within correctional facilities, designated health service facilities, or access to forensic facilities within state hospitals. The majority view among correctional administrators, though with notable reluctance, appears to be that these problems are best handled within the secure confines of correctional facilities. McCarthy (1985) reported results of a nationwide survey of mentally ill and mentally retarded offenders in corrections. Combined statistics of reporting departments classified 6% of the total inmate population as mentally ill. However, the prevalence rates varied widely from less than 1% to 12.5% (see Brodsky, 1972). Based on the average from reporting agencies, 4.2% of inmates were in specialized facilities or programs for mental illness in 1996 (C. Camp & Camp, 1997).

Specialized facilities and programs are evolving and running into the problem of cost. *Programming for Mentally Retarded and Learning Disabled Inmates: A Guide for Correctional Administrators* provides a good overview of what is needed to meet the treatment needs of this population (Coffey, Procopiow, & Miller, 1989).

Although mentally disordered offenders represent only 6% or so of the offender population, they typically receive the bulk of the available mental health resources. Even if their adaptive behavior reaches a level allowing reintegration into the broader population, they often require extensive long-term aftercare. And some mentally disordered offenders will spend most, if not all, of their incarceration in mental health housing.

One individual with a history of schizophrenia was being taken to the county courthouse for involuntary commitment proceedings by his family. While walking down the hall in the courthouse, he broke free. He then grabbed a woman who worked in the courthouse and dragged her into an elevator. He stopped the elevator between floors and attempted to rape his captive. The man was found competent to stand trial, sentenced to 40 years, and sent to prison. Soon after his arrival, while apparently trying to flee from the voices he commonly hears, he ran from his assigned area and refused all orders to return. He backed into a corner and held several correctional officers at bay for some time. (This individual was 6 feet 9 inches tall, and his weight exceeded the scale's limit of 350 pounds.) After that and for the next eight years, this man lived in a mental health management area of the department. At no time had he been completely clear of psychosis, despite massive doses of psychotropic drugs. He had a work assignment, attended group therapy, and was generally involved in the activities of the mental health unit. He was instructed to open his mouth wide when hearing voices. He complied for a while and found that he did not hear the voices when he was gaping widely. Unfortunately, he was not willing to stay compliant with this procedure. By the terms of his behavioral contract, when the voices got to be overpowering, he would put on a headset radio turned to the maximum volume he could stand. His fellow inmates tended to be reliable about reminding him to do this and, if they doubted its efficacy, retired quickly to their rooms. He frequently incorporated staff into delusions in which they tried to hurt him or make him perform sexual acts against his will. He occasionally became loud and agitated in response to delusions and confronted staff with the fact that he was going to stop them from doing "it" to him. Once the episode was over, he was usually docile and tearful, begging for help not to be that way again. Had he not been in a specialized setting, some other offender would probably have picked the wrong moment to tease him and gotten hurt. In the mental health unit, he never hurt anyone during the term of his incarceration, which was over 15 years, though he definitely made several staff and offenders nervous. He was later released, stayed on his medication, held a job, lived with his family, and adjusted to the community. Unfortunately, he died from heat stroke related probably to his job and side effects of his medication.

The techniques that would be used in a Veterans Administration or state hospital inpatient setting are largely applicable to a mental health unit within a correctional setting. However, there are some differences related to the setting and others related to the fact that the patients are also offenders.

Any individual in a setting that is, by definition, punishing can be expected to try to escape that setting. Many inmates request placement in a mental health unit, though most do not get there. Once placed in a mental health unit, nobody in his or her "right mind" would want to leave its relative safety, quiet, and sanity to be with normal inmates in a more oppressive setting. Thus, some patients pretend to work on their problems to stay in the unit but are careful to not show rapid improvement (also to stay in the unit). The perceived desirability of being in a mental health unit also creates problems for staff in screening out malingerers. One individual had been told in county jail that being "crazy" or "queer" would cause him to be placed in housing apart from the other inmates. He was well coached by another offender who had spent much of his time in mental health units and had firsthand knowledge of what symptoms impressed the "shrinks." This particular inmate took no chances and claimed to be both "queer" and "crazy." But he overplayed the crazy and was put on a sizable dose of a neuroleptic, which had the effect of making him think that he really was going crazy. In a panic, he admitted the whole scheme.

Malingering is usually detectable either because the individual gets carried away with the act and overplays the role, or because the individual gets tired of maintaining the role. However, some inmates are highly skilled in playing mentally ill (Yochelson & Samenow, 1976). Cavanaugh and Rogers (1984) provide some techniques for identifying these inmates. The most difficult manipulation to detect is that presented by inmates who have a real psychological disorder and have learned to continue or exaggerate their symptoms for secondary gain.

The second problem relating to the setting has to do with the fact that mentally disordered individuals are confined with offenders who model antisocial behaviors. Most mentally disordered offenders already have some degree of personality disorder, which may be minimal during an acute episode of psychopathology but emerge as the individual is stabilized. Those who have not previously shown antisocial personality characteristics see those behaviors apparently reinforced with pleasures and possessions. It does not take long for them to model and adopt the manipulative, sexual, and aggressive behaviors.

The third problem is that the mental health unit is often a small part of a much larger institutional system. Necessarily, the needs of the larger unit dictate schedules such as meals, movie availability, pill calls, counts, doctor and dental call, and so on. Shared facilities such as infirmaries, gyms, and mess halls may not be available at desirable times. Movement may be limited by other activities going on in the larger unit. Security concerns may become acute when inmates of different security levels are mixed or when a particularly high-security-risk inmate is seen as being in need of inpatient treatment. These problems can usually be resolved or other options developed with the cooperation of the warden but must be considered in setting up any programming.

Fourth, correctional settings often require the management of an individual for years rather than allowing for transition to another support system when the therapist and client believe the client is ready. It is usually not feasible or at least not responsible to drop inmates from treatment or urge them to find another therapist. Failures and dropouts remain to haunt the therapist on a daily basis.

The long-term presence of many of these clients raises issues of transference and countertransference to breadths and intensities that are seldom otherwise encountered outside of psychoanalysis proper. This creates a burnout danger for the therapist, who takes on a task that almost amounts to reparenting or, at least, involves long-term services to a highly demanding and sometimes psychologically primitive population. There is also a potential for physical danger as the therapist becomes incorporated into delusional systems of individuals with a record of hurting others. One female inmate with a history of chronic schizophrenia became aware of feeling "different." She hypothesized that these strange feelings were drug induced and searched her body for needle marks. When she found what she interpreted to be needle marks and was unaware of having been given an injection, she concluded that she was being injected while she slept. She began staying awake several days at a stretch, but would inevitably succumb to sleep. Upon awakening, she always found more needle marks. She concluded that I, her therapist, was living in a nearby closet and sneaking out to inject her whenever she fell asleep. She filed a cogent writ that was accepted for trial by the federal court. Ultimately, her court-appointed attorney withdrew, complaining that the offender was crazy. She was sent to the state hospital for one day for staffing and medication review.

The problems of inclusion in delusional systems, transference, and counter-transference tend to be insidious and are often recognized only in hindsight, yet there are several methods for prevention. A staffing committee rather than the individual therapist should make or at least confirm treatment decisions. Community meetings of the offenders and staff involved in residential treatment can expose covert relationships among the staff and the offenders, or between staff and individual offenders. The use of outside therapists to consult, review programs, sit on staffings, do quality assurance, and generally be involved also serves to maintain proper perspective.

Finally, like most institutions, correctional facilities operate on rules and expectations of consistent treatment. It becomes problematic at best to deal with offenders who do not fit the mold. If the policy of the department is that all offenders who are able to work do so, should offenders housed in a mental health unit be required to work? If a mentally disordered offender runs for the fence, should the officer in the tower shoot? One offender being strip-searched prior to transport to a facility with a mental health unit was asked to "bend over and spread 'em." He apparently "goosed" himself in the process and ran screaming, naked, out a door immediately under a gun tower. The officer in the tower tracked the inmate with his weapon, but quickly concluded that because the inmate was running in circles, he was not attempting to escape.

If a "crazy" breaks a rule in the hall, should the correctional officer write a disciplinary report? Correctional officers, unless they have had specialized training and experience, have difficulty responding normally to the abnormal. Similarly, psychologists have difficulty helping their clients adapt to a system that challenges their ethics and expectations about how people should be treated (for a discussion of ethical issues, see Brodsky, 1980; for a discussion of legal issues, see F. Cohen, 1985; for a discussion of applicable standards, see F. Cohen & Griset, 1985). When the mental health unit was moved to a new parent unit, a number of officers long assigned to the parent unit avoided the area unless ordered to enter it. Officers who worked for mental health were asked, "How can you work with them?" Inmates who had moved out of a mentally disordered state and had begun limit testing were "cut extra slack" by sympathetic officers. Generally, the mental health inmates were seen, in turn, as unpredictable and dangerous or as incompetent and not to be held responsible. This set of issues is one of the more difficult to resolve because the cognitive impairment of the inmate fluctuates, thus altering what can reasonably be expected from him or her. Even professional staff have problems determining levels of control and responsibility as inmates learn to use their symptoms to avoid responsibility for their actions.

The issue of expectations and rules is further complicated by the interactions of the custody and treatment environments. The psychologist may see the prison environment as not only failing to correct but, in many cases, doing harm; the harshness and oppressiveness may be seen as meeting the needs of the staff but having little to do with correcting inmates. On the other hand, security staff may see the treatment environment as overly permissive, undermining inmates with pity instead of making them get on with life, or as irrelevant to the real problems of "convicts"; some members of security staff may even see treatment as undermining the authority of officers and the order of the institution.

The conflict here is powerful and attractive to cynics. It is easy to say, Therapy is impossible in such a punitive environment. This makes it easy to form an unhelpful psychological alliance with prisoners around their perceived mistreatment. Therapists, being human, inevitably get hooked by this conflict from time to time. At such times, it may help the therapist to recall the levels of brutality and destruction that have occurred when the system has broken down (e.g., Attica, New Mexico Penitentiary) and look for ways to improve rather than undermine it. All correctional psychologists should receive security training and should provide correctional officers training related to managing human behavior.

The inequities and negative aspects of the system, both real and imagined, can and should be brought into treatment. It is possible to use misperceptions to teach reality-based thinking and to use real unfairness to teach frustration tolerance and empathy for victims. Some therapists in private practice seek "creative anxiety" to move their patients. Correctional psychologists may find this task already done for them.

OUTPATIENT PSYCHOTHERAPY

Outpatient therapy is an elective rather than a required service in most correctional settings. As long as crisis management keeps incidents from happening that would produce liability or bad press for the system, as long as security staff do not have to deal with the mentally ill and retarded offenders, and as long as there are some programs that betoken rehabilitation opportunities, there may be little or no administrative emphasis placed on treatment services for the bulk of the offender population (Lombardo, 1985). This leaves the field fairly clear to offer elective treatment and to be eclectic in approach—the very real limit being imposed by a lack of staff resources.

There is no point in listing all of the approaches. Suffice it to say that they have run the gamut from assertiveness training to Zen. Each approach has claimed some measure of success. Usually, this success has been in terms of improvement on some psychometric device or adaptation to incarceration rather than lasting changes in socially significant behavior. Most approaches have been attacked: the more humanistic for coddling criminals, the more behavior-oriented for brainwashing or depriving offenders of constitutional rights. Attempts have been made to stamp them all null and void under the "nothing works" blanket (Martinson, Lipton, & Wilks, 1975).

It is, in fact, easy to believe that nothing works when the therapist daily encounters offenders who have not benefited from treatment. In mental health centers and private practice, a therapist can at least fantasize that the client who dropped out or was terminated has undergone a healthy transformation. In a correctional setting, the failures tend to stay on while the successes leave and get on with their lives. Nor does the therapist in a correctional setting have the opportunity to select cases, as therapists do in other settings. Mental health centers and private practitioners can transfer responsibility for nontreatment, premature terminations, and failures with a mere wave of the not-motivated-for-treatment wand, and the miscreant disappears. The therapist in a correctional setting may refuse to treat or may terminate treatment because of the client's behavior, and still be held responsible for the treatment of all those whom the court has seen fit to incarcerate.

There are also factors that can work to the advantage of the therapist: correctional clients by virtue of their sentences have "time" to put into treatment; environmental factors are mostly known and maintained at an unusually stable level; external observation and reporting are system requirements; and the potential for follow-up is high. In brief, correctional facilities offer the possibility of greatly expanding the frontiers of psychotherapy, provided that the trailblazers are a hardy enough breed to survive severe trials.

Therapy in a correctional setting encounters much the same problems that therapy encounters in any setting. Some problems are more prevalent; most problems are intensified, echoing off the walls. Even so, therapy seems to work as well (Gendreau, 1996) and fail as sadly in prison as it does anywhere else. The mistakes are just more difficult to keep buried.

PROGRAMS

Programs have increasingly become the focus of treatment efforts in corrections. Regardless of the focus, programs have a number of advantages that seem to raise the chances of success over those seen in outpatient therapy. Programs provide opportunities for many more contact hours than would be feasible in outpatient treatment. Alcohol and drug programs originally adopted the community model of 28-day intensive treatment programs. This has been found to be insufficient, and emphasis is shifting toward treatment lasting six months to a year (Wexler, Falkin, & Lipton, 1990). Programs for sex offenders commonly are more than a year in duration. Therapeutic communities, treating personality disorder, usually involve the individual for more than six months and up to several years. Treatment programs are usually designed around separation from the general population. This simultaneously lessens the impact of the inmate culture and sets up an environment that offers psychological protection and permission to try new behaviors, along with positive role models.

Few programs have sufficient free-world staff. Many rely to varying degrees on inmate peer counselors. These individuals do not generate the automatic resistance that authority figures do. They are usually also adept at translating psychobabble into a language that speaks to the needs of offenders. They often have the zeal and energy of the new convert and can greatly extend the effectiveness of a therapist. At the same time, they are no more immune from corruption or abuse of power than anyone else and require careful supervision.

Programs are costly, both in terms of dollars and in terms of stress on the correctional system. That, together with the amount of staff time invested in programs, has usually led to clear mission statements and task definition. This makes it likely that the therapist and the clients, having plans and blueprints, can build a better house together than by going where the mood takes them.

Therapy programs tend to process a group of people through emotionally loaded shared experiences toward a common goal. This may produce a powerful conversion-like experience and a vehement renunciation of old deviant or self-destructive behaviors. However, the types of behaviors—drug use, deviant sex, and the constellation of antisocial personality behaviors—have such habit strength and such powerful reinforcers tied to them that short-term treatment can be expected to have only short-term effects. Treatment effects are likely to be sustained only if the individual participates in ongoing support groups, which may require a waiver of the rules limiting contacts among parolees.

The difficulties attendant in operating programs in a correctional setting are in proportion to their potential for producing real and relevant change. A program usually has the irritant effect in a correctional system that a foreign substance has in the human body. The fact that a program is good does not guarantee its success or even its survival. The following are some considerations that need to be taken into account for a program to continue to function.

It helps if the program is mandated by the federal court, state law, or strongly felt administrative needs. Programs are costly in terms of space, staff resources, and offender time. In a period of prison overcrowding, limited budgets, and doubt and cynicism about the efficacy of treatment, it is much easier to close a program than to start or expand one.

Access to offenders needs to be built into the classification system of the facility. "Good convicts" are much in demand for institutional needs. "Screwups" (jargon modified somewhat) are seen as needing straightening out (i.e., through punishment and hard work), not some soft assignment to a treatment unit. Many offenders do not have sentences long enough to allow them to complete treatment; others have sentences so long that the opportunity for them to apply some types of treatment will be years in coming.

There is a tendency for prison-based programs to get "dirty." Individuals in programs are usually involved in them over a substantial period of time. It is to be expected that, once offenders learn the program, they will try to manipulate it to their own ends and inject their value system into it. Periodic house cleanings are required to ensure that the program stays on track and that the participants stay on task. The changes that lead to a program's getting dirty tend to be mild and insidious, thus it usually requires a therapist not connected with the day-to-day operations to detect them.

Programs tend to have two major effects on staff: they provide excellent training in therapy, and they produce burnout in record time. Wherever possible, programs should provide for staff rotation or relief. Staff rotation can provide quality therapists for the other treatment areas; staff relief can be built in either by having other therapists who can cover or by closing down the program periodically to allow brief sabbaticals. These shutdown periods can be used to provide staff training and rejuvenation and allow time for program evaluation and changes.

The program must be carefully explained to correctional staff. Nobody questions the number of years it takes to earn a high school diploma or learn a professional skill, but immediate results are expected of treatment programs. Officers become suspicious of the length of time offenders are expected to stay in the program. In addition, the type of open, trusting relationship considered by therapists to form the basis for treatment is antithetical to what officers have been taught about handling "convicts." The therapist who fails to address these and similar concerns is likely to spend more time trying to overcome obstacles than doing treatment.

Public relations is essential. The political entity whose resources enable the programs to exist needs to be told frequently about the good being done by the program. It is much easier politically to allocate resources for children and the elderly than for "convicts." Other agents of the criminal justice system need accurate information about the program; these are the individuals who refer the clients, explain to offenders and their families what is going to happen in prison, and make decisions about sentencing, revocation of parole, probation, and the handling of offenders in general. Judges who hear about a program may assume that they can sentence offenders to it. Parole boards may decide to withhold parole pending completion of a program by an offender who is unmotivated or inappropriate for the program.

Three types of programs have seen fairly wide use with offenders. These are sex offender treatment, substance abuse treatment, and therapeutic communities for treating personality disorders.

Sex Offender Treatment

Sex offenders make up about 11% of the nation's prison population (Corrections Compendium, 1996a). Although this includes a grab bag of offender types, including individuals whose antisocial behavior opportunistically includes sex crimes and individuals with diagnosable paraphilias, the focus has been on pedophiles who tend to compulsively reoffend and constitute a major threat to the children of this country. There is evidence that the newer, better programs can significantly reduce recidivism and, more important, undetected reoffense (Lotke, 1996).

Sex offender program materials are available for adolescents (Kahn, 1996; Steen, 1993) and for adult offenders (Freeman-Longo & Bays, 1988; Freeman-Longo, Bays, & Bear, 1996). Dynamics of sex offending are discussed by Groth and Birnbaum (1979). Assessment and treatment strategies are presented in a book edited by Greer and Stuart (1983). Sex offender treatment, though remaining controversial (Becker & Hunter, 1992; Furby, Weinrott, & Blackshaw, 1989; Rice, Quinsey, & Harris, 1991), has shown major gains both in program numbers and treatment techniques in the past ten years. *Criminal Justice and Behavior* has dedicated two volumes to sex offender treatment (Milner, 1992; Prentky, 1994) that provide a good starting point for looking at the issues. A recent article by one of the pioneers of sex offender treatment (Marshall, 1996) provides a review of the literature and analysis of the history, current status, and future directions for sex offender treatment. The Association for the Treatment of Sexual Abusers (ATSA, P.O. Box 866, Lake Oswego, OR 97034-0140) has developed standards for practice, offers training, and tracks the evolution of the field.

Therapists who are not involved in treating paraphilias may gain considerable insight into the needs of offenders, the impact of various types of programming, the necessary duration of treatment, and reasonable expectations of change from examining the development of sex offender treatment. The successful programs appear to be those that emphasize cognitive behavioral treatment, counter cognitive distortions with victim empathy, and place a strong emphasis on relapse prevention (Laws, 1989). As in any treatment in which recovery is a process and cure is unlikely, aftercare is essential.

Chemical Dependency

Alcohol and drug treatment was brought to offender populations by Alcoholics Anonymous years before much other treatment was available, in response to a recognized need of a disproportionate number of the chemically dependent within correctional settings (U.S. Dept. of Justice, 1983a, 1983b). For years, AA was *the* correctional aftercare resource in most communities, occasionally to the detriment of AA. Regular members have stayed away out of nervousness about the number of ex-cons present at meetings; ex-offenders present to meet parole requirements are met with an environment that poisons the 12-step process.

Twelve-step programs as a required component of treatment or aftercare have been attacked in recent years *(Kerr v. Farrey)*. Though the AA language of "higher power" is intended to be theologically neutral, the spiritual component of the program is seen to be unconstitutional for the same reasons as is school prayer. This has certainly not sounded the death knell for 12-step programs, just the necessity of making sure that participation is voluntary and that the spiritual aspect is distinguished from religion. One of the elements of AA that is certainly worth emphasizing in any offender treatment is the value of support groups and mentoring (in AA terms, a sponsor). It is also my opinion that lasting change occurs from the inside; without the spiritual commitment, the will to work the program is not likely to be sustained.

The past decade has seen the proliferation of program models and material for chemical dependency treatment that have caught the attention of various agencies of the federal government. The Federal Bureau of Prisons (BOP) saw 61% of its offenders incarcerated for drug-related crimes in 1995. Lipton (1995) tapped the expertise of BOP staff to assemble a multivolume *Drug Abuse Treatment Handbook* (1994). The Substance Abuse and Mental Health Services Administration (SAMHSA) of the U.S. Department of Health and Human Services publishes a treatment-improvement protocol series, TIP, which includes *Planning for Alcohol and Other Drug Abuse Treatment for Adults in the Criminal Justice System* (TIP 17, 1995). The U.S. Department of Justice issued a research report titled *The Effectiveness of Treatment for Drug Abusers under Criminal Justice Supervision* (Lipton, 1995), which describes a number of programs and treatment approaches.

Private companies have also seen a vein worth mining. Gorski (1995) has elaborated relapse prevention and offers state-of-the-art training and material through the CENAPS Corporation (1850 Dixie Hwy., Homewood, IL 60430). Hazelden Publishing and Education (P.O. Box 176, Center City, MN 55012-0176) has developed *Design for Living,* a curriculum with videos and support material for treating chemical dependence in criminal justice settings. Kindred Publishing (1216 State St., Suite 401, Santa Barbara, CA 93101) offers videos and workbooks such as *The Price of Freedom Is Living Free.* OPEN Inc. publishes a program (Ingraham, Bell, & Rollo, 1991) that provides a hard-hitting starting point for treatment programs. The American Psychiatric Association has also published materials (Jaffe, 1993) that integrate psychological issues with the 12-step approach. Brown (1985) provides excellent information for psychotherapists working with alcoholics. An evaluation study of the Stay'n Out therapeutic community (Wexler et al., 1990) suggests that treatment for chemical dependence in a therapeutic community format can have a significant effect on parole outcome. Wexler and his associates have gathered information on chemical dependency programs over a number of years (for information: Center for Therapeutic Community Research, National Development and Research Institutes Inc., San Diego, CA). The above is intended as a point of entry in a search for program models and materials. The list is a sampler, neither inclusive nor critically reviewed. Therapists would be well advised to sample broadly and view treatment from as many perspectives as possible.

Personality Disorders

Therapeutic communities of various sorts have been tried in prison settings. Some have grown out of the work of Maxwell Jones, which has been evolving since 1947 (Jones, 1976). Asklepion communities have combined techniques evolved in Synanon drug treatment with transactional analysis, behavior modification, and others. Except for Maxwell Jones's own community, some therapeutic communities have lasted about five years (e.g., Groder's Asklepion Community at Marion, The Chino experiment; Briggs, 1980) or have become integrated into the larger correctional systems and continued there.

A therapist wishing to utilize the therapeutic community format will find few written materials to help. Most documentation has been provided by Maxwell Jones (1976, 1979) and does not portray work with offenders in correctional settings. The other body of literature (DeLeon & Beschner, 1976) relates largely to drug rehabilitation programs. This should not be viewed as minimizing the potential effectiveness of therapeutic communities. There are a sizable number of success stories from among antisocial personalities. The therapeutic community is probably the most effective modality for treating personality disorders. It is also one of the most difficult types of programs to sustain (Levinson, 1980).

As noted above, chemical dependency treatment has moved increasingly toward modified therapeutic communities. Hopefully, therapeutic communities can be developed that are focused on cognitive behavior therapy dealing with thought distortions and building relapse prevention for inmates with antisocial personality.

THERAPISTS

I have told all applicants for therapist positions in my department that they would have to work at least six months before they could expect to become effective, but if they stayed in the system for three years, they might find themselves "getting crazy." If they stayed for much longer, they might find themselves becoming institutionalized. This was based on my own experience and was usually laughed off by new staff. However, those staff members who have stayed, and many who have left, indicated that what they had taken as a joke turned out to be a fairly accurate prediction. Therapists who have remained and become effective share some common characteristics. Therapists most likely to succeed in therapy with offenders are those who can empathize without sympathy, confront without demeaning, care without carrying, direct without controlling, see manipulation as a poor coping strategy rather than a personal assault, find satisfaction in erratic progress toward limited and clearly defined goals, tolerate the ambiguities and conflicts of the setting, and accept their own limits.

Therapists who sympathize will find no shortage of offenders who love them and need a great deal of their time. Nor will they find any shortage of life events among the offender population deserving of their sympathy. They will receive much flattery and many demands for their services. In the long run, they will find themselves being used up, working *instead of* rather than *with* the offender, feeling used, being disappointed, and becoming angry with their clients.

Therapists who have difficulty confronting will be seen as sympathetic and receive much the same payoffs as just described. Therapists who confront in anger or with put-downs may effectively shape the way the offender interacts with the therapist and the group. However, the change that occurs may not be generalizable progress. For some offenders, confrontive therapy may simply represent a new external locus of control; unless it is followed by techniques for developing internal controls and learning and practicing prosocial behaviors, what it does accomplish may be lost. Angry, demeaning confrontation may have its place, like the proverbial two-by-four to get the mule's attention. But it is a poor mule trainer who does not know when to put down the two-by-four.

Caring is likely to be seen by the offender as a weakness that makes a person a good mark for a con. The natural response of most offenders to caring is, Do me something, prove that you really care. A demonstration of good faith is likely to lead to demands for further demonstrations. Rescue is a severe temptation in a correctional setting, as relatively solvable problems take on epic proportions and offer the therapist an easy route to heroic stature. The therapist who sees rescue as necessary should remember to throw a line rather than a lifeboat and avoid crushing the drowning victim.

The therapist who refuses to be directive with offender clients may never progress beyond the level of small talk or silence. Verbal interaction was more likely used in the offender's past to ask for things, than in self-disclosure, problem solving, or conflict resolution. The offender is likely to see the purpose of talking about problems as an effort to find out who is to blame. On the other hand, direction must take the shape of coaching, not controlling. Many offenders have no desire to take responsibility for their lives and would be only too happy to give control to the therapist. The best outcome of giving control over to the therapist is likely to be that the offender has someone new to blame for how screwed up things are.

In a setting in which one has no power, one is going to look for the nearest outlet and attempt to plug into it. Offenders can be counted on to attempt to manipulate the therapist to do the things they lack the energy or perceived power to do for themselves. This is not only normative behavior for a correctional setting, it is necessary for survival. The therapist can monitor this by checking what feelings are being hooked, what beliefs are being played to, and what obligations generate resentments. It may be appropriate to pull the plug. However, if the therapist is close to being as effective a manipulator as the offender, it may be feasible to bill for the power. It usually only wastes energy to get angry over manipulation, although at times it may work well to act angry.

OFFENDERS

There are characteristics in any offender groups that lend themselves to the therapy process. Therapy may proceed efficiently and effectively if the therapist understands these characteristics and how to make them work for the therapeutic process.

A free-world person seeks therapy to alleviate emotional distress, to learn to control a troublesome behavior, to deal with conflicts in a relationship, to straighten out confusion and misperceptions, and for a variety of other problems. The offender usually seeks therapy to avoid or escape the external forces of society's reaction to the offensive behavior. Therapists often think that therapy can only be effective if the person volunteers for treatment and genuinely wants to change. Actually, all therapy is probably coerced by internal discomfort, family discomfort, or societal discomfort with some set of behaviors. The fact that the leverage for treatment for offenders is external more often than not makes it no less useful as a starting point. Horses do sometimes drink when led to water. "Not motivated for treatment" is more often a therapist's excuse than a real reason for not treating an offender.

The majority of offenders have written off school early in their academic careers. Although the average claimed education level of offenders entering the Arkansas Department of Correction in 1996 was eighth to eleventh grade, depending on local pressure to stay in school, academic attainment as measured by achievement tests was more likely to be sixth or seventh grade. Over a third of the offenders coming into many departments of correction are functionally illiterate (Wilson & Herrnstein, 1985). Thus, didactic techniques are likely to be written off as "just words," unless activities, participation, role playing, and the like are built into the lessons. Pretraining can also be helpful in teaching these individuals to use therapy services effectively (Hilkey, Wilhelm, & Horne, 1982). Mentoring or tutoring is often used in programs to help the less skilled participants and to get the more skilled participants to learn by teaching.

Many offenders have great need for excitement and drama in their lives. These individuals can often be hooked by psychodrama (Schranski & Harvey,

1983) and confrontive therapies (Dies & Hess, 1971). Much energy can be directed into and appropriately released through role play. But unless these are properly planned and directed toward clear goals, they tend to become entertaining pastimes with little therapeutic gain.

Many offenders lack self-discipline and frustration tolerance; they want to see immediate results and may quickly lose interest in programs that require them to practice on their own. Thus, relaxation techniques, self-hypnosis, and meditation may produce dramatic effects initially but be dropped as the newness wears off. Therefore, it is usually necessary to build in a support group, strengthening or feedback sessions, or some other method of sustaining interest.

Offenders are often astute observers who are quick to see the games, faults, and weaknesses of others. They may be much quicker to identify some negative behavior patterns than a trained therapist. Thus, group therapy tends to be the modality of choice. Carefully supervised peer counselors may develop better therapy skills in dealing with offender clients than the supervising therapist.

These skills as astute social observers can also become liabilities. Most offenders have long histories of finding fault with others, which they use to justify their own behavior or to shift attention from their own misdeeds. These skills can also be used to find the vulnerabilities of therapists and become their ego support and reality check. It is crucial that therapists check their relationships and perspectives frequently to ensure that they are still seeing through their own eyes.

Many offenders, despite some highly romanticized and largely fictional tales, have a history of poor relationships. The interaction usually starts off with high intensity and crashes when the other person finally recognizes that his or her role is more that of a victim than a partner in a relationship. The offender then feels betrayed and concludes that people are "no damn good." This pattern then transfers to therapy but can be modulated somewhat by damping the intensity of the highs and lows. This is difficult when the therapist is alternately invited to be a hero, a punisher, and a righteously angered victim.

Cognitive distortions common to offenders act as land mines in the treatment field. A good general source for exploring these is the two-volume set of books by Yochelson and Samenow (1976). Samenow and Bussard (1994) have published a guide and workbook with accompanying videos. These materials are brief enough to use in an outpatient program and meaty enough to be a module in a more extended treatment program. *The Criminal Lifestyle* (Walters, 1990) provides an experienced practitioner's insight into offender dynamics.

A more detailed picture of the individual offender can often be developed from reviewing facility records such as disciplinary reports and seeking reality-based information from the staff who work with the offender on a daily basis. Many correctional officers hesitate to share their opinions and observations with "professionals," but a little mining of these resources is usually well worth the effort.

Usually, when confronted about a particular action, offenders do not know why they did it, or they indicate that it was the fault of the victim, a third party, or a psychoactive drug. Wherever the causes of criminal behavior are to be found, they are usually not in the explanations offered by offenders.

Similarly, having an offender recount past history, while often moving enough to be the basis of a soap opera, may provide little more than an opportunity for the offender to control the session.

CORRECTIONAL ENVIRONMENT

The correctional environment is, in some ways, a reflection of the offender. Planning occurs, but the system is mostly reactive. It has a strong tendency to victimize all who come into contact with it, staff and offender alike, with an almost total lack of empathy. Its goals, other than security, are usually unclear and often conflicting. Its means can be self-defeating. It sometimes creates high drama and excitement as the staff play cops to the offenders' robbers. And the correctional system, like the offenders it holds, usually gets public notice only by "messing up."

The prison often seems an alien, frightening, and hostile environment to newly arrived treatment staff, just as it does to new commitments. On the other hand, the injection of treatment staff, in many systems by court order, has probably been equally traumatic for some correctional systems. The tension between security and treatment generates a dialectic that ultimately benefits both systems, achieving a balance between support and opportunities for rehabilitation on the one hand, and security and discipline on the other.

Corrections departments usually operate on paramilitary models with sergeants, lieutenants, a chain of command, and the assumption of absolute loyalty and blind obedience. Correctional officers tend to assume that psychologists are naïve and unaware of the nature of offenders, likely to believe any allegation against them that an offender makes, and likely to take the offender's side in we-they controversies. The offender, on the other hand, knows who pays the psychologist's salary and may see the therapist as just another part of the system that must be avoided or manipulated. The psychologist must avoid overidentification with either side of we-they controversies, while remaining acceptable to both. This often requires clear, firm, and frequent communication as to the roles (and there are multiple roles) the psychologist is prepared to play in a correctional system.

Zimbardo's classic experiment in setting up a mock prison (Zimbardo, Haney, Banks, & Jaffe, 1975) gives some insight into the effects that pronounced differences in power have on people in a prison environment. The only analogues of such discrepancies in power seem to be found in the parent-child and master-slave relationships. These levels of paternalism and authoritarianism may not be desirable, but they are real and must be taken into consideration. This may require that the offender be taught social discrimination skills along with any other new skills. The offender who tries assertiveness training with an officer in the hall or problem-solving skills with the classification committee may be in for a difficult time.

The powerlessness of the offenders exists only in a formal, positional-power sense. The psychological power of the offender culture must be reckoned with by any therapist who hopes to facilitate changes for individuals. Security staff manage behavior largely by focusing on rule violations and removing rein-forcers, usually for a set period of time, during which positive behavior on the part of the offender cannot earn them back. Those items and behaviors that are positive reinforcers but are not guaranteed by law or policy are more likely to be dispensed by inmates than staff. Thus, for many offenders, the influence of the inmate culture may outweigh that wielded by the staff. The therapist may need to inoculate the client to resist the temptations of the inmate culture and persist in the face of ridicule, scorn, or negative attitudes of peers.

Corrections departments generally remove an offender's right to privacy along with the offender's clothing at the point of intake. Most psychologists be-lieve that therapy requires a modicum of privacy, though privacy may be more a luxury than a necessity at times. Ethics do require that an offender be told the limits of confidentiality that can be maintained in a correctional environment; usually, these include the duty to warn of planned or threatened actions that could harm self or others. In a group setting, there is often one member who will put other members' business "on the street." Most offenders who have been around know this already, and frank discussion of the problems of confidential-ity may support rather than limit openness. For some offenders, confidentiality may most clearly be conceptualized in terms of respect and their feelings about snitching.

A more important issue in confidentiality is the degree to which the actions of the therapist affect the liberty interests of the offenders. Often, offenders want the fact that they have been in treatment to go into their records, hoping that the parole board will be duly impressed by their seeking rehabilitation. Other offenders may feel stigmatized by the same treatment. Even more crucial are the psychological assessments that are done at various times during incar-ceration. Ethics require that the offenders be informed of the purpose and in-tended distribution of such assessments and their right to refuse assessment.

THE SYSTEM AS THE CLIENT

Monahan (1980) asks an astute question in the title of the volume he edited: Who is the client? It seems plausible that the therapist may ultimately do more good by helping the system become more effective than by helping the offender deal with the system. Several factors should be considered before taking on the system as a client.

Efforts to change the system should be kept separate from therapy. The of-fender may believe that the psychologist is allies with him against the system, setting up a let's-you-and-him-fight situation. At the same time, the therapist may be seen by the administration as a loose cannon or not a team player, or as choosing sides. It becomes very difficult to improve a system that views one with distrust. There is an old maxim in prison systems, If you can't get the man, get his inmate, that can lead to disciplinary action, undesirable reassignment, and the like, for inmates with whom the therapist is working.

Efforts to change the system should not be undertaken unless both the as-pect needing change and the direction of the change are clear. The therapist may need to spend a good deal of time diagnosing the problems before under-taking to "fix" them. "Facts," whether presented by staff or offenders, tend to be better reflections of those individuals' perceptions and expectations than re-ality. Never assume the first version you hear accurately portrays the situation; situations are usually much more ambiguous than they first appear. If easy fixes were available, there would be no problem to solve. Affixing blame fixes nothing.

Offenders and corrections staff tend to see themselves as highly dissimilar, and their differences often get so polarized that no resolution seems possible. The therapist who chooses sides only serves to heighten the conflict. All par-ties in corrections—inmates, officers, and even treatment staff—tend to wear gray hats. It is possible to empathize with all of them and work with the sys-tem as one would with a troubled family.

Efforts to change the system should follow good psychological techniques. In a setting where the dominant feeling is anger, it is easy to give rein to righteous indignation and condemnation. This is useful with the system about as often as it is with an individual client. The therapist who tries to punish the system for punishing the offender will seldom find the method to be corrective. The thera-pist who is willing to participate fully in an imperfect system and model posi-tive methods of dealing with people and problems can have a therapeutic impact considerably broader than his or her caseload alone. An effective thera-pist is quickly recognized by administrators and correctional officers as a pow-erful resource and can exercise considerable leverage in changing the system. A therapist seen as ineffective or undermining the safety and good order will be shut out of essential communication loops, and not last long in isolation.

There are also expectations of omniscience that systems tend to place on cor-rectional psychologists: Is it safe to move this offender to a lower security level within the institution? Is this offender that we are considering for parole safe to be back in society? The area of risk prediction is evolving (Monahan & Stead-man, 1994; Webster, Harris, Rice, Corimer, & Qinsey, 1994). Some of the best work has been done in Canada with the L-SIR (Andrews & Bonta, 1995). But it is still wise to "Just Say, No" to invitations to predict the future behavior of indi-viduals with Axis II diagnoses. If addressing the question cannot be avoided, it may be necessary to do the hedging in which mental health professionals are so well trained. It is also wise to try to shift the responsibility for competency eval-uations outside the jail or prison. Competency to be executed can become a real ethical and practical issue for a therapist whose professional life is "in the back" (of the facility, where offenders are housed).

DEFINING SUCCESS

Those who indicate that therapy with personality disorders usually fails often neglect to indicate the criteria for success. If failure is defined as failure to re-structure an individual's personality, then certainly psychotherapy, as it is legally and ethically practiced, must fail. Anyone who has ever tried to lose weight can attest to failures to restructure even this well-defined, circumscribed behavior. Eating and drinking behaviors, having their built-in reinforcers, may be appropriate models for many of the behaviors that characterize the antisocial personality. It is patently absurd to say, A house can't be built; I know because I tried all day and didn't build one. Success in any task requires understanding what the task is, selecting proper tools, and using them correctly over a period sufficient to accomplish specified goals.

The benchmark in corrections is the recidivism statistic. It is at best a poor standard in a society where fewer than 1% of illegal acts result in incarceration. But it is the political reality that determines funding and the standard against which the desirability of programs is measured. Thus, all therapists are to some degree held accountable for what their treatments contribute to the offender's probability of staying out of prison. Recidivism is usually measured over a three-year period, yet few nonlethal interventions have sustained impact over that long a period. The therapist who wishes to show treatment success should make sure that community follow-up is occurring. A strong emphasis on community corrections may well be the most effective action a correctional psychologist can take. A monograph (Lurigio, 1996) addresses many of the linkage issues with community corrections.

The therapist who wishes to continue employment must include treatment that has face validity for reducing recidivism. This is usually measured in terms of skills for "making it" and controls over deviant impulses that keep the offender from "making it." There is also a heavy element of mobilizing motivation for "making it." No matter how good the tools the therapist provides, "making it" depends on whether or not the offender chooses to use them. An active criminal with better self-esteem, more rationalizations for deviant behavior, or a more integrated personality is not an acceptable treatment product.

CONCLUSIONS (SO FAR)

Motivation need not be a problem for most offenders. The wreckage of their lives and past endeavors can be called up to provide that. The problem is a mixture of healthy and unhealthy skepticism that anything can really change.

The situation need not be a problem. One of my former professors angered me at the time by denying my request to provide a better site for an experiment. He said, "If you can demonstrate the effect only under perfect conditions, the effect is probably too trivial to be worth fooling with."

Therapists, or rather, the lack of them is a problem. There are too few universities training therapists to work with offenders (Ogloff, Tomkins, & Bersoff, 1996). There is still the stigma of correctional psychology being for those who cannot handle real jobs. And it takes an astute therapist six months or more to learn that some of the techniques learned in graduate school do not work, or worse.

Success criteria need to be explained to therapists, judges, offenders, families, and all who have an interest in the criminal justice system. Antisocial personality characteristics cannot be cured. The offender can learn controls but not quickly, easily, or cheaply. The offender, having learned these controls, continues to have the option to use them or not.

Because success is measured in terms of control, not cure, aftercare and the ongoing availability of a support group is essential for offenders with personality disorders to continue to exercise their controls in the face of so much temptation.

Independent outcome research is essential. We must find out what works, whom it works on, and the factors that can enhance its effectiveness. But if all our outcome research comes from people who have a financial interest in the process, credibility is going to be a long time coming.

Psychotherapy has not been tried and failed: we simply thought we could run a steeplechase while we were still in our toddler stage. We must clarify our goals, refine our techniques, and accept and publicly acknowledge realistic limits. We must do this quickly. The trend now is to incarcerate longer rather than correct more effectively. With longer sentences, the three strikes rule, the push to build more prisons and require a higher percentage of sentences to be served in prison, we are moving increasingly toward corrections as incapacitation and away from the notion that corrections can correct behavior. Though incapacitation is the surer bet in the short term, it is likely to have a long-term cost that our society cannot afford.

REFERENCES

Abramson, M. F. (1972). The criminalization of mentally disordered behavior: Possible side effect of a new mental health law. *Hospital and Community Psychiatry, 23,* 101–105.

Allodi, F. A., Kedward, H. B., & Robertson, M. (1977). "Insane but guilty": Psychiatric patients in jail. *Canada's Mental Health, 25,* 3–7.

Andrews, D., & Bonta, J. (1995). *L-SIR: The level of service inventory–revised.* Toronto, Canada: Multi-Health Systems.

Becker, J. V., & Hunter, J. A. (1992). Evaluation of treatment outcome for adult perpetrators of child sexual abuse. *Criminal Justice and Behavior, 19,* 74–92.

Briggs, D. (1980). An enclave of freedom: Starting a community at Chino. In H. Toch (Ed.), *Therapeutic communities, in corrections.* New York: Praeger.

Brodsky, S. L. (1972). *Psychologists in the criminal justice system.* Urbana: University of Illinois Press.

Brodsky, S. L. (1980). Ethical issues for psychologists in corrections. In J. Monahan (Ed.), *Who is the client?* Washington, DC: American Psychological Association.

Brodsky, S. L. (1982). Intervention models for mental health services in jails. *Crime and Delinquency Issues.* National Institute of Mental Health, No. 82-1181, 126–148.

Brown, S. (1985). *Treating the alcoholic: A developmental model of recovery.* New York: Wiley.

Camp, C., & Camp, G. (1997). *The corrections yearbook.* South Salem, NY: Criminal Justice Institute.

Camp, G., & Camp, C. (1985). *The corrections yearbook.* South Salem, NY: Criminal Justice Institute.

Camp, G., & Camp, C. (1996). *The corrections yearbook.* South Salem, NY: Criminal Justice Institute.

Cavanaugh, J. L., & Rogers, R. (Eds.). (1984). Malingering and deception. *Behavioral Sciences & the Law, 2,* 3–168.

Coffey, O. D., Procopiow, N., & Miller, N. (Eds.). (1989). *Programming for mentally retarded and learning disabled inmates: A guide for correctional administrators.* Washington, DC: National Institute of Corrections.

Cohen, F. (1985). Legal issues and the mentally disordered inmate. In *Source book on the mentally disordered prisoner.* Washington, DC: National Institute of Corrections.

Cohen, F., & Griset, P. (1985). Standards by legal topic. In *Source book on the mentally disordered prisoner.* Washington, DC: National Institute of Corrections.

Cohen, L. H., Claiborn, W. L., & Specter, G. A. (1983). *Crisis intervention* (2nd ed.). New York: Human Sciences Press.

Coid, J. (1984). How many psychiatric patients in prison? *British Journal of Psychiatry, 145,* 78–86.

Collins, J. J., & Schlenger, W. E. (1983). *The prevalence of psychiatric disorder among admissions to prison.* Paper presented at the American Society of Criminology, Denver.

Corrections Compendium. (1996a). 21, 5. Lincoln, NE: CEGA.

Corrections Compendium. (1996b). 21, 6. Lincoln, NE: CEGA.

Crocker, A. G., & Hodgins, S. (1997). The criminality of noninstitutionalized mental retarded persons. *Criminal Justice and Behavior, 24,* 432–454.

Cullen, F. T., Skovon, S. E., Scott, J. E., & Burton, V. S., Jr. (1990). Public support for correctional treatment: The tenacity of rehabilitative ideology. *Criminal Justice and Behavior, 17,* 6–18.

Cullen, M. (1992). *Cage your rage.* Lanham, MD: American Correctional Association.

Cullen, M., & Freeman-Longo, R. E. (1996). *Men & anger: Understanding and managing your anger for a much better life.* Brandon, VT: Safer Society Press.

DeLeon, G., & Beschner, G. M. (Eds.). (1976). *The therapeutic community: Proceedings of therapeutic communities of America.* Washington, DC: National Institute of Drug Abuse.

Denkowski, G. C., & Denkowski, K. M. (1985). The mentally retarded offender in the state prison system: Identification, prevalence, adjustment, and rehabilitation. *Criminal Justice and Behavior, 12,* 55–70.

Dies, R., & Hess, A. K. (1971). An experimental investigation of cohesiveness in marathon and conventional group psychotherapy. *Journal of Abnormal Behavior, 77,* 258–262.

Freeman-Longo, R., & Bays, L. (1988). *Who am I and why am I in treatment?* Brandon, VT: Safer Society Press.

Freeman-Longo, R., Bays, L., & Bear, E. (1996). *Empathy & compassionate action: Issues and exercises: A guided workbook for clients in treatment.* Brandon, VT: Safer Society Press.

Furby, L., Weinrott, M., & Blackshaw, L. (1989). Sex offender recidivism: A review. *Psychological Bulletin, 105,* 3–30.

Gendreau, P. (Guest Editor). (1990). Reaffirming rehabilitation [Special issue]. *Criminal Justice and Behavior, 17.*

Gendreau, P. (1996). Offender rehabilitation: What we know and what needs to be done. *Criminal Justice and Behavior, 23,* 144–161.

Gibbs, J. J. (1982). On "demons" and "Gaols": A summary and review of investigations concerning the psychological problems of jail prisoners. In C. S. Dunn & H. J. Steadman (Eds.), *Mental health services in local jails: Report of a special national workshop* (pp. 14–33). Rockville, MD: National Institute of Mental Health.

Gorski, T. T. (1995). *Chemically dependent criminal offenders: Recovery & relapse in the criminal justice system, an overview.* Homewood, IL: CENAPS.

Greer, J. G., & Stuart, I. R. (1983). *The sexual aggressor: Current perspectives on treatment.* New York: Van Nostrand-Reinhold.

Groth, A. N., & Birnbaum, H. J. (1979). *Men who rape: The psychology of the offender.* New York: Plenum Press.

Hare, R. D. (1983). Diagnosis of antisocial personality disorder in two prison populations. *American Journal of Psychiatry, 140,* 887–890.

Hayes, L. M. (1983). And darkness closes in . . . A national study of jail suicides. *Criminal Justice and Behavior, 10,* 461–484.

Hayes, L. M. (1995). *Prison suicide: An overview and guide to prevention.* Mansfield, MA: National Center of Institutions and Alternatives.

Hazelden Learning Resources on Alcohol and Other Drugs. (1997). Catalogue. Center City, MN: Author.

Hilkey, J. H., Wilhelm, C. L., & Horne, A. M. (1982). Comparative effectiveness of video tape pretraining versus no pretraining on selected process and outcome variables in group therapy. *Psychological Reports, 50*(3, pt. 2), 1151–1159.

Huggins, M. W. (1985). *Special issues in jail management for urban county sheriffs.* Paper presented to urban county sheriff's group, Dallas & Fort Worth, TX. (Available through National Institute of Corrections)

Ingraham, L., Bell, S., & Rollo, N. (1991). *Life without a crutch.* Dallas TX: Offender Preparation & Education Network.

Ivanoff, A. (1992). Background factors associated with parasuicide among male prison inmates. *Criminal Justice and Behavior, 4,* 426–436.

Jaffe, S. L. (1993). *Adult chemical dependency recovery.* Washington, DC: American Psychiatric Press.

James, J. F., Gregory, D., Jones, R. K., & Rundell, O. H. (1980). Psychiatric morbidity in prisons. *Hospital and Community Psychiatry, 31,* 674–677.

Jones, M. (1976). *Maturation of the therapeutic community.* New York: Human Sciences Press.

Jones, M. (1979). Learning as treatment. In H. Toch (Ed.), *Psychology of crime and criminal justice.* New York: Holt, Rinehart and Winston.

Kahn, T. J. (1996). *Pathways: A guided workbook for youth beginning treatment.* Brandon, VT: Safer Society Press.

Kal, E. (1977). Mental health in jail. *American Journal of Psychiatry, 134,* 463.

Laws, D. R. (1989). *Relapse prevention with sex offenders.* New York: Guilford Press.

Lester, D., & Danto, B. L. (1993). *Suicide behind bars: Prediction and prevention.* Philadelphia: Charles Press.

Levinson, R. (1980). TC or nor TC? That is the question. In H. Toch (Ed.), *Therapeutic communities in corrections.* New York: Praeger.

Levinson, R. (1984). The system that cannot say no. *American Psychologist, 39,* 811–812.

Lipton, D. S. (1995). *The effectiveness of treatment for drug abusers under criminal justice supervision.* Washington, DC: National Institute of Justice.

Lombardo, L. X. (1985). Mental health work in prisons and jails: Inmate adjustment and indigenous correctional personnel. *Criminal Justice and Behavior, 12,* 17–28.

Lotke, E. (1996). Sex offenders: Does treatment work? *Corrections Compendium, 21,* 1–3.

Lurigio, A. J. (1996). *Community corrections in America: New directions and sounder investments for person with mental illness and codisorders.* U.S. Department of Health and Human Services, Substance Abuse and Mental Health Services Administration. (Call 1-800-877-1461 for copies.)

Marshall, W. L. (1996). Assessment, treatment and theorizing about sex offenders: Developments during the past 20 years and future directions. *Criminal Justice and Behavior, 23,* 162–199.

Martinson, R., Lipton, D., & Wilks, J. (1975). *The effectiveness of correctional treatment: A survey of treatment evaluation studies.* New York: Praeger.

McCarthy, B. (1985). Mentally ill and mentally retarded offenders in corrections. In *Source book on the mentally disordered prisoner.* Washington, DC: National Institute of Corrections.

McCorkle, R. C. (1995). Gender, psychopathology, and institutional behavior: A comparison of male and female mentally ill prison inmates. *Journal of Criminal Justice, 25,* 53–61.

Milner, J. S. (Guest editor). (1992). Sexual Child Abuse [Special issue]. *Criminal Justice and Behavior, 19.*

Monahan, J. (Ed.). (1980). *Who is the client?* Washington, DC: American Psychological Association.

Monahan, J., & Steadman, H. (Eds.). (1994). *Violence and mental disorder: Developments in risk assessment.* Chicago: University of Chicago Press.

Mumola, C. J., & Beck, A. J. (1997). *Prisoners in 1996.* U.S. Department of Justice, Bureau of Justice Statistics.

National Center on Institutions and Alternative (NCIA). (1988). *Training curriculum on suicide detection and prevention in jail and lockups.* Mansfield, MA: Author.

National Institute of Corrections. (1983). *Suicide in jails.* Boulder, CO: Library Information Specialists.

National Sheriffs Association. (1984). *Suicide: The silent signals* [videotape]. Alexandria, VA.

Ogloff, J. R. P., Tomkins, A. J., & Bersoff, D. N. (1996). Education and training in psychology and law/criminal justice. *Criminal Justice and Behavior, 23,* 200–235.

Petrich, J. (1976). Rate of psychiatric morbidity in a metropolitan county jail population. *American Journal of Psychiatry, 133,* 1439–1444.

Prentky, R. A. (Guest Editor). (1994). The assessment and treatment of sex offenders [Special issue]. *Criminal Justice and Behavior, 21.*

Rice, M. E., Quinsey, V. L., & Harris, G. T. (1991). Sexual recidivism among child molesters released from a maximum security psychiatric institution. *Journal of Consulting and Clinical Psychology, 59,* 381–386.

Roth, L. H. (Ed.). (1987). *Clinical treatment of the violent person.* New York: Guilford Press.

The Safer Society Press. (1997). Catalogue. (Available from author at P. O. Box 340, Brandon, VT 05733-0340)

Samenow, S. E. (1989). *Inside the criminal mind.* CITY: Times Books.

Samenow, S. E., & Bussard, R. W. (1994). *Commitment to change: Overcoming errors in thinking.* Carpenteria, CA: FMS Productions.

Schranski, T. G., & Harvey, D. R. (1983). The impact of psychodrama and role playing in the correctional environment. *International Journal of Offender Therapy and Comparative Criminology, 27,* 243–254.

Shamsie, S. J. (1982). Antisocial adolescents: Our treatments do not work–Where do we go from here? *Annual Progress in Child Psychiatry and Child Development,* 631–647.

Sonkin, D. J. (1995). *The counselor's guide to learning to live without violence.* Volcano, CA: Volcano Press.

Sosowsky, L. (1980). Explaining increased arrest rate among mental patients. *American Journal of Psychiatry, 137,* 1602–1605.

Steadman, H. J., McCarty, D. W., & Morrisey, J. P. (1986). *Developing jail mental health services: Practice and principles.* Rockville, MD: National Institute of Mental Health.

Steadman, H. J., & Ribner, S. A. (1980). Changing perceptions of the mental health needs of inmates in local jails. *American Journal of Psychiatry, 137,* 1115–1116.

Steen, C. (1993). *The relapse prevention workbook for youth in treatment.* Brandon, VT: Safer Society Press.

Tate, D. C., Reppucci, N. D., & Mulvey, E. P. (1995). Violent delinquents: Treatment effectiveness and implications for future action. *American Psychologist, 50,* 777–781.

Teplin, L. (1983). The criminalization of the mentally ill: Speculation in search of data. *Psychological Bulletin, 94,* 54–67.

Teplin, L. (1984). Criminalizing mental disorder: The comparative arrest rate of the mentally ill. *American Psychologist, 39,* 794–803.

Teplin, L. A. (1994). Psychiatric and substance abuse disorders among male urban inmates. *American Journal of Public Health, 84,* 290–293.

Teplin, L. A. (1996). Prevalence of psychiatric disorders among incarcerated women. *Archives of General Psychiatry, 53,* 505–512.

Toch, H. (1982). The disturbed disruptive inmate: Where does the bus stop? *Journal of Psychiatry & Law, 10,* 327–349.

Toch, H., Adams, K., & Grant, J. D. (1989). *Coping: Maladaptation in prisons.* New Brunswick, NJ: Transaction.

Toch, H., Adams, K., & Greene, R. (1987). Ethnicity, disruptiveness and emotional disorder among prison inmates. *Criminal Justice and Behavior, 14,* 93–109.

Torrey, E. F., Stieber, J., Ezekiel, J., Wolfe, S. M., Sharfstein, J., Noble, J. H., & Flynn, L. M. (1992). *Criminalizing the seriously mentally ill: The abuse of jails as mental hospitals.* Washington, DC: Public Citizen's Health Research Group and the National Alliance for the Mentally Ill.

Travisono, D. N. (1984). *Directory of juvenile and adult correctional departments, institutions, agencies and paroling authorities.* College Park, MD: American Correctional Association.

U.S. Department of Health and Human Services. (1995). *Planning for alcohol and other drug abuse treatment for adults in the criminal justice system* (DHHS Publication No. (SMA) 95-309). Rockville, MD: Author.

U.S. Department of Justice. (1983a). *Prisoners and alcohol.* Washington, DC: Author.

U.S. Department of Justice. (1983b). *Prisoners and drugs.* Washington, DC: Author.

U.S. Department of Justice. (1984). *The 1983 jail census.* Washington, DC: Bureau of Justice Statistics.

Walters, G. D. (1990). *The criminal lifestyle.* Newbury Park, CA: Sage.

Webster, C. D., Harris, G. T., Rice, M. E., Corimer, C., & Quinsey, V. L. (1994). *The violence prediction scheme: Assessing dangerousness in high-risk men.* Toronto: University of Toronto Centre of Criminology.

Wexler, H. K., Falkin, G. P., & Lipton, D. S. (1990). Outcome evaluation of a prison therapeutic community. *Criminal Justice and Behavior, 17,* 71–92.

Wilson, J. Q., & Herrnstein, R. J. (1985). *Crime and human nature.* New York: Simon & Schuster.

Yochelson, S., & Samenow, S. (1976). *The criminal personality: Vol. 1. A profile for change.* New York: Aronson.

Yochelson, S., & Samenow, S. (1977). *The criminal personality: Vol. II. The change process.* New York: Aronson.

Zamble, E. (1992). Behavior and adaptation in long-term prison inmates: Descriptive longitudinal results. *Criminal Justice and Behavior, 19,* 409–425.

Zamble, E., & Porporino, F. (1990). Coping, imprisonment and rehabilitation: Some data and their implications. *Criminal Justice and Behavior, 17,* 53–70.

Zimbardo, P. G., Haney, C., Banks, W. C., & Jaffe, D. (1975). The psychology of imprisonment: Privation, power, and pathology. In D. Rosenhan & P. London (Eds.), *Theory and research in abnormal psychology* (2nd ed., pp. 270–287). New York: Holt, Rinehart and Winston.

BIBLIOGRAPHY

Kerr v. Farrey, 95 F.3d 472 (7th Cir. 1996).
Washington v. Harper, 110 S.C.T. (1990).

CHAPTER 23

Diagnosing and Treating Sexual Offenders

WILLIAM L. MARSHALL

SEXUAL OFFENDING is a significant social problem affecting the lives of many innocent victims (Marshall, in press-a). Depending on the source of the data, up to 50% of adult women will report having been sexually abused on at least one occasion, and a similar number of children also appear to have been abused (Marshall & Marshall, in press). Even when quite restrictive definitions of abuse are applied, the number of people victimized by sexual offenders remains alarmingly high. This is, then, an important social issue calling for a systematic and comprehensive response. Of course, such a response is most effective when it is based on carefully collected evidence. The present chapter addresses some of the available evidence, but it is not possible to provide a comprehensive appraisal. In particular, it is not possible to provide a detailed account of the effects on the victims, except to say that in most cases, they suffer both immediate and long-term consequences that can be quite disruptive. Accordingly, the focus is on limited aspects of the offenders and what can be done to identify their problems, their threat to reoffend, and how we can reduce that threat.

Because the diagnosis and assessment of these offenders is the critical first step in dealing with them, the greatest emphasis in what follows is on those issues. A brief overview of treatment is given, and the interested reader will be able to pursue this in the references provided in that section. Two major issues omitted from this chapter concern theoretical accounts of the etiology and maintenance of sexual offending, and attempts to reduce the variability apparent in these offenders by classification systems. Theories of sexual offending are provided in Marshall, Laws, and Barbaree (1990), and in Schwartz (1995), and the best classification system presently available is described by Knight and Prentky (1990).

DIAGNOSTIC ISSUES

CHILD MOLESTERS

The American Psychiatric Association's *Diagnostic and Statistical Manual (DSM)* first used the term "pedophilia" in *DSM-III* (American Psychiatric Association, 1980) to describe a specific subset of child molesters. Until the most recent version (i.e., *DSM-IV*), the diagnostic manual defined pedophilia in such a way that it excluded a substantial number of child molesters. Although this is not an unreasonable position, unfortunately many clinicians and researchers used the term more generically to include all child molesters, thereby causing considerable confusion. Given that most clinicians consider it necessary to evaluate and treat all child molesters, it is no wonder many have chosen to disregard *DSM* criteria. In this regard, it would have been preferable if the more diagnostically neutral term child molesters had been used as the generic descriptor rather than pedophiles. Abel, Mittelman, and Becker (1985) declared that 100% of child molesters could be diagnosed as pedophiles, but they did not make clear the basis for their diagnosis, and it does not appear that all child molesters would meet even *DSM-IV* criteria.

DSM-III-R defined pedophilia as involving "recurrent intense sexual urges and sexually arousing fantasies involving sexual activity with a prepubescent child or children" (American Psychiatric Association, 1987, p. 285). Because these criteria did not include actually engaging in sexual activities with a child, a *DSM-III-R* diagnosis of pedophilia could be applied to persons who had never committed an offense. On the other hand, unfortunately, it could not be applied to those persons who had molested a child but who were not plagued by deviant urges and fantasies. As we reported (Marshall, in press-a), an examination of our clinical files revealed no clear evidence of *recurrent* urges or fantasies in almost 60% of our nonfamilial child molesters and in over 75% of our incest offenders. Apparently, recurrent urges and fantasies are not diagnostic of all child molesters. Obviously then, a *DSM-III-R* diagnosis of pedophilia did not have relevance for treatment, for clinicians have been treating all child molesters regardless of their diagnostic status. Of course, it may be that pedophiles (properly diagnosed) are more or less responsive to treatment than are other child molesters. Again, a detailed examination of our records over the past 27 years (over 1,000 clients) revealed no differences in the reoffense rates for those offenders who could be classified as pedophiles versus those who could not. It is important to note here that our treated offenders were significantly less likely to reoffend than our untreated comparison group of sexual offenders (Marshall & Anderson, 1996; Marshall & Barbaree, 1988; Marshall & Fernandez, 1997). As a result of these and other considerations, we use the term child molesters rather than pedophiles to describe our clients to avoid diagnostic problems and also because we consider the term pedophile to be a misnomer. Translated from the Greek, it means approximately "child lover," which is hardly an appropriate description of their behavior toward children. Thus, we define the need for treatment primarily in terms of the offensive behavior rather than any possible sexual fantasies.

A significant difficulty facing diagnosticians is that child molesters are understandably reluctant to admit having deviant thoughts or feelings. Faced with this, many clinicians and researchers have for many years employed phallometry, which is presumed to produce an assessment of sexual preferences. Female offenders have not been assessed by genital measures of arousal. It is assumed that if a man displays deviant arousal during phallometric testing, then he almost certainly has deviant urges or fantasies; accordingly, he is judged to meet the criteria for a diagnosis of pedophilia (Freund & Blanchard, 1989; Freund & Watson, 1991). Pedophiles, according to this view, are those child molesters, and only those child molesters, who display sexual preferences for children at phallometric evaluation. The results of phallometric assessments, then, are seen as relevant not only to diagnosis but also to the identification of treatment targets (Marshall & Fernandez, 1997) and risk assessment (Quinsey, Harris, & Rice, 1995; Quinsey, Lalumière, Rice, & Harris, 1995).

The evidence bearing on the value of phallometrics has been reviewed by numerous authors, with almost all coming to positive conclusions (Abel & Blanchard, 1976; Freund, 1981; Murphy & Barbaree, 1994; O'Donohue & Letourneau, 1992; Rosen & Beck, 1988). However, in our recent comprehensive review (Marshall, 1997a), we were unable to find convincing evidence that the procedures were reliable, which is an essential first step in establishing the utility of any measure. It has been found that phallometric assessments differentiate nonfamilial child molesters as a group from nonoffenders (Abel, Becker, Murphy, & Flanagan, 1981; Frenzel & Lang, 1989; Freund, 1967; Freund & Blanchard, 1989; Marshall, Barbaree, & Butt, 1988; Marshall, Barbaree, & Christophe, 1986; Quinsey & Chaplin, 1988; Quinsey, Chaplin, & Carrigan, 1979), but only when the child molesters admit their problems and have multiple victims. Child molesters who are in denial or who have only a single victim display normative sexual preferences (Freund, Chan, & Coulthard, 1979; Freund & Watson, 1991), and yet these are just the clients for whom diagnostic issues are the most problematic. Even when group differences have been found between nonfamilial child molesters and comparison groups, there is clear heterogeneity among the child molesters. Indeed, we found five clearly different sets of phallometric responses among our nonfamilial offenders (Barbaree & Marshall, 1989). Familial child molesters, according to most studies, do not differ in their phallometric responses from normal males (Frenzel & Lang, 1989; Freund, Watson, & Dickey, 1991; Marshall et al., 1986; Quinsey et al., 1979).

Clearly, then, phallometric procedures will not answer all our diagnostic questions, despite the fact that *DSM* criteria continue to identify "intense sexual arousing fantasies, (and) sexual urges" (*DSM-IV*, American Psychiatric Association, 1994, p. 528) as critical to the diagnosis of pedophilia. The addition of "behaviors involving sexual activity with a prepubescent child or children" (p. 528) to the diagnostic criteria in *DSM-IV* represents a sensible change and allows for all child molesters (at least those who molest prepubescent children) to be diagnosed as pedophiles. This and other changes over the years, however, cause serious problems in integrating research over time. In addition to the habit of some researchers of using the term pedophilia as a generic descriptor, these changes make it hard to compare different studies, as it is not clear that the samples of child molesters are comparable.

There are two particular problems facing the clinician who wishes to rely on *DSM-IV* to diagnose child molester clients. According to *DSM-IV*, pedophilia should be diagnosed only if significant distress or impairment of functioning is apparent. Apparent in whom? It is generally, and correctly, assumed by almost all clinicians that the victims of child molestation suffer, so presumably it is not the victim to whom the criteria refer. Yet many (if not all) child molesters are not distressed by their actual offending, although they are distressed as a result of being caught. In any event, what child molesters might retrospectively report about their feelings when they were offending is likely to be self-serving and inaccurate. This requirement of distress, indeed, seems an absurd criterion for this population. Also, the criterion that specifies the child must be prepubescent, with the indication that this typically means age 13 years, seems arbitrary and may be difficult to determine. In many cases, clinicians have no information independent of the offender as to the victim's age, and our experience is that child molesters characteristically report that the child was older at the time of the offending than the victim claims. Even with available official information, when the victim reports the offending some time after it commenced, we are often faced with discrepant claims from the offender and the child about the child's age at the time of victimization.

RAPISTS

Absurdly, the diagnostic manual does not deem rapists (or, for that matter, child molesters who offend against postpubescent children) to have a diagnosable problem. Just why it is that a homosexual who feels uncomfortable about his or her sexual orientation should be said to have a disorder, whereas a man who repeatedly rapes women does not, is difficult to understand. The only rapists who would meet diagnostic criteria for a disorder according to *DSM-IV* are those who are sadists.

Sadists, according to *DSM-IV*, are sexually aroused by their victim's suffering (psychological or physical). Presumably, a diagnosis of sadism would be applied if the rapist admitted to being sexually excited by inflicting suffering. Rapists, however, are not usually this forthcoming, nor are they discerning about their mood state. Instead, the diagnostician must rely on inferring a sexual predilection for sadism from the rapist's behavior during the assault. This, unfortunately, presents problems. In an early study (Christie, Marshall, & Lanthier, 1979), for example, we found that 70% of rapists had inflicted gratuitous violence on their victim (i.e., violence not instrumentally aimed at gaining compliance), but when we asked them to explain this, most said it was meant to frighten the victim into silence. If they were telling the truth (and how could we possibly know), then these rapists would not be properly diagnosed as sadists. In another study, we (Marshall & Darke, 1982) found that when asked to identify their motives, 60% of rapists said they intended to humiliate their victims. If humiliating the victim sexually excited them, then these rapists would be diagnosed as sadists. But were they sexually aroused by the humiliation? In both of these examples (i.e., the use of excessive violence and the intent to humiliate), the problem is to determine whether or not these actions, in and of themselves, produced sexual arousal in the offender. Again, phallometric assessments have offered a solution, but the evidence on the value of phallometrics with rapists is even less convincing than with child molesters (Marshall, 1997a).

Early small-sample studies employing phallometry did find differences between rapists and nonrapists (Abel, Barlow, Blanchard, & Guild, 1977; Barbaree, Marshall, & Lanthier, 1979; Quinsey, Chaplin, & Upfold, 1984). More recent large-sample studies, however, have not found differences (Baxter, Barbaree, & Marshall, 1986; Hall, 1989; Langevin, Paitich, & Russon, 1985; Murphy, Krisak, Stalgaitis, & Anderson, 1984; Wormith, Bradford, Pawlak, Borzecki, & Zoher, 1988). In addition, the reliability of phallometric assessments with rapists is far too low to justify these evaluations (Barbaree, Baxter, & Marshall, 1989).

However, to illustrate the problems inherent in determining whether or not a rapist is a sadist, one particular study will serve as an example. Seto and Kubin (1996) classified rapists as sadistic or nonsadistic on the basis of their offense histories, but found no differences in the phallometric responses of these two groups. The latter results suggest the possibility that their diagnoses were inaccurate—not a possibility that these researchers entertained, however. Rapists in both groups denied any sadistic fantasies, as might be expected, but in terms of the offense behaviors described by Seto and Kubin, it appears that only one of their so-called sadists was in fact sadistic. Two others had killed their victims, but sex murderers are not always sadists; they may kill the victim accidentally, or as a result of rage, or to eliminate potential reporting. In any case, interjudge agreement on sadism was only 78%, which, in view of the rather inadequate criteria employed, does not encourage confidence in the conclusions reached by the authors. Other studies involving the identification of sadistic rapists are equally flawed, suggesting that the diagnostic criteria for sadism is not at all easy to apply.

EXHIBITIONISTS

The diagnostic manual is quite clear about exhibitionists, indicating that to meet the diagnostic criteria for this disorder, a person (typically a male) must have "recurrent, intense, sexually arousing fantasies, sexual urges, or behaviors involving the exposure of one's genitals to an unsuspecting stranger" (American Psychiatric Association, 1994, p. 526). Because all exhibitionists, by definition, engage in behaviors involving the exposure of their genitals to unsuspecting strangers, they all meet the diagnostic criteria of a paraphilia. Clinicians have always considered such offenders to need treatment, particularly because this behavior is persistent. Marshall, Eccles, and Barbaree (1991), for example, report that 57% of their untreated exhibitionists reoffended within four years of initial identification, and Maletzky (1991) found that his 770 exhibitionists averaged almost three exposures per week over an average period of 7.5 years. Thus, diagnosis and treatment are sensibly linked in exhibitionism, and the diagnosis of these offenders presents no problems.

AN ALTERNATIVE TO DIAGNOSIS

As noted earlier, most clinicians working with sexual offenders consider them all to be in need of treatment regardless of whether or not they meet diagnostic criteria for a disorder. Given the remarkably damaging effects of these offensive behaviors, and the apparent inadequacy of the diagnostic manual, this is a sensible strategy. In their work with sexual offenders, clinicians are faced with a number of issues they either must address or are asked to address. To meet these demands, clinicians must come to some conclusion regarding the nature of the problem the offender presents, and to do this, they must complete a thorough evaluation.

It is not possible in this chapter to cover all the questions asked of those who deal with sexual offenders, but one issue can be dismissed right away. There is no basis in evidence for a sexual offender clinician offering assistance in the determination of guilt or innocence. Several reviews have considered the potential value and problems that arise when such an appraisal is attempted (Barbaree & Peacock, 1995; Marshall, 1996a; Peters & Murphy, 1992; Simon & Schouten, 1992). These reviews have examined the empirical bases of a variety of procedures and have concluded that none of them is adequate to the task of determining whether an accused did or did not actually commit an offense. We have earlier seen that phallometric evaluations of nonadmitters (presumably, the only cases where the question of guilt or innocence would be raised) do not distinguish them from nonoffenders, and the same is essentially true for personality measures (Marshall, 1996a; Marshall & Hall, 1995). Responsible clinicians will, therefore, refuse to conduct appraisals aimed at determining culpability in accused sexual offenders.

Perhaps the three most important reasons to conduct a thorough assessment of sexual offenders are to (a) determine future risk to reoffend, (b) determine treatment needs, and (c) evaluate whether or not treatment has produced the desired changes. In fact, treatment providers typically expose sexual offenders to most, if not all, components of their programs, meaning that rarely is it the case that treatment is adjusted to the particular offender's needs. This may be because treatment is typically done in groups so that it is hard to implement individualized interventions, but it also arises from the fact that most clinicians seem to assume that either all sexual offenders need all treatment components, never mind what assessment tells us, or that completing a component, when they have demonstrated no deficiency relevant to that component, will not do offenders any harm. Essentially, this leaves us with just two reasons for assessing sexual offenders.

Assessing for Treatment Evaluation

The targets in these assessments should, of course, match the targets addressed in treatment. Treatment, as we will see, typically includes the following components: acceptance of responsibility, cognitive distortions, identification of victim harm, development of victim empathy, modification of deviant sexual interests, enhancement of social skills, dealing with substance abuse, and developing relapse-prevention plans. Assessments, therefore, characteristically target each of these areas, although other rather obvious features are also appraised; for example, whether or not the offender has another serious disorder (e.g., brain damage, psychosis, or depression) may affect his ability to participate in treatment, as might the offender's intellectual ability and educational attainment. Several test procedures are available that can be used to evaluate these various issues; however, interviews remain a primary source of information with these offenders. Interview strategies with sexual offenders have not been well developed, although most clinicians appear to adopt the approach suggested by W. Miller and Rollnick (1991) in their work with addicts.

Acceptance of Responsibility

Interviews appear to be the only way at present of evaluating the degree to which an offender accepts responsibility for the offenses. Rarely does a sexual offender accept full responsibility, typically deflecting responsibility onto someone else (e.g., "The victim wanted me to have sex with her"; "His mother should not have left us alone") or to some set of circumstances (e.g., "I was drunk and didn't know what I was doing"; "I hadn't had sex for a long time so I couldn't control myself"). Barbaree (1991) used Nichols and Molinder's (1984) Multiphasic Sex Inventory to identify aspects of the acceptance of responsibility; this proved to be of some value, but it is rather limited in assessing responsibility taking. A more specific instrument should be developed for this purpose.

Cognitive Distortions

It is apparent that there is considerable disagreement about what constitutes cognitive distortions. Basically, this descriptor refers to distorted perceptions or memories that are self-serving and protect the offender from taking full responsibility for his offenses. These distortions take a multitude of forms and are directed by various inappropriate attitudes and beliefs, most particularly those concerned with women or children in general and their sexuality in particular. Although the evidence is not convincing that sexual offenders have problems in all these areas, most clinicians remain convinced that these issues must be addressed in treatment. Also, the instruments that have been used to evaluate cognitive distortions are quite transparent, so it is presumed that sexual offenders simply present themselves in a positive light on these measures by endorsing only the evidently prosocial alternatives.

Abel et al. (1989) have developed and provided data on the value of a measure of cognitive distortions in child molesters. However, others have not found it to be as useful as the initial data promised (Ward, Hudson, Johnston, & Marshall, 1997). Similarly, although the measures of attitudes and beliefs about women and rape, originally described by Burt (1980), appeared to initially differentiate rapists (Burt, 1983) and rape-prone nonoffenders (Malamuth, 1984) from other males, overall, the results of such studies have not encouraged confidence in these measures. In most cases, rapists are not distinguished by their responses to tests measuring attitudes toward women, acceptance of rape myths, or hostility toward women (Marolla & Scully, 1986;

Segal & Stermac, 1984, 1990). Problems with the utility of these measures have forced most clinicians to again rely on clinical interviews to infer the attitudes, beliefs, and distortions of sexual offenders.

Victim Harm/Victim Empathy

It has typically been thought that the capacity to identify victim harm is a prerequisite to the development of victim empathy (Pithers, 1994). Measurement procedures, as a consequence, have focused on empathy, although some items on Abel et al.'s (1989) cognitive distortion scale reveal the ability to discern victim harm. Our review of the evidence on sexual offenders' capacity for empathy suggested that they do not have a general deficit in empathy, but rather are specifically deficient in empathy toward their own victim (Marshall, Hudson, Jones, & Fernandez, 1995). We take this to mean that they distort their perception of the harm they have done and as a consequence do not feel any empathy toward their victim. This means that measures of victim harm, rather than measures of empathic responding, are critical to the evaluation of sexual offenders. Unfortunately, there are no available instruments (other than the few items on Abel's scale) that directly assess the offender's understanding of the harm he has done. Once again, interviews seem the only recourse.

Deviant Sexual Interests

The value of phallometric assessments in determining the sexual preferences of sexual offenders has already been considered and found wanting. Additional, but quite important, concerns regarding phallometry are that the majority of offenders find the procedure humiliating, and the stimuli employed (either pictures depicting sexual assault on young children or graphic audiotapes describing sexual offenses) raise serious ethical problems. The ethical issues are likely to become more pronounced as victims' groups and offenders' rights groups become more aware of these procedures. Victim advocates are likely to be distressed to learn that clinicians are presenting to known sexual offenders images of women and children being victimized. Of course, subjecting clients (whoever they are) to humiliating procedures is not a wise therapeutic strategy and could only be justified if the procedures consistently and reliably produced interpretable and discriminating results. We have seen that this does not appear to be the case. Additionally, it is important to note that over 20% of all sexual offenders fail to show any arousal at phallometric testing.

Unfortunately, other alternatives to determining sexual interests (e.g., card sort tests, where the offender places preferred persons and behaviors in a separate pile; Abel & Becker, 1985) are far more open to distortion, although phallometrics are not immune to faking either (Marshall, 1997a). It has been suggested that either augmenting phallometric evaluations with concurrent polygraphic evaluations or simply employing polygraphy alone may circumvent the problem of faking (Jensen & Jewell, 1988). However, the value of polygraph testing with sexual offenders has been challenged (Lalumière & Quinsey, 1991), and there is no clear supporting evidence of its utility for more general use (Honts & Perry, 1992; Iacono & Patrick, 1987).

The basic question here is not so much the availability of reliable measures of sexual interests, but rather whether these should be aspects of assessment and treatment with sexual offenders. I (Marshall, in press-b) have challenged the value of addressing sexual preferences, and recently, I (Marshall, 1997b) provided evidence that treatment of other aspects of sexual offenders' functioning has the effect of reducing deviant interests without the necessity of specifically targeting them in treatment. We have, for the past five years, ignored these issues in our programs, and yet our relapse rates remain low (Marshall & Fernandez, 1997).

Social Skills

This is a broad descriptor that covers all aspects of social functioning, but of course it is impossible to assess every feature of social competence. Early interest among behavior therapists concerned conversational skills (Barlow, 1973), but most clinicians working with sexual offenders today appear to all but neglect this aspect of functioning. Recent interest has focused on clients' self-confidence in personal relations, their capacity for intimacy, their assertiveness, and their problems with anger.

Sexual offenders have been found to lack self-esteem in dealing with other people (Marshall, Anderson, & Champagne, 1996); the Social Self-Esteem Inventory (Lawson, Marshall, & McGrath, 1979) is a reliable and valid measure of these deficiencies. Whether self-confidence has anything to do with the origins of sexual offending or with its maintenance has yet to be determined, although it appears as an etiologic feature in several theories (e.g., Marshall & Barbaree, 1990; Williams & Finkelhor, 1990). The importance of self-confidence has more to do with effectively engaging the client in treatment (Marshall, 1996b), and so it is in that light that evaluations of self-esteem are relevant. It is quite important to have an understanding of an offender's self-confidence prior to treatment and this is not always evident at interview.

Although concerns about sexual offenders' capacity for intimacy have been noted by several authors over the years, we did not formally address this problem until 1989 (Marshall, 1989). Our suggestion was that a lack of intimacy might be due to deficient relationship skills, which might in turn encourage the man to seek sexual contacts under circumstances that do not demand these skills (e.g., by raping a woman or molesting a child). It is important to keep in mind that the reciprocal of intimacy is loneliness, which has been shown to facilitate aggression in males (Check, Perlman, & Malamuth, 1985). Subsequent research has confirmed that sexual offenders do indeed lack intimacy and experience loneliness (Bumby & Hansen, 1997; Garlick, Marshall, & Thornton, 1996; Seidman, Marshall, Hudson, & Robertson, 1994) and that they have inadequate attachment styles (Ward, Hudson, & Marshall, 1996). Fortunately, good measures of intimacy (e.g., Miller & Lefcourt's, 1982, Social Intimacy Measure) and loneliness (Russell, Peplau, & Cutrona, 1980) are available.

There have been numerous suggestions that sexual offenders have problems with assertiveness (Abel et al., 1984; Barnard, Fuller, Robbins, & Shaw,

1989; Finkelhor, 1984), although in contrast, it has also been claimed that they are angry and aggressive (e.g., Groth, 1979). The evidence on the pervasive underassertiveness and anger among sexual offenders has not presented an entirely clear picture (Stermac, Segal, & Gillis, 1990). What few studies there are have found rapists to be angry (Levine & Koenig, 1980), and nonfamilial child molesters (Knight & Prentky, 1990) and incest fathers to have problems with anger control (Paveza, 1987). Similarly, research has shown that sexual offenders tend to be underassertive (Overholser & Beck, 1986; Stermac & Quinsey, 1985), although we found that all sexual offenders displayed overassertiveness in some situations, underassertiveness in others, and appropriate assertiveness in yet other situations (Marshall, Barbaree, & Fernandez, 1995). The measure we used, the Social Response Inventory (P. Marshall, Keltner, & Marshall, 1981), allows clients to select one of five possible responses (ranging from extremely underassertive to blatantly aggressive responses) to over 40 different situations. In the Marshall, Barbaree, et al. (1995) study, we also had subjects rate the appropriateness of the behaviors, depicted in videotapes, of three males responding to a demanding acquaintance whose requests they wished to refuse. Neither the child molesters nor the rapists rated the socially appropriate response (i.e., polite but firm denial) as the most appropriate. The child molesters thought the unassertive man was the most appropriate, and the rapists considered the aggressive male to be the most appropriate. Sexual offenders, therefore, may have problems with assertiveness (i.e., be underassertive or aggressive), not necessarily because of lack of skill but perhaps because they have mistaken ideas of what constitutes appropriate social behavior.

Substance Abuse

Numerous reports indicate significant abuse or misuse of alcohol and other substances among sexual offenders (Apfelberg, Sugar, & Pfeff, 1944; Araji & Finkelhor, 1985; Lightfoot & Barbaree, 1993; Marques & Nelson, 1989; Rada, 1978). In most of these reports, unfortunately, no distinction is made between chronic substance use and the specific use of intoxicants in the context of offending. For example, it may be that chronic use erodes the offender's concerns about society's rules in a more general sense and this may allow him to begin offending without giving thought to the consequences. On the other hand, a person who carefully premeditates sexual offending may deliberately use alcohol (or some other substance) to disinhibit social constraints. In a reanalysis of data on alcohol use by sexual offenders collected in 1979 (Christie et al., 1979), Marshall (in press-a) found that some 70% of offenders were at least mildly intoxicated at the time of the offense, with slightly more than 60% having a clear and persistent drinking problem. For the most part, however, it appears that few sexual offenders are intoxicated to dysfunctional levels while they are actually engaged in their abusive behaviors. Most appear to use an intoxicant simply to facilitate offending by reducing their inhibitions, whether they are at other times substance abusers or substance-dependent.

Adequate measures of problems with alcohol or other drugs are available, although an extensive history of use is essential to get a complete picture of the problem. The Michigan Alcoholism Screening Test (Selzer, 1971) and the Drug Abuse Screening Test (Skinner, 1982) are both quite satisfactory measures.

Relapse Prevention

There are, in fact, few measures to assess the relevant facets of relapse prevention. To protect themselves against the potential for reoffending, sexual offenders need to be able to identify their offense cycle (including those emotional states and stress factors that put them at risk, as well as their typical victim-seeking and grooming strategies) and the situations that put them at risk to develop sensible plans for avoiding these problems or dealing with them should they arise in the future.

Noting that high-risk situations are essentially those in which offenders are at risk because they do not have the skills to cope with them, Miner, Day, and Nafpaktitis (1989) designed a situational competency test that measures these potential skills. The utility of this test, however, has not been convincingly demonstrated, although Marques and colleagues (Marques, in press; Marques, Day, Nelson, & West, 1994; Marques, Nelson, West, & Day, 1994) have routinely employed it and other measures relevant to reducing risk in their extensive evaluations of their treatment program. More measures pertinent to evaluating pretreatment understanding of risk need to be developed.

Other Issues

No doubt, there are many idiosyncratic features or factors that may be relevant to the full assessment of particular sexual offenders. Two that seem to be frequently salient are the offender's own history of being abused and his hormonal functioning.

A history of sexual, physical, or emotional abuse may have left the offender with many personal deficits and unresolved emotional conflicts, or it may have persuaded him that sexual abuse is normative and is not that bad after all. Obviously, a therapist would need to know this. Perhaps the best way to determine the incidence of abuse is by interview. There appears to be no doubt that a disproportionate number of sexual offenders report being abused as children (see Hanson & Slater, 1988, for a review of this literature), but there is no way to independently verify their reports and there are obvious self-serving reasons why they may exaggerate or fabricate incidents of abuse.

Hormonal evaluations are costly and, unless the facilities are readily available, it would be impractical and likely not useful to assess every sexual offender to determine whether or not his sex steroid system was functioning normally. There are reports (Bradford, 1990; Hucker & Bain, 1990; Land, 1995) clearly indicating that some, but few, sexual offenders have elevated levels of one or another of the sex steroids (not always testosterone). Well-controlled studies have demonstrated that reducing these abnormal levels has a positive therapeutic effect (Bradford, 1990, 1993), so these problems cannot be dismissed. However, as noted, we do not want to suggest that all sexual offenders should be screened for sex steroid dysfunction. Our tactic has been to refer for evaluation only those offenders who report being constantly, and irresistibly, plagued by sexual thoughts. This represents no more than 5% of our caseload.

PREDICTING RECIDIVISM

There have been a number of attempts to define those features of sexual offenders that will predict future likelihood of reoffending, but most of these have relied on clinical judgments (see review by Webster, Harris, Rice, Cormier, & Quinsey, 1994, for a discussion of the problems with clinical estimates of risk). Actuarial approaches to estimating risk to reoffend involve examining the relationship between specific variables (or sets of variables) and actual later recidivism. There is clear evidence that actuarial predictions are superior to clinical predictions (Quinsey & Maguire, 1986); in fact, there is no evidence that clinicians have any greater expertise in making such predictions than do lay people (Quinsey & Ambtman, 1979; Quinsey & Cyr, 1986). The use of actuarial bases for predicting risk to reoffend is a rather recent feature of the field of sexual offender research, and to date, there are only limited data available.

Some of the best research on this issue has been done by Quinsey and colleagues (Quinsey & Lalumière, 1996; Quinsey, Lalumière, et al., 1995; Quinsey, Rice, & Harris, 1995; Rice, Quinsey, & Harris, 1991). Quinsey, Rice, et al. (1995) examined 178 rapists and child molesters who had been released from Oak Ridge Mental Health Centre in Ontario, Canada. This institution houses sexual offenders who have either been found by the courts to be insane or for whom the courts are requesting an evaluation of sanity. Obviously, this suggests that these researchers are dealing with an unusual population of sexual offenders whom we expect to be at high risk for reoffending; essentially, that is what the recidivism data from Oak Ridge indicate. Among the 178 sexual offenders followed for an average of 50 months, 55.6% were rearrested on some charge, with 40.4% identified as having committed a violent or sexual offense and 27.5% convicted of a sexual offense. These are quite high rates of reoffending given the reliance on official records, confirming, thereby, the suggestion that this is a population of serious sexual offenders.

Quinsey, Lalumière, et al. (1995) found significant correlations between 13 variables and sexual reconviction. However, it is important to note that none of these factors on its own accounted for more than 7% of the variance in recidivism, indicating quite clearly that the use of any single predictor will be of no practical use. Interestingly, although these same authors, along with many others, emphasize the value of both Hare's (1991) Psychopathy Checklist and phallometric assessments, these two variables accounted for, respectively, 3.24% and 4.41% of the variance in recidivism. These are obviously trivial predictors on their own, and Quinsey repeatedly stresses the importance of a composite prediction index; unfortunately, not everyone heeds Quinsey's advice.

The factors that Quinsey and his colleagues have discerned as sound predictors of recidivism include prior violent convictions; prior convictions for any offenses; prior sex convictions; prior incarcerations; prior sexual offense victims (separate factors for male, female, adult, and child victims); number of male victims; never been married; the score on Hare's Psychopathy Checklist; and a deviance index derived from phallometric testing. Prior admission to Oak Ridge Centre was also a factor, although this is not likely to be relevant to clients in other settings. In addition, the observant reader will note the obvious redundancy in some of these factors. For example, prior convictions and prior incarcerations are likely to be highly correlated, so that one or the other should perhaps be dropped from a composite predictor set.

Quinsey devised a system whereby each variable (i.e., each of the 13 factors in the composite predictor set) is weighted according to both the individual subject's score on that variable and the magnitude of the relationship between that variable and the observed outcome. Using this system, Quinsey produced a summed score that was then used to sort his subjects into one of six levels of observed recidivism. This method yielded 77% accuracy in classifying Quinsey's subjects as recidivists or nonrecidivists, which was significantly better than chance (when the selection ratio is set to equal the base rate, chance would produce 44% accuracy). The probability of reoffending increased as a function of the composite score of the predictor variables. Unfortunately, a subsequent cross-validation on an independent sample did not reveal quite the same level of predictive accuracy (Rice & Harris, 1995).

The astute reader will notice that all the variables entering into Quinsey's composite predictor score are static, unchangeable factors, with the single possible exception of the deviant index. Most therapists who treat sexual offenders target deviant arousal, thereby implying that it is modifiable, although the evidence in support of this assumption is not strong (Laws & Marshall, 1991; Quinsey & Earls, 1990). Furthermore, there is no evidence that changes in deviant indices demonstrably reduce subsequent recidivism. There is, then, little or no possibility of changing an offender's risk level as estimated by Quinsey's composite index. To allow for this, Quinsey, Lalumière, et al. (1995) say that the actuarial estimate should serve as an anchor for clinical judgment "by having the clinician start with an actuarial estimate of risk and then [altering] it by examining dynamic variables such as treatment outcome" (p. 132). However, they provide no guidelines about how to determine treatment outcome (by which they apparently mean treatment-induced changes), how to assign a weight to the different features of treatment changes (e.g., does enhancing empathy get weighted as much as acceptance of responsibility, etc.), and how to combine dynamic changes with the actuarial estimates based on static factors.

In other contexts, Quinsey and his colleagues have consistently claimed that treatment of sexual offenders is not demonstrably effective (Quinsey, Harris, Rice, & Lalumière, 1993; Quinsey, Khanna, & Malcolm, 1996; Rice, Harris, & Quinsey, 1991; Rice, Harris, Quinsey, & Cyr, 1990; Rice, Quinsey, et al., 1991). In the absence of demonstrated effects it is, in fact, impossible to actuarially determine the relationship between treatment-induced changes and later success or failure. If, on the other hand, treatment is effective, then all treated clients will be normalized on whatever scores (e.g., empathy scores) measure changes. When all scores are much the same (i.e., the between-subjects variability is low), as we would expect them to be as a result of treatment, then there will be no statistical basis for predicting recidivism. In other words, whether treatment is effective or not, the clinician is left with nothing more than a guess about the influence of dynamic factors (whether changes induced by treatment, by supervision, or whatever) on estimated risk. Thus, after arguing in numerous publications (Cannon & Quinsey, 1995; Quinsey, 1980; Quinsey & Ambtman, 1979; Quinsey & Cyr, 1986; Quinsey & Lalumière, 1996; Quinsey & Maguire, 1986) that clinical judgments of risk are no better than guessing, Quinsey is recommending combining actuarial estimates with clinical judgments, which seems to eliminate the advantages of deriving the actuarial estimate. With no empirical guidelines, making a guess about the effectiveness of treatment or supervision will influence estimates of risk in quite unpredictable ways. Unfortunately, this means that unless we ignore potential treatment benefits and the estimated value of supervision, we are no further ahead than we were before. If we ignore the influence of both treatment and supervision in our estimates of risk, then we might as well save the expense of engaging in treatment and supervision and simply imprison indefinitely those sexual offenders whose risk is above some arbitrarily determined threshold. Essentially, this is what Quinsey (Quinsey et al., 1996) recently recommended regarding treatment, although, with no demonstrable evidence of its efficacy, he also strongly advocated intense supervision, including electronic monitoring.

Perhaps the most relevant point about the value of Quinsey's composite predictor is that it has been derived, as noted earlier, from a particular, and somewhat unusual, population of sexual offenders. Quinsey, Lalumière, et al. (1995) are aware of this and caution that "the actuarial scheme presented here . . . cannot be used to estimate specific recidivism probabilities for offender samples with characteristics different from those of the sample used to construct the scale" (p. 132). This is a rather circumlocutory way of saying that their actuarial predictor scheme should not be used with any sexual offenders except those at Oak Ridge Mental Health Centre or with a sample that is demonstrably equivalent, presumably meaning only sexual offenders held by reason of insanity. This, of course, excludes the majority of sexual offenders.

To make this point clear, the results of Barbaree and Marshall's (1988) recidivism study of outpatient sexual offenders revealed several factors (e.g., intelligence, socioeconomic status, age of the offender, age of the victim, number of victims of any kind, and actual or simulated intercourse) predictive of reoffending that did not appear in Quinsey's study. In addition, Barbaree and Marshall did not find prior nonsexual offenses, marital status, admissions to corrections, and number of male victims to be valuable predictors, as Quinsey had found. Both studies, however, involved relatively small numbers of subjects (particularly so in Barbaree and Marshall's study), so that the discrepancies, and for that matter the actual findings, may not be replicable with larger, more representative samples.

Hanson and Bussière (1997) conducted a meta-analysis of 61 different reports of sexual offender recidivism, all of which attempted to relate outcome to particular features of the offenders. The studies they included in their meta-analysis ranged across a variety of sexual offender populations but, with a subject pool of almost 30,000, Hansen and Bussière felt reasonably confident that the results of their study could be generalized to most samples of sexual offenders. Although their results offered some support for some of Quinsey et al.'s findings, most of the Quinsey predictors failed to satisfactorily predict outcome. This perhaps is not surprising because, in Rice and Harris's (1995) cross-replication, the composite score derived from Quinsey's factors correlated only .20 with sexual recidivism. Essentially, what Hanson and Bussière found was that the offender's prior sexual offending history, plus his responses to children on the phallometric test (but not his responses to rape), were the best predictors of subsequent success or failure. Although these factors together did not account for a remarkable amount of the variance in outcome (correlations averaged approximately .25), they satisfactorily distinguished successes from failures. Similarly, using primary sexual offense history variables, Epperson, Kaul, and Huot (1995) were able to predict sexual offending (the correlation between their composite score and outcome was $r = .27$). Thus, it appears that, in estimating risk, clinicians can rely on the offender's history of sexual abusive acts plus, where available, phallometric responses to children. However, clinicians should keep in mind that this will not provide a strong basis for prediction, except perhaps for cases at the high and low ends of the risk continuum where risk status may be rather obvious to anyone.

Our view is that caution should be exercised in the use of presently available instruments or indices of possible recidivism. In fact, it might be reasonably claimed that the empirical bases of these so-called actuarial estimates of risk is so limited that they do not yet provide a sound alternative to clinical judgment, which, in any event, must enter into an individual's estimated risk to reoffend.

TREATMENT

As our understanding of the range of problems that characterize sexual offenders has increased, so have the targets in treatment been expanded. In the late 1960s, behavior therapists, for example, assumed that sexual offending was motivated by deviant sexual preferences. Accordingly, the modification of deviant arousal was the prime, if not the only, focus of treatment (Bond & Evans, 1967). From the beginning of the 1970s, several authors suggested that social skills also need to be increased (Barlow, 1973; Marshall, 1971); shortly thereafter, treatment providers added cognitive distortions (Abel, Blanchard, & Becker, 1978) and a broad range of other targets to treatment (Marshall, Earls, Segal, & Darke, 1983). Today, the most common psychological approach to the treatment of sexual offenders involves cognitive-behavioral group therapy aimed at a comprehensive range of targets and guided by a relapse-prevention approach. It is important to note, however, that the use of pharmacological interventions are generally considered an essential adjunct to these cognitive-behavioral programs. More about that in a moment.

What follows is a brief description of the usual targets in treatment and some typical approaches to producing changes in these targets. First, however, a comment about the processes of treatment.

Process vs. Procedures

One advantage that resulted from the early challenges of behavior therapists to established approaches to treatment was the demand that all therapists make explicit the procedures they used to produce change. This had definite benefits, but it also, over time, had the drawback of convincing most behavior therapists and their progeny (i.e., cognitive-behavior therapists) that procedures were all that mattered. The skill of a therapist and client-therapist relationship features were set aside in research that focused exclusively on examining the value of particular procedures. In terms of actual practice, this led to a neglect of concern about process. As a result, a substantial number of treatment approaches with sexual offenders evolved into and remain as psychoeducational programs, where the therapist is essentially construed as and acts as a teacher (Green, 1995; Smith, 1995). The group leader in the most extreme form of these programs may do little more than lecture to the clients. Such a highly structured approach has been encouraged by the production of treatment manuals that do little more than specify the procedural aspects of treatment, as if to imply that good procedures in the hands of any therapist will be effective. Though this may be true, there is no evidence available to support the idea that procedures alone have powerful effects, and most therapists behave as though the manner in which therapeutic interventions are presented is quite important.

Some cognitive-behavioral therapists working in various fields have stressed the importance of process variables in treatment and have provided evidence of their value (Goldstein, Heller, & Sechrest, 1966; Lazarus, 1971; W. Miller & Rollnick, 1991; Wilson & Evans, 1977). I (Marshall, 1996b) have explicitly raised these issues in the treatment of sexual offenders. In that article, I emphasized the importance of treating clients with respect and enhancing their sense of self-worth and their belief in their potential for change; I also suggested that, whether intentional or not, the therapist provides a model of various kinds of behaviors. If this latter point is true, then therapists should deliberately attempt to model the kinds of behaviors and attitudes that they are trying to develop in their sexual offender clients. To date, there is little evidence concerning the value of process variables in treating sexual offenders, although I (Marshall, 1997b) have demonstrated that enhancing the self-esteem of these clients reduces their deviant sexual interests, even in the absence of targeting deviant arousal in treatment. Accordingly, researchers are encouraged to give greater attention to these factors in the future; in the meantime, we hope that clinicians who already believe in the value of process variables will continue to act accordingly, and that the procedural advocates will give serious consideration to the value of how treatment is delivered. All that follows should be understood against a background of creating a positive therapeutic environment.

Treatment Components

Acceptance of Responsibility

The majority of sexual offenders either deny any responsibility for their offending (i.e., they either claim they did not do it, or they attribute responsibility to persons or factors outside their control), or they minimize their responsibility in one way or another (Barbaree, 1991). Some treatment providers exclude from entry to treatment those sexual offenders who do not accept full, or at least substantial, responsibility. Our observations suggest that this will lead to the exclusion of many high-risk offenders and we, therefore, consider it to be our job to motivate these offenders (Marshall, in press-a). For the most part, we appear to be successful in securing the full participation in treatment of these men, and the evidence we have collected indicates that we are also successful in persuading them to accept full responsibility (Marshall, 1994).

As the first step in treatment, each offender has to provide a disclosure detailing all aspects of his abusive behavior, including the thoughts and feelings he had prior to, during, and after the offense(s). All group members (usually 8–10 in total) are asked to challenge the offender who is giving his disclosure, and the therapist models appropriately supportive but firm challenges. In this, the therapist is assisted by having available the official police account of the offense, the victim's description of what happened, and the transcript of the trial where the offender was convicted. These challenges are meant not only to diminish denial and minimizations, but also to correct faulty thinking, distorted perceptions, and inappropriate attitudes that were functionally linked to offending. Until the client changes his negative attitudes and his distorted thinking and perceptions, he cannot be said to have accepted full responsibility. This is, then, a critical and rather extensive initial component in treatment.

Empathy

Our investigations of empathy deficits (Marshall, Hudson, et al., 1995), as noted earlier, suggested that sexual offenders lack empathy primarily for their own victims rather than having a more generalized deficit. We take this to mean that they were simply distorting their view of the harm they had done. In this view, empathy training as it has typically been done with sexual offenders (see Marshall & Fernandez, in press, and Hildebran & Pithers, 1989, for descriptions of the typical treatment procedures aimed at enhancing empathy) is misplaced. It is certainly true that these procedures seem to enhance empathy (Marshall, O'Sullivan, & Fernandez, 1996; Pithers, 1994), but it may be that they are not essential to effective treatment. For instance, if it is the case that the apparent deficits in empathy toward their own victims are due to distorted perceptions of harm, then the initial part of treatment that attempts to correct distortions may be all that is necessary, so long as it includes identification of harm. We are presently evaluating this possibility, and the data so far look encouraging.

Social Functioning

The targets in this component vary considerably across programs. For example, the Vermont Treatment Program (Pithers, Martin, & Cumming, 1989) includes components that address anger, communication skills, and emotional recognition, but no explicit training in conversational or relationship skills. Maletzky (1991) targets heterosocial and heterosexual behaviors to increase success in consenting relationships; he also includes training to reduce anxiety and to increase assertiveness.

In our treatment programs, we make the acquisition of behavioral skills and appropriate attitudes, thoughts, perceptions, and feelings about adult relationships the central focus of our social skills component. Within this context, it is necessary for clients to learn the features of relationships that maximize satisfaction for both partners, and then acquire the skills (behavioral, cognitive, and affective) necessary to achieve the goal of forming effective relationships. This includes enhancement of self-confidence, overcoming blocks to intimacy (e.g., fear or avoidance of intimacy, distrust of others, poor communication), anger control, problem solving, assertiveness, and sex education.

We have described in detail elsewhere these various elements (e.g., self-esteem, relationship skills, general interpersonal skills, anger control, empathy) and the procedures and processes we employ to achieve changes on these features (Marshall, in press-c; Marshall, Bryce, Hudson, Ward, & Moth, 1996; Marshall, Champagne, Sturgeon, & Bryce, 1997). Our appraisals, as reported in these articles, have revealed positive benefits for these interventions.

Deviant Sexual Interests

We have shifted our focus over the past 27 years to markedly de-emphasizing the importance of deviant sexuality in treatment (Marshall, in press-b). We do this for several reasons, not the least of which is that this reduces the likelihood that the offenders will think of their behaviors as driven exclusively, or even primarily, by deviant sexual desires. No doubt, deviant desires play some part in their offending, but we, along with most clinicians, believe that other motives (e.g., power, control over others, desire for physical contact, desire to be admired) are more salient. Certainly, we consider that what offenders think has more to do with offending than does genital arousal. Our position is essentially that if we can have our clients develop the skills, attitudes, and feelings necessary to meet their needs in prosocial ways, they will have no need for deviant acts or fantasies. In fact, we have not addressed deviant interests directly in therapy for the past five years, and this has not affected our low recidivism rates (less than 3% have reoffended).

However, most programs do, in fact, target deviant arousal. Behavioral techniques are used to individually train offenders to eliminate deviant thoughts and increase the frequency and attractiveness of appropriate sexual fantasies. Covert sensitization (Cautela, 1967), masturbatory reconditioning (Marquis, 1970), satiation therapy (Marshall, 1979), and aversion therapy (Abel, Levis, & Clancy, 1970), have all been used to achieve the goal of altering sexual interests. Unfortunately, the evidence bearing on their value does not encourage confidence (Laws & Marshall, 1991; Quinsey & Earls, 1990; Quinsey & Marshall, 1983).

Pharmacological interventions appear to be effective in eliminating deviant desires and, when properly administered, may leave appropriate sexual interests intact (Bradford, 1990, 1993; Land, 1995). Antiandrogens, such as medroxyprogesterone acetate or cyproterone acetate, are effective in this regard, so long as the dosage does not so significantly lower testosterone levels that all sexual functioning is eliminated (Bradford & Pawlak, 1993). However, compliance can be a serious problem with the use of these agents (Langevin et al., 1979), so extreme care must be taken to prepare clients for the treatment; the use of injected rather than oral administration may increase compliance. There is also recent evidence supporting the value of serotonin-reuptake inhibitors (such as fluoxetine, buspirone, or clomipramine). Several reports (e.g., Fedoroff & Fedoroff, 1992; Kafka, 1991; Kruesi, Fine, Valladares, Phillips, & Rapoport, 1992; Perilstein, Lipper, & Friedman, 1991) have demonstrated benefits for these drugs in controlling the intrusiveness of deviant sexual fantasies and they seem to present fewer problems of compliance than do the antiandrogens. However, in our treatment programs, we have used pharmacological agents with fewer than 6% of our clients in any one year and it is usually far lower than that. In any case, pharmacological interventions should not be viewed as sole or even primary treatment agents; they are best viewed as adjunctive to comprehensive psychological treatment.

Substance Abuse

Problems with substance use, abuse, and dependence are best dealt with in specialized additional programs; the sexual offender program can serve to integrate what is learned from these interventions with the client's overall relapse-prevention plans. Substance abuse programs are based on relapse-prevention strategies developed by Marlatt and colleagues (Marlatt, 1982; Marlatt & Gordon, 1985), and the reader is referred to those sources for a more complete understanding. The next section describes the application of Marlatt's principles to the treatment of sexually deviant behavior, and this may illustrate the general approach of relapse-prevention strategies.

Relapse Prevention

Most clinicians employ a quite comprehensive approach to training sexual offenders in the use of relapse-prevention principles (Jenkins-Hall, Osborn, Anderson, Anderson, & Shockley-Smith, 1989; Marques, Day, Nelson, & Miner, 1989; Pithers, 1990). Typically, these programs train clients to understand the various and complex notions of relapse prevention and assist them in developing sound plans for avoiding future risks, and they also have a significant postdischarge supervision component. This component may involve frequent, intensive, and extended supervision by a person trained in relapse prevention, and it usually also involves follow-up treatment sessions, again for an extended period. To date, it has not been shown that such extensive postdischarge supervision and treatment adds anything to standard cognitive-behavioral treatment (Marshall & Anderson, 1996), but it may appeal to the public, politicians, and bureaucrats in the present climate that is so hostile to sexual offenders. Similarly, there is no evidence that elaborate within-treatment training of sexual offenders in the principles and concepts of relapse prevention (e.g., having clients understand notions such as the "abstinence violation effect" or the "problem of immediate gratification") is necessary or has the effect of enhancing treatment benefits.

We restrict our use of the relapse-prevention approach to having clients identify their offense cycle, develop plans to avoid or deal with unexpected occurrences of risks or precipitating problems, and define a set of warning signs that will alert themselves and others (e.g., friends, family, and probation/parole officers) that they may be moving to higher risk levels. In identifying their offense cycle, clients must generate a set of factors (e.g., anger, low self-esteem, intoxication) that put them at risk for either fantasizing about sexual abuse or enacting it. They must also identify situations or behaviors (e.g., being alone with a child; driving aimlessly, in the case of an exhibitionist or a rapist) that put them at risk and the steps they typically go through to get access to a victim, including, for example, deceiving and manipulating others, grooming a child, and convincing themselves that their preparatory actions are not aimed at offending.

Once they have identified their offense cycle, they must then develop plans for dealing more effectively with problems, for avoiding or escaping from risky situations, and for meeting their needs in prosocial ways. Finally, their warning signs are a simple product of their identified offense cycle features (e.g., beginning to feel depressed, starting to spend time alone or with children).

VALUE OF TREATMENT

There are many problems facing researchers who attempt to evaluate the effects of treatment with sexual offenders. Few of these problems arise, of course, when the task is simply to determine whether or not the goals of the treatment components have been achieved (e.g., the enhancement of self-esteem, the acceptance of responsibility, or the attainment of social skills). Difficulties arise when we wish to estimate the effects of treatment on subsequent recidivism.

Accessing official records (records held by police as well as by probation or parole officers) can be difficult, and in the United States, there may be a problem tracing ex-clients outside of the researcher's home state. For researchers working in Canada, this is not a problem, as all crimes are under federal criminal codes, and all across the country, records (including charges that have been withdrawn) are kept in a federal recording system accessible to approved researchers.

The primary problem with conducting an evaluation of treatment outcome concerns the difficulty of implementing a controlled study. The ideal requirements for such a study include, among other things, the random allocation of matched offenders, all of whom are seeking treatment, to either treatment or no-treatment. These treated and untreated offenders must then be released and followed for several years (at least four years, but preferably longer). For most sexual offenders, the failure to participate in treatment has serious implications; for example, they may be kept in prison longer, they may be transferred to a higher security prison, or they may be refused access to their children. Given these conditions, few sexual offenders can be expected to volunteer for such a study, and the motives and wits of those who do should be considered suspect. More to the point, however, is the concern that sexual offenders are hardly the ones who should be given the right to agree to such a study. The potential victims of sexual offenders are, after all, the ones who may suffer should an offender's behavior remain unchanged. Therefore, women and children, as the prime victims of sexual abuse, are the ones who should be asked to agree to the implementation of a controlled evaluation that deliberately withholds treatment from some sexual offenders. Even in the absence of any evidence that treatment might reduce reoffending, we suspect that few, if any, women and children would approve of such a controlled treatment trial unless they were coerced into supporting an untreated offender's release.

In addition, few organizations funding treatment for sexual offenders are prepared to deliberately withhold treatment from any of these dangerous men for fear of the potential public outcry that likely will follow a reoffense among the untreated men. Related to this is the fact that in most systems, untreated sexual offenders are held in custody longer than those who enter treatment. Thus, the ideal design would be seriously damaged because the treated and untreated men would thereby differ on presumably significant features— namely, the length of time in prison and no doubt resentment on the part of untreated offenders. In fact, in any ethically appropriate format, all offenders should be offered the choice of entering the controlled study, and thereby run the risk of being left untreated with all its consequences, or simply entering a regular treatment program. To deny offenders this type of choice seems unethical. In California's controlled outcome study of the treatment of sexual offenders (Marques et al., 1989), volunteers are randomly allocated to treatment or no-treatment without the option of selecting themselves out of the evaluation in order to enter treatment. Those who do not volunteer are excluded from the possibility of receiving treatment. It is surprising that prisoner advocates and civil rights lawyers have not successfully challenged the procedures of this study.

Finally, there is the problem of low base rates (i.e., the recidivism rates of untreated offenders). Untreated sexual offenders display remarkably variable recidivism rates, but in almost all cases, the rates are quite low for statistical purposes, although this is not how the public perceives it. Barbaree (1997) has calculated the statistical power necessary to discern benefits from treatment with sexual offenders. According to his calculations, with the usual base rates and a reasonably powerful treatment effect, we would need almost 1,000 subjects in an outcome study followed for up to 10 years to demonstrate the effectiveness of treatment. It is unlikely that such a study will be done in the foreseeable future, if ever.

To date, there have been a number of uncontrolled studies evaluating treatment. In the best of these, the researchers have been able to identify an approximately matched group of untreated offenders from the same setting and this has served as the comparison group. Typically, these comparison subjects were untreated simply because of the lack of resources available to the treatment providers, or because the clients could not access continued treatment. In the evaluation of our community-based program (Marshall & Barbaree, 1988), for example, many sexual offenders who expressed a desire to be treated could not attend our clinic on a regular basis because they lived too far away (some 200 miles or more). This group served as our untreated comparison group. Although this group served as a convenient comparison, it is not an ideal control because there was some overrepresentation of rural subjects in the no-treatment group compared to the treatment group. Nevertheless, it was the best we could do in the circumstances, and it is certainly better than not having any comparison group of untreated offenders.

The results of this study revealed that 8% of the nonfamilial child molesters who received treatment reoffended, whereas 18% of the untreated men reoffended. Among the exhibitionists, 12% of the treated and 24% of the untreated subjects recidivated. These recidivism figures for child molesters and exhibitionists were derived from official police records. When we accessed additional unofficial information, held in the files of the police and child protection agencies, we found evidence revealing recidivism rates for all groups that were almost three times higher than the official records showed. These unofficial data, by elevating the recidivism rates, gave us the statistical power to demonstrate treatment effects.

There are now many less than ideal studies reported in the literature of treatment outcome with sexual offenders. By far the majority of these studies reveal either lower than expected recidivism rates for treated offenders, or lower rates than a comparison group of untreated offenders. Reviews of this literature have persuaded some authors that treatment outcome with sexual offenders at the least encourages optimism (Marshall, Jones, Ward, Johnston, & Barbaree, 1991; Steele, 1995). Others remain unconvinced (Quinsey et al., 1993), although many of their arguments have been rebutted (Marshall, 1993; Marshall & Pithers, 1994).

If treatment is at best only marginally effective with sexual offenders, nevertheless the benefits to society, in terms of fewer victims and reduced financial burdens to taxpayers, are quite dramatic. It has been calculated, for example, that for every sexual offender who is successfully treated, there are more than two innocent people saved from suffering, and the taxpayer is at least $200,000 better off (Marshall, 1992; Prentky & Burgess, 1991). These data, which have been confirmed by others (McGrath, 1994; Steele, 1995), suggest that it would be negligent not to attempt to treat all sexual offenders who are going to eventually be returned to society and thereby be at risk to abuse again.

REFERENCES

Abel, G. G., Barlow, D. H., Blanchard, E. B., & Guild, D. (1977). The components of rapists' sexual arousal. *Archives of General Psychiatry, 34*, 895–903.

Abel, G. G., & Becker, J. V. (1985). *Sexual Interest Cardsort.* Atlanta: Behavioral Medicine Laboratory, Emory University.

Abel, G. G., Becker, J. V., Cunningham-Rathner, J., Rouleau, J. L., Kaplan, M., & Reich, J. (1984). *Treatment manual: The treatment of child molesters.* Atlanta: Emory University School of Medicine, Department of Psychiatry.

Abel, G. G., Becker, J. V., Murphy, W. D., & Flanagan, B. (1981). Identifying dangerous child molesters. In R. B. Stuart (Ed.), *Violent behavior: Social learning approaches to prediction, management and treatment* (pp. 116–137). New York: Brunner/Mazel.

Abel, G. G., & Blanchard, E. B. (1976). The measurement and generation of sexual arousal in male sexual deviates. In M. Hersen, R. Eisler, & P. M. Miller (Eds.), *Progress in behavior modification* (Vol. 11, pp. 99–136). New York: Academic Press.

Abel, G. G., Blanchard, E. B., & Becker, J. V. (1978). An integrated treatment program from rapists. In R. T. Rada (Ed.), *Clinical aspects of the rapist* (pp. 161–214). New York: Grune & Stratton.

Abel, G. G., Gore, D. K., Holland, C. L., Camp, N., Becker, J. V., & Rathner, J. (1989). The measurement of the cognitive distortions of child molesters. *Annals of Sex Research, 2,* 135–152.

Abel, G. G., Levis, D., & Clancy, J. (1970). Aversion therapy applied to taped sequences of deviant behavior in exhibitionists and other sexual deviations: Preliminary report. *Journal of Behavior Therapy and Experimental Psychiatry, 1,* 59–60.

Abel, G. G., Mittelman, M. S., & Becker, J. V. (1985). Sexual offenders: Results of assessments and recommendations for treatment. In M. H. Ben-Aron, S. J. Hucker, & C. D. Webster (Eds.), *Clinical criminology: Current concepts* (pp. 191–205). Toronto: M&M Graphics.

American Psychiatric Association. (1980). *Diagnostic and statistical manual of mental disorders* (3rd ed.). Washington, DC: Author.

American Psychiatric Association. (1987). *Diagnostic and statistical manual of mental disorders–revised* (Rev. 3rd ed.). Washington, DC: Author.

American Psychiatric Association. (1994). *Diagnostic and statistical manual of mental disorders* (4th ed.). Washington, DC: Author.

Apfelberg, C., Sugar, C., & Pfeff, A. Z. (1944). A psychiatric study of 250 sex offenders. *American Journal of Psychiatry, 100,* 762–769.

Araji, S., & Finkelhor, D. (1985). Explanations of pedophilia: Review of empirical research. *Bulletin of the American Academy of Psychiatry & Law, 13,* 17.

Barbaree, H. E. (1991). Denial and minimization among sex offenders: Assessment and treatment outcome. *Forum on Corrections Research, 3,* 300–333.

Barbaree, H. E. (1997). Evaluating treatment efficacy with sexual offenders: The insensitivity of recidivism studies to treatment effects. *Sexual Abuse: A Journal of Research and Treatment, 9,* 111–128.

Barbaree, H. E., Baxter, D. J., & Marshall, W. L. (1989). The reliability of the rape index in a sample of rapists and nonrapists. *Violence and Victims, 4,* 299–306.

Barbaree, H. E., & Marshall, W. L. (1988). Deviant sexual arousal, demographic and offense history variables as predictors of reoffense among child molesters and incest offenders. *Behavioral Sciences & the Law, 6,* 267–280.

Barbaree, H. E., & Marshall, W. L. (1989). Erectile responses amongst heterosexual child molesters, father-daughter incest offenders, and matched nonoffenders: Five distinct age preference profiles. *Canadian Journal of Behavioural Science, 21,* 70–82.

Barbaree, H. E., Marshall, W. L., & Lanthier, R. D. (1979). Deviant sexual arousal in rapists. *Behaviour Research and Therapy, 14,* 215–222.

Barbaree, H. E., & Peacock, E. J. (1995). Phallometric assessment of sexual preferences as an investigative tool in cases of alleged child sexual abuse. In T. Ney (Ed.), *Allegations of child sexual abuse: Assessment and case management* (pp. 242–259). New York: Brunner/Mazel.

Barlow, D. H. (1973). Increasing heterosexual responsiveness in the treatment of sexual deviation: A review of the clinical and experimental evidence. *Behavior Therapy, 4,* 655–671.

Barnard, G. W., Fuller, A. K., Robbins, L., & Shaw, T. (1989). *The child molester: An integrated approach to evaluation and treatment.* New York: Brunner/Mazel.

Baxter, D. J., Barbaree, H. E., & Marshall, W. L. (1986). Sexual responses to consenting and forced sex in a large sample of rapists and nonrapists. *Behaviour Research and Therapy, 24,* 513–520.

Bond, I., & Evans, D. (1967). Avoidance therapy: Its use in two cases of underwear fetishism. *Canadian Medical Association Journal, 96,* 1160–1162.

Bradford, J. M. W. (1990). The antiandrogen and hormonal treatment of sex offenders. In W. L. Marshall, D. R. Laws, & H. E. Barbaree (Eds.), *Handbook of sexual assault: Issues, theories, and treatment of the offender* (pp. 297–310). New York: Plenum Press.

Bradford, J. M. W. (1993). The pharmacological treatment of the adolescent sex offender. In H. E. Barbaree, W. L. Marshall, & S. M. Hudson (Eds.), *The juvenile sex offender* (pp. 278–288). New York: Guilford Press.

Bradford, J. M. W., & Pawlak, A. (1993). Double-blind placebo crossover study of cyproterone acetate in the treatment of the paraphilias. *Archives of Sexual Behavior, 22,* 383–402.

Bumby, K. M., & Hansen, D. J. (1997). Intimacy deficits, fear of intimacy, and loneliness among sexual offenders. *Criminal Justice and Behavior, 24,* 315–331.

Burt, M. R. (1980). Cultural myths and supports for rape. *Journal of Personality and Social Psychology, 38,* 217–230.

Burt, M. R. (1983). Justifying personal violence: A comparison of rapists and the general public. *Victimology, 8,* 131–150.

Cannon, C. K., & Quinsey, V. L. (1995). The likelihood of violent behavior: Predictions, postdictions, and hindsight bias. *Canadian Journal of Behavioural Science, 27,* 92–106.

Cautela, J. R. (1967). Covert sensitization. *Psychological Record, 20,* 459–468.

Check, J. V. P., Perlman, D., & Malamuth, N. M. (1985). Loneliness and aggressive behavior. *Journal of Social and Personal Relations, 2,* 243–252.

Christie, M. M., Marshall, W. L., & Lanthier, R. D. (1979). *A descriptive study of incarcerated rapists and pedophiles.* Report to the Solicitor General of Canada, Ottawa.

Epperson, D. L., Kaul, J. D., & Huot, S. J. (1995, October). *Predicting risk for recidivism for incarcerated sex offenders: Updated development on the Sex Offender Screening Tool (SOST).* Paper presented at the 14th annual conference of the Association for the Treatment of Sexual Abusers, New Orleans.

Fedoroff, J. P., & Fedoroff, I. C. (1992). Buspirone and paraphilic sexual behavior. *Journal of Offender Rehabilitation, 18,* 89–108.

Finkelhor, D. (1984). *Child sexual abuse: New theory and research.* New York: Free Press.

Frenzel, R. R., & Lang, R. A. (1989). Identifying sexual preferences in intrafamilial and extrafamilial child sexual abusers. *Annals of Sex Research, 2,* 255–275.

Freund, K. (1967). Erotic preference in pedophilia. *Behaviour Research and Therapy, 5,* 339–348.

Freund, K. (1981). Assessment of pedophilia. In M. Cook & K. Howells (Eds.), *Adult sexual interest in children* (pp. 139–179). London: Academic Press.

Freund, K., & Blanchard, R. (1989). Phallometric diagnosis of pedophilia. *Journal of Consulting and Clinical Psychology, 57,* 1–6.

Freund, K., Chan, S., & Coulthard, R. (1979). Phallometric diagnoses with "nonadmitters." *Behaviour Research and Therapy, 17,* 451–457.

Freund, K., & Watson, R. J. (1991). Assessment of the sensitivity and specificity of a phallometric test: An update of phallometric diagnosis of pedophilia. *Psychological Assessment: A Journal of Consulting and Clinical Psychology, 3,* 254–260.

Freund, K., Watson, R. J., & Dickey, R. (1991). Sex offenses against female children perpetrated by men who are not pedophiles. *Journal of Sex Research, 28,* 409–423.

Garlick, Y., Marshall, W. L., & Thornton, D. (1996). Intimacy deficits and attribution of blame among sexual offenders. *Legal and Criminological Psychology, 1,* 251–258.

Goldstein, A. P., Heller, K., & Sechrest, L. (1966). *Psychotherapy and the psychology of behavior change.* New York: Wiley.

Green, R. (1995). Psycho-educational modules. In B. K. Schwartz & H. R. Cellini (Eds.), *The sex offender: Corrections, treatment and legal practice* (pp. 13.1–13.10). Kingston, NJ: Civic Research Institute.

Groth, A. N. (1979). *Men who rape: The psychology of the offender.* New York: Plenum Press.

Hall, G. C. N. (1989). Sexual arousal and arousability in a sexual offender population. *Journal of Abnormal Psychology, 98,* 145–149.

Hanson, R. K., & Bussière, M. (1997). *Predictors of sex offender recidivism: A meta-analysis.* Unpublished report to Solicitor General of Canada, Ottawa.

Hanson, R. K., & Slater, S. (1988). Sexual victimization in the history of child sexual abusers: A review. *Annals of Sex Research, 1,* 485–499.

Hare, R. D. (1991). *Manual for the revised psychopathy checklist.* Toronto: Multi-Health Systems.

Hildebran, D., & Pithers, W. D. (1989). Enhancing offender empathy for sexual-abuse victims. In D. R. Laws (Ed.), *Relapse prevention with sex offenders* (pp. 236–243). New York: Guilford Press.

Honts, C. R., & Perry, M. V. (1992). Polygraph admissibility. *Law and Human Behavior, 16,* 357–379.

Hucker, S. J., & Bain, J. (1990). Androgenic hormones and sexual assault. In W. L. Marshall, D. R. Laws, & H. E. Barbaree (Eds.), *Handbook of sexual assault: Issues, theories, and treatment of the offender* (pp. 93–102). New York: Plenum Press.

Iacono, W. G., & Patrick, C. J. (1987). What psychologists should know about lie detection. In I. B. Weiner & A. K. Hess (Eds.), *Handbook of forensic psychology* (pp. 460–489). New York: Wiley.

Jensen, S. H., & Jewell, C. A. (1988). The sex offender experts. *The Prosecutors, 21,* 13–20.

Jenkins-Hall, K. D., Osborn, C. A., Anderson, C. S., Anderson, K. A., & Shockley-Smith, C. (1989). The center for prevention of child molestation. In D. R. Laws (Ed.), *Relapse prevention with sex offenders* (pp. 268–291). New York: Guilford Press.

Kafka, M. P. (1991). Successful treatment of paraphilic coercive disorder (a rapist) with fluoxetine hydrochloride. *British Journal of Psychiatry, 158,* 844–847.

Knight, R. A., & Prentky, R. A. (1990). Classifying sexual offenders: The development and corroboration of taxonomic models. In W. L. Marshall, D. R. Laws, & H. E. Barbaree (Eds.), *Handbook of sexual assault: Issues, theories, and treatment of the offender* (pp. 23–52). New York: Plenum Press.

Kruesi, J. M. P., Fine, S., Valladeres, L., Phillips, R. A., & Rapoport, J. L. (1992). Paraphilias: A double-blind crossover comparison of clomipramine versus dosipramine. *Archives of Sexual Behavior, 21,* 587–593.

Lalumière, M. L., & Quinsey, V. L. (1991). Polygraph testing of child molesters: Are we ready? *Violence Update, 1,* 3–11.

Land, W. B. (1995). Psychopharmacological options for sex offenders. In B. K. Schwartz & H. R. Cellini (Eds.), *The sex offender: Corrections, treatment and legal practice* (pp. 18.1–18.7). Kingston, NJ: Civic Research Institute.

Langevin, R., Paitich, D., Ramsey, G., Anderson, C., Kamrad, J., Pope, S., Geller, G., & Newman, S. (1979). Experimental studies in the etiology of genital exhibitionism. *Archives of Sexual Behavior, 8,* 307–331.

Langevin, R., Paitich, D., & Russon, A. E. (1985). Are rapists sexually anomalous, aggressive, or both? In R. Langevin (Ed.), *Erotic preference, gender identity, and aggression in men: New research studies* (pp. 13–38). Hillsdale, NJ: Erlbaum.

Laws, D. R., & Marshall, W. L. (1991). Masturbatory reconditioning: An evaluative review. *Advances in Behaviour Research and Therapy, 13,* 13–25.

Lawson, J. S., Marshall, W. L., & McGrath, P. (1979). The social self-esteem inventory. *Educational and Psychological Measurement, 39,* 803–811.

Lazarus, A. A. (1971). *Behavior therapy and beyond.* New York: McGraw-Hill.

Levine, S., & Koenig, J. (1980). *Why men rape: Interviews with convicted rapists.* New York: Macmillan.

Lightfoot, L. O., & Barbaree, H. E. (1993). The relationship between substance use and abuse and sexual offending in adolescents. In H. E. Barbaree, W. L. Marshall, & S. M. Hudson (Eds.), *The juvenile sex offender* (pp. 203–224). New York: Guilford Press.

Malamuth, N. M. (1984). Aggression against women: Cultural and individual causes. In N. M. Malamuth & E. Donnerstein (Eds.), *Pornography and sexual aggression* (pp. 19–52). Orlando, FL: Academic Press.

Maletzky, B. M. (1991). *Treating the sexual offender.* Newbury Park, CA: Sage.

Marlatt, G. A. (1982). Relapse prevention: A self-control program for the treatment of addictive behaviors. In R. B. Stuart (Ed.), *Adherence, compliance, and generalization in behavioral medicine* (pp. 329–378). New York: Brunner/Mazel.

Marlatt, G. A., & Gordon, J. R. (Eds.). (1985). *Relapse prevention.* New York: Guilford Press.

Marolla, J., & Scully, D. (1986). Attitudes toward women, violence, and rape: A comparison of convicted rapists and other felons. *Deviant Behavior, 1,* 337–355.

Marques, J. K. (in press). How to answer the question, "Does sex offender treatment work?" In W. L. Marshall & J. Frenken (Eds.), *North American and European approaches to sexual offenders: Converging trends.* Thousand Oaks, CA: Sage.

Marques, J. K., Day, D. M., Nelson, C., & Miner, M. H. (1989). The sex offender treatment and evaluation project: California's relapse prevention program. In D. R. Laws (Ed.), *Relapse prevention with sex offenders* (pp. 96–104). New York: Guilford Press.

Marques, J. K., Day, D. M., Nelson, C., & West, M. A. (1994). Effects of cognitive-behavioral treatment on sex offender recidivism: Preliminary results of a longitudinal study. *Criminal Justice and Behavior, 21,* 28–54.

Marques, J. K., & Nelson, C. (1989). Elements of high-risk situations for sex offenders. In D. R. Laws (Ed.), *Relapse prevention with sex offenders* (pp. 35–46). New York: Guilford Press.

Marques, J. K., Nelson, C., West, M. A., & Day, D. M. (1994). The relationship between treatment goals and recidivism among child molesters. *Behaviour Research and Therapy, 32,* 577–588.

Marquis, J. (1970). Orgasmic reconditioning: Changing sexual object choice through controlling masturbation fantasies. *Journal of Behavior Therapy and Experimental Psychiatry, 1,* 263–270.

Marshall, P. G., Keltner, A., & Marshall, W. L. (1981). Anxiety reduction, assertive training, and enactment of consequences: A comparative study in the modification of nonassertive and social fear. *Behavior Modification, 5,* 85–102.

Marshall, W. L. (1971). A combined treatment method for certain sexual deviations. *Behaviour Research and Therapy, 9,* 292–294.

Marshall, W. L. (1979). Satiation therapy: A procedure for reducing deviant sexual arousal. *Journal of Applied Behavior Analysis, 12,* 10–22.

Marshall, W. L. (1989). Intimacy, loneliness and sexual offenders. *Behaviour Research and Therapy, 27,* 691–503.

Marshall, W. L. (1992). The social value of treatment with sexual offenders. *Canadian Journal of Human Sexuality, 1,* 109–114.

Marshall, W. L. (1993). The treatment of sex offenders: What does the outcome data tell us? A reply to Quinsey et al. *Journal of Interpersonal Violence, 8,* 524–530.

Marshall, W. L. (1994). Treatment effects on denial and minimization in incarcerated sex offenders. *Behaviour Research and Therapy, 32,* 559–564.

Marshall, W. L. (1996a). Psychological evaluation in sexual offence cases. *Queen's Law Journal, 21,* 499–514.

Marshall, W. L. (1996b). The sexual offender: Monster, victim, or everyman? *Sexual Abuse: A Journal of Research and Treatment, 8,* 317–335.

Marshall, W. L. (1997a). *Phallometric testing with sexual offenders: Limits to its value.* Submitted for publication.

Marshall, W. L. (1997b). The relationship between self-esteem and deviant sexual arousal in nonfamilial child molesters. *Behavior Modification, 21,* 86–96.

Marshall, W. L. (in press-a). Adult sexual offenders. In A. S. Bellack & M. Hersen (Eds.) & N. Singh (Vol. ed.), *Comprehensive clinical psychology: Vol. 9. Applications in diverse populations.* Oxford, England: Elsevier Science.

Marshall, W. L. (in press-b). Sexual preferences: Are they useful in the assessment and treatment of sexual offenders? In D. Fisher, M. Cardgo, & B. Print (Eds.), *Sex offenders: Toward improved practice.* London: Whiting & Birch.

Marshall, W. L. (in press-c). Enhancing social skills and relationship skills. In M. S. Carich & S. Mussack (Eds.), *Handbook of sex offender treatment.* Orwell, VT: Safer Society Press.

Marshall, W. L., & Anderson, D. (1996). An evaluation of the benefits of relapse prevention programs with sexual offenders. *Sexual Abuse: A Journal of Research and Treatment, 8,* 209–221.

Marshall, W. L., Anderson, D., & Champagne, F. (1996). The importance of self-esteem in sexual offenders. *Psychology, Crime and Law, 3,* 81–106.

Marshall, W. L., & Barbaree, H. E. (1988). The long-term evaluation of a behavioral treatment program for child molesters. *Behaviour Research and Therapy, 26,* 499–511.

Marshall, W. L., & Barbaree, H. E. (1990). An integrated theory of sexual offending. In W. L. Marshall, D. R. Laws, & H. E. Barbaree (Eds.), *Handbook of sexual assault: Issues, theories, and treatment of the offender* (pp. 257–275). New York: Plenum Press.

Marshall, W. L., Barbaree, H. E., & Butt, J. (1988). Sexual offenders against male children: Sexual preferences. *Behaviour Research and Therapy, 26,* 383–391.

Marshall, W. L., Barbaree, H. E., & Christophe, D. (1986). Sexual offenders against female children: Sexual preferences for age of victims and type of behaviour. *Canadian Journal of Behavioural Science, 18,* 424–439.

Marshall, W. L., Barbaree, H. E., & Fernandez, Y. M. (1995). Some aspects of social competence in sexual offenders. *Sexual Abuse: A Journal of Research and Treatment, 7,* 113–127.

Marshall, W. L., Bryce, P., Hudson, S. M., Ward, T., & Moth, B. (1996). The enhancement of intimacy and the reduction of loneliness among child molesters. *Journal of Family Violence, 11,* 219–235.

Marshall, W. L., Champagne, F., Sturgeon, C., & Bryce, P. (1997). Increasing the self-esteem of child molesters. *Sexual Abuse: A Journal of Research and Treatment.*

Marshall, W. L., & Darke, J. (1982). Inferring humiliation as motivation in sexual offenses. *Treatment for Sexual Aggressives, 5,* 1–3.

Marshall, W. L., Earls, C. M., Segal, Z. V., & Darke, J. (1983). A behavioral program for the assessment and treatment of sexual aggressors. In K. Craig & R. McMahon (Eds.), *Advances in clinical behavior therapy* (pp. 148–174). New York: Brunner/Mazel.

Marshall, W. L., Eccles, A., & Barbaree, H. E. (1991). Treatment of exhibitionists: A focus on sexual deviance versus cognitive and relationship features. *Behaviour Research and Therapy, 29,* 129–135.

Marshall, W. L., & Fernandez, Y. M. (1997). Enfoques cognitivo-conductuales para las parafilias: El tratameinto de la delincuencia sexual. In V. E. Caballo (Ed.), *Manual para el tratamiento cognitivo-conductual de los trastornos psicológicos, Vol.1. Trastornos por ansiedad, sexualas, afectivos y psicóticos* (pp. 299–331). Madrid: Siglio Veintiuno de Espa–a Editores.

Marshall, W. L., & Fernandez, Y. M. (in press). Developing empathy and remorse. In M. S. Carich & S. Mussack (Eds.), *Handbook of sex offender treatment*. Orwell, VT: Safer Society Press.

Marshall, W. L., & Hall, G. C. N. (1995). The value of the MMPI in deciding forensic issues in accused sexual offenders. *Sexual Abuse: A Journal of Research and Treatment, 7,* 205–219.

Marshall, W. L., Hudson, S. M., Jones, R., & Fernandez, Y. M. (1995). Empathy in sex offenders. *Clinical Psychology Review, 15,* 99–113.

Marshall, W. L., Jones, R. L., Ward, T., Johnston, P., & Barbaree, H. E. (1991). Treatment outcome with sex offenders. *Clinical Psychology Review, 11,* 465–485.

Marshall, W. L., Laws, D. R., & Barbaree, H. E. (Eds.). (1990). *Handbook of sexual assault: Issues, theories, and treatment of the offender*. New York: Plenum Press.

Marshall, W. L., & Marshall, L. E. (in press). Child sexual molestation. In V. B. Van Hasselt & M. Hersen (Eds.), *Aggression and violence: An introductory text*. New York: Allyn & Bacon.

Marshall, W. L., O'Sullivan, C., & Fernandez, Y. M. (1996). The enhancement of victim empathy among incarcerated child molesters. *Legal and Criminological Psychology, 1,* 95–102.

Marshall, W. L., & Pithers, W. D. (1994). A reconsideration of treatment outcome with sex offenders. *Criminal Justice and Behavior, 21,* 10–27.

McGrath, R. (1994, October). *Cost effectiveness of sex offender treatment programs*. Paper presented at the annual conference of Virginia Sex Offender Providers, Hampton Beach.

Miller, R. S., & Lefcourt, H. M. (1982). The assessment of social intimacy. *Journal of Personality Assessment, 46,* 514–518.

Miller, W. R., & Rollnick, S. (1991). *Motivational interviewing: Preparing people to change addictive behavior*. New York: Guilford Press.

Miner, M. H., Day, D. M., & Nafpaktitis, M. K. (1989). Assessment of coping skills: Development of a situational competency test. In D. R. Laws (Ed.), *Relapse prevention with sex offenders* (pp. 127–136). New York: Guilford Press.

Murphy, W. D., & Barbaree, H. E. (1994). *Assessments of sex offenders by measures of erectile response: Psychometric properties and decision making*. Brandon, VT: The Safer Society Press.

Murphy, W. D., Krisak, J., Stalgaitis, S. J., & Anderson, K. (1984). The use of penile tumescence measures with incarcerated rapists: Further validity issues. *Archives of Sexual Behavior, 13,* 545–554.

Nichols, H. R., & Molinder, I. (1984). *Multiphasic sex inventory manual*. Tacoma, WA: Author.

O'Donohue, W. T., & Letourneau, E. (1992). The psychometric properties of the penile tumescence assessment of child molesters. *Journal of Psychopathology and Behavioral Assessment, 14,* 123–174.

Overholser, J. C., & Beck, S. (1986). Multimethod assessment of rapists, child molesters, and three control groups on behavioral and psychological measures. *Journal of Consulting and Clinical Psychology, 54,* 682–687.

Paveza, G. (1987, September). *Risk factors in father-daughter child sexual abuse: Findings from a case-control study*. Paper presented at the 3rd annual Family Violence Research Conference, Durham, NC.

Perilstein, R. D., Lipper, S., & Friedman, L. J. (1991). Three cases of paraphilias responsive to fluoxetine treatment. *Journal of Clinical Psychiatry, 52,* 169–170.

Peters, J. M., & Murphy, W. D. (1992). Profiling child sexual abusers: Legal considerations. *Criminal Justice and Behavior, 19,* 38–53.

Pithers, W. D. (1990). Relapse prevention with sexual aggressors: A method for maintaining therapeutic gain and enhancing external supervision. In W. L. Marshall, D. R. Laws, & H. E. Barbaree (Eds.), *Handbook of sexual assault: Issues, theories, and treatment of the offender* (pp. 343–361). New York: Plenum Press.

Pithers, W. D. (1994). Process evaluation of a group therapy component designed to enhance sex offenders' empathy for sexual abuse survivors. *Behaviour Research and Therapy, 32,* 565–570.

Pithers, W. D., Martin, G. R., & Cumming, G. F. (1989). Vermont treatment program for sexual aggressors. In D. R. Laws (Ed.), *Relapse prevention with sex offenders* (pp. 292–310). New York: Guilford Press.

Prentky, R. A., & Burgess, A. W. (1991). Rehabilitation of child molesters: A cost-benefit analysis. *American Journal of Orthopsychiatry, 60,* 108–117.

Quinsey, V. L. (1980). The base rate problem and the prediction of dangerousness: A reappraisal. *Journal of Psychiatry and Law, 8,* 329–340.

Quinsey, V. L., & Ambtman, R. (1979). Variables affecting psychiatrists' and teachers' assessments of dangerousness of mentally ill offenders. *Journal of Consulting and Clinical Psychology, 47,* 353–362.

Quinsey, V. L., & Chaplin, T. C. (1988). Penile responses of child molesters and normals to descriptions of encounters with children involving sex and violence. *Journal of Interpersonal Violence, 3,* 259–274.

Quinsey, V. L., Chaplin, T. C., & Carrigan, W. F. (1979). Sexual preferences among incestuous and nonincestuous child molesters. *Behavior Therapy, 10,* 562–565.

Quinsey, V. L., Chaplin, T. C., & Upfold, D. (1984). Sexual arousal to nonsexual violence and sadomasochistic themes among rapists and non-sex-offenders. *Journal of Consulting and Clinical Psychology, 52,* 651–657.

Quinsey, V. L., & Cyr, M. (1986). Perceived dangerousness and treatability of offenders: The effects of internal versus external attributions of crime causality. *Journal of Interpersonal Violence, 1,* 458–471.

Quinsey, V. L., & Earls, C. M. (1990). The modification of sexual preferences. In W. L. Marshall, D. R. Laws, & H. E. Barbaree (Eds.), *Handbook of sexual assault: Issues, theories, and treatment of the offender* (pp. 279–295). New York: Plenum Press.

Quinsey, V. L., Harris, G. T., & Rice, M. E. (1995). Actuarial prediction of sexual recidivism. *Journal of Interpersonal Violence, 10,* 85–105.

Quinsey, V. L., Harris, G. T., Rice, M. E., & Lalumière, M. L. (1993). Assessing treatment efficacy in outcome studies of sex offenders. *Journal of Interpersonal Violence, 8,* 512–523.

Quinsey, V. L., Khanna, A., & Malcolm, B. (1996, August). *A retrospective evaluation of the RTC Sex Offender Treatment Program.* Paper presented at the World Congress of Psychology, Montreal.

Quinsey, V. L., & Lalumière, M. L. (1996). *Assessment of sexual offenders against children.* Thousand Oaks, CA: Sage.

Quinsey, V. L., Lalumière, M. L., Rice, M. E., & Harris, G. T. (1995). Predicting sexual offenses. In J. C. Campbell (Ed.), *Assessing dangerousness: Violence by sexual offenders, batterers, and child abusers* (pp. 114–137). Thousand Oaks, CA: Sage.

Quinsey, V. L., & Maguire, A. (1986). Maximum security psychiatry patients: Actuarial and clinical prediction of dangerousness. *Journal of Interpersonal Violence, 1,* 143–171.

Quinsey, V. L., & Marshall, W. L. (1983). Procedures for reducing deviant arousal: An evaluation review. In J. G. Greer & I. R. Stuart (Eds.), *The sexual aggressor: Current perspectives on treatment* (pp. 267–289). New York: Van Nostrand-Reinholt.

Quinsey, V. L., Rice, M. E., & Harris, G. T. (1995). Actuarial prediction of sexual recidivism. *Journal of Interpersonal Violence, 10,* 85–105.

Rada, R. T. (1978). *Clinical aspects of the rapist.* New York: Grune & Stratton.

Rice, M. E., & Harris, G. T. (1995). *Cross-validation of actuarial predictors* (research report #XII-11). Pentanguishene, Ontario: Oak Ridge Mental Health Centre.

Rice, M. E., Harris, G. T., & Quinsey, V. L. (1991). Evaluation of an institution-based treatment program for child molesters. *Canadian Journal of Program Evaluation, 6,* 111–129.

Rice, M. E., Harris, G. T., Quinsey, V. L., & Cyr, M. (1990). Planning treatment programs in secure psychiatric facilities. In D. N. Weisstub (Ed.), *Law and mental health: International perspectives* (pp. 162–230). New York: Pergamon Press.

Rice, M. E., Quinsey, V. L., & Harris, G. T. (1991). Predicting sexual recidivism among treated and untreated extrafamilial child molesters released from a maximum security psychiatric institution. *Journal of Consulting and Clinical Psychology, 59,* 381–386.

Rosen, R. C., & Beck, G. (1988). *Patterns of sexual arousal: Psychophysiological processes and clinical applications.* New York: Guilford Press.

Russell, D., Peplau, L. A., & Cutrona, C. A. (1980). The Revised UCLA Loneliness Scale. *Journal of Personality and Social Psychology, 39,* 472–480.

Schwartz, B. K. (1995). Theories of sex offenses. In B. K. Schwartz & H. R. Cellini (Eds.), *The sex offender: Corrections, treatment and legal practice* (pp. 2.1–2.32). Kingston, NJ: Civic Research Institute.

Segal, Z. V., & Stermac, L. E. (1984). A measure of rapists' attitudes towards women. *International Journal of Law and Psychiatry, 7,* 437–440.

Segal, Z. V., & Stermac, L. E. (1990). The role of cognition in sexual assault. In W. L. Marshall, D. R. Laws, & H. E. Barbaree (Eds.), *Handbook of sexual assault: Issues, theories, and treatment of the offender* (pp. 161–174). New York: Plenum Press.

Seidman, B. T., Marshall, W. L., Hudson, S. M., & Robertson, P. J. (1994). An examination of intimacy and loneliness in sex offenders. *Journal of Interpersonal Violence, 9,* 518–534.

Selzer, M. L. (1971). The Michigan Alcoholism Screening Test (MAST): The quest for a new diagnostic instrument. *American Journal of Psychiatry, 127,* 1653–1658.

Seto, M. C., & Kubin, M. (1996). Criterion-related validity of a phallometric test for paraphilic rape and sadism. *Behaviour Research and Therapy, 34,* 174–183.

Simon, W. T., & Schouten, P. G. W. (1992). Problems in sexual preference testing in child sexual abuse cases: A legal and community perspective. *Journal of Interpersonal Violence, 7,* 503–516.

Skinner, H. A. (1982). The drug abuse screening test. *Addictive Behaviors, 7,* 363–371.

Smith, R. C. (1995). Sex offender program planning and implementation. In B. K. Schwartz & H. R. Cellini (Eds.), *The sex offender: Corrections, treatment and legal practice* (pp. 7.1–7.13). Kingston, NJ: Civic Research Institute.

Steele, N. (1995). Cost effectiveness of treatment. In B. K. Schwartz & H. R. Cellini (Eds.), *The sex offender: Corrections, treatment and legal practice* (pp. 4.1–4.19). Kingston, NJ: Civic Research Institute.

Stermac, L. E., & Quinsey, V. L. (1985). Social competence among rapists. *Behavioral Assessment, 8,* 171–185.

Stermac, L. E., Segal, Z. V., & Gillis, R. (1990). Social and cultural factors in sexual assault. In W. L. Marshall, D. R. Laws, & H. E. Barbaree (Eds.), *Handbook of sexual assault: Issues, theories, and treatment of the offender* (pp. 143–159). New York: Plenum Press.

Ward, T., Hudson, S. M., Johnston, L., & Marshall, W. L. (1997). Cognitive distortions in sex offenders: An integrative review. *Clinical Psychology Review, 17,* 479–507.

Ward, T., Hudson, S. M., & Marshall, W. L. (1996). Attachment style in sex offenders: A preliminary study. *Journal of Sex Research, 33,* 17–26.

Webster, C. D., Harris, G. T., Rice, M. E., Cormier, C., & Quinsey, V. L. (1994). *The violence prediction scheme: Assessing dangerousness in high-risk men.* Toronto: University of Toronto, Centre of Criminology.

Williams, L. M., & Finkelhor, D. (1990). The characteristics of incestuous fathers: A review of recent studies. In W. L. Marshall, D. R. Laws, & H. E. Barbaree (Eds.), *Handbook of sexual assault: Issues, theories, and treatment of the offender* (pp. 143–159). New York: Plenum Press.

Wilson, G. T., & Evans, I. M. (1977). The therapist-client relationship in behavior therapy. In A. S. Gurman & A. M. Razin (Eds.), *The therapist's contribution to effective psychotherapy: An empirical approach* (pp. 133–161). New York: Pergamon Press.

Wormith, J. S., Bradford, J. M. W., Pawlak, A., Borzecki, M., & Zohar, A. (1988). The assessment of deviant sexual arousal as a function of intelligence, instructional set and alcohol ingestion. *Canadian Journal of Psychiatry, 33,* 800–808.

PART SIX

PROFESSIONAL ISSUES

Practicing Principled Forensic Psychology: Legal, Ethical, and Moral Considerations

ALLEN K. HESS

The seven deadly sins: Pride,
Covetousness, Lust, Envy, Gluttony,
Anger, and Sloth
attributed to Aquinas and others

Each judge must possess seven attributes:
Wisdom, Humility, Awe, Spurning
Wealth, Love of Truth, Beloved by the
People, and A Good Reputation.
Hilkot Sanhedrin 2:7,
Babylonian Talmud

THESE TWO lists represent two approaches to principled conduct and, by extension, to principled professional practice. One approach suggests that behaving well involves avoiding sin. This view is consistent with a legal approach. The law requires few actions from people; for a person to behave legally, he or she simply needs to avoid committing a wrongful act. By this reasoning, if a person avoids the sins of pride, covetousness, and lust, sexual misconduct would not occur; avoiding pride and gluttony would end professionals practicing beyond their capabilities; and avoiding sloth would mean writing psychological reports and returning students' test papers promptly. The second approach is aspirational. It leads us to consider the higher reaches of conduct, immerses principled conduct in an interpersonal matrix, and constantly requires the examination of each act concerning its implications for the actor and the society. Both approaches are legitimate and deserve our attention. Yet, while the avoiding-of-sin approach

I am grateful to Kathryn D. Hess, Steven Walfish, Irving B. Weiner, and Peter Zachar for their helpful comments about this chapter.

allows us to achieve a profession that is adequate, the aspirational approach sets our sights on the possibility of excellence in our individual practice and for our profession.

This chapter examines the characteristics of ethics codes generally and the ethics codes applicable to forensic psychology.

ETHICS CODES

Why Have Ethics Codes?

Professions use ethics codes to regulate, educate, and inspire their practitioners (Frankel, 1989). When the government grants a monopoly to a profession, the profession assumes an obligation to practice in a way that serves the public and not merely the individual professional's appetites. Society grants privileged communication to allow individuals to consult professionals without fear that the professionals will reveal intimate disclosures. Society allows surgeons to cut into human flesh to serve the patient's medical needs. We have not granted this trust irrevocably or unconditionally. The conditions are that the profession regulate itself by developing norms, values, standards, and practices that shape the individual practitioner's behavior. The profession does not genetically produce the next generation of practitioners, but it does produce its next generation of professionals through socialization (Pavalko, 1979). Although the ultimate responsibility for ethical conduct is and must remain with the individual practitioner, the promotion of ethical conduct is the province of the profession. Professions embody these norms, values, standards, and practices in codes of ethical professional conduct, be they as short as the American Medical Association's seven principles stated in 10 sentences (Edge & Groves, 1994) or as lengthy as the 93-page American Bar Association's Model Rules of Professional Conduct (not inclusive of the equally lengthy disciplinary procedures or standards of conduct for prosecutorial, defense, and judicial functions of attorneys; West Publishing Company, 1984).

The more inclusive the process used in developing the code, the more the profession and its practitioners are likely to be morally committed to the values expressed in the code. Similarly, in light of public distrust of professions, more lay involvement in the drafting and implementation has occurred as a prophylactic to further erosion of trust. The more the profession can tolerate publicizing its code violators or publishing casebooks, the more educational and trust inducing will be its ethical procedures.

Functions

Frankel (1989) sees ethics codes as serving eight functions:

1. *As an enabling document, the code provides an ethical compass against which the practitioner can guide his or her conduct.* No matter how well intentioned a professional, he or she will experience confusion and anxiety without a framework to guide decisions.

2. *The code proclaims to the public a set of standards that the public should expect from the practitioners in the profession.*

3. Ethics codes proclaim a set of shared professional values and skills that help the profession's members enjoy a sense of pride, power, prestige, and allegiance to the profession.

4. Codes serve to educate the public and induce trust in the profession. By benefiting the public, a profession will be granted social and economic rewards. Yet ethics codes can be political devices that thwart adversaries and reduce threats to the profession's autonomy. Ethics codes protect the monopoly a profession enjoys and the values it espouses. These values typically are in the public's interest, such as the public's granting the right to surgeons to cut into human flesh or granting the client the security of privileged communication so the psychologist can delve into a person's private thoughts, feelings, and concerns. Professions enjoin practitioners to perform pro bono services to repay the public for its trust. In fact, *Schwarz v. Kogan* (1998) held that a state association can mandate pro bono services for indigent cases.

Codes are also restrictive and conserve a profession's values. They establish minimal skill levels to practice, but they also can act against the public interest by stifling creativity and fostering greed. One noteworthy neuropsychologist was on a crusade to ban the use of the Bender–Gestalt, given its poor validity in determining brain dysfunction. He wanted anyone using the Bender to be subject to ethics review and sanctions. Whatever the Bender-Gestalt's usefulness might be, banning it would be nonsensical from a scientific perspective. One would be asserting the null hypothesis and foreclosing any possibility of discovering a future use for the Bender. In fact, Schretlen, Wilkins, Van Gorp, and Bobholz (1992) found the first five Bender designs were useful in detecting feigned insanity in a group of prisoners, a use unanticipated by the neuropsychologist and undiscoverable if we had banned the Bender. One way an ethics code can be twisted to serve ignoble purposes is illustrated by a state ethics committee that passed a rule holding psychologists to be malpracticing if they did not bill the insurance company their full fee in cases where the psychologist saw the client at a reduced rate. The insurance companies informed the committee of the definitions of fraud and misrepresentation (cf. Keith-Spiegel & Koocher, 1985) and the rule was rescinded.

5. Ethics codes confer a sense of power, prestige, group solidarity, and common purpose that culminate in a sense of professional identity. Frankel (1989) describes the public trust placed in a profession's status and autonomy that flows from an ethics code. As mentioned in 4 above, this can be a double-edged sword. The profession can use ethics procedures to disarm critics and keep conflicts and embarrassments hidden, insulating the profession. One antidote to this malady is the inclusion of lay members to ethics committees and hearing panels. The degree to which the medical and legal professions in many states have only professionals on their board and hearing panels to the exclusion of respected members of the laity is the degree to which cynicism has met the panels' activities.

6. Ethics codes deter unethical behavior by using sanctions and by affirming the duty of peers to monitor misbehaving colleagues. Though ethics committees cannot levy jail time and fines on offenders, letters of reprimand, suspension, and revocation of membership in the professional society and the suspension and revocation of a state practitioner's license are severe. These sanctions have implications for a practitioner's being able to secure liability insurance, to be listed in directories and on panels that insurers reimburse, and, most pointedly for forensic psychologists, to establish credibility in court. Due to the availability of electronic databases and the growing sophistication of attorneys in challenging expert witnesses, such a sanction could be devastating to an expert witness. All these property interest losses call for ethics committees to be careful, be fair, and exercise due process on behalf of the professional in hearing complaints and to consider rehabilitative actions for the ethically impaired. Some psychology licensing boards have made the same error that university student discipline committees have committed. University committees have taken on the task of adjudicating cases of drug offenses, theft, and sexual assaults committed by students on campus when, clearly, such cases should be referred to the criminal justice system, which provides safeguards for the accused and penalties for the guilty. Having a rapist or a thief suspended from classes for a semester hardly seems like punishment. Licensing boards have taken on a prosecutorial edge since the 1970s ("Two California Attorneys," 1998). Generally, there are few provisions for safeguards for the accused, there are no guidelines for punishment that have undergone any sort of judicial and legislative review, and there is a limited array of punishments for the array of offenses such panels hear. Consequently, boards need to examine carefully whether they ought to plunge into the enforcement function or restrict their activities to education and remediation, leaving all but licensing and practice issues to the courts. A sexually predatory therapist or a lying expert witness may be more effectively punished by criminal and civil courts than by ethics boards.

7. *Practitioners find protection and support in ethics codes.* The profession and individuals can use ethical principles against improper claims by clients. One psychologist underestimated his client's maladjustment; he assigned bibliotherapy tasks beyond regular sessions, and she complained to the ethics committee of his abandoning and not adequately caring for her. The committee informed the client that bibliotherapy was a legitimate way for the psychologist to help augment sessions and the case went no further. Practitioners find codes useful when faced with unreasonable or intrusive demands by employers, bureaucrats, and other professions. Consider the prison pastoral counselor who served on disciplinary committees that heard complaints including those involving his patient-felons. Ethically and psychologically uninformed, he saw no conflict of interest in meting out punishment as a member of the disciplinary committee and in conducting psychotherapy on the same prisoners the next hour. Furthermore, he wore a prison guard's windbreaker around the prison and, bearing a shotgun, he participated in the armed hunting for escapees. Yet, he saw no reason why his clients should not see him as a benevolent, caring, trustworthy psychotherapist. A more ethically sensitive psychologist could use ethics codes to help the prison authorities understand ethical conflicts, the problems such conflicts would engender for all concerned, and how to resolve role conflicts to the benefit of all parties.

8. *Ethics codes can help adjudicate disputes both within the profession and with outside interests.* A psychologist can appeal to the judge to limit the discovery and circulation of subpoenaed materials, using ethics codes, test standards, and copyright laws safeguarding the published tests, to support the appeal (see Chapter 19 on the expert witness). This may mean that the attorney issuing the subpoena hires a psychologist to read and interpret the records and that the records are restricted in circulation so that they do not find their way into a reporter's hands.

WHAT ARE ETHICS CODES?

Ethics codes articulate the values of the profession in a set of principles. Principles are rules within an ethical system, such as the principle "First, do no harm." Whatever else physicians are about, we expect them to do no harm, notwithstanding that they may cause pain to accomplish a second principle, that of beneficence, or doing good . Standards are patterns of conduct, established by custom or authority, adherence to which fulfills the principles. Authority in psychology refers to scientific canonical knowledge. Guidelines are outlines of conduct, protocols, or procedures operationalizing the standards (Bennett, Bryant, VandenBos, & Greenwood, 1990).

PRINCIPLES, CODES, GUIDELINES, AND STANDARDS FOR FORENSIC PSYCHOLOGISTS

THE APA ETHICAL PRINCIPLES OF PSYCHOLOGISTS AND CODE OF CONDUCT (PRINCIPLES AND CODE)(APA, 1992)

There are six principles and a set of eight areas of standards in the Principles and Code. The six principles concern competence, integrity, professional and scientific responsibility, respect for people's rights and dignity, concern for others' welfare, and social responsibility. In applying the principles to cases, it becomes clear that the principles have considerable overlap and that the cases illustrating one principle frequently have applicability to other principles.

Competence

Competence requires the psychologist to offer services only in areas where he or she has had education, training, or experience. In developing areas, the psychologist should teach, educate, or provide service after taking steps to secure appropriate training, education, or experience or otherwise ensure competence in the skills and knowledge base at issue (Standard 1.04). The Speciality Guidelines for Forensic Psychologists (Guidelines)(Committee on Ethical Guidelines for Forensic Psychologists, 1991) adds knowledge and skill to the definition of competence, in keeping with the *Daubert* test (*Daubert v. Merrell Dow*, 1993). A psychologist may be expert in providing competency and insanity evaluations but may not be aware of the literature, techniques, and issues involved with a fitness-for-duty evaluation. Such an evaluation may require expertise in vocational psychology, in confidentiality issues specific to the workplace, and in prediction questions specific to job evaluations (Super, 1997).

Golding (1990) describes the testimony of Grigson, a psychiatrist, in *Barefoot v. Estelle* (1983). Grigson claimed to be able to "predict future dangerousness of an individual within reasonable medical certainty"; without seeing Barefoot, Grigson testified that Barefoot was in the "most severe category of sociopaths" and that he was "one hundred percent and absolutely [certain that] Barefoot would commit future acts of violence that would constitute a continuing threat to society" (Golding, 1990, p. 291). Cross-examination has been the mechanism that courts traditionally use to confirm or dismiss "junk science." However, cross-examination is inadequate, in that it relies on attorneys, judges, and jurors to make a determination concerning epistemological, technical, and statistical matters beyond the ability of any but other experts in the area. Golding (1990) suggests that a partial solution is to place an affirmative duty on potential experts to clarify the basis of their testimony, to show the evidence of the specific bases for the testimony rather than to passively react to attorney questions, and to describe the limits of the testimony. This may be asking the fox to guard the henhouse, but it does place responsibility and consequences on the slipshod expert.

Shuman and Greenberg (1998) offer another solution. They decry judges' dismissal of professional ethics codes and assert that many of the problems with expert testimony could be resolved by judges taking ethics codes seriously. Thus, Grigson's testimony passed judicial review but it did not pass psychiatric peer review when the American Psychiatric Association's amicus brief asserted that Grigson should not have been permitted to testify in *Barefoot v. Estelle* (1983) because it is "unethical for a psychologist to offer a professional opinion unless he/she has conducted an examination" (Shuman & Greenberg, 1998, p. 7).

Shuman and Greenberg (1998) review other instances, such as the court's accepting expert testimony in custody cases when the psychologist examined only one parent and then offered an opinion about which parent would be best for the child. This practice is unsound (one cannot make a comparative decision after seeing only one party) and is countermanded by the profession's guidelines (e.g., American Psychological Association, 1994). Shuman and Greenberg put it pithily: "It [the opinion] does not lack an adequate foundation because it is unethical, it is unethical because it lacks an adequate foundation" (p. 8).

Consider both the competence and integrity of a pair of opposing psychologists in an insanity defense case. The first psychologist testified that a borderline personality disorder led the defendant to lifelong maladaptiveness, including mood fluctuations, inappropriate anger, and poor emotional control. These, he said, prevented the defendant from conforming his conduct to the law and from distinguishing right from wrong when he stabbed to death a 74-year-old grandmother and her 4-year-old granddaughter. The psychologist offered this testimony despite the existence of a letter found in the defendant's former wife's purse outlining the steps she was to take in helping him sustain a defense. (The astute observer will note that the defendant may have been insane at the moments around the stabbings and still be planful afterward in the construction of the defense; the judge ruled the letter inadmissible due to marital privilege, though the couple divorced the year before the stabbings.) Whatever questions the expert's testimony may raise were trumped by the prosecutor's psychologist, who testified that the defendant knew the nature and quality of the charges against him (a competency issue rather than an insanity issue) and that he could distinguish right from wrong. These conclusions were based on the expert's opinion that the voices the defendant heard (not a *DSM-IV* nor a defining borderline personality characteristic found in psychopathology textbooks) were not true hallucinations because they came from *inside the defendant's head and not outside his head!* True hallucinations come from outside one's head, the psychologist opined. Although one may feel the defendant, judge, and both psychologists deserve each other, the public's view of psychology after learning about cases such as this has become increasingly cynical and distrusting of mental health experts, or, in S. J. Perelman's term, "head candlers" (after poultry farmers' practice of judging eggs by holding them up to candlelight). Did the psychologists know the legal standard for insanity? Did they select the most appropriate measures? Could they articulate their psychological test findings to the standard? Were each inclined to have his expert opinion in mind and work backward to see how the data could conform to rather than lead to the conclusion? Did their testimony have adequate foundations? Such displays fuel the distrust and hostility expressed in such scathing best sellers as Huber's *Galileo's Revenge: Junk Science in the Courtroom* (1993) and Hagen's *Whores of the Court* (1997).

Levels of Certainty

Huber (1993) and Hagen (1997) raise a set of important issues regarding the level of knowledge upon which experts base their opinions. The two psychologists in the insanity case have a well-developed methodology that they used in forming an opinion. However, they overstated the degree of certainty in applying the methodology to the particular case of the hallucinating murderer. For a century, we have refined psychological testing and defined the two components of insanity: whether there are sufficient cognitive capacities for the accused to know the nature and quality of the action at issue and, in jurisdictions using both prongs of the insanity definition, whether emotional disorders are of a magnitude to preempt the accused's cognitive capacities.

There are other areas of practice that have far less developed methodologies. For example, one key problem with jury selection is that, though we might do a good job of juror selection in terms of a person's opinions regarding the issue at trial, when the jury adjourns to the jury room, the confounding effects of the foreperson's leadership style and the particular group's dynamics might undo the psychologist's work. Thus, we might do a decent job with *juror* selection but not *jury* selection.

The forensic psychologist is well advised to have a graded system of levels of confidence in his or her conclusions, based on the level of canonical knowledge available to the expert and the degree to which that knowledge can be applied to the particular case in question. These levels can be expressed as "certain, within the bounds of the well-developed knowledge in the discipline"; "highly suggestive"; "indicative but not certain"; and "no expert opinion can be offered regarding this question." These levels should be based on both the state of knowledge in the discipline and the degree to which the case has ecological validity or is highly parallel to the knowledge base in the discipline. For example, a psychologist was asked to examine a case of Munchausen-by-proxy that a large teaching hospital alleged against a Black mother. The top medical investigators in this disorder were based at the medical center and were said to be testifying. Upon reviewing the case, the psychologist found the whole database consisted of 57 cases and that not one case of a Black woman was in this national database, rendering the "normative" reference group limited in its applicability. Several other features in the case did not make sense, including the fact that the physician who referred the case had filed the same charges against several other women whose children died under his care. The psychologist wanted to examine the physician as the possible perpetrator. When the attorney who consulted with the psychologist presented this information while deposing one of the experts on Munchausen-by-proxy, the medical center backed away from the case. Their much acclaimed Munchausen-by-proxy database was simply inadequate and irrelevant here.

Levels of certainty are a researchable forensic topic regarding at least two dimensions: the soundness of the empirical base and the degree to which the methodology fits the case at hand. Even our most developed instruments may not be revealing in a particular case and the psychologist needs to say so. Expressing levels of certainty of a knowledge base to the attorney is important when first encountering a case, and expressing both the knowledge base certainty and the certainty of findings in the particular case is important in rendering testimony whether legislatively or in a courtroom. Even when we do not have a methodology that reaches a compelling level of certainty, the court may ask for expert guidance, saying, "It is, of course, not easy to predict future behavior. The fact that such a determination is difficult, however, does not mean that it cannot be made. Indeed, prediction of future criminal conduct is an essential element in many of the decisions rendered throughout our criminal justice system. . . . What is essential is that the jury have before it all possible relevant information about the individual defendant whose fate it must determine" (*Jurek v. Texas*, 1976; pp. 274–276). The courts require all relevant information, and it is the psychologist's ethical responsibility to describe the weight that such evidence should be accorded (Golding, 1990).

Knowledge of Legal Issues

The Guidelines further oblige forensic psychologists to understand the applicable legal standards that govern the issues and procedures in which they participate and to understand the civil rights of the parties involved. If the psychologist is not knowledgeable about the charges, then an evaluation as to competence to stand trial will be compromised because the psychologist cannot adequately assess whether the defendant can understand the charges. Some charges are easily understood on their face, but others can be complex, requiring a higher level of cognitive complexity in helping to form a defense. The psychologist must weigh the defendant's cognitive abilities against the complexity of the charges and the case. The psychologist must learn about the legal standards and articulate them with the case at hand.

Role Boundaries

Regarding the second point, suppose a psychologist interviews a defendant for the prosecutor and in doing so notices the defendant in dire need of psychological support. Instead of again warning the defendant that the information is to be used in court and that the psychologist works for the prosecutor, the psychologist uses reflexive empathy rather than receptive empathy (Greenberg & Shuman, 1997; Shuman, 1993) in eliciting information. The psychologist would be operating legally, having informed the examinee. But he or she may be using a professional advantage in an ethically dubious way to gain the upper hand for the prosecutor at the expense of the civil liberties the defendant may have been psychologically and legally unable to exercise on his or her own behalf due to competence issues. Besides being found unethical, the offending psychologist may have committed a breach of duty and be legally liable.

Integrity

The APA Principles and Code (1992) call for psychologists "to be aware of their own belief systems, values, needs, and limitations and the effects of these on their work" and to "avoid improper and potentially harmful dual relationships" (p. 1599). The Guidelines anticipate *Daubert* (1993) and *Joiner v. General Electric Company* (1997) in obliging psychologists to show integrity in presenting the factual bases of their findings and the limits or confidence intervals of their data—in the words of the Court, the known or potential error rate of a technique. One's own values and their affect on a case may be more ambiguous but no less serious than one's competency to give testimony.

The area of child abuse prosecution shows how a truly devastating criminal charge can be politicized. Advocates of the alleged victim say if a victim claims abuse, it occurred; others say there may be a few child abuse incidents, but the bulk of them are fictional. That experts garner exalted status, handsome fees, and even some political advantages casts a pall that may contaminate the credibility of true believers on each side and, by extension, the reputation of the profession. The injustices experienced by the Amiraults in Massachusetts, the Little Rascals case in North Carolina, and the McMartin-Buckeys in California (Eberle, 1993) necessarily involved expert witnesses who carried a variety of agenda into the investigation. Perhaps more unsettling is the case of Margaret Kelly Michaels, who was sentenced to 47 years at age 26 for a crime that involved neither murder nor drugs. Rabinowitz (1990) details her prosecution for satanism and molestation of children in a nursery school in a then little-known case that involved such ethically questionable procedures, including misuse of psychological principles, as to outrage the conscience. Though some claim that professionals are never without their values and consequently their prejudices, yet it is qualitatively different to accept a case with some attitude toward the issues and to seek out the role of an expert witness as a way to promote a sociopolitical and personal agenda (Bruck & Ceci, 1995). One psychologist has never testified on behalf of the state, instead helping those he sees as the underclass to bring forth legal cases for which he serves as the expert witness. His fees are often paid by the court or civil liberties agencies.

Clark (1990), Golding (1990), and Hess (1998a) identify flashpoints that every expert should attend to before proceeding with a case. These include (a) whether one is using the expert role as a moral advocate versus providing objective expertise; (b) whether one is qualified by knowledge, skills, education, experience, or training to provide information to help the fact finders; (c) whether one's involvement is probative (truly informative) or prejudicial; and (d) the degree to which the adversary nature of the legal system will distort one's proffered evidence.

Diamond argued that no professional is without values and opinions (Katz, 1992). Indeed, that is a truism. However, the question is whether those values become so important to the professional that they become an interest, compromising the objective and putatively neutral position that the expert witness is supposed to bring to an examination of the evidence. Suppose a psychologist involved in child custody cases has lost custody of his own child and subsequently adopts a mission that no other man should lose custody of a child. In each case, the psychologist truly comes to believe that the father should be awarded child custody and his examinations always find for the father. The conflict of interest becomes palpable and damaging to individuals, families, and the legal process. The psychologist does have the right to believe all fathers should be awarded custody; however, the proper platform for expressing these views is as an amicus curiae or testifying to legislative bodies or forming sociopolitical action groups—not the platform of the expert witness.

Perhaps the most recent and extreme position that attacks the legal structures directly is that of the "legal criticism" and deconstructionist views. They hold that the very structure of our justice system is a product of our society's values that are fundamentally biased and destructive to those not in power. Consequently, this position might find it fitting and proper to use the expert witness role to express ideological positions. The deconstructionist position claims that because all people are value-driven and the legal process itself is conserving the prevalent values, using the system to depict the flaws in the system and to level the playing field for the powerless is not merely justified but a duty. This is an "ends justify the means" or teleological argument. That is, this view holds that whatever testimony it takes to achieve a particular sociopolitical end is justified. Another argument holds that the adversarial system through cross-examination should impeach skewed or contrived testimony. However, that assumes that introduction of such testimony is ethically questionable per se. In an individual case, truth and impartiality can suffer if the expert witness psychologist testifies to help his or her client where evidence is wanting. Also, as mentioned above, the courts cannot guarantee that attorneys have the required knowledge to know when an expert is not qualified.

On the other hand, principle-driven or deonotological philosophies hold that telling the truth as we are able is the higher duty. That is what our Principles and Code hold. Again, deconstructionists hold that being truthful is a duty imposed by the dominant culture; however, the deconstructionists may be undone by their not being able to pose alternatives. Everyone has ends he or she prefers. Some of these ends violate the ends of others. How would one propose to develop a value system other than rampant hedonism or rule of the mighty? Our legal system tries to curb hedonism and at the same time to allow each individual the pursuit of happiness within a system that preserves others' rights to happiness. The duty of the expert witness is to pursue truth—to bring a scientific perspective or at least discipline-informed view to evidence beyond the knowledge of the fact finder. To do otherwise is to invite ethics charges, to risk malpractice claims, and to commit injustices.

Wettstein, Mulvey, and Rogers (1991) provide another intriguing example of a professional's values affecting judicial proceedings. They investigated the effects of using four standards for the insanity defense and found that even if the law changes standards, the "evaluator's political ideology, professional, personal views about the insanity defense or concern about the outcome of such judgments" are reflected in clinical judgments of criminal responsibility (p. 26). In this case, politically based changes in insanity defense criteria fomented by public demand may be defeated by the inertial effect of customary practice.

The integrity principle enjoins the psychologist to examine third-party relationships. These have long been recognized as important in forensic psychology. Attorneys have a different perspective than do psychologists on what constitutes a conflicted relationship. When an attorney hires an expert, the psychologist must be certain that the attorney is not acting as an agent for the attorney's client. This has implications regarding who owns privilege and for the fee payment; that is, as an agent, the attorney can retain help in serving the client, but the client is the principal and as such is the client of the psychologist. The psychologist is advised to be sure that the attorney is the one hiring the psychologist as a principal and not as an agent; that way, the psychologist will avoid the bind of not being able to communicate with the attorney without the express consent of the client. Often, practitioners assume the attorney is the client. However, consider the case of an attorney who retained an expert, then maintained that the $18,000 fee was not his responsibility but that of his principal (his client). Although the court held otherwise, note that so far this ruling may be limited to Ohio (*Sommer v. French*, 1996).

The Kelly Flinn case, concerning the B-52 pilot who was separated from the U.S. Air Force charged with adultery and then lying, shows the need to clarify that the psychologist is retained by the attorney, that there will be limitations on the materials gleaned from interviews and tests, that the types of inference are both usable and within the bounds of scientific and professional standards, and that these issues are clear before proceeding in the case. Flinn claims that her attorney told her to see Dr. Ann Duncan, a St. Louis psychologist the attorney knew, so "we could find out more about Marc's [Zigo, the coadulter] character and have her draw up a psychological profile of me to convey how someone so successful could get into such a mess. . . . I was mad at everyone in the room. . . . Especially Dr. Duncan. I'd just found out that she had told my mother that I had chosen to fly a B-52 because it was the largest penis I could find. She also revealed to my mother the intimate details of my sex life with Marc and told her I had the social skills of a 12-year-old. I felt betrayed" (Flinn, 1997).

Attorneys often believe that a psychologist who served as a psychotherapist may be the best person to call upon as an expert witness, a conflict of roles that many psychiatrists did not recognize (Weinstock, 1986, 1989). In fact, the ABA Criminal Justice Mental Health Standards (1989) hold that a criterion for qualification as an expert in testifying about mental conditions is "a professional therapeutic or habilitative relationship with the person whose mental condition is in question" (p. 132). This is a recipe for a dual-role relationship conflict (Greenberg & Shuman, 1997). The following example shows how such a conflict can play out.

A psychologist was called by an attorney to counsel him and his wife, whose marriage was on the verge of violence and dissolution. The husband and wife wanted to see, for the sake of their young son, whether the marriage was salvageable. The psychologist agreed to see them on the condition that whatever was revealed in marital psychotherapy was not accessible to subsequent legal proceedings, explaining that any other posture would mean either or both might try to look favorable in the psychotherapist's eyes and to make the other look unfavorable, defeating any psychotherapeutic possibilities. Both said they understood and agreed to the conditions. Nevertheless, the treatment failed. Two months later, the attorney told the psychologist that he intended to subpoena the psychologist as a witness regarding the wife's instability. The psychologist reminded him of the agreement. He said it did not matter. The psychologist intimated that he would speak to the attorney's attorney first to see whether he really wanted the psychologist's testimony because the violation of the conditions would be the second of the psychologist's utterances; the first would be an appeal to the judge that the other spouse did not waive privilege. Neither statement would look good for the attorney. The attorney's attorney felt the best course was not to call the psychologist.

Attorneys are learning that the separation of therapeutic role from the expert witness role is essential for the former to work. In fact, *Jaffe v. Redmond* (1997) affirms privilege as essential for psychotherapy. An attorney might call the psychotherapist a fact witness, but perils loom when the attorney presses for expert witness testimony from the psychotherapist. Strasburger, Gutheil, and Brodsky (1997) show the irreconcilability of the two roles and the conflicts waiting for the psychologist broaching the dual-role relationship. When the roles are joined nonetheless, special care must be exercised.

The psychotherapist role may be confounded with other, non-expert witness roles. Consider the prison psychologist who conducts sex offender group psychotherapy. The explicit task set forth by the Department of Corrections was to conduct the treatment and to provide written reports on the progress of the offenders to help in determining parole planning. The ethical dilemmas include violating the offender's privacy by reporting the offender's progress regarding parole consideration and learning of offenses previously unknown to the authorities. In this case, the psychologist affirmed at the outset that the offenders knew that their general progress and the risk of reoffending, but not any specific information, would be reported. Moreover, the psychologist confirmed with the authorities that information gleaned in psychotherapy would not be forwarded nor be useful for prosecution because of the privilege that would remain, except for the general progress and risk of reoffending report. This was carefully explained to the group psychotherapy members, including the advice that should anyone bring up information in the group, including other group members, it would be shielded. Also, they were informed that should they choose to discuss material outside group sessions, the psychologist who elicits information in group psychotherapy cannot possibly guarantee confidentiality outside the group nor shield the inmate patients from real-world repercussions outside the sanctuary of psychotherapy but behind the prison walls. Psychologists who ask for personal revelations without regard to such limits to confidentiality, or without regard to their inability to control the use of the information by other group members, and who do not inform the members accordingly, are practicing unethically.

The APA integrity principle asserts, "Psychologists strive to be aware of their own belief systems, values, needs, and limitations and the effects of these on their work" (APA, 1992, p. 1599). Brown (1997) writes that "objectivity" may be simply the subjectivity of the dominant group; by declaiming the "collective professional mythology of pure empiricism and objectivity in which social constructions of reality are denied or minimized" (p. 450) and by declaring what her values are, she fosters Tikkun Olam, or a healing or making whole of the world. Golding (1990) describes a case involving the expert witness who serves as an advocate of a moral agenda rather than as an objective expert. Dr. Thomas Szasz's testimony was excluded because the court held that no matter how distinguished his qualifications may be, his immutable belief, more dogmatic than scientific, that mental illness was a myth precluded his making a relevant determination of mental illness in the case at hand (also, cf. Golding & Roesch, 1987). It does make a difference whether a psychologist determining worker's compensation believes that we all work with some degree of pain, or holds a more sympathetic view that the worker paid for what amounts to insurance and is entitled to relief from work-induced stress (Colbach, 1997). Again, all the rules of the game, from various jurisdictions' rules of evidence to the APA Code of Ethics, call for an objective rendering of professional determinations. Perhaps as an amicus curiae, consultant, or plaintiff the psychologist may espouse partisan positions, but as an expert witness a higher standard for suspension of furthering one's own values is crucial in accepting a case.

Attorneys are prone to calling on experts who are likely to share the attorney's view of the facts. Colbach (1997) suggests such safeguards as constant scrutiny by oneself, by someone like a psychotherapy supervisor, and by a data bank that records the type of cases a person takes and turns down. "If objectivity is so elusive in our current adversary system, and if changes aren't forthcoming, we would all be better off doing what I have done and giving up on court appearances" (p. 166). Given that mental health services are being (de)capitated by third-party payers and that the courtroom is providing a livelihood for a growing number of mental health professionals, this question of impartiality demands greater attention and will be revisited below.

Professional and Scientific Responsibility

The psychologist serves the best interests of the client while upholding professional standards. Who is the psychologist serving when he or she uses knowledge to help law enforcement officers shoot more accurately or elicit information in interrogation more successfully? Although these services may seem ethical, consider extending these services to federal agencies that run a school for agents from another country. How ethical would it be for psychological principles to be used to halt insurgency movements in another country? What if that country were a dictatorship? The dilemma of U.S. government agencies using psychological expertise in Project Camelot to undermine Allende's Chilean government some three decades ago confronted psychology directly (Pervin, 1984). Some of the same information-control techniques were used against Nazi Germany and Imperial Japan by the United States of America to help win World War II, so the dilemma is not easily resolved by restricting a method alone. The ethical forensic psychologist has responsibilities for how psychology is applied.

Assessment

Probably the service that lawyers request most often is testimony based on psychological testing. There are a great number of tests that are psychometrically inadequate. A perusal through Buros's *Mental Measurements Yearbooks* reveals that many tests should not be used clinically due to a failure (a) to adequately norm the test; (b) to determine ecological validity concerning the populations to which the author(s) intend the test to be applied; (c) to determine cutting scores and the error rate, or "hits" and "misses" that the cutting score yields; and (d) to ascertain reasonable reliabilities and construct concurrent, predictive, convergent, and discriminant validities.

Consider a couple contesting child custody. Both submit to psychological assessment to buttress their claims as fit parents. One spouse's psychologist uses a personality inventory that shows both the strengths and weaknesses of a person. But the other spouse's psychologist is attracted by the exaggerated advertising claims for a personality inventory and its computer scoring and interpretation options; he selects the inventory, which is designed in such a way that it is virtually impossible to be depicted as normal (Hess, 1998b). The outcome of the case will have been determined by the choice of instruments, the parental rights of one side adversely and unfairly affected simply because the parents were assessed with two different instruments.

Fisher (1995) warns of several instruments and taxonomies frequently used in child abuse assessments. The instruments have no empirical validity but rely on "the strong endorsements from experienced professionals, and from victims, offenders, and other family members" (p. 473), endorsements wholly insufficient upon which to imprison people for decades. For Weiner (1989), competent diagnosticians consider whether they are (a) describing behavior, (b) drawing inferences from behavioral descriptions to describe a state or condition, or (c) making predictions. The degrees of confidence vary with the degree of inference and with the degree to which the criterion is saturated with the traits that the tests are assessing.

Computer interpretations raise concerns. There is a degree of certainty that people attribute to computer output. A psychologist assessed an individual for disability for an insurance company. The psychologist furnished the subpoenaed protocols to the claimant's attorney but did not furnish the computer-generated narrative report he had purchased. The report said that there was psychopathology and that the profile was valid. The insuring agency challenged the report and put their own expert witness psychologist on the stand. He said the computer-generated report, from the same computerized report service, showed the claimant exaggerated psychopathology to the extent that the MMPI testing was invalid. The first psychologist compared the report he had purchased with the report the second psychologist produced at trial and found that the second psychologist had the original report retyped with the key sentence altered to fit the conclusion he thought the insuring agency wanted. The insurer lost the case, given the fraudulent psychological testimony, and the attorney pointedly told the psychologist he retained that their business was far from concluded. Whether he filed legal or ethical charges is not known, but the insuring agency's attorney learned to call the claimant's psychologist in subsequent cases.

The use of computerized assessment procedures and computer-generated narrative reports raises the same questions we confront when using any testing procedure. These include questions about the database, the applicability of the norms to the examinee, and the presentation of computer-generated reports as if they were written by the examiner (Weiner, 1989, 1995). Matarazzo (1986) captures the concern in the subtitle of his article: "Unvalidated plus all mean and no sigma." We still need to qualify our data on a case-appropriate basis. It is *not* all mean (certainty) with no sigma (qualifications to the conclusions).

Given the great number of marketed tests and the misapplication of the tests, there may be a cottage industry in consulting on cases in which the standards of practice in assessment are at issue. Test constructors have a responsibility to live up to the *Standards for Educational and Psychological Testing* (American Psychological Association, 1985). Moreover, the test user has at least as great a responsibility, and a greater legal liability, to select and use the appropriate measure, to acknowledge the many factors that limit interpretation, and to make appropriate interpretations.

In one case, a schizophrenic veteran was looking for the state office that issued his disability payments. He became confused and frustrated when a clerk in a federal office brushed him off. He pushed her desk into her. She called the police, who found the veteran walking down the street talking to himself. He went with the police with no resistance. Subsequently, a psychologist tested him for about 30 minutes while the veteran was in shackles and accompanied by two deputy sheriffs. The psychologist, who held several lucrative contracts with the state to assess inmates for criminal responsibility, reported to the court that the veteran was psychopathic and intermittently violent, ignoring the extensive history of schizophrenia that spanned most of the veteran's life and showed no criminal record, both inconsistent with a diagnosis of psychopathy. The veteran's court-appointed attorney did not request an assessment by an independent psychologist. The court deemed the veteran competent and sane, and sentenced him for criminal assault and battery to a federal penitentiary. Upon release, the veteran began procedures to overturn the conviction and expunge his record. Among the many errors in the psychological evaluation was the representation of his IQ. The psychologist had presented the Wechsler scale to the court, describing the various scales and their meanings. An examination of the test report by a consulting psychologist retained for the appeal revealed that, given the lengthy battery described in the report, and the 30-minute examination period, the original psychologist could not have administered the tests described in the time available. In fact, the original psychologist had administered only 1 of the 11 Wechsler subtests. The psychologist therefore had misrepresented the services performed, a misrepresentation that cost the veteran four and a half years of his freedom.

The ethical psychologist selects reliable and valid tests that are appropriate to the questions raised in the particular situation, administers the tests in a standardized fashion with necessary modifications accounted for in the calculation of the results and noted in reports, and renders an opinion based on the test results with the appropriate qualifying statements, including limitations of the testing, and the interpretation of the test results. In one state prison, a psychologist found the intelligence scores of inmates to be higher on the Army Beta than he had ever seen. The psychologist in charge of the state diagnostic system was proud to state that he was indignant about the stigma of prisoners consistently scoring 15 points below the general population, so he decided to free them from that handicap by not timing two of the six timed subtests on the Army Beta. Much like the Queen in *Alice in Wonderland* who decided a word meant what she decided it meant, now the prisoners would no longer be what they were but what the psychologist decided they ought to be; in one fell swoop, he eliminated the "handicap" and undermined the state's diagnostic system.

From the individual psychologist examining the individual client to systemic personnel, educational, and clinical assessment, to such general statements as Goddard's racist policies restricting immigration (Smith, 1985), much of what the psychologist has to say has been based on testing. The importance of competence in psychometry and its implications cannot be overemphasized. Eugenic theories led to the American Immigration Restriction Act of 1924, affirmed by the Supreme Court in 1927. The theories and the law were precursors of the 1935 Nuremberg Hereditary Health Law, resulting in sterilization of some 27,000 "undesirables" by 1938 (Smith, 1985). What psychologists espouse as psychologists, burnished by the patina of science, has impact and incurs responsibility.

Confronting Unethical Conduct

Whistle-blowers tend to have potent beliefs in individual responsibility, in the concept of good, and that their duty to the community of humans transcends organizational well-being (Glazer & Glazer, 1986). They persist in their quest despite demotions (Fitzgerald, who blew the whistle on the Pentagon cost overruns), transfers (Serpico, who testified about the New York City Police payoffs), and firing (Ragghianti, who made public the Tennessee Board of Pardons and Paroles payoffs), until stopped by death (Silkwood, who publicized the unsafe nuclear facility in Oklahoma). The Glazers suggest the organizational whistle-blower (a) gathers facts, (b) goes through channels, (c) does not expect the boss to solve the problem, (d) expects job insecurity and threats, (e) prepares to persist and endure, and (f) consults his or her loved ones. Additionally, the wise whistle-blower maintains true copies of records in a safe place because documentation is crucial as he or she enlists those with an interest in uncovering the wrongdoing. In keeping records, the whistle-blower may be violating gag rules, statutes, or covenants so care must be exercised in gathering evidence and a calculation must be made regarding the costs whistle-blowing will incur.

Ethics codes enjoin the professional to confront the individual who may be acting unethically and to report the wrongdoing of individuals. However, there are problems in confronting such colleagues, including the possibility that the complaining person may be acting out of self-interest (Toch, 1981) or high-handedness (Derbyshire, 1983; Rose, 1983). Given the vague nature of ethics principles, the interpretation of what is ethical can confound the process. Then, too, the complainant can be subject to countercharges, including that of defamation. Keenan (1995) surveyed first-level managers and found that knowledge of where to report unethical behavior is the most important information once the behavior is deemed unethical. He found reporting to be inhibited by fear of retaliation and that men more often report ethical misconduct.

Many organizations have set up grievance procedures so individuals can voice complaints with less fear of retribution. These procedures typically promote a sense of procedural justice that increases job performance and lowers turnover (Olson-Buchanan, 1996). However, the year following a grievance, the filers have lower promotion rates, lower performance ratings (especially if the filer won the grievance; Klaas & DeNisi, 1989), and higher job turnover rates than nonfilers (Lewin, 1987). Olson-Buchanan (1996) found that access to a grievance system reduces turnover, but that employer-employee conflict reduces the filer's objective job performance due in part to the attention demanded of the filer by the grievance and by the motivational conflict generated by the grievance process. A downward spiraling between the manager's lower performance ratings and the worker's lower performance may be interactional. Olson-Buchanan's (1996) research needs replication outside the laboratory setting, but it is informing. The studies reviewed concern business settings. Literature concerning psychologists' whistle-blowing is scant.

Respect for People's Rights and Dignity

Psychologists are to respect the rights, dignity, and worth, and within these major domains, the privacy, confidentiality, self-determination, autonomy, and cultural, individual, and role differences of people. This principle contrasts most directly with forensic psychology functions. Appelbaum (1990) finds that the partisan nature of forensic cases places the practitioner in direct conflict with these lofty goals. For example, a psychologist engages an incarcerated or incompetent client in psychotherapy only to have the client become "cured" so he or she can face charges or face punishment, including the death penalty. Has the clinician acted in the client's best interests? Has the clinician, in discharging his or her duties, acted according to beneficence and nonmaleficence, or the twin duties of doing good and doing no harm?

Regarding the dignity of the client, consider the defendant accused of murdering his girlfriend who gave damaging evidence to the police. His attorney had him tested by a psychologist as to his ability to understand the *Miranda* warning. A good part of the town and the local media attended the trial. The psychologist offered testimony regarding the defendant's IQ and cognitive abilities. The prosecuting attorney kept the psychologist on the stand, slowly asking questions such as "Now, how impaired is the defendant? Just how much can he not understand? Are you saying he is so stupid that he cannot . . . ?" The psychologist, in front of the man's parents and children, answered question after question. The good was served by the vigorous defense mounted for him by the attorney; the downside was the stripping away of dignity. The defendant may have felt positive about the acquittal, but how do we reconcile the psychologist's testimony and the principle calling for respecting others' dignity? In some cases, they may be antithetical.

Privacy, Confidentiality, and Privilege

Privacy is a matter of good taste. Traditionally, there are no enumerated rights to privacy in our Constitution. The right to privacy has developed on the basis that it is necessary in order that the enumerated rights could be exercised and that this must have been an assumed right by the Founders of our country. Thus, for social and other relations to work, we expect some privacy from others and we owe a sense of privacy to people concerning their physical and emotional matters. Privacy needs differ from person to person; one person may not want others to know of a disease, such as cancer, another person may have looser personal boundaries regarding his or her medical and other personal matters. Parents and their adolescents, and husbands and wives need to establish what is private and what they share. Social custom and personal arrangements hold that it is bad taste to disclose information from within social and personal relationships that one party thought was private; it can also result in a loss of trust and a loss of the relationship. In more formal relationships, particularly those involving a fiduciary relationship or a relationship that engenders a duty on one party's part to another, privacy becomes more legally compelling and takes the form of a duty to maintain the confidentiality of information gleaned within the relationship.

Confidentiality involves withholding information from those not entitled to it by their role relationship to the information. As a department head, I evaluate the faculty annually, and my supervisor is obliged to review these evaluations. His wife is not entitled to the evaluations. If he does not review them, he would be negligent. There are legally compelling reasons to keep confidential the information gained in a fiduciary relationship. Consider a stockbroker who gains financial information about his or her clients. Failure to keep such information confidential results in a breach of trust and legal liabilities. Breach of trust might not hold for a hairdresser who finds out and repeats gossip because the role relationship did not involve the revealing of information as a matter of course in the business.

Privilege is protection against court-compelled disclosure of information to preserve a relationship society deems important that cannot function without such a withholding of information. Tracing its origins to the 6th century practice of a gentleman not "telling on" another gentleman, privilege has been recommended by the 1973 Supreme Court in nine areas: political vote, trade secrets, state secrets, informer's identity, and in the relationships of lawyer-client, physician-patient, husband-wife, priest-penitent, and physician- and psychotherapist-patient (Bryson, 1997). However, the same Court, in *United States v. Nixon,* recognized that privileges "are not lightly created nor expansively construed, for they are in derogation of the search for the truth" (Bryson, 1997, p. 982, footnote 87), and the privileges diminish the court's abilities to hear evidence. Courts determine privilege on a case-by-case basis, weighing the relevance and the need for the information for a fair trial that allows parties the information they need to pursue truth against the harm that a breach of privilege would cause. As with other privileges, psychotherapist-patient privilege has limits and is abridged in a commitment proceeding, in a court-ordered examination, and in litigation where the patient introduces his or her condition (Bryson, 1997, footnote 50; and Federal Rules of Evidence 504). Physician-patient privilege exceptions include communications not made for purposes of diagnosis and treatment, commitments and restoration proceedings, wills and succession, insurance actions, required reports (e.g., child abuse, gunshot wounds, venereal disease), communications furthering crime or fraud, mental and physical conditions put in issue by the patient (e.g., personal injury claims), malpractice, and some or all criminal prosecutions (Federal Rule of Evidence 504). However, much of medicine can work without privilege. For example, a gunshot wound is physically obvious, although the argument can be cogently made that the wounded will be inhibited from seeking treatment knowing there is no privilege. Thus, it appears that medicine has a lower threshold for the waiver of privilege than does psychology (Bryson, 1997). Matters get even more complicated. In *Allred v. Alaska* (1976), the court distinguished between counseling and psychotherapy based on whether the aim was to uncover deep psychological processes or to make more effective use of the client's resources, the latter presumed to be accessible to the public. Yet *Jaffee v. Redmond* (1997) held that is was not the particular profession (psychiatry, psychology, or social work) but the nature of the therapeutic relationship that determined privilege.

Considering the above, the APA Code of Ethics phrase qualifying Principle D, that psychologists are "mindful that legal and other obligations may lead to inconsistency and conflict with the exercise of these rights," is hardly an exaggeration. Consistent with the Forensic Guidelines, principled psychologists must (a) clarify the relationship they are entering because the same function, such as testing, may be protected in one instance but not another; (b) be aware of applicable governing law because states as well as federal and military jurisdictions differ (in military jurisdictions, the military owns privilege and routinely can use information that would be considered privileged in civilian circumstances); (c) determine the institutional commitment to policies and procedures (one would not want to tell clients a relationship is privileged when it is not); (d) make parties aware of the limitations to privacy, confidentiality, and privilege; (e) educate support staff who are under the umbrella of the psychologist's privilege as to what they cannot divulge; (f) ensure that records are safe and are released only in circumstances abridging privilege, and that they are in a form that satisfies the court need and does not divulge information beyond the court's interest; and (g) clarify which information is protected in the particular relationship and which is not.

Group Sensibilities

It is good forensic practice to be aware of differences based on age, gender, race, national origin, religion, sexual orientation, culture, socioeconomic group membership, and even subcultural differences. The psychologist who consults on jury selection might be practicing negligently if he or she does not take into account local custom and recent events in a jurisdiction from which a jury pool will be drawn. A jury selection consultant in a California case concerning police brutality would be practicing poorly if he or she did not take into account the effects on the Los Angeles jury pool of the repeated viewing of the Rodney King videotaped beating.

In recent years, a few psychologists have been asked to help prepare witnesses so that their body language and demeanor increase their credibility. Knowledge of how the client will come across to the particular judge or jury is essential to such practice. The ethical psychologist should be mindful of the validity of the database for such a practice. Just as Weiner (1989) warned of the degree of inference when using tests to predict behavior, the ethical psychologist must make a judgment about the fit between a practice such as jury selection or preparing witnesses and the scientific soundness of the literature upon which the practice is based. Can the literature be fitted to the forensic question? Does the literature have ecological validity in the forensic setting? To what extent does the impression management literature fit the preparation of a witness's body language, dress, and vocal presentation for effective juror and jury persuasion?

Concern for Others' Welfare

Psychologists are supposed to contribute to the welfare of others in interactions with clients, students, supervisees, human research participants, and other affected people. One way to contribute is to teach about controversial topics. Miller's (1997) course immersed students in the topic of repressed memories of childhood sexual abuse. Care must be taken in the event that such activities cause turmoil in the students. Students who reveal personal material in such a course cannot be guaranteed confidentiality and must be accorded some avenues for counseling as the need arises.

One professor taught about organized crime. He showed a film with short biographies and pictures of the Detroit Mafia. When the professor taught the course again, he found the film was confiscated from the university media center by the administration. It seems that one of the students in the class asked her father about his business after seeing him named in the film as a key figure in organized crime. Other professors who conduct classroom demonstrations involving committing mock crimes or who collect survey data from the class may unwittingly be opening themselves to ethical and legal problems. For example, surveys concerning unsolved crimes, sexual practices, marital infidelity, rape, and drug abuse may make the surveyor a material witness and an accessory-after-the-fact. Such activities may be meritorious and justified for their educational value, but attention needs to be given to ethical safeguards such as being sure the data cannot be traced back to the individual respondent.

Such teaching practices can be harmful, but failure to adequately supervise forensic research and forensic clinical activities can be deadly. Tina Biggar, a student at Oakland University, had worked on a project interviewing female inmates about their awareness of HIV. The inmates complimented her about her own attractiveness and told her about the escort services that had employed them. Biggar proposed to her mentor an honors project involving interviews with prostitutes at two escort services about their sexual experiences prior to the age of 16, the use of alcohol, cigarettes, and controlled substances, and recent sexual experiences (Weinstein & Wilson, 1997). Whether her own sexual history—including a violent relationship and a teenage pregnancy—was known to her research supervisor and whether extra care should have been taken in her supervision is not documented. What is clear is that the chair of the university's Institutional Review Board (IRB) and the director of grants, contracts, and sponsored research expressed their concerns to the supervising professor, not the least of which was that contact with the escort services had begun prior to ethics review (Weinstein & Wilson, 1997, pp. 46–48). Biggar contacted the escort service through her research, dated a client, and was murdered.

Whether or not she would have traveled this path but for her research experiences is debatable. What is clear is that cons are pros. They are highly skilled at the arts of their professions, be they robbers, extortionists, or sexual predators. This creates a heightened responsibility on the part of faculty to supervise students in forensic settings and with forensic populations. The professor has a duty to manage relationships born of the research project. The student who develops a relationship with an inmate might claim the right of association. However, if an inappropriate or unwise relationship is the product of the education or research experience, the faculty has an obligation to monitor and even terminate the student in the setting and to warn the appropriate authorities. An analogous situation is when a psychotherapist develops a relationship with a patient; the treating relationship must be terminated and a period of time, perhaps a minimum of two years, must pass before the personal relationship can be said to be viable on its own. If there is a viable relationship between a student or a psychologist and a prisoner beyond a two-year period, the primacy of the professional relationship should fade, what is left may be attributed to the personal relationship that was sustained beyond the professional relationship. In human affairs, psychometric precision falls short of providing definite answers. However, the management of such affairs should not be forsaken because the rules are not clear to the supervisor. The supervisor should consult with more experienced professionals because ignorance is no excuse for negligent supervision of students.

Social Responsibility

Forensic psychologists must prevent misuse of their work. This can take a number of forms. Desperate people seek desperate solutions. A psychologist was called by an attorney wanting help with defending a student who was found cheating from another student's work. The attorney wanted to develop a theory that the cheater suffered a "wandering eyes" syndrome that caused him to scan his environment in search of answers to the test questions. The psychologist declined the case, informing the attorney that there was no sustainable literature for such a condition. Yet, expert witnesses have been used to generate defenses: the Twinkie defense, by which a defendant blamed his crime on the ingestion of Twinkies; the television influence defense, when a crime mimics a television show or movie; and the urban psychosis defense, where the everyday hassles of city living putatively culminate in the perpetrator "losing it." To be sure, progress occurs through posing novel theories, but the responsible psychologist must weigh the aggregated body of scientific knowledge that could contribute to novel defenses before accepting such case referrals.

The forensic psychologist has become increasingly involved in high-profile cases, and so there is the heady temptation to speak with the media. As a general rule, the expert witness psychologist should confine his or her reporting to the witness stand. The most apt comment in response to media inquiries is something to the effect that "We are all concerned about the issues in this case and I appreciate your concern. I have given (or will give) my testimony in court and look forward to your fine reporting of the case." When involved in forensic work, once the psychologist releases an opinion or report to the attorney or other responsible parties, the psychologist loses control of the information he or she was enjoined not to reveal. Dr. Duncan, the psychologist in the Kelly Flinn case cited above, faced just this dilemma. It appeared that she examined Lt. Flinn at the behest of Flinn's attorney or parents and owed them privilege. Some of her alleged findings were published by Lt. Flinn in *Newsweek*. Does Dr. Duncan have the right to respond to any miscasting of her findings? It appears that unless the party revealing the information travels beyond a legal threshold, such as defaming the professional, the psychologist has a duty to maintain privilege. Perhaps the question is analogous to a clinician who wants to secure the services of a collection agency but would be revealing the name of his or her clients in doing so. If clients either gave permission for such a release or voided the relationship by their actions, then limited disclosure of information might be considered. However, the threshold for answering media items should be high because the ability to offer privilege is hard-won and privilege should not be lightly discarded. Media's characterizing the psychologist's testimony in a manner distasteful to the psychologist is not grievous enough to abrogate privilege. Psychologists must be aware that the agenda of attorneys and clients might not fit the psychologist's professional code of ethics. A neuropsychologist tested a judge for dementia. The case was controversial because having a sitting justice step down is unusual and can be mired in political considerations. Thus, the psychologist proceeded with caution; confidentiality was a great concern. He was shocked to come into the seminar he was conducting on ethics to be greeted by copies of the newspaper featuring verbatim sections of his report apparently leaked by an attorney in the case. Once the psychologist releases information, he or she may have no control over the further release of the information. The principled psychologist establishes the conditions of the release of information with full regard to ethical principles that include privilege, confidentiality, the dignity of the parties in a case, and copyrights.

The media devote increasing amounts of time to topics such as infidelity, abuse, neglect, violence, and sex. Forensic psychologists participate in such shows to give their expert perspectives. Any educational value of such appearances must be weighed against the ability of the psychologist to function ethically and professionally. When the psychologist is asked for an opinion, he or she must consider whether the question is an appropriate one to answer, whether there was a chance to perform an adequate examination, whether confidentiality would be breached by the answer, whether the individual's dignity is preserved, and whether there is an opportunity to perform any necessary referrals or counseling. The psychologist must be aware that there are a number of media forums. Some are prurient, and others are educational. Psychologists perform a valuable social function when they appear on the media to explicate the scientific and professional aspects of a forensic issue or case and adhere to ethical precepts in reporting the data and their opinions. As with all the issues discussed above and with forensic and moral issues, there is a balancing of competing interests that often go begging for absolutes.

RECOMMENDATIONS

1. Practicing principled psychology involves knowing the ethics codes generally and those principles and standards most applicable to the practice in which the forensic psychologist is engaged.
2. Principled psychologists offer services in which they have achieved a level of proficiency by virtue of a combination of knowledge, skills, education, training, and experience. Thus, it may be malpractice when psychologists present a subtest score difference on psychological tests but do not keep up with testing principles such as the standard error of the differences on the measures they use.
3. Just as the psychologist practicing in the medical setting or dental school must know clinical phenomena, the language and concepts, and the professional practices of the medical or dental setting, the forensic psychologist must be conversant with the concepts, practices, and standards in the legal arena. Thus, the psychologist practicing in a setting with patients who may be harmful must know the threshold that triggers the need to warn, the literature concerning the validity of such predictions, and the applicable statutes and reporting authorities.
4. Such knowledge allows the psychologist to anticipate events that would otherwise lead to ethical and legal difficulties. Thus, the client or patient has a right to know the limits to confidentiality and to privilege before revealing information in a setting the client may have thought to be inviolate. Forensic psychologists get in trouble when they are not aware of these issues and when they operate out of a motivation that does not fit the situation.
5. The principled psychologist is mindful of the corrections dictum that if an event is not documented, it did not occur. Compiling and keeping good records securely is essential.
6. Failing to understand and evaluate the various roles the forensic client may expect can lead the psychologist to practice irresponsibly.
7. The principled psychologist seeks to understand the positions and motivations of the other parties involved.
8. When accepting a case whose issues are unfamiliar and novel or when confronted by a dilemma, the principled psychologist seeks the counsel,

and possibly the supervision, of esteemed and trusted colleagues. If the psychologist is fair to the colleague and the case, he or she will reveal the facts that the colleague needs to know to help guide the psychologist but will not reveal facts sufficient to transfer the ethical responsibility to the colleague.

9. The wise psychologist confronting forensic questions develops relationships with a few trusted attorneys so that questions with legal implications may be resolved.

10. Our professional associations need to compile casebooks to guide the practitioner to a better understanding of how the ethical principles are applied in particular instances. Our associations need to monitor the relevance and completeness of the ethics codes and update them in this rapidly developing specialty.

One can aspire to avoid the seven deadly sins, in both one's private life and in professional practice, and manage to avoid evil. However, life is not that simple. We are active agents in the world, a world that poses contradictory values. In forensic psychology, we should not merely try to avoid evil but see our practice as a way to achieve a level of excellence unparalleled by other areas of psychology. The path to principled, ethical action proposed here is that we weigh our actions on a scale of the seven positive attributes listed in this chapter's second epigraph. If the forensic psychologist acts from a basis of wisdom with humility and awe regarding the responsibilities and opportunities to do good rather than do well, he or she is on the road to principled practice. If the psychologist realizes he or she will not attain wealth through forensic work and, instead, that a love of truth serves as a nobler motivational base, the forensic psychologist will find the path to ethical practice easier to follow. The forensic psychologist who practices in accord with the seven judicious attributes will find that he or she is beloved by the people, not in the sense of popularity but in the sense of enduring respect. Finally, the principled forensic psychologist need not tell anyone how good he or she is; people will know.

REFERENCES

Allred v. Alaska, 554 P.2d 411 (Alaska, 1976).

American Bar Association. (1989). *ABA criminal justice mental health standards.* Washington, DC: Author.

American Psychological Association. (1985). *Standards for educational and psychological testing.* Washington, DC: American Psychological Association.

American Psychological Association. (1992). Ethical principles of psychologists and code of conduct. *American Psychologist, 47,* 1597–1611.

American Psychological Association. (1994). Guidelines for child custody evaluations in divorce proceedings. *American Psychologist, 49,* 677–680.

Appelbaum, P. S. (1990). The parable of the forensic psychiatrist: Ethics and the problem of doing harm. *International Journal of Law and Psychiatry, 13,* 249–259.

Barefoot v. Estelle, 463 U.S. 880 (1983).

Bennett, B. E., Bryant, B. K., VandenBos, G. R., & Greenwood, A. (1990). *Professional liability and risk management.* Washington, DC: American Psychological Association.

Brown, L. S. (1997). The private practice of subversion: Psychology as Tikkun Olam. *American Psychologist, 52,* 449–462.

Bruck, M., & Ceci, S. (1995). Amicus brief for the case of State of New Jersey v. Michaels presented by Committee of "Concerned Social Scientists." Supreme Court of New Jersey, Docket # 36,633. *Psychology, Public Policy, and Law, 1,* 272–322.

Bryson, M. R. (1997). Protecting confidential communications between a psychotherapist and patient: Jaffee v. Redmond. *Catholic University Law Review, 46,* 963–1004.

Chapple v. Ganger, 851 F. Supp. 1481 (E.D. Wash, 1994).

Clark, C. R. (1990). Agreeing to be an expert witness: Considerations of competence and role integrity. *Register Report, 16,* 4–6.

Colbach, E. M. (1997). The trouble with American forensic psychiatry. *International Journal of Offender Therapy and Comparative Criminology, 41,* 160–167.

Committee on Ethical Guidelines for Forensic Psychologists. (1991). Specialty guidelines for forensic psychologists. *Law and Human Behavior, 15,* 655–665.

Daubert v. Merrell Dow Pharmaceuticals, 113 S. Ct. 2786 (1993).

Dawes, R. M. (1994). *House of cards: Psychology and psychotherapy built on myth.* New York: Free Press.

Derbyshire, R. C. (1983). How effective in medical self-regulation? *Law and Human Behavior, 7,* 193–202.

Eberle, P. (1993). *The abuse of innocence: The McMartin preschool trial.* Buffalo, NY: Prometheus Books.

Edge, R. S., & Groves, J. R. (1994). *The ethics of health care: A guide for clinical practice.* Albany, NY: Delmar.

Fisher, C. B. (1995). American Psychological Association's 1992 ethics code and the validation of sexual abuse in day-care settings. *Psychology, Public Policy, and Law, 1,* 461–478.

Flinn, K. (1997, November, 24). *Newsweek,* pp. 57, 58. (Excerpted from *Proud to be,* by Kelly Flinn)

Frankel, M. S. (1989). Professional codes: Why, how, and with what impact? *Journal of Business Ethics, 8,* 109–115.

Glazer, M. P., & Glazer, P. M. (1986). Whistle blowing. *Psychology Today, 20,* 36–43.

Golding, S. L. (1990). Mental health professionals and the courts: The ethics of expertise. *International Journal of Law and Psychiatry, 13,* 281–307.

Golding, S. L., & Roesch, R. (1987). The assessment of criminal responsibility: A historical approach to a current controversy. In I. B. Weiner & A. K. Hess (Eds.), *The handbook of forensic psychology* (pp. 395–436). New York: Wiley.

Greenberg, S. A., & Shuman, D. W. (1997). Irreconcilable conflict between therapeutic and forensic roles. *Professional Psychology, 28,* 50–57.

Hagen, M. A. (1997). *Whores of the court: The fraud of psychiatric testimony and the rape of American justice.* New York: HarperCollins.

Hess, A. K. (1998a). Accepting forensic case referrals: Ethical and professional considerations. *Professional Psychology, 29,* 109–114.

Hess, A. K. (1998b). Review of the Millon Clinical Multiaxial Inventory, 3rd ed. *Buros' Mental Measurements Yearbook* (13th ed.). Lincoln, NE: Buros Institute.

Huber, P. W. (1993). *Galileo's revenge: Junk science in the courtroom.* New York: Basic Books.

Jaffee v. Redmond, 116 S. Ct. 1923, 1996 WL 315841 (U.S. Ill., 1997).

Joiner v. General Electric Company U.S. Court of Appeals, Eleventh Circuit, No. 94–9131 (January 13, 1997).

Jurek v. Texas, 428 U.S. 262 (1976).

Katz, J. (1992). "The fallacy of the impartial expert" revisited. *Bulletin of the American Academy of Psychiatry and the Law, 20,* 141–152.

Keenan, J. P. (1995). Whistle blowing and the first-level manager. *Journal of Social Behavior and Personality, 10,* 571–584.

Keith-Spiegel, P., & Koocher, G. P. (1985). *Ethics in psychology: Professional standards and cases.* New York: Random House.

Klass, B. S., & DeNisi, A. S. (1989). Managerial reactions to employee dissent: The impact of grievance activity on performance ratings. *Academy of Management Journal, 32,* 705–717.

Lewin, D. (1987). Dispute resolution in the nonunion firm. *Journal of Conflict Resolution, 31,* 465–502.

Matarazzo, J. D. (1986). Computerized clinical psychological test interpretations: Unvalidated plus all mean and no sigm(a). *American Psychologist, 41,* 14–24.

Miller, L. A. (1997). Teaching about repressed memories of childhood sexual abuse and eyewitness testimony. *Teaching of Psychology, 24,* 250–255.

Olson-Buchanan, J. B. (1996). Voicing discontent: What happens to the grievance filer after the grievance? *Journal of Applied Psychology, 81,* 52–63.

Pavalko, R. M. (1979). *Sociology of occupations and professions.* Itasca, IL: Peacock.

Pervin, L. A. (1984). *Current controversies and issues in personality* (2nd ed.). New York: Wiley.

Rabinowitz, D. (1990, May). From the mouths of babes to a jail cell. *Harper's Magazine, 280*(1680), 52–63.

Rose, J. (1983). Professional regulation: The current controversy. *Law and Human Behavior, 7,* 103–116.

Schretlen, D., Wilkins, S. S., Van Gorp, W. G., & Bobholz, J. H. (1992). Cross-validation of a psychological test battery to detect faked insanity. *Psychological Assessment, 4,* 77–83.

Schwarz v. Kogan, U.S. Court of Appeals, 11th Circuit, No. 96-3276 (January 12, 1998).

Shuman, D. W. (1993). The use of empathy in forensic examinations. *Ethics and Behavior, 3,* 289–302.

Shuman, D. W., & Greenberg, S. A. (1998). The role of ethical norms in the admissibility of expert testimony. *The Judge's Journal, 37,* 4–9, 42–43.

Sommer v. French, 115 Ohio App.3d 101 (1996).

Smith, J. D. (1985). *Minds made feeble: The myth and legacy of the Kallikaks.* Maryland: Aspen Systems.

Strasburger, L. H., Gutheil, T. G., & Brodsky, A. (1997). On wearing two hats: Role conflict in serving as both psychotherapist and expert witness. *American Journal of Psychiatry, 154,* 448–456.

Super, J. T. (1997). Select legal and ethical aspects of fitness for duty evaluations. *Journal of Criminal Justice, 25,* 223–229.

Toch, H. (1981). Cast the first stone? Ethics as a weapon. *Criminology, 19,* 185–194.

Two California attorneys take jabs at state licensing board. (1998, March/April). *National Psychologist* pp. 1, 2.

United States v. Nixon, 418 U.S. 683 (1974).

Weiner, I. B. (1989). On competence and ethicality in psychodiagnostic assessment. *Journal of Personality Assessment, 53,* 827–831.

Weiner, I. B. (1995). How to anticipate ethical and legal challenges in personality assessments. In J. N. Butcher (Ed.), *Clinical personality assessment: Practical applications* (pp. 95–103). New York: Oxford University Press.

Weinstein, F., & Wilson, M. (1997). *The coed call girl murder.* New York: St. Martin's Paperbacks.

Weinstock, R. (1986). Ethical concerns expressed by forensic psychiatrists. *Journal of Forensic Sciences, 31,* 596–602.

Weinstock, R. (1989). Perceptions of ethical problems by forensic psychiatrists. *Bulletin of the American Academy of Psychiatry and Law, 17,* 189–202.

West Publishing Company. (1984). *Selected statues, rules and standards on the legal profession.* St. Paul, MN: Author.

Wettstein, R. M., Mulvay, E. P., & Rogers, R. (1991). A prospective comparison of four insanity defense standards. *American Journal of Psychiatry, 148,* 21–27.

CHAPTER 25

Training in Forensic Psychology and the Law

GARY B. MELTON, MATTHEW T. HUSS, and ALAN J. TOMKINS

DURING THE past 20 years, interest in psychology and the law, and specifically forensic psychology, has undergone tremendous growth at both the student and professional levels (e.g., Bersoff et al., 1997; Ogloff, Tomkins, & Bersoff, 1996; Otto, Heilbrun, & Grisso, 1990; Tomkins & Ogloff, 1990). A proliferation of psycholegal scholarship sustains numerous professional journals (e.g., *Behavioral Sciences and the Law, Law and Human Behavior*) and several professional organizations (e.g., American Board of Forensic Psychologists; American Psychology-Law Society) (see generally, Grisso, 1991; Ogloff et al., 1996; Otto et al., 1990). In fact, efforts in the near future to identify forensic psychology as an area of specialization by the American Psychological Association could result in even more professional recognition for the field (K. Heilbrun, personal communication, December 17, 1996), which is likely, in turn, to lead to even more student interest.

It is possible that the positive attention given to forensic psychology is a reaction to the changing economic realities of clinical psychology practice within a managed care environment. Forensic psychology appears to be one of the few areas of clinical practice to thrive in recent years. In addition, both constitutional and fiscal constraints over the past 25 years have led to a trend toward decentralization of forensic services, which has resulted in an increased demand for forensic clinicians in community settings or, perhaps more precisely, for general clinicians with forensic training (see, e.g., American Bar Association, 1984; Melton, Weithorn, & Slobogin, 1985).

Despite these positive developments, not all is rosy with forensic psychology. For many years now, critics have charged researchers in the field with ignoring whole areas of law, conducting poor quality studies, and failing to make even the most basic accommodations to external validity (e.g., Loh, 1981; Melton, 1985; Monahan & Loftus, 1982; Roesch, 1990). By the same token, commentators have criticized forensic clinicians for often making conclusory judgments based on insufficient knowledge of legal standards and inadequate, perhaps an inherently inadequate, scientific foundation (e.g., Bonnie & Slobogin, 1980; Grisso, 1987; Lidz & Mulvey, 1995; Melton, Petrila, Poythress, & Slobogin, 1997; Morse, 1978, 1982a; Roesch & Golding, 1980). Legal decision makers themselves have been analogously criticized for cajoling such judgments from clinicians (e.g., Morse, 1982b; Poythress, 1978, 1982).

One response to these criticisms has been to sharpen the focus on forensic psychology training. There has emerged a recognition of the need for more specialized training, including intensive training in law as part of graduate psychology education at both the predoctoral and postdoctoral levels (Bersoff et al., 1997; Melton, 1990). Persuasive arguments have been set forth proclaiming the importance of training forensic specialists (Melton, 1994). Today, there are a number of organizational and role demands placed on forensic practice that adversely impact other aspects of mental health practice. In addition, forensic specialization is preferred because of the need to maximize legal professionals' access to forensic practice (Melton, 1994).

There has, in fact, been an increase in training in psychology and law over the past 25 years (compare Grisso, Sales, & Bayless, 1982, with Ogloff et al., 1996), although the growth has slowed in recent years despite economic and policy trends. In the 1960s, Stanford University, along with a few other schools, received funds from the Russell Sage Foundation that allowed interdisciplinary training in the social sciences and the law (Schlegel, 1995). In the early 1970s, it was the University of Nebraska that started the first fully integrated training program in law and psychology. The program was integrated in the truest sense, for students could take one interdisciplinary law/psychology course and receive credits toward both their psychology degree and their law degree (see, e.g., Grisso et al., 1982; Melton, 1990; Ogloff et al., 1996).

By the late 1970s, there were five programs that offered joint training in psychology and law at the predoctoral level, along with a few psychology programs that offered a specialty focus in psychology and law (see also Melton, 1983). Although there have been changes in the list of schools that offer psycholegal training, the number has remained small (see Bersoff et al., 1997). There are several programs that offer joint JD/PhD training (e.g., Allegheny University of the Health Sciences–Villanova University, University of Arizona, University of Nebraska–Lincoln, and the Pacific School of Psychology) and one PsyD/JD program (Widener University) (American Psychology-Law Society, 1996; see also Bersoff et al., 1997; Ogloff et al., 1996). Two programs (University of Nebraska–Lincoln and Stanford University) offer a PhD/MLS program. The master's in legal studies (MLS) is an abbreviated course of study usually equating to one year of legal course work. The JD/PhD programs also offer specialty training without the JD or MLS option. In addition, there are many other programs that offer specialty training in psychology and law culminating solely in the PhD (e.g., University of Alabama, University of British Columbia, Florida International University, University of Illinois at Chicago, University of Kansas, University of Nevada–Reno, Queen's University, Simon Fraser University, St. Louis University, Stanford University, University of Texas at El Paso, and

University of Virginia). Additional programs also offer a master's degree in forensic psychology (e.g., Castleton State College and John Jay College).

Nonetheless, programs that specialize in forensic psychology have not developed a core curriculum. A recent conference focusing on training in psychology and the law (the Villanova Conference) declined to prescribe absolute standards for training in forensic psychology (Bersoff et al., 1997). They instead identified several basic options that graduate programs should offer to forensic students that are captured within the three levels of skills, knowledge, and abilities (Bersoff et al., 1997). Many graduate programs offer at least some exposure to law and psychology. Grisso et al. (1982) found that almost 25% of graduate psychology departments offered courses in legal topics in 1978, with another 11% reporting that they were planning to develop such a course. Given that three-fourths of the psycholegal courses offered in 1978 had been offered for the first time since 1973, it is likely that a large proportion of graduate psychology programs now offer at least some education in psycholegal matters.

Thus, as we end the 20th century, forensic psychology appears to be of interest to many students and professionals, and psycholegal training is offered in many universities, though less than might be expected given the current trends. How should students and their faculty evaluate the quality of that training? Should a program in forensic psychology simply expose psychology-trained individuals to the law?

In this chapter, we consider these issues. The focus is on the merits of the various models of psycholegal training. Much of our discussion examines the various models at the predoctoral level. We also review previously identified models for forensic training at the clinical internship level as well as postdoctoral training. It should become apparent that individuals seeking training in forensic psychology have numerous training opportunities available to them at multiple levels of experience. It is important that individuals choose the paths that suit their own particular needs.

PRINCIPLES OF TRAINING

In evaluating training in psychology and law, the starting point must be an analysis of the proper goals of such training. There has been much discussion of the need for lawyers and behavioral scientists to speak with one another, to understand each other's terminology, and to reconcile differences in libertarianism-paternalism attitudes. According to such an analysis, all that is needed to integrate psychology and law is to cure a problem in communication. Just as one can facilitate communication between people of different nationalities by teaching at least one partner the language of the other, one should be able to enhance interdisciplinary work by educating at least one partner in the jargon of the other (e.g., Casey, Keilitz, & Hafemeister, 1992). Therefore, specific goals might be to ensure that psychologists know the legal meaning of insanity and that lawyers know the technical meaning of schizophrenia.

Such a view is clearly naïve. First, it overlooks the differing purposes of the two disciplines (Melton, 1994). Thus, for example, rejection of adversary procedures might increase the objectivity and comprehensiveness of mental health professionals' testimony. However, abandonment of the adversary system in mental health cases would defeat the legal system's principal purpose of the pursuit of justice, of the provision of an opportunity for each party to put its best case forward (cf. Thibaut & Walker, 1978). Moreover, a requirement of a report for the court alone in criminal cases would frustrate a defendant's ability to explore defenses and interfere with his or her Fifth Amendment rights (American Bar Association, 1984; Slobogin, 1982).

Second, learning the core concepts in the other discipline will not eliminate the fundamental disciplinary differences in philosophical assumptions (see Haney, 1980; Melton et al., 1997, Chapter 1) or style of thinking and analysis. Indeed, increased fluency of communication will illuminate such differences, not reduce them.

We do not wish to underemphasize the significance of differences in knowledge and attitudes. A mental health professional cannot give assistance to the fact finder in a legal proceeding if the clinician misunderstands the standard to be applied. Similarly, to be of significant help to legal policymakers, psychological researchers need to be aware of specific empirical questions and assumptions in the law. Nonetheless, beyond certain core knowledge, it seems that a primary need is for familiarity with the methods and philosophy of the two disciplines.

In short, behavioral scientists need enough training in relevant areas of the law to formulate relevant questions and to be able to "think like a lawyer" well enough to communicate effectively with attorneys and to analyze the policy implications and limitations of behavioral science research. On the other hand, attorneys need enough behavioral science training to be acquainted with and, most important, be able to evaluate the empirical literature relevant to legal issues and be able to collaborate in the design and implementation of policy-relevant research projects. Behavioral scientists in the area require a knowledge of basic law, particularly legal analysis; lawyers need basic research training.

This analysis of primary psycholegal training needs has two major implications for the development of training models. First, it seems that inclusion of attorneys as trainers is essential to an effective training program in law and psychology. Both disciplinary paradigmatic differences (cf. Rappaport, 1977) and core knowledge in the law are more likely to be communicated effectively by a lawyer than by a psychologist, particularly in training settings where there are opportunities for interaction only with other behavioral scientists or mental health professionals. In making such an assertion, we do not mean to imply that psychologists sophisticated in law cannot do such training. Rather, our point is that something important is lost by not including lawyers. Indeed, it is perhaps in informal conversations with lawyers that paradigmatic differences are most likely to become evident. As a general matter, lawyers also are obviously more likely to have knowledge of the relevant law, even though some psychologists may have acquired more expertise than most lawyers in particular legal specialties.

Our analysis is applicable to the training of clinical practitioners in forensic psychology as well as to the training of researchers who contribute to the development or implementation of mental health policy. Forensic clinicians need to be sensitive to differences in philosophical assumptions (e.g., the nature of voluntariness; the nature of a fact; the utility of application of group proba- bility data to individual cases) that may make translation of their findings to the legal system difficult. Moreover, although there are undoubtedly some special clinical problems inherent in forensic assessment (e.g., evaluation of claims of dissociative states; expertise in particular forms of criminal con- duct, such as sexual deviations), much of the special forensic knowledge that a generally competent clinician needs to perform forensic evaluations is purely legal (e.g., implications of the Fifth Amendment for forensic evalua- tion; clinical issues in provocation and self-defense; relevance of amnesia to competency to stand trial). Therefore, training in forensic clinical practice is best done at least partially by lawyers. In our view, their inclusion as teachers in forensic training programs is in fact more important than the inclusion of forensic clinicians, although there obviously is some expertise that senior forensic clinicians and researchers can add. Not only is sophistication in rel- evant legal issues important as a matter of professionalism of forensic clini- cians (cf. American Psychological Association, 1992, Ethical Standard 7.01), it is also ethically required to avoid invasion of clients' civil rights (cf. APA, 1992, Principle D).

In addition to the implication that interaction with, and direct training by, lawyers is essential to psycholegal training, there is a second major implication of the argument that the key to such training is an appreciation of the second discipline's methodology and core knowledge. The second implication is that having both terminal degrees is unnecessary for making a contribution to psy- cholegal studies. Indeed, expertise in one discipline with a basic knowledge in the other is probably sufficient. Whether pre- or postdegree, a concentrated program specifically on law-psychology interaction and paradigmatic differ- ences is likely to be generally as effective and certainly less costly than joint- degree programs in training scholars in psychology and law, although there may still be special benefits accruing from joint-degree opportunities for some students. We now look at each training model with respect to its special merits and liabilities.

MODELS OF TRAINING

JOINT-DEGREE PROGRAMS

Not only are two degrees unnecessary for making a contribution to psychole- gal studies, they are also insufficient. Simply having earned two degrees does not necessarily imply having integrated them. One can be a psychologist and a lawyer without being a psychologist-lawyer. Some persons earn a second de- gree as part of a career change. Others perhaps intend to integrate the disci- plines but instead lead dual careers. In reviewing JD-PhD résumés as part of faculty searches, the authors have been struck by how many jointly trained in- dividuals are psychologists by day and lawyers by night (or vice versa); they did not succeed in developing even an interdisciplinary approach to their dis- sertations or other postgraduate scholarly work.

Still other JD-PhD's achieve some minimal integration, but in a narrow, self-serving way. There are psychologists (and lawyers) who collect degrees to pad their advertisements in the yellow pages. Then there was the physician-lawyer who wrote a letter to the editor of the *Wall Street Journal* to encourage his medical colleagues to attend law school so that they might learn tax loopholes useful in managing their practice!

Of course, some of the most distinguished contributors to psycholegal studies have been JD-PhD's who achieved an integration of their dual training on their own. Nonetheless, it is intuitively clear that the likelihood of joint-degree students' becoming psychologist-lawyers (instead of psychologists and lawyers) is increased by their participation in interdisciplinary programs of training. Although some joint-degree programs have been programs only in the sense of rules permitting dual enrollment in the law school and the graduate school, most of the organized joint-degree programs do in fact have a distinctive curriculum apart from the standard requirements for the JD and the PhD degrees (Bersoff et al., 1997).

Much of our discussion will focus on the law/psychology program at the University of Nebraska–Lincoln purely for illustrative purposes. However, besides being the program that these authors are most familiar with, it is also the oldest law/psychology program in the country (Melton, 1990). Nonetheless, the Nebraska curriculum is representative in form, although the specific content of each of the joint-degree programs is unique.[1] Joint-degree students at Nebraska typically begin their graduate studies by taking standard first-year curriculum in the College of Law. Nebraska's law school, like most law schools, requires its students to be full-time during their first year, because of the crucial importance first-year courses are presumed to have in teaching students to think like lawyers. Therefore, first-year law/psychology students differ little from regular first-year law students. Indeed, the only deviation in their studies is attendance at colloquia sponsored by the law/psychology program.

It is unclear whether the first-year law curriculum should come in the first or the second year of the joint-degree curriculum. Students frequently report some difficulty in going from the first year of training in one discipline to the first year of training in the other (but see Hafemeister, Ogloff, & Small, 1990). To a certain extent, this difficulty in transition is the inherent result of doubling the stress and low status of the first year in any graduate or professional curriculum. However, there are special problems in the transition between the first year of law and the first year of psychology. Students describe their first year in law as being uncomfortable (with distant, sometimes adversarial relationships with professors), but with clear boundaries between professors and students and a high degree of anonymity, which offers a certain degree of protection.

On the other hand, the first year in graduate school is typified by collegiality inside and outside the classroom, blurring of role boundaries, and a feeling of living in a fishbowl. Thus, beyond whatever conflict is engendered by the disciplinary differences themselves, students often experience some confusion as to how they should behave as students. Given that such role disparity is apt to occur, there is some reason to support beginning the program with the first-year psychology curriculum. Some students have speculated that they might have been more active in their first-year law classes if they had begun their graduate career in psychology, where the tradition is for students to be highly involved in class discussions, indeed leading class discussions, from almost the first time they step into the classroom.

Another reason to place the first year of law school in the second year of a joint-degree curriculum is to provide some opportunities for interdisciplinary work and identification as joint-degree students from the beginning. Because all first-year law students take the same courses, there is insufficient flexibility in the first-year law curriculum to permit any interdisciplinary studies.

On the other hand, it may be unrealistic to expect students to begin to integrate their studies without a basic knowledge of legal doctrines and problems. Therefore, placing the first year of law school at the beginning of the program may maximize the early integration of studies by enabling students to look at psychology, from the beginning, in terms of potential relevance to legal issues. The initiation of study with the first year of law also avoids interruption of the first stages of the student's research program by intense, full-time course work.

As already noted, at Nebraska joint-degree students typically begin their studies in the College of Law. In the second year, the integration begins in earnest. Second-year students enroll in basic psychology courses (e.g., quantitative methods; proseminars in selected subdisciplines of psychology) and begin an interdisciplinary research program under faculty supervision. Also, they have their first exposure to interdisciplinary courses, and they participate in a law/psychology research group and attend interdisciplinary colloquia. In succeeding years, students take a mix of law, psychology, and law/psychology courses, and they collaborate with faculty members in both disciplines on research. They also occasionally obtain some teaching experience, and they can participate in practica in which they can use their dual-disciplinary skills (e.g., aide to the lieutenant governor; state legislative aide; policy planner in state agency; law clerk for public defender of respondents in civil commitment proceedings).

Most of the interdisciplinary courses are cross-listed, and students can take them for credit toward both degrees. At Nebraska, JD-PhD students are able to apply 12 credit hours of course work and 6 credit hours of research to both of their degree programs. The courses include Law and Behavioral Science (an overview of the use of social scientific evidence in the law, along with the use of psychology in litigation and the use of psychology to evaluate the law and legal processes), Mental Health Law, and Topics in Law and Psychology. The Topics course is repeatable, and its theme changes. Among the seminar topics offered in recent years are psycholegal perspectives on juries, social and domestic violence, international human rights, syndromes in the law, issues in mental health policy, distributive and procedural justice, and child development and legal policy. The interdisciplinary courses are taught by core faculty in the law/psychology program or team-taught by a law professor and a psychology professor.

Compared with other models of psycholegal training, there are three possible major advantages of joint-degree programs. First, because of their broader exposure to the law than students who obtain only a PhD, JD-PhD's may be better able to identify important issues in areas of law that psychologists have seldom explored (e.g., contracts, tax, trusts, and estates). Because psychological assumptions are not limited to criminal, juvenile, family, and mental health law, students with broad legal training should be better equipped to explore and expand the field of psycholegal research. Similarly, legal problems in the organization and delivery of mental health services are not limited to mental health law. Such topics as land use planning, corporate law, and public employment law may all have important places in the psycholegal study of the mental health system. It may not be reasonable to expect highly specialized PhD's to acquire such broad legal expertise.

Second, there may be something special about being exposed in concentrated form to both disciplines at the same time. The process of moving back and forth between thinking like a lawyer and thinking like a psychologist, discussing topics in the context of different epistemologies, may be particularly helpful in creating interdisciplinary scholarship.

Third, the possession of basic credentials in both disciplines may assist in achieving entry into diverse settings. To a certain extent, this argument is so obvious as to require no verification. Psychologists are not going to be hired to work in law firms, no matter how well they know mental health law and how skilled they are advocating patients' interests. Both guild definitions and licensing restrictions bar such employment for psychologists. Analogously, no matter how knowledgeable attorneys without PhD's are about social psychological processes and how experienced they are in inducing organizational and societal change, they are unlikely to be hired to teach courses in social and community psychology. It may also be reasonable to expect that because of their diverse training and credentials, JD-PhD's would have entry into settings traditionally the province of either psychology or law and that they would have an advantage over other applicants.

The employment advantage of JD-PhD's, however, may not be as great as one might expect intuitively. For example, one reason sometimes asserted for JD-PhD programs is the need to train psychologically sophisticated lawyers who can infiltrate law schools and shape the law's responsiveness to psychological evidence. The underlying assumption that JD-PhD's will be able easily to obtain positions on law faculties is wrong. The track into teaching law in the United States is clear. Most law professors are drawn from a few select national law schools. Law schools look for JDs who were members of Order of the Coif, signifying rank in the top 10% of one's graduating class, and law review members, usually signifying high class rank at the end of the first year of law school. Immediately after graduation, prospective teachers will maximize their chances of eventually joining the faculty of a good law school by accepting a high-status job that will provide substantial experience in legal research and writing (clerk for a respected judge, attorney in the Justice Department honors program or a federal regulatory agency, or associate in a large firm). Even when a law school has an interest in interdisciplinary studies, it is likely to choose an applicant who has the traditional credentials over a JD-PhD who has solid, but not stellar, law school grades. Indeed, a PhD without a law degree but with a record of outstanding scholarship in legally relevant areas will often have easier entree than a jointly trained person with little or no legal scholarship. Exacerbating the situation is the fact that most of the joint-degree programs are located in law schools that are not usually regarded as being on the track for producing law teachers.

As a general matter, JD-PhD's may find that they are often placed in the position of proving that they are real lawyers (or psychologists). Merely having completed the requirements for two terminal degrees and having diverse skills may not be enough. To establish credibility with their colleagues in both disciplines, joint-degree students need to establish distinguished credentials as both lawyers and psychologists. Because of the clear tracking based on law school performance, this point is especially clear in terms of building credibility as a lawyer. At Nebraska, the law/psychology program seeks to ensure that students do not just complete both the JD and the PhD and integrate them satisfactorily; they must also develop strong records in each discipline according to traditional criteria. Thus, students seeking teaching positions in law schools are encouraged to pay special attention to law grades, to join the law review, and to seek judicial clerkships. They are expected to do both substantive, lengthy legal analyses and empirical research. They are also encouraged to gain teaching experience in psychology. Even having completed such a rigorous program, JD-PhD's may have to educate potential employers as to what they can do.

Lest this analysis sound too negative, it should be pointed out that JD-PhD's *are* special (see Hafemeister et al., 1990; Melton, 1990). When they perform well in both disciplines and their integration, JD-PhD's are in demand. For example, despite the fact that Nebraska is not a school that typically leads law students into judicial clerkships and law teaching, outstanding joint-degree students have been successful in obtaining federal clerkships and obtaining law faculty positions. Nonetheless, the point is that some of the special access to positions often presumed to accompany joint degrees is contingent upon special effort and outstanding achievement in the desired career track. Thus, competing for legal opportunities involves competing with other lawyer candidates on the traditional criteria (e.g., law school grades, clerkships, and legal publications) (Campbell & Tomkins, 1992).

Even if these practical problems are overcome, students may not be sufficiently motivated to seek positions that are truly interdisciplinary. Stanford University de-emphasized its JD-PhD option for such a reason. Graduates were finding the opportunity costs of eschewing large-firm law practice (the usual career goal of Stanford lawyers) were too great; therefore, they were not really using their PhD degrees. Consequently, Stanford now emphasizes the MLS degree, a one-year law degree, as the complement to the PhD for students in psycholegal studies to ensure that they do not head to law practice. Analogously, Nebraska dropped the JD-PhD option for students majoring in clinical psychology. The clinical JD-PhD's were finding it easy to move straight from their internship into practice as clinical psychologists. Students interested in forensic clinical psychology now are steered away from the JD (though a few still successfully petition to be allowed to take the JD degree);

instead, they are encouraged to pursue a master's degree in law (the MLS degree is discussed below).

Although some legal background is useful, indeed essential, for forensic clinicians, much of law school education would be superfluous to a practicing clinical psychologist. Analogously, interdisciplinary background may be useful in legal practice; however, it is hard to imagine a situation in which lawyers in practice would use the level of behavioral science training required for a PhD. Thus, JD-PhD programs are seen by some as inefficient means of training psychologically sophisticated legal practitioners and legally sophisticated clinical psychologists. The view is that the additional clinical training required in the program and the additional year of a clinical internship make the JD-PhD a less attractive option to clinical students.

Still, many educators and students continue to subscribe to the belief that the JD is usefully integrated with the doctorate in clinical psychology (Bersoff et al., 1997). Allegheny University of the Health Sciences–Villanova and Widener programs do not subscribe to the positions taken by Nebraska and Stanford, and they continue to offer joint JD training for clinical psychology graduate students. For example, Heilbrun (K. Heilbrun, personal communication February 10, 1997) identifies the versatility of having both degrees, the ease in training clinical students already aware of the legal issues they must confront in conducting forensic assessments, and the advantage of the JD for those pursuing careers in clinical adminstration as advantages that continue to justify offering both degrees to clinical students in their program.

PhD Specialty Programs

The major differences between the joint-degree and the PhD specialty programs is one of breadth. In the latter programs, students take interdisciplinary courses, do supervised research on psycholegal topics and participate in practica, identify themselves as law/psychology students, participate in law/psychology colloquia and other activities, and work with the same faculty research sponsors as do the joint-degree students. They also take law courses, although well short of the requirements for the JD; instead, specific courses are selected to match the student's specialty interest.

The most common type of PhD specialty program is intended to produce forensic clinicians. Most programs offering a PhD specialty program in forensic psychology do not offer students any formal law degree. (For model curricula for such a program in forensic psychology alone, see, Fenster, Litwack, & Symonds, 1975, and Poythress, 1979.)

Potentially, a specialty program could be developed in any area of law/psychology interaction. Virginia offers a concentration in children, psychology, and the law. Students in such a program take courses in law that address child and family issues (e.g., juvenile law, family law, constitutional law). Similarly, a specialty program might be developed in environmental policy, psychology, and the law. Students in such a specialty program would complete course work in relevant areas of psychology (e.g., environmental psychology, behavioral toxicology) and law (e.g., environmental law, natural resources law), and they would concentrate research and practice on related topics. Whatever the specialty, the commonality is instruction in interdisciplinary methods and philosophy.

At Nebraska, the forensic specialty is taken one step beyond the kinds of specialty programs just discussed. Forensic students in Nebraska's law/psychology program are required to enter the PhD-MLS track. The MLS is a 33-credit program in law that provides students with a basic exposure to law but does not provide them with as much legal training as is needed for the JD (92 credits). The MLS program requires a core curriculum that exposes them to common law, statutory interpretation, and legal research and writing. Beyond the core curriculum, MLS students are able to pick courses that match their training interests. For example, forensic students at Nebraska might take criminal law, family law, juvenile law, and evidence, as well as the cross-registered courses in law and behavioral science, mental health law, and so forth. In addition, they complete a special core course in forensic assessment (a psychology course), and their research, practice, and internship are expected to be compatible with the forensic focus/specialty.

The major disadvantages of the PhD specialty, whether with the MLS or without, mirror the advantages of the joint-degree model. Students might miss key issues in areas of law that do not appear germane at first glance. For example, the area of law that has the most effect on family structure may be wills and trusts, not family law. Similarly, legal definitions of a family are likely to appear in zoning law, not family law. A student in a specialty on children, psychology, and the law may be less likely than a joint-degree student to be aware of such connections. It is also possible that graduates of specialty programs will have less access to policymaking positions and law school faculties than their peers who completed joint degrees.

On the other hand, students in specialty programs will have achieved mastery of a particular area of psycholegal studies and key problems in interdisciplinary scholarship and practice generally, and they will have done so with significantly less expenditure of time and money for law courses. Moreover, specialty programs provide in-depth study of a specific area. If well designed, they are structured to give all of the students' graduate work an integrated purpose. In some sense, the joint-degree student may have to be more active in finding an integrated focus of study.

The advantages and disadvantages of the PhD specialty model apply as well to similar JD programs. In such programs, law students acquire basic knowledge of psychological methods and research and theory in particular areas of psychology, and they participate in interdisciplinary seminars and research. Usually, they will complete the requirements for a master's degree or its equivalent in the process. JD specialty students seek to obtain enough psychological expertise to be collaborators in scholarship (e.g., on problems of family policy) or practitioners in areas of law in which psychology plays a major role (e.g., mental health law).

Beyond the questionable costs of JD-PhD programs as a means of training interdisciplinary practitioners, it is important to note that there are special ethical problems of dual practice. Is the counselor giving the divorcing spouse legal advice or performing psychotherapy? Can an expert have any credibility when he or she is also an attorney in the firm representing the party calling for an opinion?

In summary, there may well be some special pedagogical benefits of joint-degree programs. However, careful analysis needs to be undertaken of the particular kinds of psycholegal careers for which a program leading to both JD and PhD degrees is optimal. This analysis is ultimately empirical. There is still a limited database from which to draw inferences. Logic does dictate, though, that joint-degree programs probably are not the most cost-efficient means of training interdisciplinary practitioners.

PhD Minor

Minors in psychology and law differ from joint-degree and specialty programs in breadth, depth, and intensity. Typically, students pursuing a minor in psychology and law will not identify themselves primarily as law/psychology students. Rather, they will be working with a major professor interested in a particular aspect of psycholegal studies or taking a few interdisciplinary or law courses because of their relevance to the student's major studies or simply their interest to the student. Students completing a minor will generally not become experts in psycholegal studies but may develop sufficient competence to use their work in psychology and law fruitfully.

An analogy can be made to developmental social psychology. Such a psychologist is likely to identify himself or herself primarily as a developmentalist, but he or she will need more than incidental knowledge of social psychology, albeit less than a psychologist whose primary identification is as a social psychologist. Similarly, a social psychologist with a minor in psychology and law may see relevance of his or her work to legal problems and feel a need for background in interdisciplinary studies, even though he or she does not need or wish to become a psycholegal scholar per se. A general clinical psychologist may reasonably seek familiarity with legal issues, practice, and basic skills in forensic assessment, even though he or she has no desire to be a forensic specialist.

There is no generally accepted format for a minor in psychology and the law, and the depth of training is likely to vary substantially. In the past at Nebraska, a psycholegal minor was available. The minimum requirements for the psycholegal minor included successful completion of any three interdisciplinary courses and a comprehensive examination. Although an enterprising student could expand the minor to resemble an individualized psycholegal specialty program, our experience at Nebraska was that the majority of minors were given a false sense in regard to the depth of study needed to be credible in psycholegal analysis and to form an identification as a "law/psych" type. Consequently, Nebraska now requires students to take a master's in law if they wish to identify themselves as law/psychology students.

Predoctoral Internships

A crucial aspect of any training in forensic psychology is the clinical internship (Otto et al., 1990). In a survey conducted in 1975 (Levine, Wilson, & Sales, 1980),

55% of APA-approved internship sites reported the availability of some oppor-tunities for forensic experience. Within four years, this figure grew to 77% (Lawlor, Siskind, & Brooks, 1981), although only 33% included didactic forensic instruction, and just 10% reported that they involved attorneys in the training. Furthermore, Heilbrun and Annis (1988) surveyed forensic inpatient facilities and found that 41% had an internship program. They concluded that such facil-ities also offer potential for training in forensic psychology. A working group of the Villanova Conference identified 259 programs by the Association of Psy-chology and Postdoctoral Internship Centers as offering either major or minor training in forensic psychology (Bersoff et al., 1997). A survey of these pro-grams identified a variety of experiences, ranging from inpatient experiences with adult criminal forensic populations to outpatient, forensic neuropsychol-ogy and juvenile court experiences (Bersoff et al., 1997). Otto and Small (1989) encourage forensic internships to provide (a) familiarization with the empirical literature relevant to forensic practice, (b) familiarization with the law relevant to forensic practice, (c) the treatment and evaluation of forensic populations, and (d) the opportunity to work in the legal system through expert testimony. Predoctoral internship training is especially important for students having the depth of course work in the predoctoral forensic training programs.

Other scholars have identified two different types of forensic internship models: the specialist model and the generalist-specialist model (Otto et al., 1990). The specialist model integrates general clinical training and specializa-tion in forensic psychology in one predoctoral internship. These experiences are likely to be internships in strictly forensic settings or penal institutions (e.g., Atascadero State Hospital, Florida State Hospital, St. Elizabeth's Hospi-tal, University of North Carolina–Federal Correctional Institution–Butner). The internship experience focuses on the evaluation and treatment of foren-sic/criminal offender inpatient populations. The generalist-specialist model provides the intern with some forensic experience within a general clinical in-ternship. For example, there may be one or two forensic rotations in a full-year, four-rotation internship.

Each model has certain advantages and disadvantages over the other (Otto et al., 1990). The generalist-specialist model might necessitate a second year of training for a broad clinical experience as well as the same depth of forensic ex-perience offered in the specialist model, thereby discouraging many graduate students. The specialist model forces graduate students to specialize early on in their clinical career and assumes the broad range of clinical skills have either al-ready been learned, can be learned within the forensic setting, or are unneces-sary for forensic practice. Whichever model is chosen, the internship experience is crucial to the ongoing training of a forensic psychologist (Otto et al., 1990).

POSTDOCTORAL PROGRAMS

Postdoctoral programs differ from PhD specialty programs primarily in terms of when they occur (i. e., after, rather than during, doctoral training in psychology). Consequently, their advantages and disadvantages relative to joint-degree pro-grams are somewhat similar to those of specialty programs. Relative to specialty programs, the major disadvantage of postdoctoral study is that it delays identification as a psycholegal scholar; in so doing, there may be missed opportunities for integration of studies from the beginning. Probably the major advantage is that, because competence as a psychologist has already been achieved, there can be a year or two of immersion in attaining competence as a psycholegal scholar. The experience may, therefore, resemble joint-degree programs in the intensity of cognitive conflicts presented (and the need to resolve them).

The professional maturity of postdoctoral trainees may also enable them to use their interdisciplinary studies expeditiously. Because they will have a stronger foundation than predoctoral students in the core discipline, they should be more efficient in identifying psycholegal questions.

At Nebraska, there is an attempt to capitalize on these experiences by stimulating postdoctoral fellows to learn interdisciplinary work through their collaboration with each other. Thus, postdoctoral fellows are required to pursue the MLS degree. However, the most powerful educational experience often comes from working on research or writing projects with advanced predoctoral students, who tend to have more psycholegal sophistication than do the postdoctoral fellows at the onset of their fellowship program. Other postdoctoral opportunities also exist that provide different opportunities (see Bersoff et al., 1997 for a list of these opportunities).

CONCLUSION

Perhaps the clearest statement that can be made on the basis of this review of models of psycholegal training is that no model is clearly superior for all purposes. For example, it seems unlikely that joint-degree programs are optimal for training in a particular area of psycholegal study, but it may be that there are some advantages, substantive or practical, of joint-degree programs in training scholars who identify their primary area of concentration as psychology and law rather than a traditional subdiscipline.

Two important points follow from this general conclusion. First, before a program is established, there needs to be careful analysis of whether there is a logical relationship between the goals and the methods of training. A joint-degree model should not be adopted merely because it sounds intriguing, nor should it be rejected simply because the administrative arrangements sound cumbersome or there is uncritical espousal of pure disciplinary training, even on interdisciplinary topics. Probably, the more specific the hypotheses are about the crucial processes involved in achieving particular kinds of interdisciplinary training, the more likely a program will be designed to foster the desired integration.

Second, most of the purported pros and cons of the various models are in fact hypotheses. Now that programs are reaching sufficient maturity to follow graduates, there is an opportunity for evaluation research. The need for such research is particularly profound because of the diversity of existing programs.

At Nebraska, we have started to track the careers of our graduates. Table 25.1 provides the data for the 12 clinical psychology/forensic students (6 predoctoral students and 6 postdoctoral students) from the law/psychology program who entered the workforce between 1986 and 1997. Although the numbers are too

Table 25.1

Present Employment of Forensic Psychology Students from Nebraska
Who Entered Workforce, 1986–1997

Type of Employment	Training Track				Total
	JD PhD	PhD MLS	PhD Specialty[a]	Postdoc MLS/No MLS	
Academic: Tenure track	1	1[b]	0	1 2	5
Academic: Nontenure track (Research appointment)	0	0	1	1 2[c]	4
Forensic mental health	0	0	2	0 0	2
Community mental health	0	0	1	0 0	1
Total	1	1	4	2 4	12

[a]Specialty students, who did not take the MLS or its equivalent. The present policy at Nebraska is that all incoming students are required to pursue the MLS unless they already have a background in law or policy.

[b]Student completed the equivalent of an MLS program of studies before the MLS was officially approved by the University.

[c]Includes one postdoc who came to Nebraska with JD and PhD.

small to be dispositive, they are interesting. Only three of the students went into forensic practice, and each pursued law as a specialty rather than as a formal program of study. Even the postdoctoral students who did not pursue an MLS degree took an intensive curriculum of legal studies (or already had the JD degree). It would be interesting to compare placement data from other programs to see whether there is a correlation between more formal study of law and a career path into academia and research.

Research on the process of training would also be useful. What is it like to begin thinking like a psychologist-lawyer or a legally sophisticated psychologist? What sorts of training activities are most likely to provide such "aha" experiences? Initially, whatever the actual merits of the various models, their popularity will be contingent to a large extent on structural and ideological factors within the professions. For example, current federal policies favoring postdoctoral training will affect university willingness to enter into training in psycholegal studies.

Similarly, the conventional wisdom as to the desirability of specialization and subspecialization in predoctoral psychological training generally (e.g., whether students should be permitted or encouraged to major in clinical child psychology instead of general clinical psychology) is likely to shape departments' attitudes toward forensic specialty programs, especially if prevailing attitudes of the profession as a whole are translated into accreditation standards.

CONTINUING EDUCATION

CONTINUING EDUCATION OF SPECIALISTS

It is a cliché that professionals have a duty to stay abreast of developments in their fields. For most professionals, this obligation represents a task that they would likely fulfill anyway, simply because of interest in their work. Nonetheless, because changes in the law are often abrupt rather than gradual, forensic specialists bear a special duty to maintain a systematic continuing education program for themselves.

The significance of this duty is heightened because of the potential consequences of forensic assessments. Consider the following example. A clinician is asked to perform an evaluation pursuant to a capital sentencing proceeding. Unbeknownst to the clinician, though, the legislature has enacted a change in the standard for imposition of the death sentence, or the state supreme court has issued an opinion that clarifies the meaning of the standard. The specter of a clinician performing such an evaluation with literally life-and-death consequences without accurate knowledge of the controlling law is chilling.

Although the consequences of a psycholegal researcher's not keeping up with changes in the law relevant to his or her interests are less grave, at least in the short term, researchers also need to have up-to-date knowledge of changes in the law if their work is to retain usefulness to the law. Unless researchers systematically follow appellate opinions in their area of interest, they also may miss those golden opportunities when a court invites empirical research by suggesting in dicta that it might reach a different result if particular empirical evidence were available.

There are several ways in which forensic specialists can stay abreast of changes in the law. Probably the most efficient, although sometimes rather costly, means is to subscribe to *United States Law Week* and specialized reporters in one's area of interest (e.g., *Family Law Reporter, Mental and Physical Disability Law Reporter*). Such materials will be available in any good law library. It is also worthwhile to make a periodic trip to the law library to scan the advance sheets of appellate courts in one's jurisdiction and the session laws of the state legislature for developments relevant to one's practice. In addition to perusing the relevant law reporters, there are a number of specialized journals (e.g., *Behavioral Sciences and the Law, Bulletin of the American Academy of Psychiatry and Law, Criminal Justice and Behavior, Law and Human Behavior*,) in which forensic specialists can often read the most recent empirical and theoretical advances in their field (see generally Daniell, 1987).

Advanced workshops and symposia at professional meetings are, of course, other sources of information about current developments. One problem, though, with this source of continuing education is that, in a given jurisdiction, there may not be enough forensic specialists to warrant such formal opportunities. At least in terms of forensic clinical practice, the state department of mental health or the attorney general's office can do a real service by systematically disseminating changes in the law to the relevant practitioners. A model of such a program is at the Institute of Law, Psychiatry, and Public Policy at the University of Virginia. Under contract with the Virginia Department of Mental Health and Mental Retardation, the Institute conducts periodic workshops and consultations for clinicians who have passed a basic training course and examination in forensic assessment, as described in the following section. Similar state-university-based programs are available at other institutions (e.g., University of Massachusetts, and Florida Mental Health Institute, affiliated with the University of South Florida).

BASIC TRAINING THROUGH CONTINUING EDUCATION

It is unlikely that the university training programs will meet the demand for forensic psychologists in the foreseeable future. Besides the fact that there are still few joint-degree, PhD specialty, and postdoctoral programs, the trend is toward making forensic services a routine part of community mental health practice. There has been a recognition that most forensic evaluations can be done validly and reliably in brief outpatient assessments (Melton et al., 1985; Roesch & Golding, 1980; Slobogin, Melton, & Showalter, 1984). Given that lengthy inpatient evaluations in forensic hospitals intrude on a defendant's liberty and his or her rights to bail, a speedy trial, and effective assistance of counsel, such unnecessary hospitalization is probably unconstitutional (ABA, 1984; Melton et al., 1985). Moreover, the cost to the state of forensic mental health services for indigent defendants is much higher than necessary when the state relies on a central forensic hospital. If these points are followed to their logical conclusion, then states should move their forensic services into the community. Such a service model requires training of teams in community clinics to perform the necessary evaluations.

It is inevitable that general clinicians who do not perceive themselves as having forensic services as part of their workload will also be drawn into forensic practice on occasion, whether willfully or not, whether prepared or not. When a client becomes involved in a custody dispute or possibly subject to civil commitment or guardianship or enters treatment as a condition of probation, the mental health professional is likely to be called on to give expert opinions to the court. In view of such involvement of clinicians in the legal system, even though they were not trained as forensic psychologists in graduate school or postdoctoral study, there is a need for development of forensic knowledge and skills among general clinicians through continuing education. There is evidence that such basic training through continuing education is possible, but only under certain conditions. In an experiment mandated by the Virginia General Assembly, Melton et al. (1985) provided an eight-day training program for teams of community mental health professionals in selected centers across the state. Integral to the success of the program was that it involved institution of a community-based system with the support of the commissioner of mental health, the attorney general's office, and the state supreme court. Rather than just training clinicians, the program staff worked with state and local authorities to ensure that evaluations in the experimental communities were performed in the community clinics. The training itself involved a sophisticated mix of law, research, and clinical technique taught by an interdisciplinary faculty at the University of Virginia Institute of Law, Psychiatry, and Public Policy. The materials served as the basis for a large handbook of forensic assessment (Melton et al., 1997).

The Virginia program in fact resulted in a substantial decrease in inpatient evaluations and a corresponding large decrease in cost, without an undue net-widening effect (Melton et al., 1985). Of particular interest in the present context, though, is that the training program resulted in trainees' obtaining a level of forensic knowledge commensurate with diplomates in forensic psychology (Melton et al., 1985). The trainees were found to have knowledge of relevant law, research, and clinical technique greater than several groups of general clinicians and a sample of trial judges. Their reports were also judged superior by trial judges, prosecutors, and defense attorneys who analyzed the reports blind to the identity of the authors (Melton et al., 1985).

Within the comparison groups, level of forensic training made no difference in knowledge of forensic issues. Having taken relevant courses in graduate school, previous training programs at the UVa Institute, or continuing education workshops did not affect level of knowledge. It is thus suggested that, though training as a forensic specialist can be accomplished through a continuing education course, it will have substantial effect only if there are structures in place for actually using the new knowledge. Otherwise, there are insufficient incentives for adequately acquiring, maintaining, and expanding knowledge of forensic psychology (Grisso, 1987). An occasional workshop is unlikely to provide the depth of knowledge necessary for someone to function competently as a forensic psychologist.

CONCLUSION

Whatever the means psychologists have of obtaining training in psychology and law, the potential utility of such training seems beyond dispute at this point. The law is filled with behavioral assumptions; at its most basic is the assumption that the law in fact affects behavior (Melton, 1985). There is a need for psychologists, lawyers, and psychologist-lawyers to determine and evaluate these assumptions so that public policy can be made and implemented rationally. Similarly, insofar as a knowledge of psychology will inform adjudication of individual cases, justice demands the careful application of this knowledge. Before entering the legal system, psychologists should be educated in the nature of the inquiry and the specialized psychological knowledge and its limits relevant to the particular legal issues.

As indicated throughout this chapter, there are multiple models of acquiring the necessary training, but the optimum form and content of training is still undecided, even for particular purposes. Three graduates of law/psychology programs concluded that training in law and psychology provides unequaled training that cannot be matched by other approaches (Hafemeister et al., 1990). However, several considerations should guide prospective students in deciding on a training program.

First, and most obviously, the prospective student should be certain that the goals of the program match his or her own. Does it seek to train researchers or practitioners? What areas of psychology and law does it purport to cover? Second, the curriculum should be examined to ensure that it really offers an integration of psychology and law and that it gives due attention to the philosophical problems in applying psychology to the law. Third, is there a strong core faculty with a track record of psycholegal scholarship, and are both psychology and law faculty integrated into the program, even if they do not identify themselves primarily as psycholegal scholars? Fourth, is there a core group of students in the program? Given that learning often occurs through interaction with peers inside and outside the classroom, the availability of students with similar interests is an important consideration that is often overlooked. It is particularly important in an interdisciplinary program because of the especially acute issues in establishing a professional identity. Fifth, the prospective student should examine the reputation of the program and the department or colleges of which it is a part; for example, if a student's ultimate goal is a law school faculty position, he or she should give special attention to programs located in law schools with a national reputation.

No doubt, other considerations may be important in individual cases, including personal preferences (e.g., geographic preference). Whatever the calculus, the student who is successful in achieving admission to, and ultimately graduating from, a high-caliber program in psycholegal studies can be assured of an exciting career. The field of psycholegal studies is still sufficiently novel that an outstanding psychologist can quickly achieve visibility. And there is the possibility of substantial contribution, whether professional or scientific or both, to social welfare.

NOTE

1. The director of the Arizona program, Bruce Sales, was the first director of the Nebraska program. Amiram Elwork, the current director of the Widener program, was the former director of the Allegheny/Villanova program and also formerly associated with the Nebraska program. Both Arizona and Allegheny/Villanova follow the general format of the Nebraska program, but interdisciplinary courses and emphases differ substantially. For example, Allegheny/Villanova offers the JD-PhD only in clinical psychology. A variety of differences are present across both formal and informal interdisciplinary training programs (Bersoff et al., 1997).

REFERENCES

American Bar Association. (1984). *Criminal justice menial health standards*. Washington, DC: Author.

American Psychological Association. (1992). Ethical principles of psychologists and code of conduct. *American Psychologist, 47,* 1597–1611.

American Psychology-Law Society. (1996). *Graduate training programs in law and psychology.* Author.

Bersoff, D. N., Goodman-Delahunty, J., Grisso, T., Hans, V. P., Poythress, N. G., & Roesch, R. G. (1997). Training in law and psychology: Models from the Villanova conference. *American Psychologist, 52,* 1301–1310.

Bonnie, R. J., & Slobogin, C. (1980). The role of mental health professionals in the criminal process. The case for informed speculation. *Virginia Law Review, 66,* 421–522.

Campbell, E., & Tomkins, A. J. (1992). Gender, race, grades, and law review membership as factors in law firm decisions: An empirical study. *Journal of Contemporary Law, 18,* 211–261.

Casey, P., Keilitz, I., & Hafemeister, T. L. (1992). Toward an agenda for reform of justice and mental health systems interactions. *Law and Human Behavior, 16,* 107–128.

Daniell, D. F. (1987). Accessing legal literature. In I. B. Weiner & A. K. Hess (Eds.), *Handbook of forensic psychology.* New York: Wiley.

Fenster, C. A., Litwack, T. R., & Symonds, M. (1975). The making of a forensic psychologist: Needs and goals for doctoral training. *Professional Psychology, 4,* 457–467.

Grisso, T. (1987). The economic and scientific future of forensic psychological assessment. *American Psychologist, 42,* 831–839.

Grisso, T. (1991). A developmental history of the American Psychology–Law Society. *Law and Human Behavior, 15,* 213–231.

Grisso, T., Sales, B. D., & Bayless, S. (1982). Law-related courses and programs in graduate psychology departments. *American Psychologist, 37,* 267–278.

Hafemeister, T. L., Ogloff, J. R., & Small, M. A. (1990). Training and careers in law and psychology: The perspectives of students and graduates of dual degree programs. *Behavioral Sciences and the Law, 8,* 263–283.

Haney, C. (1980). Psychology and legal change: On the limits of a factual jurisprudence. *Law and Human Behavior, 4,* 147–199.

Heilbrun, K., & Annis, L. (1988). Research and training in forensic psychology: National survey of forensic facilities. *Professional Psychology, 19,* 211–215.

Lawlor, R. I., Siskind, G., & Brooks, I. (1981). Forensic training at internships: Update and criticism of current unspecified training models. *Professional Psychology, 12,* 400–405.

Levine, D., Wilson, K., & Sales, B. D. (1980). An exploratory assessment of APA internships with legal/forensic experiences. *Professional Psychology, 11,* 64–71.

Lidz, C. W., & Mulvey, E. P. (1995). Dangerousness: From legal definition to theoretical research. *Law and Human Behavior, 19,* 41–48.

Loh, W. (1981). Psycholegal research: Past and present. *Michigan Law Review, 79,* 659–707.

Melton, G. B. (1983). Training in psychology and law: A directory. *Division of Psychology and Law Newsletter, 3,* 1–5.

Melton, G. B. (1985). Introduction: The law and motivation. In G. B. Melton (Ed.), *Nebraska Symposium on Motivation: The law as a behavioral instrument* (Vol. 33, pp. xiii–xxvii). Lincoln: University of Nebraska Press.

Melton, G. B. (1990). Realism in psychology and humanism in law: Psycholegal studies at Nebraska. *Nebraska Law Review. 69,* 251–277.

Melton, G. B. (1994). Expert evidence: "Not for cosmic understanding." In B. D. Sales & G. R. VandenBos (Eds.), *Psychology in litigation and legislation* (pp. 57–99). Washington, DC: American Psychological Association.

Melton, G. B., Petrila, J., Poythress, N. G., Jr., & Slobogin, C. (1997). *Psychological evaluations for the courts: A handbook for mental health processionals and lawyers* (2nd ed.). New York: Guilford Press.

Melton, G. B., Weithorn, L. A., & Slobogin, C. (1985). *Community mental health centers and the courts: An evaluation of community-based forensic services.* Lincoln: University of Nebraska Press.

Monahan, J., & Loftus, E. F. (1982). The psychology of law. *Annual Review of Psychology, 33,* 441–475.

Morse, S. J. (1978). Crazy behavior, morals and science: An analysis of mental health law. *Southern California Law Review, 51,* 527–563.

Morse, S. J. (1982a). Failed explanations and criminal responsibility: Experts and the unconscious. *Virginia Law Review, 68,* 971–1084.

Morse, S. J. (1982b). Reforming expert testimony: An open response from the tower (and the trenches). *Law and Human Behavior, 6,* 45–47.

Ogloff, J. R., Tomkins, A. J., & Bersoff, D. N. (1996). Education and training in psychology and law/criminal justice: Historical foundations, present structures, and future developments. *Criminal Justice and Behavior, 23,* 200–235.

Otto, R. K., Heilbrun, K., & Grisso, T. (1990). Training and credentialing in forensic psychology. *Behavioral Sciences and the Law, 8,* 217–231.

Otto, R. K., & Small, M. A. (1989, June). *The role of internship training in forensic psychology.* Paper presented at the annual meeting of the Canadian Psychological Association, Halifax, Nova Scotia, Canada.

Poythress, N. G., Jr. (1978). Psychiatric expertise in civil commitment: Training attorneys to cope with expert testimony. *Law and Human Behavior, 2,* 1–23.

Poythress, N. G., Jr. (1979). A proposal for training in forensic psychology. *American Psychologist, 34,* 612–621.

Poythress, N. G., Jr. (1982). Concerning reform in expert testimony: An open letter from a practicing psychologist. *Law and Human Behavior, 6,* 39–43.

Rappaport, J. (1977). *Community psychology: Values, research, and action.* New York: Holt, Rinehart and Winston.

Roesch, R. (1990). From the editor. *Law and Human Behavior, 14,* 1–3.

Roesch, R., & Golding, S. (1980). *Competency to stand trial.* Urbana: University of Illinois Press.

Schlegel, J. H. (1995). *American legal realism and empirical social science.* Chapel Hill: University of North Carolina Press.

Slobogin, C. (1982). Estelle v. Smith: The constitutional contours of the forensic evaluation. *Emory Law Journal, 31,* 71–138.

Slobogin, C., Melton, G. B., & Showalter, C. (1984). Feasibility of a brief screening evaluation of mental state at the time of the offense. *Law and Human Behavior, 8,* 305–320.

Thibaut, I., & Walker, L. (1978). A theory of procedure. *California Law Review, 66,* 541–566.

Tomkins, A. J., & Ogloff, J. R. (1990). Training and career options in psychology and law. *Behavioral Sciences and the Law, 8,* 205–216.

Author Index

Subject Index